5 language VISUAL dictionary

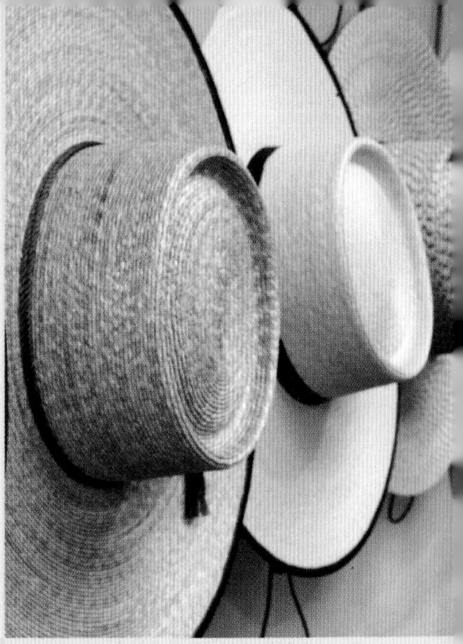

5 language VISUAL dictionary

DK

Penguin Random House

Senior Editor Angeles Gavira
Senior Art Editor Ina Stradins
US Editors Margaret Parrish, Christine Heilman
DTP Designer Rajen Shah
Production Controller Melanie Dowland
Picture Researcher Anna Grapes
Managing Editor Liz Wheeler
Managing Art Editor Phil Ormerod
Category Publisher Jonathan Metcalf

2016 Revised Edition
Editorial Pakshalika Jayaprakash, Antara Moitra, Vineetha Mokkil, Stuart Neilson, Ira Pundeer, Angela Wilkes
Design Meenal Goel, Roshni Kapur, Chhaya Sajwan, Arunesh Talapatra, Priyansha Tuli
Production Nityanand Kumar, Pankaj Sharma, Balwant Singh, Dheeraj Singh, Jacqueline Street

Designed for Dorling Kindersley by WaltonCreative.com
Art Editor Colin Walton, assisted by Tracy Musson
Designers Peter Radcliffe, Earl Neish, Ann Cannings
Picture Research Marissa Keating

Language content for Dorling Kindersley by g-and-w publishing

Translation and editing by Ana Bremón, Renate Betson, Marc Vitale, Christine Arthur

First American Edition, 2003

This edition published in the United States in 2016 by DK Publishing, 345 Hudson Street, New York, New York 10014

16 17 18 19 20 10 9 8 7 6 5 4 3 2 1
001–289026–August/2016

Published in Great Britain by Dorling Kindersley Limited.

A catalog record for this book is available from the Library of Congress.

ISBN 978-1-4654-4756-2

Printed and bound in China

A WORLD OF IDEAS:
SEE ALL THERE IS TO KNOW

www.dk.com

contents
table des matières
Inhalt
contenido
sommario

42

health
la santé
die Gesundheit
la salud
la salute

146

eating out
sortir manger
auswärts essen
comer fuera
mangiare fuori

252

leisure
le temps libre
die Freizeit
el ocio
il tempo libero

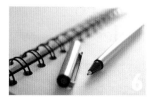

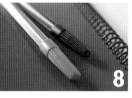

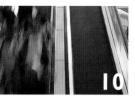

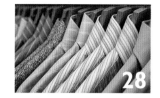

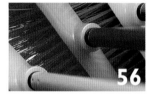

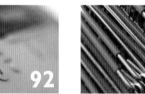

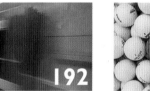

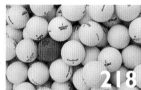

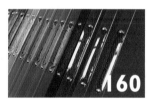

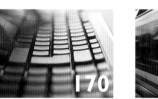

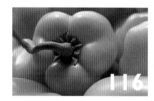

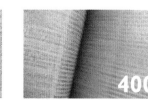

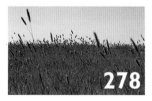

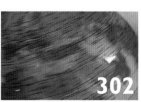

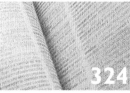

about the dictionary

The use of pictures is proven to aid understanding and the retention of information. Working on this principle, this highly-illustrated multilingual dictionary presents a large range of useful current vocabulary in five European languages.

The dictionary is divided thematically and covers most aspects of the everyday world in detail, from the restaurant to the gym, the home to the workplace, outer space to the animal kingdom. You will also find additional words and phrases for conversational use and for extending your vocabulary.

This is an essential reference tool for anyone interested in languages - practical, stimulating, and easy-to-use.

A few things to note

The five languages are always presented in the same order – English, French, German, Spanish, and Italian.

Other than in English, nouns are given with their definite articles reflecting the gender (masculine, feminine, or neuter) and number (singular or plural), for example:

seed	almonds
la graine	les amandes
der Samen	die Mandeln
la semilla	las almendras
il seme	le mandorle

Verbs are indicated by a *(v)* after the English, for example:

harvest *(v)* • récolter • ernten • recolectar • raccogliere

Each language also has its own index at the back of the book. Here you can look up a word in any of the five languages and be referred to the page number(s) where it appears. The gender is shown using the following abbreviations:

m = masculine
f = feminine
n = neuter

à propos du dictionnaire

Il est bien connu que les illustrations nous aident à comprendre et retenir l'information. Fondé sur ce principe, ce dictionnaire multilingue richement illustré présente un large éventail de vocabulaire courant et utile dans cinq langues européennes.

Le dictionnaire est divisé de façon thématique et couvre en détail la plupart des aspects du monde quotidien, du restaurant au gymnase, de la maison au lieu de travail, de l'espace au monde animal. Vous y trouverez également des mots et expressions supplémentaires pour la conversation et pour enrichir votre vocabulaire.

Il s'agit d'un outil de référence essentiel pour tous ceux qui s'intéressent aux langues – pratique, stimulant et d'emploi facile.

Quelques points à noter

Les cinq langues sont toujours présentées dans le même ordre – anglais, français, allemand, espagnol et italien.

Sauf en anglais, les noms sont donnés avec leurs articles définis qui indiquent leur genre (masculin, féminin ou neutre) et leur nombre (singulier ou pluriel):

seed	almonds
la graine	les amandes
der Samen	die Mandeln
la semilla	las almendras
il seme	le mandorle

Les verbes sont indiqués par un *(v)* après l'anglais, par exemple:

harvest *(v)* • récolter • ernten • recolectar • raccogliere

Chaque langue a également son propre index à la fin du livre. Vous pourrez y vérifier un mot dans n'importe laquelle des cinq langues et vous serez renvoyé au(x) numéro(s) de(s) page(s) où il figure. Le genre est indiqué par les abréviations suivantes:

m = masculin
f = féminin
n = neutre

über das Wörterbuch

Bilder helfen erwiesenermaßen, Informationen zu verstehen und zu behalten. Dieses mehrsprachige Wörterbuch enthält eine Fülle von Illustrationen und präsentiert gleichzeitig ein umfangreiches aktuelles Vokabular in fünf europäischen Sprachen.

Das Wörterbuch ist thematisch gegliedert und behandelt eingehend die meisten Bereiche des heutigen Alltags, vom Restaurant und Fitnesscenter, Heim und Arbeitsplatz bis zum Tierreich und Weltraum. Es enthält außerdem Wörter und Redewendungen, die für die Unterhaltung nützlich sind und das Vokabular erweitern.

Dies ist ein wichtiges Nachschlagewerk für jeden, der sich für Sprachen interessiert – es ist praktisch, anregend und leicht zu benutzen.

Einige Anmerkungen

Die fünf Sprachen werden immer in der gleichen Reihenfolge aufgeführt – Englisch, Französisch, Deutsch, Spanisch und Italienisch.

Außer für Englisch werden Substantive mit den bestimmten Artikeln, die das Geschlecht (Maskulinum, Femininum oder Neutrum) und den Numerus (Singular oder Plural) ausdrücken, angegeben, zum Beispiel:

seed	almonds
la graine	les amandes
der Samen	die Mandeln
la semilla	las almendras
il seme	le mandorle

Die Verben sind durch ein *(v)* nach dem englischen Wort gekennzeichnet:

harvest *(v)* • récolter • ernten • recolectar • raccogliere

Am Ende des Buchs befinden sich Register für jede Sprache. Sie können dort ein Wort in einer der fünf Sprachen und die jeweilige Seitenzahl nachsehen. Die Geschlechtsangabe erfolgt mit folgenden Abkürzungen:

m = Maskulinum
f = Femininum
n = Neutrum

sobre el diccionario

Está comprobado que el empleo de fotografías ayuda a la comprensión y a la retención de información. Basados en este principio, este diccionario plurilíngüe y altamente ilustrado exhibe un amplio registro de vocabulario útil y actual en cinco idiomas europeos.

El diccionario aparece dividido según su temática y abarca la mayoría de los aspectos del mundo cotidiano con detalle, desde el restaurante al gimnasio, la casa al lugar de trabajo, el espacio al reino animal. Encontrará también palabras y frases adicionales para su uso en conversación y para ampliar su vocabulario.

Este diccionario es un instrumento de referencia esencial para todo aquél que esté interesado en los idiomas; es práctico, estimulante y fácil de usar.

Algunos puntos a observar

Los cinco idiomas se presentan siempre en el mismo orden: inglés, francés, alemán, español e italiano.

A excepción del inglés, los sustantivos se muestran con sus artículos definidos reflejando el género (masculino, femenino o neutro) y el número (singular/plural):

seed	almonds
la graine	les amandes
der Samen	die Mandeln
la semilla	las almendras
il seme	le mandorle

Los verbos se indican con una *(v)* después del inglés:

harvest *(v)* • récolter • ernten • recolectar • raccogliere

Cada idioma tiene su propio índice. Aquí podrá mirar una palabra en cualquiera de los cinco idiomas y se le indicará el número de la página donde aparece. El género se indica utilizando las siguientes abreviaturas:

m = masculino
f = femenino
n = neutro

informazioni sul dizionario

È dimostrato che l'uso di immagini aiuti a capire e memorizzare le informazioni. Applicando tale principio, abbiamo realizzato questo dizionario multilingue, corredato da numerosissime illustrazioni, che presenta un ampio ventaglio di vocaboli utili in cinque lingue europee.

Il dizionario è diviso in vari argomenti ed esamina dettagliatamente molti aspetti del mondo moderno, dal ristorante alla palestra, dalla casa all'ufficio, dallo spazio al regno animale. L'opera contiene inoltre frasi e vocaboli utili per conversare e per estendere il proprio vocabolario.

È un'opera di consultazione essenziale per tutti gli appassionati delle lingue – pratica, stimolante e facile da usare.

Indicazioni

Le cinque lingue vengono presentate sempre nello stesso ordine: inglese, francese, tedesco, spagnolo e italiano.

In tutte le lingue, tranne l'inglese, i sostantivi vengono riportati con il relativo articolo determinativo, che indica il genere (maschile, femminile o neutro) e il numero (singolare o plurale), come ad esempio:

seed	almonds
la graine	les amandes
der Samen	die Mandeln
la semilla	las almendras
il seme	le mandorle

I verbi sono contraddistinti da una *(v)* dopo il vocabolo inglese, come ad esempio:

harvest *(v)* • récolter • ernten • recolectar • raccogliere

Alla fine del libro ogni lingua ha inoltre il proprio indice, che consente di cercare un vocabolo in una qualsiasi delle cinque lingue e di trovare il rimando alla pagina che gli corrisponde. Il genere è indicato dalle seguenti abbreviazioni:

m = maschile
f = femminile
n = neutro

how to use this book

Whether you are learning a new language for business, pleasure, or in preparation for a vacation abroad, or are hoping to extend your vocabulary in an already familiar language, this dictionary is a valuable learning tool which you can use in a number of different ways.

When learning a new language, look out for cognates (words that are alike in different languages) and false friends (words that *look* alike but carry significantly different meanings). You can also see where the languages have influenced each other. For example, English has imported many terms for food from other European languages but, in turn, exported terms used in technology and popular culture.

You can compare two or three languages or all five, depending on how wide your interests are.

Practical learning activities

• As you move around your home, workplace, or school, try looking at the pages which cover that setting. You could then close the book, look around you and see how many of the objects and features you can name.

• Challenge yourself to write a story, letter, or dialogue using as many of the terms on a particular page as possible. This will help you retain the vocabulary and remember the spelling. If you want to build up to writing a longer text, start with sentences incorporating 2–3 words.

• If you have a very visual memory, try drawing or tracing items from the book onto a piece of paper, then close the book and fill in the words below the picture.

• Once you are more confident, pick out words in a foreign-language index and see if you know what they mean before turning to the relevant page to check if you were right.

comment utiliser ce livre

Que vous appreniez une nouvelle langue pour les affaires, le plaisir ou pour préparer vos vacances, ou encore si vous espérez élargir votre vocabulaire dans une langue qui vous est déjà familière, ce dictionnaire sera pour vous un outil d'apprentissage précieux que vous pourrez utiliser de plusieurs manières.

Lorsque vous apprenez une nouvelle langue, recherchez les mots apparentés (mots qui se ressemblent dans différentes langues) et les faux amis (mots qui se ressemblent mais ont des significations nettement différentes). Vous pouvez aussi voir comment les langues se sont influencées. Par exemple, l'anglais a importé des autres langues européennes de nombreux termes désignant la nourriture mais, en retour, exporté des termes employés dans le domaine de la technologie et de la culture populaire.

Vous pouvez comparer deux ou trois langues ou bien toutes les cinq, selon votre intérêt.

Activités pratiques d'apprentissage

• Lorsque vous vous déplacez dans votre maison, au travail ou à l'université, essayez de regarder les pages qui correspondent à ce contexte. Vous pouvez ensuite fermer le livre, regarder autour de vous et voir combien d'objets vous pouvez nommer.

• Forcez-vous à écrire une histoire, une lettre ou un dialogue en employant le plus de termes possibles choisis dans une page. Ceci vous aidera à retenir le vocabulaire et son orthographe. Si vous souhaitez pouvoir écrire un texte plus long, commencez par des phrases qui incorporent 2 à 3 mots.

• Si vous avez une mémoire très visuelle, essayez de dessiner ou de décalquer des objets du livre sur une feuille de papier, puis fermez le livre et inscrivez les mots sous l'image.

• Une fois que vous serez plus sûr de vous, choisissez des mots dans l'index de la langue étrangère et essayez de voir si vous en connaissez le sens avant de vous reporter à la page correspondante pour vérifier.

die Benutzung des Buchs

Ganz gleich, ob Sie eine Sprache aus Geschäftsgründen, zum Vergnügen oder als Vorbereitung für einen Auslandsurlaub lernen, oder Ihr Vokabular in einer Ihnen bereits vertrauten Sprache erweitern möchten, dieses Wörterbuch ist ein wertvolles Lernmittel, das Sie auf vielfältige Art und Weise benutzen können.

Wenn Sie eine neue Sprache lernen, achten Sie auf Wörter, die in verschiedenen Sprachen ähnlich sind sowie auf falsche Freunde (Wörter, die ähnlich aussehen aber wesentlich andere Bedeutungen haben). Sie können ebenfalls feststellen, wie die Sprachen einander beeinflusst haben. Englisch hat zum Beispiel viele Ausdrücke für Nahrungsmittel aus anderen europäischen Sprachen übernommen und andererseits viele Begriffe aus der Technik und Popkultur ausgeführt.

Sie können je nach Ihrem Interesse zwei oder drei, oder auch alle fünf Sprachen miteinander vergleichen.

Praktische Übungen

• Versuchen Sie sich zu Hause, am Arbeits- oder Studienplatz den Inhalt der Seiten einzuprägen, die Ihre Umgebung behandeln. Schließen Sie dann das Buch und prüfen Sie, wie viele Gegenstände Sie in den anderen Sprachen sagen können.

• Schreiben Sie eine Geschichte, einen Brief oder Dialog und benutzen Sie dabei möglichst viele Ausdrücke von einer bestimmten Seite des Wörterbuchs. Dies ist eine gute Methode, sich das Vokabular und die Schreibweise einzuprägen. Sie können mit kurzen Sätzen von zwei bis drei Worten anfangen und dann nach und nach längere Texte schreiben.

• Wenn Sie ein visuelles Gedächtnis haben, können Sie Gegenstände aus dem Buch abzeichnen oder abpausen. Schließen Sie dann das Buch und schreiben Sie die passenden Wörter unter die Bilder.

• Wenn Sie mehr Sicherheit haben, können Sie Wörter aus einem der Fremdsprachenregister aussuchen und deren Bedeutung aufschreiben, bevor Sie auf der entsprechenden Seite nachsehen.

cómo utilizar este libro

Ya se encuentre aprendiendo un idioma nuevo por motivos de trabajo, placer, o para preparar sus vacaciones al extranjero, o ya quiera ampliar su vocabulario en un idioma que ya conoce, este diccionario es un instrumento muy valioso que podrá utilizar de distintas maneras.

Cuando esté aprendiendo un idioma nuevo, busque palabras similares en distintos idiomas y palabras que parecen similares pero que poseen significados totalmente distintos. También podrá observar cómo los idiomas se influyen unos a otros. Por ejemplo, la lengua inglesa ha importado muchos términos de comida de otras lenguas pero, a cambio, ha exportado términos empleados en tecnología y cultura popular.

Podrá comparar dos o tres idiomas o los cinco, dependiendo de cómo de amplios sean sus intereses.

Actividades prácticas de aprendizaje

- Mientras se desplaza por su casa, lugar de trabajo o colegio, intente mirar las páginas que se refieren a ese lugar. Podrá entonces cerrar el libro, mirar a su alrededor y ver cuántos objetos o características puede nombrar.
- Desafíese a usted mismo a escribir una historia, carta o diálogo empleando tantos términos de una página concreta como le sea posible. Esto le ayudará a retener vocabulario y recordar la ortografía. Si quiere ir progresando para poder escribir un texto más largo, comience con frases que incorporen 2 ó 3 palabras.
- Si tiene buena memoria visual, intente dibujar o calcar objetos del libro; luego cierre el libro y escriba las palabras correspondientes debajo del dibujo.
- Cuando se sienta más seguro, escoja palabras del índice de uno de los idiomas y vea si sabe lo que significan antes de consultar la página correspondiente para comprobarlo.

come usare questo libro

Che stiate imparando una lingua nuova a scopo di lavoro, per diletto o in preparazione per una vacanza all'estero, o desideriate estendere il vostro vocabolario in una lingua che vi è già familiare, questo dizionario è uno strumento di apprendimento prezioso che potete usare in vari modi diversi.

Quando imparate una lingua nuova, cercate le parole affini per origine (che sono quindi simili nelle varie lingue) ma occhio alle false analogie (vocaboli che sembrano uguali ma hanno significati molto diversi). Questo dizionario mostra inoltre come le lingue hanno influito l'una sull'altra (l'inglese, per esempio, ha importato dalle altre lingue europee molti vocaboli relativi agli alimenti ma ne ha esportati molti altri relativi alla tecnologia e alla cultura popolare) e vi consente di confrontare due, tre o anche tutte e cinque le lingue, a seconda di quelle che vi interessano.

Attività pratiche di apprendimento

- Girando per casa, in ufficio, a scuola, guardate le pagine relative all'ambiente in cui vi trovate, poi chiudete il libro, guardatevi attorno e cercate di ricordare il nome del maggior numero possibile di oggetti e strutture.
- Provate a scrivere un racconto, una lettera o un dialogo usando il maggior numero possibile dei vocaboli riportati su di una pagina in particolare. Vi aiuterà a memorizzare i vocaboli e a ricordare come si scrivono. Se volete scrivere testi più lunghi, cominciate con delle frasi che comprendano 2 o 3 delle parole.
- Se avete una memoria molto visiva, prendete un foglio di carta e disegnatevi o ricopiatevi le immagini che appaiono nel libro, quindi chiudete il libro e scrivete le parole sotto alle immagini.
- Quando vi sentite più sicuri, scegliete dei vocaboli dall'indice di una lingua straniera e cercate di ricordarne i significati, trovando poi le pagine corrispondenti per verificare che siano giusti.

people
les gens
die Menschen
la gente
le persone

body • le corps • der Körper • el cuerpo • il corpo

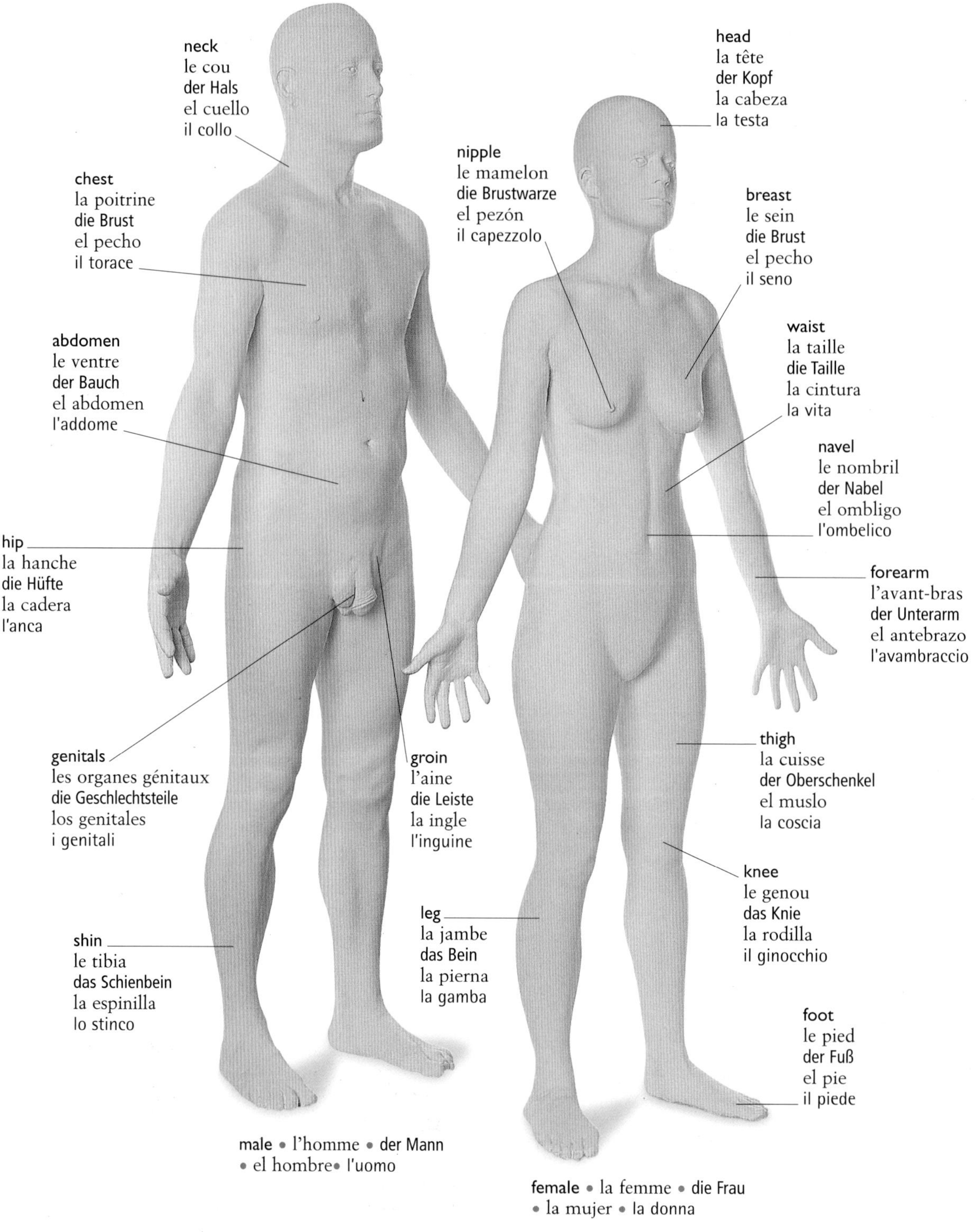

male • l'homme • der Mann • el hombre • l'uomo

female • la femme • die Frau • la mujer • la donna

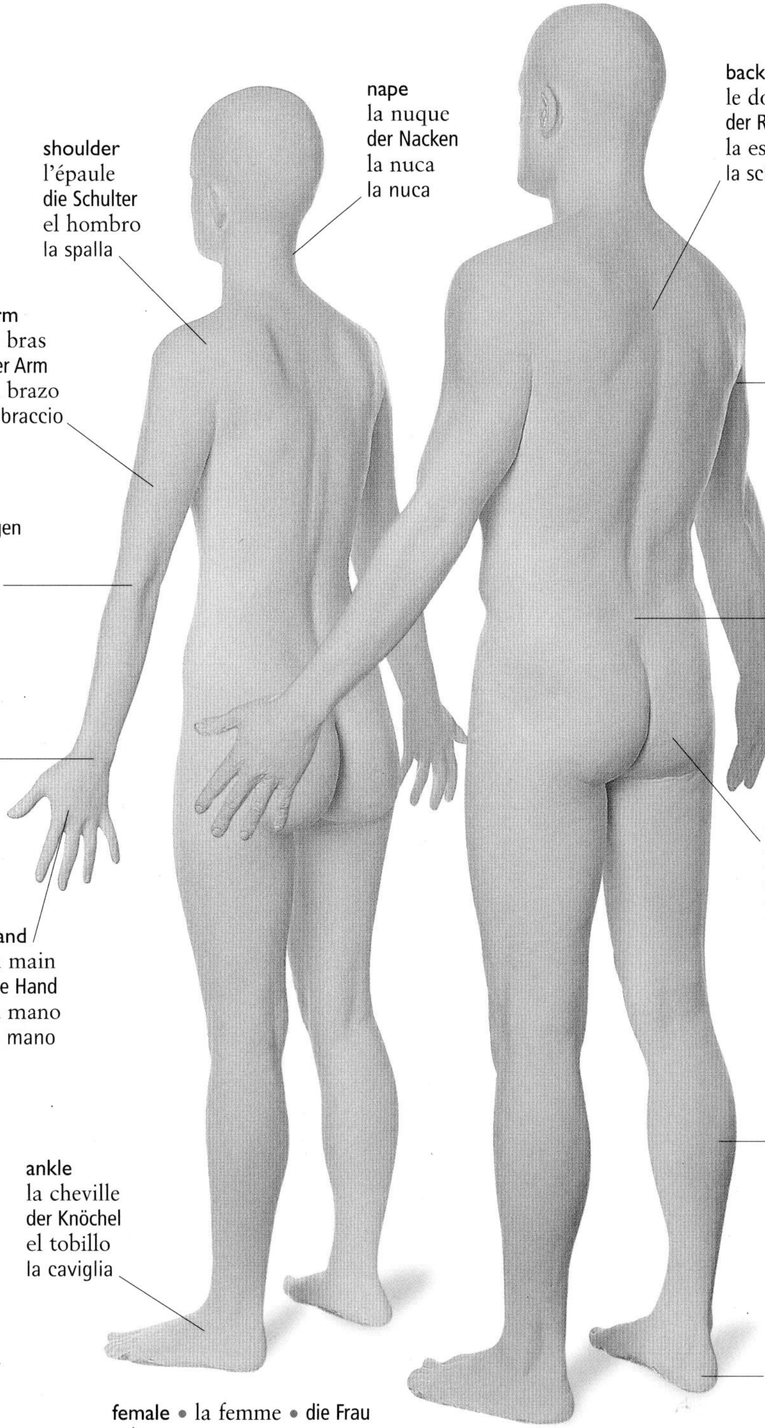

female • la femme • die Frau • la mujer • la donna

male • l'homme • der Mann • el hombre • l'uomo

face • le visage • das Gesicht • la cara • la faccia

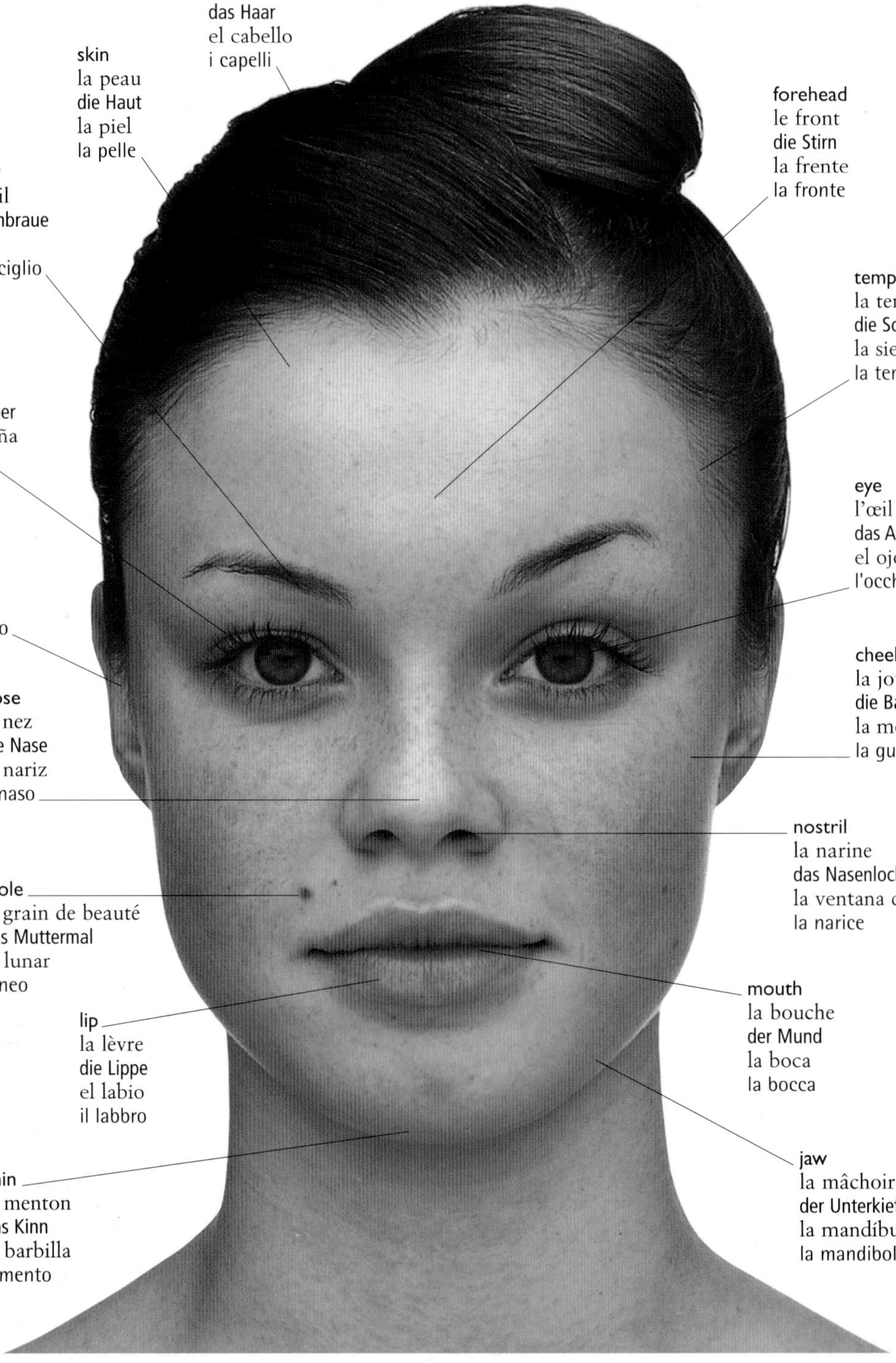
hair
les cheveux
das Haar
el cabello
i capelli
skin
la peau
die Haut
la piel
la pelle
forehead
le front
die Stirn
la frente
la fronte
eyebrow
le sourcil
die Augenbraue
la ceja
il sopracciglio
temple
la tempe
die Schläfe
la sien
la tempia
eyelash
le cil
die Wimper
la pestaña
il ciglio
eye
l'œil
das Auge
el ojo
l'occhio
ear
l'oreille
das Ohr
la oreja
l'orecchio
cheek
la joue
die Backe
la mejilla
la guancia
nose
le nez
die Nase
la nariz
il naso
nostril
la narine
das Nasenloch
la ventana de la nariz
la narice
mole
le grain de beauté
das Muttermal
el lunar
il neo
mouth
la bouche
der Mund
la boca
la bocca
lip
la lèvre
die Lippe
el labio
il labbro
jaw
la mâchoire
der Unterkiefer
la mandíbula
la mandibola
chin
le menton
das Kinn
la barbilla
il mento

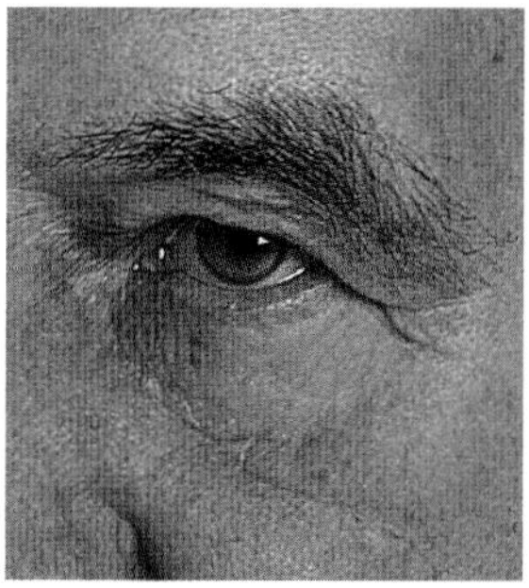

wrinkle • la ride • die Falte • la arruga • la ruga

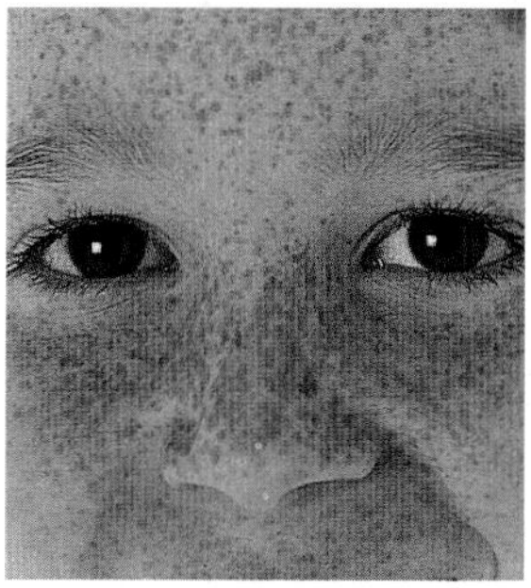

freckle • la tache de rousseur • die Sommersprosse • la peca • la lentiggine

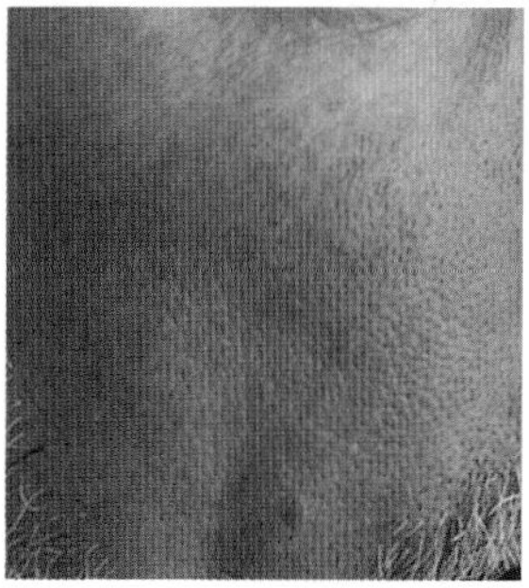

pore • le pore • die Pore • el poro • il poro

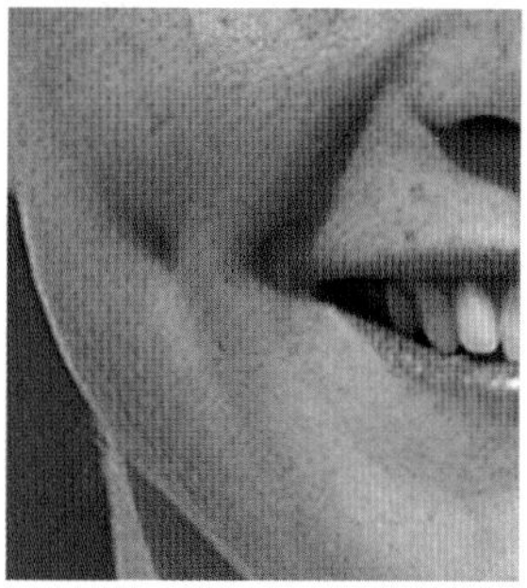

dimple • la fossette • das Grübchen • el hoyuelo • la fossetta

hand • la main • die Hand • la mano • la mano

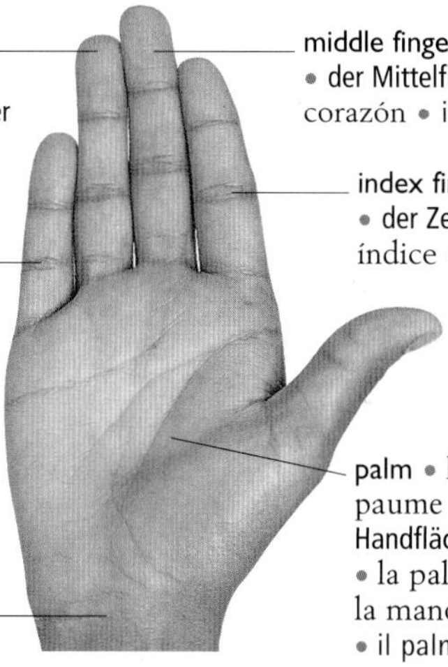

ring finger
l'annulaire
der Ringfinger
el anular
l'anulare

middle finger • le majeur • der Mittelfinger • el dedo corazón • il medio

index finger • l'index • der Zeigefinger • el índice • l'indice

little finger
l'auriculaire
der kleine Finger
el meñique
il mignolo

wrist
le poignet
das Handgelenk
la muñeca
il polso

palm • la paume • die Handfläche • la palma de la mano • il palmo

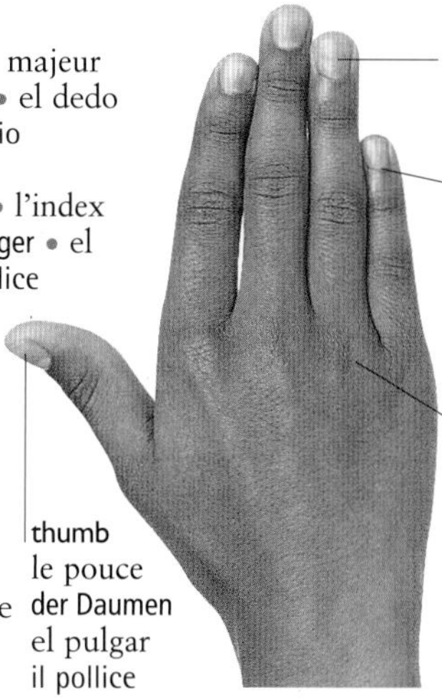

thumb
le pouce
der Daumen
el pulgar
il pollice

nail • l'ongle • der Fingernagel • la uña • l'unghia

cuticle
la cuticule
die Nagelhaut
la cutícula
la cuticola

knuckle • le nœud de l'articulation • der Handknöchel • el nudillo • la nocca

fist • le poing • die Faust • el puño • il pugno

foot • le pied • der Fuß • el pie • il piede

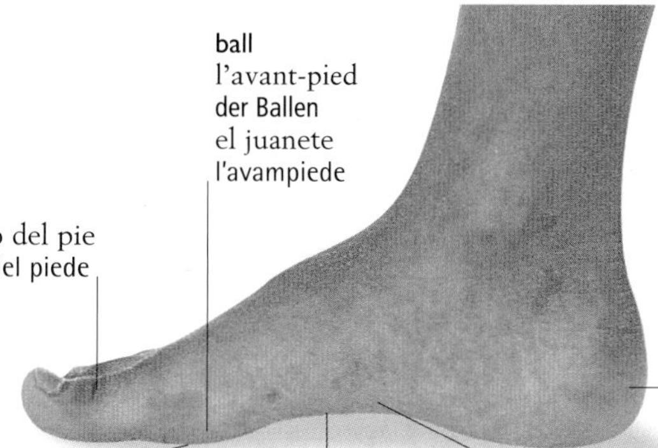

toe
l'orteil
der Zeh
el dedo del pie
il dito del piede

ball
l'avant-pied
der Ballen
el juanete
l'avampiede

heel
le talon
die Ferse
el talón
il tallone

sole
la plante du pied
die Fußsohle
la planta del pie
la pianta del piede

instep
• le cou-de-pied
• der Spann • la parte interna del pie• il collo del piede

arch
la cambrure
das Gewölbe
el arco plantar
l'arco plantare

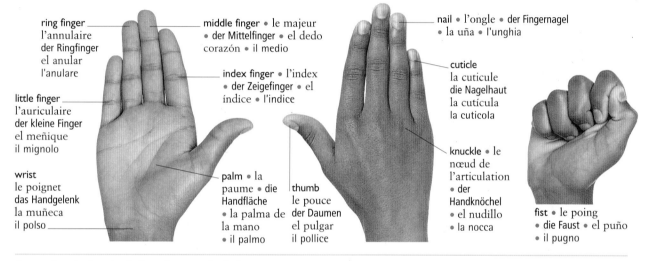

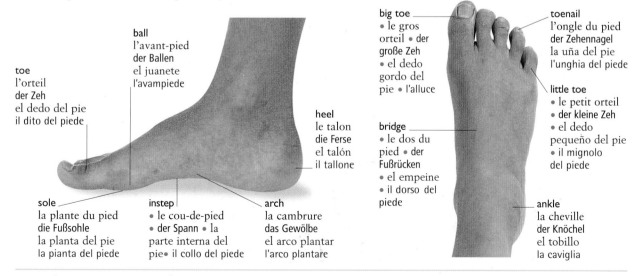

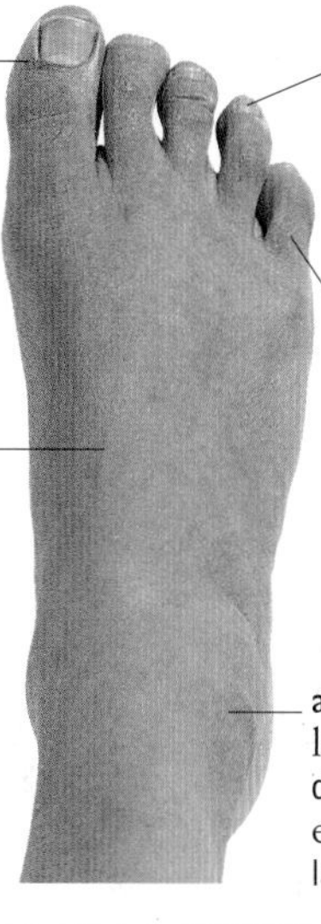

big toe
• le gros orteil • der große Zeh • el dedo gordo del pie • l'alluce

toenail
l'ongle du pied
der Zehennagel
la uña del pie
l'unghia del piede

little toe
• le petit orteil
• der kleine Zeh
• el dedo pequeño del pie
• il mignolo del piede

bridge
• le dos du pied • der Fußrücken
• el empeine
• il dorso del piede

ankle
la cheville
der Knöchel
el tobillo
la caviglia

muscles • les muscles • die Muskeln • los músculos • i muscoli

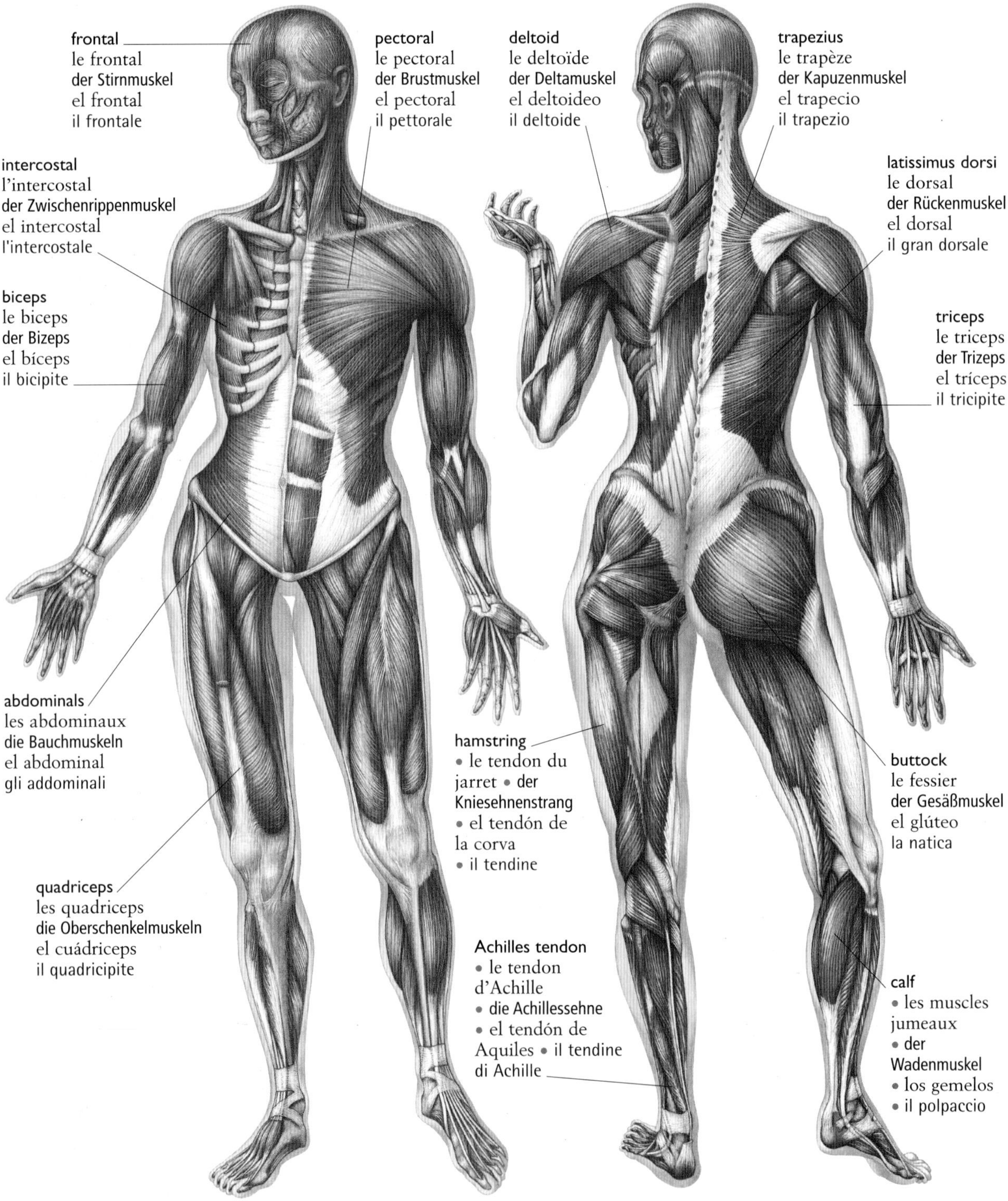
frontal
le frontal
der Stirnmuskel
el frontal
il frontale
pectoral
le pectoral
der Brustmuskel
el pectoral
il pettorale
deltoid
le deltoïde
der Deltamuskel
el deltoideo
il deltoide
trapezius
le trapèze
der Kapuzenmuskel
el trapecio
il trapezio
intercostal
l'intercostal
der Zwischenrippenmuskel
el intercostal
l'intercostale
latissimus dorsi
le dorsal
der Rückenmuskel
el dorsal
il gran dorsale
biceps
le biceps
der Bizeps
el bíceps
il bicipite
triceps
le triceps
der Trizeps
el tríceps
il tricipite
abdominals
les abdominaux
die Bauchmuskeln
el abdominal
gli addominali
hamstring
• le tendon du jarret • der Kniesehnenstrang
• el tendón de la corva
• il tendine
buttock
le fessier
der Gesäßmuskel
el glúteo
la natica
quadriceps
les quadriceps
die Oberschenkelmuskeln
el cuádriceps
il quadricipite
Achilles tendon
• le tendon d'Achille
• die Achillessehne
• el tendón de Aquiles • il tendine di Achille
calf
• les muscles jumeaux
• der Wadenmuskel
• los gemelos
• il polpaccio

skeleton • le squelette • das Skelett • el esqueleto • lo scheletro

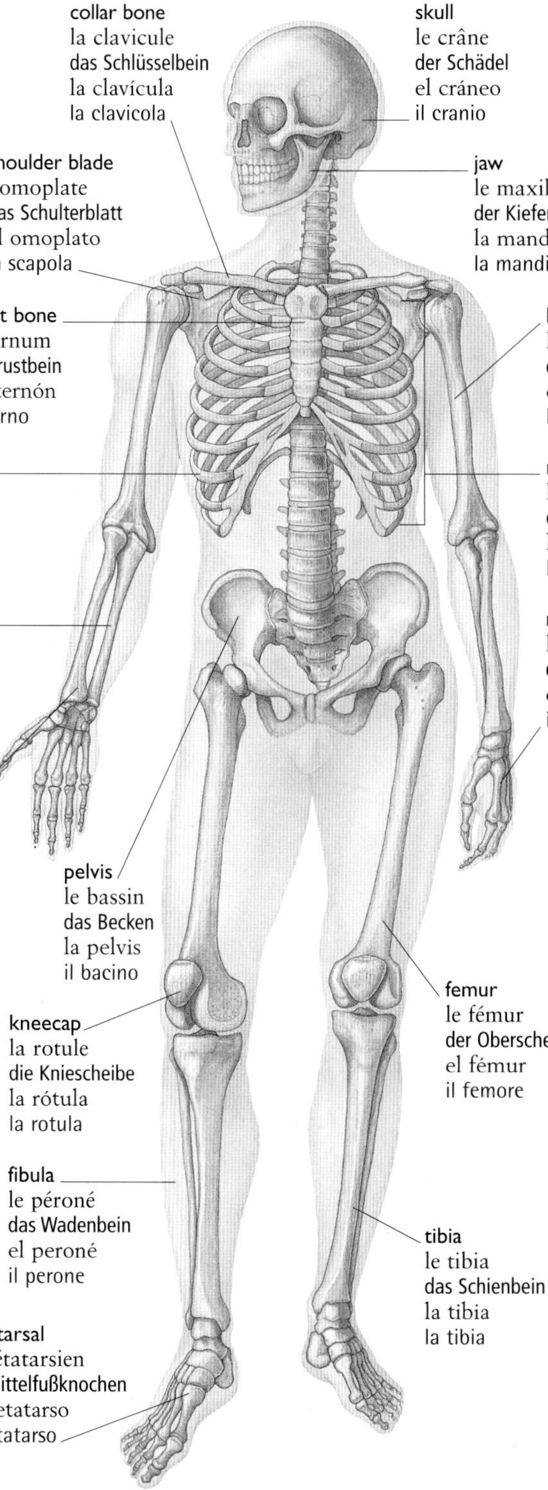

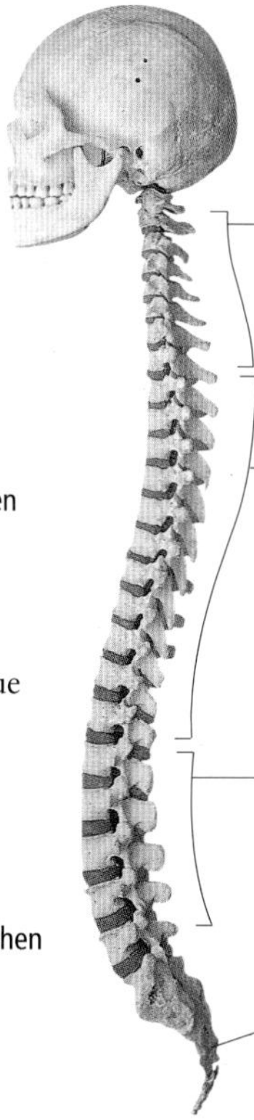

spine • la colonne vertébrale • die Wirbelsäule • la espina dorsal • la spina dorsale

joint • l'articulation • das Gelenk • la articulación • l'articolazione

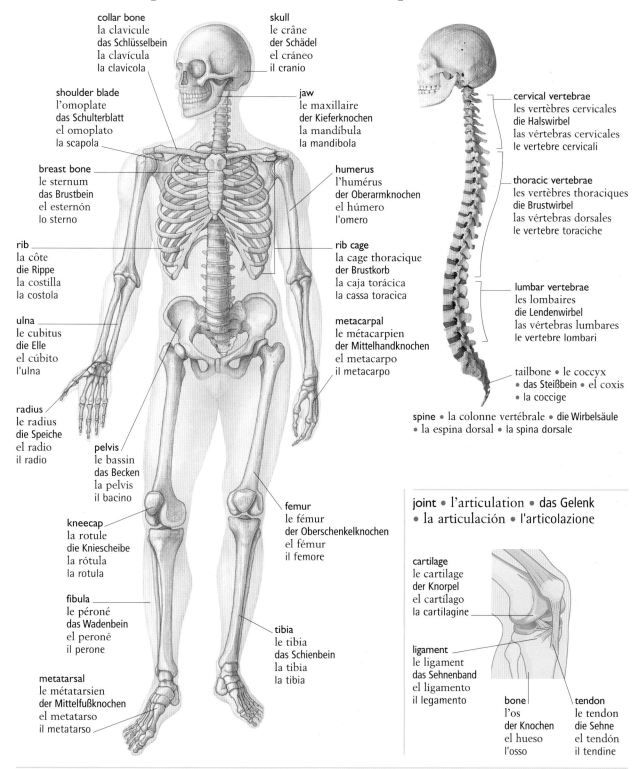

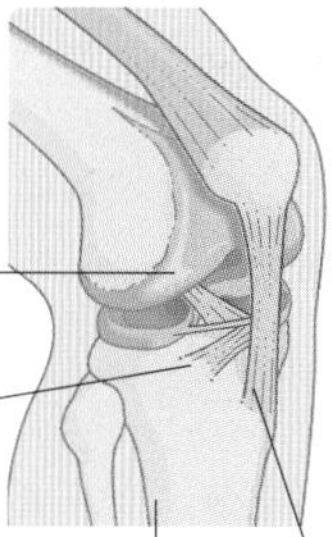

internal organs • les organes internes • die inneren Organe • los órganos internos • gli organi interni

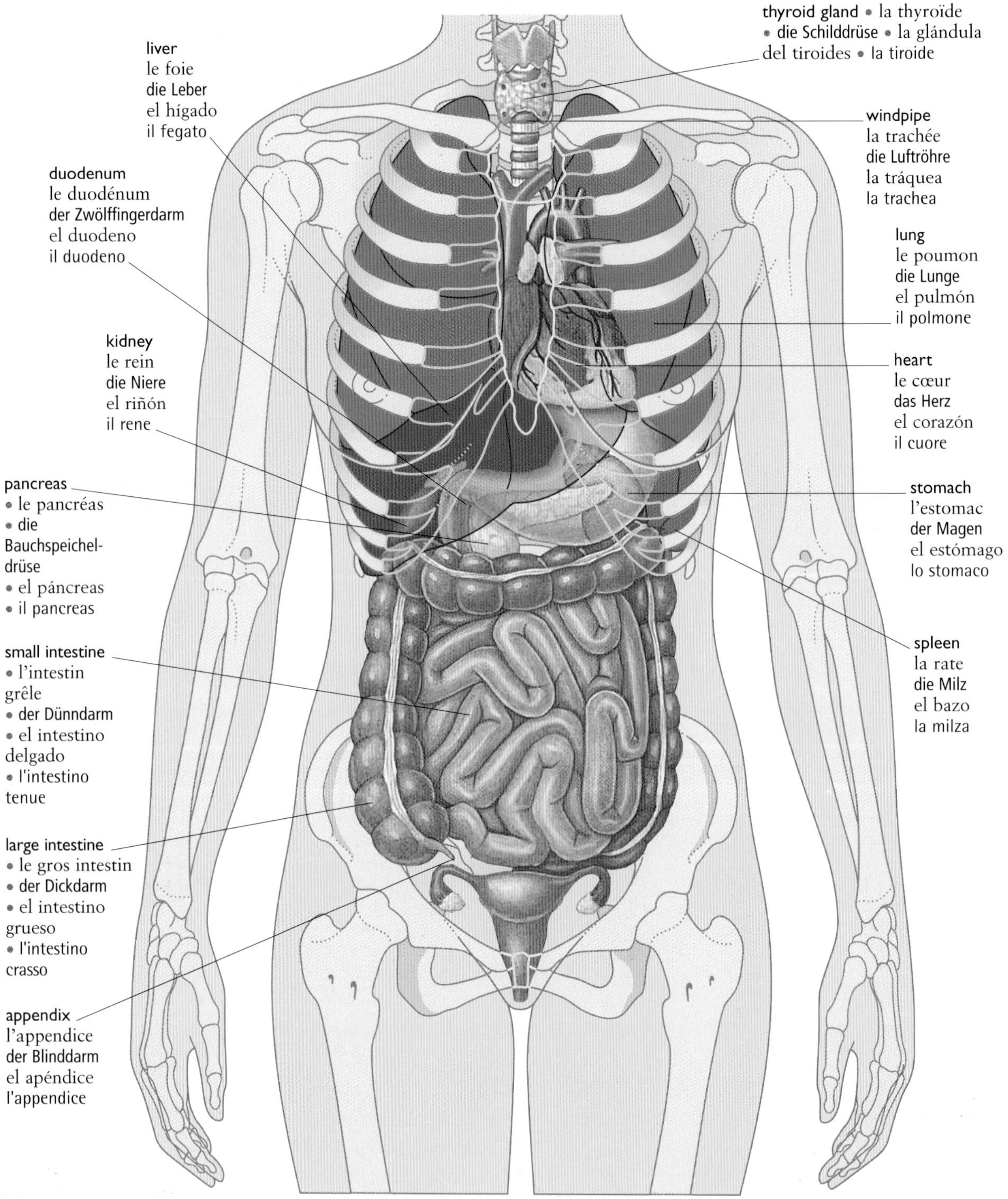

head • la tête • der Kopf • la cabeza • la testa

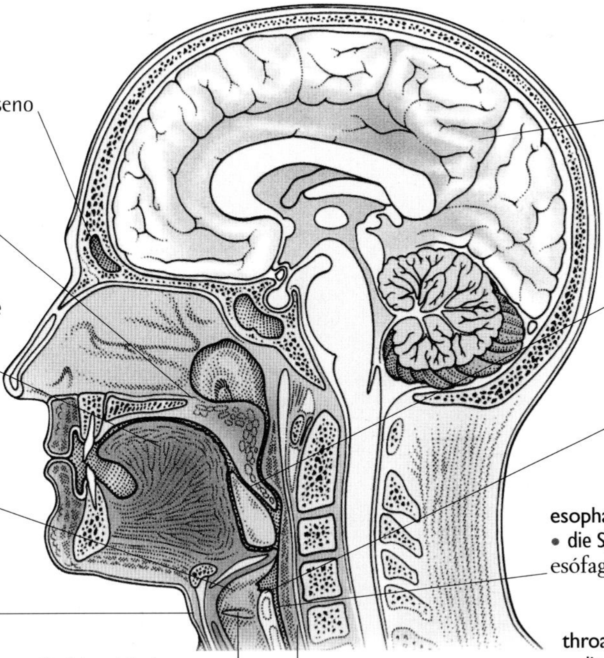

body systems • les systèmes du corps • die Körpersysteme • los sistemas • i sistemi organici

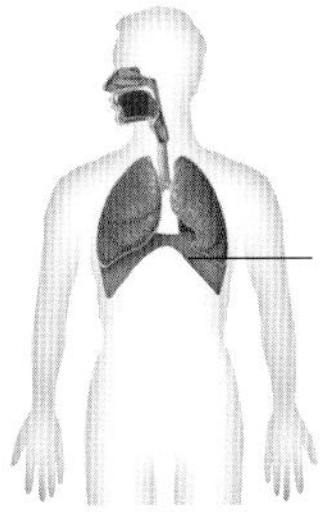

respiratory • respiratoire • das Atmungssystem • respiratorio • respiratorio

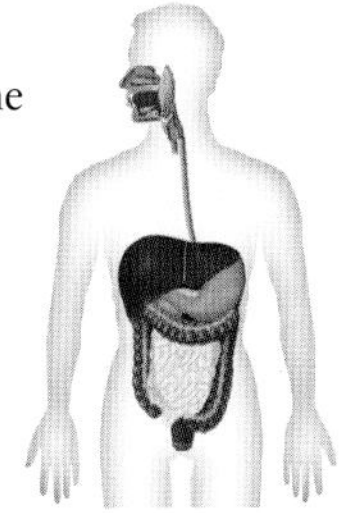

digestive • digestif • das Verdauungssystem • digestivo • digerente

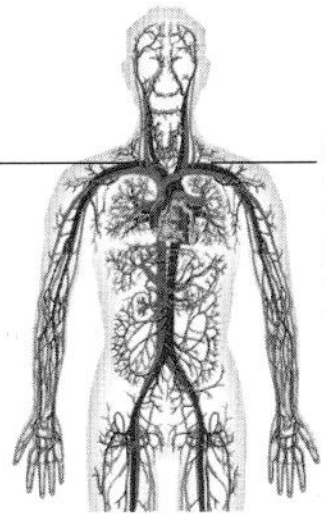

cardiovascular • cardio-vasculaire • das Herz- und Gefäßsystem • cardiovascular • cardiovascolare

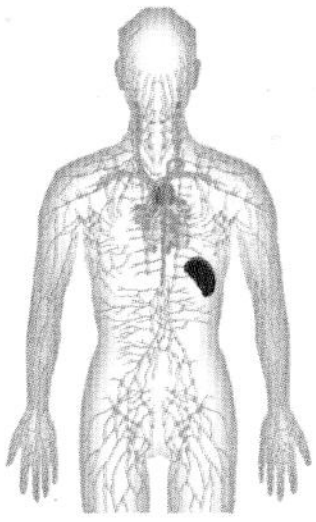

lymphatic • lymphatique • das lymphatische System • linfático • linfatico

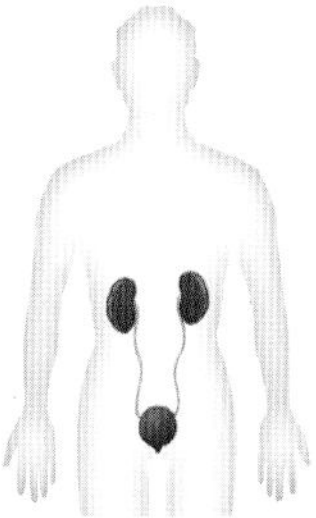

urinary • urinaire • das Harnsystem • urinario • urinario

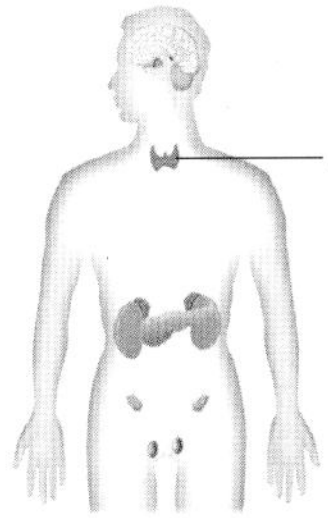

endocrine • endocrine • das endokrine System • endocrino • endocrino

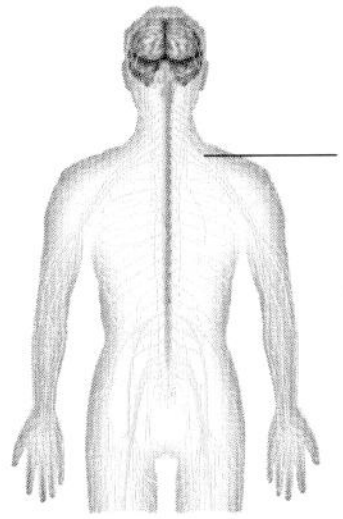

nervous • nerveux • das Nervensystem • nervioso • nervoso

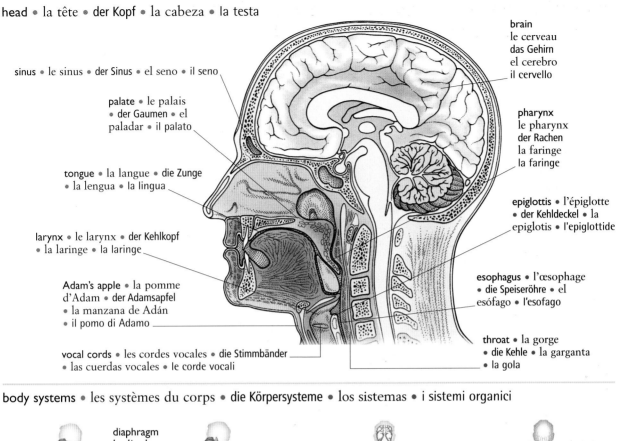

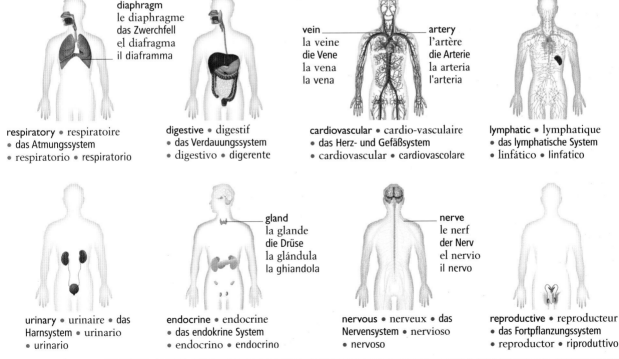

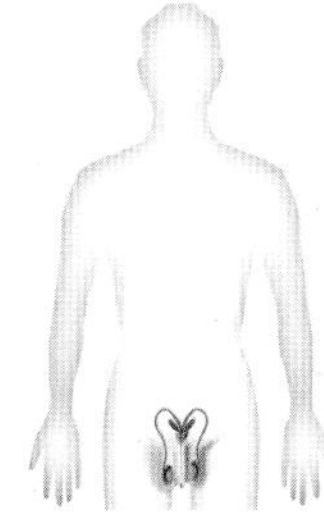

reproductive • reproducteur • das Fortpflanzungssystem • reproductor • riproduttivo

reproductive organs • les organes de reproduction • die Fortpflanzungsorgane • los órganos reproductores • gli organi riproduttivi

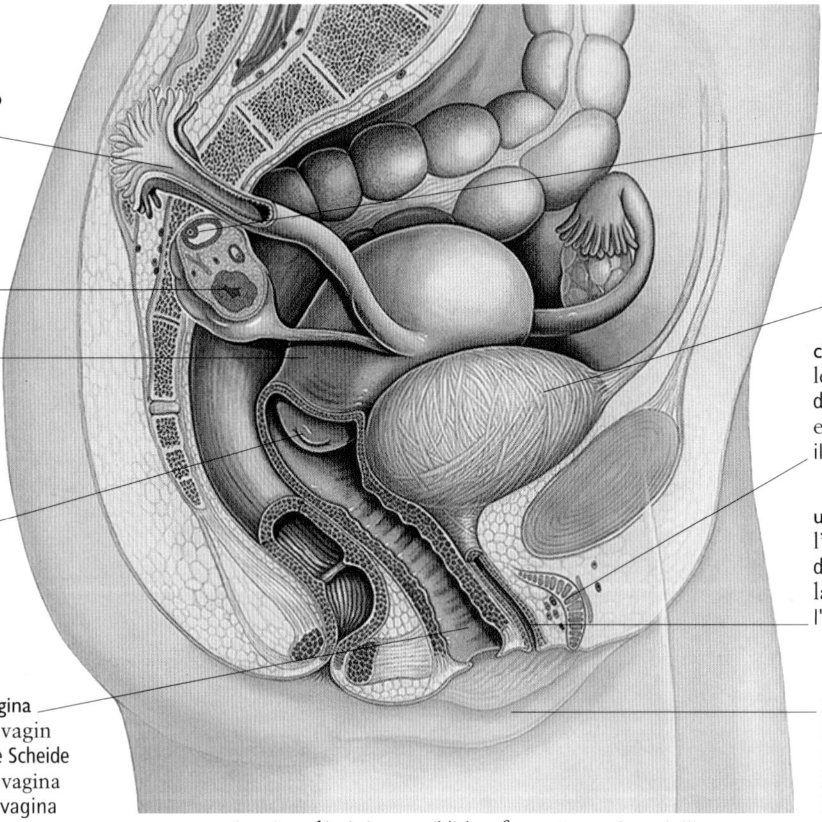

female • féminin • weiblich • femenino • femminili

reproduction • la reproduction • die Fortpflanzung • la reproducción • la riproduzione

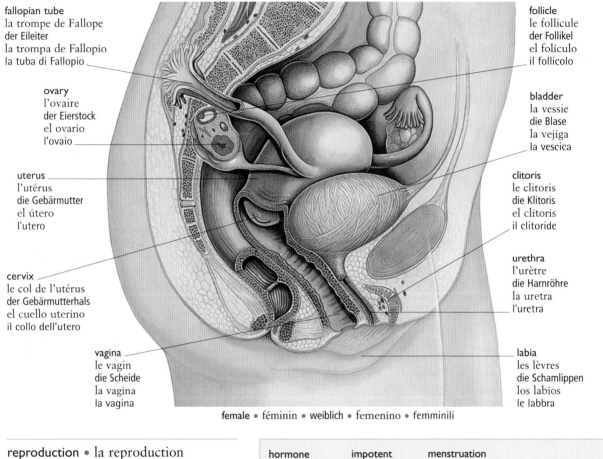

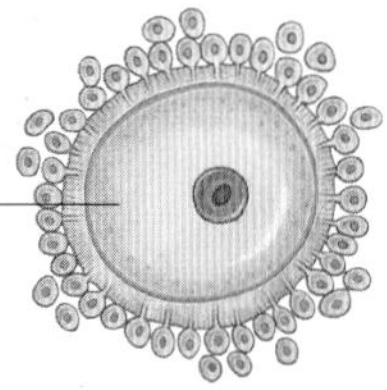

fertilization • la fertilisation • die Befruchtung • la fertilización • la fecondazione

hormone
l'hormone
das Hormon
la hormona
l'ormone

impotent
impuissant
impotent
impotente
impotente

menstruation
les règles
die Menstruation
la menstruación
la mestruazione

ovulation
l'ovulation
der Eisprung
la ovulación
l'ovulazione

fertile
fécond
fruchtbar
fértil
fecondo

intercourse
les rapports sexuels
der Geschlechtsverkehr
el coito
il coito

infertile
stérile
steril
estéril
sterile

conceive
concevoir
empfangen
concebir
concepire

sexually transmitted disease
la maladie sexuellement transmissible
die Geschlechtskrankheit
la enfermedad de transmisión sexual
la malattia sessualmente trasmessa

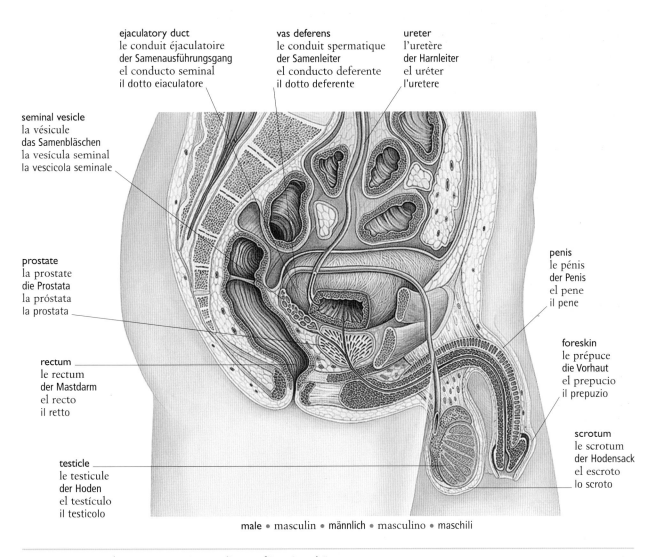

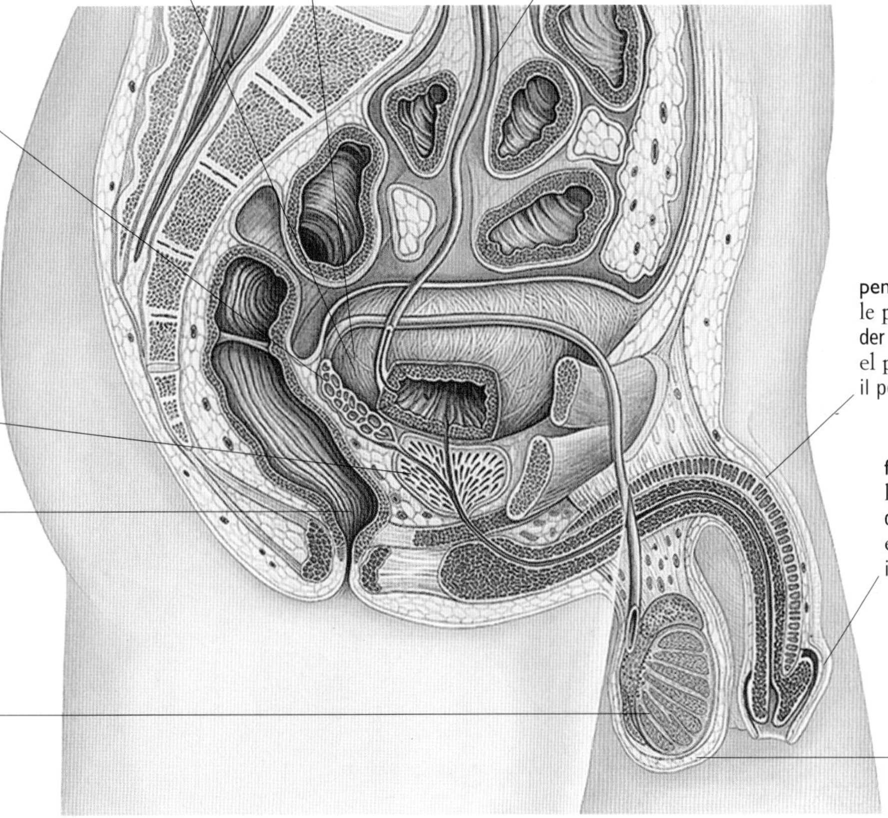

male • masculin • männlich • masculino • maschili

contraception • la contraception • die Empfängnisverhütung • la anticoncepción • la contraccezione

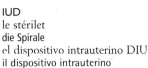

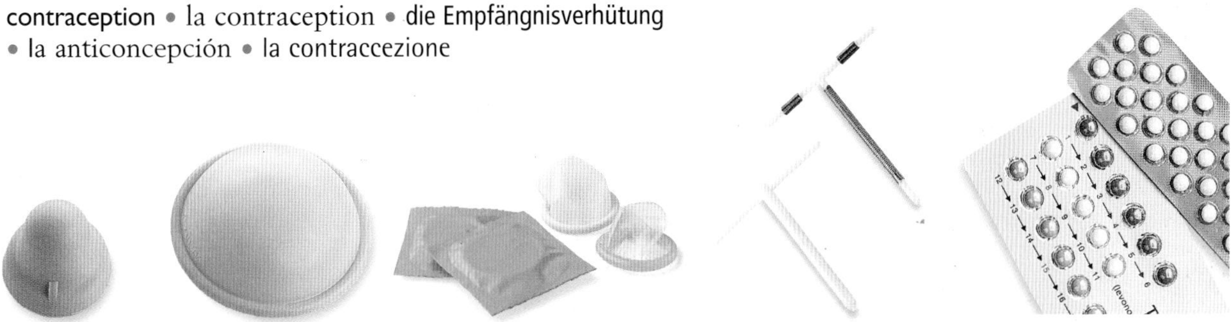

cervical cap
le pessaire
das Pessar
el anillo cervical
il cappuccio cervicale

diaphragm
le diaphragme
das Diaphragma
el diafragma
il diaframma

condom
le condom
das Kondom
el condón
il preservativo

IUD
le stérilet
die Spirale
el dispositivo intrauterino DIU
il dispositivo intrauterino

pill
la pilule
die Pille
la pastilla
la pillola

family • la famille • die Familie • la familia • la famiglia

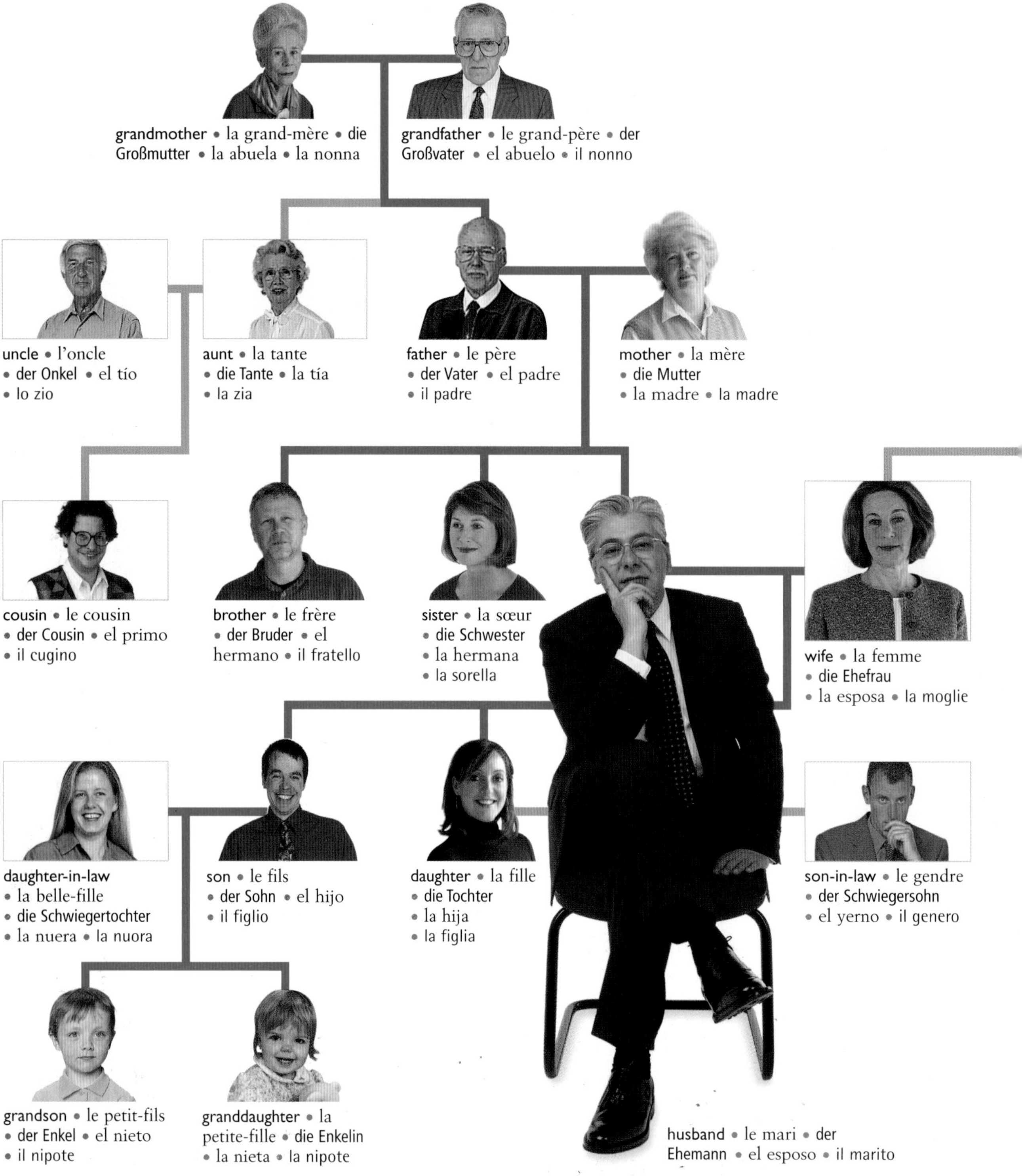
grandmother • la grand-mère • die Großmutter • la abuela • la nonna
grandfather • le grand-père • der Großvater • el abuelo • il nonno
uncle • l'oncle • der Onkel • el tío • lo zio
aunt • la tante • die Tante • la tía • la zia
father • le père • der Vater • el padre • il padre
mother • la mère • die Mutter • la madre • la madre
cousin • le cousin • der Cousin • el primo • il cugino
brother • le frère • der Bruder • el hermano • il fratello
sister • la sœur • die Schwester • la hermana • la sorella
wife • la femme • die Ehefrau • la esposa • la moglie
daughter-in-law • la belle-fille • die Schwiegertochter • la nuera • la nuora
son • le fils • der Sohn • el hijo • il figlio
daughter • la fille • die Tochter • la hija • la figlia
son-in-law • le gendre • der Schwiegersohn • el yerno • il genero
grandson • le petit-fils • der Enkel • el nieto • il nipote
granddaughter • la petite-fille • die Enkelin • la nieta • la nipote
husband • le mari • der Ehemann • el esposo • il marito

relatives les parents die Verwandten los parientes i parenti	parents les parents die Eltern los padres i genitori	grandchildren les petits-enfants die Enkelkinder los nietos i nipoti	stepmother la belle-mère die Stiefmutter la madrastra la matrigna	stepson le beau-fils der Stiefsohn el hijastro il figliastro	generation la génération die Generation la generación la generazione
grandparents les grands-parents die Großeltern los abuelos i nonni	children les enfants die Kinder los niños i bambini	stepfather le beau-père der Stiefvater el padrastro il patrigno	stepdaughter la belle-fille die Stieftochter la hijastra la figliastra	partner le/la partenaire der Partner/die Partnerin el/la compañero/-a il/la compagno/-a	twins les jumeaux die Zwillinge los gemelos i gemelli

mother-in-law • la belle-mère • die Schwiegermutter • la suegra • la suocera

father-in-law • le beau-père • der Schwiegervater • el suegro • il suocero

brother-in-law • le beau-frère • der Schwager • el cuñado • il cognato

sister-in-law • la belle-sœur • die Schwägerin • la cuñada • la cognata

niece • la nièce • die Nichte • la sobrina • la nipote

nephew • le neveu • der Neffe • el sobrino • il nipote

titles • les titres • die Anreden • los tratamientos • gli appellativi

Mr
Monsieur
Herr
Señor
Signore

Mrs
Madame
Frau
Señora
Signora

Miss
Mademoiselle
Fräulein
Señorita
Signorina

stages • les stades • die Stadien • las etapas • le fasi

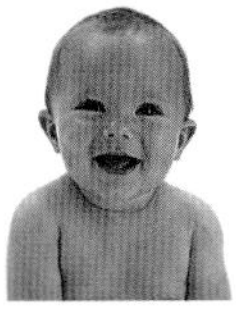

baby • le bébé • das Baby • el bebé • il bimbo

child • l'enfant • das Kind • el niño • il bambino

boy • le garçon • der Junge • el niño • il ragazzo

girl • la fille • das Mädchen • la niña • la ragazza

teenager • l'adolescente • die Jugendliche • la adolescente • l'adolescente

adult • l'adulte • der Erwachsene • el adulto • l'adulto

man • l'homme • der Mann • el hombre • l'uomo

woman • la femme • die Frau • la mujer • la donna

relationships • les relations • die Beziehungen • las relaciones • i rapporti

assistant
l'assistante
die Assistentin
la asistente
l'assistente

manager
le chef
der Chef
el jefe
il capo

business partner
l'associée
die Geschäftspartnerin
la socia
il partner di affari

employer
l'employeuse
die Arbeitgeberin
la empresaria
il datore di lavoro

employee
l'employé
der Arbeitnehmer
el empleado
il dipendente

colleague
le collègue
der Kollege
el compañero
il collega

office • le bureau • das Büro • la oficina • l'ufficio

neighbor • le voisin • der Nachbar • el vecino • il vicino

friend • l'ami • der Freund • el amigo • l'amico

acquaintance • la connaissance • der Bekannte • el conocido • il conoscente

pen pal • le correspondant • der Brieffreund • el amigo por correspondencia • l'amico di penna

boyfriend
le petit ami
der Freund
el novio
il ragazzo

girlfriend
la petite amie
die Freundin
la novia
la ragazza

couple • le couple • das Paar • la pareja • la coppia

fiancé
le fiancé
der Verlobte
el prometido
il fidanzato

fiancée
la fiancée
die Verlobte
la prometida
la fidanzata

engaged couple • les fiancés • die Verlobten • la pareja • i fidanzati

emotions • les émotions • die Gefühle • las emociones • le emozioni

smile
le sourire
das Lächeln
la sonrisa
il sorriso

happy • heureux • glücklich • contento • felice

sad • triste • traurig • triste • triste

excited • excité • aufgeregt • entusiasmado • eccitato

bored • ennuyé • gelangweilt • aburrido • annoiato

surprised • surpris • überrascht • sorprendido • sorpreso

scared • effrayé • erschrocken • asustado • spaventato

frown • le froncement de sourcils • das Stirnrunzeln • el ceño fruncido • aggrottare le sopracciglia

angry • fâché • verärgert • enfadado • arrabbiato

confused • confus • verwirrt • confuso • confuso

worried • inquiet • besorgt • preocupado • preoccupato

nervous • nerveux • nervös • nervioso • nervoso

proud • fier • stolz • orgulloso • fiero

confident • confiant • selbstsicher • seguro de sí mismo • fiducioso

embarrassed • gêné • verlegen • avergonzado • imbarazzato

shy • timide • schüchtern • tímido • timido

upset consterné bestürzt triste turbato	**laugh** *(v)* rire lachen reír ridere	**sigh** *(v)* soupirer seufzen suspirar sospirare	**shout** *(v)* crier schreien gritar gridare
shocked choqué schockiert horrorizado scioccato	**cry** *(v)* pleurer weinen llorar piangere	**faint** *(v)* s'évanouir in Ohnmacht fallen desmayarse svenire	**yawn** *(v)* bâiller gähnen bostezar sbadigliare

life events • les événements de la vie • die Ereignisse des Lebens • los acontecimientos de una vida • gli avvenimenti della vita

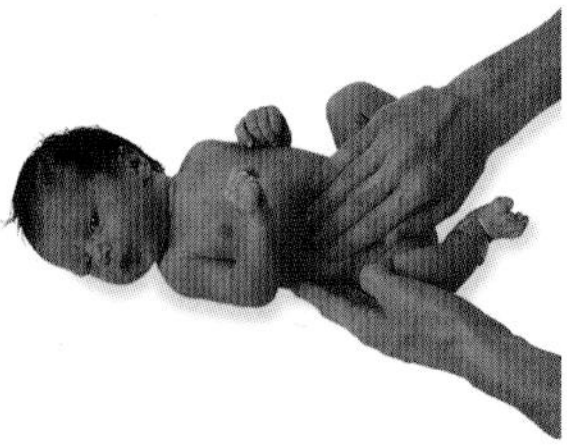

be born *(v)* • naître • geboren werden • nacer • nascere

start school *(v)* • commencer à l'école • zur Schule kommen • empezar el colegio • iniziare la scuola

make friends *(v)* • faire des amis • sich befreunden • hacer amigos • fare amicizia

graduate *(v)* • obtenir sa licence • graduieren • graduarse • laurearsi

get a job *(v)* • trouver un emploi • eine Stelle bekommen • conseguir un trabajo • trovare un lavoro

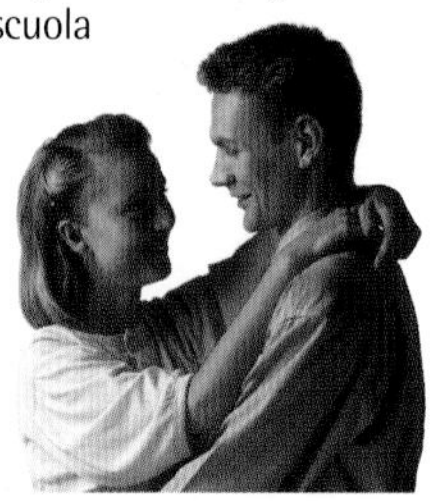

fall in love *(v)* • tomber amoureux • sich verlieben • enamorarse • innamorarsi

get married *(v)* • se marier • heiraten • casarse • sposarsi

have a baby *(v)* • avoir un bébé • ein Baby bekommen • tener un hijo • avere un bambino

wedding • le mariage • die Hochzeit • la boda • il matrimonio

divorce • le divorce • die Scheidung • el divorcio • il divorzio

funeral • l'enterrement • das Begräbnis • el funeral • il funerale

christening
le baptême
die Taufe
el bautizo
il battesimo

bar mitzvah
la bar-mitsvah
die Bar Mizwa
el bar mitzvah
il bar mitzvah

anniversary
l'anniversaire de mariage
der Hochzeitstag
el aniversario
l'anniverario

emigrate *(v)*
émigrer
emigrieren
emigrar
emigrare

retire *(v)*
prendre sa retraite
in den Ruhestand treten
retirarse
andare in pensione

die *(v)*
mourir
sterben
morir
morire

make a will *(v)*
faire son testament
sein Testament machen
hacer testamento
fare testamento

birth certificate
l'acte de naissance
die Geburtsurkunde
el acta de nacimiento
il certificato di nascita

wedding reception
le repas de noces
die Hochzeitsfeier
el banquete de boda
il ricevimento nuziale

honeymoon
le voyage de noces
die Hochzeitsreise
la luna de miel
il viaggio di nozze

celebrations • les fêtes • die Feste • las celebraciones • le celebrazioni

birthday party
la fête
die Geburtstagsfeier
la fiesta de cumpleaños
la festa di compleanno

card
la carte
die Karte
la tarjeta
il biglietto d'auguri

birthday • l'anniversaire • der Geburtstag • el cumpleaños • il compleanno

present
le cadeau
das Geschenk
el regalo
il regalo

Christmas • le Noël • das Weihnachten • la Navidad • il Natale

New Year • le Nouvel An • das Neujahr • el Año Nuevo • il Capodanno

carnival • le carnaval • der Karneval • el carnaval • il carnevale

procession
le défilé
der Umzug
el desfile
la processione

ribbon
le ruban
das Band
la cinta
il nastro

Thanksgiving • la fête de Thanksgiving • der Thanksgiving Day • el día de Acción de Gracias • il Giorno del Ringraziamento

Easter • Pâques • das Ostern • la Pascua • la Pasqua

Halloween • la veille de la Toussaint • das Halloween • el día de Halloween • la Festa de Halloween

festivals • les fêtes • die Feste • los festivales • le feste

Passover • la Pâque • das Passah • la Pascua judía • la Pasqua ebraica

Ramadan • le Ramadan • der Ramadan • el Ramadán • il Ramadan

Diwali • la Diwali • das Diwali • el Diwali • il Diwali

appearance
l’apparence
die äußere Erscheinung
la apariencia
l’aspetto

children's clothing • les vêtements d'enfants • die Kinderkleidung • la ropa de niño • gli abiti per il bambino

baby • le bébé • das Baby • el bebé • il bimbo

snowsuit • la combinaison de neige • der Schneeanzug • el traje de invierno • la tutina da neve

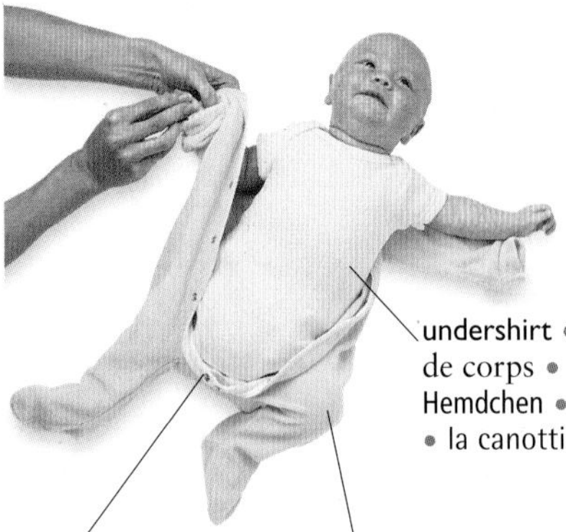

undershirt • le tricot de corps • das Hemdchen • la camiseta • la canottiera

snap
le bouton-pression
der Druckknopf
el botón
il bottone automatico

onesize • la grenouillère • der Strampelanzug • el mameluco • la tutina

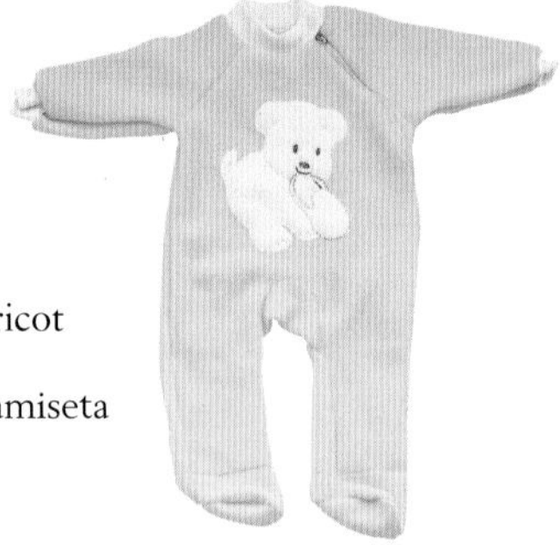

sleeper • le pyjama • der Schlafanzug • el mameluco • il pigiamino

romper suit • la combinaison-short • der Spielanzug • el mameluco sin pies • il pagliaccetto

bib • le bavoir • das Lätzchen • el babero • il bavaglino

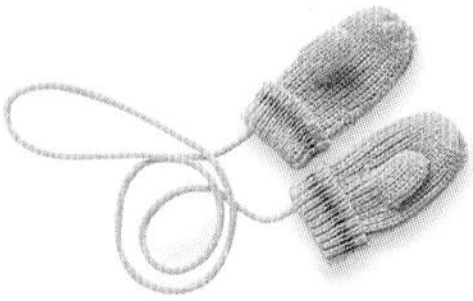

mittens • les moufles • die Babyhandschuhe • los guantes • i guanti

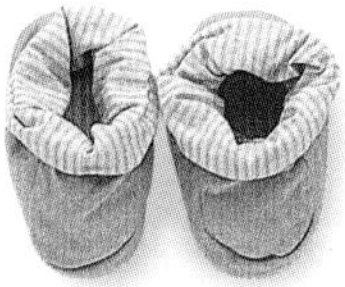

booties • les chaussons • die Babyschuhe • las botas • le scarpette

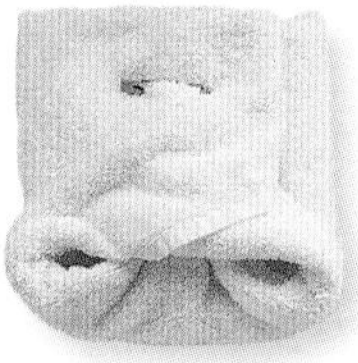

cloth diaper • la couche éponge • die Stoffwindel • el pañal de felpa • il pannolino di spugna

disposable diaper • la couche jetable • die Wegwerfwindel • el pañal desechable • il pannolino usa e getta

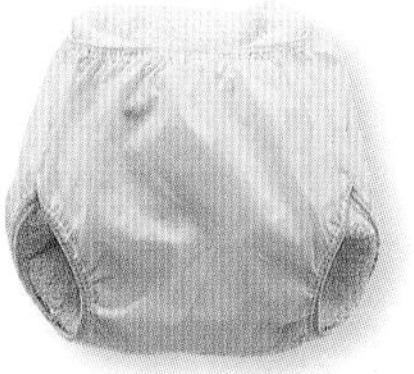

plastic underpants • la culotte en plastique • das Gummihöschen • el calzón de plástico • le mutande di plastica

toddler • le petit enfant • das Kleinkind • el niño pequeño • il bambino piccolo

sun hat • le chapeau de soleil • der Sonnenhut • el gorro para el sol • il cappello per il sole

apron • le tablier • die Schürze • el delantal • il grembiulino

shorts
le bermuda
die Shorts
los shorts
i pantaloncini

overalls • la salopette • die Latzhose • los panatalones con peto • la salopette

t-shirt
le t-shirt
das T-Shirt
la playera
la maglietta

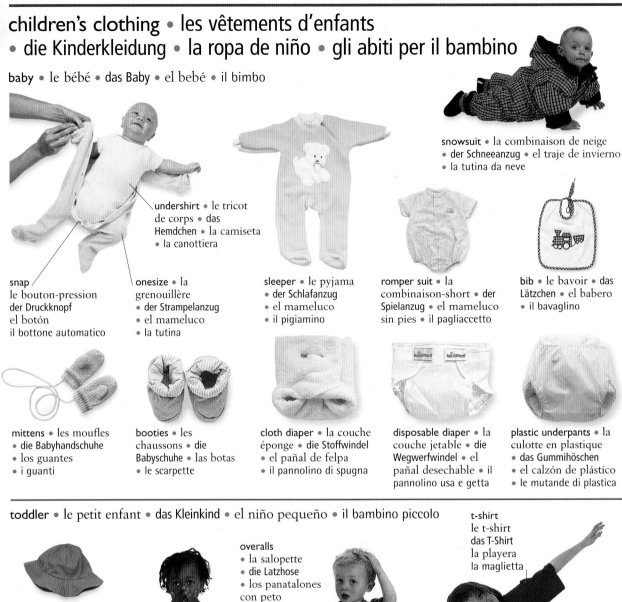

skirt
la jupe
der Rock
la falda
la gonna

child • l'enfant • das Kind • el niño • il bambino

dress • la robe • das Kleid • el vestido • il vestito

sandals
les sandales
die Sandalen
los huaraches
i sandali

summer • l'été • der Sommer • el verano • l'estate

hood
la capuche
die Kapuze
la capucha
il cappuccio

raincoat • l'imperméable • der Regenmantel • el impermeable • l'impermeabile

jeans
le jean
die Jeans
los jeans
i jeans

backpack
le sac à dos
der Rucksack
la mochila
lo zaino

fall • l'automne • der Herbst • el otoño • l'autunno

toggle
le bouton
der Knebelknopf
el broche
l'olivetta

duffel coat • le duffel-coat • der Dufflecoat • el abrigo • il montgomery

scarf
l'écharpe
der Schal
la bufanda
la sciarpa

parka
l'anorak
der Anorak
la chamarra
l'eskimo

galoshes
• les bottes de caoutchouc
• die Gummistiefel
• las botas de agua • le galosce

winter • l'hiver • der Winter • el invierno • l'inverno

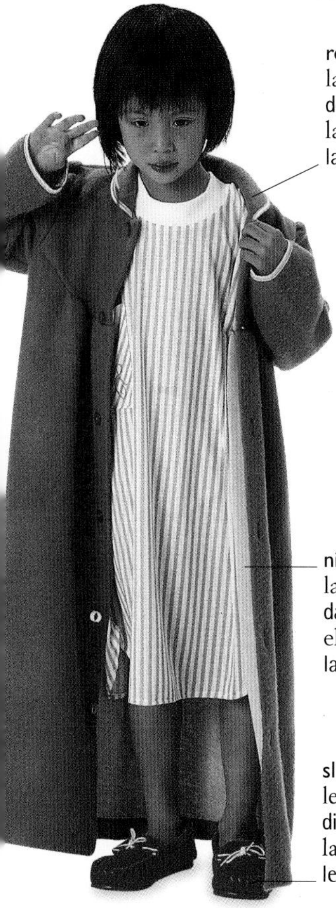

robe
la robe de chambre
der Morgenrock
la bata
la vestaglia

nightgown
la chemise de nuit
das Nachthemd
el camisón
la camicia da notte

slippers
les pantoufles
die Hausschuhe
las pantuflas
le pantofole

nightwear • les vêtements de nuit • die Nachtwäsche • la ropa para dormir • gli indumenti per la notte

logo
le logo
das Logo
el logotipo
il distintivo

sneakers
les baskets
die Sportschuhe
los tenis
le scarpe da ginnastica

soccer uniform • la tenue de foot • der Fußballdress • el uniforme del equipo • la tenuta da calcio

warm-up suit • le survêtement • der Trainingsanzug • los pants • la tuta

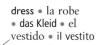

leggings • les leggings • die Leggings • las mallas • il pantacollant

natural fiber la fibre naturelle die Naturfaser la fibra natural la fibra naturale	Is it machine washable? C'est lavable en machine? Ist es waschmaschinenfest? ¿Se puede lavar en lavadora? È lavabile in lavatrice?
synthetic synthétique synthetisch sintético sintetico	Will this fit a two-year-old? C'est la taille pour deux ans? Passt das einem Zweijährigen? ¿Le quedará a un niño de dos años? È la taglia giusta per un bambino di due anni?

men's clothing • les vêtements pour hommes • die Herrenkleidung • la ropa de caballero • l'abbigliamento da uomo

collar
le col
der Kragen
el cuello
il colletto

tie
la cravate
die Krawatte
la corbata
la cravatta

jacket
la veste
die Jacke
la chaqueta
la giacca

cuff
la manchette
die Manschette
el puño
il polsino

pants
le pantalon
die Hose
el saco
i pantaloni

button
le bouton
der Knopf
el botón
il bottone

leather shoes • les chaussures en cuir • die Lederschuhe • los zapatos de piel • le scarpe di cuoio

business suit • le costume der Straßenanzug • el traje • l'abito

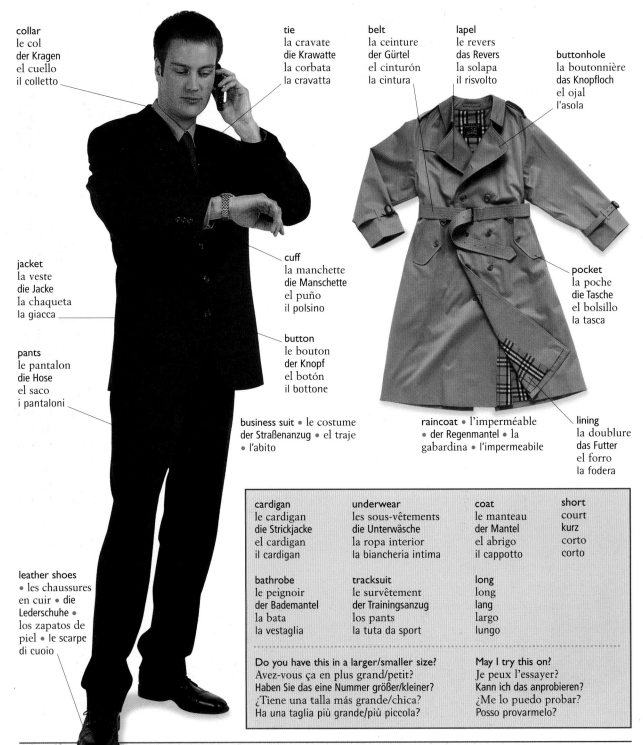

belt
la ceinture
der Gürtel
el cinturón
la cintura

lapel
le revers
das Revers
la solapa
il risvolto

buttonhole
la boutonnière
das Knopfloch
el ojal
l'asola

pocket
la poche
die Tasche
el bolsillo
la tasca

lining
la doublure
das Futter
el forro
la fodera

raincoat • l'imperméable • der Regenmantel • la gabardina • l'impermeabile

cardigan le cardigan die Strickjacke el cardigan il cardigan	underwear les sous-vêtements die Unterwäsche la ropa interior la biancheria intima	coat le manteau der Mantel el abrigo il cappotto	short court kurz corto corto
bathrobe le peignoir der Bademantel la bata la vestaglia	tracksuit le survêtement der Trainingsanzug los pants la tuta da sport	long long lang largo lungo	

Do you have this in a larger/smaller size?
Avez-vous ça en plus grand/petit?
Haben Sie das eine Nummer größer/kleiner?
¿Tiene una talla más grande/chica?
Ha una taglia più grande/più piccola?

May I try this on?
Je peux l'essayer?
Kann ich das anprobieren?
¿Me lo puedo probar?
Posso provarmelo?

blazer • le blazer • der Blazer • el saco • il blazer

sport coat • la veste de sport • das Sportjackett • el saco sport • la giacca sportiva

vest • le gilet • die Weste • el chaleco • il gilet

v-neck
l'encolure en V
der V-Ausschnitt
el cuello en V
il collo a V

crew neck
le col rond
der runde Ausschnitt
el cuello redondo
il girocollo

t-shirt
le t-shirt
das T-Shirt
la camiseta
la maglietta

jeans • le jean • die Jeans • los pantalones vaqueros • i jeans

parka • l'anorak • der Anorak • el chaquetón • il giaccone

sweatshirt • le sweat-shirt • das Sweatshirt • la sudadera • la felpa

shirt • la chemise • das Hemd • la camisa • la camicia

sweater • le pullover • der Pullover • el suéter • il maglione

pajamas • le pyjama • der Schlafanzug • la piyama • il pigiama

undershirt • le tricot de corps • das Unterhemd • la camiseta de tirantes • la canottiera

casual wear • les vêtements sport • die Freizeitkleidung • la ropa casual • il casual

shorts • le short • die Shorts • los shorts • i calzoncini

briefs • le slip • der Slip • los calzoncillos • lo slip

boxer shorts • le caleçon • die Boxershorts • los boxers • i boxer

socks • les chaussettes • die Socken • los calcetines • i calzini

women's clothing • les vêtements pour femmes • die Damenkleidung • la ropa de dama • l'abbigliamento da donna

jacket
la veste
die Jacke
el saco
la giacca

sleeve
la manche
der Ärmel
la manga
la manica

hem
l'ourlet
der Saum
el dobladillo
l'orlo

shoes
les chaussures
die Schuhe
los zapatos
le scarpe

seam
la couture
die Naht
la costura
la cucitura

skirt
la jupe
der Rock
la falda
la gonna

knee-length
à genou
knielang
hasta la rodilla
al ginocchio

hose
le collant
die Strumpfhose
las pantimedias
il collant

formal • habillé • formell • de vestir • formale

strapless
sans bretelles
trägerlos
sin tirantes
senza spalline

ankle length
long
knöchellang
largo
alla caviglia

evening dress • la robe du soir • das Abendkleid • el traje de noche • l'abito da sera

sleeveless
sans manches
ärmellos
sin mangas
senza maniche

dress • la robe • das Kleid • el vestido • il vestito

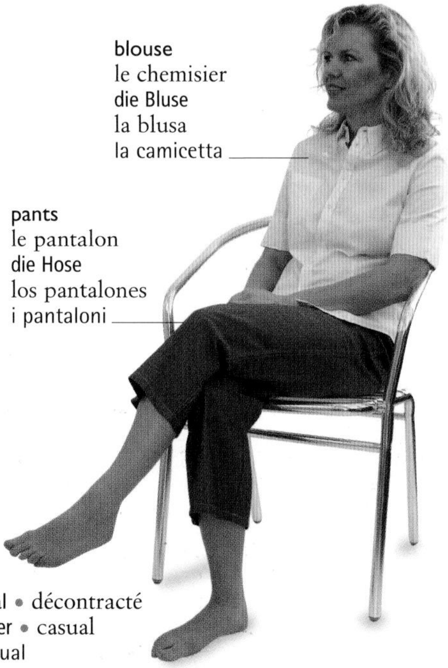

blouse
le chemisier
die Bluse
la blusa
la camicetta

pants
le pantalon
die Hose
los pantalones
i pantaloni

casual • décontracté • leger • casual • casual

lingerie • la lingerie • die Unterwäsche • la lencería • la biancheria intima

robe • le peignoir • der Morgenmantel • la bata • la vestaglia

slip • le caraco • der Unterrock • el fondo • la sottoveste

camisole • la camisole • das Mieder • la camisola • il corpetto

bustier • la guêpière • das Bustier • el corsé con liguero • la guêpière

stocking • le bas • der Strumpf • la media • la calza

panty hose • le collant • die Strumpfhose • las pantimedias • il collant

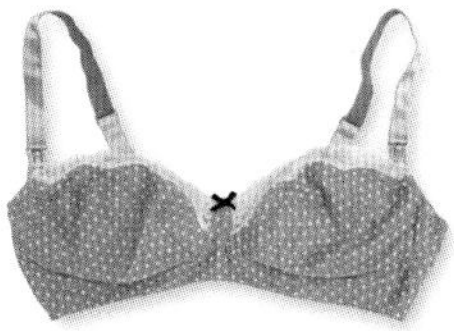

bra • le soutien-gorge • der Büstenhalter • el brassiere • il reggiseno

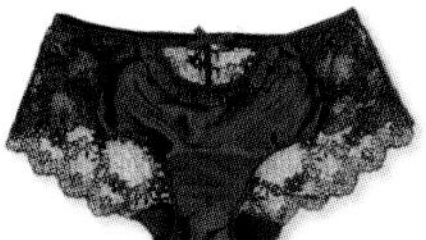

underpants • le slip • der Slip • las pantaletas • lo slip

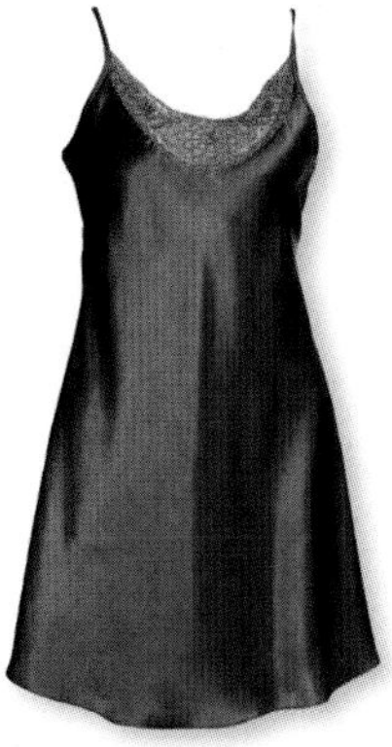

nightgown • la chemise de nuit • das Nachthemd • el camisón • la camicia da notte

wedding • le mariage • die Hochzeit • la boda • il matrimonio

wedding dress • la robe de mariée • das Hochzeitskleid • el vestido de novia • l'abito da sposa

corset
le corset
das Korsett
el corsé
il busto

garter belt
la jarretière
das Strumpfband
la liga
la giarrettiera

shoulder pad
l'épaulette
das Schulterpolster
la hombrera
la spallina

waistband
la ceinture
der Rockbund
la cinturilla
il girovita

tailored
ajusté
gut geschnitten
entallado
attillato

halter neck
dos-nu
rückenfrei
con los hombros al aire
scollo all'Americana

sports bra
le soutient-gorge sport
der Sport-BH
el brassiere deportivo
il reggiseno sportivo

underwire
à armature
mit Formbügeln
con varillas
con armatura

accessories • les accessoires • die Accessoires • los accesorios • gli accessori

cap • la casquette • die Mütze • la gorra • il berretto

hat • le chapeau • der Hut • el sombrero • il cappello

scarf • le foulard • das Halstuch • la mascada • il foulard

buckle
la boucle
die Gürtelschnalle
la hebilla
la fibbia

belt • la ceinture • der Gürtel • el cinturón • la cintura

handle
le manche
der Griff
el mango
il manico

tip
la pointe
die Spitze
la punta
la punta

umbrella • le parapluie • der Regenschirm • el paraguas • l'ombrello

handkerchief • le mouchoir • das Taschentuch • el pañuelo • il fazzoletto

bow tie • le nœud papillon • die Fliege • el moño • la farfalla

tiepin • l'épingle de cravate • die Krawattennadel • el alfiler de corbata • il fermacravatta

gloves • les gants • die Handschuhe • los guantes • i guanti

jewelry • les bijoux • der Schmuck • las joyas • i gioielli

pendant • le pendentif • der Anhänger • el colguije • il pendaglio

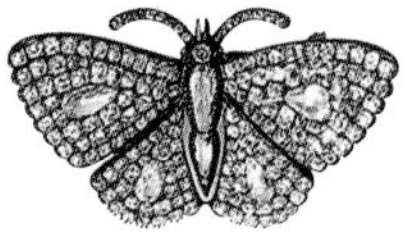

brooch • la broche • die Brosche • el prendedor • la spilla

cufflink • le bouton de manchette • der Manschettenknopf • las mancuernillas • il gemello

link
le maillon
das Glied
el eslabón
la maglia

bracelet • le bracelet • das Armband • la pulsera • il bracciale

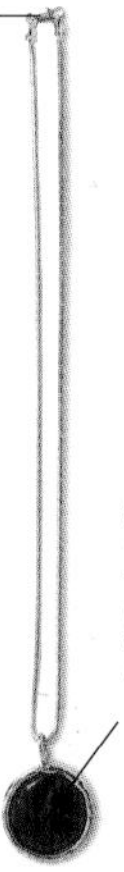

clasp
le fermoir
der Verschluss
el broche
il fermaglio

stone
la pierre
der Edelstein
la piedra
la pietra

chain • la chaîne • die Kette • la cadena • la catena

strand of pearls
le rang de perles
die Perlenkette
el collar de perlas
il filo di perle

earring • la boucle d'oreille • der Ohrring • el arete • l'orecchino

ring
la bague
der Ring
el anillo
l'anello

necklace
le collier
die Halskette
el collar
la collana

watch • la montre • die Uhr • el reloj • l'orologio da polso

jewelry box • la boîte à bijoux • der Schmuckkasten • el joyero • il cofanetto portagioie

bags • les sacs • die Taschen • las bolsas • le borse

wallet • le portefeuille • die Brieftasche • la cartera • il portafoglio

change purse • le porte-monnaie • das Portemonnaie • el monedero • il portamonete

clasp
le fermoir
der Verschluss
el cierre
la cinghia

shoulder bag • le sac à bandoulière • die Umhängetasche • la bolsa • la borsa a tracolla

shoulder strap
la bretelle
der Schulterriemen
la correa
la bretella

backpack • le sac à dos • der Rucksack • la mochila • lo zainetto

duffle bag • le fourre-tout • die Reisetasche • la bolsa de viaje • la sacca da viaggio

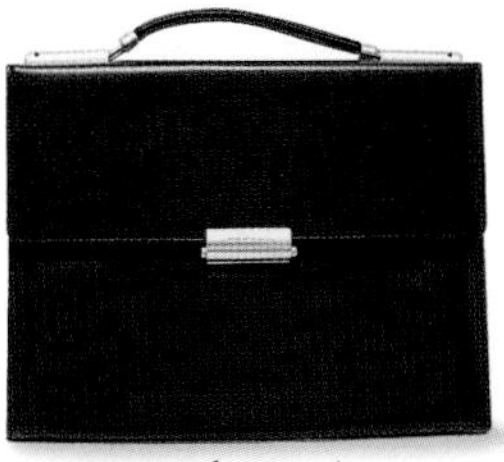

briefcase • la serviette • die Aktentasche • el maletín • la valigetta

handles
les poignées
die Griffe
las asas
i manici

handbag • le sac à main • die Handtasche • la bolsa de mano • la borsetta

shoes • les chaussures • die Schuhe • los zapatos • le scarpe

eyelet
l'œillet
die Öse
el ojal
l'occhiello

lace
le lacet
der Schnürsenkel
la agujeta
il laccio

tongue
la languette
die Zunge
la lengüeta
la lingua

sole
la semelle
die Sohle
la suela
la suola

heel
le talon
der Absatz
el tacón
il tacco

lace-up • la chaussure lacée • der Schnürschuh • el zapato de agujetas • la scarpa con i lacci

boot • la botte • der Stiefel • la bota • lo stivale

walking boot
le pataugas
der Wanderschuh
la bota de trekking
la scarpa da trekking

sneaker • la basket • der Sportschuh • el tenis • la scarpa da ginnastica

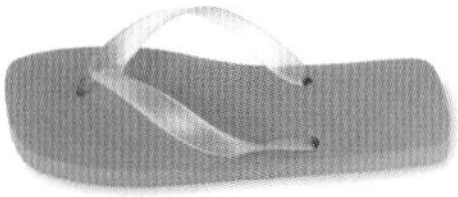

flip-flop • la tong • die Strandsandale • la chancla • l'infradito

brogue • le richelieu der Herrenhalbschuh • el zapato de caballero • la scarpa da uomo

high heel shoe • la chaussure à talon • der Schuh mit hohem Absatz • el zapato de tacón • la scarpa con il tacco alto

wedge • la chaussure compensée • der Keilschuh • la cuña • la zeppa

sandal • la sandale die Sandale • la sandalia • il sandalo

slip-on • le mocassin der Slipper • el mocasín • il mocassino

pump • la ballerina • der Pumps • la bailarina • la ballerina

hair • les cheveux • das Haar • el cabello • i capelli

comb
le peigne
der Kamm
el peine
il pettine

comb (v) • peigner • kämmen • peinar • pettinare

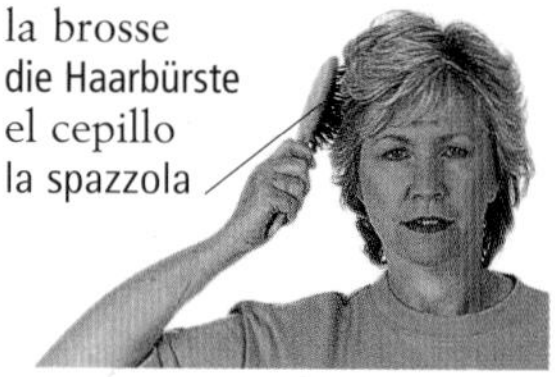

brush
la brosse
die Haarbürste
el cepillo
la spazzola

brush (v) • brosser • bürsten • cepillar • spazzolare

rinse (v) • rincer • ausspülen • enjuagar • sciacquare

hairdresser
la coiffeuse
die Friseurin
la estilista
la parrucchiera

sink
le lavabo
das Waschbecken
el lavabo
il lavandino

client
la cliente
die Kundin
la cliente
la cliente

wash (v) • laver • waschen • lavar • lavare

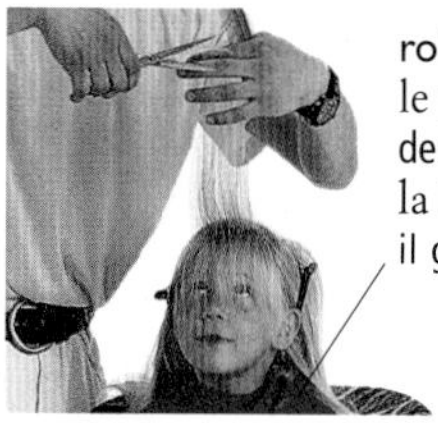

robe
le peignoir
der Frisierumhang
la bata
il grembiule

cut (v) • couper • schneiden • cortar • tagliare

blowdry (v) • sécher • föhnen • secar con la secadora • asciugare con il phon

set (v) • faire une mise en plis • legen • marcar • mettere in piega

accessories • les accessoires • die Frisierartikel • los accesorios • gli accessori

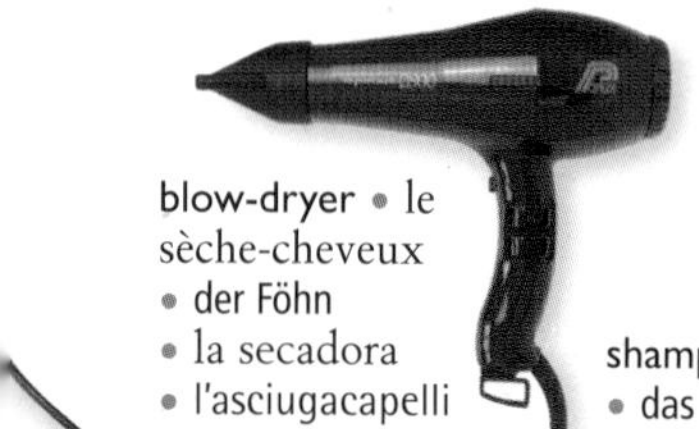

blow-dryer • le sèche-cheveux • der Föhn • la secadora • l'asciugacapelli

shampoo • le shampoing • das Shampoo • el champú • lo shampoo

conditioner • le conditionneur • die Haarspülung • el acondicionador • il balsamo

gel • le gel • das Haargel • el gel • il gel

hairspray • la laque • das Haarspray • la laca • la lacca

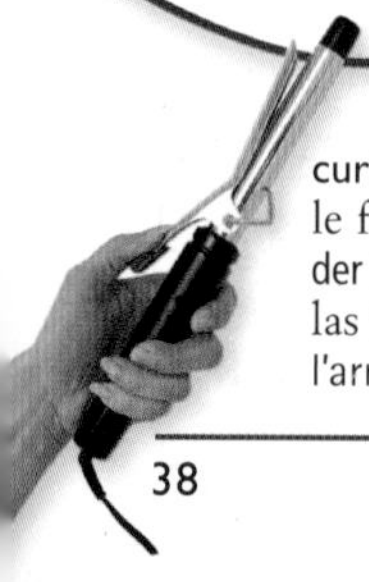

curling iron
le fer à friser
der Lockenstab
las tenazas
l'arricciacapelli

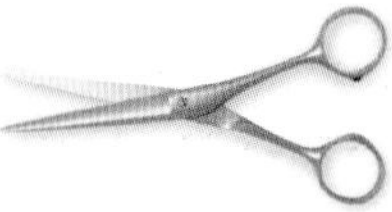

scissors • les ciseaux • die Schere • las tijeras • le forbici

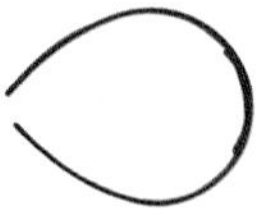

headband • le serre-tête • der Haarreif • la diadema • il cerchietto

hair straightener • le fer à lisser • der Haarglätter • la plancha de pelo • la piastra per i capelli

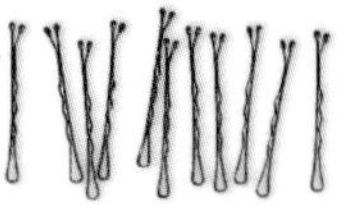

bobby pin • la pince à cheveux • die Haarklammer • el pasador • la forcina

styles • les coiffures • die Frisuren • los estilos • le acconciature

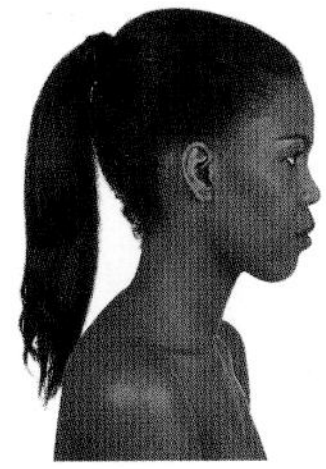
ponytail • la queue de cheval • der Pferdeschwanz • la cola de caballo • la coda di cavallo

braid • la natte • der Zopf • la trenza • la treccia

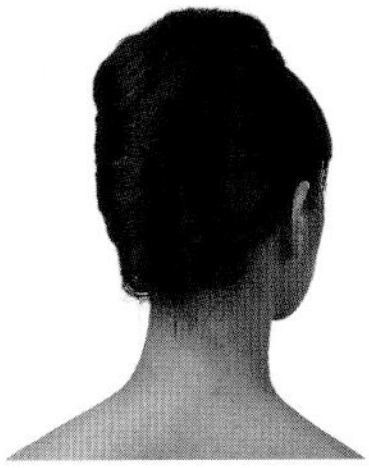
French twist • le rouleau • die Hochfrisur • el chongo francés • la piega alla francese

bun • le chignon • der Haarknoten • el chongo • la crocchia

pigtails • les couettes • die Schwänzchen • las coletas • i codini

bob • au carré • der Bubikopf • el príncipe valiente • il caschetto

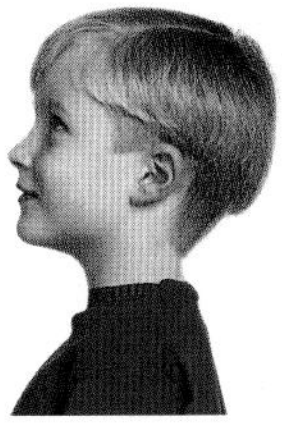
crop • la coupe courte • der Kurzhaarschnitt • el pelo corto • la sfumatura alta

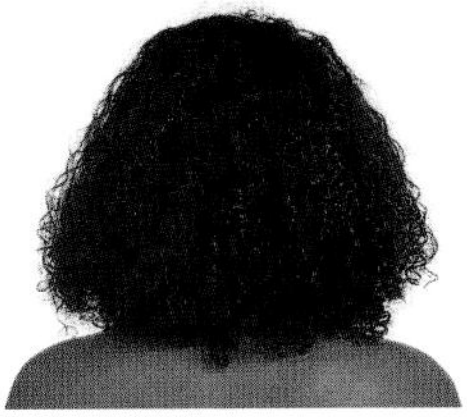
curly • frisé • kraus • rizado • ricci

perm • la permanente • die Dauerwelle • la permanente • la permanente

straight • raide • glatt • lacio • lisci

roots
les racines
die Wurzeln
las raíces
le radici

highlights • les reflets • die Strähnen • las luces • i colpi di sole

bald • chauve • kahl • calvo • calvo

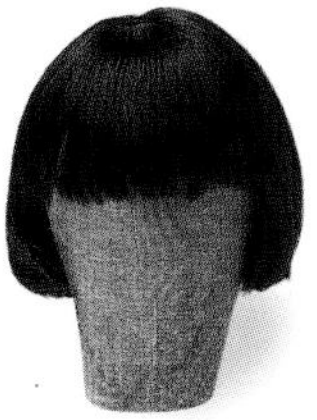
wig • la perruque • die Perücke • la peluca • la parrucca

colors • les couleurs • die Haarfarben • los colores • i colori

blonde • blond • blond • güero • biondo

brunette • châtain • brünett • castaño • bruno

auburn • auburn • rotbraun • rojizo • castano

red • roux • rot • pelirrojo • rosso

black • noir • schwarz • negro • nero

gray • gris • grau • gris • grigio

white • blanc • weiß • blanco • bianco

dyed • teint • gefärbt • teñido • tinto

hair band
la bande de cheveux
das Haarband
la goma del pelo
l'elastico

trim *(v)*
rafraîchir
nachschneiden
despuntar
spuntare

barber
le coiffeur
der Herrenfriseur
el peluquero
il barbiere

dandruff
les pellicules
die Schuppen
la caspa
la forfora

split ends
les fourches
der Haarspliss
la orzuela
le doppie punte

greasy
gras
fettig
graso
grassi

dry
sec
trocken
seco
secchi

normal
normal
normal
normal
normali

scalp
le cuir chevelu
die Kopfhaut
el cuero cabelludo
il cuoio capelluto

straighten *(v)*
décrêper
glätten
alaciar
lisciare

beauty • la beauté • die Schönheit • la belleza • la bellezza

makeup • le maquillage • das Make-up • el maquillaje • il trucco

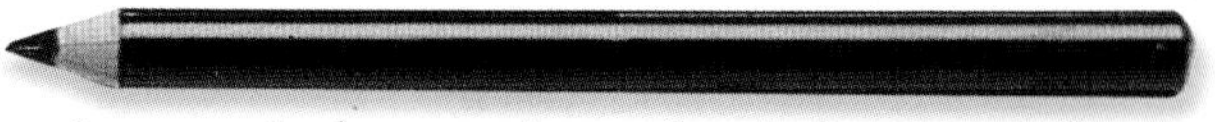

eyebrow pencil • le crayon à sourcils • der Augenbrauenstift • el lápiz de cejas • la matita per le sopracciglia

eyebrow brush • la brosse à sourcils • das Brauenbürstchen • el cepillo para las cejas • la spazzolina per le sopracciglia

tweezers • la pince à épiler • die Pinzette • las pinzas • le pinzette

lip gloss • le brillant à lèvres • das Lipgloss • el brillo de labios • il lucidalabbra

lip brush • le pinceau à lèvres • der Lippenpinsel • el pincel de labios • il pennello per le labbra

lip liner • le crayon à lèvres • der Lippenkonturenstift • el lápiz de labios • la matita per le labbra

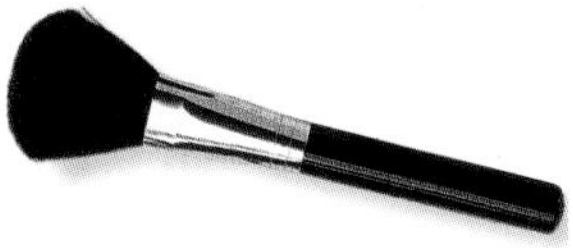

brush • le pinceau • der Puderpinsel • la brocha • il pennello

concealer • le correcteur • der Korrekturstift • el lápiz corrector • il correttore

compact • le poudrier • die Puderdose • la polvera • il portacipria

beauty treatments • les soins de beauté • die Schönheitsbehandlungen • los tratamientos de belleza • i trattamenti di bellezza

face pack • le masque de beauté • die Gesichtsmaske • la mascarilla • la maschera di bellezza

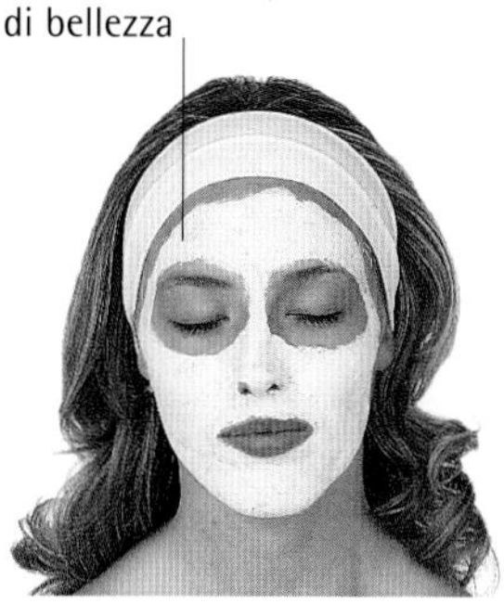

facial • le soin du visage • die Gesichtsbehandlung • la limpieza de cutis • il trattamento per il viso

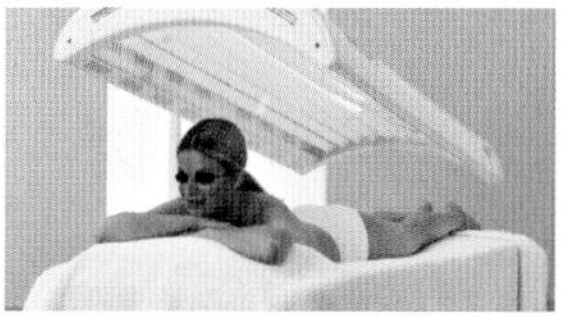

sunbed • le lit U.V. • die Sonnenbank • la cama de rayos ultravioletas • il lettino solare

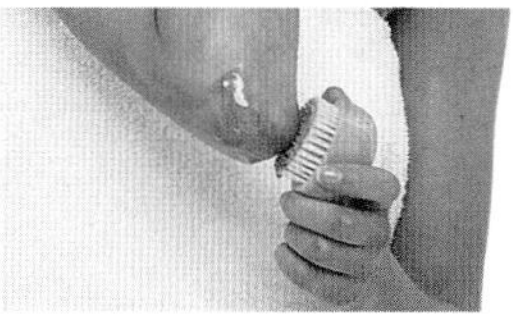

exfoliate (*v*) • exfolier • die Haut schälen • exfoliar • esfoliare

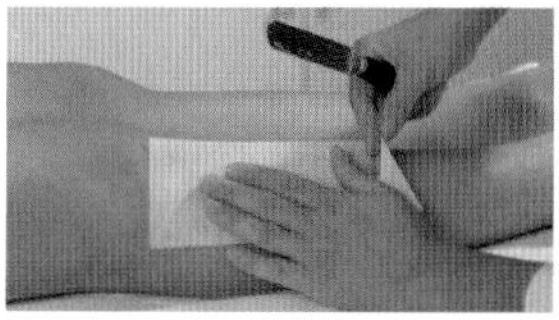

wax • l'épilation • die Enthaarung • la depilación a la cera • la ceretta

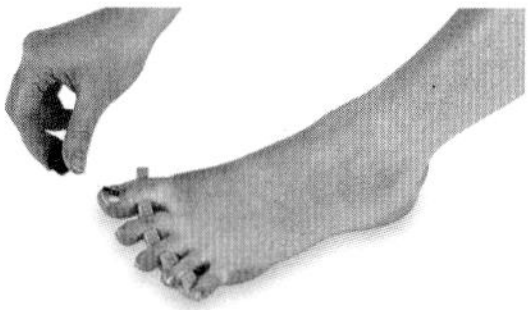

pedicure • la pédicurie • die Pediküre • la pedicura • la pedicure

manicure • la manicure • die Maniküre • la manicura • la manicure

nail file • la lime à ongles • die Nagelfeile • la lima de uñas • la limetta

nail polish remover
le dissolvant
der Nagellackentferner
el quitaesmalte
l'acetone

nail polish • le vernis à ongles • der Nagellack • el esmalte de uñas • lo smalto per unghie

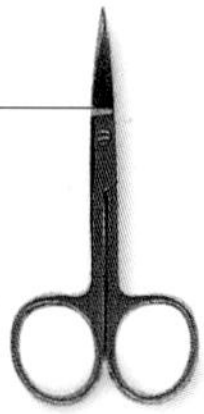

nail scissors • les ciseaux à ngles • die Nagelschere • las tijeras de uñas • le forbicine per le unghie

nail clippers
le coupe-ongles
der Nagelknipser
el cortaúñas
il tagliaunghie

toiletries • les accessoires de toilette • die Toilettenartikel • los artículos de tocador • gli articoli da toilette

cleanser • le démaquillant • der Reiniger • la crema limpiadora • il latte detergente

toner • le tonique • das Gesichtswasser • el tónico • la lozione tonificante

moisturizer • la crème hydratante • die Feuchtigkeitscreme • la crema hidratante • la crema idratante

self-tanning lotion • l'autobronzant • die Selbstbräunungscreme • la crema bronceadora • la crema autoabbronzante

perfume
le parfum
das Parfum
el perfume
il profumo

eau de toilette • l'eau de toilette • das Eau de Toilette • el agua de colonia • l'acqua di colonia

complexion le teint der Teint el cutis la carnagione	oily gras fettig graso grasso	tan le bronzage die Sonnenbräune el bronceado l'abbronzatura
fair clair hell claro chiaro	sensitive sensible empfindlich sensible sensibile	tattoo le tatouage die Tätowierung el tatuaje il tatuaggio
dark foncé dunkel moreno scuro	hypoallergenic hypoallergénique hypoallergen hipoalergénico ipoallergenico	cotton balls les boules de coton die Wattebällchen las bolas de algodón i batuffoli di ovatta
dry sec trocken seco secco	shade le ton der Farbton el tono la tonalità	antiwrinkle antirides Antifalten- antiarrugas antirughe

health
la santé
die Gesundheit
la salud
la salute

illness • la maladie • die Krankheit • la enfermedad • la malattia

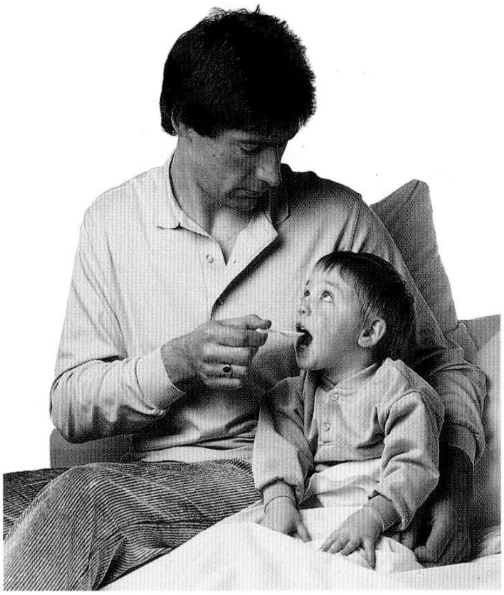

fever • la fièvre • das Fieber • la fiebre • la febbre

headache • le mal de tête • die Kopfschmerzen • el dolor de cabeza • il mal di testa

nosebleed • le saignement de nez • das Nasenbluten • la hemorragia nasal • l'emorragia nasale

cough • la toux • der Husten • la tos • la tosse

sneeze • l'éternuement • das Niesen • el estornudo • lo starnuto

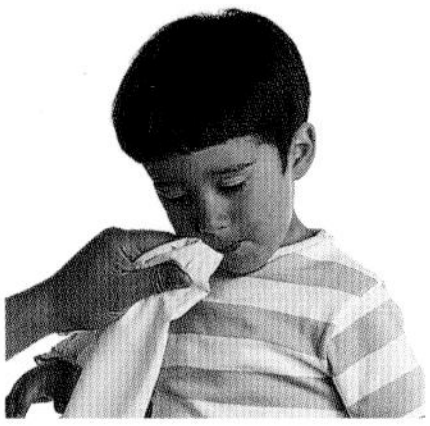

cold • le rhume • die Erkältung • el resfriado • il raffreddore

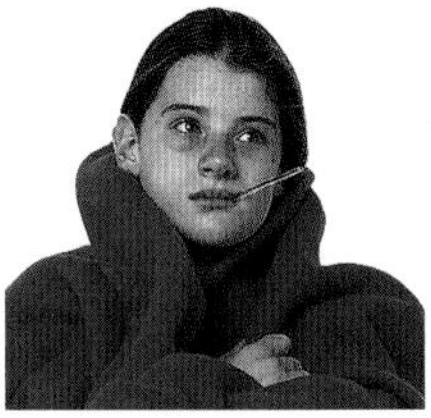

the flu • la grippe • die Grippe • la gripe • l'influenza

inhaler
l'inhalateur
der Inhalationsapparat
el inhalador
l'inalatore

asthma • l'asthme • das Asthma • el asma • l'asma

cramps • les crampes • die Krämpfe • los calambres • i crampi

nausea • la nausée • die Übelkeit • la náusea • la nausea

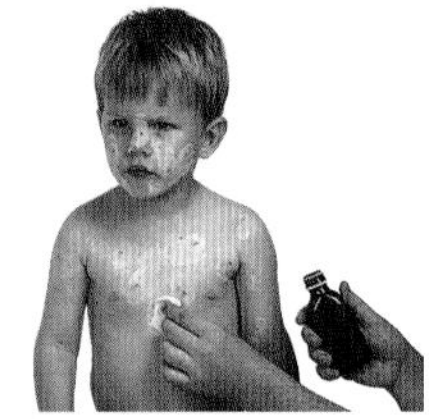

the chickenpox • la varicelle • die Windpocken • la varicela • la varicella

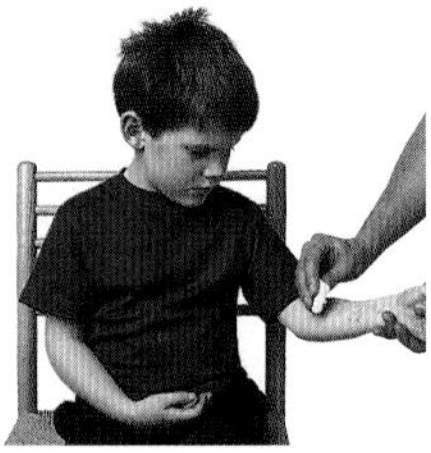

rash • l'éruption • der Hautausschlag • el sarpullido • lo sfogo

heart attack la crise cardiaque der Herzinfarkt el ataque cardiaco l'infarto	diabetes le diabète die Zuckerkrankheit la diabetes il diabete	eczema l'eczéma das Ekzem el eccema l'eczema	chill le refroidissement die Verkühlung el resfriado l'infreddatura	vomit *(v)* vomir sich übergeben vomitar vomitare	diarrhea la diarrhée der Durchfall la diarrea la diarrea
stroke l'attaque der Schlaganfall la aplopejía l'ictus	hay fever le rhume des foins der Heuschnupfen la fiebre del heno la febbre da fieno	infection l'infection die Infektion la infección l'infezione	stomach ache le mal d'estomac die Magenschmerzen el dolor de estómago il mal di stomaco	epilepsy l'épilepsie die Epilepsie la epilepsia l'epilessia	measles la rougeole die Masern el sarampión il morbillo
blood pressure la tension der Blutdruck la presión arterial la pressione sanguina	allergy l'allergie die Allergie la alergia l'allergia	virus le virus der Virus el virus il virus	faint *(v)* s'évanouir in Ohnmacht fallen desmayarse svenire	migraine la migraine die Migräne la migraña l'emicrania	mumps les oreillons der Mumps las paperas gli orecchioni

doctor • le médecin • der Arzt • el doctor • il medico

consultation • la consultation • die Konsultation • la consulta • la visita

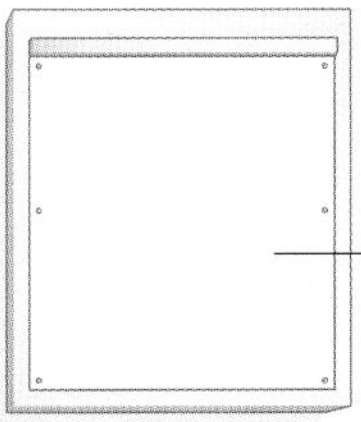

x-ray viewer
la lampe de radio
der Röntgenbildbetrachter
el lector de rayos X
il negatoscopio

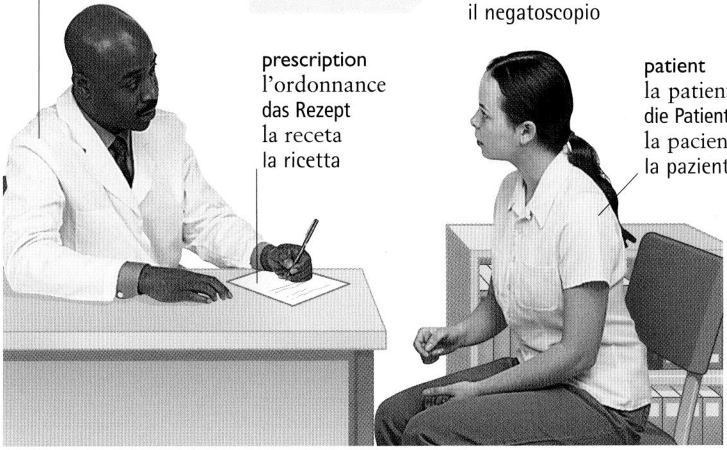

doctor
le médecin
der Arzt
el doctor
il medico

prescription
l'ordonnance
das Rezept
la receta
la ricetta

patient
la patiente
die Patientin
la paciente
la paziente

nurse
l'infirmière
die Krankenschwester
la enfermera
l'infermiera

scales • la balance • die Personenwaage • la báscula • la bilancia

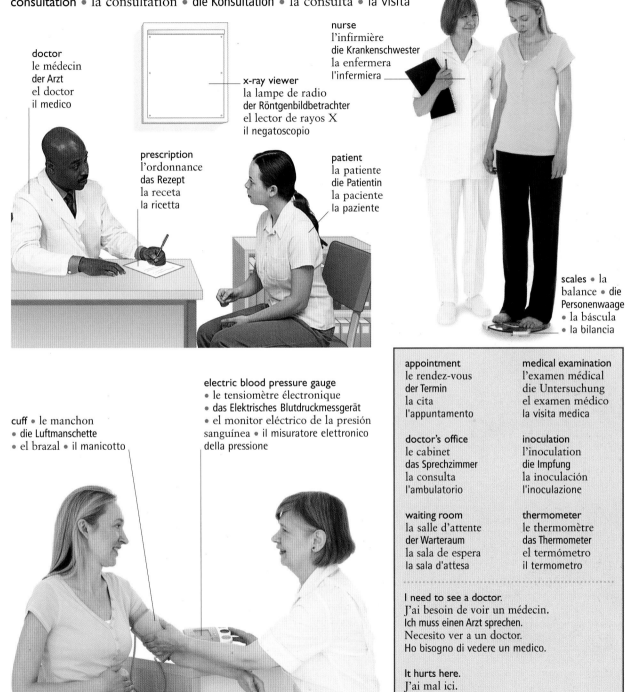

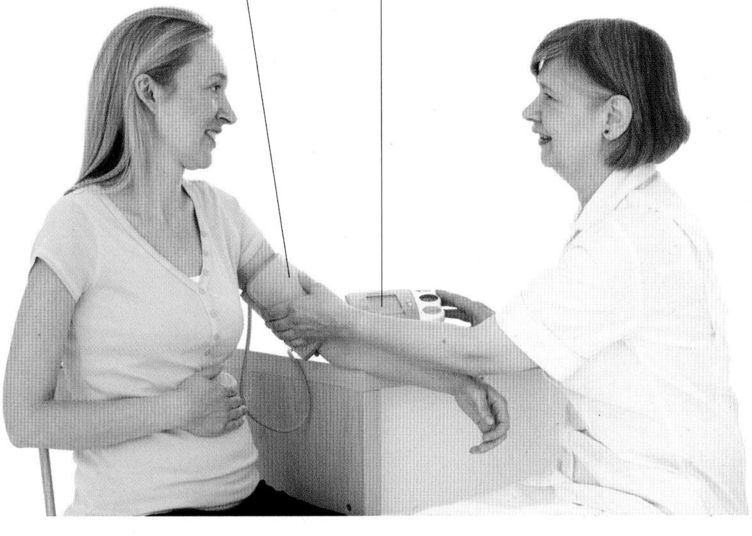

cuff • le manchon • die Luftmanschette • el brazal • il manicotto

electric blood pressure gauge • le tensiomètre électronique • das Elektrisches Blutdruckmessgerät • el monitor eléctrico de la presión sanguínea • il misuratore elettronico della pressione

appointment
le rendez-vous
der Termin
la cita
l'appuntamento

doctor's office
le cabinet
das Sprechzimmer
la consulta
l'ambulatorio

waiting room
la salle d'attente
der Warteraum
la sala de espera
la sala d'attesa

medical examination
l'examen médical
die Untersuchung
el examen médico
la visita medica

inoculation
l'inoculation
die Impfung
la inoculación
l'inoculazione

thermometer
le thermomètre
das Thermometer
el termómetro
il termometro

I need to see a doctor.
J'ai besoin de voir un médecin.
Ich muss einen Arzt sprechen.
Necesito ver a un doctor.
Ho bisogno di vedere un medico.

It hurts here.
J'ai mal ici.
Es tut hier weh.
Me duele aquí.
Ho un dolore qui.

injury • la blessure • die Verletzung • la lesión • la ferita

sprain • l'entorse • die Verstauchung • la torcedura • la slogatura

sling
l'écharpe
die Schlinge
el cabestrillo
la fascia a tracolla

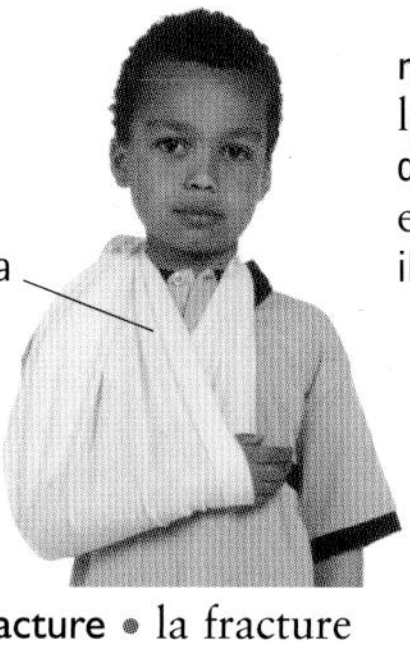

fracture • la fracture • die Fraktur • la fractura • la frattura

neck brace
la minerve
die Halskrawatte
el collarín
il collare

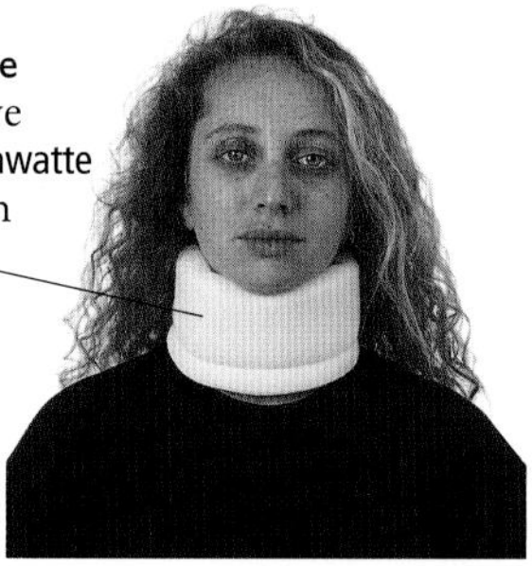

whiplash • le coup du lapin • das Schleudertrauma • el tirón en el cuello • il colpo di frusta

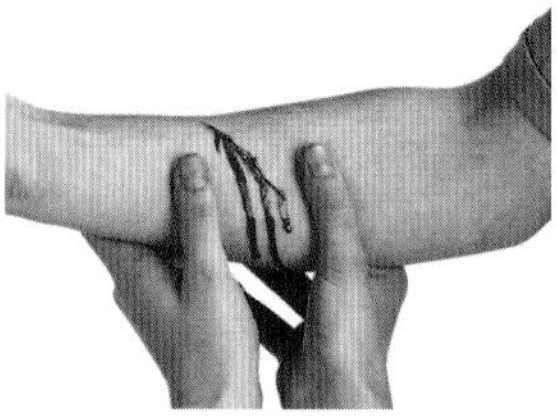

cut • la coupure • der Schnitt • la cortada • il taglio

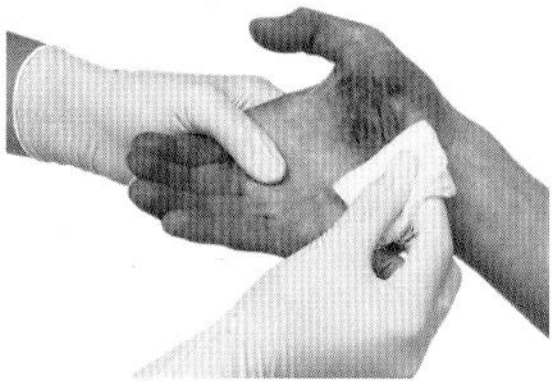

graze • l'écorchure • die Abschürfung • la raspada • la sbucciatura

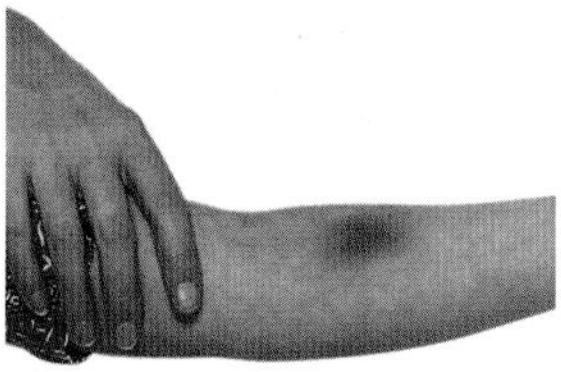

bruise • la contusion • die Prellung • el moretón • il livido

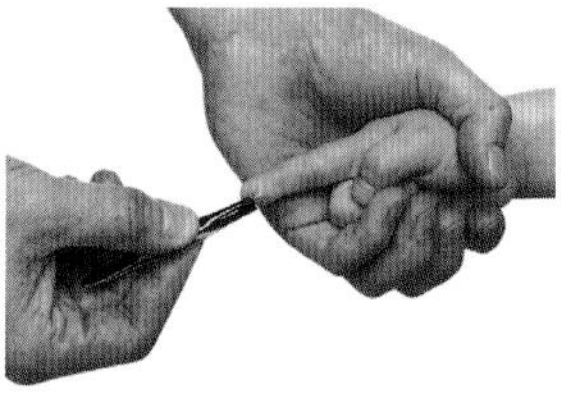

splinter • l'écharde • der Splitter • la astilla • la scheggia

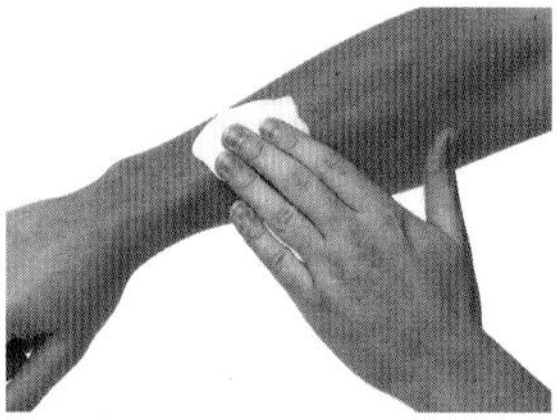

sunburn • le coup de soleil • der Sonnenbrand • la ardida • la scottatura

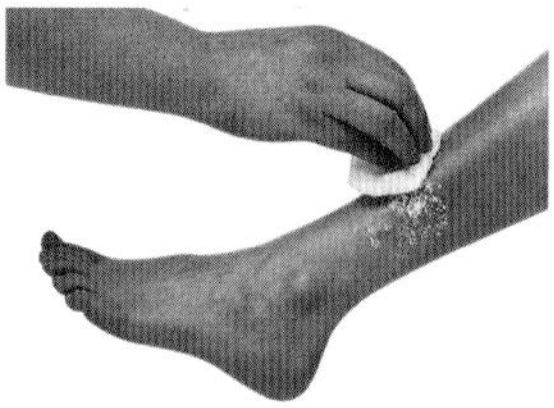

burn • la brûlure • die Brandwunde • la quemadura • l'ustione

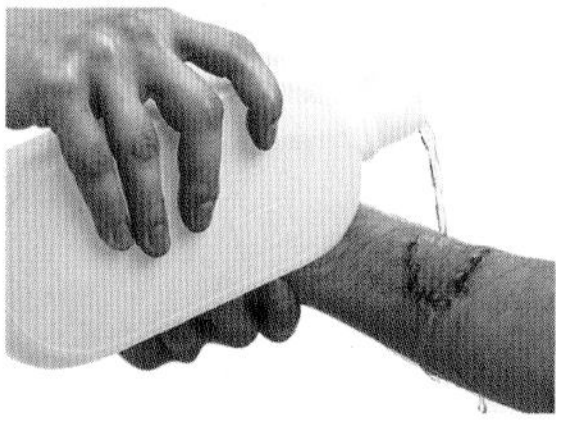

bite • la morsure • der Biss • el mordisco • il morso

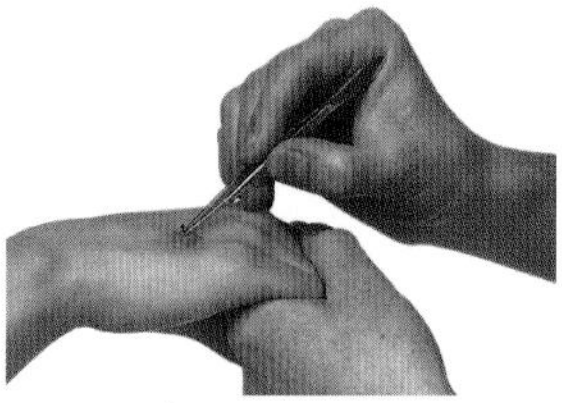

sting • la piqûre • der Stich • la picadura • la puntura

accident l'accident der Unfall el accidente l'incidente	hemorrhage l'hémorragie die Blutung la hemorragia l'emorragia	concussion la commotion cérébrale die Gehirnerschütterung la conmoción la commozione cerebrale	Will he/she be all right? Est-ce qu'il/elle va se remettre? Wird er/sie es gut überstehen? ¿Se pondrá bien? Si rimetterà?
emergency l'urgence der Notfall la emergencia l'emergenza	blister l'ampoule die Blase la ampolla la vescica	head injury le traumatisme crânien die Kopfverletzung la lesión en la cabeza la ferita alla testa	Please call an ambulance. Appelez une ambulance s'il vous plaît. Rufen Sie bitte einen Krankenwagen. Por favor llame a una ambulancia. Chiami un'ambulanza, per favore.
wound la blessure die Wunde la herida la ferita	poisoning l'empoisonnement die Vergiftung el envenenamiento l'avvelenamento	electric shock le choc électrique der elektrische Schlag el shock eléctrico la scossa elettrica	Where does it hurt? Où avez-vous mal? Wo haben Sie Schmerzen? ¿Dónde le duele? Dove le fa male?

first aid • les premiers secours • die erste Hilfe • los primeros auxilios • il pronto soccorso

ointment • la pommade • die Salbe • la pomada • la pomata

adhesive bandage • le pansement • das Pflaster • la tirita • il cerotto

safety pin
l'épingle de sûreté
die Sicherheitsnadel
el seguro
la spilla da balia

bandage
le bandage
die Bandage
la venda
la benda

painkillers
les analgésiques
die Schmerztabletten
los analgésicos
gli antidolarifici

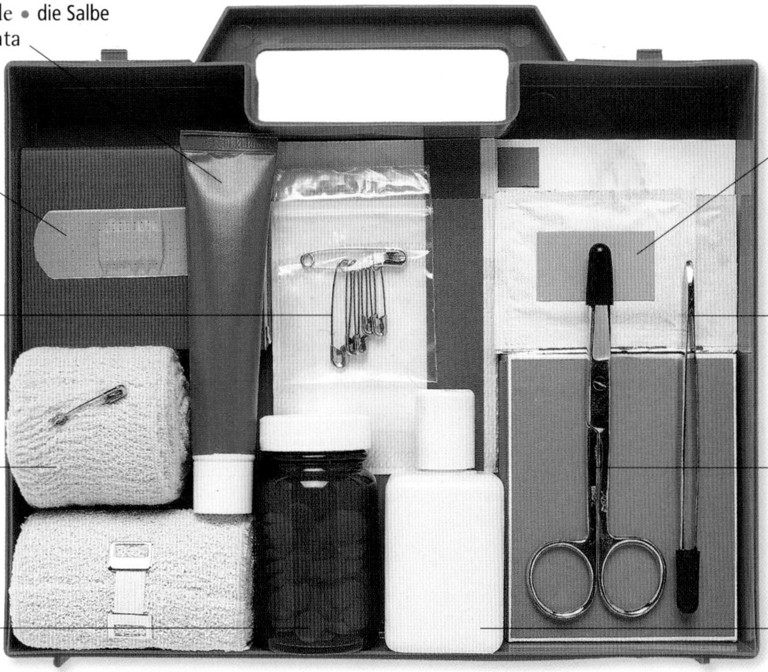

antiseptic wipe
la serviette antiseptique
das Desinfektionstuch
la toallita antiséptica
la salvietta antisettica

tweezers
la pince fine
die Pinzette
las pinzas
le pinzette

scissors
les ciseaux
die Schere
las tijeras
le forbici

antiseptic
l'antiseptique
das Antiseptikum
el desinfectante
il disinfettante

first aid kit • la trousse de premiers secours • der Erste-Hilfe-Kasten • el botiquín • la cassetta di pronto soccorso

gauze • la gaze • die Gaze • la gasa • la garza

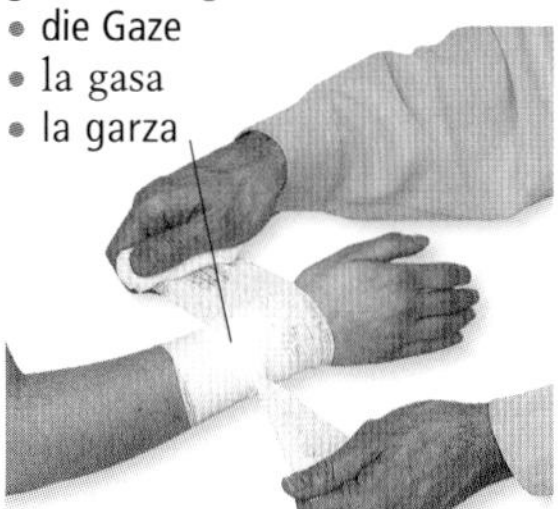

dressing • le pansement • der Verband • el vendaje • la bendatura

splint • l'attelle • die Schiene • la tablilla • la stecca

adhesive tape
le sparadrap
das Leukoplast
la tela adhesiva
il nastro adesivo

resuscitation • la réanimation • die Wiederbelebung • la reanimación • la rianimazione

shock le choc der Schock el shock lo shock	pulse le pouls der Puls el pulso le pulsazioni	choke *(v)* étouffer ersticken ahogarse soffocare	Can you help? Est-ce que vous pouvez m'aider? Können Sie mir helfen? ¿Me puede ayudar? Può aiutarmi?
unconscious sans connaissance bewusstlos inconsciente privo di sensi	breathing la respiration die Atmung la respiración la respirazione	sterile stérile steril estéril sterile	Do you know first aid? Pouvez-vous donner les soins d'urgence? Beherrschen Sie die Erste Hilfe? ¿Sabe primeros auxilios? Sa dare pronto soccorso?

hospital • l'hôpital • das Krankenhaus • el hospital • l'ospedale

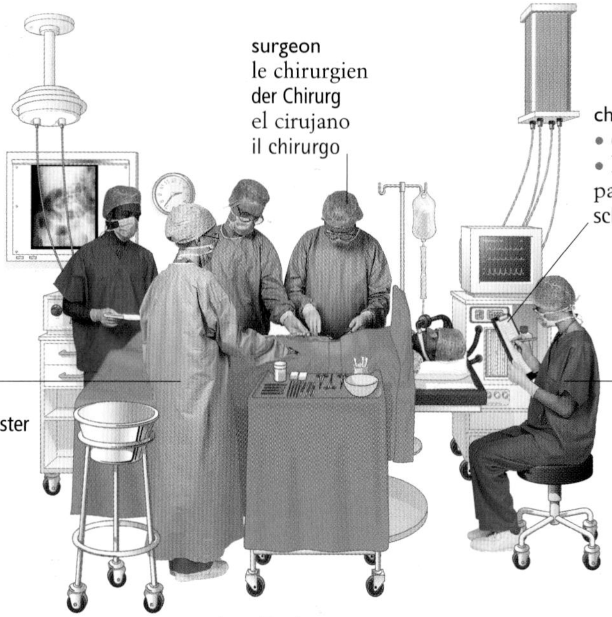

operating room • la salle d'opération • der Operationssaal • el quirófano • la sala operatoria

blood test • l'analyse de sang • die Blutuntersuchung • el análisis de sangre • l'analisi del sangue

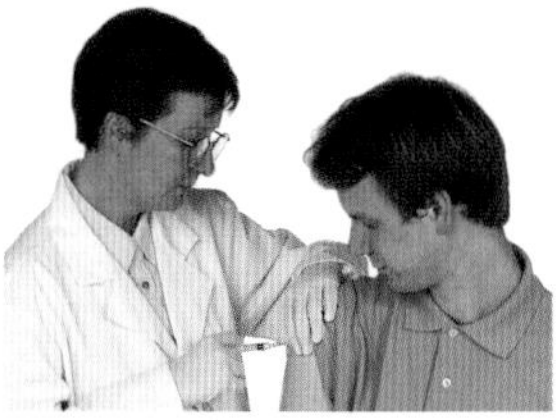

injection • l'injection • die Spritze • la inyección • l'iniezione

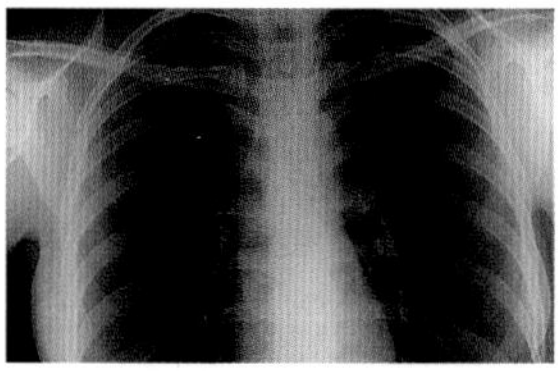

x-ray • la radio • die Röntgenaufnahme • la radiografía • la radiografia

gurney • le chariot • die fahrbare Liege • la camilla • la lettiga

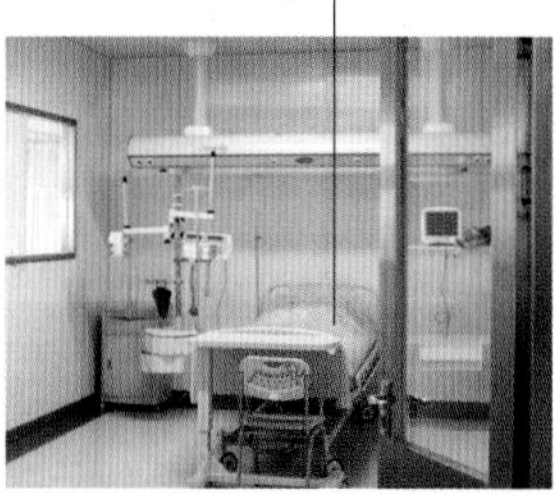

emergency room • la salle des urgences • die Notaufnahme • la sala de urgencias • la sala emergenze

call button • le bouton d'appel • der Rufknopf • el timbre • il pulsante di chiamata

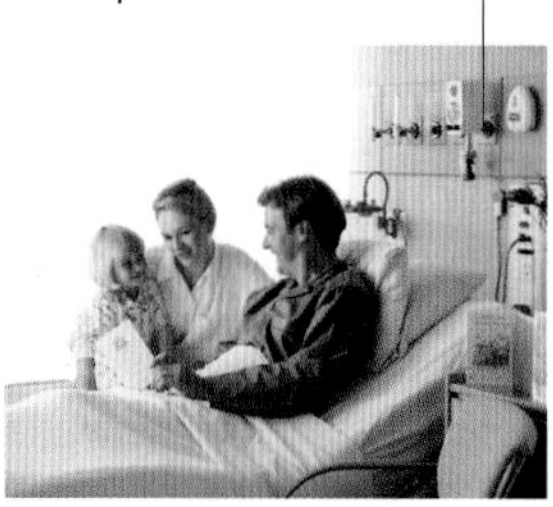

ward • la salle • die Krankenhausstation • la planta • il reparto

wheelchair • la chaise roulante • der Rollstuhl • la silla de ruedas • la sedia a rotelle

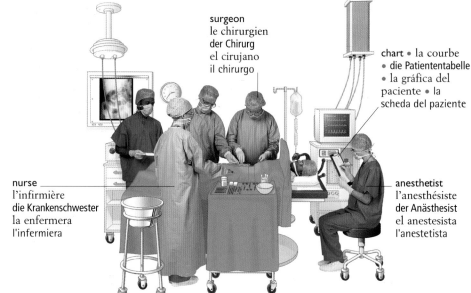

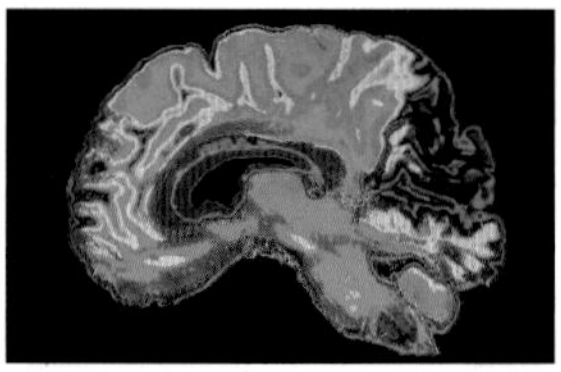

scan • la scanographie • der CT-Scan • el ultrasonido • l'ecografia

operation l'opération die Operation la operación l'operazione	discharged renvoyé entlassen dado de alta dimesso	visiting hours les heures de visite die Besuchszeiten las horas de visita l'orario delle visite	maternity ward la maternité die Entbindungsstation la sala de maternidad il reparto maternità	intensive care unit le service de soins intensifs die Intensivstation la unidad de cuidados intensivos il reparto di cura intensiva
admitted admis aufgenommen internado ricoverato	clinic la clinique die Klinik la clínica la clinica	children's ward la pédiatrie die Kinderstation la sala de pediatría il reparto pediatrico	private room la chambre privée das Privatzimmer la habitación privada la camera privata	outpatient le malade en consultation externe der ambulante Patient el paciente externo il paziente esterno

departments • les services • die Abteilungen • los servicios • i reparti

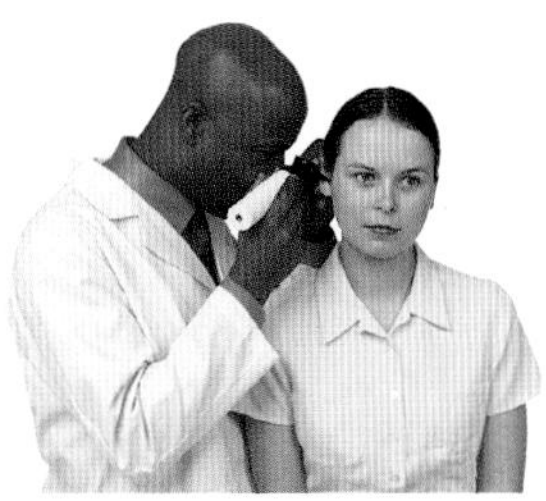

Ear, Nose, and Throat • l'O.R.L. • die HNO-Abteilung • la otorrinonaringología • l'otorinolaringologia

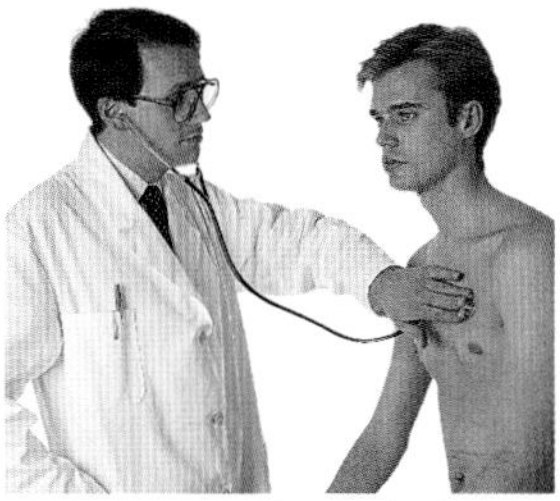

cardiology • la cardiologie • die Kardiologie • la cardiología • la cardiologia

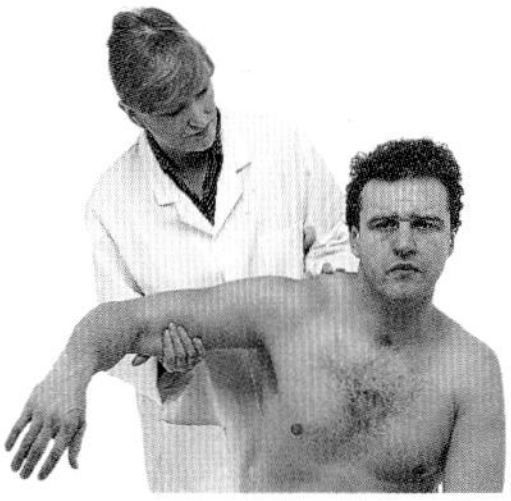

orthopedics • l'orthopédie • die Orthopädie • la ortopedia • l'ortopedia

gynecology • la gynécologie • die Gynäkologie • la ginecología • la ginecologia

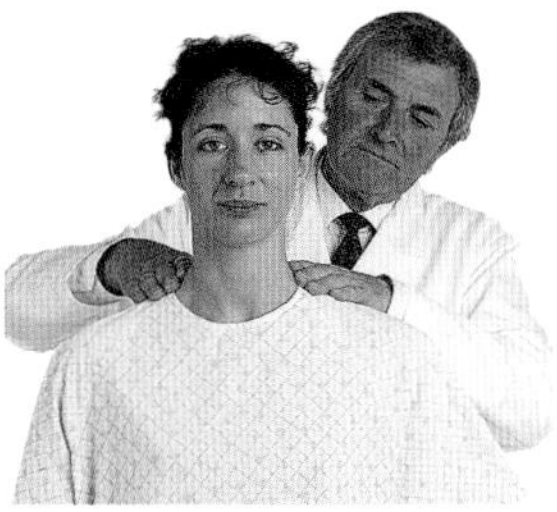

physiotherapy • la kinésithérapie • die Physiotherapie • la fisioterapia • la fisioterapia

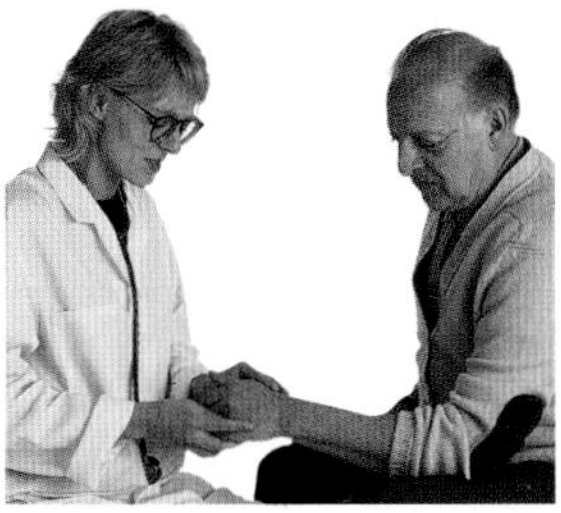

dermatology • la dermatologie • die Dermatologie • la dermatología • la dermatologia

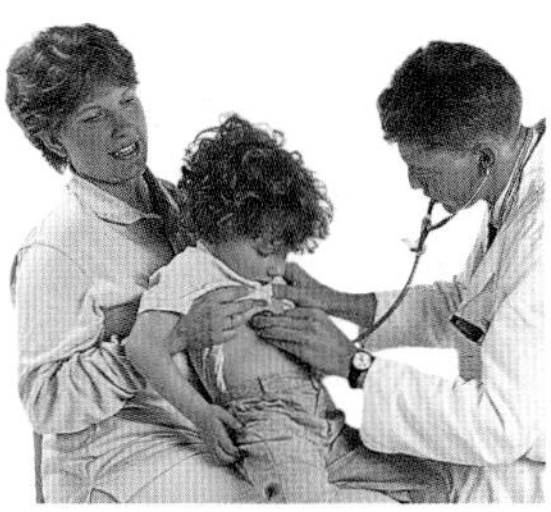

pediatrics • la pédiatrie • die Pädiatrie • la pediatría • la pediatria

radiology • la radiologie • die Radiologie • la radiología • la radiologia

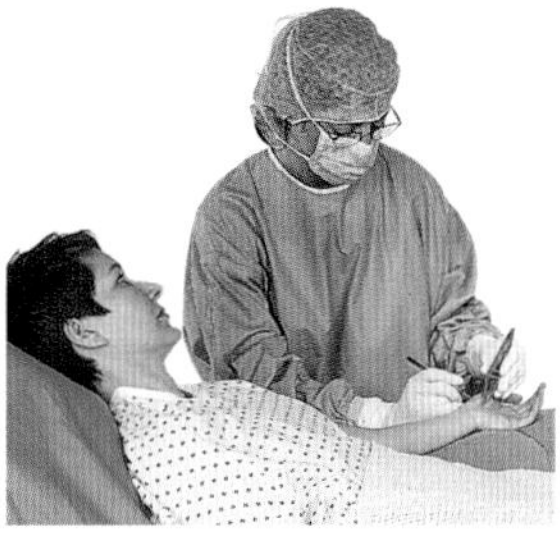

surgery • la chirurgie • die Chirurgie • la cirugía • la chirurgia

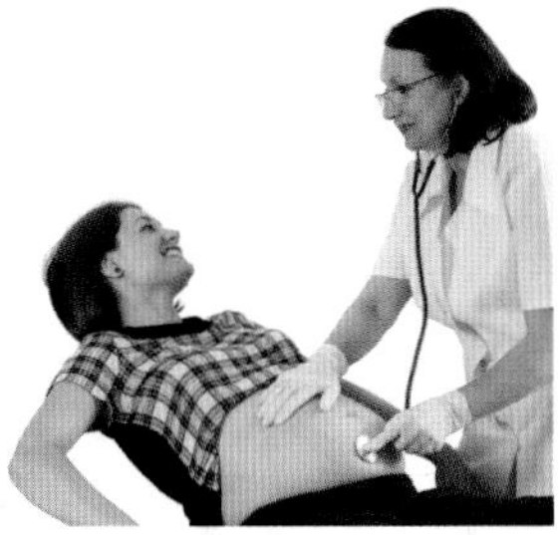

maternity • la maternité • die Entbindungsstation • la maternidad • la maternità

psychiatry • la psychiatrie • die Psychiatrie • la psiquiatría • la psichiatria

ophthalmology • l'ophtalmologie • die Ophthalmologie • la oftalmología • l'oftalmologia

neurology
la neurologie
die Neurologie
la neurología
la neurologia

urology
l'urologie
die Urologie
la urología
l'urologia

plastic surgery
la chirurgie esthétique
die plastische Chirurgie
la cirugía plástica
la chirurgia plastica

pathology
la pathologie
die Pathologie
la patología
la patologia

result
le résultat
das Ergebnis
el resultado
il risultato

oncology
l'oncologie
die Onkologie
la oncología
l'oncologia

endocrinology
l'endocrinologie
die Endokrinologie
la endocrinología
l'endocrinologia

referral
l'orientation d'un patient
die Überweisung
la referencia
mandare da uno specialista

test
l'analyse
die Untersuchung
el análisis
l'analisi

consultant
le spécialiste
der Facharzt
el especialista
lo specialista

dentist • le dentiste • der Zahnarzt • el dentista • il dentista

tooth • la dent • der Zahn • el diente • il dente

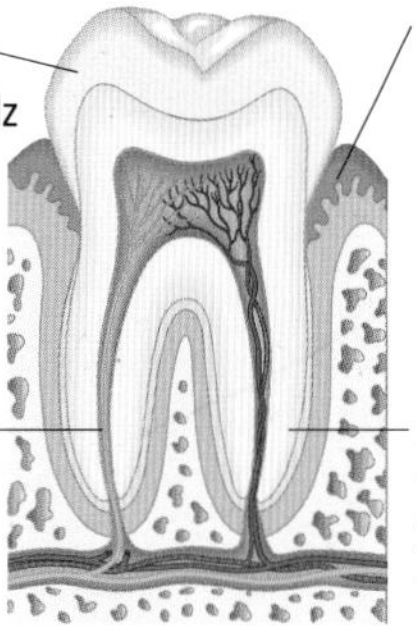

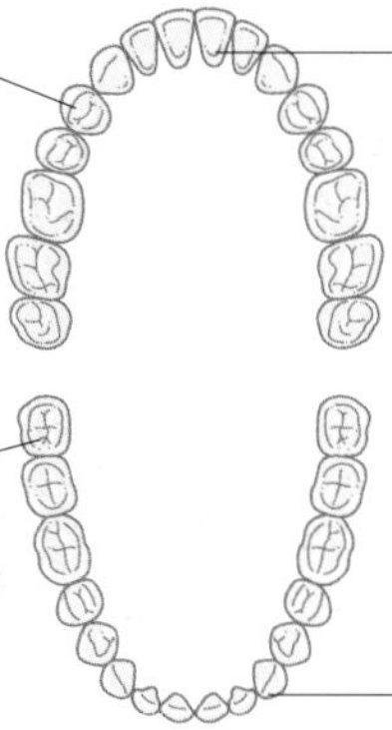

toothache
la rage de dents
die Zahnschmerzen
el dolor de muelas
il mal di denti

drill
la fraise
der Bohrer
el torno del dentista
il trapano

plaque
la plaque
der Zahnbelag
la placa bacteriana
la placca

dental floss
le fil dentaire
die Zahnseide
el hilo dental
il filo dentale

decay
la carie
die Karies
la caries
la carie

extraction
l'extraction
die Extraktion
la extracción
l'estrazione

filling
le plombage
die Zahnfüllung
el empaste
l'otturazione

crown
la couronne
die Krone
la corona
la capsula

check-up • la visite de contrôle • der Check-up • la revisión • il controllo

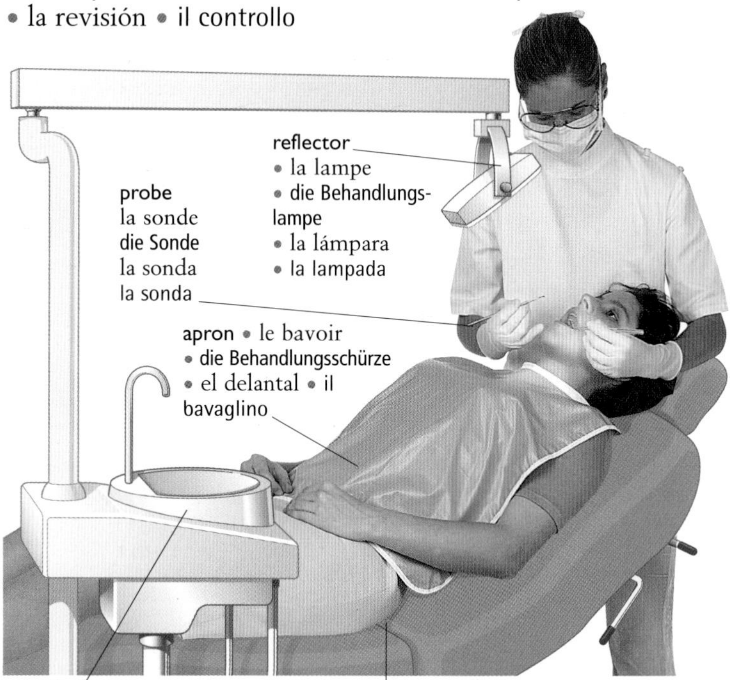

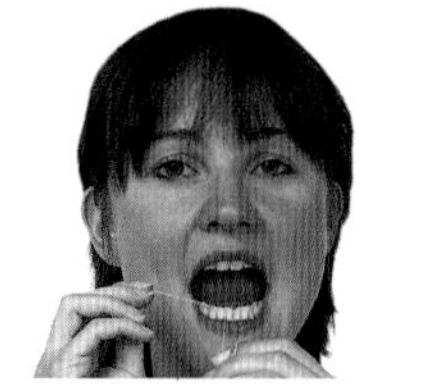

floss (v) • utiliser le fil dentaire • mit Zahnseide reinigen • usar el hilo dental • usare il filo dentale

brush (v) • brosser • bürsten • cepillarse los dientes • spazzolare

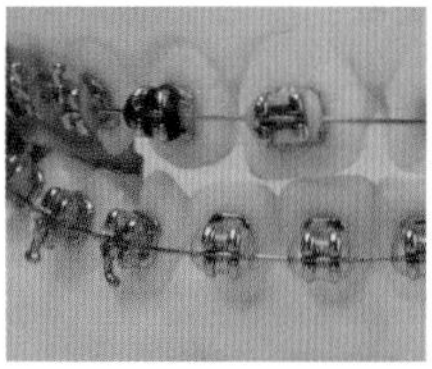

braces • l'appareil dentaire • die Zahnspange • los frenos • l'apparecchio correttore

dental x-ray • la radio dentaire • die Röntgenaufnahme • los rayos x dentales • la radiografia dentale

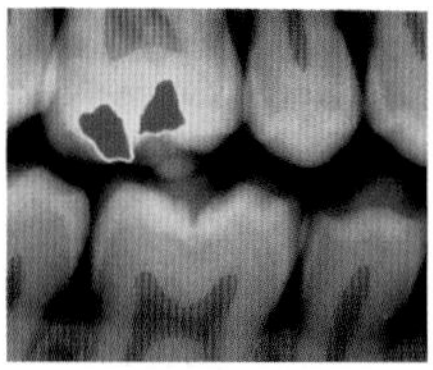

x-ray film • la radio • das Röntgenbild • la radiografía • la pellicola radiografica

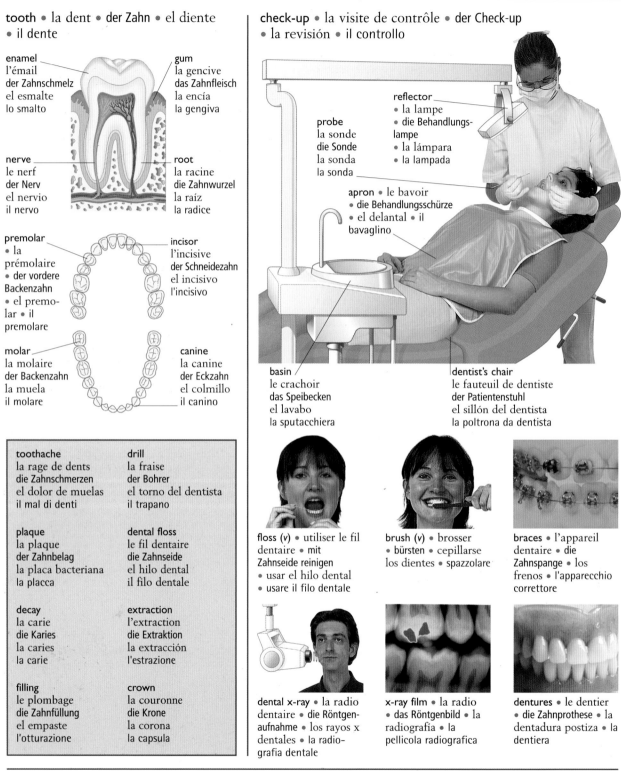

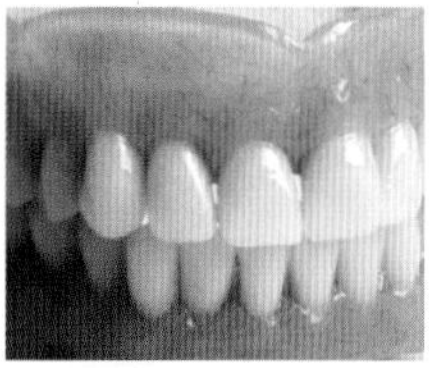

dentures • le dentier • die Zahnprothese • la dentadura postiza • la dentiera

optician • l'opticien • der Augenoptiker • el óptico • l'oculista

case
l'etui
das Futteral
el estuche
la custodia

lens
le verre
das Glas
el cristal
la lente

frame
la monture
das Brillengestell
la montura
la montatura

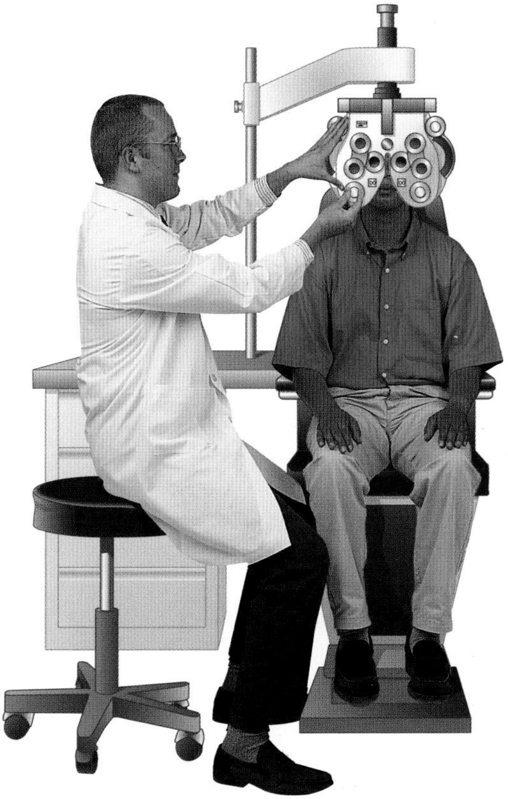

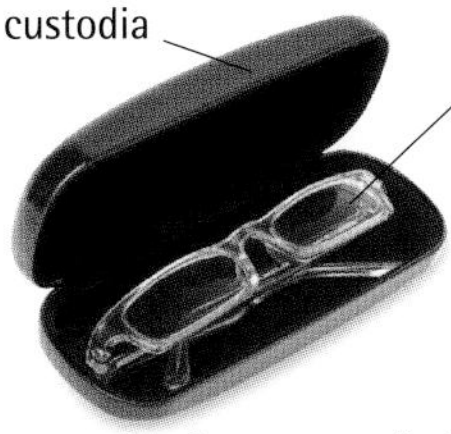

glasses • les lunettes • die Brille • los lentes • gli occhiali

sunglasses • les lunettes de soleil • die Sonnenbrille • los lentes obscuros • gli occhiali da sole

cleaning fluid
la solution nettoyante
das Reinigungsmittel
el líquido limpiador
la soluzione per la pulizia

disinfectant solution
la solution désinfectante
das Desinfektionsmittel
la solución desinfectante
la soluzione disinfettante

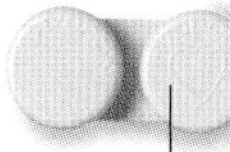

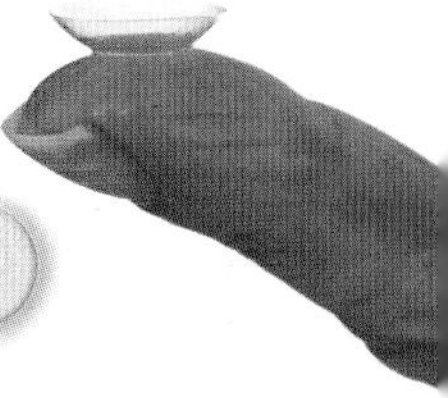

lens case
• l'étui à lentilles
• der Kontaktlinsenbehälter
• el estuche para los pupilentes
• la custodia per le lenti

eye test • l'examen de la vue • der Sehtest • el examen de ojos • l'esame della vista

contact lenses • les lentilles de contact • die Kontaktlinsen • los pupilentes • le lenti a contatto

eye • l'œil • das Auge • el ojo • l'occhio

eyebrow
le sourcil
die Augenbraue
la ceja
il sopracciglio

pupil
la pupille
die Pupille
la pupila
la pupilla

lens
le cristallin
die Linse
el cristalino
il cristallino

cornea • la cornée • die Hornhaut • la córnea • la cornea

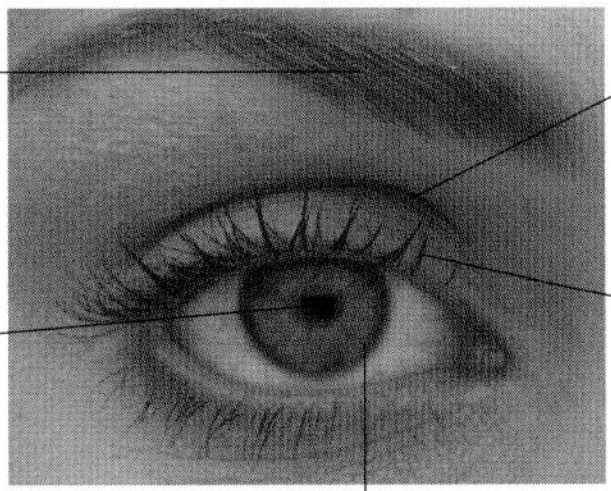

iris • l'iris • die Iris • el iris • l'iride

eyelid
la paupière
das Lid
el párpado
la palpebra

eyelash
le cil
die Wimper
la pestaña
il ciglio

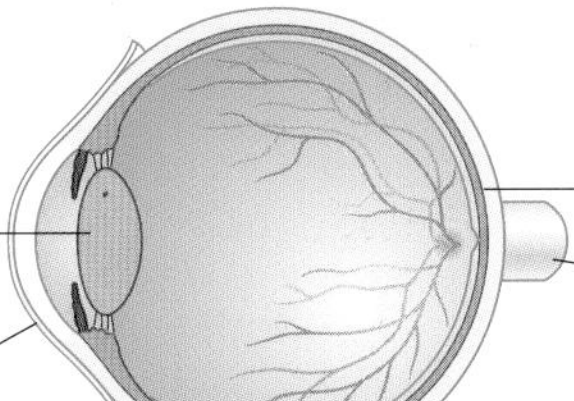

retina
la rétine
die Netzhaut
la retina
la retina

optic nerve
le nerf optique
der Sehnerv
el nervio óptico
il nervo ottico

vision la vue die Sehkraft la vista la vista	**astigmatism** l'astigmatisme der Astigmatismus el astigmatismo l'astigmatismo
diopter la dioptrie die Dioptrie la dioptría la diottria	**farsighted** la presbytie die Weitsichtigkeit la hipermetropía la presbiopia
tear la larme die Träne la lágrima la lacrima	**nearsighted** la myopie die Kurzsichtigkeit la miopía la miopia
cataract la cataracte der graue Star la catarata la cataratta	**bifocal** bifocal Bifokal- bifocal bifocale

pregnancy • la grossesse • die Schwangerschaft • el embarazo • la gravidanza

pregnancy test • le test de grossesse • der Schwangerschaftstest • la prueba del embarazo • il test di gravidanza

scan
l'échographie
die Ultraschallaufnahme
el ultrasonido
l'ecografia

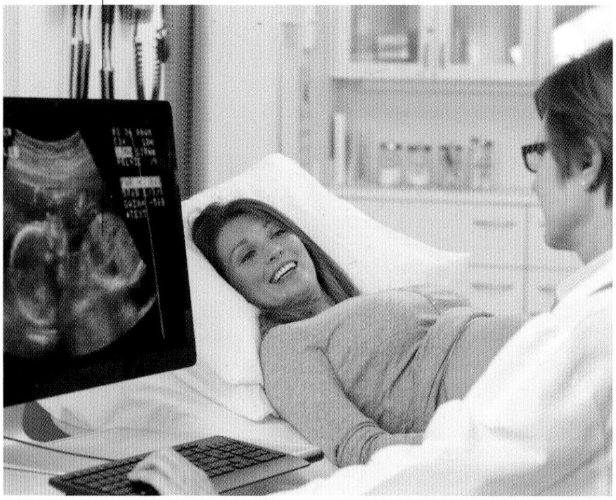

ultrasound • les ultrasons • der Ultraschall • el ultrasonido • l'ultrasuono

umbilical cord
le cordon ombilical
die Nabelschnur
el cordón umbilical
il cordone ombelicale

placenta
le placenta
die Plazenta
la placenta
la placenta

cervix
le col de l'utérus
der Gebärmutterhals
el cuello uterino
la cervice

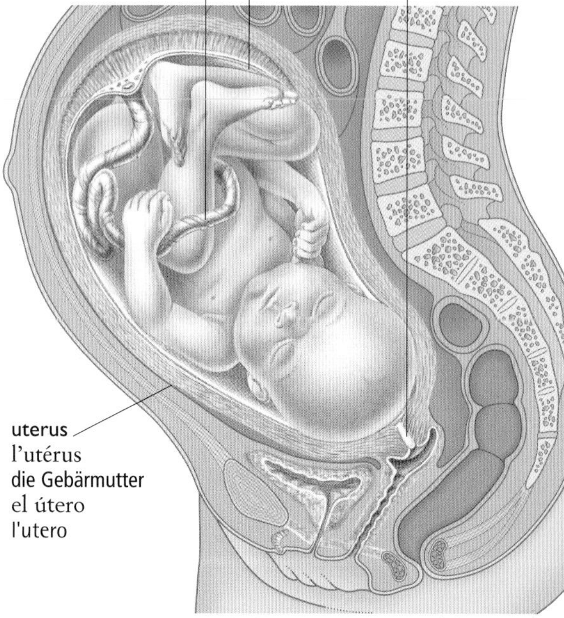

uterus
l'utérus
die Gebärmutter
el útero
l'utero

fetus • le fœtus • der Fetus • el feto • il feto

ovulation l'ovulation der Eisprung la ovulación l'ovulazione	antenatal prénatal vorgeburtlich prenatal prenatale	amniotic fluid le liquide amniotique das Fruchtwasser el líquido amniótico il liquido amniotico	dilation la dilatation die Erweiterung la dilatación la dilatazione	stitches les points de suture die Naht las puntadas i punti	breech par le siège Steiß- de espaldas podalico
conception la conception die Empfängnis la concepción il concepimento	trimester le trimestre das Trimester el trimestre il trimestre	amniocentesis l'amniocentèse die Amniozentese la amniocentesis l'amniocentesi	epidural la péridurale die Periduralanästhesie la epidural l'epidurale	delivery l'accouchement die Entbindung el parto il parto	premature prématuré vorzeitig prematuro prematuro
pregnant enceinte schwanger embarazada incinta	embryo l'embryon der Embryo el embrión l'embrione	contraction la contraction die Wehe la contracción la contrazione	cesarean section la césarienne der Kaiserschnitt la cesárea il taglio cesareo	birth la naissance die Geburt el nacimiento la nascita	gynecologist le gynécologue der Gynäkologe el ginecólogo il ginecologo
expectant enceinte schwanger embarazada in stato interessante	womb l'utérus die Gebärmutter la matriz l'utero	break water *(v)* perdre les eaux das Fruchtwasser geht ab romper aguas rompere le acque	episiotomy l'épisiotomie der Dammschnitt la episiotomía l'episiotomia	miscarriage la fausse couche die Fehlgeburt el aborto espontáneo l'aborto spontaneo	obstetrician l'obstétricien der Geburtshelfer el obstetra l'ostetrico

childbirth • la naissance • die Geburt • el parto • il parto

drip • la perfusion • die Tropfinfusion • el suero • la flebo

midwife
la sage-femme
die Hebamme
la partera
l'ostetrica

monitor
le moniteur
der Monitor
el monitor
il monitor

catheter
le cathéter
der Katheter
el catéter
il catetere

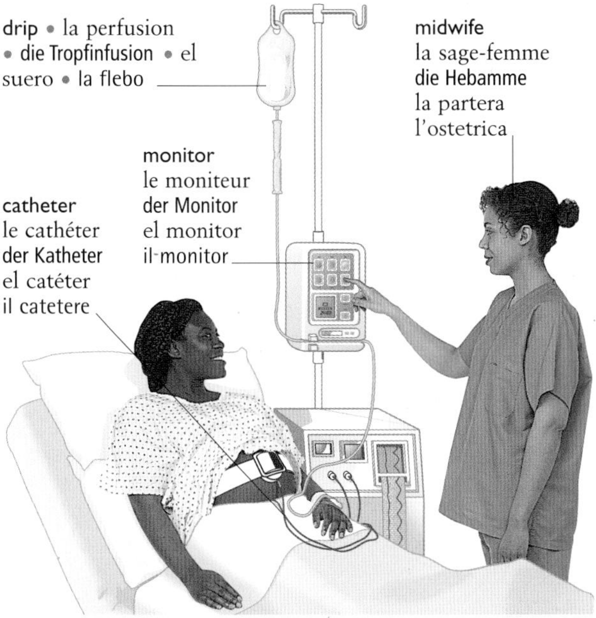

induce labor *(v)* • déclencher l'accouchement • die Geburt einleiten • inducir el parto • indurre il travaglio

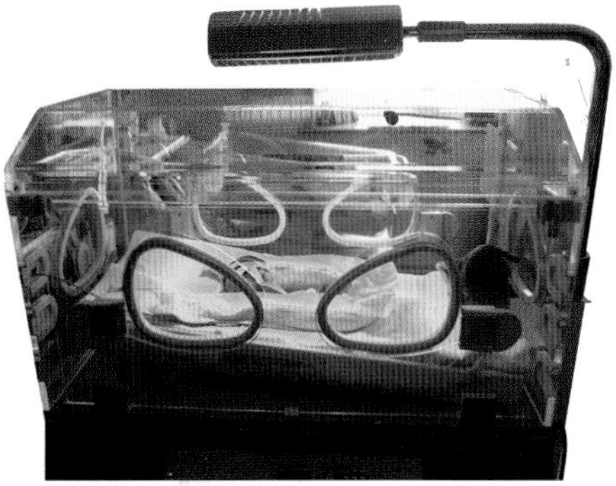

incubator • la couveuse • der Brutkasten • la incubadora • l'incubatrice

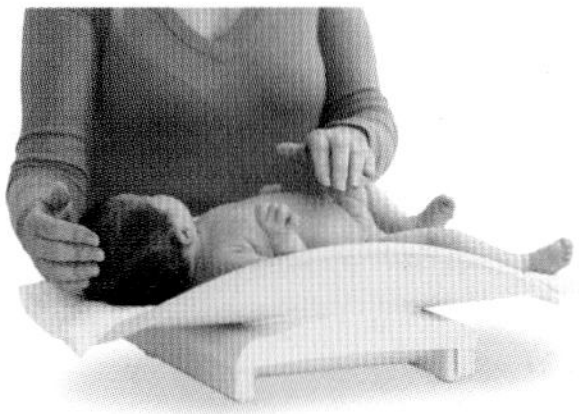

birth weight • le poids de naissance • das Geburtsgewicht • el peso al nacer • il peso alla nascita

forceps • le forceps • die Geburtszange • los fórceps • il forcipe

suction cup • la ventouse • die Saugglocke • la ventosa • la ventosa

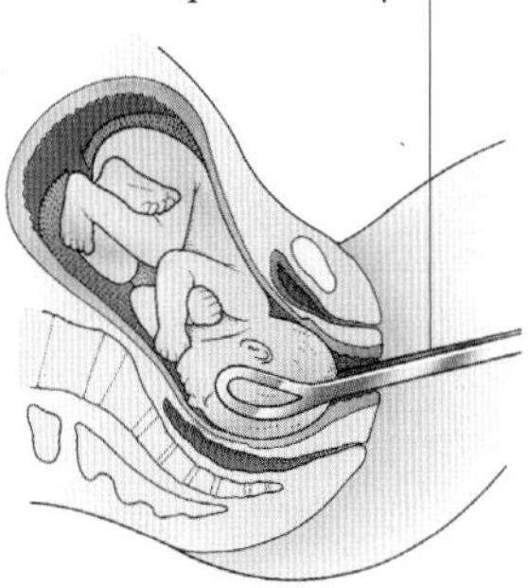

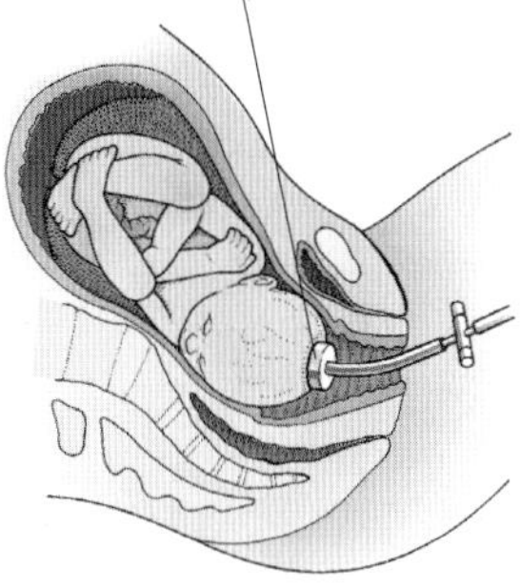

assisted delivery • l'accouchement assisté • die assistierte Entbindung • el parto asistido • il parto assistito

identity tag • le bracelet d'identité • das Erkennungsetikett • la pulsera de identificación • la targhetta d'identità

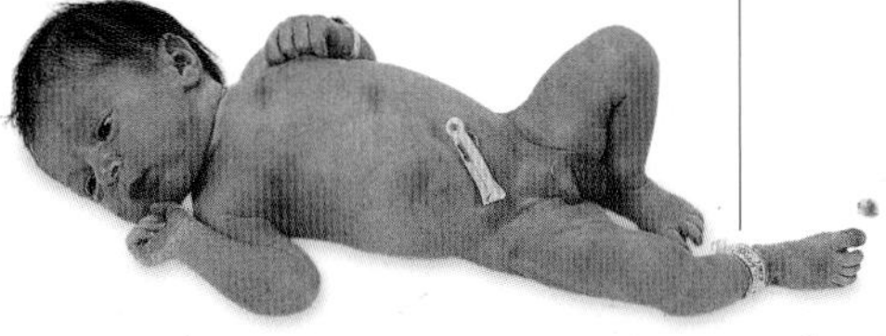

newborn baby • le nouveau-né • das Neugeborene • el recién nacido • il neonato

nursing • l'allaitement • das Stillen • la lactancia • l'allattamento

breast pump • la pompe à lait • die Brustpumpe • el tiraleches • la pompa tiralatte

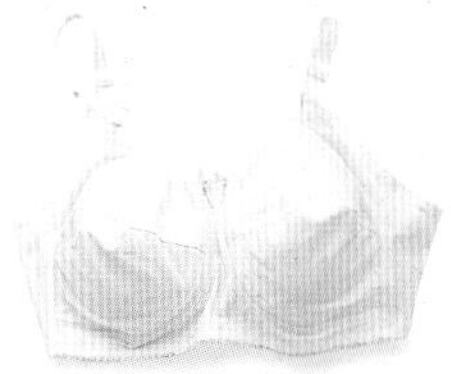

nursing bra • le soutien-gorge d'allaitement • der Stillbüstenhalter • el brassiere para la lactancia • il reggiseno da allattamento

breastfeed *(v)* • donner le sein • stillen • amamantar • allattare al seno

pads • les coussinets • die Einlagen • los discos protectores • le coppe

alternative therapy • les thérapies alternatives • die Alternativtherapien • las terapias alternativas • le terapie alternative

yoga • le yoga • das Yoga • el yoga • lo yoga

massage • le massage • die Massage • el masaje • il massaggio

shiatsu • le shiatsu • das Shiatsu • el shiatsu • lo shiatsu

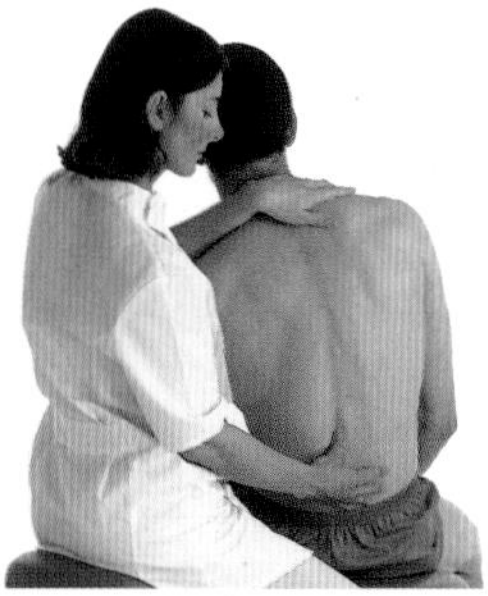

chiropractic • la chiropractie • die Chiropraktik • la quiropráctica • la chiropratica

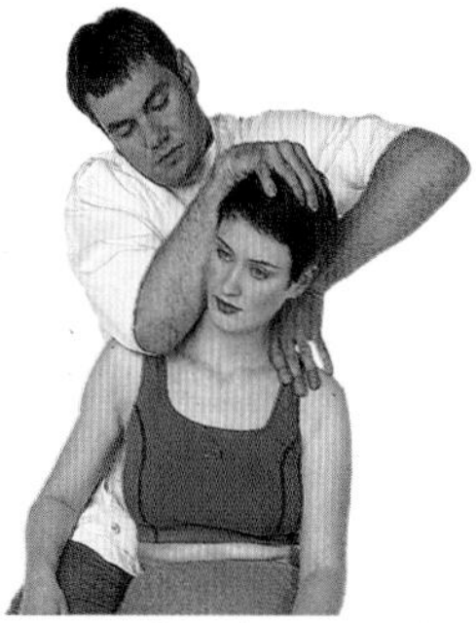

osteopathy • l'ostéopathie • die Osteopathie • la osteopatía • l'osteopatia

reflexology • la réflexiologie • die Reflexzonenmassage • la reflexología • la riflessologia

meditation • la méditation • die Meditation • la meditación • la meditazione counselor • le conseiller • der Berater • el terapeuta • l'assistente socio-psicologico

group therapy • la thérapie de groupe • die Gruppentherapie • la terapia de grupo • la terapia di gruppo

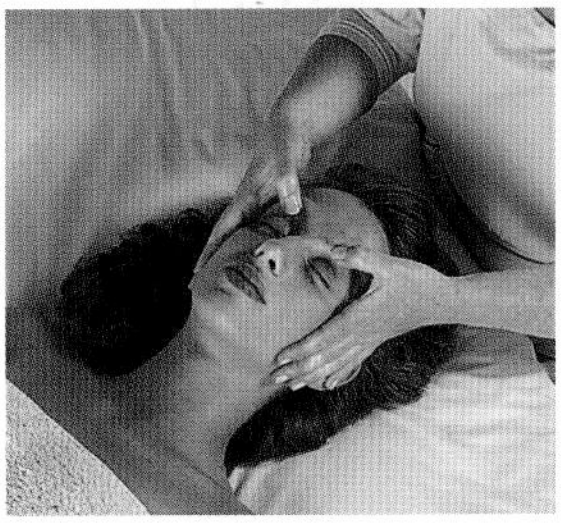

reiki • le reiki • das Reiki • el reiki • il reiki

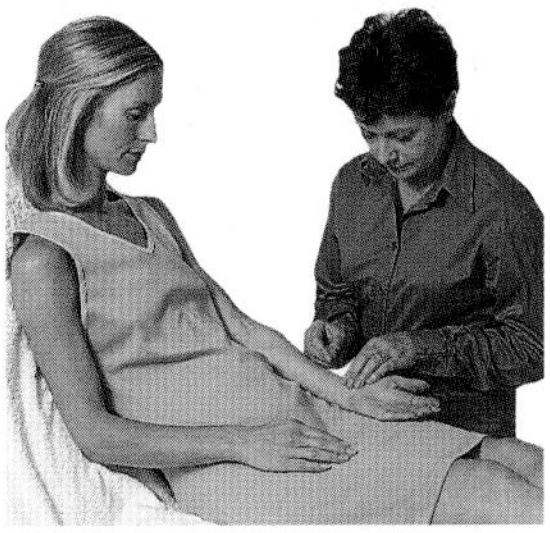

acupuncture • l'acuponcture • die Akupunktur • la acupuntura • l'agopuntura

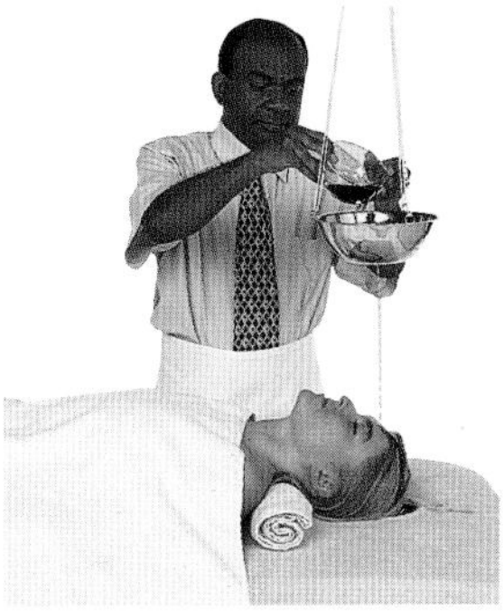

ayurveda • la médecine ayurvédique • das Ayurveda • la ayurveda • la medicina aiurvedica

hypnotherapy • l'hypnothérapie • die Hypnotherapie • la hipnoterapia • l'ipnositerapia

herbalism • l'herboristerie • die Kräuterheilkunde • el herbolario • l'erbalismo

essential oils • les huiles essentielles • die ätherischen Öle • los aceites esenciales • gli oli essenziali

aromatherapy • l'aromathérapie • die Aromatherapie • la aromaterapia • l'aromaterapia

homeopathy • l'homéopathie • die Homöopathie • la homeopatía • l'omeopatia

acupressure • l'acupression • die Akupressur • la acupresión • l'agopressione

therapist • la thérapeute • die Therapeutin • la terapeuta • la terapista

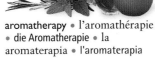

psychotherapy • la psychothérapie • die Psychotherapie • la psicoterapia • la psicoterapia

crystal healing	naturopathy	relaxation	herb
la guérison par cristaux	la naturopathie	la relaxation	l'herbe
die Kristalltherapie	die Naturheilkunde	die Entspannung	das Heilkraut
la cristaloterapia	la naturopatía	la relajación	la hierba
la cristalloterapia	la naturopatia	il rilassamento	l'erba
hydrotherapy	feng shui	stress	supplement
l'hydrothérapie	le feng shui	le stress	le supplément
die Wasserbehandlung	das Feng Shui	der Stress	die Ergänzung
la hidroterapia	el feng shui	el estrés	el suplemento
l'idroterapia	il feng shui	lo stress	l'integratore

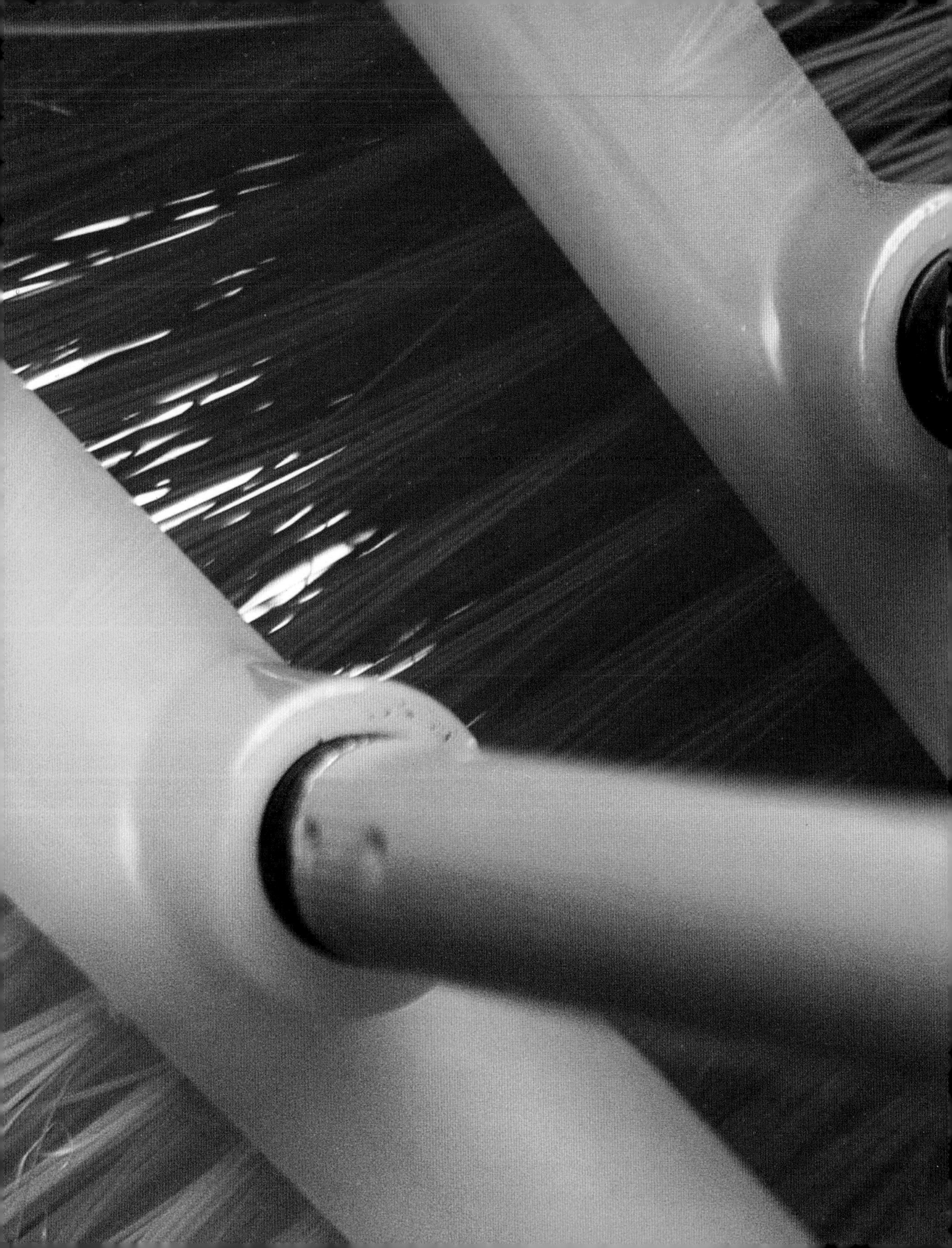

home
la maison
das Haus
la casa
la casa

house • la maison • das Haus • la casa • la casa

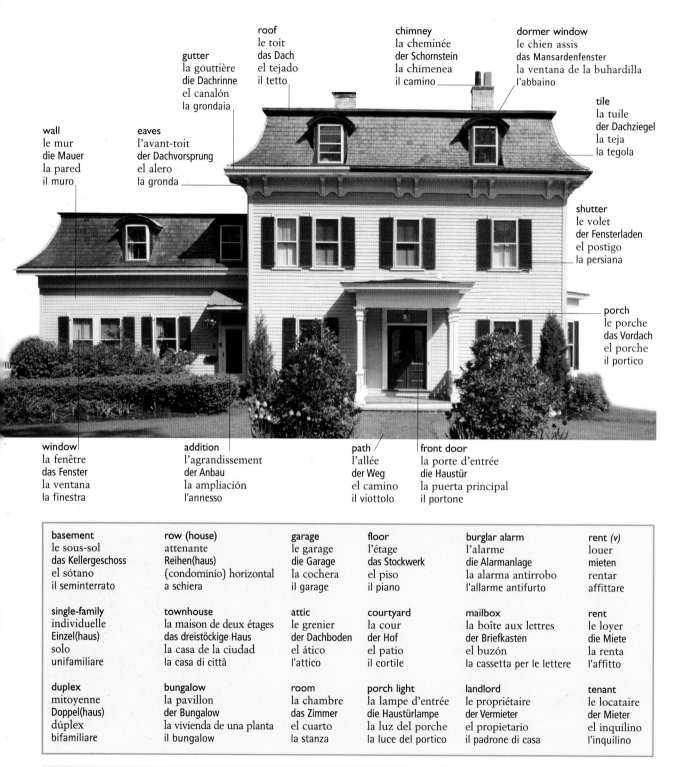

basement le sous-sol das Kellergeschoss el sótano il seminterrato	**row (house)** attenante Reihen(haus) (condominio) horizontal a schiera	**garage** le garage die Garage la cochera il garage	**floor** l'étage das Stockwerk el piso il piano	**burglar alarm** l'alarme die Alarmanlage la alarma antirrobo l'allarme antifurto	**rent** *(v)* louer mieten rentar affittare
single-family individuelle Einzel(haus) solo unifamiliare	**townhouse** la maison de deux étages das dreistöckige Haus la casa de la ciudad la casa di città	**attic** le grenier der Dachboden el ático l'attico	**courtyard** la cour der Hof el patio il cortile	**mailbox** la boîte aux lettres der Briefkasten el buzón la cassetta per le lettere	**rent** le loyer die Miete la renta l'affitto
duplex mitoyenne Doppel(haus) dúplex bifamiliare	**bungalow** la pavillon der Bungalow la vivienda de una planta il bungalow	**room** la chambre das Zimmer el cuarto la stanza	**porch light** la lampe d'entrée die Haustürlampe la luz del porche la luce del portico	**landlord** le propriétaire der Vermieter el propietario il padrone di casa	**tenant** le locataire der Mieter el inquilino l'inquilino

entrance • l'entrée • der Eingang • la entrada • l'ingresso

hand rail
la main courante
das Geländer
el pasamanos
il corrimano

landing
le palier
der Treppenabsatz
el descanso
il pianerottolo

banister
la rampe
das Treppengeländer
el barandal
la ringhiera

staircase
l'escalier
die Treppe
la escalera
le scale

hallway • le vestibule • die Diele • el vestíbulo • l'entrata

doorbell • la sonnette • die Türklingel • el timbre •il campanello

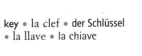

doormat • le paillasson • der Fußabtreter • el tapete • lo zerbino

door knocker • le marteau de porte • der Türklopfer • la aldaba • il battente

door chain • la chaîne de sûreté • die Türkette • la cadena • la catenella

key • la clef • der Schlüssel • la llave • la chiave

lock • la serrure • das Schloss • la cerradura • la serratura

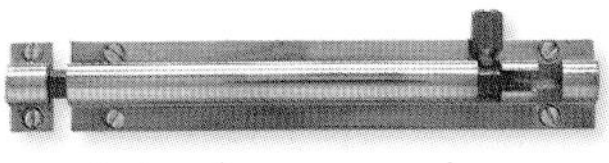

bolt • le verrou • der Türriegel • el cerrojo • il chiavistello

apartment • l'appartement • die Wohnung • el departamento • l'appartamento

balcony • le balcon • der Balkon • el balcón • il balcone

apartment block • l'immeuble • der Wohnblock • el edificio • il palazzo

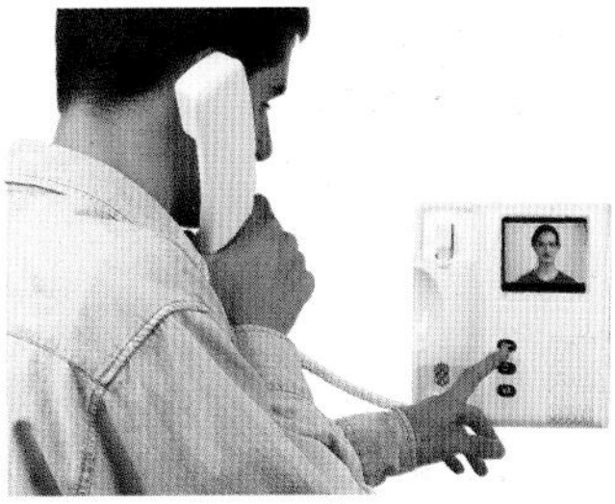

intercom • l'interphone • die Sprechanlage • el interfono • il citofono

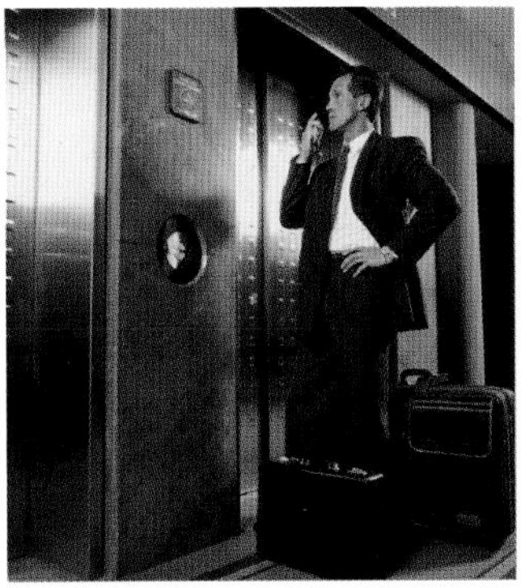

elevator • l'ascenseur • der Fahrstuhl • el elevador • l'ascensore

internal systems • les systèmes domestiques • die Hausanschlüsse • las instalaciones internas • i sistemi interni

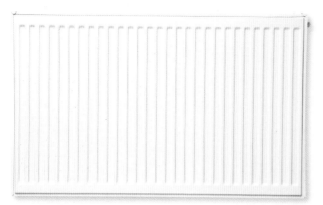

radiator • le radiateur • der Heizkörper • el radiador • il calorifero

space heater • l'appareil de chauffage • der Heizofen • el calentador • la stufa

blade • l'aile • der Flügel • el aspa • la pala

fan • le ventilateur • der Ventilator • el ventilador • il ventilatore

portable heater • le convecteur • der Heizlüfter • el calentador de convección • la stufa a convezione

electricity • l'électricité • die Elektrizität • la electricidad • l'elettricità

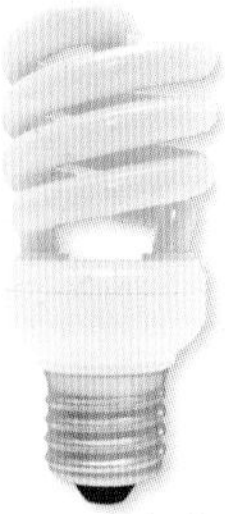

energy saving bulb • l'ampoule basse consommation • die Energiesparbirne • la bombilla de ahorro de energía • la lampadina a risparmio energetico

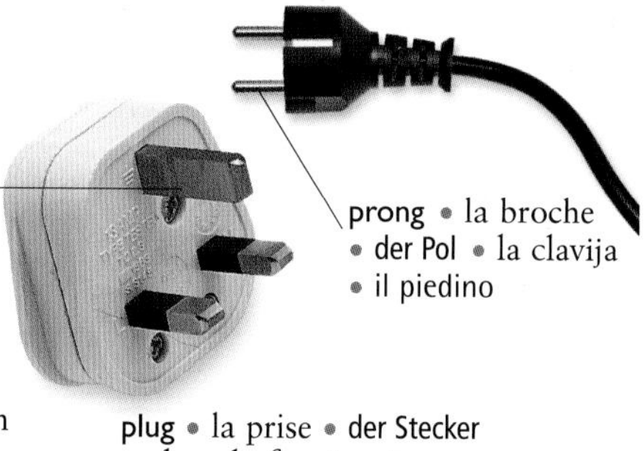

ground • la mise à la terre • die Erdung • la toma de tierra • la messa a terra

prong • la broche • der Pol • la clavija • il piedino

plug • la prise • der Stecker • el enchufe • la spina

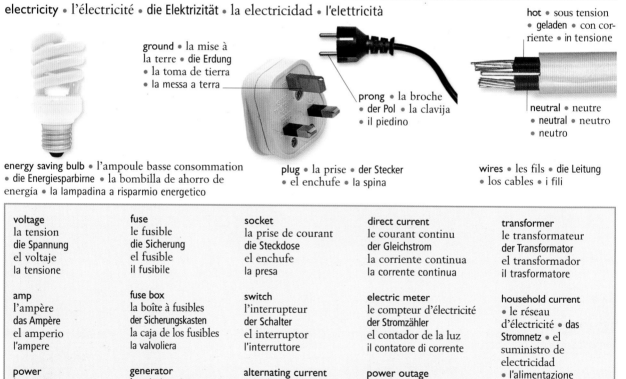

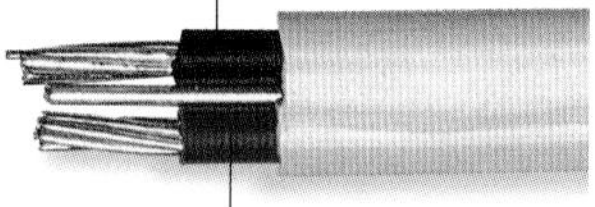

hot • sous tension • geladen • con corriente • in tensione

neutral • neutre • neutral • neutro • neutro

wires • les fils • die Leitung • los cables • i fili

voltage la tension die Spannung el voltaje la tensione	fuse le fusible die Sicherung el fusible il fusibile	socket la prise de courant die Steckdose el enchufe la presa	direct current le courant continu der Gleichstrom la corriente continua la corrente continua	transformer le transformateur der Transformator el transformador il trasformatore
amp l'ampère das Ampère el amperio l'ampere	fuse box la boîte à fusibles der Sicherungskasten la caja de los fusibles la valvoliera	switch l'interrupteur der Schalter el interruptor l'interruttore	electric meter le compteur d'électricité der Stromzähler el contador de la luz il contatore di corrente	household current • le réseau d'électricité • das Stromnetz • el suministro de electricidad • l'alimentazione di rete
power le courant der Strom la corriente eléctrica l'elettricità	generator la génératrice der Generator el generador il generatore	alternating current le courant alternatif der Wechselstrom la corriente alterna la corrente alternata	power outage la coupure de courant der Stromausfall el corte de luz l'interruzione di corrente	

plumbing • la plomberie • die Installation • la fontanería • l'impianto idraulico

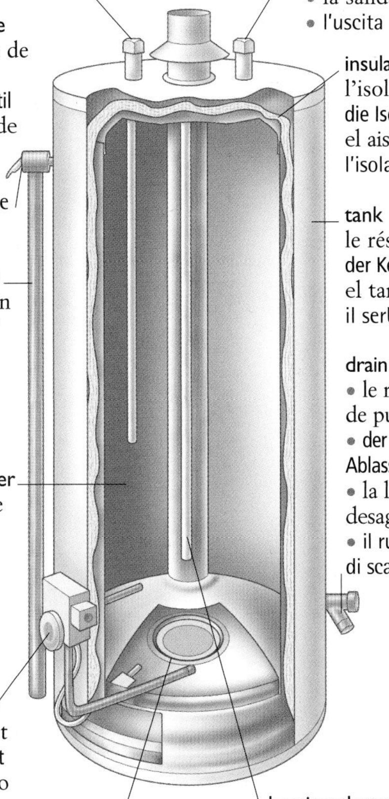

inlet • l'arrivée • die Zuleitung • la toma • l'entrata

pressure valve • la soupape de sûreté • das Sicherheitsventil • la válvula de la presión • la valvola della pressione

overflow pipe • le trop-plein • der Überlauf • el tubo de desagüe • il tubo di troppopieno

water chamber • la chambre d'eau • der Wasserraum • el tanque del agua • il serbatoio dell'acqua

thermostat
le thermostat
der Thermostat
el termostato
il termostato

burner • le brûleur à gaz • der Gasbrenner • el quemador • il ruciatore a gas

outlet • la sortie • der Auslass • la salida • l'uscita

insulation
l'isolation
die Isolierung
el aislamiento
l'isolamento

tank
le réservoir
der Kessel
el tanque
il serbatoio

drain valve • le robinet de purge • der Ablasshahn • la llave del desagüe • il rubinetto di scarico

heating element
la résistance
das Heizelement
la resistencia
l'elemento riscaldante

boiler • la chaudière • der Boiler • la caldera • lo scaldaacqua

sink • l'évier • die Spüle • el fregador • l'acquaio

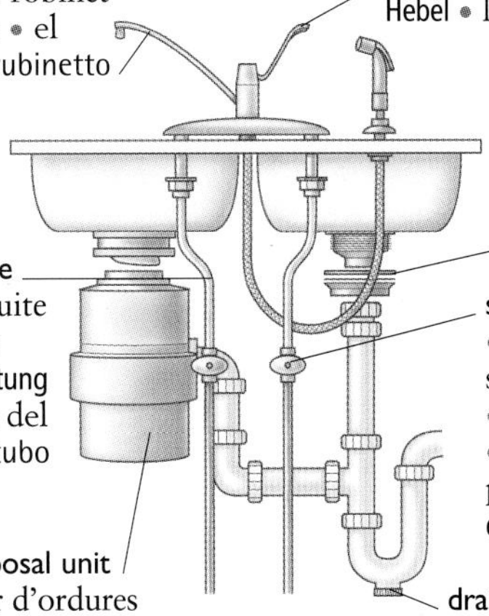

faucet • le robinet • der Hahn • el grifo • il rubinetto

supply pipe • la conduite d'amenée • die Zuleitung • la toma del agua • il tubo dell'acqua

waste disposal unit
le broyeur d'ordures
der Müllschlucker
el triturador de basuras
il macinatore di rifiuti

lever • la manette • der Hebel • la palanca • la leva

gasket
le joint
die Dichtung
la junta
la guarnizione

shutoff valve • le robinet de sectionnement • der Absperrhahn • la llave de paso • il rubinetto di arresto

drain • le tuyau d'écoulement • der Abfluss • el desagüe • lo scolo

toilet • les W.-C. • das WC • el retrete • il water

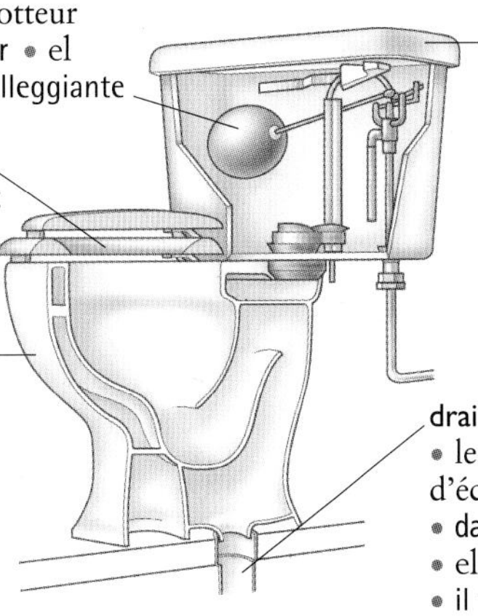

float ball • le flotteur • der Schwimmer • el flotador • il galleggiante

seat • le siège • der Toilettensitz • la tapa • il sedile

bowl
la cuvette
das Becken
la taza
la tazza

tank • la chasse-d'eau • der Spülkasten • el depósito • la cassetta

drain • le tuyau d'écoulement • das Abflussrohr • el desagüe • il tubo di scolo

waste disposal • l'enlèvement de déchets • die Abfallentsorgung • la eliminación de desechos • lo smaltimento dei rifiuti

bottle
la bouteille
die Flasche
la botella
la bottiglia

recycling bin • la boîte à déchets recyclables • der Recyclingbehälter • el cubo para reciclar • il contenitore di riciclaggio

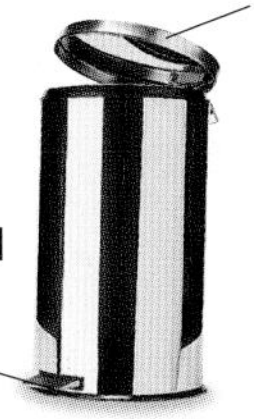

pedal
la pédale
der Trethebel
el pedal
il pedale

lid
le couvercle
der Deckel
la tapa
il coperchio

trash can • la poubelle • der Abfalleimer • el cubo de la basura • la pattumiera

sorting unit • la boîte de tri • die Abfallsortiereinheit • el armario para clasificar la basura • l'unità di smistamento

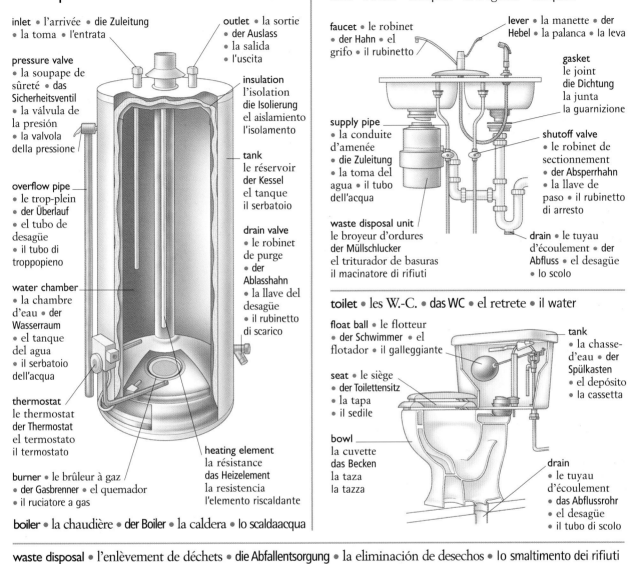

organic waste • les déchets bios • der Bio-Abfall • los desperdicios orgánicos • i rifiuti organici

living room • le salon • das Wohnzimmer • la sala • il salotto

wall light
l'applique
die Wandlampe
el arbotante
l'applique

fireplace
la cheminée
der Kamin
la chimenea
il caminetto

ceiling
le plafond
die Decke
el techo
il soffitto

vase
le vase
die Vase
el jarrón
il vaso

pillow
le coussin
das Sofakissen
el cojín
il cuscino

lamp
la lampe
die Lampe
la lámpara
la lampada

coffee table
la table basse
der Couchtisch
la mesa de centro
il tavolino

sofa
le canapé
das Sofa
el sofá
il divano

floor
le sol
der Fußboden
el piso
il pavimento

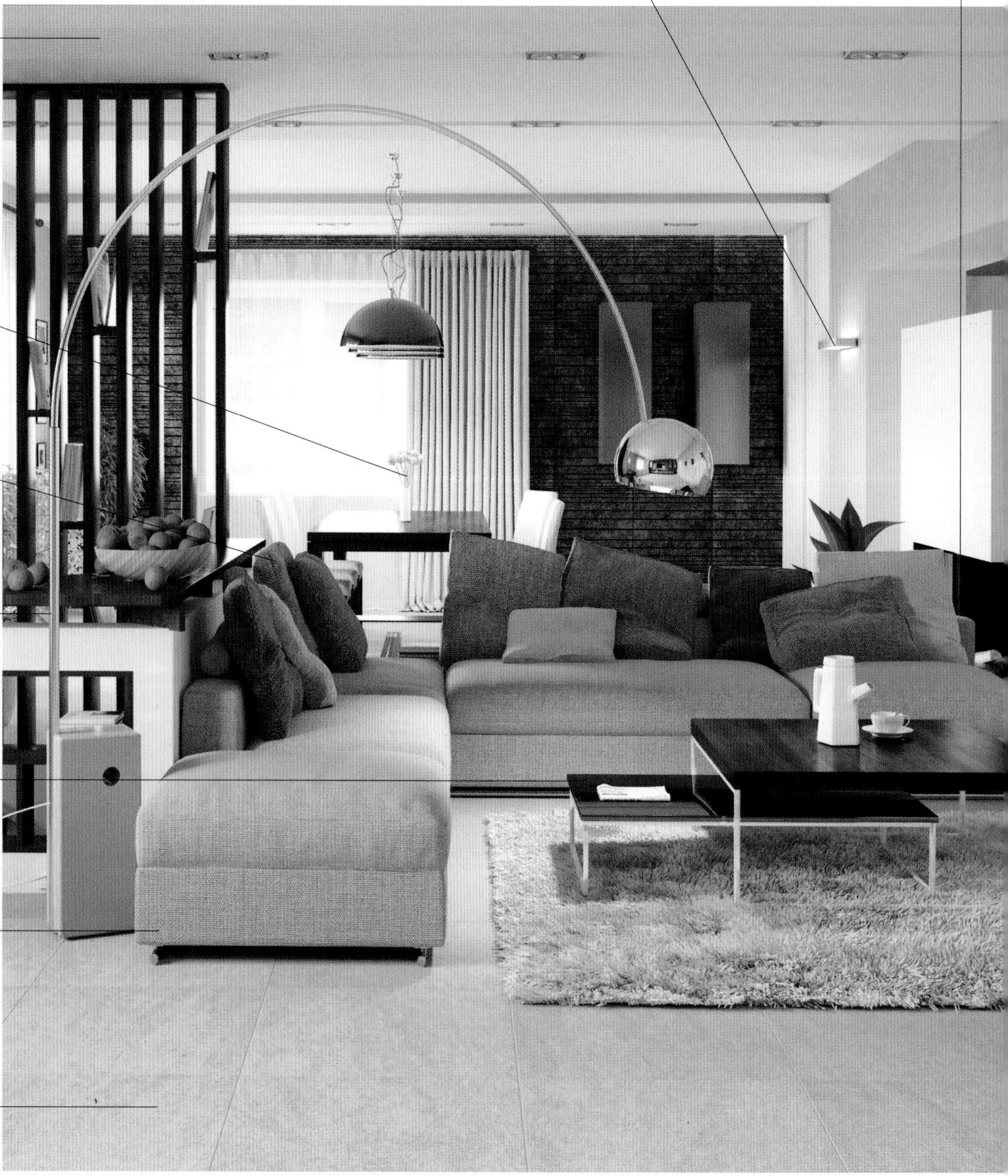

frame
le cadre
der Bilderrahmen
el marco
la cornice

painting
le tableau
das Gemälde
el cuadro
il quadro

curtain • le rideau • der Vorhang • la cortina • la tenda

net curtain • le brise-bise • die Gardine • el visillo • la tendina

venetian blind • le store vénitien • die Jalousie • la persiana • la veneziana

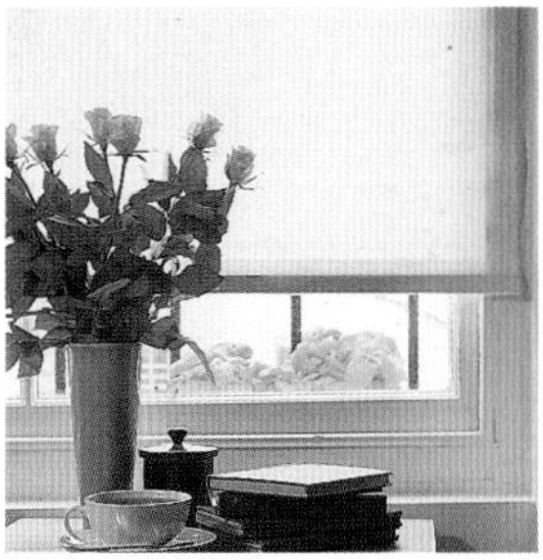

roller blind • le store • das Rollo • el estor • l'avvolgibile

molding • la moulure • der Stuck • la moldura • la cornice

armchair • le fauteuil • der Sessel • el sillón • la poltrona

bookshelf
la bibliothèque
das Bücherregal
el librero
la libreria

sofabed
le canapé-lit
die Bettcouch
el sofá-cama
il divano letto

rug
le tapis
der Teppich
el tapete
il tappeto

study • le bureau • das Arbeitszimmer • el estudio • lo studio

dining room • la salle à manger • das Esszimmer • el comedor • la sala da pranzo

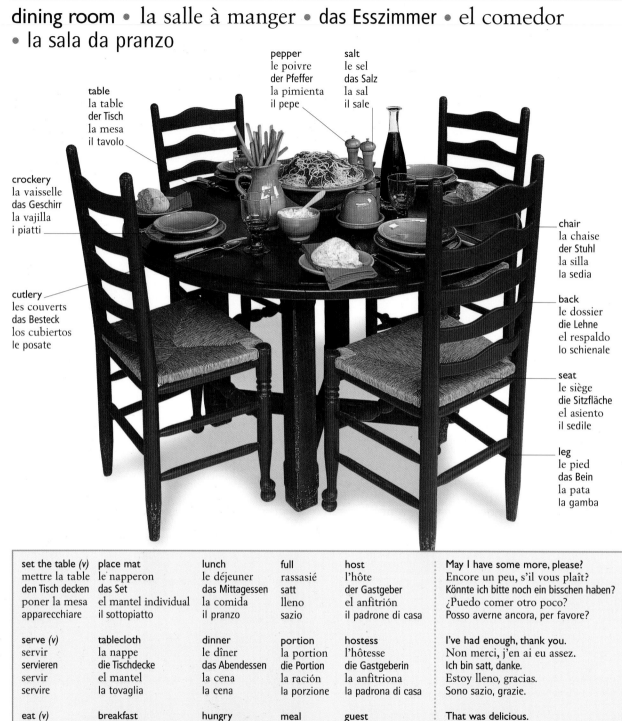

set the table *(v)* mettre la table den Tisch decken poner la mesa apparecchiare	**place mat** le napperon das Set el mantel individual il sottopiatto	**lunch** le déjeuner das Mittagessen la comida il pranzo	**full** rassasié satt lleno sazio	**host** l'hôte der Gastgeber el anfitrión il padrone di casa	**May I have some more, please?** Encore un peu, s'il vous plaît? Könnte ich bitte noch ein bisschen haben? ¿Puedo comer otro poco? Posso averne ancora, per favore?
serve *(v)* servir servieren servir servire	**tablecloth** la nappe die Tischdecke el mantel la tovaglia	**dinner** le dîner das Abendessen la cena la cena	**portion** la portion die Portion la ración la porzione	**hostess** l'hôtesse die Gastgeberin la anfitriona la padrona di casa	**I've had enough, thank you.** Non merci, j'en ai eu assez. Ich bin satt, danke. Estoy lleno, gracias. Sono sazio, grazie.
eat *(v)* manger essen comer mangiare	**breakfast** le petit déjeuner das Frühstück el desayuno la colazione	**hungry** (avoir) faim hungrig hambriento affamato	**meal** le repas das Essen la comida il pasto	**guest** l'invité der Gast el invitado l'ospite	**That was delicious.** C'était délicieux. Das war lecker. Estaba riquísimo. Era squisito.

crockery and cutlery • la vaisselle et les couverts • das Geschirr und das Besteck • la vajilla y los cubiertos • le stovigle e le posate

mug • la grande tasse • der Becher • la taza • la tazza

coffee cup • la tasse à café • die Kaffeetasse • la taza de café • la tazzina da caffè

teaspoon • la cuiller à café • der Teelöffel • la cucharilla de café • il cucchiaino

teacup • la tasse à thé • die Teetasse • la taza de té • la tazza da tè

plate • l'assiette • der Teller • el plato • il piatto

bowl • le bol • die Schüssel • el plato sopero • la ciotola

French press • la cafetière • die Cafetière • la cafetera de émbolo • la caffettiera

teapot • la théière • die Teekanne • la tetera • la teiera

pitcher • le pot • das Kännchen • la jarra • la brocca

egg cup • le coquetier • der Eierbecher • la taza para el huevo • il portauovo

tumbler
le verre
das Wasserglas
el vaso
il bicchiere

wine glass • le verre à vin • das Weinglas • la copa de vino• il calice da vino

glassware • la verrerie • die Glaswaren • la cristalería • la cristalleria

napkin ring
le rond de serviette
der Serviettenring
el servilletero
il portatovagliolo

dessert plate
l'assiette à dessert
der Beilagenteller
el plato del pan
il piattino

dinner plate
l'assiette plate
der Essteller
el plato
il piatto piano

soup bowl
l'assiette à soupe
der Suppenteller
el plato sopero
il piatto fondo

soup spoon • la cuiller à soupe • der Suppenlöffel • la cuchara sopera • il cucchiaio da minestra

napkin
la serviette
die Serviette
la servilleta
il tovagliolo

fork • la fourchette • die Gabel • el tenedor • la forchetta

spoon
la cuiller
der Löffel
la cuchara
il cucchiaio

knife
le couteau
das Messer
el cuchillo
il coltello

place setting • le couvert • das Gedeck • el lugar en la mesa • il coperto

kitchen • la cuisine • die Küche • la cocina • la cucina

shelves
l'étagère
das Küchenregal
los estantes
le mensole

splashback
le revêtement
der Spritzschutz
el frente de la cocina
l'alzatina paraspruzzi

faucet
le robinet
der Wasserhahn
el grifo
il rubinetto

sink
l'évier
das Spülbecken
el fregadero
il lavandino

drawer
le tiroir
die Schublade
el cajón
il cassetto

ventilation hood
la hotte
der Dunstabzug
el extractor
la cappa

ceramic stovetop • la table de cuisson céramique • das Glaskeramikkochfeld • la placa vitrocerámica • il fornello di ceramica

countertop • le plan de travail • die Arbeitsfläche • la plancha • il piano di lavoro

oven • le four • der Backofen • el horno • il forno

cabinet
le placard
der Küchenschrank
la gaveta
l'armadietto

appliances • les appareils ménagers • die Küchengeräte • los electrodomésticos • gli elettrodomestici

microwave oven • le micro-ondes • die Mikrowelle • el microondas • il forno a microonde

tea kettle • la bouilloire électrique • der Elektrokessel • la jarra para hervir • il bollitore

toaster • le grille-pain • der Toaster • el tostador • il tostapane

work bowl
le bol du mixeur
die Mixerschüssel
el recipiente
il recipiente

blade
la lame
das Messer
la cuchilla
la lama

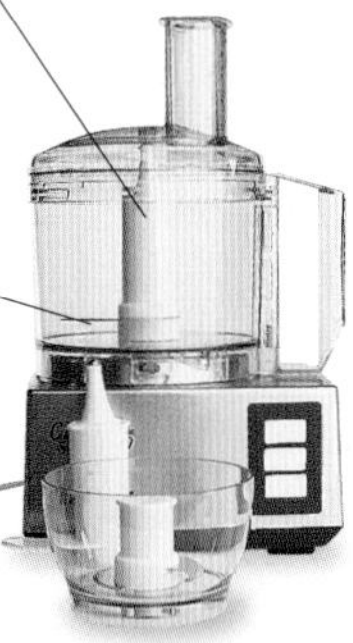

food processor • le robot ménager • die Küchenmaschine • el multimezclador • il tritatutto

lid
le couvercle
der Deckel
la tapa
il coperchio

blender • le mixeur • der Mixer • la licuadora • il frullatore

dishwasher • le lave-vaisselle • die Spülmaschine • la lavavajilla • la lavastoviglie

ice maker • le freezer • das Eisfach • la máquina de los hielos • il fabbricaghiaccio

refrigerator
le frigidaire
der Kühlschrank
el refrigerador
il frigorifero

shelf
la clayette
der Rost
la charola
la mensola

freezer
le congélateur
das Gefrierfach
el congelador
il congelatore

crisper • le bac à légumes • das Gemüsefach • el cajón de las verduras • il cassetto per la verdura

refrigerator-freezer • le réfrigérateur-congélateur • der Gefrier-Kühlschrank • el refrigerador congelador • il frigocongelatore

stove la table de cuisson das Kochfeld la hornilla il piano di cottura	freeze *(v)* congeler einfrieren congelar congelare
draining board l'égouttoir das Abtropfbrett el escurridor lo scolapiatti	defrost *(v)* décongeler auftauen descongelar scongelare
burner le brûleur der Brenner el quemador il fornello	steam *(v)* cuire à la vapeur dämpfen cocer al vapor cuocere al vapore
garbage can la poubelle der Mülleimer el bote de basura la pattumiera	sauté *(v)* sauter anbraten saltear saltare in padella

cooking • la cuisine • das Kochen • cocinar • cucinare

peel *(v)* • éplucher • schälen • pelar • sbucciare

slice *(v)* • couper • schneiden • cortar • affettare

grate *(v)* • râper • reiben • rallar • grattugiare

pour *(v)* • verser • gießen • vaciar • versare

mix *(v)* • mélanger • verrühren • mezclar • mescolare

whisk *(v)* • battre • schlagen • batir • sbattere

boil *(v)* • bouillir • kochen • hervir • bollire

fry *(v)* • frire • braten • freír • friggere

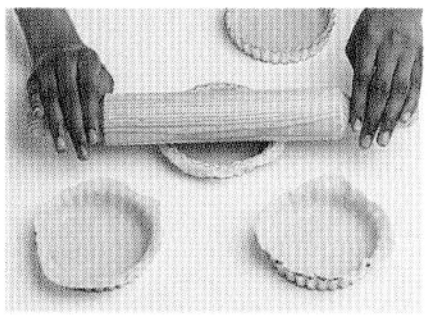

roll *(v)* • abaisser à rouleau • ausrollen • amasar con el rodillo • spianare

stir *(v)* • remuer • rühren • remover • rimestare

simmer *(v)* • mijoter • köcheln lassen • cocer a fuego lento • cuocere a fuoco lento

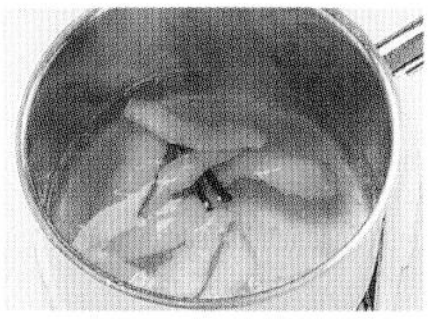

poach *(v)* • pocher • pochieren • escalfar • affogare

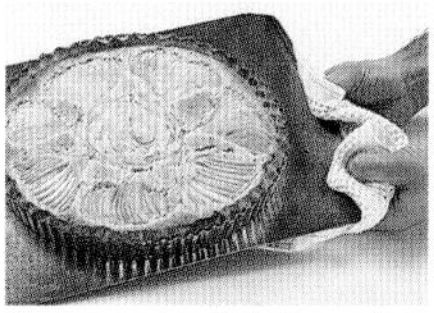

bake *(v)* • cuire au four • backen • hornear • cuocere al forno

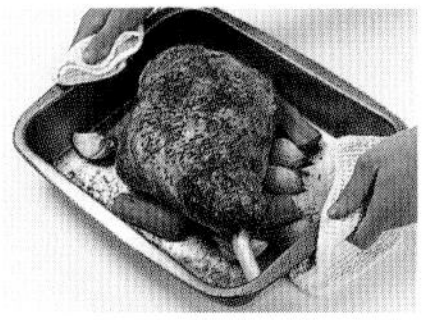

roast *(v)* • rôtir • braten • asar • arrostire

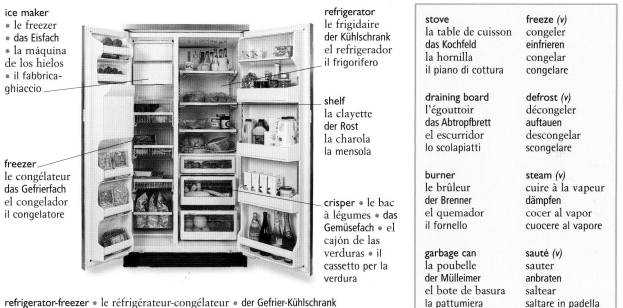

grill *(v)* • griller • grillen • asar a la parrilla • cuocere alla griglia

kitchenware • les ustensiles de cuisine • die Küchengeräte • los utensilios de cocina • gli utensili da cucina

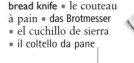

cutting board
la planche à hacher
das Hackbrett
la tabla para cortar
il tagliere

bread knife • le couteau à pain • das Brotmesser • el cuchillo de sierra • il coltello da pane

paring knife
le couteau de cuisine
das Küchenmesser
el cuchillo de cocina
il coltello da cucina

meat cleaver • le fendoir • das Hackmesser • el hacha de cocina • la mannaia

knife sharpener • l'aiguisoir • der Messerschärfer • el afilador • l'affilacoltelli

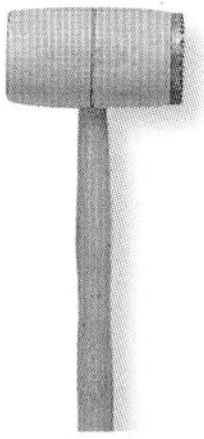

meat tenderizer • l'écrase-viande • der Fleischklopfer • el mazo de cocina • il martello

skewer • la broche • der Spieß • el pincho • lo spiedino

peeler • l'épluche-légume • der Schäler • el pelador • il pelapatate

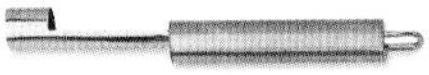

apple corer
le vide-pomme
der Apfelstecher
el descorazonador
il cavatorsoli

grater • la râpe • die Reibe • el rallador • la grattugia

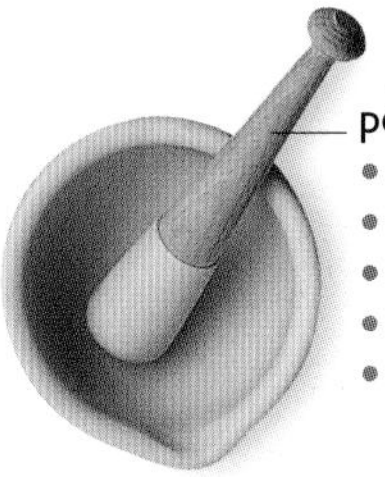

pestle • le pilon • der Stößel • la mano de • mortero • il pestello

mortar • le mortier • der Mörser • el mortero • il mortaio

masher • le presse-purée • der Kartoffelstampfer • el machacador • lo schiacciapatate

can opener • l'ouvre-boîte • der Dosenöffner • el abrelatas • l'apriscatole

bottle opener
l'ouvre-bouteille
der Flaschenöffner
el destapador
l'apribottiglie

garlic press • le presse-ail • die Knoblauchpresse • el exprimidor de ajos • lo spremiaglio

serving spoon • la cuiller à servir • der Servierlöffel • la cuchara de servir • il cucchiaio da portata

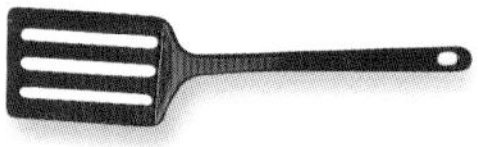

fish spatula • la truelle • der Pfannenwender • la pala • la paletta forata

colander • la passoire • das Sieb • el escurridor • lo scolapasta

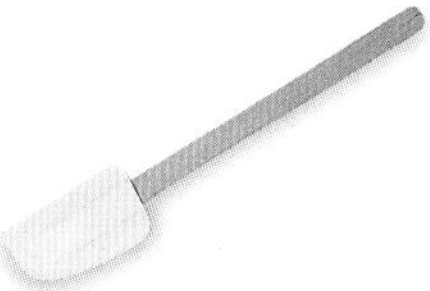

spatula • la spatule • der Spachtel • la espátula • la spatola

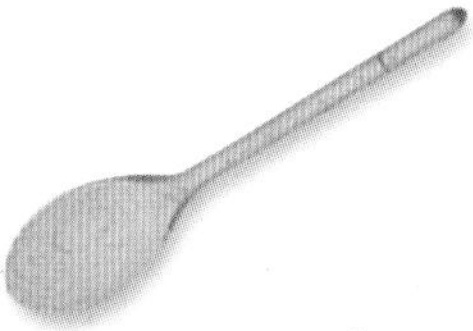

wooden spoon • la cuiller en bois • der Holzlöffel • la cuchara de madera • il cucchiaio di legno

mesh skimmer
l'écumoire
der Schaumlöffel
la espumadera
la schiumarola

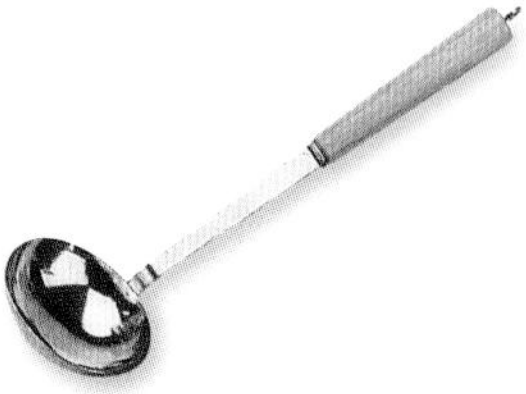

ladle • la louche • der Schöpflöffel • el cucharón • il mestolo

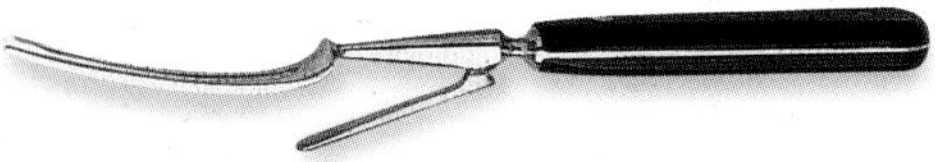

carving fork • la fourchette à découper • die Tranchiergabel • el trinche • il forchettone

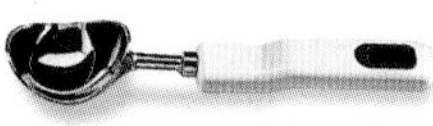

ice-cream scoop • la cuiller à glace • der Portionierer • la cuchara para helado • il cucchiaio dosatore

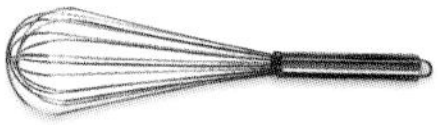

whisk • le fouet • der Schneebesen • el globo para batir • la frusta

strainer • la passoire • das Sieb • el colador • il colino

lid • le couvercle • der Deckel • la tapa • il coperchio

nonstick • anti-adhérent • kunststoffbeschichtet • antiadherente • antiaderente

frying pan • la poêle • die Bratpfanne • la sartén • la padella

saucepan • la casserole • der Kochtopf • la cacerola • la pentola

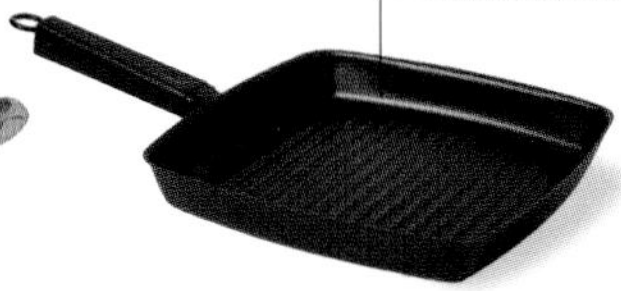

griddle • le gril • das Grillblech • la parrilla • la padella per grigliare

wok • le wok • der Wok • el wok • il wok

earthenware dish • le fait-tout • der Schmortopf • la olla de barro • la casseruola di terracotta

glass • en verre • Glas- • de cristal • di vetro

mixing bowl • le grand bol • die Rührschüssel • la ensaladera • la scodella

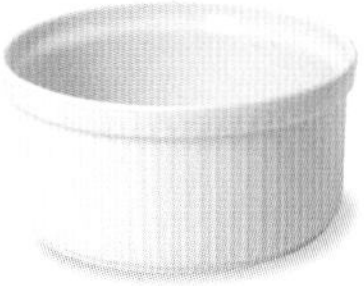

soufflé dish • le moule à soufflé • die Souffléform • el molde para suflé • lo stampo per soufflé

ovenproof • allant au four • feuerfest • resistente al horno • pirofilo

gratin dish • le plat à gratin • die Auflaufform • la fuente para gratinar • il piatto da gratin

ramekin • le ramequin • das Auflaufförmchen • el molde individual • lo stampo

casserole dish • la cocotte • die Kasserolle • la cazuela • la casseruola

baking cakes • la pâtisserie • das Kuchenbacken • la repostería • la cottura dei dolci

scales • la balance • die Haushaltswaage • la báscula de cocina • la bilancia

measuring cup • le pot gradué • der Messbecher • la taza medidora • il bricco misuratore

cake pan • le moule à gâteaux • die Kuchenform • el molde para pastel • lo stampo per dolci

pie pan • la tourtière • die Pastetenform • el molde redondo • lo stampo per torte

flan pan • le moule à tarte • die Obstkuchenform • la flanera • lo stampo per flan

pastry brush • le pinceau à pâtisserie • der Backpinsel • la brocha de cocina • il pennello da cucina

rolling pin • le rouleau pâtissier • das Nudelholz • el rodillo de cocina • il matterello

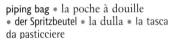

piping bag • la poche à douille • der Spritzbeutel • la dulla • la tasca da pasticciere

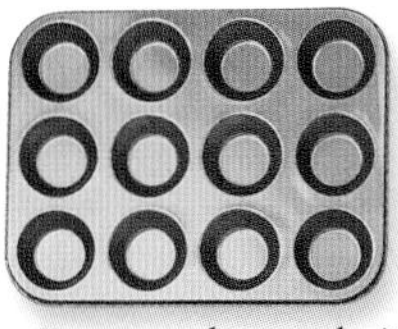

muffin pan • le moule à muffins • die Törtchenform • el molde para panqués • la teglia per pasticcini

cookie sheet • la plaque à gâteaux • das Kuchenblech • la charola de horno • la placca da forno

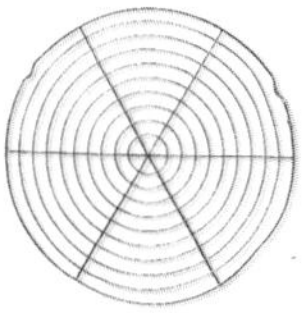

cooling rack • la grille de refroidissement • das Abkühlgitter • la rejilla • la gratella

oven mitt • le gant isolant • der Topfhandschuh • el guante de cocina • il guanto da forno

apron • le tablier • die Schürze • el delantal • il grembiule

bedroom • la chambre • das Schlafzimmer • la recámara • la camera da letto

wardrobe
l'armoire
der Kleiderschrank
el armario
l'armadio

bedside lamp
la lampe de chevet
die Nachttischlampe
la lámpara del buró
l'abat-jour

headboard
la tête de lit
das Kopfende
la cabecera
la testata

nightstand
la table de nuit
der Nachttisch
el buró
il comodino

chest of drawers
la commode
die Kommode
la cómoda
il cassettone

drawer
le tiroir
die Schublade
el cajón
il cassetto

bed
le lit
das Bett
la cama
il letto

mattress
le matelas
die Matratze
el colchón
il materasso

bedspread
le couvre-lit
die Tagesdecke
la colcha
il copriletto

pillow
l'oreiller
das Kopfkissen
la almohada
il guanciale

hot-water bottle • la bouillotte • die Wärmflasche • la bolsa de agua caliente • la borsa calda

clock radio • le radio-réveil • der Radiowecker • la radio despertador • la radiosveglia

alarm clock • le réveil • der Wecker • el reloj despertador • la sveglia

box of tissues • la boîte de kleenex • die Papiertaschentuchschachtel • la caja de pañuelos desechables • la scatola di fazzolettini

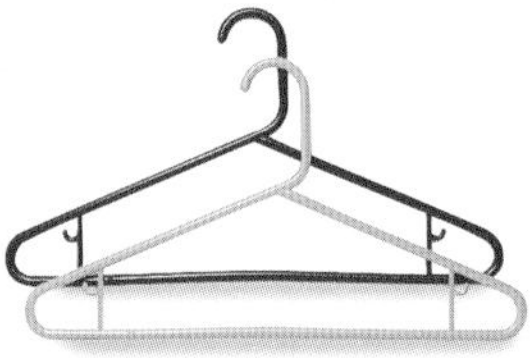

coat hanger • le cintre • der Kleiderbügel • el gancho • la gruccia

mirror
le miroir
der Spiegel
el espejo
lo specchio

vanity table
la coiffeuse
der Frisiertisch
el tocador
la toeletta

floor
le sol
der Fußboden
el suelo
il pavimento

bed linen • le linge de lit • die Bettwäsche • la ropa de cama • la biancheria da letto

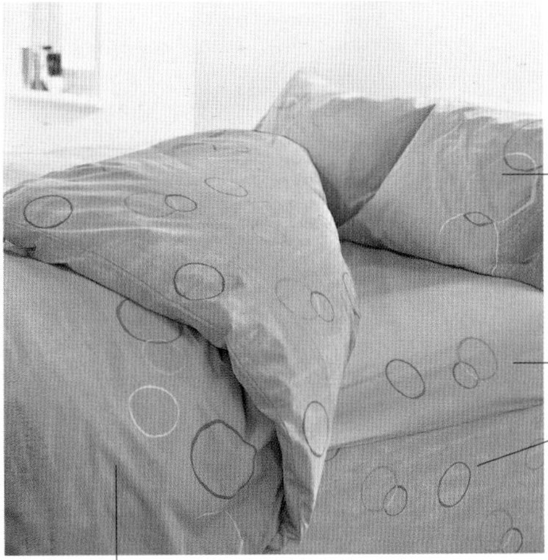

pillowcase
la taie d'oreiller
der Kissenbezug
la funda de la almohada
la federa

sheet
le drap
das Bettlaken
la sábana
il lenzuolo

valance
la frange de lit
der Volant
el cubrecanapé
la balza

comforter
la couette
die Bettdecke
el edredón
il piumone

quilt
l'édredon
die Steppdecke
la colcha
la trapunta

blanket
la couverture
die Decke
la cobija
la coperta

single bed
le lit simple
das Einzelbett
la cama individual
il letto singolo

double bed
le grand lit
das Doppelbett
la cama matrimonial
il letto matrimoniale

electric blanket
la couverture chauffante
die Heizdecke
la cobija eléctrica
la termocoperta

footboard
le pied de lit
das Fußende
el pie de la cama
la pedana del letto

box spring
le ressort
die Sprungfeder
el resorte
la molla

carpet
le tapis
der Teppich
el tapete
il tappeto

insomnia
l'insomnie
die Schlaflosigkeit
el insomnio
l'insonnia

go to bed *(v)*
se coucher
ins Bett gehen
acostarse
andare a letto

go to sleep *(v)*
s'endormir
einschlafen
dormirse
addormentarsi

wake up *(v)*
se réveiller
aufwachen
despertarse
svegliarsi

get up *(v)*
se lever
aufstehen
levantarse
alzarsi

make the bed *(v)*
faire le lit
das Bett machen
hacer la cama
fare il letto

set the alarm *(v)*
mettre le réveil
den Wecker stellen
poner el despertador
mettere la sveglia

snore *(v)*
ronfler
schnarchen
roncar
russare

closet
l'armoire encastrée
der Einbauschrank
el armario empotrado
l'armadio a muro

bathroom • la salle de bain • das Badezimmer • el baño • la stanza da bagno

towel rack
le porte-serviettes
der Handtuchhalter
el toallero
il portasciugamani

shower door
la porte de douche
die Duschtür
la puerta de la regadera
la porta della doccia

cold faucet
le robinet d'eau froide
der Kaltwasserhahn
la llave de agua fría
il rubinetto dell'acqua fredda

hot faucet
le robinet d'eau chaude
der Heißwasserhahn
la llave de agua caliente
il rubinetto dell'acqua calda

shower head
le pommeau de douche
der Duschkopf
la piña de la regadera
il soffione della doccia

sink
le lavabo
das Waschbecken
el lavabo
il lavandino

stopper
la bonde
der Stöpsel
el tapón
il tappo

shower
la douche
die Dusche
la regadera
la doccia

drain
le tuyau d'écoulement
der Abfluss
el desagüe
lo scolo

toilet seat
le siège des toilettes
der Toilettensitz
la tapa del excusado
il sedile

toilet
les toilettes
die Toilette
el excusado
il water

toilet brush
la brosse
die Toilettenbürste
la escobilla del excusado
la spazzola da water

bathtub • la baignoire • die Badewanne • la tina • la vasca

bidet • le bidet • das Bidet • el bidé • il bidè

medicine cabinet
la pharmacie de ménage
die Hausapotheke
el botiquín
l'armadietto dei medicinali

bathmat
le tapis de bain
die Badematte
el tapete de baño
lo scendibagno

toilet paper
le rouleau de papier hygiénique
die Rolle Toilettenpapier
el rollo de papel higiénico
la carta igienica

shower curtain
le rideau de douche
der Duschvorhang
la cortina de la regadera
la tenda da doccia

take a shower *(v)*
prendre une douche
duschen
bañarse
farsi la doccia

take a bath *(v)*
prendre un bain
baden
darse un baño
farsi il bagno

dental hygiene • l'hygiène dentaire • die Zahnpflege • la higiene dental • l'igiene dentale

toothbrush • la brosse à dents • die Zahnbürste • el cepillo de dientes • lo spazzolino da denti

toothpaste • le dentifrice • die Zahnpasta • la pasta de dientes • il dentifricio

mouthwash • l'eau dentifrice • das Mundwasser • el enjuague bucal • il collutorio

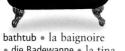

dental floss
le fil dentaire
die Zahnseide
el hilo dental
il filo interdentale

sponge • l'éponge • der Schwamm • la esponja • la spugna

pumice stone • la pierre ponce • der Bimsstein • la piedra pómez • la pomice

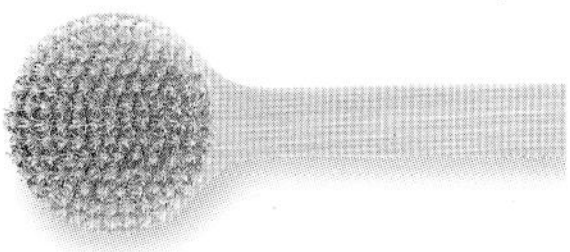

back brush • la brosse pour le dos • die Rückenbürste • el cepillo para la espalda • la spazzola

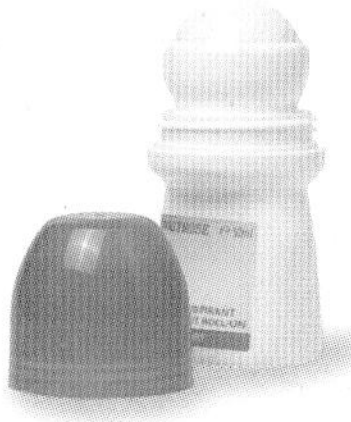

deodorant • le déodorant • das Deo • el desodorante • il deodorante

soap dish
le porte-savon
die Seifenschale
la jabonera
il portasapone

soap • le savon • die Seife • el jabón • il sapone

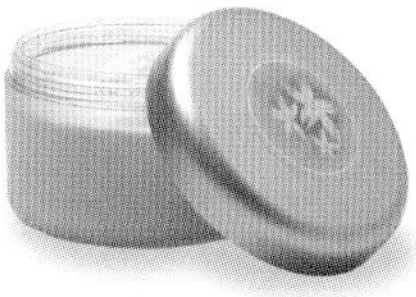

face cream • la crème pour le visage • die Gesichtscreme • la crema para la cara • la crema per il viso

shower gel
le gel douche
das Duschgel
el shampoo para el cuerpo
il gel per doccia

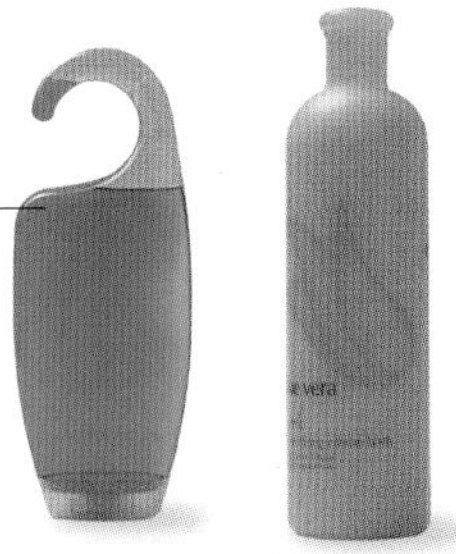

bubble bath • le bain moussant • das Schaumbad • el gel de baño • il bagnoschiuma

hand towel
la serviette
das Handtuch
la toalla de mano
l'asciugamano piccolo

bath towel
la serviette de bain
das Badetuch
la toalla de baño
l'asciugamano grande

towels • les serviettes • die Handtücher • las toallas • gli asciugamani

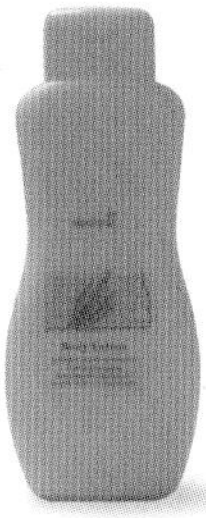

body lotion • la lotion pour le corps • die Körperlotion • la crema para el cuerpo • la lozione per il corpo

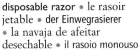

talcum powder • le talc • der Körperpuder • el talco • il talco

bathrobe • le peignoir • der Bademantel • la bata • l'accappatoio

shaving • le rasage • das Rasieren • el afeitado • la rasatura

electric razor
le rasoir électrique
der Elektrorasierer
la rasuradora
il rasoio elettrico

shaving cream • la mousse à raser • der Rasierschaum • la espuma de afeitar • la schiuma da barba

disposable razor • le rasoir jetable • der Einwegrasierer • la navaja de afeitar desechable • il rasoio monouso

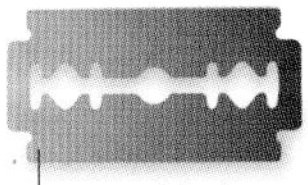

razor blade
la lame de rasoir
die Rasierklinge
la hoja de afeitar
la lametta

aftershave • l'after-shave • das Rasierwasser • el aftershave • il dopobarba

nursery • la chambre d'enfants • das Kinderzimmer • la habitación de los niños • la camera dei bambini

baby care • les soins de bébé • die Säuglingspflege • el cuidado del bebé • l'igiene del neonato

sponge
l'éponge
der Schwamm
la esponja
la spugna

diaper rash cream • la crème pour l'érythème • die Wundsalbe • la crema para las rozaduras • la pomata antirossore

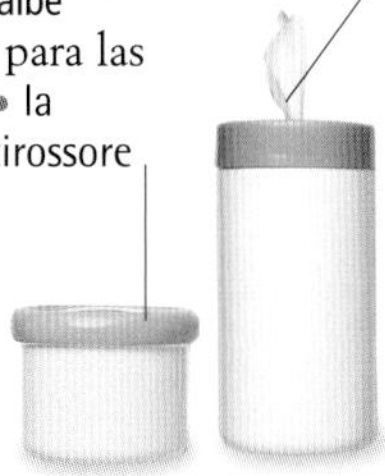

wet wipe • la serviette humide • das Erfrischungstuch • la toallita húmeda • la salviettina umidificata

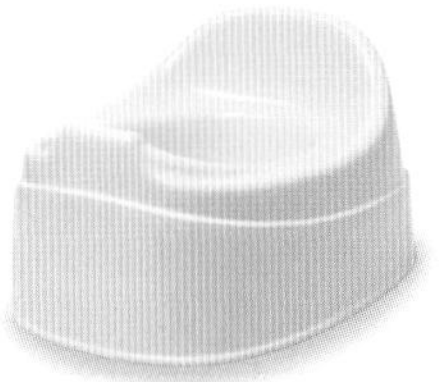

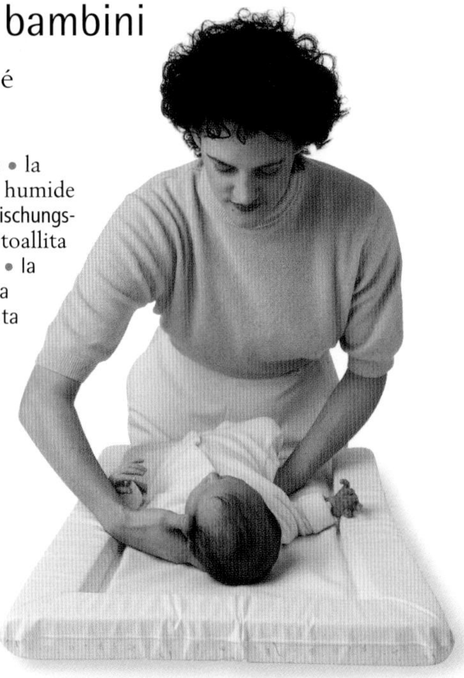

baby bath • la baignoire en plastique • die Babywanne • la tina de plástico • la vaschetta

potty • le pot • das Töpfchen • el orinal • il vasino

changing mat • le matelas à langer • die Wickelmatte • el cambiador • il materassino

sleeping • le coucher • das Schlafen • la hora de dormir • dormire

mobile
le mobile
das Mobile
el móvil
la giostrina

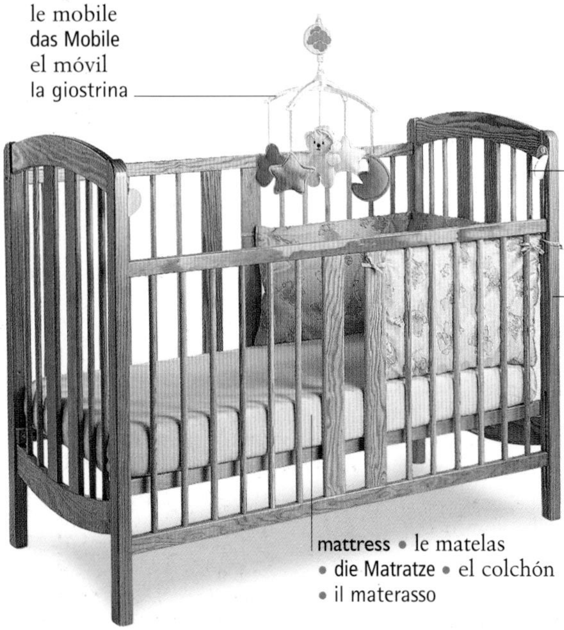

bars
les barreaux
die Gitterstäbe
los barrotes
le sbarre

bumper
le protège-barreaux
der Kopfschutz
el protector
il paracolpi

mattress • le matelas • die Matratze • el colchón • il materasso

crib • le lit d'enfant • das Kinderbett • la cuna • il lettino

sheet
le drap
das Laken
la sábana
il lenzuolo

blanket • la couverture • die Decke • la cobija • la coperta

fleece • la couverture laineuse • die Flauschdecke • el vellón • la felpa

bedding • la literie • das Bettzeug • la ropa de cama • la biancheria da letto

rattle • le hochet • die Rassel • la sonaja • il sonaglio

bassinet • le moïse • das Körbchen • el moisés • il portabebè

playing • le jeu • das Spielen • los juegos • il gioco

doll • la poupée • die Puppe • la muñeca • la bambola

stuffed toy • le jouet en peluche • das Kuscheltier • el muñeco de peluche • il giocattolo di pezza

dollhouse • la maison de poupée • das Puppenhaus • la casa de muñecas • la casa delle bambole

playhouse • la maison pliante • das Spielhaus • la casa de juguete • la casa da gioco

teddy bear • l'ours en peluche • der Teddy • el oso de peluche • l'orsacchiotto

toy
le jouet
das Spielzeug
el juguete
il giocattolo

toy basket • le panier à jouets • der Spielzeugkorb • el cesto de los juguetes • il cesto dei giocattoli

ball
la balle
der Ball
la pelota
la palla

playpen • le parc • der Laufstall • el corral • il box

safety • la sécurité • die Sicherheit • la seguridad • la sicurezza

child latches • la serrure de sécurité • die Kindersicherung • el cierre de seguridad • il fermo di sicurezza

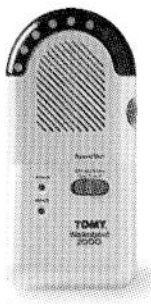

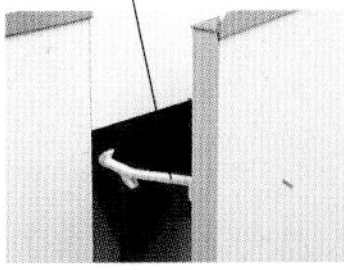

baby monitor • le moniteur • die Babysprechanlage • el intercomunicador • l'interfono

stair gate • la barrière d'escalier • das Treppengitter • la barrera de seguridad • lo sbarramento

eating • le manger • das Essen • la comida • il pasto

high chair • la chaise haute • der Kinderstuhl • la periquera • il seggiolone

nipple • la tétine • der Sauger • el chupón • la tettarella

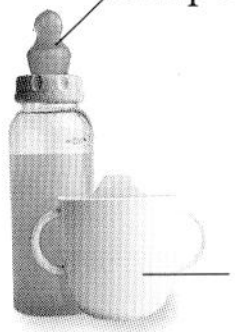

drinking cup
la tasse
der Babybecher
la taza
la tazza per bere

bottle • le biberon • die Babyflasche • la mamila • il biberon

going out • la sortie • das Ausgehen • el paseo • la passeggiata

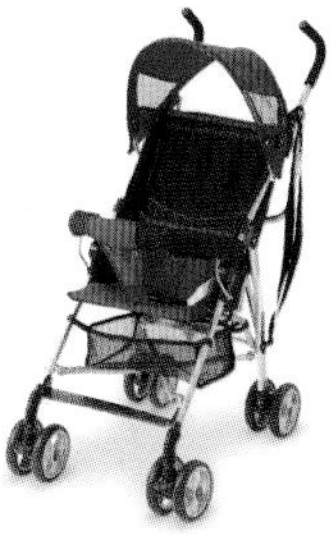

stroller • la poussette • der Sportwagen • la carriola • il passeggino

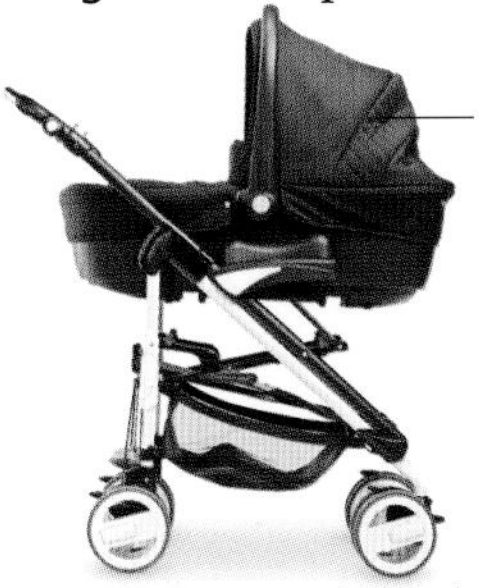

hood
la capote
das Verdeck
la capota
la capote

baby carriage • le landau • der Kinderwagen • la carriola • la carrozzina

carrier • le couffin • das Tragebettchen • el bambineto • la culla portatile

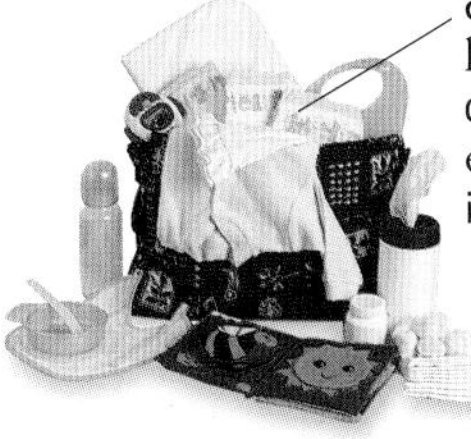

diaper
la couche
die Windel
el pañal
il pannolino

diaper bag • le sac • die Babytasche • la pañalera • la borsa per il cambio

baby sling • le porte-bébé • die Babytrageschlinge • la cangurera • il marsupio

utility room • la buanderie • der Allzweckraum • la lavandería • la lavanderia

laundry • le linge • die Wäsche • la colada • il bucato

dirty laundry
le linge sale
die schmutzige Wäsche
la ropa sucia
i panni sporchi

laundry basket • le panier à linge • der Wäschekorb • el cesto de la ropa sucia • il cesto della biacheria da lavare

washing machine • le lave-linge • die Waschmaschine • la lavadora • la lavatrice

washer-dryer • le lave-linge séchant • der Waschtrockner • la lavadora secadora • la lavasciuga

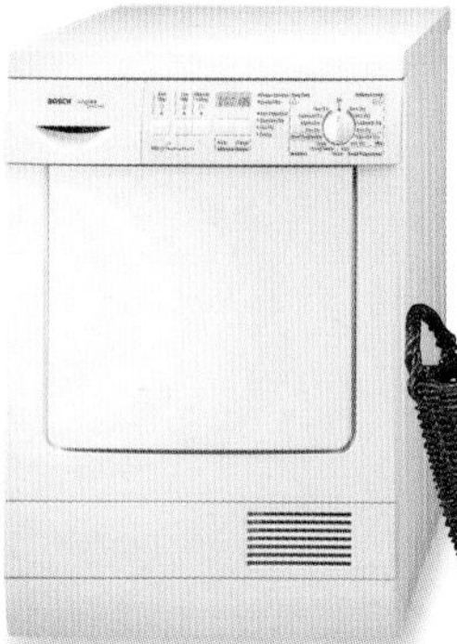

tumble dryer • le sèche-linge • der Trockner • la secadora • l'asciugabiancheria

clean clothes
le linge propre
die saubere Wäsche
la ropa limpia
i vestiti puliti

linen basket • le panier à linge • der Wäschekorb • el cesto de la ropa para planchar • il cesto della biancheria pulita

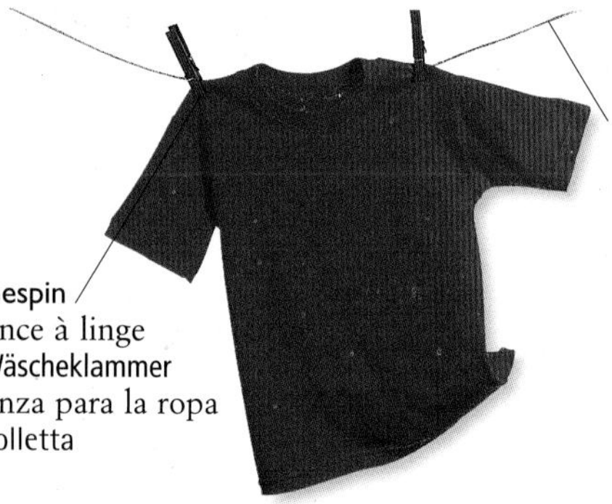

clothesline
la corde à linge
die Wäscheleine
el tendedero
la corda per bucato

clothespin
la pince à linge
die Wäscheklammer
la pinza para la ropa
la molletta

dry (v) • sécher • trocknen • secar • asciugare

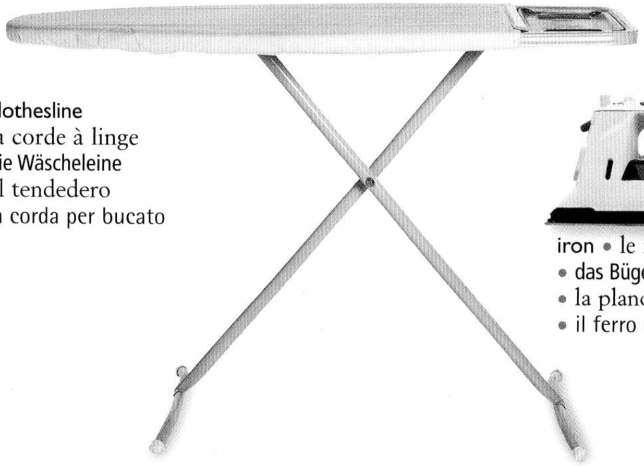

ironing board • la planche à repasser • das Bügelbrett • el burro de la plancha • l'asse da stiro

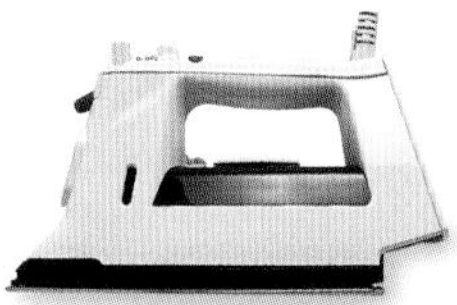

iron • le fer à repasser • das Bügeleisen • la plancha • il ferro da stiro

load (v) charger füllen cargar caricare	spin (v) essorer schleudern centrifugar centrifugare	iron (v) repasser bügeln planchar stirare	How do I operate the washing machine? Comment fonctionne le lave-linge? Wie benutze ich die Waschmaschine? ¿Cómo funciona la lavadora? Come funziona la lavatrice?
rinse (v) rincer spülen aclarar sciacquare	spin dryer l'essoreuse die Wäscheschleuder la centrífuga la centrifuga	fabric conditioner le produit assouplissant der Weichspüler el suavizante l'ammorbidente	What is the setting for colors/whites? Quel est le programme pour les couleurs/le blanc? Welches Programm nehme ich für farbige/weiße Wäsche? ¿Cuál es el programa para la ropa de color/blanca? Qual è il programma per i tessuti colorati/bianchi?

cleaning equipment • l'équipement d'entretien • die Reinigungsartikel • el equipo de limpieza • gli accessori per la pulizia

suction hose • le tuyau flexible • der Saugschlauch • el tubo de la aspiradora • il tubo di aspirazione

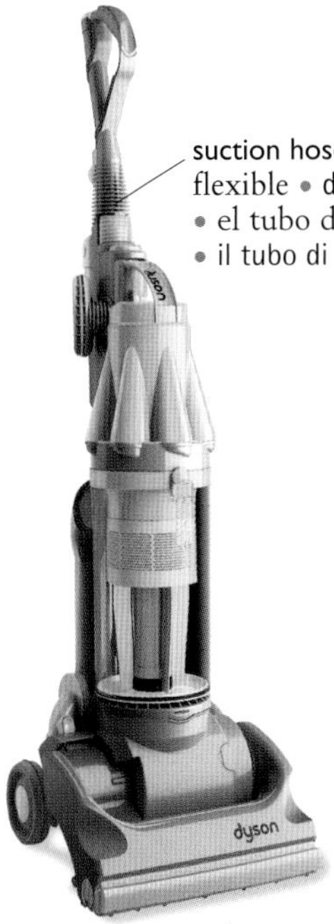

vacuum cleaner • l'aspirateur • der Staubsauger • la aspiradora • l'aspirapolvere

pail
le seau
der Eimer
el cubo
il secchio

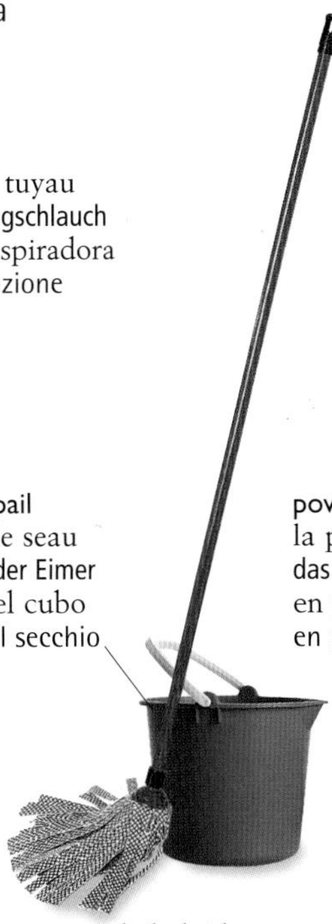

mop • le balai laveur • der Mopp • el trapeador • la scopa lavapavimenti

brush
la balayette
der Handfeger
el cepillo
la spazzola

dustpan • la pelle • die Müllschaufel • el recogedor • la paletta

bleach • l'eau de Javel • das Reinigungsmittel • la lejía • la varechina

powder
la poudre
das Pulver
en polvo
en polvere

liquid
le liquide
die Flüssigkeit
líquido
liquido

detergent • le détergent • das Waschmittel • el detergente • il detergente

dust cloth • le chiffon • das Staubtuch • el sacudidor • lo spolverino

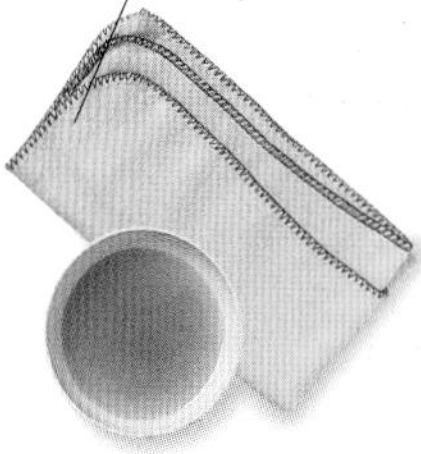

polish • la cire • die Politur • la cera • la cera

activities • les activités • die Tätigkeiten • las acciones • le attività

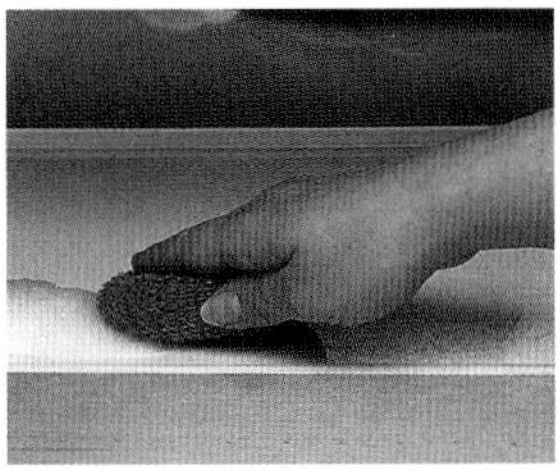

clean *(v)* • nettoyer • putzen • limpiar • pulire

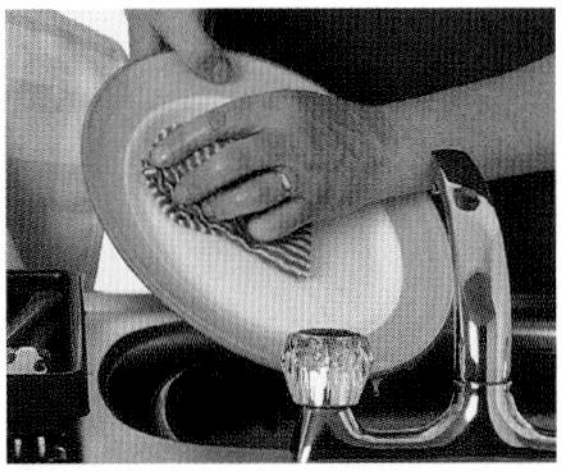

wash *(v)* • laver • spülen • fregar • lavare

wipe *(v)* • essuyer • wischen • trapear • asciugare

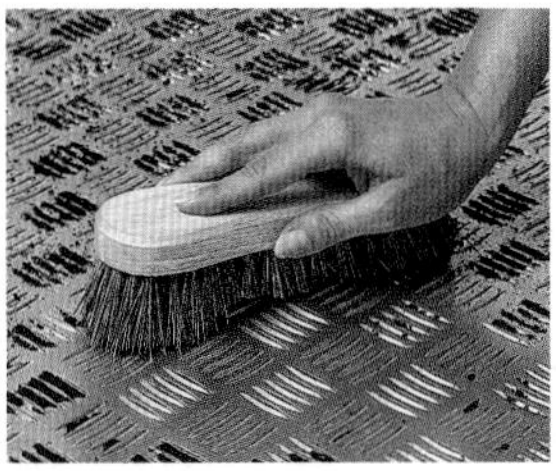

scrub *(v)* • laver à la brosse • schrubben • restregar • fregare

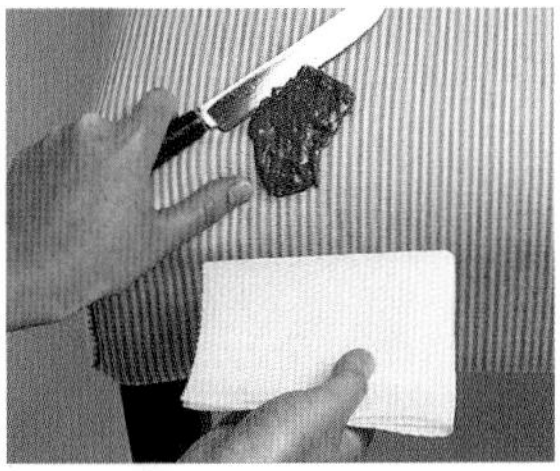

scrape *(v)* • racler • kratzen • raspar • raschiare

broom
le balai
der Besen
la escoba
la scopa

sweep *(v)* • balayer • fegen • barrer • spazzare

dust *(v)* • épousseter • Staub wischen • sacudir • spolverare

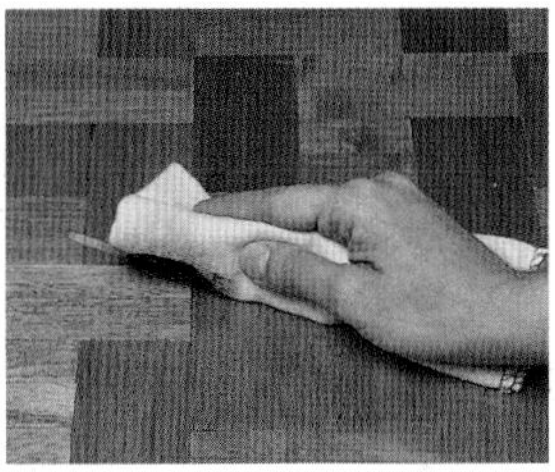

polish *(v)* • cirer • polieren • pulir • lucidare

workshop • l'atelier • die Heimwerkstatt • el taller • il laboratorio

chuck
le mandrin
das Bohrfutter
el cabezal
il mandrino

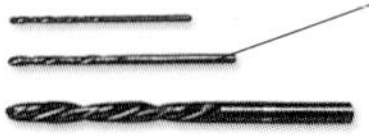

drill bit
la mèche
der Bohrer
la broca
la punta

jigsaw • la scie sauteuse • die Stichsäge • la sierra de vaivén • la sega da traforo

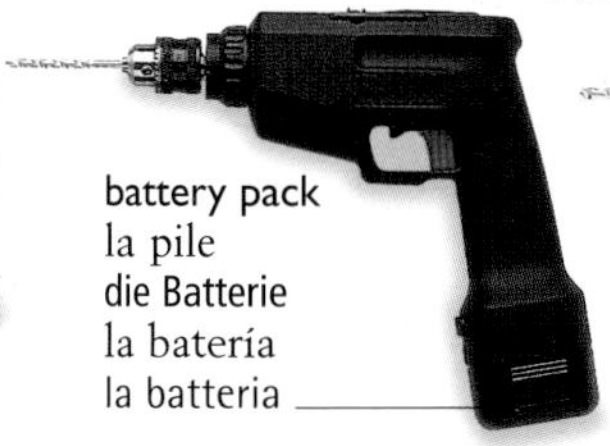

battery pack
la pile
die Batterie
la batería
la batteria

rechargeable drill • la perceuse rechargeable • der Bohrer mit Batteriebetrieb • el taladro inalámbrico • il trapano ricaricabile

electric drill • la perceuse électrique • der Elektrobohrer • el taladro eléctrico • il trapano elettrico

glue gun • le pistolet à colle • die Leimpistole • la pistola para encolar • la pistola per colla

clamp • le serre-joint • die Zwinge • la abrazadera • il morsetto

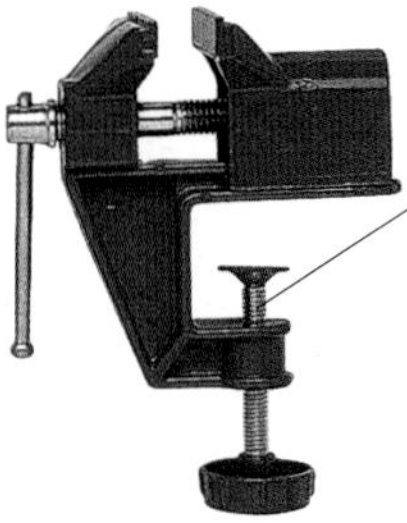

vise • l'étau • der Schraubstock • el tornillo de banco • la morsa

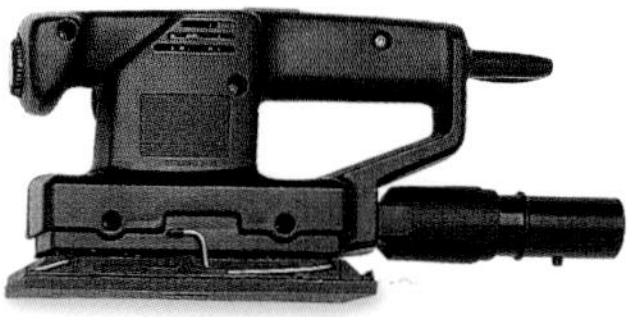

sander • la ponceuse • die Schleifmaschine • la lijadora • la levigatrice

blade • la lame • das Blatt • la cuchilla • la lama

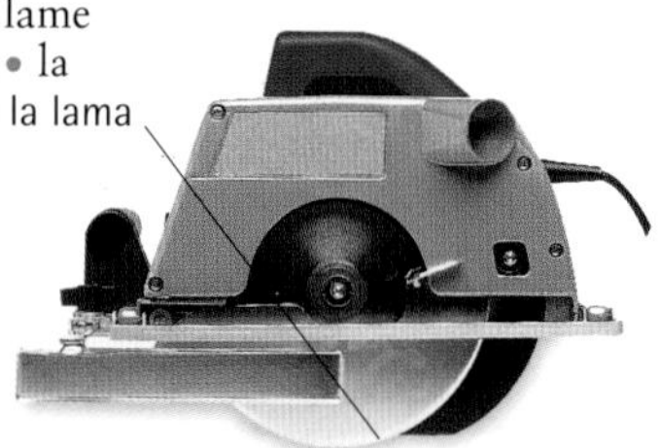

circular saw • la scie circulaire • die Kreissäge • la sierra circular • la sega circolare

workbench • l'établi • die Werkbank • el banco de trabajo • il banco da lavoro

wood glue
la colle à bois
der Holzleim
el pegamento de carpintero
la colla da legno

router
la guimbarde
der Grundhobel
la guimbarda
la contornitrice

wood shavings
les copeaux
die Holzspäne
las virutas de madera
i trucioli

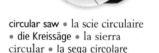

tool rack
• le porte-outils
• das Werkzeuggestell
• el organizador de las herramientas
• la rastrelliera per gli arnesi

bit brace
le vilebrequin
die Bohrwinde
el taladro manual
il girabacchino

extension cord
le prolongateur
die Verlängerungsschnur
la extensión
la prolunga

techniques • les techniques • die Fertigkeiten • las técnicas • le tecniche

cut *(v)* • découper • schneiden • cortar • tagliare

saw *(v)* • scier • sägen • serrar • segare

drill *(v)* • percer • bohren • taladrar • forare

hammer *(v)* • marteler • hämmern • clavar • martellare

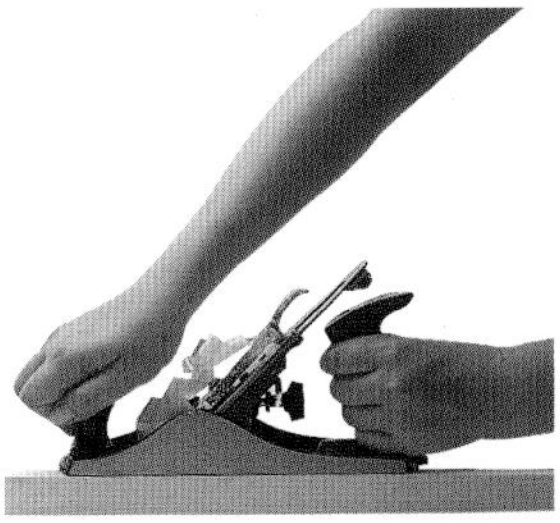

plane *(v)* • raboter • hobeln • cepillar • piallare

turn *(v)* • tourner • drechseln • tornear • tornire

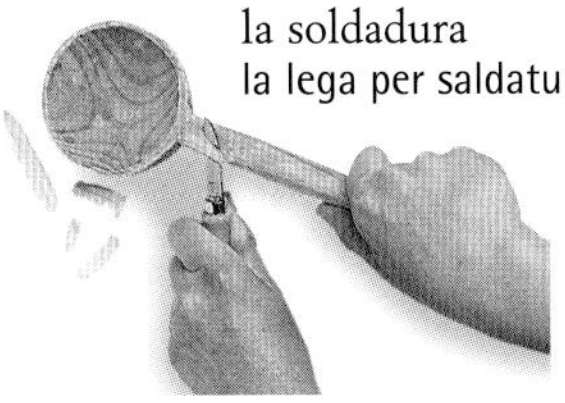

carve *(v)* • sculpter • schnitzen • tallar • incidere

solder
la soudure
der Lötzinn
la soldadura
la lega per saldatura

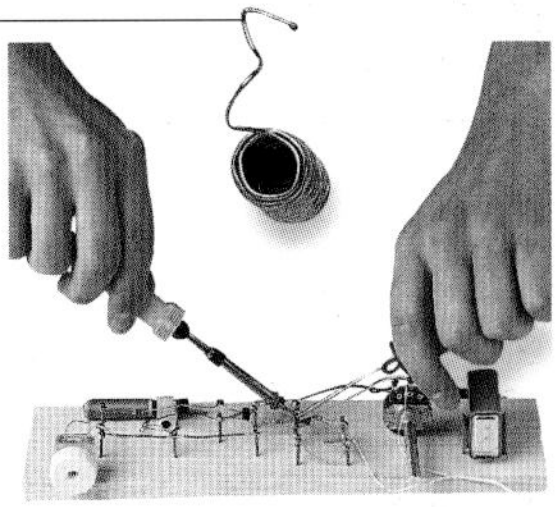

solder *(v)* • souder • löten • soldar • saldare

materials • les matériaux • die Materialien • los materiales • i materiali

medium-density fiberboard
le médium
die MDF-Platte
el tablero de densidad media
l'MDF

plywood
le contreplaqué
das Sperrholz
el contrachapado
il compensato

chipboard
l'aggloméré
das Spanholz
el aglomerado
il truciolato

hardboard • l'isorel • die Hartfaserplatte • el cartón madera • la masonite

softwood • le bois tendre • das Weichholz • la madera de pino • il legno dolce

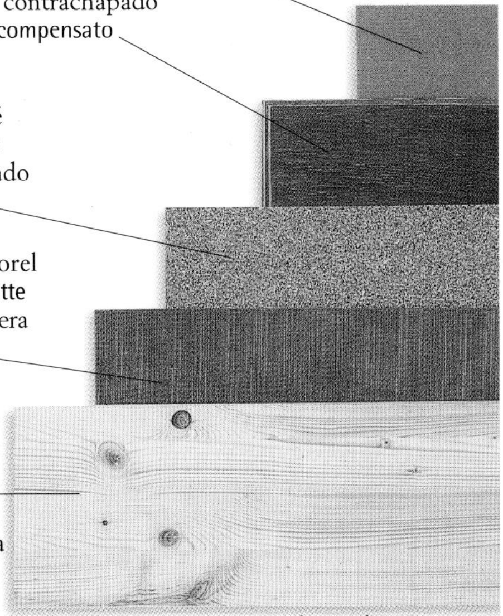

wood • le bois • das Holz • la madera • il legno

hardwood
le bois dur
das Hartholz
la madera noble
il legno duro

varnish
le vernis
der Lack
el barniz
la lacca

woodstain • la couleur pour bois • die Beize • el tinte para madera • il mordente per legno

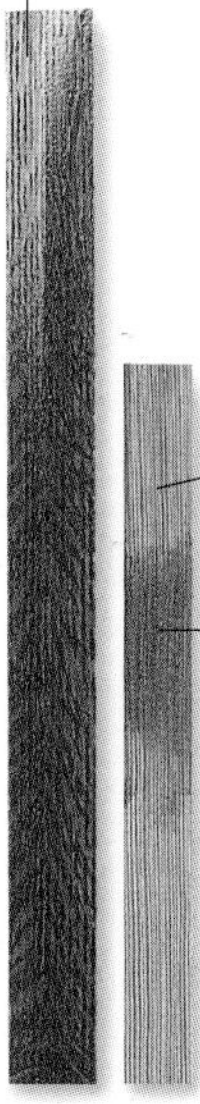

wire
le fil de fer
der Draht
el alambre
il filo

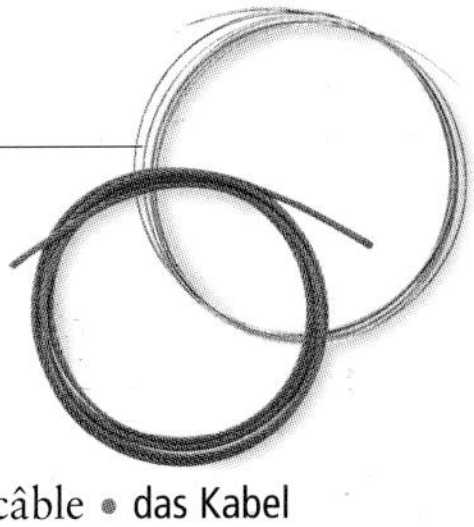

cable • le câble • das Kabel • el cable • il cavo

stainless steel
l'inox
der rostfreie Stahl
el acero inoxidable
l'acciaio inossidabile

galvanized
galvanisé
galvanisiert
galvanizado
zincato

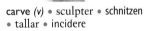

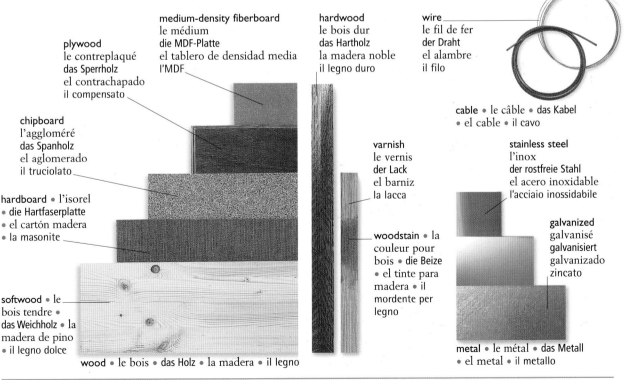

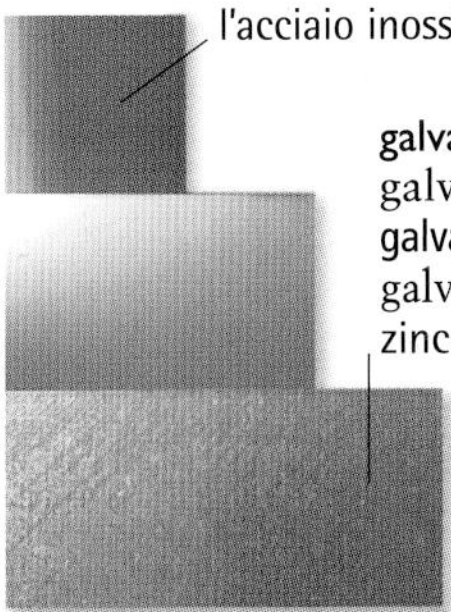

metal • le métal • das Metall • el metal • il metallo

toolbox • la boîte à outils • der Werkzeugkasten • la caja de las herramientas • la scatola degli attrezzi

wrench la clef der Schraubenschlüssel la llave de boca la chiave

adjustable wrench • la clef à molette • der verstellbare Schraubenschlüssel • la llave inglesa • la chiave regolabile

hammer • le marteau • der Hammer • el martillo • il martello

needle-nose pliers • la pince plate • die Flachzange • las pinzas de alambre • le pinze ad ago

socket wrench • la clef à pipe • der Steckschlüssel • la llave de tubo • la chiave a tubo

screwdriver bits • les embouts de tournevis • die Schraubenziehereinsätze • los cabezales de destornillador • la punte per cacciavite

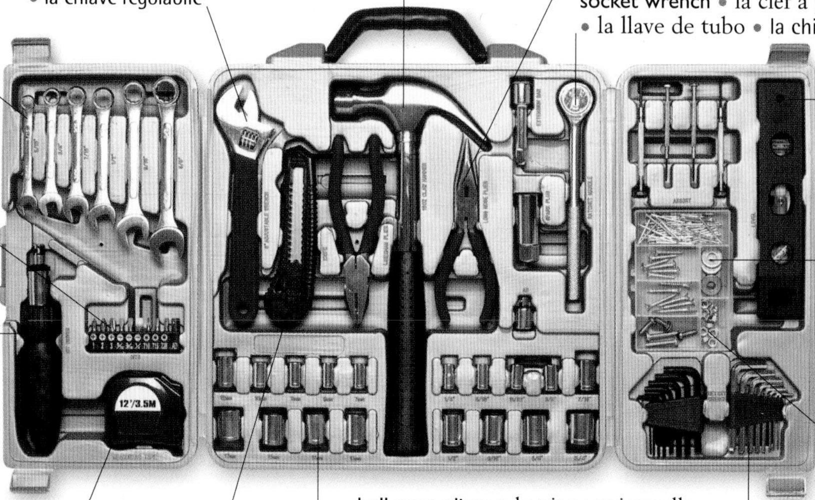

level le niveau die Wasserwaage el nivel la livella

washer le joint der Dichtungsring la rondana la rondella

screwdriver le tournevis der Schraubenzieher el destornillador il cacciavite

nut l'écrou die Mutter la tuerca il dado

tape measure • le mètre • das Metermaß • la cinta métrica • il metro

utility knife le couteau der Schneider el cúter il coltello

bull-nose pliers • la pince universelle • die Kombinationszange • los alicates • le pinze tonde

socket • la douille • die Tülle • el encaje • la bussola

Allen wrench • la clef • der Schlüssel • la llave • la chiave

drill bits • les forets • die Bohrer • las brocas • le punte

metal bit • le foret à métaux • der Metallbohrer • la broca para metal • la punta per metalli

spade bit • le foret à bois plat • der Flachholzbohrer • la broca para madera • la punta piana per legno

reamer l'alésoir die Reibahle el escariador l'alesatore

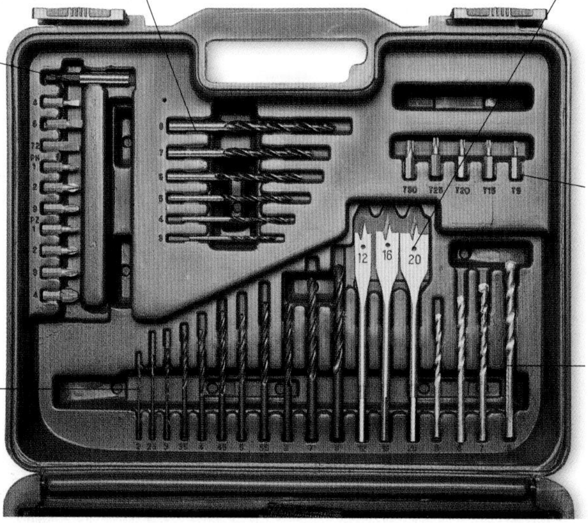

wood bits • les forets de bois • die Holzbohrer • las brocas para madera • le punte da falegnameria

security bit le foret de sécurité der Sicherheitsbohrer la broca de seguridad la punta di sicurezza

masonry bit le foret de maçonnerie der Mauerwerkbohrer la broca de albañilería la punta per muratura

Phillips screwdriver • le tournevis cruciforme • der Kreuzschlitzschraubenzieher • el destornillador de cruz • il cacciavite a croce

head • la tête • der Nagelkopf • la cabeza • la testa

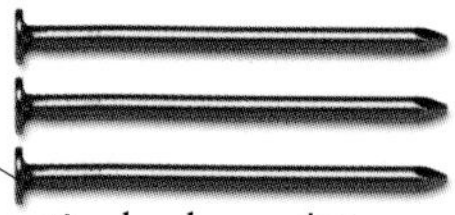

nail • le clou • der Nagel • el clavo • il chiodo

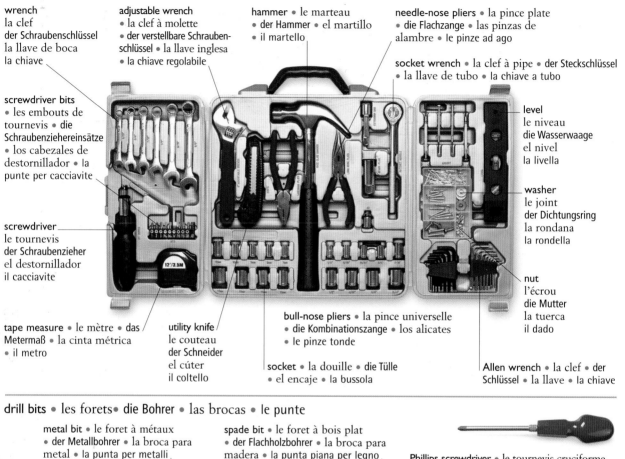

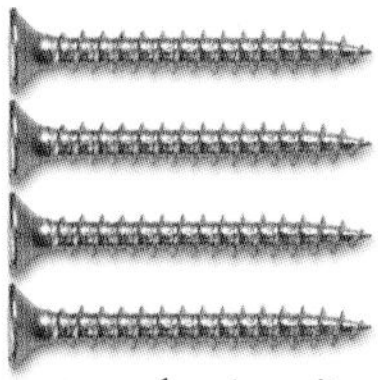

screw • la vis • die Schrauben • el tornillo • la vite

wire stripper • la pince à dénuder • die Entisolierzange • el pelacables • la pinza spelafilo

wire cutter • la pince coupante • der Drahtschneider • el cortaalambres • la pinza tagliafilo

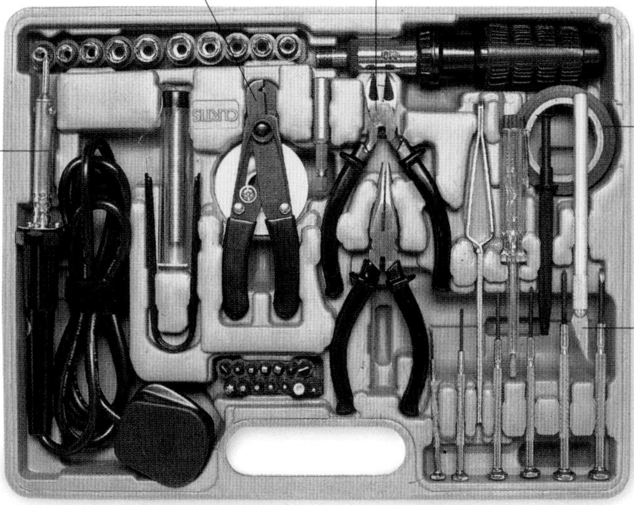

soldering iron
le fer à souder
der Lötkolben
el soldador
il saldatoio

electrical tape
le ruban isolant
das Isolierband
la cinta aislante
il nastro isolante

hobby knife
le scalpel
das Skalpell
el escalpelo
il bisturi

fretsaw • la scie à chantourner • die Schweifsäge • la sierra de calar • la sega da traforo

solder
la soudure
der Lötzinn
la soldadura
le lega per saldatura

tenon saw • la scie à dosseret • die Profilsäge • el serrucho de costilla • la sega per tenoni

safety goggles • les lunettes de sécurité • die Schutzbrille • las gafas de seguridad • gli occhiali protettivi

plane • le rabot • der Hobel • el cepillo • la pialla

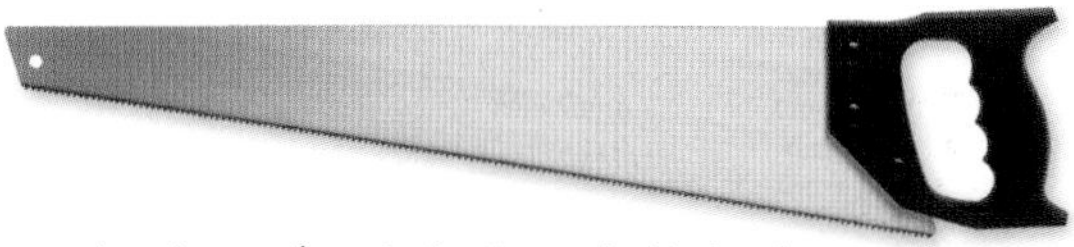

handsaw • la scie égoïne • der Fuchsschwanz • el serrucho • il seghetto

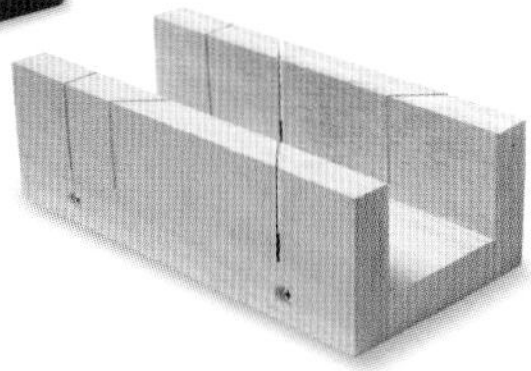

miter block • la boîte à onglets • die Gehrungslade • la caja para cortar en inglete • la cassetta guidalama per ugnature

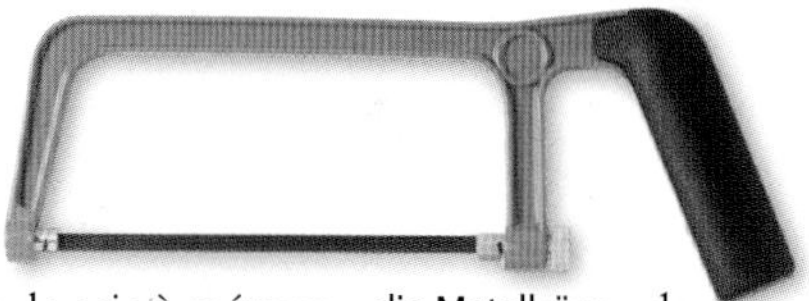

hacksaw • la scie à métaux • die Metallsäge • la sierra para metales • il seghetto per metalli

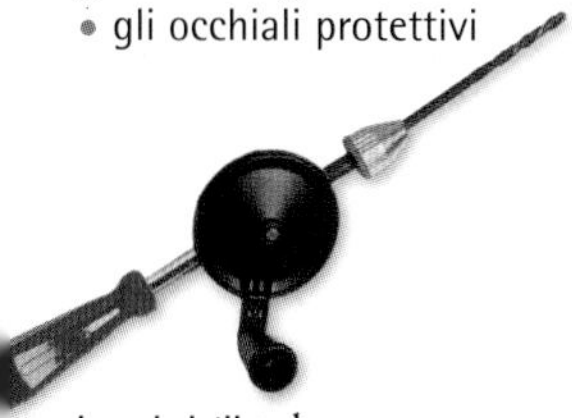

hand drill • la perceuse manuelle • der Handbohrer • el taladro manual • il trapano manuale

steel wool • la paille de fer • die Stahlwolle • la lana de acero • la lana d'acciaio

sandpaper • le papier de verre • das Schmirgelpapier • el papel de lija • la carta vetrata

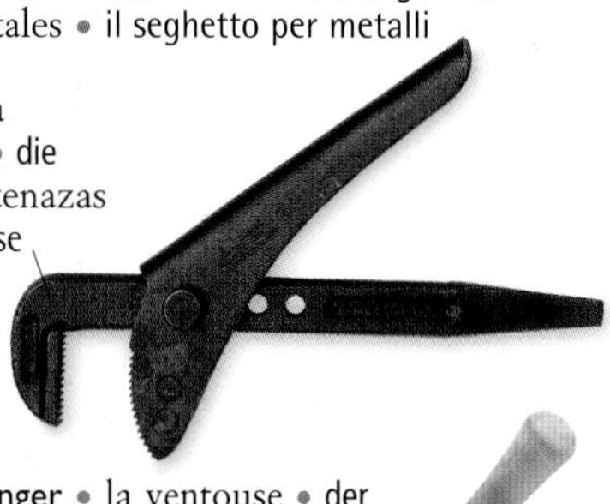

pipe wrench • la clef serre-tube • die Rohrzange • las tenazas • la chiave inglese

chisel • le burin • der Meißel • el formón • lo scalpello

sharpening stone • la pierre à aiguiser • der Wetzstahl • la piedra afiladora • l'affilatore

pipe cutter • le coupe-tube • der Rohrabschneider • el cortatuberías • il tagliatubi

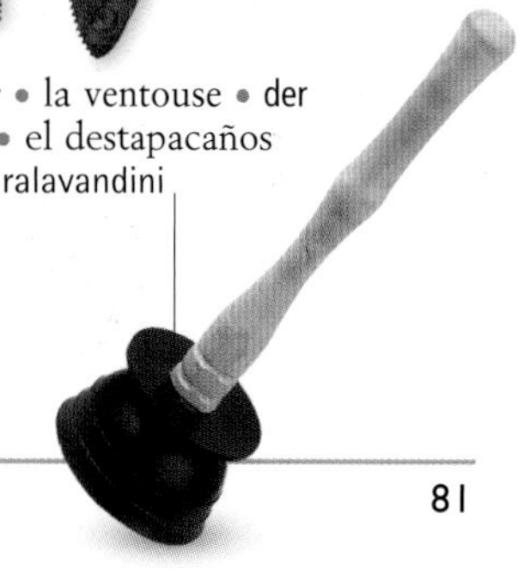

plunger • la ventouse • der Sauger • el destapacaños • lo sturalavandini

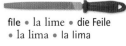

file • la lime • die Feile • la lima • la lima

decorating • la décoration • das Tapezieren • la decoración • la decorazione

scissors • les ciseaux • die Tapezierschere • las tijeras • le forbici

craft knife • le cutter • das Tapeziermesser • el cúter • il coltello da pacchi

plumb line • le fil à plomb • das Senkblei • la plomada • il filo a piombo

scraper • le grattoir • der Spachtel • la espátula • il raschietto

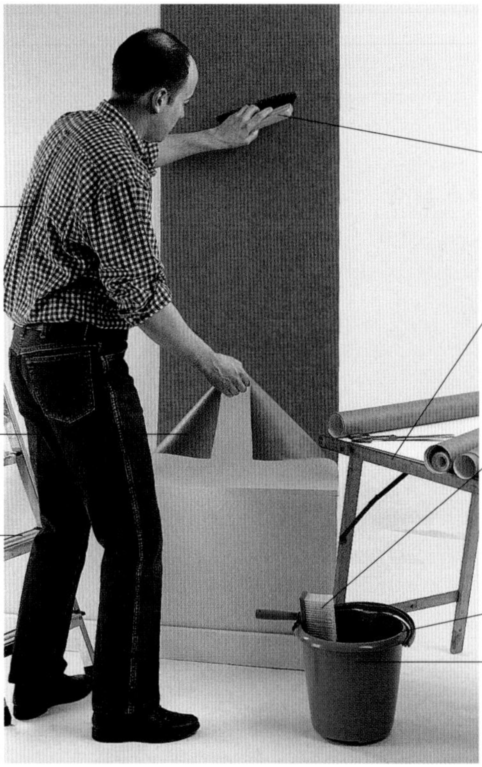

decorator
le tapissier décorateur
der Tapezierer
el pintor
il decoratore

wallpaper
le papier peint
die Tapete
el papel tapiz
la carta da parati

stepladder
l'escabeau
die Trittleiter
la escalera de mano
la scala a libretto

wallpaper brush
• la brosse à tapisser
• die Tapezierbürste
• la brocha de tapicero
• la spazzola

pasting table
la table à encoller
der Tapeziertisch
la mesa de encolar
il tavolo da lavoro

pasting brush
la brosse à encoller
die Kleisterbürste
la brocha de encolar
il pennello da colla

wallpaper paste • la colle à tapisser • der Tapetenkleister • el pegamento para tapizar • la colla da parati

bucket
le seau
der Eimer
la cubeta
il secchio

wallpaper (v) • tapisser • tapezieren • tapizar • tappezzare

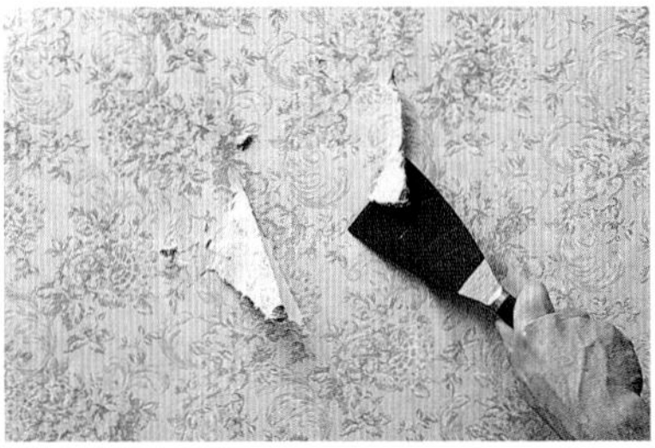

strip (v) • décoller • abziehen • despegar • staccare

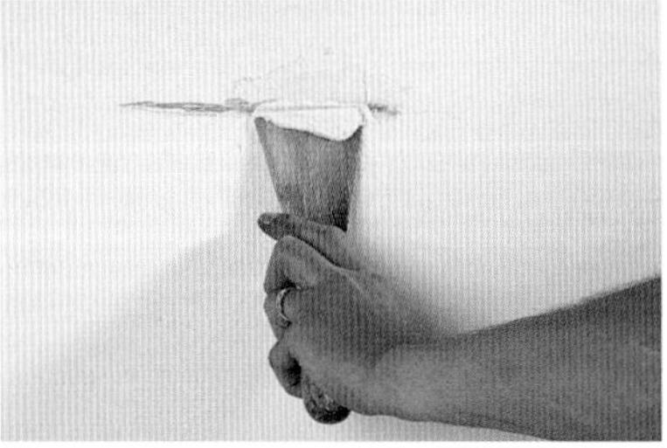

fill (v) • mastiquer • spachteln • rellenar • otturare

sand (v) • poncer • schmirgeln • lijar • scartavetrare

plaster (v) • plâtrer • verputzen • enyesar • intonacare

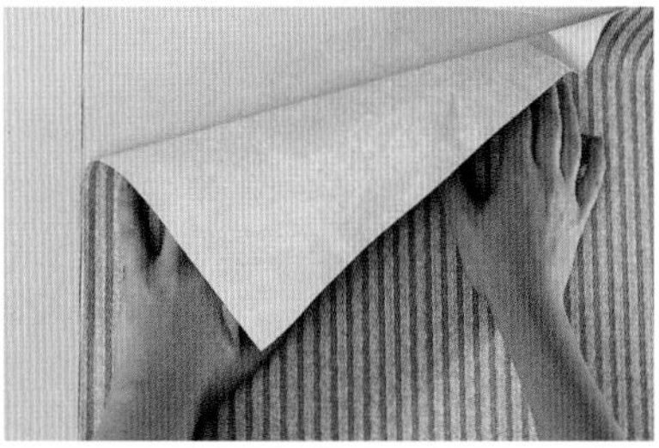

hang (v) • poser • anbringen • empapelar • incollare

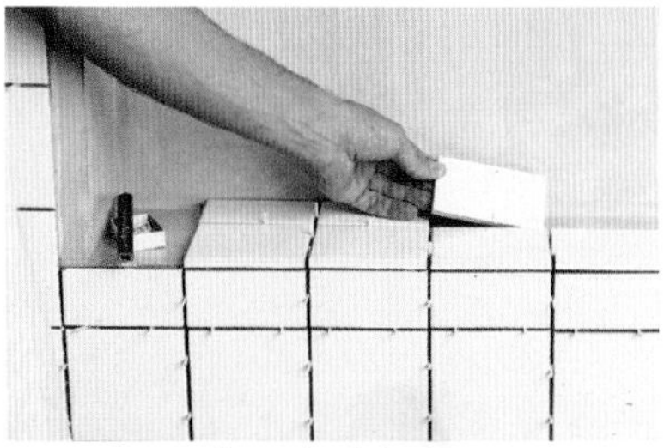

tile (v) • carreler • kacheln • poner azulejos • piastrellare

brush
la brosse
die Streichbürste
la brocha
il pennello

paint can
le pot de peinture
der Farbtopf
la lata de pintura
il barattolo di vernice

coveralls
les bleus
der Overall
el overol
la tuta

oilcloth
la couverture de protection
das Abdecktuch
el protector
il telo di protezione

paint *(v)* • peindre • anstreichen • pintar • dipingere

roller
le rouleau
der Roller
el rodillo
il rullo

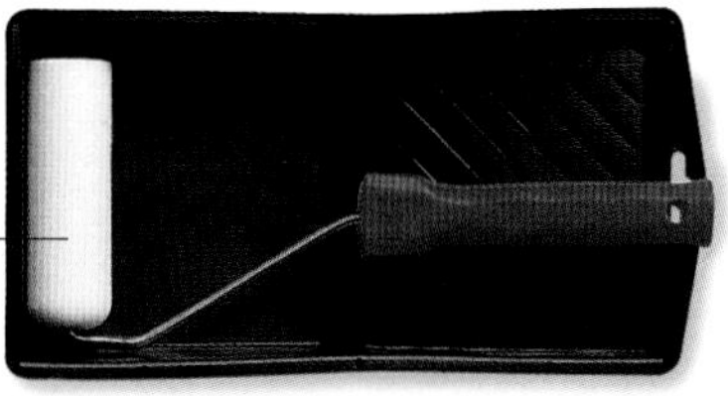

paint tray • le bac à peinture • die Wanne • la bandeja para la pintura • la vaschetta per la vernice

paint • la peinture • die Farbe • la pintura • la vernice

sponge • l'éponge • der Schwamm • la esponja • la spugna

masking tape • le papier cache • das Abdeckband • el masking tape • il nastro adesivo coprente

sandpaper • le papier de verre • das Schmirgelpapier • el papel de lija • la carta vetrata

filler • le mastic • die Spachtelmasse • el mastique • lo stucco

turpentine
la térébenthine
das Terpentin
la trementina
la trementina

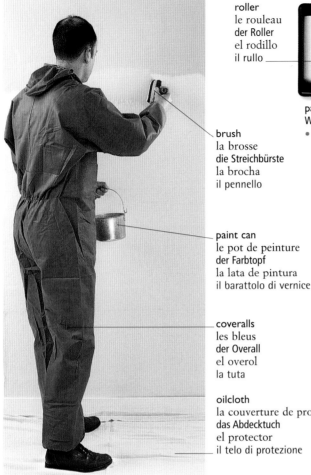

paint thinner • le white-spirit • das Verdünnungsmittel • el aguarrás • l'acquaragia

plaster le plâtre der Gips el yeso l'intonaco	gloss brillant Glanz- con brillo lucido	embossed paper le papier gaufré das Relieftapete el papel estampado en relieve la carta a rilievo	base coat la couche de fond die Grundierung la primera mano la mano di fondo	sealant l'enduit das Versiegelungsmittel el sellador il sigillante
varnish le vernis der Lack el barniz la vernice trasparente	matte mat matt mate opaco	lining paper le papier d'apprêt das Einsatzpapier el papel de apresto la carta di fondo	top coat la dernière couche der Deckanstrich la última mano la mano finale	solvent le solvant das Lösungsmittel el solvente il solvente
latex paint la peinture mate die Emulsionsfarbe la pintura al agua la pittura	stencil le pochoir die Schablone la plantilla lo stampino	primer l'apprêt die Grundfarbe la base la vernice di base	preservative l'agent de conservation der Schutzanstrich el conservante il conservante	grout le mastic der Fugenkitt el cemento blanco la malta

garden • le jardin • der Garten • el jardín • il giardino

garden styles • les styles de jardin • die Gartentypen • los estilos de jardín • i tipi di giardino

patio garden • le patio • der Patio • el patio con jardín • il giardino a patio

roof garden • le jardin sur le toit • der Dachgarten • el jardín en la azotea • il giardino pensile

rock garden • la rocaille • der Steingarten • la rocalla • il giardino di rocce

formal garden • le jardin à la française • der architektonische Garten • el jardín clásico • il giardino all'italiana

courtyard • la cour • der Hof • el patio • il cortile

English garden • le jardin paysan • der Bauerngarten • el jardín campestre • il giardino all'inglese

herb garden • le jardin d'herbes aromatiques • der Kräutergarten • el jardín de plantas herbáceas • il giardino di erbe

water garden • le jardin d'eau • der Wassergarten • el jardín acuático • il giardino acquatico

garden features • les ornements de jardin • die Gartenornamente • los adornos para el jardín • gli ornamenti per il giardino

hanging basket • le panier suspendu • die Blumenampel • la cesta colgante • il cesto sospeso

trellis • le treillis • das Spalier • la enredadera • il graticcio

arbor • la pergola • die Pergola • la pérgola • la pergola

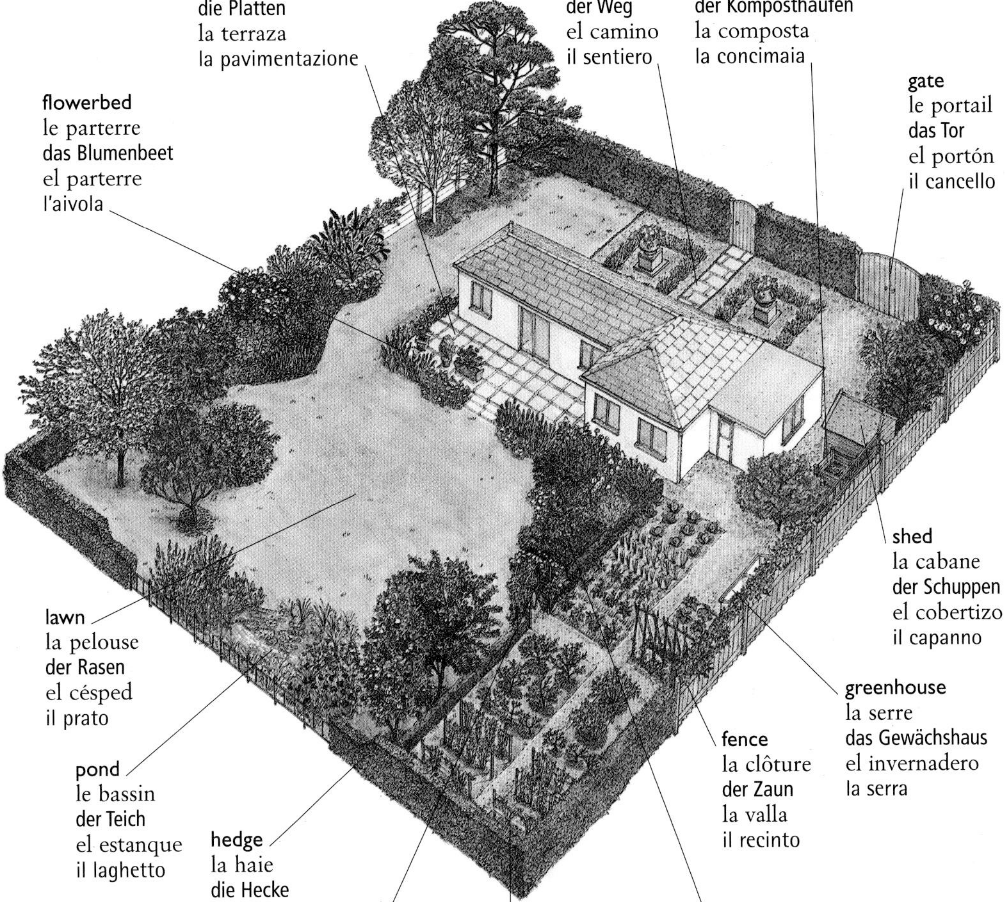

deck • les planches • die Planken • el entarimado • il tavolato

fountain • la fontaine • der Springbrunnen • la fuente • la fontana

soil • le sol • der Boden • la tierra • il terreno

topsoil • la terre • die Erde • la capa superior de la tierra • lo strato superficiale

sand • le sable • der Sand • la arena • la sabbia

chalk • la chaux • der Kalk • la creta • il calcare

silt • le vase • der Schlick • el cieno • il limo

clay • l'argile • der Lehm • la arcilla • l'argilla

garden plants • les plantes de jardin • die Gartenpflanzen • las plantas de jardín • le piante da giardino

types of plants • les genres de plantes • die Pflanzenarten • los tipos de plantas • i tipi di piante

annual • annuel • einjährig • anual • annuale

biennial • bisannuel • zweijährig • bienal • biennale

perennial • vivace • mehrjährig • perenne • perenne

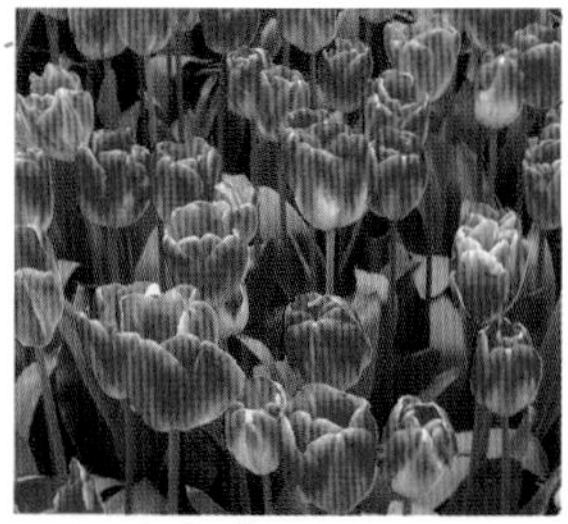
bulb • le bulbe • die Zwiebel • el bulbo • il bulbo

fern • la fougère • der Farn • el helecho • la felce

cattail • le jonc • die Binse • el junco • il giunco

bamboo • le bambou • der Bambus • el bambú • il bambù

weeds • les mauvaises herbes • das Unkraut • las malas hierbas • le erbacce

herb • l'herbe • das Kraut • la hierba • le erbe aromatica

water plant • la plante aquatique • die Wasserpflanze • la planta acuática • la pianta acquatica

tree • l'arbre • der Baum • el árbol • l'albero

palm • le palmier • die Palme • la palmera • la palma

conifer • le conifère • der Nadelbaum • la conífera • la conifera

evergreen • à feuilles persistantes • immergrün • de hoja perenne • sempreverde

deciduous • à feuilles caduques • der Laubbaum • de hoja caduca • a foglie caduche

topiary • la topiaire • der Formschnitt • las plantas podadas con formas • l'arte topiaria

alpine • la plante alpestre • die Alpenpflanze • la planta alpestre • le piante da roccia

succulent • la plante grasse • die Fettpflanze • la planta suculenta • la pianta grassa

cactus • le cactus • der Kaktus • el cactus • il cactus

potted plant • la plante en pot • die Topfpflanze • la planta de maceta • la pianta da vaso

shade plant • la plante d'ombre • die Schattenpflanze • la planta de sombra • la pianta d'ombra

climber
la plante grimpante
die Kletterpflanze
la planta trepadora
il rampicante

flowering shrub
l'arbuste à fleurs
der Zierstrauch
el arbusto de flor
l'arbusto da fiore

ground cover • la couverture du sol • der Bodendecker • la planta para cubrir suelo • la pianta copriterreno

creeper
la plante rampante
die Kriechpflanze
la planta trepadora
la pianta strisciante

ornamental
ornemental
Zier-
ornamental
ornamentale

grass
l'herbe
das Gras
el pasto
l'erba

gardening tools • les outils de jardin • die Gartengeräte • las herramientas de jardinería • gli attrezzi da giardino

compost • le terreau • die Komposterde • la composta • il terriccio

seeds • les graines • die Samen • las semillas • i semi

bone meal • la cendre d'os • die Knochenasche • la harina de huesos • la farina di ossa

gravel • le gravier • der Kies • la grava • la ghiaia

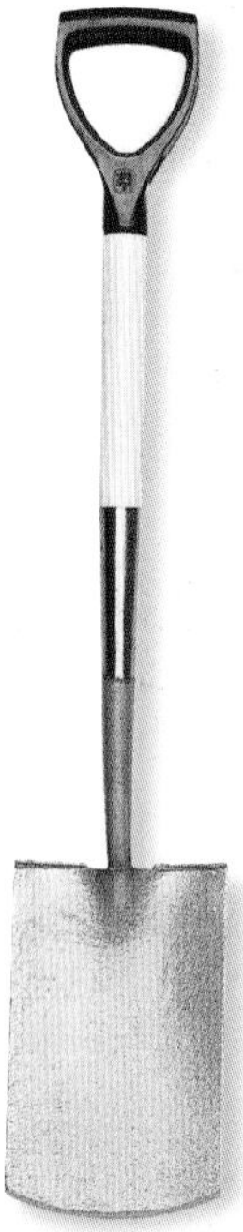

shovel • la bêche • der Spaten • la pala • la vanga

fork • la fourche • die Gabel • el trinche • il forcone

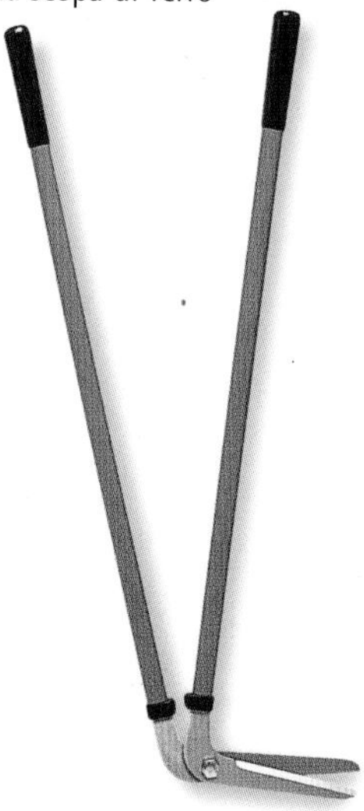

long-handled shears • la grande cisaille • die Schere • la podadora de mango largo • le forbici tagliabordi

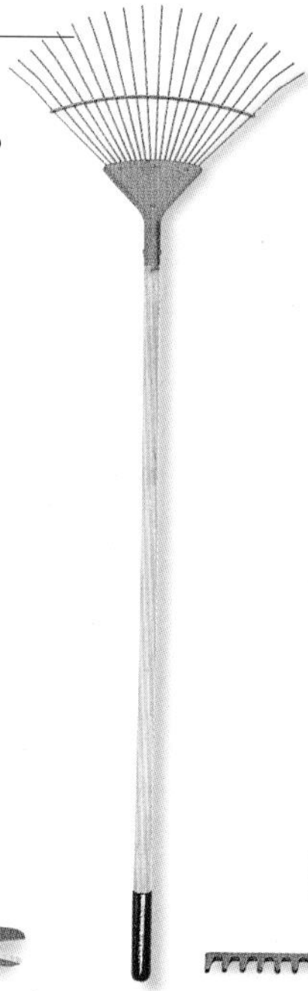

lawn rake
le balai à gazon
der Laubrechen
el rastrillo para el pasto
la scopa di ferro

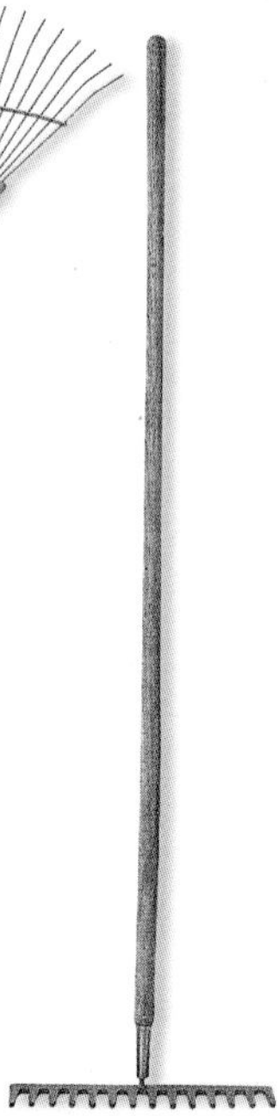

rake • le râteau • der Rechen • el rastrillo • il rastrello

hoe • la houe • die Hacke • el azadón • la zappa

gardening basket • le panier de jardinier • der Gartenkorb • la cesta de jardinero • il cestello

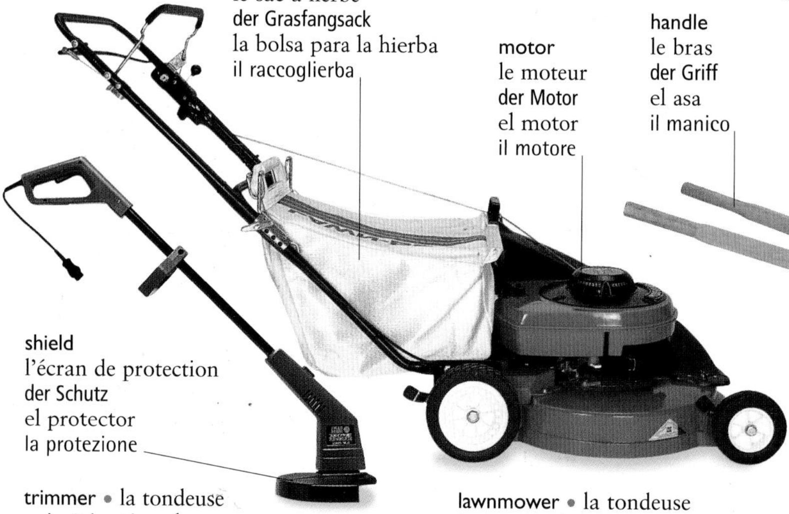

shield
l'écran de protection
der Schutz
el protector
la protezione

trimmer • la tondeuse • der Schneider • la cortadora • il tagliabordi

grass bag
le sac à herbe
der Grasfangsack
la bolsa para la hierba
il raccoglierba

motor
le moteur
der Motor
el motor
il motore

lawnmower • la tondeuse à gazon • der Rasenmäher • la podadora • il tosaerba

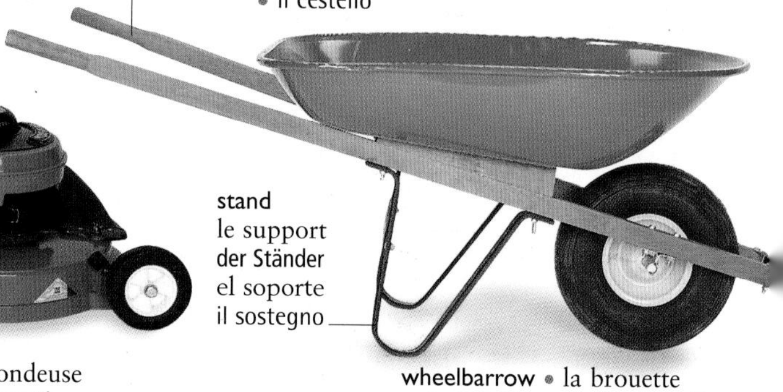

handle
le bras
der Griff
el asa
il manico

stand
le support
der Ständer
el soporte
il sostegno

wheelbarrow • la brouette • der Schubkarren • la carretilla • la carriola

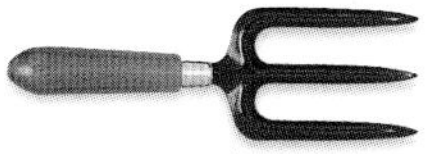

hand fork • la petite fourche • die Handgabel • el trinche • la forchetta

trowel • le déplantoir • die Pflanzschaufel • la pala pequeña • la paletta

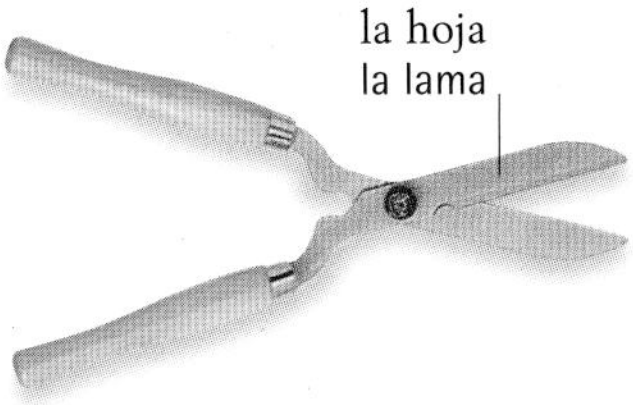

blade
la lame
das Messer
la hoja
la lama

shears • la cisaille • die Heckenschere • las tijeras • le forbici da giardino

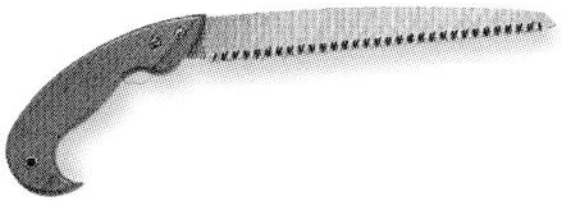

hand saw • la scie à main • die Handsäge • la sierra de mano • la sega

pruning shears • le sécateur • die Rosenschere • las podadoras • la cesoia

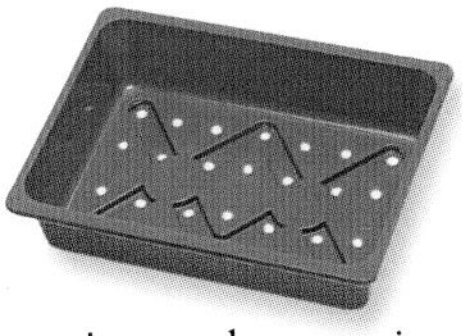

seed tray • le germoir • der Setzkasten • el semillero • il semenzaio

pesticide
le pesticide
das Pestizid
el pesticida
il pesticida

gardening gloves
les gants de jardinage
die Gartenhandschuhe
los guantes de jardín
i guanti da giardinaggio

twine
la ficelle
der Zwirn
el hilo de bramante
lo spago

labels
les étiquettes
die Pflanzenschildchen
las etiquetas
le etichette

twist ties
les attaches
die Befestigungen
el alambre
le fettucce

ring ties
les anneaux
die Ringbefestigungen
las anillas
gli anelli

canes
les cannes
die Gartenstöcke
las cañas
le canne

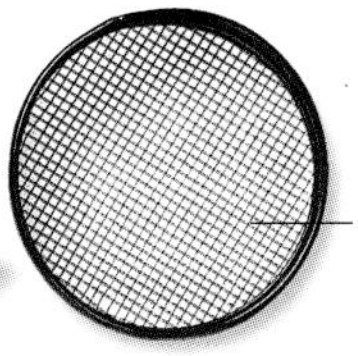

sieve
le tamis
das Sieb
la criba
il setaccio

plant pot
le pot à fleurs
der Blumentopf
la maceta
il vaso da fiori

rubber boots • les bottes • die Gummistiefel • las botas de goma • le galosce

watering • l'arrosage • das Gießen • el riego • l'annaffiatura

watering can
l'arrosoir
die Gießkanne
la regadera
l'annaffiatoio

rose • la pomme • die Brause • la piña • la rosa

spray gun • le vaporisateur • die Gartenspritze • el pulverizador • il diffusore

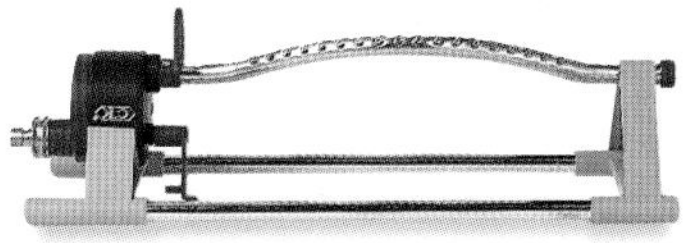

sprinkler • l'arroseur • der Rasensprenger • el aspersor • l'irrigatore

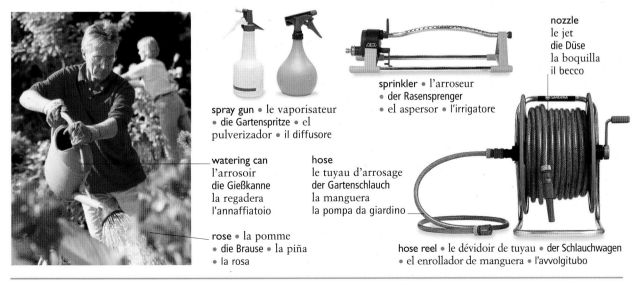

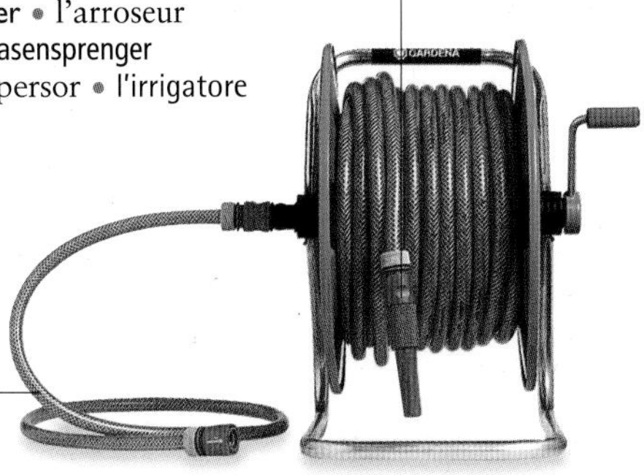

nozzle
le jet
die Düse
la boquilla
il becco

hose
le tuyau d'arrosage
der Gartenschlauch
la manguera
la pompa da giardino

hose reel • le dévidoir de tuyau • der Schlauchwagen • el enrollador de manguera • l'avvolgitubo

gardening • le jardinage • die Gartenarbeit • la jardinería • il giardinaggio

mow *(v)* • tondre • mähen • cortar el césped • tagliare l'erba

turf *(v)* • gazonner • mit Rasen bedecken • poner césped • ricoprire di zolle erbose

spike *(v)* • piquer • stechen • hacer agujeros con el trinche • inforcare

rake *(v)* • ratisser • harken • rastrillar • rastrellare

trim *(v)* • tailler • stutzen • podar • spuntare

dig *(v)* • bêcher • graben • cavar • scavare

sow *(v)* • semer • säen • sembrar • seminare

top dress *(v)* • fumer en surface • mit Kopfdünger düngen • abonar en la superficie • concimare a spandimento

water *(v)* • arroser • gießen • regar • annaffiare

train (v) • palisser • ziehen • guiar • far crescere

deadhead (v) • enlever les fleurs fanées • köpfen • quitar las flores muertas • togliere i fiori appassiti

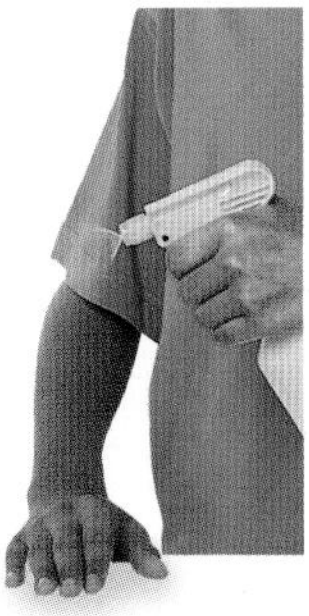

spray (v) • asperger • sprühen • rociar • spruzzare

stake (v) • mettre un tuteur • hochbinden • apuntalar • legare a un tutore

graft (v) • greffer • pfropfen • injertar • innestare

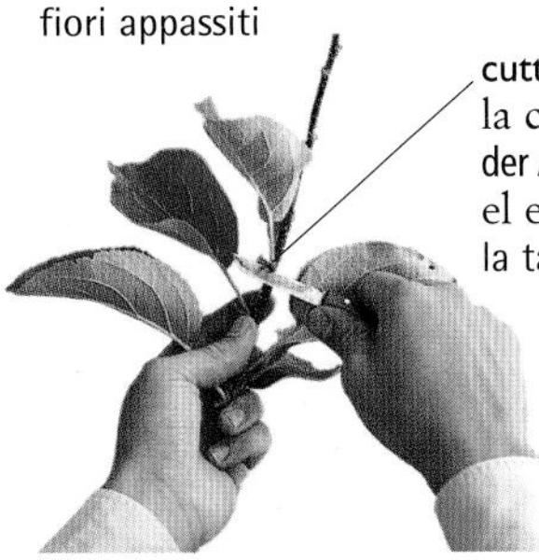

propagate (v) • propager • vermehren • propagar • propagare

prune (v) • élaguer • beschneiden • podar • potare

transplant (v) • transplanter • umpflanzen • transplantar • trapiantare

weed (v) • désherber • jäten • escardar • sradicare le erbacce

mulch (v) • pailler • mulchen • cubrir la tierra • coprire con strato protettivo

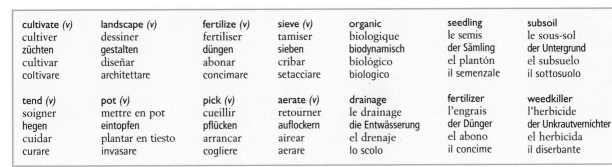

harvest (v) • récolter • ernten • cosechar • raccogliere

cultivate (v) cultiver züchten cultivar coltivare	landscape (v) dessiner gestalten diseñar architettare	fertilize (v) fertiliser düngen abonar concimare	sieve (v) tamiser sieben cribar setacciare	organic biologique biodynamisch biológico biologico	seedling le semis der Sämling el plantón il semenzale	subsoil le sous-sol der Untergrund el subsuelo il sottosuolo
tend (v) soigner hegen cuidar curare	pot (v) mettre en pot eintopfen plantar en tiesto invasare	pick (v) cueillir pflücken arrancar cogliere	aerate (v) retourner auflockern airear aerare	drainage le drainage die Entwässerung el drenaje lo scolo	fertilizer l'engrais der Dünger el abono il concime	weedkiller l'herbicide der Unkrautvernichter el herbicida il diserbante

JKL
5
TUV
8
7
0

services
les services
die Dienstleistungen
los servicios
i servizi

emergency services • les services d'urgence • die Notdienste • los servicios de emergencia • i servizi di emergenza

ambulance • l'ambulance • der Krankenwagen • la ambulancia • l'ambulanza

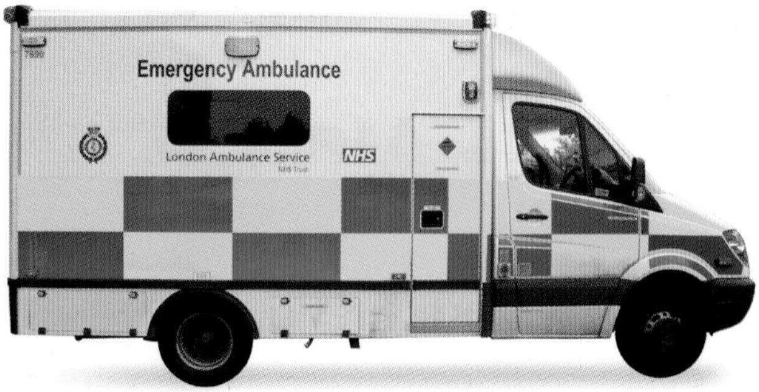

ambulance • l'ambulance • der Krankenwagen • la ambulancia • l'ambulanza

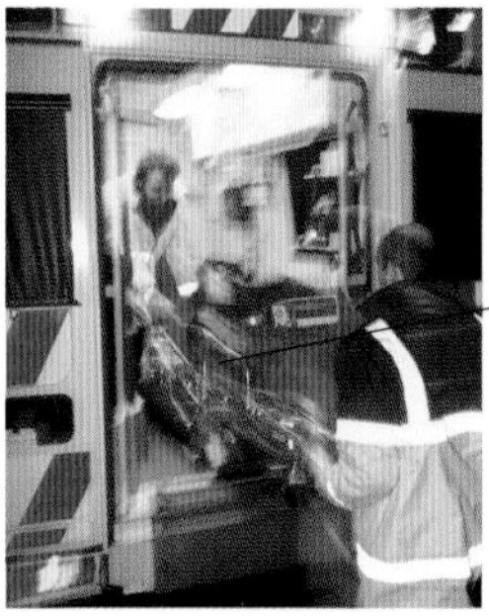

stretcher
le brancard
die Tragbahre
la camilla
la barella

paramedic • l'infirmier du SAMU • der Rettungssanitäter • el paramédico • il paramedico

police • la police • die Polizei • la policía • la polizia

badge
le badge
die Kennmarke
la placa
il distintivo

uniform
l'uniforme
die Uniform
el uniforme
l'uniforme

nightstick
la matraque
der Gummiknüppel
la macana
il manganello

gun
le pistolet
die Pistole
la pistola
la pistola

handcuffs
les menottes
die Handschellen
las esposas
le manette

police officer • le policier • der Polizist • el policía • l'agente

lights
les feux
das Licht
las luces
le luci

siren
la sirène
die Sirene
la sirena
la sirena

police car • la voiture de police • das Polizeiauto • la patrulla • l'auto della polizia

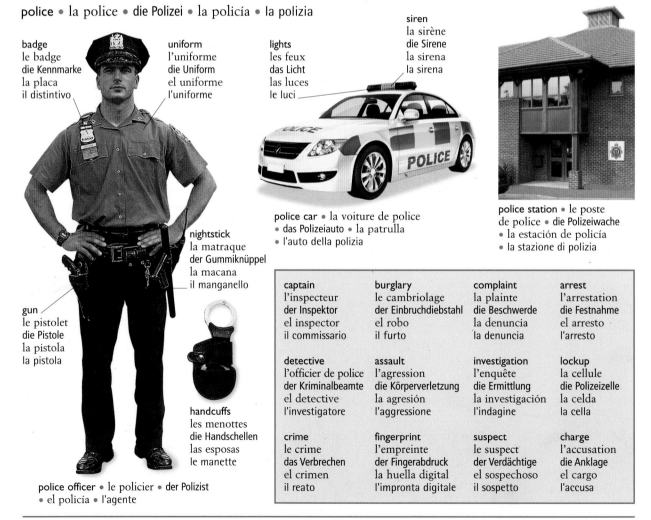

police station • le poste de police • die Polizeiwache • la estación de policía • la stazione di polizia

captain l'inspecteur der Inspektor el inspector il commissario	**burglary** le cambriolage der Einbruchdiebstahl el robo il furto	**complaint** la plainte die Beschwerde la denuncia la denuncia	**arrest** l'arrestation die Festnahme el arresto l'arresto
detective l'officier de police der Kriminalbeamte el detective l'investigatore	**assault** l'agression die Körperverletzung la agresión l'aggressione	**investigation** l'enquête die Ermittlung la investigación l'indagine	**lockup** la cellule die Polizeizelle la celda la cella
crime le crime das Verbrechen el crimen il reato	**fingerprint** l'empreinte der Fingerabdruck la huella digital l'impronta digitale	**suspect** le suspect der Verdächtige el sospechoso il sospetto	**charge** l'accusation die Anklage el cargo l'accusa

fire department • les pompiers • die Feuerwehr • los bomberos • i vigili del fuoco

smoke
la fumée
der Rauch
el humo
il fumo

hose
le tuyau
der Schlauch
la manguera
l'idrante

helmet • la casque • der Schutzhelm • el casco • il casco

cherry picker
la nacelle
der Auslegerkorb
la cesta
la gabbia

water jet
le jet d'eau
der Wasserstrahl
el chorro de agua
il getto d'acqua

firefighters • les sapeurs-pompiers • die Feuerwehrleute • los bomberos • i vigili del fuoco

boom
la flèche
der Ausleger
el brazo
il braccio

ladder
l'échelle
die Leiter
la escalera
la scala

cab
la cabine
die Fahrerkabine
la cabina
la cabina

fire • l'incendie • der Brand • el incendio • l'incendio

fire station • le poste d'incendie • die Feuerwache • la estación de bomberos • la caserma dei vigili del fuoco

fire escape • l'escalier de secours • die Feuertreppe • la escalera de incendios • la scala di sicurezza

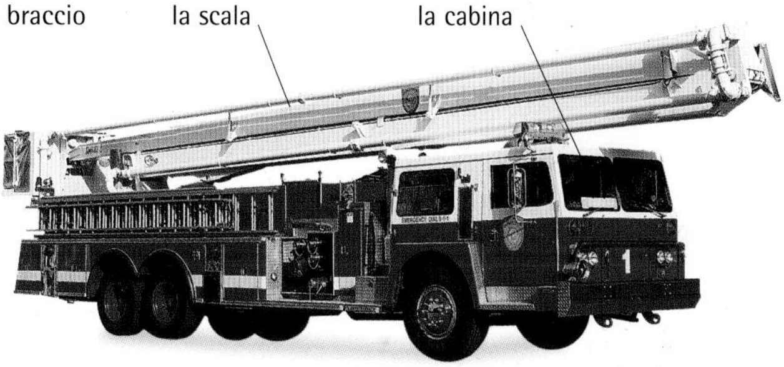

fire engine • la voiture de pompiers • das Löschfahrzeug • el carro de bomberos • l'autopompa

smoke alarm • le détecteur de fumée • der Rauchmelder • el detector de humo • l'allarme antifumo

fire alarm • l'avertisseur d'incendie • der Feuermelder • la alarma contra incendios • l'allarme antincendio

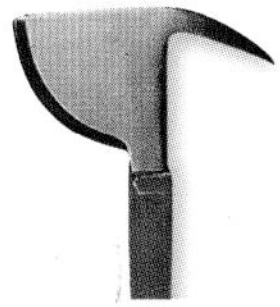

ax • la hache • das Beil • el hacha • l'ascia

fire extinguisher • l'extincteur • der Feuerlöscher • el extintor • l'estintore

hydrant • la borne d'incendie • der Hydrant • la bomba de agua • l'idrante

I need the police/fire department/ambulance.	There's a fire at...	There's been an accident.	Call the police!
La police/les pompiers/une ambulance, s'il vous plaît.	Il y a un incendie à...	Il y a eu un accident.	Appelez la police!
Die Polizei/die Feuerwehr/einen Krankenwagen, bitte.	Es brennt in...	Es ist ein Unfall passiert.	Rufen Sie die Polizei!
Necesito la policía/los bomberos/una ambulancia.	Hay un incendio en...	Ha habido un accidente.	¡Llame a la policía!
Ho bisogno della polizia/dei vigili del fuoco/di un'ambulanza.	C'è un incendio a...	C'è stato un incidente.	Chiamate la polizia!

bank • la banque • die Bank • el banco • la banca

customer
le client
der Kunde
el cliente
il cliente

window
le guichet
der Schalter
la ventanilla
lo sportello

teller
le caissier
der Kassierer
el cajero
il cassiere

brochures
les dépliants
die Broschüren
los folletos
i dépliants

counter
le comptoir
der Schalter
el mostrador
il banco

deposit slips
les fiches de versement
die Einzahlungsscheine
las fichas de depósito
i moduli di versamento

branch manager
• le directeur d'agence
• der Filialleiter • el gerente del banco • il direttore

debit card
la carte bancaire
die EC-Karte
la tarjeta de débito
la carta di debito

credit card • la carte de crédit • die Kreditkarte
• la tarjeta de crédito
• la carta di credito

stub
le talon
der Abschnitt
la matriz
la matrice

account number
le numéro de compte
die Kontonummer
el número de cuenta
il numero di conto

signature
la signature
die Unterschrift
la firma
la firma

amount
le montant
der Betrag
la cantidad
l'importo

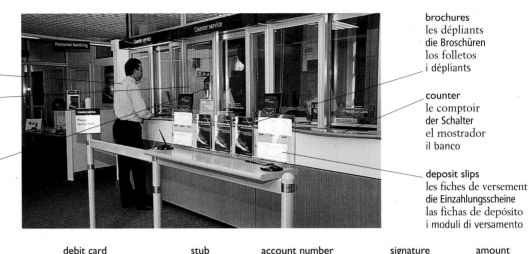

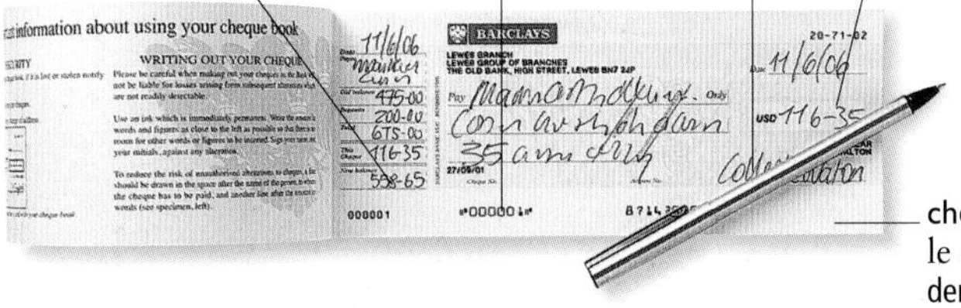

check
le chèque
der Scheck
el cheque
l'assegno

checkbook • le carnet de chèques
• das Scheckheft • el talonario de cheques
• il libretto degli assegni

savings l'épargne die Spareinlagen los ahorros i risparmi	mortgage l'hypothèque die Hypothek la hipoteca l'ipoteca	payment le paiement die Zahlung el pago il pagamento	deposit *(v)* verser einzahlen depositar versare	checking account le compte courant das Girokonto la cuenta corriente il conto corrente
tax l'impôt die Steuer los impuestos l'imposta	line of credit le découvert die Kontoüberziehung el sobregiro lo scoperto	automatic bill payment le prélèvement der Einzugsauftrag el débito directo l'addebito diretto	direct deposit le virement bancaire die Banküberweisung la transferencia bancaria il bonifico bancario	savings account le compte d'épargne das Sparkonto la cuenta de ahorros il conto di risparmio
loan le prêt das Darlehen el préstamo il prestito	interest rate le taux d'intérêt der Zinssatz la tasa de interés il tasso d'interesse	withdrawal slip la fiche de retrait das Abhebungsformular la ficha de retiro il modulo di prelievo	service charge les frais bancaire die Bankgebühr la comisión del banco la commissione bancaria	pin number le code secret der PIN-Kode el pin il pin

coin
la pièce
die Münze
la moneda
la moneta

bill
le billet
der Schein
el billete
la banconota

money • l'argent • das Geld • el dinero • il denaro

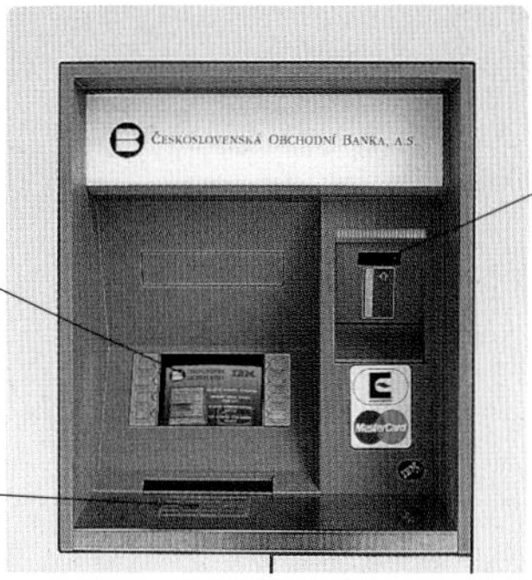

screen
l'écran
der Bildschirm
la pantalla
lo schermo

keypad
le clavier
das Tastenfeld
el teclado
la tastiera

card reader
la fente
der Kartenschlitz
la ranura de la tarjeta
la fessura per la carta

ATM • le distributeur • der Geldautomat • el cajero automático • la cassa automatica

foreign currency • les devises étrangères • die ausländische Währung • las divisas • la valuta estera

currency exchange • le bureau de change • die Wechselstube • la oficina de cambio • l'ufficio di cambio

traveler's check
le traveller
der Reisescheck
el cheque de viajero
il travel cheque

exchange rate
le taux de change
der Wechselkurs
el tipo de cambio
il tasso di cambio

finance • la finance • die Geldwirtschaft • las finanzas • la finanza

financial advisor • la conseillère financière • die Finanzberaterin • la asesora financiera • la consulente finanziaria

stock price
le prix des actions
der Aktienpreis
el valor de las acciones
il corso per azione

stockbroker
l'agent de la bourse
der Börsenmakler
el agente de bolsa
il broker

stock exchange • la bourse • die Börse • la bolsa de valores • la borsa valori

cash (*v*)
encaisser
einlösen
cobrar
incassare

denomination
la valeur
der Nennwert
la denominación
la denominazione

commission
la commission
die Provision
la comisión
la commissione

investment
l'investissement
die Kapitalanlage
la inversión
l'investimento

securities
les titres
die Wertpapiere
las acciones
i titoli

stocks
les actions
die Aktien
las acciones
le azioni

dividends
les dividendes
die Gewinnanteile
los dividendos
i dividendi

accountant
le comptable
der Wirtschaftsprüfer
el contador
il contabile

portfolio
le portefeuille
das Portefeuille
la cartera
il portafoglio

equity
l'action
die Stammaktie
el patrimonio neto
il capitale netto

Can I change this, please?
Est-ce que je peux changer ça, s'il vous plaît?
Könnte ich das bitte wechseln?
¿Podría cambiar esto por favor?
Posso cambiare questo?

What's today's exchange rate?
Quel est le taux de change aujourd'hui?
Wie ist der heutige Wechselkurs?
¿Cómo está el tipo de cambio hoy?
Qual è il tasso di cambio oggi?

communications • les communications • die Kommunikation • las comunicaciones • le comunicazioni

postal worker
le postier
der Postbeamte
el empleado de correos
l'impiegato delle poste

window
le guichet
der Schalter
la ventanilla
lo sportello

scale
la balance
die Waage
la báscula
la bilancia

counter
le guichet
der Schalter
el mostrador
il banco

post office • la poste • die Post • la oficina de correos • l'ufficio postale

mail carrier • le facteur • der Briefträger • el cartero • il postino

postmark
le tampon de la poste
der Poststempel
el matasellos
il timbro postale

stamp
le timbre
die Briefmarke
el timbre
il francobollo

address
l'adresse
die Adresse
la dirección
l'indirizzo

zip code
le code postal
die Postleitzahl
el código postal
il codice di avviamento postale

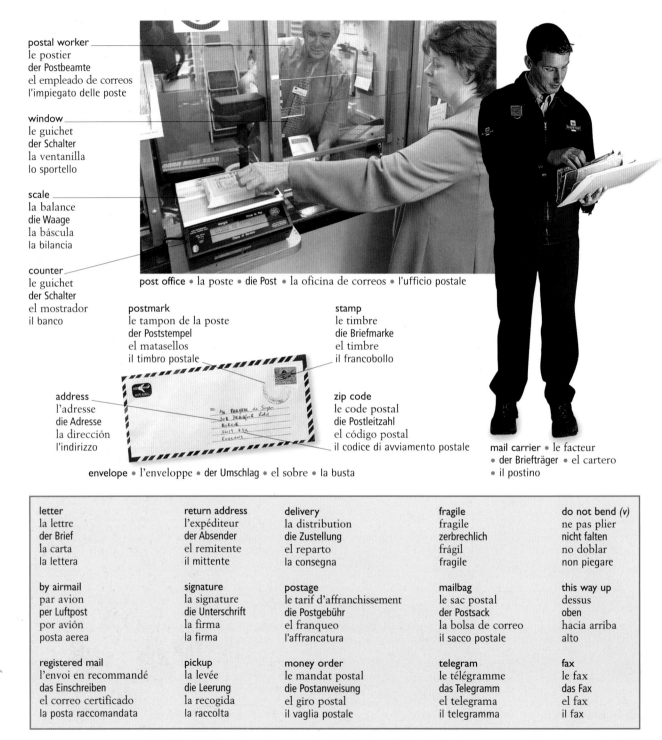

envelope • l'enveloppe • der Umschlag • el sobre • la busta

letter la lettre der Brief la carta la lettera	return address l'expéditeur der Absender el remitente il mittente	delivery la distribution die Zustellung el reparto la consegna	fragile fragile zerbrechlich frágil fragile	do not bend *(v)* ne pas plier nicht falten no doblar non piegare
by airmail par avion per Luftpost por avión posta aerea	signature la signature die Unterschrift la firma la firma	postage le tarif d'affranchissement die Postgebühr el franqueo l'affrancatura	mailbag le sac postal der Postsack la bolsa de correo il sacco postale	this way up dessus oben hacia arriba alto
registered mail l'envoi en recommandé das Einschreiben el correo certificado la posta raccomandata	pickup la levée die Leerung la recogida la raccolta	money order le mandat postal die Postanweisung el giro postal il vaglia postale	telegram le télégramme das Telegramm el telegrama il telegramma	fax le fax das Fax el fax il fax

mailbox • la boîte aux lettres • der Briefkasten • el buzón • la buca delle lettere

letter slot • la boîte aux lettres • der Hausbriefkasten • el buzón • la cassetta delle lettere

parcel • le colis • das Paket • el paquete • il pacco

courier • le service de messagerie • der Kurierdienst • la mensajería • il corriere

telephone • le téléphone • das Telefon • el teléfono • il telefono

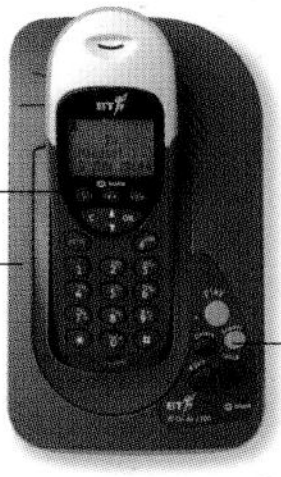

handset
le combiné
der Hörer
el auricular
il ricevitore

base station
la base
die Basis
la base
la base

answering machine
le répondeur
der Anrufbeantworter
la contestadora
la segreteria telefonica

cordless phone • le téléphone sans fil • das schnurlose Telefon • el teléfono inalámbrico • il telefono senza fili

video phone • le visiophone • das Fernsehtelefon • el videoteléfono • il videotelefono

phone booth • la cabine téléphonique • die Telefonzelle • la cabina telefónica • la cabina telefonica

smartphone • le smartphone • das Smartphone • el teléfono inteligente • lo smartphone

keypad
le clavier
das Tastenfeld
el teclado
la tastiera

mobile phone • le portable • das Handy • el teléfono móvil • il telefonino

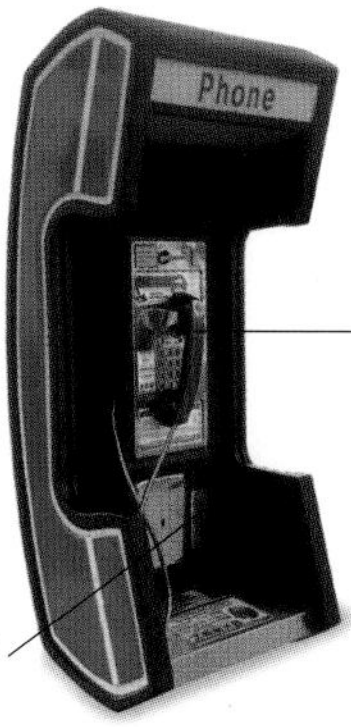

receiver
le combiné
der Hörer
el auricular
il ricevitore

coin return
le rendu de monnaie
die Münzrückgabe
las monedas devueltas
le monete non utilizzate

payphone • le téléphone public • der Münzfernsprecher • el teléfono público • il telefono pubblico

app
l'appli
die app
la aplicación
l'app

passcode
le mot de passe
der passcode
la clave de acceso
il codice d'accesso

dial *(v)*
composer
wählen
marcar
comporre

answer *(v)*
répondre
abheben
contestar
rispondere

text
le SMS
die SMS
el mensaje de texto (SMS)
il messaggio (SMS)

voice message
le message vocal
die Sprachmitteilung
el mensaje de voz
il messaggio vocale

operator
le téléphoniste
die Vermittlung
el operador
l'operatore

busy
occupé
besetzt
ocupado
occupato

disconnected
coupé
unterbrochen
desconectado
staccato

Can you give me the number for...?
Pouvez-vous me donner le numéro pour…?
Können Sie mir die Nummer für…geben?
¿Me podría dar el número de…?
Può darmi il numero per...?

What is the area code for...?
Quel est l'indicatif pour…?
Was ist die Vorwahl für…?
¿Cuál es el prefijo de larga distancia para llamar a…?
Qual è il prefisso per...?

hotel • l'hôtel • das Hotel • el hotel • l'albergo

lobby • le hall • die Empfangshalle • el lobby • l'ingresso

guest
le client
der Gast
el huésped
l'ospite

room key
la clef de la chambre
der Zimmerschlüssel
la llave de la habitación
la chiave della camera

messages
les messages
die Nachrichten
los mensajes
i messaggi

pigeonhole
le casier
das Fach
la casilla
la casella

receptionist
la réceptionniste
die Empfangsdame
la recepcionista
l'addetta alla ricezione

register
le registre
das Gästebuch
el registro
il registro

counter
le comptoir
der Schalter
el mostrador
il banco

reception • la réception • der Empfang • la recepción • la ricezione

luggage
les bagages
das Gepäck
el equipaje
il bagaglio

luggage rack
le diable
der Kofferkuli
el diablito
il carrello

porter • le porteur • der Hoteldiener • el botones • il facchino

elevator • l'ascenseur • der Fahrstuhl • el elevador • l'ascensore

room number • le numéro de chambre • die Zimmernummer • el número de la habitación • il numero della camera

rooms • les chambres • die Zimmer • los habitaciones • le camere

single room • la chambre simple • das Einzelzimmer • la habitación sencilla • la camera singola

double room • la chambre double • das Doppelzimmer • la habitación doble • la camera doppia

twin room • la chambre à deux lits • das Zweibettzimmer • la habitación con dos camas individuales • la camera a due letti

private bathroom
la salle de bain privée
das Privatbadezimmer
el baño privado
il bagno privato

services • les services • die Dienstleistungen • los servicios • i servizi

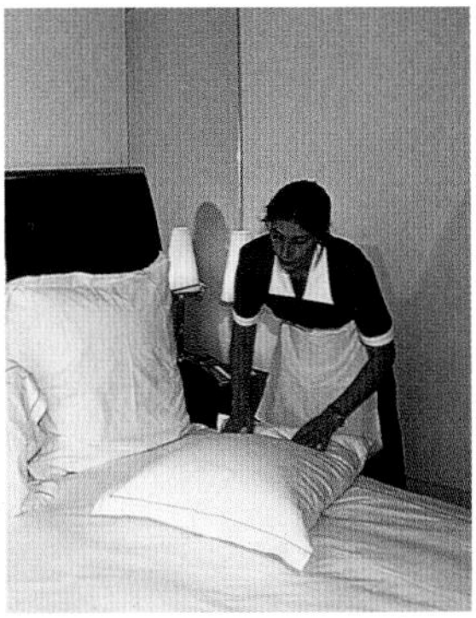

maid service • le service de ménage • die Zimmerreinigung • el servicio de limpieza • il servizio di pulizia

laundry service • le service de blanchisserie • der Wäschedienst • el servicio de lavandería • il servizio di lavanderia

breakfast tray • le plateau à petit déjeuner • das Frühstückstablett • la charola del desayuno • il vassoio della colazione

room service • le service d'étage • der Zimmerservice • el servicio de habitaciones • il servizio in camera

minibar • le minibar • die Minibar • el minibar • il minibar

restaurant • le restaurant • das Restaurant • el restaurante • il ristorante

gym • la salle de sport • der Fitnessraum • el gimnasio • la palestra

swimming pool • la piscine • das Schwimmbad • la piscina • la piscina

full board
la pension complète
die Vollpension
la pensión completa
la pensione completa

half board
la demi-pension
die Halbpension
la media pensión
la mezza pensione

bed and breakfast
la chambre avec le petit déjeuner
die Übernachtung mit Frühstück
la habitación con desayuno incluido
la pensione con colazione

Do you have any vacancies?
Avez-vous une chambre de libre?
Haben Sie ein Zimmer frei?
¿Tiene alguna habitación libre?
Avete una camera libera?

I have a reservation.
J'ai une réservation.
Ich habe ein Zimmer reserviert.
Tengo una reservación.
Ho una prenotazione

I'd like a single room.
Je voudrais une chambre simple.
Ich möchte ein Einzelzimmer.
Quiero una habitación sencilla.
Vorrei una camera singola

I'd like a room for three nights.
Je voudrais une chambre pour trois nuits.
Ich möchte ein Zimmer für drei Nächte.
Quiero una habitación para tres días.
Vorrei una camera per tre notti.

What is the charge per night?
C'est combien par nuit?
Was kostet das Zimmer pro Nacht?
¿Cuánto cuesta la habitación por día?
Quanto costa la camera a notte?

When do I have to vacate the room?
Quand est-ce que je dois quitter la chambre?
Wann muss ich das Zimmer räumen?
¿Cuándo tengo que dejar la habitación?
Quando devo lasciare la stanza?

shopping
les courses
der Einkauf
las compras
gli acquisti

shopping mall • le centre commercial • das Einkaufszentrum • el centro comercial • il centro commerciale

children's department
le rayon enfants
die Kinderabteilung
el departamento de niños
il reparto bambini

luggage department
le rayon bagages
die Gepäckabteilung
el departamento de equipajes
il reparto bagagli

shoe department
le rayon chaussures
die Schuhabteilung
el departamento de zapatería
il reparto calzature

store directory
le guide
die Anzeigetafel
el directorio
la guida al negozio

sales clerk
le vendeur
der Verkäufer
el vendedor
il commesso

rest room
les toilettes
die Toiletten
los baños
le toilettes

fitting rooms
les cabines d'essayage
die Anprobe
los probadores
i camerini

baby changing room
les soins de bébés
der Wickelraum
el cuarto para cambiar a los bebés
spazio co fasciatoio

customer services
le service après-vente
der Kundendienst
el servicio al cliente
l'assistenza ai clienti

How much is this?
C'est combien?
Was kostet das?
¿Cuánto cuesta esto?
Quanto costa questo?

May I exchange this?
Est-ce que je peux changer ça?
Kann ich das umtauschen?
¿Puedo cambiar esto?
Posso cambiare questo?

department store • le grand magasin • das Kaufhaus • las tiendas departamentales • il grande magazzino

menswear • les vêtements pour hommes • die Herrenbekleidung • la ropa de caballero • l'abbigliamento da uomo

womenswear • les vêtements pour femmes • die Damenoberbekleidung • la ropa de dama • l'abbigliamento da donna

lingerie • la lingerie • die Damenwäsche • la lencería • la biancheria intima

perfumes • la parfumerie • die Parfümerie • la perfumería • la profumeria

cosmetics • la beauté • die Schönheitspflege • los cosméticos • la bellezza

linens • le linge de maison • die Wäsche • los blancos • la biancheria

home furnishings • l'ameublement • die Möbel • el mobiliario para el hogar • l'arredamento per la casa

notions • la mercerie • die Kurzwaren • la mercería • la merceria

kitchenware • la vaisselle • die Küchengeräte • los artículos de cocina • gli articoli da cucina

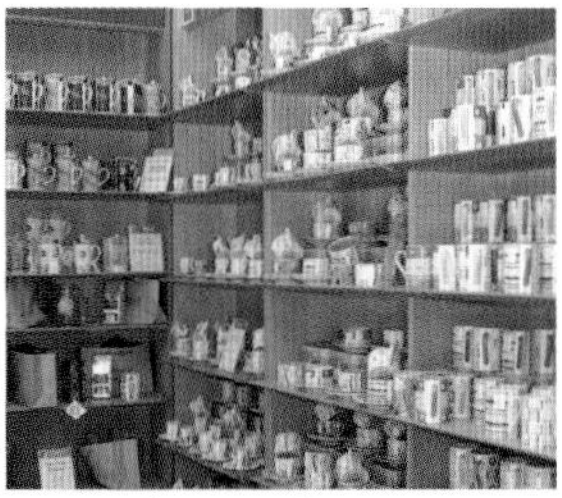

china • la porcelaine • das Porzellan • las vajillas • la porcellana

electronics l'électroménager die Elektroartikel los aparatos eléctricos gli articoli elettronici

lighting • l'éclairage • die Lampen • la iluminación • l'illuminazione

sportswear • les articles de sport • die Sportartikel • los artículos deportivos • gli articoli sportivi

toys • les jouets • die Spielwaren • la juguetería • i giocattoli

stationery • la papeterie • die Scheibwaren • la papelería • la cancelleria

groceries • l'alimentation • die Lebensmittelabteilung • los abarrotes • il reparto alimentari

supermarket • le supermarché • der Supermarkt • el supermercado • il supermercato

aisle • l'allée • der Gang • el pasillo • il passaggio

shelf • l'ètàgere • das Warenregal • el estante • lo scaffale

checkout counter
le tapis roulant
das Laufband
la banda transportadora
il nastro convogliatore

cashier
le caissier
der Kassierer
el cajero
il cassiere

offers
les promotions
die Angebote
las ofertas
le offerte

checkout • la caisse • die Kasse • la caja • la cassa

customer
le client
der Kunde
el cliente
il cliente

cash register
la caisse
die Kasse
la caja
la cassa

shopping bag
la sac à provisions
die Einkaufstasche
la bolsa
la busta della spesa

groceries
les provisions
die Lebensmittel
la compra
la spesa

grocery cart • le caddie • der Einkaufswagen • el carrito • il carrello

handle
l'anse
der Henkel
el asa
il manico

basket • le panier • der Einkaufskorb • la canasta • il cestino

780863 185779

bar code • le code barres • der Strichkode • el código de barras • il codice a barre

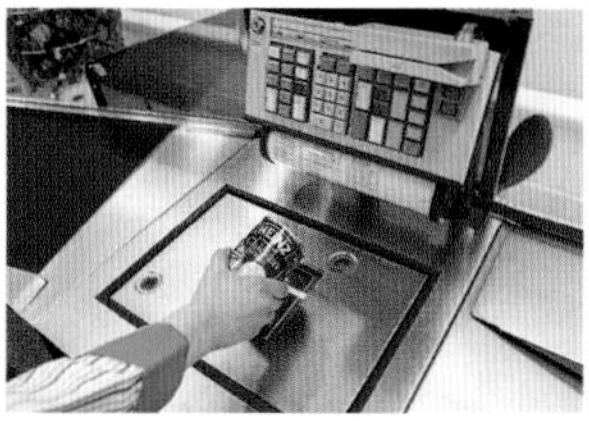

scanner • le lecteur optique • der Scanner • el escáner • il lettore ottico

bakery • la boulangerie • die Backwaren • la panadería • il pane

dairy • la crémerie • die Milchprodukte • los lácteos • i latticini

breakfast cereals
les céréales
die Getreideflocken
los cereales
i cereali da colazione

canned goods
les conserves
die Konserven
las conservas
lo scatolame

candies • la confiserie • die Süßwaren • la dulcería • i dolci

vegetables • les légumes • das Gemüse • la verdura • le verdure

fruits • les fruits • das Obst • la fruta • la frutta

meat and poultry • la viande et la volaille • das Fleisch und das Geflügel • la carne y las aves • la carne e il pollame

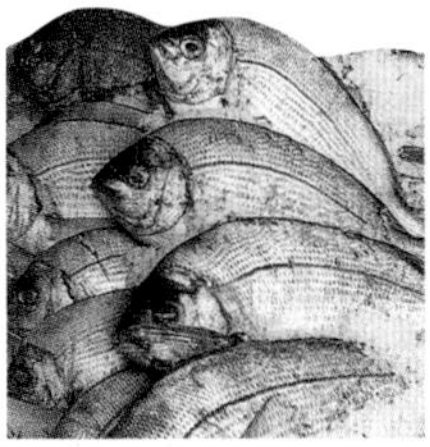

fish • le poisson • der Fisch • el pescado • il pesce

deli • la charcuterie • die Feinkost • la charcutería • i salumi

frozen food • les produits surgelés • die Gefrierware • los congelados • i surgelati

prepared food
les plats cuisinés
die Fertiggerichte
los platos preparados
i cibi pronti

drinks • les boissons • die Getränke • las bebidas • le bibite

household products • les produits d'entretien • die Haushaltswaren • los productos de limpieza • i casalinghi

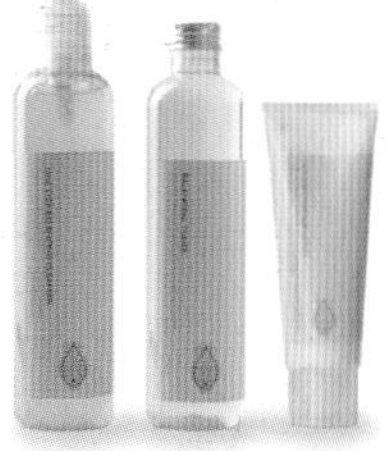

toiletries • les articles de toilette • die Toilettenartikel • los artículos de aseo • gli articoli da toilette

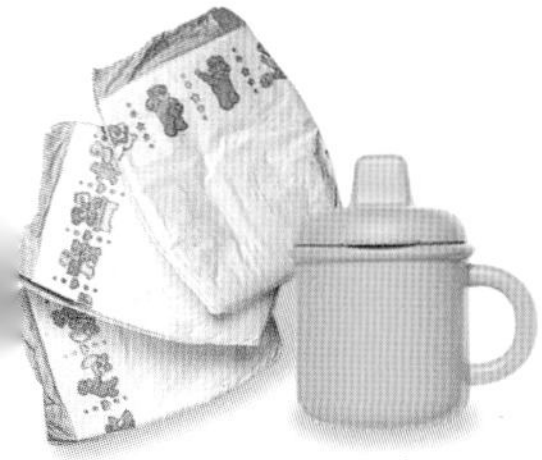

baby products • les articles pour bébés • die Babyprodukte • los artículos para el bebé • i prodotti per bambini

electrical goods
l'électroménager
die Elektroartikel
los electrodomésticos
gli articoli elettrici

pet food • la nourriture pour animaux • das Tierfutter • la comida para animales • il cibo per animali

magazines • les magazines • die Zeitschriften • las revistas • le riviste

chemist • la pharmacie • die Apotheke • la farmacia • la farmacia

dental care
le soin dentaire
die Zahnpflege
el cuidado dental
i prodotti per i denti

feminine hygiene
l'hygiène féminine
die Monatshygiene
la higiene femenina
l'igiene femminile

deodorants
les déodorants
die Deos
los desodorantes
i deodoranti

vitamins
les cachets de vitamines
die Vitamintabletten
las vitaminas
le vitamine

pharmacy
l'officine
die Apotheke
el dispensario
il dispensario

pharmacist
le pharmacien
der Apotheker
el farmacéutico
il farmacista

cough medicine
le médicament pour la toux
das Hustenmedikament
el jarabe para la tos
la medicina per la tosse

herbal remedies
l'herboristerie
das Kräuterheilmittel
los remedios naturistas
i rimedi fitoterapaci

skin care
les soins de la peau
die Hautpflege
el cuidado de la piel
i prodotti per la pelle

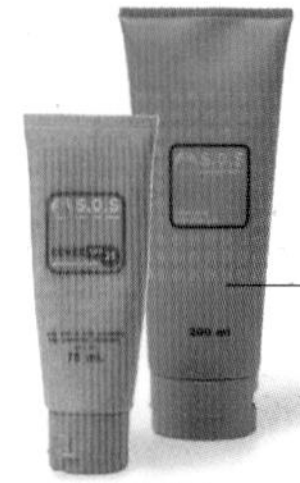

aftersun care • l'après-soleil • die After-Sun-Lotion • la crema para después del sol • il doposole

sunscreen • l'écran solaire • die Sonnenschutzcreme • la crema protectora • la crema schermo

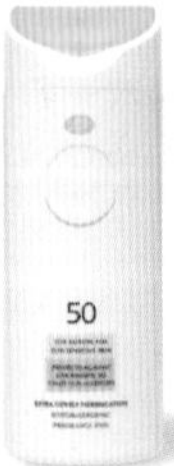

sun block • l'écran total • der Sonnenblock • la crema protectora total • la crema schermo totale

insect repellent • le produit anti-insecte • das Insektenschutzmittel • el repelente de insectos • l'insettifugo

wet wipe • la serviette humide • das Reinigungstuch • la toallita húmeda • la salviettina umidificata

tissue • le kleenex • das Papiertaschentuch • el pañuelo desechable • il fazzolettino

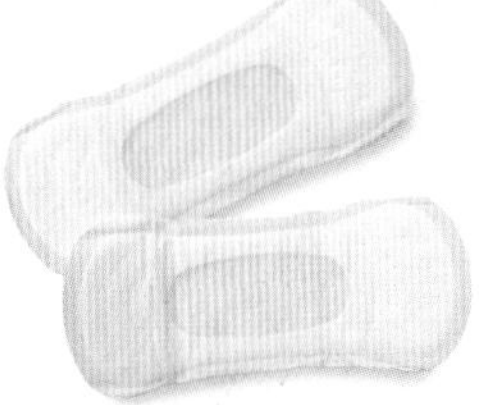

sanitary napkin • la serviette hygiénique • die Damenbinde • las toallas femeninas • l'assorbente

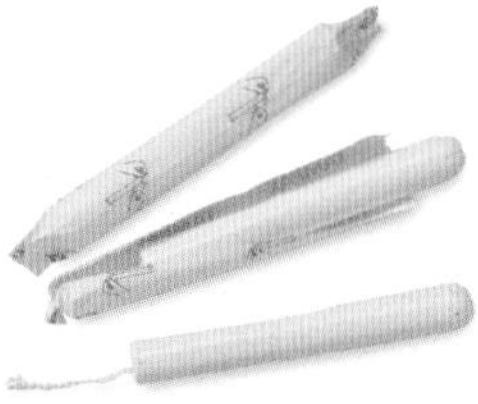

tampon • le tampon • der Tampon • el tampón • il tampone

panty liner • le protège-slip • die Slipeinlage • el pantiprotector • i salvaslip

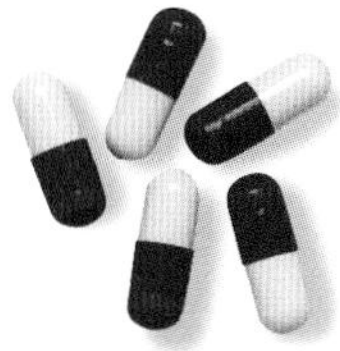

capsule • la capsule • die Kapsel • la cápsula • la capsula

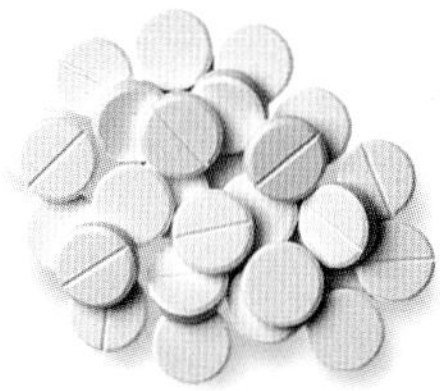

pill • la pilule • die Pille • la píldora • la compressa

measuring spoon
la cuiller pour mesurer
der Messlöffel
la cuchara medidora
il cucchiaio dosatore

syrup • le sirop • der Saft • el jarabe • lo sciroppo

instructions
le mode d'emploi
die Gebrauchsanweisung
el modo de empleo
le istruzioni

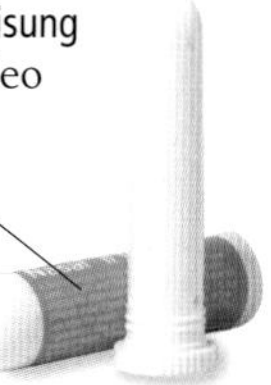

inhaler • l'inhalateur • der Inhalierstift • el inhalador • l'inalatore

cream • la crème • die Creme • la crema • la pomata

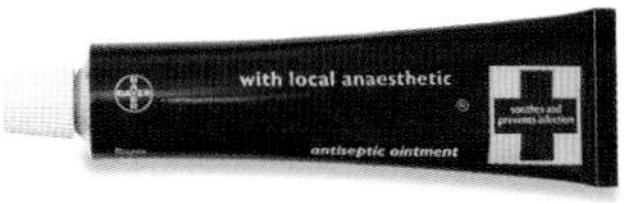

ointment • la pommade • die Salbe • la pomada • l'unguento

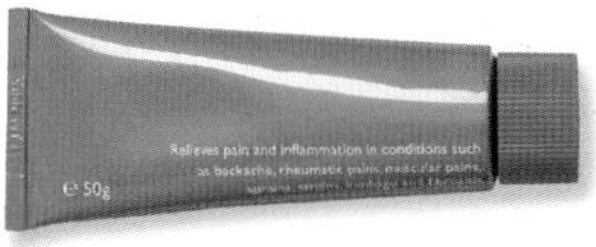

gel • le gel • das Gel • el gel • il gel

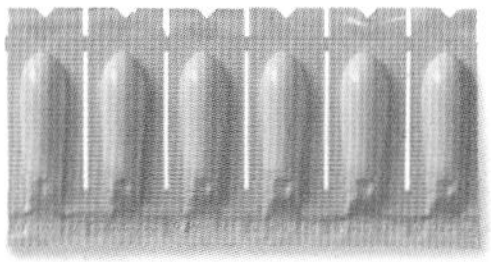

suppository • le suppositoire • das Zäpfchen • el supositorio • la supposta

eye dropper
le compte-gouttes
der Tropfer
el gotero
il contagocce

eye drops • les gouttes • die Tropfen • las gotas • le gocce

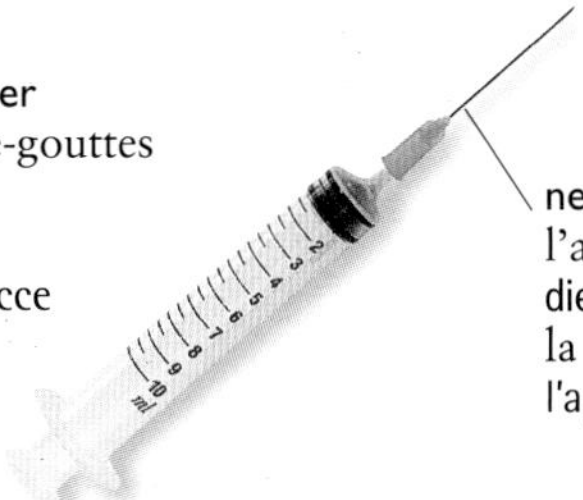

needle
l'aiguille
die Nadel
la aguja
l'ago

syringe • la seringue • die Spritze • la jeringa • la siringa

spray • le spray • der Spray • el spray • lo spray

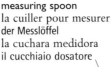

powder • la poudre • der Puder • los polvos • la polvere

iron le fer das Eisen el hierro il ferro	**multivitamins** le médicament multivitamine das Multivitaminmittel el complejo vitamínico la multivitamina	**disposable** jetable Wegwerf- desechable monouso	**medicine** le médicament das Medikament el medicamento la medicina	**painkiller** l'analgésique das Schmerzmittel el analgésico l'antidolorifico
calcium le calcium das Kalzium el calcio il calcio	**side-effects** les effets secondaires die Nebenwirkungen los efectos secundarios gli effetti collaterali	**soluble** soluble löslich soluble solubile	**laxative** le laxatif das Abführmittel el laxante il lassativo	**sedative** le sédatif das Beruhigungsmittel el calmante il sedativo
magnesium le magnésium das Magnesium el magnesio il magnesio	**expiration date** la date d'expiration das Verfallsdatum la fecha de caducidad la data di scadenza	**dosage** la posologie die Dosierung la dosis il dosaggio	**diarrhea** la diarrhée der Durchfall la diarrea la diarrea	**sleeping pill** le somnifère die Schlaftablette el somnífero il sonnifero
insulin l'insuline das Insulin la insulina l'insulina	**travel sickness pills** les cachets antinaupathiques die Reisekrankheitstabletten las píldoras para el mareo le pasticche per il mal d'auto	**medication** la médication die Verordnung la medicación il medicamento	**throat lozenge** la pastille pour la gorge die Halspastille la pastilla para la garganta la pasticca per la gola	**anti-inflammatory** l'anti-inflammatoire der Entzündungshemmer el antiinflamatorio l'antinfiammatorio

florist • le fleuriste • das Blumengeschäft • la florería • il fioraio

flowers
les fleurs
die Blumen
las flores
i fiori

lily
le lis
die Lilie
la azucena
il giglio

acacia
l'acacia
die Akazie
la acacia
l'acacia

carnation
l'œillet
die Nelke
el clavel
il garofano

potted plant
la plante en pot
die Topfpflanze
la maceta
la pianta da vaso

gladiolus
le glaïeul
die Gladiole
la gladiola
il gladiolo

iris
l'iris
die Iris
el iris
l'iris

daisy
la marguerite
die Margerite
la margarita
la margherita

chrysanthemum
le chrysanthème
die Chrysantheme
el crisantemo
il crisantemo

gypsophila
la gypsophile
das Schleierkraut
la nube
la gipsofila

stocks • la giroflée • die Levkoje • el alhelí • la violacciocca

gerbera • le gerbera • die Gerbera • la gerbera • la gerbera

foliage • le feuillage • die Blätter • el follaje • il fogliame

rose • la rose • die Rose • la rosa • la rosa

freesia • le freesia • die Freesie • la fresia • la fresia vase • le vase • die Blumenvase • el florero • il vaso

orchid • l'orchidée • die Orchidee • la orquídea • l'orchidea

peony • la pivoine • die Pfingstrose • la peonía • la peonia

bunch
la botte
der Strauß
el ramo
il mazzetto

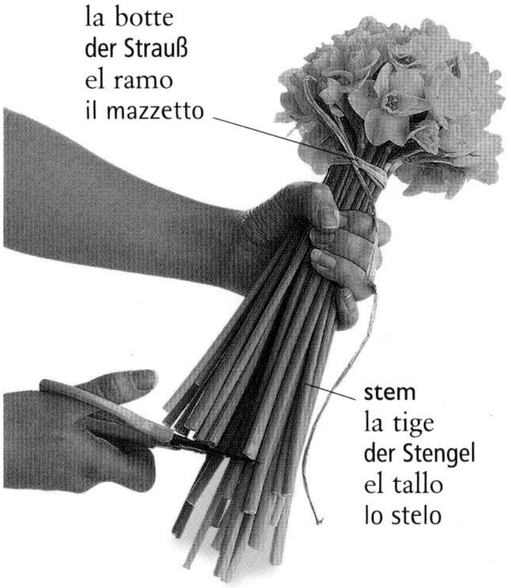

stem
la tige
der Stengel
el tallo
lo stelo

daffodil • la jonquille • die Osterglocke • el narciso • il narciso

bud
le bourgeon
die Knospe
el capullo
il bocciolo

wrapping
l'emballage
das Einwickelpapier
la envoltura
l'incarto

tulip • la tulipe • die Tulpe • el tulipán • il tulipano

arrangements • les compositions florales • die Blumenarrangements • los arreglos • gli arrangiamenti

ribbon
le ruban
das Band
la cinta
il nastro

bouquet • le bouquet • das Bukett • el ramo • il mazzo di fiori

dried flowers • les fleurs séchées • die Trockenblumen • las flores secas • i fiori secchi

pot-pourri • le pot-pourri • das Duftsträußchen • el popurrí • il pot-pourri

wreath • la couronne • der Kranz • la corona • la corona

garland • la guirlande de fleurs • die Blumengirlande • la guirnalda • la ghirlanda

May I have a bunch of... please.
Je voudrais un bouquet de..., SVP.
Ich möchte einen Strauß..., bitte.
¿Me da un ramo de... por favor?
Mi dà un mazzo di... per favore?

May I have them wrapped?
Pouvez-vous les emballer?
Können Sie die Blumen bitte einwickeln?
¿Me los puede envolver?
Me li può incartare?

May I attach a message?
Je peux y attacher un message?
Kann ich eine Nachricht mitschicken?
¿Puedo poner un mensaje?
Posso allegare un messaggio?

How long will these last?
Elles tiennent combien de temps?
Wie lange halten sie?
¿Cuánto tiempo durarán éstos?
Quanto dureranno?

Are they fragrant?
Est-ce qu'elles sentent bon?
Duften sie?
¿Huelen?
Sono profumati?

Would you send them to....?
Pouvez-vous les envoyer à...?
Können Sie die Blumen an... schicken?
¿Los puede enviar a...?
Li può mandare a...?

newsstand • le marchand de journaux • der Zeitungshändler • los tabacos y las revistas • l'edicola

cigarettes
les cigarettes
die Zigaretten
los cigarros
le sigarette

pack of cigarettes
le paquet de cigarettes
das Päckchen Zigaretten
la cajetilla de cigarros
il pacchetto di sigarette

stamps
les timbres
die Briefmarken
los timbres
i francobolli

postcard • la carte postale • die Postkarte • la tarjeta postal • la cartolina

comic • la bande dessinée • das Comicheft • la historieta • il giornalino a fumetti

magazine • le magazine • die Zeitschrift • la revista • la rivista

newspaper • le journal • die Zeitung • el periódico • il giornale

smoking • fumer • das Rauchen • fumar • fumare

tobacco • le tabac • der Tabak • el tabaco • il tabacco

lighter • le briquet • das Feuerzeug • el encendedor • l'accendino

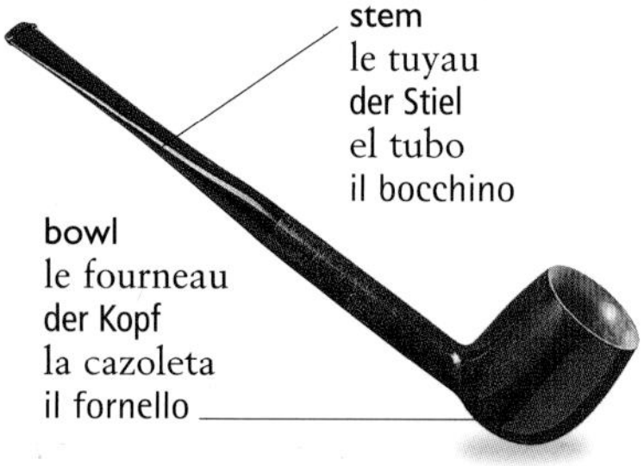

stem
le tuyau
der Stiel
el tubo
il bocchino

bowl
le fourneau
der Kopf
la cazoleta
il fornello

pipe • la pipe • die Pfeife • la pipa • la pipa

cigar • le cigare• die Zigarre • el puro • il sigaro

candy store • le confiseur • der Konditor • la dulcería • il confettiere

box of chocolates
la boîte de chocolats
die Schachtel Pralinen
la caja de chocolates
la scatola di cioccolatini

snack bar
la friandise
die Nascherei
la barrita
la merendina

potato chips
les chips
die Chips
las papas fritas
le patatine

candy store • la confiserie • das Süßwarengeschäft • la dulcería • il negozio di dolciumi

milk chocolate le chocolat au lait die Milchschokolade el chocolate de leche il cioccolato al latte	caramel le caramel der Karamell el caramelo il caramello
dark chocolate le chocolat noir die bittere Schokolade el chocolate negro il cioccolato fondente	truffle la truffe der Trüffel la trufa il tartufo
white chocolate le chocolat blanc die weiße Schokolade el chocolate blanco il cioccolato bianco	cookie le biscuit der Keks la galleta il biscotto
pick and mix les bonbons assortis die bunte Mischung los dulces a granel la caramelle assortite	hard candy les bonbons die Bonbons los caramelos duros le caramelle

confectionery • la confiserie • die Süßwaren • los dulces • i dolciumi

chocolate • le chocolat • die Praline • el chocolate • il cioccolatino

chocolate bar • la tablette de chocolat • die Tafel Schokolade • la tablilla de chocolate • la tavoletta di cioccolata

hard candy • les bonbons • die Bonbons • los caramelos duros • le caramelle

lollipop • la sucette • der Lutscher • la paleta • il lecca lecca

toffee • le caramel • das Toffee • el toffee • la caramella mou

nougat • le nougat • der Nugat • el turrón • il torrone

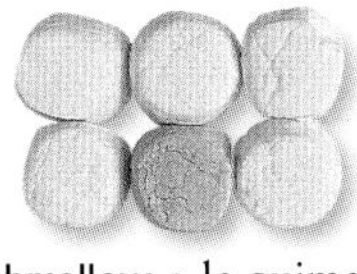

marshmallow • la guimauve • das Marshmallow • el malvarisco • la caramella gommosa

mint • le bonbon à la menthe • das Pfefferminz • la pastilla de menta • la mentina

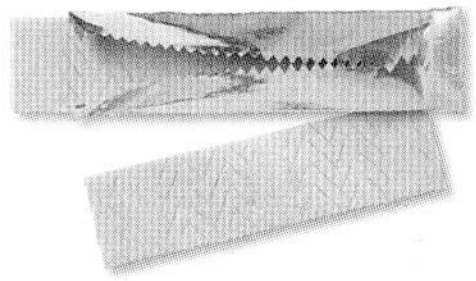

chewing gum • le chewing-gum • der Kaugummi • el chicle • la gomma da masticare

jellybean • la dragée à la gelée • der Geleebonbon • el caramelo blando • la caramella di gelatina

gumdrop • le bonbon au fruit • der Fruchtgummi • la gomita • la caramella alla frutta

licorice • le réglisse • die Lakritze • el regaliz • la liquirizia

other stores • les autres magasins • andere Geschäfte • las otras tiendas • gli altri negozi

bakery • la boulangerie • die Bäckerei • la panadería • il panificio

cake shop • la pâtisserie • die Konditorei • la confitería • la pasticceria

butcher shop • la boucherie • die Metzgerei • la carnicería • la macelleria

fish counter • la poissonnerie • das Fischgeschäft • la pescadería • la pescheria

produce stand • le marchand de légumes • der Gemüseladen • la verdulería • il fruttivendolo

grocery store • l'épicerie • das Lebensmittelgeschäft • los abarrotes • la drogheria

shoe store • le magasin de chaussures • das Schuhgeschäft • la zapatería • il negozio di calzature

hardware store • la quincaillerie • die Eisenwarenhandlung • la ferretería • il negozio di ferramenta

antique store • le magasin d'antiquités • der Antiquitätenladen • la tienda de antigüedades • il negozio di antiquariato

gift store • la boutique de cadeaux • der Geschenkartikelladen • la tienda de regalos • il negozio di articoli da regalo

travel agency • l'agence de voyage • das Reisebüro • la agencia de viajes • l'agenzia di viaggi

jewelry store • la bijouterie • das Juweliergeschäft • la joyería • la gioielleria

bookstore • la librairie • der Buchladen • la librería • la libreria

record store • le magasin de disques • das Plattengeschäft • la tienda de discos • il negozio di dischi

liquor store • le magasin de vins et spiritueux • die Weinhandlung • la tienda de licores • il negozio di liquori

pet store • l'animalerie • die Tierhandlung • la tienda de mascotas • il negozio di animali

furniture store • le magasin de meubles • das Möbelgeschäft • la mueblería • il negozio di mobili

boutique • la boutique • die Boutique • la boutique • la boutique

realty office
l'agent immobilier
der Immobilienmakler
la agencia inmobiliaria
l'agenzia immobiliare

garden center
la pépinière
das Gartencenter
el vivero
il centro di giardinaggio

dry cleaner
le pressing
die Reinigung
la tintorería
il lavasecco

laundromat
la laverie automatique
der Waschsalon
la lavandería
la lavanderia

camera store
le magasin d'appareils photos
das Fotogeschäft
la tienda de fotografía
il negozio di articoli fotografici

second-hand store
le marchand d'occasion
der Gebrauchtwarenhändler
la tienda de artículos usados
il negozio dell'usato

health food store
le magasin bio
das Reformhaus
la tienda naturista
il negozio dietetico

art store
la boutique d'art
die Kunsthandlung
la galería de arte
il negozio di articoli per l'arte

tailor shop • le tailleur • die Schneiderei • la sastrería • la sartoria

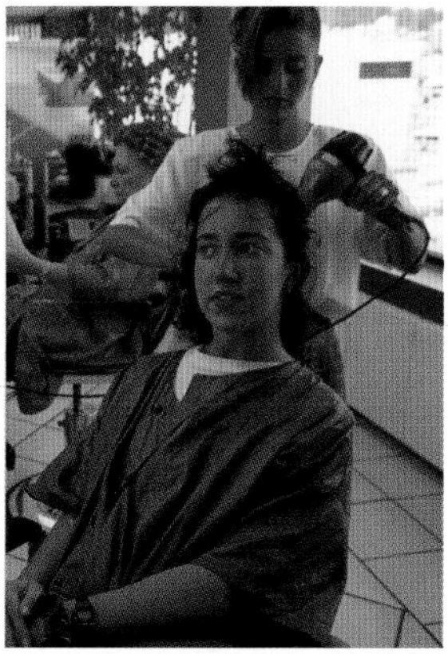

hair salon • le salon de coiffure • der Frisiersalon • la estética • il parrucchiere

market • le marché • der Markt • el mercado • il mercato

food
la nourriture
die Nahrungsmittel
los alimentos
il cibo

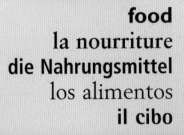

meat • la viande • das Fleisch • la carne • la carne

pork le porc das Schweinefleisch el cerdo il maiale	venison la venaison das Wild el venado il cervo	offal les abats die Innereien las asaduras le frattaglie	free range de ferme aus Freilandhaltung de granja ruspante	red meat la viande rouge das rote Fleisch la carne roja la carne rossa
beef le bœuf das Rindfleisch la vaca il manzo	rabbit le lapin das Kaninchen el conejo il coniglio	cured salé gepökelt curado stagionato	organic naturel biologisch kontrolliert orgánico biologico	lean meat la viande maigre das magere Fleisch la carne magra la carne magra
veal le veau das Kalbfleisch la ternera il vitello	tongue la langue de bœuf die Zunge la lengua la lingua	smoked fumé geräuchert ahumado affumicato	white meat la viande blanche das weiße Fleisch la carne blanca la carne bianca	cooked meat la viande cuite das gekochte Fleisch el fiambre la carne cotta

cuts • les morceaux de viande • die Fleischsorten • los cortes • i tagli

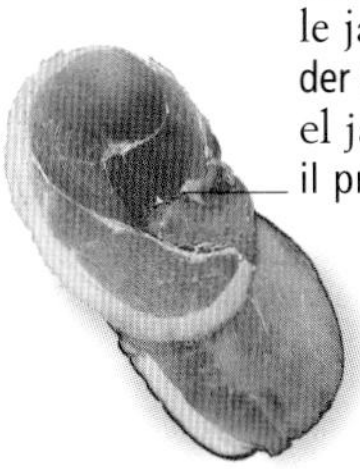

ham
le jambon
der Schinken
el jamón
il prosciutto

slice • la tranche • die Scheibe • la rebanada • la fetta

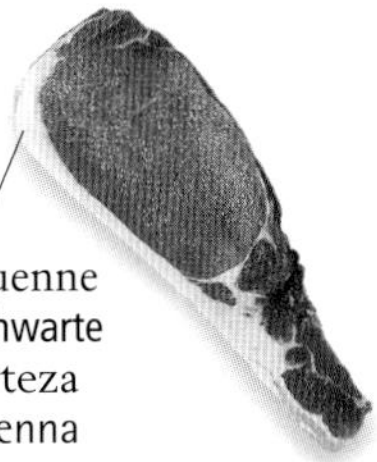

rind
la couenne
die Schwarte
la corteza
la cotenna

rasher • la tranche de lard • die Speckscheibe • la rebanada • la fetta

ground beef • la viande hachée • das Hackfleisch • la carne molida • la carne macinata

fillet • le filet • das Filet • el solomillo • il filetto

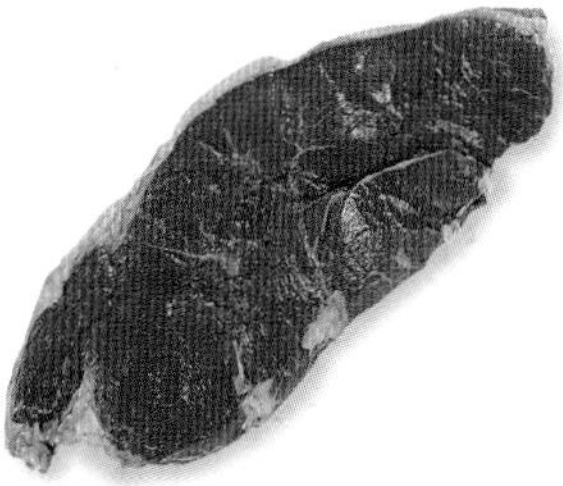

rump steak • le rumsteck • das Rumpsteak • el filete de cadera • la bistecca di culaccio

sirloin steak • le bifteck d'aloyau • das Lendensteak • el filete de lomo • il controfiletto di manzo

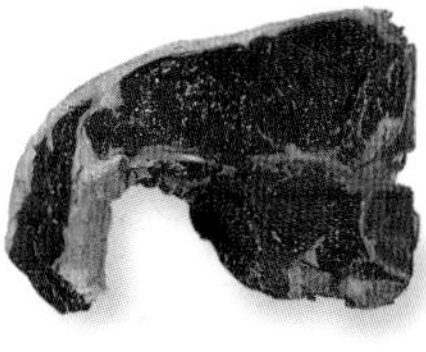

rib • la côte de bœuf • das Rippenstück • la costilla • la costata

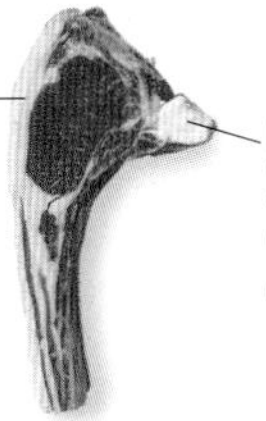

fat
le gras
das Fett
la grasa
il grasso

bone
l'os
der Knochen
el hueso
l'osso

chop • la côtelette • das Kotelett • la chuleta • la costoletta

joint • le gigot • die Keule • el asado • l'arrosto

kidney
le rognon
die Niere
el riñón
il rognone

heart • le cœur • das Herz • el corazón • il cuore

poultry • la volaille • das Geflügel • las aves • il pollo

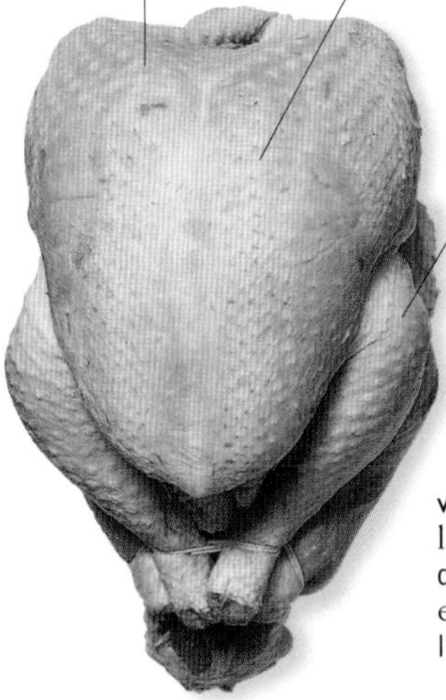

skin
la peau
die Haut
la piel
la pelle

breast
le blanc
die Brust
la pechuga
il petto

thigh
la cuisse
der Schenkel
el muslo
la coscia

turkey • la dinde • die Pute • el pavo • il tacchino

dressed chicken
le poulet préparé
das bratfertige Huhn
el pollo preparado
il pollo preparato

wing
l'aile
der Flügel
el ala
l'ala

chicken • le poulet • das Hähnchen • el pollo • il pollo

game
le gibier
das Wild
la carne de caza
la cacciagione

pheasant • le faisan • der Fasan • el faisán • il fagiano

leg
la cuisse
das Bein
la pierna
la zampa

quail • la caille • die Wachtel • la codorniz • la quaglia

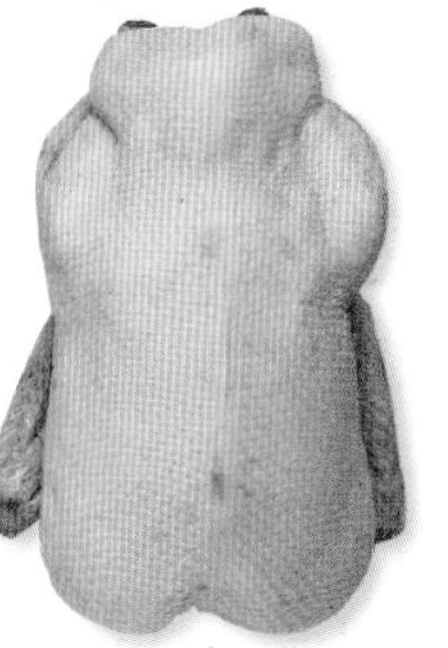

duck • le canard • die Ente • el pato • l'anatra

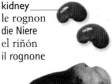

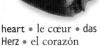

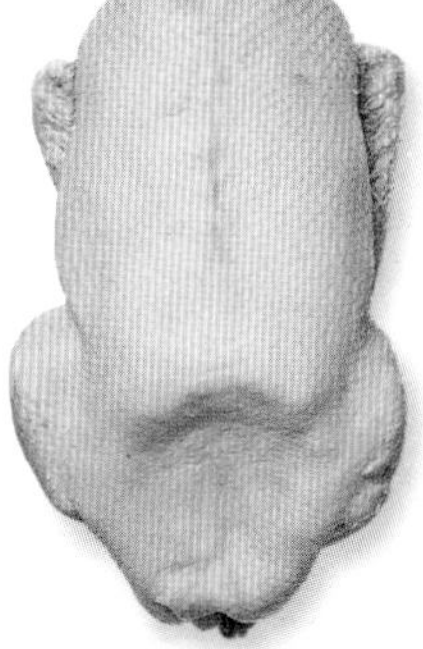

goose • l'oie • die Gans • el ganso • l'oca

fish • le poisson • der Fisch • el pescado • il pesce

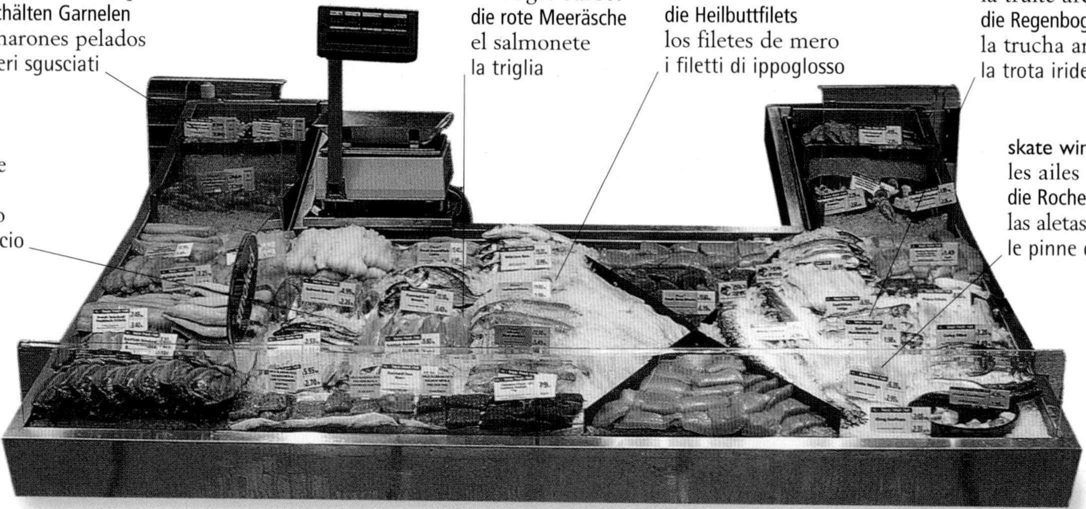

peeled shrimp
les crevettes décortiquées
die geschälten Garnelen
los camarones pelados
i gamberi sgusciati

ice
la glace
das Eis
el hielo
il ghiaccio

red mullet
le rouget barbet
die rote Meeräsche
el salmonete
la triglia

halibut fillets
les filets de flétan
die Heilbuttfilets
los filetes de mero
i filetti di ippoglosso

rainbow trout
la truite arc-en-ciel
die Regenbogenforelle
la trucha arco iris
la trota iridea

skate wings
les ailes de raie
die Rochenflügel
las aletas de raya
le pinne di razza

fish seller • la poissonnerie • das Fischgeschäft • la pescadería • la pescheria

monkfish • la lotte • die Quappe • el rape • la rana pescatrice

mackerel • le maquereau • die Makrele • la caballa • lo sgombro

trout • la truite • die Forelle • la trucha • la trota

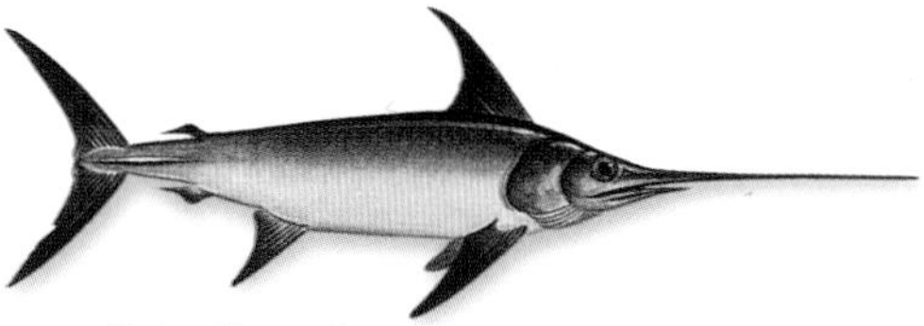

swordfish • l'espadon • der Schwertfisch • el pez espada • il pesce spada

Dover sole • la sole • die Seezunge • el lenguado • la sogliola di Dover

lemon sole • la limande-sole • die Rotzunge • la platija • la sogliola limanda

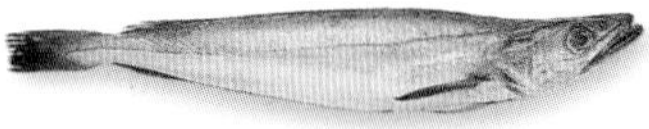

haddock • l'aiglefin • der Schellfisch • el abadejo • l'eglefino

sardine • la sardine • die Sardine • la sardina • la sardina

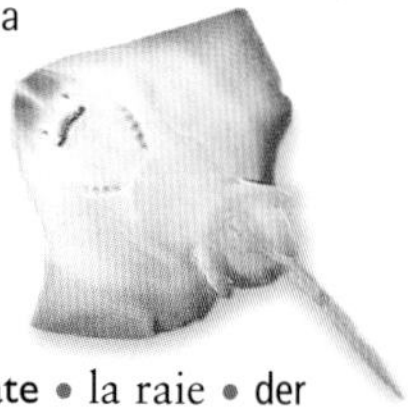

skate • la raie • der Rochen • la raya • la razza

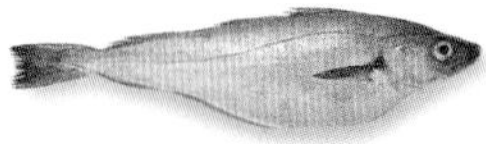

silver hake • le merlan • der Weißfisch • la pescadilla • il merlano

sea bass • le bar • der Seebarsch • la lubina • la spigola

salmon • le saumon • der Lachs • el salmón • il salmone

cod • la morue • der Kabeljau • el bacalao • il merluzzo

sea bream • la daurade • der Seebrassen • el besugo • l'orata

tuna • le thon • der Tunfisch • el atún • il tonno

seafood • les fruits de mer • die Meeresfrüchte • el marisco • i frutti di mare

scallop
la coquille Saint-Jacques
die Jakobsmuschel
la vieira
il pettine

lobster
le homard
der Hummer
la langosta
l'aragosta

crab
le crabe
die Krabbe
el cangrejo
il granchio

prawn
la crevette
die Garnele
el camarón
il gambero

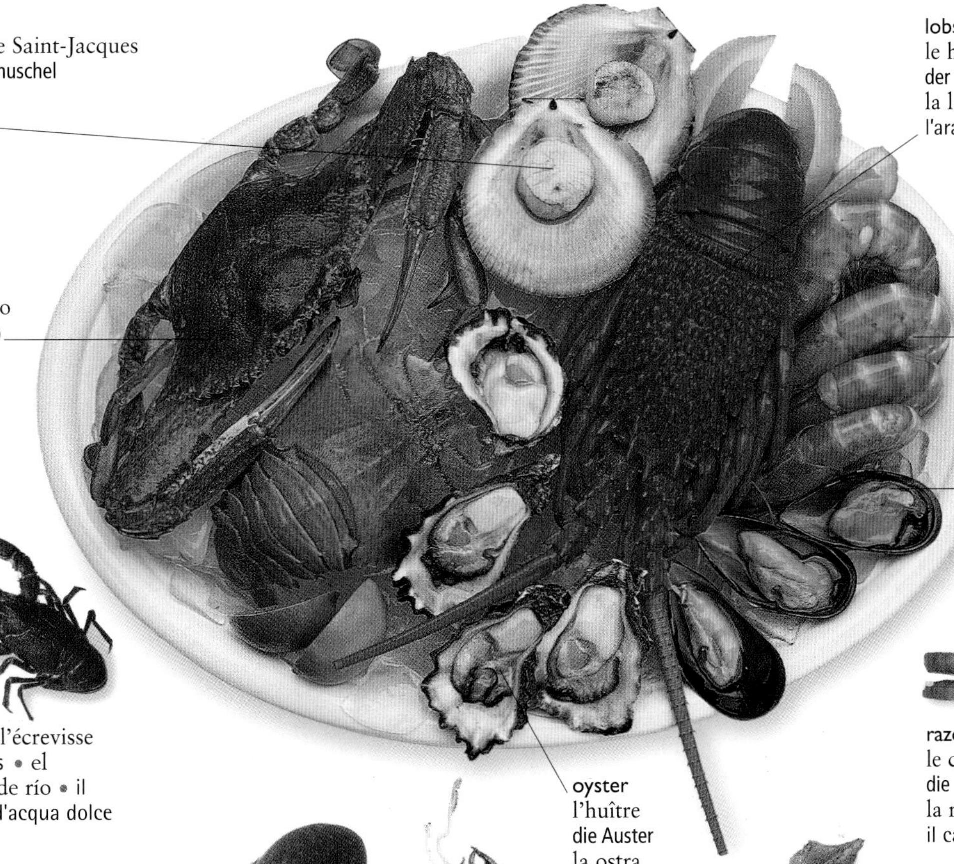

mussel
la moule
die Miesmuschel
el mejillón
la cozza

crayfish • l'écrevisse • der Krebs • el cangrejo de río • il gambero d'acqua dolce

razor shell
le couteau
die Scheidenmuschel
la navaja
il cannolicchio

oyster
l'huître
die Auster
la ostra
l'ostrica

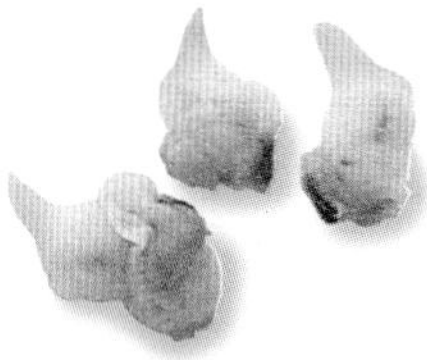

cockle • la coque • die Herzmuschel • el berberecho • il cardio

octopus • la pieuvre • der Seepolyp • el pulpo • il polpo

cuttlefish • la seiche • die Sepie • la sepia • la seppia

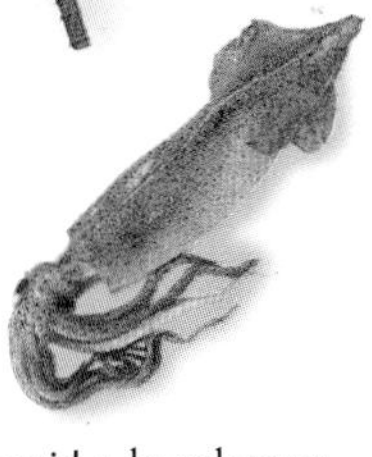

squid • le calamar • der Tintenfisch • el calamar • il calamaro

clam • le clam • die Venusmuschel • la almeja • la vongola

frozen	cleaned	smoked	descaled	filleted	steak	tail	bone	scale
surgelé	préparé	fumé	écaillé	en filets	la tranche	la queue	l'arête	l'écaille
tiefgefroren	zubereitet	geräuchert	entschuppt	filetiert	die Schnitte	der Schwanz	die Gräte	die Schuppe
congelado	limpio	ahumado	sin escamas	en filetes	la rodaja	la cola	la espina	la escama
congelato	pulito	affumicato	desquamato	a filetti	la trancia	la coda	la spina	la squama

fresh	salted	skinned	boned	fillet	loin
frais	salé	sans peau	sans arêtes	le filet	la longe
frisch	gesalzen	enthäutet	entgrätet	das Filet	die Lende
fresco	salado	sin piel	sin espinas	el filete	el lomo
fresco	salato	spellato	spinato	il filetto	il lombo

Can you clean it for me?
Pouvez-vous le préparer pour moi?
Können Sie ihn mir fertig zubereiten?
¿Me lo puede limpiar?
Me lo pulisce?

vegetables 1 • les légumes 1 • das Gemüse 1 • las verduras 1 • la verdura 1

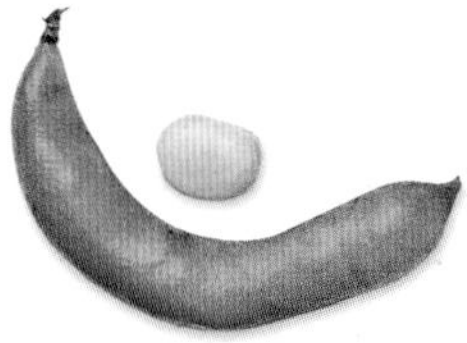

fava bean • la fève • die dicke Bohne • la haba • la fava

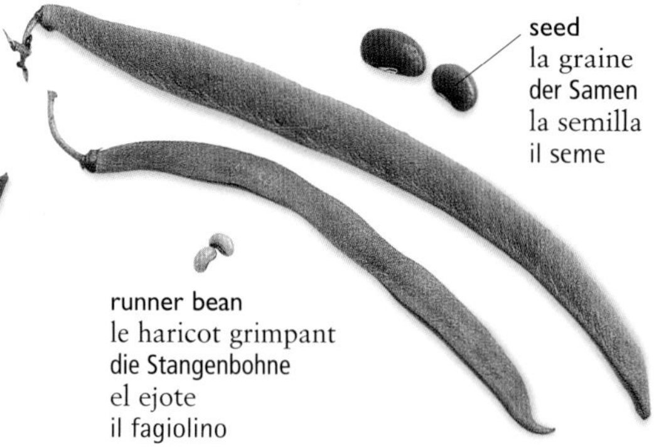

seed
la graine
der Samen
la semilla
il seme

runner bean
le haricot grimpant
die Stangenbohne
el ejote
il fagiolino

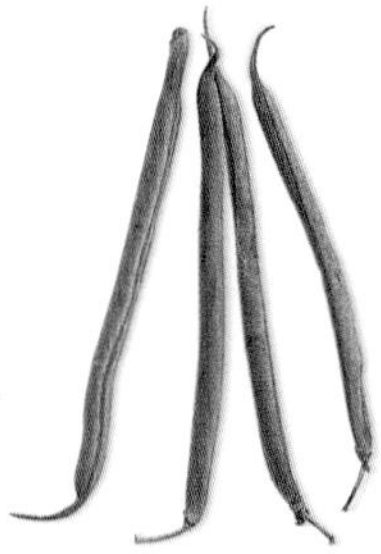

green bean • le haricot vert • die grüne Bohne • el ejote • il fagiolino

pea • le petit pois • die grüne Erbse • el chícharo • il pisello

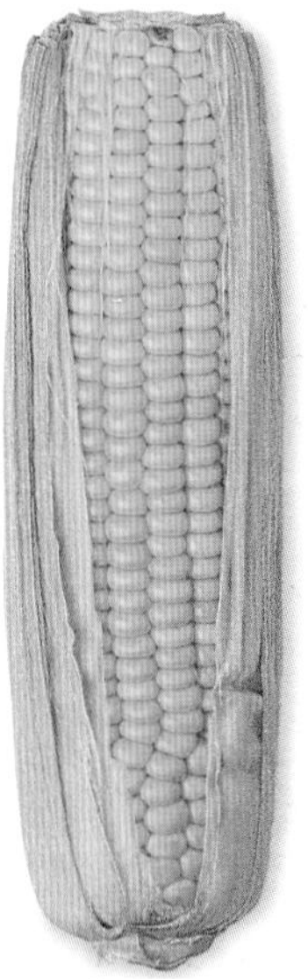

corn • le maïs • der Mais • el maíz dulce • il granturco

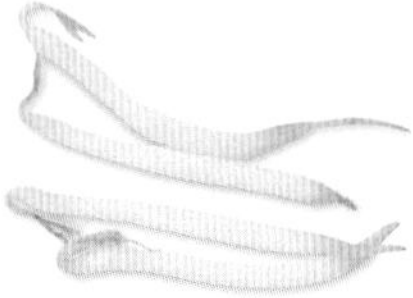

bean sprout • le germe de soja • die Sojabohnensprosse • el germinado de soja • il germoglio di soia

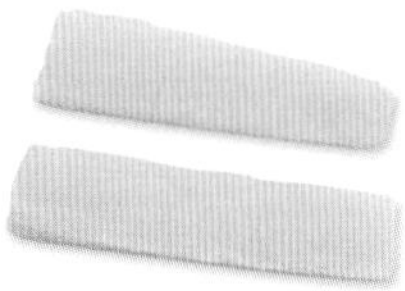

bamboo • le bambou • der Bambus • el bambú • il bambù

pod
la gousse
die Schote
la vaina
il baccello

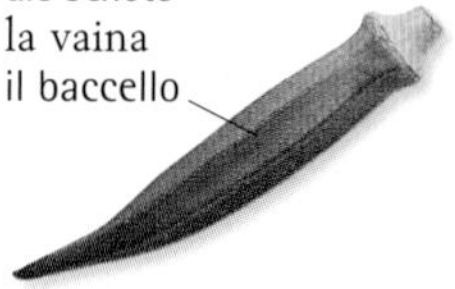

okra • l'okra • die Okra • el quingombó • l'okra

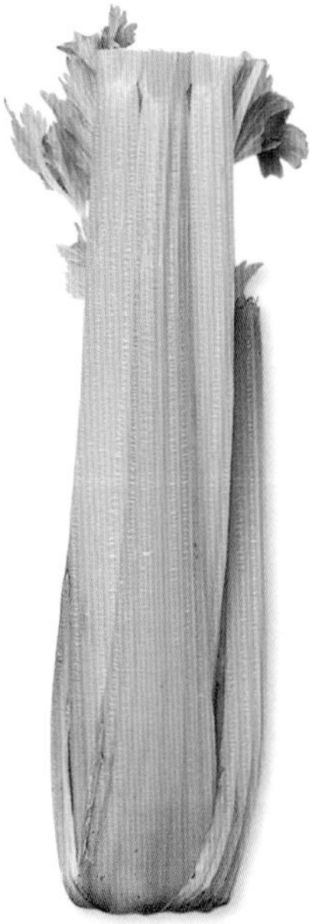

celery • le céleri • der Stangensellerie • el apio • il sedano

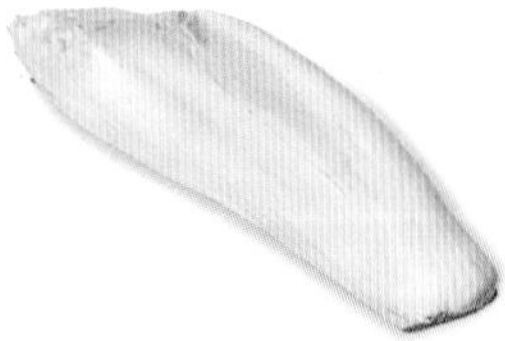

chicory • l'endive • der Chicorée • la endibia • la cicoria

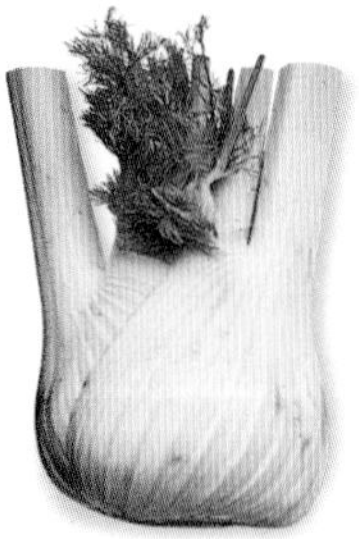

fennel • le fenouil • der Fenchel • el hinojo • il finocchio

palm hearts • les cœurs de palmier • die Palmherzen • los palmitos • i cuori di palma

leaf la feuille das Blatt la hoja la foglia	floret la fleurette das Röschen la cabezuela il germoglio	tip la pointe die Spitze la punta la punta	organic biologique biodynamisch biológico biologico
stalk le trognon der Strunk el tallo lo stelo	kernel le grain der Kern la almendra il nocciolo	heart le cœur das Herz el corazón il cuore	plastic bag le sac en plastique die Plastiktüte la bolsa de plástico la busta di plastica

Do you sell organic vegetables?
Est-ce que vous vendez des légumes bios?
Verkaufen Sie Biogemüse?
¿Vende verduras orgánicas?
Vendete verdure biologiche?

Are these grown locally?
Est-ce qu'ils sont cultivés dans la région?
Werden sie in dieser Gegend angebaut?
¿Son productos locales?
Queste sono della zona?

arugula • la roquette • die Rauke • la roqueta • la rucola

watercress • le cresson • die Brunnenkresse • el berro • il crescione

radicchio • le radicchio • der Radicchio • el radicchio • il radicchio

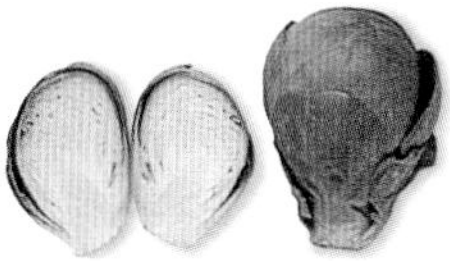
Brussels sprout • le chou de Bruxelles • der Rosenkohl • la col de bruselas • il cavolino di Bruxelles

swiss chard • la bette • der Mangold • la acelga • la bietola

kale • le chou frisé • der Grünkohl • la col rizada • il cavolo riccio

sorrel • l'oseille • der Garten-Sauerampfer • la acedera • l'acetosa

endive • la chicorée • die Endivie • la escarola • l'indivia

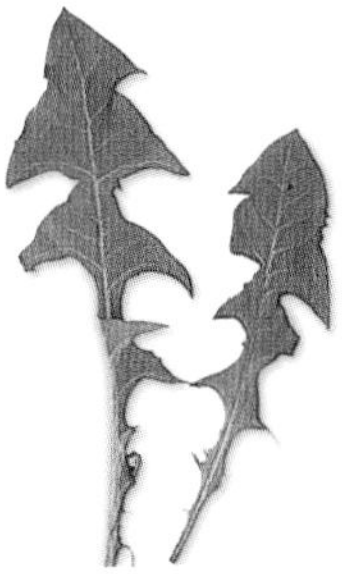
dandelion • le pissenlit • der Löwenzahn • el diente de león • il dente di leone

spinach • les épinards • der Spinat • la espinaca • gli spinaci

kohlrabi • le chou-rave • der Kohlrabi • el colinabo • il cavolo rapa

bok choy • le chou chinois • der Chinakohl • la acelga china • la bieta

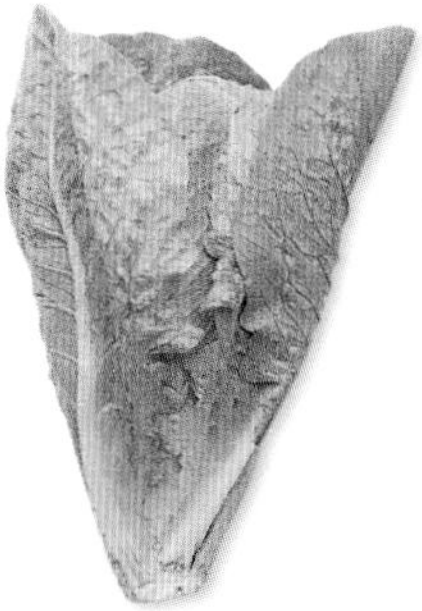
lettuce • la laitue • der Salat • la lechuga • la lattuga

broccoli • le brocoli • der Brokkoli • el brócoli • il broccolo

cabbage • le chou • der Kohl • la col • il cavolo

young cabbage • le chou précoce • der Frühkohl • la berza • la verza

vegetables 2 • les légumes 2 • das Gemüse 2 • las verduras 2 • le verdure 2

cherry tomato
la tomate cerise
die Kirschtomate
el jitomate cherry
il pomodoro cigliegino

carrot
la carotte
die Karotte
la zanahoria
la carota

breadfruit
le fruit de l'arbre à pain
die Brotfrucht
el fruto del pan
il frutto dell'albero del pane

new potato
la pomme de terre nouvelle
die neue Kartoffel
la papa nueva
la patata novella

celeriac
le céleri
der Sellerie
el apio-nabo
il sedano rapa

taro root
le taro
die Tarowurzel
la raíz del taro
la radice di taro

water chestnut
la châtaigne d'eau
die Wasserkastanie
la castaña de agua
la castagna d'acqua

cassava
le manioc
der Maniok
la mandioca
la cassava

frozen
surgelé
tiefgefroren
congelado
congelato

raw
cru
roh
crudo
crudo

hot (*spicy*)
épicé
scharf
picante
piccante

sweet
sucré
süß
dulce
dolce

bitter
amer
bitter
amargo
amaro

firm
ferme
fest
firme
sodo

pulp
la pulpe
das Fleisch
la pulpa
la polpa

root
la racine
die Wurzel
la raíz
la radice

May I have one kilo of potatoes please?
Puis-je avoir un kilo de pommes de terre s'il vous plaît?
Könnte ich bitte ein Kilo Kartoffeln haben?
¿Me da un kilo de papas, por favor?
Mi dà un chilo di patate per favore?

What's the price per kilo?
C'est combien le kilo?
Was kostet ein Kilo?
¿Cuánto vale el kilo?
Quanto costa al chilo?

What are those called?
Ils s'appellent comment?
Wie heißen diese?
¿Cómo se llaman?
Quelli come si chiamano?

sweet potato
la patate douce
die Süßkartoffel
el camote
la patata dolce

yam • l'igname • die Jamswurzel • el ñame • l'igname

beet • la betterave • die Rote Bete • el betabel • la barbabietola

rutabaga • le rutabaga • die Kohlrübe • el nabo sueco • la rapa svedese

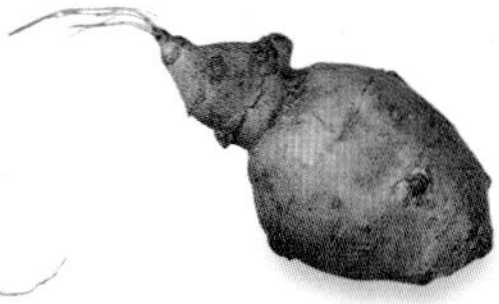

Jerusalem artichoke
le topinambour
der Topinambur
el topinambur
il topinambur

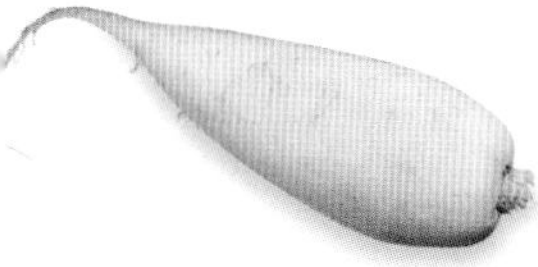

horseradish • le raifort • der Meerrettich • el rábano picante • il rafano

parsnip • le panais • die Pastinake • la chirivía • la pastinaca

ginger • le gingembre • der Ingwer • el jengibre • lo zenzero

eggplant • l'aubergine • die Aubergine • la berenjena • la melanzana

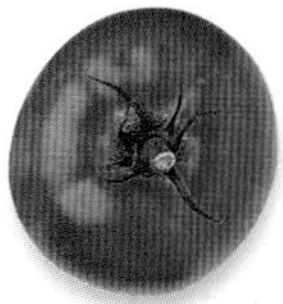

tomato • la tomate • die Tomate • el jitomate • il pomodoro

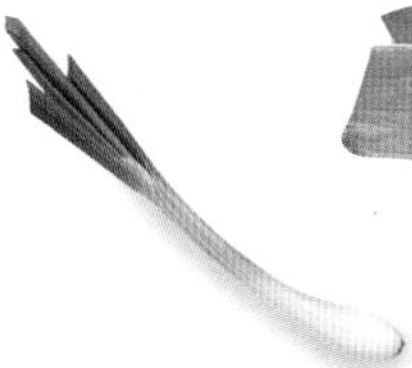

scallion • la ciboule • die Frühlingszwiebel • el cebollín • la cipollina

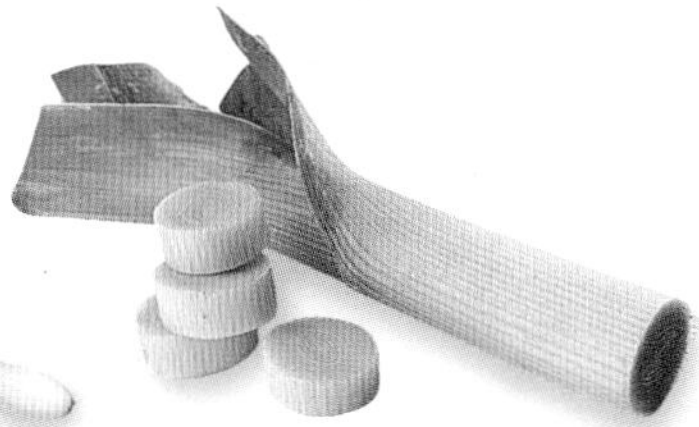

leek • le poireau • der Lauch • el puerro • il porro

shallot • l'échalote • die Schalotte • el chalote • lo scalogno

clove
la gousse
die Zehe
el diente
lo spicchio

garlic • l'ail • der Knoblauch • el ajo • l'aglio

truffle
la truffe
die Trüffel
la trufa
il tartufo

mushroom • le champignon • der Pilz • el champiñón • il fungo

cucumber • le concombre • die Gurke • el pepino • il cetriolo

zucchini • la courgette • die Zucchini • la calabacita • la zucchina

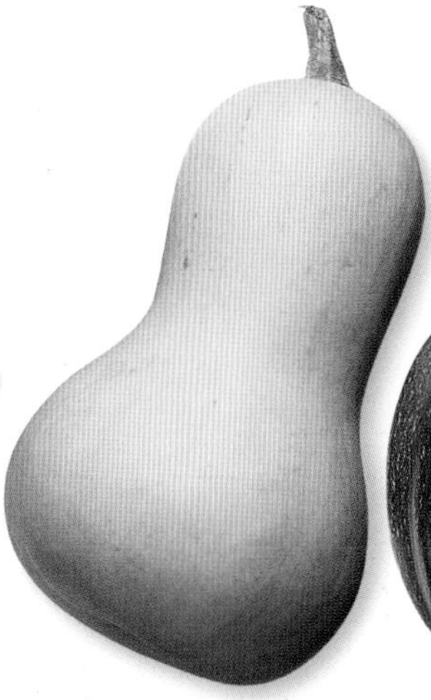

butternut squash
la courge musquée
der Butternuss-kürbis
la calabaza
la zucca Butternut

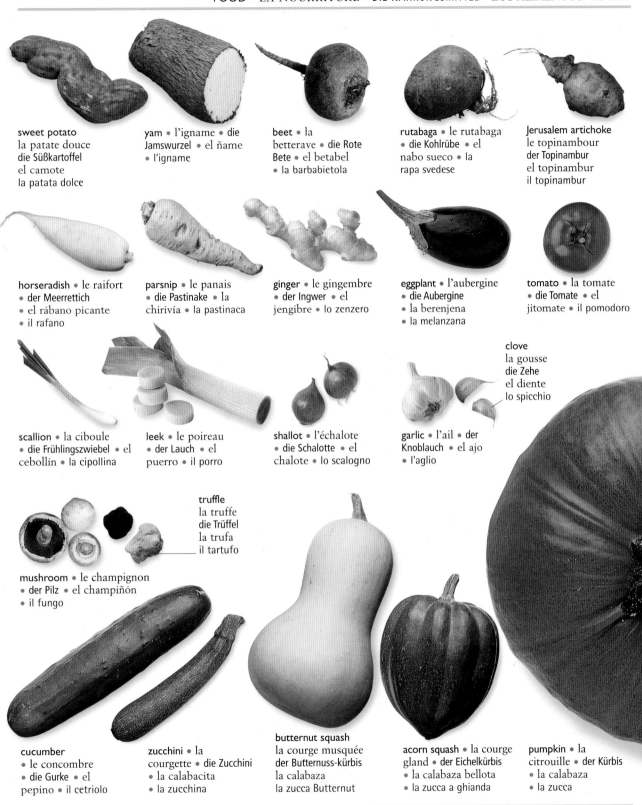

acorn squash • la courge gland • der Eichelkürbis • la calabaza bellota • la zucca a ghianda

pumpkin • la citrouille • der Kürbis • la calabaza • la zucca

fruit I • le fruit 1 • das Obst 1 • la fruta 1 • la frutta 1

citrus fruit • les agrumes • die Zitrusfrüchte • los cítricos • gli agrumi

orange • l'orange • die Orange • la naranja • l'arancio

clementine • la clémentine • die Klementine • la mandarina clementina • la clementina

tangelo • le tangelo • die Tangelo • el ugli • il mapo

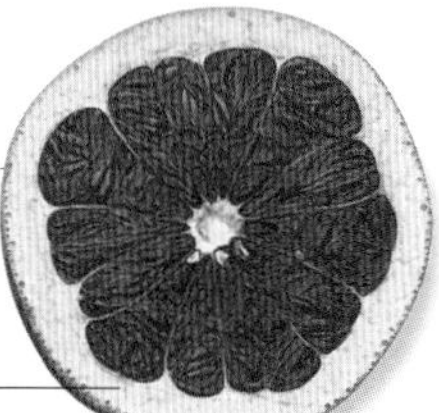

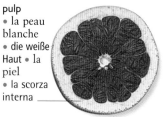

pulp • la peau blanche • die weiße Haut • la piel • la scorza interna

grapefruit • le pamplemousse • die Grapefruit • la toronja • il pompelmo

tangerine • la mandarine • die Mandarine • la mandarina • il mandarino

segment le quartier der Schnitz el gajo lo spicchio

satsuma • la satsuma • die Satsuma • la mandarina satsuma • il satsuma

zest le zeste die Schale la cáscara la scorza

lime • le citron vert • die Limone • la lima • la limetta

lemon • le citron • die Zitrone • el limón • il limone

kumquat • le kumquat • die Kumquat • la naranja china • l'arancino cinese

stone fruit • les fruits à noyau • das Steinobst • la fruta con hueso • la frutta con nocciolo

peach • la pêche • der Pfirsich • el durazno • la pesca

nectarine • la nectarine • die Nektarine • la nectarina • la pesca noce

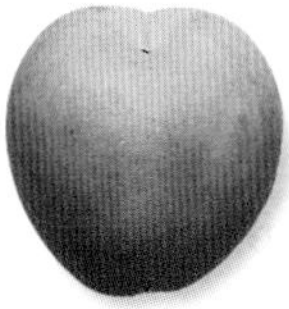

apricot • l'abricot • die Aprikose • el chabacano • l'albicocca

plum • la prune • die Pflaume • la ciruela • la prugna

cherry • la cerise • die Kirsche • la cereza • la ciliegia

pear • la poire • die Birne • la pera • la pera

apple • la pomme • der Apfel • la manzana • la mela

basket of fruit • la corbeille de fruits • der Obstkorb • el frutero • il cestino di frutta

berries and melons • les fruits rouges et les melons • das Beerenobst und die Melonen • las bayas y los melones • i frutti di bosco e i meloni

strawberry • la fraise • die Erdbeere • la fresa • la fragola

raspberry • la framboise • die Himbeere • la frambuesa • il lampone

melon • le melon • die Melone • el melón • il melone

grapes • les raisins • die Weintrauben • la uva • l'uva

blackberry • la mûre • die Brombeere • la zarzamora • la mora

redcurrant • la groseille • die Johannisbeere • la grosella • il ribes rosso

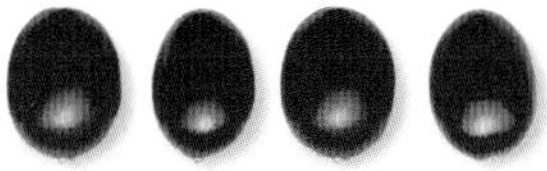

cranberry • la canneberge • die Preiselbeere • el arándano rojo • l'ossicocco

blackcurrant • le cassis • die schwarze Johannisbeere • la grosella negra • il ribes nero

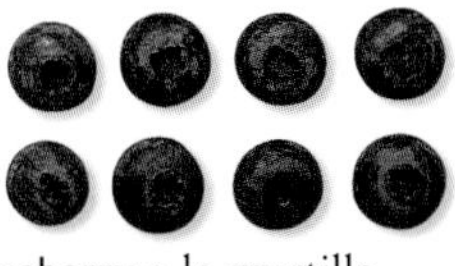

blueberry • la myrtille • die Heidelbeere • el arándano • il mirtillo

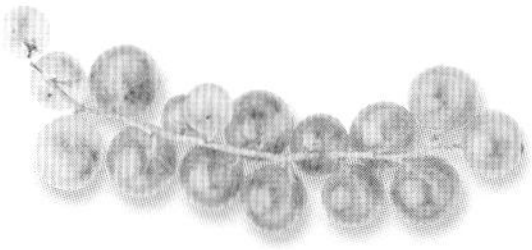

white currant • la groseille blanche • die weiße Johannisbeere • la grosella blanca • il ribes bianco

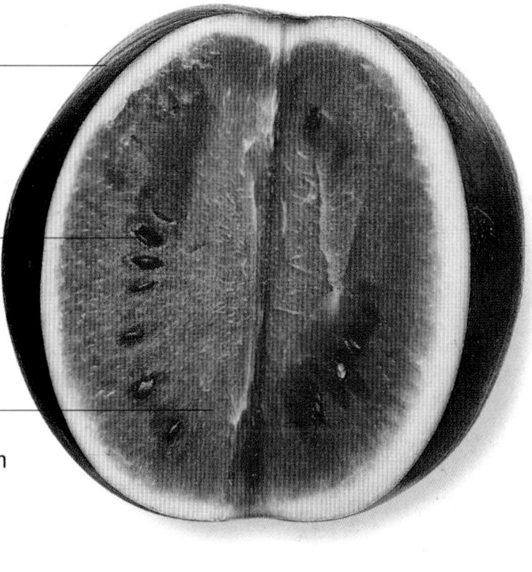

rind
l'écorce
die Schale
la cáscara
la buccia

seed
le pépin
der Kern
la semilla
il seme

flesh
la pulpe
das Fruchtfleisch
la pulpa
la polpa

watermelon • la pastèque • die Wassermelone • la sandía • l'anguria

loganberry • la loganberry • die Loganbeere • la frambuesa Logan • la mora-lampone

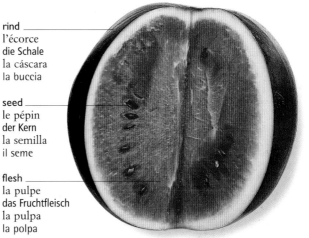

gooseberry • la groseille à maquereau • die Stachelbeere • el capulín • l'uva spina

rhubarb	**sour**	**crisp**	**seedless**	**Are they ripe?**
la rhubarbe	aigre	croquant	sans pépins	Est-ce qu'ils sont mûrs?
der Rhabarber	sauer	knackig	kernlos	Sind sie reif?
el ruibarbo	amargo	fresco	sin semillas	¿Están maduros?
il rabarbaro	agre	croccante	senza semi	Sono maturi?
fiber	**fresh**	**rotten**	**juice**	**May I try one?**
la fibre	frais	pourri	le jus	Je peux goûter?
die Faser	frisch	faul	der Saft	Könnte ich eine probieren?
la fibra	fresco	podrido	el jugo	¿Puedo probar uno?
la fibra	fresco	marcio	il succo	Posso assaggiarne uno?
sweet	**juicy**	**pulp**	**core**	**How long will they keep?**
sucré	juteux	la pulpe	le trognon	Ils se gardent combien de temps?
süß	saftig	das Fruchtmark	das Kerngehäuse	Wie lange halten sie sich?
dulce	jugoso	la pulpa	el corazón	¿Hasta cuándo durarán?
dolce	sugoso	la polpa	il torsolo	Per quanto tempo si mantengono?

fruit 2 • les fruits 2 • das Obst 2 • la fruta 2 • la frutta 2

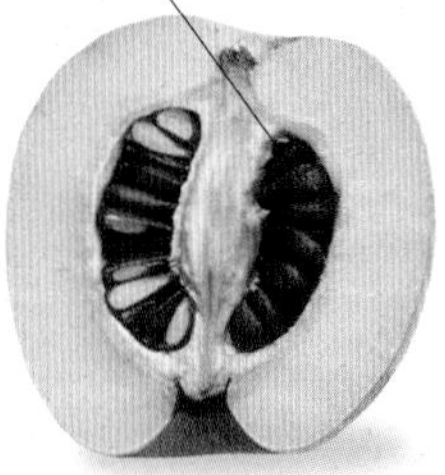

quince • le coing • die Quitte • el membrillo • la mela cotogna

passion fruit • le fruit de la passion • die Passionsfrucht • el maracuyá • il frutto della passione

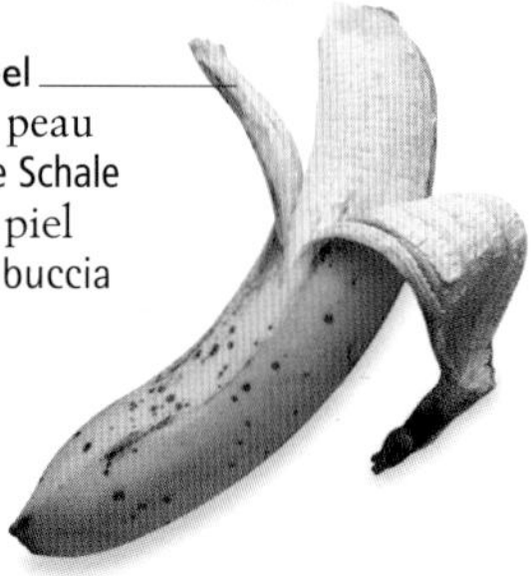

banana • la banane • die Banane • el plátano • la banana

guava • la goyave • die Guave • la guayaba • la guaiava

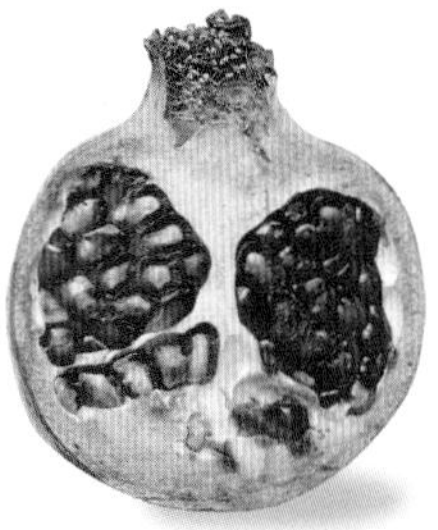

pomegranate • la grenade • der Granatapfel • la granada • la melagrana

persimmon • le kaki • die Kaki • el caqui • il cachi

feijoa • le feijoa • die Feijoa • la feijoa • il feijoa

prickly pear • la figue de Barbarie • die Kaktusfeige • la tuna • il fico d'india

star fruit • la carambole • die Sternfrucht • la carambola • la carambola

tamarillo • le tamarillo • die Tamarillo • el tomate de árbol • il tamarillo

nuts and dried fruit • les noix et les fruits secs • die Nüsse und das Dörrobst • los frutos secos • le noci e la frutta secca

pine nut • le pignon • die Piniennuss • el piñón • il pinolo

pistachio • la pistache • die Pistazie • el pistache • il pistacchio

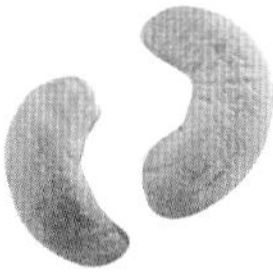

cashew nut • la noix de cajou • die Cashewnuss • la nuez de la India • l'anacardio

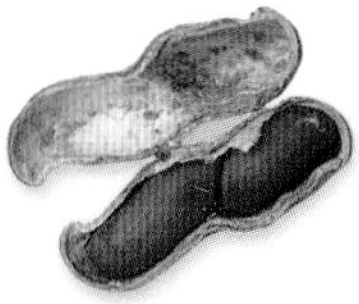

peanut • la cacahouète • die Erdnuss • el cacahuete • l'arachide

hazelnut • la noisette • die Haselnuss • la avellana • la nocciola

Brazil nut • la noix du Brésil • die Paranuss • la nuez de Brasil • la mandorla brasiliana

pecan • la noix pacane • die Pecannuss • la nuez • la noce pecan

almond • l'amande • die Mandel • la almendra • la mandorla

walnut • la noix • die Walnuss • la nuez de Castilla • la noce

chestnut • le marron • die Esskastanie • la castaña • la castagna

macadamia
le macadamia
die Macadamianuss
la noce di macadamia
caramellato per intero

fig • la figue • die Feige • el higo • il fico

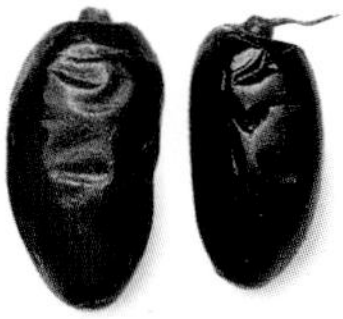

date • la datte • die Dattel • el dátil • il dattero

prune • le pruneau • die Backpflaume • la ciruela pasa • la prugna secca

shell
la coquille
die Schale
la cáscara
il guscio

flesh
la chair
das Fruchtfleisch
la pulpa
la polpa

coconut • la noix de coco • die Kokosnuss • el coco • la noce di cocco

sultana • le raisin de Smyrne • die Sultanine • la pasa sultana • l'uva sultanina

raisin • le raisin sec • die Rosine • la pasa • l'uvetta

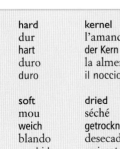

currant • le raisin de Corinthe • die Korinthe • la pasa de Corinto • l'uva passa

green vert grün verde verde	**hard** dur hart duro duro	**kernel** l'amande der Kern la almendra il nocciolo	**salted** salé gesalzen salado salato	**roasted** grillé geröstet tostado arrostito	**tropical fruit** les fruits tropicaux die Südfrüchte las frutas tropicales la frutta tropicale	**shelled** décortiqué geschält pelado sgusciato
ripe mûr reif maduro maturo	**soft** mou weich blando morbido	**dried** séché getrocknet desecado essiccato	**raw** cru roh crudo crudo	**seasonal** de saison Saison- de temporada stagionale	**candied fruit** le fruit confit die kandierten Früchte la fruta escarchada la frutta candita	**whole** complet ganz entero intero

grains and pulses • les céréales et les légumes secs • die Getreidearten und die Hülsenfrüchte • los granos y las legumbres • le granaglie e i legumi secchi

grains • les céréales • das Getreide • los granos • le granaglie

wheat • le blé • der Weizen • el trigo • il grano

oats • l'avoine • der Hafer • la avena • l'avena

barley • l'orge • die Gerste • la cebada • l'orzo

millet • le millet • die Hirse • el mijo • il miglio

corn • le maïs • der Mais • el maíz • il mais

quinoa • le quinoa • die Reismelde • la quinoa • la quinoa

seed	la graine	der Samen	la semilla	il seme
husk	la balle	die Hülse	la cáscara	la pula
kernel	le grain	der Kern	el grano	il seme
dry	sec	trocken	seco	secco
fresh	frais	frisch	fresco	fresco
fragranced	parfumé	aromatisch	perfumado	profumato
cereal	la céréale	die Getreideflocken	los cereales	il cereale
soak *(v)*	laisser tremper	einweichen	poner a remojo	mettere a bagno
easy-to-cook	facile à cuisiner	leicht zu kochen	de fácil cocción	cottura facile
whole-grain	complet	Vollkorn-	integral	integrale
long-grain	à grains longs	Langkorn-	largo	a chicco lungo
short-grain	à grains ronds	Rundkorn-	corto	a chicco corto

rice • le riz • der Reis • el arroz • il riso

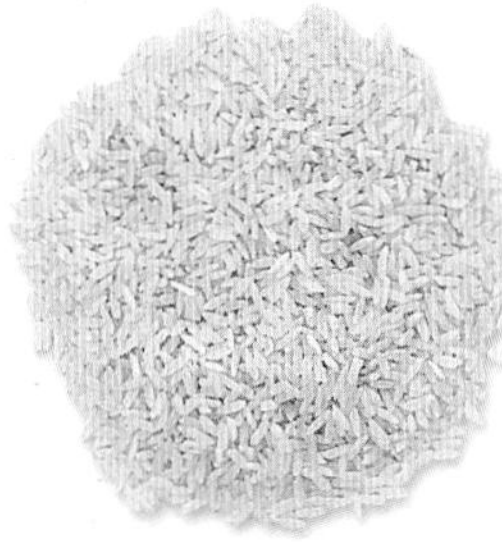
white rice • le riz blanc • der weiße Reis • el arroz largo • il riso bianco

brown rice • le riz complet • der Naturreis • el arroz integral • il riso integrale

wild rice • le riz sauvage • der Wasserreis • el arroz salvaje • il riso selvatico

dessert rice • le riz rond • der Milchreis • el arroz bomba • il riso da budino

processed grains • les céréales traitées • die verarbeiteten Getreidearten • los granos procesados • i cereali trattati

couscous • le couscous • der Kuskus • el cuscús • il cuscus

cracked wheat • le blé écrasé • der Weizenschrot • el trigo partido • il grano spezzato

semolina • la semoule • der Grieß • la sémola • la semola

bran • le son • die Kleie • el salvado • la crusca

beans and peas • les haricots et les pois • die Bohnen und die Erbsen • los frijoles y los chícharos • i fagioli e i piselli

lima beans • les gros haricots blancs • die Mondbohnen • el frijol blanco • i fagioli bianchi

navy beans • les haricots blancs • die weißen Bohnen • el frijol blanco chico • i fagioli cannellini

kidney beans • les haricots rouges • die roten Bohnen • el frijol rojo • i fagioli di Spagna

adzuki beans • les adzukis • die Adzukibohnen • el frijol morado • i fagioli aduki

fava beans • les fèves • die Saubohnen • las habas • le fave

soybeans • les graines de soja • die Sojabohnen • la semilla de soja • i semi di soia

black-eyed peas • les haricots à œil noir • die Teparybohnen • el frijol de ojo negro • i fagioli dall'occhio nero

pinto beans • les haricots pinto • die Pintobohnen • el frijol pinto • i fagioli borlotti

mung beans • les haricots mung • die Mungbohnen • el frijol mung • i fagioli mung

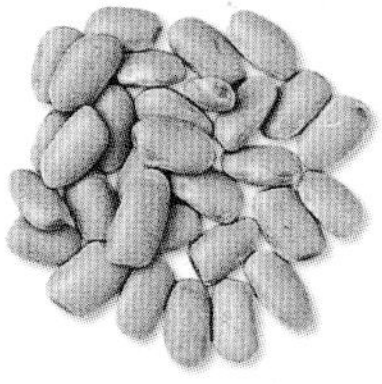

flageolet beans • les flageolets • die französischen Bohnen • el frijol flageolet • i fagioli nani

brown lentils • les lentilles • die braunen Linsen • la lenteja castellana • le lenticchie marroni

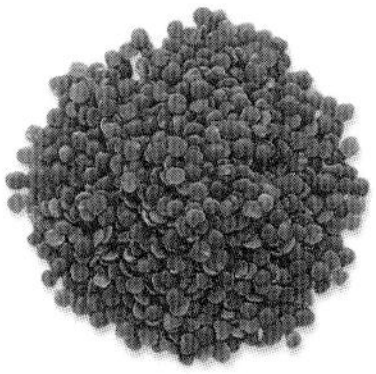

red lentils • les lentilles rouges • die roten Linsen • la lenteja roja • le lenticchie rosse

peas • les petits pois • die grünen Erbsen • los chícharos • i piselli

chick peas • les pois chiches • die Kichererbsen • los garbanzos • i ceci

split peas • les pois cassés • die getrockneten Erbsen • los chícharos secos • i piselli spaccati

seeds • les graines • die Körner • las semillas • i semi

pumpkin seed • la graine de potiron • der Kürbiskern • la pepita de calabaza • il seme di zucca

mustard seed • le grain de moutarde • das Senfkorn • la semilla de mostaza • il seme di mostarda

caraway • la graine de carvi • der Kümmel • el carvi • il seme di carvi

sesame seed • la graine de sésame • das Sesamkorn • la semilla de sésamo • il seme di sesamo

sunflower seed • la graine de tournesol • der Sonnenblumenkern • la semilla de girasol • il seme di girasole

herbs and spices • les herbes et les épices • die Kräuter und Gewürze • las hierbas y las especias • le erbe aromatiche e le spezie

spices • les épices • die Gewürze • las especias • le spezie

vanilla • la vanille • die Vanille • la vainilla • la vaniglia

nutmeg • la noix de muscade • die Muskatnuss • la nuez moscada • la noce moscata

mace • le macis • die Muskatblüte • la macis • il macis

turmeric • le curcuma • die Kurkuma • la cúrcuma • la curcuma

cumin • le cumin • der Kreuzkümmel • el comino • il cumino

bouquet garni • le bouquet garni • die Kräutermischung • el ramillete aromático • il mazzetto odoroso

allspice • le poivre de la Jamaïque • der Piment • la pimienta de Jamaica • il pepe della Giamaica

peppercorn • le grain de poivre • das Pfefferkorn • la pimienta en grano • il grano di pepe

fenugreek • le fenugrec • der Bockshornklee • el heno griego • il fieno greco

chili • le piment • der Chili • el chile piquín • il peperoncino rosso

saffron • le safran • der Safran • el azafrán • lo zafferano

cardamom • la cardamome • der Kardamom • el cardamono • il cardamomo

curry powder • la poudre de curry • das Currypulver • el curry en polvo • la polvere di curry

whole
en morceaux
ganz
entero
intero

crushed
écrasé
zerstoßen
machacado
tritato

ground
en poudre
gemahlen
molido
macinato

flakes
en flocons
geraspelt
a hojuelas
a scaglie

paprika • le paprika • der Paprika • el pimentón • la paprica

garlic • l'ail • der Knoblauch • el ajo • l'aglio

sticks
les bâtons
die Stangen
las rajas
i bastoncini

cinnamon • la cannelle • der Zimt • la canela • la cannella

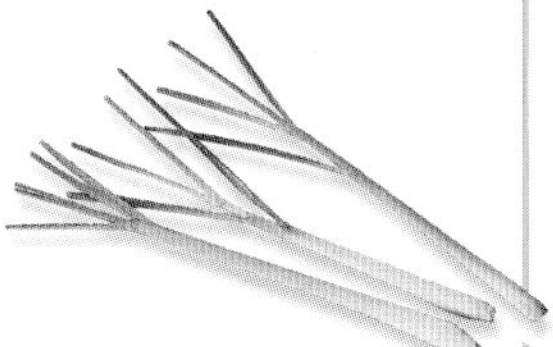

lemon grass • la citronnelle • das Zitronengras • la citronela • la citronella

cloves • le clou de girofle • die Gewürznelke • los clavos • i chiodi di garofano

star anise • l'anis étoilé • der Sternarnis • el anís estrellado • l'anice stellato

ginger • le gingembre • der Ingwer • el jengibre • lo zenzero

herbs • les herbes • die Kräuter • las hierbas • le erbe aromatiche

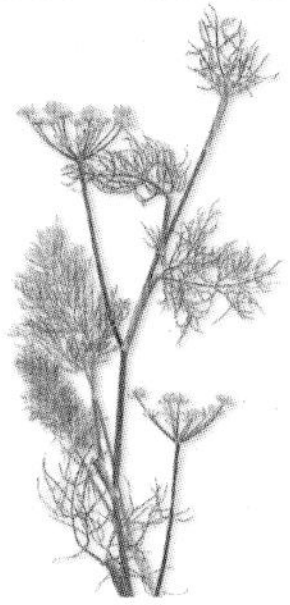

fennel • le fenouil • der Fenchel • el hinojo • il finocchio

fennel seeds
les graines de fenouil
die Fenchelsamen
las semillas de hinojo
i semi di finocchio

bay leaf • la feuille de laurier • das Lorbeerblatt • el laurel • l'alloro

parsley • le persil • die Petersilie • el perejil • il prezzemolo

chives • la ciboulette • der Schnittlauch • los cebollinos • l'erba cipollina

mint • la menthe • die Minze • la menta • la menta

thyme • le thym • der Thymian • el tomillo • il timo

sage • la sauge • der Salbei • la salvia • la salvia

tarragon • l'estragon • der Estragon • el estragón • il dragoncello

marjoram • la marjolaine • der Majoran • la mejorana • la maggiorana

basil • le basilic • das Basilikum • la albahaca • il basilico

oregano • l'origan • der Oregano • el orégano • l'origano

coriander • la coriandre • der Koriander • el cilantro • il coriandolo

dill • l'aneth • der Dill • el eneldo • l'aneto

rosemary • le romarin • der Rosmarin • el romero • il rosmarino

bottled foods • les aliments en bouteilles • die Nahrungsmittel in Flaschen • los alimentos embotellados • i cibi imbottigliati

walnut oil • l'huile de noix • das Walnussöl • el aceite de nueces • l'olio di noce

grapeseed oil • l'huile de pépins de raisin • das Traubenkernöl • el aceite de semillas de uva • l'olio di semi d'uva

almond oil • l'huile d'amande • das Mandelöl • el aceite de almendras • l'olio di mandorla

cork • le bouchon • der Korken • el corcho • il tappo

sunflower oil • l'huile de tournesol • das Sonnenblumenöl • el aceite de girasol • l'olio di semi di girasole

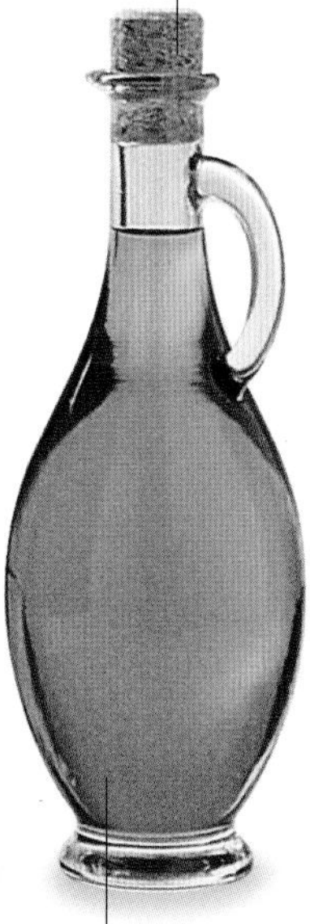

sesame seed oil • l'huile de sésame • das Sesamöl • el aceite de sésamo • l'olio di sesamo

hazelnut oil • l'huile de noisette • das Haselnussöl • el aceite de avellanas • l'olio di noccioline

olive oil • l'huile d'olive • das Olivenöl • el aceite de oliva • l'olio d'oliva

herbs • les herbes • die Kräuter • las hierbas • le erbe aromatiche

flavored oil • l'huile parfumée • das aromatische Öl • el aceite aromatizado • l'olio aromatizzato

oils • les huiles • die Öle • los aceites • gli oli

sweet spreads • les produits à tartiner • der süße Aufstrich • las conservas dulces • le confetture

jar • le pot • das Glas • el tarro • il barattolo

honeycomb • le gâteau de miel • die Honigwabe • el panal • il favo

set honey • le miel solide • der feste Honig • la miel cristalizada • il miele condensato

lemon curd • la pâte à tartiner au citron • der Zitronenaufstrich • la crema de limón • la crema al limone

raspberry jam • la confiture de framboises • die Himbeerkonfitüre • la mermelada de frambuesa • la marmellata di lamponi

marmalade • la confiture d'oranges • die Orangenmarmelade • la mermelada de naranja • la marmellata di agrumi

clear honey • le miel liquide • der flüssige Honig • la miel líquida • il miele sciolto

maple syrup • le sirop d'érable • der Ahornsirup • la miel de maple • lo sciroppo d'acero

condiments and spreads • les condiments • die Würzen • los condimentos • condimenti e cibi da spalmare

mayonnaise • la mayonnaise • die Majonäse • la mayonesa • la maionese

cider vinegar
le vinaigre de cidre
der Apfelweinessig
el vinagre de sidra
l'aceto di sidro

balsamic vinegar
le vinaigre balsamique
der Gewürzessig
el vinagre balsámico
l'aceto balsamico

malt vinegar
le vinaigre de malt
der Malzessig
el vinagre de malta
l'aceto di malto

wine vinegar
le vinaigre de vin
der Weinessig
el vinagre de vino
l'aceto di vino

vinegar • le vinaigre • der Essig • el vinagre • l'aceto

chutney • le chutney • das Chutney • el chutney • il chutney

bottle
la bouteille
die Flasche
la botella
la bottiglia

ketchup • le ketchup • der Ketchup • la catsup • il ketchup

sauce • la sauce • die Soße • la salsa • la salsa

English mustard • la moutarde anglaise • der englische Senf • la mostaza inglesa • la senape

French mustard • la moutarde française • der französische Senf • la mostaza francesa • la mostarda

wholegrain mustard • la moutarde en grains • der grobe Senf • la mostaza en grano • la mostarda con semi

peanut butter • le beurre de cacahouètes • die Erdnussbutter • la crema de cacahuete • il burro di arachidi

chocolate spread • la pâte à tartiner au chocolat • der Schokoladenaufstrich • el chocolate para untar • la cioccolata spalmabile

sealed jar • le bocal scellé • das Einmachglas • el tarro hermético • il barattolo a chiusura ermetica

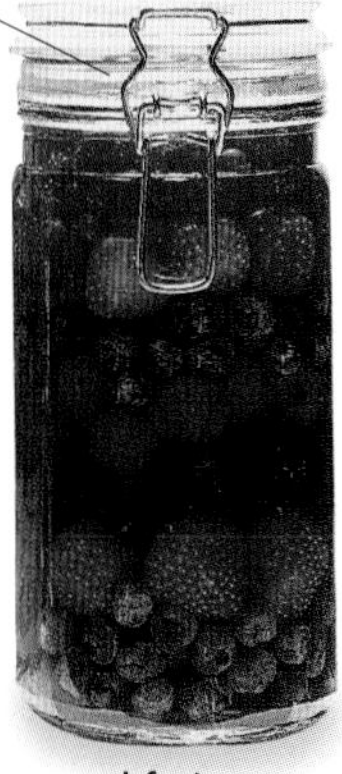

preserved fruit
les fruits en bocaux
das eingemachte Obst
la fruta en conserva
la conserva di frutta

vegetable oil
l'huile végétale
das Pflanzenöl
el aceite vegetal
l'olio vegetale

corn oil
l'huile de maïs
das Maiskeimöl
el aceite de maíz
l'olio di mais

peanut oil
l'huile d'arachide
das Erdnussöl
el aceite de cacahuete
l'olio di arachide

canola oil
l'huile de colza
das Rapsöl
el aceite de colza
l'olio di colza

cold-pressed oil
l'huile pressée à froid
das kaltgepresste Öl
el aceite de presión en frío
l'olio spremuto a freddo

dairy products • les produits laitiers • die Milchprodukte • los productos lácteos • i latticini

cheese • le fromage • der Käse • el queso • il formaggio

rind
la croûte
die Rinde
la corteza
la crosta

semihard cheese
le fromage à pâte pressée non cuite
der mittelharte Käse
el queso semicurado
il formaggio semiduro

grated cheese
le fromage râpé
der geriebene Käse
el queso rallado
il formaggio grattugiato

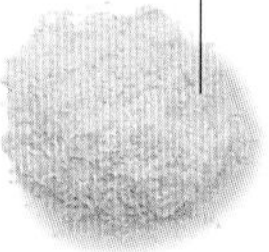

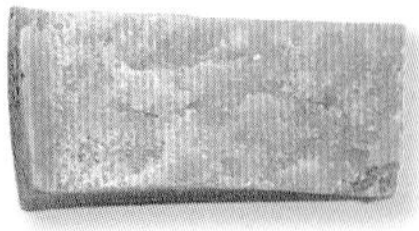

hard cheese • le fromage à pâte pressée cuite • der Hartkäse • el queso curado • il formaggio duro

semisoft cheese • le fromage à pâte semi-molle • der halbfeste Käse • el queso cremoso semicurado • il formaggio semimorbido

cottage cheese • le cottage • der Hüttenkäse • el requesón • il formaggio molle fresco

blue cheese • le bleu • der Blauschimmelkäse • el queso azul • il formaggio erborinato

cream cheese • le fromage à la crème • der Rahmkäse • el queso cremoso • il formaggio cremoso

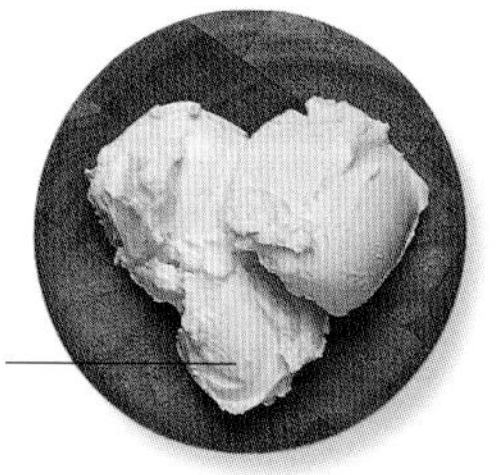

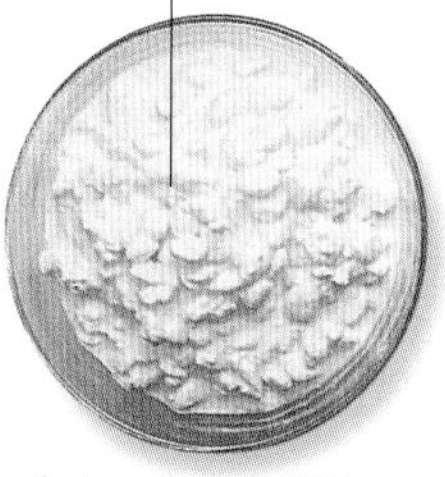

soft cheese • le fromage à pâte molle • der Weichkäse • el queso cremoso • il formaggio morbido

fresh cheese • le fromage frais • der Frischkäse • el queso fresco • il formaggio fresco

milk • le lait • die Milch • la leche • il latte

whole milk
le lait entier
die Vollmilch
la leche entera
il latte intero

reduced-fat milk
le lait demi-écrémé
die Halbfettmilch
la leche semidescremada
il latte parzialmente scremato

fat-free milk
le lait écrémé
die Magermilch
la leche descremada
il latte scremato

cow's milk • le lait de vache • die Kuhmilch • la leche de vaca • il latte di mucca

milk carton
le carton de lait
die Milchtüte
el cartón de leche
il cartone di latte

goat's milk • le lait de chèvre • die Ziegenmilch • la leche de cabra • il latte di capra

condensed milk
le lait condensé
die Kondensmilch
la leche condensada
il latte condensato

butter • le beurre • die Butter • la mantequilla • il burro

margarine • la margarine • die Margarine • la margarina • la margarina

cream • la crème • die Sahne • la crema • la panna

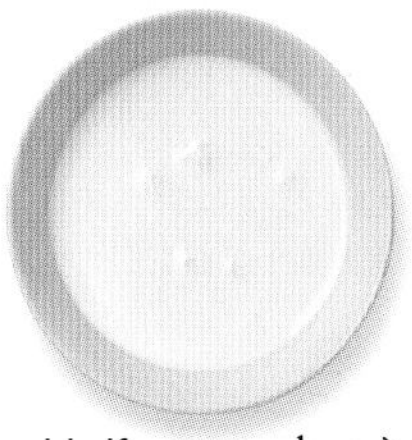
half-and-half cream • la crème allégée • die fettarme Sahne • la crema líquida • la panna liquida

whipping cream
la crème épaisse
die Schlagsahne
la crema para batir
la panna densa

whipped cream
la crème fouettée
die Schlagsahne
la crema batida
la panna montata

sour cream
la crème fraîche
die saure Sahne
la crema ácida
la panna acida

yogurt
le yaourt
der Joghurt
el yogurt
lo yogurt

ice cream
la glace
das Eis
el helado
il gelato

eggs • les œufs • die Eier • los huevos • le uova

soft-boiled egg • l'œuf à la coque • das gekochte Ei • el huevo tibio • l'uovo alla coque

goose egg • l'œuf d'oie • das Gänseei • el huevo de ganso • l'uovo d'oca

hen's egg • l'œuf de poule • das Hühnerei • el huevo de gallina • l'uovo di gallina

quail egg • l'œuf de caille • das Wachtelei • el huevo de codorniz • l'uovo di quaglia

duck egg • l'œuf de cane • das Entenei • el huevo de pato • l'uovo di anatra

pasteurized pasteurisé pasteurisiert pasteurizado pastorizzato	fat-free sans matières grasses fettfrei sin grasa senza grassi	salted salé gesalzen salado salato	sheep's milk le lait de brebis die Schafmilch la leche de oveja il latte di pecora	lactose le lactose die Laktose la lactosa il lattosio	milkshake le milk-shake der Milchshake la malteada il frullato
unpasteurized non pasteurisé unpasteurisiert sin pasteurizar non pastorizzato	powdered milk le lait en poudre das Milchpulver la leche en polvo il latte in polvere	unsalted non salé ungesalzen sin sal senza sale	buttermilk le babeurre die Buttermilch el suero de la leche il siero di latte	homogenized homogénéisé homogenisiert homogeneizado omogeneizzato	frozen yogurt le yaourt surgelé der gefrorene Joghurt el yogurt helado lo yogurt gelato

breads and flours • les pains et la farine • das Brot und das Mehl • el pan y las harinas • il pane e le farine

bakery • la boulangerie • die Bäckerei • la panadería • il panificio

making bread • faire du pain • Brot backen • haciendo pan • fare il pane

white flour • la farine blanche • das Weizenmehl • la harina blanca • la farina bianca

whole-wheat flour • la farine complète • das Roggenmehl • la harina morena • la farina nera

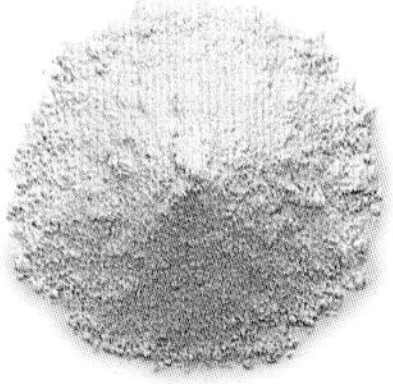

stone-ground flour • la farine brute • das Vollkornmehl • la harina integral • la farina integrale

yeast • la levure • die Hefe • la levadura • il lievito

sift *(v)* • tamiser • sieben • cernir • setacciare

mix *(v)* • mélanger • verrühren • mezclar • mescolare

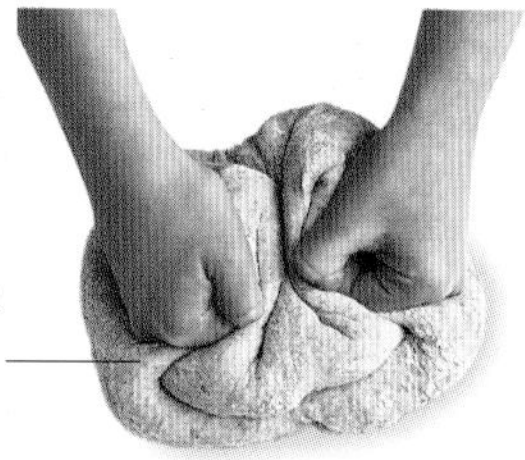

knead *(v)* • pétrir • kneten • amasar • impastare

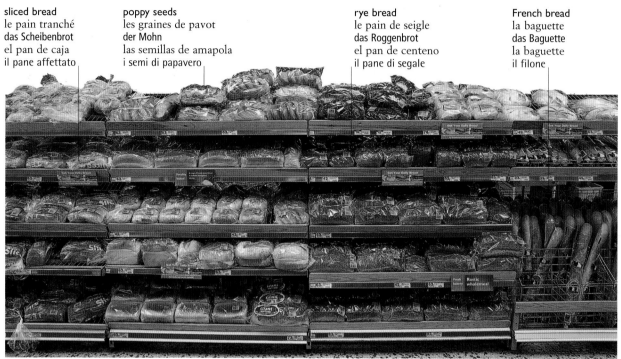

bake *(v)* • faire cuir au four • backen • hornear • cuocere al forno

white bread • le pain blanc • das Weißbrot • el pan blanco • il pane bianco

brown bread • le pain bis • das Graubrot • el pan negro • il pane nero

whole-wheat bread • le pain de son • das Vollkornbrot • el pan integral • il pane integrale

multigrain bread • le pain complet • das Mehrkornbrot • el pan con grano • il pane di granaio

corn bread • le pain de maïs • das Maisbrot • el pan de maíz • il pane di mais

soda bread • le pain à la bicarbonate de soude • das Sodabrot • el pan al bicarbonato sódico • il pane lievitato con bicarbonato di sodio

sourdough bread • le pain au levain • das Sauerteigbrot • el pan fermentado • il pane di lievito naturale

flat bread • le pain plat • das Fladenbrot • el pan sin levadura • la schiacciata

bagel • le petit pain américain • das Hefebrötchen • la dona • il bagel

bun • le petit pain rond • das weiche Brötchen • el bollo • la pagnotella

roll • le petit pain • das Brötchen • el panecillo • il panino

fruit bread • le pain aux raisins secs • das Rosinenbrot • el pan de frutas • il pane alla frutta

seeded bread • le pain aux graines • das Körnerbrot • el pan con semillas • il pane con semi

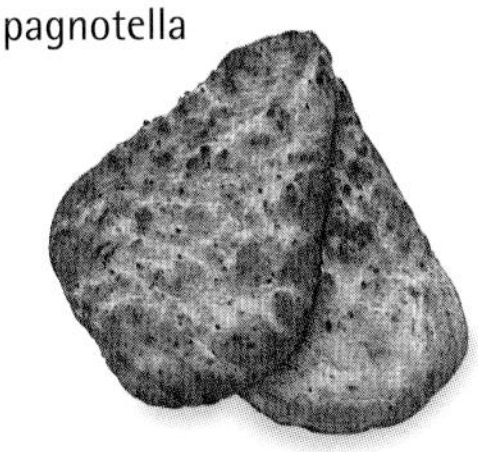

naan bread • le naan • der Naan • el naan • il naan

pita bread • le pita • das Pitabrot • la pita • la pita

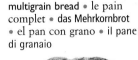

crispbread • le biscuit scandinave • das Knäckebrot • el pan danés • i crackers

self-rising flour
la farine avec la levure
das Mehl mit Backpulver
la harina con levadura
la farina autolievitante

all-purpose flour
la farine sans levure
das Mehl ohne Backpulver
la harina blanca
la farina semplice

prove *(v)*
lever
gehen lassen
levar
riposare

breadcrumbs
la chapelure
das Paniermehl
el pan molido
le briciole

slicer
la machine à couper
der Brotschneider
el rebanador
l'affettatrice

bread flour
la farine traitée
das angereicherte Mehl
la harina para pan
la farina per il pane

rise *(v)*
se lever
aufgehen
subir
lievitare

glaze *(v)*
glacer
glasieren
glasear
glassare

flute
la flûte
die Flöte
la barra
il filoncino

baker
le boulanger
der Bäcker
el panadero
il panettiere

cakes and desserts • les gâteaux et les desserts • Kuchen und Nachspeisen • la repostería • i dolci e i dessert

éclair
l'éclair
das Eclair
el profiterol
il bignè ripieno

profiterole pastry
la pâte à choux
der Brandteig
la masa de profiteroles
l'éclair

cream
la crème
die Sahne
la crema
la panna

puff pastry
la pâte feuilletée
der Blätterteig
el hojaldre
la pasta sfoglia

filling
la garniture
die Füllung
el relleno
il ripieno

filo dough
la pâte de filo
der Blätterteig
la masa brisa
la pasta filo

fruit cake
le cake
der englische Kuchen
el plum-cake
il dolce alla frutta

chocolate coated
enrobé de chocolat
mit Schokolade überzogen
cubierto de chocolate
ricoperto di cioccolato

fruit pie
la tarte aux fruits
das Obsttortelett
la tartaleta de fruta
la crostatina

muffin
le muffin
der Muffin
el muffin
il muffin

meringue
la meringue
das Baiser
el merengue
la meringa

sponge cake
la madeleine
das Biskuittörtchen
la magdalena
il pan di Spagna

cakes • les gâteaux • das Gebäck • los pasteles • i dolci

pastry cream
la crème pâtissière
die Konditorcreme
la crema pastelera
la crema pasticcera

chocolate cake
le gâteau au chocolat
die Schokoladentorte
el pastel de chocolate
la torta al cioccolato

bun
le petit gâteau
das Teilchen
el bollo
la focaccina

custard
la crème anglaise
der Vanillepudding
las natillas
la crema

pastry
la pâte
der Teig
la masa
la pasta

slice
la tranche
das Stück
la rebanada
la fetta

rice pudding
le riz au lait
der Milchreis
el arroz con leche
il budino di riso

celebration
la fête
die Feier
la celebración
la festa

May I have a slice please?
Est-ce que je peux avoir une tranche s'il vous plaît?
Könnte ich bitte ein Stück haben?
¿Puedo tomar una rebanada?
Posso avere una fetta?

chocolate chip • les pépites de chocolat • das Schokoladenstückchen • los chips de chocolate • il biscotto con scaglie di cioccolato

florentine • le florentine • der Florentiner • la florentina • il biscotto alle noci

cookies • les biscuits • die Kekse • las galletas • i biscotti

lady fingers
les boudoirs
die Löffelbiskuits
las soletillas
i savoiardi

trifle • le diplomate • das Trifle • el postre de soletillas, gelatina de frutas y crema • la zuppa inglese

mousse • la mousse • die Mousse • el mousse • il mousse

sorbet • le sorbet • das Sorbett • el sorbete • il sorbetto

custard pie • la tarte à la crème • die Sahnetorte • el pastel de crema • la torta alla crema

crème caramel • la crème caramel • der Karamellpudding • el flan • il crème caramel

special occasion cakes • les gâteaux de fête • die festlichen Kuchen • los pasteles para celebraciones • le torte per celebrazioni

top tier
l'étage supérieur
der obere Kuchenteil
el último piso
il piano superiore

ribbon
le ruban
das Band
el listón
il nastro

bottom tier
l'étage inférieur
der untere Kuchenteil
el primer piso
il piano inferiore

icing
le glaçage
der Zuckerguss
la alcorza
la glassa

marzipan
la pâte d'amandes
das Marzipan
el mazapán
il marzapane

wedding cake • le gâteau de mariage • die Hochzeitstorte • el pastel de bodas • la torta nuziale

decoration
la décoration
die Dekoration
la decoración
la decorazione

birthday candles
les bougies d'anniversaire
die Geburtstagskerzen
las velas de cumpleaños
le candeline

blow out *(v)*
souffler
ausblasen
apagar
soffiare

birthday cake • le gâteau d'anniversaire • der Geburtstagskuchen • el pastel de cumpleaños • la torta di compleanno

delicatessen • la charcuterie • die Feinkost • la charcutería • la salumeria

spicy sausage
le saucisson piquant
die pikante Wurst
el fiambre
la salsiccia piccante

oil
l'huile
das Öl
el aceite
l'olio

vinegar
le vinaigre
der Essig
el vinagre
l'aceto

salami • le salami • die Salami • el salami • il salame

pepperoni • le pepperoni • die Pepperoniwurst • el salchichón • il salame piccante

quiche • la quiche • die Quiche • la quiche • lo sformato

uncooked meat
la viande non cuite
das frische Fleisch
la carne fresca
la carne cruda

counter
le comptoir
die Theke
el mostrador
il banco

pâté • le pâté • die Pastete • el paté • il pâté

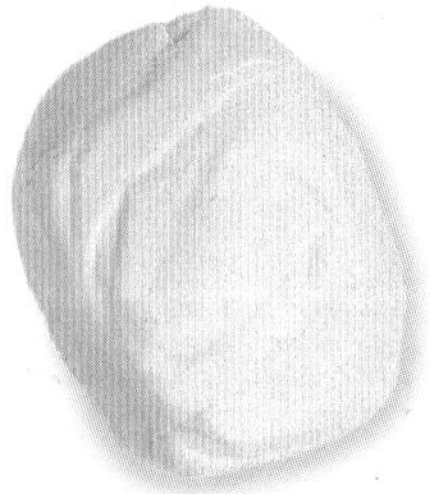

mozzarella • la mozzarella • der Mozzarella • la mozzarella • la mozzarella

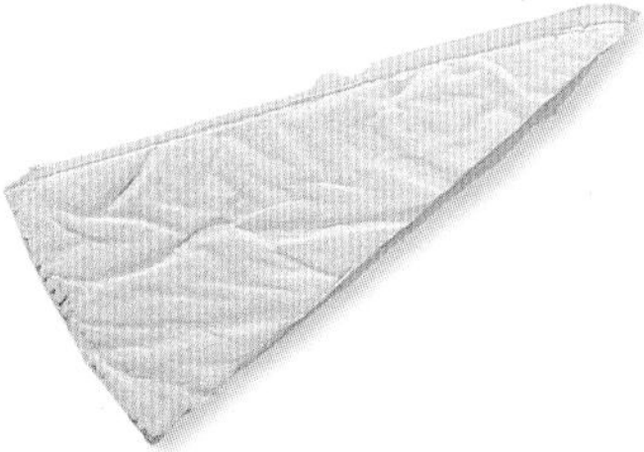

brie • le brie • der Brie • el brie • il brie

goat's cheese • le fromage de chèvre • der Ziegenkäse • el queso de cabra • il formaggio di capra

cheddar • le cheddar • der Cheddar • el cheddar • il cheddar

parmesan • le parmesan • der Parmesan • el parmesano • il parmigiano

camembert • le camembert • der Camembert • el camembert • il camembert

rind
la croûte
die Rinde
la corteza
la scorza

edam • l'édam • der Edamer • el queso de bola • l'edam

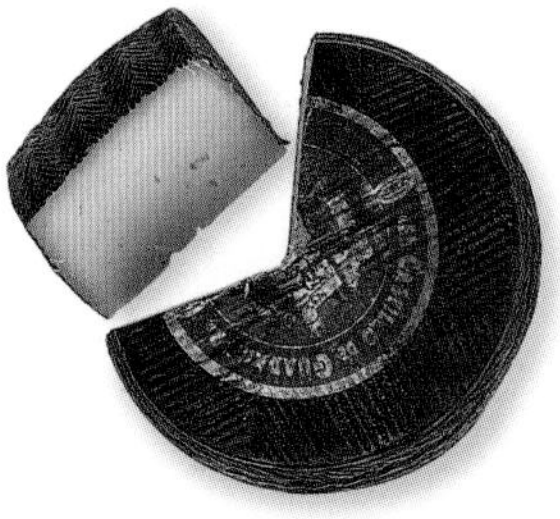

manchego • le manchego • der Manchego • el manchego • il manchego

meat pies • les pâtés en croûte • die Pasteten • los pasteles de carne • i pasticci di carne

cooked meat
la viande cuite
das gekochte Fleisch
el fiambre
la carne cotta

ham • le jambon • der Schinken • el jamón • il prosciutto

roll
le petit pain
das Brötchen
el panecillo
il panino

black olive
l'olive noire
die schwarze Olive
la aceituna negra
l'oliva nera

chili
le piment
die Peperoni
el chile piquín
il peperoncino

sauce
la sauce
die Soße
la salsa
la salsa

green olive
l'olive verte
die grüne Olive
la aceituna verde
l'oliva verde

sandwich counter • le comptoir sandwichs • die Sandwichtheke • el mostrador de bocadillos • la paninoteca

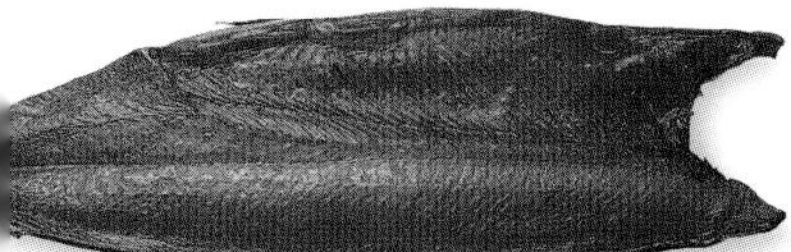

smoked fish • le poisson fumé • der Räucherfisch • el pescado ahumado • il pesce affumicato

capers • les câpres • die Kapern • las alcaparras • i capperi

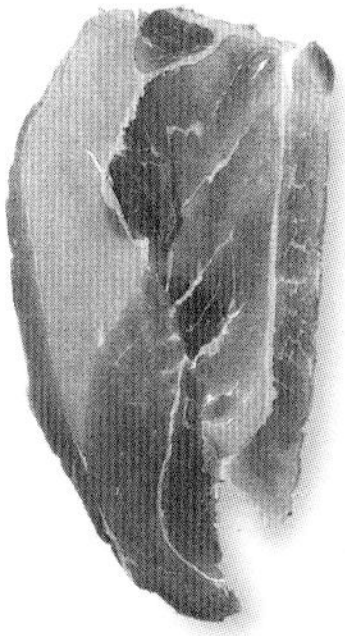

prosciutto • le prosciutto • der Prosciutto • el jamón serrano • il prosciutto crudo

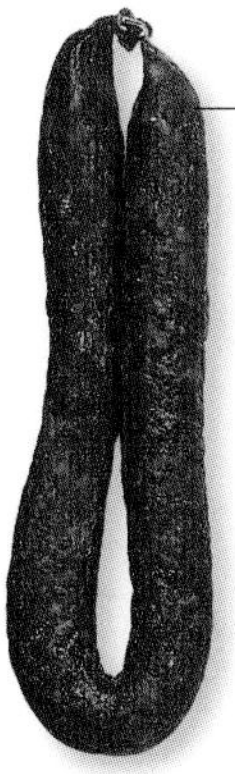

chorizo • le chorizo • die Chorizo • el chorizo • il chorizo

stuffed olive • l'olive fourrée • die gefüllte Olive • la aceituna rellena • l'oliva ripiena

in oil • à l'huile • in Öl • en aceite • sott'olio

in brine • en saumure • in Lake • en salmuera • in salamoia

marinated • mariné • mariniert • marinado • marinato

salted • salé • gepökelt • salado • salato

smoked • fumé • geräuchert • ahumado • affumicato

cured • séché • getrocknet • curado • trattato

Take a number, please.
Prenez un numéro, s'il vous plaît.
Nehmen Sie bitte eine Nummer.
Tome un número, por favor.
Prenda un numero, per favore.

Can I try some of that, please?
Est-ce que je peut goûter un peu de ça, s'il vous plaît?
Kann ich bitte etwas davon probieren?
¿Puedo probar un poco de eso?
Posso assaggiare un po' di quello, per favore?

May I have six slices of that, please?
Je voudrais six tranches, s'il vous plaît.
Ich hätte gerne sechs Scheiben davon, bitte.
¿Me pone seis rebanadas de aquél?
Mi dà sei fette di quello, per favore?

drinks • les boissons • die Getränke • las bebidas • le bevande

water • l' eau • das Wasser • el agua • l'acqua

tap water • l'eau du robinet • das Leitungswasser • el agua de la llave • l'acqua dal rubinetto

bottled water
l'eau en bouteille
das Flaschenwasser
el agua embotellada
l'acqua in bottiglia

sparkling
gazeux
mit Kohlensäure
con gas
frizzante

noncarbonated
non gazeux
ohne Kohlensäure
sin gas
naturale

mineral water • l'eau minérale • das Mineralwasser • el agua mineral • l'acqua minerale

tonic water • le tonic • das Tonicwater la tónica • l'acqua tonica

soda water • le soda • das Sodawasser • la soda • la soda

hot drinks • les boissons chaudes • die heißen Getränke • las bebidas calientes • le bevande calde

teabag • le sachet de thé • der Teebeutel • la bolsita de té • la bustina di tè

loose leaf tea • les feuilles de thé • die Teeblätter • el té en hoja • il tè sciolto

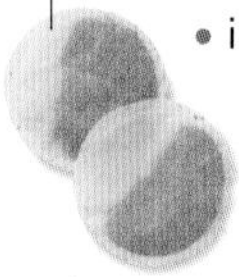

tea • le thé • der Tee • el té • il tè

beans • les grains • die Bohnen • los granos • i chicchi

ground coffee
le café moulu
der gemahlene Kaffee
el café molido
il caffè macinato

coffee • le café • der Kaffee • el café • il caffè

hot chocolate • le chocolat chaud • die heiße Schokolade • el chocolate caliente • il cioccolato caldo

malted drink • la boisson maltée • das Malzgetränk • la bebida malteada • la bevanda al malto

soft drinks • les boissons non alcoolisées • die alkoholfreien Getränke • los refrescos • le bibite

straw • la paille • der Strohhalm • el popote • la cannuccia

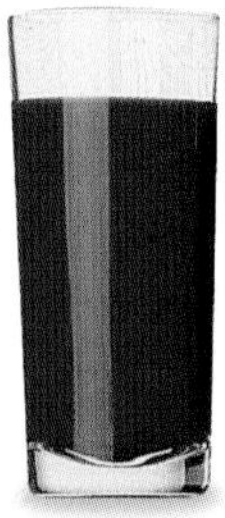

tomato juice • le jus de tomate • der Tomatensaft • el jugo de tomate • il succo di pomodoro

grape juice • le jus de raisin • der Traubensaft • el jugo de uva • il succo d'uva

lemonade • la limonade • die Limonade • la limonada • la limonata

orangeade • l'orangeade • die Orangeade • la naranjada • l'aranciata

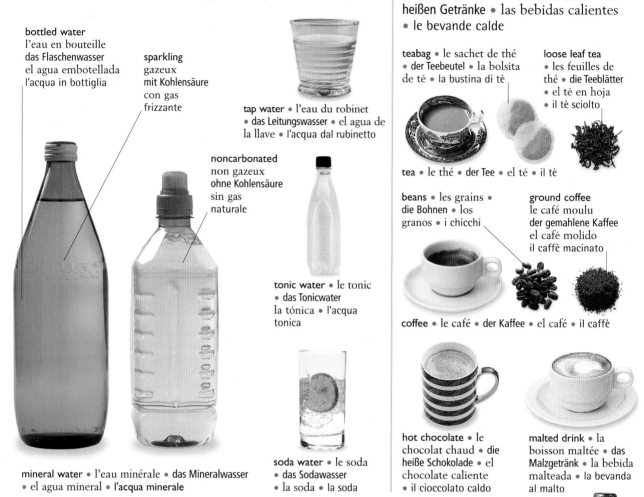

cola • le coca • die Cola • la cola • la coca

alcoholic drinks • les boissons alcoolisées • die alkoholischen Getränke • las bebidas alcohólicas • le bevande alcoliche

gin • le gin • der Gin • la ginebra • il gin

can
la boîte
die Dose
la lata
la lattina

beer • la bière • das Bier • la cerveza • la birra

hard cider • le cidre • der Apfelwein • la sidra • il sidro

bitter • la bière anglaise • das halbdunkle Bier • la cerveza amarga • la birra amara

stout • la bière brune • der Stout • la cerveza negra • la birra scura

vodka • la vodka • der Wodka • el vodka • la vodka

whiskey • le whisky • der Whisky • el whisky • il whisky

rum • le rhum • der Rum • el ron • il rum

brandy • le brandy • der Weinbrand • el brandy • il brandy

port • le porto • der Portwein • el oporto • il porto

dry • sec • trocken • seco • secco

sherry • le sherry • der Sherry • el vino de jerez • lo sherry

campari • le campari • der Campari • el campari • il Campari

liqueur • la liqueur • der Likör • el licor • il liquore

tequila • la téquila • der Tequila • el tequila • la tequila

champagne • le champagne • der Champagner • el champán • lo champagne

rosé
rosé
rosé
rosado
rosé

white
blanc
weiß
blanco
bianco

red
rouge
rot
tinto
rosso

wine • le vin • der Wein • el vino • il vino

eating out
sortir manger
auswärts essen
comer fuera
mangiare fuori

café • le café • das Café • la cafetería • il caffè

menu
le menu
die Speisekarte
la carta
il menù

awning
le store
die Markise
el toldo
la tenda

sidewalk café • la terrasse de café • das Straßencafé • la cafetería con mesas fuera • il bar all'aperto

umbrella
le parasol
der Sonnenschirm
la sombrilla
l'ombrellone

terrace café • la terrasse de café • das Terrassencafé • la terraza • il bar con terrazza

server
le serveur
der Kellner
el mesero
il cameriere

coffee machine
le percolateur
die Kaffeemaschine
la máquina del café
la macchina del caffè

table
la table
der Tisch
la mesa
il tavolo

snack bar • le snack • die Snackbar • el bar • lo snack bar

coffee • le café • der Kaffee • el café • il caffè

coffee with cream
le crème
der Kaffee mit Milch
el café con leche
il caffè macchiato

black coffee
le noir
der schwarze Kaffee
el café solo
il caffè nero

filter coffee • le café filtre • der Filterkaffee • el café de cafetera eléctrica • il caffè filtrato

espresso • l'expresso • der Espresso • el expreso • l'espresso

cocoa powder
le chocolat en poudre
das Kakaopulver
la cocoa
la polvere di cacao

froth
la mousse
der Schaum
la espuma
la schiuma

cappuccino • le cappuccino • der Cappuccino • el cappuccino • il cappuccino

iced coffee • le café glacé • der Eiskaffee • el café con hielo • il caffè freddo

tea • le thé • der Tee • el té • il tè

camomile tea • la camomille • der Kamillentee • la manzanilla • la camomilla

green tea • le thé vert • der grüne Tee • el té verde • il tè verde

herbal tea
la tisane
der Kräutertee
el té de hierbas
il tè alle erbe

tea with milk • le thé au lait • der Tee mit Milch • el té con leche • il tè con latte

black tea • le thé nature • der schwarze Tee • el té solo • il tè nero

tea with lemon • le thé au citron • der Tee mit Zitrone • el té con limón • il tè al limone

mint tea • l'infusion de menthe • der Pfefferminztee • la menta poleo • il tè alla menta

iced tea • le thé glacé • der Eistee • el té con hielo • il tè freddo

juices and milkshakes • les jus et milk-shakes • die Säfte und Milchshakes • los jugos y las malteadas • le spremute e i frappé

orange juice • le jus d'orange • der Orangensaft • el jugo de naranja • il succo d'arancia

apple juice • le jus de pomme • der Apfelsaft • el jugo de manzana • il succo di mela

pineapple juice
le jus d'ananas
der Ananassaft
el jugo de piña
il succo d'ananas

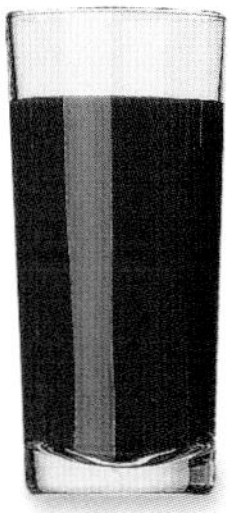

tomato juice • le jus de tomate • der Tomatensaft • el jugo de tomate • il succo di pomodoro

chocolate milkshake
le milk-shake au chocolat
der Schokoladenmilchshake
la malteada de chocolate
il frappé al cioccolato

strawberry milkshake
le milk-shake à la fraise
der Erdbeermilchshake
la malteada de fresa
il frappé alle fragole

coffee milkshake
le milk-shake au café
der Kaffeemilchshake
la malteada de café
il frappé al caffè

food • la nourriture • das Essen • la comida • il cibo

brown bread
le pain bis
das Graubrot
el pan integral
il pane integrale

toasted sandwich • le sandwich grillé • der getoastete Sandwich • el sandwich tostado • il tramezzino tostato

salad • la salade • der Salat • la ensalada • l'insalata

scoop
la boule
die Kugel
la bola
la pallina

ice cream • la glace • das Eis • el helado • il gelato

pastry • la pâtisserie • das Gebäck • el pan dulce • la pasta

bar • le bar • die Bar • el bar • il bar

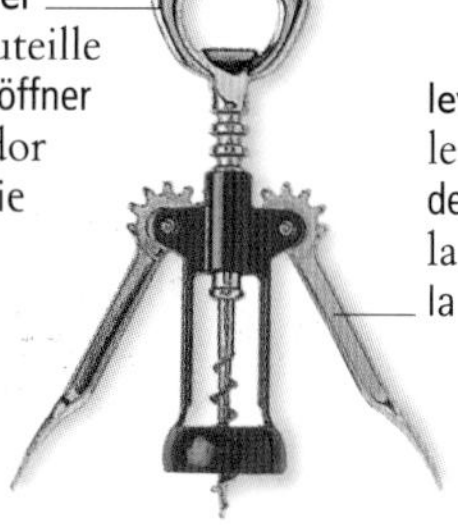

corkscrew • le tire-bouchon • der Korkenzieher • el sacacorchos • il cavatappi

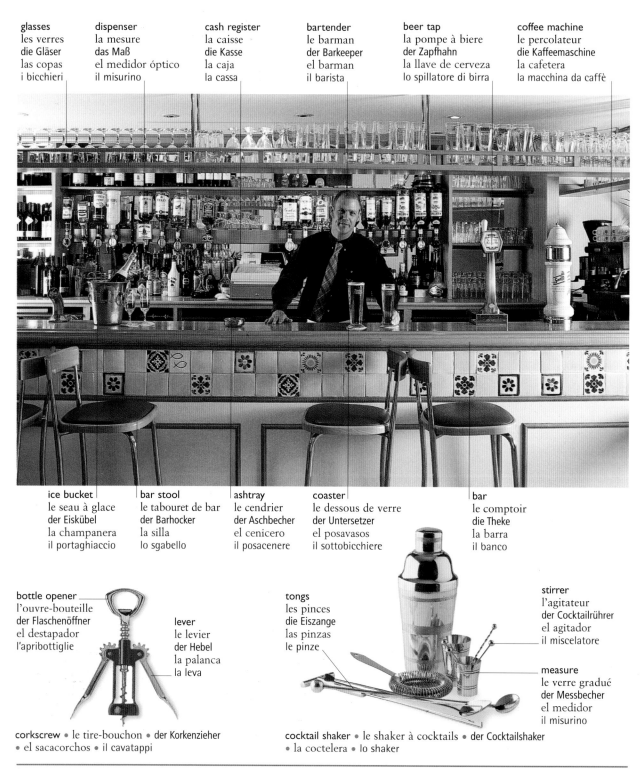

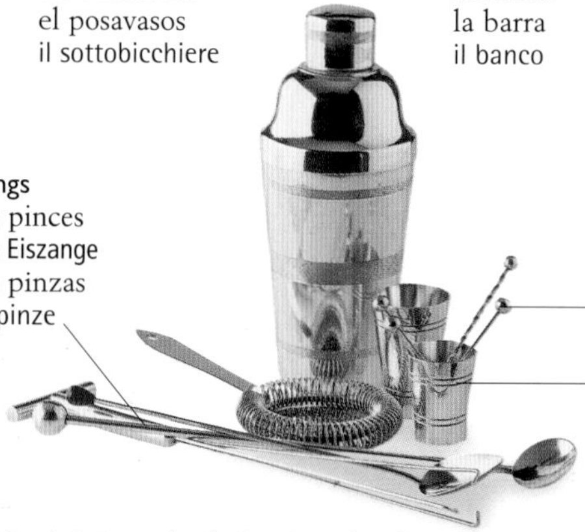

cocktail shaker • le shaker à cocktails • der Cocktailshaker • la coctelera • lo shaker

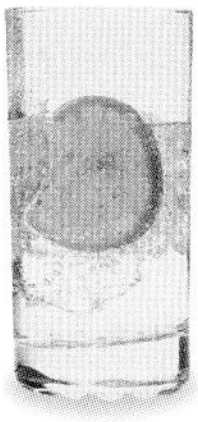

gin and tonic • le gin tonic • der Gin Tonic • el gin tonic • il gin tonic

pitcher
le pichet
der Krug
la jarra
la brocca

scotch and water • le scotch à l'eau • der Scotch mit Wasser • el whiskey escocés con agua • il whisky con acqua

ice cube
le glaçon
der Eiswürfel
el cubito de hielo
il cubetto di ghiaccio

rum and coke • le rhum coca • der Rum mit Cola • la cuba libre • il rum con coca cola

vodka and orange • la vodka à l'orange • der Wodka mit Orangensaft • el desarmador • la vodka all'arancia

martini • le martini • der Martini • el martini • il martini

cocktail • le cocktail • der Cocktail • el cóctel • il cocktail

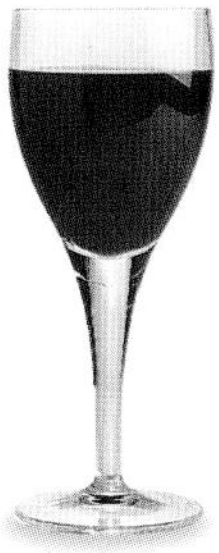

wine • le vin • der Wein • el vino • il vino

beer • la bière • das Bier • la cerveza • la birra

a shot • un coup • ein Schuss • un trago • un bicchiere

single
simple
einfach
sencillo
singolo

double
double
doppelt
doble
doppio

measure • la mesure • das Maß • la medida • la misura

without ice • sans glaçons • ohne Eis • sin hielo • liscio

ice and lemon
citron et glaçons
Eis und Zitrone
con hielo y limón
con ghiaccio e limone

with ice • avec des glaçons • mit Eis • con hielo • con ghiaccio

bar snacks • les amuse-gueule • die Knabbereien • la botana • gli stuzzichini

potato chips • les chips • die Kartoffelchips • las papas fritas • le patatine

almonds
les amandes
die Mandeln
las almendras
le mandorle

cashews
• les noix de cajou
• die Cashewnüsse
• las nueces de la India
• gli anacardi

peanuts
les cacahouètes
die Erdnüsse
los cacahuetes
le noccioline americane

nuts • les noix • die Nüsse • los frutos secos • le noccioline

olives • les olives • die Oliven • las aceitunas • le olive

restaurant • le restaurant • das Restaurant • el restaurante • il ristorante

table setting
le couvert
das Gedeck
el cubierto
il coperto

assistant chef
le commis
der Hilfskoch
el ayudante del chef
l'aiuto cuoco

chef
le chef de cuisine
der Küchenchef
el chef
il cuoco

kitchen • la cuisine • die Küche • la cocina • la cucina

glass
le verre
das Glas
la copa
il bicchiere

tray
le plateau
das Tablett
la charola
il vassoio

server • le garçon • der Kellner • el mesero • il cameriere

lunch menu le menu du déjeuner das Mittagsmenü el menú de la comida il menù del pranzo	specials les spécialités die Spezialitäten los platillos del día i piatti del giorno	price le prix der Preis el precio il prezzo	tip le pourboire das Trinkgeld la propina la mancia	buffet le buffet das Buffet el buffet il buffet	salt le sel das Salz la sal il sale
dinner menu le menu du soir das Abendmenü el menú de la cena il menù della cena	à la carte à la carte à la carte a la carta a la carte	check l'addition die Rechnung la cuenta il conto	service charge included service compris Bedienung inbegriffen servicio incluido servizio compreso	bar le bar die Bar el bar il bar	pepper le poivre der Pfeffer la pimienta il pepe
wine list la carte des vins die Weinkarte la lista de vinos la lista dei vini	dessert cart le plateau à desserts der Dessertwagen el carrito de los postres il carrello dei dolci	receipt le reçu die Quittung el recibo la ricevuta	service charge not included service non compris ohne Bedienung servicio no incluido servizio non compreso	customer le client der Kunde el cliente il cliente	

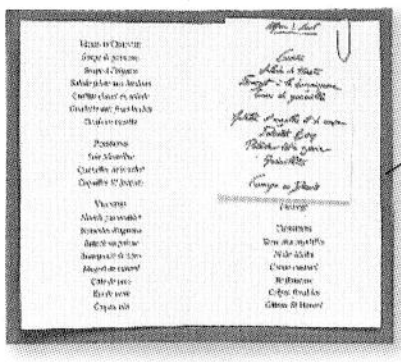

menu • la carte • die Speisekarte • la carta • il menù

child's meal • le menu d'enfant • die Kinderportion • el menú para niños • il menù per bambini

order *(v)* • commander • bestellen • ordenar • ordinare

pay *(v)* • payer • bezahlen • pagar • pagare

courses • les plats • die Gänge • los platos • le portate

apéritif • l'apéritif • der Aperitif • el aperitivo • l'aperitivo

appetizer • l'entrée • die Vorspeise • la entrada • l'antipasto

soup • la soupe • die Suppe • la sopa • la minestra

main course • le plat principal • das Hauptgericht • el plato principal • il piatto principale

side order • l'accompagnement • die Beilage • el acompañamiento • il contorno

dessert • le dessert • der Nachtisch • el postre • il dessert

coffee • le café • der Kaffee • el café • il caffè

A table for two, please.
Une table pour deux, s'il vous plaît.
Einen Tisch für zwei Personen, bitte.
Una mesa para dos, por favor.
Un tavolo per due, per favore.

Can I see the menu/wine list, please?
La carte/la carte des vins, s'il vous plaît.
Die Speisekarte/Weinkarte, bitte.
¿Podría ver la carta/lista de vinos, por favor?
Posso vedere il menù\la lista dei vini, per favore?

Is there a prix fixe menu?
Avez-vous un menu à prix fixe?
Haben Sie ein Tagesmenü?
¿Hay menú del día?
C'è un menù a prezzo fisso?

Do you have any vegetarian dishes?
Avez vous des plats végétariens?
Haben Sie vegetarische Gerichte?
¿Tiene platos vegetarianos?
Avete dei piatti vegetariani?

Could I have the check/a receipt, please?
L'addition/un reçu, s'il vous plaît.
Könnte ich bitte die Rechnung/eine Quittung haben?
¿Me podría traer la cuenta/un recibo?
Posso avere il conto\una ricevuta per favore?

Can we pay separately?
Pouvons-nous payer chacun notre part?
Können wir getrennt zahlen?
¿Podemos pagar por separado?
Possiamo pagare separatamente?

Where are the rest rooms, please?
Où sont les toilettes, s'il vous plaît?
Wo sind die Toiletten, bitte?
¿Dónde están los baños, por favor?
Dove sono i bagni per favore?

fast food • la restauration rapide • der Schnellimbiss • la comida rápida • il fast food

burger
le hamburger
der Hamburger
la hamburguesa
l'hamburger

straw
la paille
der Strohhalm
el popote
la cannuccia

soft drink
la boisson non-alcoolisée
das alkoholfreie Getränk
el refresco
la bibita

french fries
les frites
die Pommes frites
las papas fritas
le patate fritte

paper napkin
la serviette en papier
die Papierserviette
la servilleta de papel
il tovagliolo di carta

tray
le plateau
das Tablett
la charola
il vassoio

burger meal • le hamburger avec des frites • der Hamburger mit Pommes frites • la hamburguesa con papas fritas • il pasto con hamburger

pizza • la pizza • die Pizza • la pizza • la pizza

price list • le tarif • die Preisliste • la lista de precios • il listino

canned drink
la boisson en boîte
das Dosengetränk
el refresco en lata
la bibita in lattina

delivery • la livraison à domicile • die Lieferung ins Haus • la entrega a domicilio • la consegna a domicilio

hot-dog stand • le marchand de hot-dogs • der Imbissstand • el puesto • il venditore ambulante

pizzeria
la pizzeria
die Pizzeria
la pizzería
la pizzeria

fast food restaurant
le restaurant rapide
die Imbissstube
el restaurant de hamburguesas
il fastfood

menu
la carte
die Speisekarte
el menú
il menù

eat in
manger sur place
hier essen
para comer en el local
mangiare sul posto

carry out
à emporter
zum Mitnehmen
para llevar
da asporto

reheat *(v)*
réchauffer
aufwärmen
recalentar
riscaldare

ketchup
le ketchup
der Tomatenketchup
la catsup
la salsa di pomodoro

Can I have that to go, please?
À emporter, s'il vous plaît.
Ich möchte das mitnehmen.
¿Me lo pone para llevar?
Me lo dà da asporto?

Do you deliver?
Est-ce que vous livrez à domicile?
Liefern Sie ins Haus?
¿Entregan a domicilio?
Consegnate a domocilio?

hamburger • le hamburger • der Hamburger • la hamburguesa • l'hamburger

chicken burger • le hamburger au poulet • der Chickenburger • la hamburguesa de pollo • l'hamburger di pollo

veggie burger • le hamburger végétarien • der vegetarische Hamburger • la hamburguesa vegetariana • l'hamburger vegetariano

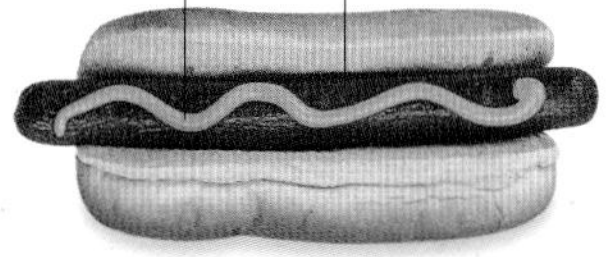

hot dog • le hot-dog • das Hot Dog • el hot dog • l'hot dog

sub • le sandwich • der Sandwich • el bocadillo • il tramezzino

club sandwich • le sandwich mixte • der Klubsandwich • el club sandwich • il tramezzino a strati

open-face sandwich • le canapé • das belegte Brot • el sandwich abierto • il tramezzino aperto

wrap • le taco • das gefüllte Fladenbrot • el taco • la piadina

kabob • le kébab • der Kebab • el alambre • il kebab

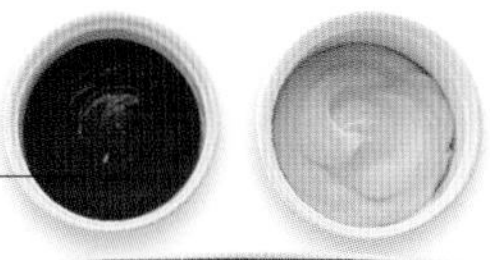

chicken nuggets • les beignets de poulet • die Hähnchenstückchen • los nuggets de pollo • i bocconcini di pollo

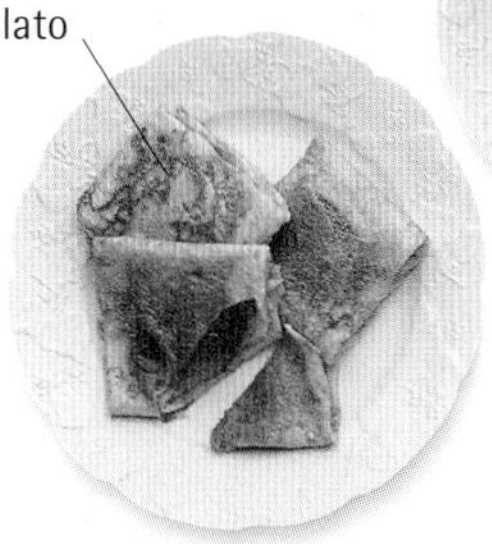

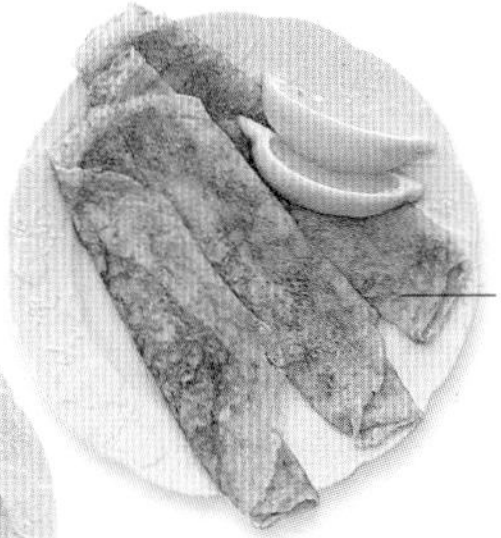

crepes • les crêpes • die Crêpes • la crêpe • la crêpe

fish and chips • le poisson avec des frites • der Bratfisch mit Pommes frites • el pescado con papas fritas • il pesce con patatine

ribs • les côtes • die Rippen • las costillas • le costolette

fried chicken • le poulet frit • das gebratene Hähnchen • el pollo frito • il pollo fritto

pizza • la pizza • die Pizza • la pizza • la pizza

breakfast • le petit déjeuner • das Frühstück • el desayuno • la colazione

milk
le lait
die Milch
la leche
il latte

cereal
les céréales
die Getreideflocken
los cereales
il cereale

jam
la confiture
die Konfitüre
la mermelada
la marmellata

dried fruit
les fruit secs
das Dörrobst
la fruta seca
la frutta secca

ham
le jambon
der Schinken
el jamón
il prosciutto

cheese
le fromage
der Käse
el queso
il formaggio

crispbread
le biscuit scandinave
das Knäckebrot
la galleta de centeno
il pane biscottato

breakfast buffet • le buffet du petit déjeuner • das Frühstücksbuffet • el buffet de desayuno • il buffet della colazione

marmalade
la confiture d'oranges
die Orangenmarmelade
la mermelada de naranja
la marmellata di agrumi

pâté
le pâté
die Pastete
el paté
il pâté

butter
le beurre
die Butter
la mantequilla
il burro

fruit juice
le jus de fruit
der Obstsaft
el jugo de frutas
il succo di frutta

coffee
le café
der Kaffee
el café
il caffè

breakfast table • la table du petit déjeuner • der Frühstückstisch • la mesa del desayuno • il tavolo della colazione

croissant
le croissant
das Croissant
el croissant
il cornetto

hot chocolate
le chocolat chaud
die Schokolade
el chocolate caliente
la cioccolata calda

tea
le thé
der Tee
el té
il tè

drinks • les boissons • die Getränke • las bebidas • le bevande

brioche • la brioche • die Brioche • el pan dulce • la brioche

bread • le pain • das Brot • el pan • il pane

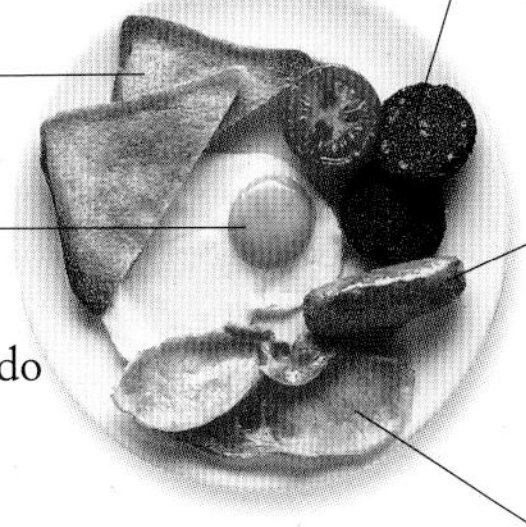

English breakfast • le petit déjeuner anglais • das englische Frühstück • el desayuno inglés • la colazione all'inglese

smoked herring • les kippers • die Räucherheringe • los arenques ahumados • le aringhe affumicate

french toast • le pain perdu • das in Ei gebratene Brot • el pan francés • il pane fritto all'uovo

soft-boiled egg • l'œuf à la coque • das gekochte Ei • el huevo tibio • l'uovo alla coque

scrambled eggs • les œufs brouillés • das Rührei • los huevos revueltos • le uova strapazzate

crepes • les crêpes • die Pfannkuchen • las crepas • le crêpes

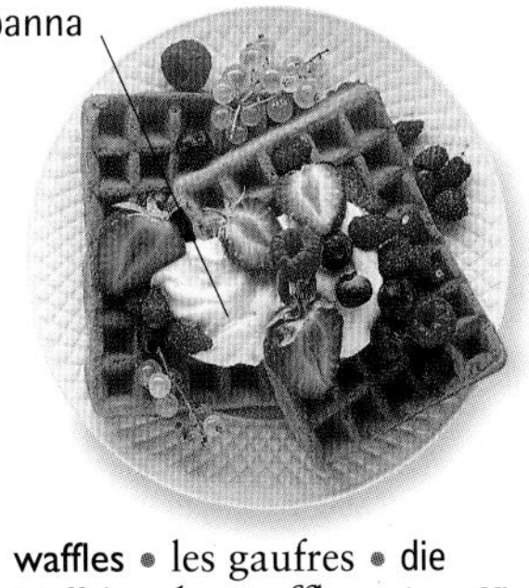

waffles • les gaufres • die Waffeln • los waffles • i waffle

oatmeal • le porridge • der Porridge • la avena • il porridge

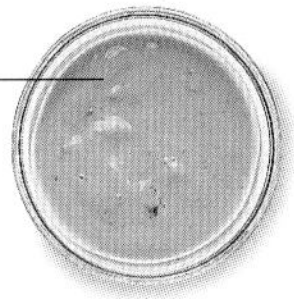

fresh fruit • les fruits • das Obst • la fruta fresca • la frutta fresca

dinner • le repas • die Hauptmahlzeit • la comida principal • la cena

soup • le potage • die Suppe • la sopa • la minestra

broth • le bouillon • die Brühe • el caldo • la zuppa

stew • le ragoût • der Eintopf • el guiso • lo stufato

curry • le curry • das Curry • el curry • il curry

roast • le rôti • der Braten • el asado • l'arrosto

pie • la tourte • die Pastete • la empanada • il pasticcio

soufflé • le soufflé • das Soufflé • el soufflé • il soufflé

kabob • le chiche-kébab • der Schaschlik • la brocheta • lo spiedino

meatballs • les boulettes de viande • die Fleischklöße • las albóndigas • le polpette

omelet • l'omelette • das Omelett • la omelette • la frittata

noodles • les nouilles • die Nudeln • los fideos • i taglierini

stir fry • le sauté • das Schnellbratgericht • el revuelto • la frittura

pasta • les pâtes • die Nudeln • la pasta • la pasta

rice • le riz • der Reis • el arroz • il riso

tossed salad • la salade composée • der gemischte Salat • la ensalada mixta • l'insalata mista

green salad • la salade verte • der grüne Salat • la ensalada verde • l'insalata verde

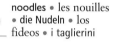

dressing • la vinaigrette • die Salatsoße • el aderezo • il condimento

techniques • la préparation • die Zubereitung • las técnicas • i metodi

stuffed • farci • gefüllt • relleno • farcito

in sauce • en sauce • in Soße • en salsa • al sugo

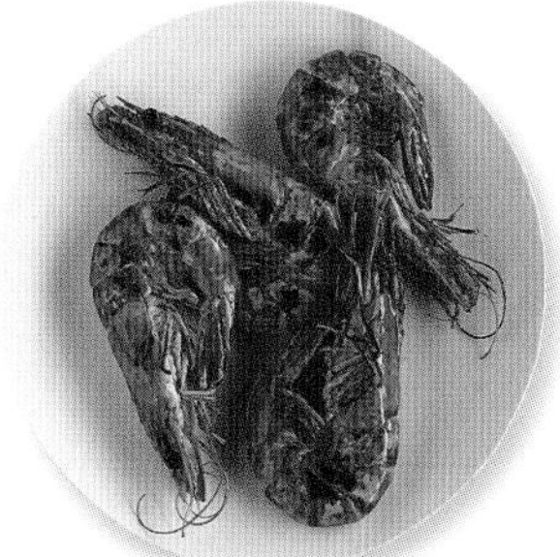

grilled • grillé • gegrillt • a la plancha • alla griglia

marinated • mariné • mariniert • adobado • marinato

poached • poché • pochiert • escalfado • affogato

mashed • en purée • püriert • hecho puré • schiacciato

baked • cuit • gebacken • al horno • cotto al forno

pan fried • sauté • kurzgebraten • frito con poco aceite • fritto in padella

fried • frit • gebraten • frito • fritto

pickled • macéré • eingelegt • en vinagre • sottaceto

smoked • fumé • geräuchert • ahumado • affumicato

deep fried • frit • frittiert • frito con mucho aceite • fritto in olio abbondante

in syrup • au sirop • in Saft • en almíbar • allo sciroppo

dressed • assaisonné • angemacht • sazonado • condito

steamed • cuit à la vapeur • gedämpft • al vapor • al vapore

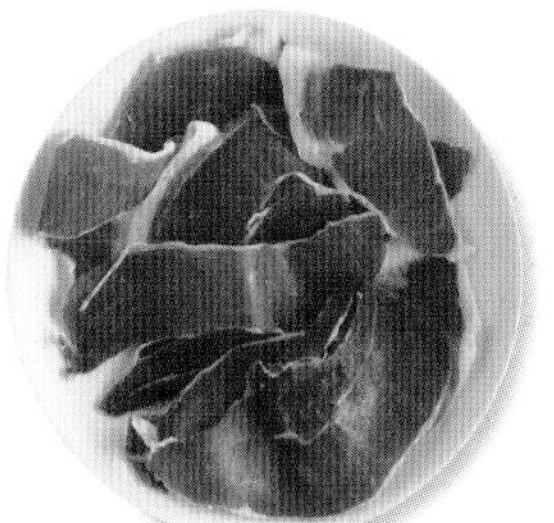

cured • séché • getrocknet • curado • stagionato

study
l’étude
das Lernen
el estudio
lo studio

school • l'école • die Schule • la escuela • la scuola

chalkboard
le tableau
die Tafel
el pizarrón
la lavagna

teacher
l'institutrice
die Lehrerin
la maestra
l'insegnante

pupil
l'élève
der Schüler
el alumno
l'alunno

desk
le pupitre
das Pult
el pupitre
il banco

chalk
la craie
die Kreide
el gis
il gesso

classroom • la salle de classe • das Klassenzimmer • el salón • l'aula

book bag
le cartable
die Schultasche
la mochila
la cartella

schoolgirl • l'écolière • das Schulmädchen • la colegiala • la scolara

schoolboy • l'écolier • der Schuljunge • el colegial • lo scolaro

history l'histoire die Geschichte la historia la storia	art l'art die Kunst el arte l'arte	physics la physique die Physik la física la fisica
geography la géographie die Erdkunde la geografía la geografia	music la musique die Musik la música la musica	chemistry la chimie die Chemie la química la chimica
literature la littérature die Literatur la literatura la letteratura	math les mathématiques die Mathematik las matemáticas la matematica	biology la biologie die Biologie la biología la biologia
languages les langues die Sprachen los idiomas le lingue	science les sciences die Naturwissenschaft la ciencia la scienza	physical education l'éducation physique der Sport la educación física l'educazione fisica

activities • les activités • die Aktivitäten • las actividades • le attività

read *(v)* • lire • lesen • leer • leggere

write *(v)* • écrire • schreiben • escribir • scrivere

spell *(v)* • épeler • buchstabieren • deletrear • scandire

draw *(v)* • dessiner • zeichnen • dibujar • disegnare

digital projector • le projecteur numérique • der Digitalprojektor • el proyector digital • il proiettore digitale

nib
la plume
die Feder
la punta
la punta

pen • le stylo • der Füller • la pluma • la penna

colored pencil
le crayon de couleur
der Buntstift
el color
la matita colorata

pencil • le crayon • der Bleistift • el lápiz • la matita

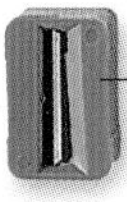

pencil sharpener
le taille-crayon
der Spitzer
el sacapuntas
il temperamatite

eraser • la gomme • der Radiergummi • la goma • la gomma

notebook • le cahier • das Heft • el cuaderno • il quaderno

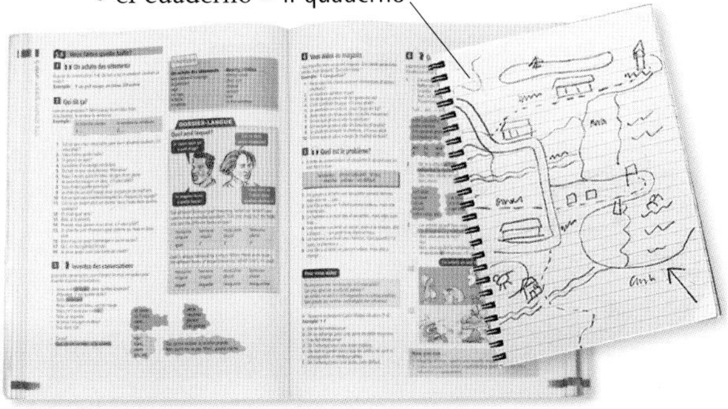

textbook • le livre • das Schulbuch • el libro de texto • il libro di testo

pencil case • la trousse • das Federmäppchen • el estuche • l'astuccio

ruler • la règle • das Lineal • la regla • il righello

question *(v)* • questionner • fragen • preguntar • domandare

answer *(v)* • répondre • antworten • contestar • rispondere

discuss *(v)* • discuter • diskutieren • discutir • discutere

learn *(v)* • apprendre • lernen • aprender • imparare

principal le directeur der Schulleiter el director il preside	answer la réponse die Antwort la respuesta la risposta	grade la note die Note la calificación il livello
class la leçon die Stunde la lección la lezione	homework les devoirs die Hausaufgabe la tarea i compiti	year la classe die Klasse el año la classe
take notes *(v)* prendre des notes Notizen machen tomar apuntes prendere appunti	essay la rédaction der Aufsatz la redacción il tema	dictionary le dictionnaire das Wörterbuch el diccionario il dizionario
question la question die Frage la pregunta la domanda	examination l'examen die Prüfung el examen l'esame	encyclopedia l'encyclopédie das Lexikon la enciclopedia l'enciclopedia

math • les mathématiques • die Mathematik • las matemáticas • la matematica

shapes • les formes • die Formen • las formas • le forme

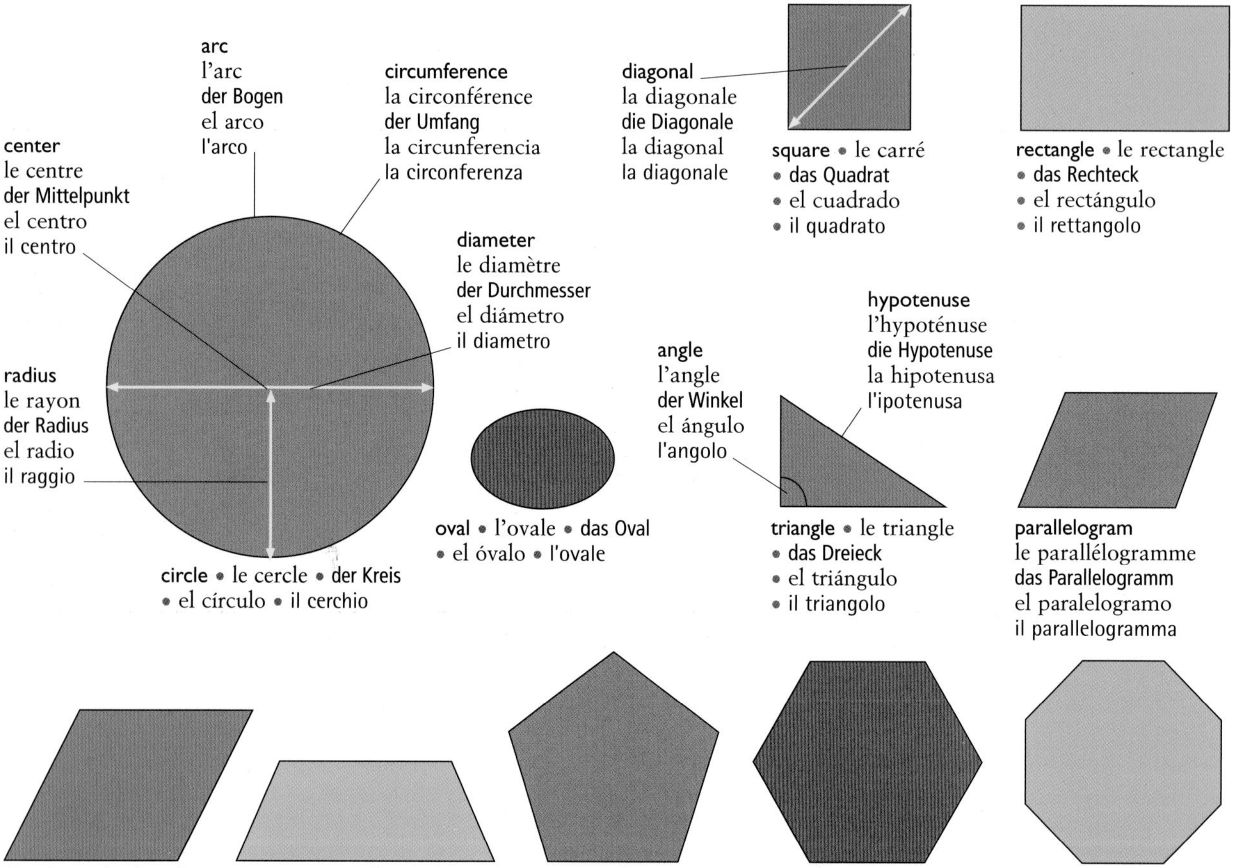

circle • le cercle • der Kreis • el círculo • il cerchio

oval • l'ovale • das Oval • el óvalo • l'ovale

square • le carré • das Quadrat • el cuadrado • il quadrato

rectangle • le rectangle • das Rechteck • el rectángulo • il rettangolo

triangle • le triangle • das Dreieck • el triángulo • il triangolo

parallelogram
le parallélogramme
das Parallelogramm
el paralelogramo
il parallelogramma

rhombus • le rhombe • der Rhombus • el rombo • il rombo

trapezium • le trapèze • das Trapez • el trapecio • il trapezio

pentagon • le pentagone • das Fünfeck • el pentágono • il pentagono

hexagon • l'hexagone • das Sechseck • el hexágono • l'esagono

octagon • l'octogone • das Achteck • el octágono • l'ottagono

solids • les solides • die Körper • los cuerpos geométricos • i solidi

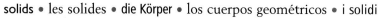

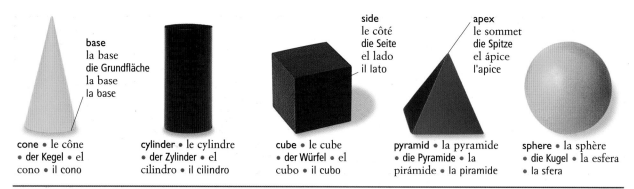

cone • le cône • der Kegel • el cono • il cono

cylinder • le cylindre • der Zylinder • el cilindro • il cilindro

cube • le cube • der Würfel • el cubo • il cubo

pyramid • la pyramide • die Pyramide • la pirámide • la piramide

sphere • la sphère • die Kugel • la esfera • la sfera

lines • les lignes • die Linien • las líneas • le linee

straight • droit • gerade • recto • dritta

parallel • parallèle • parallel • paralelo • parallela

perpendicular • perpendiculaire • senkrecht • perpendicular • perpendicolare

curved • courbe • gekrümmt • curvo • curva

measurements • les mesures • die Maße • las medidas • le misure

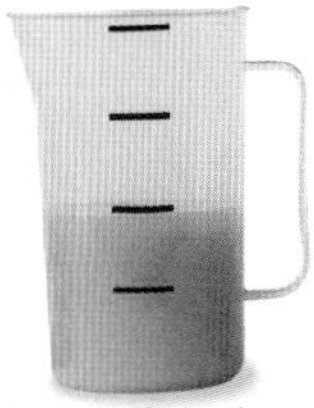

volume • le volume • das Volumen • el volumen • il volume

numerator
le numérateur
der Zähler
el numerador
il numeratore

denominator
le dénominateur
der Nenner
el denominador
il denominatore

fraction • la fraction • der Bruch • la fracción • la frazione

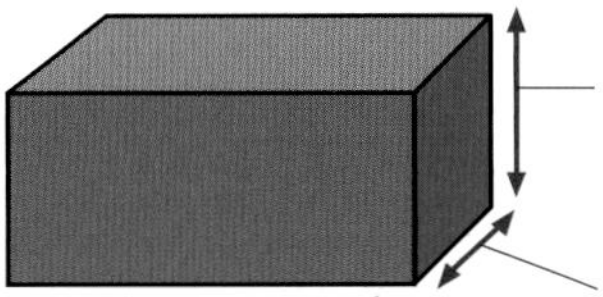

height
la hauteur
die Höhe
la altura
l'altezza

depth
la profondeur
die Tiefe
la profundidad
la profondità

dimensions • les dimensions • die Abmessungen • las dimensiones • le dimensioni

width
la largeur
die Breite
la anchura
la larghezza

length
la longueur
die Länge
la longitud
la lunghezza

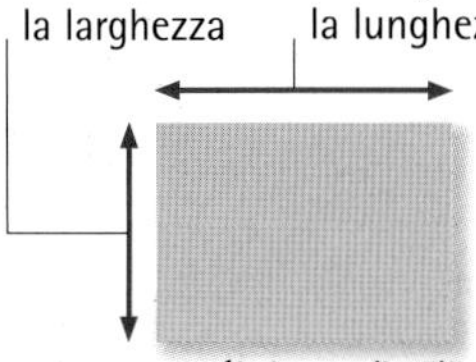

area • l'aire • die Fläche • el área • la superficie

equipment • l'équipement • die Ausrüstung • los materiales • l'attrezzatura

set square • l'équerre • das Zeichendreieck • la escuadra • la squadra

protractor • le rapporteur • der Winkelmesser • el transportador • il goniometro

ruler • la règle • das Lineal • la regla • il righello

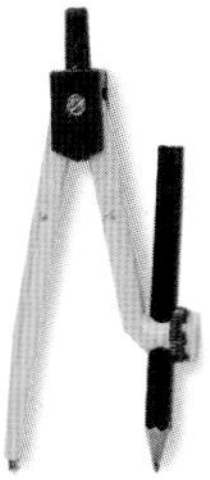

compass • le compas • der Zirkel • el compás • il compasso

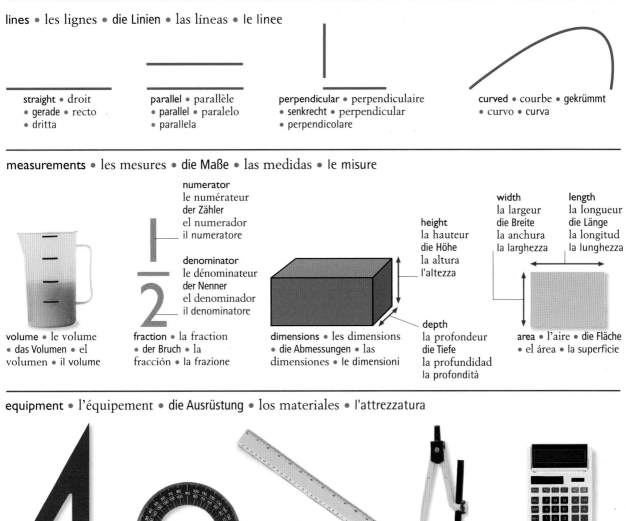

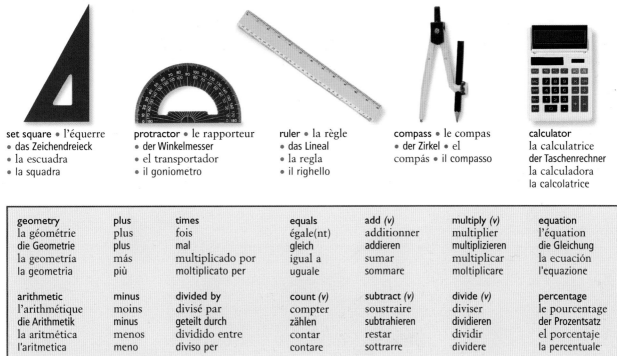

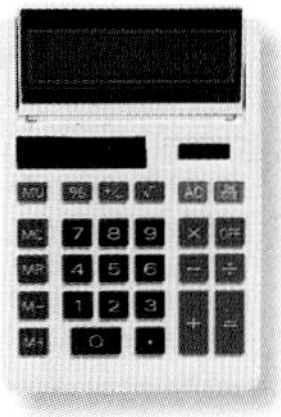

calculator
la calculatrice
der Taschenrechner
la calculadora
la calcolatrice

geometry la géométrie die Geometrie la geometría la geometria	**plus** plus plus más più	**times** fois mal multiplicado por moltiplicato per	**equals** égale(nt) gleich igual a uguale	**add** *(v)* additionner addieren sumar sommare	**multiply** *(v)* multiplier multiplizieren multiplicar moltiplicare	**equation** l'équation die Gleichung la ecuación l'equazione
arithmetic l'arithmétique die Arithmetik la aritmética l'aritmetica	**minus** moins minus menos meno	**divided by** divisé par geteilt durch dividido entre diviso per	**count** *(v)* compter zählen contar contare	**subtract** *(v)* soustraire subtrahieren restar sottrarre	**divide** *(v)* diviser dividieren dividir dividere	**percentage** le pourcentage der Prozentsatz el porcentaje la percentuale

science • la science • die Wissenschaft • las ciencias • la scienza

laboratory • le laboratoire • das Labor • el laboratorio • il laboratorio

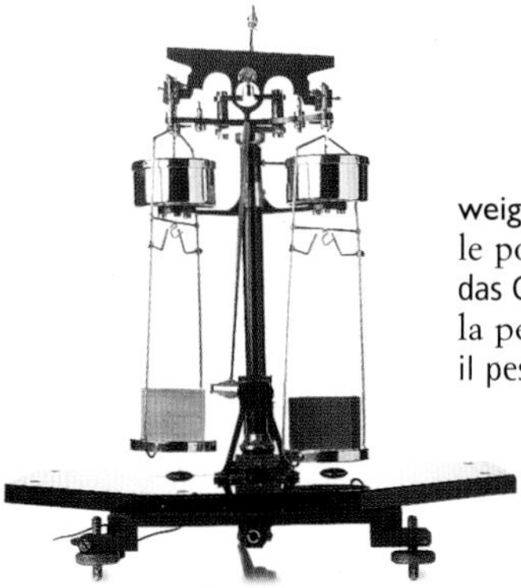

scales • la balance • die Laborwaage • la báscula • la bilancia

weight
le poids
das Gewicht
la pesa
il peso

spring balance • la balance à ressort • die Federwaage • la balanza de muelle • la bilancia a molla

crucible • le creuset • der Tiegel • el crisol • il crogiolo

bunsen burner
le bec Bunsen
der Bunsenbrenner
el mechero Bunsen
il becco Bunsen

tripod • le trépied • der Dreifuß • el trípode • il treppiede

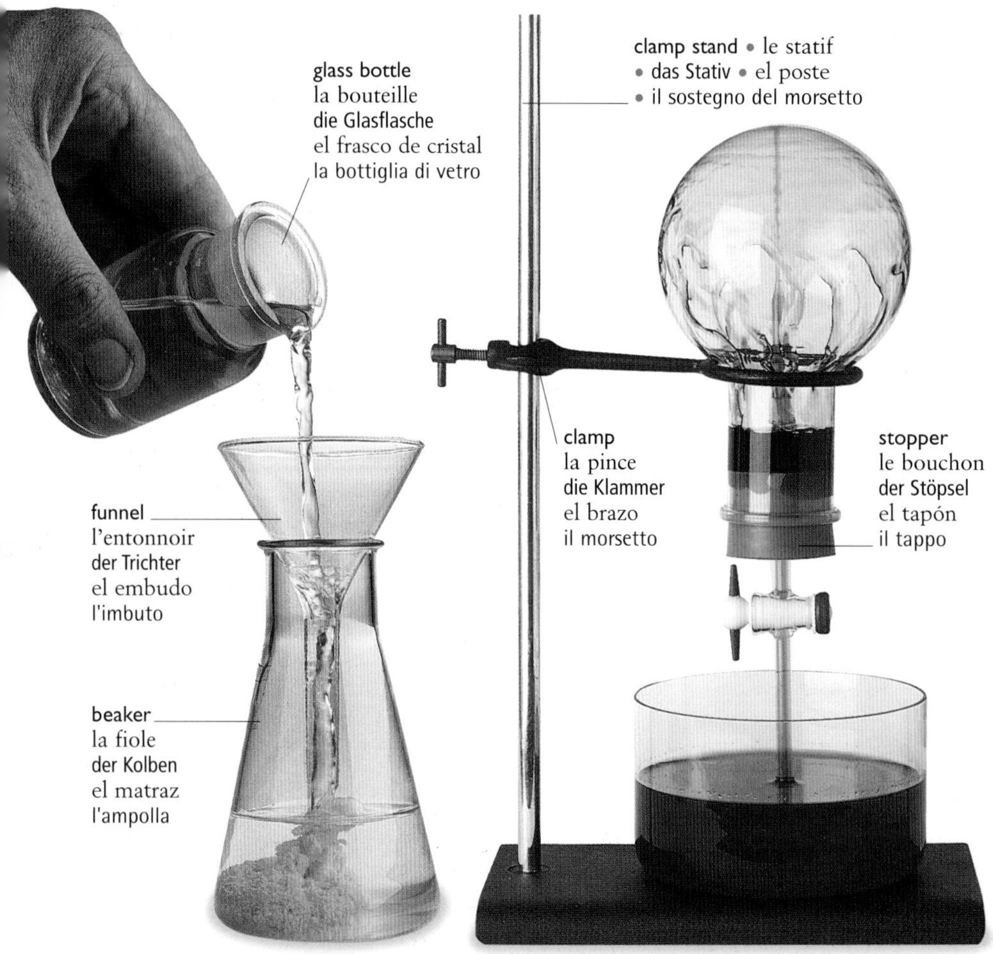

glass bottle
la bouteille
die Glasflasche
el frasco de cristal
la bottiglia di vetro

clamp stand • le statif • das Stativ • el poste • il sostegno del morsetto

funnel
l'entonnoir
der Trichter
el embudo
l'imbuto

clamp
la pince
die Klammer
el brazo
il morsetto

stopper
le bouchon
der Stöpsel
el tapón
il tappo

beaker
la fiole
der Kolben
el matraz
l'ampolla

experiment • l'expérience • der Versuch • el experimento • l'esperimento

test tube
l'éprouvette
das Reagenzglas
el tubo de ensayo
la provetta

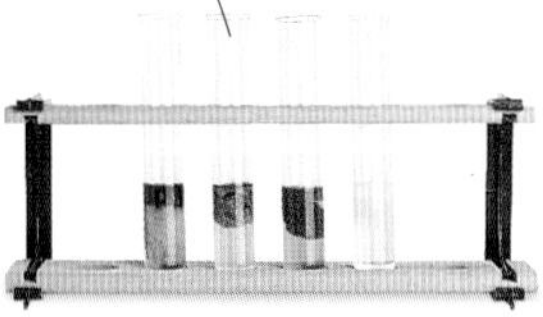

rack • le support • das Gestell • el portatubos • la rastrelliera

timer • le chronomètre • der Zeitmesser • el cronómetro • il cronometro

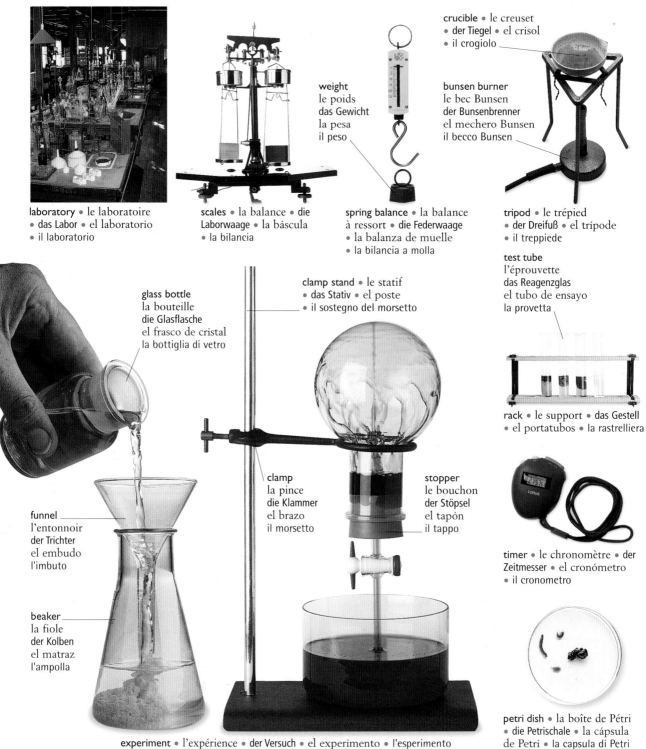

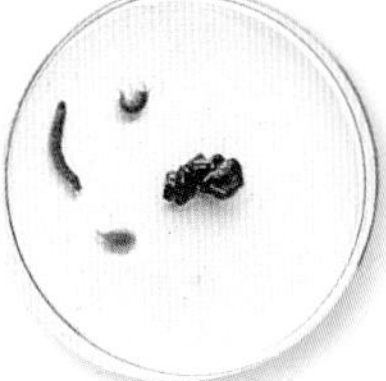

petri dish • la boîte de Pétri • die Petrischale • la cápsula de Petri • la capsula di Petri

thermometer • le thermomètre • das Thermometer • el termómetro • il termometro

syringe • la seringue • die Spritze • la jeringa • la siringa

tweezers • la pince fine • die Pinzette • las pinzas • le pinzette

scalpel • le scalpel • das Skalpell • el bisturí • il bisturi

dropper • le compte-gouttes • der Tropfer • el gotero • il contagocce

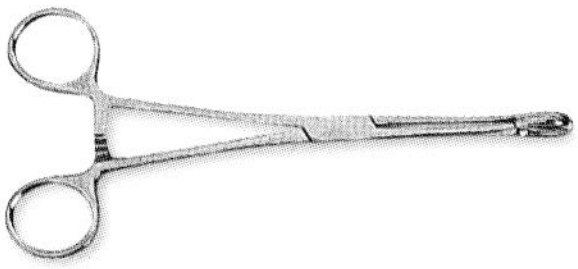

forceps • le forceps • die Zange • los fórceps • il forcipe

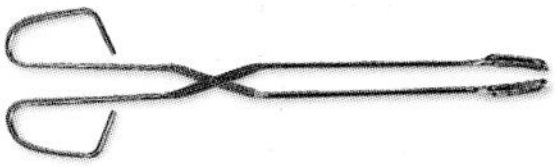

tongs • la pince • die Greifzange • las tenazas • le tenaglie

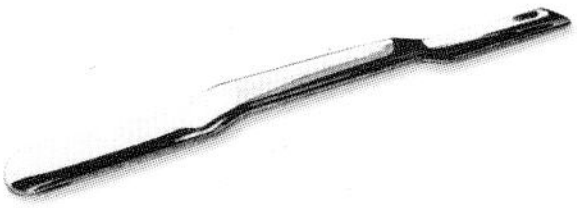

spatula • la spatule • der Spatel • la espátula • la spatola

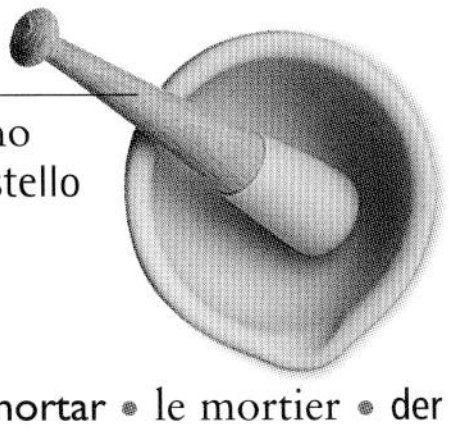

pestle • le pilon • die Keule • la mano de mortero • il pestello

mortar • le mortier • der Mörser • el mortero • il mortaio

filter paper • le papier filtre • das Filterpapier • el filtro de papel • il filtro di carta

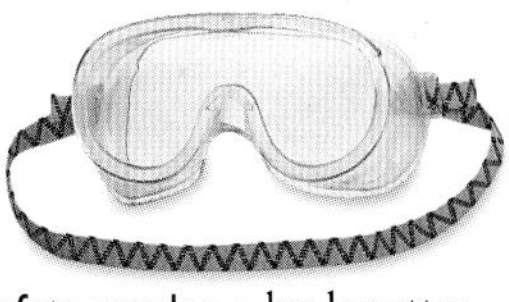

safety goggles • les lunettes de protection • die Schutzbrille • las gafas protectoras • gli occhiali protettivi

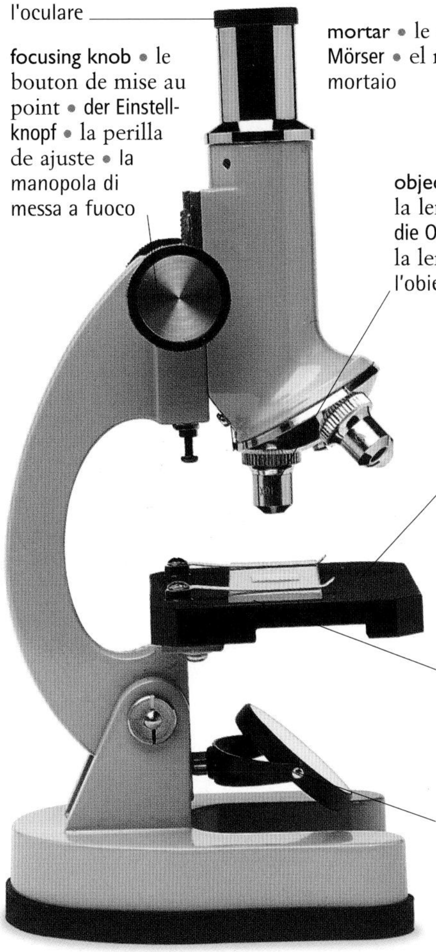

eyepiece • l'oculaire das Okular • el ocular l'oculare

focusing knob • le bouton de mise au point • der Einstellknopf • la perilla de ajuste • la manopola di messa a fuoco

objective lens la lentille de l'objectif die Objektivlinse la lente del objectivo l'obiettivo

stage la platine der Tisch la platina il ripiano

slide le porte-objet der Objektträger el portaobjetos la lastrina

mirror le miroir der Spiegel el espejo lo specchio

microscope • le microscope • das Mikroskop • el microscopio • il microscopio

pipette • la pipette • die Pipette • la pipeta • la pipetta

glass rod la tige de verre das Glasstäbchen la varilla de cristal la bacchetta di vetro

beaker • le bécher • das Becherglas • el vaso de precipitados • il becher

magnet • l'aimant • der Magnet • el imán • la calamita

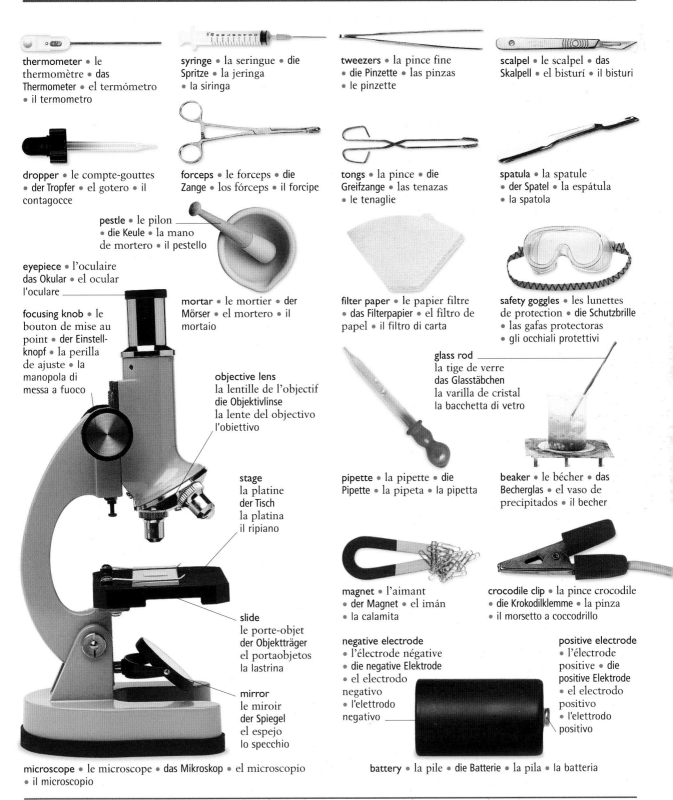

crocodile clip • la pince crocodile • die Krokodilklemme • la pinza • il morsetto a coccodrillo

negative electrode • l'électrode négative • die negative Elektrode • el electrodo negativo • l'elettrodo negativo

positive electrode • l'électrode positive • die positive Elektrode • el electrodo positivo • l'elettrodo positivo

battery • la pile • die Batterie • la pila • la batteria

college • l'enseignement supérieur • die Hochschule • la enseñanza superior • l'università

admissions office
le secrétariat
das Sekretariat
la secretaría
l'ufficio iscrizioni

dining room
• le restaurant universitaire
• die Mensa
• el comedor
• il refettorio

health center
• le service de santé • die Gesundheitsfürsorge
• el centro de salud • l'ambulatorio

playing field
• le terrain de sport • der Sportplatz
• el campo deportivo • il campo sportivo

residence hall
• la résidence universitaire
• das Studentenheim
• la residencia estudiantil
• la casa dello studente

campus • le campus • der Campus • el campus • il campus

librarian
la bibliothécaire
die Bibliothekarin
la bibliotecaria
la bibliotecaria

checkout desk • le service de prêt • die Ausleihe • el mostrador de préstamos • il banco prestiti

bookshelf
les rayons
das Bücherregal
el librero
lo scaffale

periodical
le périodique
das Periodikum
el periódico
il periodico

journal
la revue
die Zeitschrift
la revista
la rivista

library • la bibliothèque • die Bibliothek • la biblioteca • la biblioteca

library card
la carte de lecteur
der Leserausweis
la credencial
il tesserino

reading room
la salle de lecture
der Lesesaal
la sala de lecturas
la sala di lettura

reading list
les ouvrages recommandés
die Literaturliste
la lista de lecturas
la lista dei libri

due date
la date de retour
das Rückgabedatum
la fecha de devolución
la data di restituzione

inquiries
les renseignements
die Auskunft
la información
il banco informazioni

borrow *(v)*
emprunter
ausleihen
coger prestado
prendere in prestito

reserve *(v)*
réserver
vorbestellen
reservar
prenotare

loan
le prêt
die Ausleihe
el préstamo
il prestito

renew *(v)*
renouveler
verlängern
renovar
rinnovare

book
le livre
das Buch
el libro
il libro

title
le titre
der Titel
el título
il titolo

aisle
le couloir
der Gang
el pasillo
la corsia

undergraduate • l'étudiant • der Student • el estudiante • lo studente universitario

professor • l'assistant • der Dozent • el profesor • il docente

lecture hall • la salle de cours • der Hörsaal • el auditorio • l'aula

graduate • la licenciée • die Graduierte • la licenciada • la laureata

gown • la robe • die Robe • la toga • la toga

graduation ceremony • la cérémonie de la remise des diplômes • die Graduierungsfeier • la ceremonia de graduación • la consegna delle lauree

schools • les écoles • die Fachhochschulen • las escuelas • le scuole

model
le modèle
das Modell
la modelo
la modella

art school • l'école des beaux arts • die Kunsthochschule • la escuela de Bellas Artes • la scuola d'arte

music school • le Conservatoire • die Musikhochschule • el conservatorio • il conservatorio

dance school • l'école de danse • die Tanzakademie • la academia de danza • l'accademia di danza

scholarship
la bourse
das Stipendium
la beca
la borsa di studio

diploma
le diplôme
das Diplom
el diploma
il diploma

degree
la licence
der akademische Grad
la carrera
la laurea

postgraduate
de troisième cycle
postgraduiert
posgrado
di perfezionamento

research
la recherche
die Forschung
la investigación
la ricerca

master's degree
la maîtrise
der Magister
la mestría
il master

doctorate
le doctorat
die Promotion
el doctorado
il dottorato

thesis
la thèse
die Dissertation
la tesis
la tesi

dissertation
la dissertation
die Examensarbeit
la tesina
la dissertazione

department
l'U.F.R.
der Fachbereich
el departamento
il dipartimento

law
le droit
die Rechtswissenschaft
el derecho
il diritto

engineering
les études d'ingénieur
der Maschinenbau
la ingeniería
l'ingegneria

medicine
la medecine
die Medizin
la medicina
la medicina

zoology
la zoologie
die Zoologie
la zoología
la zoologia

physics
la physique
die Physik
la física
la fisica

philosophy
la philosophie
die Philosophie
la filosofía
la filosofia

economics
les sciences économiques
die Wirtschaftswissenschaft
las ciencias económicas
l'economia

political science
les sciences politiques
die Politologie
la política
la politica

literature
la littérature
die Literatur
la literatura
la letteratura

art history
l'histoire d'art
die Kunstgeschichte
la historia del arte
la storia dell'arte

work
le travail
die Arbeit
el trabajo
il lavoro

office 1 • le bureau 1 • das Büro 1 • la oficina 1 • l'ufficio 1

office • le bureau • das Büro • la oficina • l'ufficio

in-tray
la corbeille arrivée
die Ablage für Eingänge
la bandeja de entrada
il vassoio in arrivo

monitor
le moniteur
der Bildschirm
la pantalla
il monitor

desktop organizer
le porte-crayons
der Stifthalter
el portaplumas
il portapenne

notebook
le carnet
das Notizbuch
el cuaderno
il blocco

out-tray
la corbeille départ
die Ablage für Ausgänge
la bandeja de salida
il vassoio in partenza

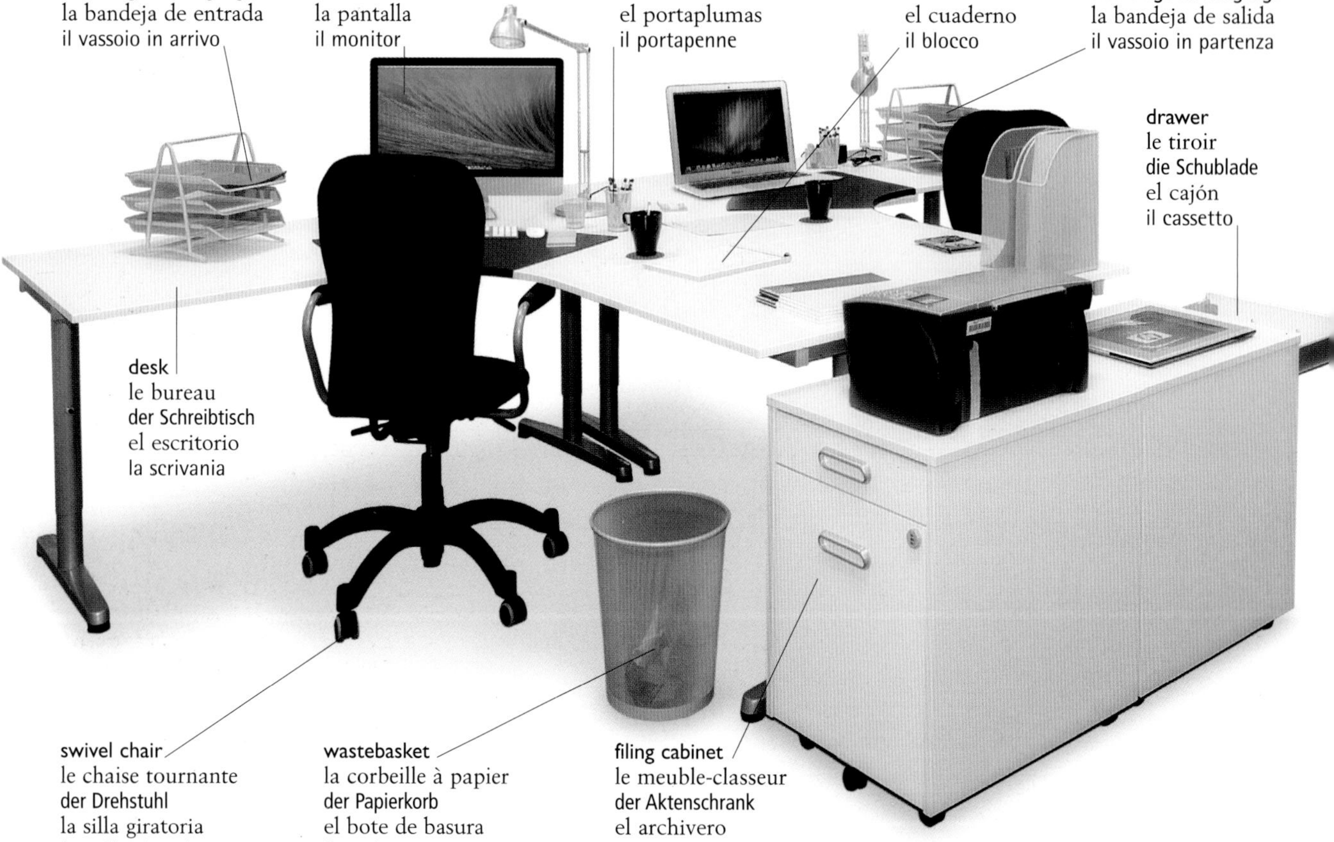

drawer
le tiroir
die Schublade
el cajón
il cassetto

desk
le bureau
der Schreibtisch
el escritorio
la scrivania

swivel chair
le chaise tournante
der Drehstuhl
la silla giratoria
la sedia girevole

wastebasket
la corbeille à papier
der Papierkorb
el bote de basura
il cestino

filing cabinet
le meuble-classeur
der Aktenschrank
el archivero
lo schedario

office equipment • l'équipement de bureau • die Büroausstattung • el equipo de oficina • l'apparecchiature da ufficio

paper tray • le magasin à papier • der Papierbehälter • la bandeja para el papel • la contenitore per la carta

printer • l'imprimante • der Drucker • la impresora • la stampante

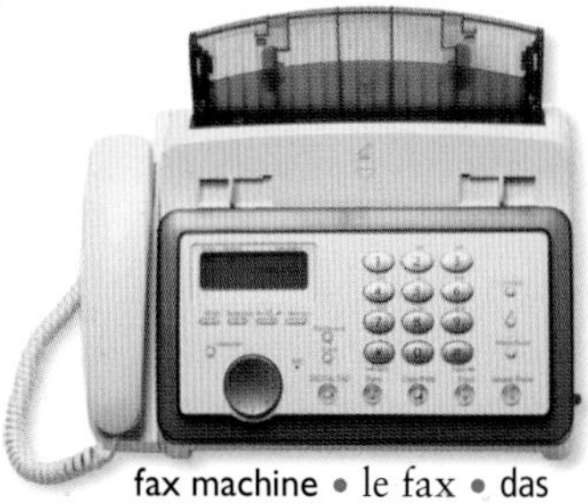

fax machine • le fax • das Faxgerät • el fax • il fax

print *(v)*
imprimer
drucken
imprimir
stampare

enlarge *(v)*
agrandir
vergrößern
ampliar
ingrandire

copy *(v)*
photocopier
kopieren
fotocopiar
copiare

reduce *(v)*
réduire
verkleinern
reducir
ridurre

I need to make some copies.
J'ai besoin de faire des photocopies.
Ich möchte fotokopieren.
Necesito sacar unas copias.
Devo fare delle copie.

office supplies • les fournitures de bureau • der Bürobedarf • la papelería • gli articoli di cancelleria

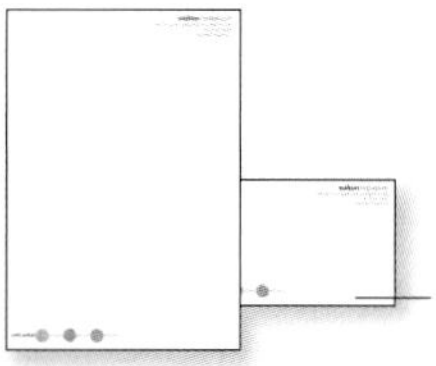

compliments slip • la fiche compliments • der Empfehlungszettel • la tarjeta membretada • il foglietto di omaggio

letterhead • l'en-tête • der Geschäftsbogen • el membrete • la carta intestata

envelope • l'enveloppe • der Briefumschlag • el sobre • la busta

box file
le dossier-classeur
der Aktenordner
la caja archivador
la scatola d'archivio

clipboard • le clipboard • das Klemmbrett • la tabla con portapapeles • il portablocco con fermaglio

notepad • le bloc-notes • der Notizblock • la libreta • il blocco per appunti

tab • l'étiquette • der Kartenreiter • el rótulo • l'etichetta

hanging file • le dossier suspendu • der Hängeordner • el colgante • la cartella sospesa

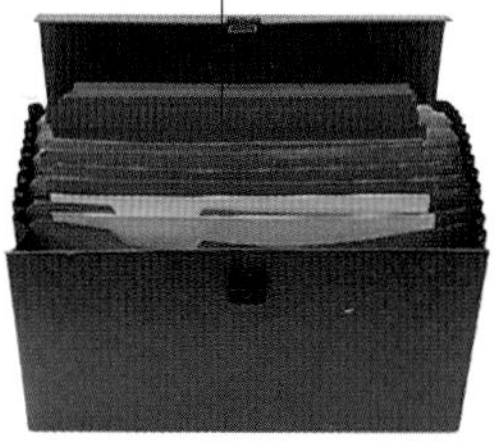

divider
la fiche intercalaire
der Teiler
el divisor
il divisore

accordion file • le porte-dossiers • der Fächerordner • la carpeta de acordeón • il portacarte a fisarmonica

binder file
le classeur à levier
der Leitz-Ordner
la carpeta de argollas
il raccoglitore a leva

personal organizer • l'agenda • der Terminkalender • la agenda • l'agenda

staples
les agrafes
die Klammern
las grapas
i punti

stapler • l'agrafeuse • der Hefter • la engrapadora • la cucitrice

adhesive tape • le scotch • der Tesafilm • la cinta scotch • il nastro adesivo

tape dispenser • le dévidoir de scotch • der Tesafilmhalter • el portacinta • il dispenser

hole punch • le perforateur • der Locher • la perforadora • il perforatore

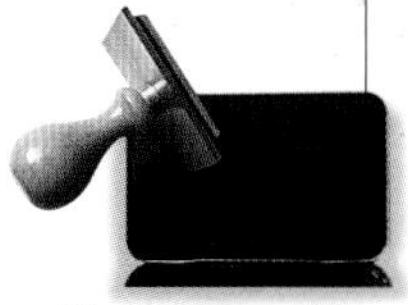

ink pad
le tampon encreur
das Stempelkissen
el cojín de la tinta
il tampone di inchiostro

rubber stamp • le cachet • der Stempel • el sello • il timbro umido

rubber band • l'élastique • das Gummiband • la liga • l'elastico

bulldog clip • la pince à dessin • die Papierklammer • la pinza • la molletta

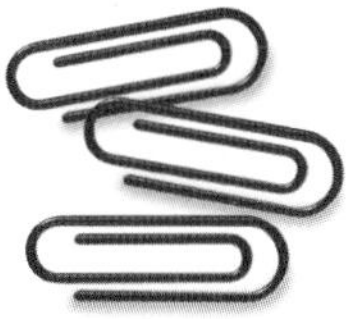

paper clip • le trombone • die Büroklammer • el clip • la grappetta

thumbtack
la punaise
der Reißnagel
la chinche
la puntina

bulletin board • le panneau d'affichage • die Pinnward • el corcho • il tabellone

office 2 • le bureau 2 • das Büro 2 • la oficina 2 • l'ufficio 2

flipchart
le tableau à feuilles mobiles
das Flipchart
el pizarrón
la lavagna a fogli

minutes
le compte rendu
das Protokoll
la minuta
il verbale

easel
le chevalet
das Gestell
el caballete
il cavalletto

report
le rapport
der Bericht
el reporte
la relazione

manager
le directeur
der Manager
el gerente
il direttore

proposal
la proposition
das Angebot
la propuesta
la proposta

executive
le cadre
der leitende Angestellte
el ejecutivo
il dirigente

meeting • le réunion • die Sitzung • la junta • la riunione

meeting room la salle de conférence der Sitzungsraum la sala de juntas la sala da riunione	**attend** *(v)* assister à teilnehmen asistir partecipare
agenda l'ordre du jour die Tagesordnung el orden del día l'ordine del giorno	**chair** *(v)* présider den Vorsitz führen presidir presiedere

What time is the meeting?
La conférence est à quelle heure?
Um wie viel Uhr ist die Sitzung?
¿A qué hora es la junta?
A che ora è la riunione?

What are your office hours?
Quelles sont vos heures de bureau?
Was sind Ihre Geschäftszeiten?
¿Cuál es su horario de oficina?
Qual è il vostro orario di lavoro?

speaker
le conférencier
der Sprecher
el orador
il relatore

presentation • la présentation • die Präsentation • la presentación • la presentazione

business • les affaires • das Geschäft • los negocios • gli affari

business lunch • le déjeuner d'affaires • das Arbeitsessen • la comida de negocios • il pranzo di lavoro

businessman
l'homme d'affaires
der Geschäftsmann
el hombre de negocios
l'uomo d'affari

businesswoman
la femme d'affaires
die Geschäftsfrau
la mujer de negocios
la donna d'affari

business trip • le voyage d'affaires • die Geschäftsreise • el viaje de negocios • il viaggio d'affari

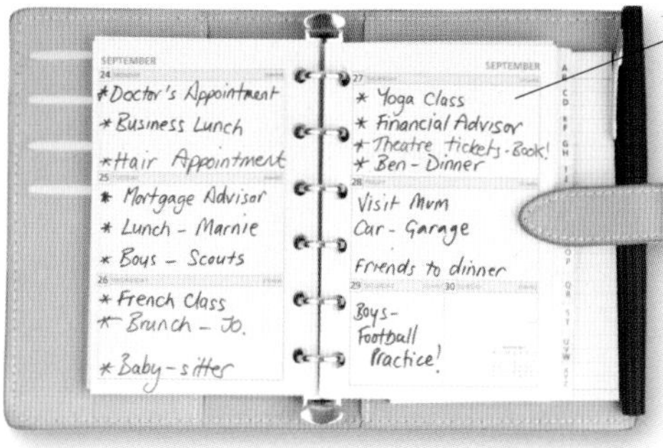

appointment
le rendez-vous
der Termin
la cita
l'appuntamento

date book • l'agenda • der Terminkalender • la agenda • l'agenda

client • le client • der Kunde • el cliente • il cliente

managing director • le directeur général • der Generaldirektor • el director general • l'amministratore delegato

business deal • le contrat • das Geschäftsabkommen • el trato • l'accordo di affari

company
la société
die Firma
la empresa
la società

head office
le siège social
die Zentrale
la oficina central
la sede centrale

branch
la succursale
die Zweigstelle
la sucursal
la succursale

staff
le personnel
das Personal
el personal
il personale

payroll
le livre de paie
die Lohnliste
la nómina
il libro paga

salary
le salaire
das Gehalt
el sueldo
lo stipendio

accounting department
la comptabilité
die Buchhaltung
el departamento de contabilidad
l'ufficio contabilità

marketing department
le service marketing
die Marketingabteilung
el departamento de márketing
l'ufficio marketing

sales department
le service des ventes
die Verkaufsabteilung
el departamento de ventas
l'ufficio vendite

legal department
le service du contentieux
die Rechtsabteilung
el departamento legal
l'ufficio legale

customer service department
le service après-vente
die Kundendienstabteilung
el departamento de atención al cliente
l'ufficio di assistenza al cliente

human resources department
le service de ressources humaines
die Personalabteilung
el departamento de recursos humanos
l'ufficio del personale

computer • l'ordinateur • der Computer • la computadora • il computer

printer
l'imprimante
der Drucker
la impresora
la stampante

scanner
le scanneur
der Scanner
el escáner
lo scanner

screen
l'écran
der Bildschirm
la pantalla
lo schermo

laptop • le portable • der Laptop • el ordenador portátil • il computer portatile

speaker • le haut-parleur • der Lautsprecher • la bocina • l'altoparlante

key
la touche
die Taste
la tecla
il tasto

keyboard • le clavier • die Tastatur • el teclado • la tastiera

mouse • la souris • die Maus • el ratón • il mouse

hardware • le matériel • die Hardware • el hardware • l'hardware

memory stick • la clé USB • der Memorystick • la llave de memoria • la chiavetta USB

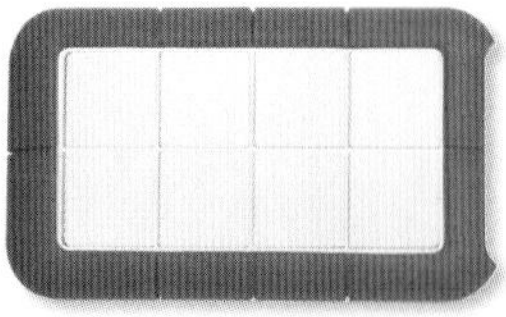

external hard drive
le disque dur externe
die Externe Festplatte
el disco duro externo
il disco rigido esterno

memory
la mémoire
der Speicher
la memoria
la memoria

RAM
la RAM
das RAM
el RAM
la RAM

bytes
les bytes
die Bytes
los bytes
i byte

system
le système
das System
el sistema
il sistema

software
le logiciel
die Software
el software
il software

application
l'application
die Anwendung
la aplicación
l'applicazione

program
le programme
das Programm
el programa
il programma

network
le réseau
das Netzwerk
la red
la rete

server
le serveur
der Server
el servidor
il server

port
le port
der Port
el puerto
la porta

power cable
le câble électrique
das Stromkabel
el cable de alimentación
il cavo di alimentazione

processor
le processeur
der Prozessor
el precesador
il processare

iPad© • l'iPad • das iPad • el iPad • l'iPad

smartphone • le smartphone • das Smartphone • el teléfono inteligente • lo smartphone

desktop • le bureau • das Desktop • el escritorio • il desktop

file • le fichier • die Datei • el archivo • il file

folder • le dossier • der Ordner • la carpeta • la cartella

trash • la poubelle • der Papierkorb • el basurero • il cestino

menubar
la barre de menus
der Menübalken
la barra del menú
la barra del menu

font • la police • die Schriftart • la fuente • il carattere

icon • l'icône • das Symbol • el icono • l'icona

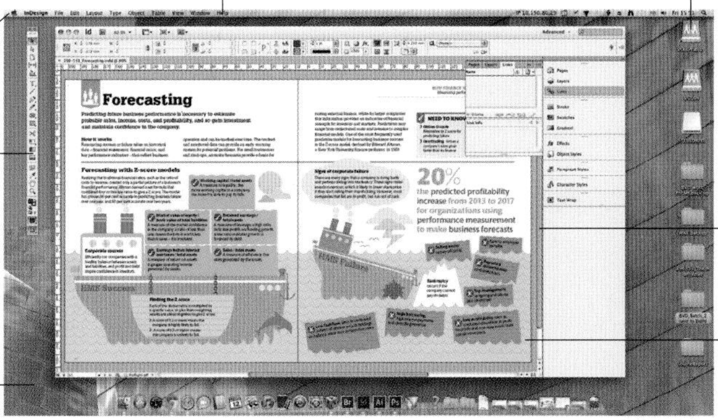

toolbar • la barre d'outils • die Werkzeugleiste • la barra de herramientas • la barra degli strumenti

scrollbar • la barre de défilement • der Scrollbalken • la barra de desplazamiento • la barra di scorrimento

window • la fenêtre • das Fenster • la ventana • la finestra

wallpaper • le papier peint • die Tapete • el fondo • lo sfondo

Internet • l'internet • das Internet • el internet • Internet

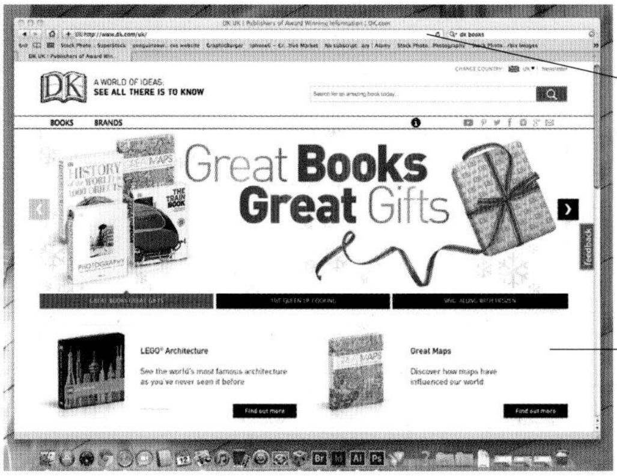

browser
le navigateur
der Browser
el navegador
il browser

website
le site web
die Web-Site
el sitio web
il sito web

browse *(v)* • naviguer • browsen • navegar • navigare

email • le courrier électronique • die E-Mail • el correo electrónico • la posta elettronica

email address • l'adresse e-mail • die E-Mail-Adresse • la dirección electrónico • l'indirizzo e-mail

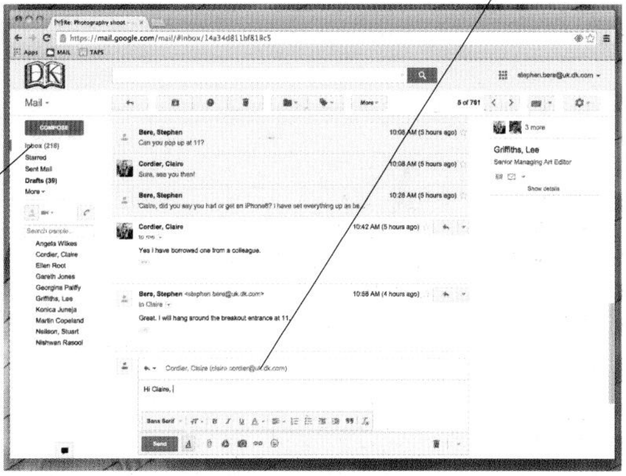

inbox • la boîte de réception • die Inbox • la bandeja de entrada • la posta in arrivo

connect *(v)* connecter verbinden conectar collegare	service provider le fournisseur d'accès der Serviceprovider el proveedor de servicios il fornitore di servizi	log on *(v)* entrer einloggen entrar en el sistema collegarsi	download *(v)* télécharger herunterladen bajar scaricare	send *(v)* envoyer senden enviar spedire	save *(v)* sauvegarder sichern guardar salvare
install *(v)* installer installieren instalar installare	email account le compte de courrier électronique das E-Mail-Konto la cuenta de correo l'account di posta elettronica	online en ligne online en línea in rete	attachment le document attaché der Anhang el documento adjunto l''allegato	receive *(v)* recevoir erhalten recibir ricevere	search *(v)* chercher suchen buscar cercare

media • les médias • die Medien • los medios de comunicación • i mass media

television studio • le studio de télévision • das Fernsehstudio • el estudio de televisión • lo studio televisivo

set
le plateau
die Studioeinrichtung
el plató
il set

host
le présentateur
der Moderator
el presentador
il presentatore

light
l'éclairage
die Beleuchtung
el reflector
la lampada

camera
la caméra
die Kamera
la cámara
la telecamera

camera crane
la grue de caméra
der Kamerakran
la grúa de la cámara
il carrello della telecamera

cameraman
le cameraman
der Kameramann
el camarógrafo
il cameraman

channel la chaîne der Kanal el canal il canale	documentary le documentaire der Dokumentarfilm el documental il documentario	press la presse die Presse la prensa la stampa	soap le feuilleton die Seifenoper la telenovela la telenovela	cartoon le dessin animé der Zeichentrickfilm las caricaturas il cartone animato	live en direct live en directo in diretta
programming la programmation die Programmgestaltung la programación la programmazione	news les nouvelles die Nachrichten el noticiario il telegiornale	television series la série télévisée die Fernsehserie la serie televisiva le serie televisiva	game show le jeu télévisé die Spielshow el concurso il gioco a premi	prerecorded en différé vorher aufgezeichnet pregrabado in differita	broadcast *(v)* émettre senden transmitir trasmettere

interviewer • l'interviewer • **der Interviewer** • el entrevistador • l'intervistatore

reporter • la reporter • **die Reporterin** • la reportera • la cronista

teleprompter • le télésouffleur • **der Teleprompter** • el teleprompter • il gobbo

anchor • la présentatrice • **die Nachrichtensprecherin** • la presentadora de las noticias • la presentatrice

actors • les acteurs • **die Schauspieler** • los actores • gli attori

sound boom • la perche • **der Mikrophongalgen** • el micrófono de aire • la giraffa

clapper board • la claquette • **die Klappe** • la pizarra • il ciac

film set • le décor de cinéma • **das Set** • el plató de rodaje • il set

radio • la radio • das Radio • la radio • la radio

sound technician
l'ingénieur du son
der Tonmeister
el técnico de sonido
il tecnico del suono

mixing desk
le pupitre de mixage
das Mischpult
la consola
il piano di mixaggio

microphone
le microphone
das Mikrophon
el micrófono
il microfono

recording studio • le studio d'enregistrement • **das Tonstudio** • el estudio de grabación • lo studio di registrazione

radio station
la station de radio
die Rundfunkstation
la estación de radio
il canale radiofonico

DJ
le D.J.
der DJ
el DJ
il DJ

broadcast
l'émission
die Sendung
la transmisión
la trasmissione

wavelength
la longueur d'ondes
die Wellenlänge
la longitud de onda
la lunghezza d'onda

long wave
les grandes ondes
die Langwelle
la onda larga
l'onda lunga

analog
analogique
analog
analógica
analogica

digital
numérique
digital
digital
digitale

frequency
la fréquence
die Frequenz
la frecuencia
la frequenza

volume
le volume
die Lautstärke
el volumen
il volume

tune *(v)*
régler
einstellen
sintonizar
sintonizzare

law • le droit • das Recht • el derecho • la legge

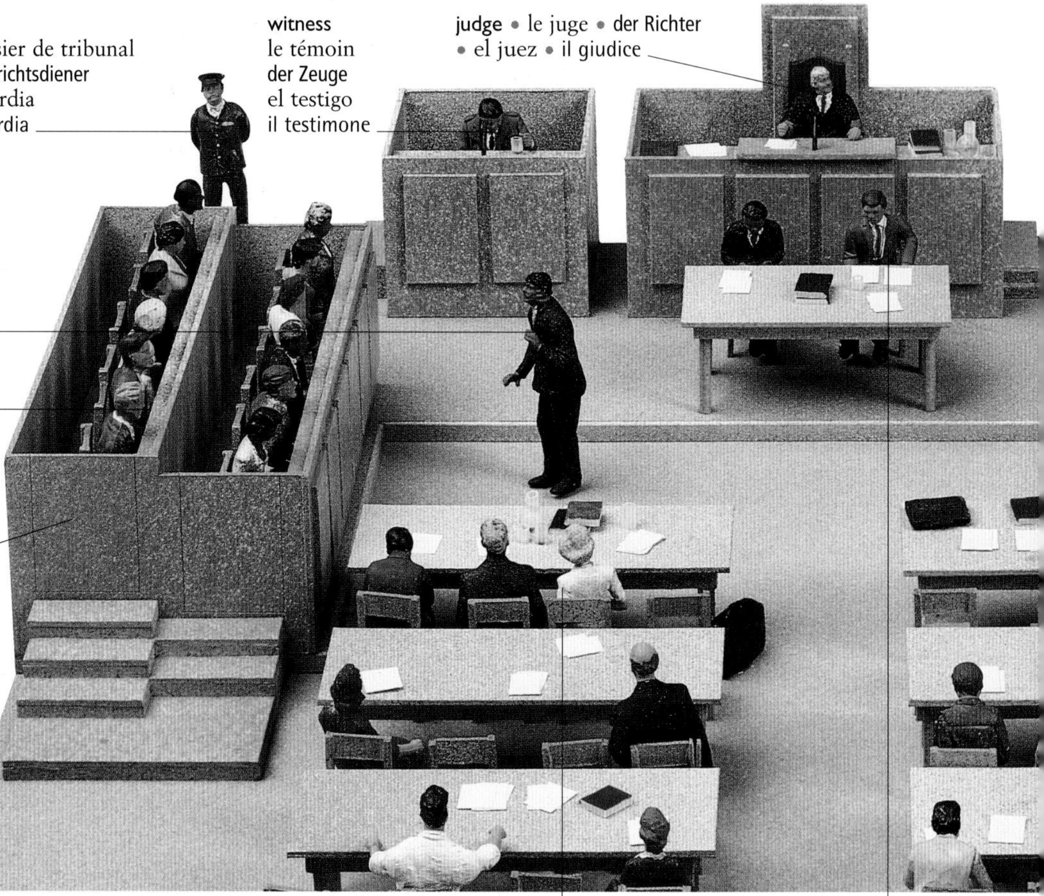

courtroom • la salle de tribunal • der Gerichtssaal • la sala del tribunal • l'aula del tribunale

lawyer's office le cabinet das Anwaltsbüro el bufete lo studio dell'avvocato	summons l'assignation die Vorladung la citación la citazione	writ l'acte judiciaire die Verfügung la orden judicial l'ordine	court case la cause der Rechtsfall el juicio il procedimento
legal advice le conseil juridique die Rechtsberatung la asesoría jurídica la consulenza legale	statement la déposition die Aussage la declaración la dichiarazione	court date la date du procès der Gerichtstermin la fecha del juicio la data di comparizione	charge l'accusation die Anklage el cargo l'imputazione
client le client der Klient el cliente il cliente	warrant le mandat der Haftbefehl la orden judicial il mandato	plea le plaidoyer das Plädoyer cómo se declara el acusado la petizione	accused l'accusé der Angeklagte el acusado l'accusato

court reporter
le sténographe
der Gerichtsstenograf
la taquígrafa
lo stenografo

defense • la défense • die Verteidigung • la defensa • la difesa

defendant • l'accusé • der Angeklagte • el acusado • l'imputato

suspect
le suspect
der Verdächtige
el sospechoso
la persona suspetta

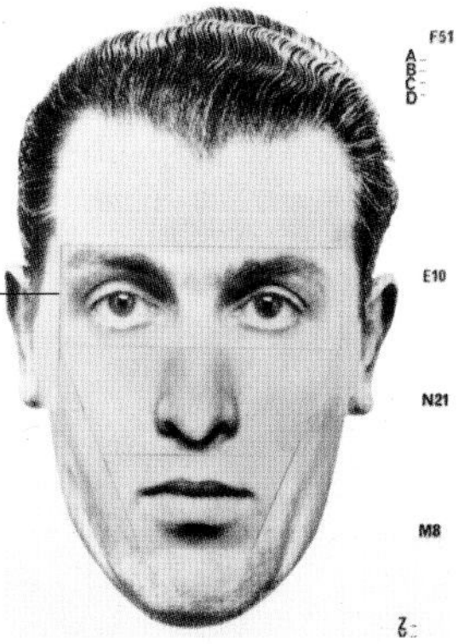

facial composite • le portrait-robot • das Phantombild • el retrato hablado • il fotofit

criminal
le criminel
der Straftäter
el criminal
il criminale

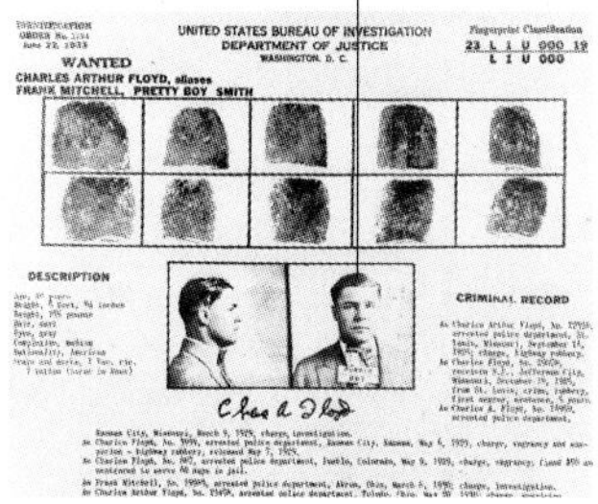

criminal record • le casier judiciare • das Strafregister • los antecedentes • la fedina penale

prison guard • le gardien de prison • der Gefängniswärter • el celador • la guardia carceraria

cell • la cellule • die Gefängniszelle • la celda • la cella

prison • la prison • das Gefängnis • la cárcel • il carcere

evidence la preuve das Beweismittel la evidencia la prova	guilty coupable schuldig culpable colpevole	bail la caution die Kaution la fianza la cauzione	I want to see a lawyer. Je voudrais voir un avocat. Ich möchte mit einem Anwalt sprechen. Quiero ver a un abogado. Voglio vedere un avvocato.
verdict le verdict das Urteil el veredicto il verdetto	acquitted acquitté freigesprochen absuelto assolto	appeal l'appel die Berufung la apelación il ricorso	Where is the courthouse? Où est le palais de justice? Wo ist das Gericht? ¿Dónde está el juzgado? Dov'è il palazzo di giustizia?
innocent innocent unschuldig inocente innocente	sentence la condamnation das Strafmaß la sentencia la sentenza	parole la liberté conditionnelle die Haftentlassung auf Bewährung la libertad condicional la libertà condizionale	Can I post bail? Est-ce que je peux verser la caution? Kann ich die Kaution leisten? ¿Puedo pagar la fianza? Posso versare una cauzione?

farm 1 • la ferme 1 • der Bauernhof 1 • la granja 1 • la fattoria 1

farmer
le fermier
der Bauer
el granjero
l'agricoltore

farmland
les terres cultivées
das Ackerland
las tierras de labranza
il terreno agricolo

farmyard
la cour de ferme
der Hof
el corral
l'aia

outbuilding
la dépendence
das Nebengebäude
el cobertizo
il capanno

farmhouse
la maison d'habitation
das Bauernhaus
la casa de labranza
il casolare

field
le champ
das Feld
el campo
il campo

barn
la grange
die Scheune
el granero
il granaio

vegetable garden
le potager
der Gemüsegarten
el huerto
l'orto

hedge
la haie
die Hecke
el seto
la siepe

gate
la barrière
das Tor
la puerta
il cancello

fence
la clôture
der Zaun
la cerca
il recinto

pasture
le pré
die Weide
el pasto
il pascolo

livestock
les bestiaux
das Vieh
el ganado
il bestiame

cultivator
le cultivateur
der Kultivator
el cultivador
l'aratro

tractor • le tracteur • der Traktor • el tractor • il trattore

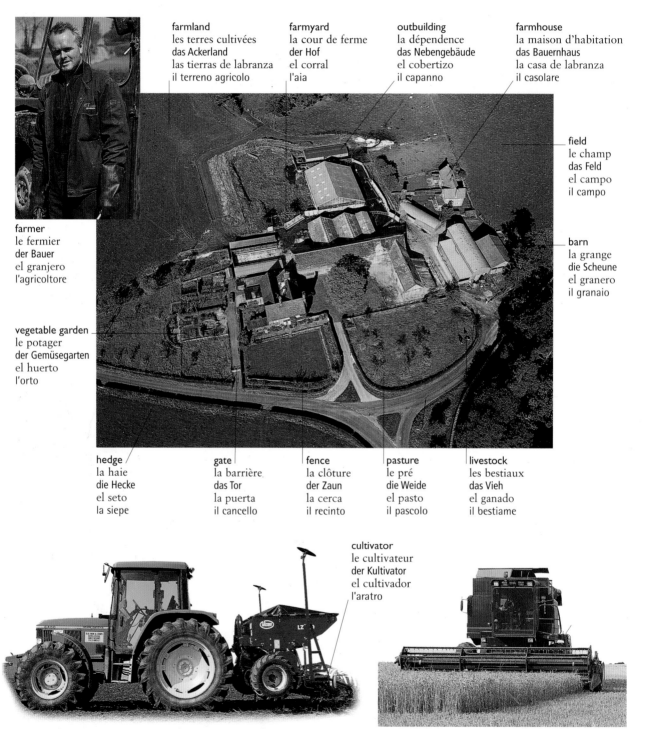

combine • la moissonneuse-batteuse • der Mähdrescher • la cosechadora • la mietitrebbia

types of farms • les exploitations agricoles • die landwirtschaftlichen Betriebe • los tipos de granja • i tipi di fattoria

crop farm • la ferme de culture • der Ackerbaubetrieb • la granja de tierras cultivables • l'azienda agricola

dairy farm • la ferme laitière • der Betrieb für Milchproduktion • la vaquería • il caseificio

sheep farm • la ferme d'élevage de moutons • die Schaffarm • la granja de ganado ovino • l'allevamento di pecore

poultry farm • la ferme d'aviculture • die Hühnerfarm • la granja avícola • l'azienda avicola

pig farm • la ferme d'élevage porcin • die Schweinefarm • la granja de ganado porcino • l'allevamento di maiali

fish farm • le centre de pisciculture • die Fischzucht • el criadero de peces • il vivaio ittico

fruit farm • l'exploitation fruitière • der Obstanbau • la granja de frutales • l'azienda ortofrutticola

vineyard • la vigne • der Weinberg • el viñedo • il vigneto

actions • les activités • die Tätigkeiten • las actividades • le attività

plow *(v)* • labourer • pflügen • arar • arare

sow *(v)* • semer • säen • sembrar • seminare

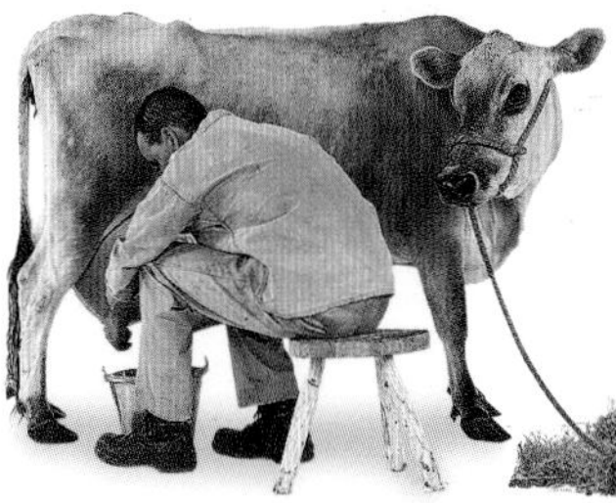

milk *(v)* • traire • melken • ordeñar • mungere

feed *(v)* • donner à manger • füttern • alimentar • dar da mangiare

water *(v)* • arroser • bewässern • regar • irrigare

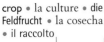

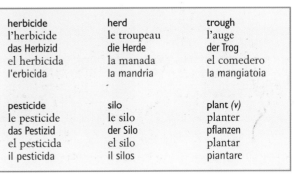

harvest *(v)* • récolter • ernten • recolectar • raccogliere

herbicide	herd	trough
l'herbicide	le troupeau	l'auge
das Herbizid	die Herde	der Trog
el herbicida	la manada	el comedero
l'erbicida	la mandria	la mangiatoia
pesticide	**silo**	**plant *(v)***
le pesticide	le silo	planter
das Pestizid	der Silo	pflanzen
el pesticida	el silo	plantar
il pesticida	il silos	piantare

farm 2 • la ferme 2 • der Bauernhof 2 • la granja 2 • la fattoria 2

crops • les cultures • die Feldfrüchte • los cultivos • le colture

wheat • le blé • der Weizen • el trigo • il grano

corn • le maïs • der Mais • el maíz • il granturco

barley • l'orge • die Gerste • la cebada • l'orzo

rapeseed • le colza • der Raps • la colza • la colza

sunflower • le tournesol • die Sonnenblume • el girasol • il girasole

hay • le foin • das Heu • el heno • il fieno

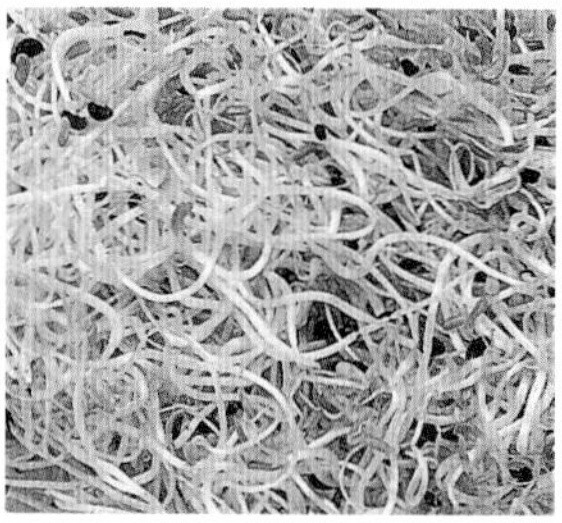

alfalfa • la luzerne • die Luzerne • la alfalfa • l'alfalfa

tobacco • le tabac • der Tabak • el tabaco • il tabacco

rice • le riz • der Reis • el arroz • il riso

tea • le thé • der Tee • el té • il tè

coffee • le café • der Kaffee • el café • il caffè

scarecrow • l'épouvantail • die Vogelscheuche • el espantapájaros • lo spaventapasseri

flax • le lin • der Flachs • el lino • il lino

sugarcane • la canne à sucre • das Zuckerrohr • la caña de azúcar • la canna da zucchero

cotton • le coton • die Baumwolle • el algodón • il cotone

livestock • le bétail • das Vieh • el ganado • il bestiame

piglet • le porcelet • das Ferkel • el chanchito • il maialino

pig • le cochon • das Schwein • el puerco • il maiale

calf
le veau
das Kalb
el ternero
il vitello

cow • la vache • die Kuh • la vaca • la mucca

bull • le taureau • der Stier • el toro • il toro

sheep • le mouton • das Schaf • la oveja • la pecora

lamb • l'agneau • das Lamm • el cordero • l'agnello

kid
le chevreau
das Zicklein
el cabrito
il capretto

goat • la chèvre • die Ziege • la cabra • la capra

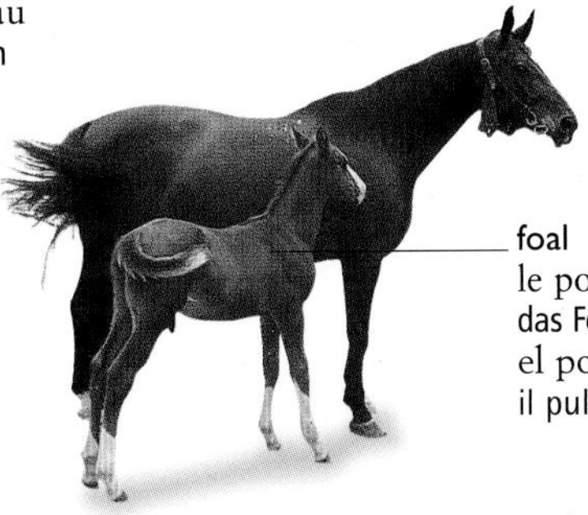

foal
le poulain
das Fohlen
el potro
il puledro

horse • le cheval • das Pferd • el caballo • il cavallo

donkey • l'âne • der Esel • el burro • l'asino

chick • le poussin • das Küken • el pollito • il pulcino

chicken • le poulet • das Huhn • la gallina • la gallina

rooster • le coq • der Hahn • el gallo • il gallo

turkey • le dindon • der Truthahn • el guajolote • il tacchino

duckling
le caneton
das Entenküken
el patito
l'anatroccolo

duck • le canard • die Ente • el pato • l'anatra

stable • l'écurie • der Stall • el establo • la stalla

pen • l'enclos • der Pferch • el redil • il recinto

chicken coop • le poulailler • der Hühnerstall • el gallinero • il pollaio

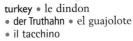

pigsty • la porcherie • der Schweinestall • el chiquero • il porcile

construction • la construction • der Bau • la construcción • l'edilizia

construction site • le chantier • die Baustelle • la obra • il cantiere

build *(v)* • construire • bauen • construir • costruire

construction worker • le maçon • der Bauarbeiter • el albañil • il muratore

cement mixer • la bétonnière • die Betonmischmaschine • la mezcladora de cemento • la betoniera

materials • les matériaux • das Material • los materiales • i materiali

brick • la brique • der Ziegelstein • el ladrillo • il mattone

timber • le bois • das Bauholz • la madera • il legno

roof tile • la tuile • der Dachziegel • la teja • la tegola

cinder block • le bloc de béton • der Betonblock • el bloque de hormigón • il blocco di calcestruzzo

tools • les outils • die Werkzeuge • las herramientas • gli attrezzi

mortar • le mortier • der Mörtel • la argamasa • la malta

trowel • la truelle • die Kelle • la paleta • la cazzuola

spirit level • le niveau à bulle • die Wasserwaage • el nivel • la livella

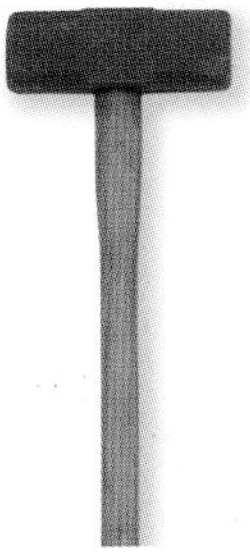

sledgehammer • le marteau de forgeron • der Vorschlaghammer • el mazo • la mazza

handle
le manche
der Stiel
el mango
il manico

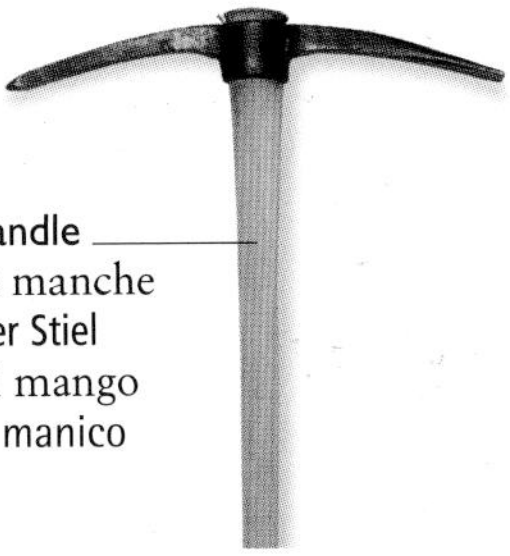

pickax • la pioche • die Spitzhacke • el zapapico • il piccone

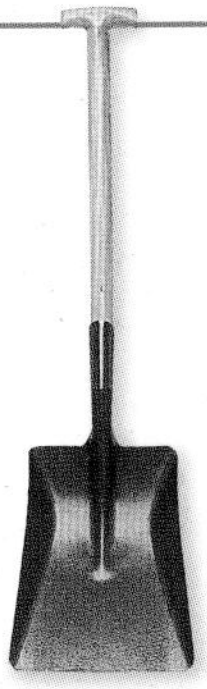

shovel • la pelle • die Schaufel • la pala • la pala

machinery • les machines • die Maschinen • la maquinaria • i macchinari

steam roller • le rouleau compresseur • die Walze • la aplanadora • il rullo compressore

dump truck • le tombereau • der Kipper • el camión de volteo • il camion con cassone ribaltabile

support • le support • die Stütze • el soporte • il supporto

hook
le crochet
der Haken
el gancho
il gancio

crane • la grue • der Kran • la grúa • la gru

roadwork • les travaux • die Straßenarbeiten • las obras viales • i lavori stradali

tarmac
le macadam goudronné
der Asphalt
el asfalto
il catrame

cone
le cône
der Leitkegel
el cono
il birillo

pneumatic drill • le marteau-piqueur • der Pressluftbohrer • el martillo neumático • il martello pneumatico

resurfacing
le revêtement
der Neubelag
el revestimiento
la riasfaltatura

mechanical digger • la pelle mécanique • der Bagger • la pala mecánica • l'escavatrice meccanica

occupations 1 • les professions 1 • die Berufe 1 • los profesiones 1 • i mestieri 1

carpenter • le menuisier • der Schreiner • el carpintero • il falegname

electrician • l'électricien • der Elektriker • el electricista • l'elettricista

plumber • le plombier • der Klempner • el plomero • l'idraulico

construction worker • le maçon • der Bauhandwerker • el albañil • il muratore

gardener • le jardinier • der Gärtner • el jardinero • il giardiniere

vacuum cleaner
l'aspirateur
der Staubsauger
la aspiradora
l'aspirapolvere

cleaner • le nettoyeur • der Gebäudereiniger • el empleado de la limpieza • l'addetto alle pulizie

mechanic • le mécanicien • der Mechaniker • el mecánico • il meccanico

butcher • le boucher • der Metzger • el carnicero • il macellaio

hairdresser • le coiffeur • der Friseur • el estilista • il parrucchiere

fishmonger • la marchande de poissons • die Fischhändlerin • la pescadera • la pescivendola

greengrocer • le marchand de légumes • der Gemüsehändler • el frutero • il fruttivendolo

florist • la fleuriste • die Floristin • la florista • la fioraia

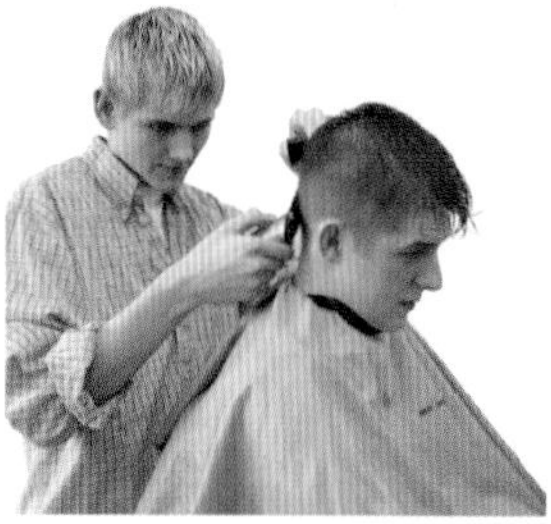

barber • le coiffeur • der Friseur • el peluquero • il barbiere

jeweler • le bijoutier • der Juwelier • el joyero • il gioielliere

sales assistant • l'employée de magasin • die Verkäuferin • la vendedora • la commessa

realtor • l'agent immobilier • die Immobilienmaklerin • la agente inmobiliario • l'agente immobiliare

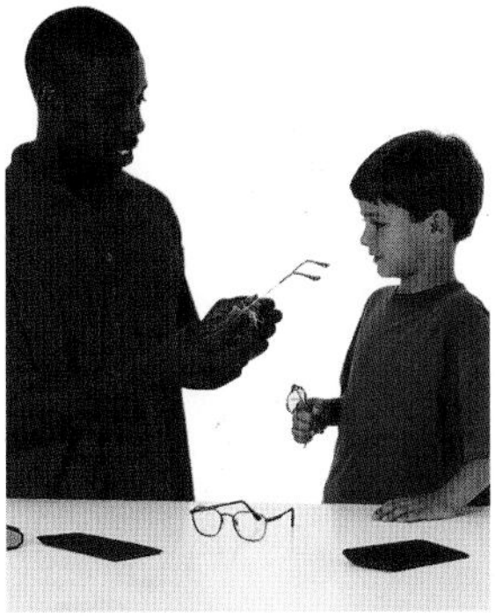

optician • l'opticien • der Optiker • el optometrista • l'ottico

mask
la masque
die Maske
la mascarilla
la mascherina

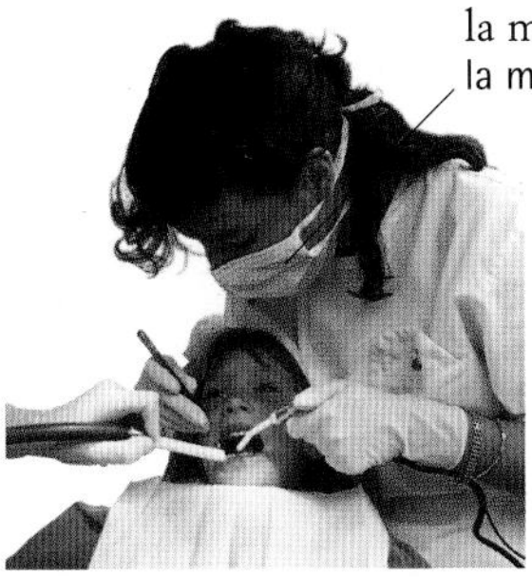

dentist • la dentiste • die Zahnärztin • la dentista • la dentista

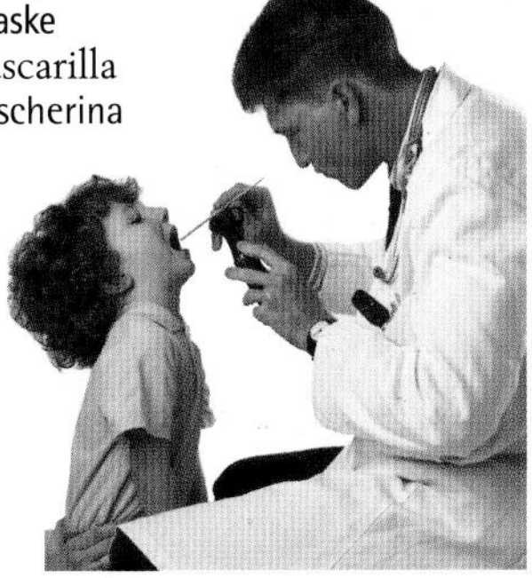

doctor • le docteur • der Arzt • el médico • il medico

pharmacist • la pharmacienne • die Apothekerin • la farmacéutica • la farmacista

nurse • l'infirmière • die Krankenschwester • la enfermera • l'infermiera

vet • la vétérinaire • die Tierärztin • la veterinaria • la veterinaria

farmer • le fermier • der Bauer • el agricultor • l'agricoltore

fisherman • le pêcheur • der Fischer • el pescador • il pescatore

machine gun
• la mitrailleuse
• das Maschinengewehr
• la metralleta
• la mitragliatrice

soldier • le soldat • der Soldat • el soldado • il soldato

uniform
l'uniforme
die Uniform
el uniforme
la divisa

policeman • le policier • der Polizist • el policía • il poliziotto

identity card
• le badge
• das Abzeichen
• la placa de identificación
• il distintivo

security guard • le garde • der Wächter • el guardia de seguridad • la guardia di sicurezza

sailor • le marin • der Seemann • el marino • il marinaio

fireman • le pompier • der Feuerwehrmann • el bombero • il vigile del fuoco

occupations 2 • les professions 2 • die Berufe 2 • las profesiones 2 • i mestieri 2

lawyer • l'avocat • der Rechtsanwalt • el abogado • l'avvocato

accountant • le comptable • der Wirtschaftsprüfer • el contador • il commercialista

architect • l'architecte • der Architekt • el arquitecto • l'architetto

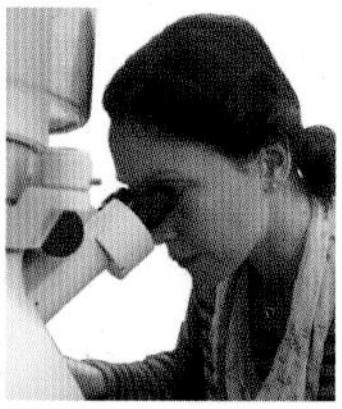

scientist • la scientifique • die Wissenschaftlerin • la cientifica • la scienziata

teacher • l'institutrice • die Lehrerin • la maestro • l'insegnante

librarian • le bibliothécaire • der Bibliothekar • el bibliotecario • il bibliotecario

receptionist • la réceptionniste • die Empfangsdame • la recepcionista • l'addetta alla ricezione

mail carrier • le facteur • der Briefträger • el cartero • il postino

bus driver • le conducteur de bus • der Busfahrer • el chófer • l'autista

truck driver • le camionneur • der Lastwagenfahrer • el chófer • il camionista

taxi driver • le chauffeur de taxi • der Taxifahrer • el taxista • il tassista

pilot • le pilote • der Pilot • el piloto • il pilota

flight attendant • l'hôtesse de l'air • die Flugbegleiterin • la sobrecargo • l'assistente di volo

travel agent • l'agent de voyages • die Reisebürokauffrau • la agente de viajes • l'agente di viaggio

chef • le chef • der Koch • el chef • il cuoco

musician • le musicien • der Musiker • el músico • il musicista

tutu
le tutu
das Ballettröckchen
el tutú
il tutù

dancer • la danseuse • die Tänzerin • la bailarina • la ballerina

actor • l'acteur • der Schauspieler • el actor • l'attore

singer • la chanteuse • die Sängerin • la cantante • la cantante

waitress • la serveuse • die Kellnerin • la mesera • la cameriera

barman • le barman • der Barkeeper • el barman • il barista

sportsman • le sportif • der Sportler • el deportista • l'atleta

sculptor • le sculpteur • der Bildhauer • el escultor • lo scultore

painter • la peintre • die Malerin • la pintora • la pittrice

photographer • le photographe • der Fotograf • el fotógrafo • il fotografo

anchor • le présentatrice • die Nachrichtensprecherin • la presentadora • l'annunciatrice

notes
les notes
die Notizen
las notas
gli appunti

journalist • le journaliste • der Journalist • el periodista • il giornalista

editor • la rédactrice • die Redakteurin • la redactora • la redattrice

designer • la dessinateur • der Designer • el diseñador • il disegnatore

seamstress • la couturière • die Damenschneiderin • la modista • la costumista

tailor • le couturier • der Schneider • el sastre • il sarto

transportation

le transport

der Verkehr

el transporte

i trasporti

roads • les routes • die Straßen • las carreteras • le strade

highway
l'autoroute
die Autobahn
la autopista
l'autostrada

toll booth
le poste de péage
die Mautstelle
la caseta de cobro
il casello

road markings
les signalisations
die Straßenmarkierungen
las señales de piso
la segnaletica orizzontale

entrance ramp
la bretelle d'accès
die Zufahrtsstraße
la entrada
la rampa di accesso

one-way
à sens unique
Einbahn-
de sentido único
a senso unico

divider
l'îlot directionnel
die Verkehrsinsel
la línea divisoria
la linea divisoria

junction
le carrefour
die Kreuzung
el crucero
lo svincolo

traffic light
les feux
die Verkehrsampel
el semáforo
il semaforo

truck
le camion
der Lastwagen
el camión
il camion

median strip
le terre-plein
der Mittelstreifen
el muro de división
la banchina spartitraffico

inside lane • la file de droite • die rechte Spur • el carril de baja • la corsia interna

middle lane
la voie centrale
die mittlere Spur
el carril central
la corsia centrale

outside lane
• la voie de dépassement
• die Überholspur
• el carril izquierdo
• la corsia esterna

exit ramp
la bretelle de sortie
die Ausfahrts
la rampa de salida
la rampa di uscita

traffic
la circulation
der Verkehr
el tránsito
il traffico

overpass
l'autopont
die Überführung
el puente
il cavalcavia

hard shoulder
l'accotement stabilisé
der Seitenstreifen
el acotamiento
la corsia d'emergenza

underpass
le passage inférieur
die Unterführung
el paso a desnivel
il sottopassaggio

crosswalk
le passage clouté
der Fußgängerüberweg
el paso de peatones
il passaggio pedonale

emergency phone • le téléphone de secours • die Notrufsäule • el teléfono de emergencia • il telefono per emergenze

disabled parking place • le parking réservé aux personnes handicapées • der Behindertenparkplatz • el estacionamiento para minusválidos • il parcheggio per disabili

traffic jam • l'embouteillage • der Verkehrsstau • el tráfico • l'ingorgo

satnav • le GPS • das Navi • el navegador por satélite • il navigatore satellitare

parking meter
le parc-mètre
die Parkuhr
el parquímetro
il parchimetro

traffic policeman • l'agent de la circulation • der Verkehrspolizist • el policía de tránsito • il vigile urbano

rotary — le rond-point / der Kreisverkehr / la glorieta / la rotatoria

reverse *(v)* — faire marche arrière / rückwärts fahren / meter reversa / fare marcia indietro

tow away *(v)* — remorquer / abschleppen / remolcar / rimorchiare

detour — la déviation / die Umleitung / la desviación / la deviazione

drive *(v)* — conduire / fahren / manejar / guidare

divided highway — la route à quatre voies / die Schnellstraße / la autovía / la carreggiata doppia

park *(v)* — garer / parken / estacionar / parcheggiare

roadworks — les travaux / die Straßenbaustelle / las obras / i lavori stradali

Is this the road to...? — C'est la route pour...? / Ist dies die Straße nach...? / ¿Es ésta la carretera hacia...? / È questa la strada per ...?

pass *(v)* — doubler / überholen / rebasar / sorpassare

guardrail — la glissière de sécurité / die Leitplanke / el muro de contención / il guardrail

Where can I park? — Où peut-on se garer? / Wo kann ich parken? / ¿Dónde me puedo estacionar? / Dove posso parcheggiare?

road signs • les panneaux routiers • die Verkehrsschilder • las señales de tráqnsito • i cartelli stradali

no entry
sens interdit
keine Einfahrt
prohibido el paso
ingresso vietato

speed limit
la limitation de vitesse
die Geschwindig-keitsbegrenzung
el límite de velocidad
il limite di velocità

hazard
danger
Gefahr
peligro
pericolo

no stopping
arrêt interdit
halten verboten
prohibido parar
sosta vietata

no right turn
interdit de tourner à droite
rechts abbiegen verboten
no dar vuelta a la derecha
svolta a destra vietata

bus • le bus • der Bus • el autobús • l'autobus

driver's seat
le siège du conducteur
der Fahrersitz
el asiento del conductor
il sedile dell'autista

handrail
la poignée
der Haltegriff
la barandilla
la maniglia

automatic door
la porte automatique
die Automatiktür
la puerta automática
la porta a soffietto

front wheel
la roue avant
das Vorderrad
la rueda delantera
la ruota anteriore

luggage hold
le compartiment à bagages
das Gepäckfach
el portaequipaje
il bagagliaio

door • la porte • die Tür • la puerta • la porta

bus • le car • der Reisebus • el autocar • il pullman

types of buses • les types de bus • die Bustypen • los tipos de autobuses • i tipi di autobus

route number
le numéro de bus
die Liniennummer
el número de ruta
il numero del percorso

driver
le conducteur
der Fahrer
el chófer
l'autista

double-decker bus • le bus à deux étages • der Doppeldecker • el autobús de dos pisos • l'autobus a due piani

tram • le tramway • die Straßenbahn • el tranvía • il tram

streetcar • le trolleybus • der Obus • el trolebús • il filobus

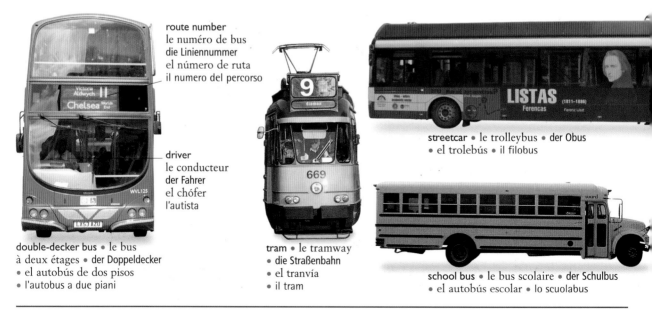

school bus • le bus scolaire • der Schulbus • el autobús escolar • lo scuolabus

rear wheel
la roue arrière
das Hinterrad
la rueda trasera
la ruota posteriore

window
la fenêtre
das Fenster
la ventanilla
il finestrino

stop button • le bouton d'arrêt • der Halteknopf • el botón de parada • il pulsante di chiamata

bus ticket • le ticket • der Fahrschein • el boleto de autobús • il biglietto

bell • la sonnette • die Klingel • el timbre • il campanello

bus station • la gare routière • der Busbahnhof • la estación de autobuses • l'autostazione

bus stop • l'arrêt de bus • die Bushaltestelle • la parada de autobús • la fermata dell'autobus

fare	wheelchair access
le prix du ticket	l'accès aux handicapés
der Fahrpreis	der Rollstuhlzugang
la tarifa	la rampa para sillas de ruedas
la tariffa	l'accesso per sedie a rotelle
timetable	**bus shelter**
l'horaire	l'abribus
der Fahrplan	das Wartehäuschen
el horario	la marquesina
l'orario	la pensilina
Do you stop at...?	**Which bus goes to...?**
Vous stoppez à...?	C'est quel bus pour aller à...?
Halten Sie am...?	Welcher Bus fährt nach...?
¿Para usted en...?	¿Qué autobús va a...?
Ferma a...?	Qual è l'autobus per...?

minibus • le minibus • der Kleinbus • el microbús • il pulmino

shuttle bus • la navette • der Zubringer • el autobús directo • la navetta

tourist bus • le bus de touristes • der Touristenbus • el autobús turístico • il pullman

car 1 • la voiture 1 • das Auto 1 • el carro 1 • l'automobile 1

exterior • l'extérieur • das Äußere • el exterior • l'esterno

mirror
le rétroviseur
der Seitenspiegel
el espejo lateral
lo specchietto laterale

windshield
le pare-brise
die Windschutzscheibe
el parabrisas
il parabrezza

rearview mirror
le rétroviseur
der Rückspiegel
el espejo retrovisor
lo specchietto retrovisore

windshield wiper
l'essuie-glace
der Scheibenwischer
el limpiaparabrisas
il tergicristallo

door
la porte
die Autotür
la puerta
lo sportello

hood
le capot
die Motorhaube
el cofre
il cofano

trunk
le coffre
der Kofferraum
la cajuela
il bagagliaio

turn signal
le clignotant
der Blinker
la direccional
la freccia

license plate
la plaque d'immatriculation
das Nummernschild
la matrícula
la targa

bumper
le pare-chocs
die Stoßstange
la defensa
il paraurti

headlight
le phare
der Scheinwerfer
el faro
i fari anabbaglianti

wheel
la roue
das Rad
la rueda
la ruota

tire
le pneu
der Reifen
la llanta
il pneumatico

luggage
les bagages
das Gepäck
el equipaje
i bagagli

roof rack • la galerie • der Dachgepäckträger • la baca • il portabagagli

tailgate • le hayon • die Hecktür • la puerta abatible • il portellone

seat belt • la ceinture de sécurité • der Sicherheitsgurt • el cinturón de seguridad • la cintura di sicurezza

child seat • le siège d'enfant • der Kindersitz • la silla para niños • il seggiolino per bambino

types • les modèles • die Wagentypen • los modelos • i tipi

electric car • la voiture électrique • das Elektroauto • el coche eléctrico • l'automobile elettrica

hatchback • la berline à hayon • die Fließhecklimousine • el carro de cinco puertas • l'auto a cinque porte

sedan • la berline • die Limousine • el carro familiar • la berlina

station wagon • le break • der Kombiwagen • la camioneta • l'auto familiare

convertible • la décapotable • das Kabriolett • el convertible • l'auto decappottabile

sports car • le cabriolet sport • das Sportkabriolett • el carro deportivo • l'auto sportiva

minivan • la voiture à six places • die Großraumlimousine • la minivan • la monovolume

four-wheel drive • la quatre-quatre • der Geländewagen • la doble tracción • il fuoristrada

vintage • la voiture d'époque • das Vorkriegsmodell • el auto de época • l'auto d'epoca

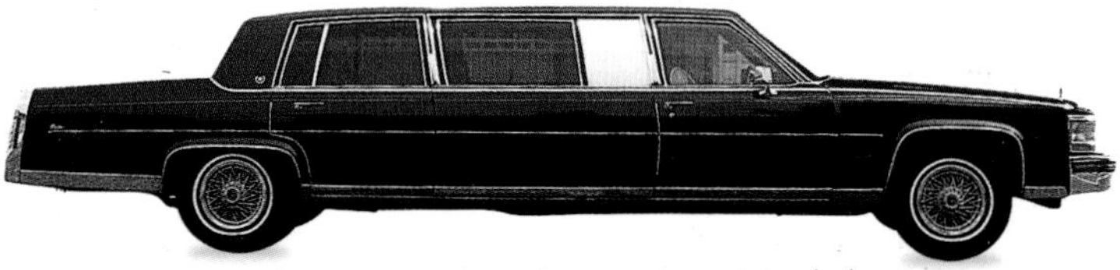

limousine • la limousine • die verlängerte Limousine • la limousine • la limousine

gas station • la station-service • die Tankstelle • la gasolinera • la stazione di servizio

gas pump
la pompe
die Zapfsäule
la bomba
la pompa di benzina

price
le tarif
der Benzinpreis
el precio
il prezzo

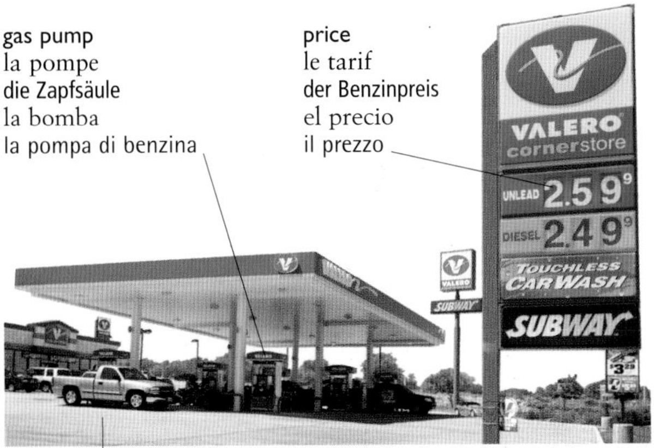

forecourt
l'aire de stationnement
der Tankstellenplatz
la zona de abastecimiento
l'area di stazionamento

oil
l'huile
das Öl
el aceite
l'olio

leaded
avec plomb
verbleit
con plomo
piombata

car wash
le lave-auto
die Autowaschanlage
el auto-lavado
l'autolavaggio

gasoline
l'essence
das Benzin
la gasolina
la benzina

diesel
le diesel
der Diesel
el diesel
il diesel

antifreeze
l'antigel
das Frostschutzmittel
el anticongelante
l'antigelo

unleaded
sans plomb
bleifrei
sin plomo
senza piombo

garage
le garage
die Werkstatt
el taller
il garage

windshield wiper fluid
le lave-glace
die Scheibenwaschanlage
el líquido limpiaparabrisas
il detegente per vetri

Fill it up, please.
Le plein, s'il vous plaît.
Voll tanken, bitte.
Llénelo por favor.
Il pieno per favore.

car 2 • la voiture 2 • das Auto 2 • el carro 2 • l'automobile 2

interior • l'intérieur • die Innenausstattung • el interior • l'interno

backseat
le siège arrière
der Rücksitz
el asiento trasero
il sedile posteriore

armrest
l'accoudoir
die Armstütze
el reposabrazos
il bracciolo

headrest
le repose-tête
die Kopfstütze
el reposacabezas
il poggiatesta

door lock
le verrouillage
die Türverriegelung
el seguro
la sicura

handle
la poignée
der Türgriff
la manija
la maniglia

two-door
à deux portes
zweitürig
dos puertas
a due porte

four-door
à quatre portes
viertürig
de cuatro puertas
a quattro porte

automatic
automatique
mit Automatik
automático
automatico

brake
le frein
die Bremse
el freno
il freno

accelerator
l'accélérateur
das Gaspedal
el acelerador
l'acceleratore

three-door
à trois portes
dreitürig
de tres puertas
a tre porte

manual
manuel
mit Handschaltung
manual
manuale

ignition
l'allumage
die Zündung
el encendido
l'accensione

clutch
l'embrayage
die Kupplung
el embrague
la frizione

air-conditioning
la climatisation
die Klimaanlage
el aire acondicionado
l'aria condizionata

Can you tell me the way to…?
Pouvez-vous m'indiquer la route pour…?
Wie komme ich nach…?
¿Me puede decir cómo se va a…?
Può indicarmi la strada per…?

Where is the parking lot?
Où est le parking?
Wo ist hier ein Parkplatz?
¿Dónde hay un estacionamiento?
Dov'è il parcheggio?

Can I park here?
On peut se garer ici?
Kann ich hier parken?
¿Se puede estacionar aquí?
Posso parcheggiare qui?

controls • les commandes • die Armaturen • los controles • i comandi

steering wheel
le volant
das Lenkrad
el volante
il volante

horn
le klaxon
die Hupe
el claxon
il clacson

dashboard
le tableau de bord
das Armaturenbrett
el tablero
il cruscotto

hazard lights
les feux de détresse
die Warnlichter
las luces de emergencia
le luci intermittenti

satellite navigation
le navigateur par satellite
das GPS-System
la navegación por satélite
la navigazione via satellite

left-hand drive • la conduite à gauche • die Linkssteuerung • el volante a la izquierda • la guida a sinistra

temperature gauge
le thermomètre
die Temperaturanzeige
el indicador de temperatura
la spia della temperatura

tachometer
le compte-tours
der Drehzahlmesser
el tacómetro
il contagiri

speedometer
le compteur
der Tachometer
el velocímetro
il contachilometri

fuel gauge
la jauge d'essence
die Kraftstoffanzeige
el indicador de la gasolina
la spia del carburante

car stereo
la stéréo
die Autostereoanlage
la radio del coche
l'autoradio

heater controls
la manette de chauffage
der Heizungsregler
la calefacción
i comandi per il riscaldamento

gearshift
le levier de vitesses
der Schalthebel
la palanca de velocidades
la leva del cambio

right-hand drive • la conduite à droite • die Rechtssteuerung • el volante a la derecha • la guida a destra

light switch
l'interrupteur feux
der Lichtschalter
la palanca de luces
l'interruttore per le luci

odometer
l'odomètre
der Kilometerzähler
el odómetro
l'odometro

air bag
l'airbag
der Airbag
la bolsa de aire
l'airbag

car 3 • la voiture 3 • das Auto 3 • el carro 3 • l'automobile 3

mechanics • la mécanique • die Mechanik • la mecánica • la meccanica

washer fluid reservoir
le réservoir de lave-glace
der Scheibenputzmittelbehälter
el depósito del limpiaparabrisas
il serbatoio del liquido lavavetri

dipstick
la jauge d'huile
der Ölmessstab
la varilla del nivel del aceite
l'indicatore di livello dell'olio

air filter
le filtre à air
der Luftfilter
el filtro del aire
il filtro dell'aria

brake fluid reservoir
le réservoir de liquide de frein
der Bremsflüssigkeitsbehälter
el depósito del líquido de frenos
il serbatoio del liquido per i freni

battery
la batterie
die Batterie
la batería
la batteria

bodywork
la carrosserie
die Karosserie
la chapa
la carrozzeria

coolant reservoir • le réservoir de liquide de refroidissement • der Kühlmittelbehälter • el depósito del líquido refrigerante • il serbatoio per il liquido refrigerante

cylinder head
la culasse
der Zylinderkopf
la culata
la testa del cilindro

pipe
le tuyau
das Rohr
el tubo
il tubo

sunroof
le toit ouvrant
das Schiebedach
el quemacocos
il tettuccio

radiator
le radiateur
der Kühler
el radiador
il radiatore

fan
le ventilateur
der Ventilator
el ventilador
il ventilatore

engine
le moteur
der Motor
el motor
il motore

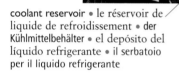

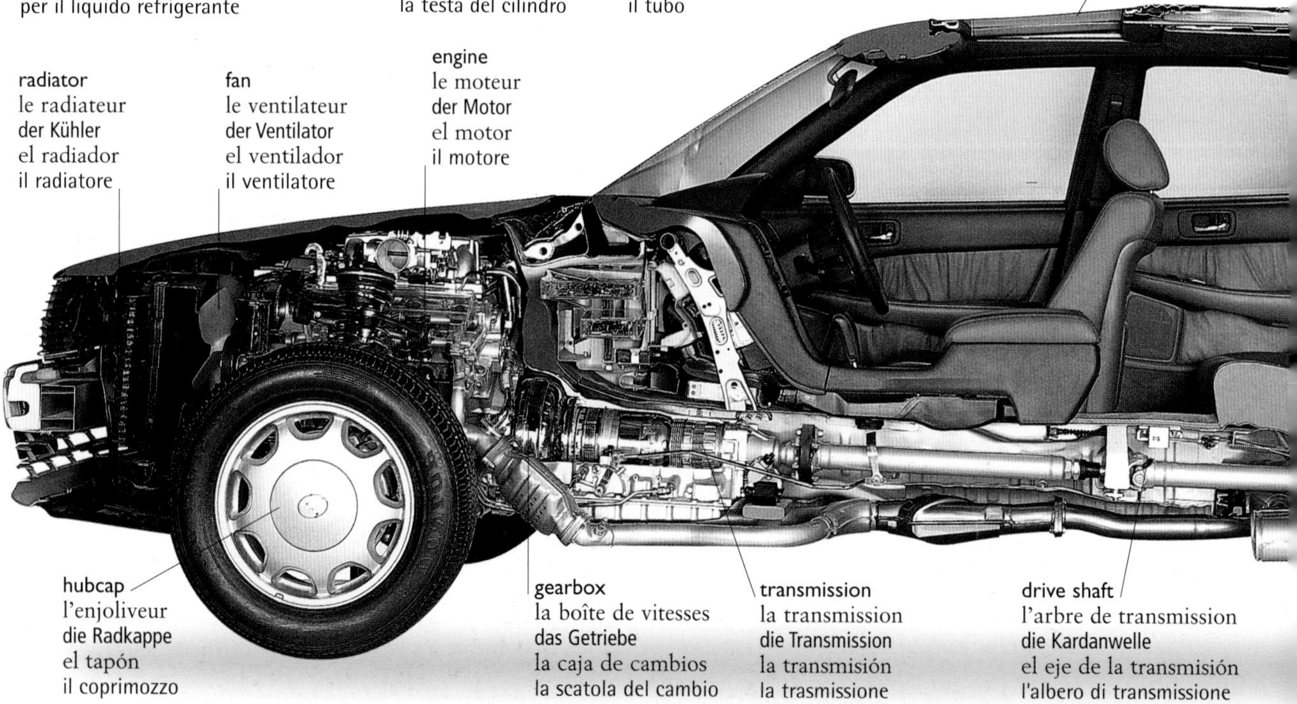

hubcap
l'enjoliveur
die Radkappe
el tapón
il coprimozzo

gearbox
la boîte de vitesses
das Getriebe
la caja de cambios
la scatola del cambio

transmission
la transmission
die Transmission
la transmisión
la trasmissione

drive shaft
l'arbre de transmission
die Kardanwelle
el eje de la transmisión
l'albero di transmissione

flat tire • la crevaison • die Reifenpanne • la ponchadura • la foratura

spare tire
la roue de secours
das Ersatzrad
la llanta de refacción
la ruota di scorta

tire iron
la manivelle
der Radschlüssel
la llave
la chiave

lug nuts
les écrous de roue
die Radmuttern
los birlos
i bulloni della ruota

jack
le cric
der Wagenheber
el gato
il cric

change a tire *(v)* • changer une roue • ein Rad wechseln • cambiar una llanta • cambiare una ruota

roof
le toit
das Dach
el techo
il tetto

suspension
la suspension
die Aufhängung
la suspensión
la sospensione

muffler
le silencieux
der Auspufftopf
el silenciador
il silenziatore

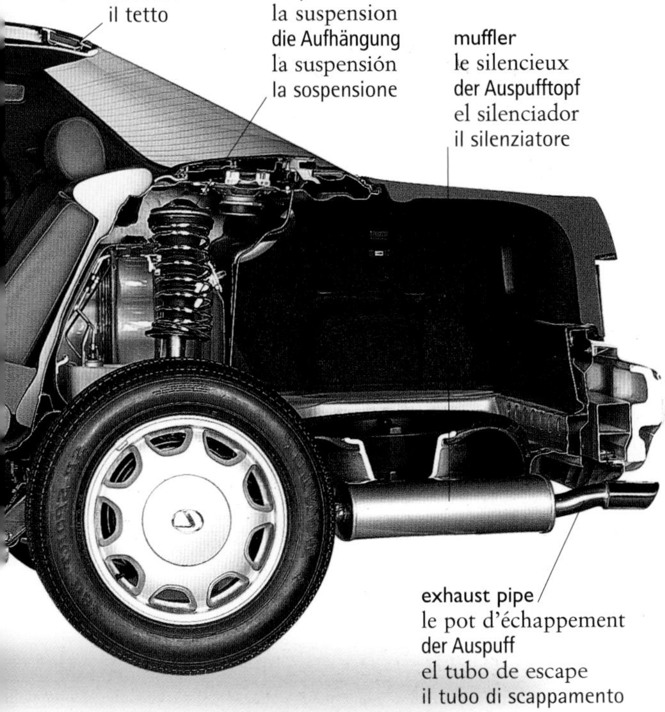

exhaust pipe
le pot d'échappement
der Auspuff
el tubo de escape
il tubo di scappamento

car accident
l'accident de voiture
der Autounfall
el accidente de carro
l'incidente stradale

breakdown
la panne
die Panne
la avería
il guasto

insurance
l'assurance
die Versicherung
el seguro
l'assicurazione

tow truck
la dépanneuse
der Abschleppwagen
la grúa
il carro attrezzi

mechanic
le mécanicien
der Mechaniker
el mecánico
il meccanico

tire pressure
la pression des pneus
der Reifendruck
la presión del neumático
la pressione dei pneumatici

fuse box
le porte-fusibles
der Sicherungskasten
la caja de fusibles
la scatola dei fusibili

spark plug
la bougie
die Zündkerze
la bujía
la candela

fan belt
la courroie de ventilateur
der Keilriemen
la banda del ventilador
la cinghia della ventola

gas tank
le réservoir d'essence
der Benzintank
el tanque de la gasolina
il serbatoio della benzina

cam belt
la courroie de cames
der Nockenriemen
la banda del disco
la cinghia della camma

turbocharger
le turbocompresseur
der Turbolader
el turbo
il tubocompressore

distributor
le distributeur
der Verteiler
el distribuidor
il distributore

timing
le réglage de l'allumage
die Einstellung
el ralentí
la messa in fase

chassis
le châssis
das Chassis
el chasis
il telaio

parking brake
le frein à main
die Handbremse
el freno de mano
il freno a mano

alternator
l'alternateur
die Lichtmaschine
el alternador
l'alternatore

My car has broken down.
Ma voiture est en panne.
Ich habe eine Panne.
Se descompuso el carro.
Sono in panne.

My car won't start.
Ma voiture ne démarre pas.
Mein Auto springt nicht an.
El carro no arranca.
La mia macchina non parte.

motorcycle • la moto • das Motorrad • la motocicleta • la motocicletta

turn signal
le clignotant
der Blinker
la direccional
la freccia

speedometer • le compteur • der Tachometer • el velocímetro • il contachilometri

brake
le frein
die Bremse
el freno
il freno

horn
le klaxon
die Hupe
el claxon
il clacson

clutch
l'embrayage
die Kupplung
el embrague
la frizione

throttle
l'accélérateur
der Gashebel
el acelerador
l'acceleratore

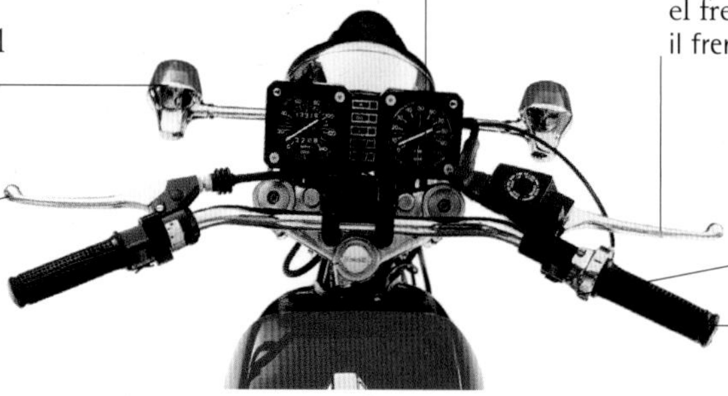

controls • les commandes • die Steuerung • los controles • i comandi

helmet
le casque
der Motorradhelm
el casco
il casco

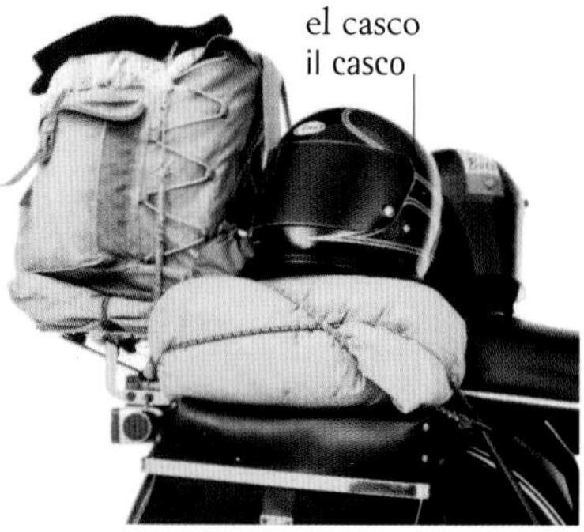

carrier • le porte-bagages • der Gepäckträger • el portaequipaje • il portapacchi

passenger seat
le siège arrière
der Soziussitz
el asiento trasero
il sellino posteriore

seat
la selle
der Sitz
el asiento
il sedile

engine
le moteur
der Motor
el motor
il motore

fuel tank
le réservoir d'essence
der Kraftstofftank
el tanque de la gasolina
il serbatoio

reflector
le réflecteur
das Katzenauge
el reflector
il riflettore

taillight
le feu arrière
das Bremslicht
la luz trasera
il fanale posteriore

exhaust pipe
le pot d'échappement
das Auspuffrohr
el tubo de escape
il tubo di scappamento

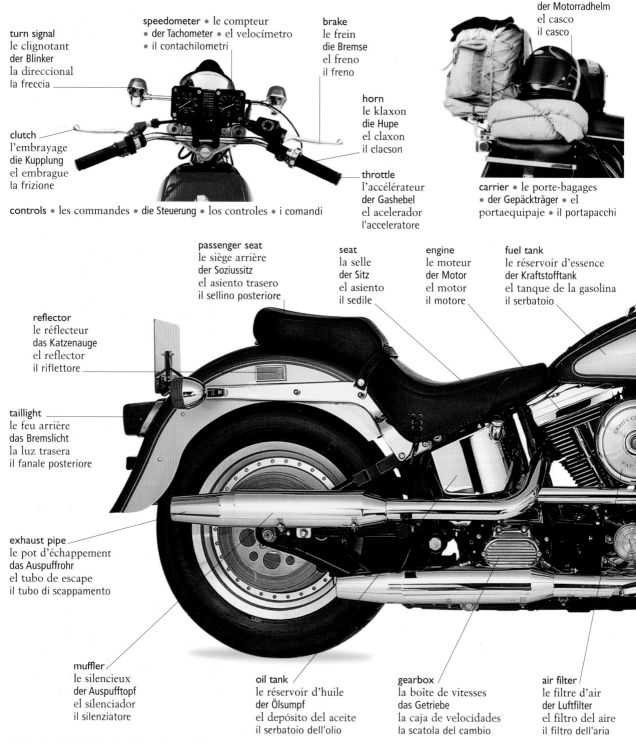

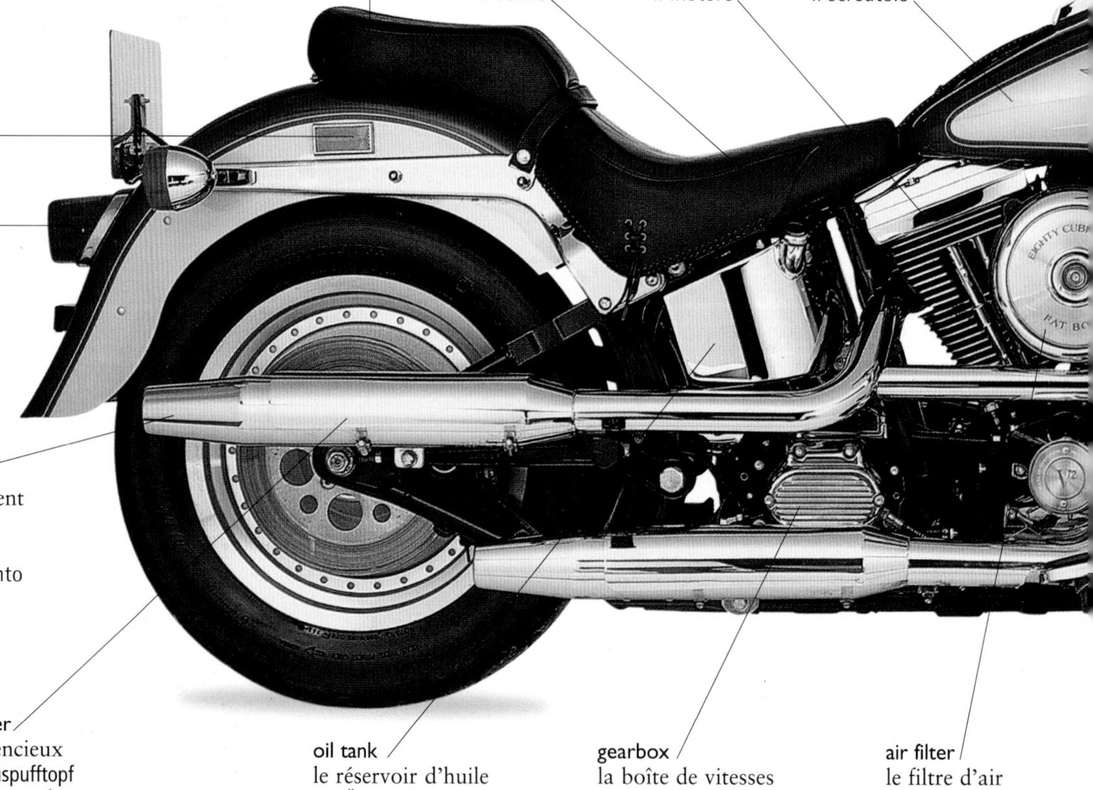

muffler
le silencieux
der Auspufftopf
el silenciador
il silenziatore

oil tank
le réservoir d'huile
der Ölsumpf
el depósito del aceite
il serbatoio dell'olio

gearbox
la boîte de vitesses
das Getriebe
la caja de velocidades
la scatola del cambio

air filter
le filtre d'air
der Luftfilter
el filtro del aire
il filtro dell'aria

visor
la visière
das Visier
la visera
la visiera

reflector strap
la bande fluorescente
der Leuchtstreifen
la cinta reflectante
la fascia rifrangente

leathers
le vêtement en cuir
der Lederanzug
el traje de cuero
la tuta di pelle

kneepad
la genouillère
der Knieschützer
la rodillera
il paraginocchio

clothing • les vêtements • die Kleidung • el equipo • l'abbigliamento

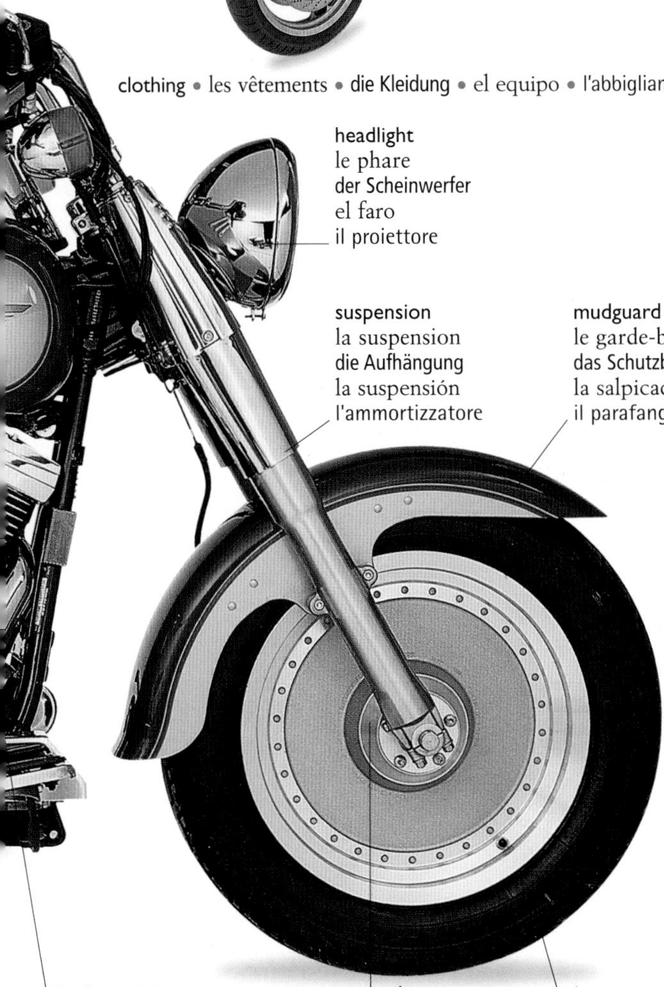

headlight
le phare
der Scheinwerfer
el faro
il proiettore

suspension
la suspension
die Aufhängung
la suspensión
l'ammortizzatore

mudguard
le garde-boue
das Schutzblech
la salpicadera
il parafango

brake pedal
la pédale de frein
das Bremspedal
el pedal de los frenos
il pedale del freno

axle
l'essieu
die Achse
el eje
l'asse

tire
le pneu
der Reifen
la llanta
il pneumatico

types • les types • die Typen • los tipos • i tipi

racing bike • la moto de course • die Rennmaschine • la moto de carreras • la moto da corsa

windshield • le pare-brise • die Windschutzscheibe • el parabrisas • il parabrezza

tourer • la moto routière • der Tourer • la moto de carretera • la moto da turismo

dirt bike • la moto tout-terrain • das Geländemotorrad • la motocross • la moto da cross

stand • la béquille • der Motorradständer • el soporte • il cavalletto

scooter • le scooter • der Roller • la vespa • il motorino

bicycle • la bicyclette • das Fahrrad • la bicicleta • la bicicletta

tandem • le tandem • das Tandem • el tándem • il tandem

racing bike • le vélo de course • das Rennrad • la bicicleta de carreras • la bicicletta da corsa

mountain bike • le vélo tout-terrain • das Mountainbike • la bicicleta de montaña • la mountain bike

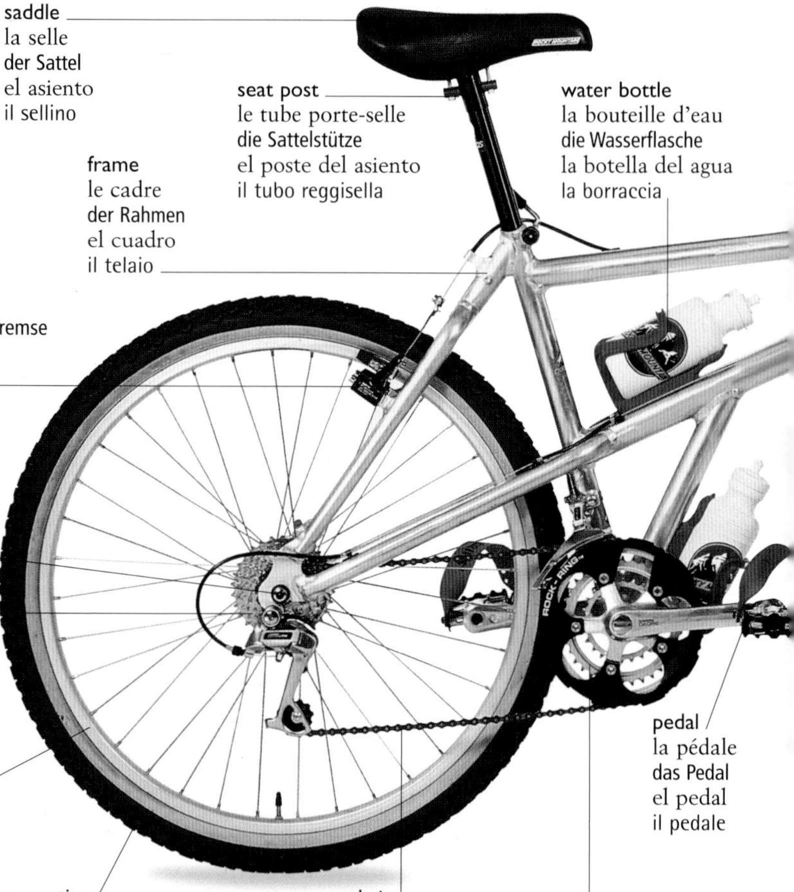

saddle
la selle
der Sattel
el asiento
il sellino

seat post
le tube porte-selle
die Sattelstütze
el poste del asiento
il tubo reggisella

water bottle
la bouteille d'eau
die Wasserflasche
la botella del agua
la borraccia

frame
le cadre
der Rahmen
el cuadro
il telaio

brake
le frein
die Felgenbremse
el freno
il freno

hub
le moyeu
die Nabe
el eje
il mozzo

gears
les vitesses
die Gänge
los cambios
le marce

pedal
la pédale
das Pedal
el pedal
il pedale

rim
la jante
die Felge
el rin
il cerchione

tire
le pneu
der Reifen
la llanta
il pneumatico

chain
la chaîne
die Fahrradkette
la cadena
la catena

cog
la roue dentée
das Zahnrad
la estrella
la ruota dentata

touring bike • le vélo de randonnée • das Tourenfahrrad • la bicicleta de paseo • la bicicletta da turismo

helmet
le casque
der Fahrradhelm
el casco
il casco

road bike • le vélo de ville • das Straßenrad • la bicicleta de pista • la bicicletta da strada

cycle lane • la piste cyclable • der Fahrradweg • el carril de bicicletas • la pista ciclabile

crossbar • la barre • die Stange • el tubo superior • la canna

handlebar
le guidon
die Lenkstange
el manubrio
il manubrio

gear lever
le levier de vitesse
der Schalthebel
la palanca de cambio
la leva del cambio

brake lever
le levier de frein
der Bremsgriff
los frenos
la leva del freno

fork
la fourche
die Gabel
las tijeras
la forcella

spoke
le rayon
die Speiche
el rayo
il raggio

wheel
la roue
das Rad
la llanta
la ruota

valve
la valve
das Ventil
el pivote
la valvola

tread
la bande de roulement
das Reifenprofil
la banda de rodadura
il battistrada

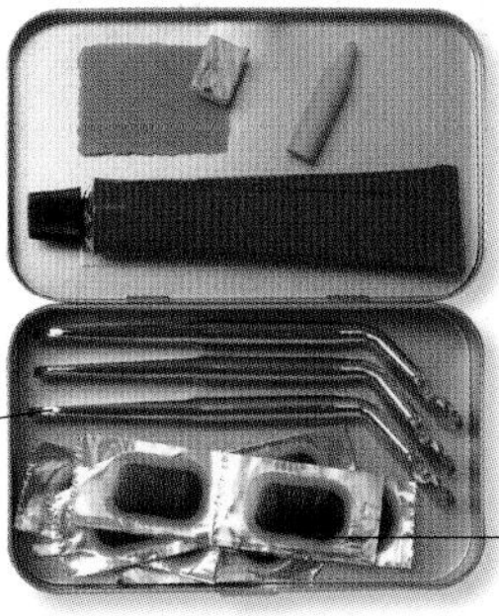

tire lever • le démonte-pneu • der Reifenschlüssel • la palanca de la llanta • la leva per il pneumatico

patch
la rustine
der Flicken
el parche
la toppa

repair kit • la boîte d'outils • der Reparaturkasten • el kit de reparaciones • il kit per riparazioni

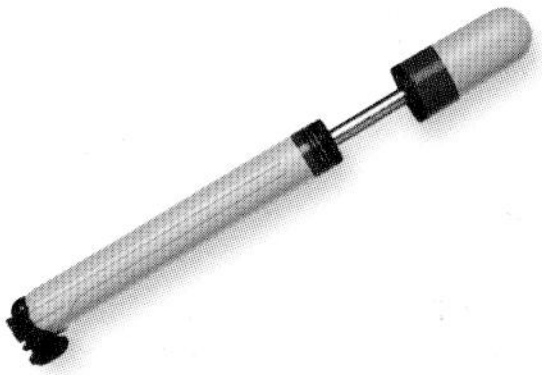

pump • la pompe • die Luftpumpe • la bomba • la pompa

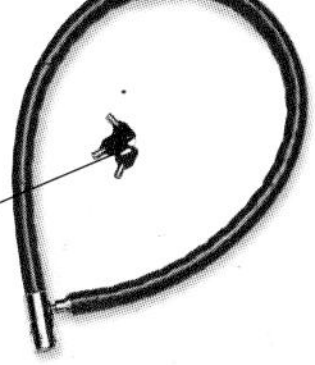

key
la clef
der Schlüssel
la llave
la chiave

lock • l'antivol • das Fahrradschloss • el candado • il lucchetto

inner tube • la chambre à air • der Schlauch • la cámara • la camera d'aria

child seat • le siège d'enfant • der Kindersitz • la silla para el niño • il seggiolino per bambino

light le phare die Fahrradlampe el faro il fanale	**kickstand** la béquille der Fahrradständer la patilla de apoyo il cavalletto	**brake block** le patin de frein die Bremsbacke la goma del freno il blocca freni	**basket** le panier der Korb la canastilla il cestello	**toe clip** le cale-pied der Rennbügel el calzapié il fermapiedi	**change gear** *(v)* changer de vitesse schalten cambiar de velocidad cambiare marcia
rear light le feu arrière das Rücklicht el faro trasero il fanale posteriore	**stabilizers** les roues d'entraînement die Stützräder las ruedas de apoyo le rotelle	**cable** le câble das Kabel el cable il cavo	**dynamo** la dynamo der Dynamo la dinamo la dinamo	**toe strap** la lanière der Riemen la banda del calzapié il cinghietto	**brake** *(v)* freiner bremsen frenar frenare
reflector le cataphote der Rückstrahler el reflector il catarifrangente	**bike rack** la galerie à vélo der Fahrradständer el rack para bicicletas il posteggio per bici	**sprocket** le pignon das Kettenzahnrad el engrane il dente	**flat tire** la crevaison die Reifenpanne la ponchadura la foratura	**pedal** *(v)* pédaler treten pedalear pedalare	**cycle** *(v)* faire du vélo Rad fahren andar en bicicleta andare in bici

train • le train • der Zug • el tren • il treno

carriage
la voiture
der Wagen
el vagón
il vagone

platform
le quai
der Bahnsteig
el andén
il binario

cart
le caddie
der Kofferkuli
el carrito
il carrello

platform number
le numéro de voie
die Gleisnummer
el número de andén
il numero del binario

commuter
le voyageur
der Pendler
el viajero de cercanías
il pendolare

train station • la gare • der Bahnhof • la estación de tren • la stazione ferroviaria

types of train • les types de trains • die Zugtypen • los tipos de tren • i tipi di treno

steam train • le train à vapeur • die Dampflokomotive • el tren de vapor • il treno a vapore

engine
la locomotive
die Lokomotive
la locomotora
la locomotiva

conducter's cabin
la cabine du conducteur
der Führerstand
la cabina del conductor
la cabina del conducente

rail
le rail
die Schiene
el riel
la rotaia

diesel train • le train diesel • die Diesellokomotive • el tren diesel • il treno diesel

electric train • le train électrique • die Elektrolokomotive • el tren eléctrico • il treno elettrico

high-speed train • le train à grande vitesse • der Hochgeschwindigkeitszug • el tren de alta velocidad • il treno ad alta velocità

monorail • le monorail • die Einschienenbahn • el monorriel • la monorotaia

subway • le métro • die U-Bahn • el metro • la metropolitana

tram • le tram • die Straßenbahn • el tranvía • il tram

freight train • le train de marchandises • der Güterzug • el tren de carga • il treno merci

luggage rack • le porte-bagages • die Gepäckablage • el portaequipajes • il portabagagli

window
la fenêtre
das Zugfenster
la ventanilla
il finestrino

track
la voie ferrée
das Gleis
la vía
il binario

door
la porte
die Tür
la puerta
la porta

seat
le siège
der Sitz
el asiento
il sedile

compartment • le compartiment • das Abteil • el compartimento • lo scompartimento

ticket barrier • le portillon • die Eingangssperre • la barrera • la barriera

dining car • la voiture-restaurant • der Speisewagen • el vagón restaurante • il vagone ristorante

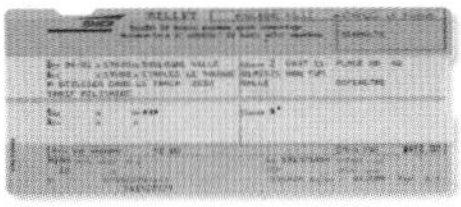

ticket • le billet • die Fahrkarte • el boleto • il biglietto

public address system • le haut-parleur • der Lautsprecher• el altavoz • il sistema di avviso ai passeggeri

schedule
l'horaire
der Fahrplan
el horario
l'orario

concourse • le hall de gare • die Bahnhofshalle • el vestíbulo • l'atrio

sleeping compartment • le compartiment-couchettes • das Schlafabteil • el cochecama • lo scompartimento a cuccette

railroad network
le réseau ferroviaire
das Bahnnetz
la red ferroviaria
la rete ferroviaria

inter-city train
le rapide
der Intercity
el tren intercity
il treno intercity

rush hour
l'heure de pointe
die Stoßzeit
la hora pico
l'ora di punta

underground map
le plan de métro
der U-Bahnplan
el plano del metro
la mappa della metropolitana

delay
le retard
die Verspätung
el retraso
il ritardo

fare
le prix
der Fahrpreis
el precio
la tariffa

ticket office
le guichet
der Fahrkartenschalter
la taquilla
la biglietteria

ticket inspector
le contrôleur
der Schaffner
el checador
il controllore

change *(v)*
changer
umsteigen
cambiar
cambiare

live rail
le rail conducteur
die stromführende Schiene
el riel electrificado
il binario elettrificato

signal
le signal
das Signal
la señal
il segnale

emergency lever
la manette de secours
der Nothebel
la palanca de emergencia
la leva di emergenza

aircraft • l'avion • das Flugzeug • el avión • l'aeroplano

airliner • l'avion de ligne • das Verkehrsflugzeug • el avión de pasajeros • l'aereo di linea

nose
le nez
der Bug
la nariz
il muso

cockpit
le cockpit
das Cockpit
la cabina de pilotaje
la cabina di pilotaggio

engine
le réacteur
das Triebwerk
el motor
il motore

fuselage
le fuselage
der Rumpf
el fuselaje
la fusoliera

wing
l'aile
die Tragfläche
el ala
l'ala

tail
la queue
das Heck
la cola
la coda

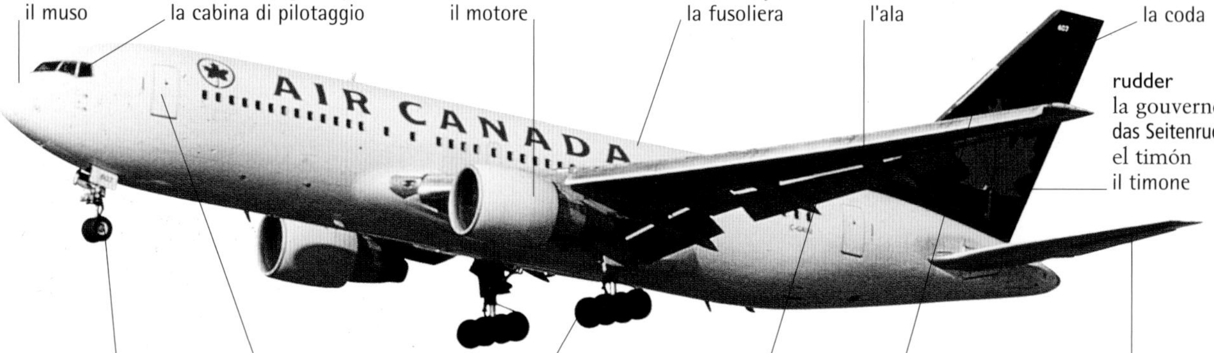

rudder
la gouverne
das Seitenruder
el timón
il timone

nosewheel
la roue de nez
das Bugfahrwerk
el tren delantero
la ruota anteriore

exit
la sortie
der Ausgang
la salida
l'uscita

landing gear
le train d'atterrissage
das Hauptfahrwerk
el tren de aterrizaje
il carrello d'atterraggio

aileron
l'aileron
das Querruder
el alerón
l'alettone

fin
la dérive
das Seitenleitwerk
la aleta
l'aletta

tailplane
l'empennage
das Höhenleitwerk
el estabilizador
lo stabilizzatore

cabin • la cabine • die Kabine • la cabina • la cabina

emergency exit
la sortie de secours
der Notausgang
la salida de emergencia
l'uscita di emergenza

flight attendant
l'hôtesse de l'air
die Flugbegleiterin
la sobrecargo
l'assistente di volo

overhead bin
le casier à bagages
das Gepäckfach
el compartimento portaequipajes
il compartimento portabagagli

window
le hublot
das Fenster
la ventanilla
il finestrino

seat
le siège
der Sitz
el asiento
il sedile

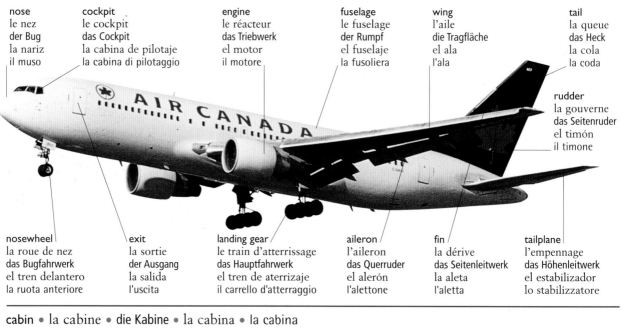

air vent
le ventilateur
die Luftdüse
el ventilador
la ventola per l'aria

reading light
la liseuse
die Leselampe
la luz de lectura
la luce di lettura

row
la rangée
die Reihe
la fila
la fila

tray-table
la tablette
der Klapptisch
la mesa plegable
il vassoio

armrest
l'accoudoir
die Armlehne
el descansabrazos
il bracciolo

aisle
le couloir
der Gang
el pasillo
il corridoio

seat back
le dossier
die Rückenlehne
el respaldo
lo schienale

hot-air balloon • la montgolfière • der Heißluftballon • el globo aerostático • la mongolfiera

ultralight • l'U.L.M. • das Ultraleichtflugzeug • el ultraligero • l'aereo biposto

glider • le planeur • das Segelflugzeug • el planeador • l'aliante

biplane • le biplan • der Doppeldecker • el biplano • il biplano

propeller
l'hélice
der Propeller
la hélice
l'elica

light aircraft • l'avion léger • das Leichtflugzeug • la avioneta • l'aereo da diporto

sea plane • l'hydravion • das Wasserflugzeug • el hidroavión • l'idrovolante

private jet • le jet privé • der Privatjet • el jet privado • l'aereo privato

fighter plane • le chasseur • das Jagdflugzeug • el caza • l'aereo da caccia

missile
le missile
die Rakete
el misil
il missile

rotor blade
la pale de rotor
das Rotorblatt
el aspa
la lama rotante

helicopter • l'hélicoptère • der Hubschrauber • el helicóptero • l'elicottero

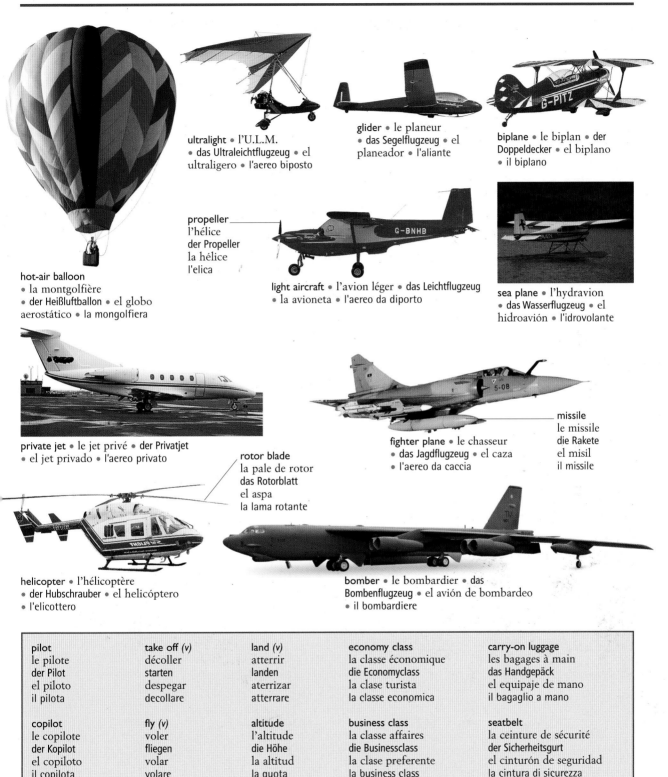

bomber • le bombardier • das Bombenflugzeug • el avión de bombardeo • il bombardiere

pilot le pilote der Pilot el piloto il pilota	take off *(v)* décoller starten despegar decollare	land *(v)* atterrir landen aterrizar atterrare	economy class la classe économique die Economyclass la clase turista la classe economica	carry-on luggage les bagages à main das Handgepäck el equipaje de mano il bagaglio a mano
copilot le copilote der Kopilot el copiloto il copilota	fly *(v)* voler fliegen volar volare	altitude l'altitude die Höhe la altitud la quota	business class la classe affaires die Businessclass la clase preferente la business class	seatbelt la ceinture de sécurité der Sicherheitsgurt el cinturón de seguridad la cintura di sicurezza

airport • l'aéroport • der Flughafen • el aeropuerto • l'aeroporto

apron
l'aire de stationnement
das Vorfeld
la pista de estacionamiento
l'area di stazionamento

baggage trailer
le porte-bagages
der Gepäckanhänger
el remolque del equipaje
il carrello portabagagli

terminal
le terminal
der Terminal
la terminal
il terminal

service vehicle
le véhicule de service
das Versorgungsfahrzeug
el vehículo de servicio
il veicolo di servizio

jetway
la passerelle
die Fluggastbrücke
la pasarela
il passaggio pedonale

airliner • l'avion de ligne • das Verkehrsflugzeug • el avión de línea • l'aereo di linea

runway
la piste
die Start- und Landebahn
la pista
la pista

international flight
le vol international
der Auslandsflug
el vuelo internacional
il volo internazionale

domestic flight
le vol domestique
der Inlandsflug
el vuelo nacional
il volo nazionale

connection
la correspondance
die Flugverbindung
la conexión
la coincidenza

flight number
le numéro de vol
die Flugnummer
el número de vuelo
il numero del volo

immigration
l'immigration
die Passkontrolle
migración
l'immigrazione

customs
la douane
der Zoll
la aduana
la dogana

excess baggage
l'excédent de bagages
das Übergepäck
el exceso de equipaje
il bagaglio in eccedenza

baggage carousel
le tapis roulant
das Gepäckband
la banda transportadora
il nastro trasportatore

security
la sécurité
die Sicherheitsvorkehrungen
la seguridad
la sicurezza

x-ray machine
la machine de rayons x
die Gepäckröntgenmaschine
la máquina de rayos x
l'apparecchio a raggi x

travel brochure
la brochure de vacances
der Urlaubsprospekt
el folleto de viajes
l'opuscolo vacanze

vacation
les vacances
der Urlaub
las vacaciones
la vacanza

make a flight reservation *(v)*
faire une réservation de vol
einen Flug buchen
reservar un vuelo
prenotare un volo

check in *(v)*
enregistrer
einchecken
hacer check-in
fare il check-in

control tower
la tour de contrôle
der Kontrollturm
la torre de control
la torre di controllo

carry-on luggage
les bagages à main
das Handgepäck
el equipaje de mano
il bagaglio a mano

luggage
les bagages
das Gepäck
el equipaje
il bagaglio

cart
le chariot
der Kofferkuli
el carrito
il carrello

check-in desk • l'enregistrement des bagages • der Abfertigungsschalter • el mostrador de check-in • il banco accettazione

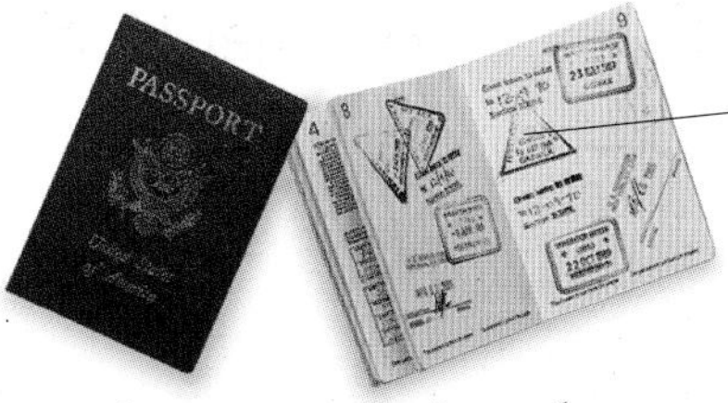

visa
le visa
das Visum
la visa
il visto

passport • le passeport • der Pass • el pasaporte • il passaporto

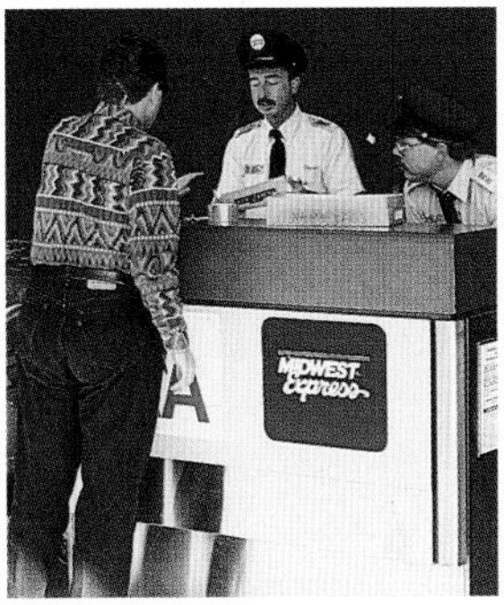

passport control • le contrôle de passeports • die Passkontrolle • el control de pasaportes • il controllo passaporti

boarding pass
la carte d'embarquement
die Bordkarte
la tarjeta de embarque
la carta d'imbarco

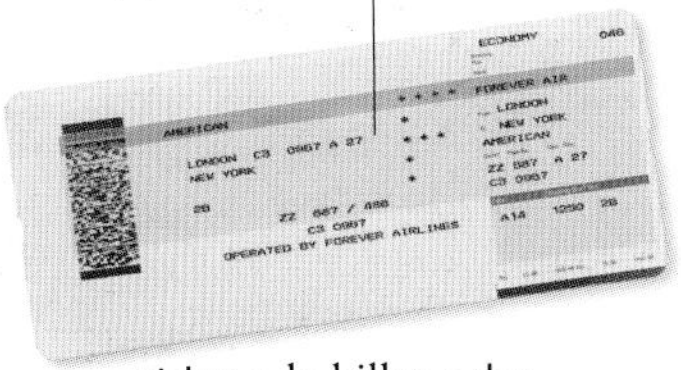

ticket • le billet • das Flugticket • el boleto • il biglietto

gate number • le numéro de la porte d'embarquement • die Gatenummer • el número de puerta de embarque • il numero dell'uscita

departure lounge • la salle de départ • die Abflughalle • la sala de embarque • la sala delle partenze

departures
les départs
der Abflug
las salidas
le partenze

destination
la destination
das Reiseziel
el destino
la destinazione

arrivals
les arrivées
die Ankunft
las llegadas
gli arrivi

information screen • l'écran d'information • die Fluginformationsanzeige • la pantalla informativa • il pannello degli orari

duty-free store
la boutique hors taxes
der Duty-free-Shop
el duty-free
il negozio duty free

baggage claim
le retrait des bagages
die Gepäckausgabe
la recogida de equipajes
il ricupero bagagli

taxi stand
la station de taxis
der Taxistand
el sitio de taxis
il posteggio dei taxi

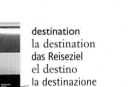

car rental
la location de voitures
der Autoverleih
la renta de carros
l'autonoleggio

ship • le navire • das Schiff • el barco • la nave

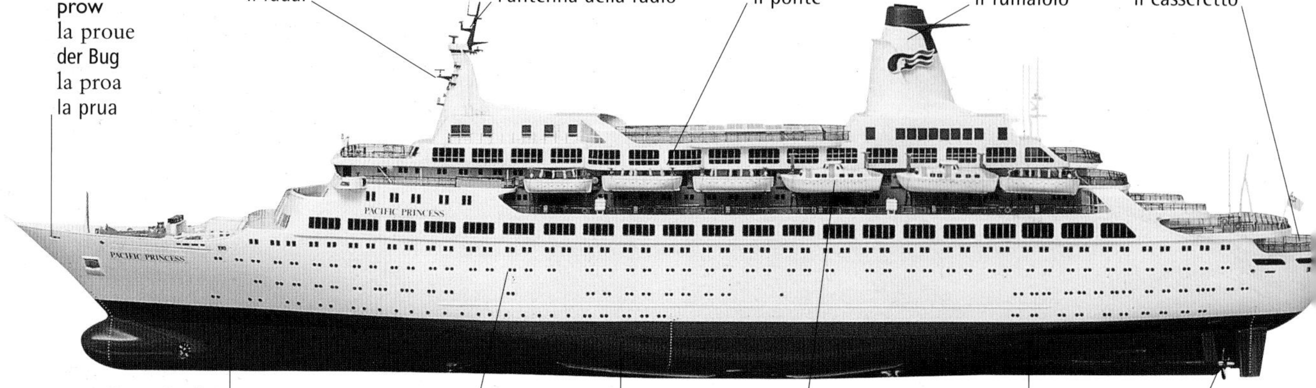

ocean liner • le paquebot • der Ozeandampfer • el transatlántico • la nave da crociera

bridge • la passerelle de commandement • die Kommandobrücke • el puente • il ponte di comando

engine room • la salle des moteurs • der Maschinenraum • la sala de máquinas • la sala macchine

cabin • la cabine • die Kabine • el camarote • la cabina

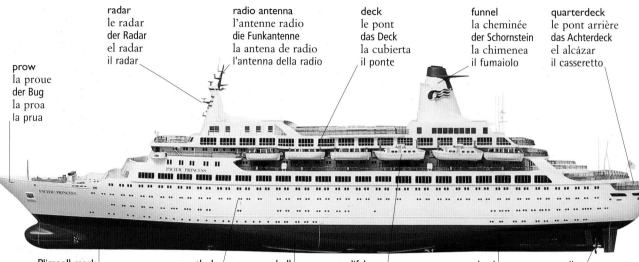

galley • la cuisine • die Kombüse • la cocina • la cucina di bordo

dock
le dock
das Dock
el muelle
il bacino

port
le port
der Hafen
el puerto
il porto

gangway
la passerelle
die Landungsbrücke
la pasarela
la passerella

anchor
l'ancre
der Anker
el ancla
l'ancora

bollard
le bollard
der Poller
el noray
la colonna d'ormeggio

windlass
le guindeau
die Ankerwinde
el cabrestante
il mulinello

captain
le capitaine
der Kapitän
el capitán
il capitano

speedboat
le runabout
das Rennboot
la lancha de motor
il motoscafo

rowboat
la barque
das Ruderboot
la barca de remos
la barca a remi

canoe
le canoë
das Kanu
la piragua
la canoa

other ships • autres bateaux • andere Schiffe • otras embarcaciones • altre imbarcazioni

ferryboat • le ferry • die Fähre • el ferry • il traghetto

outboard motor
le hors-bord
der Außenbordmotor
el motor fueraborda
il motore fuoribordo

inflatable dinghy • le dinghy pneumatique • das Schlauchboot • la zodiac • il gommone

hydrofoil • l'hydroptère • das Tragflügelboot • el hidrodeslizador • l'aliscafo

yacht • le yacht • die Jacht • el yate • lo yacht

catamaran • le catamaran • der Katamaran • el catamarán • il catamarano

tugboat • le remorqueur • der Schleppdampfer • el remolcador • il rimorchiatore

hovercraft • l'aéroglisseur • das Luftkissenboot • el aerodeslizador • l'hovercraft

container ship • le navire porte-conteneurs • das Containerschiff • el barco carguero • la nave porta container

rigging
le gréement
die Takelung
las jarcias
il sartiame

sailboat • le voilier • das Segelboot • el barco de vela • la barca a vela

hold
la cale
der Frachtraum
la bodega
la stiva

freighter • le cargo • das Frachtschiff • el buque de carga • la nave da trasporto

oil tanker • le pétrolier • der Öltanker • el buque tanque • la petroliera

aircraft carrier • le porte-avions • der Flugzeugträger • el portaaviones • la portaerei

battleship • le navire de guerre • das Kriegsschiff • el barco de guerra • la nave da guerra

conning tower
le kiosque
der Kommandoturm
la falsa torre
la torretta di comando

submarine • le sous-marin • das U-Boot • el submarino • il sottomarino

port • le port • der Hafen • el puerto • il porto

warehouse
l'entrepôt
das Warenlager
la bodega
il magazzino

crane
la grue
der Kran
la grúa
la gru

forklift
le chariot élévateur
der Gabelstapler
la carretilla elevadora
il carrello elevatore

access road
la route d'accès
die Zufahrtsstraße
la vía de acceso
la strada di accesso

customs house
le bureau des douanes
das Zollamt
las aduanas del puerto
l'ufficio della dogana

container
le conteneur
der Container
el contenedor
il container

dock
le dock
das Dock
la dársena
il bacino

quay
le quai
der Kai
el muelle
la banchina

cargo
la cargaison
die Fracht
la carga
il carico

ferry terminal
le terminal de ferrys
der Fährterminal
la terminal del ferry
il terminale dei traghetti

ferryboat
le ferry
die Fähre
el ferry
il traghetto

containerport • le port de conteneurs • der Containerhafen • el muelle comercial • il porto per container

ticket office
le guichet
der Fahrkartenschalter
la ventanilla de boletos
la biglietteria

passenger
le passager
der Passagier
el pasajero
il passeggero

passenger port • le port de passagers • der Passagierhafen • el muelle de pasajeros • il porto per passeggeri

net
le filet
das Netz
la red
la rete

fishing boat
le bateau de pêche
das Fischerboot
el barco pesquero
la barca da pesca

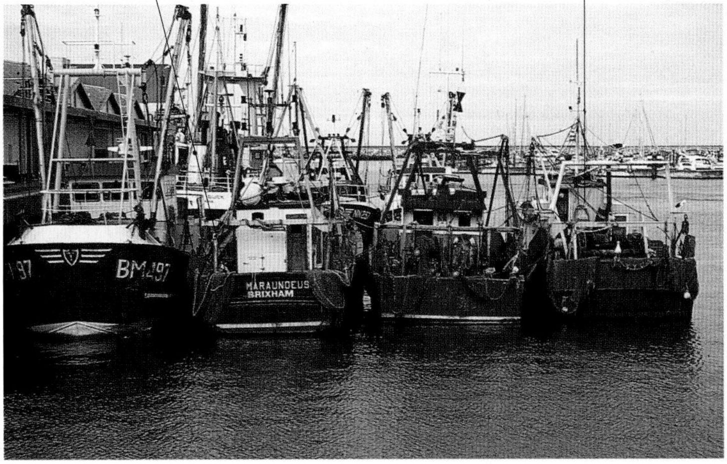

fishing port • le port de pêche • der Fischereihafen • el puerto pesquero • il porto da pesca

mooring
les amarres
die Verankerung
el punto de amarre
l'ormeggio

marina • la marina • die Marina • el puerto deportivo • il porto turistico

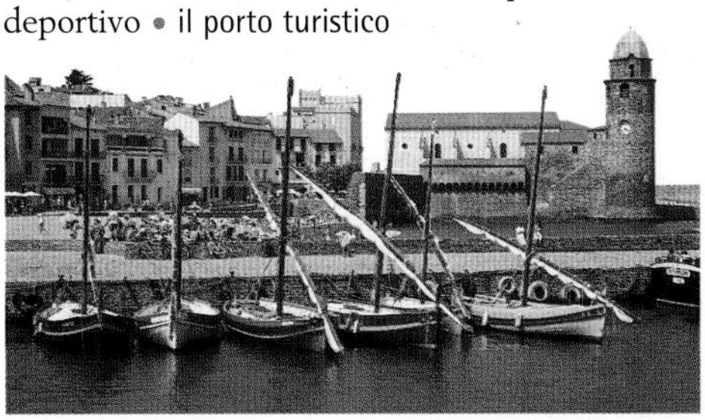

harbor • le port • der Hafen • el puerto • il porto

pier • l'embarcadère • der Pier • el embarcadero • il pontile

jetty • la jetée • der Landungssteg • el espigón • il molo

shipyard • le chantier naval • die Werft • el astillero • il cantiere navale

lantern
le feu
die Laterne
la lámpara
la luce

lighthouse • le phare • der Leuchtturm • el faro • il faro

buoy • la bouée • die Boje • la boya • la boa

coast guard
le garde-côte
die Küstenwache
el guardacostas
il guardacoste

harbormaster
le capitaine de port
der Hafenmeister
el capitán del puerto
il capitano di porto

drop anchor *(v)*
jeter l'ancre
den Anker werfen
anclar
mollare l'ancora

dry dock
la cale sèche
das Trockendock
el dique seco
il bacino di carenaggio

moor *(v)*
mouiller
festmachen
amarrar
ormeggiare

dock *(v)*
se mettre à quai
anlegen
atracar
entrare in bacino

board *(v)*
embarquer
an Bord gehen
embarcar
imbarcare

disembark *(v)*
débarquer
von Bord gehen
desembarcar
sbarcare

set sail *(v)*
prendre la mer
auslaufen
zarpar
salpare

ULTRA
3
DUNLOP
DDH III
4
DUNLOP
MOLITOR
TOUR
EDITION
1
ProStaff
4
GOLF CLUB
TOP-FLITE
HOT XL
4
ProStaff
4
RAM TOUR
1
MAXFLI
TOP-FLITE
STRATA
3
DISTANCE

sports
les sports
der Sport
los deportes
gli sport

football • le football américain • der Football • el fútbol americano • il football americano

goalpost
le poteau
der Torpfosten
el poste de la portería
la porta

sideline
la ligne de touche
die Seitenlinie
la línea de banda
la linea laterale

referee
le juge de ligne
der Linienrichter
el juez de línea
il giudice di linea

goal line
la ligne de but
die Torlinie
la línea de gol
la linea del gol

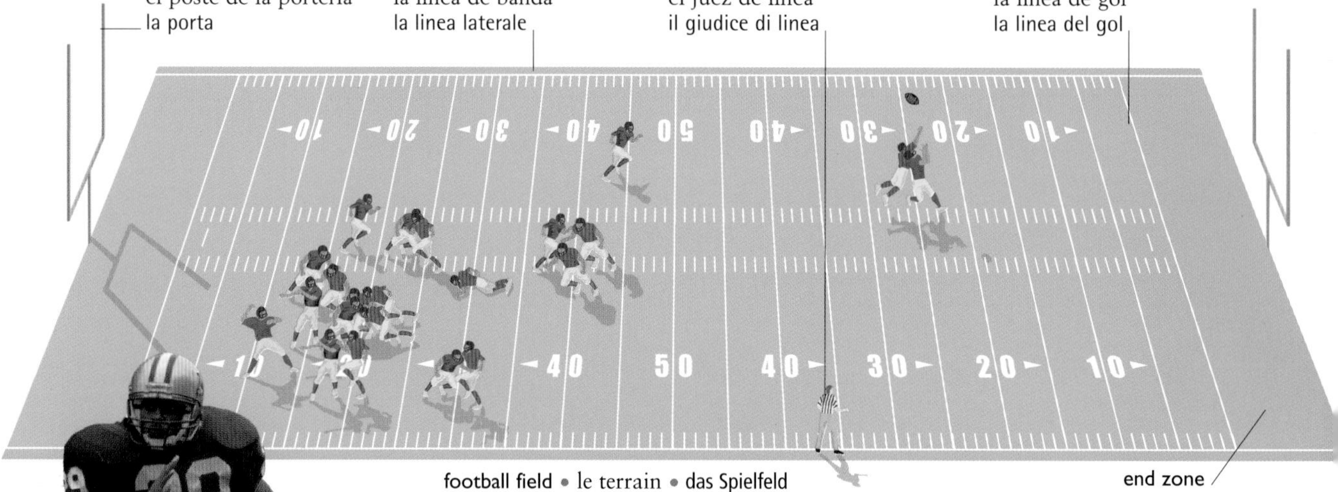

football field • le terrain • das Spielfeld • el campo • il campo

end zone
la zone de fond
die Endzone
la zona final
il fondo campo

football
le ballon
der Football
el balón
il pallone

cleat
la botte
der Stiefel
los tenis
lo scarpino

football player • le joueur de football • der Footballspieler • el jugador • il giocatore

pads
les protections
das Polster
las rodilleras
le ginocchiere

helmet
le casque
der Helm
el casco
il casco

tackle (*v*) • tacler • angreifen • taclear • placcare

pass (*v*) • faire une passe • den Ball abgeben • pasar • passare

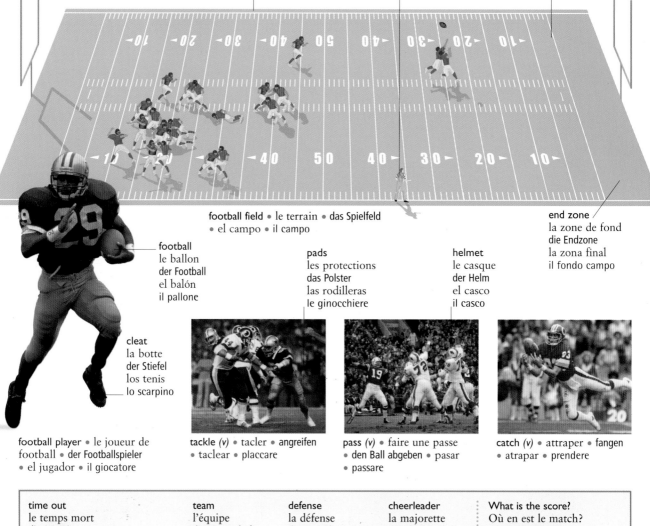

catch (*v*) • attraper • fangen • atrapar • prendere

time out le temps mort die Auszeit el tiempo fuera il time-out	team l'équipe die Mannschaft el equipo la squadra	defense la défense die Verteidigung la defensa la difesa	cheerleader la majorette der Cheerleader la porrista la cheerleader	What is the score? Où en est le match? Wie ist der Stand? ¿Cómo van? A quanto stanno?
fumble la prise de ballon maladroite das unsichere Fangen des Balls el balón perdido il fumble	attack l'attaque der Angriff el ataque l'attacco	score le score der Spielstand la puntuación il punteggio	touchdown le but der Touchdown el intento il touch-down	Who is winning? Qui est-ce qui gagne? Wer gewinnt? ¿Quién va ganando? Chi vince?

rugby • le rugby • das Rugby • el rugby • il rugby

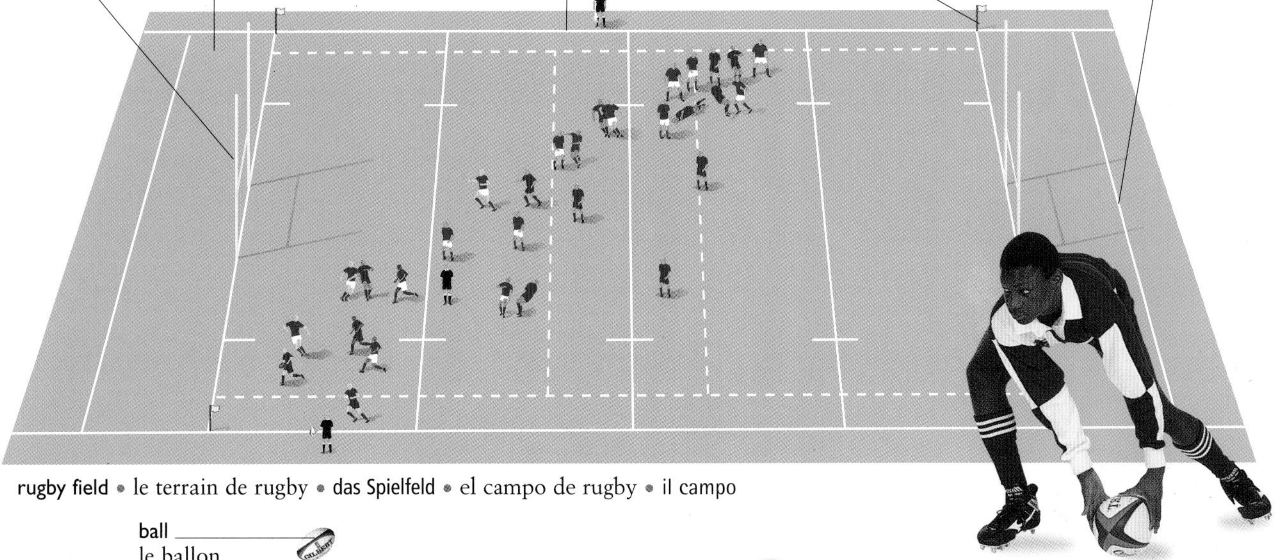

rugby field • le terrain de rugby • das Spielfeld • el campo de rugby • il campo

throw *(v)* • lancer • werfen • lanzar • tirare

kick *(v)* • botter • kicken • patear • calciare

pass *(v)* • faire une passe • den Ball abgeben • pasar • passare

tackle *(v)* • tacler • angreifen • taclear • placcare

try • l'essai • der Versuch • el intento • la meta

ruck • la mêlée ouverte • das offene Gedränge • la abierta • il ruck

scrum • la mêlée • das Gedränge • la cerrada • la mischia

soccer • le football • der Fußball • el fútbol • il calcio

soccer player • le joueur de foot • der Fußballspieler • el futbolista • il calciatore

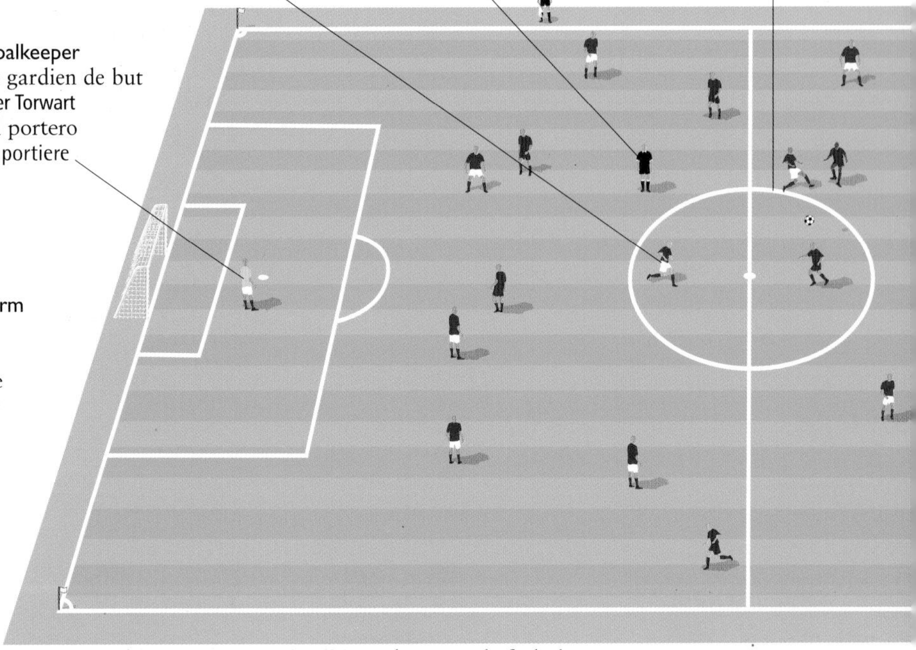

soccer field • le terrain • das Fußballfeld • el campo de fútbol • il campo di calcio

goal • le but • das Tor • el gol • il gol

dribble *(v)* • dribbler • dribbeln • regatear • dribblare

head *(v)* • faire une tête • köpfen • cabecear • colpire di testa

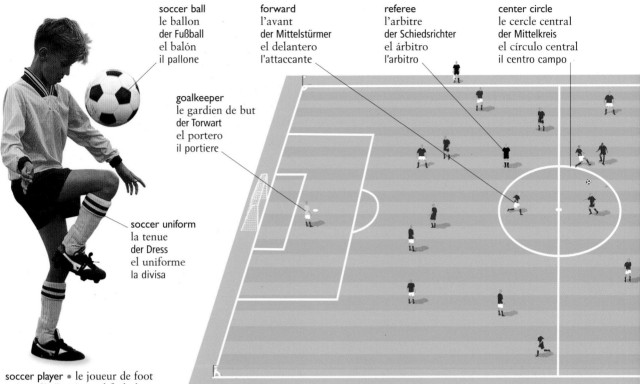

free kick • le coup franc • der Freistoß • el tiro libre • il calcio di punizione

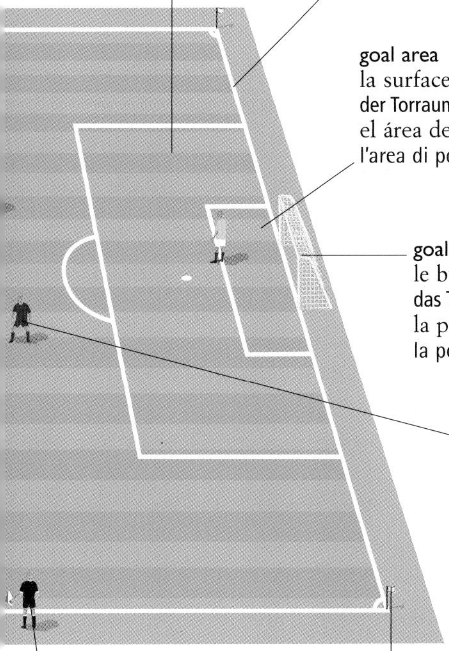

penalty area
la surface de réparation
der Strafraum
el área de penalty
l'area di rigore

goal line
la ligne de but
die Torlinie
la línea de meta
la linea di fondo

goal area
la surface de but
der Torraum
el área de meta
l'area di porta

goal
le but
das Tor
la portería
la porta

defender
le défenseur
der Verteidiger
el defensa
il difensore

linesman
le juge de ligne
der Linienrichter
el juez de línea
il guardialinee

corner flag
le drapeau de coin
die Eckfahne
la bandera de esquina
la bandierina

throw-in • la rentrée en touche • der Einwurf • el saque de banda • la rimessa in gioco

kick *(v)* • botter • kicken • patear • calciare

cleat
la botte
der Fußballschuh
los tacos
lo scarpino

pass *(v)* • faire une passe • den Ball abgeben • mandar un pase • passare

shoot *(v)* • shooter • schießen • tirar • tirare

save *(v)* • sauver • halten • parar • parare

tackle *(v)* • tacler • angreifen • hacer una entrada • contrastare

stadium le stade das Stadion el estadio lo stadio	**foul** la faute das Foul la falta il fallo	**yellow card** le carton jaune die gelbe Karte la tarjeta amarilla il cartellino giallo	**league** le championnat die Liga la liga il campionato	**extra time** la prolongation die Verlängerung el tiempo extra il tempo supplementare
score a goal *(v)* marquer un but ein Tor schießen marcar un gol segnare	**corner** le corner der Eckball el tiro de esquina il calcio d'angolo	**offside** l'hors-jeu das Abseits el fuera de juego il fuorigioco	**draw** l'egalité das Unentschieden el empate il pareggio	**substitute** le remplaçant der Ersatzspieler el reserva il sostituto
penalty le penalty der Elfmeter el penalty il rigore	**red card** le carton rouge die rote Karte la tarjeta roja il cartellino rosso	**send off** l'expulsion der Platzverweis la expulsión l'espulsione	**halftime** la mi-temps die Halbzeit el descanso l'intervallo	**substitution** le remplacement die Auswechslung el cambio la sostituzione

hockey • le hockey • das Hockey • el hockey • l'hockey

ice hockey • le hockey sur glace • das Eishockey • el hockey sobre hielo • l'hockey su ghiaccio

goal line
la ligne de but
die Torlinie
la línea de meta
la linea della porta

attack zone
la zone d'attaque
die Angriffszone
la zona de ataque
l'area di attacco

neutral zone
la zone neutre
die neutrale Zone
la zona neutral
l'area neutrale

defending zone
la zone de défense
die Verteidigungszone
la zona de defensa
l'area di difesa

goal keeper
le gardien de but
der Torwart
el portero
il portiere

goal
le but
das Tor
la portería
la porta

face-off circle
le cercle de mise en jeu
der Anspielkreis
el círculo de face-off
il circolo di confronto

center circle
le cercle central
der Mittelkreis
el círculo central
il cerchio centrale

ice hockey rink • la patinoire • die Eisfläche • la pista de hockey sobre hielo • la pista da hockey su ghiaccio

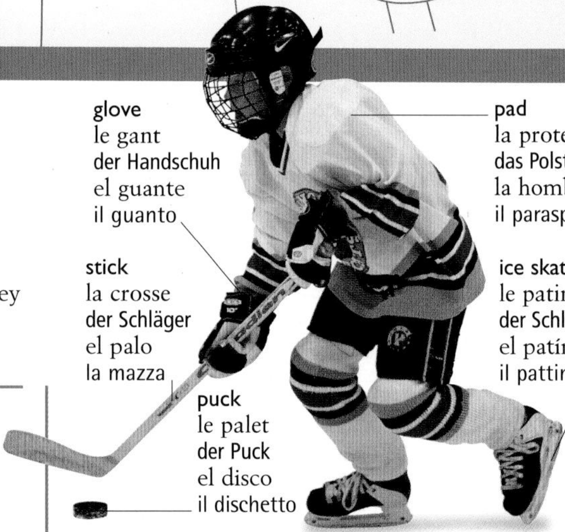

glove
le gant
der Handschuh
el guante
il guanto

pad
la protection
das Polster
la hombrera
il paraspalla

stick
la crosse
der Schläger
el palo
la mazza

ice skate
le patin à glace
der Schlittschuh
el patín de cuchilla
il pattino

puck
le palet
der Puck
el disco
il dischetto

ice hockey player • le hockeyeur • der Eishockeyspieler • el jugador de hockey sobre hielo • il giocatore di hockey su ghiaccio

field hockey • le hockey • das Hockey • el hockey sobre pasto • l'hockey sull'erba

hockey stick
la crosse de hockey
der Hockeyschläger
el palo de hockey
la mazza da hockey

ball
la balle
der Hockeyball
la pelota
la pallina

skate *(v)* • patiner • Schlittschuh laufen • patinar • pattinare

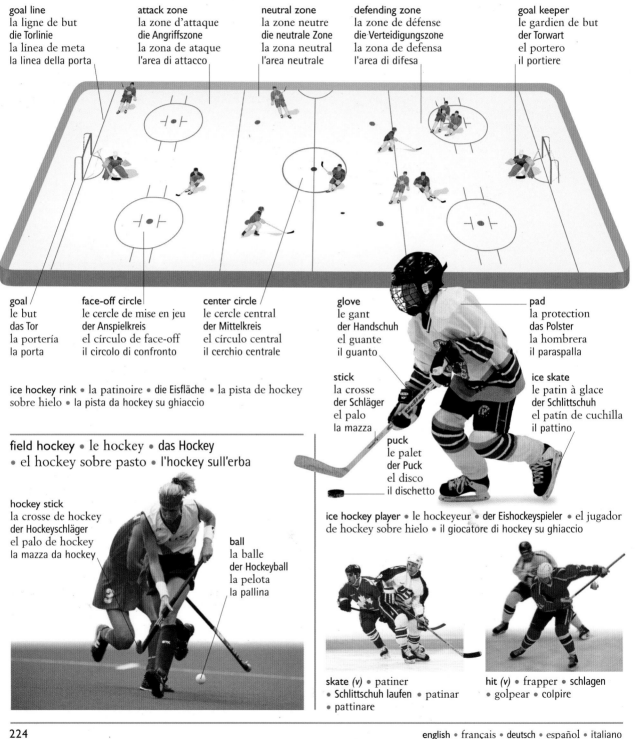

hit *(v)* • frapper • schlagen • golpear • colpire

cricket • le cricket • das Kricket • el críquet • il cricket

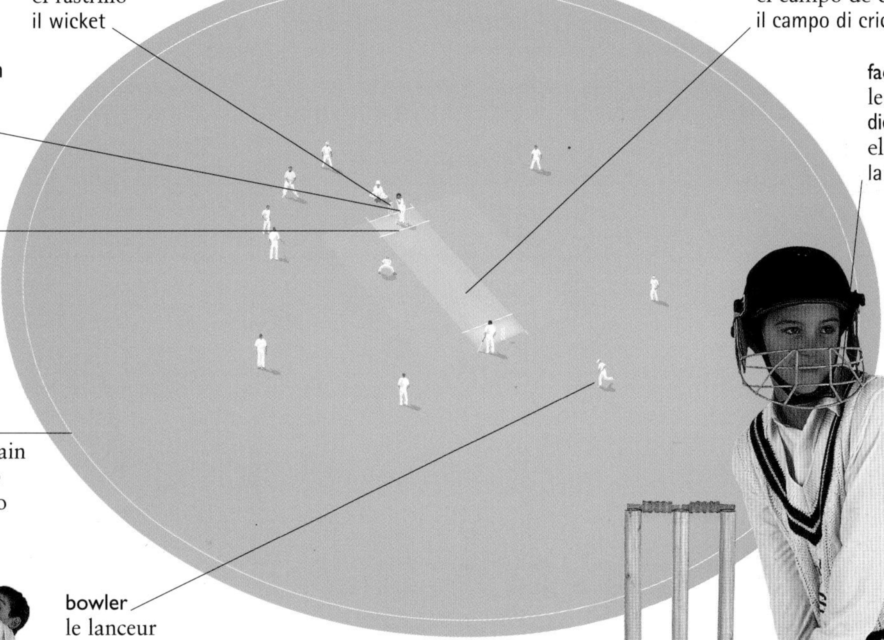

wicket
le guichet
das Krickettor
el rastrillo
il wicket

pitch
le terrain de cricket
die Spielbahn
el campo de críquet
il campo di cricket

batsman
le batteur
der Schlagmann
el bateador
il battitore

face mask
le masque protecteur
die Gesichtsschutzmaske
el protector de la cara
la maschera protettiva

crease • la ligne d'envoi • die Wurflinie • la línea del bateador • la linea

boundary line
la limite du terrain
die Spielfeldgrenze
la línea de fondo
il limite

bowler
le lanceur
der Werfer
el lanzador
il lanciatore

stump
le piquet
der Stab
el palo
il piolo

leg pad • la jambière • das Polster • el protector de la pierna • il parastinchi

bat
la batte
das Schlagholz
el bate
la mazza

cricket player • le jouer de cricket • der Kricketspieler • el jugador de críquet • il giocatore di cricket

bowl *(v)* lancer • werfen • lanzar • lanciare

bat *(v)* • frapper • schlagen • batear • colpire

cricket ball
la balle de criquet
der Kricketball
la pelota de críquet
la pallina da cricket

field *(v)* • attraper • fangen • interceptar y devolver • difendere

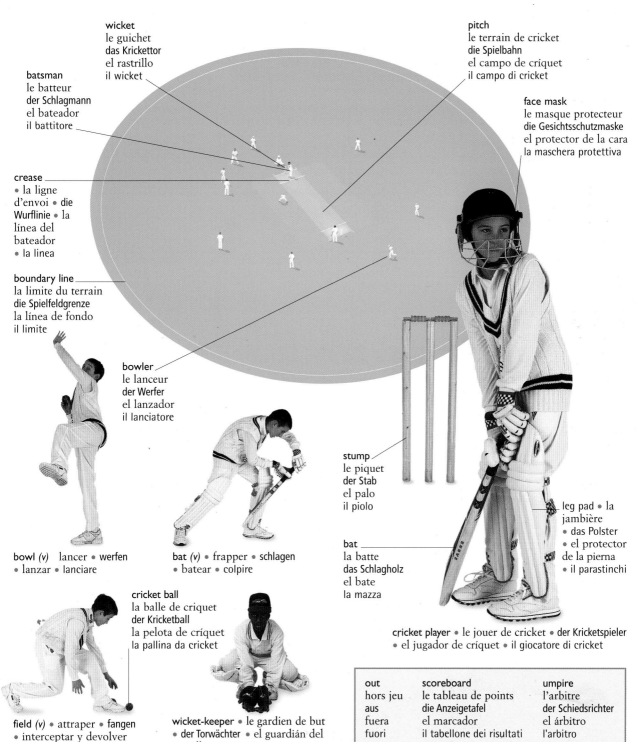

wicket-keeper • le gardien de but • der Torwächter • el guardián del rastrillo • il ricevitore

out	scoreboard	umpire
hors jeu	le tableau de points	l'arbitre
aus	die Anzeigetafel	der Schiedsrichter
fuera	el marcador	el árbitro
fuori	il tabellone dei risultati	l'arbitro

basketball • le basket • der Basketball • el baloncesto • la pallacanestro

sideline
la ligne de touche
die Seitenlinie
la línea de banda
la linea laterale

referee
l'arbitre
der Schiedsrichter
el árbitro
l'arbitro

center circle
le cercle central
der Mittelkreis
el círculo central
il dischetto

free-throw line
la ligne de lancer franc
die Freiwurflinie
la línea de tiro libre
la linea di tiro libero

endline
la ligne de bout
die Endlinie
la línea de fondo
la linea di fondo

court • le terrain • das Spielfeld • la cancha • il campo

centerline
la ligne de centre
die Mittellinie
la línea central
la linea di centrocampo

three-point line
la ligne de trois points
die Dreipunktlinie
la línea de tres puntos
la linea dei tre punti

number
le numéro
die Spielernummer
el número
il numero

ball
le ballon
der Basketball
el balón
il pallone

basketball player • le joueur de basket • der Basketballspieler • el jugador de baloncesto • il giocatore di pallacenestro

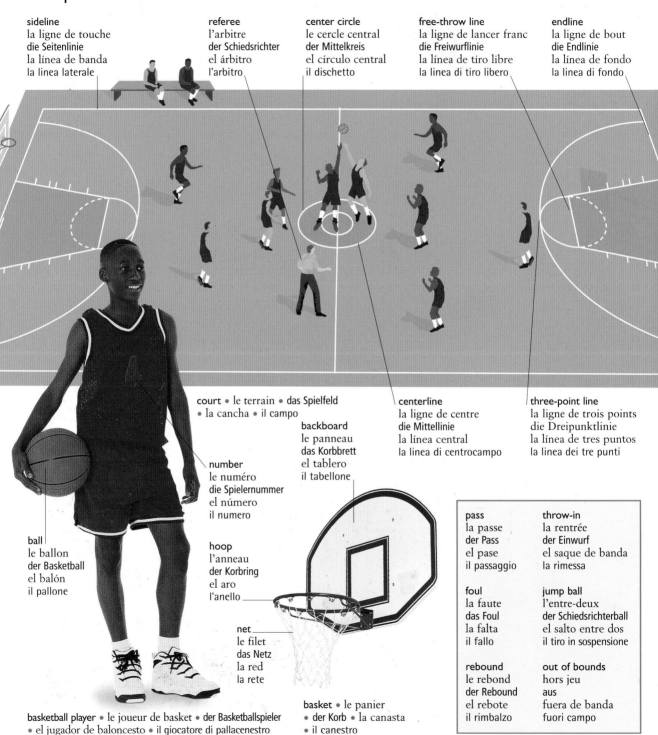

backboard
le panneau
das Korbbrett
el tablero
il tabellone

hoop
l'anneau
der Korbring
el aro
l'anello

net
le filet
das Netz
la red
la rete

basket • le panier • der Korb • la canasta • il canestro

pass la passe der Pass el pase il passaggio	**throw-in** la rentrée der Einwurf el saque de banda la rimessa
foul la faute das Foul la falta il fallo	**jump ball** l'entre-deux der Schiedsrichterball el salto entre dos il tiro in sospensione
rebound le rebond der Rebound el rebote il rimbalzo	**out of bounds** hors jeu aus fuera de banda fuori campo

actions • les actions • die Aktionen • las acciones • le azioni

throw *(v)* • lancer • werfen • lanzar • tirare

catch *(v)* • attraper • fangen • cachar • acchiappare

shoot *(v)* • tirer • schießen • tirar • tirare

jump *(v)* • sauter • springen • saltar • saltare

cover *(v)* • marquer • decken • marcar • marcare

block *(v)* • bloquer • blocken • bloquear • bloccare

dribble *(v)* • faire rebondir • springen lassen • botar • rimbalzare

dunk *(v)* • faire un dunk • einen Dunk spielen • marcar • segnare

volleyball • le volley • der Volleyball • el vóleibol • la pallavolo

block *(v)*
bloquer
blocken
bloquear
contrastare

net
le filet
das Netz
la red
la rete

dig *(v)*
• faire une manchette
• baggern
• recibir
• difendere

referee
l'arbitre
der Schiedsrichter
el árbitro
l'arbitro

knee support
la genouillère
der Knieschützer
la rodillera
la ginocchiera

court • le terrain • das Spielfeld • la cancha • il campo

baseball • le baseball • der Baseball • el béisbol • il baseball

field • le terrain • das Spielfeld • el campo • il campo

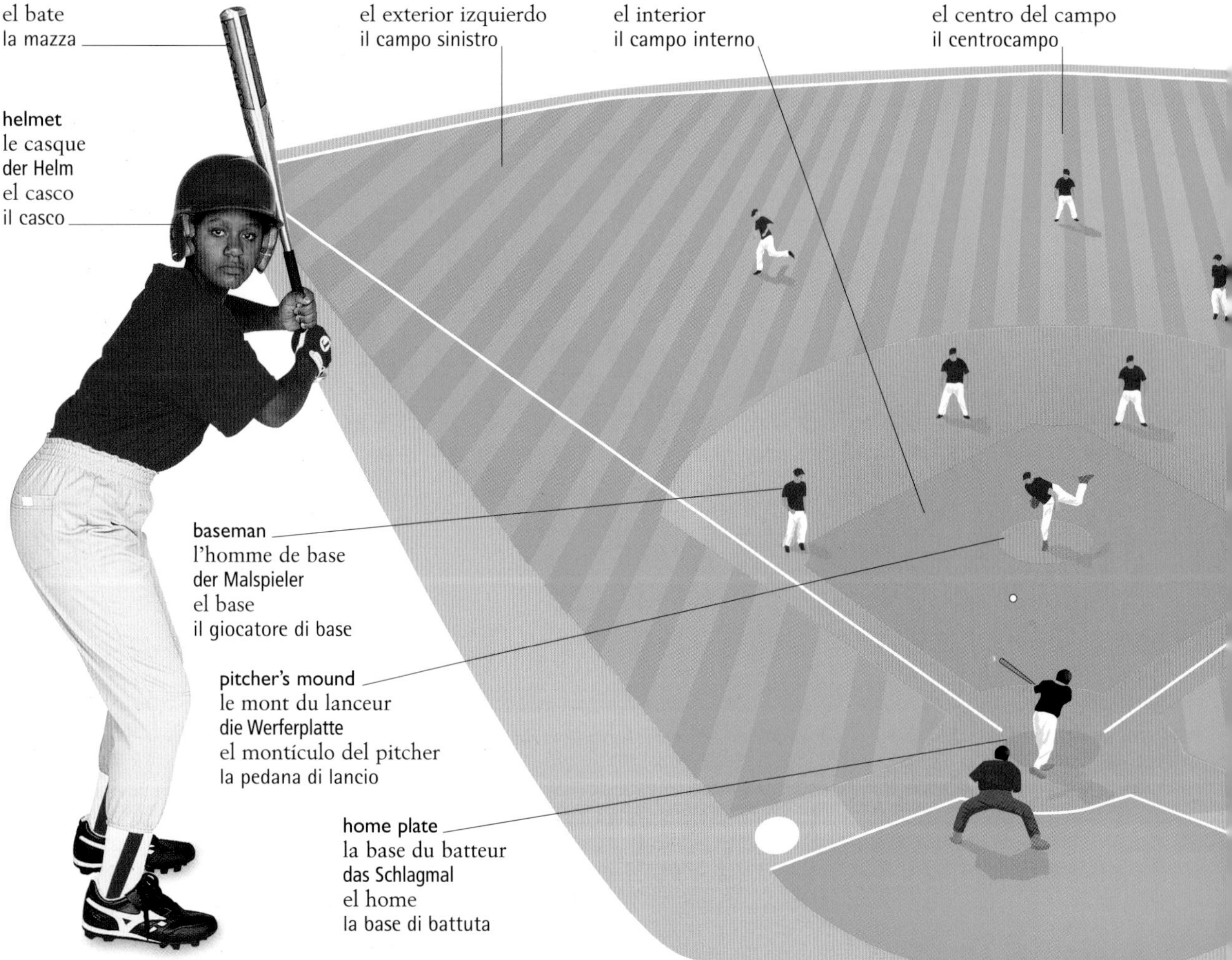

batter • le batteur • der Schlagmann • el bateador • il battitore

inning le tour de batte das Inning el turno il turno di battuta	safe sauf in Sicherheit safe salvo	strike le coup manqué der Schlagfehler el strike lo strike
run le point der Lauf la carrera il giro	out hors jeu aus fuera fuori	foul ball la fausse balle der ungültige Schlag el foul il fallo

glove • le gant • der Handschuh • la manopla • il guantone

mask • le masque • die Schutzmaske • la careta • la maschera

outfield
le champ extérieur
das Außenfeld
el exterior
il campo esterno

right field
le champ droit
das rechte Feld
el exterior derecho
il campo destro

foul line
la ligne de pénalité
die Foullinie
la línea de falta
la linea di fallo

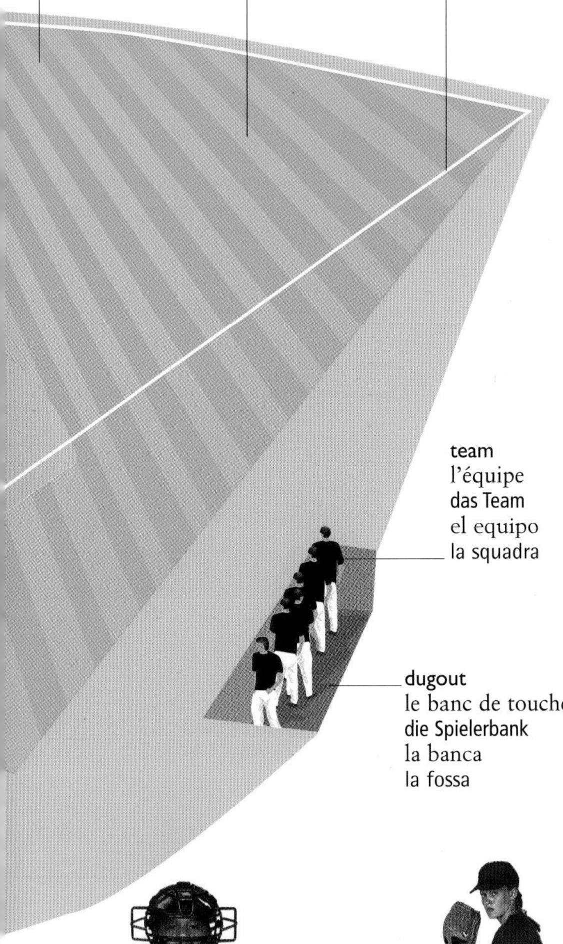

team
l'équipe
das Team
el equipo
la squadra

dugout
le banc de touche
die Spielerbank
la banca
la fossa

catcher • le receveur • der Fänger • el catcher • il ricevitore

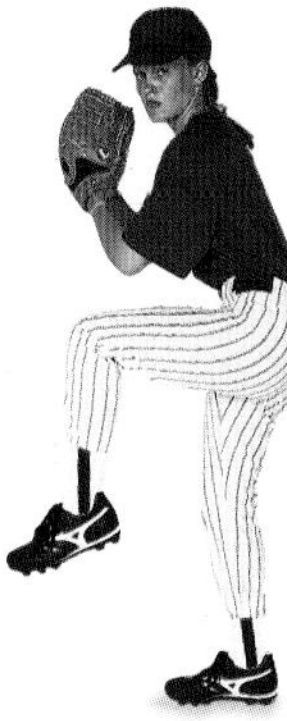

pitcher • le lanceur • der Werfer • el pitcher • il pitcher

actions • les actions • die Aktionen • las acciones • le azioni

throw *(v)* • lancer • werfen • lanzar • lanciare

catch *(v)* • attraper • fangen • atrapar • acchiappare

run *(v)* • courir • rennen • correr • correre

field *(v)* • être en défense • als Fänger spielen • defender • difendere

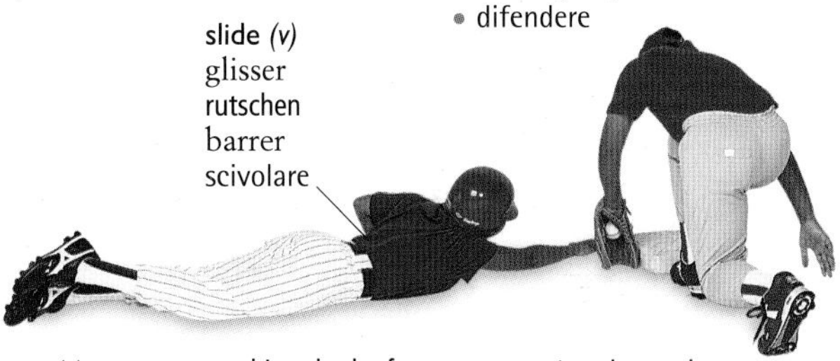

slide *(v)*
glisser
rutschen
barrer
scivolare

tag *(v)* • courser • hinterherlaufen • perseguir • inseguire

pitch *(v)*
lancer
werfen
lanzar
servire

bat *(v)*
batter
schlagen
batear
battere

umpire
l'arbitre
der Schiedsrichter
el umpire
l'arbitro

play *(v)* • jouer • spielen • jugar • giocare

tennis • le tennis • das Tennis • el tenis • il tennis

handle
le manche
der Griff
el mango
l'impugnatura

head
la tête
der Kopf
la cabeza
la testa

string
la corde
die Saite
la cuerda
la corda

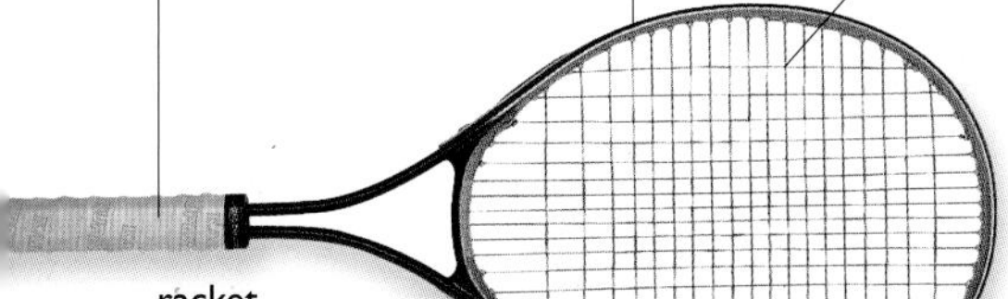

racket • la raquette • der Tennisschläger • la raqueta • la racchetta

umpire
l'arbitre
der Schiedsrichter
el juez de silla
l'arbitro

baseline • la ligne de fond • die Grundlinie • la línea de fondo • la linea di fondo

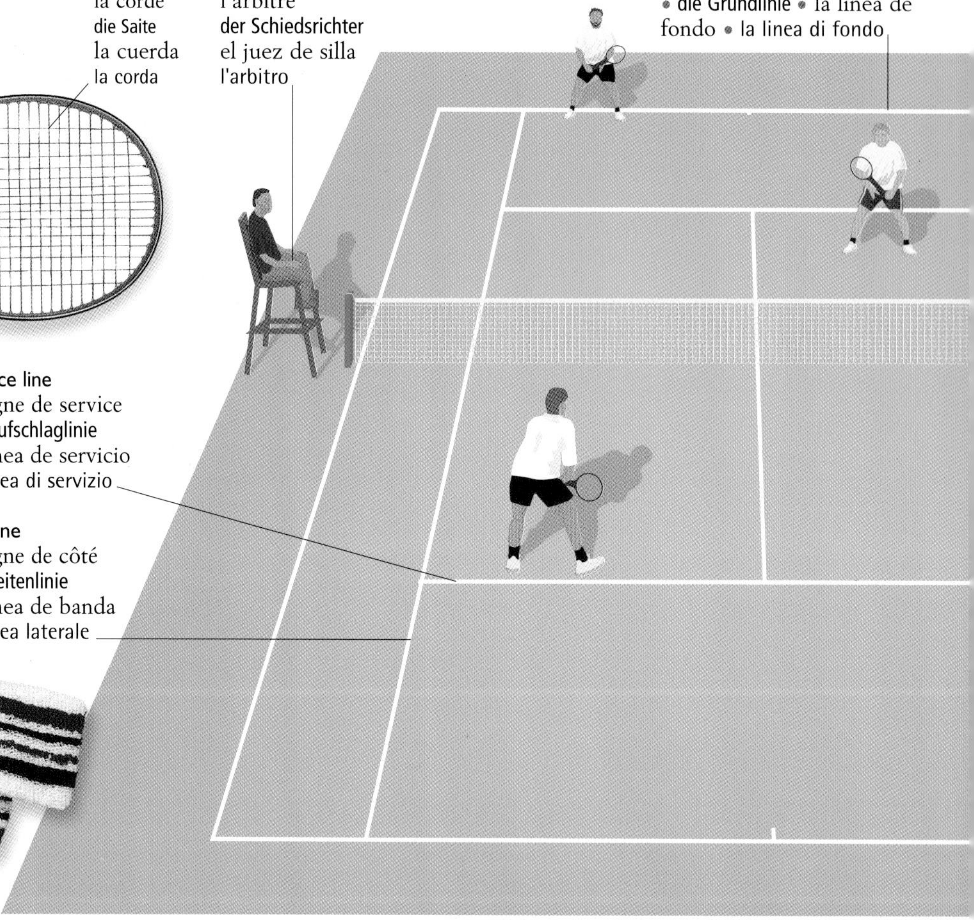

service line
la ligne de service
die Aufschlaglinie
la línea de servicio
la linea di servizio

sideline
la ligne de côté
die Seitenlinie
la línea de banda
la linea laterale

tennis court • le court de tennis • der Tennisplatz • la pista de tenis • il campo

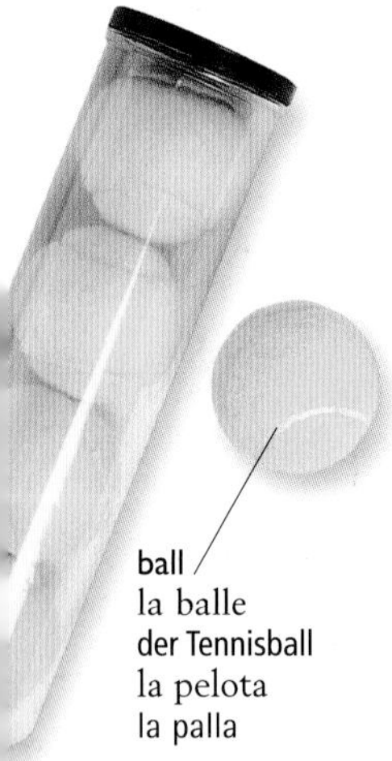

ball
la balle
der Tennisball
la pelota
la palla

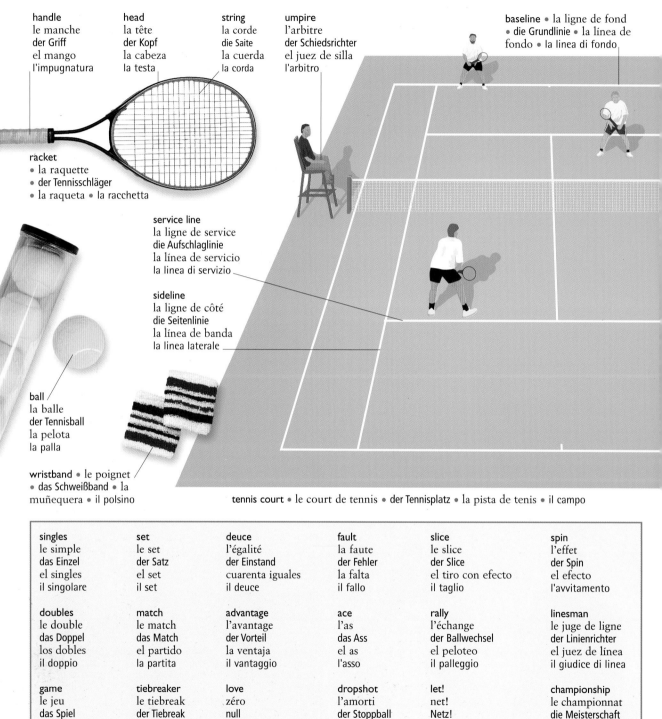

wristband • le poignet • das Schweißband • la muñequera • il polsino

singles le simple das Einzel el singles il singolare	**set** le set der Satz el set il set	**deuce** l'égalité der Einstand cuarenta iguales il deuce	**fault** la faute der Fehler la falta il fallo	**slice** le slice der Slice el tiro con efecto il taglio	**spin** l'effet der Spin el efecto l'avvitamento
doubles le double das Doppel los dobles il doppio	**match** le match das Match el partido la partita	**advantage** l'avantage der Vorteil la ventaja il vantaggio	**ace** l'as das Ass el as l'asso	**rally** l'échange der Ballwechsel el peloteo il palleggio	**linesman** le juge de ligne der Linienrichter el juez de línea il giudice di linea
game le jeu das Spiel el juego il gioco	**tiebreaker** le tiebreak der Tiebreak el tiebreak il tiebreak	**love** zéro null nada a zero	**dropshot** l'amorti der Stoppball la dejada la smorzata	**let!** net! Netz! ¡red! colpo nullo!	**championship** le championnat die Meisterschaft el campeonato il campionato

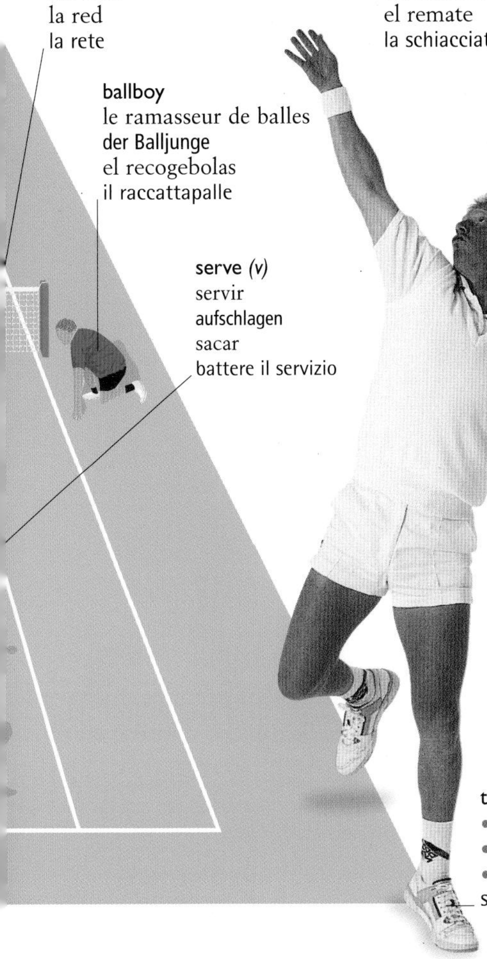

net
le filet
das Netz
la red
la rete

smash
le smash
der Schmetterball
el remate
la schiacciata

ballboy
le ramasseur de balles
der Balljunge
el recogebolas
il raccattapalle

serve *(v)*
servir
aufschlagen
sacar
battere il servizio

tennis shoes • les tennis • die Tennisschuhe • los tenis • le scarpe da tennis

player • le joueur • der Tennisspieler • el jugador • il tennista

strokes • les coups • die Schläge • los golpes • i colpi

serve • le service • der Aufschlag • el servicio • il servizio

volley • la volée • der Volley • la volea • la volée

return • le retour • der Return • el resto • il ritorno

lob • le lob • der Lob • el globo • il pallonetto

forehand • le coup droit • die Vorhand • el derecho • il dritto

backhand • le revers • die Rückhand • el revés • il rovescio

racket games • les jeux de raquette • die Schlägerspiele • los juegos de raqueta • i giochi con la racchetta

shuttlecock
le volant
der Federball
el gallo
il volano

badminton • le badminton • das Badminton • el bádminton • il badminton

bat • la raquette • der Tischtennisschläger • la raqueta • la racchetta

table tennis • le tennis de table • das Tischtennis • el ping-pong • il ping pong

squash • le squash • das Squash • el squash • lo squash

racquetball • le racquetball • das Racquetball • el racketball • il racquetball

golf • le golf • das Golf • el golf • il golf

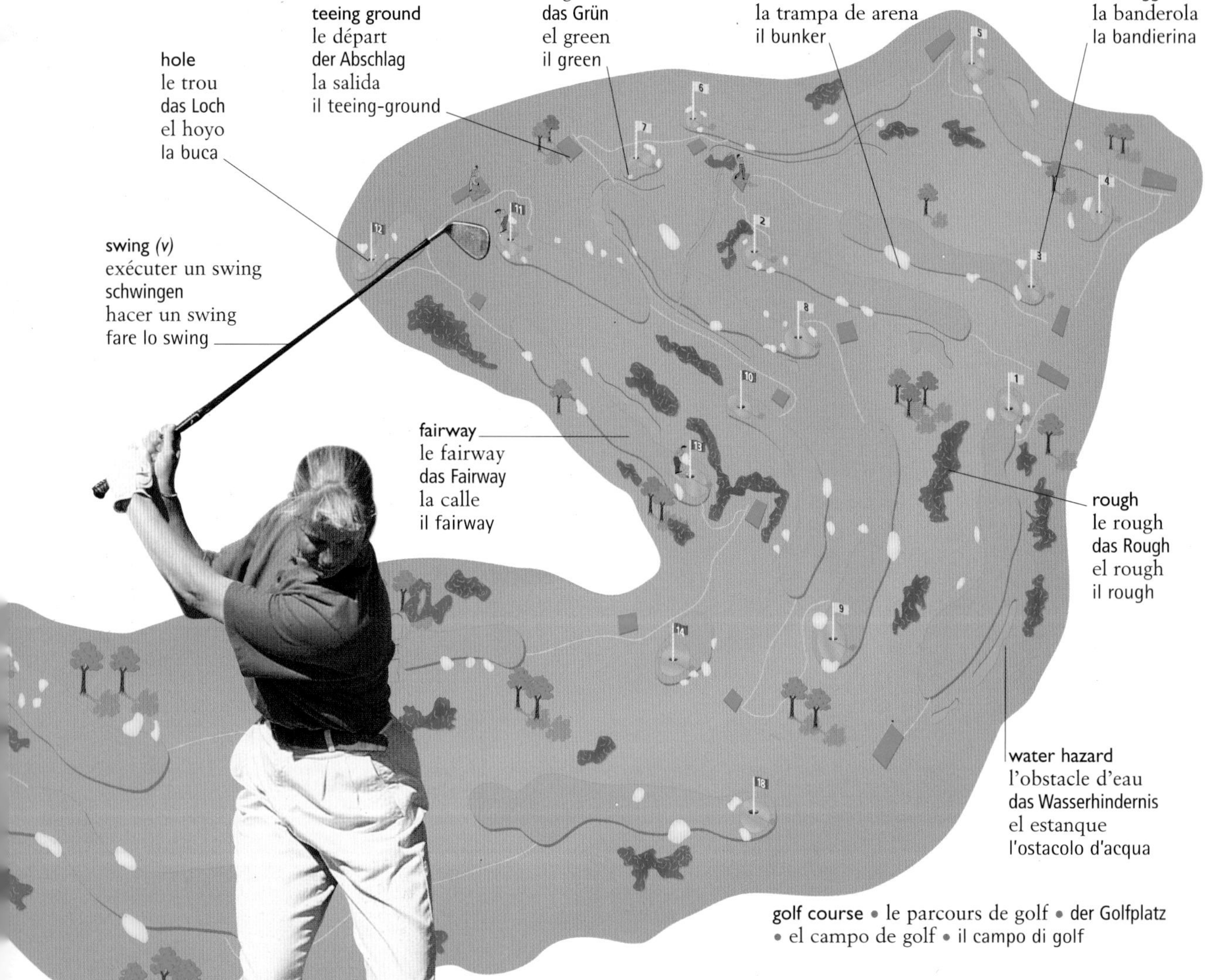

hole
le trou
das Loch
el hoyo
la buca

teeing ground
le départ
der Abschlag
la salida
il teeing-ground

green
le green
das Grün
el green
il green

bunker
le bunker
der Bunker
la trampa de arena
il bunker

flag
le drapeau
die Flagge
la banderola
la bandierina

swing (*v*)
exécuter un swing
schwingen
hacer un swing
fare lo swing

fairway
le fairway
das Fairway
la calle
il fairway

rough
le rough
das Rough
el rough
il rough

water hazard
l'obstacle d'eau
das Wasserhindernis
el estanque
l'ostacolo d'acqua

golf course • le parcours de golf • der Golfplatz • el campo de golf • il campo di golf

stance
la position
die Haltung
la postura
la posizione

golfer • la joueuse de golf • die Golferin • la golfista • la golfista

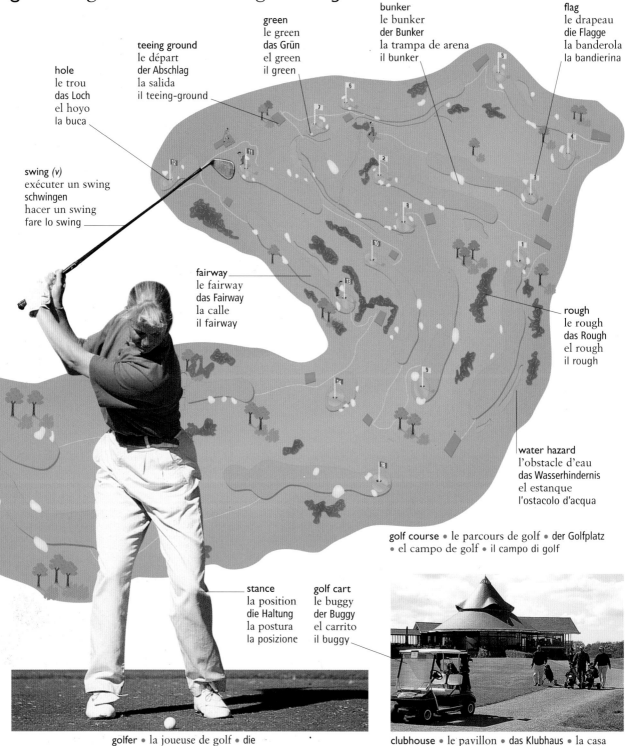

golf cart
le buggy
der Buggy
el carrito
il buggy

clubhouse • le pavillon • das Klubhaus • la casa club • la sede del circolo

equipment • l'équipement • die Ausrüstung • el equipo • le attrezzature

golf ball
la balle de golf
der Golfball
la bola de golf
la pallina da golf

tee • le tee • der Aufsatz • el tee • il tee

golf bag
le sac de golf
die Golftasche
la bolsa de golf
la sacca da golf

bag cart • le caddie • der Caddie • el carrito de golf • il carrellino

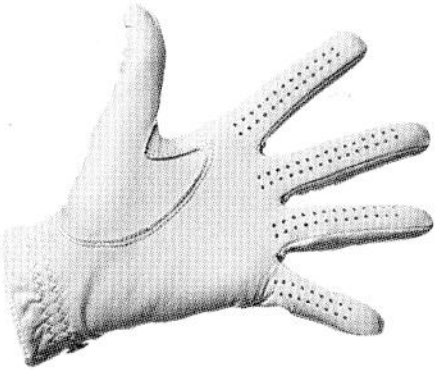

glove • le gant • der Handschuh • el guante • il guanto

spikes
les pointes
die Spikes
los spikes
i chiodi

golf shoe • la chaussure de golf • der Golfschuh • el zapato de golf • la scarpa da golf

actions • les actions • die Aktionen • las acciones • le azioni

tee-off *(v)* • partir du tee • vom Abschlag spielen • salir • cominciare la partita

drive *(v)* • driver • driven • hacer un drive • colpire a distanza

putt *(v)* • putter • einlochen • tirar al hoyo con un putter • colpire leggermente

chip *(v)* • cocher • chippen • hacer un chip • colpire da vicino

golf clubs • les clubs de golf • die Golfschläger • los palos de golf • le mazze da golf

wood • le bois • das Holz • la madera • la mazza di legno

putter • le putter • der Putter • el putter • il putter

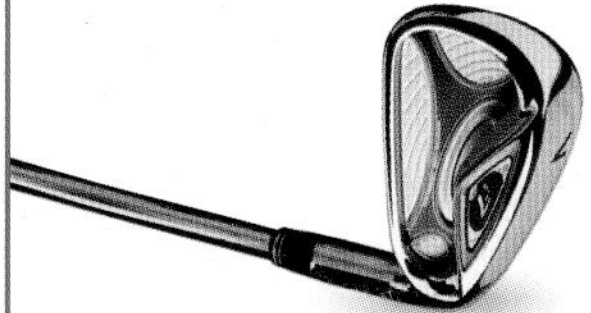

iron • le fer • das Eisen • el fierro • la mazza di ferro

wedge • la cale • das Wedge • el wedge • la mazza ricurva

par	over par	handicap	caddy	stroke	backswing
le par	le over par	le handicap	le caddie	le coup	le swing en arrière
das Par	das Überpar	das Golfhandicap	der Caddie	der Schlag	der Durchschwung
el par	el sobre par	el handicap	el caddy	el golpe	el backswing
il par	l'overpar	l'handicap	il caddy	il colpo	il back-swing
under par	hole in one	tournament	spectators	practice swing	line of play
le under par	le trou en un	le tournoi	les spectateurs	le swing d'essai	la ligne de jeu
das Unterpar	das Hole-in-One	das Golfturnier	die Zuschauer	der Übungsschwung	die Spielbahn
el bajo par	el hoyo en uno	el torneo	los espectadores	el swing de práctica	la línea de juego
l'underpar	la buca in uno	il torneo	gli spettatori	lo swing di pratica	la linea di gioco

track and field • l'athlétisme • die Leichtathletik • el atletismo • l'atletica

lane
le couloir
die Bahn
el carril
la corsia

track
la piste
die Rennbahn
la pista
la pista

finish line
la ligne d'arrivée
die Ziellinie
la línea de meta
il traguardo

starting line
la ligne de départ
die Startlinie
la línea de salida
la linea di partenza

field • le terrain • das Feld • el campo • il campo

starting block
le bloc de départ
der Startblock
el cajón de salida
la pedana di partenza

sprinter • le sprinter • der Sprinter • el esprinter • il velocista

discus • le disque • das Diskuswerfen • el lanzamiento de disco • il lancio del disco

athlete
l'athlète
die Leichtathletin
la atleta
l'atleta

shotput • le lancement du poids • das Kugelstoßen • el lanzamiento de bala • il lancio del peso

javelin • le javelot • das Speerwerfen • el lanzamiento de jabalina • il lancio del giavellotto

race la course das Rennen la carrera la gara	record le record der Rekord el récord il primato	photo finish le photo-finish das Fotofinish la foto final il fotofinish	pole vault le saut à la perche der Stabhochsprung el salto con pértiga il salto con l'asta
time le temps die Zeit el tiempo il tempo	break a record *(v)* battre un record einen Rekord brechen batir un récord battere un primato	marathon le marathon der Marathon la maratón la maratona	personal best le record personnel die persönliche Bestleistung la marca personal il primato personale

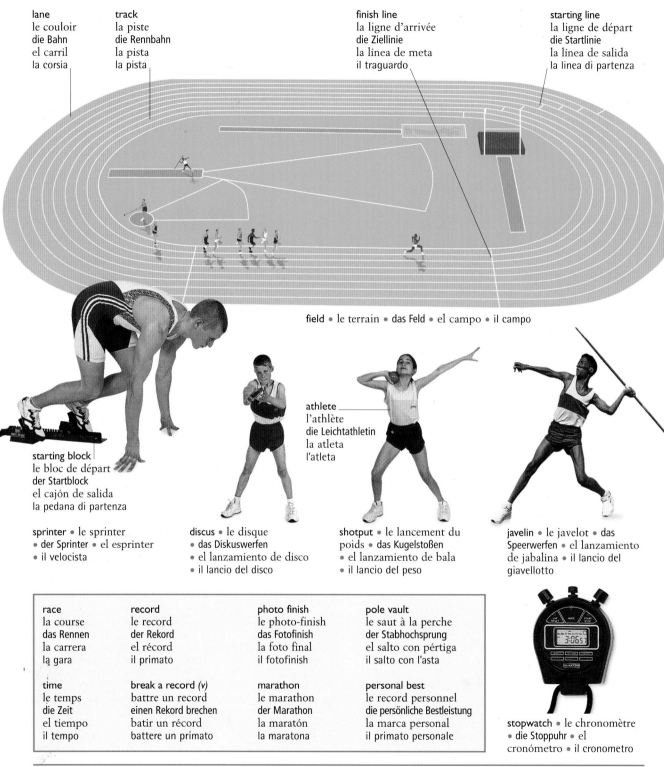

stopwatch • le chronomètre • die Stoppuhr • el cronómetro • il cronometro baton • le bâton • der Stab • el relevo • il testimone

relay race • le relais • der Staffellauf • la carrera de relevos • la staffetta

bar • la barre • die Latte • la barra • la sbarra

high jump • le saut en hauteur • der Hochsprung • el salto de altura • il salto in alto

long jump • le saut en longueur • der Weitsprung • el salto de longitud • il salto in lungo

hurdles • les haies • der Hürdenlauf • la carrera de vallas • la corsa a ostacoli

gymnastics • la gymnastique • das Turnen • la gimnasia • la ginnastica

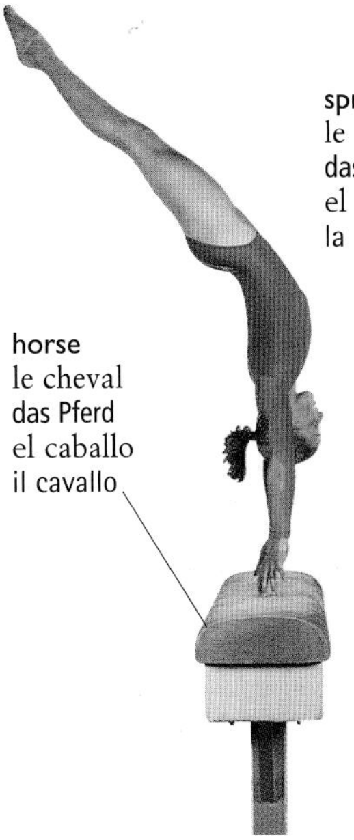

horse
le cheval
das Pferd
el caballo
il cavallo

vault • le saut • der Sprung • el salto • il volteggio

springboard
le tremplin
das Sprungbrett
el trampolín
la pedana elastica

somersault • le salto • der Salto • el salto mortal • la capriola

mat • le tapis • die Matte • el tapete • la pedana

floor exercises • les exercises au sol • das Bodenturnen • los ejercicios de piso • la ginnastica a corpo libero

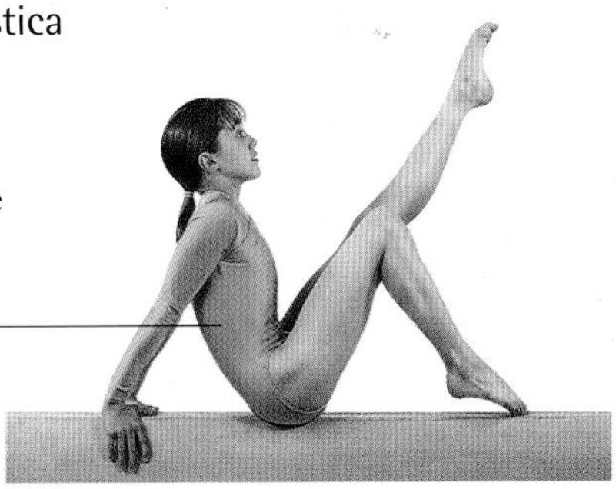

gymnast
la gymnaste
die Turnerin
la gimnasta
la ginnasta

beam • la poutre • der Schwebebalken • la viga de equilibrio • la trave

cartwheel • la cabriole • die Bodenakrobatik • la voltereta • la ruota

ribbon • le drapeau • das Gymnastikband • el listón • il nastro

rhythmic gymnastics • la gymnastique rythmique • die rhythmische Gymnastik • la gimnasia rítmica • la ginnastica ritmica

horizontal bar la barre fixe das Reck la barra fija la sbarra	asymmetric bars les barres asymétriques der Stufenbarren las barras asimétricas le sbarre asimmetriche	rings les anneaux die Ringe las argollas gli anelli	medals les médailles die Medaillen las medallas le medaglie	silver l'argent das Silber la plata l'argento
parallel bars les barres parallèles der Barren las barras paralelas le parallele	pommel horse le cheval d'arçons das Seitpferd el caballo con arcos il cavallo	podium le podium das Siegerpodium el podio il podio	gold l'or das Gold el oro l'oro	bronze le bronze die Bronze el bronce il bronzo

combat sports • les sports de combat • der Kampfsport • los deportes de combate • gli sport da combattimento

tae kwon do • le taekwondo • das Taekwondo • el taekwondo • il tae kwondo

karate • le karaté • das Karate • el karate • il karate

judo • le judo • das Judo • el judo • il judo

aikido • l'aïkido • das Aikido • el aikido • l'aikido

kendo • le kendo • das Kendo • el kendo • il kendo

kung fu • le kung-fu • das Kung-Fu • el kung fu • il kung fu

kickboxing • la boxe thaïlandaise • das Kickboxen • el full contact • il kickboxing

wrestling • la lutte • das Ringen • la lucha libre • la lotta greco-romana

boxing • la boxe • das Boxen • el boxeo • il pugilato

actions • les actions • die Techniken • los movimientos • le mosse

fall • la chute • das Fallen • la caída • la scivolata

hold • la prise • der Griff • el agarre • la presa

throw • la projection • der Wurf • el derribo • la proiezione

pin • l'immobilisation • das Fesseln • la inmovilización • la caduta

kick • le coup de pied • der Seitfußstoß • la patada • il calcio

punch • le coup de poing • der Stoß • el puñetazo • il pugno

strike • le coup • der Angriff • el golpe • il colpo

jump • le saut • der Sprung • el salto • il salto

block • le blocage • der Block • el bloqueo • la parata

chop • le coup • der Hieb • el golpe • il colpo di taglio

boxing ring le ring der Boxring el ring il ring	round le round die Runde el round il round	fist le poing die Faust el puño il pugno	black belt la ceinture noire der schwarze Gürtel el cinturón negro la cintura nera	capoeira la capoeira das Capoeira la capoeira la capoeira
boxing gloves les gants de boxe die Boxhandschuhe los guantes de boxeo i guantoni	bout le combat der Kampf el combate l'incontro	knockout le knock-out der Knockout el K.O. il k.o	self-defense l'autodéfense die Selbstverteidigung la defensa personal l'autodifesa	sumo wrestling le sumo das Sumo el sumo il sumo
mouth guard le protège-dents der Mundschutz el protegedientes il paradenti	sparring l'entraînement das Sparren el entrenamiento l'allenamento	punching bag le punching-bag der Sandsack el saco de arena il sacco	martial arts les arts martiaux die Kampfsportarten las artes marciales le arti marziali	tai-chi le taï chi das Tai Chi el tai-chi il tai-chi

swimming • la natation • der Schwimmsport • la natación • il nuoto

equipment • l'équipement • die Ausrüstung • el equipo • l'attrezzatura

swim band • la brassière • der Schwimmflügel • el flotador de brazo • il bracciolo

nose clip
la pince pour le nez
die Nasenklemme
la pinza para la nariz
la molletta per il naso

goggles • les lunettes protectrices • die Schwimmbrille • los goggles • gli occhialetti

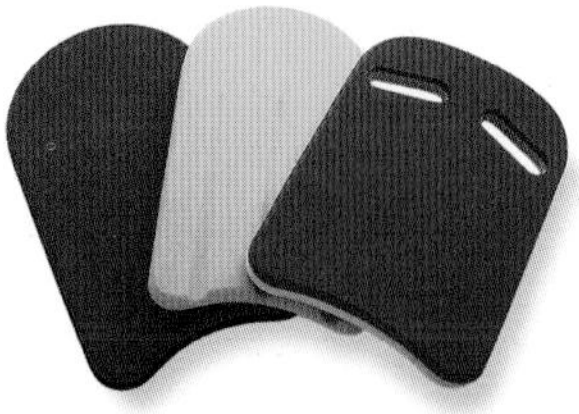

kickboard • la planche • das Schwimmfloß • la tabla • la tavoletta

swimsuit • le maillot de bain • der Badeanzug • el traje de baño • il costume da bagno

lane
le couloir
die Bahn
el carril
la corsia

water
l'eau
das Wasser
el agua
l'acqua

starting block
le plot de départ
der Startblock
el cajón de salida
il podio di partenza

swimming pool • la piscine • das Schwimmbecken • la alberca • la piscina

swimming cap • le bonnet de natation • die Badekappe • la gorra • la cuffia

trunks • le slip de bain • die Badehose • el traje de baño • il costume da bagno

swimmer • le nageur • der Schwimmer • el nadador • il nuotatore

diving board
le tremplin
das Sprungbrett
el trampolín
il trampolino

diver
le plongeur
der Springer
el clavadista
il tuffatore

dive *(v)* • plonger • springen • tirarse un clavado • tuffarsi

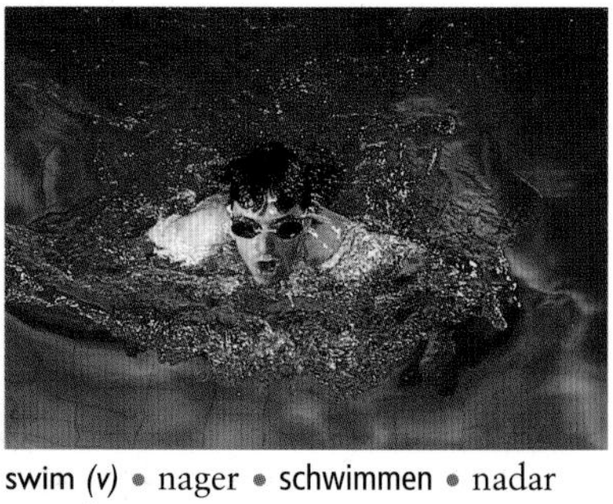

swim *(v)* • nager • schwimmen • nadar • nuotare

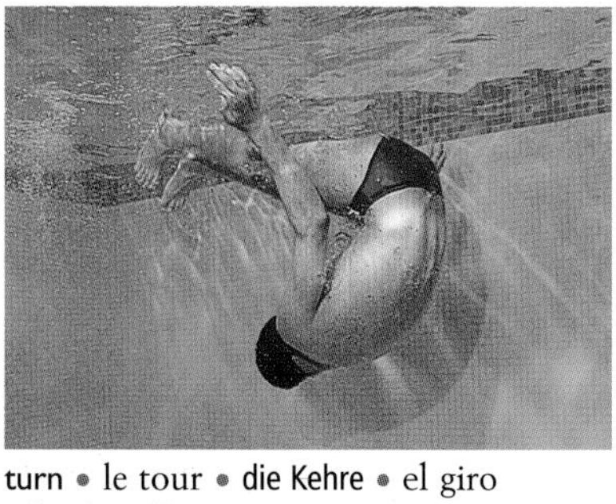

turn • le tour • die Kehre • el giro • la giravolta

styles • les styles • die Schwimmstile • los estilos • gli stili

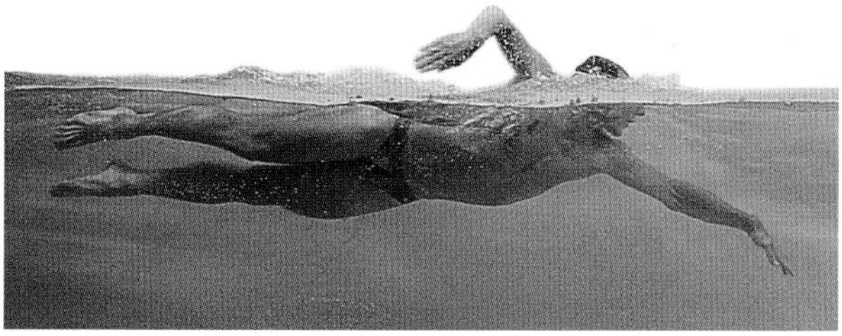

front crawl • le crawl • das Kraulen • el crol • lo stile libero

breaststroke • la brasse • das Brustschwimmen • el pecho • la rana

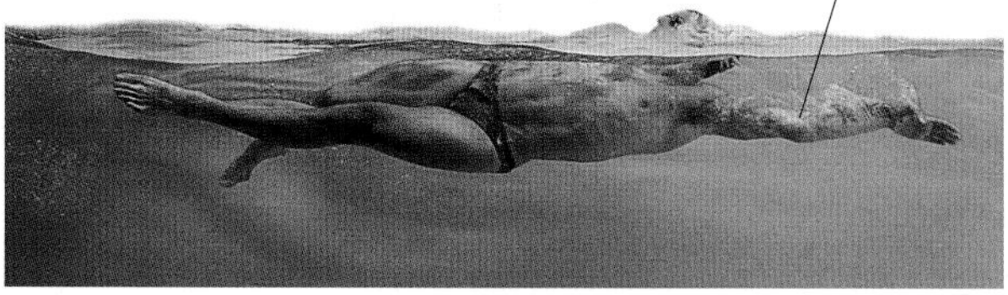

backstroke • la nage sur le dos • das Rückenschwimmen • el dorso • il dorso

butterfly • le papillon • der Butterfly • la mariposa • la farfalla

scuba diving • la plongée • das Tauchen • el buceo • il nuoto subacqueo

dive le plongeon der Sprung el clavado il tuffo	racing dive le départ plongé der Startsprung el clavado de salida il tuffo di rincorsa	lockers les casiers die Schließfächer las taquillas gli armadietti	water polo le water-polo der Wasserball el waterpolo la pallanuoto	shallow end le petit bassin das flache Ende la zona poco profunda la parte bassa	cramp la crampe der Krampf el calambre il crampo
high dive le plongeon de haut vol der Turmsprung el clavado il tuffo alto	tread water *(v)* nager sur place Wasser treten hacer agua tenersi a galla	lifeguard le maître nageur der Bademeister el salvavidas il bagnino	deep end le grand bassin das tiefe Ende la zona profunda la parte profonda	synchronized swimming la nage synchronisée das Synchronschwimmen el nado sincronizado il nuoto sincronizzato	drown *(v)* se noyer ertrinken ahogarse annegare

sailing • la voile • der Segelsport • la vela • la vela

compass • le compas • der Kompass • la brújula • la bussola

anchor • l'ancre • der Anker • el ancla • l'ancora

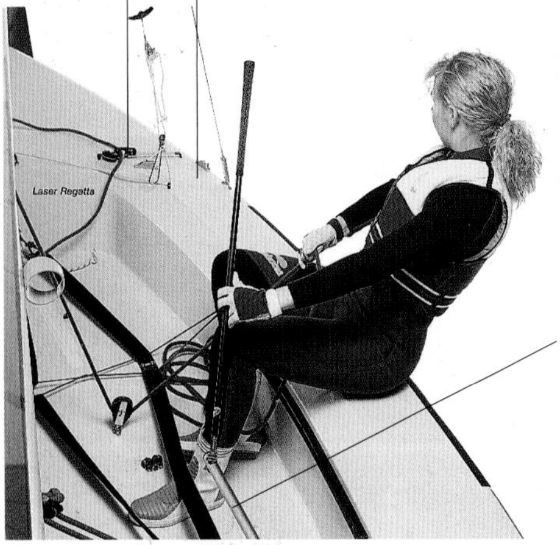

navigate *(v)* • naviguer • navigieren • navegar • navigare

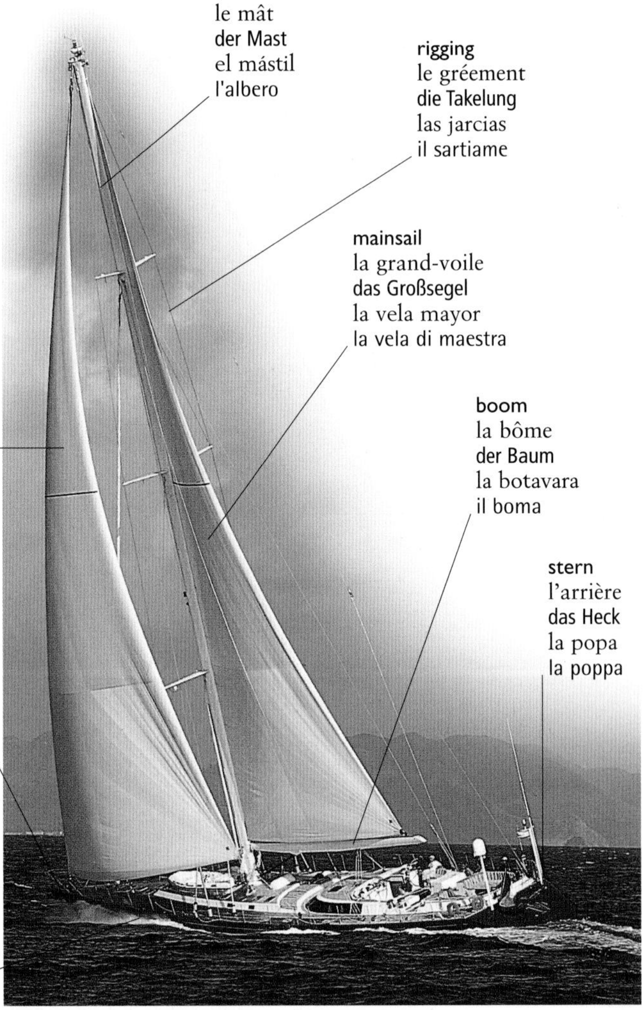

yacht • le yacht • die Segeljacht • el yate • lo yacht

safety • la sécurité • die Sicherheit • la seguridad • la sicurezza

flare • la fusée éclairante • die Leuchtrakete • la bengala • il razzo illuminante

life preserver • la bouée de sauvetage • der Rettungsring • el salvavidas • il salvagente

life jacket • le gilet de sauvetage • die Schwimmweste • el chaleco salvavidas • il giubbotto di salvataggio

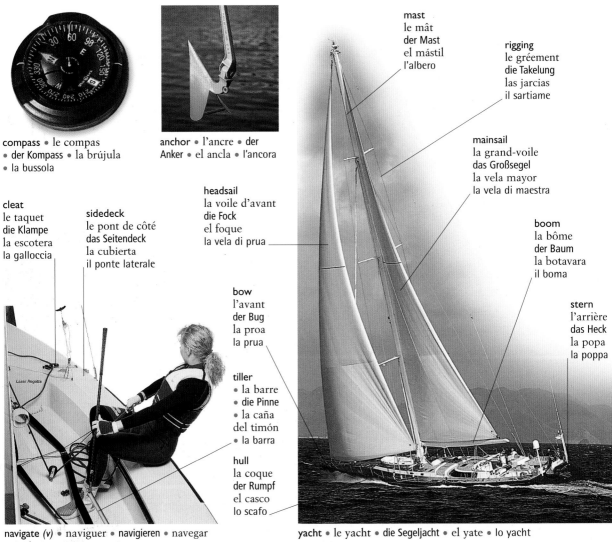

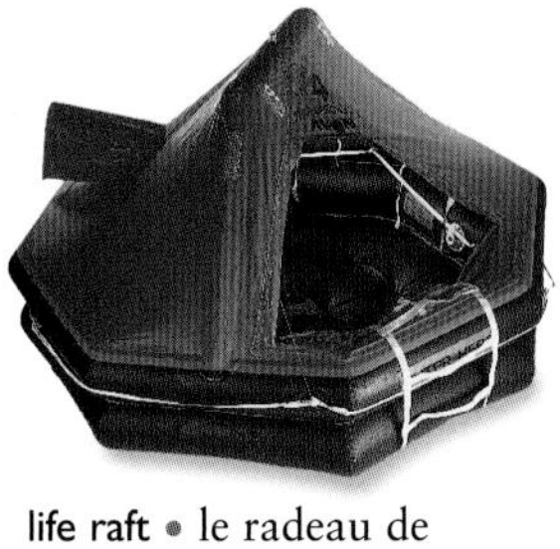

life raft • le radeau de sauvetage • das Rettungsboot • la balsa salvavidas • la zattera di salvataggio

watersports • les sports aquatiques • der Wassersport • los deportes acuáticos • gli sport acquatici

rower
le rameur
der Ruderer
el remero
il rematore

oar
la rame
das Ruder
el remo
il remo

row (v) • ramer • rudern • remar • remare

kayak
le kayak
das Kajak
el kayak
il kayak

paddle
la pagaie
das Paddel
el remo
la pagaia

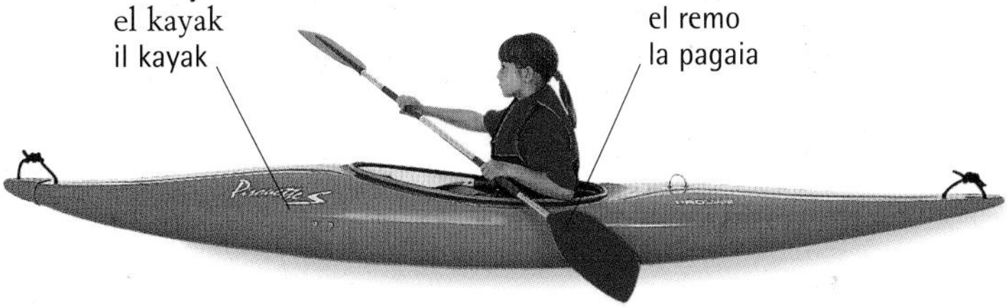

kayaking • le canoë • der Kanusport • el canotaje • il canottaggio

sail
la voile
das Segel
la vela
la vela

windsurfer
le planchiste
der Windsurfer
el windsurfista
il windsurf

board
la planche
das Surfbrett
la tabla
la tavola

footstrap
la bride
die Fußschlaufe
la cinta para el pie
la presa per il piede

windsurfing • la planche à voile • das Windsurfing • el windsurf • il windsurfing

surfboard • la planche • das Surfbrett • la tabla de surf • il surf

surfing • le surf • das Wellenreiten • el surfing • il surfing

waterski • le ski • der Wasserski • el esquí • lo sci

waterskiing • le ski nautique • das Wasserski • el esquí acuático • lo sci d'acqua

speedboating • le motonautisme • der Schnellbootsport • la carrera de lanchas • la corsa in motoscafo

rafting • le rafting • das Rafting • el rafting • rafting

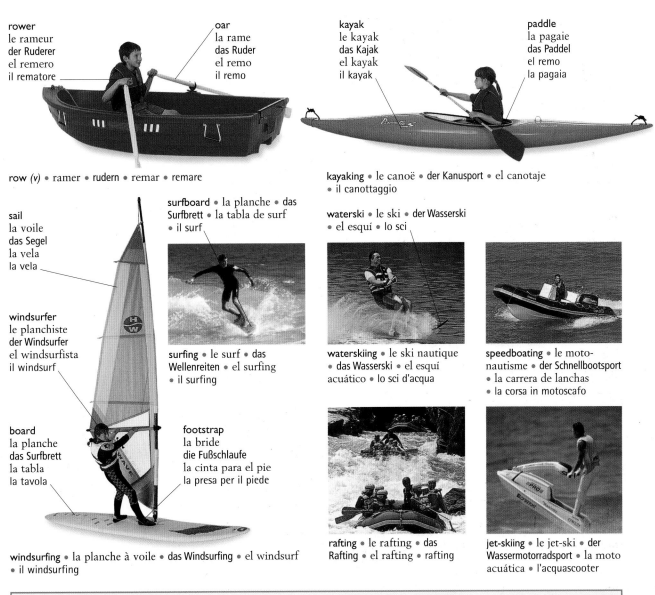

jet-skiing • le jet-ski • der Wassermotorradsport • la moto acuática • l'acquascooter

waterskier le skieur nautique der Wasserskifahrer el esquiador acuático lo sciatore d'acqua	crew l'équipage die Crew la tripulación l'equipaggio	wind le vent der Wind el viento il vento	surf l'écume die Brandung la rompiente la cresta dell'onda	sheet l'écoute die Schot la escota la scotta	centerboard la dérive das Schwert la orza il centro della tavola
surfer le surfeur der Surfer el surfista il surfista	tack (v) louvoyer aufkreuzen virar bordeggiare	wave la vague die Welle la ola l'onda	rapids les rapides das Wildwasser los rápidos le rapide	rudder le gouvernail das Ruder el timón il timone	capsize (v) chavirer kentern volcar capovolgersi

horseback riding • l'équitation • der Reitsport • la equitación • l'equitazione

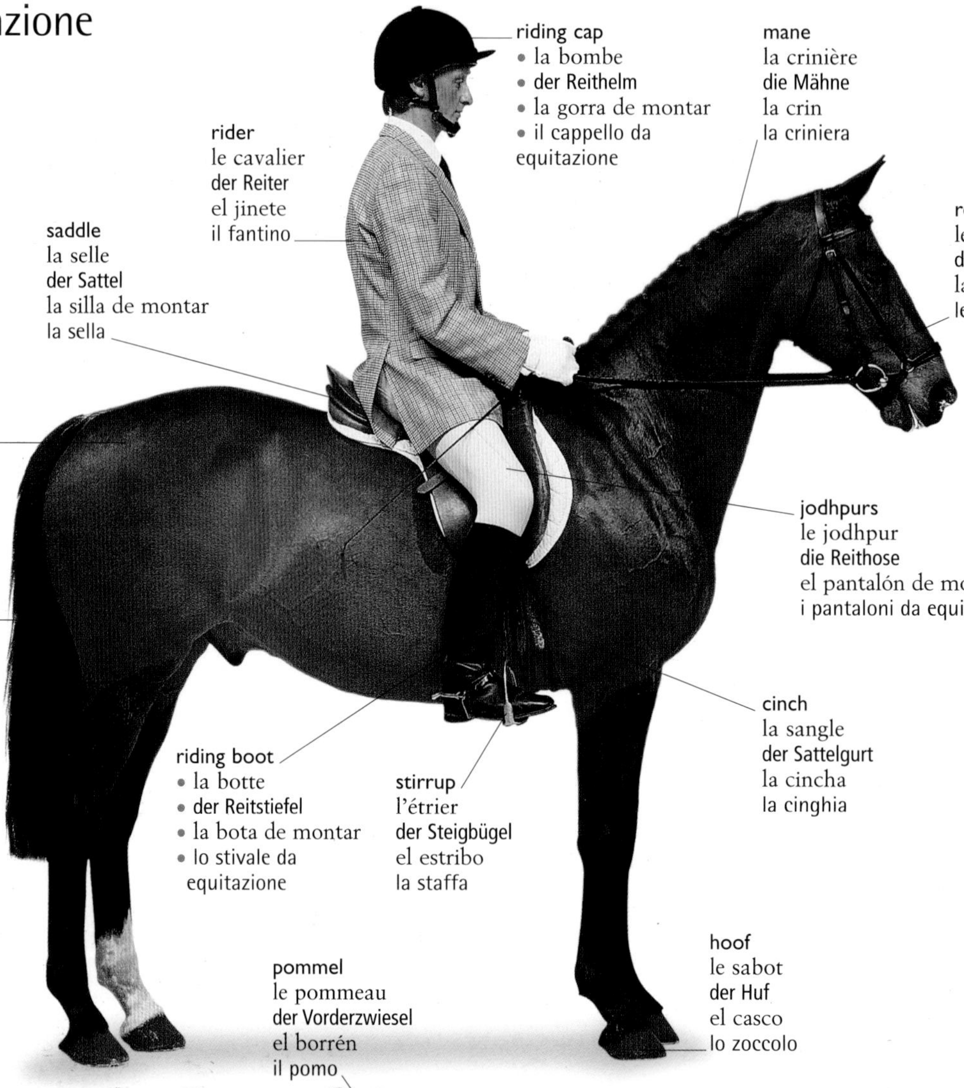

horseshoe • le fer à cheval • das Hufeisen • la herradura • il ferro da cavallo

sidesaddle • la selle de femme • der Damensattel • la silla de montar de escaramuza • la sella da signora

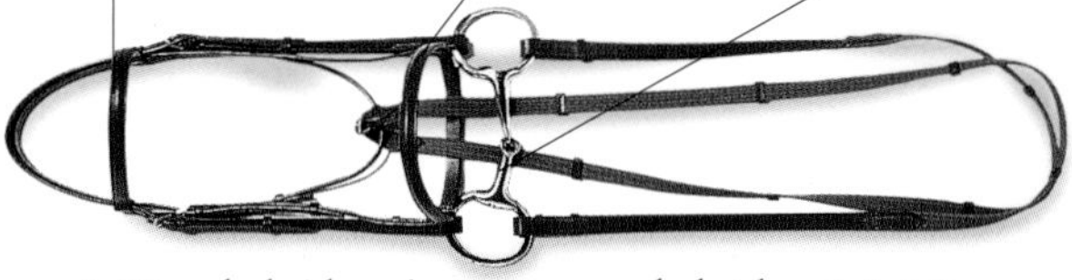

bridle • la bride • das Zaumzeug • la brida • la briglia

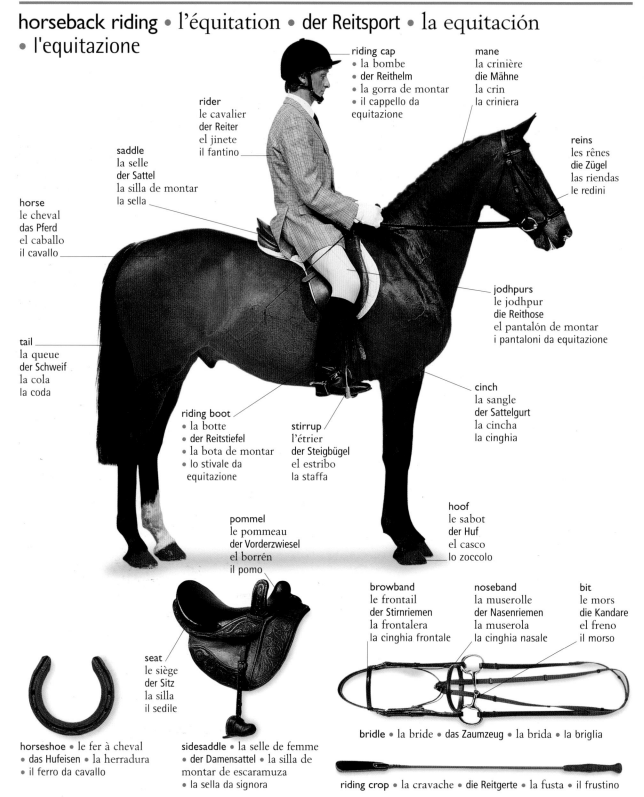

riding crop • la cravache • die Reitgerte • la fusta • il frustino

events • les courses • die Veranstaltungen • las modalidades • le corse

racehorse • le cheval de course • das Rennpferd • el caballo de carreras • il cavallo da corsa

horse race • la course de chevaux • das Pferderennen • la carrera de caballos • la corsa di cavalli

fence • l'obstacle • das Hindernis • la valla • l'ostacolo

steeplechase • le steeple • das Jagdrennen • la carrera de obstáculos • il concorso ippico

harness race • la course de trot • das Trabrennen • la carrera al trote • la corsa al trotto

rodeo • le rodéo • das Rodeo • el rodeo • il rodeo

show jumping • le jumping • das Springreiten • el concurso de saltos • il concorso di salto a ostacoli

carriage race • la course attelée • das Zweispännerrennen • la carrera de carrozas • la corsa di carrozze

trekking • la randonnée • das Trekking • el paseo • l'escursione a cavallo

dressage • le dressage • das Dressurreiten • la doma y monta • il dressage

polo • le polo • das Polo • el polo • il polo

walk le pas der Schritt el paso il passo	canter le petit galop der Kanter el medio galope il piccolo galoppo	jump le saut der Sprung el salto il salto	halter le licou das Halfter el cabestro la cavezza	paddock l'enclos die Koppel el cercado il recinto	flat race la course de plat das Flachrennen la carrera sin obstáculos la corsa in piano
trot le trot der Trab el trote il trotto	gallop le galop der Galopp el galope il galoppo	groom le valet d'écurie der Stallbursche el mozo de cuadra il palafreniere	stable l'écurie der Pferdestall la cuadra la stalla	arena l'arène der Turnierplatz el ruedo l'arena	racecourse le champs de courses die Rennbahn el hipódromo l'ippodromo

fishing • la pêche • der Angelsport • la pesca • la pesca

sinker • le plomb • das Gewicht • el plomo • il peso

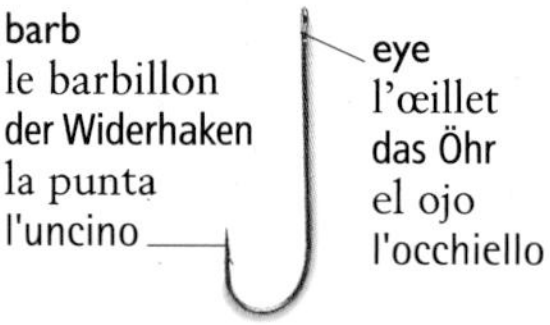

fishhook • l'hameçon • der Angelhaken • el anzuelo • l'amo

bait • l'amorce • der Köder • el cebo • l'esca

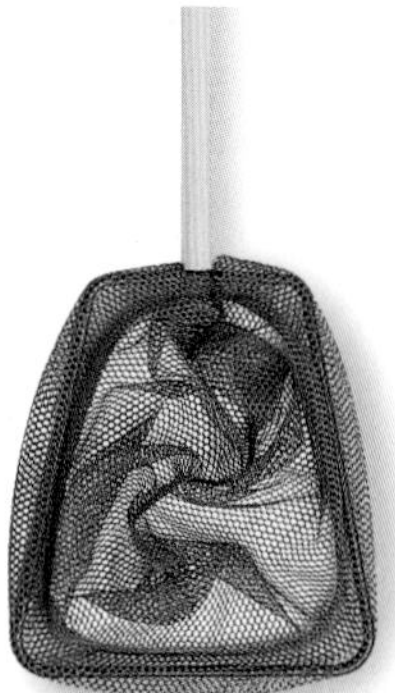

landing net • l'épuisette • der Kescher • la red para recoger • la retina

float • le flotteur • die Pose • el flotador • il galleggiante

fly • la mouche • die Fliege • la mosca • la mosca

lure • l'appât • der Köderhaken • el señuelo • l'esca

tackle box • la boîte d'équipement • der Spinnerkasten • la caja de aparejos • la scatola degli attrezzi

keep net • la bourriche • der Setzkescher • la red para las capturas • la rete da pesca

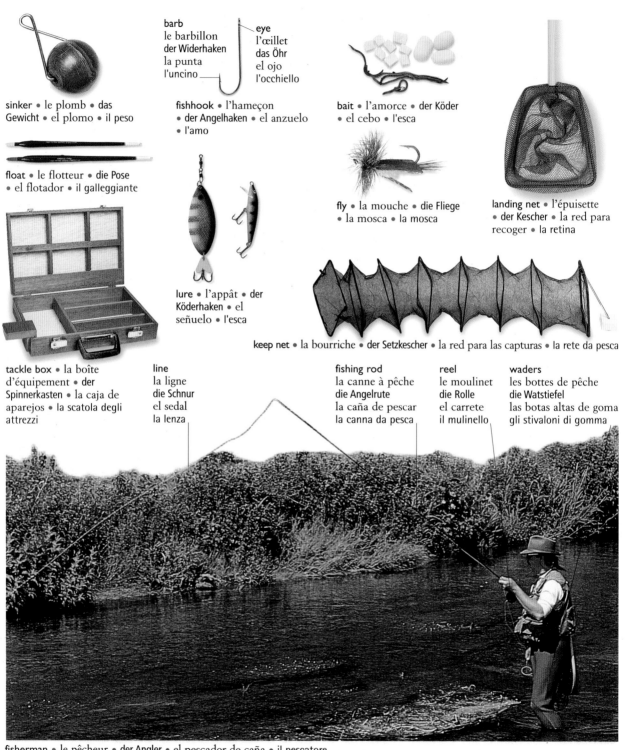

fisherman • le pêcheur • der Angler • el pescador de caña • il pescatore

types of fishing • les genres de pêche • die Fischfangarten • los tipos de pesca • i tipi di pesca

freshwater fishing • la pêche en eau douce • das Süßwasserangeln • la pesca en agua dulce • la pesca in acqua dolce

fly fishing • la pêche à la mouche • das Fliegenangeln • la pesca con mosca • la pesca con la mosca

sport fishing • la pêche sportive • das Sportangeln • la pesca deportiva • la pesca sportiva

deep sea fishing • la pêche hauturière • die Hochseefischerei • la pesca de altura • la pesca il alto mare

surfcasting • la pêche au lancer en mer • das Brandungsangeln • la pesca en la orilla • la pesca dalla riva

activities • les activités • die Aktivitäten • las acciones • le attività

cast *(v)* • lancer • auswerfen • lanzar • lanciare

catch *(v)* • attraper • fangen • atrapar • prendere

reel in *(v)* • ramener • einholen • recoger • tirare con il mulinello

net *(v)* • prendre au filet • mit dem Netz fangen • atrapar con la red • pescare con la rete

release *(v)* • lâcher • loslassen • soltar • rilasciare

bait *(v)* amorcer ködern cebar fornire di esca	**tackle** le matériel de pêche die Angelgeräte los aparejos l'attrezzatura	**rain clothes** l'imperméable die Regenhaut la ropa impermeable i sovrapantaloni	**fishing license** le permis de pêche der Angelschein la licencia de pesca la licenza di pesca	**creel** le panier de pêche der Fischkorb la nasa la nassa
bite *(v)* mordre anbeißen picar abboccare	**spool** le tambour die Rolle el carrete la bobina	**pole** la perche die Stake la pértiga la canna da pesca	**marine fishing** la pêche maritime die Seefischerei la pesca en alta mar la pesca in mare	**spearfishing** la pêche sous-marine das Speerfischen la pesca con arpón la pesca con la fiocina

skiing • le ski • der Skisport • el esquí • lo sci

ski slope • la pente de ski • der Skihang • la pista • la pista da sci

chairlift
le télésiège
der Sessellift
la telesilla
la seggiovia

cable car
la télécabine
der Kabinenlift
la góndola
la funivia

glove
le gant
der Handschuh
el guante
il guanto

ski pole
le bâton de ski
der Skistock
el bastón
il bastone da sci

ski run • la piste de ski • die Skipiste• la pista de esquí• la pista da sci

ski jacket
la veste de ski
die Skijacke
el chaqueta de esquí
lo scarpone da sci

edge • la carre • die Kante • el canto • la lama

tip • la pointe • die Spitze • la punta • la punta

ski • le ski • der Ski • el esquí • lo sci

skier • la skieuse • die Skiläuferin • la esquiadora • la sciatrice

ski boot • la chaussure de ski • der Skistiefel • la bota de esquí • lo scarpone da sci

safety barrier
la barrière de sécurité
die Sicherheitssperre
la barrera de seguridad
la transenna di sicurezza

events • les épreuves • die Disziplinen • las modalidades • le gare

downhill skiing • la descente • der Abfahrtslauf • el descenso • la discesa

gate • la porte • das Tor • el poste • la porta

slalom • le slalom • der Slalom • el slálom • lo slalom

ski jump • le saut • der Skisprung • el salto • il salto

cross-country skiing • le ski de randonnée • der Langlauf • el esquí de fondo • lo sci di fondo

winter sports • les sports d'hiver • der Wintersport • los deportes de invierno • gli sport invernali

ice climbing • l'escalade en glace • das Eisklettern • la escalada en hielo • l'arrampicata su ghiaccio

ice skating • le patinage • das Eislaufen • el patinaje sobre hielo • il pattinaggio su ghiaccio

skate
le patin à glace
der Schlittschuh
el patín
il pattino

figure skating • le patinage artistique • der Eiskunstlauf • el patinaje artístico • il pattinaggio artistico

goggles • les lunettes de ski • die Skibrille • los goggles • gli occhiali

snowboarding • le surf des neiges • das Snowboarding • el snowboarding • lo snowboard

bobsled • le bobsleigh • der Bobsport • el bobsleigh • il bob

luge • la luge • das Rennrodeln • el luge • lo slittino

snowmobile • l'autoneige • das Schneemobil • la moto de nieve • la motoslitta

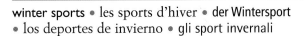

sledding • la luge • das Schlittenfahren • tirarse en trineo • la corsa su slitta

alpine skiing
le ski alpin
die alpine Kombination
el esquí alpino
lo sci alpino

giant slalom
le slalom géant
der Riesenslalom
el slálom gigante
lo slalom gigante

off-piste
hors piste
abseits der Piste
fuera de pista
fuoripista

curling
le curling
das Curling
el curling
il curling

dogsledding
le traîneau à chiens
das Hundeschlittenfahren
el trineo con perros
la corsa su slitta trainata da cani

speed skating
le patinage de vitesse
das Eisschnelllauf
el patinaje de velocidad
il pattinaggio di velocità

biathlon
le biathlon
das Biathlon
el biatlón
il biathlon

avalanche
l'avalanche
die Lawine
la avalancha
la valanga

other sports • les autres sports • die anderen Sportarten • los otros deportes • gli altri sport

gliding • le vol plané • das Segelfliegen • el vuelo sin motor • il volo a vela

hang-gliding • le deltaplane • das Drachenfliegen • el vuelo con ala delta • il volo in deltaplano

rock climbing • l'escalade • das Klettern • la escalada • l'alpinismo in parete

parachuting • le parachutisme • das Fallschirmspringen • el paracaidismo • il paracadutismo

parasailing • le parapente • das Gleitschirmfliegen • el parapente • il parapendio

skydiving • le saut en chute libre • das Fallschirmspringen • el paracaidismo en caída libre • il paracadutismo libero

rappeling • le rappel • das Abseilen • el rappel • la cordata

bungee jumping • le saut à l'élastique • das Bungeejumping • el salto bungee • il bungee jumping

rally driving • le rallye • das Rallyefahren • el rally • il rally

race-car driver
le coureur automobile
der Rennfahrer
el piloto de carreras
il pilota da corsa

auto racing • la course automobile • der Rennsport • el automovilismo • l'automobilismo

motocross • le motocross • das Motocross • el motocross • il motocross

motorbike racing • la course de moto • das Motorradrennen • el motociclismo • il motociclismo

skateboard
la planche à roulettes
das Skateboard
la patineta
la tavola da skateboard

skateboarding • la planche à roulettes • das Skateboardfahren • andar en patineta • lo skate board

inline skating • le patin en ligne • das inlineskaten • el patinaje en línea • il pattinaggio in linea

stick
la crosse
der Lacrosseschläger
el palo
la mazza

lacrosse • le lacrosse • das Lacrosse • el lacrosse • il lacrosse

mask
le masque
die Maske
la máscara
la maschera

foil
le fleuret
das Florett
el florete
il fioretto

fencing • l'escrime • das Fechten • la esgrima • la scherma

pin • la quille • der Kegel • el pino • il birillo

bowling • le bowling • das Bowling • el boliche • il bowling

bowling ball • la boule de bowling • die Bowlingkugel • la bola de boliche • la palla da bowling

arrow
la flèche
der Pfeil
la flecha
la freccia

quiver
le carquois
der Köcher
el carcaj
la faretra

bow • l'arc • der Bogen • el arco• l'arco

archery • le tir à l'arc • das Bogenschießen • el tiro con arco • il tiro con l'arco

target • la cible • die Zielscheibe • la diana • il bersaglio

target shooting • le tir à cible • das Scheibenschießen • el tiro • il tiro al bersaglio

pool • le billard américain • das Poolbillard • el pool • il biliardo

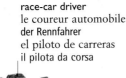

snooker • le billard • das Snooker • el billar • lo snooker

fitness • le conditionnement physique • die Fitness • la forma física • il fitness

gym machine • l'appareil de gym • das Fitnessgerät • la máquina de ejercicios • la macchina per esercizi

bench • le banc • die Bank • el banco • la panca

exercise bike • le vélo d'entraînement • das Trainingsrad • la bicicleta • la cyclette

free weights
les poids
die Gewichte
las pesas
i manubri

bar
la barre
die Stange
la barra
la sbarra

gym • le gymnase • das Fitnesscenter • el gimasio • la palestra

rowing machine • la machine à ramer • die Rudermaschine • la máquina de remos • il vogatore

treadmill • la tapis roulant • das Laufband • la banda caminadora • il treadmill

elliptical trainer • la machine de randonnée • die Langlaufmaschine • la máquina de cross • il cross trainer

personal trainer • l'entraîneuse individuelle • die private Fitnesstrainerin • la entrenadora personal • l'istruttore individuale

step machine • l'escalier d'entraînement • die Tretmaschine • la máquina de step • la macchina per step

swimming pool • la piscine • das Schwimmbecken • la alberca • la piscina

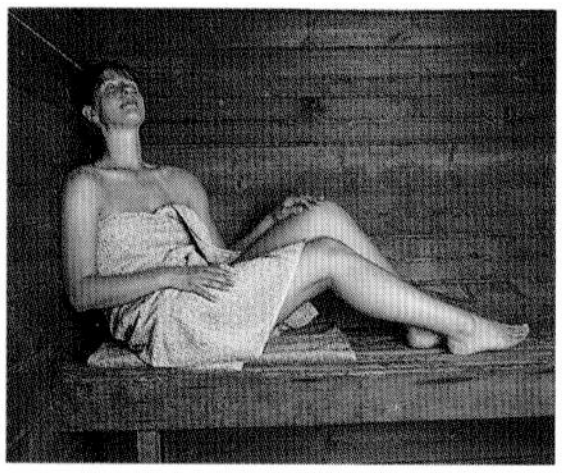

sauna • le sauna • die Sauna • el sauna • la sauna

exercises • les exercices • die Übungen • los ejercicios • gli esercizi

stretch • l'étirement • das Strecken • el estiramiento • lo stretching

lunge • la fente en avant • der Ausfall • la flexión con estiramiento • lo stiramento

tights
le collant
die Strumpfhose
los leotardos
il collant

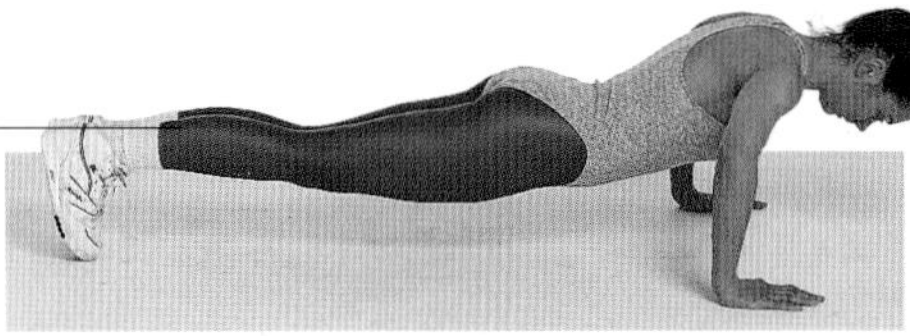

push-up • la traction • der Liegestütz • la flexión • le flessioni

squat • la flexion de jambes • die Kniebeuge • ponerse en cuclillas • lo squat

sit-up • le redressement assis • das Rumpfheben • el abdominal • gli addominali

dumbbell
l'haltère
die Hantel
la pesa
il manubrio

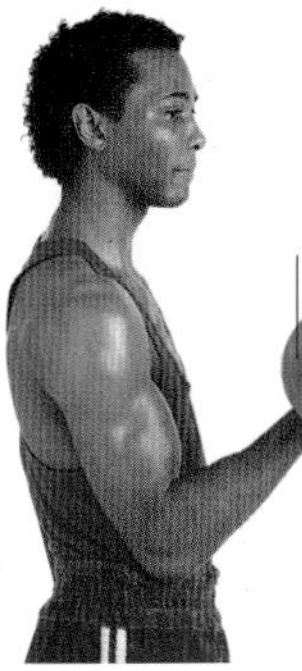

bicep curl • l'exercise pour les biceps • die Bizepsübung • el ejercicio de bíceps • le alzate con il manubrio

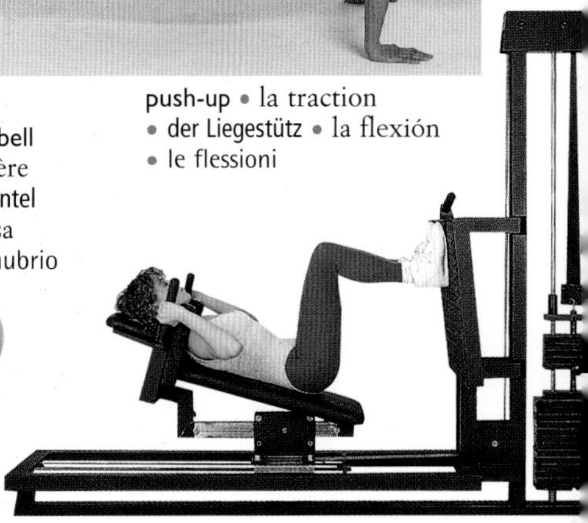

leg press • la traction pour les jambes • der Beinstütz • los ejercicios de piernas • la pressa per le gambe

chest press • l'exercice pour la poitrine • die Brustübung • los ejercicios pectorales • la pressa per pettorali

running shoes
• les baskets
• die Trainingsschuhe • las zapatillas
• gli scarponcini

weight bar
la barre à poids
die Gewichthantel
la barra de pesas
il bilanciere

weight training • l'entraînement poids et haltères • das Krafttraining • el levantamiento de pesas • l'addestramento ai pesi

vest
le tricot de corps
das Unterhemd
la camiseta de tirantes
la canottiera

jogging • le jogging • das Jogging • el jogging • il footing

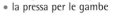

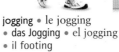

pilates • le pilates • das Pilates • el pilates • il pilates

train *(v)* s'entraîner trainieren entrenar allenarsi	jog in place *(v)* jogger sur place auf der Stelle joggen correr en parada correre sul posto	extend *(v)* étendre ausstrecken estirar stendere	boxercise l'aéroboxe die Boxgymnastik la gimnasia prepugilística la ginnastica prepugilistica	jumping rope le saut à la corde das Seilspringen saltar a la comba saltare con la corda
warm up *(v)* s'échauffer sich aufwärmen calentar riscaldarsi	flex *(v)* fléchir beugen flexionar flettere	pull up *(v)* tirer hochziehen levantar sollevare	circuit training l'entraînement en circuit das Zirkeltraining la tabla de gimnasia l'allenamento in circuito	

leisure

le temps libre

die Freizeit

el ocio

il tempo libero

theater • le théâtre • das Theater • el teatro • il teatro

stage • la scène • die Bühne • el escenario • il palcoscenico

seating • les places • die Bestuhlung • las butacas • le poltrone

play
la pièce de théâtre
das Theaterstück
la obra
l'opera teatrale

cast
la distribution
die Besetzung
el reparto
il cast

actor
l'acteur
der Schauspieler
el actor
l'attore

actress
l'actrice
die Schauspielerin
la actriz
l'attrice

director
le metteur en scène
der Regisseur
el director
il regista

producer
le metteur en scène
der Regisseur
el productor
il produttore

script
le texte
das Rollenheft
el guión
il copione

backdrop
la toile de fond
der Prospekt
el telón de fondo
il fondale

opening night
la première
die Premiere
el estreno
la prima

intermission
l'entracte
die Pause
el entreacto
l'intervallo

program
le programme
das Programm
el programa
il programma

orchestra pit
la fosse d'orchestre
der Orchestergraben
el foso de la orquesta
il golfo mistico

concert • le concert • das Konzert • el concierto • il concerto

musical • la comédie musicale • das Musical • el musical • il musical

costume
le costume
das Theaterkostüm
el vestuario
il costume

ballet • le ballet • das Ballett • el ballet • il balletto

opera • l'opéra • die Oper • la ópera • l'opera

usher
le placeur
der Platzanweiser
el acomodador
la maschera

classical music
la musique classique
die klassische Musik
la música clásica
la musica classica

musical score
la partition
die Noten
la partitura
la partitura musicale

soundtrack
la bande sonore
die Tonspur
la banda sonora
la colonna sonora

applaud *(v)*
applaudir
applaudieren
aplaudir
applaudire

encore
le bis
die Zugabe
el bis
il bis

I'd like two tickets for tonight's performance.
Je voudrais deux billets pour la représentation de ce soir.
Ich möchte zwei Karten für die Aufführung heute Abend.
Quisiera dos entradas para la sesión de esta noche.
Vorrei due biglietti per lo spettacolo di stasera.

What time does it start?
Ça commence à quelle heure?
Um wie viel Uhr beginnt die Aufführung?
¿A qué hora empieza?
A che ora inizia?

movies • le cinéma • das Kino • el cine • il cinema

popcorn
le pop-corn
das Popcorn
las palomitas
il popcorn

box office
la caisse
die Kasse
la taquilla
la biglietteria

lobby
le foyer
das Foyer
el vestíbulo
l'atrio

poster
l'affiche
das Plakat
el póster
il poster

movie theater • la salle de cinéma • der Kinosaal • el cine • il cinema

screen • l'écran • die Leinwand • la pantalla • lo schermo

comedy
la comédie
die Komödie
la comedia
la commedia

thriller
le thriller
der Thriller
la película de suspenso
il thriller

horror movie
le film d'horreur
der Horrorfilm
la película de miedo
il film di orrore

Western
le western
der Western
la película de vaqueros
il western

romance
la comédie romantique
der Liebesfilm
la película romántica
il film d'amore

science fiction movie
le film de science-fiction
der Science-Fiction-Film
la película de ciencia ficción
il film di fantascienza

adventure
le film d'aventures
der Abenteuerfilm
la película de aventuras
il film di avventura

animated movie
le film d'animation
der Zeichentrickfilm
la película de dibujos animados
il film di animazione

orchestra • l'orchestre • das Orchester • la orquesta • l'orchestra

strings • les cordes • die Saiteninstrumente • la cuerda • le corde

harp
la harpe
die Harfe
el arpa
l'arpa

conductor
le chef d'orchestre
der Dirigent
el director de orquesta
il direttore di orchestra

double bass
le contrebasse
der Kontrabass
el contrabajo
il contrabbasso

violin
le violon
die Geige
el violín
il violino

podium
le podium
das Podium
el podio
il podio

viola
l'alto
die Bratsche
la viola
la viola

cello
le violoncelle
das Cello
el violoncelo
il violoncello

score
la partition
die Noten
la partitura
lo spartito

bass clef
la clé de fa
der Bassschlüssel
la clave de fa
la chiave di basso

piano • le piano • das Klavier • el piano • il pianoforte

treble clef
la clé de sol
der Violinschlüssel
la clave de sol
la chiave di sol

note
la note
die Note
la nota
la nota

staff
la portée
das Liniensystem
el pentagrama
il pentagramma

notation • la notation • die Notation • la notación • l'annotazione

overture
l'ouverture
die Ouvertüre
la obertura
l'ouverture

symphony
la symphonie
die Symphonie
la sinfonía
la sinfonia

sonata
la sonate
die Sonate
la sonata
la sonata

instruments
les instruments
die Musikinstrumente
los instrumentos
gli strumenti

rest
le silence
das Pausenzeichen
la pausa
la pausa

pitch
le ton
die Tonhöhe
el tono
il tono

sharp
la dièse
das Kreuz
sostenido
il diesis

flat
le bémol
das B
bemol
il bemolle

natural
le bécarre
das Auflösungszeichen
natural
naturale

bar
la barre de mesure
der Taktstrich
la barra
la battuta

scale
la gamme
die Tonleiter
la escala
la scala

baton
la baguette
der Taktstock
la batura
la bacchetta

woodwind • les bois • die Holzblasinstrumente • el viento-madera • gli strumenti a fiato

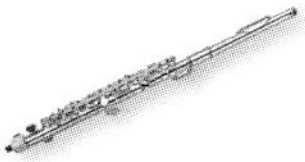

piccolo • le piccolo • die Pikkoloflöte • el flautín • il piffero

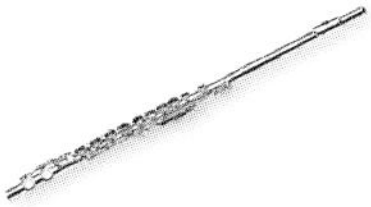

flute • la flûte traversière • die Querflöte • la flauta • il flauto

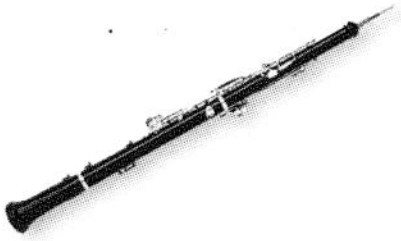

oboe • le hautbois • die Oboe • el oboe • l'oboe

English horn • le cor anglais • das Englischhorn • el corno inglés • il corno inglese

clarinet • la clarinette • die Klarinette • el clarinete • il clarinetto

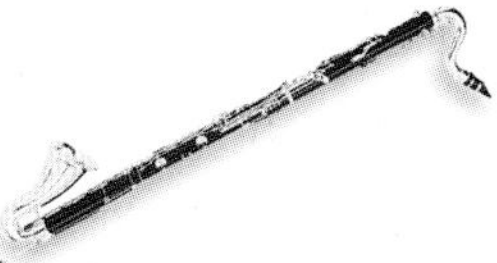

bass clarinet • la clarinette basse • die Bassklarinette • el clarinete bajo • il clarinetto basso

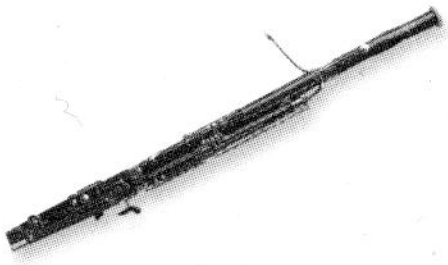

bassoon • le basson • das Fagott • el fagote • il fagotto

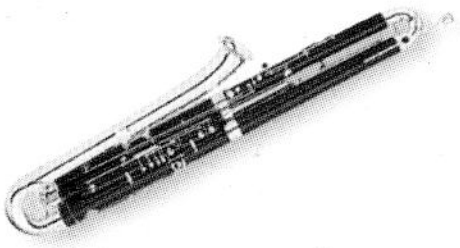

double bassoon • le contrebasson • das Kontrafagott • el contrafagote • il controfagotto

saxophone • le saxophone • das Saxophon • el saxofón • il sassofono

percussion • la percussion • die Schlaginstrumente • la percusión • la percussione

kettledrum • la timbale • die Kesselpauke • el timbal • il timpano

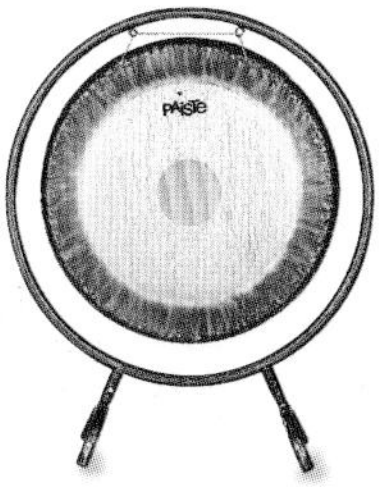

gong • le gong • der Gong • el gong • il gong

vibraphone • le vibraphone • das Vibraphon • el vibráfono • il vibrafono

foot pedal • les pédales • das Fußpedal • el pedal • i pedali

bongos • les bongos • die Bongos • los bongos • i bongo

snare drum • la caisse claire • die kleine Trommel • el tambor pequeño • il tamburo militare

cymbals • les cymbales • das Becken • los platillos • i cembali

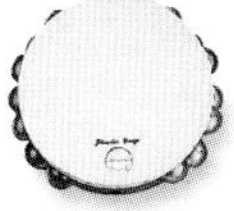

tambourine
le tambour
das Tamburin
el pandero
il tamburino

triangle
le triangle
der Triangel
el triángulo
il triangolo

maracas
les maracas
die Maracas
las maracas
i maracas

brass • les cuivres • die Blechblasinstrumente • el viento-metal • gli ottoni

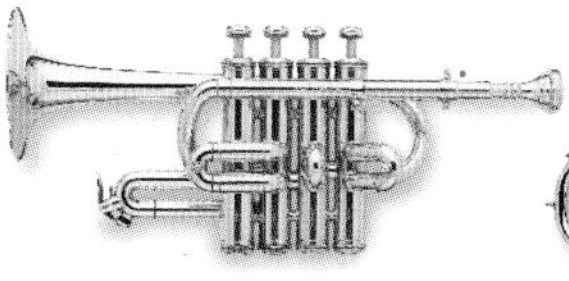

trumpet • la trompette • die Trompete • la trompeta • la tromba

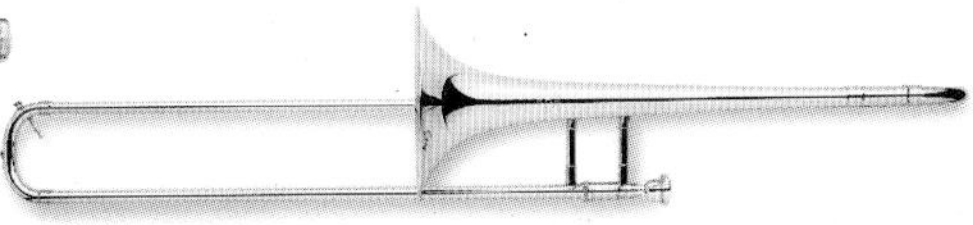

trombone • le trombone • die Posaune • el trombón de varas • il trombone

French horn • le cor • das Horn • el corno de caza • il corno

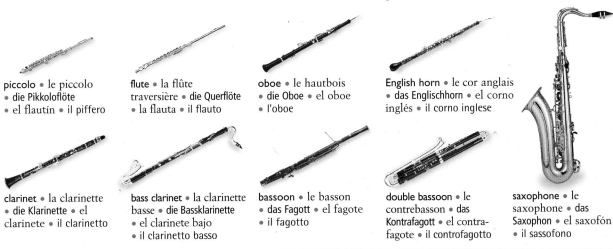

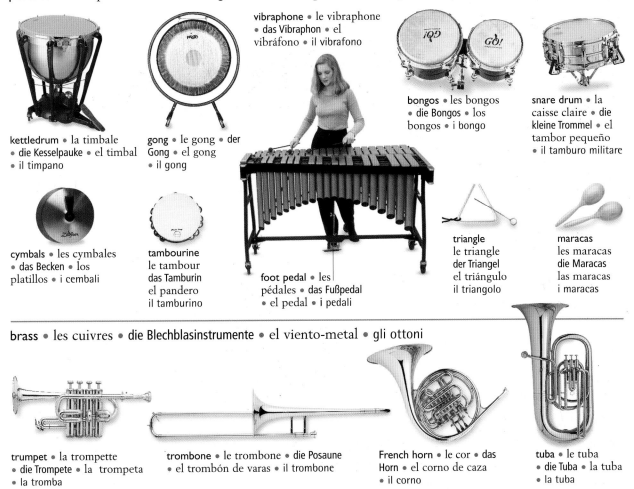

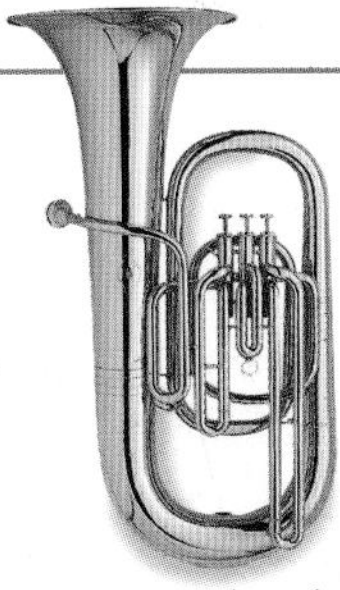

tuba • le tuba • die Tuba • la tuba • la tuba

concert • le concert • das Konzert • el concierto • il concerto

rock concert • le concert de rock • das Rockkonzert • el concierto de rock • il concerto rock

instruments • les instruments • die Instrumente • los instrumentos • gli strumenti

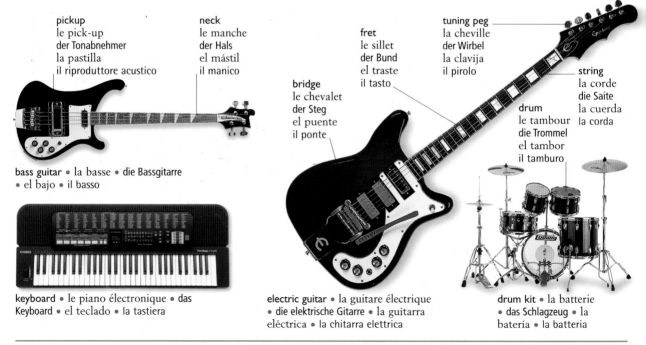

bass guitar • la basse • die Bassgitarre • el bajo • il basso

keyboard • le piano électronique • das Keyboard • el teclado • la tastiera

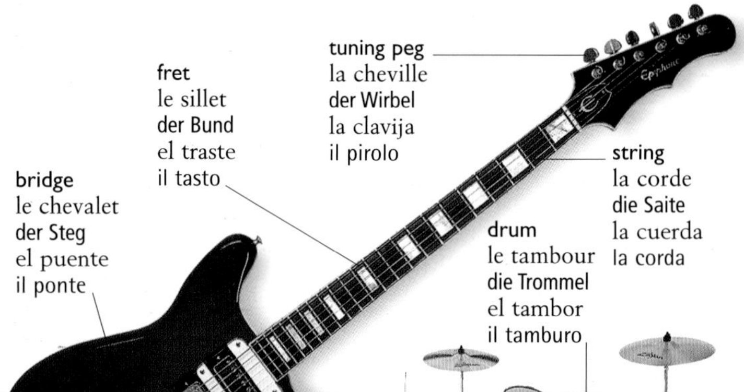

electric guitar • la guitare électrique • die elektrische Gitarre • la guitarra eléctrica • la chitarra elettrica

drum kit • la batterie • das Schlagzeug • la batería • la batteria

musical styles • les styles de musique • die Musikstile • los estilos musicales • gli stili musicali

jazz • le jazz • der Jazz • el jazz • il jazz

blues • le blues • der Blues • el blues • il blues

punk • la musique punk • die Punkmusik • el punk • il punk

folk music • la musique folk • der Folk • la música folklórica • la musica folk

pop • la pop • der Pop • el pop • il pop

dance • la dance • die Tanzmusik • la música de baile • la musica da ballo

rap • le rap • der Rap • el rap • il rap

heavy metal • la heavy métal • das Heavymetal • el heavy metal • l'heavy metal

classical music • la musique classique • die klassische Musik • la música clásica • la musica classica

song	lyrics	melody	beat	reggae	country	spotlight
la chanson	les paroles	la mélodie	le beat	le reggae	la country	le projecteur
das Lied	der Text	die Melodie	der Beat	der Reggae	die Countrymusic	der Scheinwerfer
la canción	la letra	la melodía	el ritmo	el reggae	la música country	el reflector
la canzone	il testo	la melodia	il ritmo	il reggae	il country	il proiettore

sightseeing • le tourisme • die Besichtigungstour • el turismo • il turismo

tourist
le touriste
der Tourist
el turista
il turista

tourist attraction • l'attraction touristique • die Touristenattraktion • la atracción turística • il luogo d'interesse turistico

itinerary
l'itinéraire
die Route
el itinerario
l'itinerario

open-top
à impériale
mit offenem Oberdeck
descubierto
scoperto

tour bus • le bus touristique • der Stadtrundfahrtbus • el autobús turístico • il pullman turistico

tour guide
la guide
die Fremdenführerin
la guía turística
la guida turistica

figurine • la statuette • die Figur • la estatuilla • la statuina

guided tour • la tour guidé • die Führung • la visita guiada • la visita guidata

souvenirs • les souvenirs • die Andenken • los recuerdos • i ricordi

open ouvert geöffnet abierto aperto	guidebook le guide der Reiseführer la guía del viajero la guida	camcorder le caméscope der Camcorder la cámara de vídeo la videocamera	left à gauche links la izquierda a sinistra
closed fermé geschlossen cerrado chiuso	film la pellicule der Film la película la pellicola	camera l'appareil photo die Kamera la cámara fotográfica la macchina fotografica	right à droite rechts la derecha a destra
admission charge le prix d'entrée das Eintrittsgeld el precio de entrada la tariffa d'ingresso	batteries les piles die Batterien las pilas le batterie	directions les directions die Richtungsangaben las indicaciones le indicazioni	straight ahead tout droit geradeaus recto dritto

Where is…?
Où est…?
Wo ist…?
¿Dónde está…?
Dov'è...?

I'm lost.
Je me suis perdu.
Ich habe mich verlaufen.
Estoy perdido.
Mi sono perso.

Can you tell me the way to….?
Pour aller à…, s'il vous plaît?
Können Sie mir sagen, wie ich nach… komme?
¿Podría decirme cómo se va a…?
Mi può dire come si arriva a...?

attractions • les attractions • die Sehenswürdigkeiten • los lugares de interés • i luoghi d'interesse

painting
le tableau
das Gemälde
el cuadro
il quadro

exhibit
l'objet exposé
das Ausstellungsstück
la muestra
l'oggetto

art gallery • le musée d'art • die Kunstgalerie • la galería de arte • la galleria d'arte

monument • le monument • das Monument • el monumento • il monumento

exhibition • l'exposition • die Ausstellung • la exposición • l'esposizione

museum • le musée • das Museum • el museo • il museo

famous ruin
la ruine célèbre
die berühmte Ruine
la ruina famosa
la rovina famosa

historic building • le monument historique • das historische Gebäude • el edificio histórico • l'edificio storico

casino • le casino • das Kasino • el casino • il casinò

garden • le parc • der Park • los jardines • i giardini

national park • le parc national • der Nationalpark • el parque nacional • il parco nazionale

information • l'information • die Information • la información • l'informazione

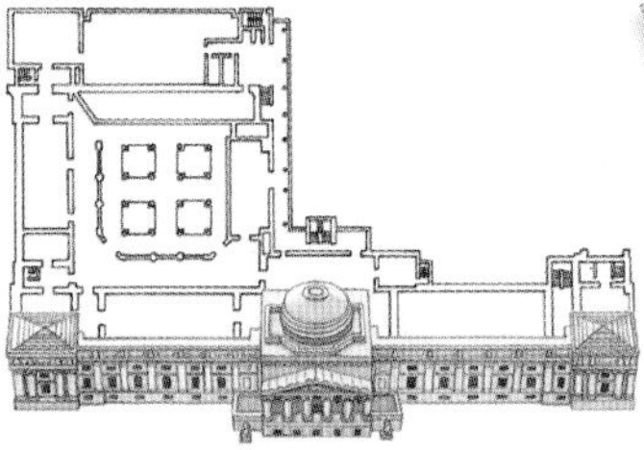

floor plan • le plan • der Grundriss • el plano de la planta • la pianta del piano

map • le plan • der Stadtplan • el mapa • la mappa

times
les heures
die Zeiten
las horas
gli orari

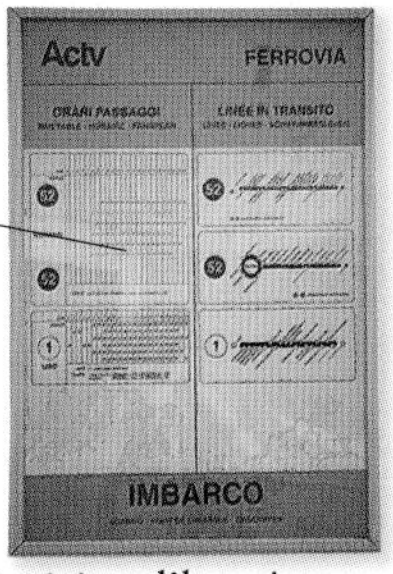

schedule • l'horaire • der Fahrplan • el horario • l'orario

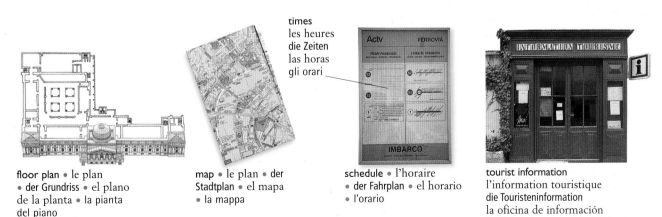

tourist information
l'information touristique
die Touristeninformation
la oficina de información
l'ufficio informazioni turistiche

outdoor activities • les activités de plein air • die Aktivitäten im Freien • las actividades al aire libre • le attività all'aria aperta

park • le parc • der Park • el parque • il parco

fair • la foire • der Jahrmarkt • la feria • il luna park

amusement park • le parc d'attractions • der Vergnügungspark • el parque de diversiones • il parco a tema

wildlife park • la réserve • der Safaripark • el safari park • lo zoosafari

zoo • le zoo • der Zoo • el zoológico • lo zoo

activities • les activités • die Aktivitäten • las actividades • le attività

cycling • le vélo • das Radfahren • el ciclismo • il ciclismo

jogging • le jogging • das Jogging • el jogging • il footing

skateboarding • la planche à roulette • das Skateboardfahren • la patineta • lo skateboard

rollerblading • le roller • das Inlinerfahren • el patinaje • il pattinaggio

riding trail • la piste cavalière • der Reitweg • el sendero para caballos • il sentiero per cavalli

bird watching • l'observation des oiseaux • das Vogelbeobachten • la ornitología • l'ornitologia

horseback riding • l'équitation • das Reiten • la equitación • l'equitazione

hiking • la randonnée • das Wandern • la caminata • l'escursionismo

hamper • le panier à pique-nique • der Picknickkorb • la canasta • la cesta

picnic • le pique-nique • das Picknick • el picnic • il picnic

playground • le terrain de jeux • der Spielplatz • el área de juegos • il parco giochi

sandbox • le bac à sable • der Sandkasten • el cajón de arena • la fossa di sabbia

wading pool • la pataugeoire • das Planschbecken • la alberca de plástico • la piscina gonfiabile

swing • la balançoire • die Schaukel • los columpios • l'altalena

climber • la cage à poules • das Klettergerüst • el changuero • la struttura per arrampicarsi

seesaw • la bascule • die Wippe • el subibaja • il bilanciere

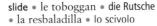

slide • le toboggan • die Rutsche • la resbaladilla • lo scivolo

beach • la plage • der Strand • la playa • la spiaggia

hotel
l'hôtel
das Hotel
el hotel
l'albergo

beach umbrella
le parasol
der Sonnenschirm
la sombrilla
l'ombrellone

beach hut
la cabine de plage
das Strandhäuschen
la caseta
la cabina

sand
le sable
der Sand
la arena
la sabbia

wave
la vague
die Welle
la ola
l'onda

sea
la mer
das Meer
el mar
il mare

beach bag
le sac de plage
die Strandtasche
la bolsa de playa
la borsa da spiaggia

bikini • le bikini • der Bikini • el bikini • il bikini

sunbathe *(v)* • prendre un bain de soleil • sonnenbaden • asolear • prendere il sole

lifeguard
le maître nageur
der Rettungsschwimmer
el salvavidas
il bagnino

lifeguard tower • la tour de surveillance • der Rettungsturm • la torre de vigilancia • la torre di sorveglianza

windbreak • le pare-vent • der Windschutz • la barrera contra el viento • il paravento

boardwalk • la promenade • die Promenade • el paseo marítimo • il lungomare

deck chair • le transat • der Liegestuhl • el asoleadero • la sedia a sdraio

sunglasses • les lunettes de soleil • die Sonnenbrille • los lentes obscuros • gli occhiali da sole

sun hat • le chapeau de plage • der Sonnenhut • el sombrero para el sol • il cappello da spiaggia

suntan lotion • la lotion solaire • die Sonnenmilch • el bronceador • la crema abbronzante

sunblock • l'écran total • der Sonnenblock • la crema protectora • la crema protettiva

beach ball • le ballon de plage • der Wasserball • la pelota de playa • il pallone da spiaggia

inflatable ring • la bouée • der Schwimmreifen • la llanta • la ciambella

swimsuit
le maillot de bain
der Badeanzug
el traje de baño
il costume da bagno

shovel
la pelle
der Schaufel
la pala
la paletta

pail
le seau
der Eimer
la cubeta
il secchiello

sandcastle
le château de sable
die Sandburg
el castillo de arena
il castello di sabbia

shell
le coquillage
die Muschel
la concha
la conchiglia

beach towel • la serviette de plage • das Strandtuch • la toalla de playa • l'asciugamano da spiaggia

camping • le camping • das Camping • el camping • il campeggio

campsite • le terrain de camping • der Campingplatz • el camping • il campeggio

camp (*v*) camper zelten acampar campeggiare	site l'emplacement der Zeltplatz el lugar il posteggio	picnic bench le banc à pique-nique die Picknickbank la mesa de picnic il tavola da picnic	charcoal le charbon de bois die Holzkohle el carbón vegetal la carbonella
manager's office le bureau du chef die Campingplatzverwaltung la oficina del director l'ufficio del direttore	pitch a tent (*v*) monter une tente ein Zelt aufschlagen poner una tienda piantare una tenda	hammock le hamac die Hängematte la hamaca l'amaca	firelighter l'allume-feu der Feueranzünder la pastilla para fogatas l'esca per il fuoco
sites available les emplacements de libre Zeltplätze frei hay lugares libres le piazzole disponibili	tent pole le mât die Zeltstange el tubo de la tienda il palo	camper van l'autocaravane das Wohnmobil el cámper il camper	light a fire (*v*) allumer un feu ein Feuer machen encender una fogata accendere un fuoco
full complet voll lleno completo	cot le lit de camp das Faltbett el catre de campaña il lettino da campeggio	trailer la remorque der Anhänger el remolque il rimorchio	campfire le feu de camp das Lagerfeuer la fogata il fuoco

frame
le cadre
das Gestänge
la estructura
la struttura

ground cloth
le tapis de sol
der Zeltboden
el suelo aislante
il telo isolante

backpack
le sac à dos
der Rucksack
la mochila
lo zaino

thermos
le thermos
die Thermosflasche
el termo
il thermos

water bottle
la bouteille d'eau
die Wasserflasche
la cantimplora
la borraccia

tent • la tente • das Zelt • la tienda de campaña • la tenda

insect repellent • le spray contre les insectes • der Insektenspray • el repelente de insectos • l'insettifugo

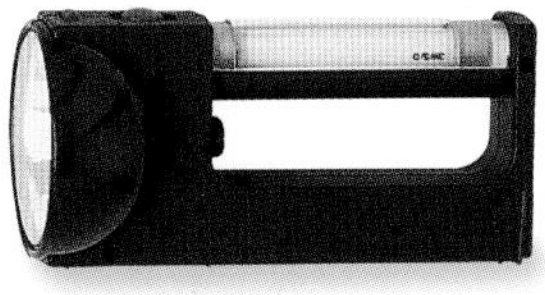

flashlight • la lampe torche • die Taschenlampe • la linterna • la torcia

mosquito net
la moustiquaire
das Moskitonetz
el mosquitero
la zanzariera

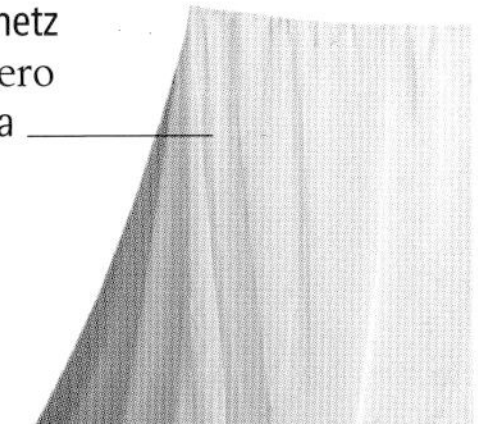

thermal underwear
les sous-vêtements thermiques
die Thermowäsche
la ropa térmica
gli indumenti termici

hiking boots • les chaussures de marche • die Wanderschuhe • las botas de trekking • le scarpe da escursionismo

rain clothes • l'imperméable • die Regenhaut • la manga • gli indumenti impermeabili

sleeping bag • le sac de couchage • der Schlafsack • el saco de dormir • il sacco a pelo

sleeping mat
le tapis de sol
die Schlafmatte
la esterilla
il materassino

camp stove • le réchaud • der Gasbrenner • la estufilla • il fornelletto da campeggio

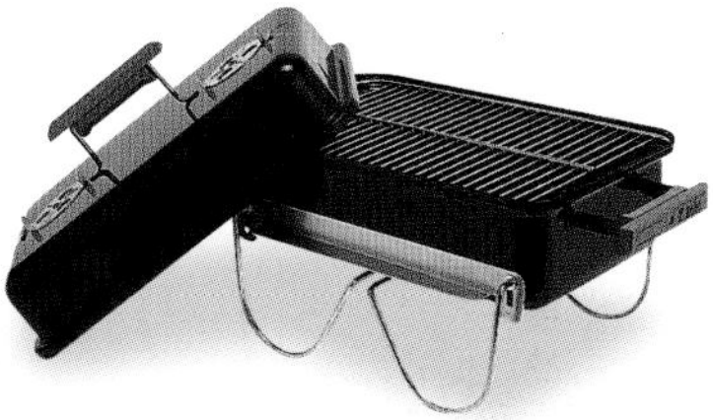

grill • le barbecue • der Grill • la parrilla • la griglia per barbecue

air mattress • le matelat pneumatique • die Luftmatratze • la colchoneta • il materassino ad aria

home entertainment • les distractions à la maison • die Privatunterhaltung • el entretenimiento en el hogar • gli intrattenimenti in casa

digital radio • la radio numérique • das Digitalradio • la radio digital • la radio digitale

iPod© • l'iPod • der iPod • el iPod • l'iPod

DVD • le DVD • die DVD-Platte • el disco de DVD • il disco DVD

DVD player • le lecteur DVD • der DVD-Spieler • el reproductor de DVD • il lettore di DVD

record player
le tourne-disque
der Plattenspieler
el tocadiscos
il giradischi

CD player
le lecteur CD
der CD-Spieler
el lector de discos compactos
il lettore di CD

radio
la radio
das Radio
la radio
la radio

amplifier
l'amplificateur
der Verstärker
el amplificador
l'amplificatore

headphones
les écouteurs
die Kopfhörer
los audífonos
le cuffie

stereo rack
l'étagère
das Rack
el mueble
il supporto

stereo system • la chaîne hi-fi • die Hi-Fi-Anlage • el equipo de alta fidelidad • l'impianto stereo

speaker
le baffle
die Box
la bocina
l'altoparlante

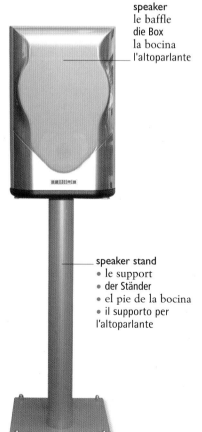

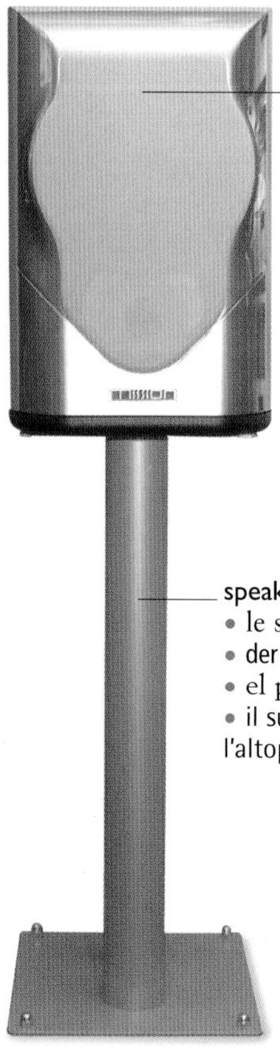

speaker stand • le support • der Ständer • el pie de la bocina • il supporto per l'altoparlante

DTV box • le box • die Digitale box • la sintonizador digital • il decoder

screen
l'écran
der Bildschirm
la pantalla
lo schermo

eyecup
l'œilleton
die Okularmuschel
el borde del ocular
l'oculare

camcorder • le caméscope • der Camcorder • la cámara de video • la videocamera

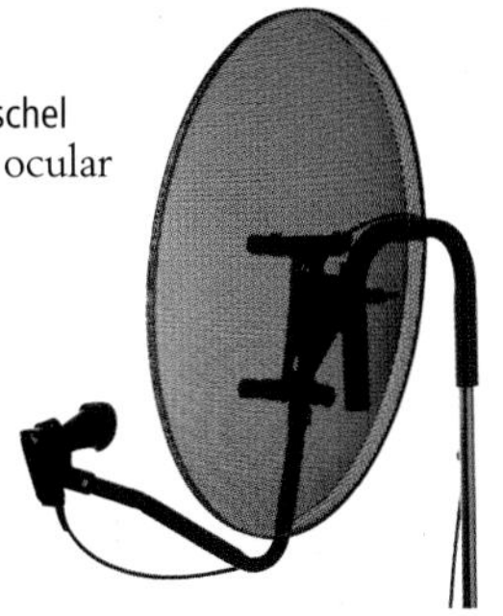

satellite dish • l'antenne parabolique • die Satellitenschüssel • la antena parabólica • l'antenna parabolica

flatscreen TV • la télévision à écran plat • der Flachbildfernseher • el televisor de pantalla • la TV a schermo piatto

console
la console
das Pult
la consola
la console

controller
la commande
der Steuerhebel
los controles
il comando

video game • le jeu vidéo • das Videospiel • el videojuego • il videogioco

fast-forward • l'avance rapide • der Vorlauf • el avance rápido • l'avanzamento veloce

pause
la pause
die Pause
la pausa
la pausa

record
• l'enregistrement
• die Aufnahme
• el botón para grabar • la registrazione

volume
le volume
die Lautstärke
el volumen
il volume

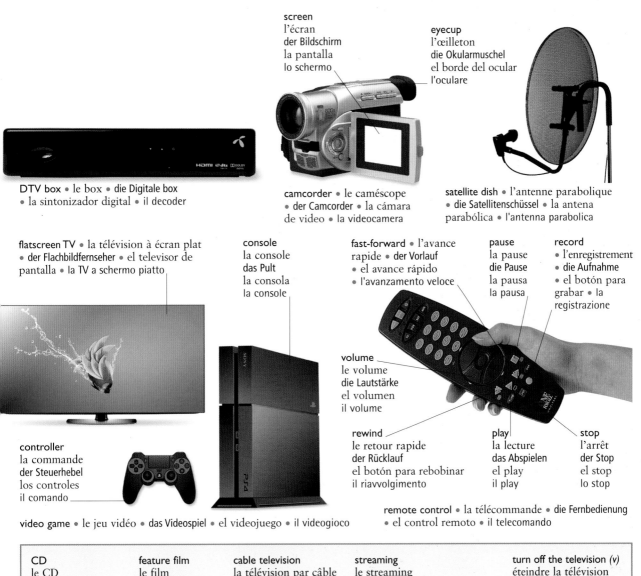

rewind
le retour rapide
der Rücklauf
el botón para rebobinar
il riavvolgimento

play
la lecture
das Abspielen
el play
il play

stop
l'arrêt
der Stop
el stop
lo stop

remote control • la télécommande • die Fernbedienung • el control remoto • il telecomando

CD le CD die CD-Platte el disco compacto il compact disc	feature film le film der Spielfilm la película il lungometraggio	cable television la télévision par câble das Kabelfernsehen la televisión por cable la televisione via cavo	streaming le streaming das Streaming la transmisión por secuencias lo streaming	turn off the television *(v)* éteindre la télévision den Fernseher abschalten apagar la televisión spegnere la televisione
Wi-fi le wifi WLAN el wi-Fi Wifi	advertisement la publicité die Werbung el anuncio la pubblicità	program le programme das Programm el programa il programma	turn on the television *(v)* allumer la télévision den Fernseher einschalten encender la televisión accendere la televisione	tune the radio *(v)* régler la radio das Radio einstellen sintonizar la radio sintonizzare la radio
high-definition haute définition hochauflösend alta definición alta definizione (HD)	digital numérique digital digital digitale	change channels *(v)* changer de chaîne den Kanal wechseln cambiar de canal cambiare canale	watch television *(v)* regarder la télévision fernsehen ver la televisión guardare la televisione	stereo stéréo stereo estéreo stereo

photography • la photographie • die Fotografie • la fotografía • la fotografia

shutter release
le déclencheur
der Auslöser
el disparador
il pulsante di scatto

aperture dial
le réglage de l'ouverture
der Blendenregler
el obturador
il regolatore di esposizione

lens
l'objectif
die Linse
el lente
l'obiettivo

SLR camera • l'appareil réflex mono-objectif • die Spiegelreflexkamera • la cámara réflex • la macchina fotografica SLR

filter • le filtre • der Filter • el filtro • il filtro

lens cap • le bouchon d'objectif • die Schutzkappe • la tapa del lente • il copriobiettivo

flash gun • le flash compact • der Elektronenblitz • el flash electrónico • il flash

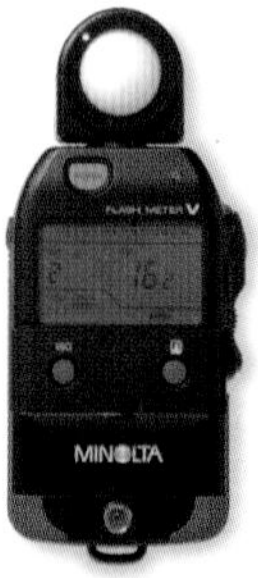

light meter • le posemètre • der Belichtungsmesser • el fotómetro • l'esposimetro

zoom lens • le zoom • das Zoom • el zoom • lo zoom

tripod • le trépied • das Stativ • el tripié • il treppiede

types of camera • les types d'appareils photo • die Fotoapparattypen • los tipos de cámara • i tipi di macchina fotorafica

polaroid camera • le Polaroid® • die Polaroidkamera • la cámara Polaroid • la macchina fotografica Polaroid

flash
le flash
der Blitz
el flash
il flash

digital camera • l'appareil numérique • die Digitalkamera • la cámara digital • la macchina fotografica digitale

cameraphone • le photophone • das Kamera-Handy • el teléfono con cámara • il telefono con macchina fotografica

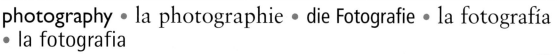

disposable camera • l'appareil jetable • die Einwegkamera • la cámara desechable • la macchina fotografica usa e getta

photograph (v) • photographier • fotografieren • fotografiar • fotografare

film spool
le rouleau de pellicule
die Filmspule
el carrete
il rullino

film • la pellicule • der Film • el rollo • la pellicola

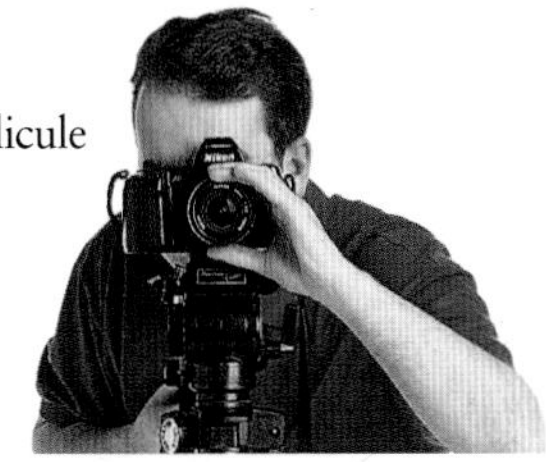

focus (v) • mettre au point • einstellen • enfocar • mettere a fuoco

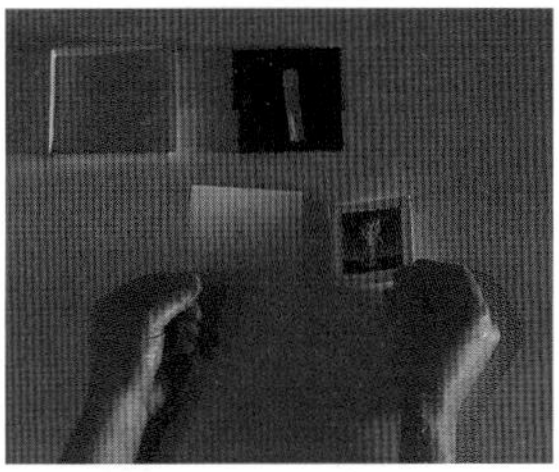

develop (v) • développer • entwickeln • revelar • sviluppare

negative • le négatif • das Negativ • el negativo • il negativo

landscape • paysage • quer • apaisado • orizzontale

portrait • portrait • hoch • en formato vertical • verticale

photograph • la photo • das Foto • la fotografía • la fotografia

photo album • l'album de photos • das Fotoalbum • el álbum de fotos • l'album fotografico

picture frame • le cadre de photo • der Fotorahmen • el portarretratos • la cornice

problems • les problèmes • die Probleme • los problemas • i difetti

underexposed • sous-exposé • unterbelichtet • subexpuesto • sottoesposto

overexposed • surexposé • überbelichtet • sobreexpuesto • sovraesposto

out of focus • flou • unscharf • desenfocado • sfocato

red eye • la tache rouge • die Rotfärbung der Augen • los ojos rojos • l'occhio rosso

viewfinder
le viseur
der Bildsucher
el visor
il mirino

camera case
le sac d'appareil photo
die Kameratasche
la funda de la cámara
la custodia

exposure
la pose
die Belichtung
la exposición
l'esposizione

darkroom
la chambre noire
die Dunkelkammer
el cuarto oscuro
la camera oscura

print
l'épreuve
der Abzug
la foto (revelada)
la fotografia (sviluppata)

mat
mat
matt
mate
opaco

gloss
brilliant
hochglanz
con brillo
lucido

enlargement
l'agrandissement
die Vergrößerung
la ampliación
l'ingrandimento

I'd like this film processed.
Pourriez-vous faire développer cette pellicule?
Könnten Sie diesen Film entwickeln lassen?
Me gustaría revelar este rollo.
Vorrei far sviluppare questo rullino.

games • les jeux • die Spiele • los juegos • i giochi

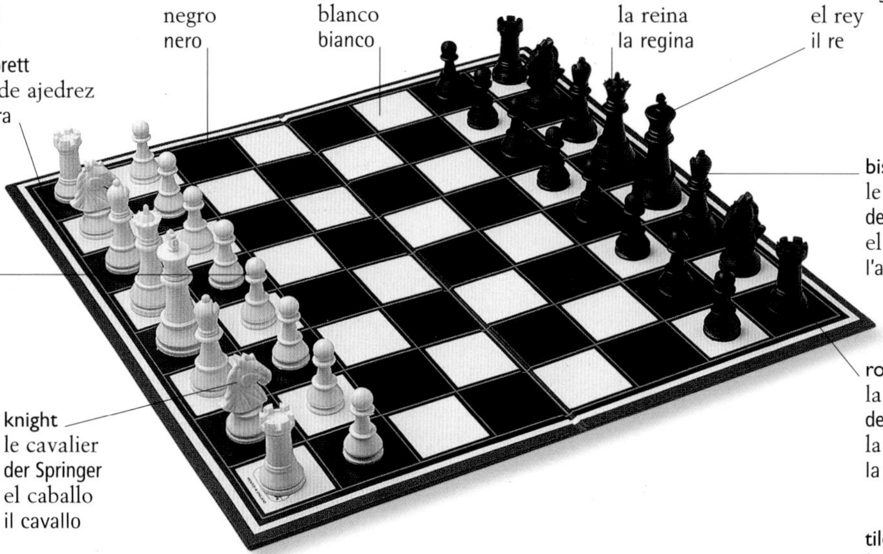

chess • les échecs • das Schach • el ajedrez • gli scacchi

checkers • les dames • das Damespiel • las damas • la dama

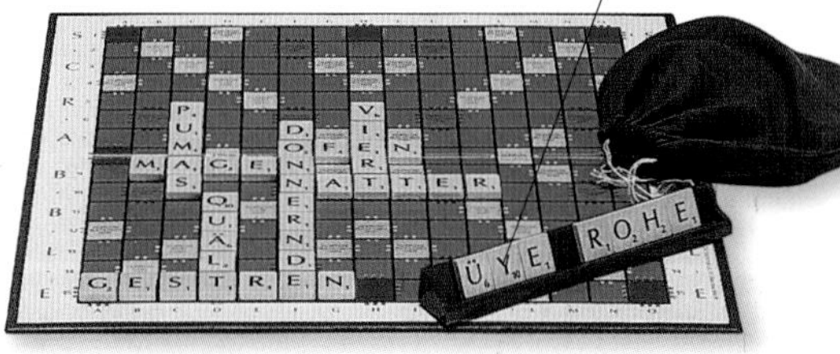

scrabble • le scrabble • das Scrabble • el scrabble • lo scrabble

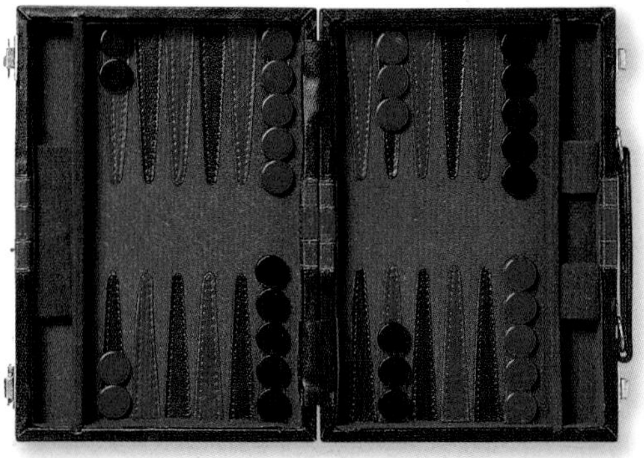

backgammon • le trictrac • das Backgammon • el backgammon • il tric trac (la tavola reale)

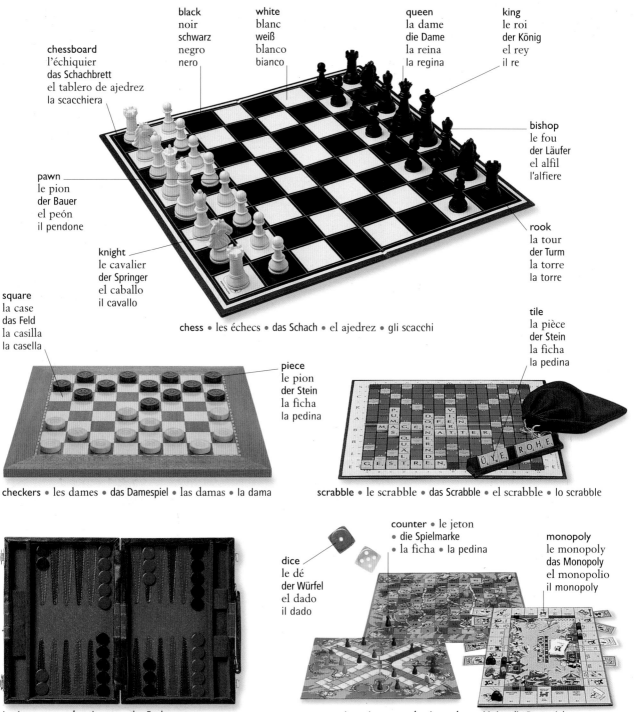

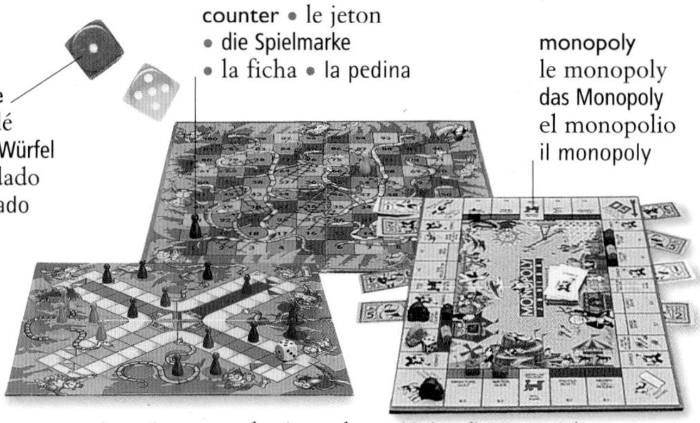

board games • les jeux de société • die Brettspiele • los juegos de mesa • i giochi da tavolo

stamp collecting • la philatélie • das Briefmarkensammeln • la filatelia • la filatelia

jigsaw puzzle • le puzzle • das Puzzle • el rompecabezas • il puzzle

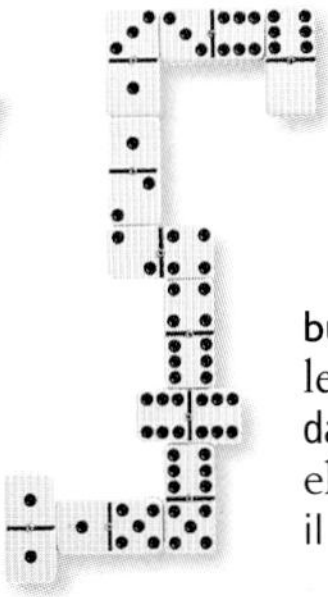

dominoes • les dominos • das Domino • el dominó • il domino

dartboard
la cible
die Dartscheibe
la diana
il bersaglio

bullseye
le mille
das Bull's Eye
el blanco
il centro

darts • les fléchettes • das Darts • los dardos • le freccette

joker
le joker
der Joker
el comodín
il jolly

jack
le valet
der Bube
el joto
il fante

queen
la dame
die Dame
la reina
la regina

king
le roi
der König
el rey
il re

ace • l'as • das Ass • el as • l'asso

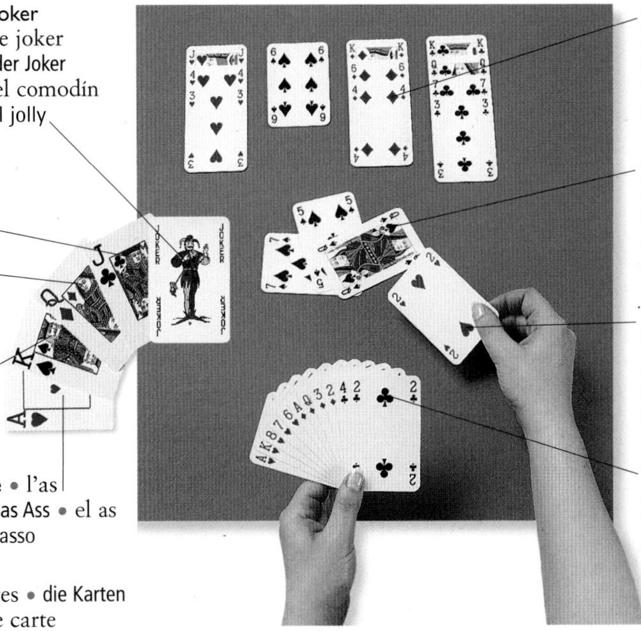

diamond
le carreau
das Karo
el diamante
il quadro

spade
le pique
das Pik
la espada
la picca

heart
le cœur
das Herz
el corazón
il cuore

club
le trèfle
das Kreuz
el trébol
il fiore

cards • les cartes • die Karten • las cartas • le carte

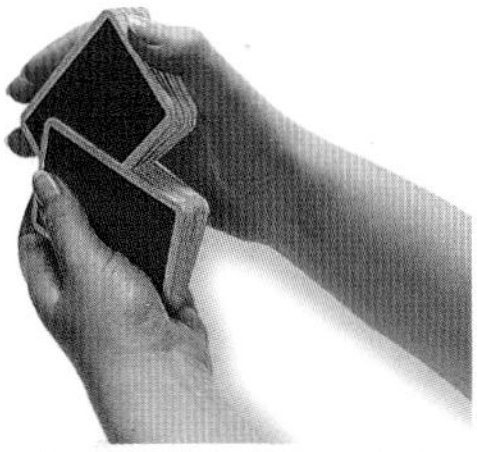

shuffle *(v)* • battre • mischen • barajar • mescolare

deal *(v)* • donner • geben • repartir • distribuire

move le coup der Zug el turno la mossa	win *(v)* gagner gewinnen ganar vincere	loser le perdant der Verlierer el perdedor il perdente	point le point der Punkt el punto il punto	bridge le bridge das Bridge el bridge il bridge	Whose turn is it? C'est à qui de jouer? Wer ist dran? ¿A quién le toca? A chi tocca?
play *(v)* jouer spielen jugar giocare	winner le gagnant der Gewinner el ganador il vincitore	game le jeu das Spiel la partida il gioco	score la marque das Spielergebnis la puntuación il punteggio	deck of cards le jeu de cartes das Kartenspiel la baraja il mazzo di carte	It's your move. C'est à toi de jouer. Du bist dran. Te toca a ti. Tocca a te.
player le joueur der Spieler el jugador il giocatore	lose *(v)* perdre verlieren perder perdere	bet le pari die Wette la apuesta la scommessa	poker le poker das Poker el póquer il poker	suit la couleur die Farbe el palo il colore	Roll the dice. Jette le dé. Würfle. Tira los dados. Tira i dadi.

arts and crafts 1 • les arts et métiers 1 • das Kunsthandwerk 1 • las manualidades 1 • arte e artigianato 1

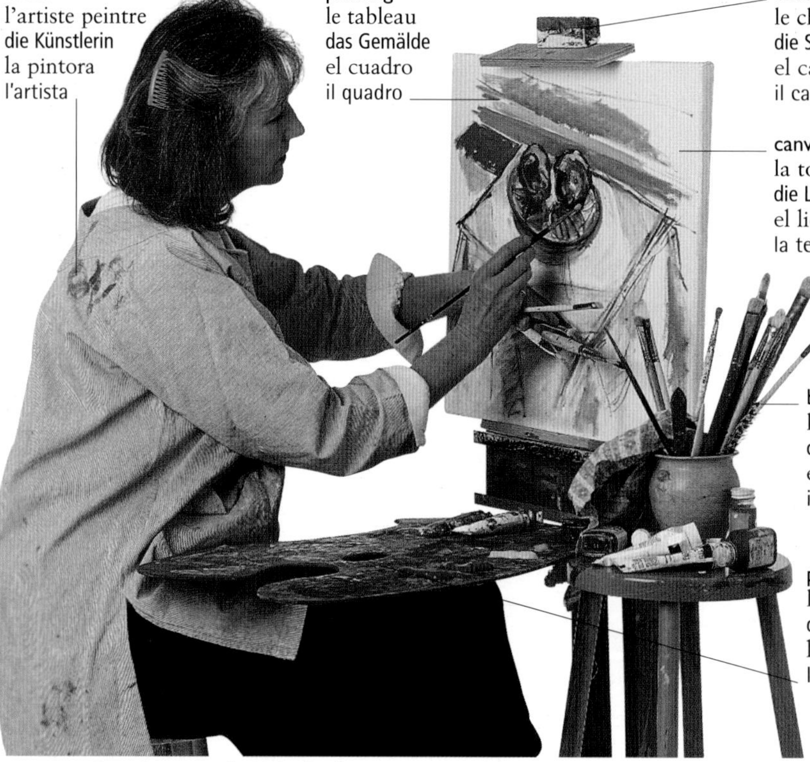

painting • la peinture • die Malerei • la pintura • la pittura

colors • les couleurs • die Farben • los colores • i colori

red • rouge • rot • rojo • rosso

blue • bleu • blau • azul • blu

yellow • jaune • gelb • amarillo • giallo

green • vert • grün • verde • verde

orange • orange • orange • naranja • arancione

purple • violet • lila • morado • viola

white • blanc • weiß • blanco • bianco

black • noir • schwarz • negro • nero

gray • gris • grau • gris • grigio

pink • rose • rosa • rosa • rosa

brown • marron • braun • marrón • marrone

indigo • indigo • indigoblau • azul añil • indaco

paints • les couleurs • die Farben • las pinturas • la vernice

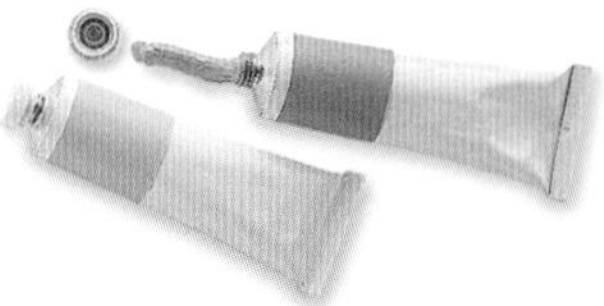

oil paints • les couleurs à l'huile • die Ölfarben • las pinturas al óleo • i colori ad olio

watercolors • la couleur à l'eau • die Aquarellfarbe • las acuarelas • gli acquarelli

pastels • les pastels • die Pastellstifte • los pasteles • i pastelli

acrylic paint • l'acrylique • die Acrylfarbe • la pintura acrílica • i colori acrilici

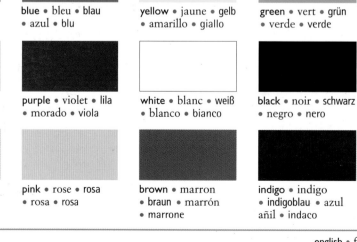

poster paint • la gouache • die Plakatfarbe • la témpera • la tempera

other crafts • les autres arts • andere Kunstfertigkeiten • las otras manualidades • altri lavori artigianali

sketchbook
le carnet à croquis
der Skizzenblock
el bloc de dibujo
il blocco per schizzi

sketch
le croquis
die Skizze
el boceto
lo schizzo

ink
l'encre
die Druckfarbe
la tinta
l'inchiostro

pencil
le crayon
der Bleistift
el lápiz
la matita

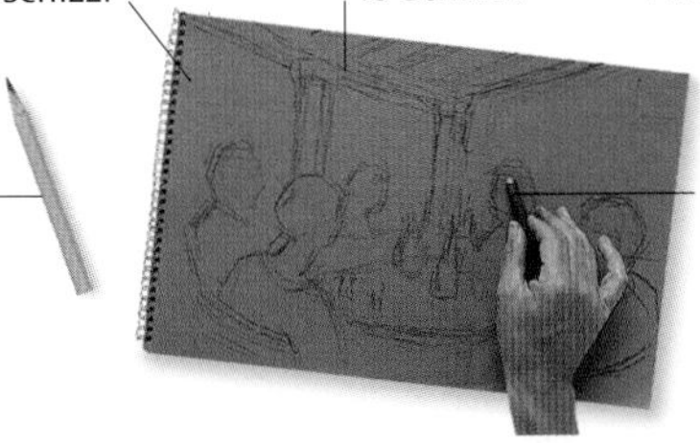

charcoal
le fusain
der Kohlestift
el carboncillo
il carboncino

drawing • le dessin • das Zeichnen • el dibujo • il disegno

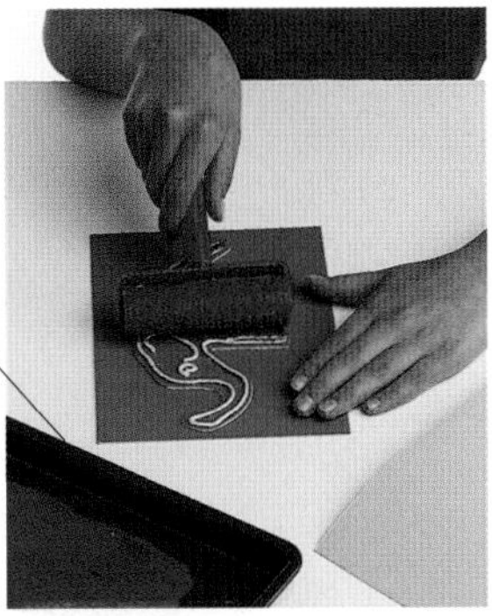

printing • l'imprimerie • das Drucken • la impresión • la stampa

engraving • la gravure • das Gravieren • el grabado • l'incisione

stone
la pierre
der Stein
la piedra
la pietra

mallet
le maillet
der Schlegel
el mazo
il martello

chisel
le burin
der Meißel
el cincel
lo scalpello

wood
le bois
das Holz
la madera
il legno

sculpting • la sculpture • die Bildhauerei • la escultura • la scultura

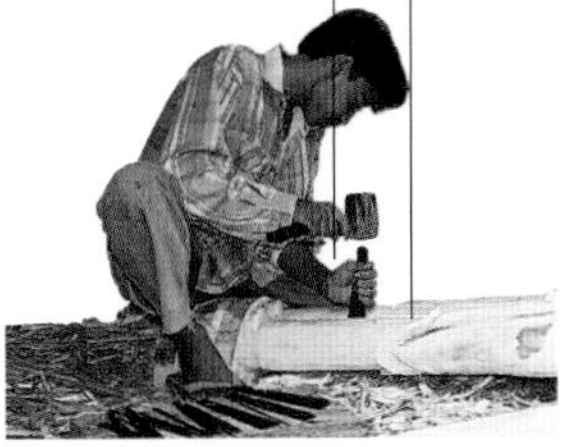

woodworking • la sculpture sur bois • die Holzarbeit • la talla en madera • la falegnameria

modeling tool • la spatule • das Modellierholz • la herramienta para modelar • l'attrezzo per modellare

potter's wheel
le tour de potier
die Drehscheibe
el torno de alfarero
il tornio da vasaio

clay
l'argile
der Ton
la arcilla
l'argilla

pottery • la poterie • die Töpferei • la cerámica • la ceramica

glue
la colle
der Klebstoff
el pegamento
la colla

cardboard
le carton
die Pappe
la cartulina
il cartone

collage • le collage • die Collage • el collage • il collage

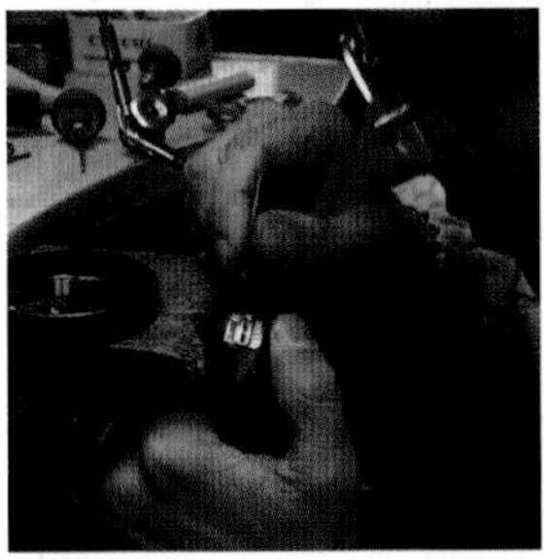

jewelry making • la joaillerie • die Juwelierarbeit • la orfebrería • l'oreficeria

papier-mâché • le papier mâché • das Papiermaché • el papel maché • la cartapesta

origami • l'origami • das Origami • la papiroflexia • l'origami

model-making • le modélisme • der Modellbau • el modelismo • il modellismo

arts and crafts 2 • les arts et métiers 2 • das Kunsthandwerk 2 • las manualidades 2 • arte e artigianato 2

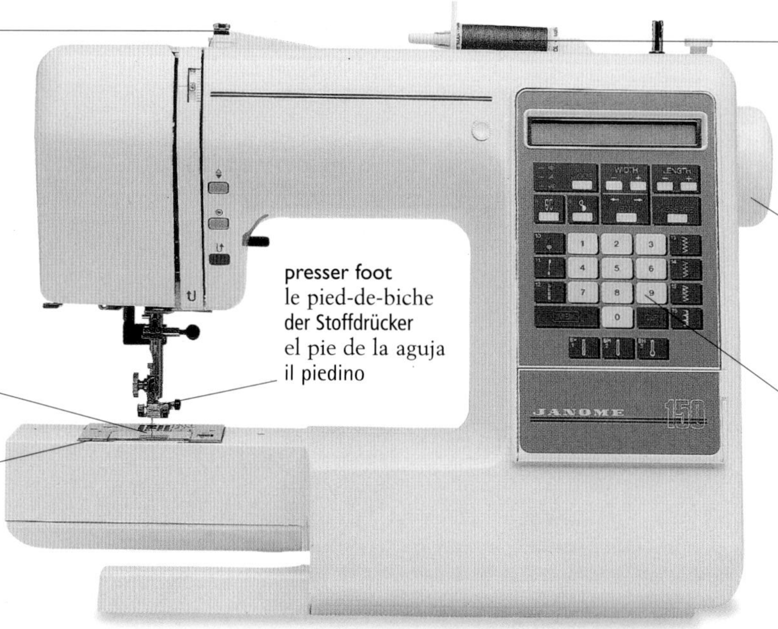

thread guide
le guide de fil
der Fadenleiter
la guía del hilo
il guidafilo

needle
l'aiguille
die Nadel
la aguja
l'ago

presser foot
le pied-de-biche
der Stoffdrücker
el pie de la aguja
il piedino

needle plate
la platine
die Stichplatte
la placa de la aguja
la piastrina dell'ago

thread reel
la bobine de fil
der Spuler
el carrete de hilo
il rocchetto del filo

balance wheel
le balancier
das Handrad
la rueda de ajuste
la ruota

stitch selector
le sélecteur de point
der Stichwähler
el selector de puntada
il selezionatore dei punti

sewing machine • la machine à coudre • die Nähmaschine • la máquina de coser • la macchina da cucire

scissors • les ciseaux • die Schere • las tijeras • le forbici

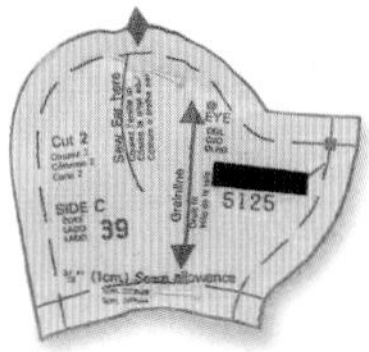

pattern • le patron • das Schnittmuster • el patrón • il modello

pincushion
la pelote à épingles
das Nadelkissen
el alfiletero
il puntaspilli

pin
l'épingle
die Stecknadel
el alfiler
lo spillo

sewing basket • la corbeille à couture • der Nähkorb • el costurero • la cesta del cucito

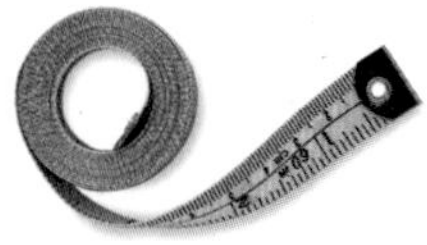

tape measure • le centimètre • das Zentimetermaß • la cinta métrica • il metro

material • le tissu • der Stoff • la tela • la stoffa

bobbin • la bobine • die Spule • la bobina • la bobina

thread
le fil
das Garn
el hilo
il filo

eye
l'œillet
die Öse
la hembra
l'occhiello

hook • l'agrafe • der Haken • el macho • il gancio

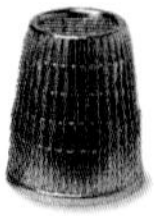

thimble • le dé à coudre • der Fingerhut • el dedal • il ditale

tailor's chalk • la craie de tailleur • die Schneiderkreide • el jaboncillo • il gesso

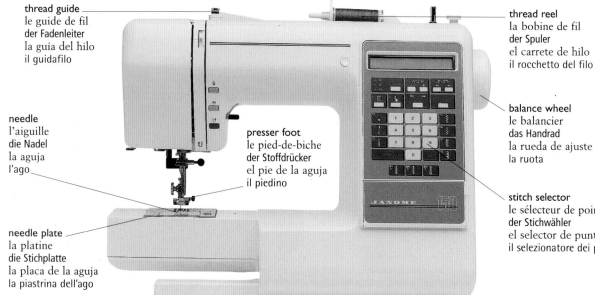

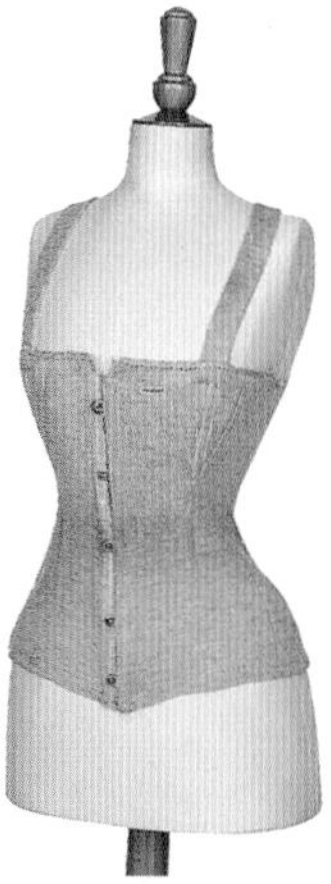

tailor's dummy • le mannequin • die Schneiderpuppe • el maniquí • il manichino

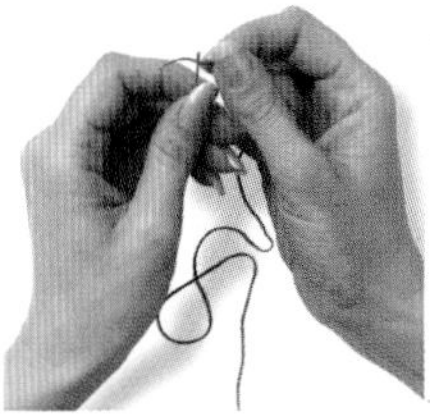

thread *(v)* • zenfiler • einfädeln • ensartar • infilare

stitch
le point
der Stich
la puntada
il punto

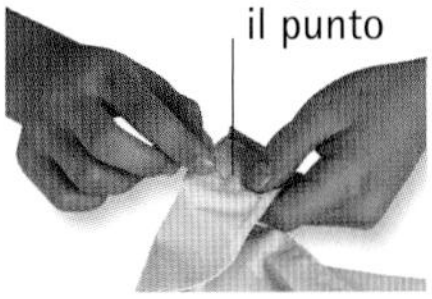

sew *(v)* • coudre • nähen • coser • cucire

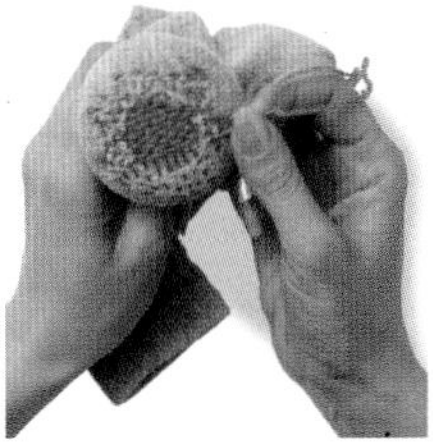

darn *(v)* • repriser • stopfen • zurcir • rammendare

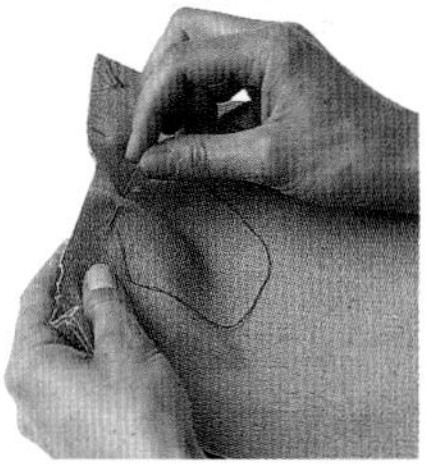

tack *(v)* • bâtir • heften • hilvanar • imbastire

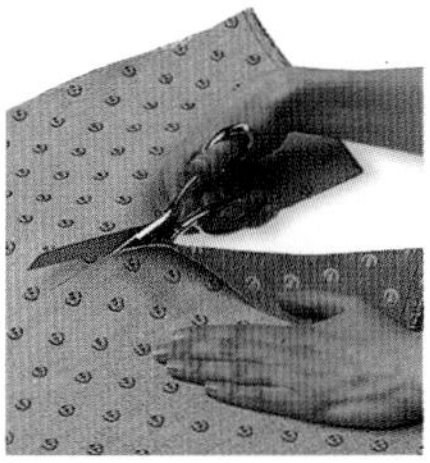

cut *(v)* • couper • schneiden • cortar • tagliare

needlepoint • la tapisserie • die Tapisserie • el bordado en cañamazo • lil mezzopunto

embroidery • la broderie • die Stickerei • el bordado • il ricamo

crochet hook
le crochet
der Häkelhaken
la aguja de ganchillo
l'uncinetto

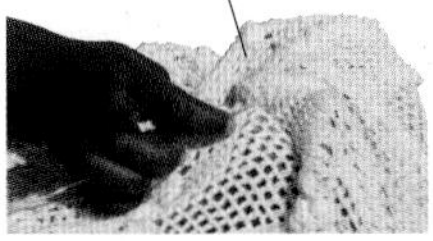

crochet • le crochet • das Häkeln • el ganchillo • il lavoro all'uncinetto

macramé • le macramé • das Makramee • el macramé • il macramè

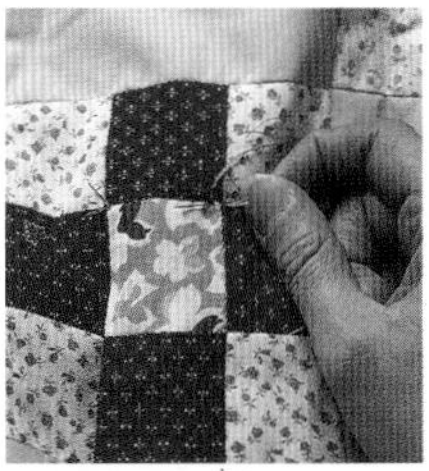

patchwork • le patchwork • das Patchwork • la labor de retales • il patchwork

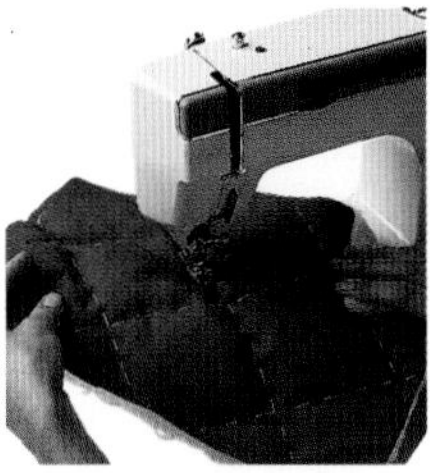

quilting • le ouatage • das Wattieren • el acolchado • il trapunto

lace bobbin • le fuseau • der Klöppel • el bolillo • la spoletta

lace-making • la dentelle • die Spitzenklöppelei • la labor de encaje • la fabbricazione dei merletti

loom • le métier à tisser • der Webstuhl • el telar • il telaio

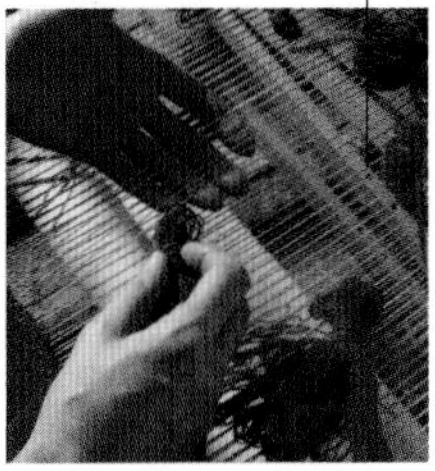

weaving • le tissage • die Weberei • tejer • la tessitura

knitting needle
l'aiguille à tricoter
die Stricknadel
la aguja de tejer
il ferro da calza

knitting • le tricot • das Stricken • la labor de punto • il lavoro a maglia

yarn
la laine
die Wolle
la lana
la lana

skein • l'écheveau • der Strang • la madeja • la matassa

unpick *(v)*
défaire
auftrennen
descoser
scucire

fabric
le tissu
der Stoff
la tela
il tessuto

cotton
le coton
die Baumwolle
el algodón
il cotone

linen
le lin
das Leinen
el lino
il lino

polyester
le polyester
das Polyester
el poliéster
il poliestere

nylon
le nylon
das Nylon
el nailon
il nailon

silk
la soie
die Seide
la seda
la seta

designer
le styliste
der Modedesigner
el diseñador
lo stilista

fashion
la mode
die Mode
la moda
la moda

zipper
la fermeture éclair
der Reißverschluss
la cremallera
la chiusura lampo

environment
l’environnement
die Umwelt
el medio ambiente
l'ambiente

space • l'espace • der Weltraum • el espacio • lo spazio

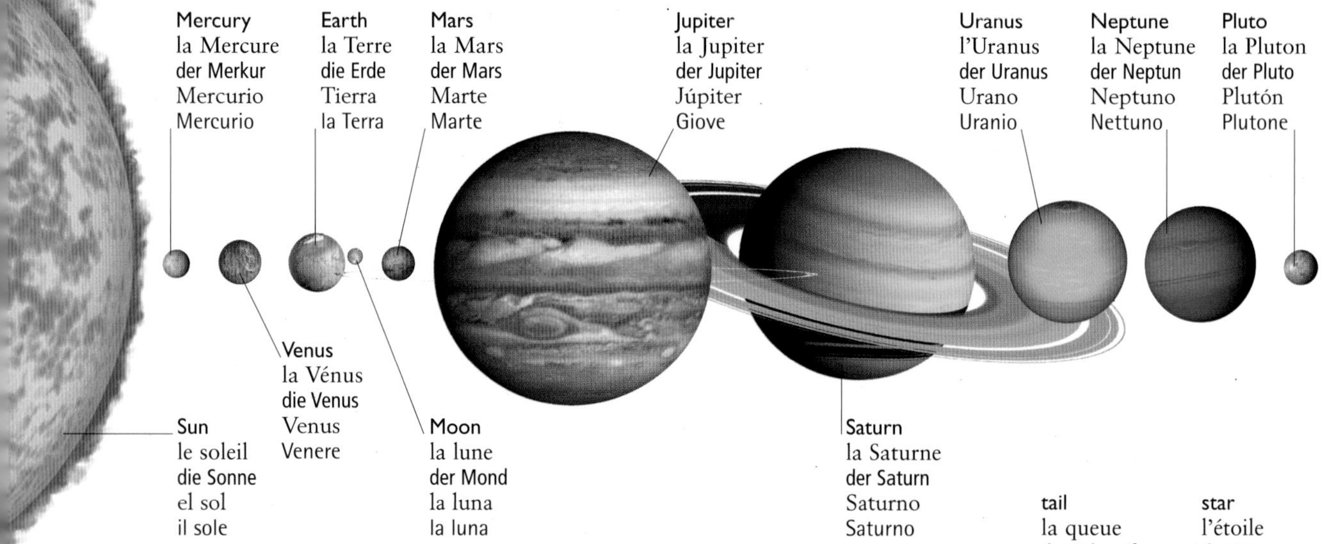

solar system • le sytème solaire • das Sonnensystem • el sistema solar • il sistema solare

galaxy • la galaxie • die Galaxie • la galaxia • la galassia

nebula • la nébuleuse • der Nebelfleck • la nebulosa • la nebulosa

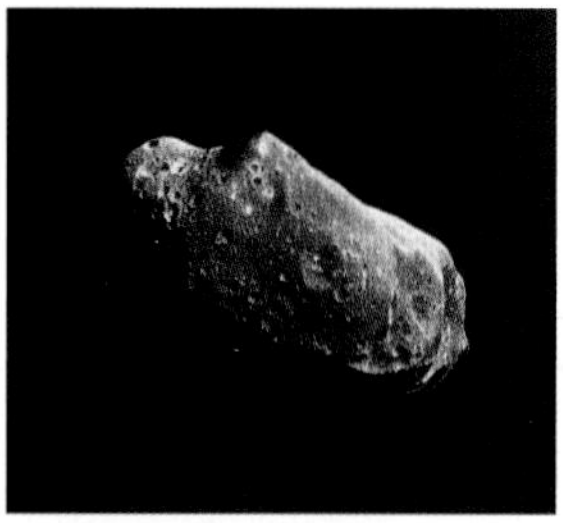

asteroid • l'astéroïde • der Asteroid • el asteroide • l'asteroide

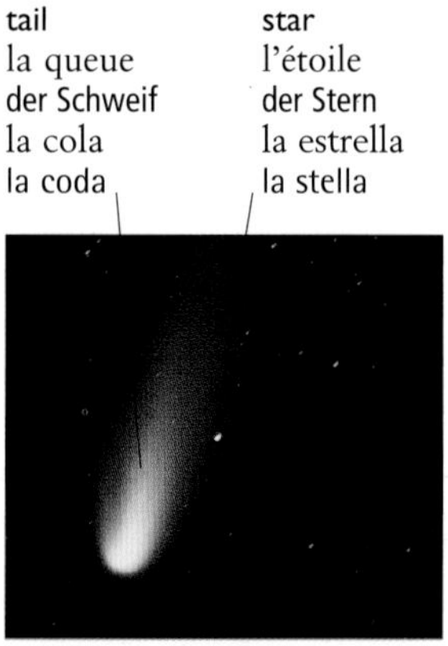

comet • la comète • der Komet • el cometa • la cometa

universe
l'univers
das Universum
el universo
l'universo

black hole
le trou noir
das schwarze Loch
el agujero negro
il buco nero

full moon
la pleine lune
der Vollmond
la luna llena
la luna piena

orbit
l'orbite
die Umlaufbahn
la órbita
l'orbita

planet
la planète
der Planet
el planeta
il pianeta

new moon
la nouvelle lune
der Neumond
la luna nueva
la luna nuova

gravity
la pesanteur
die Schwerkraft
la gravedad
la gravità

meteor
le météore
der Meteor
el meteorito
la meteora

crescent moon
le croissant de lune
die Mondsichel
la media luna
la mezzaluna

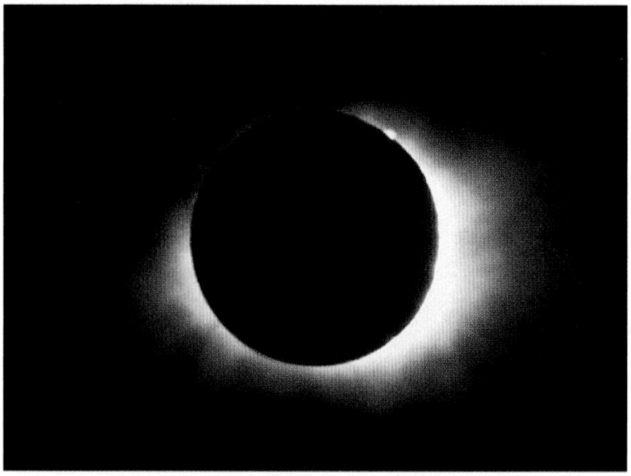

eclipse • l'éclipse • die Finsternis • el eclipse • l'eclisse

space exploration • l'exploration spatiale • die Raumforschung • la exploración espacial • l'esplorazione dello spazio

space shuttle • la navette spatiale • die Raumfähre • el transbordador espacial • lo shuttle

space suit
le scaphandre spatial
der Raumanzug
el traje espacial
la tuta spaziale

thruster
la fusée d'orientation
die Steuerrakete
el propulsor
il reattore

radar
le radar
der Radar
el radar
il radar

crew hatch • le sas d'équipage • die Besatzungsluke • la escotilla • lo sportello dell'equipaggio

booster
l'accélérateur
der Booster
el lanzacohetes
il lanciarazzi

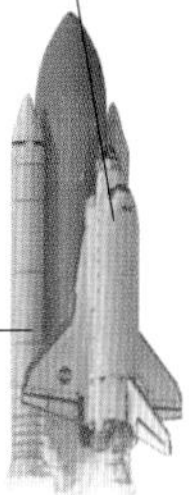

launch • le lancement • der Abschuss • el lanzamiento • il lancio

astronaut • l'astronaute • der Astronaut • el astronauta • l'astronauta

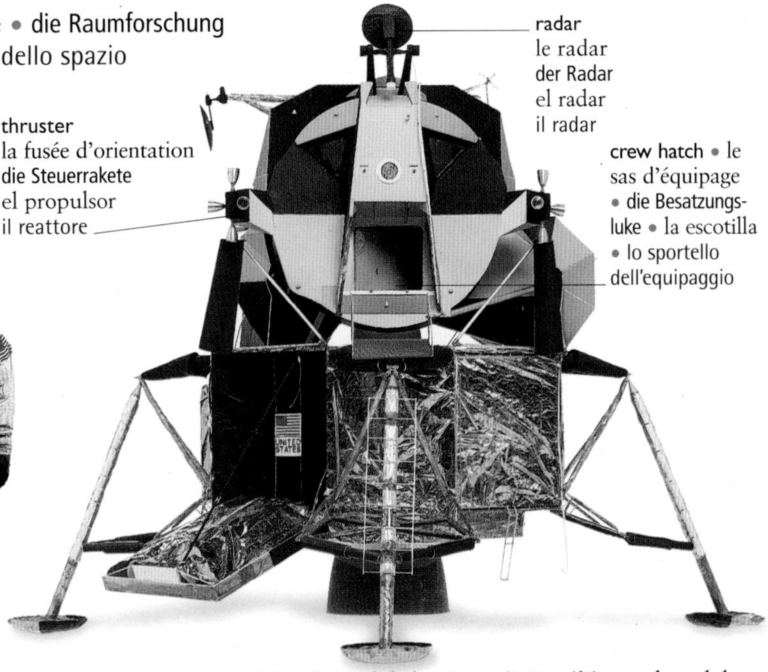

lunar module • le module lunaire • die Mondfähre • el módulo lunar • il modulo lunare

launch pad • la rampe de lancement • die Abschussrampe • la rampa de lanzamiento • la rampa di lancio

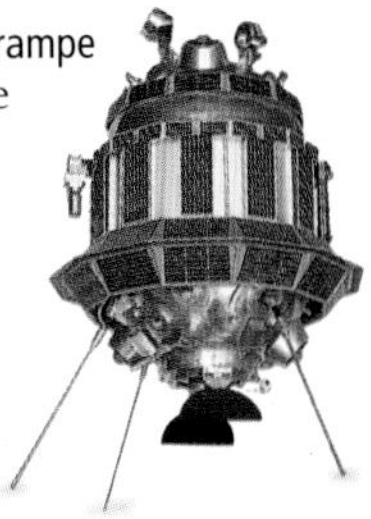

satellite • le satellite • der Satellit • el satélite • il satellite

space station • la station spatiale • die Raumstation • la estación espacial • la stazione spaziale

astronomy • l'astronomie • die Astronomie • la astronomía • l'astronomia

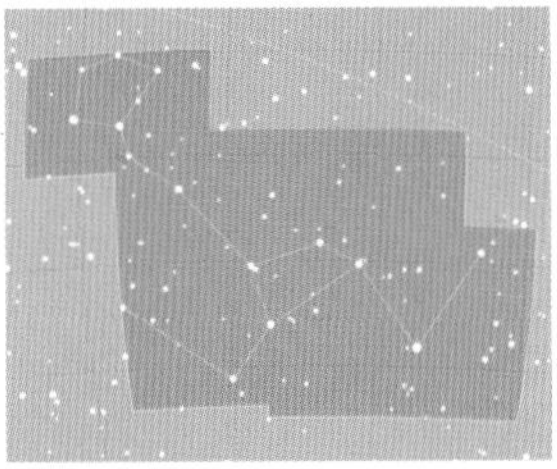

constellation • la constellation • das Sternbild • la constelación • la costellazione

binoculars • les jumelles • das Fernglas • los prismáticos • il binocolo

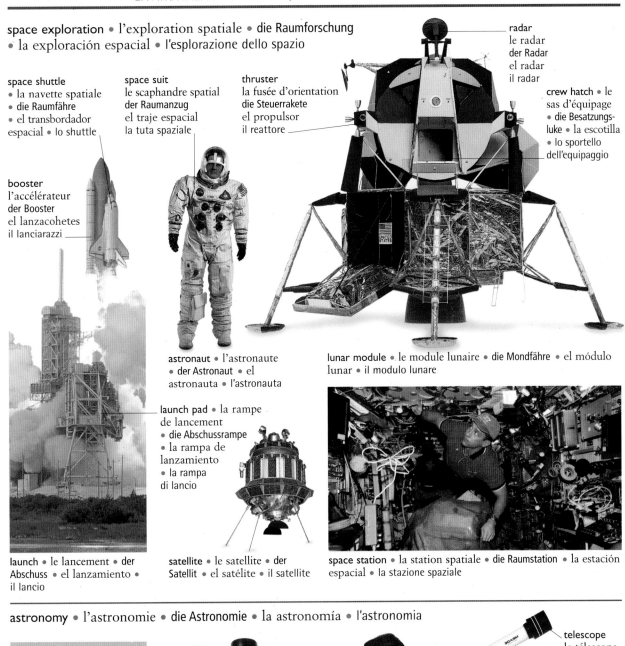

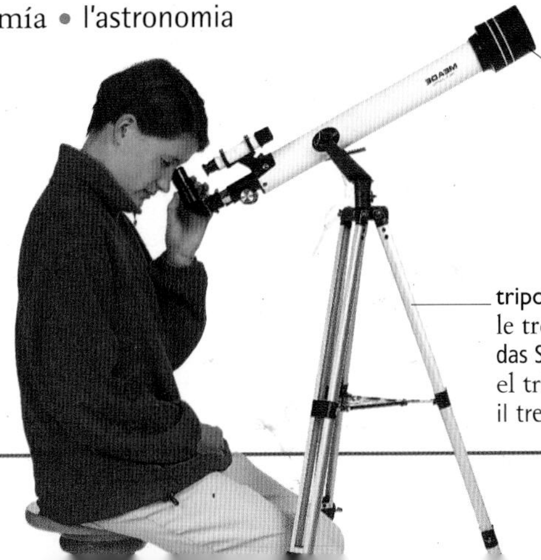

telescope
le télescope
das Teleskop
el telescopio
il telescopio

tripod
le trépied
das Stativ
el trípode
il treppiede

Earth • la terre • die Erde • la Tierra • la Terra

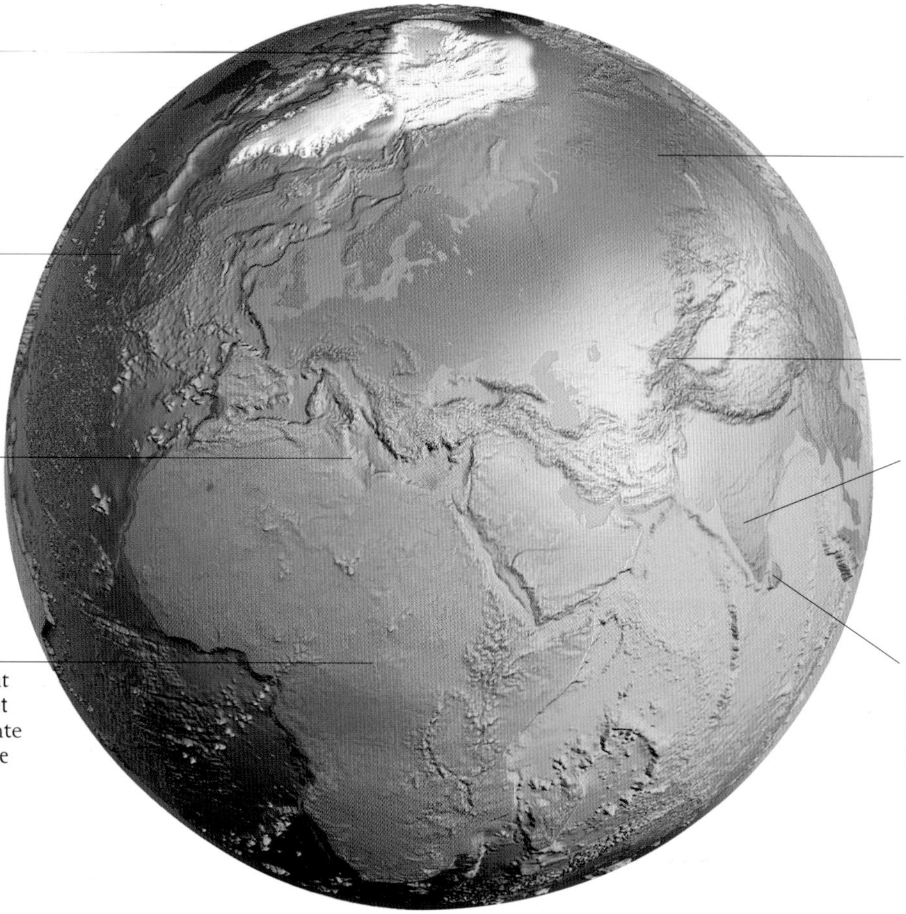

planet • la planète • der Planet • el planeta • il pianeta

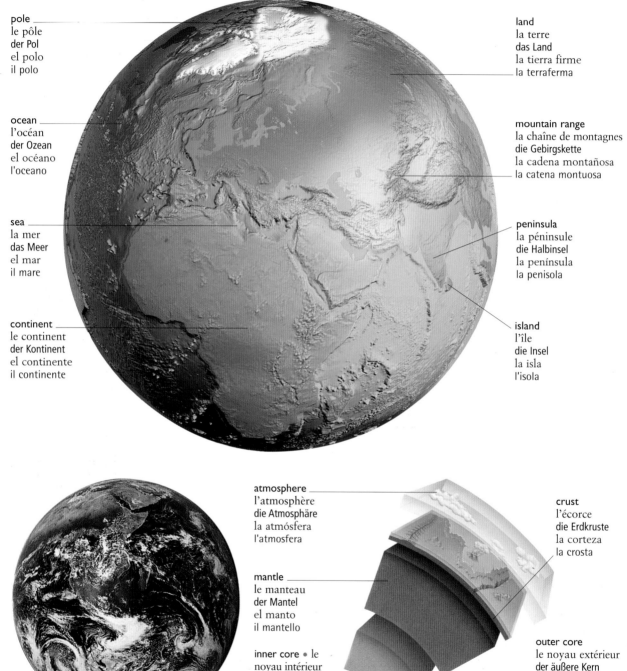

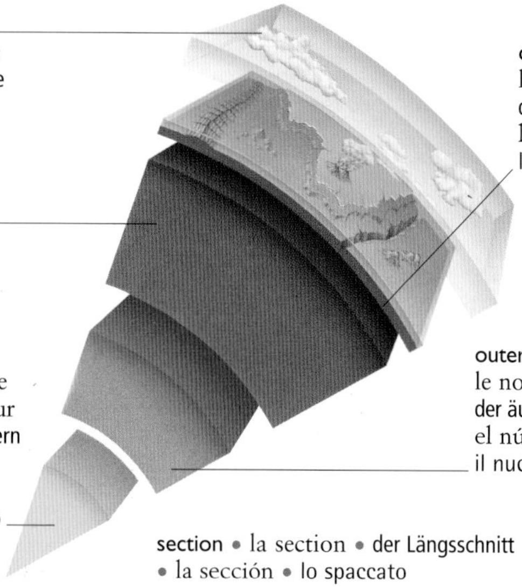

section • la section • der Längsschnitt • la sección • lo spaccato

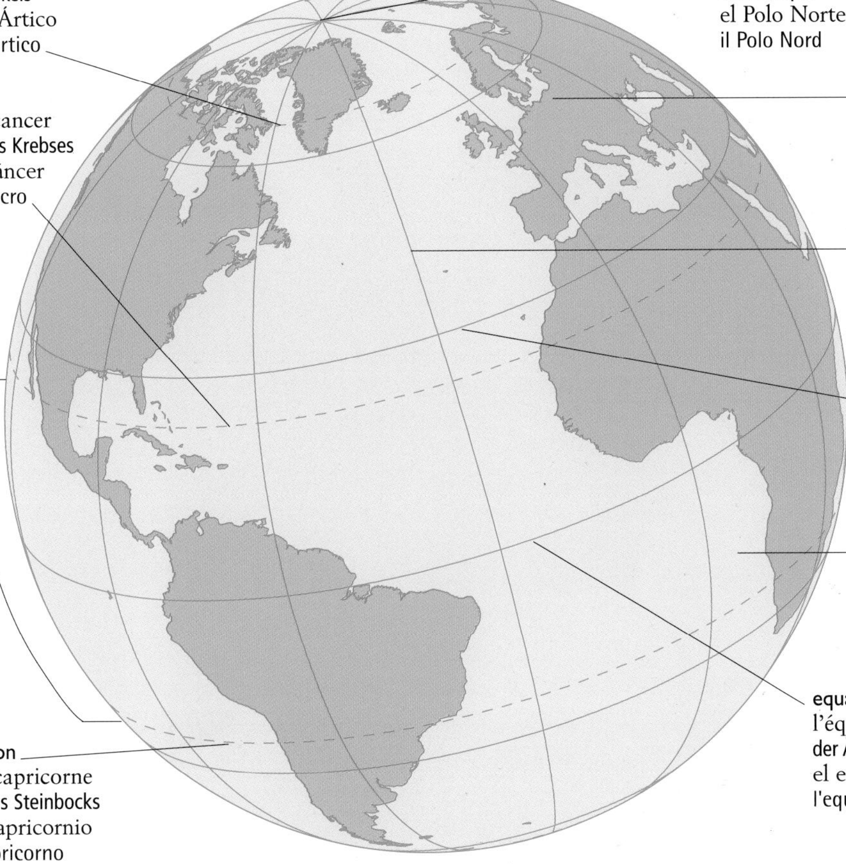

zones • les zones • die Erdzonen • las zonas • le zone

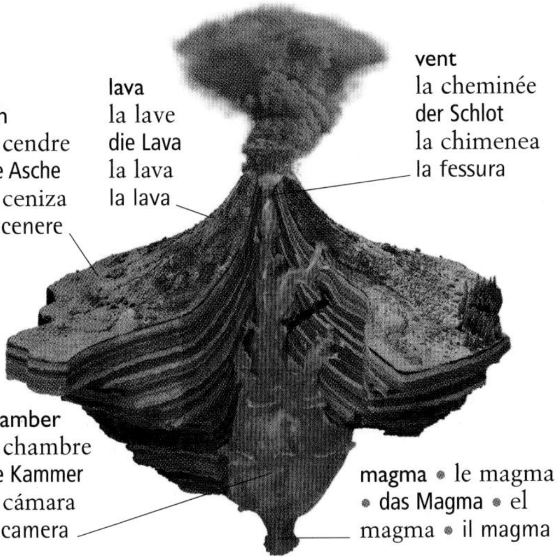

volcano • le volcan • der Vulkan • el volcán • il vulcano

crater • le cratère • der Krater • el cráter • il cratere

earthquake
le tremblement
das Erdbeben
el terremoto
il terremoto

plate
la plaque
die Platte
la placa
la zolla

erupt *(v)*
entrer en éruption
ausbrechen
hacer erupción
eruttare

tremor
le tremblement
das Beben
el temblor
il tremore

landscape • le paysage • die Landschaft • el paisaje • il paesaggio

mountain
la montagne
der Berg
la montaña
la montagna

slope
la pente
der Hang
la ladera
la pendice

bank
la rive
das Ufer
la orilla
la riva

river
la rivière
der Fluss
el río
il fiume

rapids
les rapides
die Stromschnellen
los rápidos
le rapide

rocks
les rochers
die Felsen
las rocas
le rocce

glacier • le glacier • der Gletscher • el glaciar • il ghiacciaio

valley • la vallée • das Tal • el valle • la valle

hill • la colline • der Hügel • la colina • la collina

plateau • le plateau • das Plateau • la meseta • l'altipiano

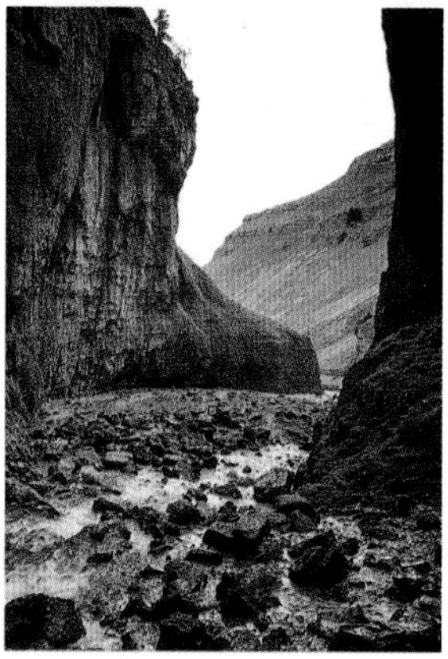

gorge • la gorge • die Schlucht • el desfiladero • la gola

cave • la caverne • die Höhle • la cueva • la caverna

plain • la plaine • die Ebene • la llanura • la pianura

desert • le désert • die Wüste • el desierto • il deserto

forest • la forêt • der Wald • el bosque • la foresta

wood • le bois • der Wald • el bosque • il bosco

rain forest • la forêt tropicale • der Regenwald • la selva tropical • la foresta pluviale

swamp • le marais • der Sumpf • el pantano • la palude

meadow • le pré • die Wiese label • el prado • il pascolo

grassland • la prairie • das Grasland • la pradera • la prateria

waterfall • la cascade • der Wasserfall • la cascada • la cascata

stream • le ruisseau • der Bach • el arroyo • il torrente

lake • le lac • der See • el lago • il lago

geyser • le geyser • der Geysir • el géiser • il geyser

coast • la côte • die Küste • la costa • la costa

cliff • la falaise • die Klippe • el acantilado • la scogliera

coral reef • le récif de corail • das Korallenriff • el arrecife de coral • la barriera corallina

estuary • l'estuaire • die Flussmündung • el estuario • l'estuario

weather • le temps • das Wetter • el tiempo • il tempo

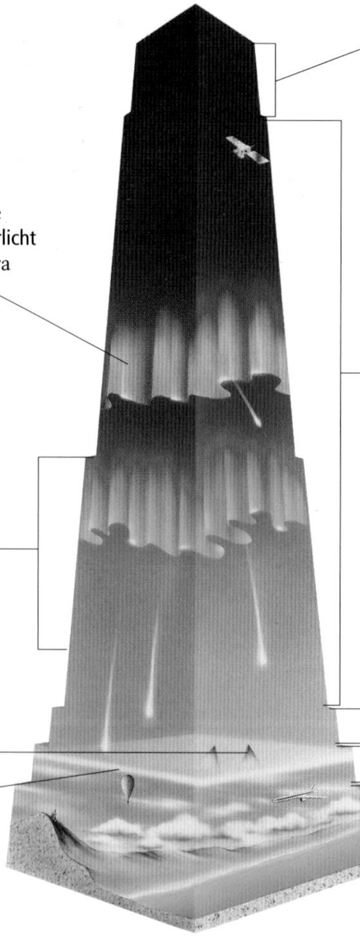

atmosphere • l'atmosphère • die Atmosphäre • la atmósfera • l'atmosfera

sunshine • le soleil • der Sonnenschein • el sol • la luce del sole

wind • le vent • der Wind • el viento • il vento

sleet la neige fondue der Schneeregen el aguanieve il nevischio	shower l'averse der Schauer el chubasco il rovescio	hot (très) chaud heiß caluroso caldo	dry sec trocken seco secco	windy venteux windig ventoso ventoso	I'm hot/cold. J'ai chaud/froid. Mir ist heiß/kalt. Tengo calor/frío. Ho caldo/freddo.
hail la grêle der Hagel el granizo la grandine	sunny ensoleillé sonnig soleado soleggiato	cold froid kalt frío freddo	wet humide nass lluvioso piovoso	gale la tempête der Sturm el temporal la bufera	It's raining. Il pleut. Es regnet. Está lloviendo. Sta piovendo.
thunder le tonnerre der Donner el trueno il tuono	cloudy nuageux bewölkt nublado nuvoloso	warm chaud warm cálido tiepido	humid humide feucht húmedo umido	temperature la température die Temperatur la temperatura la temperatura	It's ... degrees. Il fait ... degrés. Es sind ... Grad. Estamos a ... grados. Fa ... gradi.

cloud • le nuage • die Wolke • la nube • la nuvola

rain • la pluie • der Regen • la lluvia • la pioggia

lightning • l'éclair • der Blitz • el relámpago • il fulmine

storm • l'orage • das Gewitter • la tormenta • la tempesta

mist • la brume • der feine Nebel • la neblina • la foschia

fog • le brouillard • der dichte Nebel • la niebla • la nebbia

rainbow • l'arc-en-ciel • der Regenbogen • el arcoiris • l'arcobaleno

snow • la neige • der Schnee • la nieve • la neve

frost • le givre • der Raureif • la escarcha • il gelo

icicle • le glaçon • der Eiszapfen • el carámbano • il ghiacciolo

ice • la glace • das Eis • el hielo • il ghiaccio

freeze • le gel • der Frost • la helada • la gelata

hurricane • l'hurricane • der Hurrikan • el huracán • l'uragano

tornado • la tornade • der Tornado • el tornado • il tornado

monsoon • la mousson • der Monsun • el monzón • il monsone

flood • l'inondation • die Überschwemmung • la inundación • l'inondazione

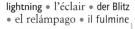

rocks • les roches • das Gestein • las rocas • le rocce

igneous • igné • eruptiv • ígneo • igneo

granite • le granit • der Granit • el granito • il granito

obsidian • l'obsidienne • der Obsidian • la obsidiana • l'ossidiana

basalt • le basalte • der Basalt • el basalto • il basalto

pumice • la pierre ponce • der Bimsstein • la piedra pómez • la pomice

sedimentary • sédimentaire • sedimentär • sedimentario • sedimentario

sandstone • le grès • der Sandstein • la piedra arenisca • l'arenaria

limestone • le calcaire • der Kalkstein • la piedra caliza • il calcare

chalk • la craie • die Kreide • la tiza • il gesso

flint • le silex • der Feuerstein • el pedernal • la selce

conglomerate
le conglomérat
das Konglomerat
el conglomerado
il conglomerato

coal • le charbon • die Kohle • el carbón • il carbone

metamorphic • métamorphique • metamorph • metamórfico • metamorfico

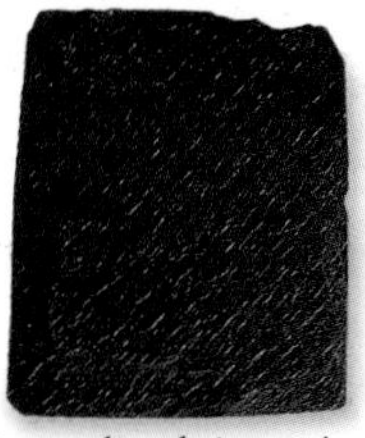

slate • l'ardoise • der Schiefer • la pizarra • l'ardesia

schist • le schiste • der Glimmers • el esquisto • lo scisto

gneiss • le gneiss • der Gneis • el gneis • lo gneiss

marble • le marbre • der Marmor • el mármol • il marmo

gems • les gemmes • die Schmucksteine • las gemas • le gemme

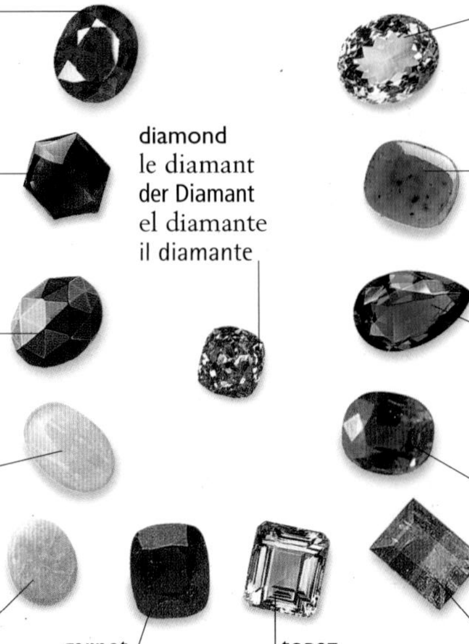

ruby
le rubis
der Rubin
el rubí
il rubino

amethyst
l'améthyste
der Amethyst
la amatista
l'ametista

jet
le jais
der Jett
el azabache
il giaietto

opal
l'opale
der Opal
el ópalo
l'opale

diamond
le diamant
der Diamant
el diamante
il diamante

aquamarine
l'aigue-marine
der Aquamarin
la aguamarina
l'acquamarina

jade
le jade
der Jade
el jade
la giada

emerald
l'émeraude
der Smaragd
la esmeralda
lo smeraldo

sapphire
le saphir
der Saphir
el zafiro
lo zaffiro

moonstone
la pierre de lune
der Mondstein
la adularia
la lunaria

garnet
le grenat
der Granat
el granate
il granato

topaz
le topaze
der Topas
el topacio
il topazio

tourmaline
la toumaline
der Turmalin
la turmalina
la tormalina

minerals • les minéraux • die Mineralien • los minerales • i minerali

quartz • le quartz • der Quarz • el cuarzo • il quarzo

mica • le mica • der Glimmer • la mica •

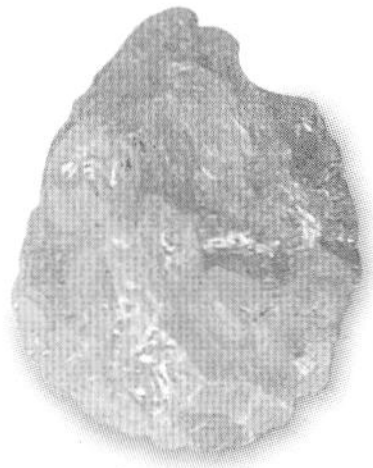
sulfur • le soufre • der Schwefel • el azufre • lo zolfo

hematite • l'hématite • der Hämatit • la hematita • l'ematite

calcite • la calcite • der Kalzit • la calcita • la calcite

malachite
la malachite
der Malachit
la malaquita
la malachite

turquoise • la turquoise • der Türkis • la turquesa • il turchese

onyx • l'onyx • der Onyx • el ónix • l'onice

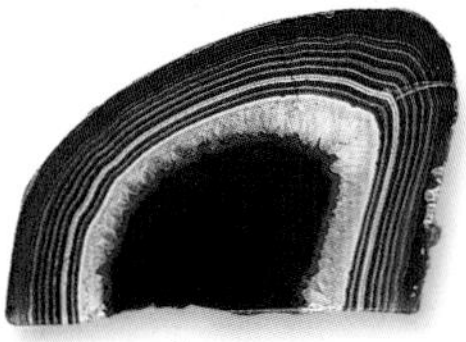
agate • l'agate • der Achat • el ágata • l'agata

graphite • le graphite • der Graphit • el grafito • la grafite

metals • les métaux • die Metalle • los metales • i metalli

gold • l'or • das Gold • el oro • l'oro

silver • l'argent • das Silber • la plata • l'argento

platinum • le platine • das Platin • el platino • il platino

nickel • le nickel • das Nickel • el níquel • il nichel

iron • le fer • das Eisen • el hierro • il ferro

copper • le cuivre • das Kupfer • el cobre • il rame

tin • l'étain • das Zinn • el estaño • lo stagno

aluminum • l'aluminium • das Aluminium • el aluminio • l'alluminio

mercury • le mercure • das Quecksilber • el mercurio • il mercurio

zinc • le zinc • das Zink • el zinc • lo zinco

animals 1 • les animaux 1 • die Tiere 1 • los animales 1 • gli animali 1

mammals • les mammifères • die Säugetiere • los mamíferos • i mammiferi

rabbit • le lapin • das Kaninchen • el conejo • il coniglio

hamster • le hamster • der Hamster • el hámster • il criceto

whiskers
les poils
die Schnurrhaare
los bigotes
i baffi

mouse • la souris • die Maus • el ratón • il topo

tail
la queue
der Schwanz
la cola
la coda

rat • le rat • die Ratte • la rata • il ratto

hedgehog • le hérisson • der Igel • el erizo • il riccio

squirrel • l'écureuil • das Eichhörnchen • la ardilla • lo scoiattolo

bat • la chauve-souris • die Fledermaus • el murciélago • il pipistrello

raccoon • le raton laveur • der Waschbär • el mapache • il procione

fox • le renard • der Fuchs • el zorro • la volpe

wolf • le loup • der Wolf • el lobo • il lupo

puppy
le chiot
der Welpe
el cachorro
il cucciolo

dog • le chien • der Hund • el perro • il cane

kitten
le chaton
das Kätzchen
el gatito
il gattino

cat • le chat • die Katze • el gato • il gatto

otter • la loutre • der Otter • la nutria • la lontra

pup
le bébé-phoque
das Junge
la cría
il cucciolo

seal • le phoque • die Robbe • la foca • la foca

sea lion • l'otarie • der Seelöwe • el león marino • il leone marino

flipper
la nageoire
die Flosse
la aleta
la pinna

walrus • le morse • das Walross • la morsa • il tricheco

blowhole
l'évent
das Atemloch
el orificio nasal
lo sfiatatoio

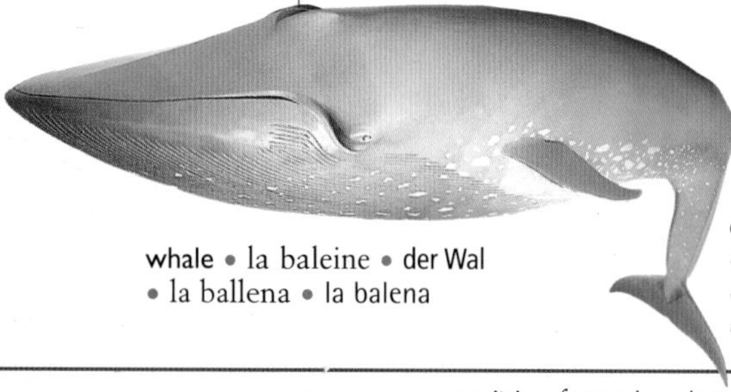

whale • la baleine • der Wal • la ballena • la balena

dolphin • le dauphin • der Delphin • el delfín • il delfino

deer • le cerf • der Hirsch • el ciervo • il cervo

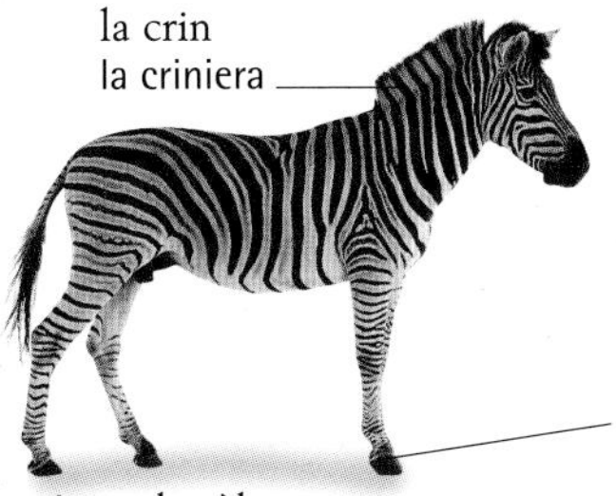

zebra • le zèbre • das Zebra • la cebra • la zebra

giraffe • la girafe • die Giraffe • la jirafa • la giraffa

camel • le chameau • das Kamel • el camello • il cammello

hippopotamus • le hippopotame • das Nilpferd • el hipopótamo • l'ippopotamo

elephant • l'éléphant • der Elefant • el elefante • l'elefante

rhinoceros • le rhinocéros • das Nashorn • el rinoceronte • il rinoceronte

tiger • le tigre • der Tiger • el tigre • la tigre

lion • le lion • der Löwe • el león • il leone

monkey • le singe • der Affe • el chango • la scimmia

gorilla • le gorille • der Gorilla • el gorila • il gorilla

koala • le koala • der Koalabär • el koala • il koala

kangaroo • le kangourou • das Känguru • el canguro • il canguro

bear • l'ours • der Bär • el oso • l'orso

polar bear • l'ours blanc • der Eisbär • el oso polar • l'orso polare

panda • le panda • der Pandabär • el oso panda • il panda

animals 2 • les animaux 2 • die Tiere 2 • los animales 2 • gli animali 2

birds • les oiseaux • die Vögel • las aves • gli uccelli

canary • le canari • der Kanarienvogel • el canario • il canarino

sparrow • le moineau • der Spatz • el gorrión • il passero

hummingbird • le colibri • der Kolibri • el colibrí • il colibrì

swallow • l'hirondelle • die Schwalbe • la golondrina • la rondine

crow • le corbeau • die Krähe • el cuervo • la cornacchia

pigeon • le pigeon • die Taube • la paloma • il piccione

woodpecker • le pic • der Specht • el pájaro carpintero • il picchio

falcon • le faucon • der Falke • el halcón • il falco

owl • la chouette • die Eule • el búho • il gufo

gull • la mouette • die Möwe • la gaviota • il gabbiano

eagle • l'aigle • der Adler • el águila • l'aquila

pelican • le pélican • der Pelikan • el pelícano • il pellicano

flamingo • le flamant • der Flamingo • el flamenco • il fenicottero

stork • la cigogne • der Storch • la cigüeña • la cicogna

crane • la grue • der Kranich • la grulla • la gru

penguin • le pingouin • der Pinguin • el pingüino • il pinguino

ostrich • l'autruche • der Strauß • el avestruz • lo struzzo

goose • l'oie • die Gans • la oca • l'oca

swan • le cygne • der Schwan • el cisne • il cigno

peacock • le paon • der Pfau • el pavo real • il pavone

pheasant • le faisan • der Fasan • el faisán • il fagiano

turkey • le dindon • der Truthahn • el guajolote • il tacchino

beak le bec der Schnabel el pico il becco

cockatoo le cacatoès der Kakadu la cacatúa il cacatoa

feather la plume die Feder la pluma la piuma

wing l'aile der Flügel el ala l'ala

claw la griffe die Kralle la garra l'artiglio

parrot • le perroquet • der Papagei • el loro • il pappagallo

reptiles • les reptiles • die Reptilien • los reptiles • i rettili

scales • les écailles • die Schuppen • las escamas • le scaglie

alligator • l'alligator • der Alligator • el caimán • l'alligatore

lizard • le lézard • die Eidechse • el lagarto • la lucertola

iguana • l'iguane • der Leguan • la iguana • l'iguana

shell la carapace der Panzer el caparazón il guscio

turtle • la tortue marine • die Wasserschildkröte • el galápago • la testuggine

tortoise • la tortue • die Schildkröte • la tortuga • la tartaruga

snake • le serpent • die Schlange • la serpiente • il serpente

snout le museau die Schnauze el hocico il muso

crocodile • le crocodile • das Krokodil • el cocodrilo • il coccodrillo

animals 3 • les animaux 3 • die Tiere 3 • los animales 3 • gli animali 3

amphibians • les amphibiens • die Amphibien • los anfibios • gli anfibi

frog • la grenouille • der Frosch • la rana • la rana

toad • le crapaud • die Kröte • el sapo • il rospo

tadpole • le têtard • die Kaulquappe • el renacuajo • il girino

salamander • la salamandre • der Salamander • la salamandra • la salamandra

fish • les poissons • die Fische • los peces • i pesci

eel • l'anguille • der Aal • la anguila • l'anguilla

shark • le requin • der Haifisch • el tiburón • lo squalo

sea horse • l'hippocampe • das Seepferd • el caballito de mar • il cavalluccio marino

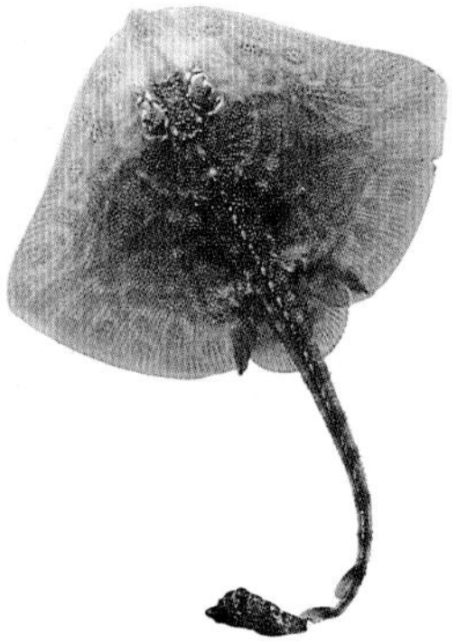

skate • la raie • der Glattrochen • la raya • la razza

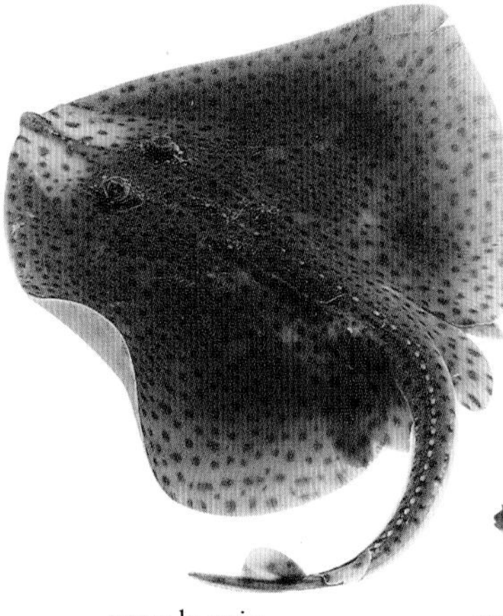

ray • la raie • der Rochen • la raya • il trigone

goldfish • le poisson rouge • der Goldfisch • el pez de colores • il pesce rosso

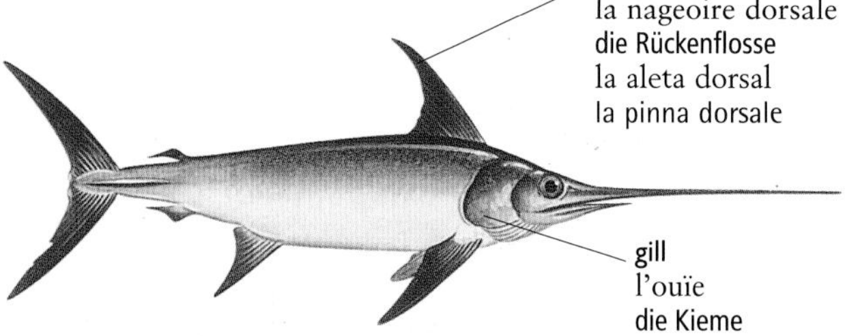

swordfish • l'espadon • der Schwertfisch • el pez espada • il pesce spada

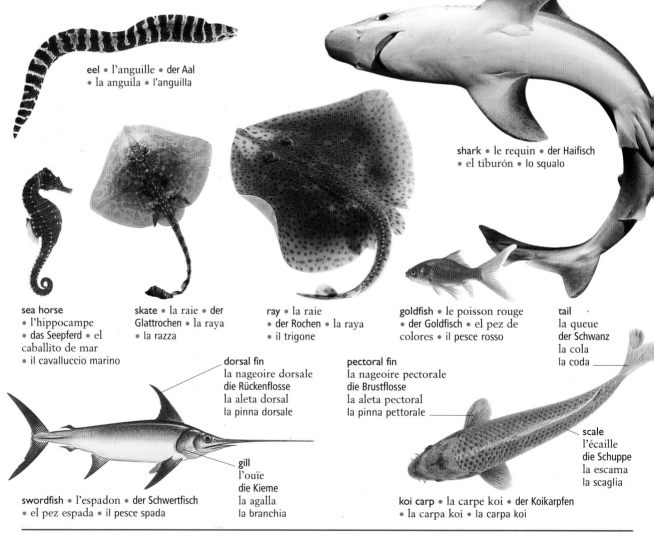

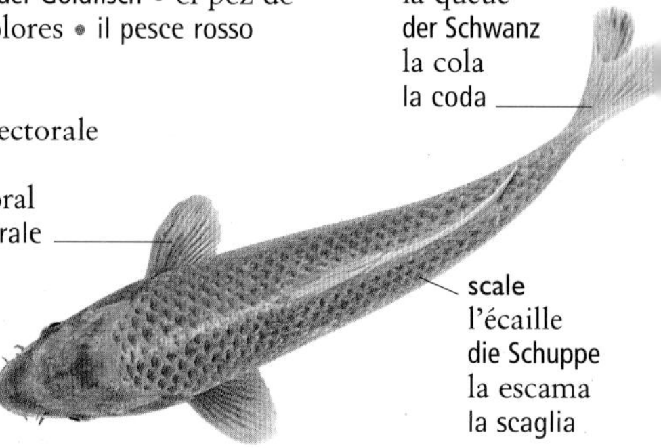

koi carp • la carpe koi • der Koikarpfen • la carpa koi • la carpa koi

invertebrates • les invertébrés • die Wirbellosen • los invertebrados • gli invertebrati

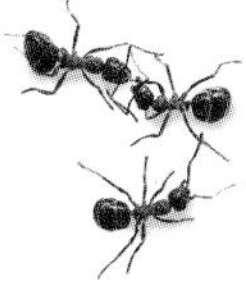

ant • la fourmi • die Ameise • la hormiga • la formica

termite • la termite • die Termite • la termita • la termite

bee • l'abeille • die Biene • la abeja • l'ape

wasp • la guêpe • die Wespe • la avispa • la vespa

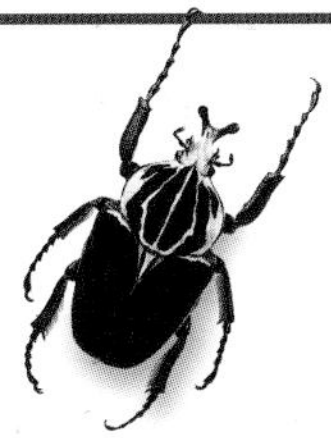

beetle • le scarabée • der Käfer • el escarabajo • lo scarafaggio

cockroach • le cafard • der Kakerlak • la cucaracha • la blatta

moth • le papillon • die Motte • la polilla • la falena

butterfly • le papillon • der Schmetterling • la mariposa • la farfalla

cocoon • le cocon • der Kokon • el capullo • il bozzolo

caterpillar • la chenille • die Raupe • la oruga • il bruco

cricket • le grillon • die Grille • el grillo • il grillo

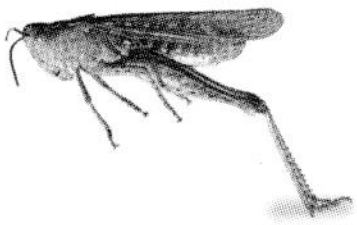

grasshopper
la sauterelle
die Heuschrecke
el saltamontes
la cavalletta

praying mantis
la mante religieuse
die Gottesanbeterin
la mantis religiosa
la mantide religiosa

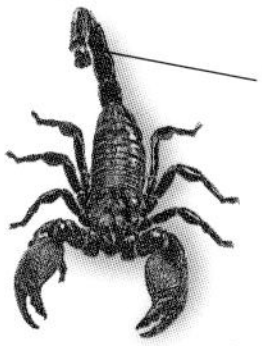

scorpion • le scorpion • der Skorpion • el alacrán • lo scorpione

centipede • le mille-pattes • der Tausendfüßer • el ciempiés • il millepiedi

dragonfly • la libellule • die Libelle • la libélula • la libellula

fly • la mouche • die Fliege • la mosca • la mosca

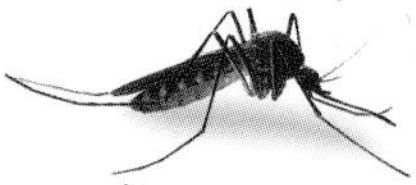

mosquito • le moustique • die Stechmücke • el mosquito • la zanzara

ladybug • la coccinelle • der Marienkäfer • la catarina • la coccinella

spider • l'araignée • die Spinne • la araña • il ragno

slug • la limace • die Wegschnecke • la babosa • la lumaca

snail • l'escargot • die Schnecke • el caracol • la chiocciola

worm • le ver • der Wurm • el gusano • il verme

starfish • l'étoile de mer • der Seestern • la estrella de mar • la stella di mare

mussel • la moule • die Muschel • el mejillón • la cozza

crab • le crabe • der Krebs • el cangrejo • il granchio

lobster • le homard • der Hummer • la langosta • l'aragosta

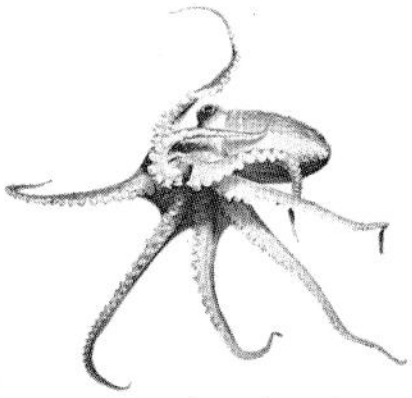

octopus • la pieuvre • der Krake • el pulpo • la piovra

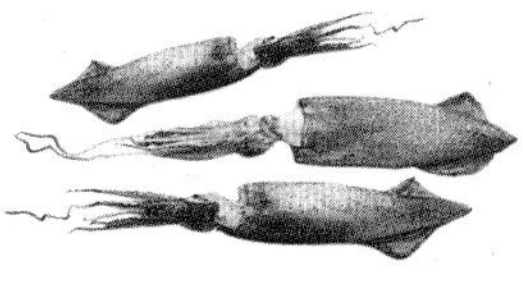

squid • le calmar • der Tintenfisch • el calamar • il calamaro

jellyfish • la méduse • die Qualle • la medusa • la medusa

plants • les plantes • die Pflanzen • las plantas • le piante

tree • l'arbre • der Baum • el árbol • l'albero

branch
la branche
der Ast
la rama
il ramo

bark
l'écorce
die Rinde
la corteza
la corteccia

root
la racine
die Wurzel
la raíz
la radice

trunk
le tronc
der Stamm
el tronco
il tronco

oak • le chêne • die Eiche • el roble • la quercia

leaf
la feuille
das Blatt
la hoja
la foglia

twig
la brindille
der Zweig
la ramita
il ramoscello

willow • le saule • die Weide • el sauce • il salice

poplar • le peuplier • die Pappel • el álamo • il pioppo

eucalyptus • l'eucalyptus • der Eukalyptus • el eucalipto • l'eucalipto

larch • le mélèze • die Lärche • el alerce • il larice

beech • le hêtre • die Buche • la haya • il faggio

birch • le bouleau • die Birke • el abedul • la betulla

pine • le pin • die Kiefer • el pino • il pino

cedar • le cèdre • die Zeder • el cedro • il cedro

maple • l'érable • der Ahorn • el arce • l'acero

elm • l'orme • die Ulme • el olmo • l'olmo

lime • le tilleul • die Linde • el tilo • il tiglio

berry
la baie
die Beere
la baya
la bacca

holly • le houx • die Stechpalme • el acebo • l'agrifoglio

palm • le palmier • die Palme • la palmera • la palma

flowering plant • la plante à fleurs • die blühende Pflanze • la planta de flor • la pianta da fiori

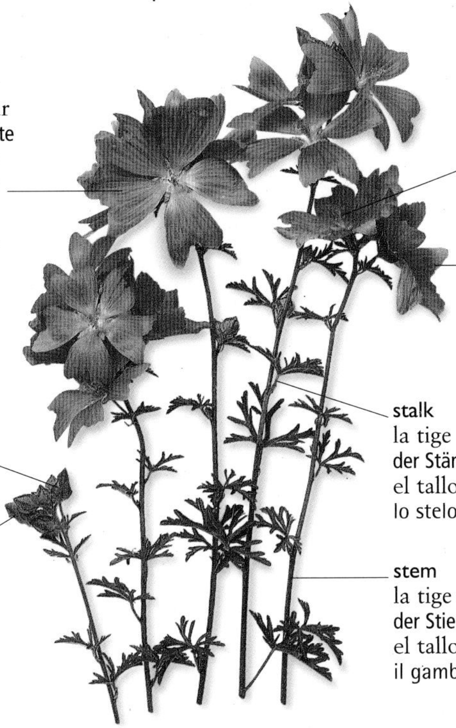

buttercup • la renoncule • der Hahnenfuß • el ranúnculo • il ranuncolo

daisy • la pâquerette • das Gänseblümchen • la margarita • la margherita

thistle • le chardon • die Distel • el cardo • il cardo

dandelion • le pissenlit • der Löwenzahn • el diente de león • il dente di leone

heather • la bruyère • das Heidekraut • el brezo • l'erica

poppy • le coquelicot • der Klatschmohn • la amapola • il papavero

foxglove • la digitale • der Fingerhut • la dedalera • la digitale

honeysuckle • le chèvrefeuille • das Geißblatt • la madreselva • il caprifoglio

sunflower • le tournesol • die Sonnenblume • el girasol • il girasole

clover • le trèfle • der Klee • el trébol • il trifoglio

bluebells • les jacinthes des bois • die Sternhyazinthen • los narcisos silvestres • i giacinti di bosco

primrose • la primevère • die Schlüsselblume • la prímula • la primula

lupins • les lupins • die Lupinen • el lupino • i lupini

nettle • l'ortie • die Nessel • la ortiga • l'ortica

town • la ville • die Stadt • la ciudad • la città

street
la rue
die Straße
la calle
la strada

curb
le bord du trottoir
die Bordkante
el borde de la banqueta
il ciglio

street corner
le coin de la rue
die Straßenecke
la esquina
l'angolo della strada

store
le magasin
der Laden
la tienda
il negozio

intersection
le carrefour
die Kreuzung
el crucero
il crocevia

one-way system
la voie à sens unique • die Einbahnstraße • la calle de sentido único • il senso unico

sidewalk
le trottoir
der Bürgersteig
la banqueta
il marciapiede

office block
• l'immeuble de bureaux • das Bürogebäude • el edificio de oficinas • il complesso di uffici

apartment block
• l'immeuble
• der Wohnblock
• el edificio de apartamentos
• il caseggiato

alley
la ruelle
die Gasse
el callejón
il vicolo

parking lot
le parking
der Parkplatz
el estacionamiento
il parcheggio

street sign
le panneau de signalisation
das Straßenschild
la señal de tráfico
il segnale stradale

traffic post
la borne
der Poller
la baliza
la colonnina

street light
le lampadaire
die Straßenlaterne
el farol
il lampione

buildings • les bâtiments • die Gebäude • los edificios • gli edifici

town hall • la mairie • das Rathaus • el palacio municipal • il municipio

library • la bibliothèque • die Bibliothek • la biblioteca • la biblioteca

movie theater • le cinéma • das Kino • el cine • il cinema

theater • le théâtre • das Theater • el teatro • il teatro

university • l'université • die Universität • la universidad • l'università

school • l'école • die Schule • la escuela • la scuola

skyscraper • le gratte-ciel • der Wolkenkratzer • el rascacielos • il grattacielo

areas • les environs • die Wohngegend • las zonas • le zone

industrial park • la zone industrielle • das Industriegebiet • la zona industrial • la zona industriale

city • la ville • die Stadt • la ciudad • la città

suburb • la banlieue • der Vorort • el suburbio • la periferia

village • le village • das Dorf • el pueblo • il villaggio

pedestrian zone la zone piétonnière die Fußgängerzone la zona peatonal la zona pedonale	side street la rue transversale die Seitenstraße la calle lateral la via laterale	manhole la bouche d'égout der Kanalschacht la coladera il tombino	gutter le caniveau der Rinnstein la alcantarilla la cunetta	church l'église die Kirche la iglesia la chiesa
avenue l'avenue die Allee la avenida il viale	square la place der Platz la plaza la piazza	bus stop l'arrêt de bus die Bushaltestelle la parada de autobús la fermata dell'autobus	factory l'usine die Fabrik la fábrica la fabbrica	drain l'égout der Kanal el drenaje il canale di scolo

architecture • l'architecture • die Architektur • la arquitectura • l'archittettura

buildings and structures • les bâtiments et structures • die Gebäude und Strukturen • los edificios y las estructuras • edifici e strutture

skyscraper • le gratte-ciel • der Wolkenkratzer • el rascacielos • il grattacielo

turret
la tourelle
der Mauerturm
el torreón
la torre

moat
la douve
der Burggraben
el foso
il fossato

castle • le château • die Burg • el castillo • il castello

church • l'église • die Kirche • la iglesia • la chiesa

dome
le dôme
die Kuppel
la cúpula
la cupola

mosque • la mosquée • die Moschee • la mezquita • la moschea

temple • le temple • der Tempel • el templo • il tempio

vault
la voûte
das Gewölbe
la bóveda
la volta

synagogue • la synagogue • die Synagoge • la sinagoga • la sinagoga

dam • le barrage • der Staudamm • el embalse • la diga

bridge • le pont • die Brücke • el puente • il ponte

spire
la flèche
die Turmspitze
la aguja
la spira

finial
le fleuron
die Kreuzblume
el florón
il pinnacolo

gable
le pignon
der Giebel
el frontón
il frontone

tower
la tour
der Turm
la torre
la torretta

cornice
la corniche
das Gesims
la cornisa
il cornicione

pillar
la colonne
die Säule
la columna
la colonna

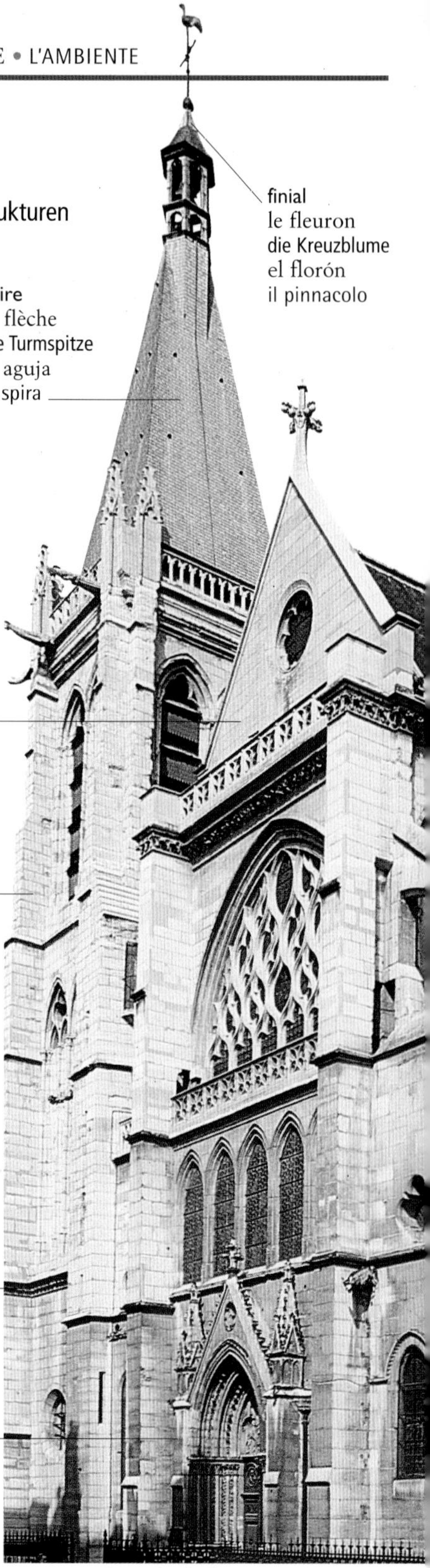

cathedral • la cathédrale • die Kathedrale • la catedral • la cattedrale

styles • les styles • die Baustile • los estilos • gli stili

Gothic • gothique • gotisch • gótico • gotico

architrave
l'architrave
der Architrav
el arquitrabe
l'architrave

Renaissance • Renaissance • Renaissance- • Renacimiento • Rinascimento

baroque • baroque • barock • barroco • barocco

choir
le chœur
der Chor
el coro
il coro

rococo • rococo • Rokoko- • rococó • rococò

arch
l'arc
der Bogen
el arco
l'arco

frieze
la frise
der Fries
el friso
il fregio

buttress
le contrefort
der Strebepfeiler
el contrafuerte
il contrafforte

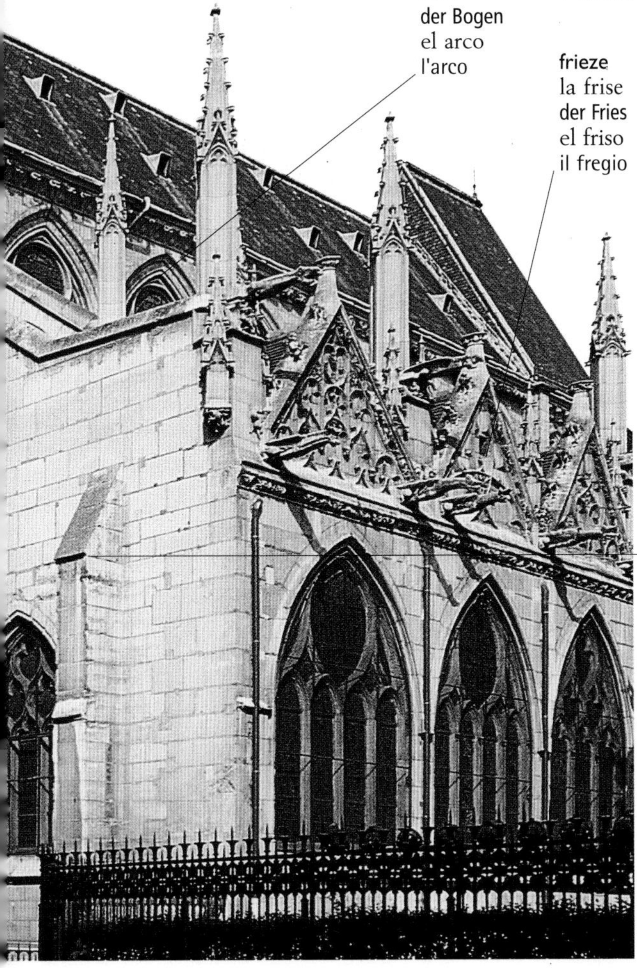

pediment
le fronton
das Giebeldreieck
el frontón
il frontone

neoclassical • néoclassique • klassizistisch • neoclásico • neoclassico

art nouveau • art nouveau • der Jugendstil • el estilo modernista • l'art nouveau

art deco • art déco • Art-déco- • art decó • art déco

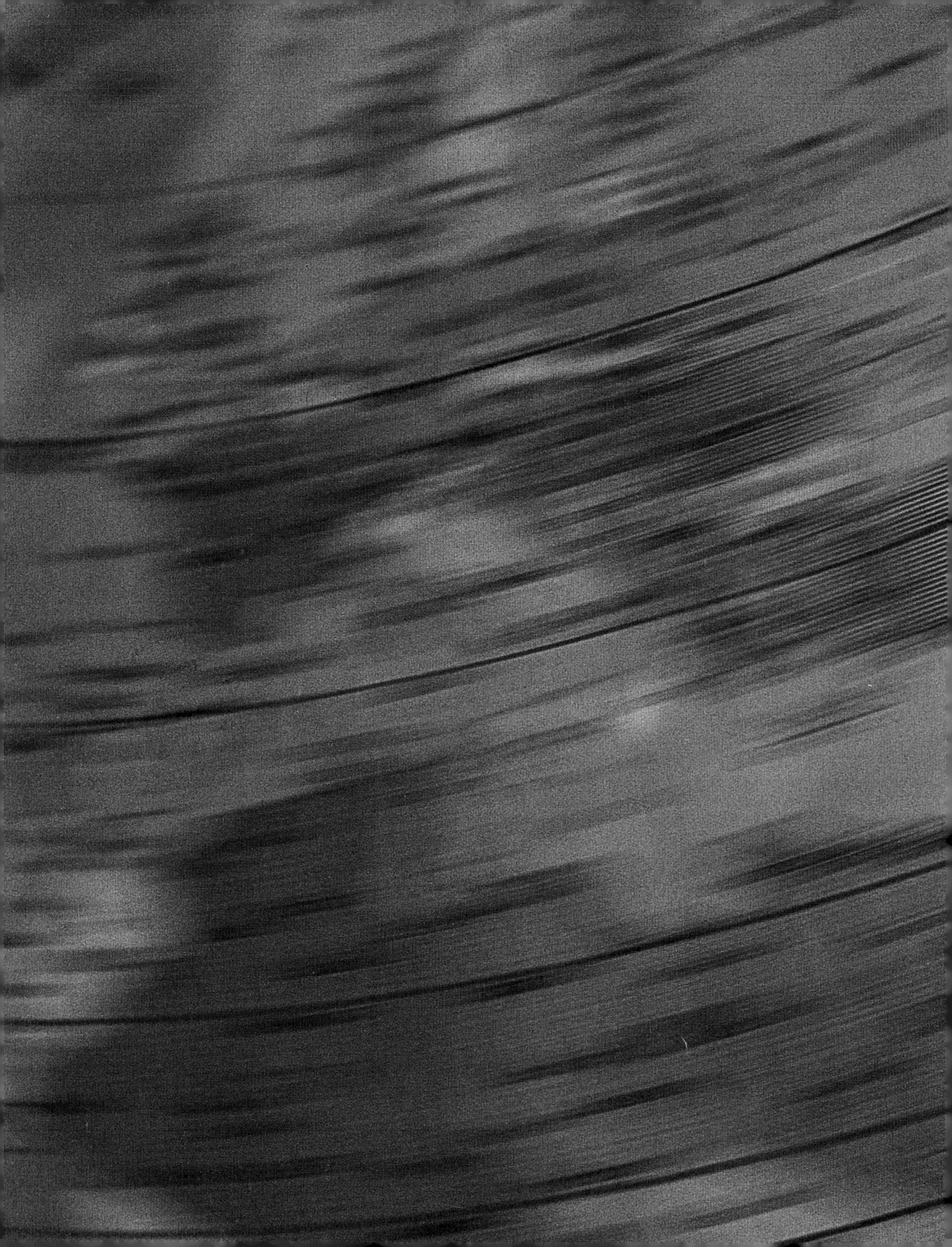

reference
l'information
die Information
los datos
i dati

time • l'heure • die Uhrzeit • el tiempo • l'ora

minute hand
la grande aiguille
der Minutenzeiger
el minutero
la lancetta dei minuti

hour hand
la petite aiguille
der Stundenzeiger
la manecilla de la hora
la lancetta delle ore

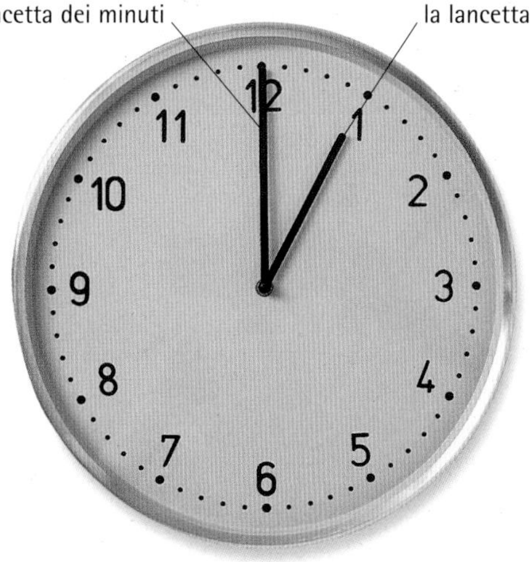

clock • l'horloge • die Uhr • el reloj • l'orologio

second la seconde die Sekunde el segundo il secondo	now maintenant jetzt ahora adesso	a quarter of an hour un quart d'heure eine Viertelstunde un cuarto de hora un quarto d'ora
minute la minute die Minute el minuto il minuto	later plus tard später más tarde più tardi	twenty minutes vingt minutes zwanzig Minuten veinte minutos venti minuti
hour l'heure die Stunde la hora l'ora	half an hour une demi-heure eine halbe Stunde media hora una mezzora	forty minutes quarante minutes vierzig Minuten cuarenta minutos quaranta minuti

What time is it?
Quelle heure est-il?
Wie spät ist es?
¿Qué hora es?
Che ore sono?

It's three o'clock.
Il est trois heures.
Es ist drei Uhr.
Son las tres en punto.
Sono le tre.

five after one • une heure cinq • fünf nach eins • la una y cinco • l'una e cinque

ten after one • une heure dix • zehn nach eins • la una y diez • l'una e dieci

quarter after one • une heure et quart • Viertel nach eins • la una y cuarto • l'una e un quarto

twenty after one • une heure vingt • zwanzig nach eins • la una y veinte • l'una e venti

second hand • la trotteuse • der Sekundenzeiger • el segundero • la lancetta dei secondi

twenty-five after one • une heure vingt-cinq • fünf vor halb zwei • la una y veinticinco • l'una e venticinque

one-thirty • une heure trente • ein Uhr dreißig • la una y media • l'una e trente

twenty-five to two • deux heures moins vingt-cinq • fünf nach halb zwei • las veinticinco para las dos • le due meno venticinque

twenty to two • deux heures moins vingt • zwanzig vor zwei • las veinte para las dos • le due meno venti

quarter to two • deux heures moins le quart • Viertel vor zwei • el cuarto para las dos • le due meno un quarto

ten to two • deux heures moins dix • zehn vor zwei • las diez para las dos • le due meno dieci

five to two • deux heures moins cinq • fünf vor zwei • las cinco para las dos • le due meno cinque

two o'clock • deux heures • zwei Uhr • las dos en punto • le due

night and day • la nuit et le jour • die Nacht und der Tag • la noche y el día • la notte e il giorno

midnight • le minuit • die Mitternacht • la medianoche • la mezzanotte

sunrise • le lever du soleil • der Sonnenaufgang • el amanecer • il sorgere del sole

dawn • l'aube • die Morgendämmerung • el alba • l'alba

morning • le matin • der Morgen • la mañana • il mattino

sunset • le coucher du soleil • der Sonnenuntergang • el atardecer • il tramonto

noon • le midi • der Mittag • el mediodía • il mezzogiorno

dusk • le crépuscule • die Abenddämmerung • el anochecer • l'imbrunire

evening • le soir • der Abend • la noche • la sera

afternoon • l'après-midi • der Nachmittag • la tarde • il pomeriggio

early tôt früh temprano presto	You're early. Tu es en avance. Du bist früh. Llegas temprano. Sei in anticipo.	Please be on time. Sois à l'heure, s'il te plaît. Sei bitte pünklich. Por favor, sé puntual. Per favore, vieni in orario.	What time does it end? Ça finit à quelle heure? Wann ist es zu Ende? ¿A qué hora termina? A che ora finisce?
on time à l'heure pünktlich puntual in orario	You're late. Tu es en retard. Du hast dich verspätet. Llegas tarde. Sei in ritardo.	I'll see you later. À tout à l'heure. Bis später. Hasta luego. A più tardi.	How long will it last? Ça dure combien de temps? Wie lange dauert es? ¿Cuánto dura? Quanto durerà?
late tard spät tarde tardi	I'll be there soon. J'y arriverai bientôt. Ich werde bald dort sein. Llegaré dentro de poco. Arrivo subito.	What time does it start? Ça commence à quelle heure? Wann fängt es an? ¿A qué hora comienza? A che ora inizia?	It's getting late. Il se fait tard. Es ist schon spät. Se está haciendo tarde. Si sta facendo tardi.

calendar • le calendrier • der Kalender • el calendario • il calendario

month • le mois • der Monat • el mes • il mese

year • l'an • das Jahr • el año • l'anno

January
janvier
Januar
enero
gennaio

2010

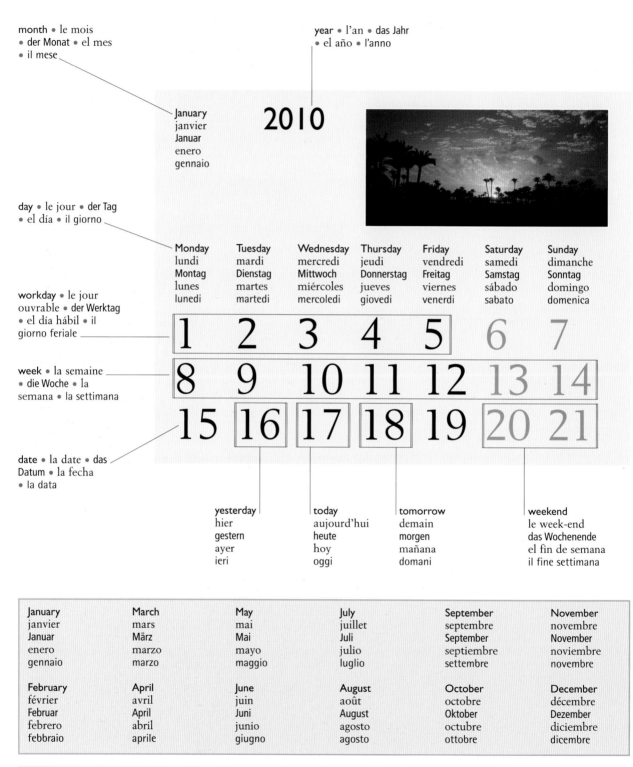

day • le jour • der Tag • el día • il giorno

Monday lundi Montag lunes lunedi	Tuesday mardi Dienstag martes martedi	Wednesday mercredi Mittwoch miércoles mercoledi	Thursday jeudi Donnerstag jueves giovedi	Friday vendredi Freitag viernes venerdi	Saturday samedi Samstag sábado sabato	Sunday dimanche Sonntag domingo domenica
1	2	3	4	5	6	7
8	9	10	11	12	13	14
15	16	17	18	19	20	21

workday • le jour ouvrable • der Werktag • el día hábil • il giorno feriale

week • la semaine • die Woche • la semana • la settimana

date • la date • das Datum • la fecha • la data

yesterday
hier
gestern
ayer
ieri

today
aujourd'hui
heute
hoy
oggi

tomorrow
demain
morgen
mañana
domani

weekend
le week-end
das Wochenende
el fin de semana
il fine settimana

January janvier Januar enero gennaio	March mars März marzo marzo	May mai Mai mayo maggio	July juillet Juli julio luglio	September septembre September septiembre settembre	November novembre November noviembre novembre
February février Februar febrero febbraio	April avril April abril aprile	June juin Juni junio giugno	August août August agosto agosto	October octobre Oktober octubre ottobre	December décembre Dezember diciembre dicembre

years • les ans • die Jahre • los años • gli anni

1900 nineteen hundred • mille neuf cents • neunzehnhundert • mil novecientos • millenovecento

1901 nineteen hundred and one • mille neuf cent un • neunzehnhunderteins • mil novecientos uno • millenovecentouno

1910 nineteen ten • mille neuf cent dix • neunzehnhundertzehn • mil novecientos diez • millenovecentodieci

2000 two thousand • deux mille • zweitausend • dos mil • duemila

2001 two thousand and one • deux mille un • zweitausendeins • dos mil uno • duemilauno

seasons • les saisons • die Jahreszeiten • las estaciones • le stagioni

spring • le printemps • der Frühling • la primavera • la primavera

summer • l'été • der Sommer • el verano • l'estate

fall • l'automne • der Herbst • el otoño • l'autunno

winter • l'hiver • der Winter • el invierno • l'inverno

century • le siècle • das Jahrhundert • el siglo • il secolo

decade • la décennie • das Jahrzehnt • la década • la decade

millennium • le millénaire • das Jahrtausend • el milenio • il millennio

two weeks • quinze jours • vierzehn Tage • quince días • quindici giorni

this week • cette semaine • diese Woche • esta semana • questa settimana

last week • la semaine dernière • letzte Woche • la semana pasada • la settimana scorsa

next week • la semaine prochaine • nächste Woche • la semana que viene • la settimana prossima

the day before yesterday • avant-hier • vorgestern • anteayer • l'altroieri

the day after tomorrow • après-demain • übermorgen • pasado mañana • il dopodomani

weekly • hebdomadaire • wöchentlich • semanalmente • settimanale

monthly • mensuel • monatlich • mensual • mensile

annual • annuel • jährlich • anual • annuo

What's the date today?
Quelle est la date aujourd'hui?
Welches Datum haben wir heute?
¿Qué día es hoy?
Oggi che giorno è?

It's February seventh, two thousand and two.
C'est le sept février deux mille deux.
Heute ist der siebte Februar zweitausendzwei.
Es el siete de febrero del dos mil dos.
È il sette febbraio, duemiladue.

numbers • les nombres • die Zahlen • los números • i numeri

0 zero • zéro • null • cero • zero

1 one • un • eins • uno • uno

2 two • deux • zwei • dos • due

3 three • trois • drei • tres • tre

4 four • quatre • vier • cuatro • quattro

5 five • cinq • fünf • cinco • cinque

6 six • six • sechs • seis • sei

7 seven • sept • sieben • siete • sette

8 eight • huit • acht • ocho • otto

9 nine • neuf • neun • nueve • nove

10 ten • dix • zehn • diez • dieci

11 eleven • onze • elf • once • undici

12 twelve • douze • zwölf • doce • dodici

13 thirteen • treize • dreizehn • trece • tredici

14 fourteen • quatorze • vierzehn • catorce • quattordici

15 fifteen • quinze • fünfzehn • quince • quindici

16 sixteen • seize • sechzehn • dieciséis • sedici

17 seventeen • dix-sept • siebzehn • diecisiete • diciassette

18 eighteen • dix-huit • achtzehn • dieciocho • diciotto

19 nineteen • dix-neuf • neunzehn • diecinueve • diciannove

20 twenty • vingt • zwanzig • veinte • venti

21 twenty-one • vingt et un • einundzwanzig • veintiuno • ventuno

22 twenty-two • vingt-deux • zweiundzwanzig • veintidós • ventidue

30 thirty • trente • dreißig • treinta • trenta

40 forty • quarante • vierzig • cuarenta • quaranta

50 fifty • cinquante • fünfzig • cincuenta • cinquanta

60 sixty • soixante • sechzig • sesenta • sessanta

70 seventy • soixante-dix • siebzig • setenta • settanta

80 eighty • quatre-vingt • achtzig • ochenta • ottanta

90 ninety • quatre-vingt-dix • neunzig • noventa • novanta

100 one hundred • cent • hundert • cien • cento

110 one hundred and ten • cent dix • hundertzehn • ciento diez • centodieci

200 two hundred • deux cents • zweihundert • doscientos • duecento

300 three hundred • trois cents • dreihundert • trescientos • trecento

400 four hundred • quatre cents • vierhundert • cuatrocientos • quattrocento

500 five hundred • cinq cents • fünfhundert • quinientos • cinquecento

600 six hundred • six cents • sechshundert • seiscientos • seicento

700 seven hundred • sept cents • siebenhundert • setecientos • settecento

800 eight hundred • huit cents • achthundert • ochocientos • ottocento

900 nine hundred • neuf cents • neunhundert • novecientos • novecento

1000 one thousand • mille • tausend • mil • mille

10,000 ten thousand • dix mille • zehntausend • diez mil • diecimila

20,000 twenty thousand • vingt mille • zwanzigtausend • veinte mil • ventimila

50,000 fifty thousand • cinquante mille • fünfzigtausend • cincuenta mil • cinquantamila

55,500 fifty-five thousand five hundred • cinqante-cinq mille cinq cents • fünfundfünfzigtausend-fünfhundert • cincuenta y cinco mil quinientos • cinquantacinquemilacinquecento

100,000 one hundred thousand • cent mille • hunderttausend • cien mil • centomila

1,000,000 one million • un million • eine Million • un millón • un milione

1,000,000,000 one billion • un milliard • eine Milliarde • mil millones • un miliardo

first
premier
erster
primero
primo

second
deuxième
zweiter
segundo
secondo

third
troisième
dritter
tercero
terzo

fourth • quatrième • vierter • cuarto • quarto

fifth • cinquième • fünfter • quinto • quinto

sixth • sixième • sechster • sexto • sesto

seventh • septième • siebter • séptimo • settimo

eighth • huitième • achter • octavo • ottavo

ninth • neuvième • neunter • noveno • nono

tenth • dixième • zehnter • décimo • decimo

eleventh • onzième • elfter • undécimo • undicesimo

twelfth • douzième • zwölfter • duodécimo • dodicesimo

thirteenth • treizième • dreizehnter • decimotercero • tredicesimo

fourteenth • quatorzième • vierzehnter • decimocuarto • quattordicesimo

fifteenth • quinzième • fünfzehnter • decimoquinto • quindicesimo

sixteenth • seizième • sechzehnter • decimosexto • sedicesimo

seventeenth • dix-septième • siebzehnter • decimoséptimo • diciassettesimo

eighteenth • dix-huitième • achtzehnter • décimo octavo • diciottesimo

nineteenth • dix-neuvième • neunzehnter • décimo noveno • diciannovesimo

twentieth • vingtième • zwanzigster • vigésimo • ventesimo

twenty-first • vingt et unième • einundzwanzigster • vigésimo primero • ventunesimo

twenty-second
vingt-deuxième
zweiundzwanzigster
vigésimo segundo
ventiduesimo

twenty-third • vingt-troisième • dreiundzwanzigster • vigésimo tercero • ventitreesimo

thirtieth • trentième • dreißigster • trigésimo • trentesimo

fortieth • quarantième • vierzigster • cuadragésimo • quarantesimo

fiftieth • cinquantième • fünfzigster • quincuagésimo • cinquantesimo

sixtieth • soixantième • sechzigster • sexagésimo • sessantesimo

seventieth • soixante-dixième • siebzigster • septuagésimo • settantesimo

eightieth • quatre-vingtième • achtzigster • octogésimo • ottantesimo

ninetieth • quatre-vingt-dixième • neunzigster • nonagésimo • novantesimo

one hundredth • centième • hundertster • centésimo • centesimo

weights and measures • les poids et mesures • die Maße und Gewichte • los pesos y las medidas • i pesi e le misure

area • la superficie • die Fläche • el área • la superficie

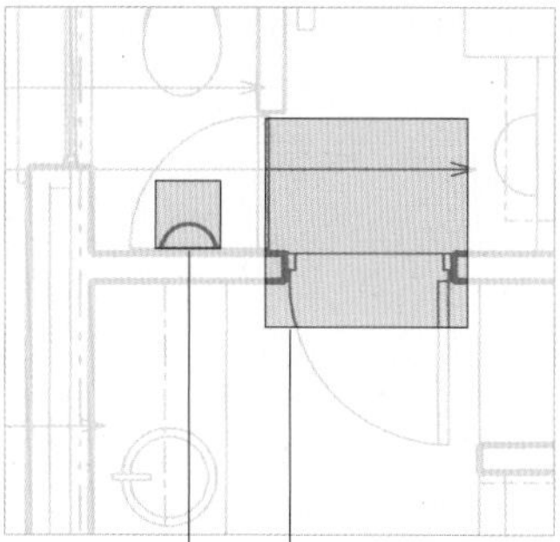

square foot
le pied carré
der Quadratfuß
el pie cuadrado
il piede quadro

square meter
le mètre carré
der Quadratmeter
el metro cuadrado
il metro quadro

distance • la distance • die Entfernung • la distancia • la distanza

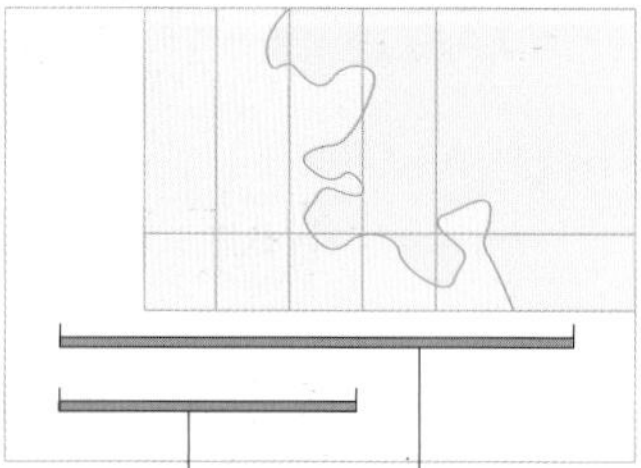

kilometer
le kilomètre
der Kilometer
el kilómetro
il chilometro

mile
le mile
die Meile
la milla
il miglio

pan • le plateau • die Waagschale • la bandeja • il piatto

pound
la livre
das Pfund
la libra
la libbra

ounce
l'once
die Unze
la onza
l'oncia

kilogram
le kilogramme
das Kilogramm
el kilogramo
il chilogrammo

gram
le gramme
das Gramm
el gramo
il grammo

scale • la balance • die Waage • la báscula • la bilancia

yard le yard das Yard la yarda la iarda	ton la tonne die Tonne la tonelada la tonnellata	measure *(v)* mesurer messen medir misurare
metre le mètre der Meter el metro il metro	milligram le milligramme das Milligramm el miligramo il milligrammo	weigh *(v)* peser wiegen pesar pesare

length • la longueur • die Länge • la longitud • la lunghezza

foot • le pied • der Fuß • el pie • il piede

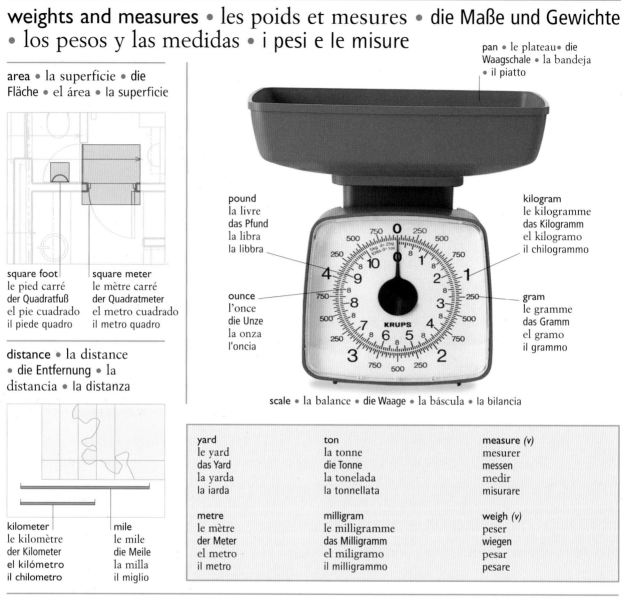

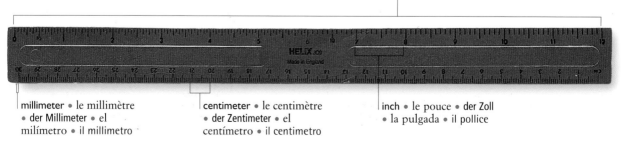

millimeter • le millimètre • der Millimeter • el milímetro • il millimetro

centimeter • le centimètre • der Zentimeter • el centímetro • il centimetro

inch • le pouce • der Zoll • la pulgada • il pollice

capacity • la capacité • das Fassungsvermögen • la capacidad • la capacità

half-liter • le demi-litre • der halbe Liter • el medio litro • il mezzo litro

pint • la pinte • das Pint • la pinta • la pinta

milliliter
le millilitre
der Milliliter
el mililitro
il millilitro

measuring cup • le pot gradué • der Messbecher • la jarra graduada • la brocca graduata

volume • le volume • das Volumen • el volumen • il volume

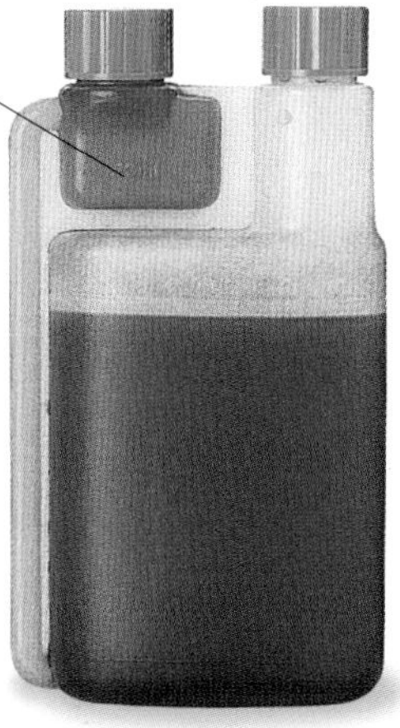

liquid measure • la mesure pour les liquides • das Flüssigkeitsmaß • la medida de capacidad • la misura di liquido

gallon
le gallon
die Gallone
el galón
il gallone

quart
deux pintes
das Quart
el cuarto de galón
il quarto di gallone

liter
le litre
der Liter
el litro
il litro

container • le récipient • der Behälter • el recipiente • il contenitore

carton • le carton • die Tüte • el tetrabrik • il cartone

bag • le paquet • das Päckchen • el paquete • il pacchetto

bottle • la bouteille • die Flasche • la botella • la bottiglia

sack • le sac • der Beutel • la bolsa • il sacchetto

tub • le pot • die Dose • la tarrina • la vaschetta

jar • le pot • das Glas • el tarro • il barattolo

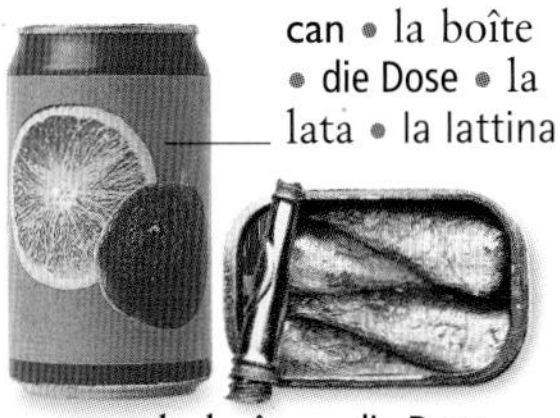

can • la boîte • die Dose • la lata • la lattina

tin • la boîte • die Dose • la lata • la scatoletta

spray bottle • le pulvérisateur • die Spritze • el pulverizador • il nebulizzatore

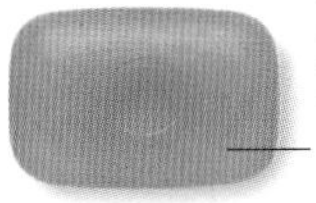

bar
le pain
das Stück
la pastilla
la saponetta

tube • le tube • die Tube • el tubo • il tubetto

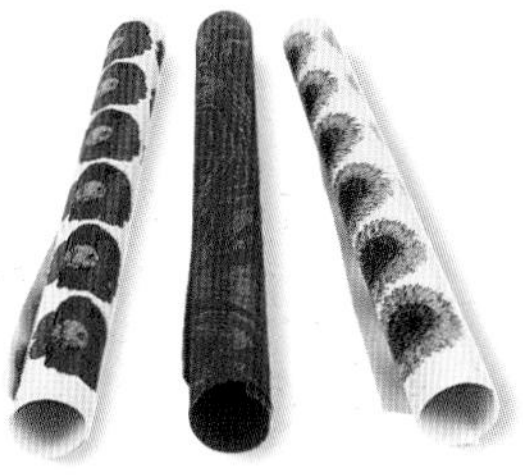

roll • le rouleau • die Rolle • el rollo • il rotolo

pack • le paquet • das Päckchen • la cajetilla • il pacchetto

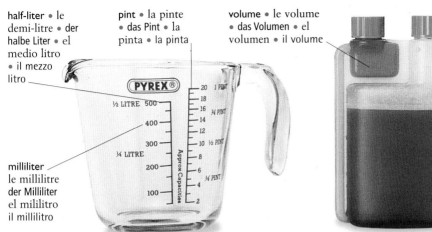

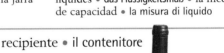

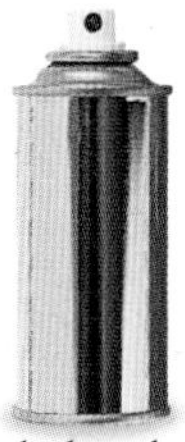

spray can • la bombe • die Sprühdose • el spray • la bomboletta spray

world map • la carte du monde • die Weltkarte • el mapamundi • il mappamondo

North Sea
la mer du Nord
die Nordsee
el Mar del Norte
il Mare del Nord

Arctic Ocean
l'océan Arctique
das Nordpolarmeer
el Océano Ártico
l'Oceano Artico

Rocky Mountains
les Rocheuses
die Rocky Mountains
las Montañas Rocosas
le Montagne Rocciose

Caribbean Sea
la mer des Antilles
das Karibische Meer
el Mar Caribe
il Mar dei Caraibi

Amazonia
l'Amazonie
Amazonien
el Amazonas
l'Amazzonia

Pacific Ocean
l'océan Pacifique
der Pazifische Ozean
el Océano Pacífico
l'Oceano Pacifico

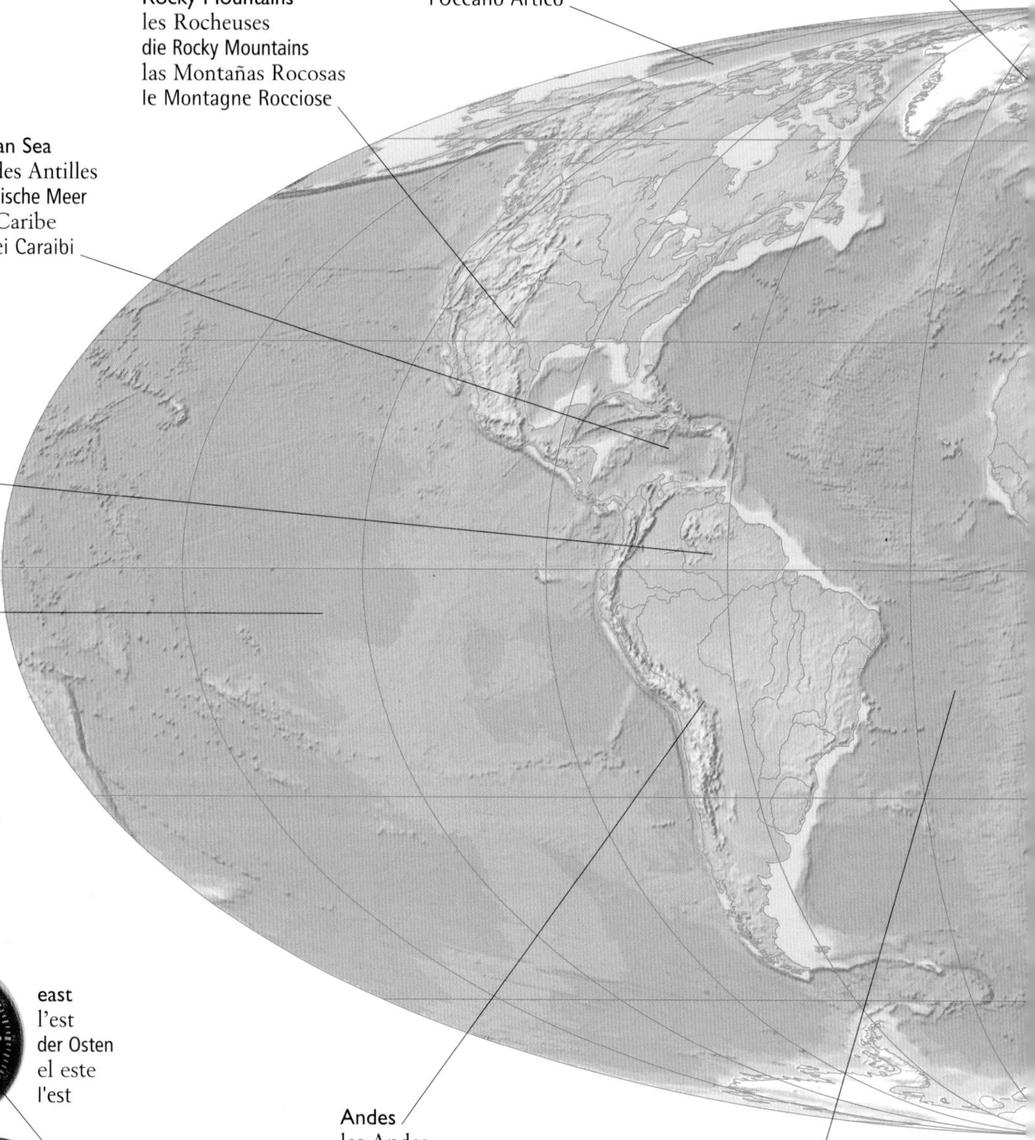

north
le nord
der Norden
el norte
il nord

west
l'ouest
der Westen
el oeste
l'ovest

east
l'est
der Osten
el este
l'est

compass
la boussole
der Kompass
la brújula
la bussola

south
le sud
der Süden
el sur
il sud

Andes
les Andes
die Anden
los Andes
le Ande

Atlantic Ocean
l'océan Atlantique
der Atlantische Ozean
el Océano Atlántico
l'Oceano Atlantico

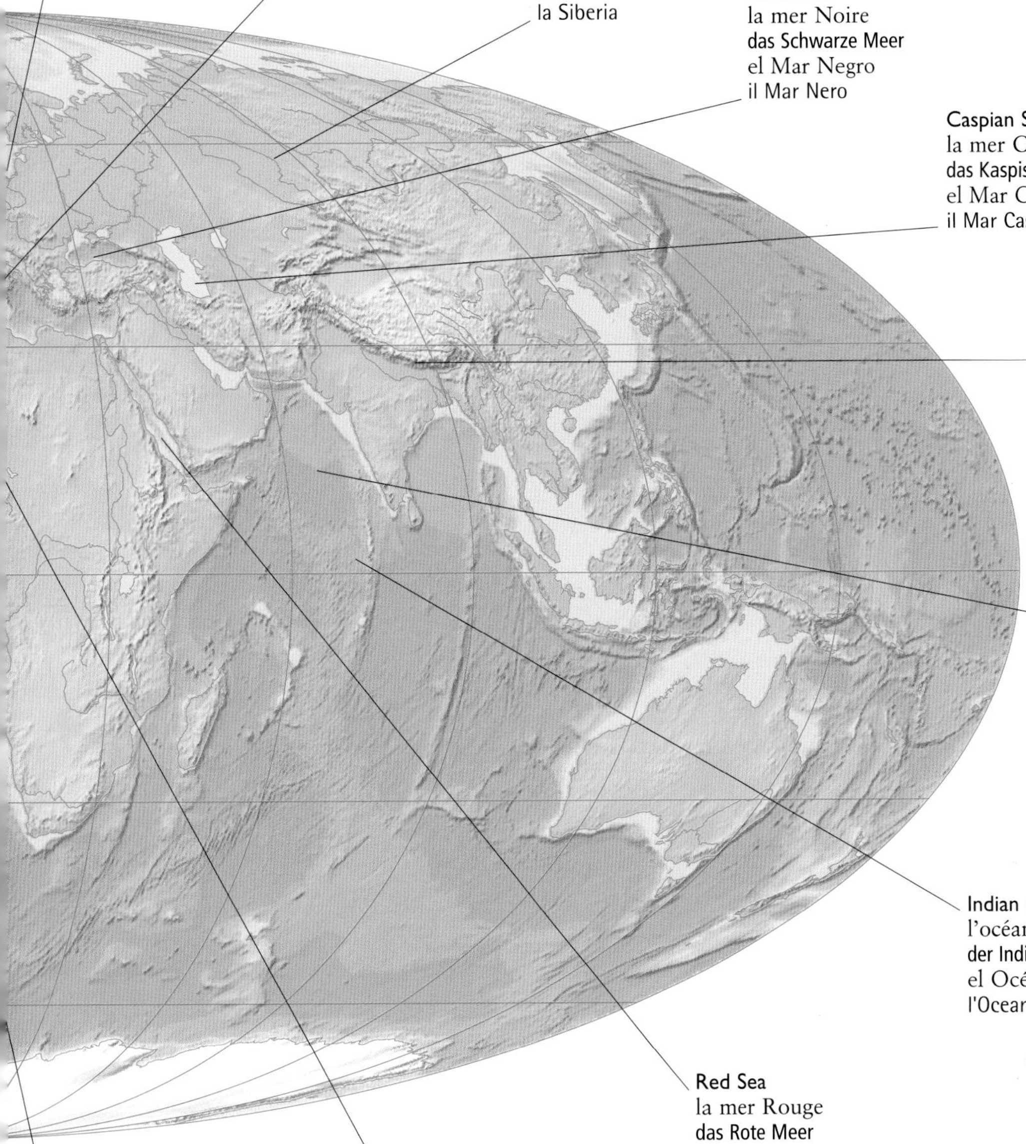
Baltic Sea
la mer Baltique
die Ostee
el Mar Báltico
il Mar Baltico
Mediterranean Sea
la Méditerranée
das Mittelmeer
el Mar Mediterráneo
il Mar Mediterraneo
Siberia
la Sibérie
Sibirien
Siberia
la Siberia
Black Sea
la mer Noire
das Schwarze Meer
el Mar Negro
il Mar Nero
Caspian Sea
la mer Caspienne
das Kaspische Meer
el Mar Caspio
il Mar Caspio
Himalayas
l'Himalaya
der Himalaja
el Himalaya
l'Himalaia
Arabian Sea
la mer d'Arabie
das Arabische Meer
el Mar de Omán
il Mare Arabico
Indian Ocean
l'océan Indien
der Indische Ozean
el Océano Índico
l'Oceano Indiano
Red Sea
la mer Rouge
das Rote Meer
el Mar Rojo
il Mar Rosso
Sahara Desert
le Sahara
die Sahara
el Sáhara
il Sahara
Southern Ocean
l'océan Austral
das Südpolarmeer
el Océano Antártico
l'Oceano Antartico

North and Central America • l'Amérique du Nord et centrale • Nord- und Mittelamerika • América del Norte y Central • l'America del Nord e Centrale

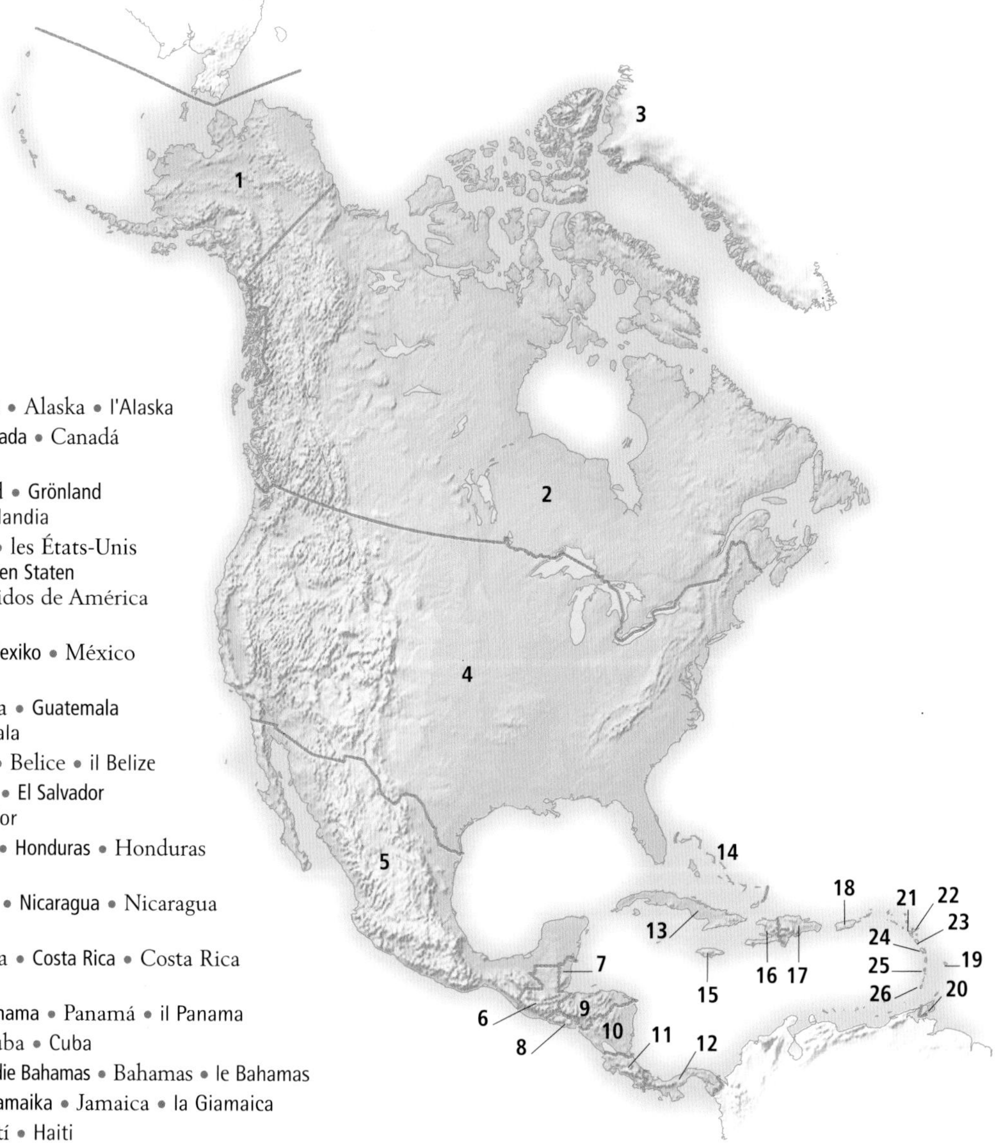

1 **Alaska** • l'Alaska • **Alaska** • Alaska • l'Alaska
2 **Canada** • le Canada • **Kanada** • Canadá • il Canada
3 **Greenland** • le Groenland • **Grönland** • Groenlandia • la Groenlandia
4 **United States of America** • les États-Unis d'Amérique • **die Vereinigten Staten von Amerika** • Estados Unidos de América • gli Stati Uniti d'America
5 **Mexico** • le Mexique • **Mexiko** • México • il Messico
6 **Guatemala** • le Guatemala • **Guatemala** • Guatemala • il Guatemala
7 **Belize** • le Bélize • **Belize** • Belice • il Belize
8 **El Salvador** • Le Salvador • **El Salvador** • El Salvador • l'El Salvador
9 **Honduras** • le Honduras • **Honduras** • Honduras • l'Honduras
10 **Nicaragua** • le Nicaragua • **Nicaragua** • Nicaragua • il Nicaragua
11 **Costa Rica** • le Costa Rica • **Costa Rica** • Costa Rica • il Costa Rica
12 **Panama** • le Panama • **Panama** • Panamá • il Panama
13 **Cuba** • Cuba • **Kuba** • Cuba • Cuba
14 **Bahamas** • les Bahamas • **die Bahamas** • Bahamas • le Bahamas
15 **Jamaica** • la Jamaïque • **Jamaika** • Jamaica • la Giamaica
16 **Haiti** • Haïti • **Haiti** • Haití • Haiti
17 **Dominican Republic** • la République dominicaine • **die Dominikanische Republik** • República Dominicana • la Repubblica Dominicana
18 **Puerto Rico** • la Porto Rico • **Puerto Rico** • Puerto Rico • Puerto Rico
19 **Barbados** • la Barbade • **Barbados** • Barbados • Barbados
20 **Trinidad and Tobago** • la Trinité-et-Tobago • **Trinidad und Tobago** • Trinidad y Tobago • Trinidad e Tobago
21 **St. Kitts and Nevis** • Saint-Kitts-et-Nevis • **Saint Kitts und Nevis** • Saint Kitts y Nevis • Saint Kitts-Nevis
22 **Antigua and Barbuda** • Antigua-et-Barbuda • **Antigua und Barbuda** • Antigua y Barbuda • Antigua e Barbuda
23 **Dominica** • la Dominique • **Dominica** • Dominica • Dominica
24 **St. Lucia** • Sainte-Lucie • **Saint Lucia** • Santa Lucía • Saint Lucia
25 **St. Vincent and the Grenadines** • Saint-Vincent-et-les-Grenadines • **Saint Vinzent und die Grenadinen** • San Vicente y las Granadinas • Saint Vincent e Grenadine
26 **Grenada** • la Grenade • **Grenada** • Granada • Grenada

South America • l'Amérique du Sud • Südamerika • América del Sur • l'America del Sud

1 **Venezuela** • le Venezuela • **Venezuela** • Venezuela • il Venezuela
2 **Colombia** • la Colombie • **Kolumbien** • Colombia • la Colombia
3 **Ecuador** • l'Équateur • **Ecuador** • Ecuador • l'Ecuador
4 **Peru** • le Pérou • **Peru** • Perú • il Perù
5 **Galápagos Islands** • les îles Galapagos • **die Galapagosinseln** • las Islas Galápagos • le Isola Galapagos
6 **Guyana** • la Guyane • **Guyana** • Guyana • la Guyana
7 **Suriname** • le Surinam • **Suriname** • Suriname • il Suriname
8 **French Guiana** • la Guyane française • **Französisch-Guayana** • la Guayana Francesa • la Guyana Francese
9 **Brazil** • le Brésil • **Brasilien** • Brasil • il Brasile
10 **Bolivia** • la Bolivie • **Bolivien** • Bolivia • la Bolivia
11 **Chile** • le Chili • **Chile** • Chile • il Cile
12 **Argentina** • l'Argentine • **Argentinien** • Argentina • l'Argentina
13 **Paraguay** • le Paraguay • **Paraguay** • Paraguay • il Paraguay
14 **Uruguay** • l'Uruguay • **Uruguay** • Uruguay • l'Uruguay
15 **Falkland Islands** • les îles Malouines • **die Falklandinseln** • las Malvinas • le Isola Falkland

continent le continent **der Kontinent** el continente il continente	**province** la province **die Provinz** la provincia la provincia	**zone** la zone **die Zone** la zona la zona
country le pays **das Land** el país il paese	**territory** le territoire **das Territorium** el territorio il territorio	**district** le district **der Bezirk** el distrito il distretto
nation la nation **die Nation** la nación la nazione	**principality** la principauté **das Fürstentum** el principado il principato	**region** la région **die Region** la región la regione
state l'État **der Staat** el estado lo stato	**colony** la colonie **die Kolonie** la colonia la colonia	**capital** la capitale **die Hauptstadt** la capital la capitale

Europe • l'Europe • Europa • Europa • l'Europa

1 **Ireland** • l'Irlande • Irland • Irlanda • l'Irlanda

2 **United Kingdom** • le Royaume-Uni • das Vereinigte Königreich • Reino Unido • il Regno Unito

3 **Portugal** • le Portugal • Portugal • Portugal • il Portogallo

4 **Spain** • l'Espagne • Spanien • España • la Spagna

5 **Balearic Islands** • les Baléares • die Balearen • las Islas Baleares • le Isole Baleari

6 **Andorra** • l'Andorre • Andorra • Andorra • Andorra

7 **France** • la France • Frankreich • Francia • la Francia

8 **Belgium** • la Belgique • Belgien • Bélgica • il Belgio

9 **Netherlands** • les Pays-Bas • die Niederlande • los Países Bajos • i Paesi Bassi

10 **Luxembourg** • le Luxembourg • Luxemburg • Luxemburgo • il Lussemburgo

11 **Germany** • l'Allemagne • Deutschland • Alemania • la Germania

12 **Denmark** • le Danemark • Dänemark • Dinamarca • la Danimarca

13 **Norway** • la Norvège • Norwegen • Noruega • la Norvegia

14 **Sweden** • la Suède • Schweden • Suecia • la Svezia

15 **Finland** • la Finlande • Finnland • Finlandia • la Finlandia

16 **Estonia** • l'Estonie • Estland • Estonia • l'Estonia

17 **Latvia** • la Lettonie • Lettland • Letonia • la Lettonia

18 **Lithuania** • la Lituanie • Litauen • Lituania • la Lituania

19 **Kaliningrad** • Kaliningrad • Kaliningrad • Kaliningrado • Kaliningrad

20 **Poland** • la Pologne • Polen • Polonia • la Polonia

21 **Czech Republic** • la République tchèque • die Tschechische Republik • República Checa • la Repubblica Ceca

22 **Austria** • l'Autriche • Österreich • Austria • l'Austria

23 **Liechtenstein** • le Liechtenstein • Liechtenstein • Liechtenstein • il Liechtenstein

24 **Switzerland** • la Suisse • die Schweiz • Suiza • la Svizzera

25 **Italy** • l'Italie • Italien • Italia • l'Italia

26 **Monaco** • Monaco • Monaco • Mónaco • Monaco

27 **Corsica** • la Corse • Korsika • Córcega • la Corsica

28 **Sardinia** • la Sardaigne • Sardinien • Cerdeña • la Sardegna

29 **San Marino** • le Saint-Marin • San Marino • San Marino • San Marino

30 **Vatican City** • la Cité du Vatican • die Vatikanstadt • la Ciudad del Vaticano • la Città del Vaticano

31 **Sicily** • la Sicile • Sizilien • Sicilia • la Sicilia

32 **Malta** • Malte • Malta • Malta • Malta

33 **Slovenia** • la Slovénie • Slowenien • Eslovenia • la Slovenia

34 **Croatia** • la Croatie • Kroatien • Croacia • la Croazia

35 **Hungary** • la Hongrie • Ungarn • Hungría • l'Ungheria

36 **Slovakia** • la Slovaquie • die Slowakei • Eslovaquia • la Slovacchia

37 **Ukraine** • l'Ukraine • die Ukraine • Ucrania • l'Ucraina

38 **Belarus** • la Bélarus • Weißrussland • Belarús • la Bielorussia

39 **Moldova** • la Moldavie • Moldawien • Moldavia • la Moldavia

40 **Romania** • la Roumanie • Rumänien • Rumanía • la Romania

41 **Serbia** • la Serbie • Serbien • Serbia • la Serbia

42 **Bosnia and Herzogovina** • la Bosnie-Herzégovine • Bosnien und Herzegowina • Bosnia y Herzegovina • la Bosnia ed Erzegovina

43 **Albania** • l'Albanie • Albanien • Albania • l'Albania

44 **Macedonia** • la Macédonie • Mazedonien • Macedonia • la Macedonia

45 **Bulgaria** • la Bulgarie • Bulgarien • Bulgaria • la Bulgaria

46 **Greece** • la Grèce • Griechenland • Grecia • la Grecia

47 **Kosovo** • le Kosovo • Kosovo • Kosovo • il Kosovo

48 **Montenegro** • le Montenegro • Montenegro • Montenegro • Montenegro

49 **Iceland** • l'Islande • Island • Islandia • l'Islanda

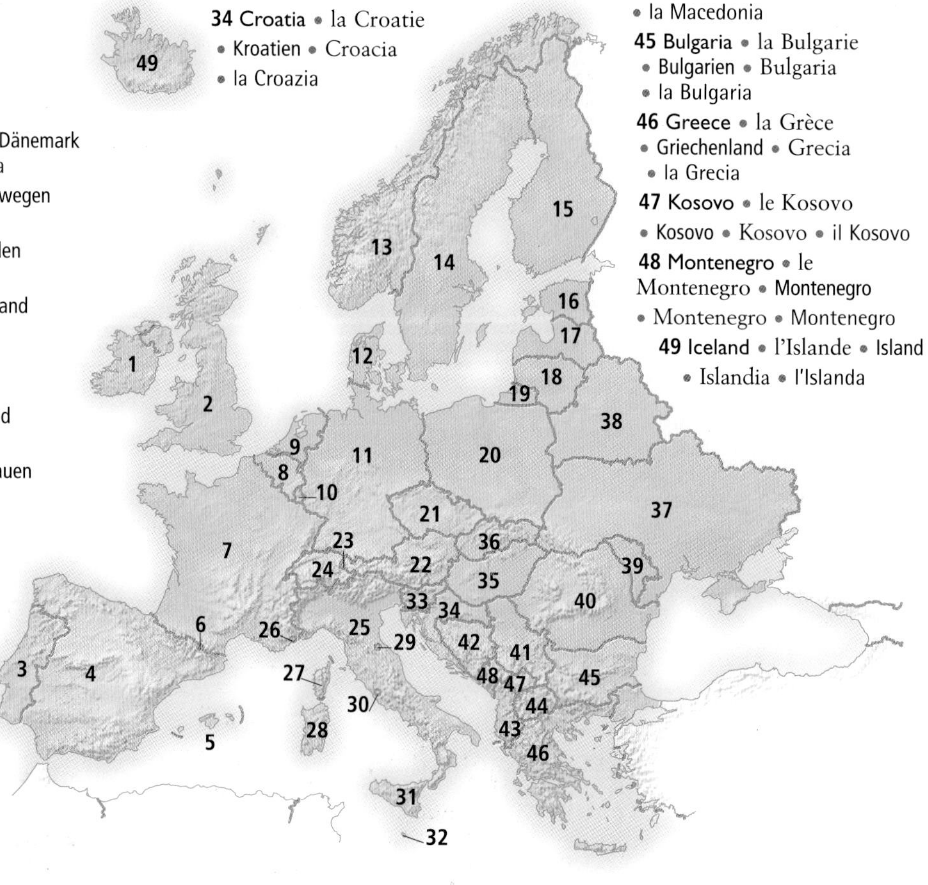

Africa • l'Afrique • Afrika • África • l'Africa

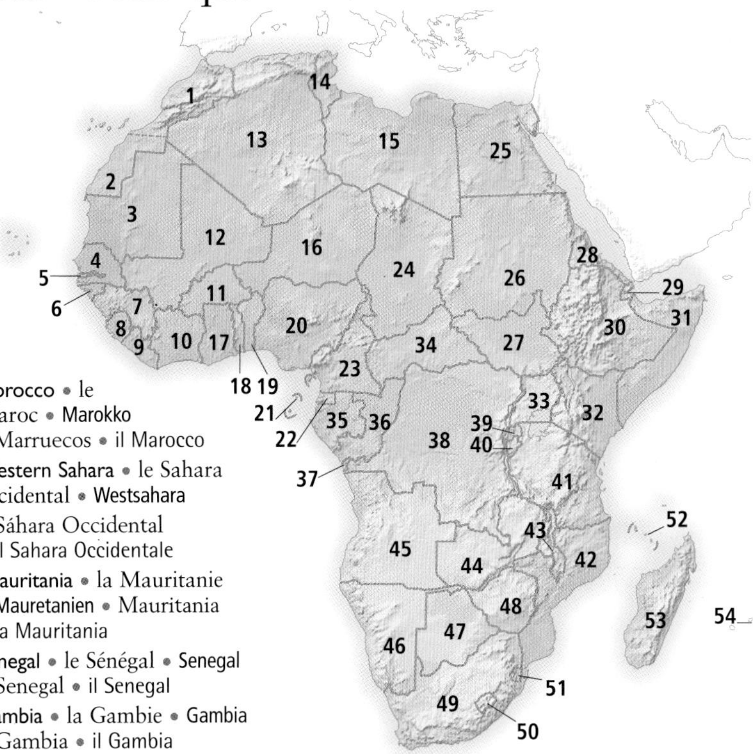

1 Morocco • le Maroc • Marokko • Marruecos • il Marocco

2 Western Sahara • le Sahara occidental • Westsahara • Sáhara Occidental • il Sahara Occidentale

3 Mauritania • la Mauritanie • Mauretanien • Mauritania • la Mauritania

4 Senegal • le Sénégal • Senegal • Senegal • il Senegal

5 Gambia • la Gambie • Gambia • Gambia • il Gambia

6 Guinea-Bissau • la Guinée-Bissau • Guinea-Bissau • Guinea-Bissau • la Guinea-Bissau

7 Guinea • la Guinée • Guinea • Guinea • la Guinea

8 Sierra Leone • la Sierra Leone • Sierra Leone • Sierra Leona • Sierra Leone

9 Liberia • le Libéria • Liberia • Liberia • la Liberia

10 Ivory Coast • la Côte d'Ivoire • Elfenbeinküste • Costa de Marfil • la Costa d'Avorio

11 Burkina Faso • le Burkina • Burkina Faso • Burquina Faso • il Burkina Faso

12 Mali • le Mali • Mali • Malí • il Mali

13 Algeria • l'Algérie • Algerien • Argelia • l'Algeria

14 Tunisia • la Tunisie • Tunesien • Túnez • la Tunisia

15 Libya • la Libye • Libyen • Libia • la Libia

16 Niger • le Niger • Niger • Níger • il Niger

17 Ghana • le Ghana • Ghana • Ghana • il Ghana

18 Togo • le Togo • Togo • Togo • il Togo

19 Benin • le Bénin • Benin • Benin • il Benin

20 Nigeria • le Nigéria • Nigeria • Nigeria • la Nigeria

21 São Tomé and Principe • Sao Tomé-et-Principe • São Tomé und Príncipe • Santo Tomé y Príncipe • São Tomé e Príncipe

22 Equatorial Guinea • la Guinée equatoriale • Äquatorialguinea • Guinea Ecuatorial • la Guinea Equatoriale

23 Cameroon • le Cameroun • Kamerun • Camerún • il Camerun

24 Chad • le Tchad • Tschad • Chad • il Ciad

25 Egypt • l'Égypte • Ägypten • Egipto • l'Egitto

26 Sudan • le Soudan • der Sudan • Sudán • il Sudan

27 South Sudan • le Soudan du Sud • Südsudan • Sudán del Sur • il Sudan del Sud

28 Eritrea • l'Érythrée • Eritrea • Eritrea • l'Eritrea

29 Djibouti • Djibouti • Dschibuti • Djibouti • Gibuti

30 Ethiopia • l'Éthiopie • Äthiopien • Etiopía • l'Etiopia

31 Somalia • la Somalie • Somalia • Somalia • la Somalia

32 Kenya • le Kenya • Kenia • Kenya • il Kenya

33 Uganda • l'Ouganda • Uganda • Uganda • l'Uganda

34 Central African Republic • la République centrafricaine • die Zentralafrikanische Republik • República Centroafricana • la Repubblica Centrafricana

35 Gabon • le Gabon • Gabun • Gabón • il Gabon

36 Congo • le Congo • Kongo • Congo • il Congo

37 Cabinda (Angola) • Cabinda • Kabinda • Cabinda • Cabinda

38 Democratic Republic of the Congo • la République démocratique du Congo • die Demokratische Republik Kongo • República Democrática del Congo • la Repubblica Democratica del Congo

39 Rwanda • le Rwanda • Ruanda • Rwanda • il Ruanda

40 Burundi • le Burundi • Burundi • Burundi • il Burundi

41 Tanzania • la Tanzanie • Tansania • Tanzania • la Tanzania

42 Mozambique • le Mozambique • Mosambik • Mozambique • il Mozambico

43 Malawi • le Malawi • Malawi • Malawi • il Malawi

44 Zambia • la Zambie • Sambia • Zambia • lo Zambia

45 Angola • l'Angola • Angola • Angola • l'Angola

46 Namibia • la Namibie • Namibia • Namibia • la Namibia

47 Botswana • le Botswana • Botsuana • Botswana • il Botswana

48 Zimbabwe • le Zimbabwe • Simbabwe • Zimbabwe • lo Zimbabwe

49 South Africa • l'Afrique du Sud • Südafrika • Sudáfrica • il Sud Africa

50 Lesotho • le Lesotho • Lesotho • Lesotho • il Lesotho

51 Swaziland • le Swaziland • Swasiland • Swazilandia • lo Swaziland

52 Comoros • les Comores • die Komoren • Comoros • le Comore

53 Madagascar • Madagascar • Madagaskar • Madagascar • il Madagascar

54 Mauritius • l'île Maurice • Mauritius • Mauricio • Mauritius

Asia • l'Asie • Asien • Asia • l'Asia

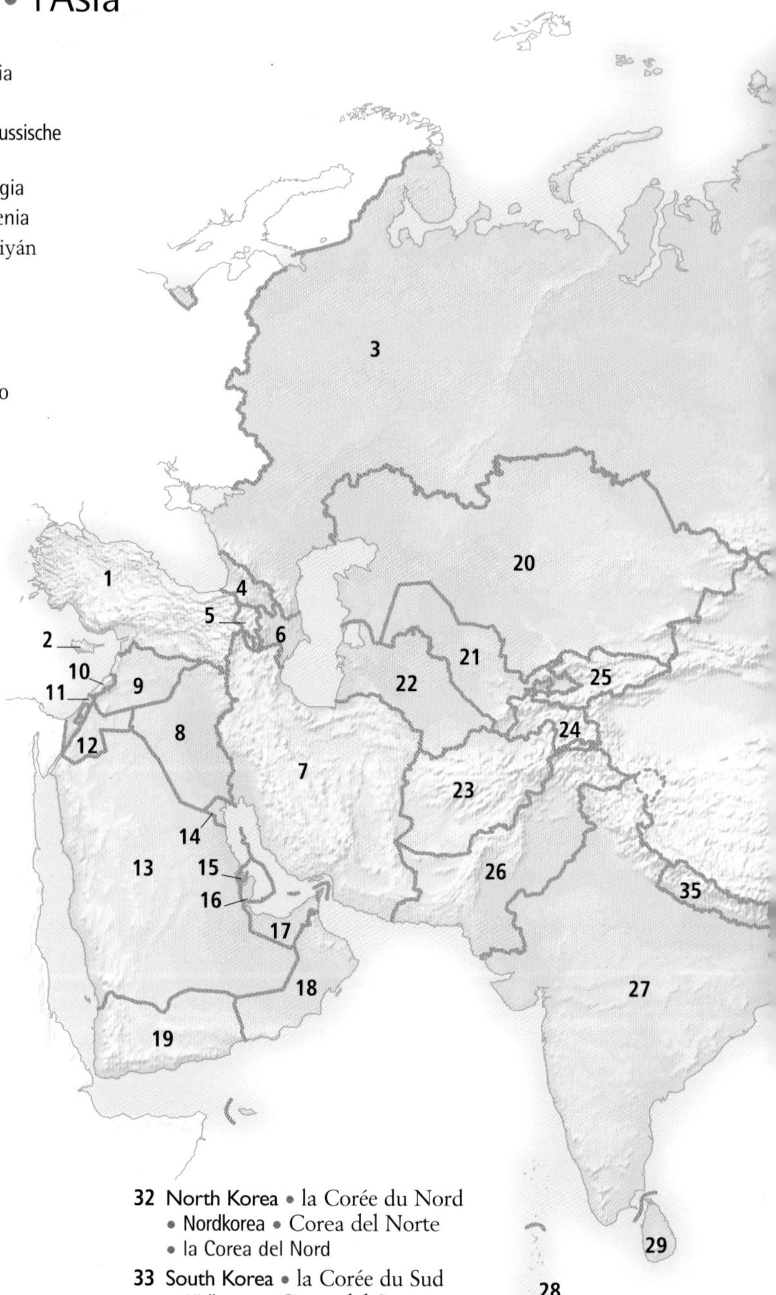

1 Turkey • la Turquie • die Türkei • Turquía • la Turchia

2 Cyprus • Chypre • Zypern • Chipre • Cipro

3 Russian Federation • la Fédération de Russie • die Russische Föderation • Federación Rusa • la Federazione Russa

4 Georgia • la Géorgie • Georgien • Georgia • la Georgia

5 Armenia • l'Arménie • Armenien • Armenia • l'Armenia

6 Azerbaijan • l'Azerbaïdjan • Aserbaidschan • Azerbaiyán • l'Azerbaigian

7 Iran • l'Iran • der Iran • Irán • l'Iran

8 Iraq • l'Irak • der Irak • Iraq • l'Iraq

9 Syria • la Syrie • Syrien • Siria • la Siria

10 Lebanon • le Liban • der Libanon • Líbano • il Libano

11 Israel • Israël • Israel • Israel • l'Israele

12 Jordan • la Jordanie • Jordanien • Jordania • la Giordania

13 Saudi Arabia • l'Arabie Saoudite • Saudi-Arabien • Arabia Saudita • l'Arabia Saudita

14 Kuwait • le Koweït • Kuwait • Kuwait • il Kuwait

15 Bahrein • le Bahreïn • Bahrain • Bahrein • il Bahrain

16 Qatar • le Qatar • Katar • Qatar • il Qatar

17 United Arab Emirates • les Émirats arabes unis • Vereinigte Arabische Emirate • Emiratos Árabes Unidos • gli Emirati Arabi Uniti

18 Oman • l'Oman • Oman • Omán • l'Oman

19 Yemen • le Yémen • der Jemen • Yemen • lo Yemen

20 Kazakhstan • le Kasakhastan • Kasachstan • Kazajstán • il Kazakistan

21 Uzbekistan • l'Ouzbékistan • Usbekistan • Uzbekistán • l'Uzbekistan

22 Turkmenistan • le Turkmenistan • Turkmenistan • Turkmenistán • il Turkmenistan

23 Afghanistan • l'Afghanistan • Afghanistan • Afganistán • l'Afghanistan

24 Tajikistan • le Tadjikistan • Tadschikistan • Tayikistán • il Tagikistan

25 Kyrgyzstan • le Kirghizistan • Kirgisistan • Kirguistán • il Kirghizistan

26 Pakistan • le Pakistan • Pakistan • Pakistán • il Pakistan

27 India • l'Inde • Indien • India • l'India

28 Maldives • les Maldives • die Malediven • Maldivas • le Maldive

29 Sri Lanka • Sri Lanka • Sri Lanka • Sri Lanka • lo Sri Lanka

30 China • la Chine • China • China • la Cina

31 Mongolia • la Mongolie • die Mongolei • Mongolia • la Mongolia

32 North Korea • la Corée du Nord • Nordkorea • Corea del Norte • la Corea del Nord

33 South Korea • la Corée du Sud • Südkorea • Corea del Sur • la Corea del Sud

34 Japan • le Japon • Japan • Japón • il Giappone

35 Nepal • le Népal • Nepal • Nepal • il Nepal

36 Bhutan • le Bhoutan • Bhutan • Bhutan • il Bhutan

37 Bangladesh • le Bangladesh • Bangladecsh • Bangladesh • il Bangladesh

Australasia • l'Australasie • Australien und Ozeanien • Australasia • l'Oceania

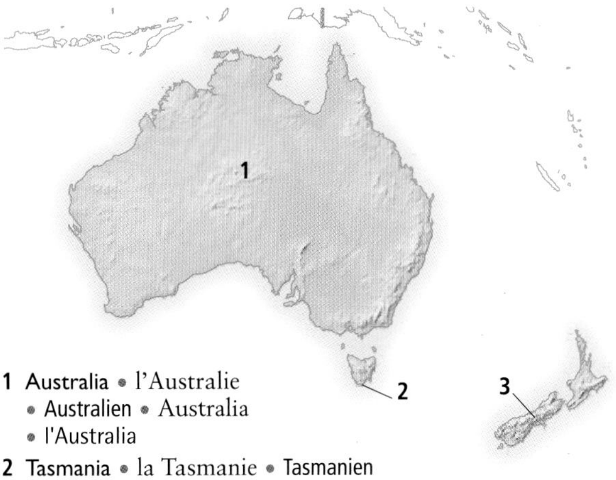

1 **Australia** • l'Australie • Australien • Australia • l'Australia

2 **Tasmania** • la Tasmanie • Tasmanien • Tasmania • la Tasmania

3 **New Zealand** • la Nouvelle-Zélande • Neuseeland • Nueva Zelandia • la Nuova Zelanda

38 **Burma (Myanmar)** • la Birmanie (le Myanmar) • Birma (Myanmar) • Birmania (Myanmar) • la Birmania (il Myanmar)

39 **Thailand** • la Thaïlande • Thailand • Tailandia • la Tailandia

40 **Laos** • le Laos • Laos • Laos • il Laos

41 **Viet Nam** • le Vietnam • Vietnam • Viet Nam • il Vietnam

42 **Cambodia** • le Cambodge • Kambodscha • Camboya • la Cambogia

43 **Malaysia** • la Malaisie • Malaysia • Malasia • la Malaysia

44 **Singapore** • Singapour • Singapur • Singapur • Singapore

45 **Indonesia** • l'Indonésie • Indonesien • Indonesia • l'Indonesia

46 **Brunei** • le Brunei • Brunei • Brunei • Brunei

47 **Philippines** • les Philippines • die Philippinen • Filipinas • le Filippine

48 **East Timor** • le Timor oriental • Ost-Timor • Timor Oriental • Timor Est

49 **Papua New Guinea** • la Papouasie-Nouvelle-Guinée • Papua-Neuguinea • Papua Nueva Guinea • la Papua Nuova Guinea

50 **Solomon Islands** • les îles Saloman • die Salomonen • Islas Salomón • le Isole Salomone

51 **Vanuatu** • Vanuatu • Vanuatu • Vanuatu • Vanuatu

52 **Fiji** • Fidji • Fidschi • Fiji • Figi

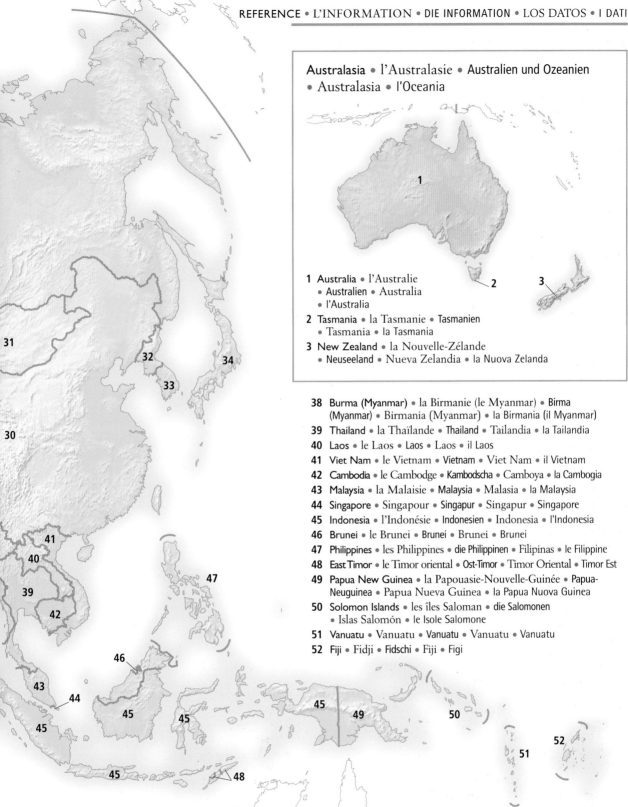

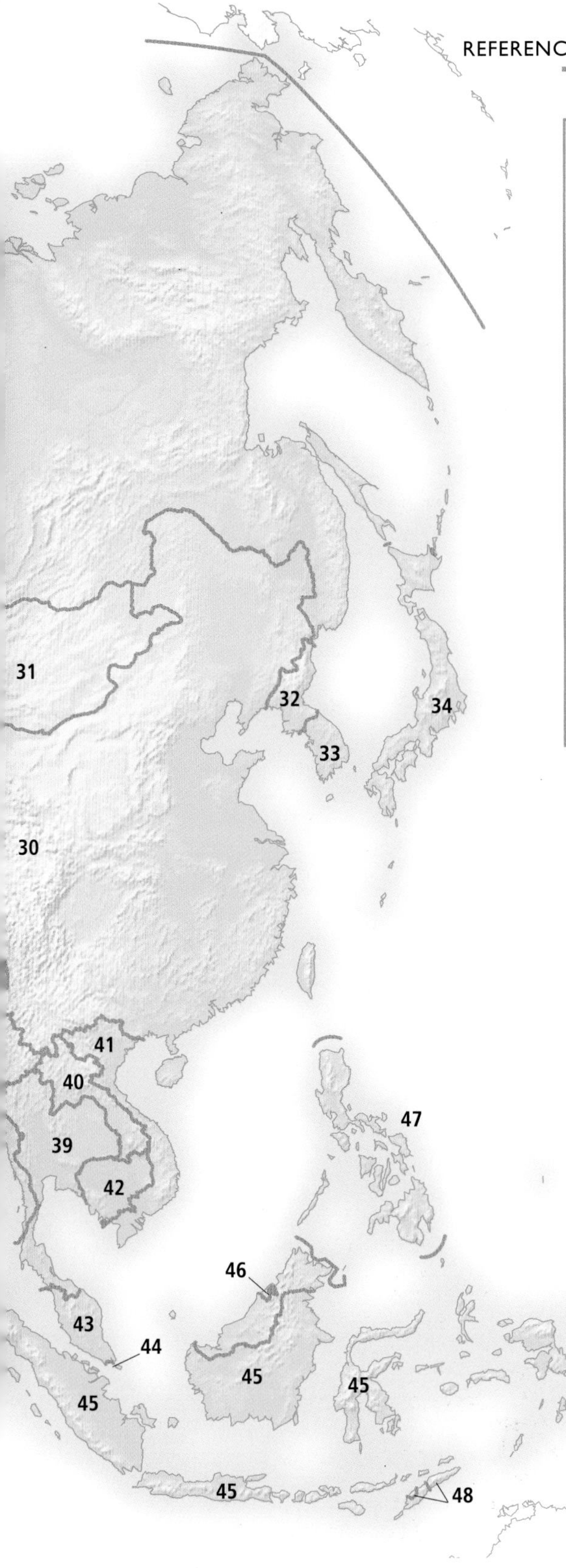

particles and antonyms • particules et antonymes • Partikeln und Antonyme • partículas y antónimos • particelle e antonimi

to
à
zu, nach
a, hacia
a

from
de
von, aus
de, desde
da

over
au-dessus de
über
encima de
sopra

under
sous
unter
debajo de
sotto

in front of
devant
vor
delante de
davanti

behind
derrière
hinter
detrás de
dietro

onto
sur
auf
sobre
sopra

into
dans
in
dentro de
dentro

in
dans
in
en
dentro

out
dehors
aus
fuera
fuori

above
au-dessus de
über
sobre
sopra

below
au-dessous de
unter
bajo
sotto

inside
à l'intérieur de
innerhalb
dentro
all'interno

outside
à l'extérieur de
außerhalb
fuera
all'esterno

up
en haut
hinauf
arriba
su

down
en bas
hinunter
abajo
giù

at
à
an, bei
en
a

beyond
au-delà de
jenseits
más allá de
oltre

through
à travers
durch
a través de
attraverso

around
autour de
um
alrededor de
attorno

on top of
sur
auf
encima de
in cima

beside
à côté de
neben
al lado de
accanto

between
entre
zwischen
entre
tra

opposite
en face de
gegenüber
en frente de
di fronte

near
près de
nahe
cerca
vicino

far
loin de
weit
lejos
lontano

with
avec
mit
con
con

without
sans
ohne
sin
senza

before
avant
vor
antes
prima

after
après
nach
después
dopo

by
avant
bis
antes de
entro

until
jusqu'à
bis
hasta
fino

for
pour
für
para
per

toward
vers
zu
hacia
verso

along
le long de
entlang
por
lungo

across
à travers
über
al otro lado de
attraverso

large grand groß grande grande	small petit klein pequeño piccolo	hot chaud heiß caliente caldo	cold froid kalt frío freddo
wide large breit ancho largo	narrow étroit schmal estrecho stretto	open ouvert offen abierto aperto	closed fermé geschlossen cerrado chiuso
tall grand groß alto alto	short court kurz bajo basso	full plein voll lleno pieno	empty vide leer vacío vuoto
high haut hoch alto alto	low bas niedrig bajo basso	new neuf neu nuevo nuovo	old vieux alt viejo vecchio
thick épais dick grueso spesso	thin mince dünn delgado sottile	light clair hell claro chiaro	dark foncé dunkel oscuro scuro
light léger leicht ligero leggero	heavy lourd schwer pesado pesante	easy facile leicht fácil facile	difficult difficile schwer difícil difficile
hard dur hart duro duro	soft mou weich blando morbido	free libre frei libre libero	occupied occupé besetzt ocupado occupato
wet humide nass húmedo bagnato	dry sec trocken seco asciutto	beginning le début der Anfang el principio l'inizio	end la fin das Ende el final la fine
good bon gut bueno buono	bad mauvais schlecht malo cattivo	strong fort stark fuerte forte	weak faible schwach débil debole
fast rapide schnell rápido veloce	slow lent langsam lento lento	fat gros dick gordo grasso	thin mince dünn delgado magro

useful phrases • phrases utiles • praktische Redewendungen • frases útiles • frasi utili

essential phrases • phrases essentielles • wesentliche Redewendungen • frases esenciales • frasi essenziali

Yes
Oui
Ja
Sí
Sì

No
Non
Nein
No
No

Maybe
Peut-être
Vielleicht
Quizá
Forse

Please
S'il vous plaît
Bitte
Por favor
Per favore

Thank you
Merci
Danke
Gracias
Grazie

You're welcome.
De rien.
Bitte sehr.
De nada.
Prego.

Excuse me.
Pardon.
Entschuldigung.
Perdone.
Permesso.

I'm sorry .
Je suis désolé.
Es tut mir Leid.
Lo siento.
Mi dispiace.

Don't
Ne... pas
Nicht
No
No

OK
D'accord
Okay
Okay
D'accordo

That's fine.
Très bien.
In Ordnung.
Está bien.
Vabbene.

That's correct.
C'est juste.
Das ist richtig.
Está bien.
È giusto.

That's wrong.
C'est faux.
Das ist falsch.
Está mal.
È sbagliato.

greetings • salutations • Begrüßungen • saludos • saluti

Hello
Bonjour
Guten Tag
Hola
Buongiorno

Goodbye
Au revoir
Auf Wiedersehen
Adiós
Arrivederci

Good morning
Bonjour
Guten Morgen
Buenos días
Buongiorno

Good afternoon
Bonjour
Guten Tag
Buenas tardes
Buon pomeriggio

Good evening
Bonsoir
Guten Abend
Buenas noches
Buona sera

Good night
Bonne nuit
Gute Nacht
Buenas noches
Buona notte

How are you?
Comment allez-vous?
Wie geht es Ihnen?
¿Cómo está?
Come sta?

My name is...
Je m'appelle...
Ich heiße...
Me llamo...
Mi chiamo...

What is your name?
Vous vous appelez comment?
Wie heißen Sie?
¿Cómo se llama?
Come si chiama?

Whis is his/her name?
Il/Elle s'appelle comment?
Wie heißt er/sie?
¿Cómo se llama?
Come si chiama lui/lei?

May I introduce...
Je vous présente...
Darf ich... vorstellen
Le presento a...
Le posso presentare...

This is...
C'est...
Das ist...
Este es...
Le presento...

Pleased to meet you
Enchanté
Angenehm
Encantado de conocerle
Piacere di conoscerla

See you later
À tout à l'heure
Bis später
Hasta luego
A più tardi

signs • panneaux • Schilder • letreros • insegne

Tourist information
Office de tourisme
Touristen-Information
Información
Ufficio informazioni turistiche

Entrance
Entrée
Eingang
Entrada
Entrata

Exit
Sortie
Ausgang
Salida
Uscita

Emergency exit
Sortie de secours
Notausgang
Salida de emergencia
Uscita di emergenza

Push
Poussez
Drücken
Empuje
Spingere

Danger
Danger
Lebensgefahr
Peligro
Pericolo

No smoking
Défense de fumer
Rauchen verboten
Prohibido fumar
Vietato fumare

Out of order
En panne
Außer Betrieb
Fuera de servicio
Guasto

Opening times
Heures d'ouverture
Öffnungszeiten
Horario de apertura
Orario di apertura

Free admission
Entrée gratuite
Eintritt frei
Entrada libre
Ingresso libero

Knock before entering
Frappez avant d'entrer
Bitte anklopfen
Llame antes de entrar
Bussare prima di entrare

Keep off the grass
Défense de marcher sur la pelouse
Betreten des Rasens verboten
Prohibido pisar el pasto
Non calpestare l'erba

help • assistance • Hilfe • ayuda • aiuto

Can you help me?
Pouvez-vous m'aider?
Können Sie mir helfen?
¿Me puede ayudar?
Mi può aiutare?

I don't understand.
Je ne comprends pas.
Ich verstehe nicht.
No entiendo.
Non capisco

I don't know.
Je ne sais pas.
Ich weiß nicht.
No lo sé.
Non lo so

Do you speak English, French…?
Vous parlez anglais, français…?
Sprechen Sie Englisch, Französisch…?
¿Habla inglés, francés…?
Parla inglese, francese...?

I speak English, Spanish…
Je parle anglais, espagnol…
Ich spreche Englisch, Spanisch…
Hablo inglés, español…
Parlo inglese, spagnolo...

Please speak more slowly.
Parlez moins vite, s'il vous plaît.
Sprechen Sie bitte langsamer.
Hable más despacio, por favor.
Parli più lentamente.

Please write it down for me.
Écrivez-le pour moi, s'il vous plaît.
Schreiben Sie es bitte für mich auf.
¿Me lo puede escribir?
Me lo scriva, per favore.

I have lost…
J'ai perdu…
Ich habe… verloren
He perdido…
Ho perso...

directions • directions • Richtungsangaben • indicaciones • indicazioni

I am lost.
Je me suis perdu.
Ich habe mich verlaufen.
Estoy perdido.
Mi sono perso/a.

Where is the…?
Où est le/la…?
Wo ist der/die/das…?
¿Dónde está el/la…?
Dov'è il/la...?

Where is the nearest…?
Où est le/la…le/la plus proche?
Wo ist der/die/das nächste…?
¿Dónde está el/la… más cercano/a?
Dov'è il/la ... più vicino/a?

Where are the toilets?
Où sont les toilettes?
Wo sind die Toiletten?
¿Dónde están los baños?
Dov'è il bagno?

How do I get to…?
Pour aller à…?
Wie komme ich nach…?
¿Cómo voy a…?
Come si arriva a...?

To the right
À droite
Nach rechts
A la derecha
A destra

To the left.
À gauche
Nach links
A la izquierda
A sinistra

Straight ahead
Tout droit
Geradeaus
Todo recto
Sempre dritto

How far is…?
C'est loin…?
Wie weit ist…?
¿A qué distancia está…?
Quant'è lontano...?

accommodation • logement • Unterkunft • alojamiento • alloggio

I have a reservation.
J'ai réservé une chambre.
Ich habe ein Zimmer reserviert.
Tengo una reservación.
Ho una prenotazione.

What time is breakfast?
Le petit déjeuner est à quelle heure?
Wann gibt es Frühstück?
¿A qué hora es el desayuno?
A che ora è la colazione?

Where is the dining room?
Où est la salle à manger?
Wo ist der Speisesaal?
¿Dónde está el comedor?
Dov'è la sala da pranzo?

eating and drinking • nourriture et boissons • Essen und Trinken • comida y bebida • cibo e bevande

Cheers!
À la vôtre!
Zum Wohl!
¡Salud!
Salute!

It's delicious/awful.
C'est délicieux/terrible.
Es ist köstlich/scheußlich.
Está buenísimo/malísimo.
È buonissimo/disgustoso.

I don't drink/smoke.
Je ne bois/fume pas.
Ich trinke/rauche nicht.
Yo no bebo/fumo.
Non bevo/fumo.

I don't eat meat.
Je ne mange pas de la viande.
Ich esse kein Fleisch.
Yo no como carne.
Non mangio la carne.

No more for me, thank you.
Je n'en veux plus, merci.
Nichts mehr, danke.
Ya no más, gracias.
Per me basta, grazie.

May I have some more?
Encore un peu, s'il vous plaît.
Könnte ich noch etwas mehr haben?
¿Puedo repetir?
Posso prenderne ancora?

May we have the check?
L'addition, s'il vous plaît.
Wir möchten bitte zahlen.
¿Me trae la cuenta?
Il conto, per favore.

Can I have a receipt?
Je voudrais un reçu.
Ich hätte gerne eine Quittung.
¿Me da un recibo?
Mi dà una ricevuta?

No-smoking area
Partie non-fumeurs
Nichtraucherbereich
Área de no fumar
Area riservata i non fumatori

English index • index anglais • englisches Register • índice inglés • indice inglese

A

à la carte 152
a shot 151
abdomen 12
abdominals 16
above 320
acacia 110
accelerator 200
access road 216
accessories 36, 38
accident 46
accordion file 173
account number 96
accountant 97, 190
accounting department 175
accused 180
ace 230, 273
Achilles tendon 16
acorn squash 125
acquaintance 24
acquitted 181
across 320
acrylic paints 274
actions 237, 229, 227, 233, 183
activities 263, 245, 162, 77
actor 254, 191
actors 179
actress 254
acupressure 55
acupunture 55
Adam's apple 19
add *v* 165
addition 58
address 98
adhesive bandage 47
adhesive tape 47, 173
adjustable wrench 80
admission charge 260
admissions office 168
admitted 48
adzuki beans 131
adult 23
advantage 230
adventure 255
advertisement 269
aerate *v* 91
Afghanistan 318
Africa 317
after 320
afternoon 305
aftershave 73
aftersun care 108
agate 289
agenda 174
aikido 236
aileron 210
air bag 201
air cylinder 239
air filter 202, 204
air letter 98
air mattress 267
air vent 210
air-conditioning 200
aircraft 210
aircraft carrier 215
airliner 210, 212
airport 212
aisle 106, 168, 210, 254
alarm clock 70
Alaska 314
Albania 316
alcoholic drinks 145
alfalfa 184
Algeria 317
Allen wrench 80
allergy 44
alley 298
all-purpose flour 139
allspice 132
almond 129
almond oil 134
almonds 151
along 320
alpine 87
alpine skiing 247
alternating current 60
alternative therapy 54
alternator 203
altitude 211
aluminum 289
Amazonia 312
ambulance 94
amethyst 288
amniocentesis 52
amniotic fluid 52
amount 96
amp 60
amphibians 294
amplifier 268
amusement park 262
analog 179
anchor 179, 191, 214, 240
Andes 312
Andorra 316
anesthetist 48
angle 164
angler 244
Angola 317
angry 25
animals 290, 292, 294
animated movie 255
ankle 13, 15
ankle-length 34
anniversary 26
annual 86, 307
answer 163
answer *v* 99, 163
answering machine 99
ant 295
antenatal 52
antenna 295
antifreeze 199, 203
Antigua and Barbuda 314
anti-inflammatory 109
antique store 114
antiseptic 47
antiseptic wipe 47
antiwrinkle 41
antler 291
apartment 59
apartment block 59, 298
apéritif 153
aperture dial 270
apex 165
app 99
appeal 181
appearance 30
appendix 18
appetizer 153
applaud *v* 255
apple 126
apple corer 68
apple juice 149
appliances 66
application 176
appointment 45, 175
apricot 126
April 306
apron 30, 50, 69, 212
aquamarine 288
Arabian Sea 313
arbor 84
arc 164
arch 15, 85, 301
archery 249
architect 190
architecture 300
architrave 301
Arctic circle 283
Arctic Ocean 312
area 165, 310
areas 299
arena 243
Argentina 315
arithmetic 165
arm 13
armchair 63
Armenia 318
armpit 13
armrest 200, 210
aromatherapy 55
around 320
arrangements 111
arrest 94
arrivals 213
arrow 249
art 162
art deco 301
art gallery 261
art history 169
art nouveau 301
art school 169
art store 115
artery 19
artichoke 124
artist 274
arts and crafts 274, 276
arugula 123
ash 283
ashtray 150
Asia 318
asparagus 124
assault 94
assistant 24
assistant chef 152
assisted delivery 53
asteroid 280
asthma 44
astigmatism 51
astronaut 281
astronomy 281
asymmetric bars 235
at 320
athlete 234
Atlantic Ocean 312
ATM 97
atmosphere 282, 286
atrium 104
attachment 177
attack 220
attack zone 224
attend *v* 174
attic 58
attractions 261
auburn 39
audience 254
August 306
aunt 22
aurora 286
Australasia 319
Australia 319
Austria 316
auto racing 249
automatic 200
automatic bill payment 96
automatic door 196
avalanche 247
avenue 299
avocado 128
awning 148
ax 95
axle 205
ayurveda 55
Azerbaijan 318

B

baby 23, 30
baby bath 74
baby carriage 75
baby care 74
baby changing room 104
baby monitor 75
baby products 107
baby sling 75
back 13
back brush 73
backboard 226
backdrop 254
backgammon 272
backhand 231
backpack 31, 37, 267
backseat 200
backstroke 239
backswing 233
bacon 118, 157
bad 321
badge 94
badminton 231
bag 311
bag cart 233
bagel 139
baggage carousel 212
baggage claim 213
baggage trailer 212
bags 37
Bahamas 314
Bahrain
bail 181
bailiff 180
bait 244
bait *v* 245
bake *v* 67, 138
baked 159
baker 139
bakery 107, 114, 138
baking 69
balance wheel 276
balcony 59, 254
bald 39
bale 184
Balearic Islands 316
ball 15, 75, 221,224, 226, 228, 230
ballboy 231
ballet 255
balsamic vinegar 135
Baltic Sea 313
bamboo 86,122
banana 128
bandage 47
Bangladesh 318
banister 59
bank 96, 284
bar 150, 152, 235, 250, 256, 311
bar code 106
bar mitzvah 26
bar snacks 151
bar stool 150
barb 244
Barbardos 314
barber 39, 188
bark 296
barley 130, 184
barman 191
barn 182
baroque 301
bars 74
bartender 150
basalt 288
base 164, 229
base coat 83
base station 99
baseball 228
baseline 230
baseman 228
basement 58
basil 133
basin 50
basket 106, 207, 226
basket of fruit 126
basketball 226
basketball player 226
bass clarinet 257
bass clef 256
bass guitar 258
bassoon 257
bat 225, 228, 231, 290
bat *v* 225, 229
bath towel 73
bathmat 72
bathrobe 32
bathrobe 73
bathroom 72
bathtub 72
baton 235, 256
batsman 225
batter 228
batteries 260
battery 167, 202
battery pack 78
battleship 215
bay leaf 133
be born *v* 26
beach 264
beach bag 264
beach ball 265
beach hut 264
beach towel 265

beach umbrella 264
beak 293
beaker 166, 167
beam 186, 235
bean sprout 122
beans 131, 144
bear 291
beat 259
beauty 40
beauty treatments 41
bed 70
bed and breakfast 101
bed linen 71
bedding 74
bedroom 70
bedside lamp 70
bedspread 70
bee 295
beech 296
beef 118
beer 145,151
beer tap 150
beet 125
beetle 295
before 320
beginning 321
behind 320
Belarus 316
Belgium 316
Belize 314
bell 197
below 320
belt 32, 36, 236
bench 250, 262
Benin 317
berry 296
beside 320
bet 273
between 320
beyond 320
Bhutan 318
biathlon 247
bib 30
bicep curl 251
biceps 16
bicycle 206
bidet 72
biennial 86
bifocal 51
big toe 15
bike rack 207
bikini 264
bill 97
binder file 173
binoculars 281
biology 162
biplane 211
birch 296
bird watching 263
birds 292
birth 52
birth certificate 26
birth weight 53
birthday 27
birthday cake 141
birthday candles 141
birthday party 27
bishop 272
bit 242
bit brace 78
bite 46
bite *v* 245
bitter 124, 145
black 39, 272, 274
black belt 237
black coffee 148
black hole 280
black olive 143
Black Sea 313
black tea 149
blackberry 127
blackcurrant 127
black-eyed peas 131
bladder 20
blade 60, 66, 78, 89
blanket 71, 74
blazer 33
bleach 77
blender 66
blister 46
block 237
block *v* 227
blonde 39
blood pressure 44
blood sausage 157
blood test 48
blouse 34
blow out *v* 141
blow-dry *v* 38
blow-dryer 38
blowhole 290
blue 274
blue cheese 136
bluebells 297
blueberry 127
blues 259
blush 40
board 241
board games 272
board *v* 217
boardwalk 265
boarding pass 213
bob 39
bobbin 276
bobby pin 38
bobsled 247
body 12
body lotion 73
body systems 19
bodywork 202
boil *v* 67
bok choy 123
Bolivia 315
bollard 214
bolt 59
bomber 211
bone 17, 119, 121
bone meal 88
boned 121
bongos 257
book 168
book bag 162
bookshelf 63, 168
bookstore 115
boom 95, 240
booster 281
boot 37
booties 30
bored 25
borrow *v* 168
Bosnia and Herzegovina 316
Botswana 317
bottle 61, 75, 135, 311
bottle opener 68, 150
bottled foods 134
bottled water 144
bottom tier 141
boundary line 225
bouquet 35, 111
bouquet garni 132
bout 237
boutique 115
bow 240, 249
bow tie 36
bowl 61, 65, 112
bowl *v* 225
bowler 225
bowling 249
bowling ball 249
box 254
box file 173
box of chocolates 113
box of tissues 70
box office 255
box spring 71
boxer shorts 33
boxercise 251
boxing 236
boxing gloves 237
boxing ring 237
boy 23
boyfriend 24
bra 35
bracelet 36
braces 50
braid 39
brain 19
brake 200, 204, 206
brake block 207
brake fluid reservoir 202
brake lever 207
brake pedal 205
brake *v* 207
bran 130
branch 175, 296
branch manager 96
brandy 145
brass 256
Brazil 315
brazil nut 129
bread 157
bread flour 139
bread knife 68
breadcrumbs 139
breadfruit 124
breads 138
break a record *v* 234
break water *v* 52
breakdown 203
breakfast 64, 156
breakfast buffet 156
breakfast cereals 107
breakfast table 156
breakfast tray 101
breast 12, 119
breast pump 53
breastbone 17
breastfeed *v* 53
breaststroke 239
breathing 47
breech 52
brick 187
bridge 15, 214, 258, 273, 300
bridle 242
Brie 142
briefcase 37
briefs 33, 35
brioche 157
broadcast 179
broadcast *v* 178
broccoli 123
brochure 175
brochures 96
brogan 37
bronze 235
brooch 36
broom 77
broth 158
brother 22
brother-in-law 23
browband 242
brown 274
brown bread 139, 149
brown lentils 131
brown rice 130
browse *v* 177
browser 177
bruise 46
Brunei 319
brunette 39
brush 38, 40, 77, 83, 274
brush *v* 38, 50
Brussels sprout 122
bubble bath 73
buckle 36
bud 111, 297
buffet 152
build *v* 186
buildings 299
bulb 86
Bulgaria 316
bull 185
bulldog clip 173
bulletin board 173
bull-nose pliers 80
bullseye 273
bumper 74, 198
bun 39, 139, 140, 155
bunch 111
bungalow 58
bungee jumping 248
bunker 232
bunsen burner 166
buoy 217
burger 154
burger meal 154
burglar alarm 58
burglary 94
Burkina Faso 317
Burma (Myanmar) 318
burn 46
burner 61, 67
Burundi 317
bus 196
bus driver 190
bus shelter 197
bus station 197
bus stop 197, 299
bus ticket 197
buses 196
business 175
business class 211
business deal 175
business lunch 175
business partner 24
business suit 32
business trip 175
businessman 175
businesswoman 175
bustier 35
busy 99
butcher 118, 188
butcher shop 114
butter 137, 156
buttercup 297
butterfly 239, 295
buttermilk 137
butternut squash 125
buttock 13, 16
button 32
buttonhole 32
buttress 301
by 320
by airmail 98
bytes 176

C

cab 95
cabbage 123
cabin 210, 214
Cabinda 317
cabinet 66
cable 79, 207
cable car 246
cable television 269
cactus 87
caddy 233
café 148, 262
cake pan 69
cake shop 114
cakes 140
calcite 289
calcium 109
calculator 165
calendar 306
calf 13, 16, 185
call button 48
calyx 297
cam belt 203
Cambodia 318
camcorder 260, 269
camel 291
Camembert 142
camera 178, 260, 270
camera case 271
camera crane 178
camera store 115
cameraman 178
cameraphone 270
Cameroon 317
camisole 35
camomile tea 149
camp stove 267
camp *v* 266
campari 145
camper 266
camper van 266
campfire 266
campground 266
camping 266
campus 168
can 145, 311
can opener 68
Canada 314
canary 292
candied fruit 129
candies 107
candy 113
candy store 113
cane 91
canes 89
canine 50
canned drink 154
canned goods 107
canoe 214
canola oil 135
canter 243
canvas 274
cap 36
capacity 311
Cape gooseberry 128
capers 143
capital 315
capoeira 237
capsize *v* 241
capsule 109
captain 214
captain 94
capuccino 148

car 198, 200
car accident 203
car rental 213
car stereo 201
car wash 198
caramel 113
caraway 131
card 27
card reader 97
cardamom 132
cardboard 275
cardigan 32
cardiology 49
cardiovascular 19
cards 273
cargo 216
Caribbean Sea 312
carnation 110
carnival 27
carpenter 188
carpet 71
carriage 208
carriage race 243
carrier (nursery) 75
carrier (motorcycle) 204
carrot 124
carry out 154
carry-on luggage 211, 213
cart 208, 213
cartilage 17
carton 311
cartoon 178
cartwheel 235
carve *v* 79
carving fork 68
case 51
cash register 106, 150
cash *v* 97
cashew nut 129
cashews 151
cashier 106
casino 261
Caspian Sea 313
cassava 124
casserole dish 69
cast 254
cast *v* 245
castle 300
casual 34
cat 290
catamaran 215
cataract 51
catch *v* 220, 227, 229, 245
catcher 229
caterpillar 295
cathedral 300
catheter 53
cattail 86
cauliflower 124
cave 284
CD 269
CD player 268
cedar 296
ceiling 62
celebration 140
celebrations 27
celeriac 124
celery 122
cell 181
cello 256
cellular phone 99
cement 186
cement mixer 186
center 164
center circle 222, 224, 226
center field 228
center line 226
centerboard 241
centimeter 310
centipede 295
Central Afrian Republic 317
century 307
cereal 130, 156
cervical cap 21
cervical vertebrae 17
cervix 20, 52
cesarean section 52
Chad 317
chain 36, 206
chair 64
chair *v* 174
chairlift 246
chalk 85, 162, 288
chalkboard 162
chamber 283
champagne 145
championship 230
change a tire *v* 203
change channels *v* 269
change gear *v* 207
change purse 37
change *v* 209
changing mat 74
channel 178
charcoal 266, 275
charge 94, 180
chart 48
chassis 203
check 96, 152
checkbook 96
checkers 272
check-in desk 213
check-in *v* 212
checking account 96
checkout 106
checkout counter 106
checkout desk 168
check-up 50
Cheddar 142
cheek 14
cheerleader 220
cheese 136, 156
chef 152, 190
chef's hat 190
chemist 108
chemistry 162
cherry 126
cherry picker 95
cherry tomato 124
chess 272
chessboard 272
chest 12
chest of drawers 70
chest press 251
chestnut 129
chewing gum 113
chick 185
chick peas 131
chicken 119, 185
chicken burger 155
chicken coop 185
chicken nuggets 155
chicken pox 44
chicory 122
child 23, 31
child latches 75
child seat 198, 207
child's meal 153
childbirth 53
children 23
children's clothing 30
children's department 104
children's ward 48
Chile 315
chili 124, 132
chili 143
chill 44
chimney 58
chin 14
china 105
China 318
chip *v* 233
chipboard 79
chiropractic 54
chisel 81, 275
chives 133
chocolate 113
chocolate bar 113
chocolate cake 140
chocolate chip 141
chocolate coated 140
chocolate milkshake 149
chocolate spread 135
choir 301
choke *v* 47
chop 119, 237
chorizo 143
christening 26
Christmas 27
chrysanthemum 110
chuck 78
church 298, 300
chutney 134
cider vinegar 135
cigar 112
cigarettes 112
cinch 242
cinder block 187
cinnamon 133
circle 165
circuit training 251
circular saw 78
circumference 164
cistern 61
citrus fruit 126
city 299
clam 121
clamp 78, 166
clamp stand 166
clapper board 179
clarinet 257
clasp 36
clasp 37
class 163
classical music 255, 259
classroom 162
claw 291
clay 85, 275
clean clothes 76
clean *v* 77
cleaned 121
cleaner 188
cleaning equipment 77
cleaning fluid 51
cleanser 41
clear honey 134
cleat 220, 223
cleat 240
clementine 126
client 38, 175, 180
cliff 285
climber 263
climber 87
clinic 48
clipboard 173
clitoris 20
clock radio 70
closed 260, 321
closet 71
cloth diaper 30
clothesline 76
clothespin 76
clothing 205
cloud 287
cloudy 286
clove 125
clover 297
cloves 133
club 273
club sandwich 155
clubhouse 232
clutch 200, 204
coal 288
coast 285
coast guard 217
coaster 150
coat 32
coat hanger 70
cockatoo 293
cockle 121
cockpit 210
cockroach 295
cocktail 151
cocktail shaker 150
cocoa powder 148
coconut 129
cocoon 295
cod 120
coffee 144, 148, 153, 156, 184
coffee cup 65
coffee machine 148, 150
coffee milkshake 149
coffee spoon 153
coffee table 62
coffee with cream 148
cog 206
coin 97
coin return 99
cola 144
colander 68
cold 44, 286, 321
cold faucet 72
cold-pressed oil 135
collage 275
collar 32
collarbone 17
colleague 24
college 168
Colombia 315
colony 315
colored pencil 163
colors 39, 274
comb 38
comb *v* 38
combat sports 236
combine 182
comedy 255
comet 280
comforter 71
comic 112
commission 97
communications 98
commuter 208
Comoros 317
compact 40
company 175
compartment 209
compass 165, 312, 240
complaint 94
complexion 41
compliments slip 173
compost 88
compost heap 85
computer 176
concealer 40
conceive *v* 20
conception 52
concert 255, 258
concourse 209
concussion 46
condensed milk 136
conditioner 38
condom 21
conducter's cabin 208
conductor 256
cone 164, 187
confectionery 113
confident 25
confused 25
conglomerate 288
Congo 317
conifer 86
connect *v* 177
connection 212
conning tower 215
console 269
constellation 281
construction 186
construction site 186
construction worker 186, 188
consultant 49
consultation 45
contact lenses 51
container 216, 311
container ship 215
containerport 216
continent 282, 315
contraception 21, 52
contraction 52
control tower 212
controller 269
controls 201, 204
convertible 199
cooked meat 118, 143
cookie 113
cookie sheet 69
cookies 141
cooking 67
coolant reservoir 202
cooling rack 69
copilot 211
copper 289
copy *v* 172
coral reef 285
cordless phone 99
core 127
coriander 133
cork 134
corkscrew 150
corn 122, 124, 130, 184
corn bread 139
corn oil 135
cornea 51
corner 223
corner flag 223
cornice 300
corset 35
Corsica 316
cosmetics 105
Costa Rica 314
costume 255
cot 266
cottage cheese 136
cotton 184, 277
cotton balls 41
cough 44
cough medicine 108
counselor 55
count *v* 165
counter 96, 98, 100, 142, 272

countertop 66
country 259, 315
couple 24
courier 99
courses 153
court 226
court case 180
court date 180
court official 180
courtroom 180
courtyard 58, 84
couscous 130
cousin 22
cover v 227
coveralls 83
cow 185
cow's milk 136
crab 121, 295
cracked wheat 130
crafts 275
cramp 239
cramps 44
cranberry 127
crane 187, 216, 292
crater 283
crayfish 121
cream 109, 137, 140
cream cheese 136
crease 225
credit card 96
creel 245
creeper 87
crème caramel 141
crepes 155, 157
crescent moon 280
crew 241
crew hatch 281
crew neck 33
crib 74
cricket 225, 295
cricket ball 225
cricket player 225
crime 94
criminal 181
criminal record 181
crisp 127
crispbread 139, 156
crisper 67
Croatia 316
crochet 277
crochet hook 277
crockery 64
crockery and cutlery 65
crocodile 293
crocodile clip 167
croissant 156
crop 39, 183
crop farm 183
crops 184
crossbar 207, 222
cross-country skiing 247
crosswalk 195
crow 292
crown 50
crucible 166
crushed 132
crust 139, 282
cry v 25
crystal healing 55
Cuba 314
cube 164
cucumber 125
cuff 32, 45
cufflink 36
cultivate v 91
cultivator 182
cumin 132
curb 298
cured 118, 159, 143
curling 247
curling iron 38
curly 39
currant 129
currency exchange 97
curry 158
curry powder 132
curtain 63, 254
curved 165
custard 140
custard pie 141
customer 96, 104, 106, 152
customer service department 175
customer services 104
customs 212
customs house 216
cut 46
cut v 38, 79, 277
cuticle 15
cutlery 64
cuts 119
cutting 91
cutting board 68
cuttlefish 121
cycle lane 206
cycle v 207
cycling 263
cylinder 164
cylinder head 202
cymbals 257
Cyprus 316
Czech Republic 316

D

daffodil 111
dairy 107
dairy farm 183
dairy products 136
daisy 110, 297
dam 300
dance 259
dance school 169
dancer 191
dandelion 123, 297
dandruff 39
dark 41, 321
dark chocolate 113
darkroom 271
darn v 277
dartboard 273
darts 273
dashboard 201
date 129, 306
date book 175
daughter 22
daughter-in-law 22
dawn 305
day 305, 306
dead ball line 221
deadhead v 91
deal v 273
debit card 96
decade 307
decay 50
December 306
deciduous 86
decimal 165
deck 214
deck 85
deck chair 265
deck of cards 273
decorating 82
decoration 141
decorator 82
deep end 239
deep fried 159
deep sea fishing 245
deer 291
defendant 181
defender 223
defending zone 224
defense 181, 220
defrost v 67
degree 169
delay 209
deli 107
delicatessen 142
delivery 52, 98, 154
deltoid 16
Democratic Republic of the Congo 317
Denmark 316
denomination 97
denominator 165
dental care 108
dental floss 50, 72
dental hygiene 72
dental x-ray 50
dentist 50, 189
dentist's chair 50
dentures 50
deodorant 73
deodorants 108
department 169
department store 105
departments 49
departure lounge 213
departures 213
deposit slips 96
deposit v 96
depth 165
dermatology 49
descaled 121
desert 285
designer 191, 277
desk 162, 172
desktop 177
dessert 153
dessert cart 152
dessert plate 65
dessert rice 130
desserts 140
destination 213
detective 94
detergent 77
detour 195
deuce 230
develop v 271
diabetes 44
diagonal 164
dial v 99
diameter 164
diamond 273, 288
diaper 75
diaper bag 75
diaper rash cream 74
diaphragm 19, 21
diarrhea 44, 109
dice 272
dictionary 163
die v 26
diesel 199
diesel train 208
difficult 321
dig v 90, 227
digestive 19
digital 179, 269
digital camera 270
digital projector 163
digital radio 268
dilation 52
dill 133
dimensions 165
dimple 15
dining car 209
dining room 64, 168
dinner 64, 158
dinner menu 152
dinner plate 65
diopter 51
diploma 169
dipstick 202
direct current 60
direct deposit 96
directions 260
director 254
dirt bike 205
dirty laundry 76
disabled parking place 195
discharged 48
disconnected 99
discus 234
discuss v 163
disembark v 217
dishwasher 66
disinfectant solution 51
dispenser 150
disposable 109
disposable camera 270
disposable diaper 30
disposable razor 73
dissertation 169
distance 310
distributor 203
district 315
dive 239
dive v 238
diver 238
divide v 165
divided by 165
divided highway 195
dividends 97
divider 173, 194
diving board 238
divorce 26
Diwali 27
DJ 179
Djibouti 317
do not bend v 98
dock 214, 216
dock v 217
doctor 45, 189
doctor's office 45
doctorate 169
documentary 178
dog 290
dogsledding 247
doll 75
dollhouse 75
dolphin 290
dome 300
domestic flight 212
Dominica 314
Dominican Republic 314
dominoes 273
donkey 185
door 196, 198, 209
door chain 59
door knob 59
door knocker 59
door lock 200
doorbell 59
doormat 59
dormer 58
dorsal fin 294
dosage 109
double 151
double bass 256
double bassoon 257
double bed 71
double room 100
double-decker bus 196
doubles 230
dough 138
Dover sole 120
down 320
downhill skiing 247
download v 177
dragonfly 295
drain 61
drain 61, 72, 299
drain board 67
drain valve 61
drainage 91
draw 223
draw v 162
drawer 66, 70, 172
drawing 275
dress 31, 34
dressage 243
dressed 159
dressed chicken 119
dressing 47, 158
dribble v 223
dribble v 227
dried 129
dried flowers 111
dried fruit 156
drill 50
drill bit 78
drill bits 80
drill v 79
drinking cup 75
drinking fountain 262
drinks 107, 144, 156
drip 53
drive shaft 202
drive v 195, 233
driver 196
driver's seat 196
drop anchor v 217
dropper 167
dropshot 230
drown v 239
drum 258
drum kit 258
drummer 258
dry 39, 41, 130, 145, 286, 321
dry cleaner 115
dry dock 217
dry v 76
DTV box 269
duck 119, 185
duck egg 137
duckling 185
due date 168
duffel coat 31
duffle bag 37
dugout 229
dumbbell 251
dump truck 187
dunk v 227
duodenum 18
duplex 58
dusk 305
dust cloth 77
dust v 77
dustpan 77
duty-free store 213
DVD 269

DVD player 268
dyed 39
dynamo 207

E

eagle 292
ear 14
Ear Nose and Throat 49
early
earring 36
Earth 280, 282
earthenware dish 69
earthquake 283
easel 174, 274
east 312
East Timor 319
Easter 27
easy 321
easy-to-cook 130
eat in 154
eat *v* 64
eating 75
eau de toilette 41
eaves 58
éclair 140
eclipse 280
economics 169
economy class 211
Ecuador 315
eczema 44
Edam 142
edge 246
editor 191
eel 294
egg 20
egg white 137
eggcup 65, 137
eggplant 125
eggs 137
Egypt 317
eight 308
eight hundred 308
eighteen 308
eighteenth 309
eighth 309
eightieth 309
eighty 308
ejaculatory duct 21
El Salvador 314
elbow 13
electric blanket 71
electric blood pressure gauge 45
electric car 199
electric drill 78
electric guitar 258
electric meter 60
electric razor 73
electric shock 46
electric train 208
electrical goods 107
electrical tape 81
electrician 188
electricity 60
electronics 105
elephant 291
elevator 59, 100, 104
eleven 308
eleventh 309
elliptical trainer 250
elm 296
email 98, 177
email account 177
email address 177
embarrassed 25
embossed paper 83
embroidery 277
embryo 52
emerald 288
emergency 46
emergency exit 210
emergency lever 209
emergency phone 195
emergency room 48
emergency services 94
emigrate *v* 26
emotions 25
employee 24
employer 24
empty 321
enamel 50
encore 255
encyclopedia 163
end 321
end zone 220
endive 123
endline 226
endocrine 19
endocrinology 49
energy-saving bulb 60
engaged couple 24
engine 202, 204, 208, 210
engine room 214
engineering 169
English breakfast 157
English garden 84
English horn 257
english mustard 135
engraving 275
enlarge *v* 172
enlargement 271
entrance 59
entrance ramp 194
envelope 98, 173
environment 280
epidural 52
epiglottis 19
epilepsy 44
episiotomy 52
equals 165
equation 165
equator 283
equipment 165
equipment 233, 238
Equitorial Guinea 317
equity 97
eraser 163
Eritrea 317
erupt *v* 283
escalator 104
esophagus 19
espresso 148
essay 163
essential oils 55
Estonia 316
estuary 285
Ethiopia 317
eucalyptus 296
Europe 316
evening 305
evening dress 34
events 243, 247
evergreen 86
evidence 181
examination 163
excess baggage 212
exchange rate 97
excited 25
excuse me 322
executive 174
exercise bike 250
exercises 251
exfoliate *v* 41
exhaust pipe 203, 204
exhibit *v* 261
exhibition 261
exit 210
exit ramp 194
exosphere 286
expectant 52
experiment 166
expiration date 109
exposure 271
extend *v* 251
extension cord 78
exterior 198
external hard drive 176
extra time 223
extraction 50
eye 14, 51, 244, 276
eye dropper 109
eye drops 109
eye shadow 40
eye test 51
eyebrow 14, 51
eyebrow brush 40
eyebrow pencil 40
eyecup 269
eyelash 14, 51
eyelet 37
eyelid 51
eyeliner 40
eyepiece 167

F

fabric 277
fabric conditioner 76
face 14
face cream 73
face mask 225
face pack 41
face powder 40
face-off circle 224
facial 41
facial composite 181
factory 299
faint *v* 25, 44
fair 41, 262
fairway 232
falcon 292
Falkland Islands 315
fall 237
fall 31, 307
fall in love *v* 26
Fallopian tube 20
family 22
famous ruin 261
fan 60, 202
fan belt 203
fans 258
far 320
fare 197, 209
farm 182, 183, 184
farmer 182, 189
farmhouse 182
farmland 182
farmyard 182
farsighted 51
fashion 277
fast 321
fast food 154
fast food restaurant 154
fast-forward 269
fat 119, 321
fat-free 137
fat-free milk 136
father 22
father-in-law 23
faucet 61, 66
fault 230
fava bean 122
fava beans 131
fax 98
fax machine 172
feather 293
feature film 269
February 306
feed *v* 183
feijoa 128
female 12, 20
feminine hygene 108
femur 17
fence 85, 182, 243
fencing 249
feng shui 55
fennel 122, 133
fennel seeds 133
fenugreek 132
fern 86
ferry terminal 216
ferryboat 215, 216
fertilization 20
fertilize *v* 91
fertilizer 91
festivals 27
fetus 52
fever 44
fiancé 24
fiancée 24
fiber 127
fibula 17
field 182, 222, 228, 234
field hockey 224
field *v* 225, 229
fifteen 308
fifteenth 309
fifth 309
fiftieth 309
fifty 308
fifty five thousand, five hundred 309
fifty thousand 309
fig 129
fighter plane 211
figure skating 247
figurine 260
Fiji 319
file 81, 177
filing cabinet 172
fill *v* 82
filler 83
fillet 119, 121
filleted 121
filling 50, 140, 155
film 260, 271
film chamber 270
film set 179
film spool 271
filo dough 140
filter 270
filter coffee 148
filter paper 167
fin 210
finance 97
financial advisor 97
fingerprint 94
finial 300
finish line 234
Finland 316
fire 95
fire alarm 95
fire department 95
fire engine 95
fire escape 95
fire extinguisher 95
fire station 95
firefighters 95
firelighter 266
fireman 189
fireplace 63
firm 124
first 309
first aid 47
first aid kit 47
fish 107, 120, 294
fish and chips 155
fish counter 114
fish farm 183
fish seller 120
fish spatula 68
fisherman 189
fishhook 244
fishing 244, 245
fishing boat 217
fishing license 245
fishing port 217
fishing rod 244
fishmonger 188
fist 15, 237
fitness 250
fitting room 104
five 308
five hundred 308
flag 221, 232
flageolet beans 131
flakes 132
flamingo 292
flan pan 69
flare 240
flash 270
flash gun 270
flashlight 267
flat 256
flat race 243
flat tire 203, 207
flatbread 139
flatscreen TV 269
flavored oil 134
flax 184
fleece 74
flesh 127, 129
flex *v* 251
flight attendant 190
flight attendant 210
flight number 213
flint 288
flipchart 174
flip-flop 37
flipper 239, 290
float 244
float ball 61
flock 183
flood 287
floor 58, 62, 71
floor exercises 235
floor plan 261
florentine 141
floret 122
florist 110, 188
floss *v* 50
flours 138
flower 297
flowerbed 85, 90
flowering plant 297
flowering shrub 87
flowers 110
flu 44
flute 139, 257
fly 244, 295
fly fishing 245

fly sheet 266
fly v 211
foal 185
focus v 271
focusing knob 167
fog 287
foil 249
folder 177
foliage 110
folk music 259
follicle 20
font 177
food 118, 130, 149
food processor 66
foot 12, 15, 310
football 220
football field 220
football player 220
footboard 71
footpath 262
foot pedal 257
footstrap 241
for 320
forceps 53, 167
forearm 12
forecourt 199
forehand 231
forehead 14
foreign currency 97
foreskin 21
forest 285
fork 65, 88, 153, 207
forklift 186, 216
formal 34
formal garden 84
formal gardens 262
fortieth 309
forty 308
forty minutes
forward 222
foul 222, 226
foul ball 228
foul line 229
foundation 40
fountain 85
four 308
four hundred 308
four-door 200
fourteen 308
fourteenth 309
fourth 309
four-wheel drive 199
fox 290
foxglove 297
fraction 165
fracture 46
fragile 98
fragranced 130
frame 51, 62, 206, 230, 267
France 316
freckle 15
free 321
free kick 222
free range 118
free weights 250
freesia 110
free-throw line 226
freeze 287
freeze v 67
freezer 67
freight train 208
freighter 215
French twist 39
French bread 138
French fries 154
French Guiana 315
French horn 257
french mustard 135
French press 65
French toast 157
frequency 179
fresh 121, 127, 130
fresh cheese 136
fresh fruit 157
freshwater fishing 245
fret 258
fretsaw 81
Friday 306
fried 159
fried chicken 155
fried egg 157
friend 24
frieze 301
frog 294
from 320
front crawl 239
front door 58
front wheel 196
frontal 16
frost 287
froth 148
frown 25
frozen 121, 124
frozen food 107
frozen yogurt 137
fruit 126, 128
fruit bread 139
fruit cake 140
fruit farm 183
fruit juice 127, 156
fruit pie 140
fruit yogurt 157
fruits 107
fry v 67
frying pan 69
fuel gauge 201
fuel tank 204
full 64, 266, 321
full board 101
full moon 280
fumble 220
funeral 26
funnel 166, 214
furniture store 115
furrow 183
fuse 60
fuse box 60, 203
fuselage 210

G

gable 300
Gabon 317
Galápagos Islands 315
galaxy 280
gale 286
galley 214
gallon 311
gallop 243
galoshes 31
galvanized 79
Gambia 317
game 119, 230, 273
game show 178
games 272
gangway 214
garage 58, 199, 203
garbage can 67
garden 84, 261
garden center 115
garden features 84
garden plants 86
garden styles 84
gardener 188
gardening 90
gardening basket 88
gardening gloves 89
gardening tools 88
garland 111
garlic 125, 132
garlic press 68
garnet 288
garter belt 35
garters 35
gas pump 199
gas station 199
gas tank 203
gasket 61
gasoline 199
gate 85, 182, 247
gate number 213
gauze 47, 167
gear lever 207
gearbox 202, 204
gears 206
gearshift 201
gel 38, 109
gems 288
generation 23
generator 60
genitals 12
geography 162
geometry 165
Georgia 318
gerbera 110
Germany 316
get a job v 26
get married v 26
get up v 71
geyser 285
Ghana 317
giant slalom 247
gift store 114
gill 294
gin 145
gin and tonic 151
ginger 125, 133
giraffe 291
girder 186
girl 23
girlfriend 24
glacier 284
gladiolus 110
gland 19
glass 69, 152
glass bottle 166
glass rod 167
glasses 51, 150
glassware 64
glaze v 139
glider 211, 248
gliding 248
gloss 83, 271
glove 224, 228, 233, 236, 246
gloves 36
glue 275
glue gun 78
gneiss 288
go to bed v 71
go to sleep v 71
goal 221, 223, 224
goal area 223
goal line 220, 223, 224
goalkeeper 222, 224
goalpost 220, 222
goat 185
goat's cheese 142
goat's milk 136
goggles 238, 247
going out 75
gold 235, 289
goldfish 294
golf 232
golf bag 233
golf ball 233
golf cart 232
golf clubs 233
golf course 232
golf shoe 233
golfer 232
gong 257
good 321
good afternoon 322
good evening 322
good morning 322
good night 322
goodbye 322
goose 119, 293
goose egg 137
gooseberry 127
gorge 284
gorilla 291
Gothic 301
gown 38
grade 163
graduate 169
graduate v 26
graduation ceremony 169
graft v 91
grains 130
gram 310
grandchildren 23
granddaughter 22
grandfather 22
grandmother 22
grandparents 23
grandson 22
granite 288
grape juice 144
grapefruit 126
grapeseed oil 134
graphite 289
grass 86, 262
grass bag 88
grasshopper 295
grassland 285
grate v 67
grated cheese 136
grater 68
gratin dish 69
gravel 88
gravity 280
gray 39, 274
graze 46
greasy 39
Greece 316
green 129, 232, 274
green bean 122
green olive 143
green salad 158
green tea 149
greengrocer 188
greenhouse 85
Greenland 314
Grenada 314
griddle 69
grill 267
grill v 67
grilled 159
grip 78
groceries 105, 106
grocery cart 106
grocery store 114
groin 12
groom 243
ground 132
ground 60
ground beef 119
ground cloth 267
ground coffee 144
ground cover 87
ground floor 104
group therapy 55
grout 83
guard 236
guardrail 195
Guatemala 314
guava 128
guest 64, 100
guidebook 260
guided tour 260
guilty 181
Guinea 317
Guinea-Bissau 317
guitarist 258
gull 292
gum 50
gumdrop 113
gun 94
gurney 48
gutter 58, 299
guy rope 266
Guyana 315
gym 101, 250
gym machine 250
gymnast 235
gymnastics 235
gynecologist 52
gynecology 49
gypsophila 110

H

hacksaw 81
haddock 120
hail 286
hair 14, 38
hair band 39
hair dye 40
hair salon 115
hair straightener 38
hairdresser 38, 188
hairspray 38
Haiti 314
half an hour 304
half board 101
half-and-half 137
half-liter 311
halftime 223
hallibut fillets 120
Halloween 27
hallway 59
halter 243
halter neck 35
ham 119, 143, 156
hammer 80
hammer v 79
hammock 266
hamper 263
hamster 290
hamstring 16
hand 13, 15
hand drill 81
hand fork 89
hand rail 59
hand saw 89
hand towel 73
handbag 37
handcuffs 94
handicap 233
handkerchief 36

handle 36, 88, 106, 187, 200, 230
handle 61
handlebar 207
handles 37
handrail 196
handsaw 80
handset 99
hang *v* 82
hang-glider 248
hang-gliding 248
hanging basket 84
hanging file 173
happy 25
harbor 217
harbormaster 217
hard 129, 321
hard candy 113
hard cheese 136
hard cider 145
hard hat 186
hard shoulder 194
hardboard 79
hardware 176
hardware store 114
hardwood 79
harness race 243
harp 256
harvest *v* 91, 183
hat 36
hatchback 199
have a baby *v* 26
Hawaii 314
hay 184
hay fever 44
hazard 195
hazard lights 201
hazelnut 129
hazelnut oil 134
head 12, 19, 81, 230
head injury 46
head office 175
head *v* 222
headache 44
headband 38
headboard 70
headlight 198, 205
headphones 268
headrest 200
headsail 240
health 44
health center 168
health food store 115
heart 18, 119, 122, 273
heart attack 44
heater controls 201
heather 297
heating element 61
heavy 321
heavy metal 259
hedge 85, 90, 182
hedgehog 290
heel 13, 15, 37
height 165
helicopter 211
hello 322
helmet 95, 204, 206, 220, 224, 228
hem 34
hematite 289
hemorrhage 46
hen's egg 137
herb 55, 86
herb garden 84
herbaceous border 85
herbal remedies 108
herbal tea 149
herbalism 55
herbicide 183
herbs 133, 134
herbs & spices 132
herd 183
hexagon 164
high 321
high chair 75
high-definition 269
high dive 239
high heel shoe 37
high jump 235
high speed train 208
highlights 39
highway 194
hiking 263
hiking boots 267
hill 284
Himalayas 313
hip 12
hippopotamus 291
historic building 261
history 162
hit *v* 224
hobby knife 81
hockey 224
hockey stick 224
hoe 88
hold 215, 237
hole 232
hole in one 233
hole punch 173
holly 296
home 58
home entertainment 268
home furnishings 105
home plate 228
homeopathy 55
homework 163
homogenized 137
Honduras 314
honeycomb 135
honeymoon 26
honeysuckle 297
hood 198
hood 31, 75
hoof 242, 291
hook 187, 276
hoop 226, 277
horizontal bar 235
hormone 20
horn 201, 204, 291
horror movie 255
horse 185, 235, 242
horseback riding 242, 263
horserace 243
horseradish 125
horseshoe 242
hose 89
hose 95
hose reel 89
hospital 48
host 64, 178
hostess 64
hot 60, 124, 286, 321
hot chocolate 144
hot cocoa 156
hot dog 155
hot drinks 144
hot faucet 72
hot-air balloon 211
hot-dog stand 154
hotel 100, 264
hot-water bottle 70
hour 304
hour hand 304
house 58
household current 60
household products 107
hovercraft 215
hub 206
hubcap 202
hull 214, 240
human resources department 175
humerus 17
humid 286
hummingbird 292
hump 291
hundred 308
hundred and ten 308
hundred thousand 308
hundredth 309
Hungary 316
hungry 64
hurdles 235
hurricane 287
husband 22
husk 130
hydrant 95
hydrofoil 215
hydrotherapy 55
hypnotherapy 55
hypoallergenic 41
hypotenuse 164

I

ice 120, 287
ice and lemon 151
ice bucket 150
ice climbing 247
ice cream 137, 149
ice cube 151
ice hockey 224
ice hockey player 224
ice hockey rink 224
Iceland 317
ice maker 67
ice skate 224
ice-cream scoop 68
iced coffee 148
iced tea 149
ice-skating 247
icicle 287
icing 141
icon 177
identity card 189
identity tag 53
igneous 288
ignition 200
iguana 293
illness 44
immigration 212
impotent 20
in 320
in brine 143
in front of 320
in oil 143
in sauce 159
in syrup 159
inbox 177
inch 310
incisor 50
incubator 53
index finger 15
India 318
Indian Ocean 312
indigo 274
Indonesia 319
induce labor *v* 53
industrial park 299
infection 44
infertile 20
infield 228
inflatable dinghy 215
inflatable ring 265
information 261
information screen 213
in-goal area 221
inhaler 44, 109
injection 48
injury 46
ink 275
ink pad 173
inlet 61
inline skating 249
inner core 282
inner tube 207
inning 228
innocent 181
inoculation 45
inquiries 168
insect repellent 108, 267
inside 320
inside lane 194
insomnia 71
install *v* 177
instep 15
instructions 109
instruments 256, 258
insulation 61
insulin 109
insurance 203
intensive care unit 48
inter-city train 209
intercom 59
intercostal 16
intercourse 20
interest rate 96
interior 200
intermissionl 254
internal systems 60
international flight 212
Internet 177
intersection 298
interviewer 179
into 320
in-tray 172
invertebrates 295
investigation 94
investment 97
ionosphere 286
iPad© 176
iPod© 268
Iran 318
Iraq 318
Ireland 316
iris 51, 110
iron 76, 109, 233, 289
iron *v* 76
ironing board 76
island 282
Israel 318
Italy 316
itinerary 260
IUD 21
Ivory Coast 317

J

jack 203, 273
jacket 32, 34
jade 288
jam 134, 156
Jamaica 314
January 306
Japan 318
jar 134, 311
javelin 234
jaw 14, 17
jazz 259
jeans 31
jelly bean 113
jellyfish 295
Jerusalem artichoke 125
jet 288
jet-skiing 241
jetty 217
jetway 212
jeweler 188
jewelry 36
jewelry box 36
jewelry making 275
jewelry store 114
jigsaw 78
jigsaw puzzle 273
jodhpurs 242
jog in place 251
jogging 251, 263
joint 17, 119
joker 273
Jordan 318
journal 168
journalist 190
judge 180
judo 236
juices and milkshakes 149
juicy 127
July 306
jump 237, 243
jump ball 226
jump *v* 227
jumping rope 251
junction 194
June 306
Jupiter 280
jury 180
jury box 180

K

kabob 155, 158
kale 123
kangaroo 291
karate 236
Kaliningrad 316
kayak 241
kayaking 241
Kazakhstan 318
keel 214
keep net 244
kendo 236
Kenya 317
kernel 122, 129, 130
ketchup 135, 154
kettledrum 257
key 59, 176, 207
keyboard 176, 258
keypad 97. 99
kick 237, 239
kick *v* 221, 223
kickboard 238
kickboxing 236
kickstand 207
kid 185
kidney 18, 119
kidney beans 131
kilogram 310
kilometer 310
king 272, 273
king prawn 121
kitchen 66, 152
kitchenware 68, 105
kitten 290
kiwifruit 128

knead v 138
knee 12
knee support 227
kneecap 17
knee-length 34
kneepad 205
knickers 35
knife 65
knife sharpener 68, 118
knight 272
knitting 277
knitting needle 277
knockout 237
knuckle 15
koala 291
kohlrabi 123
koi carp 294
Kosovo 316
kumquat 126
kung fu 236
Kuwait 318
Kyrgyzstan 318

L

labels 89
labia 20
laboratory 166
lace 35, 37
lace bobbin 277
lace making 277
lace-up 37
lacrosse 249
lactose 137
ladder 95, 186
ladle 68
lady fingers 141
ladybug 295
lake 285
lamb 118, 185
lamp 62
land 282
land v 211
landing 59
landing gear 210
landing net 244
landlord 58
landscape 271, 284
landscape v 91
lane 234, 238
languages 162
lantern 217
Laos 318
lapel 32
laptop 176
larch 296
large 321
large intestine 18
larynx 19
last week 307
lat 16
late 305
later 304
latex paint 83
latitude 283
Latvia 316
laugh v 25
launch 281
launch pad 281
laundromat 115
laundry 76
laundry basket 76
laundry service 101
lava 283
law 169, 180
lawn 85, 90
lawn rake 88
lawnmower 88, 90
lawyer 180, 190
lawyer's office 180
laxative 109
lead singer 258
leaded 199
leaf 122, 296
league 223
lean meat 118
learn v 163
leather shoes 32
leathers 205
Lebanon 318
lecture hall 169
lecturer 169
leek 125
left 260
left field 228
left-hand drive 201
leg 12, 119
leg pad 225
leg press 251
legal advice 180
legal department 175
leggings 31
leisure 258, 254, 264
lemon 126
lemon curd 134
lemon grass 133
lemon sole 120
lemonade 144
length 165, 310
lens 270
lens (eye) 51
lens (glasses) 51
lens cap 270
lens case 51
Lesotho 317
let! 231
letter 98
letter slot 99
letterhead 173
lettuce 123
level 80
lever 150
Liberia 317
librarian 168, 190
library 168, 299
library card 168
Libya 317
license plate 198
licorice 113
lid 61, 66
Liechtenstein 316
life events 26
life jacket 240
life preserver 240
life raft 240
lifeboat 214
lifeguard 239, 265
lifeguard tower 265
ligament 17
light 178, 207, 321
light a fire v 266
light aircraft 211
light meter 270
light switch 201
lighter 112
lighthouse 217
lighting 105
lightning 287
lights 94
lily 110
lima beans 131
lime 126, 296
limestone 288
limousine 199
line 244
line of credit 96
line of play 233
linen 277
linen basket 76
linens 105
lines 165
linesman 223, 230
lingerie 35, 105
lining 32
lining paper 83
link 36
lintel 186
lion 291
lip 14
lip brush 40
lip gloss 40
lip liner 40
lipstick 40
liqueur 145
liquid 77
liquid measure 311
liquor store 115
liter 311
literature 162, 169
Lithuania 316
little finger 15
little toe 15
live 178
live rail 209
liver 18, 118
livestock 183, 185
living room 62
lizard 293
load v 76
loaf 139
loan 96, 168
lob 230
lobby 100, 255
lobster 121, 295
lock 59, 207
lockers 239
lockup 94
log on v 177
loganberry 127
logo 31
loin 121
lollipop 113
long 32
long jump 235
long wave 179
long-grain 130
long-handled shears 88
longitude 283
loom 277
loose leaf tea 144
lose v 273
loser 273
lotion 109
lottery tickets 112
love 230
low 321
luge 247
luggage 100, 198, 213
luggage department 104
luggage hold 196
luggage rack 100
luggage rack 209
lumbar vertebrae 17
lunar module 281
lunch 64
lunch menu 152
lung 18
lunge 251
lupins 297
lure 244
Luxembourg 316
lychee 128
lymphatic 19
lyrics 259

M

macadamia 129
mace 132
Macedonia 316
machine gun 189
machinery 187
mackerel 120
macramé 277
Madagascar 317
magazine 112
magazines 107
magma 283
magnesium 109
magnet 167
maid service 101
mail carrier 98, 190
mailbag 98, 190
mailbox 58, 99
mailbox 99
main course 153
mainsail 240
make a flight reservation v 212
make a will v 26
make friends v 26
make the bed v 71
makeup 40
making bread 138
malachite 288
Malawi 317
Malaysia 318
Maldives 318
male 12, 21
Mali 317
mallet 78, 275
malt vinegar 135
Malta 316
malted drink 144
mammals 290
man 23
manager 24, 174
manager's office 266
managing director 175
Manchego 142
mane 242, 291
mango 128
mangosteen 128
manhole 299
manicure 41
mantle 282
manual 200
map 261
maple 296
maple syrup 134
maracas 257
marathon 234
marble 288
March 306
margarine 137
marina 217
marinated 143, 159
marine fishing 245
marjoram 133
market 115
marketing department 175
marmalade 134, 156
Mars 280
marshmallow 113
martial arts 237
martini 151
marzipan 141
mascara 40
mashed 159
masher 68
mask 189, 228, 236, 239, 249
masking tape 83
masonry bit 80
massage 54
mast 240
master's degree 169
mat 54, 83, 235, 271
match 230
material 276
materials 79, 187
maternity 49
maternity ward 48
math 162, 164
mattress 70, 74
Mauritiana 317
Mauritius 317
May 306
maybe 322
mayonnaise 135
meadow 285
meal 64
measles 44
measure 150, 151
measure v 310
measurements 165
measuring cup 69, 311
measuring spoon 109
meat 119
meat and poultry 106
meat cleaver 68
meat pies 143
meat tenderizer 68
meatballs 158
meathook 118
mechanic 188, 203
mechanical digger 187
mechanics 202
medals 235
media 178
median strip 194
medical examination 45
medication 109
medicine 109, 169
medicine cabinet 72
meditation 54
Mediterranean Sea 313
medium-density fiberboard 79
meeting 174
meeting room 174
melody 259
melon 127
memory 176
memory stick 176
men's clothing 32
menstruation 20
menswear 105
menu 148, 153, 154
menubar 177
Mercury 280
mercury 289
meringue 140
mesh skimmer 68
mesophere 286
messages 100
metacarpal 17
metal 79
metal bit 80
metals 289
metamorphic 288
metatarsal 17
meteor 280
meter 310

Mexico 314
mezzanine 254
mica 289
microphone 179, 258
microscope 167
microwave oven 66
middle finger 15
middle lane 194
midnight
midwife 53
migraine 44
mile 310
milk 136, 156
milk carton 136
milk chocolate 113
milk v 183
milkshake 137
millennium 307
millet 130
milligram 310
milliliter 311
millimeter 310
mineral 144
minerals 289
minibar 101
minibus 197
mini-dress 34
minivan 199
mint 113, 133
mint tea 149
minus 165
minute 304
minute hand 304
minutes 174
mirror 40, 71, 167, 198
miscarriage 52
Miss 23
missile 211
mist 287
miter block 81
mittens 30
mix v 67, 138
mixing desk 179
moat 300
mobile 74
model 169, 190
modeling tool 275
model-making 275
moisturizer 41
molar 50
molding 63
Moldova 316
mole 14
Monaco 316
Monday 306
money 97
Mongolia 318
monitor 172
monitor 53
monkey 291
monkfish 120
monopoly 272
monorail 208
monsoon 287
month 306
monthly 307
monument 261
Moon 280
moonstone 288
moor v 217
mooring 217
mop 77
morning 305
Morocco 317
mortar 68, 167, 187
mortgage 96
bassinet 74
mosque 300
mosquito 295
mosquito net 267
moth 295
mother 22
mother-in-law 23
motocross 249
motor 88
motorbike racing 249
motorcycle 204
mountain 284
mountain bike 206
mountain range 282
mouse 176, 290
mousse 141
mouth 14
mouth guard 237
mouthwash 72
move 273
movie theater 255, 299
movies 255
mow v 90
Mozambique 317
mozzarella 142
Mr. 23
Mrs. 23
mudguard 205
muffin 140
muffin pan 69
muffler 203, 204
mug 65
mulch v 91
multigrain bread 139
multiply v 165
multivitamin tablets 109
mumps 44
mung beans 131
muscles 16
museum 261
mushroom 125
music 162
music school 169
musical 255
musical score 255
musical styles 259
musician 191
mussel 121, 295
mustard 155
mustard seed 131
Myanmar 318

N

naan bread 139
nail 15, 80
nail clippers 41
nail file 41
nail polish 41
nail polish remover 41
nail scissors 41
Namibia 317
nape 13
napkin 65
napkin ring 65
narrow 321
nation 315
national park 261
natural 256
natural fibre 31
naturopathy 55
nausea 44
navel 12
navigate v 240
navy beans 131
near 320
nearsighted 51
nebula 280
neck 12, 258
neck brace 46
necklace 36
nectarine 126
needle 109, 276
needle plate 276
needle-nose pliers 80
needlepoint 277
negative 271
negative electrode 167
neighbor 24
neoclassical 301
Nepal 318
nephew 23
Neptune 280
nerve 19, 50
nervous 19, 25
net 217, 222, 226, 227, 231
net curtain 63
net v 245
Netherlands 316
nettle 297
network 176
neurology 49
neutral 60
neutral zone 224
new 321
new moon 280
new potato 124
New Year 27
New Zealand 319
newborn baby 53
news 178
newspaper 112
newsstand 112
next week 306
Nicaragua 314
nickel 289
niece 23
Niger 317
Nigeria 317
night 305
nightgown 31, 35
nightstand 70
nightstick 94
nightwear 31
nine 308
nine hundred 308
nineteen 308
nineteen hundred 307
nineteen hundred and one 307
nineteen ten 307
nineteenth 309
ninetieth 309
ninety 308
ninth 309
nipple 12
nipple 75
no 322
no entry 195
no right turn 195
no stopping 195
non-carbonated 144
nonstick 69
noodles 158
noon 305
normal 39
north 312
North and Central America 314
North Korea 318
North pole 283
North Sea 312
northern hemisphere 283
Norway 316
nose 14, 210
nose clip 238
noseband 242
nosebleed 44
nosewheel 210
nostril 14
notation 256
note 256
notebook 163, 172
notepad 173
notes 191
notions 105
nougat 113
November 306
now 304
nozzle 89
number 226
numbers 308
numerator 165
nurse 45, 48, 189
nursery 74
nursing 53
nursing bra 53
nut 80
nutmeg 132
nuts 151
nuts and dried fruit 129
nylon 277

O

oak 296
oar 241
oatmeal 157
oats 130
objective lens 167
oboe 257
obsidian 288
obstetrician 52
occupations 188, 190
occupied 321
ocean 282
ocean liner 215
octagon 164
October 306
octopus 121, 295
odometer 201
offal 118
offers 106
office 24, 172, 174
office block 298
office equipment 172
office supplies 173
off-piste 247
offside 223
oil 142, 199
oil paints 274
oil tank 204
oil tanker 215
oilcloth 83
oils 134
oily 41
ointment 47, 109
okra 122
old 321
olive oil 134
olives 151
Oman 318
omelet 158
on time 305
on top of 320
oncology 49
one 308
one billion 309
one million 309
one thousand 309
onesize 30
one-way 194
one-way system 298
onion 124
online 177
onto 320
onyx 289
opal 288
open 260, 321
open-face sandwich 155
opening night 254
open-top 260
opera 255
operating room 48
operation 48
operator 99
ophthalmology 49
opponent 236
opposite 320
optic nerve 51
optician 51, 189
orange 126, 274
orange juice 148
orangeade 144
orbit 280
orchestra 254, 256
orchestra pit 254
orchestra seats 254
orchid 111
order v 153
oregano 133
organic 91, 118, 122
organic waste 61
origami 275
ornamental 87
orthopedics 49
osteopathy 54
ostrich 292
otter 290
ounce 310
out 225, 228, 320
out of bounds 226
out of focus 271
outboard motor 215
outbuilding 182
outdoor activities 262
outer core 282
outfield 229
outlet 61
outpatient 48
outside 320
outside lane 194
out-tray 172
oval 164
ovary 20
oven 66
oven mitt 69
ovenproof 69
over 320
over par 233
overalls 30
overexposed 271
overflow pipe 61
overhead bin 210
overpass 194
overture 256
ovulation 20, 52
owl 292
oyster 121
ozone layer 286

P

Pacific Ocean 312
pack 311
pack of cigarettes 112
pad 224
paddle 241

paddock 242
pads 53, 220
pail 77, 82, 265
painkiller 109
painkillers 47
paint 83
paint can 83
paint thinner 83
paint tray 83
paint *v* 83
painter 191
painting 62, 261, 274
paints 274
pajamas 33
Pakistan 318
palate 19
palette 274
pallet 186
palm 15, 86, 296
palm hearts 122
pan 310
pan fried 159
Panama 314
pancreas 18
panda 291
pants 32, 34
panty liner 108
pantyhose 251
papaya 128
paper clip 173
paper napkin 154
paper tray 172
papier-maché 275
paprika 132
Papua New Guinea 319
par 233
parachute 248
parachuting 248
Paraguay 315
parallel 165
parallel bars 235
parallelogram 164
paramedic 94
parasailing 248
parcel 99
parents 23
paring knife 68
park 262
park *v* 195
parka 31, 33
parking brake 203
parking lot 298
parking meter 195
Parmesan 142
parole 181
parrot 293
parsley 133
parsnip 125
partner 23
pass 226
pass *v* 195, 220, 223
passcode 99
passenger 216
passenger port 216
passenger seat 204
passion fruit 128
Passover 27
passport 213
passport control 213
pasta 158
pastels 274
pasteurized 137
pasting brush 82
pasting table 82
pastry 140, 149
pastry brush 69
pastry cream 140
pasture 182
patch 207
patchwork 277
pâté 142, 156
path 58, 85
pathology 49
patient 45
patio 85
patio garden 85
pattern 276
pause 269
pawn 272
pay phone 99
pay *v* 153
payment 96
payroll 175
pea 122
peach 126, 128
peacock 293
peanut 129
peanut butter 135
peanut oil 135
peanuts 151
pear 127
peas 131
pecan 129
pectoral 16
pectoral fin 294
pedal 61, 206
pedal *v* 207
pedestrian zone 299
pediatrics 49
pedicure 41
pediment 301
peel 128
peel *v* 67
peeled shrimp 120
peeler 68
pelican 292
pelvis 17
pen 163, 185
pen holder 172
pen pal 24
penalty 222
penalty area 223
pencil 163, 275
pencil case 163
pencil sharpener 163
pendant 36
penguin 292
peninsula 282
penis 21
pentagon 164
peony 111
people 12, 16
pepper 64, 124, 152
peppercorn 132
pepperoni 142
percentage 165
percussion 257
perennial 86
perfume 41
perfumes 105
periodical 168
perm 39
perpendicular 165
persimmon 128
personal best 234
personal organizer 173, 175
personal trainer 250
Peru 315
pesticide 89, 183
pestle 68, 167
pet food 107
pet store 115
petal 297
petri dish 166
pharmacist 108, 189
pharmacy 108
pharynx 19
pheasant 119, 293
Phillips screwdriver 81
philosophy 169
Phlippines 319
phone booth 99
photo album 271
photo finish 234
photograph 271
photograph *v* 271
photographer 191
photography 270
physical education 162
physics 162, 169
physiotherapy 49
piano 256
piccolo 257
pick and mix 113
pick *v* 91
pickax 187
pickled 159
pickup 258
pick-up 98
picnic 263
picnic bench 266
picture frame 271
pie 158
pie pan 69
piece 272
pier 217
pig 185
pig farm 183
pigeon 292
pigeonhole 100
piglet 185
pigsty 185
pigtails 39
Pilates 251
pill 21, 109
pillar 300
pillow 62, 70
pillowcase 71
pilot 190, 211
pin 237, 249, 276
pin number 96
pincushion 276
pine 296
pine nut 129
pineapple 128
pineapple juice 149
pink 274
pint 311
pinto beans 131
pipe 112, 202
pipe cutter 81
pipe wrench 81
pipette 167
piping bag 69
pistachio 129
pit 128
pita bread 139
pitch 225, 256
pitch a tent *v* 266
pitch *v* 229
pitcher 151, 229
pitcher 65
pitcher's mound 228
pizza 154
pizzeria 154
place mat 64
place setting 65
placenta 52
plain 285
plane 81
plane *v* 79
planet 280, 282
plant pot 89
plant *v* 183
plants 86, 296
plaque 50
plaster 83
plaster *v* 82
plastic bag 122
plastic surgery 49
plastic underpants 30
plate 283
plateau 284
platform 208
platform number 208
platinum 289
play 254, 269
play *v* 229, 273
player 221, 231, 273
playground 263
playhouse 75
playing 75
playing field 168
playpen 75
plea 180
please 322
Plimsoll mark 214
plow *v* 183
plug 60
plum 126
plumb line 82
plumber 188
plumbing 61
plunger 81
plus 165
Pluto 280
plywood 79
pneumatic drill 187
poach *v* 67
poached 159
pocket 32
pod 122
podium 235, 256
point 273
poisoning 46
poker 273
Poland 316
polar bear 291
polaroid camera 270
pole 245, 282
pole vault 234
police 94
police car 94
police officer 94
police station 94
policeman 189
polish 77
polish *v* 77
political science 169
polo 243
polyester 277
pomegranate 128
pommel 242
pommel horse 235
pond 85
ponytail 39
pool 249
pop 259
popcorn 255
poplar 296
poppy 297
poppy seeds 138
porch 58
porch light 58
pore 15
pork 118
port 145, 176, 214, 216
portable heater 60
porter 100
portfolio 97
porthole 214
portion 64
portrait 271
Portugal 316
positive electrode 167
post office 98
postage 98
money order 98
postal worker 98
postcard 112
poster 255
poster paint 274
postgraduate 169
postmark 98
pot *v* 91
potato 124
potato chips 113, 151
potpourri 111
potted plant 110
potted plant 87
potter's wheel 275
pottery 275
potty 74
pouch 291
poultry 119
poultry farm 183
pound 310
pour *v* 67
powder 77, 109
powder puff 40
powdered milk 137
power 60
power cable 176
power outage 60
practice swing 233
praying mantis 295
pregnancy 52
pregnancy test 52
pregnant 52
premature 52
premolar 50
prepared food 107
prerecorded 178
prescription 45
present 27
presentation 174
preservative 83
preserved fruit 134
press 178
presser foot 276
pressure valve 61
price 152, 199
price list 154
prickly pear 128
primer 83
primrose 297
principal 163
principality 315
print 271
print *v* 172
printer 172, 176
printing 275
prison 181
prison guard 181
private bathroom 100
private jet 211
private room 48
probe 50
problems 271
processed grains 130

english

procession 27
processor 176
produce stand 114
producer 254
profiterole pastry 140
program 176
program 254, 269
programming 178
prong 60
propagate *v* 91
propeller 211, 214
proposal 174
prosciutto 143
prosecution 180
prostate 21
protractor 165
proud 25
prove *v* 139
province 315
prow 215
prune 129
prune *v* 91
pruning shears 89
psychiatry 49
psychotherapy 55
public address system 209
puck 224
Puerto Rico 314
puff pastry 140
pull up *v* 251
pulp 124, 126, 127
pulse 47
pulses 130
pumice 288
pumice stone 73
pump 37, 207
pumpkin 125
pumpkin seed 131
punch 237
punching bag 237
pup 290
pupil 51, 162
puppy 290
purple 274
push-up 251
putt *v* 233
putter 233
pyramid 164

Q

Qatar 318
quadriceps 16
quail 119
quail egg 137
quart 311
quarter of an hour 304
quarterdeck 214
quartz 289
quay 216
queen 272, 273
question 163
question *v* 163
quiche 142
quilt 71
quilting 277
quince 128
quinoa 130
quiver 249

R

rabbit 118, 290
raccoon 290
race 234
race-car driver 249
racecourse 243
racehorse 243
racing bike 205, 206
racing dive 239
rack 166, 268
racket 230
racket games 231
racquetball 231
radar 214, 281
radiator 60, 202
radicchio 123
radio 179, 268
radio antenna 214
radio station 179
radiology 49
radish 124
radius 17, 164
rafter 186
rafting 241
rail 208
railroad network 209
rain 287
rain clothes 245, 267
rain forest 285
rainbow 287
rainbow trout 120
raincoat 31, 32
raisin 129
rake 88
rake *v* 90
rally 230
rally driving 249
RAM 176
Ramadan 26
ramekin 69
rap 259
rapeseed 184
rapids 240, 284
rappeling 248
rash 44
rasher 119
raspberry 127
raspberry jam 134
rat 290
rattle 74
raw 124, 129
ray 294
razor blade 73
razor shell 121
read *v* 162
reading light 210
reading list 168
reading room 168
realtor 189
realty office 115
reamer 80
rear light 207
rear wheel 197
rearview mirror 198
receipt 152
receive *v* 177
receiver 99
reception 100
receptionist 100, 190
rechargeable drill 78
record 234, 269
record player 268
record store 115
recording studio 179
rectangle 164
rectum 21
recycling bin 61
red 39, 145, 274
red card 223
red eye 271
red lentils 131
red meat 118
red mullet 120
Red Sea 313
reduce *v* 172
reduced-fat milk 136
reel 244
reel in *v* 245
referee 220
referee 222, 226
referral 49
reflector 50, 204, 207
reflector strap 205
reflexology 54
refrigerator 67
refrigerator-freezer 67
reggae 259
region 315
register 100
registered mail 98
regulator 239
reheat *v* 154
reiki 55
reins 242
relationships 24
relatives 23
relaxation 55
relay race 235
release *v* 245
remote control 269
Renaissance 301
renew *v* 168
rent 58
rent *v* 58
repair kit 207
report 174
reporter 179
reproduction 20
reproductive 19
reproductive organs 20
reptiles 293
research 169
reserve *v* 168
residence hall 168
respiratory 19
rest 256
rest room 104, 266
restaurant 101, 152
result 49
resurfacing 187
resuscitation 47
retina 51
retire *v* 26
return 231
return address 98
reverse *v* 195
rewind 269
rhinoceros 291
rhombus 164
rhubarb 127
rhythmic gymnastics 235
rib 17, 119
rib cage 17
ribbon 27
ribbon 39, 111, 141, 235
ribs 155
rice 130, 158, 184
rice pudding 140
rider 242
riding boot 242
riding cap 242
riding crop 242
riding trail 263
rigging 215, 240
right 260
right field 229
right-hand drive 201
rim 206
rind 119, 127, 136, 142
ring 36
ring finger 15
ring ties 89
rings 235
rinse *v* 38, 76
ripe 129
rise *v* 139
river 284
road bike 206
road markings 194
road signs 195
roads 194
roadwork 187, 195
roast 158
roast *v* 67
roasted 129
roasting tin 69
robe 31, 35, 38
rock climbing 248
rock concert 258
rock garden 84
rocks 284, 288
Rocky Mountains 312
rococo 301
rodeo 243
roll 139, 143, 311
roll *v* 67
roller 83
roller blind 63
roller coaster 262
rollerblading 263
rolling pin 69
romance 255
Romania 316
romper suit 30
roof 58, 203
roof garden 84
roof rack 198
roof tile 187
rook 272
room 58
room key 100
room number 100
room service 101
rooms 100
rooster 185
root 50, 124, 296
roots 39
rope 248
rosé 145
rose 89, 110
rosemary 133
rotary 195
rotor blade 211
rotten 127
rough 232
round 237
route number 196
router 78
row 210, 254
row (house) 58
row *v* 241
rowboat 214
rower 241
rowing machine 250
rubber band 173
rubber boots 89
rubber stamp 173
ruby 288
ruck 221
rudder 210, 241
rug 63
rugby 221
rugby field 221
rugby uniform 221
ruler 163, 165
rum 145
rum and coke 151
rump steak 119
run 228
run *v* 228
runner bean 122
running shoes 251
runway 212
rush hour 209
Russian Federation 318
rutabaga 125
Rwanda 317
rye bread 138

S

sack 311
sad 25
saddle 206, 242
safe 228
safety 75, 240
safety barrier 246
safety goggles 81, 167
safety pin 47
saffron 132
sage 133
Sahara Desert 313
sail 241
sailboat 215
sailing 240
sailor 189
salad 149
salamander 294
salami 142
salary 175
sales assistant 188
sales clerk 104
sales department 175
salmon 120
salt 64, 152
salted 121, 129, 137, 143
San Marino 316
sand 85, 264
sand *v* 82
sandal 37
sandals 31
sandbox 263
sandcastle 265
sander 78
sandpaper 81, 83
sandstone 288
sandwich counter 143
sanitary napkin 108
Sao Tome and Principe 317
sapphire 288
sardine 120
Sardinia 316
satellite 281
satellite dish 269
satellite navigation 201
satnav 195
satsuma 126
Saturday 306
Saturn 280
sauce 134, 143, 155
saucepan 69
Saudi Arabia 318
sauna 250
sausage 155, 157
sausages 118
sauté *v* 67
save *v* 177, 223
savings 96
savings account 97
savory 155
saw *v* 79
saxophone 257

scaffolding 186
scale 98, 121, 256, 294, 310
scales 45, 69, 118, 166, 212, 293
scallion 125
scallop 121
scalp 39
scalpel 167
scan 48, 52
scanner 106, 176
scarecrow 184
scared 25
scarf 31, 36
schedule (transportation) 209
schedule (leisure) 261
schist 288
scholarship 169
school 162, 299
school bus 196
schoolboy 162
schoolgirl 162
schools 169
science 162, 166
science fiction movie 255
scientist 190
scissors 38, 47, 82, 276
scoop 149
scooter 205
score 220, 256, 273
score a goal v 223
scoreboard 225
scorpion 295
scotch and water 151
scrabble 272
scrambled eggs 157
scrape v 77
scraper 82
screen 59, 97, 176, 255, 269
screw 80
screwdriver 80
screwdriver bits 80
script 254
scrollbar 177
scrotum 21
scrub v 77
scrum 221
scuba diving 239
sculpting 275
sculptor 191
sea 264, 282
sea bass 120
sea bream 120
sea horse 294
sea lion 290
seafood 121
seal 290
sealant 83
sealed jar 135
seam 34
seamstress 191
seaplane 211
search v 177
seasonal 129
seasons 306
seat 61, 204, 209, 210, 242, 254
seat back 210
seat belt 198, 211
seat post 206
seating 254
second 304, 309
second floor 104
second floor 104
second hand 304
second-hand store 115
section 282
securities 97
security 212
security bit 80
security guard 189
sedan 199
sedative 109
sedimentary 288
seed 122, 127, 130
seed tray 89
seeded bread 139
seedless 127
seedling 91
seeds 88, 131
seesaw 263
segment 126
self-defense 237
self-rising flour 139
self-tanning lotion 41
semihard cheese 136
seminal vesicle 21
semisoft cheese 136
semolina 130
send off 223
send v 177
Senegal 317
sensitive 41
sentence 181
September 306
series 179
serve 231
serve v 64, 231
server 148, 152
server 176
service charge 96
service charge included 152
service charge not included 152
service line 230
service provider 177
service vehicle 212
serving spoon 68
sesame seed 131
sesame seed oil 134
set 178, 230, 254
set honey 134
set sail v 217
set square 165
set the alarm v 71
set the table v 64
set v 38
seven 308
seven hundred 308
seventeen 308
seventeenth 309
seventh 309
seventieth 309
seventy 308
sew v 277
sewing basket 276
sewing machine 276
sexually transmitted disease 20
shade 41
shade plant 87
shallot 125
shallow end 239
shampoo 38
shapes 164
share price 97
shark 294
sharp 256
sharpening stone 81
shaving 73
shaving cream 73
shears 89
shed 84
sheep 185
sheep farm 183
sheep's milk 137
sheet 71, 74, 241
shelf 67, 106
shell 129, 137, 265, 293
shelled 129
shelves 66
sherry 145
shiatsu 54
shield 88
shin 12
ship 214
ships 215
shipyard 217
shirt 33
shock 47
shocked 25
shoe department 104
shoe store 114
shoes 34, 37
shoot v 223, 227
shopping 104
shopping bag 106
shopping mall 104
short 32, 321
short-grain 130
shorts 30, 33
shotput 234
shoulder 13
shoulder bag 37
shoulder blade 17
shoulder pad 35
shoulder strap 37
shout v 25
shovel 265
shovel 88, 187
show jumping 243
shower 72, 286
shower curtain 72
shower door 72
shower gel 73
shower head 72
showers 266
shuffle v 273
shutoff valve 61
shutter 58
shutter release 270
shuttle bus 197
shuttlecock 231
shy 25
Siberia 313
Sicily 316
side 164
side order 153
side street 299
sidedeck 240
side-effects 109
sideline 220
sideline 226, 230
sidesaddle 242
sidewalk 298
sidewalk cafe 148
Sierra Leone 317
sieve 89
sieve v 91
sift v 138
sigh v 25
sightseeing 260
sign 104
signal 209
signature 96, 98
silk 277
silo 183
silt 85
silver 235, 289
silver hake 120
simmer v 67
Singapore 319
singer 191
single 151
single bed 71
single room 100
single-family 58
singles 230
sink 38, 61, 66
sink 72
sinker 244
sinus 19
siren 94
sirloin steak 119
sister 22
sister-in-law 23
site 266
sites available 266
sit-up 251
six 308
six hundred 308
sixteen 308
sixteenth 309
sixth 309
sixtieth 309
sixty 308
skate 120, 247, 294
skate v 224
skate wings 120
skateboard 249
skateboarding 249, 263
skein 277
skeleton 17
sketch 275
sketchbook 275
skewer 68
ski 246
ski boot 246
ski jacket 246
ski jump 247
ski pole 246
ski run 246
ski slope 246
skier 246
skiing 246
skin 14, 119
skin care 108
skinned 121
skirt 30, 34
skull 17
skydiving 248
skyscraper 299, 300
slalom 247
slate 288
sledding 247
sledgehammer 187
sleeper 30
sleeping 74
sleeping bag 267
sleeping compartment 209
sleeping mat 267
sleeping pill 109
sleet 286
sleeve 34
sleeveless 34
slice 119, 139, 140, 230
slice v 67
sliced bread 138
slicer 139
slide 167, 263
slide v 229
sling 46
slip 35
slip-on 37
slippers 31
slope 284
Slovakia 316
Slovenia 316
slow 321
slug 295
small 321
small intestine 18
small of back 13
smartphone 99, 176
smash 231
smile 25
smoke 95
smoke alarm 95
smoked 118, 121, 143, 159
smoked fish 143
smoked herring 156
smoking 112
snack bar 113, 148
snail 295
snake 293
snap 30
snare drum 257
sneaker 37
sneakers 31,
sneeze 44
snooker 249
snore v 71
snorkel 239
snout 293
snow 287
snowboarding 247
snowmobile 247
snowsuit 30
soak v 130
soap 73, 178
soap dish 73
soccer 222
soccer ball 222
soccer field 222
soccer player 222
soccer uniform 31, 222
socket 60, 80
socket wrench 80
socks 33
soda bread 139
soda water 144
sofa 62
sofabed 63
soft 129, 321
soft cheese 136
soft drink 154
soft drinks 144
soft-boiled egg 137, 157
software 176
softwood 79
soil 85
solar system 280
solder 79, 80
solder v 79
soldering iron 81
soldier 189
sole 15, 37
solids 164
Soloman Islands 319
soluble 109
solvent 83
Somalia 317
somersault 235
son 22
sonata 256
song 259
son-in-law 22
sorbet 141
sorrel 123
sorting unit 61
soufflé 158
soufflé dish 69

sound boom 179
sound technician 179
soundtrack 255
soup 153, 158
soup bowl 65
soup spoon 65
sour 127
sour cream 137
sourdough bread 139
south 312
South Africa 317
southern hemisphere 283
Southern Ocean 313
South Korea 318
South Sudan 317
souvenirs 260
sow *v* 90, 183
soybeans 131
space 280
space exploration 281
space heater 60
space shuttle 281
space station 281
space suit 281
spade 273
spade bit 80
Spain 316
spare tire 203
spark plug 203
sparkling 144
sparring 237
sparrow 292
spatula 68, 167
speaker 174, 176, 258, 268
speaker stand 268
spearfishing 245
special occasion cakes 141
specials 152
spectators 233
speed limit 195
speed skating 247
speedboat 214
speedboating 241
speedometer 201, 204
spell *v* 162
sperm 20
sphere 164
spices 132
spicy sausage 142
spider 295
spike *v* 90
spikes 233
spin 230
spin dryer 76
spin *v* 76
spinach 123
spine 17
spire 300
spirit level 187
splashback 66
spleen 18
splint 47
splinter 46
split ends 39
split peas 131
spoke 207
sponge 73, 74, 83
sponge cake 140
spool 245
spoon 65
sport coat 33
sport fishing 245
sports 220, 236, 248
sports car 198
sportsman 191
sportswear 33, 105
spotlight 259
sprain 46
spray 109
spray bottle 311
spray can 311
spray gun 89
spray *v* 91
spring 307
spring balance 166
springboard 235
sprinkler 89
sprinter 234
sprocket 207
spy hole 59
square 164, 272, 299
square foot 310
square meter 310
squash 124
squash 231
squat 251
squid 121, 295
squirrel 290
Sri Lanka 318
St. Kitts and Nevis 314
St. Lucia 314
St. Vincent and the Grenadines 314
stabilizers 207
stable 185, 243
stadium 223
staff 175, 256
stage 167, 254
stages 23
stainless steel 79
stair gate 75
staircase 59
stake 90
stake *v* 91
stalk 122, 297
stamen 297
stamp 98
stamp collecting 273
stamps 112
stance 232
stand 88, 205
stanley knife 82
stapler 173
staples 173
star 280
star anise 133
star fruit 128
starfish 295
start school *v* 26
starting block 234, 238
starting line 234
state 315
statement 180
station wagon 199
stationery 105
steak 121
steam train 208
steam *v* 67
steamed 159
steel wool 81
steeplechase 243
steering wheel 201
stem 111, 112, 297
stencil 83
stenographer 181
step machine 250
stepdaughter 23
stepfather 23
stepladder 82
stepmother 23
stepson 23
stereo 269
stereo system 268
sterile 47
stern 240
stethoscope 45
stew 158
stick 224, 249
sticks 133
sting 46, 295
stir fry 158
stir *v* 67
stirrer 150
stirrup 242
stitch 277
stitch selector 276
stitches 52
stock broker 97
stock exchange 97
stocking 35
stocks 97, 110
stomach 18
stomach ache 44
stone 36, 275
stone fruit 126
stone-ground flour 138
stop 269
stop button 197
stopper 166
stopper 72
stopwatch 234
store 298
store directory 104
stores 114
stork 292
storm 287
stout 145
stove 67
stovetop 66
straight 39, 165
straight ahead 260
straighten *v* 39
strainer 68
strand of pearls 36
strap 35
strapless 34
stratosphere 286
straw 144, 154
strawberry 127
strawberry milkshake 149
stream 285
streaming 269
stream roller 187
street 298
street corner 298
street light 298
street sign 298
streetcar 196,
stress 55
stretch 251
stretcher 94
strike 228, 237
string 230, 258
strings 256
strip *v* 82
stroke 44, 233, 239
strokes 231
stroller 75
strong 321
stub 96
study 63, 162
stuffed 159
stuffed olive 143
stuffed toy 75
stump 225
styles 39, 239, 301
sub 155
submarine 215
subsoil 91
substitute 223
substitution 223
subtract *v* 165
suburb 299
subway 208
succulent 87
suction cup 53
suction hose 77
Sudan 317
sugarcane 184
suit 273
sulfur 289
sultana 129
summer 31, 307
summons 180
sumo wrestling 237
Sun 280
sun hat 30, 265
sunbathe *v* 264
sunbed 41
sunblock 108, 265
sunburn 46
Sunday 306
sunflower 184, 297
sunflower oil 134
sunflower seed 131
sunglasses 51, 265
sunny 286
sunrise 305
sunroof 202
sunscreen 108
sunset 305
sunshine 286
suntan lotion 265
supermarket 106
supplement 55
supply pipe 61
support 187
suppository 109
surf 241
surfboard 241
surfcasting 245
surfer 241
surfing 241
surgeon 48
surgery 48
Suriname 315
surprised 25
suspect 94, 181
suspension 203, 205
swallow 292
swamp 285
swan 293
Swaziland 317
sweater 33
sweatshirt 33
Sweden 316
sweep *v* 77
sweet 124, 127, 155
sweet potato 125
sweet spreads 134
swim band 238
swim *v* 238
swimmer 238
swimming 238
swimming cap 238
swimming pool 101, 238, 250
swimsuit 238, 265
swing 263
swing *v* 232
swiss chard 123
switch 60
Switzerland 316
swivel chair 172
sword 236
swordfish 120, 294
symphony 256
synagogue 300
synchronized swimming 239
synthetic 31
Syria 318
syringe 109, 167
syrup 109
system 176

T

tab 173
table 64, 148
table tennis 231
tablecloth 64
tachometer 201
tack *v* 241, 277
tackle 245
tackle box 244
tackle *v* 220, 223
tadpole 294
tae kwon do 236
tag *v* 229
tai chi 236
tail 121, 210, 242, 280, 290, 294
tailbone 17
tailgate 198
taillight 204
tailor 191
tailor shop 115
tailor's chalk 276
tailor's dummy 276
tailored 35
tailplane 210
Taiwan 319
Tajikistan 318
take a bath *v* 72
take a shower *v* 72
take notes *v* 163
take off *v* 211
talcum powder 73
tall 321
tambourine 257
tampon 108
tan 41
tandem 206
tangelo 126
tangerine 126
tank 61
Tanzania 317
tap water 144
tape deck 268
tape dispenser 173
tape measure 80, 276
target 249
target shooting 249
tarmac 187
taro root 124
tarragon 133
Tasmania 319
tattoo 41
tax 96
taxi driver 190
taxi stand 213
tea 144, 149, 184
tea kettle 66
tea with lemon 149
tea with milk 149
teabag 144
teacher 162, 191
teacup 65
team 220, 229
teapot 65
tear 51

teaspoon 65
techniques 79, 159
teddy bear 75
tee 233
teeing ground 232
teenager 23
tee-off *v* 233
telegram 98
telephone 99
teleprompter 179
telescope 281
television 268
television series 178
television studio 178
teller 96
temperature 286
temperature gauge 201
temple 14, 300
ten 308
ten thousand 309
tenant 58
tend *v* 91
tendon 17
tennis 230
tennis court 230
tennis shoes 231
tenon saw 81
tent 267
tent peg 266
tent pole 266
tenth 309
tequila 145
terminal 212
termite 295
terrace café 148
territory 315
test 49
test tube 166
testicle 21
text 99
textbook 163
Thailand 318
thank you 322
Thanksgiving 27
the day after tomorrow 307
the day before yesterday 307
theater 254, 299
therapist 55
thermal underwear 35, 267
thermometer 45, 167
thermos flask 267
thermosphere 286
thermostat 61
thesis 169
thick 321
thigh 12, 119
thimble 276
thin 321
third 309
thirteen 308
thirteenth 309
thirtieth 309
thirty 308
this way up 98
this week 307
thistle 297
thoracic vertebrae 17
thread 276
thread guide 276
thread reel 276
thread *v* 277
three 308
three hundred 308
three-door 200
three-point line 226
thriller 255
throat 19
throat lozenge 109
throttle 204
through 320
throw 237
throw *v* 221, 227, 229
throw-in 223, 226
thruster 281
thumb 15
thumb tack 173
thunder 286
Thursday 306
thyme 133
thyroid gland 18
tibia 17
ticket 209, 213
ticket barrier 209
ticket inspector 209
ticket office 209, 216
tie 32
tiebreaker 230
tiepin 36
tiger 291
tile 58, 272
tile *v* 82
tiller 240
timber 187
time 234, 304
time out 220
timer 166
times 165, 261
timetable 197
timing 203
tin 289, 311
tip 36, 122, 246
tire 198, 205, 206
tire iron 203
tire lever 207
tire pressure 203
tissue 108
title 168
titles 23
to 320
toad 294
toast 157
toasted sandwich 149
toaster 66
tobacco 112, 184
today 306
toddler 30
toe 15
toe clip 207
toe strap 207
toenail 15
toffee 113
toggle 31
Togo 317
toilet 61
toilet 72
toilet brush 72
toilet paper 72
toilet seat 72
toiletries 41, 107
toll booth 194
tomato 125, 157
tomato juice 144, 149
tomorrow 306
ton 310
toner 41
tongs 150, 167
tongue 19, 37, 118
tonic water 144
tool rack 78
toolbar 177
toolbelt 186
toolbox 80
tools 187
tooth 50
toothache 50
toothbrush 72
toothpaste 72
top coat 83
top dress *v* 90
top tier 141
topaz 288
topiary 87
topping 155
topsoil 85
tornado 287
tortoise 293
tossed salad 158
touch line 221
touchdown 221
tour bus 260
tour guide 260
tourer 205
touring bike 206
tourist 260
tourist attraction 260
tourist bus 197
tourist information 261
tourmaline 288
tournament 233
tow away *v* 195
tow truck 203
toward 320
towel rack 72
towels 73
tower 300
town 298
town hall 299
townhouse 58
toy 75
toy basket 75
toys 105
track 208, 234
track and field 234
tractor 182
traffic 194
traffic jam 195
traffic light 194
traffic policeman 195
traffic post 298
trailer 266
train 35, 208
train station 208
train *v* 91, 251
tram 208
transfer 223
transformer 60
transmission 202
transplant *v* 91
transportation 194
trapezium 164
trapezius 16
trash 177
trash can 61
travel agency 114
travel agent 190
travel brochure 212
travel sickness pills 109
traveler's check 97
tray 152, 154
tray-table 210
tread 207
tread water *v* 239
treadmill 250
treble clef 256
tree 86, 296
trekking 243
trellis 84
tremor 283
triangle 164, 257
triceps 16
trifle 141
trim *v* 39, 90
trimester 52
trimmer 88
Trinidad and Tobago 314
tripod 166, 270, 281
trolley bus 196
trombone 257
tropic of Cancer 283
tropic of Capricorn 283
tropical fruit 128
tropics 283
troposphere 286
trot 243
trough 183
trout 120
trowel 89, 187
truck 194
truck driver 190
truffle 113, 125
trumpet 257
trunk 198, 291, 296
trunks 238
try 221
t-shirt 30, 33, 54
tub 311
tuba 257
tube 311
Tuesday 306
tugboat 215
tulip 111
tumble dryer 76
tumbler 65
tuna 120
tune the radio *v* 269
tune *v* 179
tuning peg 258
Tunisia 317
turbocharger 203
turf *v* 90
turkey 119, 185, 293
Turkey 316
Turkmenistan 318
turmeric 132
turn 238
turn off the television *v* 269
turn on the television *v* 269
turn signal 198, 204
turn *v* 79
turnip 124
turpentine 83
turquoise 289
turret 300
turtle 293
tusk 291
tutu 191
tweezers 40, 47, 167
twelfth 309
twelve 308
twentieth 309
twenty 308
twenty minutes 304
twenty thousand 309
twenty-first 309
twenty-one 308
twenty-second 309
twenty-third 309
twenty-two 308
twig 296
twin room 100
twine 89
twins 23
twist ties 89
two 308
two hundred 308
two o'clock 304
two thousand 307
two thousand and one 307
two weeks 307
two-door 200
types 199, 205
types of buses 196
types of camera 270
types of farms 183
types of fishing 245
types of plants 86
types of train 208

U

Uganda 317
Ukraine 316
ulna 17
ultralight 211
ultrasound 52
ultraviolet rays 286
umbilical cord 52
umbrella 36
umbrella stand 59
umpire 225, 229, 230
uncle 22
unconscious 47
uncooked meat 142
under 320
under par 233
underexposed 271
undergraduate 169
underground map 209
underpass 194
undershirt 33, 35, 251
underwear 32, 35
underwire 35
uniform 94, 189
United Arab Emirates 318
United Kingdom 316
United States of America 314
universe 280
university 299
unleaded 199
unpasteurised 137
unpick *v* 277
unsalted 137
until 320
up 320
upper balcony 254
upset 25
Uranus 280
ureter 21
urethra 20
urinary 19
urology 49
Uruguay 315
usher 255
uterus 20, 52
utility knife 80
utility room 76
Uzbekistan 318

V

vacation 212
vacuum cleaner 77, 188
vagina 20
valance 71
valley 284
valve 207
vanilla 132
vanity table 71
Vanuatu 319
varnish 79, 83
vas deferens 21
vase 63, 111

Vatican City 316
vault 235, 300
veal 118
vegetable garden 85, 182
vegetable oil 135
vegetables 107, 122, 124
veggie burger 155
veil 35
vein 19
venetian blind 63
Venezuela 315
venison 118
vent 283
ventilation hood 66
Venus 280
verdict 181
vest 33, 251
vet 189
vibraphone 257
video game 269
video phone 99
Viet Nam 318
viewfinder 271
village 299
vine 183
vinegar 135, 142
vineyard 183
vintage 199
viola 256
violin 256
virus 44
visa 213
vise 78
vision 51
visiting hours 48
visor 205
vitamins 108
v-neck 33
vocal cords 19
vodka 145
vodka and orange 151
voice message 99
volcano 283
volley 231
volleyball 227
voltage 60
volume 165, 179, 269, 311
vomit *v* 44

W

waders 244
wading pool 263
waffles 157
waist 12
waistband 35
waiting room 45
waitress 191
wake up *v* 71
walk 243
walking boot 37
wall 58, 186, 222
wall light 62
wallet 37
wallpaper 82, 177
wallpaper brush 82
wallpaper paste 82
wallpaper *v* 82
walnut 129
walnut oil 134
walrus 290
ward 48
wardrobe 70
warehouse 216
warm 286
warm up *v* 251
warm-up suit 31, 32
warrant 180
wash *v* 38, 77
washer 80
washer fluid reservoir 202
washer-dryer 76
washing machine 76
wasp 295
waste disposal 61, 266
waste disposal unit 61
wastebasket 172
watch 36
watch television *v* 269
water 144, 238
water bottle 206, 267
water chamber 61
water chestnut 124
water garden 84
water hazard 232
water heater 61
water jet 95
water plant 86
water polo 239
water ski 241
water sports 241
water *v* 90, 183
watercolors 274
watercress 123
waterfall 285
watering 89
watering can 89
watermelon 127
waterskier 241
waterskiing 241
wave 241, 264
wavelength 179
wax 41
weak 321
weather 286
weaving 277
website 177
wedding 26. 35
wedding cake 141
wedding dress 35
wedding reception 26
wedge 37, 233
Wednesday 306
weed killer 91
weed *v* 91
weeds 86
week 306
weekend 306
weekly 307
weigh *v* 310
weight 166
weight bar 251
weight belt 239
weight training 251
west 312
Western 255
Western sahara 317
wet 286, 321
wet wipe 75, 108
wetsuit 239
whale 290
wheat 130, 184
wheel 198, 207
lug nuts 203
wheelbarrow 88
wheelchair 48
wheelchair access 197
whiplash 46
whipped cream 137
whipped cream 157
whipping cream 137
whisk 68
whisk *v* 67
whiskers 290
whiskey 145
white 39, 145, 272, 274
white bread 139
white chocolate 113
white currant 127
white flour 138
white meat 118
white rice 130
whole 129, 132
whole milk 136
whole-grain 131
wholegrain mustard 135
whole-wheat bread 139
whole-wheat flour 138
wicket 225
wicket-keeper 225
wide 321
width 165
wife 22
Wi-Fi 269
wig 39
wild rice 130
wildlife park 262
willow 296
win *v* 273
wind 241, 286
windbreak 265
windlass 214
window 58, 96, 98, 177, 186, 197, 209, 210
windpipe 18
windshield 198, 205
windshield wiper 198
windshield wiper fluid 199
windsurfer 241
windsurfing 241
windy 286
wine 145, 151
wine glass 65
wine list 152
wine vinegar 135
wing 119, 210, 293
wings 254
winner 273
winter 31, 307
winter sports 247
wipe *v* 77
wire 79
wire cutter 80
wire stripper 81
wires 60
with 320
withdrawal slip 96
without 320
witness 180
wok 69
wolf 290
woman 23
womb 52
women's clothing 34
womenswear 105
wood 79, 233, 275, 285
wood bits 80
wood glue 78
wood shavings 78
wooden spoon 68
woodpecker 292
woodstain 79
woodwind 257
woodworking 275
work 172
work bowl 66, 69
workbench 78
workday 306
workshop 78
world map 312
worm 295
worried 25
wound 46
wrap 155
wrapping 111
wreath 111
wrench 80
wrestling 236
wrinkle 15
wrist 13, 15
wristband 230
writ 180
write *v* 162

X

x-ray 48
x-ray film 50
x-ray machine 212
x-ray viewer 45

Y

yacht 215
yam 125
yard 310
yarn 277
yatch 240
yawn *v* 25
year 163, 306
yeast 138
yellow 274
yellow card 223
Yemen 318
yes 322
yesterday 306
yoga 54
yogurt 137
yolk 137, 157
young cabbage 123
you're welcome 322
Yugoslavia 316

Z

Zambia 317
zebra 291
zero 308
zest 126
Zimbabwe 317
zinc 289
zip code 98
zipper 277
zone 315
zones 283
zoo 262
zoology 169
zoom lens 270
zucchini 125

French index • index français • französisches Register • índice francés • indice francese

A

à 320
à armature 35
à côté de 320
à deux portes 200
à droite 260
à emporter 154
à feuilles caduques 86
à feuilles persistantes 86
à gauche 260
à genou 34
à grains longs 130
à grains ronds 130
à impériale 260
à l'extérieur de 320
à l'heure 305
à l'intérieur de 320
à la carte 152
à l'huile 143
à quatre portes 200
à sens unique 194
à travers 320
à trois portes 200
abaisser à rouleau 67
abats *m* 118
abdominaux *m* 16
abeille *f* 295
abribus *m* 197
abricot *m* 126
acacia *m* 110
accélérateur *m* 200, 204
accès aux handicapés *m* 197
accessoires *m* 36, 38
accessoires de toilette *m* 41
accident *m* 46
accident de voiture *m* 203
accompagnement *m* 153
accotement stabilisé *m* 194
accouchement *m* 52
accouchement assisté *m* 53
accoudoir *m* 200, 210
accusation *f* 94, 180
accusé *m* 180, 181
acquitté 181
acrylique *m* 274
acte de naissance *m* 26
acte judiciaire *m* 180
acteur *m* 191, 254
acteurs *m* 179
action *f* 97
actions *f* 97, 233, 227, 229, 237
activités *f* 77, 162, 183, 245, 263
actrice *f* 254
acuponcture *f* 55
acupression *f* 55
addition *f* 152
additionner 165
admis 48
adolescente *f* 23
adresse e-mail *f* 177
adulte *m* 23
adversaire *f* 236
adzukis *m* 131
aéroboxe *m* 251
aéroglisseur *m* 215
aéroport *m* 212
affaires *f* 175
affiche *f* 255
Afghanistan 318
Afrique 317
Afrique du Sud 317
after-shave *m* 73
agate *f* 289
agence de voyage *f* 114
agenda *m* 173, 175
agenda électronique *m* 175
agent de conservation *m* 83
agent de la bourse *m* 97
agent de la circulation *m* 195
agent de voyage *m* 190
agent immobilier *m* 115, 189
aggloméré *m* 79
agitateur *m* 150
agneau *m* 118, 185
agrafe *f* 276
agrafes *f* 173
agrafeuse *f* 173
agrandir 172
agrandissement *m* 58, 271
agression *f* 94
agrumes *m* 126
aigle *m* 292
aiglefin *m* 120
aigre 127
aigue-marine *f* 288
aiguille *f* 109, 276
aiguille à tricoter *f* 277
aiguisoir *m* 68
aïkido *m* 236
ail *m* 125, 132
aile *f* 60, 119, 210, 293
aileron *m* 210
ailes de raie *f* 120
aimant *m* 167
aine *f* 12
airbag *m* 201
aire *f* 165
aire de stationnement *f* 199, 212
aisselle *f* 13
ajusté 35
alarme *f* 58
Alaska 314
Albanie 316
album de photos *m* 271
alésoir *m* 80
Algérie 317
alimentation *f* 105
aliments en bouteille *m* 134
allaitement *m* 53
allant au four 69
allée *f* 58, 85, 106, 254
Allemagne 316
allergie *f* 44
alligator *m* 293
allonge *f* 118
allumage *m* 200
allume-feu *m* 266
allumer la télévision 269
allumer un feu 266
alternateur *m* 203
altitude *f* 211
alto *m* 256
aluminium *m* 289
amande *f* 129
amandes *f* 151
amarres *f* 217
Amazonie *f* 312
amer 124
Amérique centrale 314
Amérique du Nord 314
améthyste *f* 288
ameublement *m* 105
ami *m* 24
amniocentèse *f* 52
amorce *f* 244
amorcer 245
amorti *m* 230
ampère *m* 60
amphibiens *m* 294
amplificateur *m* 268
ampoule *f* 46
ampoule basse consommation *f* 60
amuse-gueule *m* 151
an *m* 306
analgésique *m* 109
analgésiques *m* 47
analogique 179
analyse *f* 49
analyse de sang *f* 48
ananas *m* 128
ancre *f* 214, 240
Andes *f* 312
Andorre 316
âne *m* 185
anesthésiste *m* 48
aneth *f* 133
angle *m* 164
Angola 317
anguille *f* 294
animalerie *f* 115
animaux *m* 292, 294
anis *m* 133
anneau *m* 226
anneaux *m* 89, 235
anniversaire *m* 27
anniversaire de mariage *m* 26
annuel 86, 307
annulaire *m* 15
anorak *m* 31, 33
anse *f* 106
antenne *f* 295
antenne parabolique *f* 269
antenne radio *f* 214
anti-adhérent 69
antigel *m* 199, 203
Antigua-et-Barbuda 314
anti-inflammatoire *m* 109
antirides 41
antiseptique *m* 47
antivol *m* 207
août *m* 306
apéritif *m* 153
appareil de chauffage *m* 60
appareil de gym *m* 250
appareil dentaire *m* 50
appareil jetable *m* 270
appareil photo *m* 260
appareil photo APS *m* 270
appareils électriques *m* 105
appareils ménagers *m* 66
apparence *f* 30
appartement *m* 59
appât *m* 244
appel *m* 181
appendice *m* 18
applaudir 255
appli *m* 99
application *f* 176
applique *f* 62
apprendre 163
apprêt *m* 83
après 320
après-demain 307
après-midi *f* 305
après-soleil *m* 108
Arabie Saoudite 318
araignée *f* 295
arbitre *m* 222, 225, 226, 229, 230
arbre *m* 86, 296
arbre de transmission *m* 202
arbuste à fleurs *m* 87
arc *m* 164, 249, 300
arceau *m* 85
arc-en-ciel *m* 287
architecte *m* 190
architecture *f* 300
architrave *f* 301
ardoise *f* 288
arène *f* 243
arête *f* 121
argent *m* 97, 235, 289
Argentine 315
argile *f* 85, 275
arithmétique *f* 165
Arménie 318
armoire *f* 70
armoire encastrée *f* 71
aromathérapie *f* 55
arrestation *f* 94
arrêt *m* 269
arrêt de bus *m* 197, 299
arrêt interdit 195
arrière *m* 240
arrivée *f* 61
arrivées *f* 213
arrosage *m* 89
arroser 90, 183
arroseur *m* 89
art *m* 162
art déco 301
art nouveau 301
artère *f* 19
artichaut *m* 124
articles de sport *m* 105
articles de toilette *m* 107
articles pour bébés *m* 107
articulation *f* 17
articulation du doigt *f* 15
artiste peintre *f* 274
arts et métiers *m* 274, 276
arts martiaux *m* 237
as *m* 230, 273
ascenseur *m* 59, 100, 104
Asie 318
asperge *f* 124
asperger 91
aspirateur *m* 77, 188
assaisonné 159
assiette à dessert *f* 65
assiette à soupe *f* 65
assiette plate *f* 65
assignation *f* 180
assistant *m* 169
assistante *f* 24
assister à 174
associée *f* 24
astéroïde *m* 280
asthme *m* 44
astigmatisme *m* 51
astronaute *m* 281
astronomie *f* 281
atelier *m* 78
athlète *m* 234
athlétisme *m* 234
atmosphère *f* 282, 286
atrium *m* 104
attaches *f* 89
attaque *f* 44, 220
attelle *f* 47
attenante 58
atterrir 211
attraction touristique *f* 260
attractions *f* 261
attraper 225, 227, 229, 220, 245
au carré 39
au revoir 322
au sirop 159
aube *f* 305
aubergine *f* 125
auburn 39
au-delà de 320
au-dessous de 320
au-dessus de 320
auge *f* 183
aujourd'hui 306
auriculaire *m* 15
aurore *f* 286
Australasie 319
Australie 319
autobronzant *m* 41
autocaravane *f* 266
autodéfense *f* 237
automatique 200
automne *m* 31, 307
autoneige *m* 247
autopont *m* 194
autoroute *f* 194
autour de 320
autres arts *m* 275
autres bateaux *m* 215
autres magasins *m* 114
autres sports *m* 248
Autriche 316
autruche *f* 292
aux pépites de chocolats 141
avalanche *f* 247
avance rapide *f* 269
avant 320
avant *m* 240
avant *m* 222
avantage *m* 230
avant-bras *m* 12
avant-hier 307
avant-toit *m* 58
avec 320
avec plomb 199
avenue *f* 299
averse *f* 286
avertisseur d'incendie *m* 95
avion *m* 210
avion de ligne *m* 210, 212

français

avion léger *m* 211
avion supersonique *m* 211
avocat *m* 128, 180, 190
avoine *f* 130
avoir faim 64
avoir un bébé 26
avril *m* 306
avtivités de plein air *f* 262
Azerbaïdjan 318

B

babeurre *m* 137
bac à légumes *m* 67
bac à peinture *m* 83
bac à sable *m* 263
bacon *m* 118, 157
badge *m* 94,189
badminton *m* 231
baffle *m* 268
bagages *m* 100, 198, 213
bagages à main *m* 211, 213
bague *f* 36
baguette *f* 138, 256
Bahamas 314
Bahreïn 318
baie *f* 296
baignoire *f* 72
baignoire en plastique *f* 74
bâiller 25
bain moussant *m* 73
balai *m* 77
balai à gazon *m* 88
balai laveur *m* 77
balance *f* 45, 69, 98, 118, 166, 212, 310
balance à ressort *f* 166
balancier *m* 276
balançoire *f* 263
balayer 77
balayette *f* 77
balcon *m* 59, 254
Baléares 316
baleine *f* 290
balle *f* 75, 130, 184, 224, 228, 230
balle de criquet *f* 225
balle de golf *f* 233
ballerina *f* 37
ballet *m* 255
ballon *m* 221, 220, 222, 226
ballon de plage *m* 265
ballon lancé *m* 226
bambou *m* 86, 122
banane *f* 128
banc *m* 250, 262
banc à pique-nique *m* 266
banc de touche *m* 229
banc des jurés *m* 180
bandage *m* 47
bande de cheveux *f* 39
bande de roulement *f* 207
bande dessinée *f* 112
bande fluorescente *f* 205
bande sonore *f* 255
Bangladesh 318
banlieue *f* 299
banque *f* 96
baptême *m* 26
bar *m* 120, 150, 152
Barbade 314
barbecue *m* 267
barbillon *m* 244
barman *m* 150, 191
bar-mitsvah *f* 26
baroque 301
barque *f* 214
barrage *m* 300
barre *f* 207, 235, 240, 250
barre à poids *f* 251
barre d'outils *f* 177
barre de défilement *f* 177
barre de menus *f* 177
barre de mesure *f* 256
barre fixe *f* 235
barre transversale *f* 222
barreaux *m* 74
barres asymétriques *f* 235
barres parallèles *f* 235
barrière *f* 182
barrière d'escalier *f* 75
barrière de sécurité *f* 246
bas 321
bas *m* 35
basalte *m* 288
bascule *f* 263
base *f* 99, 164, 229
base du batteur *f* 228
baseball *m* 228
basilic *m* 133
basket *m* 226
basket *f* 37
baskets *m* 251
baskets *f* 31
bassin *m* 17, 85
basson *m* 257
bateau de pêche *m* 217
bâtiments *m* 299
bâtir 277
bâton *m* 235
bâton de ski *m* 246
bâtons *m* 133
batte *f* 225, 228
batter 229
batterie *f* 202, 258
batteur *m* 225, 228
battre 67, 273
battre un record 234
bavoir *m* 30, 50
beat *m* 259
beau-fils *m* 23
beau-frère *m* 23
beau-père *m* 23
beauté *f* 40, 105
bébé *m* 23, 30
bébé-phoque *m* 290
bec *m* 293
bec Bunsen *m* 166
bécarre *m* 256
bêche *f* 88
bécher *m* 167
bêcher 90
beignets de poulet *m* 155
Bélarus 316
Belgique 316
Bélize 314
belle-fille *f* 22, 23
belle-mère *f* 23
belle-sœur *f* 23
bémol *m* 256
Bénin 317
béquille *f* 205, 207
berline *f* 199
berline à hayon *f* 199
bermuda *m* 30
bestiaux *m* 183, 185
bétonnière *f* 186
bette *f* 123
betterave *f* 125
beurre *m* 137, 156
beurre de cacahouètes *m* 135
Bhoutan 318
biathlon *m* 247
biberon *m* 75
bibliothécaire *m* 190
bibliothécaire *f* 168
bibliothèque *f* 63, 168, 299
biceps *m* 16
bicyclette *f* 206
bidet *m* 72
bière *f* 145, 151
bière anglaise *f* 145
bière brune *f* 145
bifocal 51
bifteck d'aloyau *m* 119
bijouterie *f* 114
bijoutier *m* 188
bijoux *m* 36
bikini *m* 264
billard *m* 249
billard américain *m* 249
billet *m* 97, 209, 213
billets de loterie *m* 112
biologie *f* 162
biologique 91, 122
biplan *m* 211
Birmanie 318
bis *m* 255
bisannuel 86
biscuit *m* 113
biscuit scandinave *m* 139, 156
biscuits *m* 141
blanc 39, 145, 272, 274
blanc *m* 119
blanc d'œuf *m* 137
blazer *m* 33
blé *m* 130, 184
blé écrasé *m* 130
blessure *f* 46
bleu 274
bleu *m* 136
bleus *m* 82
bloc de béton *m* 187
blocage *m* 237
bloc-note 173
blond 39
bloquer 227
blues *m* 259
bobine *f* 276
bobine de fil *f* 276
bobsleigh *m* 247
bocal scellé *m* 135
bœuf *m* 118
bois *m* 79, 187, 233, 257, 275, 285
bois dur *m* 79
bois tendre *m* 79
boisson en boîte *f* 154
boisson maltée *f* 144
boisson non alcoolisée *f* 154
boissons *f* 107, 144, 156
boissons alcoolisées *f* 145
boissons chaudes *f* 144
boissons non alcoolisées *f* 144
boîte *f* 145, 311
boîte à bijoux *f* 36
boîte à déchets recyclables *f* 61
boîte à fusibles *f* 60
boîte à onglets *f* 81
boîte à outils *f* 80
boîte aux lettres *f* 58, 99
boîte d'équipement *f* 244
boîte de chocolats *f* 113
boîte de kleenex *f* 70
boîte de réception *f* 177
boîte de tri *f* 61
boîte de vitesses *f* 202, 204
boîte d'outils *f* 207
bol *m* 65
bol du mixeur *m* 66
Bolivie 315
bollard *m* 214
bombardier *m* 211
bombe *f* 242, 311
bôme *m* 240
bon 321
bonbon à la menthe *m* 113
bonbon au fruit *m* 113
bonbons *m* 113
bonbons assortis *m* 113
bonde *f* 72
bongos *m* 257
bonjour 322
bonne nuit 322
bonnet de natation *m* 238
bonsoir 322
bord du trottoir *m* 298
bordure de plantes herbacées *f* 85
bordure de plantes mixtes *f* 85
borne *f* 298
borne d'incendie *f* 95
Bosnie-Herzégovine 316
bosse *f* 291
Botswana 317
botte *f* 37, 111, 220, 223, 242
botter 221, 223
bottes *f* 89
bottes de caoutchouc *f* 31
bottes de pêche *f* 244
bouche *f* 14
bouche de l'égout *f* 299
boucher *m* 118, 188
boucherie *f* 114
bouchon *m* 134, 166
bouchon d'objectif *m* 270
boucle *f* 36
boucle d'oreille *f* 36
boudin *m* 157
boudoirs *m* 141
bouée *f* 217, 265
bouée de sauvetage *f* 240
bougie *f* 203
bougies d'anniversaire *f* 141
bouillir 67
bouilloire électrique *f* 66
bouillon *m* 158
bouillotte *f* 70
boulanger *m* 139
boulangerie *f* 107, 114, 138
boule *f* 149
boule de bowling *f* 249
bouleau *m* 296
boules de coton *f* 41
boulettes de viande *f* 158
bouquet *m* 35, 111
bouquet garni *m* 132
bourgeon *m* 111
bourriche *f* 244
bourse *f* 97, 169
boussole *f* 312
bouteille *f* 61, 135, 166, 311
bouteille d'eau *f* 206, 267
bouteille d'air *f* 239
boutique *f* 115
boutique d'art *f* 115
boutique de cadeaux *f* 114
boutique hors taxes *f* 213
bouton *m* 31, 32, 297
bouton d'appel *m* 48
bouton d'arrêt *m* 197
bouton de manchette *m* 36
bouton de mise au point *m* 167
bouton de porte *m* 59
boutonnière *f* 32
bouton-pression *m* 30
bowling *m* 249
box *m* 269
boxe *f* 236
boxe thaïlandaise *f* 236
bracelet *m* 36
bracelet d'identité *m* 53
brancard *m* 94
branche *f* 296
brandy *m* 145
bras *m* 13, 88
brassard *m* 45
brasse *f* 239
brassière *f* 238
break *m* 199
Brésil 315
bretelle *f* 35, 37
bretelle d'accès *f* 194
bretelle de sortie *f* 194
bride *f* 241, 242
bridge *m* 273
brie *m* 142
brillant 83
brillant à lèvres *m* 40
brilliant 271
brindille *f* 296
brioche *f* 157
brique *f* 187
briquet *m* 112
brise-bise *m* 63
broche *f* 36, 60, 68
brochure *f* 175
brochure de vacances *f* 212
brocoli *m* 123
broderie *f* 277
bronzage *m* 41
bronze *m* 235
brosse *f* 38, 72, 83
brosse à dents *f* 72
brosse à encoller *f* 82
brosse à sourcils *f* 40
brosse à tapisser *f* 82
brosse pour le dos *f* 73
brosser 38, 50
brouette *f* 88
brouillard *m* 287
broyeur d'ordures *m* 61
brûleur *m* 67
brûleur à gaz *m* 61
brulure *f* 46
brume *f* 287
Brunei 319
bruyère *f* 297
buanderie *f* 76
buffet *m* 152
buffet du petit déjeuner *m* 156
buggy *m* 232
bulbe *m* 86
Bulgarie 316
bunker *m* 232
bureau 172
bureau *m* 24, 63, 174, 177
bureau de change *m* 97
bureau des douanes *m* 216
bureau du chef *m* 266
burin *m* 81, 275
Burkina 317

français

Burundi 317
bus *m* 196
bus à deux étages *m* 196
bus de touristes *m* 197
bus scolaire *m* 196
bus touristique *m* 260
but *m* 221, 223, 224
bytes *m* 176

C

cabane *f* 84
cabin d'essayage *f* 104
Cabinda 317
cabine *f* 95, 210, 214
cabine de plage *f* 264
cabine du conducteur *f* 208
cabine téléphonique *f* 99
cabinet *m* 45, 180
câble *m* 79, 207
câble électrique *m* 176. 209
cabriole *f* 235
cabriolet sport *m* 198
cacahouète *f* 129
cacahouètes *f* 151
cacao *m* 156
cacatoès *m* 293
cachet 173
cachets antinaupathiques *m* 109
cachets de vitamines *m* 108
cactus *m* 87
caddie *m* 106, 208, 233
cadeau *m* 27
cadre *m* 62, 174, 206, 230, 267
cadre de photo *m* 271
cafard *m* 295
café *m* 144, 148, 153, 156, 184, 262
café filtre *m* 148
café glacé *m* 148
café moulu *m* 144
cafetière *f* 65
cage à poules *f* 263
cage thoracique *f* 17
cahier *m* 163
caille *f* 119
caisse *f* 106, 150, 255
caisse claire *f* 257
caissier *m* 96, 106
cake *m* 140
calamar *m* 121
calcaire *m* 288
calcite *f* 289
calcium *m* 109
calculatrice *f* 165
cale *f* 215, 233
cale sèche *f* 217
caleçon *m* 33
calendrier *m* 306
cale-pied *m* 207
calice *m* 297
calmar *m* 295
Cambodge 318
cambriolage *m* 94
cambrure *f* 15
camembert *m* 142
caméra *f* 178
cameraman *m* 178
Cameroun 317
caméscope *m* 260, 269
camion *m* 194
camionneur *m* 190
camisole *f* 35
camomille *f* 149
Campari *m* 145
camper 266
camping *m* 266
campus *m* 168
Canada 314
canapé *m* 62, 155
canapé-lit *m* 63
canard *m* 119, 185
canari *m* 292
caneton *m* 185
canine *f* 50
caniveau *m* 299
canne *f* 91
canne à pêche *f* 244
canne à sucre *f* 184
canneberge *f* 127
cannelle *f* 133
cannes *f* 89
canoë *m* 214, 241
canot de sauvetage *m* 214
capacité *f* 311
capitaine *m* 214
capitaine de port *m* 217
capitale *f* 315
capoeira *m* 237
capot *m* 198
capote *f* 75
cappuccino *m* 148
câpres *f* 143
capsule *f* 109
capuche *f* 31
car *m* 196
caractéristiques *f* 282
carambole *f* 128
caramel *m* 113
carapace *f* 293
caravane *f* 266
cardamome *f* 132
cardigan *m* 32
cardiologie *f* 49
cardio-vasculaire 19
cargaison *f* 216
cargo *m* 215
carie *f* 50
carnaval *m* 27
carnet 172
carnet à croquis *m* 275
carnet de chèques *m* 96
carotte *f* 124
carpe koi *f* 294
carquois *m* 249
carre *f* 246
carré *m* 164
carreau *m* 273
carrefour *m* 194, 298
carreler 82
carrosserie *f* 202
cartable *m* 162
carte *f* 27, 153, 154
carte bancaire *f* 96
carte d'embarquement *f* 213
carte de crédit *f* 96
carte de lecteur *f* 168
carte des vins *f* 152
carte du monde *f* 312
carte postale *f* 112
cartilage *m* 17
carton *m* 275, 311
carton de lait *m* 136
carton jaune *m* 223
carton rouge *m* 223
cascade *f* 285
case *f* 272
casier *m* 100
casier à bagages *m* 210
casier judiciaire *m* 181
casiers *m* 239
casino *m* 261
casque *m* 95, 204, 206, 220, 224, 228
casque de sécurité *m* 186
casquette *f* 36
casserole *f* 69
cassis *m* 127
catamaran *m* 215
cataphote *m* 207
cataracte *f* 51
cathédrale *f* 300
cathéter *m* 53
cause *f* 180
caution *f* 181
cavalier *m* 242, 272
caverne *f* 284
CD *m* 269
cèdre *m* 296
ceinture *f* 32, 35, 36, 236
ceinture à outils *f* 186
ceinture de plomb *f* 239
ceinture de sécurité *f* 198
ceinture de sécurité *f* 211
ceinture noire *f* 237
céleri *m* 122, 124
cellule *f* 94, 181
cendre *f* 283
cendres d'os *f* 88
cendrier *m* 150
cent 308
cent dix 308
cent mille 308
centième 309
centimètre *m* 276, 310
centre *m* 164
centre commercial *m* 104
centre de pisciculture *m* 183
cerceau *m* 277
cercle *m* 165
cercle central *m* 222, 224, 226
cercle de jeu *m* 224
cercle polaire arctique *m* 283
céréale *f* 130
céréales *f* 107, 130
céréales traitées *f* 130
cérémonie de la remise des diplômes *f* 169
céréales *f* 156
cerf *m* 291
cerise *f* 126
cerveau *m* 19
césarienne *f* 52
cette semaine 307
chaîne *f* 36, 178, 206, 269
chaîne de montagnes *f* 282
chaîne de sûreté *f* 59
chaîne hi-fi *f* 268
chair *f* 127, 129
chaise *f* 64
chaise haute *f* 75
chaise roulante *f* 48
chaise tournante 172
chambre *f* 58, 70, 283
chambre à air *f* 207
chambre à deux lits *f* 100
chambre d'enfants *f* 74
chambre d'eau *f* 61
chambre double *f* 100
chambre noire *f* 271
chambre privée *f* 48
chambre simple *f* 100
chambres *f* 100
chameau *m* 291
champ *m* 182
champ central *m* 228
champ droit *m* 229
champ extérieur *m* 229
champ gauche *m* 228
champ intérieur *m* 228
champagne *m* 145
champignon *m* 125
championnat *m* 223, 230
champs de courses *m* 243
changer de chaîne 269
changer de vitesse 207
changer une roue 203
chanson *f* 259
chanteur *m* 258
chanteuse *f* 191
chantier *m* 186
chantier naval *m* 217
chapeau *m* 36
chapeau de plage *m* 265
chapeau de soleil *m* 30
chapelure *f* 139
charbon *m* 288
charbon de bois *m* 266
charcuterie *f* 107, 142
chardon *m* 297
charger 76
chariot *m* 48, 213
chariot de levage *m* 186
chariot élévateur *m* 216
chasse-d'eau *f* 61
chasseur *m* 211
châssis *m* 203
chat *m* 290
châtaigne d'eau *f* 124
châtain 39
château *m* 300
chateau de sable *m* 265
chaton *m* 290
chaud 286, 321
chaudière *f* 61
chauffeur de taxi *m* 190
chaussettes *f* 33
chaussons *m* 30
chaussure *f* 233
chaussure compensée *f* 37
chaussure à talon *f* 37
chaussure de ski *f* 246
chaussure lacée *f* 37
chaussures *f* 34, 37
chaussures de marche *f* 267
chaussures en cuir *f* 32
chauve 39
chauve-souris *f* 290
chaux *f* 85
chavirer 241
cheddar *m* 142
chef *m* 24, 190
chef d'orchestre *m* 256
chef de cuisine *m* 152
cheminée *f* 58, 63, 214, 283
chemise *f* 33
chemise de nuit *f* 31, 35
chemisier *m* 34
chêne *m* 296
chenille *f* 295
chèque *m* 96
chercher 177
cheval *m* 185, 235, 242
cheval d'arçons *m* 235
cheval de course *m* 243
chevalet *m* 174, 258, 274
cheveux *m* 14, 38
cheville *f* 13, 15, 259
chèvre *m* 185
chevreau *m* 185
chèvrefeuille *m* 297
chevron *m* 186
chewing-gum *m* 113
chiche-kébab *m* 158
chicorée *f* 123
chien *m* 290
chien assis *m* 58
chiffon *m* 77
chignon *m* 39
Chili 315
chimie *f* 162
Chine 318
chiot *m* 290
chips *f* 113, 151
chiropractie *f* 54
chirurgie *f* 48
chirurgien *m* 48
chiurgie esthétique *f* 49
choc *m* 47
choc électrique *m* 46
chocolat *m* 113
chocolat au lait *m* 113
chocolat blanc *m* 113
chocolat chaud *m* 144
chocolat en poudre *m* 148
chocolat noir *m* 113
chœur *m* 301
choqué 25
chorizo *m* 143
chou *m* 123
chou chinois *m* 123
chou de Bruxelles *m* 122
chou frisé *m* 123
chou précoce *m* 123
chouette *f* 292
chou-fleur *m* 124
chou-rave *m* 123
chronomètre *m* 166, 234
chrysanthème *m* 110
chute *f* 237
chutney *m* 134
Chypre 316
cible *f* 249, 273
ciboule *f* 125
ciboulette *f* 133
cidre *m* 145
cigare *m* 112
cigarettes *f* 112
cigogne *f* 292
cil *m* 14, 51
ciment *m* 186
cinéma *m* 255, 299
cinq 308
cinq cents 308
cinqante-cinq mille cinq cents 309
cinquante 308
cinquante mille 309
cinquantième 309
cinquième 309
cintre *m* 70
circonférence *f* 164
circulation *f* 194
cire *f* 77
cirer 77
cisaille *f* 89
ciseaux *m* 38, 47, 82, 276
ciseaux à ongles *m* 41
Cité du Vatican *f* 316
citron *m* 126
citron et glaçons 151
citron vert *m* 126
citronnelle *f* 133
citrouille *f* 125
clair 41, 321
clam *f* 121
claquette *f* 179

français

clarinette *f* 257
clarinette basse *f* 257
classe *f* 163
classe affaires *f* 211
classe économique *f* 211
classeur à levier 173
clavicule *f* 17
clavier 97, 99, 176
clayette *f* 67
clé de fa *f* 256
clé de sol *f* 256
clef *f* 59, 80, 207
clef à molette *f* 80
clef à pipe *f* 80
clef de la chambre *f* 100
clef serre-tube *f* 81
clementine *f* 126
clé USB *f* 176
client *m* 96, 100, 104, 106, 152, 175, 180
cliente *f* 38
clignotant *m* 198, 204
climatisation *f* 200
clinique *f* 48
clipboard 173
clitoris *m* 20
clôture *f* 85, 182
clou *m* 80
clou de girofle *m* 133
clubs de golf *m* 233
coccinelle *f* 295
coccyx *m* 17
cocher 233
cochon *m* 185
cockpit *m* 210
cocktail *m* 151
cocon *m* 295
cocotte *f* 69
cocquille *f* 129
code barres *m* 106
code postal *m* 98
code secret *m* 96
cœur *m* 18, 119, 122, 273
cœurs de palmier *m* 122
coffre *m* 198
coiffeur *m* 39, 188
coiffeuse *f* 38, 71
coiffures *f* 39
coin de la rue *m* 298
coing *m* 128
col *m* 32
col de l'utérus *m* 20
col de l'utérus *m* 52
col rond *m* 33
cola *m* 144
colibri *m* 292
colis *m* 99
collage *m* 275
collant *m* 35, 251
colle *f* 275
colle à bois *f* 78
colle à tapisser *f* 82
collègue *m* 24
collier *m* 36
colline *f* 284
Colombie 315
colonie 315
colonne *f* 300
colonne vertébrale *f* 17
colza *m* 184
combat *m* 237
combinaison *f* 35
combinaison de neige *f* 30
combinaison de plongée *f* 239
combinaison-short *f* 30
combiné *m* 99
comédie *f* 255
comédie musicale *f* 255
comédie romantique *f* 255
comète *f* 280
commande *f* 269
commander 153
commandes *f* 201, 204
commencer à l'école 26
commis *m* 152
commission *f* 97
commode *f* 70
commotion cérébrale *f* 46
communications *f* 98
Comores 317
compartiment *m* 209
compartiment à bagages *m* 196
compartiment-couchettes *m* 209
compas *m* 165, 240
complet 129, 131, 266
composer 99
compositions florales *f* 111
comptabilité *f* 175
comptable *m* 97, 190
compte courant *m* 96
compte de courrier électronique *m* 177
compte d'épargne *m* 97
compte rendu *m* 174
compte-gouttes *m* 109, 167
compter 165
compte-tours *m* 201
compteur *m* 201, 204
compteur de vues *m* 270
compteur d'électricité *m* 60
comptoir *m* 96, 100, 142, 150
comptoir sandwichs *m* 143
conception *f* 52
concert *m* 255, 258
concert de rock *m* 258
concevoir 20
concombre *m* 125
condamnation *f* 181
conditionnement physique *m* 250
conditionneur *m* 38
condom *m* 21
conducteur *m* 196
conducteur de bus *m* 190
conduit éjaculatoire *m* 21
conduit spermatique *m* 21
conduite à droite *f* 201
conduite à gauche *f* 201
conduite d'amenée *f* 61
cône *m* 164, 187
conférencier *m* 174
confiant 25
confiserie *f* 107, 113
confiseur *m* 113
confiture *f* 134, 156
confiture de framboises *f* 134
confiture d'oranges *f* 134, 156
confus 25
congélateur *m* 67
congeler 67
conglomérat *m* 288
Congo 317
conifère *m* 86
connaissance *m* 24
connecter 177
conseil juridique *m* 180
conseillère *f* 55
conseillère financière *f* 97
Conservatoire *m* 169
conserves *f* 107
console *f* 269
constellation *f* 281
consterné 25
construction *f* 186
construire 186
consultation *f* 45
conteneur *m* 216
continent *m* 282, 315
contraception *f* 21, 52
contraction *f* 52
contrat *m* 175
contrebasse *f* 256
contrebasson *m* 257
contrefort *m* 301
contreplaqué *m* 79
contrôle de passeports *m* 213
contrôleur *m* 209
contusion *f* 46
convecteur *m* 60
copeaux *m* 78
copilote *m* 211
coq *m* 185
coque *f* 121, 214, 240
coquelicot *m* 297
coquetier *m* 65, 137
coquillage *m* 265
coquille *f* 137
coquille Saint-Jacques *f* 121
cor *m* 257
cor anglais *m* 257
corbeau *m* 292
corbeille *f* 254
corbeille à couture *f* 276
corbeille à papier 172
corbeille arrivée 172
corbeille de fruits *f* 126
corbeille départ 172
corde *f* 248, 258, 266
corde à linge *f* 76
cordes *f* 256
cordes vocales *f* 19
cordon ombilical *m* 52
Corée du Nord 318
Corée du Sud 318
coriandre *f* 133
corne 293
cornée *f* 51
corner *m* 223
corniche *f* 300
corps *m* 12
correcteur *m* 40
correspondance *f* 212
correspondant *m* 24
Corse 316
corset *m* 35
Costa Rica 314
costume *m* 255
costume *m* 32
côte *f* 17, 285
côté *m* 164
côte de bœuf *f* 119
Côte d'Ivoire 317
côtelette *f* 119
côtes *f* 155
coton *m* 184, 277
cottage *m* 136
cou *m* 12
couche *f* 75
couche de fond *f* 83
couche d'ozone *f* 286
couche éponge *f* 30
couche jetable *f* 30
coucher *m* 74
coucher du soleil *m* 305
coude *m* 13
cou-de-pied *m* 15
coudre 277
couenne *f* 119
couette *f* 71
couettes *f* 39
couffin *m* 75
couleur *f* 273
couleur à l'eau *f* 274
couleur pour bois *f* 79
couleurs *f* 39, 274
couleurs à l'huile *f* 274
coulisses *f* 254
couloir *m* 168, 210, 234, 238
country *f* 259
coup *m* 151, 233, 237, 273
coup de pied *m* 237, 239
coup de poing *m* 237
coup de soleil *m* 46
coup droit *m* 231
coup du lapin *m* 46
coup franc *m* 222
coup manqué *m* 228
coupable 181
coupe *f* 91
coupé 99
coupe courte *f* 39
coupe-ongles *m* 41
couper 38, 67, 277
coupe-tube *m* 81
couple *m* 24
coups *m* 231
coupure *f* 46
coupure de courant *f* 60
cour *f* 58, 84
cour de ferme *f* 182
courant *m* 60
courant alternatif *m* 60
courant continu *m* 60
courbe 165
courbe *f* 48
coureur automobile *m* 249
courge *f* 124, 125
courge musquée *f* 125
courgette *f* 125
courir 228
couronne *f* 50, 111
courrier électronique *m* 177
courroie de cames *f* 203
courroie de ventilateur *f* 203
course *f* 234
course attelée *f* 243
course automobile *f* 249
course de chevaux *f* 243
course de moto *f* 249
course de plat *f* 243
course de trot *f* 243
courser 229
courses *f* 104, 243
court 321
court de tennis *m* 230
couscous *m* 130
cousin *m* 22
coussin *m* 62
coussinets *m* 53
couteau *m* 65, 80, 121
couteau à pain *m* 68
couteau de cuisine *m* 68
couture *f* 34
couturier *m* 191
couturière *f* 191, 277
couvercle *m* 61, 66
couvert *m* 65
couverts *m* 64
couverture *f* 71, 74
couverture chauffante *f* 71
couverture de protection *f* 83
couverture du sol *f* 87
couverture laineuse *f* 74
couveuse *f* 53
couvre-lit *m* 70
crabe *m* 121, 295
crachoir *m* 50
craie *f* 162, 288
craie de tailleur *f* 276
crampe *f* 239
crampes *f* 44
crâne *m* 17
crapaud *m* 294
cratère *m* 283
cravache *f* 242
cravate *f* 32
crawl *m* 239
crayon *m* 163, 275
crayon à lèvres *m* 40
crayon à sourcils *m* 40
crayon de couleur *m* 163
crème *f* 109, 137, 140, 157
crème *m* 148
crème allégée *f* 137
crème anglaise *f* 140
crème caramel *f* 141
crème épaisse *f* 137
crème fouettée *f* 137
crème fraîche *f* 137
crème hydratante *f* 41
crème pâtissière *f* 140
crème pour le visage *f* 73
crème pour l'érythème *f* 74
crémerie *f* 107
crêpes *f* 155, 157
crépuscule *m* 305
cresson *m* 123
creuset *m* 166
creux des reins *m* 13
crevaison *f* 203, 207
crevette *f* 121
crevettes décortiquées *f* 120
cric *m* 203
cricket *m* 225
crier 25
crime *m* 94
criminel *m* 181
crinière *f* 242, 291
crise cardiaque *f* 44
cristallin *m* 51
Croatie 316
crochet *m* 187, 277
crocodile *m* 293
croissant *m* 156
croissant de lune *m* 280
croquant 127
croquis *m* 275
crosse *f* 224, 249
crosse de hockey *f* 224
croûte *f* 136, 139, 142
cru 124, 129
Cuba 314
cube *m* 164
cubitus *m* 17
cueillir 91
cuiller *f* 65
cuiller à café *f* 65, 153
cuiller à glace *f* 68
cuiller à servir *f* 68
cuiller à soupe *f* 65

cuiller en bois *f* 68
cuiller pour mesurer *f* 109
cuir chevelu *m* 39
cuire à la vapeur 67
cuire au four 67
cuisine *f* 66, 67, 152, 214
cuisse *f* 12, 119
cuit 159
cuit à la vapeur 159
cuivre *m* 289
cuivres *m* 256
culasse *f* 202
culotte en plastique *f* 30
cultivateur *m* 182
cultiver 91
culture *f* 183
cultures *f* 184
cumin *m* 132
curcuma *m* 132
curling *m* 247
curry *m* 158
cutter *m* 82
cuvette *f* 61
cygne *m* 293
cylindre *m* 164
cymbales *f* 257

D

d'accord 322
dame *f* 272, 273
dames *f* 272
dance *f* 259
Danemark 316
danger *m* 195
dans 320
danseuse *f* 191
dard *m* 295
date *f* 306
date d'expiration *f* 109
date de retour *f* 168
date du procès *f* 180
datte *f* 129
dauphin *m* 290
daurade *f* 120
de 320
dé *m* 272
dé à coudre *m* 276
de ferme 118
de rien 322
de saison 129
de troisième cycle 169
débarquer 217
début *m* 321
décapotable *f* 199
décembre *m* 306
décennie *f* 307
déchets bios *m* 61
déclencher l'accouchement 53
déclencheur *m* 270
décoller 82, 211
décongeler 67
décontracté 34
décor *m* 254
décor de cinéma *m* 179
décoration *f* 82, 141
décortiqué 129
découper 79
découvert *m* 96
décrêper 39
défaire 277
défense *f* 181, 220, 291
défenseur *m* 223
défilé *m* 27
dehors 320
déjeuner *m* 64
déjeuner d'affaires *m* 175
deltaplane *m* 248
deltoïde *m* 16
demain 306
démaquillant *m* 41
demi-heure 304
demi-litre *m* 311
demi-pension *f* 101
démonte-pneu *m* 207
dénominateur *m* 165
dent *f* 50
dentelle *f* 35, 277
dentier *m* 50
dentifrice *m* 72
dentiste *f* 189
dentiste *m* 50
déodorant *m* 73
déodorants *m* 108
dépanneuse *f* 203
départ *m* 232
départ plongé *m* 239
départs *m* 213
dépendance *f* 182
déplantoir *m* 89
dépliants *m* 96
déposition *f* 180
dérive *f* 210, 241
dermatologie *f* 49
dernière couche *f* 83
derrière 320
descente *f* 247
désert *m* 285
désherber 91
dessert *m* 153
desserts *m* 140
dessin *m* 275
dessin animé *m* 178
dessinateur *m* 191
dessiner 91, 162
dessous de verre *m* 150
dessus 98
destination *f* 213
détecteur de fumée *m* 95
détergent *m* 77
deux 308
deux cents 308
deux heures 304
deux mille 307
deux mille un 307
deux pintes 311
deuxième 309
deuxième étage *m* 104
deuxième galerie *f* 254
devant 320
développer 271
déviation *f* 195
dévidoir de scotch 173
dévidoir de tuyau *m* 89
devises étrangères *f* 97
devoirs *m* 163
diabète *m* 44
diable *m* 100
diagonale *f* 164
diamant *m* 288
diamètre *m* 164
diaphragme *m* 21, 19
diarrhée *f* 44, 109
dictionnaire *m* 163
dièse *m* 256
diesel *m* 199
difficile 321
digestif 19
digitale *f* 297
dilatation *f* 52
dimanche *m* 306
dimensions *f* 165
dinde *f* 119
dindon *m* 185, 293
dîner *m* 64
dinghy pneumatique *m* 215
dioptrie *f* 51
diplomate *m* 141
diplôme *m* 169
directeur *m* 163, 174
directeur d'agence *m* 96
directeur général *m* 175
directions *f* 260
disc-jockey *m* 179
discuter 163
disque *m* 234
disque dur externe *m* 176
dissertation *f* 169
dissolvant *m* 41
distance *f* 310
distractions à la maison *f* 268
distributeur *m* 97, 203
distribution *f* 98, 254
district *m* 315
dividendes *f* 97
divisé par 165
diviser 165
divorce *m* 26
Diwali *f* 27
dix 308
dix mille 309
dix-huit 308
dix-huitième 309
dixième 309
dix-neuf 308
dix-neuvième 309
dix-sept 308
dix-septième 309
Djibouti 317
dock *m* 214, 216
docteur *m* 189
doctorat *m* 169
document attaché *m* 177
documentaire *m* 178
dôme *m* 300
Dominique 314
dominos *m* 273
donner 273
donner à manger 183
donner le sein 53
dorsal *m* 16
dos *m* 13
dos du pied *m* 15
dos-nu 35
dossier *m* 210
dossier *m* 177
dossier suspendu 173
dossier-classeur 173
douane *f* 212
double *m* 230
double 151
double toit *m* 266
doubler 195
doublure *f* 32
douche *f* 72
douches *f* 266
douille *f* 69, 80
douve *f* 300
douze 308
douzième 309
dragée à la gelée *f* 113
drainage *m* 91
drap *m* 71, 74
drapeau *m* 221, 232, 235
drapeau de coin *m* 223
dressage *m* 243
dribbler 223
driver 233
droit *m* 169, 180
droite 165
drummer *m* 258
duffel-coat *m* 31
dumper *m* 187
duodénum *m* 18
dur 129, 321
DVD *m* 269
dynamo *f* 207

E

eau *f* 144, 238
eau de Javel
eau de toilette *f* 41
eau dentifrice *f* 72
eau du robinet *m* 144
eau en bouteille *f* 144
eau minérale *f* 144
écaille *f* 121, 294
écaillé 121
écailles *f* 293
échafaudage *m* 186
échalote *f* 125
échange *m* 230
écharde *f* 46
écharpe *f* 31, 46
échecs *m* 272
échelle *f* 95, 186
écheveau *m* 277
échiquier *m* 272
échographie *f* 52
éclair *m* 140, 287
éclairage *m* 105, 178
éclipse *f* 280
école *f* 162, 299
école de danse *f* 169
école des beaux arts *f* 169
écoles *f* 169
écolier *m* 162
écolière *f* 162
écorce *f* 127, 282, 296
écorchure *f* 46
écoute *f* 241
écouteurs *m* 268
écran *m* 97, 176, 255, 269
écran d'information *m* 213
écran de protection *m* 88
écran de soleil *m* 108
écran total *m* 108, 265
écrasé 132
écrase-viande *m* 68
écrevisse *f* 121
écrire 162
écrou *m* 80
écrous de roue *m* 203
écume *f* 241
écumoire *f* 68
écureuil *m* 290
écurie *f* 185, 243
eczéma *m* 44
édam *m* 142
édredon *m* 71
éducation physique *f* 162
effet *m* 230
effets secondaires *m* 109
effrayé 25
égale 165
égalité *f* 223, 230
église *f* 298, 300
égout *m* 299
égouttoir *m* 67
Égypte 317
élaguer 91
élastique 173
électricien *m* 188
électricité *f* 60
électrode négative *f* 167
électrode positive *f* 167
électroménager *m* 107
éléphant *m* 291
élève *m* 162
e-mail *m* 98
émail *m* 50
emballage *m* 111
embarcadère *f* 217
embarquer 217
embouteillage *m* 195
embouts de tournevis *m* 80
embrayage *m* 200, 204
embryon *m* 52
émeraude *f* 288
émettre 178
émigrer 26
Émirats arabes unis 318
émission *f* 179
émotions *f* 25
empennage *m* 210
emplacement *m* 266
emplacements de libre 266
employé *m* 24
employée de magasin *f* 188
employeuse *f* 24
empoisonnement *m* 46
empreintes *f* 94
emprunter 168
en bas 320
en différé 178
en direct 178
en face de 320
en filets 121
en flocons 132
en haut 320
en ligne 177
en morceaux 132
en poudre 132
en purée 159
en sauce 159
en saumure 143
en verre 69
encaisser 97
enceinte 52
enclos *m* 185, 242
encolure en V *f* 33
encre *f* 275
encyclopédie *f* 163
endive *f* 122
endocrine 19
endocrinologie *f* 49
enduit *m* 83
enfant *m* 23
enfant *m* 31
enfants *m* 23
enfiler 277
engrais *m* 91
enjoliveur *m* 202
enlèvement de déchets *m* 61
enlever les fleurs fanées 91
ennuyé 25
enquête *f* 94
enregistrement des bagages *m* 213
enregistrer 212, 269
enrobé de chocolat 140
enseigne *f* 104
enseignement supérieur *m* 168
ensoleillé 286
enterrement *m* 26
en-tête 173
entonnoir *m* 166

entorse *f* 46
entracte *m* 254
entraînement *m* 237
entraînement en circuit *m* 251
entraînement poids et haltères *m* 251
entraîneuse *f* 250
entre 320
entrée *f* 58, 59, 153
entrepôt *m* 216
entrer 177
entrer en éruption 283
enveloppe 173
enveloppe *f* 98
environnement *m* 280
environs *m* 299
envoi en recommandé *m* 98
envoyer 177
éouffer 47
épais 321
épargne *f* 96
épaule *f* 13
épaulette *f* 35
épeler 162
épicé 124
épicerie *f* 114
épices *f* 132
épiglotte *f* 19
épilation *f* 41
épilepsie *f* 44
épinards *m* 123
épingle *f* 276
épingle de cravate *f* 36
épingle de sûreté *f* 47
épisiotomie *f* 52
épluche-légume *m* 68
éplucher 67
éponge *f* 73, 74, 83
épousseter 77
épouvantail *m* 184
épreuve *f* 271
épreuves *f* 247
éprouvette *f* 166
épuisette *f* 244
Équateur 315
équateur *m* 283
équation *f* 165
équerre *f* 165
équipage *m* 241
equipe *f* 220, 229
équipement *m* 165, 233, 238
équipement de bureau 172
équipement d'entretien *m* 77
équitation *f* 242, 263
érable *m* 296
éruption *f* 44
Érythrée 317
escabeau *m* 82
escalade *f* 248
escalade en glace *f* 247
escalator *m* 104
escalier *m* 59
escalier de secours *m* 95
escalier d'entraînement 250
escargot *m* 295
escrime *f* 249
espace *m* 280
espadon *m* 120, 294
Espagne 316
essai *m* 221
essence *f* 199
essieu *m* 205
essorer 76
essoreuse *f* 76
essuie-glace *m* 198
essuyer 77
est *m* 312
estomac *m* 18
Estonie 316
estragon *m* 133
estuaire *m* 285
établi *m* 78
étage inférieur *m* 141
étage supérieur *m* 141
étagère *f* 66, 106, 268
étain *m* 289
étamine *f* 297
État *m* 315
États-Unis d'Amérique 314
étau *m* 78
été *m* 31, 307
éteindre la télévision 269
étendre 251
éternuement *m* 44
Éthiopie 317
étiquette 173
étiquettes *f* 89
étirement *m* 251
étoile *f* 280
étoile de mer *f* 295
être en défense 229
étrier *m* 242
étroit 321
étude *f* 162
études d'ingénieur *f* 169
étudiant *m* 169
etui *m* 51
étui à lentilles *m* 51
eucalyptus *m* 296
Europe 316
événements de la vie *m* 26
évent *m* 290
évier *m* 61, 66
examen *m* 163
examen de la vue *m* 51
examen médical *m* 45
excédent de bagages *m* 212
excité 25
exécuter un swing 232
exercice pour la poitrine *m* 251
exercice pour les biceps *m* 251
exercices *m* 251
exercices au sol *m* 235
exercices Pilates *m* 251
exfolier 41
exosphère *f* 286
expéditeur *m* 98
expérience *f* 166
exploitation fruitière *f* 183
exploitations agricoles *f* 183
exploration spatiale *f* 281
exposition *f* 261
expresso *m* 148
expulsion *f* 223
extérieur *m* 198
extincteur *m* 95
extraction *f* 50
eye-liner *m* 40

F

faché 25
facile 321
facile à cuisiner 130
facteur *m* 98, 190
faible 321
fair du pain 138
faire cuire au four 138
faire des amis 26
faire du vélo 207
faire le lit 71
faire marche arrière 195
faire rebondir 227
faire son testament 26
faire un dunk 227
faire un vœu 140
faire une manchette 227
faire une mise en plis 38
faire une passe 220, 223
faire une réservation de vol 212
faire une tête 222
fairway *m* 232
faisan *m* 119, 293
fait-tout *m* 69
falaise *f* 285
famille *f* 22
fans *m* 258
farci 159
fard à joues *m* 40
fard à paupières *m* 40
farine *f* 138
farine avec la levure chimique *f* 139
farine blanche *f* 138
farine brute *f* 138
farine complète *f* 138
farine sans levure chimique *f* 139
farine traitée *f* 139
faucon *m* 292
fausse couche *f* 52
faute *f* 222, 226, 230
fauteuil *m* 63, 254
fauteuil de dentiste *m* 50
fax *m* 98
Fédération de Russie 318
féminin 20
femme *f* 12, 22, 23
femme d'affaires *f* 175
fémur *m* 17
fendoir *m* 68
fenêtre *f* 58, 177, 186, 197, 209
feng shui *m* 55
fenouil *m* 122, 133
fente *f* 97
fente avant *f* 251
fenugrec *m* 132
fer *m* 109, 233, 289
fer à cheval *m* 242
fer à friser *m* 38
fer à lisser *m* 38
fer à repasser *m* 76
fer à souder *m* 81
ferme *f* 182, 184
ferme 124
fermé 260, 321
ferme d'aviculture *f* 183
ferme de culture *f* 183
ferme d'élevage de moutons *f* 183
ferme d'élevage porcin *f* 183
ferme laitière *f* 183
fermeture éclair *f* 277
fermier *m* 182, 189
fermoir *m* 36
ferry *m* 215, 216
fertilisation *f* 20
fertiliser 91
fesse *f* 13
fessier *m* 16
fête *f* 140
fête de Thanksgiving *f* 27
fêtes *f* 27
feu *m* 217
feu arrière *m* 204, 207
feu de camp *m* 266
feuillage *m* 110
feuille *f* 122, 296
feuille de laurier *f* 133
feuilles de thé *f* 144
feux *m* 94, 194
feux de détresse *m* 201
fève *f* 122
fèves *f* 131
février *m* 306
fiancé *m* 24
fiancée *f* 24
fiancés *m* 24
fibre *f* 127
fibre naturelle *f* 31
ficelle *f* 89
fiche compliments 173
fiche de retrait *f* 96
fiche intercalaire 173
fiches de versement *m* 96
fichier *m* 177
Fidji 319
fier 25
fièvre *f* 44
figue *f* 129
figue de Barbarie *f* 128
fil *m* 276
fil à plomb *m* 82
fil de fer *m* 79
fil dentaire *m* 50, 72
file de droite *f* 194
filet *m* 119, 121, 217, 222, 226, 227, 231
filets de flétan *m* 120
fille *f* 22, 23
film *m* 178, 269
film d'aventure *m* 255
film d'horreur *m* 255
film d'animation *m* 255
film de science-fiction *m* 255
fils *m* 22, 60
filtre *m* 270
filtre à air *m* 202
filtre d'air *m* 204
fin *f* 321
finance *f* 97
Finlande 316
fiole *f* 166
flageolets *m* 131
flamant *m* 292
flanc *m* 284
flash *m* 270
flash compact *m* 270
flèche *f* 95, 249, 300
fléchettes *f* 273
fléchir 251
fleur *f* 297
fleuret *m* 249
fleurette *f* 122
fleuriste *f* 188
fleuriste *m* 110
fleuron *m* 300
fleurs *f* 110
fleurs séchées *f* 111
flexion de jambes *f* 251
florentin *m* 141
flotteur *m* 61, 244
flou 271
flûte *f* 139, 257
fœtus *m* 52
foie *m* 18, 118
foin *m* 184
foire *f* 262
fois 165
follicule *m* 20
foncé 41, 321
fond de teint *m* 40
fontaine *f* 85
fontaine publique *f* 262
foot *m* 222
football américain *m* 220
forceps *m* 53, 167
forêt *f* 285
foret à bois plat *m* 80
foret à métaux *m* 80
foret de maçonnerie *m* 80
foret de sécurité *m* 80
forêt tropicale *f* 285
forets *m* 80
forets de bois *m* 80
formes *f* 164
fort 321
fosse d'orchestre *f* 254
fossette *f* 15
fou *m* 272
fouet *m* 68
fougère *f* 86
foulard *m* 36
four *m* 66
fourche *f* 88, 207
fourches *f* 39
fourchette *f* 65, 153
fourchette à découper *f* 68
fourmi *f* 295
fourneau *m* 112
fournitures de bureau 173
fourre-tout *m* 37
foyer *m* 255
fraction *f* 165
fracture *f* 46
fragile 98
frais 121, 127, 130
frais bancaires *m* 96
fraise *f* 50, 127
framboise *f* 127
France 316
frange de lit *f* 71
frapper 224, 225
freesia *m* 110
freezer *m* 67
frein *m* 204
frein *m* 200, 206
frein à main *m* 203
freiner 207
fréquence *f* 179
frère *m* 22
friandise *f* 113
frigidaire *m* 67
frire 67
frise *f* 301
frisé 39
frit 159
frites *f* 154
froid 286, 321
fromage *m* 136, 156
fromage à la crème *m* 136
fromage à pâte molle *m* 136
fromage à pâte pressée cuite *m* 136
fromage à pâte pressée non cuite *m* 136
fromage à pâte semi-molle *m* 136
fromage de chèvre *m* 142
fromage frais *m* 136
fromage râpé *m* 136
froncement de sourcils *m* 25
front *m* 14
frontail *m* 242

français

frontal *m* 16
fronton *m* 301
fruit confit *m* 129
fruit de feijoa *m* 128
fruit de l'arbre à pain *m* 124
fruit de la passion *m* 128
fruits *m* 107, 126, 128, 157
fruits à noyau *m* 126
fruits de mer *m* 121
fruits en bocaux *m* 134
fruits secs *m* 156
fruits tropicaux *m* 128
fumé 118, 121, 143, 159
fumée *f* 95
fumer 112
fumer en surface 90
fusain *m* 275
fuseau *m* 277
fusée d'orientation *f* 281
fusée éclairante *f* 240
fuselage *m* 210
fusible *m* 60
fusil *m* 118

G

Gabon 317
gagnant *m* 273
gagner 273
galaxie *f* 280
galerie *f* 198
galerie à vélo *f* 207
gallon *m* 311
galop *m* 243
galvanisé 79
Gambie 317
gamme *f* 256
gant *m* 224, 228, 233, 236, 246
gant isolant *m* 69
gants *m* 36
gants de boxe *m* 237
gants de jardinage *m* 89
garage *m* 58, 199, 203
garçon *m* 23, 152
garde *m* 189
garde-boue *m* 205
garde-côte *m* 217
gardien de but *m* 222
gardien de guichet *m* 225
gardien de prison *f* 181
gare *f* 208
gare routière *f* 197
garer 195
garniture *f* 140, 155
gâteau au chocolat *m* 140
gâteau d'anniversaire *m* 141
gâteau de mariage *m* 141
gâteau de miel *m* 135
gâteaux *m* 140
gâteaux de fête *m* 141
gaufres *f* 157
gaze *f* 47
gazeux 144
gazonner 90
gel *m* 38, 109, 287
gel douche *m* 73
gemmes *f* 288
gencive *f* 50
gendre *m* 22
gêné 25
génération *f* 23
génératrice *f* 60
genou *m* 12
genouillère *f* 227
genres de pêche *m* 245
genres de plantes *m* 86
gens 12, 16
géographie *f* 162
géométrie *f* 165
Géorgie 318
gerbera *m* 110
germe de soja *m* 122
germoir *m* 89
geyser *m* 285
Ghana 317
gibier *m* 119
gigot *m* 119
gilet *m* 33
gilet de sauvetage *m* 240
gin *m* 145
gin tonic *m* 151
gingembre *m* 125, 133
girafe *f* 291
giroflée *f* 110
givre *m* 287
glaçage *m* 141
glace *f* 120, 137, 149, 287
glacer 139
glacier *m* 284
glaçon *m* 151, 287
glaïeul *m* 110
glande *f* 19
glisser 229
glissière de sécurité *f* 195
gneiss *m* 288
golf *m* 232
gomme *f* 163
gong *m* 257
gorge *f* 19, 284
gorille *m* 291
gotique 301
gouache *f* 274
gourde amère *f* 124
gousse *f* 122, 125
gouttes *f* 109
gouttière *f* 58
gouvernail *m* 241
gouverne *f* 210
goyave *f* 128
GPS *m* 195
grain *m* 122, 130
grain de beauté *m* 14
grain de moutarde *m* 131
grain de poivre *m* 132
graine *f* 122, 130
graine de carvi *f* 131
graine de potiron *f* 131
graine de sésame *f* 131
graine de tournesol *f* 131
graines *f* 88, 131
graines de fenouil *f* 133
graines de pavot *f* 138
graines de soja *f* 131
grains *m* 144
gramme *m* 310
grand 321
grand bassin *m* 239
grand bol *m* 69
grand lit *m* 71
grand magasin *m* 105
grande aiguille *f* 304
grande cisaille *f* 88
grande tasse *f* 65
grandes ondes *f* 179
grand-mère *f* 22
grand-père *m* 22
grands-parents *m* 23
grand-voile *f* 240
grange *f* 182
granite *m* 288
graphite *m* 289
gras *m* 119
gras 39, 41
gratte-ciel *m* 299, 300
grattoir *m* 82
gravier *m* 88
gravure *f* 275
Grèce 316
gréement *m* 215, 240
green *m* 232
greffer 91
greffier *m* 180
grêle *f* 286
Grenade 314
grenade *f* 128
grenat *m* 288
grenier *m* 58
grenouille *f* 294
grenoullière *f* 30
grès *m* 288
griffe *f* 291
gril *m* 69
grillé 129, 159
grille de refroidissement *f* 69
grille-pain *m* 66
griller 67
grillon *m* 295
grippe *f* 44
gris 39, 274
Groenland 314
gros 321
gros haricots blancs *m* 131
gros intestin *m* 18
gros orteil *m* 15
groseille à maquereau *f* 127
groseille blanche *f* 127
grossesse *f* 52
grue *f* 187, 216, 292
grue de caméra *f* 178
Guatemala 314
guêpe *f* 295
guêpière *f* 35
guérison par cristaux *f* 55
gueule *f* 293
guichet *m* 96, 98, 209, 216, 225
guide *m* 104, 260
guide *f* 260
guide de fil *m* 276
guidon *m* 207
guimauve *f* 113
guimbarde *f* 78
guindeau *m* 214
Guinée 317
Guinée équatoriale 317
Guinée-Bissau 317
guirlande de fleurs *f* 111
guitare basse *f* 258
guitare électrique *f* 258
Guyane 315
Guyane française 315
gymnase *m* 250
gymnaste *f* 235
gymnastique *f* 235
gymnastique rythmique *f* 235
gynécologie *f* 49
gynécologue *m* 52
gypsophile *f* 110

H

habillé 34
hache *f* 95
haie *f* 85, 90, 182
haies *f* 235
Haïti 314
hall *m* 100
hall de gare *m* 209
haltère *m* 251
hamac *m* 266
hamburger *m* 154
hamburger au poulet *m* 155
hamburger avec des frites *m* 154
hamburger végétarien *m* 155
hameçon *m* 244
hamster 290
hanche *f* 12
handicap *m* 233
haricot grimpant *m* 122
haricot vert *m* 122
haricots *m* 131
haricots blancs *m* 131
haricots mung *m* 131
haricots pinto *m* 131
haricots rouges *m* 131
harpe *f* 256
haut 321
haute définition 269
haut parleur *m* 176
hautbois *m* 257
hauteur *f* 165
haut-parleur *m* 209
Hawaii 314
hayon *m* 198
heavy métal *f* 259
hebdomadaire 307
hebicide *m* 91
hélice *f* 211, 214
hélicoptère *m* 211
hématite *f* 289
hémisphère nord *m* 283
hémisphère sud *m* 283
hémorragie *f* 46
herbe *f* 55, 86
herbes *f* 133, 134
herbes et les épices *f* 132
herbicide *m* 183
herboristerie *f* 55, 108
hérisson *m* 290
hêtre *m* 296
heure *f* 304
heure de pointe *f* 209
heures *f* 261
heures de visite *f* 48
heureux 25
hexagone *m* 164
hier 306
Himalaya *m* 313
hippocampe *m* 294
hippopotame *m* 291
hirondelle *f* 292
histoire *f* 162
histoire d'art *f* 169
hiver *m* 31, 307
hochet *m* 74
hockey *m* 224
hockey sur glace *m* 224
hockeyeur *m* 224
homard *m* 121, 295
homéopathie *f* 55
homme *m* 12, 23
homme d'affaires *m* 175
homme de base *m* 228
homogénéisé 137
Honduras 314
Hongrie 316
hôpital *m* 48
horaire *m* 197, 209, 261
horloge *f* 304
hormone *f* 20
hors jeu 225, 226, 228
hors piste 247
hors-bord *m* 215
hors-jeu *m* 223
hot-dog *m* 155
hôte *m* 64
hôtel *m* 100, 264
hôtesse *f* 64
hôtesse de l'air *f* 190, 210
hotte *f* 66
houe *f* 88
houppette *f* 40
houx *m* 296
hublot *m* 210, 214
huile *f* 142, 199
huile d'amande *f* 134
huile d'arachide *f* 135
huile d'olive *f* 134
huile de colza *f* 135
huile de maïs *f* 135
huile de noisette *f* 134
huile de noix *f* 134
huile de pépins de raisin *f* 134
huile de sésame *f* 134
huile de tournesol *f* 134
huile parfumée *f* 134
huile pressée à froid *f* 135
huile végétale *f* 135
huiles *f* 134
huiles essentielles *f* 55
huissier *m* 180
huit 308
huit cents 308
huitième 309
huître *m* 121
humérus *m* 17
humide 321, 286
hurricane *m* 287
hydravion *m* 211
hydroptère *m* 215
hydrothérapie *f* 55
hygiène dentaire *f* 72
hygiène féminine *f* 108
hypnothérapie *f* 55
hypoallergénique 41
hypoténuse *f* 164
hypothèque *f* 96

I

icône *f* 177
igname *f* 125
igné 288
iguane *m* 293
île *f* 282
île Maurice 317
îles Galapagos 315
îles Malouines 315
îles Salomon 319
immeuble *m* 59, 298
immeuble de bureaux *m* 298
immigration *f* 212
immobilisation *f* 237
imperméable *m* 31, 32, 245, 267
impôt *m* 96
imprimante *f* 172, 176
imprimer 172
imprimerie *f* 275
impuissant 20
incendie *m* 95
incisive *f* 50
Inde 318
index *m* 15
individuelle 58
Indonésie 319
infection *f* 44
infirmier du SAMU *m* 94
infirmière *f* 45, 48, 189

français

information *f* 261
information touristique *f* 261
infusion de menthe *f* 149
ingénieur du son *m* 179
inhalateur *m* 44, 109
injection *f* 48
innocent 181
inoculation *f* 45
inondation *f* 287
inox *m* 79
inquiet 25
insomnie *f* 71
inspecteur *m* 94
installer 177
institutrice *f* 162, 190
instruments *m* 256, 258
insuline *f* 109
intercostal *m* 16
interdit de tourner à droite 195
intérieur *m* 200
internet *m* 177
interphone *m* 59
interrupteur *m* 60
interrupteur feux *m* 201
interviewer *m* 179
intestin grêle *m* 18
invertébrés *m* 295
investissement *m* 97
invité *m* 64
ionosphère *f* 286
iPad *m* 176
iPod *m* 268
Irak 318
Iran 318
iris *m* 51, 110
Irlande 316
Islande 316
isolation *f* 61
isorel *m* 79
Israël 318
Italie 316
itinéraire *m* 260

J

jacinthes des bois *f* 297
jade *m* 288
jais *m* 288
Jamaïque 314
jambe *f* 12
jambière *f* 224, 225
jambon *m* 119, 143, 156
jante *f* 206
janvier *m* 306
Japon 318
jardin *m* 84
jardin à la française *m* 84
jardin d'eau *m* 84
jardin d'herbes aromatiques *m* 84
jardin paysan *m* 84
jardin sur le toit *m* 84
jardinage *m* 90
jardinier *m* 188
jardins à la française *m* 262
jarretelle *f* 35
jarretière *f* 35
jauge d'essence *f* 201
jauge d'huile *f* 202
jaune 274
jaune d'œuf *m* 137, 157
javelot *m* 234
jazz *m* 259
jean *m* 31, 33
jet *m* 89
jet d'eau *m* 95
jet privé *m* 211
jetable 109
jetée *f* 217
jeter l'ancre 217
jeton *m* 272
jet-ski *m* 241
jeu *m* 75, 230, 273
jeu de cartes *m* 273
jeu télévisé *m* 178
jeu vidéo *m* 269
jeudi *m* 306
jeux *m* 272
jeux de raquette *m* 231
jeux de société *m* 272
joaillerie *f* 275
jodhpur *m* 242
jogger sur place 251
jogging *m* 251, 263
joint *m* 61, 80
jointoiement *m* 187
joker *m* 273
jonc *m* 86
jonquille *f* 111
Jordanie 318
joue *f* 14
jouer 229, 273
jouer de cricket *m* 225
jouet *m* 75
jouet en peluche *m* 75
jouets *m* 105
joueur *m* 221, 231, 273
joueur de basket *m* 226
joueur de foot *m* 222
joueur de football *m* 220
joueuse de golf *f* 232
jour *m* 306
jour ouvrable *m* 306
journal *m* 112
journaliste *m* 190
judas *m* 59
judo *m* 236
juge *m* 180
juge de ligne *m* 220, 223, 230
juillet *m* 306
juin *m* 306
jumeaux *m* 23
jumelles *f* 281
jumping *m* 243
jupe *f* 30, 34
Jupiter *f* 280
jury *m* 180
jus *m* 127
jus d'ananas *m* 149
jus de fruit *m* 156
jus de pomme *m* 149
jus de raisin *m* 144
jus de tomate *m* 144, 149
jus d'orange *m* 148
jus et milk-shakes *m* 149
jusqu'à 320
juteux 127

K

kaki *m* 128
Kaliningrad 316
kangourou *m* 291
karaté *m* 236
Kasakhastan 318
kébab *m* 155
kendo *m* 236
Kenya 317
ketchup *m* 135, 154
kilogramme *m* 310
kilomètre *m* 310
kinésithérapie *f* 49
kiosque *m* 215
kippers *m* 157
Kirghizistan 318
kiwi *m* 128
klaxon *m* 201, 204
kleenex *m* 108
knock-out *m* 237
koala *m* 291
Koweït 318
kumquat *m* 126
kung-fu *m* 236

L

laboratoire *m* 166
labourer 183
lac *m* 285
lacet *m* 37
lâcher 245
lacrosse *m* 249
lactose *m* 137
laine *f* 277
laisser tremper 130
lait *m* 136, 156
lait condensé *m* 136
lait de brebis *m* 137
lait de chèvre *m* 136
lait de vache *m* 136
lait demi-écrémé *m* 136
lait écrémé *m* 136
lait en poudre *m* 137
lait entier *m* 136
laitue *f* 123
lame *f* 66, 78, 89
lame de rasoir *f* 73
lampadaire *m* 298
lampe *f* 50, 62
lampe de chevet *f* 70
lampe de radio *f* 45
lampe d'entrée *f* 58
lampe torche *f* 267
lancement *m* 281
lancement du poids *m* 234
lancer 221, 225, 227, 229, 245
lanceur *m* 225, 229, 281
landau *m* 75
langue *f* 19
langue de bœuf *f* 118
langues *f* 162
languette *f* 37
lanière *f* 207
Laos 318
lapin *m* 118, 290
laque *f* 38
large 321
largeur *f* 165
larme *f* 51
larynx *m* 19
latitude *f* 283
lavabo *m* 38, 72
lave *f* 283
lave-auto *m* 198
lave-glace *m* 199
lave-linge *m* 76
lave-linge séchant 76
laver 38, 77
laver à la brosse 77
laverie automatique *f* 115
lave-vaisselle *m* 66
laxatif *m* 109
le Kosovo 316
le long de 320
Le Salvador 314
leçon *f* 163
lecteur CD *m* 268
lecteur DVD *m* 268
lecteur optique *m* 106
lecture *f* 269
léger 321
leggings 31
légumes *m* 107, 122, 124
légumes secs *m* 130
lent 321
lentille de l'objectif *f* 167
lentilles *f* 131
lentilles de contact *f* 51
lentilles rouges *f* 131
Lesotho 317
Lettonie 316
lettre *f* 98
lettre par avion 98
levée *f* 98
lever 139
lever du soleil *m* 305
levier *m* 150
levier de frein *m* 207
levier de vitesse *m* 207
levier de vitesses *m* 201
lèvre *f* 14
lèvres *f* 20
levure *f* 138
lézard *m* 293
Liban 318
libellule *f* 295
Libéria 317
liberté conditionnelle *f* 181
librairie *f* 115
libre 321
Libye 317
licence *f* 169
licenciée *f* 169
licou *m* 243
Liechtenstein 316
ligament *m* 17
ligne *f* 244
ligne d'arrivée *f* 234
ligne de bout *f* 226
ligne de but *f* 220, 223, 224
ligne de centre *f* 226
ligne de côté *f* 230
ligne de départ *f* 234
ligne de fond *f* 230
ligne de jeu *f* 233
ligne de lancer franc *f* 226
ligne de pénalité *f* 229
ligne de service *f* 230
ligne de touche *f* 220, 221, 226
ligne de trois points *f* 226
ligne d'envoi *f* 225
ligne du ballon mort *f* 221
lignes *f* 165
limace *f* 295
limande-sole *f* 120
lime *f* 81
lime à ongles *f* 41
limitation de vitesse *f* 195
limite du terrain *f* 225
limonade *f* 144
limousine *f* 199
lin *m* 184, 277
linge *m* 76
linge de lit *m* 71
linge de maison *m* 105
linge propre *m* 76
linge sale *m* 76
lingerie *f* 35, 105
linteau *m* 186
lion *m* 291
liqueur *f* 145
liquide *m* 77
liquide amniotique *m* 52
lire 162
lis *m* 110
liseuse *f* 210
lit *m* 70
lit d'enfant *m* 74
lit de camp *m* 266
lit simple *m* 71
lit U.V. *m* 41
litchi *m* 128
literie *f* 74
litre *m* 311
littérature *f* 162, 169
Lituanie 316
livraison à domicile *f* 154
livre *f* 310
livre *m* 163, 168
lob *m* 230
locataire *m* 58
location de voitures *f* 213
locomotive *f* 208
loganberry *f* 127
loge *f* 254
logement du film *m* 270
logiciel *m* 176
logo *m* 31
loin de 320
lombaires *f* 17
long 34
longe *f* 121
longitude *f* 283
longueur *f* 165, 310
longueur d'ondes *f* 179
lotion *f* 109
lotion pour le corps *f* 73
lotion solaire *f* 265
lotte *f* 120
louche *f* 68
louer 58
loup *m* 290
lourd 321
loutre *f* 290
louvoyer 241
loyer *m* 58
luge *f* 247
lundi *m* 306
lune *f* 280
lunettes *f* 51, 247
lunettes de protection *f* 167
lunettes de sécurité *f* 81
lunettes de soleil *f* 51, 265
lunettes protectrices *f* 238
lupins *m* 297
lutte *f* 236
Luxembourg 316
luzerne *f* 184
lymphatique 19

M

macadam goudronné *m* 187
macadamia *f* 129
Macédoine 316
macéré 159
machine à coudre *f* 276
machine à couper *f* 139
machine à ramer *f* 250
machine de randonnée *f* 250
machine de rayons X *f* 212
machines *f* 187
mâchoire *f* 14
macis *m* 132
maçon *m* 186, 188
macramé *m* 277
Madagascar 317
Madame *f* 23
madeleine *f* 140
Mademoiselle *f* 23

magasin *m* 298
magasin à papier 172
magasin bio *m* 115
magasin d'antiquités *m* 114
magasin d'appareils photos *m* 115
magasin de chaussures *m* 114
magasin de disques *m* 115
magasin de meubles *m* 115
magasin de vins et spiritueux *m* 115
magazine *m* 112
magazines *m* 107
magma *m* 283
magnésium *m* 109
mai *m* 306
maillet *m* 275
maillon *m* 36
maillot *m* 222
maillot de bain *m* 238, 265
maillot de rugby *m* 221
main *f* 13, 15
maintenant 304
mairie *f* 299
maïs *m* 122, 124, 130, 184
maison *f* 58
maison de deux étages *f* 58
maison de poupée *f* 75
maison d'habitation *f* 182
maison pliante *f* 75
maître nageur *m* 239, 265
maîtrise *f* 169
majeur *m* 15
majorette *f* 220
mal de tête *m* 44
mal d'estomac *m* 44
malachite *f* 288
malade en consultation externe *m* 48
maladie *f* 44
maladie sexuellement transmissible *f* 20
Malaisie 318
Malawi 317
Maldives 318
Mali 317
Malte 316
mamelon *m* 12
mammifères *m* 290
manche *m* 34, 36, 187, 230, 258
manchego *m* 142
manchette *f* 32
mandarine *f* 126
mandat *m* 180
mandat postal *m* 98
mandrin *m* 78
manette *f* 61
manette de chauffage *f* 201
manette de secours *f* 209
manger 64
manger *m* 75
manger sur place 154
mangoustan *m* 128
mangue *f* 128
manicure *f* 41
manioc *m* 124
manivelle *f* 203
mannequin *m* 276
mante religieuse *f* 295
manteau *m* 32, 282
manuel 200
maquereau *m* 120
maquette *f* 190
maquillage *m* 40
maracas *m* 257
marais *m* 285
marathon *m* 234
marbre *m* 288
marchand de hot-dogs *m* 154
marchand de journaux *m* 112
marchand de légumes *m* 114, 188
marchand d'occasion *m* 115
marchande de poissons *f* 188
marché *m* 115
mardi *m* 306
margarine *f* 137
marguerite *f* 110
mari *m* 22
mariage *m* 26, 35
marin *m* 189
marina *f* 217
mariné 143, 159
marjolaine *f* 133
Maroc 317
marque *f* 273
marque de flottaison en charge *f* 214
marquer 227
marquer un but 223
marron 274
marron *m* 129
mars *m* 306
Mars *f* 280
marteau *m* 80
marteau de forgeron *m* 187
marteau de porte *m* 59
marteau-piqueur *m* 187
marteler 79
martini *m* 151
mascara *m* 40
masculin 21
masque *m* 189, 228, 236, 239, 249
masque de beauté *m* 41
masque protecteur *m* 225
massage *m* 54
mastic *m* 83
mastiquer 82
mat 83, 271
mât *m* 240, 266
match *m* 230
matelas *m* 70, 74
matelas à langer *m* 74
matelas pneumatique *m* 267
matériaux *m* 79, 187
matériel *m* 176
matériel de pêche *m* 245
maternité *f* 48, 49
mathématiques *f* 162, 164
matin *m*
matraque *f* 94
Mauritanie 317
mauvais 321
mauvais point *m* 228
mauvaises herbes *f* 86
maxillaire *m* 17
mayonnaise *f* 135
mécanicien *m* 188
mécanique *f* 202
mèche *f* 78
médailles *f* 235
médecin *m* 45
medecine *f* 169
médecine ayurvédique *f* 55
médias *m* 178
médicament *m* 109
médicament multivitamine *m* 109
médicament pour la toux *m* 108
médication *f* 109
méditation *f* 54
Méditerranée *f* 313
médium *m* 79
méduse *f* 295
mélanger 67, 138
mêlée *f* 221
mêlée ouverte *f* 221
mélèze *m* 296
mélodie *f* 259
melon *m* 127
mémoire *f* 176
menottes *f* 94
mensuel 307
menthe *f* 133
menton *m* 14
menu *m* 148
menu du déjeuner *m* 152
menu du soir *m* 152
menu enfant *m* 153
menuisier *m* 188
mer *f* 264, 282
mer Baltique *f* 313
mer Caspienne *f* 313
mer d'Arabie *f* 313
mer des Caraïbes *f* 312
mer du Nord *f* 312
mer Noire *f* 313
mer Rouge *f* 313
mercerie *f* 105
merci 322
mercredi *m* 306
mercure *m* 289
Mercure *f* 280
mère *f* 22
meringue *f* 140
merlan *m* 120
mésosphère *f* 286
message vocal *m* 99
messages *m* 100
mesure *f* 150, 151
mesure pour les liquides *f* 311
mesurer 310
mesures *f* 165
métacarpien *m* 17
métal *m* 79
métamorphique *m* 288
métatarsien *m* 17
métaux *m* 289
météore *m* 280
métier à tisser *m* 277
mètre *m* 80, 310
mètre carré *m* 310
métro *m* 209
metteur en scène *m* 254
mettre en pot 91
mettre la table 64
mettre le réveil 71
mettre un tuteur 91
meuble-classeur 172
Mexique 314
mica *m* 289
micro *m* 258
micro-ondes *m* 66
microphone *m* 179
microscope *m* 167
midi *m* 305
miel liquide *m* 134
miel solide *m* 134
migraine *f* 44
mijoter 67
mile *m* 310
milk-shake *m* 137
milk-shake à la fraise *m* 149
milk-shake au chocolat *m* 149
mille 309
mille *m* 273
mille neuf cent dix 307
mille neuf cent un 307
mille neuf cents 307
millénaire *m* 307
mille-pattes *m* 295
millet *m* 130
milliard *m* 309
milligramme *m* 310
millilitre *m* 311
millimètre *m* 310
million *m* 309
mince 321
minéraux *m* 289
minerve *f* 46
minibar *m* 101
minibus *m* 197
minijupe *f* 34
minuit *m* 305
minute *f* 304
miroir *m* 40, 71, 167
mise à la terre *f* 60
mise au point *f* 271
missile *m* 211
mi-temps *f* 223
mitoyenne 58
mitrailleuse *f* 189
mixeur *m* 66
mobile *m* 74
mocassin *m* 37
mode *f* 277
mode d'emploi *m* 109
modèle *m* 169
modèles *m* 199
modélisme *m* 275
module lunaire *m* 281
moineau *m* 292
moins 165
mois *m* 306
moïse *m* 74
moissonneuse-batteuse *f* 182
molaire *f* 50
Moldavie 316
mollet *m* 13, 16
Monaco 316
Mongolie 318
moniteur *m* 53, 75, 172
Monopoly *m* 272
monorail *m* 208
Monsieur *m* 23
mont du lanceur *m* 228
montagne *f* 284
montagnes russes *f* 262
montant *m* 96
monter une tente 266
montgolfière *f* 211
montre *f* 36
monture *f* 51
monument *m* 261
monument historique *m* 261
morceaux de viande *m* 119
mordre 245
mors *m* 242
morse *m* 290
morsure *f* 46
mortier *m* 68, 167, 187
morue *f* 120
mosquée *f* 300
mot de passe *m* 99
moteur *m* 88, 202, 204
moto *f* 204
moto de course *f* 205
moto routière *f* 205
moto tout-terrain *f* 205
motocross *m* 249
motonautisme *m* 241
mou 129, 321
mouche *f* 244, 295
mouchoir *m* 36
mouette *f* 292
moufles *f* 30
mouiller 217
moule *f* 121, 295
moule à gâteaux *f* 69
moule à muffins *m* 69
moule à soufflé *m* 69
moule à tarte *m* 69
moulinet *m* 244
moulure *f* 63
mourir 26
mousse *f* 141, 148
mousse à raser *f* 73
mousson *f* 287
moustiquaire *f* 267
moustique *m* 295
moutarde *f* 155
moutarde anglaise *f* 135
moutarde en grains *f* 135
moutarde française *f* 135
mouton *m* 185
moyeu *m* 206
Mozambique 317
mozzarella *f* 142
muffin *m* 140
multiplier 165
mur *m* 58, 186
mûr 129
mûre *f* 127
muscles *m* 16
musée *m* 261
musée d'art *m* 261
muserolle *f* 242
musicien *m* 191
musique *f* 162
musique classique *f* 255, 259
musique folk *f* 259
myopie *f* 51
myrtille *f* 127

N

naan *m* 139
nacelle *f* 95
nage *f* 239
nage sur le dos *f* 239
nage synchronisée *f* 239
nageoire 290
nageoire dorsale *f* 294
nageoire pectorale *f* 294
nager 238
nager sur place 239
nageur *m* 238
naissance *f* 52, 53
naître 26
Namibie 317
nappe *f* 64
narine *f* 14
natation *f* 238
nation *m* 315
natte *f* 39
naturel 118
naturopathie *f* 55
nausée *f* 44
navet *m* 124
navette *f* 197
navette spatiale *f* 281

français

navigateur *m* 177
navigateur satellite *m* 201
naviguer 177, 240
navire *m* 214
navire de guerre *m* 215
navire porte-conteneurs *m* 215
ne pas plier 98
nébuleuse *f* 280
nectarine *f* 126
négatif *m* 271
neige *f* 287
neige fondue *f* 286
néoclassique 301
Népal 318
Neptune *f* 280
nerf *m* 50, 19
nerf optique *m* 51
nerveux 19, 25
nettoyer 77
nettoyeur *m* 188
neuf 308, 321
neuf cents 308
neurologie *f* 49
neutre 60
neuvième 309
neveu *m* 23
nez *m* 14, 210
Nicaragua 314
nickel *m* 289
nièce *f* 23
niévés *m* 131
Niger 317
Nigéria 317
niveau *m* 80
niveau à bulle *m* 187
Noël *m* 27
nœud papillon *m* 36
noir 39, 272, 274
noir *m* 148
noisette *f* 129
noix *f* 129, 151
noix de cajou *f* 129, 151
noix de coco *f* 129
noix de muscade *f* 132
noix du Brésil *f* 129
noix et les fruits secs f, *m* 129
noix pacane *f* 129
nombres *m* 308
nombril *m* 12
non 322
non gazeux 144
non pasteurisé 137
non salé 137
nord *m* 312
normal 39
Norvège 316
notation *f* 256
note *f* 163, 256
notes *f* 191
nougat *m* 113
nouilles *f* 158
nourriture *f* 118, 130, 149
nourriture pour animaux *f* 107
nouveau-né *m* 53
Nouvel An *m* 27
nouvelle lune *f* 280
nouvelles *f* 178
Nouvelle-Zélande 319
novembre *m* 306
noyau extérieur *m* 282
noyau intérieur *m* 282
nuage *m* 287
nuageux 286
nuit *f* 305
numérateur *m* 165
numérique 179, 269
numéro *m* 226
numéro de bus *m* 196
numéro de chambre *m* 100
numéro de compte *m* 96
numéro de la porte d'embarquement *m* 213
numéro de voie *m* 208
numéro de vol *m* 213
nuque *f* 13
nylon *m* 277

O

O.R.L. *f* 49
objectif *m* 270
objet exposé *m* 261
observation des oiseaux *f* 263
obsidienne *f* 288
obstacle *m* 243
obstacle d'eau *m* 232
obstétricien *m* 52
obtenir sa licence 26
occupé 99
océan *m* 282
océan Arctique *m* 312
océan Atlantique *m* 312
océan Austral *m* 313
océan Indien *m* 312
océan Pacifique *m* 312
octobre *m* 306
octogone *m* 164
oculaire *m* 167
odomètre *m* 201
œil *m* 14, 51
œillet *m* 37, 110, 244, 276
œilleton *m* 269
œsophage *m* 19
œuf à la coque *m* 137, 157
œuf de caille *m* 137
œuf de cane *m* 137
œuf de poule *m* 137
œuf d'oie *m* 137
œuf sur le plat *m* 157
œufs *m* 137
œufs brouillés *m* 157
officier de police *m* 94
officine *f* 108
oie *f* 119, 293
oignon *m* 124
oiseaux *m* 292
okra *m* 122
olive fourrée *f* 143
olive noire *f* 143
olive verte *f* 143
olives *f* 151
Oman 318
omelette *f* 158
omoplate *f* 17
once *f* 310
oncle *m* 22
oncologie *f* 49
ongle *m* 15
ongle du pied *m* 15
onyx *m* 289
onze 308
onzième 309
opale *f* 288
opéra *m* 255
opération *f* 48
ophtalmologie *f* 49
opticien *m* 51, 189
or *m* 235, 289
orage *m* 287
orange 274
orange *f* 126
orangeade *f* 144
orbite *f* 280
orchestre *m* 254, 256
orchidée *f* 111
ordinateur *m* 176
ordonnance *f* 45
ordre du jour *m* 174
oreille *f* 14
oreiller *m* 70
oreillons *m* 44
organes de reproduction *m* 20
organes génitaux 12
orge *f* 130, 184
orientation d'un patient *m* 49
origami *m* 275
origan *m* 133
orme *m* 296
ornemental 87
ornements de jardin *m* 84
orteil *m* 15
orthopédie *f* 49
ortie *f* 297
os *m* 17, 119
oseille *f* 123
ostéopathie *f* 54
otarie *f* 290
ouatage *m* 277
ouest *m* 312
Ouganda *m* 317
oui 322
ouïe *f* 294
ourlet *m* 34
ours *m* 291
ours blanc *m* 291
ours en peluche *m* 75
outils *m* 187
outils de jardin *m* 88
ouvert 260, 321
ouverture *f* 256
ouvrages recommandés *m* 168
ouvre-boîte *m* 68
ouvre-bouteille *m* 68, 150
Ouzbékistan 318
ovaire *m* 20
ovale *m* 164
over par *m* 233
ovulation *f* 20, 52
ovule *m* 20

P

pagaie *f* 241
paie *f* 175
paiement *m* 96
paillasson *m* 59
paille *f* 144, 154
paille de fer *f* 81
pailler 91
pain *m* 139, 157, 311
pain à la bicarbonate de soude *m* 139
pain au levain *m* 139
pain aux graines *m* 139
pain aux raisins secs *m* 139
pain bis *m* 139, 149
pain blanc *m* 139
pain complet *m* 139
pain de maïs *m* 139
pain de seigle *m* 138
pain de son *m* 139
pain perdu *m* 157
pain plat *m* 139
pain tranché *m* 138
pains *m* 138
Pakistan 318
palais *m* 19
pale de rotor *f* 211
palet *m* 224
palette *f* 186, 274
palier *m* 59
palisser 91
palme *f* 239
palmier *m* 86, 296
pamplemousse *m* 126
panais *m* 125
Panama 314
pancréas *m* 18
panda *m* 291
panier *m* 106, 207, 226
panier à jouets *m* 75
panier à linge *m* 76
panier à pique-nique *m* 263
panier de jardinier *m* 88
panier de pêche *m* 245
panier suspendu *m* 84
panne *f* 195, 203
panneau *m* 226
panneau d'affichage 173
panneau de signalisation *m* 298
panneaux routiers *m* 195
pansement *m* 47
pantalon *m* 32, 34
pantoufles *f* 31
paon *m* 293
papaye *f* 128
papeterie *f* 105
papier cache *m* 83
papier d'apprêt *m* 83
papier de verre *m* 81, 83
papier filtre *m* 167
papier gaufré *m* 83
papier mâché *m* 275
papier peint *m* 82, 177
papillon *m* 239, 295
Papouasie-Nouvelle-Guinée 319
paprika *m* 132
Pâque *f* 27
paquebot *m* 215
pâquerette *f* 297
Pâques *f* 27
paquet *m* 311
paquet de cigarettes *m* 112
par *m* 233
par avion 98
parachute *m* 248
parachutisme *m* 248
Paraguay 315
parallèle 165
parallélogramme *m* 164
parapente *m* 248
parapluie *m* 36
parasol *m* 264
parc *m* 75, 261, 262
parc d'attractions *m* 262
parc national *m* 261
parcomètre *m* 195
parcours de golf *m* 232
pare-brise *m* 198, 205
pare-chocs *m* 198
parents *m* 23
pare-vent *m* 265
pardon 322
parfum *m* 41
parfumé 130
parfumerie *f* 105
pari *m* 273
parking *m* 298
parking réserve aux personnes handicapées *m* 195
parmesan *m* 142
paroles *f* 259
partenaire m, *f* 23
parterre *m* 85, 90
partir du tee 233
partition *f* 255, 256
pas *m* 243
passage clouté *m* 195
passage inférieur *m* 194
passager *m* 216
passe *f* 226
passeport *m* 213
passerelle *f* 212, 214
passoire *f* 68
pastels *m* 274
pastèque *f* 127
pasteurisé 137
pastille pour la gorge *f* 109
patate douce *f* 125
pataugas *m* 37
pataugeoire *f* 263
patchwork *m* 277
pâte *f* 138, 140
pâté *m* 142, 156
pâte à choux *f* 140
pâte à tartiner au chocolat *f* 135
pâte à tartiner au citron *f* 134
pâte d'amandes *f* 141
pâte de filo *f* 140
pâte feuilletée *f* 140
pâtes *f* 158
pâtés en croûte *m* 143
pathologie *f* 49
patient *m* 45
patin à glace *m* 224, 247
patin de frein *m* 207
patinage *m* 247
patinage artistique *m* 247
patinage de vitesse *m* 247
patin en ligne *m* 249
patiner 224
patinoire *f* 224
patio *m* 85
pâtisserie *f* 69, 114, 149
patron *m* 276
paume *f* 15
paupière *f* 51
pause *f* 269
pavé *m* 85
pavillon *m* 58, 232
payer 153
pays *m* 315
paysage *m* 284
paysage 271
Pays-Bas 316
peau *f* 14, 119, 128
peau blanche *f* 126
pêche *f* 126, 128, 244
pêche à la mouche *f* 245
pêche au lancer en mer *f* 245
pêche en eau douce *f* 245
pêche hauturière *f* 245
pêche maritime *f* 245
pêche sous-marine *f* 245
pêche sportive *f* 245
pêcheur *m* 189, 244
pectoral *m* 16
pédale *f* 61, 206, 257
pédale de frein *f* 205

français

pédaler 207
pédiatrie *f* 48, 49
pédicurie *f* 41
peigne *m* 38
peigner 38
peignoir *m* 32, 35, 38, 73
peindre 83
peintre *m* 191
peinture *f* 83, 274
peinture mate *f* 83
pélican *m* 292
pelle *f* 77, 187, 265
pelle mécanique *f* 187
pellicule *f* 260, 271
pellicules *f* 39
pelote à épingles *f* 276
pelouse *f* 85, 90, 262
penalty *m* 222
pendentif *m* 36
péninsule *f* 282
pénis *m* 21
pension complète *f* 101
pentagone *m* 164
pente de ski *f* 246
pépin *m* 128, 127
pépinière *f* 115
pepperoni *m* 142
percer 79
perceuse électrique *f* 7
perceuse manuelle *f* 81
perceuse rechargeable *f* 78
perche *f* 179, 245
percolateur *m* 148, 150
percussion *f* 257
perdant *m* 273
perdre 273
perdre les eaux 52
père *m* 22
perforateur 173
perfusion *f* 53
pergola *f* 84
péridurale *f* 52
périodique *m* 168
permanente *f* 39
permis de pêche *m* 245
péroné *f* 17
Pérou 315
perpendiculaire 165
perroquet *m* 293
perruque *f* 39
persil *m* 133
personnel *m* 175
pesanteur *f* 280
peser 310
pessaire *m* 21
pesticide *m* 89, 183
pétale *m* 297
petit 321
petit ami *m* 24
petit bassin *m* 239
petit déjeuner *m* 64, 156
petit déjeuner anglais *m* 156
petit enfant *m* 30
petit galop *m* 243
petit gâteau *m* 140
petit orteil *m* 15
petit pain *m* 139, 143, 155
petit pain américain *m* 139
petit pain rond *m* 139
petit pois *m* 122
petite aiguille *f* 304
petite amie *f* 24
petite fourche *f* 89
petite peau *f* 15
petite-fille *f* 22
petit-fils *m* 22
petits pois *m* 131
petits-enfants *m* 23
pétrir 138
pétrolier *m* 215
peuplier *m* 296
peut-être 322
phare *m* 198, 205, 207, 217
pharmacie de ménage *f* 72
pharmacien *m* 108
pharmacienne *f* 189
pharynx *m* 19
philatélie *f* 273
Philippines 319
philosophie *f* 169
phoque *f* 290
photo *f* 271
photocopier 172
photo-finish *m* 234
photographe *m* 191
photographie *f* 270
photographier 271
photophone *m* 270
physalis *f* 128
physique *f* 162, 169
piano *m* 256
piano électronique *m* 258
pic *m* 292
piccolo *m* 257
pichet *m* 151
pick-up *m* 258
pièce *f* 97, 272
pièce de théâtre *f* 254
pied *m* 12, 15, 310
pied carré *m* 310
pied du lit *m* 71
pierre *f* 36, 275
pierre à aiguiser *f* 81
pierre de lune *f* 288
pierre ponce *f* 73, 288
pieuvre *f* 121, 295
pigeon *m* 292
pignon *m* 129, 207, 300
pilates *m* 251
pile *f* 78, 167
piles *f* 260
pillule *f* 109
pilon *m* 68, 167
pilote *m* 190, 211
pilule *f* 21
piment *m* 124, 132, 143
pin *m* 296
pince *f* 166, 167
pince à cheveux *f* 38
pince à dénuder *f* 81
pince à dessin 173
pince à épiler *f* 40
pince à linge *f* 76
pince coupante *f* 80
pince crocodile *f* 167
pince fine *f* 47, 167
pince plate *f* 80
pince pour le nez *f* 238
pince universelle *f* 80
pinceau *m* 40, 274
pinceau à lèvres *m* 40
pinceau à pâtisserie *m* 69
pinces *f* 150
pingouin *m* 292
pinte *f* 311
pioche *f* 187
pion *m* 272
pipe *f* 112
pipette *f* 167
pique *m* 273
pique-nique *m* 263
piquer 90
piquet *m* 225, 266
piqûre *f* 46
piscine *f* 101, 238, 250
pissenlit *m* 123, 297
pistache *f* 129
piste *f* 212, 234
piste cavalière *f* 263
piste cyclable *f* 206
piste de ski *f* 246
pistolet *m* 94
pistolet à colle *m* 78
pita *m* 139
pivoine *f* 111
pizza *f* 154
pizzeria *f* 154
placard *m* 66
place *f* 299
placenta *m* 52
places *f* 254
placeur *m* 255
plafond *m* 62
plage *f* 264
plaidoyer *m* 180
plaine *f* 285
plainte *f* 94
plan *m* 261
plan de métro *m* 209
plan de travail *m* 66
planche *f* 238, 241
planche à hacher *f* 68
planche à repasser *f* 76
planche à roulette *f* 249, 263
planche à voile *f* 241
planches *f* 85
planchiste *m* 241
planète *f* 280, 282
planeur *m* 211, 248
plante à fleurs *f* 297
plante alpestre *f* 87
plante aquatique *f* 86
plante d'ombre *f* 87
plante du pied *f* 15
plante en pot *f* 110
plante en pot *f* 87
plante grasse *f* 87
plante grimpante *f* 87
plante rampante *f* 87
planter 183
plantes *f* 296
plantes de jardin *f* 86
plaque *f* 50, 283
plaque à gâteaux *f* 69
plaque d'immatriculation *f* 198
plat à gratin *m* 69
plat à rôtir *m* 69
plat principal *m* 153
plateau *m* 152, 154, 178, 284, 310
plateau à desserts *m* 152
plateau à petit déjeuner *m* 101
platine *m* 289
platine *f* 167, 276
platine magnétophone *f* 268
plâtre *m* 83
plâtrer 82
plats *m* 153
plats cuisinés *m* 107
plein 321
pleine lune *f* 280
pleurer 25
plomb *m* 244
plombage *m* 50
plomberie *f* 61
plombier *m* 188
plongée *f* 239
plongeon *m* 239
plongeon de haut vol *m* 239
plonger 238
plongeur *m* 238
plot de départ *m* 238
pluie *f* 287
plume *f* 163, 293
plus 165
plus tard 304
Pluton *m* 280
pneu *m* 198, 205, 206
poche *f* 32, 293
pocher 67
pochoir *m* 83
podium *m* 235, 256
poêle *f* 69
poids *m* 166, 250
poids de naissance *m* 53
poignée *f* 196, 200
poignées *f* 37
poignet *m* 13, 15, 230
poing *m* 15, 237
point *m* 228, 273, 277
pointe *f* 37, 122, 246
pointes *f* 233
points de suture *m* 52
poire *f* 127
poireau *m* 125
pois *m* 131
pois cassés *m* 131
pois chiches *m* 131
poisson *m* 107, 120
poisson avec des frites *m* 155
poisson fumé 143
poisson rouge *m* 294
poissonnerie *f* 114, 120
poissons *m* 294
poitrine *f* 12
poivre *m* 64, 152
poivre de la Jamaïque *f* 132
poivron *m* 124
poker *m* 273
Polaroid® *m* 270
pôle *m* 282
pôle nord *m* 283
police *f* 94, 177
policier *m* 94, 189
polo *m* 243
Pologne 316
polyester *m* 277
pommade *f* 47, 109
pomme *f* 126
pomme d'Adam *f* 19
pomme de terre *f* 124
pomme de terre nouvelle *f* 124
pommeau *m* 242
pommeau de douche *m* 72
pommes *f* 89
pompe *f* 199, 207
pompe à bière *f* 150
pompe à lait *f* 53
pompier *m* 189
pompiers *m* 95
poncer 82
ponceuse *f* 78
pont *m* 214, 300
pont arrière *m* 214
pont de commandement *m* 214
pont de côté *m* 240
pop *f* 259
pop-corn *m* 255
porc *m* 118
porcelaine *f* 105
porcelet *m* 185
porche *m* 58
porcherie *f* 185
pore *m* 15
porridge *m* 157
port *m* 176, 214, 216, 217
port de conteneurs *m* 216
port de passagers *m* 216
port de pêche *m* 217
portable *m* 99, 176
portail *m* 85
porte *f* 196, 198, 209, 247
porte automatique *f* 196
porte d'entrée *f* 58
porte de douche *f* 72
porte vitrée *f* 59
porte-avions *m* 215
porte-bagages *m* 204, 209, 212
porte-bébé *m* 75
porte-crayons 172
porte-dossiers 173
portée *f* 256
portefeuille *m* 37, 97
porte-fusibles *m* 203
porte-monnaie *m* 37
porte-objet *m* 167
porte-outils *m* 78
porte-parapluies *m* 59
porte-savon *m* 73
porte-serviettes *m* 72
porteur *m* 100
portillon *m* 209
portion *f* 64
porto *m* 145
Porto Rico 314
portrait 271
portrait-robot *m* 181
Portugal 316
pose *f* 271
posemètre *m* 270
poser 82
position *f* 232
posologie *f* 109
poste *f* 98
poste de péage *m* 194
poste de police *m* 94
poste d'incendie *m* 95
postier *m* 98
pot *m* 65, 74, 134, 311
pot à fleurs *m* 89
pot d'échappement *m* 204
pot de peinture *m* 83
pot d'échappement *m* 203
pot gradué *m* 69, 311
potage *m* 158
potager *m* 85, 182
poteau *m* 220, 222
poterie *f* 275
pot-pourri *m* 111
poubelle *f* 61, 67, 177
pouce *m* 15, 310
poudre *f* 40, 77, 109
poudre de curry *f* 132
poudrier *m* 40
poulailler *m* 185
poulain *m* 185
poulet *m* 119, 185
poulet frit *m* 155
poulet préparé *m* 119
pouls *m* 47
poumon *m* 18

français

poupée *f* 75
pour 320
pourcentage *m* 165
pourri 127
poussette *f* 75
poussin *m* 185
poutre *f* 186, 235
prairie *f* 285
pré *m* 182, 285
prélèvement *m* 96
prématuré 52
premier 309
premier étage *m* 104
première *f* 254
premiers secours *m* 47
prémolaire *f* 50
prénatal 52
prendre au filet 245
prendre des notes 163
prendre la mer 217
prendre sa retraite 26
prendre un bain 72
prendre un bain de soleil 264
prendre une douche 72
préparation *f* 159
préparé 121
prépuce *m* 21
près de 320
presbytie *f* 51
présentateur *m* 178
présentation *f* 174
présentatrice *f* 179, 191
présider 174
presse-ail *m* 68
presse-pied *m* 276
presse-purée *m* 68
pressing *m* 115
pression des pneus *f* 203
prêt *m* 96, 168
preuve *f* 181
prie 321
primevère *f* 297
principauté *f* 315
printemps *m* 307
prise *f* 60, 237
prise de courant *f* 60
prise maladroite du ballon *f* 220
prison *f* 181
prix *m* 152, 209
prix d'entrée *m* 260
prix des actions *m* 97
prix du ticket *m* 197
problèmes *m* 271
produit anti-insecte *m* 108
produit assouplissant *m* 76
produits à tartiner *m* 134
produits d'entretien *m* 107
produits laitiers *m* 136
produits surgelés *m* 107
professions *f* 188, 190
profondeur *f* 165
programmation *f* 178
programme *m* 176, 254
projecteur *m* 259
projecteur numérique *m* 163
projection *f* 237
prolongateur *m* 78
prolongation *f* 223
promenade *f* 265
promotions *f* 106
propager 91
proposition *f* 174
propriétaire *m* 58
prosciutto *m* 143
prostate *f* 21
protections *f* 220
protège-barreaux *m* 74
protège-dents *m* 237
protège-slip *m* 108
protège-tête *m* 236
proue *f* 215
province *f* 315
provisions *f* 106
prune *f* 126
pruneau *m* 129
psychiatrie *f* 49
psychothérapie *f* 55
public *m* 254
publicité *f* 269
pullover *m* 33
pulpe *f* 124, 127
pulvérisateur *m* 311
punaise 173
punching-bag *m* 237
pupille *f* 51
pupitre *m* 162
pupitre de mixage *m* 179
putter 233
putter *m* 233
puzzle *m* 273
pyjama *m* 30, 33
pyramide *f* 164

Q

Qatar 318
quadriceps *m* 16
quai *m* 208, 216
quarante 308
quarante minutes 304
quarantième 309
quart d'heure 304
quartier *m* 126
quartz *m* 289
quatorze 308
quatorzième 309
quatre 308
quatre cents 308
quatre-quatre *f* 199
quatre-vingt 308
quatre-vingt-dix 308
quatre-vingt-dixième 309
quatre-vingtième 309
quatrième 309
question *f* 163
questionner 163
queue *f* 121, 210, 242, 280, 290, 294
queue de cheval *f* 39
quiche *f* 142
quille *f* 214, 249
quincaillerie *f* 114
quinoa *m* 130
quinze 308
quinze jours 307
quinzième 309

R

rabot *m* 81
raboter 79
racine *f* 50, 124, 296
racines *f* 39
racler 77
racquetball *m* 231
radar *m* 214, 281
radeau de sauvetage *m* 240
radiateur *m* 60, 202
radicchio *m* 123
radio *f* 48, 50, 179, 268
radio dentaire *f* 50
radiologie *f* 49
radio numérique *m* 268
radio-réveil *m* 70
radis *m* 124
radius *m* 17
rafraîchir 39
rafting *m* 241
rage de dents *f* 50
ragout *m* 158
raide 39
raie *f* 120, 294
raifort *m* 125
rail *m* 208
rail conducteur *m* 209
raisin de Corinthe *m* 129
raisin de Smyrne *m* 129
raisin sec *m* 129
rallye *m* 249
RAM *f* 176
ramadan *m* 26
ramasseur de balles *m* 231
rambarde *f* 59
rame *f* 241
ramener 245
ramequin *m* 69
ramer 241
rameur *m* 241
rampe *f* 59
rampe de lancement *f* 281
ramure *f* 291
randonnée *f* 243, 263
rang de perles *m* 36
rangée *f* 210, 254
rap *m* 259
râpe *f* 68
râper 67
rapide 321
rapide *m* 209
rapides *m* 240, 284
rappel *m* 248
rapport *m* 174
rapporteur *m* 165
rapports sexuels *m* 20
raquette *f* 230, 231
rasage *m* 73
rasoir électrique *m* 73
rasoir jetable *m* 73
rassasié 64
rat *m* 290
rate *f* 18
râteau *m* 88
ratisser 90
raton laveur *m* 290
rayon *m* 164, 207
rayon bagages *m* 104
rayon chaussures *m* 104
rayon enfants *m* 104
rayons *m* 168
rayons ultraviolets *m* 286
réacteur *m* 210
réanimation *f* 47
rebond *m* 227
réception *f* 100
réceptionniste *f* 100, 190
receveur *m* 229
recevoir 177
réchaud *m* 269
réchauffer 154
recherche *f* 169
récif de corail *m* 285
récipient *m* 311
récipient Petri *m* 166
récolter 91, 183
record *m* 234
record personnel *m* 234
rectangle *m* 164
rectum *m* 21
reçu *m* 152
rédaction *f* 163
rédactrice *f* 191
redressement assis *m* 251
réduire 172
réflecteur *m* 204
reflets *m* 39
réflexiologie *f* 54
réfrigérateur-congélateur *m* 67
refroidissement *m* 44
regarder la télévision 269
reggae *m* 259
région *f* 315
registre *m* 100
réglage de l'allumage *m* 203
règle *f* 163, 165
régler 179
régler la radio 269
règles *f* 20
réglisse *m* 113
régulateur *m* 239
reiki *f* 55
rein *m* 18
relais *m* 235
relations *f* 24
relaxation *f* 55
remorque *f* 266
remorquer 195
remorqueur *m* 215
remplaçant *m* 223
remplacement *m* 223
remuer 67
Renaissance 301
renard *m* 290
rendez-vous *m* 45, 175
rendu de monnaie *m* 99
rênes *f* 242
renoncule *f* 297
renouveler 168
renseignements *m* 168
rentrée en touche *f* 223, 226
rentrée en touche *f*
renvoyé 48
repas *m* 64, 158
repas de noces *m* 26
répasser 76
répondeur *m* 99
répondre 163
réponse *f* 163
reporter *f* 179
repose-tête *m* 200
repriser 277
reproducteur 19
reproduction *f* 20
reptiles *m* 293
République centrafricaine 317
République démocratique du Congo 317
République dominicaine 314
République tchèque 316
requin *m* 294
réseau *m* 176
réseau d'électricité *m* 60
réseau ferroviaire *m* 209
réserve *f* 262
réserver 168
réservoir *m* 61
réservoir d'huile *m* 204
réservoir de lave-glace *m* 202
réservoir de liquide de freins *m* 202
réservoir de liquide de refroidissement *m* 202
réservoir d'essence *m* 203, 204
résidence universitaire *f* 168
résistance *f* 61
respiration *f* 47
respiratoire 19
ressort *m* 71
restaurant *m* 101, 152
restaurant rapide *m* 154
restaurant universitaire *m* 168
restauration rapide *f* 154
résultat *m* 49
retard *m* 209
rétine *f* 51
retour *m* 231
retour rapide *m* 269
retourner 91
retrait des bagages 213
rétroviseur *m* 198
réunion *f* 174
réveil *m* 70
revers *m* 32, 231
revêtement *m* 66, 187
revue *f* 168
rez-de-chaussée *m* 104
rhinocéros *m* 291
rhombe *m* 164
rhubarbe *f* 127
rhum *m* 145
rhum coca *m* 151
rhume *m* 44
rhume des foins *m* 44
richelieu *m* 37
ride *f* 15
rideau *m* 63, 254
rideau de douche *m* 72
rincer 38, 76
ring *m* 237
rire 25
rive *f* 284
rivière *f* 284
riz *m* 130, 158, 184
riz à grains ronds *m* 130
riz blanc *m* 130
riz complet *m* 130
riz sauvage *m* 130
robe *f* 31, 34, 169
robe de chambre *f* 31
robe de mariée *f* 35
robe du soir *f* 34
robinet *m* 61, 66
robinet d'eau chaude *m* 72
robinet d'eau froide *m* 72
robinet de purge *m* 61
robinet de sectionnement *m* 61
robot ménager *m* 66
rocaille *f* 84
rochers *m* 284
roches *f* 288
Rocheuses *f* 312
rococo 301
rodéo *m* 243
rognon *m* 119
roi *m* 272, 273
roller *m* 263
romarin *m* 133
rond de serviette *m* 65
rond-point *m* 195
ronfler 71
roquette *f* 123
rose 274
rose *f* 110
rosé 145
rôti *m* 158
rôtir 67
rotule *f* 17

roue *f* 198, 207
roue arrière *f* 197
roue avant *f* 196
roue de nez *f* 210
roue de secours *f* 203
roue dentée *f* 206
roues d'entraînement *f* 207
rouge 145, 274
rouge à lèvres *m* 40
rougeole *f* 44
rouget barbet *m* 120
rough *m* 232
rouleau *m* 39, 83, 311
rouleau compresseur *m* 187
rouleau de papier hygiénique *m* 72
rouleau de pellicule *m* 271
rouleau pâtissier *m* 69
Roumanie 316
round *m* 237
route à quatre voies *f* 195
route d'accès *f* 216
routes *f* 194
roux 39
Royaume-Uni *m* 316
ruban *m* 27, 39, 111, 141
ruban isolant *m* 81
rubis *m* 288
rue *f* 298
rue transversale *f* 299
ruelle *f* 298
rugby *m* 221
ruine célèbre *f* 261
ruisseau *m* 285
rumsteck *m* 119
runabout *m* 214
rustine *f* 207
rutabaga *m* 125
Rwanda 317

S

sable *m* 85, 264
sabot *m* 291
sabot *m* 242
sabre *m* 236
sac *m* 75, 311
sac à bandoulière *m* 37
sac à dos *m* 31, 37, 267
sac à l'herbe *m* 88
sac à main *m* 37
sac à provisions *m* 106
sac d'appareil photo *m* 271
sac de couchage *m* 267
sac de golf *m* 233
sac de plage *m* 264
sac en plastique *m* 122
sac postal *m* 98, 190
sachet de thé *m* 144
sacs *m* 37
safran *m* 132
sage-femme *f* 53
Sahara *m* 313
Sahara occidental *m* 317
saignement de nez *m* 44
Sainte-Lucie 314
Saint-Kitts-et-Nevis 314
Saint-Marin 316
Saint-Vincent-et-les-Grenadines 314
saisons *f* 306
salade *f* 149
salade composée *f* 158
salade verte *f* 158
salaire *m* 175
salamandre *f* 294
salami *m* 142
salé 118, 121, 129, 137, 143, 155
salle *f* 48
salle à manger *f* 64
salle d'opération *f* 48
salle d'attente *f* 45
salle de bain *f* 72
salle de bain privée *f* 100
salle de cinéma *f* 255
salle de classe *f* 162
salle de conférence *f* 174
salle de cours *f* 169
salle de départ *f* 213
salle de lecture *f* 168
salle de sport *f* 101
salle de tribunal *f* 180
salle des moteurs *f* 214
salle des urgences *f* 48
salon *m* 62
salon de coiffeur *m* 115
salopette *f* 30
salto *m* 235
samedi *m* 306
sandale *f* 37
sandales *f* 31
sandwich *m* 155
sandwich grillé *m* 149
sandwich mixte *m* 155
sangle *f* 242
sans 320
sans arêtes 121
sans bretelles 34
sans connaissance 47
sans manches 34
sans matières grasses 137
sans peau 121
sans pépins 127
sans plomb 199
santé *f* 44
Sao Tomé-et-Principe 317
sapeurs-pompiers *m* 95
saphir *m* 288
Sardaigne 316
sardine *f* 120
sas d'équipage *m* 281
satellite *m* 281
satsuma *f* 126
Saturne *f* 280
sauce *f* 134, 143, 155
saucisse *f* 155, 157
saucisses *m* 118
saucisson piquant *m* 142
sauf 228
sauge *f* 133
saule *m* 296
saumon *m* 120
sauna *m* 250
saut *m* 235, 237, 243, 247
saut à l'élastique *m* 248
saut à la corde *m* 251
saut à la perche *m* 234
saut en chute libre *m* 248
saut en hauteur *m* 235
saut en longueur *m* 235
sauté 159
sauté *m* 158
sauter 67, 227
sauterelle *f* 295
sauvegarder 177
sauver 223
savon *m* 73
saxophone *m* 257
scalpel *m* 81, 167
scanner *m* 176
scanographie *f* 48
scaphandre spatial *m* 281
scarabée *m* 295
scène *f* 254, 258
schiste *m* 288
scie à chantourner *f* 81
scie à dosseret *f* 81
scie à main *f* 89
scie circulaire *f* 78
scie égoïne *f* 80
scie sauteuse *f* 78
science *f* 166
sciences *f* 162
sciences économiques *f* 169
sciences politiques *f* 169
scientifique *f* 190
scier 79
scooter *m* 205
score *m* 220
scorpion *m* 295
scotch 173
scotch à l'eau *m* 151
Scrabble *m* 272
scrotum *m* 21
sculpter 79
sculpteur *m* 191
sculpture *f* 275
sculpture sur bois *f* 275
se coucher 71
se lever 71, 139
se marier 26
se mettre à quai 217
se noyer 239
se réveiller 71
seau *m* 77, 82, 265
seau à glace *m* 150
sec 39, 41, 130, 145, 286, 321
sécateur *m* 89
s'échauffer 251
séché 129, 143, 159
sèche-cheveux *m* 38
sèche-linge *m* 76
sécher 38, 76
seconde *f*
secrétariat *m* 168
section *f* 282
sécurité *f* 75, 212, 240
sédatif *m* 109
sédimentaire 288
seiche *f* 121
sein *m* 12
seize 308
seizième 309
sel *m* 64, 152
sélecteur de point *m* 276
selle *f* 204, 206, 242
selle de femme *f* 242
semaine *f* 306
semaine dernière 307
semaine prochaine 306
semelle *f* 37
semer 90, 183
semis *m* 91
semoule *f* 130
s'endormir 71
Sénégal 317
sens interdit 195
sensible 41
sentier *m* 262
s'entraîner 251
sept 308
sept cents 308
septembre *m* 306
septième 309
série télévisée *f* 178, 179
seringue *f* 109, 167
serpent *m* 293
serre *f* 85
serre-joint *m* 78
serrure *f* 59
serrure de sécurité *f* 75
serveur *m* 148, 176
serveur d'accès *m* 177
serveuse *f* 191
service *m* 231
service après-vente *m* 104, 175
service compris 152
service de blanchisserie *m* 101
service de ménage *m* 101
service de messagerie *m* 99
service de prêt *m* 168
service de ressources humaines *m* 175
service de santé *m* 168
service de soins intensifs *m* 48
service des ventes *m* 175
service d'étage *m* 101
service du contentieux *m* 175
service marketing *m* 175
service non compris 152
services *m* 49
services d'urgence *m* 94, 99
serviette *f* 37, 65, 73
serviette antiseptique *f* 47
serviette de bain *f* 73
serviette de plage *f* 265
serviette en papier *f* 154
serviette humide *f* 75, 108
serviette hygiénique *f* 108
serviettes *f* 73
servir 64
set *m* 230
set de table *m* 64
s'évanouir 25, 44
shaker à cocktails *m* 150
shampoing *m* 38
sherry *m* 145
shiatsu *m* 54
shooter 223
short *m* 33
Sibérie *f* 313
Sicile 316
siècle *m* 307
siège *m* 52, 61, 209, 210, 242
siège arrière *m* 200, 204
siège d'enfant *m* 198, 207
siège des toilettes *m* 72
siège du conducteur *m* 196
siège social *m* 175
Sierra Leone 317
sierra para metales *f* 81
signal *m* 209
signalisations *f* 194
signature *f* 96, 98
s'il vous plaît 322
silence *m* 256
silencieux *m* 203, 204
silex *m* 288
sillet *m* 258
sillon *m* 183
silo *m* 183
simple *m* 230
simple 151
Singapour 319
singe *m* 291
sinus *m* 19
sirène *f* 94
sirop *m* 109
sirop d'érable *m* 134
site web *m* 177
six 308
six cents 308
sixième 309
ski *m* 241, 246
ski alpin *m* 247
ski de randonnée *m* 247
ski nautique *m* 241
skieur nautique *m* 241
skieuse *f* 246
slalom *m* 247
slalom géant *m* 247
slice *m* 230
slip *m* 33, 35
slip de bain *m* 238
Slovaquie 316
Slovénie 316
smartphone *m* 99, 176
smash *m* 231
SMS *m* 99
snack *m* 148
soap-opéra *m* 178
société *f* 175
soda *m* 144
sœur *f* 22
soigner 91
soin dentaire *m* 108
soin du visage *m* 41
soins de beauté *m* 41
soins de bébé *m* 74, 104
soins de la peau *m* 108
soir *m* 305
soixante 308
soixante-dix 308
soixante-dixième 309
soixantième 309
sol *m* 62, 71, 85
soldat *m* 189
sole *f* 120
soleil *m* 280, 286
solides *m* 164
soluble 109
solution désinfectante *f* 51
solution nettoyante *f* 51
solvant *m* 83
Somalie 317
sommet *m* 165, 284
somnifère *m* 109
son *m* 130
sonate *f* 256
sonde *f* 50
sonnette *f* 59, 197
sorbet *m* 141
sortie *f* 61, 75, 210
sortie de secours *f* 210
Soudan 317
Soudan du Sud 317
souder 79
soudure *f* 79, 80
soufflé *m* 158
souffler 141
soufre *m* 289
soupape de sûreté *f* 61
soupe *f* 153
soupirer 25
sourcil *m* 14, 51
sourire *m* 25
souris *f* 290
souris *f* 176
sous 320
sous tension 60
sous-exposé 271
sous-marin *m* 215
sous-sol *m* 58, 91
soustraire 165

français

sous-vêtements *m* 32
sous-vêtements thermiques *m* 35, 267
soutien-gorge *m* 35
soutient-gorge d'allaitement *m* 53
souvenirs *m* 260
sparadrap *m* 47
spatule *f* 68, 167, 275
spécialiste *m* 49
spécialités *f* 152
spectateurs *m* 233
sperme *m* 20
sphère *f* 164
sportif *m* 191
sports *m* 220, 236
sports aquatiques *m* 241
sports d'hivers *m* 247
sports de combat *m* 236
spray *m* 109
spray contre les insectes *m* 267
sprinter *m* 234
squash *m* 231
squelette *m* 17
Sri Lanka 318
stade *m* 223
stades *m* 23
starting block *m* 234
statif *m* 166
station de radio *f* 179
station de taxis *f* 213
station spatiale *f* 281
station-service *f* 199
statuette *f* 260
steeple *m* 243
sténographe *m* 181
stéréo 269
stéréo *f* 201
stérile 47, 20
stérilet *m* 21
sternum *m* 17
stéthoscope *m* 45
store *m* 63, 148
store vénitien *m* 63
stratosphère *f* 286
streaming *m* 269
stress *m* 55
studio d'enregistrement *m* 179
studio de télévision *m* 178
styles *m* 239, 301
styles de jardin *m* 84
styles de musique *m* 259
styliste *m* 277
stylo *m* 163
succursale *f* 175
sucette *f* 113
sucré 124, 127, 155
sud *m* 312
Suède 316
Suisse *f* 316
sumo *m* 237
superficie *f* 310
supermarché *m* 106
supplément *m* 55
support *m* 88, 166, 187, 268
suppositoire *m* 109
sur 320
surexposé 271
surf *m* 241
surf des neiges *m* 247
surface de but *f* 221, 223
surface de réparation *f* 223
surfeur *m* 241
surgelé 121, 124
Surinam 315
surpris 25
survêtement *m* 31, 32
suspect *m* 94, 181
suspension *f* 203, 205
Swaziland 317
sweat-shirt *m* 33
swing d'essai *m* 233
swing en arrière *m* 233
symphonie *f* 256
synagogue *f* 300
synthétique 31
Syrie 318
système *m* 176
système solaire *m* 280
systèmes domestiques *m* 60
systèmes du corps *m* 19

T

tabac *m* 112, 184
table *f* 64, 148
table à encoller *f* 82
table basse *f* 62
table de cuisson *f* 67
table de cuisson vitrocéramique *f* 66
table de nuit *f* 70
table du petit déjeuner *f* 156
tableau *m* 62, 162, 261, 274
tableau à feuilles mobiles *m* 174
tableau de bord *m* 201
tableau des points *m* 225
tablette *f* 210
tablette de chocolat *f* 113
tablier *m* 30, 69
tabouret de bar *m* 150
tache de rousseur *f* 15
tache rouge *f* 271
tacler 220, 223
taco *m* 155
Tadjikistan 318
taekwondo *m* 236
taï chi *m* 236
taie d'oreiller *f* 71
taille *f* 12
taille-crayon *m* 163
tailler 90
tailleur *m* 115
Taiwan 319
talc *m* 73
talon *m* 13, 15, 37, 96
tambour *m* 245, 257
tamis *m* 89
tamiser 91, 138
tampon *m* 108
tampon de la poste *m* 98
tampon encreur 173
tandem *m* 206
tangelo *m* 126
tante *f* 22
Tanzanie *f* 317
tapis *m* 54, 63, 71, 235
tapis de bain *m* 72
tapis de sol *m* 267
tapis roulant *m* 106, 212, 250
tapisser 82
tapisserie *f* 277
tapissier décorateur *m* 82
taquet *m* 240
tard 305
tarif *m* 154, 199
tarif d'affranchissement *m* 98
taro *m* 124
tarte *f* 141
tarte à la crème *f* 141
tarte aux fruits *f* 140
tas de compost *m* 85
Tasmanie 319
tasse *f* 75
tasse à café *f* 65
tasse à thé *f* 65
tatouage *m* 41
taureau *m* 185
taux d'intérêt *m* 96
taux de change *m* 97
Tchad 317
techniques *f* 79
tee *m* 233
teint *m* 41
teint 39
teinture de cheveux *f* 40
télécabine *f* 246
télécharger 177
télécommande *f* 269
télégramme *m* 98
téléphone *m* 99
téléphone de secours *m* 195
téléphone public *m* 99
téléphone sans fil *m* 99
téléphoniste *m* 99
téléprompteur *m* 179
télescope *m* 281
télésiège *m* 246
télévision *f* 268
télévision à écran plat *f* 269
télévision par câble *f* 269
témoin *m* 180
tempe *f* 14
température *f* 286
tempête *f* 286
temple *m* 300
temps *m* 234, 286
temps libre *m* 254, 258, 264
temps mort *m* 220
tendon *m* 17
tendon d'Achille *m* 16
tendon du jarret *m* 16
tennis *m* 230, 231
tennis de table *m* 231
tensiomètre électronique *m* 45
tension *f* 44, 60
tente *f* 267
tenue de foot *f* 31
téquila *f* 145
térébenthine *f* 83
terminal *m* 212
terminal de ferrys *m* 216
termite *f* 295
terrain *m* 220, 222, 226, 228, 234
terrain de camping *m* 266
terrain de cricket *m* 225
terrain de jeux *m* 263
terrain de rugby *m* 221
terrain de sport *m* 168
terrasse de café *f* 148
terrasse de café *f* 148
terre *f* 85, 282
Terre *f* 280
terreau *m* 88
terre-plein *m* 194
terres cultivées *f* 182
territoire *m* 315
test de grossesse *m* 52
testicule *m* 21
têtard *m* 294
tête *f* 12, 19, 81, 230
tête du lit *f* 70
tétine *f* 75
texte *m* 254
texto *m* 99
Thaïlande 318
thé *m* 144, 149, 184
thé au citron *m* 149
thé au lait *m* 149
thé glacé *m* 149
thé nature *m* 149
thé vert *m* 149
théâtre *m* 254, 299
théière *f* 65
thénar *m* 15
thérapeute *f* 55
thérapie de groupe *f* 55
thérapies alternatives *f* 54
thermomètre *m* 44, 167, 201
thermos *m* 267
thermosphère *f* 286
thermostat *m* 61
thèse *f* 169
thon *m* 120
thriller *m* 255
thym *m* 133
thyroïde *f* 18
tibia *m* 12, 17
ticket *m* 197
tiebrake *m* 230
tige *f* 111, 297
tige de verre *f* 167
tigre *m* 291
tilleul *m* 296
timbale *f* 257
timbre *m* 98
timbres *m* 112
timide 25
Timor oriental 319
tioir *m* 70
tir à cible *m* 249
tir à l'arc *m* 249
tire-bouchon *m* 150
tirer 227, 251
tiroir *m* 66, 172
tisane *f* 149
tissage *m* 277
tissu *m* 276, 277
titre *m* 168
titres *m* 23, 97
toast *m* 157
toboggan *m* 263
Togo *m* 317
toile *f* 274
toile de fond *f* 254
toile métallique *f* 167
toilettes *f* 72, 104, 266
toit *m* 58, 203
toit ouvrant *m* 202
tomate *f* 125, 157
tomate cerise *f* 124
tomber amoureux 26
ton *m* 41, 256
tondeuse *f* 88, 90
tondeuse à gazon *f* 88
tondre 90
tong *f* 37
tonic *m* 144
tonique *m* 41
tonne *f* 310
tonnerre *m* 286
topaze *m* 288
topiaire *f* 87
topinambour *m* 125
toque *f* 190
tornade *f* 287
tortue *f* 293
tortue marine *f* 293
tôt 305
touche *f* 176
tour *f* 272, 301
tour *m* 238
tour de batte *m* 228
tour de contrôle *f* 212
tour de potier *m* 275
tour de surveillance *f* 265
tour guidé *m* 260
tourelle *f* 300
tourisme *m* 260
touriste *m* 260
tourmaline *f* 288
tourne-disque *m* 268
tourner 79
tournesol *m* 184, 297
tournevis *m* 80
tournevis cruciforme *m* 81
tournois *m* 233
tourte *f* 158
tourtière *f* 69
tout droit 260
toux *f* 44
trachée *f* 18
tracteur *m* 182
traction *f* 251
traction pour les jambes *f* 251
train *m* 208
train à grande vitesse *m* 208
train à vapeur *m* 208
train d'atterrissage *m* 210
train de marchandises *m* 208
train diesel *m* 208
train électrique *m* 208
traîne *f* 35
traîneau à chiens *m* 247
traire 183
tram *m* 208
tramway *m* 196
tranche *f* 119, 121, 139, 140
tranche de lard *f* 119
transat *m* 265
transfert *m* 223
transformateur *m* 60
transmission *f* 202
transplanter 91
transport *m* 194
trapèze *m* 16, 164
traumatisme crânien *m* 46
travail 172
travaux *m* 187, 195
traveller *m* 97
trèfle *m* 273, 297
treillis *m* 84
treize 308
treizième 309
tremblement *m* 283
tremplin *m* 235, 238
trente 308
trentième 309
trépied *m* 166, 270, 281
très chaud 286
triangle *m* 164, 257
triceps *m* 16
tricot *m* 277
tricot de corps *m* 33
trictrac *m* 272
trimestre *m* 52
Trinité-et-Tobago 314
triste 25

trognon *m* 122, 127
trois 308
trois cents 308
troisième 309
trolleybus *m* 196
trombone *m* 257
trombone 173
trompe *f* 291
trompe de Fallope *f* 20
trompette *f* 257
tronc *m* 296
tropique du cancer *f* 283
tropique du capricorne *f* 283
tropiques *f* 283
troposphère *f* 286
trop-plein *m* 61
trot *m* 243
trotteuse *f* 304
trottoir *m* 298
trou *m* 232
trou en un *m* 233
trou noir *m* 280
troupeau *m* 183
trousse *f* 163
trousse de premiers secours *f* 47
trouver un emploi 26
truelle *f* 68, 187
truffe *f* 113, 125
truite *f* 120
truite arc-en-ciel *f* 120
t-shirt *m* 30, 33, 54
tuba *m* 239, 257
tube *m* 230, 311
tube porte-selle *m* 206
tuile *f* 58, 187
tulipe *f* 111
Tunisie *f* 317
turbocompresseur *m* 203
Turkmenistan 318
Turquie *f* 316
turquoise *f* 289
tuteur *m* 90
tutu *m* 191
tuyau *m* 95, 112, 202
tuyau d'arrosage *m* 89
tuyau d'écoulement *m* 61, 72
tuyau flexible *m* 77
types *m* 205
types d'appareils photo *m* 270
types de bus *m* 196
types de trains *m* 208

U

U.F.R. *f* 169
U.L.M. *m* 211
Ukraine *f* 316
ultrasons *m* 52
un 308
under par *m* 233
uniforme *m* 94, 189
univers *m* 280
université *f* 299
Uranus *f* 280
uretère *m* 21
urètre *m* 20
urgence *f* 46
urinaire 19
urologie *f* 49
Uruguay 315
usine *f* 299
ustensiles de cuisine *m* 68, 105
utérus *m* 20, 52
utiliser le fil dentaire 50

V

vacances *f* 212
vaccination *f* 45
vache *f* 185
vagin *m* 20
vague *f* 241, 264
vaisselle *f* 64
vaisselle et les couverts *f* 65
valet *m* 273
valet d'écurie *m* 243
valeur *f* 97
vallée *f* 284
valve *f* 207
vanille *f* 132
Vanuatu 319
vaporisateur *m* 89
varicelle *f* 44
vase *m* 63, 85, 111
veau *m* 118, 185
véhicule de service *m* 212
veille de la Toussaint *f* 27
veine *f* 19
vélo *m* 263
vélo de course *m* 206
vélo de randonnée *m* 206
vélo de ville *m* 206
vélo d'entraînement *m* 250
vélo tous terrains *m* 206
venaison *f* 118
vendeur *m* 104
vendredi *m* 306
Venezuela 315
vent *m* 241, 286
venteux 286
ventilateur *m* 60, 202, 210
ventouse *f* 53, 81
ventre *m* 12
Vénus *f* 280
ver *m* 295
verdict *m* 181
vernis *m* 79, 83
vernis à ongles *m* 41
verre *m* 51, 65, 152
verre à vin *m* 65
verre gradué *m* 150
verrerie *f* 64
verres *m* 150
verrou *m* 59
verrouillage *m* 200
vers 320
verser 67, 96
vert 129, 274
vertèbres cervicales *f* 17
vertèbres thoraciques *f* 17
vésicule *f* 21
vessie *f* 20
veste *f* 32, 34
veste de ski *f* 246
veste de sport *f* 33
vestibule *m* 59
vêtement en cuir *m* 205
vêtements *m* 205
vêtements de nuit *m* 31
vêtements pour enfants *m* 30
vêtements pour femmes *m* 34, 105
vêtements pour hommes *m* 32, 105
vêtements sport *m* 33
vétérinaire *f* 189
viande *f* 119
viande blanche *f* 118
viande cuite *f* 118, 143
viande et la volaille *f* 106
viande hachée *f* 119
viande maigre *f* 118
viande non cuite *f* 142
viande rouge *f* 118
vibraphone *m* 257
vide 321
vide-pomme *m* 68
Vietnam 318
vieux 321
vigne *f* 183
vilebrequin *m* 78
village *m* 299
ville *f* 298, 299
vin *m* 145, 151
vinaigre *m* 135, 142
vinaigre balsamique *m* 135
vinaigre de cidre *m* 135
vinaigre de malt *m* 135
vinaigre de vin *m* 135
vinaigrette *f* 158
vingt 308
vingt et un 308
vingt et unième 309
vingt mille 309
vingt minutes
vingt-deux 308
vingt-deuxième 309
vingtième 309
vingt-troisième 309
violet 274
violon *m* 256
violoncelle *m* 256
virement *m* 96
virus *m* 44
vis *f* 80
visa *m* 213
visage *m* 14
viseur *m* 271
visière *f* 205
visiophone *m* 99
visite de contrôle *m* 50
vitesses *f* 206
vivace 86
vodka *f* 145
vodka à l'orange *f* 151
voie à sens unique *f* 298
voie centrale *f* 194
voie de dépassement *f* 194
voie ferrée *f* 208
voile *f* 240, 241
voile *m* 35
voile d'avant *f* 240
voilier *m* 215
voisin *m* 24
voiture *f* 198, 200, 208
voiture à six places *f* 199
voiture de police *f* 94
voiture de pompiers *f* 95
voiture d'époque *f* 199
voiture électrique *f* 199
voiture-restaurant *f* 209
vol domestique *m* 212
vol international *m* 212
vol plané *m* 248
volaille *f* 119
volant *m* 201, 231
volcan *m* 283
voler 211
volet *m* 58
vollée *f* 231
volley *m* 227
volume *m* 165, 179, 269, 311
vomir 44
voûte *f* 300
voyage d'affaires *m* 175
voyage de noces *m* 26
voyageur *m* 208
vue *f* 51

W

W.-C. *m* 61
water-polo *m* 239
week-end *m* 306
western *m* 255
whisky *m* 145
white-spirite *m* 83
wifi *m* 269
wok *m* 69

Y

yacht *m* 215, 240
yaourt *m* 137
yaourt aux fruits *m* 157
yaourt surgelé *m* 137
yard *m* 310
Yémen 318
yoga *m* 54
Yougoslavie 316

Z

Zambie *f* 317
zèbre *m* 291
zéro 230, 308
zeste *m* 126
Zimbabwe *m* 317
zinc *m* 289
zone *f* 315
zone d'attaque *f* 224
zone de défense *f* 224
zone de fond *f* 220
zone industrielle *f* 299
zone neutre *f* 224
zone piétonnière *f* 299
zones *f* 283
zoo *m* 262
zoologie *f* 169
zoom *m* 270

français

German index • index allemand • deutsches Register • índice alemán • indice tedesco

A

à la carte 152
Aal *m* 294
Abdeckband *n* 83
Abdecktuch *n* 83
Abend *m* 305
Abenddämmerung *f* 305
Abendessen *n* 64
Abendkleid *n* 34
Abendmenü *n* 152
Abenteuerfilm *m* 255
Abfahrtslauf *m* 247
Abfalleimer *m* 61
Abfallentsorgung *f* 61
Abfallsortiereinheit *f* 61
Abfertigungsschalter *m* 213
Abflug *m* 213
Abflughalle *f* 213
Abfluss *m* 61, 72
Abflussrohr *n* 61
Abführmittel *n* 109
abheben 99
Abhebungsformular *m* 96
Abkühlgitter *n* 69
Ablage für Ausgänge *f* 172
Ablage für Eingänge *f* 172
Ablasshahn *m* 61
Ableger *m* 91
Abmessungen *f* 165
Absatz *m* 37
Abschlag *m* 232
abschleppen 195
Abschleppwagen *m* 203
Abschnitt *m* 96
Abschürfung *f* 46
Abschuss *m* 281
Abschussrampe *f* 281
Abseilen *n* 248
Abseits *n* 223
abseits der Piste 247
Absender *m* 98
Absperrhahn *m* 61
Abspielen *n* 269
Abteil *n* 209
Abteilungen *f* 49
Abtropfbrett *n* 67
Abzeichen *n* 189
abziehen 82
Abzug *m* 271
Accessoires *n* 36
Achat *m* 289
Achillessehne *f* 16
Achse *f* 205
Achselhöhle *f* 13
acht 308
Achteck *n* 164
achter 309
Achterdeck *n* 214
achthundert 308
achtzehn 308
achtzehnter 309
achtzig 308
achtzigster 309
Ackerbaubetrieb *m* 183
Ackerland *n* 182
Acrylfarbe *f* 274
Adamsapfel *m* 19
addieren 165
Adler *m* 292
Adresse *f* 98
Adzukibohnen *f* 131
Affe *m* 291
Afghanistan 318
Afrika 317
After-Sun-Lotion *f* 108
Ägypten 317
Ahorn *m* 296
Ahornsirup *m* 134
Aikido *n* 236
Airbag *m* 201
akademische Grad *m* 169
Akazie *f* 110
Aktenordner *m* 173
Aktenschrank *m* 172
Aktentasche *f* 37
Aktien *f* 97
Aktienpreis *m* 97
Aktionen *f* 227, 229, 233
Aktivitäten *f* 162, 245, 263
Aktivitäten im Freien *f* 262
Akupressur *f* 55
Akupunktur *f* 55
Alarmanlage *f* 58
Alaska 314
Albanien 316
Algerien 317
alkoholfreie Getränk *n* 154
alkoholfreien Getränke *n* 144
alkoholischen Getränke *n* 145
Allee *f* 299
Allergie *f* 44
Alligator *m* 293
Allzweckraum *m* 76
Alpenpflanze *f* 87
alpine Kombination *f* 247
als Fänger spielen 229
alt 321
Alternativtherapien *f* 54
Aluminium *n* 289
Amazonien 312
ambulante Patient *m* 48
Ameise *f* 295
Amethyst *m* 288
Amniozentese *f* 52
Ampère *n* 60
Amphibien *f* 294
an Bord gehen 217
an, bei 320
analog 179
Ananas *f* 128
Ananassaft *m* 149
Anästhesist *m* 48
Anbau *m* 58
anbeißen 245
anbraten 67
anbringen 82
Anden 312
Andenken *n* 260
andere Geschäfte *n* 114
andere Kunstfertigkeiten *f* 275
andere Schiffe *n* 215
andere Sportarten *f* 248
Andorra 316
Anfang *m* 321
Angebot *n* 174
Angebote *n* 106
Angeklagte *m* 180, 181
Angelgeräte *n* 245
Angelhaken *m* 244
Angelrute *f* 244
Angelschein *m* 245
Angelsport *m* 244
angemacht 159
angereicherte Mehl *n* 139
Angler *m* 244
Angola 317
angreifen 220, 223
Angriff *m* 220, 237
Angriffszone *f* 224
Anhang *m* 177
Anhänger *m* 36, 266
Anker *m* 214, 240
Ankerwinde *f* 214
Anklage *f* 94, 180
Ankunft *f* 213
anlegen 217
Anorak *m* 31, 33
Anprobe *f* 104
Anreden *f* 23
Anrufbeantworter *m* 99
Anspielkreis *m* 224
anstreichen 83
Antifalten- 41
Antigua und Barbuda 314
Antiquitätenladen *m* 114
Antiseptikum *n* 47
Antwort *f* 163
antworten 163
Anwaltsbüro *n* 180
Anwendung *f* 176
Anzeigetafel *f* 104, 225
Aperitif *m* 153
Apfel *m* 126
Apfelsaft *m* 149
Apfelstecher *m* 68
Apfelwein *m* 145
Apfelweinessig *m* 135
Apotheke *f* 108
Apotheker *m* 108
Apothekerin *f* 189
App *f* 99
Apparat *m* 99
applaudieren 255
Aprikose *f* 126
April *m* 306
Aquamarin *m* 288
Aquarellfarbe *f* 274
Äquator *m* 283
Äquatorialguinea 317
Arabische Meer *n* 313
Arbeit *f* 172
Arbeitgeberin *f* 24
Arbeitnehmer *m* 24
Arbeitsessen *n* 175
Arbeitsfläche *f* 66
Arbeitszimmer *n* 63
Architekt *m* 190
architektonische Garten *m* 84
Architektur *f* 300
Architrav *m* 301
Argentinien 315
Arithmetik *f* 165
Arm *m* 13
Armaturen *f* 201
Armaturenbrett *n* 201
Armband *n* 36
Ärmel *m* 34
ärmellos 34
Armenien 318
Armlehne *f* 210
Armstütze *f* 200
Aromatherapie *f* 55
aromatisch 130
aromatische Öl *n* 134
Art-déco- 301
Arterie *f* 19
Artischocke *f* 124
Arzt *m* 45, 189
Aschbecher *m* 150
Asche *f* 283
Aserbaidschan 318
Asien 318
Asphalt *m* 187
Ass *n* 230, 273
Assistentin *f* 24
assistierte Entbindung *f* 53
Ast *m* 296
Asteroid *m* 280
Asthma *n* 44
Astigmatismus *m* 51
Astronaut *m* 281
Astronomie *f* 281
Atemloch *n* 290
ätherischen Öle *n* 55
Äthiopien 317
Atlantische Ozean *m* 312
Atmosphäre *f* 282, 286
Atmung *f* 47
Atmungssystem *n* 19
Atrium *n* 104
Aubergine *f* 125
auf 320
auf der Stelle joggen 251
aufgehen 139
aufgenommen 48
aufgeregt 25
Aufhängung *f* 203, 205
aufkreuzen 241
Auflaufform *f* 69
Auflaufförmchen *n* 69
auflockern 91
Auflösungszeichen *n* 256
Aufnahme *f* 269
Aufsatz *m* 163, 233
Aufschlag *m* 231
aufschlagen 231
Aufschlaglinie *f* 230
aufstehen 71
auftauen 67
auftrennen 277
aufwachen 71
aufwärmen 154
Auge *n* 14, 51
Augenbraue *f* 14, 51
Augenbrauenstift *m* 40
Augenoptiker *m* 51
August *m* 306
aus 225, 226, 228, 320
aus Freilandhaltung 118
ausblasen 141
ausbrechen 283
Ausfahrt *f* 194
Ausfall *m* 251
Ausgang *m* 210
Ausgehen *n* 75
Auskunft *f* 168
ausländische Währung *f* 97
Auslandsflug *m* 212
Auslass *m* 61
auslaufen 217
Ausleger *m* 95
Auslegerkorb *m* 95
Ausleihe *f* 168
Ausleihe *m* 168
ausleihen 168
Auslöser *m* 270
Auspuff *m* 203
Auspuffrohr *n* 204
Auspufftopf *m* 203
ausrollen 67
Ausrüstung *f* 165, 233, 238
Aussage *f* 180
Außenbordmotor *m* 215
Außenfeld *n* 229
Außentür *f* 59
Äussere *n* 198
äussere Erscheinung *f* 30
äussere Kern *m* 282
außerhalb 320
ausspülen 38
Ausstellung *f* 261
Ausstellungsstück *n* 261
ausstrecken 251
Auster *f* 121
Australien 319
Australien und Ozeanien 319
Auswechslung *f* 223
auswerfen 245
Auszeit *f* 220
Auto *n* 198, 200
Autobahn *f* 194
Automatiktür *f* 196
Autostereoanlage *f* 201
Autotür *f* 198
Autounfall *m* 203
Autoverleih *m* 213
Autowaschanlage *f* 198
Avocado *f* 128
Ayurveda *n* 55

B

Baby *n* 23, 30
Babybecher *m* 75
Babyflasche *f* 75
Babyhandschuhe *m* 30
Babyprodukte *n* 107
Babyschuhe *m* 30
Babysprechanlage *f* 75
Babytasche *f* 75
Babytrageschlinge *f* 75
Babywanne *f* 74
Bach *m* 285
Backe *f* 14
backen 67, 138
Backenzahn *m* 50
Bäcker *m* 139
Bäckerei *f* 114, 138
Backgammon *n* 272
Backofen *m* 66
Backpflaume *f* 129
Backpinsel *m* 69
Backwaren *f* 107
Badeanzug *m* 238, 265
Badehose *f* 238
Badekappe *f* 238
Bademantel *m* 32, 73
Badematte *f* 72
Bademeister *m* 239
baden 72
Badetuch *n* 73

deutsch

Badewanne *f* 72
Badezimmer *n* 72
Badminton *n* 231
Bagger *m* 187
baggern 227
Baguette *n* 138
Bahamas 314
Bahn *f* 234, 238
Bahnhof *m* 208
Bahnhofshalle *f* 209
Bahnnetz *m* 209
Bahnsteig *m* 208
Bahrein 318
Baiser *n* 140
Balearen 316
Balken *m* 186
Balkon *m* 59, 254
Ball *m* 75
Ballen *m* 15, 184
Ballett *n* 255
Balletttröckchen *n* 191
Balljunge *m* 231
Ballwechsel *m* 230
Bambus *m* 86, 122
Banane *f* 128
Band *n* 27, 39, 47, 141
Bandage *f* 47
Bangladesch 318
Bank *f* 96, 250, 262
Bankgebühr *f* 96
Banküberweisung *f* 96
Bar *f* 150, 152
Bär *m* 291
Bar Mizwa *f* 26
Barbados 314
Barhocker *m* 150
Barkeeper *m* 150, 191
barock 301
Barren *m* 235
Basalt *m* 288
Baseball *m* 228
Basilikum *n* 133
Basketball *m* 226
Basketballspieler *m* 226
Bassgitarre *f* 258
Bassklarinette *f* 257
Bassschlüssel *m* 256
Batterie *f* 78, 167, 202
Batterien *f* 260
Bau *m* 186
Bauarbeiter *m* 186
Bauch *m* 12
Bauchmuskeln *m* 16
Bauchspeicheldrüse *f* 18
bauen 186
Bauer *m* 182, 189, 272
Bauerngarten *m* 84
Bauernhaus *n* 182
Bauernhof *m* 182, 184
Bauhandwerker *m* 188
Bauholz *n* 187
Baum *m* 86, 240, 296
Baumwolle *f* 184, 277
Baustelle *f* 186
Baustile *m* 301
Beat *m* 259
Beben *n* 283
Becher *m* 65
Becherglas *n* 167
Becken *n* 17, 61, 257
Bedienung inbegriffen 152
Beere *f* 296
Befestigungen *f* 89
Befruchtung *f* 20
Begräbnis *n* 26
Behälter *m* 311
Behandlungslampe *f* 50
Behandlungsschürze *f* 50
Behindertenparkplatz *m* 195
Beil *n* 95
Beilage *f* 153
Beilagenteller *m* 65
Bein *n* 12, 64
Beinstütz *m* 251
Beize *f* 79
Bekannte *m* 24
belegt 321
belegte Brot *n* 155
Beleuchtung *f* 178
Belgien 316
Belichtung *f* 271
Belichtungsmesser *m* 270
Belize 314
Benin 317
Benzin *n* 199
Benzinpreis *m* 199
Benzintank *m* 203
Beraterin *f* 55
Berg *m* 284
Berg-und-Talbahn *f* 262
Bericht *m* 174
Berufe *m* 188, 190
Berufung *f* 181
Beruhigungsmittel *n* 109
berühmte Ruine *f* 261
Besatzungsluke *f* 281
beschneiden 91
Beschwerde *f* 94
Besen *m* 77
besetzt 99, 321
Besetzung *f* 254
Besichtigungstour *f* 260
besorgt 25
Besteck *n* 64
bestellen 153
Bestuhlung *f* 254
bestürzt 25
Besuchszeiten *f* 48
Betonblock *m* 187
Betonmischmaschine *f* 186
Betrag *m* 96
Betrieb für Milchproduktion *m* 183
Bett *n* 70
Bettcouch *f* 63
Bettdecke *f* 71
Bettlaken *n* 71
Bettwäsche *f* 71
Bettzeug *n* 74
beugen 251
Beutel *m* 291, 311
bewässern 183
Beweismittel *n* 181
bewölkt 286
bewusstlos 47
bezahlen 153
Beziehungen *f* 24
Bezirk *m* 315
Bhutan 318
Biathlon *n* 247
Bibliothek *f* 168, 299
Bibliothekar *m* 190
Bibliothekarin *f* 168
Bidet *n* 72
Biene *f* 295
Bier *n* 145, 151
Bifokal- 51
Bikini *m* 264
Bilderrahmen *m* 62
Bildhauer *m* 191
Bildhauerei *f* 275
Bildschirm *m* 97, 172, 176, 269
Bildsucher *m* 271
Bimsstein *m* 73, 288
Binse *f* 86
Bio-Abfall *m* 61
biodynamisch 91, 122
Biologie *f* 162
biologisch kontrolliert 118
Birke *f* 296
Birma 318
Birne *f* 126
bis 320
Biskuittörtchen *n* 140
Biss *m* 46
bitter 124
bittere Schokolade *f* 113
Bizeps *m* 16
Bizepsübung *f* 251
Blase *f* 46
Blatt *n* 78, 122, 296
Blätter *n* 110
Blätterteig *m* 140
blau 274
Blauschimmelkäse *m* 136
Blazer *m* 33
Blechblasinstrumente *n* 256
bleifrei 199
Bleigürtel *m* 239
Bleistift *m* 163, 275
Blendenregler *m* 270
Blinddarm *m* 18
Blinker *m* 198, 204
Blitz *m* 270, 287
Block *m* 237
blocken 227
blond 39
Blues *m* 259
blühende Pflanze *f* 297
Blumen *f* 110
Blumenampel *f* 84
Blumenarrangements *n* 111
Blumenbeet *n* 85, 90
Blumengeschäft *n* 110
Blumengirlande *f* 111
Blumenkohl *m* 124
Blumentopf *m* 89
Blumenvase *f* 111
Bluse *f* 34
Blutdruck *m* 44
Blüte *f* 297
Blütenblatt *n* 297
Blutung *f* 46
Blutuntersuchung *f* 48
Blutwurst *f* 157
Bob *m* 247
Bockshornklee *m* 132
Boden *m* 85
Bodenakrobatik *f* 235
Bodendecker *f* 87
Bodenturnen *n* 235
Bogen *m* 85, 164, 249, 300
Bogenschießen *n* 249
Bohnen *f* 131, 144
bohren 79
Bohrer *m* 50, 78, 80
Bohrer mit Batteriebetrieb *m* 78
Bohrfutter *m* 78
Bohrwinde *f* 78
Boiler *m* 61
Boje *f* 217
Bolivien 315
Bombenflugzeug *n* 211
Bonbons *m* 113
Bongos *m* 257
Booster *m* 281
Bordkante *f* 298
Bordkarte *f* 213
Börse *f* 97
Börsenmakler *m* 97
Bosnien und Herzegowina 316
Botsuana 317
Boutique *f* 115
Bowling *n* 249
Bowlingkugel *f* 249
Box *f* 268
Boxen *n* 236
Boxershorts 33
Boxgymnastik *f* 251
Boxhandschuhe *m* 237
Boxring *m* 237
Brand *m* 95
Brandteig *m* 140
Brandung *f* 241
Brandungsangeln *n* 245
Brandwunde *f* 46
Brasilien 315
Braten *m* 158
braten 67
Bratenblech *n* 69
bratfertige Huhn *n* 119
Bratfisch mit Pommes frites *m* 155
Bratpfanne *f* 69
Bratsche *f* 256
Brauenbürstchen *n* 40
braun 274
braunen Linsen *f* 131
Brause *f* 89
breit 321
Breite *f* 165
Breitengrad *m* 283
Bremsbacke *f* 207
Bremse *f* 200, 204
bremsen 207
Bremsflüssigkeitsbehälter *m* 202
Bremshebel *m* 207
Bremslicht *n* 204
Bremspedal *n* 205
Brenner *m* 67
Brettspiele *n* 272
Bridge *n* 273
Brie *m* 142
Brief *m* 98
Brieffreund *m* 24
Briefkasten *m* 58, 99
Briefmarke *f* 98
Briefmarken *f* 112
Briefmarkensammeln *n* 273
Brieftasche *f* 37
Briefträger *m* 98, 190
Briefumschlag *m* 173
Brille *f* 51
Brillengestell *n* 51
Brioche *f* 157
Brokkoli *m* 123
Brombeere *f* 127
Bronze *f* 235
Brosche *f* 36
Broschüre *f* 175
Broschüren *n* 96
Brot *n* 138, 157
Brot backen 138
Brötchen *n* 139, 143, 155
Brotfrucht *f* 124
Brotmesser *n* 68
Brotschneider *m* 139
browsen 177
Browser *m* 177
Bruch *m* 165
Brücke *f* 300
Bruder *m* 22
Brühe *f* 158
Brunei 319
brünett 39
Brunnenkresse *f* 123
Brust *f* 12, 119
Brustbein *n* 17
Brustflosse *f* 294
Brustkorb *m* 17
Brustmuskel *m* 16
Brustpumpe *f* 53
Brustschwimmen *n* 239
Brustübung *f* 251
Brustwarze *f* 12
Brustwirbel *m* 17
Brutkasten *m* 53
Bube *m* 273
Bubikopf *m* 39
Buch *n* 168
Buche *f* 296
Bücherregal *n* 63, 168
Buchhaltung *f* 175
Buchladen *m* 115
buchstabieren 162
Buffet *n* 152
Bug *m* 210, 215, 240
Bügelbrett *n* 76
Bügeleisen *n* 76
bügeln 76
Bugfahrwerk *n* 210
Buggy *m* 232
Bühne *f* 254, 258
Bühnenbild *n* 254
Bukett *n* 35, 111
Bulgarien 316
Bullauge *n* 214
Bull's eye *n* 273
Bund *m* 258
Bungalow *m* 58
Bungeejumping *n* 248
Bunker *m* 232
Bunsenbrenner *m* 166
bunte Mischung *f* 113
Buntstift *m* 163
Burg *f* 300
Bürgersteig *m* 298
Burggraben *m* 300
Burkina Faso 317
Büro *n* 24, 172, 174
Büroausstattung *f* 172
Bürobedarf *m* 173
Bürogebäude *n* 298
Büroklammer *f* 173
bürsten 38, 50
Burundi 317
Bus *m* 196
Busbahnhof *m* 197
Busfahrer *m* 190
Bushaltestelle *f* 197, 299
Businessclass *f* 211
Büstenhalter *m* 35
Bustier *n* 35
Bustypen *m* 196
Butter *f* 137, 156
Butterfly *m* 239
Buttermilch *f* 137
Butternusskürbis *m* 125
Bytes *n* 176

C

Caddie *m* 233
Café *n* 148, 262
Cafetière *f* 65
Camcorder *m* 260, 269
Camembert *m* 142
Campari *m* 145
Camping *n* 266
Campingplatz *m* 266
Campingplatzverwaltung *f* 266
Campus *m* 168

deutsch

Capoeira *n* 237
Cappuccino *m* 148
Cashewnuss *f* 129
Cashewnüsse *f* 151
CD-Platte *f* 269
CD-Spieler *m* 268
Cello *n* 256
Champagner *m* 145
Chassis *n* 203
Check-up *m* 50
Cheddar *m* 142
Cheerleader *m* 220
Chef *m* 24
Chemie *f* 162
Chickenburger *m* 155
Chicorée *m* 122
Chile 315
Chili *m* 132
China 318
Chinakohl *m* 123
chippen 233
Chips *m* 113
Chiropraktik *f* 54
Chirurg *m* 48
Chirurgie *f* 48
Chor *m* 301
Chorizo *f* 143
Chrysantheme *f* 110
Chutney *n* 134
Cockpit *n* 210
Cocktail *m* 151
Cocktailrührer *m* 150
Cocktailshaker *m* 150
Cola *f* 144
Collage *f* 275
Comicheft *n* 112
Computer *m* 176
Container *m* 216
Containerhafen *m* 216
Containerschiff *n* 215
Costa Rica 314
Couchtisch *m* 62
Countrymusic *f* 259
Cousin *m* 22
Creme *f* 109
Crêpes *f* 155
Crew *f* 241
Croissant *n* 156
Curling *n* 247
Curry *n* 158
Currypulver *n* 132

D

Dach *n* 58, 203
Dachboden *m* 58
Dachgarten *m* 84
Dachgepäckträger *m* 198
Dachrinne *f* 58
Dachsparren *m* 186
Dachvorsprung *m* 58
Dachziegel *m* 58, 187
Dame *f* 272, 273
Damenbinde *f* 108
Damenkleidung *f* 34
Damenoberbekleidung *f* 105
Damensattel *m* 242
Damenschneiderin *f* 191
Damenwäsche *f* 105
Damespiel *n* 272
Dammschnitt *m* 52
dämpfen 67
Dampflokomotive *f* 208
Dänemark 316
Darlehen *n* 96
Darts *n* 273
Dartscheibe *f* 273
das Bett machen 71
das Fruchtwasser geht ab 52
das Radio einstellen 269
Datei *f* 177
Dattel *f* 129
Datum *n* 306
Daumen *m* 15
Deck *n* 214
Deckanstrich *m* 83
Decke *f* 62, 71, 74
Deckel *m* 61, 66, 69
decken 227
Degen *m* 236
Dekoration *f* 141
Delphin *m* 290
Deltamuskel *m* 16
Demokratische Republik Kongo 317
den Anker werfen 217
den Ball abgeben 220, 223
den Fernseher abschalten 269
den Fernseher einschalten 269
den Kanal wechseln 269
den Tisch decken 64
den Vorsitz führen 174
den Wecker stellen 71
Deo *n* 73
Deos *m* 108
Dermatologie *f* 49
Designer *m* 191
Desinfektionsmittel *n* 51
Desinfektionstuch *n* 47
Desktop *n* 177
Dessertwagen *m* 152
Deutschland 316
Dezember *m* 306
Diagonale *f* 164
Diamant *m* 288
Diaphragma *n* 21
dichte Nebel *m* 287
Dichtung *f* 61
Dichtungsring *m* 80
dick 321
Dickdarm *m* 18
dicke Bohne *f* 122
die Geburt einleiten 53
Diele *f* 59
Dienstag *m* 306
Diesel *m* 199
Diesellokomotive *f* 208
digital 179, 269
Digitale Box *f* 269
Digitalkamera *f* 270
Digitalprojektor *m* 163
Digitalradio *n* 268
Dill *m* 133
Dioptrie *f* 51
Diplom *n* 169
Dirigent *m* 256
Diskjockey *m* 179
Diskuswerfen *n* 234
diskutieren 163
Dissertation *f* 169
Distel *f* 297
Disziplinen *f* 247
dividieren 165
Diwali *n* 27
Dock *n* 214, 216
Dokumentarfilm *m* 178
Dominica 314
Dominikanische Republik 314
Domino *n* 273
Donner *m* 286
Donnerstag *m* 306
Doppel *n* 230
Doppel(haus) 58
Doppelbett *n* 71
Doppeldecker *m* 196, 211
doppelt 151
Doppelzimmer *n* 100
Dorf *n* 299
Dörrobst *n* 156
Dose *f* 145, 311
Dosengetränk *n* 154
Dosenöffner *m* 68
Dosierung *f* 109
Dozent *m* 169
Drachen *m* 248
Drachenfliegen *n* 248
Draht *m* 79
Drahtnetz *n* 167
Drahtschneider *m* 80
drechseln 79
Drehscheibe *f* 275
Drehstuhl *m* 172
Drehzahlmesser 201
drei 308
Dreieck *n* 164
Dreifuß *m* 166
dreihundert 308
Dreipunktlinie *f* 226
dreißig 308
dreißigster 309
dreistöckige Haus *n* 58
dreitürig 200
dreiundzwanzigster 309
dreizehn 308
dreizehnter 309
Dress *m* 222
Dressurreiten *n* 243
dribbeln 223
dritter 309
driven 233
Drucken *n* 275
drucken 172
Drucker *m* 172, 176
Druckfarbe *f* 275
Druckknopf *m* 30
Druckluftflasche *f* 239
Drüse *f* 19
Dschibuti 317
Duffelcoat *m* 31
Duftsträußchen *n* 111
düngen 91
Dünger *m* 91
dunkel 41, 321
Dunkelkammer *f* 271
dünn 321
Dünndarm *m* 18
Dunstabzug *m* 66
durch 320
Durchfall *m* 44, 109
Durchmesser *m* 164
Durchschwung *m* 233
Dusche *f* 72
Duschen *f* 266
duschen 72
Duschgel *n* 73
Duschkopf *m* 72
Duschtür *f* 72
Duschvorhang *m* 72
Düse *f* 89
Duty-free-Shop *m* 213
DVD-Platte *f* 269
DVD-Spieler *m* 268
Dynamo *m* 207

E

Eau de Toilette *n* 41
Ebene *f* 285
EC-Karte *f* 96
Eckball *m* 223
Eckfahne *f* 223
Eckzahn *m* 50
Eclair *n* 140
Economyclass *f* 211
Ecuador 315
Edamer *m* 142
Edelstein *m* 36
Ehefrau *f* 22
Ehemann *m* 22
Ei *n* 20
Eiche *f* 296
Eichelkürbis *m* 125
Eichhörnchen *n* 290
Eidechse *f* 293
Eier *n* 137
Eierbecher *m* 65, 137
Eierschale *f* 137
Eierstock *m* 20
Eigelb *n* 137, 157
Eileiter *m* 20
Eimer *m* 77, 82, 265
ein Baby bekommen 26
ein Feuer machen 266
ein Rad wechseln 203
ein Tor schießen 223
ein Zelt aufschlagen 266
Einbahn- 194
Einbahnstraße *f* 298
Einbauschrank *m* 71
Einbruchdiebstahl *m* 94
einchecken 212
eine halbe Stunde 304
eine Stelle bekommen 26
eine Viertelstunde 304
einen Dunk spielen *m* 227
einen Flug buchen 212
einen Rekord brechen 234
einfach 151
einfädeln 277
einfrieren 67
Eingang *m* 59
Eingangssperre *f* 209
eingelegt 159
eingemachte Obst *n* 134
einholen 245
einjährig 86
Einkauf *m* 104
Einkaufskorb *m* 106
Einkaufstasche *f* 106
Einkaufswagen *m* 106
Einkaufszentrum *n* 104
Einlagen *f* 53
einlochen 233
einloggen 177
einlösen 97
Einmachglas *n* 135
eins 308
Einsatzpapier *n* 83
Einschienenbahn *f* 208
einschlafen 71
Einschreiben *n* 98
Einstand *m* 230
einstellen 179
Einstellknopf *m* 167
Einstellung *f* 203, 271
eintausend 309
Eintopf *m* 158
eintopfen 91
Eintrittsgeld *n* 260
einundzwanzig 308
einundzwanzigster 309
Einwegkamera *f* 270
Einwegrasierer *m* 73
einweichen 130
Einwickelpapier *n* 111
Einwurf *m* 223, 226
einzahlen 96
Einzahlungsscheine *m* 96
Einzel *n* 230
Einzel(haus) 58
Einzelbett *n* 71
Einzelzimmer *n* 100
Einzugsauftrag *m* 96
Eis *n* 120, 137, 149, 287
Eis und Zitrone 151
Eisbär *m* 291
Eisen *n* 109, 233, 289
Eisenwarenhandlung *f* 114
Eisfach *n* 67
Eisfläche *f* 224
Eishockey *n* 224
Eishockeyspieler *m* 224
Eiskaffee *m* 148
Eisklettern *n* 247
Eiskübel *m* 150
Eiskunstlauf *m* 247
Eislaufen *n* 247
Eisprung *m* 20, 52
Eisschnelllauf *m* 247
Eistee *m* 149
Eiswürfel *m* 151
Eiszange *f* 150
Eiszapfen *m* 287
Eiweiß *n* 137
Ekzem *n* 44
El Salvador 314
Elefant *m* 291
Elektriker *m* 188
elektrische Gitarre *f* 258
elektrische Schlag *m* 46
Elektrisches Blutdruckmessgerät *n* 45
Elektrizität *f* 60
Elektroartikel *m* 105, 107
Elektroauto *n* 199
Elektrobohrer *m* 78
Elektrokessel *m* 66
Elektrolokomotive *f* 208
Elektronenblitz *m* 270
Elektrorasierer *m* 73
elf 308
Elfenbeinküste 317
Elfmeter *m* 222
elfter 309
Ellbogen *m* 13
Elle *f* 17
Eltern 23
E-Mail *f* 98, 177
E-Mail-Adresse *f* 177
E-Mail-Konto *n* 177
Embryo *m* 52
emigrieren 26
Empfang *m* 100
empfangen 20
Empfängnis *f* 52
Empfängnisverhütung *f* 21, 52
Empfangsdame *f* 100, 190
Empfangshalle *f* 100
Empfehlungszettel *m* 173
empfindlich 41
Emulsionsfarbe *f* 83
Ende *n* 321
Endivie *f* 123
Endlinie *f* 226
endokrine System *n* 19
Endokrinologie *f* 49
Endzone *f* 220
Energiesparbirne *f* 60
englische Frühstück *n* 157
englische Kuchen *m* 140
englische Senf *m* 135
Englischhorn *n* 257

deutsch

Enkel *m* 22
Enkelin *f* 22
Enkelkinder *n* 23
Entbindung *f* 52
Entbindungsstation *f* 48, 49
Ente *f* 119, 185
Entenei *n* 137
Entenküken *n* 185
Entfernung *f* 310
entgrätet 121
Enthaarung *f* 41
enthäutet 121
Entisolierzange *f* 81
entlang 320
entlassen 48
entschuppt 121
Entspannung *f* 55
Entwässerung *f* 91
entwickeln 271
Entzündungshemmer *m* 109
Epilepsie *f* 44
Erbsen *f* 131
Erdbeben *n* 283
Erdbeere *f* 127
Erdbeermilchshake *m* 149
Erde *f* 85, 280, 282
Erdgeschoss *n* 104
Erdkruste *f* 282
Erdkunde *f* 162
Erdnuss *f* 129
Erdnussbutter *f* 135
Erdnüsse *f* 151
Erdnussöl *n* 135
Erdung *f* 60
Erdzonen *f* 283
Ereignisse des Lebens *n* 26
Erfrischungstuch *n* 75
Ergänzung *f* 55
Ergebnis *n* 49
erhalten 177
Eritrea 317
Erkältung *f* 44
Erkennungsetikett *n* 53
Ermittlung *f* 94
ernten 91, 183
Ersatzrad *n* 203
Ersatzspieler *m* 223
erschrocken 25
erste Etage *f* 104
erste Hilfe *f* 47
Erste-Hilfe-Kasten *m* 47
erste Rang *m* 254
erster 309
ersticken 47
ertrinken 239
eruptiv 288
Erwachsene *m* 23
Erweiterung *f* 52
Esel *m* 185
Espresso *m* 148
Essen *n* 64, 75, 149
essen 64
Essig *m* 135, 142
Esskastanie *f* 129
Essteller *m* 65
Esszimmer *n* 64
Estland 316
Estragon *m* 133
Eukalyptus *m* 296
Eule *f* 292
Europa 316
Examensarbeit *f* 169
Exosphäre *f* 286
Externe Festplatte *f* 176
Extraktion *f* 50
Eyeliner *m* 40

F

Fabrik *f* 299
Fach *n* 100
Facharzt *m* 49
Fachbereich *m* 169
Fächerordner *m* 173
Fachhochschulen *f* 169
Fadenleiter *m* 276
Fagott *n* 257
Fahne *f* 221
fahrbare Liege *f* 48
Fähre *f* 215, 216
fahren 195
Fahrer *m* 196
Fahrerkabine *f* 95
Fahrersitz *m* 196
Fahrkarte *f* 209
Fahrkartenschalter *m* 209, 216
Fahrplan *m* 197, 209, 261
Fahrpreis *m* 197, 209
Fahrrad *n* 206
Fahrradhelm *m* 206
Fahrradkette *f* 206
Fahrradlampe *f* 207
Fahrradschloss *n* 207
Fahrradständer *m* 207
Fahrradweg *m* 206
Fahrschein *m* 197
Fahrstuhl *m* 59, 100, 104
Fährterminal *m* 216
Fairway *n* 232
Falke *m* 292
Falklandinseln 315
Fallen *n* 237
Fallschirm *m* 248
Fallschirmspringen *n* 248
Faltbett *n* 266
Falte *f* 15
Familie *f* 22
fangen 220, 225, 227, 229, 245
Fänger *m* 229
Fans *m* 258
Farbe *f* 83, 273
Farben *f* 274
Farbton *m* 41
Farbtopf *m* 83
Farn *m* 86
Fasan *m* 119, 293
Faser *f* 127
Fassungsvermögen *n* 311
faul 127
Faust *f* 15, 237
Fax *n* 98
Faxgerät *n* 172
Februar *m* 306
Fechten *n* 249
Feder *f* 163, 293
Federball *m* 231
Federhalter *m* 172
Federmäppchen *n* 163
Federwaage *f* 166
fegen 77
Fehler *m* 230
Fehlgeburt *f* 52
Feier *f* 140
Feige *f* 129
Feijoa *f* 128
Feile *f* 81
feine Nebel *m* 287
Feinkost *f* 107, 142
Feld *n* 182, 234, 272
Feldauslinie *f* 221
Feldfrucht *f* 183
Feldfrüchte *f* 184
Felge *f* 206
Felgenbremse *f* 206
Felsen *m* 284
Fenchel *m* 122, 133
Fenchelsamen *m* 133
Feng Shui *n* 55
Fenster *n* 58, 177, 186, 197, 210
Fensterladen *m* 58
Ferkel *n* 185
Fernbedienung *f* 269
Fernglas *n* 281
fernsehen 269
Fernseher *m* 268
Fernsehserie *f* 178, 179
Fernsehstudio *n* 178
Fernsehtelefon *n* 99
Ferse *f* 13, 15
Fertiggerichte *n* 107
Fertigkeiten *f* 79
Fesseln *n* 237
fest 124
Feste *n* 27
feste Honig *m* 134
festlichen Kuchen *m* 141
festmachen 217
Festnahme *f* 94
Feststation *f* 99
Fett *n* 119
fettarme Sahne *f* 137
fettfrei 137
fettig 39, 41
Fettpflanze *f* 87
Fetus *m* 52
feucht 286
Feuchtigkeitscreme *f* 41
Feueranzünder *m* 266
feuerfest 69
Feuerlöscher *m* 95
Feuermelder *m* 95
Feuerstein *m* 288
Feuertreppe *f* 95
Feuerwache *f* 95
Feuerwehr *f* 95
Feuerwehrleute 95
Feuerwehrmann *m* 189
Feuerzeug *n* 112
Fidschi 319
Fieber *n* 44
Figur *f* 260
Filet *n* 119, 121
filetiert 121
Filialleiter *m* 96
Film *m* 260, 271
Filmfach *n* 270
Filmspule *f* 271
Filter *m* 270
Filterkaffee *m* 148
Filterpapier *n* 167
Finanzberaterin *f* 97
Fingerabdruck *m* 94
Fingerhut *m* 276, 297
Fingernagel *m* 15
Finnland 316
Finsternis *f* 280
Firma *f* 175
Fisch *m* 107, 120
Fische *m* 294
Fischer *m* 189
Fischerboot *n* 217
Fischereihafen *m* 217
Fischfangarten *f* 245
Fischgeschäft *n* 114, 120
Fischhändlerin *f* 188
Fischkorb *m* 245
Fischzucht *f* 183
Fitness *f* 250
Fitnesscenter *n* 250
Fitnessgerät *n* 250
Fitnessraum *m* 101
Flachbildfernseher *m* 269
Fläche *f* 165, 310
flache Ende *n* 239
Flachholzbohrer *m* 80
Flachrennen *n* 243
Flachs *m* 184
Flachzange *f* 80
Fladenbrot *n* 139
Flagge *f* 232
Flamingo *m* 292
Flasche *f* 61, 135, 311
Flaschenöffner *m* 68, 150
Flaschenwasser *n* 144
Flauschdecke *f* 74
Fledermaus *f* 290
Fleisch *n* 119, 124
Fleisch und das Geflügel *n* 106
Fleischerhaken *m* 118
Fleischklopfer *m* 68
Fleischklöße *m* 158
Fleischsorten *f* 119
Flicken *m* 207
Fliege *f* 36, 244, 295
fliegen 211
Fliegenangeln *n* 245
Fließhecklimousine *f* 199
Flipchart *n* 174
Florentiner *m* 141
Florett *n* 249
Floristin *f* 188
Flosse *f* 290
Flöte *f* 139
Flugbegleiterin *f* 190, 210
Flügel *m* 60, 119, 293
Fluggastbrücke *f* 212
Flughafen *m* 212
Fluginformationsanzeige *f* 213
Flugnummer *f* 213
Flugticket *n* 213
Flugverbindung *f* 212
Flugzeug *n* 210
Flugzeugträger *m* 215
Fluss *m* 284
flüssige Honig *m* 134
Flüssigkeit *f* 77
Flüssigkeitsmaß *n* 311
Flussmündung *f* 285
Fock *f* 240
Fohlen *n* 185
Föhn *m* 38
föhnen 38
Folk *m* 259
Follikel *m* 20
Football *m* 220
Footballspieler *m* 220
Forelle *f* 120
formell 34
Formen *f* 164
Formschnitt *m* 87
Forschung *f* 169
Fortpflanzung *f* 20
Fortpflanzungsorgane *n* 20
Fortpflanzungssystem *n* 19
Foto *n* 271
Fotoalbum *n* 271
Fotoapparattypen *m* 270
Fotofinish *n* 234
Fotogeschäft *n* 115
Fotograf *m* 191
Fotografie *f* 270
fotografieren 271
Fotorahmen *m* 271
Foul *n* 222, 226
Foullinie *f* 229
Foyer *n* 255
Fracht *f* 216
Frachtraum *m* 215
Frachtschiff *n* 215
Frage *f* 163
fragen 163
Fraktur *f* 46
Frankreich 316
französische Senf *m* 135
französischen Bohnen *f* 131
Französisch-Guyana 315
Frau *f* 12, 23
Fräulein *n* 23
Freesie *f* 110
frei 321
freigesprochen 181
Freistoß *m* 222
Freitag *m* 306
Freiwurflinie *f* 226
Freizeit *f* 254, 258, 264
Freizeitkleidung *f* 33
Fremdenführerin *f* 260
Frequenz *f* 179
Freund *m* 24
Freundin *f* 24
Fries *m* 301
frisch 121, 127, 130
frische Fleisch *n* 142
Frischkäse *m* 136
Friseur *m* 188
Friseurin *f* 38
Frisierartikel *m* 38
Frisiersalon *m* 115
Frisiertisch *m* 71
Frisierumhang *m* 38
Frisuren *f* 39
frittiert 159
Frosch *m* 294
Frost *n* 287
Frostschutzmittel *n* 199, 203
Früchtejoghurt *m* 157
Fruchtfleisch *n* 127, 129
Fruchtgummi *m* 113
Fruchtmark *n* 127
Fruchtwasser *n* 52
früh 305
Frühkohl *m* 123
Frühling *m* 307
Frühlingszwiebel *f* 125
Frühstück *n* 64, 156
Frühstücksbuffet *n* 156
Frühstücksspeck *m* 157
Frühstückstablett *n* 101
Frühstückstisch *m* 156
Fuchs *m* 290
Fuchsschwanz *m* 80
Fugenkitt *m* 83
Fühler *m* 295
Führerstand *m* 208
Führung *f* 260
füllen 76
Füller *m* 163
Füllung *f* 140, 155
fünf 308
Fünfeck *n* 164
fünfhundert 308
fünfter 309
fünfundfünfzigtausend-
fünfhundert 309
fünfzehn 308
fünfzehnter 309
fünfzig 308
fünfzigster 309
fünfzigtausend 309
Funkantenne *f* 214
für 320
Furche *f* 183

deutsch

Fürstentum *n* 315
Fuß *m* 12, 15, 310
Fußabtreter *m* 59
Fußball *m* 222
Fußball *m* 222
Fußballdress *m* 31
Fußballfeld *n* 222
Fußballschuh *m* 223
Fußballspieler *m* 222
Fußboden *m* 62, 71
Fußende *n* 71
Fußgängerüberweg *m* 195
Fußgängerzone *f* 299
Fußpedal *n* 257
Fußrücken *m* 15
Fußschlaufe *f* 241
Fußsohle *f* 15
Fußweg *m* 262
Futter *n* 32
Futteral *n* 51
füttern 183

G

Gabel *f* 65, 88, 153, 207
Gabelstapler *m* 186, 216
Gabun 317
gähnen 25
Galapagosinseln 315
Galaxie *f* 280
Gallone *f* 311
Galopp *m* 243
galvanisiert 79
Gambia 317
Gang *m* 106, 168, 210, 254
Gänge *m* 153, 206
Gans *f* 119, 293
Gänseei *n* 137
ganz 129, 132
Garage *f* 58
Gardine *f* 63
Garn *n* 276
Garnele *f* 121
Garten *n* 84
Gartenanlagen *f* 262
Gartenarbeit *f* 90
Gartencenter *n* 115
Gartengeräte *n* 88
Gartenhandschuhe *m* 89
Gartenkorb *m* 88
Gartenkürbis *m* 124
Gartenornamente *n* 84
Gartenpflanzen *f* 86
Garten-Sauerampfer *m* 123
Gartenschlauch *m* 89
Gartenspritze *f* 89
Gartenstöcke *m* 89
Gartentypen *m* 84
Gärtner *m* 188
Gasbrenner *m* 61, 267
Gashebel *m* 204
Gaspedal *n* 200
Gasse *f* 298
Gast *m* 100
Gästebuch *n* 100
Gastgeber *m* 64
Gastgeberin *f* 64
Gatenummer *f* 213
Gaumen *m* 19
Gaze *f* 47
Gebäck *n* 140, 149
gebacken 159
Gebärmutter *f* 20, 52
Gebärmutterhals *m* 20, 52
Gebäude *n* 299
Gebäudereiniger *m* 188
geben 273
Gebirgskette *f* 282
gebogen 165
geboren werden 26
gebratene Hähnchen *n* 155
Gebrauchsanweisung *f* 109
Gebrauchtwarenhändler *m* 115
Geburt *f* 52, 53
Geburtsgewicht *n* 53
Geburtshelfer *m* 52
Geburtstag *m* 27
Geburtstagsfeier *f* 27
Geburtstagskerzen *f* 141
Geburtstagskuchen *m* 141
Geburtsurkunde *f* 26
Geburtszange *f* 53
gedämpft 159
Gedeck *n* 65
Gedränge *n* 221
Gefahr *f* 195
Gefängnis *n* 181
Gefängniswärter *m* 181
Gefängniszelle *f* 181
gefärbt 39
Geflügel *n* 119
Gefrierfach *n* 67
Gefrier-Kühlschrank *m* 67
Gefrierware *f* 107
gefrorene Joghurt *m* 137
Gefühle *n* 25
gefüllt 159
gefüllte Fladenbrot *n* 155
gefüllte Olive *f* 143
gegenüber 320
Gegner *f* 236
gegrillt 159
Gehalt *n* 175
gehen lassen 139
Gehirn *n* 19
Gehirnerschütterung *f* 46
Gehrungslade *f* 81
Geige *f* 256
Geißblatt *n* 297
gekochte Ei *n* 137, 157
gekochte Fleisch *n* 118, 143
gekrümmt 165
Gel *n* 109
geladen 60
Geländemotorrad *n* 205
Geländer *n* 59
Geländewagen *m* 199
gelangweilt 25
gelb 274
gelbe Karte *f* 223
Geld *n* 97
Geldautomat *m* 97
Geldwirtschaft *f* 97
Geleebonbon *m* 113
Gelenk *n* 17
gemahlen 132
gemahlene Kaffee *m* 144
Gemälde *n* 62, 261, 274
gemischte Salat *m* 158
Gemüse *n* 107, 122, 124
Gemüsefach *n* 67
Gemüsegarten *m* 85, 182
Gemüsehändler *m* 188
Gemüseladen *m* 114
Generaldirektor *m* 175
Generation *f* 23
Generator *m* 60
geöffnet 260
Geometrie *f* 165
Georgien 318
Gepäck *n* 100, 198, 213
Gepäckablage *f* 209
Gepäckabteilung *f* 104
Gepäckanhänger *m* 212
Gepäckausgabe *f* 213
Gepäckband *n* 212
Gepäckfach *n* 196, 210
Gepäckröntgenmaschine *f* 212
Gepäckträger *m* 204
Gepäckwaage *f* 212
gepökelt 118, 143
gerade 165
geradeaus 260
geraspelt 132
geräuchert 118, 121, 143, 159
Gerbera *f* 110
Gerichtsdiener *m* 180
Gerichtssaal *m* 180
Gerichtsstenograf *m* 181
Gerichtstermin *m* 180
geriebene Käse *m* 136
geröstet 129
Gerste *f* 130, 184
Gerüst *n* 186
gesalzen 121, 129, 137
Gesäßmuskel *m* 16
Geschäft *n* 175
Geschäftsabkommen *n* 175
Geschäftsbogen *m* 173
Geschäftsfrau *f* 175
Geschäftsmann *m* 175
Geschäftspartnerin *f* 24
Geschäftsreise *f* 175
geschält 129
geschälten Garnelen *f* 120
Geschenk *n* 27
Geschenkartikelladen *m* 114
Geschichte *f* 162
Geschirr *n* 64
Geschirr und das Besteck *n* 65
Geschlechtskrankheit *f* 20
Geschlechtsteile 12
Geschlechtsverkehr *m* 20
geschlossen 260. 321
Geschwindigkeitsbegrenzung *f* 195
Geschworenen *m* 180
Geschworenenbank *f* 180
Gesicht *n* 14
Gesichtsbehandlung *f* 41
Gesichtscreme *f* 73
Gesichtsmaske *f* 41
Gesichtspuder *m* 40
Gesichtsschutzmaske *f* 225
Gesichtswasser *n* 41
Gesims *n* 300
gespaltenen Haarspitzen *f* 39
gestalten 91
Gestänge *n* 267
Gestein *n* 288
Gestell *n* 166, 174
gestern 306
Gesundheit *f* 44
Gesundheitsfürsorge *f* 168
geteilt durch 165
getoastete Sandwich *m* 149
Getränke *n* 107, 144, 156
Getreide *n* 130
Getreideflocken *f* 107, 130, 156
Getriebe *n* 202, 204
getrocknet 129, 143, 159
getrockneten Erbsen *f* 131
Gewächshaus *n* 85
Geweih *n* 291
Gewicht *n* 166, 244
Gewichte *n* 250
Gewichthantel *f* 251
Gewinnanteile *m* 97
gewinnen 273
Gewinner *m* 273
Gewitter *n* 287
Gewölbe *n* 15, 300
Gewürze *n* 132
Gewürzessig *m* 135
Gewürznelke *f* 133
Geysir *m* 285
Ghana 317
Giebel *m* 300
Giebeldreieck *n* 301
gießen 67, 90
Gießen *n* 89
Gießkanne *f* 89
Gin *m* 145
Gin Tonic *m* 151
Gips *m* 83
Giraffe *f* 291
Girokonto *n* 96
Gitarrist *m* 258
Gitterstäbe *m* 74
Gladiole *f* 110
Glanz- 83
Glas *n* 51, 134, 152, 311
Glas- 69
Gläser *n* 150
Glasflasche *f* 166
glasieren 139
Glaskeramikkochfeld *n* 66
Glasstäbchen *n* 167
Glaswaren *f* 64
glatt 39
glätten 39
Glattrochen *m* 294
gleich 165
Gleichstand *m* 230
Gleichstrom *m* 60
Gleichung *f* 165
Gleis *n* 208
Gleisnummer *f* 208
Gleitschirmfliegen *n* 248
Gletscher *m* 284
Glied *n* 36
Glimmer *m* 289
glücklich 25
Gneis *m* 288
Gold *n* 235, 289
Goldfisch *m* 294
Golf *n* 232
Golfball *m* 233
Golferin *f* 232
Golfhandicap *n* 233
Golfplatz *m* 232
Golfschläger *m* 233
Golftasche *f* 233
Golfturnier *n* 233
Gong *m* 257
Gorilla *m* 291
gotisch 301
Gottesanbeterin *f* 295
GPS-System *n* 201
graben 90
graduieren 26
Graduierte *f* 169
Graduierungsfeier *f* 169
Gramm *n* 310
Granat *m* 288
Granatapfel *m* 128
Granit *m* 288
Grapefruit *f* 126
Graphit *m* 289
Gras *n* 86, 262
Grasfangsack *m* 88
Grasland *n* 285
Gräte *f* 121
grau 39, 274
Graubrot *n* 139, 149
graue Star *m* 51
Gravieren *n* 275
Greifzange *f* 167
Grenada 314
Griechenland 316
Grieß *m* 130
Griff *m* 36, 88, 230, 237
Griffe *m* 37
Grill *m* 267
Grillblech *n* 69
Grille *f* 295
grillen 67
Grippe *f* 44
grobe Senf *m* 135
Grönland 314
groß 321
große Zeh *m* 15
Großeltern 23
Großmutter *f* 22
Großraumlimousine *f* 199
Großsegel *n* 240
Großvater *m* 22
Grübchen *n* 15
grün 129, 274
Grün *n* 232
Grundfläche *f* 164
Grundhobel *m* 78
Grundierfarbe *f* 83
Grundierung *f* 40, 83
Grundlinie *f* 230
Grundriss *m* 261
grüne Bohne *f* 122
grüne Erbse *f* 122
grüne Olive *f* 143
grüne Salat *m* 158
grüne Tee *m* 149
grünen Erbsen *f* 131
Grünkohl *m* 123
Gruppentherapie *f* 55
Guatemala 314
Guave *f* 128
Guinea 317
Guinea-Bissau 317
Gummiband *n* 173
Gummihose *f* 30
Gummiknüppel *m* 94
Gummistiefel *m* 31, 89
Gurke *f* 125
Gürtel *m* 32, 36, 236
Gürtelschnalle *f* 36
gut 321
gut geschnitten 35
Güterzug *m* 208
Guyana 315
Gymnastikband *n* 235
Gynäkologe *m* 52
Gynäkologie *f* 49

H

Haar *n* 14, 38
Haarband *n* 39
Haarbürste *f* 38
Haarfärbemittel *n* 40
Haarfarben *f* 39
Haarglätter *m* 38
Haargel *n* 38
Haarklammer *f* 38
Haarknoten *m* 39
Haarreif *m* 38
Haarspray *n* 38
Haarspülung *f* 38
Hackbrett *n* 68
Hacke *f* 88
Hackfleisch *n* 119
Hackmesser *n* 68
Hafen *m* 214, 216, 217

deutsch

Hafenmeister *m* 217
Hafer *m* 130
Haftbefehl *m* 180
Haftentlassung auf Bewährung *f* 181
Hagel *m* 286
Hahn *m* 61, 185
Hähnchen *n* 119
Hähnchenstückchen *n* 155
Hahnenfuß *m* 297
Haifisch *m* 294
Haiti 314
Häkelhaken *m* 277
Häkeln *n* 277
Haken *m* 187, 276
halbdunkle Bier *n* 145
halbe Liter *m* 311
halbfeste Käse *m* 136
Halbfettmilch *f* 136
Halbinsel *f* 282
Halbpension *f* 101
Halbzeit *f* 223
Halfter *n* 243
Halloween *n* 27
Hals *m* 12, 258
Halskette *f* 36
Halskrawatte *f* 46
Halspastille *f* 109
Halstuch *n* 36
Halswirbel *m* 17
Haltegriff *m* 196
Halteknopf *m* 197
halten 223
Halten verboten 195
Haltung *f* 232
Hämatit *m* 289
Hamburger *m* 154
Hamburger mit Pommes frites *m* 154
Hammer *m* 80
hämmern 79
Hamster *m* 290
Hand *f* 13, 15
Handbohrer *m* 81
Handbremse *f* 203
Handfeger *m* 77
Handfläche *f* 15
Handgabel *f* 89
Handgelenk *n* 13, 15
Handgepäck *n* 211, 213
Handknöchel *m* 15
Handrad *n* 276
Handsäge *f* 89
Handschellen *f* 94
Handschuh *m* 224, 228, 233, 236, 246
Handschuhe *m* 36
Handtasche *f* 37
Handtuch *n* 73
Handtücher *n* 73
Handtuchhalter *m* 72
Handy *n* 99
Hang *m* 284
Hängematte *f* 266
Hängeordner *m* 173
Hantel *f* 251
Hardware *f* 176
Harfe *f* 256
harken 90
Harnblase *f* 20
Harnleiter *m* 21
Harnröhre *f* 20
Harnsystem *n* 19
hart 129, 321
Hartfaserplatte *f* 79
Hartholz *n* 79
Hartkäse *m* 136
Haselnuss *f* 129
Haselnussöl *n* 134
Hauptfahrwerk *n* 210
Hauptgericht *n* 153
Hauptmahlzeit *f* 158
Hauptstadt *f* 315
Haus *n* 58
Hausanschlüsse *m* 60
Hausapotheke *f* 72
Hausaufgaben *f* 163
Haushaltswaage *f* 69
Haushaltswaren *f* 107
Hausschuhe *m* 31
Haustür *f* 58
Haustürlampe *f* 58
Haut *f* 14, 119
Hautausschlag *m* 44
Hautpflege *f* 108
Hawaii 314
Heavymetal *n* 259
Hebamme *f* 53
Hebel *m* 61, 150
Heck *n* 198, 210, 240
Hecke *f* 85, 90, 182
Heckenschere *f* 89
Hefe *f* 138
Hefebrötchen *n* 139
Heft *n* 163
heften 277
Hefter *m* 173
hegen 91
Heidekraut *n* 297
Heidelbeere *f* 127
Heilbuttfilets *n* 120
Heilkräuter *n* 55
Heimwerkstatt *f* 78
heiraten 26
heiß 286, 321
heiße Schokolade *f* 144
heißen Getränke *n* 144
Heißluftballon *m* 211
Heißwasserhahn *m* 72
Heizdecke *f* 71
Heizelement *n* 61
Heizkörper *m* 60
Heizlüfter *m* 60
Heizofen *m* 60
Heizungsregler *m* 201
hell 41, 321
Helm *m* 204, 220, 228
Hemd *n* 33
Henkel *m* 106
Herbizid *n* 183
Herbst *m* 31, 307
Herde *f* 183
Hering *m* 266
Herr *m* 23
Herrenbekleidung *f* 105
Herrenfriseur *m* 39
Herrenhalbschuh *m* 37
Herrenkleidung *f* 32
herunterladen 177
Herz *n* 18, 119, 122, 273
Herz- und Gefäßsystem *n* 19
Herzinfarkt *m* 44
Herzmuschel *f* 121
Heu *n* 184
Heuschnupfen *m* 44
Heuschrecke *f* 295
heute 306
Hieb *m* 237
hier essen 154
Hi-Fi-Anlage *f* 268
Hilfskoch *m* 152
Himalaja *m* 313
Himbeere *f* 127
Himbeerkonfitüre *f* 134
hinauf 320
Hindernis *n* 243
hinter 320
Hinterbacke *f* 13
hinterherlaufen 229
Hinterrad *n* 197
hinunter 320
Hirsch *m* 291
Hirse *f* 130
historische Gebäude *n* 261
HNO-Abteilung *f* 49
Hobel *m* 81
hobeln 79
hoch 271, 321
hochauflösend 269
hochbinden 91
Hochfrisur *f* 39
Hochgeschwindigkeitszug *m* 208
Hochglanz- 271
Hochschule *f* 168
Hochseefischerei *f* 245
Hochsprung *m* 235
Höchstlademarke *f* 214
Hochzeit *f* 26, 35
Hochzeitsfeier *f* 26
Hochzeitskleid *n* 35
Hochzeitsreise *f* 26
Hochzeitstag *m* 26
Hochzeitstorte *f* 141
hochziehen 251
Höcker *m* 291
Hockey *n* 224
Hockeyball *m* 224
Hockeyschläger *m* 224
Hoden *m* 21
Hodensack *m* 21
Hof *m* 58, 84, 182
Höhe *f* 165, 211
Höhenleitwerk *n* 210
Höhle *f* 284
Hole-in-One *n* 233
Holz *n* 79, 233, 275
Holzarbeit *f* 275
Holzblasinstrumente *n* 257
Holzbohrer *m* 80
Holzkohle *f* 266
Holzleim *m* 78
Holzlöffel *m* 68
Holzspäne *m* 78
homogenisiert 137
Homöopathie *f* 55
Honduras 314
Honigwabe *f* 135
Hörer *m* 99
Hormon *n* 20
Horn *n* 257, 291
Hornhaut *f* 51
Horrorfilm *m* 255
Hörsaal *m* 169
Hose *f* 32, 34
Hot Dog *n* 155
Hotel *n* 100, 264
Hoteldiener *m* 100
Hubschrauber *m* 211
Huf *m* 242, 291
Hufeisen *n* 242
Hüfte *f* 12
Hügel *m* 284
Huhn *n* 185
Hühnerbein *n* 119
Hühnerei *n* 137
Hühnerfarm *f* 183
Hühnerstall *m* 185
Hülse *f* 130
Hülsenfrüchte *f* 130
Hummer *m* 121, 295
Hund *m* 290
hundert 308
hundertster 309
hunderttausend 308
hundertzehn 308
Hundeschlittenfahren *n* 247
hungrig 64
Hupe *f* 201, 204
Hürdenlauf *m* 235
Hurrikan *m* 287
Husten *m* 44
Hustenmedikament *n* 108
Hut *m* 36
Hüttenkäse *m* 136
Hydrant *m* 95
Hypnotherapie *f* 55
hypoallergen 41
Hypotenuse *f* 164
Hypothek *f* 96

I

Ich möchte fotokopieren 172
Igel *m* 290
Imbissstand *m* 154
Imbissstube *f* 154
immergrün 86
Immobilienmakler *m* 115
Immobilienmaklerin *f* 189
impotent 20
in 320
in den Ruhestand treten 26
indigoblau 274
in Ei gebratene Brot *n* 157
in Lake 143
in Ohnmacht fallen 25, 44
in Öl 143
in Saft 159
in Sicherheit 228
in Soße 159
Inbox *f* 177
Indien 318
Indische Ozean *m* 312
Indonesien 319
Industriegebiet *n* 299
Infektion *f* 44
Information *f* 261
Ingwer *m* 125, 133
Inhalationsapparat *m* 44
Inhalierstift *f* 109
Inlandsflug *m* 212
Inlinerfahren *n* 263
Inlineskaten *n* 249
Innenausstattung *f* 200
Innenfeld *n* 228
innere Kern *m* 282
Innereien 118
innerhalb 320
Inning *n* 228
ins Bett gehen 71
Insektenschutzmittel *n* 108
Insektenspray *m* 267
Insel *f* 282
Inspektor *m* 94
Installation *f* 61
installieren 177
Instrumente *n* 258
Insulin *n* 109
Intensivstation *f* 48
Intercity *m* 209
Internet *n* 177
Interviewer *m* 179
Ionosphäre *f* 286
iPad *n* 176
iPod *m* 268
Irak 318
Iran 318
Iris *f* 51, 110
Irland 316
Island 316
Isolierband *n* 81
Isolierung *f* 61
Israel 318
Italien 316

J

Jacht *f* 215
Jacke *f* 32, 34
Jade *m* 288
Jagdflugzeug *n* 211
Jagdrennen *n* 243
Jahr *n* 306
Jahreszeiten *f* 306
Jahrhundert *n* 307
jährlich 307
Jahrmarkt *m* 262
Jahrtausend *n* 307
Jahrzehnt *n* 307
Jakobsmuschel *f* 121
Jalousie *f* 63
Jamaika 314
Jamswurzel *f* 125
Januar *m* 306
Japan 318
jäten 91
Jazz *m* 259
Jeans *f* 31, 33
Jemen 318
jenseits 320
Jett *m* 288
jetzt
Jogging *n* 251, 263
Joghurt *m* 137
Joker *m* 273
Jordanien 318
Journalist *m* 190
Judo *n* 236
Jugendliche *f* 23
Jugendstil *m* 301
Jugoslawien 316
Juli *m* 306
Junge *m* 23, 290
Juni *m* 306
Jupiter *m* 280
Juwelier 188
Juwelierarbeit *f* 275
Juweliergeschäft *n* 114

K

Kabel *n* 79, 207
Kabelfernsehen *n* 269
Kabeljau *m* 120
Kabinda 317
Kabine *f* 210, 214
Kabinenlift *m* 246
Kabriolett *n* 199
kacheln 82
Käfer *m* 295
Kaffee *m* 144, 148, 153, 156, 184
Kaffee mit Milch *m* 148
Kaffeelöffel *m* 153
Kaffeemaschine *f* 148, 150
Kaffeemilchshake *m* 149
Kaffeetasse *f* 65
kahl 39
Kai *m* 216
Kaiserschnitt *m* 52
Kakadu *m* 293
Kakaopulver *n* 148

deutsch

Kakerlak *m* 295
Kaktus *m* 87
Kaktusfeige *f* 128
Kalb *n* 185
Kalbfleisch *n* 118
Kalender *m* 306
Kaliningrad 316
Kalk *m* 85
Kalkstein *m* 288
kalt 286, 321
kaltgepresste Öl *n* 135
Kaltwasserhahn *m* 72
Kalzit *m* 289
Kalzium *n* 109
Kambodscha 318
Kamel *n* 291
Kamera *f* 178, 260
Kamera-Handy *n* 270
Kamerakran *m* 178
Kameramann *m* 178
Kameratasche *f* 271
Kamerun 317
Kamillentee *m* 149
Kamin *m* 63
Kamm *m* 38
kämmen 38
Kammer *f* 283
Kampf *m* 237
Kampfsport *m* 236
Kampfsportarten *f* 237
Kanada 314
Kanal *m* 178, 269, 299
Kanalschacht *m* 299
Kanarienvogel *m* 292
Kandare *f* 242
kandierten Früchte *f* 129
Känguru *n* 291
Kaninchen *n* 118, 290
Kännchen *n* 65
Kante *f* 246
Kanter *m* 243
Kanu *n* 214
Kanusport *m* 241
Kapern *f* 143
Kapitalanlage *f* 97
Kapitän *m* 214
Kapsel *f* 109
Kapstachelbeere *f* 128
Kapuze *f* 31
Kapuzenmuskel *m* 16
Karamell *m* 113
Karamellpudding *m* 142
Karate *n* 236
Kardamom *m* 132
Kardanwelle *f* 202
Kardiologie *f* 49
Karibische Meer *n* 312
Karies *f* 50
Karneval *m* 27
Karo *n* 273
Karosserie *f* 202
Karotte *f* 124
Karte *f* 27
Karten *f* 273
Kartenreiter *m* 173
Kartenschlitz *m* 97
Kartenspiel *n* 273
Kartoffel *f* 124
Kartoffelchips *m* 151
Kartoffelstampfer *m* 68
Kasachstan 318
Käse *m* 136, 156
Kasino *n* 261
Kaspische Meer *n* 313
Kasse *f* 106, 150, 255
Kasserolle *f* 69
Kassierer *m* 96, 106
Katamaran *m* 215
Katar 318
Kathedrale *f* 300
Katheter *m* 53
Kätzchen *n* 290
Katze *f* 290
Katzenauge *n* 204
Kaufhaus *n* 105
Kaugummi *m* 113
Kaulquappe *f* 294
Kaution *f* 181
Kajak *n* 241
Kebab *m* 155
Kegel *m* 164, 249
Kehldeckel *m* 19
Kehle *f* 19
Kehlkopf *m* 19
Kehre *f* 238
Keilriemen *m* 203
Keilschuh *m* 37
keine Einfahrt 195
Keks *m* 113, 141
Kelch *m* 297
Kelle *f* 187
Kellergeschoss *n* 58
Kellner *m* 148, 152
Kellnerin *f* 191
Kendo *n* 236
Kenia 317
Kennmarke *f* 94
kentern 241
Kern *m* 122, 127, 128, 129, 130
Kerngehäuse *n* 127
kernlos 127
Kescher *m* 244
Kessel *m* 61
Kesselpauke *f* 257
Ketchup *m* 135
Kette *f* 36
Kettenzahnrad *n* 207
Keule *f* 119, 167, 228
Keyboard *n* 258
Kichererbsen *f* 131
Kickboxen *n* 236
kicken 221, 223
Kiefer *f* 296
Kieferknochen *m* 17
Kiel *m* 214
Kieme *f* 294
Kies *m* 88
Kilogramm *n* 310
Kilometer *m* 310
Kilometerzähler *m* 201
Kind *n* 23, 31
Kinder *n* 23
Kinderabteilung *f* 104
Kinderbett *n* 74
Kinderkleidung *f* 30
Kinderportion *f* 153
Kindersicherung *f* 75
Kindersitz *m* 198, 207
Kinderstation *f* 48
Kinderstuhl *m* 75
Kinderwagen *m* 75
Kinderzimmer *n* 74
Kinn *n* 14
Kinnlade *f* 14
Kino *n* 255, 299
Kinosaal *m* 255
Kipper *m* 187
Kirche *f* 298, 300
Kirgisistan 318
Kirsche *f* 126
Kirschtomate *f* 124
Kissenbezug *m* 71
Kiwi *f* 128
Klammer *f* 166
Klammern *f* 173
Klampe *f* 240
Klappe *f* 179
Klapptisch *m* 210
Klarinette *f* 257
Klasse *f* 163
Klassenzimmer *n* 162
klassische Musik *f* 255, 259
klassizistisch 301
Klatschmohn *m* 297
Klaue *f* 291
Klavier *n* 256
Klebstoff *m* 275
Klee *m* 297
Kleid *n* 31, 34
Kleiderbügel *m* 70
Kleiderschrank *m* 70
Kleidung *f* 205
Kleie *f* 130
klein 321
Kleinbus *m* 197
kleine Finger *m* 15
kleine Trommel *f* 257
kleine Zeh *m* 15
Kleinkind *n* 30
Kleisterbürste *f* 82
Klementine *f* 126
Klemmbrett *n* 173
Klempner *m* 188
Klettergerüst *n* 263
Klettern *n* 248
Kletterpflanze *f* 87
Klient *m* 180
Klimaanlage *f* 200
Klinge *f* 89
Klingel *f* 197
Klinik *f* 48
Klippe *n* 285
Klitoris *f* 20
Klöppel *m* 277
Klubhaus *n* 232
Klubsandwich *m* 155
Knabbereien *f* 151
Knäckebrot *n* 139, 156
knackig 127
Knebelknopf *m* 31
kneten 138
Knie *n* 12
Kniebeuge *f* 251
knielang 34
Kniescheibe *f* 17
Knieschützer *m* 205, 227
Kniesehnenstrang *m* 16
Knoblauch *m* 125, 132
Knoblauchpresse *f* 68
Knöchel *m* 13, 15
knöchellang 34
Knochen *m* 17, 119
Knochenasche *f* 88
Knockout *m* 237
Knopf *m* 32
Knopfloch *n* 32
Knorpel *m* 17
Knospe *f* 111, 297
Koalabär *m* 291
Koch *m* 190
köcheln lassen 67
kochen 67
Kochen *n* 67
Köcher *m* 249
Kochfeld *n* 67
Kochmütze *f* 190
Kochtopf *m* 69
Köder *m* 244
Köderhaken *m* 244
ködern 245
Kofferkuli *m* 100, 208, 213
Kofferraum *m* 198
Kohl *m* 123
Kohle *f* 288
Kohlestift *m* 275
Kohlrabi *m* 123
Kohlrübe *f* 125
Koikarpfen *m* 294
Kokon *m* 295
Kokosnuss *f* 129
Kolben *m* 166
Kolibri *m* 292
Kollege *m* 24
Kolonie 315
Kolumbien 315
Kombinationszange *f* 80
Kombiwagen *m* 199
Kombüse *f* 214
Komet *m* 280
Kommandobrücke *f* 214
Kommandoturm *m* 215
Kommode *f* 70
Kommunikation *f* 98
Komödie *f* 255
Komoren 317
Kompass *m* 240, 312
Komposterde *f* 88
Komposthaufen *m* 85
Kondensmilch *f* 136
Konditor *m* 113
Konditorcreme *f* 140
Konditorei *f* 114
Kondom *n* 21
Konfitüre *f* 134, 156
Konglomerat *n* 288
Kongo 317
König *m* 272, 273
Königsberg 316
Konserven *f* 107
Konsultation *f* 45
Kontaktlinsen *f* 51
Kontaktlinsenbehälter *m* 51
Kontinent *m* 282, 315
Kontonummer *f* 96
Kontoüberziehung *f* 96
Kontrabass *m* 256
Kontrafagott *n* 257
Kontrollturm *m* 212
Konzert *n* 255, 258
Kopf *m* 12, 19, 112, 230
köpfen 91, 222
Kopfende *n* 70
Kopfhaut *f* 39
Kopfhörer *m* 268
Kopfkissen *n* 70
Kopfschmerzen *m* 44
Kopfschutz *m* 74, 236
Kopfstütze *f* 200
Kopfverletzung *f* 46
kopieren 172
Kopilot *m* 211
Koppel *f* 242
Korallenriff *n* 285
Korb *m* 207, 226
Korbbrett *n* 226
Körbchen *n* 74
Korbring *m* 226
Koriander *m* 133
Korinthe *f* 129
Korken *m* 134
Korkenzieher *m* 150
Körner *n* 131
Körnerbrot *n* 139
Körper *m* 12, 164
Körperlotion *f* 73
Körperpuder *m* 73
Körpersysteme *n* 19
Körperverletzung *f* 94
Korrekturstift *m* 40
Korsett *n* 35
Korsika 316
Kosovo 316
Kotelett *n* 119
Krabbe *f* 121
Kraftstoffanzeige *f* 201
Kraftstofftank *m* 204
Krafttraining *n* 251
Kragen *m* 32
Krähe *f* 292
Kralle *f* 293
Krampf *m* 239
Krämpfe *m* 44
Kran *m* 187, 216
Kranich *m* 292
Krankenhaus *n* 48
Krankenhausstation *f* 48
Krankenschwester *f* 45, 48, 189
Krankenwagen *m* 94
Krankheit *f* 44
Kranz *m* 111
Krater *m* 283
kratzen 77
Kraulen *n* 239
kraus 39
Kraut *n* 86
Kräuter *n* 133, 134
Kräuter und Gewürze *n* 132
Kräutergarten *m* 84
Kräuterheilkunde *f* 55
Kräuterheilmittel *n* 108
Kräutermischung *f* 132
Kräutertee *m* 149
Krawatte *f* 32
Krawattennadel *f* 36
Krebs *m* 121, 295
Kreditkarte *f* 96
Kreide *f* 162, 288
Kreis *m* 165
Kreissäge *f* 78
Kreisverkehr *m* 195
Kreuz *n* 13, 256, 273
Kreuzblume *f* 300
Kreuzkümmel *m* 132
Kreuzschlitzschraubenzieher *m* 81
Kreuzung *f* 194, 298
Kricket *n* 225
Kricketball *m* 225
Kricketspieler *m* 225
Krickettor *n* 225
Kriechpflanze *f* 87
Kriegsschiff *n* 215
Kriminalbeamte *m* 94
Kristalltherapie *f* 55
Kroatien 316
Krokodil *n* 293
Krokodilklemme *f* 167
Krone *f* 50
Kröte *f* 294
Krug *m* 151
Kruste *f* 139
Kuba 314
Küche *f* 66, 152
Kuchen *m* 141
Kuchen backen *n* 69
Kuchenblech *n* 69
Küchenchef *m* 152
Kuchenform *f* 69
Küchengeräte *n* 66, 68, 105

deutsch

Küchenmaschine *f* 66
Küchenmesser *n* 68
Küchenregal *n* 66
Küchenschrank *m* 66
Kugel *f* 149, 164
Kugelstoßen *n* 234
Kuh *f* 185
Kühler *m* 202
Kühlmittelbehälter *m* 202
Kühlschrank *m* 67
Kuhmilch *f* 136
Küken *n* 185
Kulisse *f* 254
Kultivator *m* 182
Kümmel *m* 131
Kumquat *f* 126
Kunde *m* 96, 104, 106, 152, 175
Kundendienst *m* 104
Kundendienstabteilung *f* 175
Kundin *f* 38
Kung-Fu *n* 236
Kunst *f* 162
Kunstgalerie *f* 261
Kunstgeschichte *f* 169
Kunsthandlung *f* 115
Kunsthandwerk *n* 274, 276
Kunsthochschule *f* 169
Künstlerin *f* 274
kunststoffbeschichtet 69
Kupfer *n* 289
Kuppel *f* 300
Kupplung *f* 200, 204
Kürbiskern *m* 131
Kurierdienst *m* 99
Kurkuma *f* 132
kurz 32, 321
kurz gebraten 159
Kurzhaarschnitt *m* 39
Kurzsichtigkeit *f* 51
Kurzwaren *f* 105
Kuscheltier *n* 75
Kuskus *m* 130
Küste *f* 285
Küstenwache *f* 217
Kuwait 318

L

Labor *n* 166
Laborwaage *f* 166
lächeln 25
lachen 25
Lachs *m* 120
Lack *m* 79, 83
Lacrosse *n* 249
Lacrosseschläger *m* 249
Laden *m* 298
Lagerfeuer *n* 266
Laib *m* 139
Laken *n* 74
Lakritze *f* 113
Laktose *f* 137
Lamm *n* 118, 185
Lampe *f* 62
Lampen *f* 105
Land *n* 282, 315
landen 211
Landschaft *f* 284
Landungsbrücke *f* 214
Landungssteg *m* 217
landwirtschaftlichen Betriebe *m* 183
lang 32
Länge *f* 165, 310
Längengrad *m* 283
Langkorn- 130
Langlauf *m* 247
Langlaufmaschine *f* 250
langsam 321
Längsschnitt *m* 282
Langwelle *f* 179
Laos 318
Laptop *m* 176
Lärche *f* 296
Lastwagen *m* 194
Lastwagenfahrer *m* 190
Laterne *f* 217
Latte *f* 235
Lätzchen *n* 30
Latzhose *f* 30
Laubbaum *m* 86
Laubrechen *m* 88
Lauch *m* 125
Lauf *m* 228
Laufband *n* 106, 250
Läufer *m* 272
Laufstall *m* 75
Lautsprecher *m* 176, 209, 258
Lautstärke *f* 179, 269
Lava *f* 283
Lawine *f* 247
Leadsänger *m* 258
Lebensmittel *n* 106
Lebensmittelabteilung *f* 105
Lebensmittelgeschäft *n* 114
Leber *f* 18, 118
Lederanzug *m* 205
Lederschuhe *m* 32
leer 321
Leerung *f* 98
legen 38
leger 34
Leggings *f* 31
Leguan *m* 293
Lehm *m* 85
Lehne *f* 64
Lehrerin *f* 162, 190
leicht 321
Leichtathlet *m* 234
Leichtathletik *f* 234
Leichtflugzeug *n* 211
Leimpistole *f* 78
Leinen *n* 277
Leinwand *f* 255, 274
Leiste *f* 12
leitende Angestellte *m* 174
Leiter *f* 95, 186
Leitkegel *m* 187
Leitplanke *f* 195
Leitung *f* 60
Leitungswasser *n* 144
Leitz-Ordner *m* 173
Lende *f* 121
Lendensteak *n* 119
Lendenwirbel *m* 17
Lenkrad *n* 201
Lenkstange *f* 207
lernen 163
Lernen *n* 162
Leselampe *f* 210
lesen 162
Leserausweis *m* 168
Lesesaal *m* 168
Lesotho 317
Lettland 316
letzte Woche 307
Leuchtrakete *f* 240
Leuchtstreifen *m* 205
Leuchtturm *m* 217
Leukoplast *n* 47
Levkoje *f* 110
Lexikon *n* 163
Libanon 318
Libelle *f* 295
Liberia 317
Libyen 317
Licht *n* 94
Lichtmaschine *f* 203
Lichtschalter *m* 201
Lid *n* 51
Lidschatten *m* 40
Liebesfilm *m* 255
Liechtenstein 316
Lied *n* 259
Lieferung ins Haus *f* 154
Liegestuhl *m* 265
Liegestütz *m* 251
Liga *f* 223
Likör *m* 145
Lilie *f* 110
Limonade *f* 144
Limone *f* 126
Limousine *f* 199
Linde *f* 296
Lineal *n* 163, 165
Linien *f* 165
Liniennummer *f* 196
Linienrichter *m* 220, 223, 230
Liniensystem *n* 256
linke Feld *n* 228
links 260
Linkssteuerung *f* 201
Linse *f* 51, 270
Lipgloss *m* 40
Lippe *f* 14
Lippenkonturenstift *m* 40
Lippenpinsel *m* 40
Lippenstift *m* 40
Litauen 316
Liter *m* 311
Literatur *f* 162, 169
Literaturliste *f* 168
Litschi *f* 128
live 178
Lob *m* 230
Loch *n* 232
Locher *m* 173
Lockenstab *m* 38
Löffel *m* 65
Löffelbiskuits *n* 141
Loganbeere *f* 127
Loge *f* 254
Logo *n* 31
Lohnliste *f* 175
Lokomotive *f* 208
Lorbeerblatt *n* 133
Löschfahrzeug *n* 95
loslassen 245
löslich 109
Lösungsmittel 83
löten 79
Lotion *f* 109
Lötkolben *m* 81
Lottoscheine *m* 112
Lötzinn *m* 79, 80
Löwe *m* 291
Löwenzahn *m* 123, 297
Luftdüse *f* 210
Luftfilter *m* 202, 204
Luftkissenboot *n* 215
Luftmanschette *f* 45
Luftmatratze *f* 267
Luftpostbrief *m* 98
Luftpumpe *f* 207
Luftröhre *f* 18
Lunge *f* 18
Lungenautomat *m* 239
Lupinen *f* 297
Lutscher *m* 113
Luxemburg 316
Luzerne *f* 184
lymphatische System *n* 19

M

Macadamianuss *f* 129
Madagaskar 317
Mädchen *n* 23
Magen *m* 18
Magenschmerzen *m* 44
magere Fleisch *n* 118
Magermilch *f* 136
Magister *m* 169
Magma *n* 283
Magnesium *n* 109
Magnet *m* 167
Mähdrescher *m* 182
mähen 90
Mähne *f* 242, 291
Mai *m* 306
Mais *m* 122, 124, 130, 184
Maisbrot *n* 139
Maiskeimöl *n* 135
Majonäse *f* 135
Majoran *m* 133
Make-up *n* 40
Makramee *n* 277
Makrele *f* 120
Mal *n* 229
mal 165
Malachit *m* 288
Malawi 317
Malaysia 318
Malediven 318
Malerei *f* 274
Malerin *f* 191
Mali 317
Malspieler *m* 228
Malta 316
Malzessig *m* 135
Malzgetränk *n* 144
Manager *m* 174
Manchego *m* 142
Mandarine *f* 126
Mandel *f* 129
Mandeln *f* 151
Mandelöl *n* 134
Mango *f* 128
Mangold *m* 123
Mangostane *f* 128
Maniküre *f* 41
Maniok *m* 124
Mann *m* 12, 23
männlich 21
Mannschaft *f* 220
Mansarde *f* 58
Mansardenfenster *n* 58
Manschette *f* 32
Manschettenknopf *m* 36
Mantel *m* 32, 282
Maracas *f* 257
Marathon *m* 234
Margarine *f* 137
Margerite *f* 110, 297
Marienkäfer *m* 295
Marina *f* 217
mariniert 143, 159
Marketingabteilung *f* 175
Markise *f* 148
Markt *m* 115
Marmor *m* 288
Marokko 317
Mars *m* 280
Marshmallow *n* 113
Martini *m* 151
März *m* 306
Marzipan *n* 141
Maschinen *f* 187
Maschinenbau *m* 169
Maschinengewehr *n* 189
Maschinenraum *m* 214
Masern *f* 44
Maske *f* 189, 236, 249
Maß *n* 150, 151
Massage *f* 54
Maße *n* 165
Mast *m* 240
Mastdarm *m* 21
Match *n* 230
Material *n* 187
Materialien *n* 79
Mathematik *f* 162, 164
Matratze *f* 70, 74
matt 83, 271
Matte *f* 54, 235
Mauer *f* 58, 186, 222
Mauerturm *m* 300
Mauerwerkbohrer *m* 80
Mauretanien 317
Mauritius 317
Maus *f* 176, 290
Mautstelle *f* 194
Mazedonien 316
MDF-Platte *f* 79
Mechanik *f* 202
Mechaniker *m* 188, 203
Medaillen *f* 235
Medien *f* 178
Medikament *n* 109
Meditation *f* 54
Medizin *f* 169
Meer *n* 264, 282
Meeresfrüchte *f* 121
Meerrettich *m* 125
Mehl *n* 138
Mehl mit Backpulver *n* 139
Mehl ohne Backpulver *n* 139
mehrjährig 86
Mehrkornbrot *n* 139
Meile *f* 310
Meißel *m* 81, 275
Meisterschaft *f* 230
melken 183
Melodie *f* 259
Melone *f* 127
Memorystick *m* 176
Mensa *f* 168
Menschen *m* 12, 16, 39
Menstruation *f* 20
Menübalken *m* 177
Merkur *m* 280
Mesosphäre *f* 286
Messbecher *m* 69, 150, 311
messen 310
Messer *n* 65, 66
Messerschärfer *m* 68, 118
Messlöffel *m* 109
Metall *n* 79
Metallbohrer *m* 80
Metalle *n* 289
Metallsäge *f* 81
metamorph 288
Meteor *m* 280
Meter *m* 310
Metermaß *n* 80
Metzger *m* 118, 188
Metzgerei *f* 114
Mexiko 314
Mieder *n* 35
Miesmuschel *f* 121
Miete *f* 58

deutsch

mieten 58
Mieter *m* 58
Migräne *f* 44
Mikrophon *n* 179, 258
Mikrophongalgen *m* 179
Mikroskop *n* 167
Mikrowelle *f* 66
Milch *f* 136, 156
Milchprodukte *n* 107, 136
Milchpulver *n* 137
Milchreis *m* 130, 140
Milchschokolade *f* 113
Milchshake *m* 137
Milchtüte *f* 136
Milliarde 309
Milligramm *n* 310
Milliliter *m* 311
Millimeter *m* 310
Million 309
Milz *f* 18
Mineralien *n* 289
Mineralwasser *n* 144
Minibar *f* 101
minirock *m* 34
minus 165
Minute *f*
Minutenzeiger *m*
Minze *f* 133
mischen 273
Mischpult *n* 179
mit 320
mit Automatik 200
mit Formbügeln 35
mit Handschaltung 200
mit Kohlensäure 144
mit Kopfdünger düngen 90
mit offenem Oberdeck 260
mit Rasen bedecken 90
mit Schokolade überzogen 140
mit Schokoladenstückchen 141
mit Zahnseide reinigen 50
Mittag *m* 305
Mittagessen *n* 64
Mittagsmenü *n* 152
Mittelfeld *n* 228
Mittelfinger *m* 15
Mittelfußknochen *m* 17
Mittelhandknochen *m* 17
mittelharte Käse *m* 136
Mittelkreis *m* 222, 224, 226
Mittellinie *f* 226
Mittelmeer *n* 313
Mittelpunkt *m* 164
Mittelstreifen *m* 194
Mittelstürmer *m* 222
Mitternacht *f* 305
mittlere Spur *f* 194
Mittwoch *m* 306
Mixer *m* 66
Mixerschüssel *f* 66
Möbel *n* 105
Möbelgeschäft *n* 115
Mobile *n* 74
Mode *f* 277
Modedesigner *m* 277
Modell *n* 169, 190
Modellbau *m* 275
Modellierholz *n* 275
Moderator *m* 178
Mohn *m* 138
Moldawien 316
Monaco 316
Monat *m* 306
monatlich 307
Monatshygiene *f* 108
Mond *m* 280
Mondbohnen *f* 131
Mondfähre *f* 281
Mondsichel *f* 280
Mondstein *m* 288
Mongolei 318
Monitor *m* 53
Monopoly *n* 272
Monsun *m* 287
Montag *m* 306
Monument *n* 261
Mopp *m* 77
Morgen *m* 305
morgen 306
Morgendämmerung *f* 305
Morgenmantel *m* 35
Morgenrock *m* 31
Mörser *m* 68, 167
Mörtel *m* 187
Mosambik 317
Moschee *f* 300
Moskitonetz *n* 267
Motocross *n* 249
Motor *m* 88, 202, 204
Motorhaube *f* 198
Motorrad *n* 204
Motorradrennen *n* 249
Motorradständer *m* 205
Motte *f* 295
Mountainbike *n* 206
Mousse *f* 141
Möwe *f* 292
Mozzarella *m* 142
Muffin *m* 140
mulchen 91
Mülleimer *m* 67, 266
Müllschaufel *f* 77
Müllschlucker *m* 61
multiplizieren 165
Multivitaminmittel *n* 109
Mumps *m* 44
Mund *m* 14
Mundschutz *m* 237
Mundwasser *n* 72
Mungbohnen *f* 131
Münze *f* 97
Münzfernsprecher *m* 99
Münzrückgabe *f* 99
Muschel *f* 265
Museum *n* 261
Musical *n* 255
Musik *f* 162
Musiker *m* 191
Musikhochschule *f* 169
Musikinstrumente *n* 256
Musikstile *f* 259
Muskatblüte *f* 132
Muskatnuss *f* 132
Muskeln *m* 16
Mutter *f* 22, 80
Muttermal *n* 14
Mütze *f* 36
Myanmar 318

N

Naan *m* 139
Nabe *f* 206
Nabel *m* 12
Nabelschnur *f* 52
nach 320
Nachbar *m* 24
Nachmittag *m* 305
Nachrichten *f* 100, 178
Nachrichtensprecherin *f* 179, 191
nachschneiden 39
Nachspeisen *f* 140
nächste Woche 307
Nacht *f* 305
Nachthemd *n* 31, 35
Nachttisch *m* 70, 153
Nachttischlampe *f* 70
Nachtwäsche *f* 31
Nacken *m* 13
Nadel *f* 109, 276
Nadelbaum *m* 86
Nadelkissen *n* 276
Nagel *m* 80
Nagelfeile *f* 41
Nagelhaut *f* 15
Nagelknipser *m* 41
Nagelkopf *m* 81
Nagellack *m* 41
Nagellackentferner *m* 41
Nagelschere *f* 41
nahe 320
nähen 277
Näherin *f* 277
Nähkorb *m* 276
Nähmaschine *f* 276
Nahrungsmittel *n* 118, 130
Nahrungsmittel in Flaschen *n* 134
Naht *f* 34, 52
Namibia 317
Nascherei *f* 113
Nase *f* 14
Nasenbluten *n* 44
Nasenklemme *f* 238
Nasenloch *n* 14
Nasenriemen *m* 242
Nashorn *n* 291
nass 286, 321
Nation *f* 315
Nationalpark *m* 261
Naturfaser *f* 31
Naturheilkunde *f* 55
Naturreis *m* 130
Naturwissenschaft *f* 162
Navi *n* 195
navigieren 240
Nebelfleck *m* 280
neben 320
Nebengebäude *n* 182
Nebenwirkungen *f* 109
Neffe *m* 23
Negativ *n* 271
negative Elektrode *f* 167
Nektarine *f* 126
Nelke *f* 110
Nenner *m* 165
Nennwert *m* 97
Nepal 318
Neptun *m* 280
Nerv *m* 19, 50
Nervensystem *n* 19
nervös 25
Nessel *f* 297
Netz *n* 217, 226, 227, 231
netzen 245
Netzhaut *f* 51
Netzwerk *n* 176
neu 321
Neubelag *m* 187
neue Kartoffel *f* 124
Neugeborene *n* 53
Neujahr *n* 27
Neumond *m* 280
neun 308
neunhundert 308
neunter 309
neunzehn 308
neunzehnhundert 307
neunzehnhunderteins 307
neunzehnhundertzehn 307
neunzehnter 309
neunzig 308
neunzigster 309
Neurologie *f* 49
Neuseeland 319
neutral 60
neutrale Zone *f* 224
Nicaragua 314
nicht falten 98
Nichte *f* 23
Nickel *m* 289
Niederlande 316
niedrig 321
Niere *f* 18, 119
Niesen *n* 44
Niger 317
Nigeria 317
Nilpferd *n* 291
Nockenriemen *m* 203
Nord- und Mittelamerika 314
Norden *m* 312
Nordkorea 318
nördliche Halbkugel *f* 283
nördliche Polarkeis *m* 283
Nordpol *m* 283
Nordpolarmeer *n* 312
Nordsee *f* 312
normal 39
Norwegen 316
Notation *f* 256
Notaufnahme *f* 48
Notausgang *m* 210
Note *f* 163, 256
Noten *f* 255, 256
Notfall *m* 46
Nothebel *m* 209
Notizblock *m* 173
Notizbuch *n* 172
Notizen *f* 191
Notizen machen 163
Notrufsäule *f* 195
November *m* 306
Nudelholz *n* 69
Nudeln *f* 158
Nugat *m* 113
null 230, 308
Nummernschild *n* 198
Nüsse *f* 151
Nüsse und das Dörrobst f, *n* 129
Nylon *n* 277

O

oben 98
Oberarmknochen *m* 17
obere Kuchenteil *m* 141
Oberschenkel *m* 12
Oberschenkelknochen *m* 17
Oberschenkelmuskeln *m* 16
Objektivlinse *f* 167
Objektträger *m* 167
Oboe *f* 257
Obsidian *m* 288
Obst *n* 107, 126, 128, 157
Obstanbau *m* 183
Obstkorb *m* 126
Obstkuchenform *f* 69
Obstsaft *m* 156
Obsttortelette *n* 140
Obus *m* 196
offen 321
offene Gedränge *n* 221
ohne 320
ohne Bedienung 152
ohne Kohlensäure 144
Ohr *n* 14
Öhr *n* 244
Ohrring *m* 36
Okra *f* 122
Oktober *m* 306
Okular *n* 167
Okularmuschel *f* 269
Öl *n* 142, 199
Öle *n* 134
Ölfarben *f* 274
Oliven *f* 151
Olivenöl *n* 134
Ölmessstab *m* 202
Ölsumpf *m* 204
Öltanker *m* 215
Oman 318
Omelett *n* 158
Onkel *m* 22
Onkologie *f* 49
online 177
Onyx *m* 289
Opal *m* 288
Oper *f* 255
Operation *f* 48
Operationssaal *m* 48
Ophthalmologie *f* 49
Optiker *m* 189
orange 274
Orange *f* 126
Orangeade *f* 144
Orangenmarmelade *f* 134, 156
Orangensaft *m* 148
Orchester *n* 254, 256
Orchestergraben *m* 254
Orchidee *f* 111
Ordner *m* 177
Oregano *m* 133
Origami *n* 275
Orthopädie *f* 49
Öse *f* 37, 276
Osten *m* 312
Osteopathie *f* 54
Osterglocke *f* 111
Ostern *n* 27
Österreich 316
Ostsee *f* 313
Ost-Timor 319
Otter *m* 290
Ouvertüre *f* 256
Oval *n* 164
Overall *m* 82
Ozean *m* 282
Ozeandampfer *m* 215
Ozonschicht *f* 286

P

Paar *n* 24
Päckchen *n* 311
Päckchen Zigaretten *n* 112
Packung *f* 311
Paddel *n* 241
Pädiatrie *f* 49
Paket *n* 99
Pakistan 318
Palette *f* 186, 274
Palme *f* 86, 296
Palmherzen *n* 122
Panama 314
Pandabär *m* 291
Paniermehl *n* 139
Panzer *m* 293
Papagei *m* 293
Papaya *f* 128
Papierbehälter *m* 172
Papierklammer *f* 173
Papierkorb *m* 172, 177
Papiermaché *n* 275
Papierserviette *f* 154

Papiertaschentuch *n* 108
Papiertaschentuchschachtel *f* 70
Pappe *f* 275
Pappel *f* 296
Paprika *f* 124
Paprika *m* 132
Papua-Neuguinea 319
Par *n* 233
Paraguay 315
parallel 165
Parallelogramm *n* 164
Paranuss *f* 129
Parfum *n* 41
Parfümerie *f* 105
Park *m* 261, 262
parken 195
Parkett *n* 254
Parkplatz *m* 298
Parkuhr *f* 195
Parmesan *m* 142
Partner *m* 23
Partnerin *f* 23
Parümerie *f* 105
Pass *m* 213, 226
Passagier *m* 216
Passagierhafen *m* 216
Passah *n* 27
Passcode *m* 99
Passionsfrucht *f* 128
Passkontrolle *f* 212, 213
Pastellstifte *m* 274
Pastete *f* 142, 156, 158
Pasteten *f* 143
Pastetenform *f* 69
pasteurisiert 137
Pastinake *f* 125
Patchwork *n* 277
Pathologie *f* 49
Patientenstuhl *m* 50
Patiententabelle *f* 48
Patientin *f* 45
Patio *m* 85
Pause *f* 254, 269
Pausenzeichen *n* 256
Pazifische Ozean *m* 312
Pecannuss *f* 129
Pedal *n* 206
Pediküre *f* 41
Peeling *n* 41
Pelikan *m* 292
Pendler *m* 208
Penguin *m* 292
Penis *m* 21
Peperoni *f* 124, 143
Pepperoni *f* 142
per Luftpost 98
Pergola *f* 84
Periduralanästhesie *f* 52
Periodikum *n* 168
Perlenkette *f* 36
Persimone *f* 128
Personal *n* 175
Personalabteilung *f* 175
Personenwaage *f* 45
persönliche Bestleistung *f* 234
Peru 315
Perücke *f* 39
Pessar *n* 21
Pestizid *n* 89, 183
Petersilie *f* 133
Petrischale *f* 166
Pfannenwender *m* 68
Pfannkuchen *m* 157
Pfau *m* 293
Pfeffer *m* 64, 152
Pfefferkorn *n* 132
Pfefferminz *n* 113
Pfefferminztee *m* 149
Pfeife *f* 112
Pfeil *m* 249
Pferch *m* 185
Pferd *n* 185, 235, 242
Pferderennen *n* 243
Pferdeschwanz *m* 39
Pferdestall *m* 243
Pfingstrose *f* 111
Pfirsich *m* 126, 128
pflanzen 183
Pflanzen *f* 296
Pflanzenarten *f* 86
Pflanzenöl *n* 135
Pflanzenschildchen *n* 89
Pflanzschaufel *f* 89
Pflaster *n* 47
Pflaume *f* 126
pflücken 91
pflügen 183
pfropfen 91
Pfund *n* 310
Phantombild *n* 181
Philippinen 319
Philosophie *f* 169
Physik *f* 162, 169
Physiotherapie *f* 49
Picknick *n* 263
Picknickbank *f* 266
Picknickkorb *m* 263
Pier *m* 217
Pik *n* 273
pikante Wurst *f* 142
Pikkoloflöte *f* 257
Pilates *n* 251
Pille *f* 21, 109
Pilot *m* 190, 211
Pilz *m* 125
Piment *m* 132
Piniennuss *f* 129
PIN-Kode *m* 96
Pinne *f* 240
Pinnwand *f* 173
Pinsel *m* 274
Pint *n* 311
Pintobohnen *f* 131
Pinzette *f* 40, 47, 167
Pipette *f* 167
Pistazie *f* 129
Pistole *f* 94
Pitabrot *n* 139
Pizza *f* 154
Pizzabelag *m* 155
Pizzeria *f* 154
Plädoyer *n* 180
Plakat *n* 255
Plakatfarbe *f* 274
Planet *m* 280, 282
Planken *f* 85
Planschbecken *n* 263
Plastiktüte *f* 122
plastische Chirurgie *f* 49
Plateau *n* 284
Platin *n* 289
Platte *f* 283
Platten *f* 85
Plattengeschäft *n* 115
Plattenspieler *m* 268
Platz *m* 299
Platzanweiser *m* 255
Platzverweis *m* 223
Plazenta *f* 52
plus 165
Pluto *m* 280
pochieren 67
pochiert 159
Podium *n* 256
Poker *n* 273
Pol *m* 60, 282
Polarlicht *n* 286
Polaroidkamera *f* 270
Polen 316
polieren 77
Politologie *f* 169
Politur *f* 77
Polizei *f* 94
Polizeiauto *n* 94
Polizeiwache *f* 94
Polizeizelle *f* 94
Polizist *m* 94, 189
Poller *m* 214, 298
Polo *n* 243
Polster *n* 220, 224, 225
Polyester *n* 277
Pommes frites 154
Poolbillard *n* 249
Pop *m* 259
Popcorn *n* 255
Pore *f* 15
Porridge *m* 157
Port *m* 176
Portefeuille *n* 97
Portemonnaie *n* 37
Portion *f* 64
Portionierer *m* 68
Portugal 316
Portwein *m* 145
Porzellan *n* 105
Posaune *f* 257
Pose *f* 244
positive Elektrode *f* 167
Post *f* 98
Postanweisung *f* 98
Postbeamte *m* 98
Postgebühr *f* 98
postgraduierte 169
Postkarte *f* 112
Postleitzahl *f* 98
Postsack *m* 98
Poststempel *m* 98
Posttasche *f* 190
Praline *f* 113
Präsentation *f* 174
Preis *m* 152
Preiselbeere *f* 127
Preisliste *f* 154
Prellung *f* 46
Premiere *f* 254
Presse *f* 178
Pressluftbohrer *m* 187
Privatbadezimmer *n* 100
private Fitnesstrainerin *f* 250
Privatjet *m* 211
Privatunterhaltung *f* 268
Privatzimmer *n* 48
Probleme *n* 271
Profilsäge *f* 81
Programm *n* 176, 254, 269
Programmgestaltung *f* 178
Promenade *f* 265
Promotion *f* 169
Propeller *m* 211
Prosciutto *f* 143
Prospekt *m* 254
Prostata *f* 21
Protokoll *n* 174
Protokollführer *m* 180
Provinz *f* 315
Provision *f* 97
Prozentsatz *m* 165
Prozessor *m* 176
Prüfung *f* 163
Psychiatrie *f* 49
Psychotherapie *f* 55
Publikum *n* 254
Puck *m* 224
Puder *m* 109
Puderdose *f* 40
Puderpinsel *m* 40
Puderquaste *f* 40
Puderrouge *n* 40
Puerto Rico 314
Pullover *m* 33
Puls *m* 47
Pult *n* 162, 269
Pulver *n* 77
Pumps *m* 37
Punkmusik *f* 259
pünktlich
Pupille *f* 51
Puppe *f* 75
Puppenhaus *n* 75
püriert 159
Pute *f* 119
Putter *m* 233
putzen 77
Puzzle *n* 273
Pyramide *f* 164

Q

Quadrat *n* 164
Quadratfuß *m* 310
Quadratmeter *m* 310
Qualle *f* 295
Quappe *f* 120
Quart *n* 311
Quarz *m* 289
Quecksilber *n* 289
quer 271
Querflöte *f* 257
Querlatte *f* 222
Querruder *n* 210
Quiche *f* 142
Quitte *f* 128
Quittung *f* 152

R

Rachen *m* 19
Rack *n* 268
Racquetball *n* 231
Rad *n* 198, 207
Rad fahren 207
Radar *m* 214, 281
Radfahren *n* 263
Radicchio *m* 123
Radiergummi *m* 163
Radieschen *n* 124
Radio *n* 179, 268
Radiologie *f* 49
Radiowecker *m* 70
Radius *m* 164
Radkappe *f* 202
Radmuttern *f* 203
Radschlüssel *m* 203
Rafting *n* 241
Rahmen *m* 206, 230
Rahmkäse *m* 136
Rakete *f* 211
Rallyefahren *n* 249
RAM *n* 176
Ramadan *m* 26
Rap *m* 259
Raps *m* 184
Rapsöl *n* 135
Rasen *m* 85, 90
Rasenmäher *m* 88, 90
Rasenrandschere *f* 88
Rasensprenger *m* 89
Rasieren *n* 73
Rasierklinge *f* 73
Rasierschaum *m* 73
Rasierwasser *n* 73
Rassel *f* 74
Rathaus *n* 299
Ratte *f* 290
Rauch *m* 95
Rauchen *n* 112
Räucherfisch *m* 143
Räucherheringe *m* 157
Rauchmelder *m* 95
Raumanzug *m* 281
Raumfähre *f* 281
Raumforschung *f* 281
Raumstation *f* 281
Raupe *f* 295
Raureif *m* 287
Reagenzglas *n* 166
Rebound *m* 227
Rechen *m* 88
Rechnung *f* 152
Recht *n* 180
rechte Feld *n* 229
rechte Spur *f* 194
Rechteck *n* 164
rechte Spur *f* 194
rechts 260
rechts abbiegen verboten 195
Rechtsabteilung *f* 175
Rechtsanwalt *m* 180, 190
Rechtsberatung *f* 180
Rechtsfall *m* 180
Rechtssteuerung *f* 201
Rechtswissenschaft *f* 169
Reck *n* 235
Recyclingbehälter *m* 61
Redakteurin *f* 191
Reflexzonenmassage *f* 54
Reformhaus *n* 115
Regen *m* 287
Regenbogen *m* 287
Regenbogenforelle *f* 120
Regenhaut *f* 245, 267
Regenmantel *m* 31, 32
Regenschirm *m* 36
Regenwald *m* 285
Reggae *m* 259
Region *f* 315
Regisseur *m* 254
Reibahle *f* 80
Reibe *f* 68
reiben 67
reif 129
Reifen *m* 198, 205, 206
Reifendruck *m* 203
Reifenpanne *f* 203, 207
Reifenprofil *n* 207
Reifenschlüssel *m* 207
Reihe *f* 210, 254
Reihen(haus) 58
Reiki *n* 55
Reiniger *m* 41
Reinigung *f* 115
Reinigungsartikel *m* 77
Reinigungsmittel *n* 51, 77
Reinigungstuch *n* 108
Reis *m* 130, 158, 184
Reisebüro *n* 114
Reisebürokauffrau *f* 190
Reisebus *m* 196
Reiseführer *m* 260
Reisekrankheitstabletten *f* 109
Reisescheck *m* 97
Reisetasche *f* 37

deutsch

Reiseziel *n* 213
Reismelde *f* 130
Reißnagel *m* 173
Reißverschluss *m* 277
Reiten *n* 263
Reiter *m* 242
Reitgerte *f* 242
Reithelm *m* 242
Reithose *f* 242
Reitsport *m* 242
Reitstiefel *m* 242
Reitweg *m* 263
Rekord *m* 234
Reliefpapier *n* 83
Renaissance- 301
Rennbahn *f* 234, 243
Rennboot *n* 214
Rennbügel *m* 207
Rennen *n* 234
rennen 228
Rennfahrer *m* 249
Rennmaschine *f* 205
Rennpferd *n* 243
Rennrad *n* 206
Rennrodeln *n* 247
Rennsport *m* 249
Reparaturkasten *m* 207
Reporterin *f* 179
Reproduktion *f* 20
Reptilien *n* 293
Restaurant *n* 101, 152
Rettungsboot *n* 214, 240
Rettungsring *m* 240
Rettungssanitäter *m* 94
Rettungsschwimmer *m* 265
Rettungsturm *m* 265
Return *m* 231
Revers *n* 32
Rezept *n* 45
Rhabarber *m* 127
Rhombus *m* 164
rhythmische Gymnastik *f* 235
Richter *m* 180
Richtungsangaben *f* 260
Riemen *m* 207
Riesenslalom *m* 247
Rinde *f* 136, 142, 296
Rindfleisch *n* 118
Ring *m* 36
Ringbefestigungen *f* 89
Ringe *m* 235
Ringen *n* 236
Ringfinger *m* 15
Rinnstein *m* 299
Rippe *f* 17, 126
Rippen *f* 155
Rippenstück *n* 119
Robbe *f* 290
Robe *f* 169
Rochen *m* 120, 294
Rochenflügel *m* 120
Rock *m* 30, 34
Rockbund *m* 35
Rockkonzert *n* 258
Rocky Moutains 312
Rodeo *n* 243
Roggenbrot *n* 138
Roggenmehl *n* 138
roh 124, 129
Rohr *n* 202
Rohrabschneider *m* 81
Rohrzange *f* 81
Rokoko- 301
Rolle *f* 244, 245, 311
Rolle Toilettenpapier *f* 72
Rollenheft *n* 254
Roller *m* 83, 205
Rollo *n* 63
Rollstuhl *m* 48
Rollstuhlzugang *m* 197
Rolltreppe *f* 104
Röntgenaufnahme *f* 48, 50
Röntgenbild *n* 50
Röntgenbildbetrachter *m* 45
rosa 274
Röschen *n* 122
Rose *f* 110
rosé 145
Rosenkohl *m* 122
Rosenschere *f* 89
Rosine *f* 129
Rosinenbrot *n* 139
Rosmarin *m* 133
Rost *m* 67
rostfreie Stahl *m* 79
rot 39, 145, 274
rotbraun 39
Rote Bete *f* 125
rote Fleisch *n* 118
rote Karte *f* 223
Rote Meer *n* 313
rote Meeräsche *f* 120
roten Bohnen *f* 131
roten Linsen *f* 131
Rotfärbung der Augen *f* 271
Rotorblatt *n* 211
Rotzunge *f* 120
Rough *n* 232
Route *f* 260
Ruanda 317
Rübe *f* 124
Rubin *m* 288
Rücken *m* 13
Rückenbürste *f* 73
Rückenflosse *f* 294
rückenfrei 35
Rückenlehne *f* 210
Rückenmuskel *m* 16
Rückenschwimmen *n* 239
Rückgabedatum *n* 168
Rückhand *f* 231
Rücklauf *m* 269
Rücklicht *n* 207
Rucksack *m* 31, 37, 267
Rücksitz *m* 200
Rückspiegel *m* 198
Rückstrahler *m* 207
rückwärts fahren 195
Ruder *n* 241
Ruderboot *n* 214
Ruderer *m* 241
Rudermaschine *f* 250
rudern 241
Rufknopf *m* 48
Rugby *n* 221
Rugbyball *m* 221
Rugbyspieler *m* 221
Rugbytrikot *n* 221
Rührei *n* 157
rühren 67
Rührschüssel *f* 69
Rukula *m* 123
Rum *m* 145
Rum mit Cola *m* 151
Rumänien 316
Rumpf *m* 210, 214, 240
Rumpfheben *n* 251
Rumpsteak *n* 119
Runde *f* 237
runde Ausschnitt *m* 33
Rundfunkstation *f* 179
Rundkorn- 130
Rüssel *m* 291
Russische Föderation 318
Rutsche *f* 263
rutschen 229

S

säen 90, 183
Safaripark *m* 262
Safran *m* 132
Saft *m* 109, 127
Säfte und Milchshakes *m* 149
saftig 127
sägen 79
Sahara *f* 313
Sahne *f* 137, 140, 157
Sahnetorte *f* 141
Saint Kitts und Nevis 314
Saint Lucia 314
Saint Vinzent und die Grenadinen 314
Saison- 129
Saite *f* 230, 258
Saiteninstrumente *n* 256
Salamander *m* 294
Salami *f* 142
Salat *m* 123, 149
Salatsoße *f* 158
Salbe *f* 47, 109
Salbei *m* 133
Salomonen 319
Salto *m* 235
Salz *n* 64, 152
salzig 155
Sambia 317
Samen *m* 88, 122, 130
Samenausführungsgang *m* 21
Samenbläschen *n* 21
Samenleiter *m* 21
Sämling *m* 91
Samstag *m* 306
San Marino 316
Sand *m* 85, 264
Sandale *f* 37
Sandalen *f* 31
Sandburg *f* 265
Sandkasten *m* 263
Sandsack *m* 237
Sandstein *m* 288
Sandwich *m* 155
Sandwichtheke *f* 143
Sängerin *f* 191
Sao Tomé und Príncipe 317
Saphir 288
Sardine *f* 120
Sardinien 316
Satellit *m* 281
Satellitenschüssel *f* 269
Satsuma *f* 126
satt 64
Sattel *m* 206, 242
Sattelgurt *m* 242
Sattelstütze *f* 206
Saturn *m* 280
Satz *m* 230
saubere Wäsche *f* 76
Saubohnen *f* 131
Saudi-Arabien 318
sauer 127
Sauerteigbrot *n* 139
Sauger *m* 75, 81
Säugetiere *n* 290
Saugglocke *f* 53
Säuglingspflege *f* 74
Saugschlauch *m* 77
Säule *f* 300
Saum *m* 34
Sauna *f* 250
saure Sahne *f* 137
Saxophon *n* 257
Scan *m* 48
Scanner *m* 106, 176
Schablone *f* 83
Schach *n* 272
Schachbrett *n* 272
Schachtel Pralinen *f* 113
Schädel *m* 17
Schaf *n* 185
Schaffarm *f* 183
Schaffner *m* 209
Schafsmilch *f* 137
Schal *m* 31
Schale *f* 126, 127, 128, 129
schälen 67
Schäler *m* 68
Schalldämpfer *m* 204
Schalotte *f* 125
schalten 207
Schalter *m* 60, 96, 98, 100
Schalthebel *m* 201, 207
Schamlippen *f* 20
scharf 124
Schaschlik *m* 158
Schattenpflanze *f* 87
Schauer *m* 286
Schaufel *f* 187
Schaukel *f* 263
Schaum *m* 148
Schaumbad *n* 73
Schaumlöffel *m* 68
Schauspieler *m* 179, 191, 254
Schauspielerin *f* 254
Scheck *m* 96
Scheckheft *n* 96
Scheibe *f* 119, 139
Scheibenbrot *n* 138
Scheibenputzmittelbehälter *m* 202
Scheibenschießen *n* 249
Scheibenwaschanlage *f* 199
Scheibenwischer *m* 198
Scheide *f* 20
Scheidenmuschel *f* 121
Scheidung *f* 26
Schein *m* 97
Scheinwerfer *m* 198, 205, 259
Schellfisch *m* 120
Schenkel *m* 119
Schere *f* 38, 47, 276
Scheune *f* 182
Schiebedach *n* 202
Schiedsrichter *m* 222, 225, 226, 229, 230
Schiedsrichterball *m* 226
Schiefer *m* 288
Schienbein *n* 12, 17
Schiene *f* 47, 208
schießen 223, 227
Schiff *n* 214
Schiffsschraube *f* 214
Schilddrüse *f* 18
Schildkröte *f* 293
Schinken *m* 119, 143, 156
Schirmständer *m* 59
Schlafabteil *n* 209
Schlafanzug *m* 30, 33
Schläfe *f* 14
Schlafen *n* 74
Schlaflosigkeit *f* 71
Schlafmatte *f* 267
Schlafmittel *n* 109
Schlafsack *m* 267
Schlafzimmer *n* 70
Schlag *m* 233
Schlaganfall *m* 44
Schläge *m* 231
schlagen 67, 224, 225, 229
Schläger *m* 224
Schlägerspiele *n* 231
Schlagfehler *m* 228
Schlagholz *n* 225
Schlaginstrumente *n* 257
Schlagmal *n* 228
Schlagmann *m* 225, 228
Schlagsahne *f* 137
Schlagzeug *n* 258
Schlagzeuger *m* 258
Schlange *f* 293
Schlauch *m* 95, 207
Schlauchboot *n* 215
Schlauchwagen *m* 89
schlecht 321
Schlegel *m* 275
Schleier *m* 35
Schleierkraut *n* 110
Schleifmaschine *f* 78
Schleppdampfer *m* 215
Schleppe *f* 35
schleudern 76
Schleudertrauma *n* 46
Schlick *m* 85
Schließfächer *n* 239
Schlinge *f* 46
Schlittenfahren *n* 247
Schlittschuh *m* 224, 247
Schlittschuh laufen 224
Schloss *n* 59
Schlot *m* 283
Schlucht *f* 284
Schlüssel *m* 59, 80, 207
Schlüsselbein *n* 17
Schlüsselblume *f* 297
schmal 321
Schmerzmittel *n* 109
Schmerztabletten *f* 47
Schmetterball *m* 231
Schmetterling *m* 295
schmirgeln 82
Schmirgelpapier *n* 81, 83
Schmortopf *m* 69
Schmuck *m* 36
Schmuckkasten *m* 36
Schmucksteine *m* 288
schmutzige Wäsche *f* 76
Schnabel *m* 293
schnarchen 71
Schnauze *f* 293
Schnecke *f* 295
Schnee *m* 287
Schneeanzug *m* 30
Schneebesen *m* 68
Schneemobil *n* 247
Schneeregen *m* 286
schneiden 38, 67, 79, 277
Schneider *m* 80, 88, 191
Schneiderei *f* 115
Schneiderkreide *f* 276
Schneiderpuppe *f* 276
Schneidezahn *m* 50
schnell 321
schnell zubereitet 130
Schnellbootsport *n* 241
Schnellbratgericht *n* 158
Schnellimbiss *m* 154
Schnellstraße *f* 195
Schnitt *m* 46
Schnitte *f* 121
Schnittlauch *m* 133
Schnittmuster *n* 276

deutsch

schnitzen 79
Schnorchel *m* 239
Schnur *f* 244
schnurlose Telefon *n* 99
Schnurrhaare *n* 290
Schnürschuh *m* 37
Schnürsenkel *m* 37
Schock *m* 47
schockiert 25
Schokolade *f* 156
Schokoladenaufstrich *m* 135
Schokoladenmilchshake *m* 149
Schokoladentorte *f* 140
Schönheit *f* 40
Schönheitsbehandlungen *f* 41
Schönheitspflege *f* 105
Schöpflöffel *m* 68
Schornstein *m* 58, 214
Schot *f* 241
Schote *f* 122
Schraube *f* 80
Schraubenschlüssel *m* 80
Schraubenzieher *m* 80
Schraubenziehereinsätze *m* 80
Schraubstock *m* 78
schreiben 162
Schreibtisch *m* 172
Schreibwaren *f* 105
schreien 25
Schreiner *m* 188
Schriftart *f* 177
Schritt *m* 243
schrubben 77
Schubkarren *m* 88
Schublade *f* 66, 70, 172
schüchtern 25
Schuh *m* 233
Schuh mit hohem Absatz *m* 37
Schuhabteilung *f* 104
Schuhe *m* 34, 37
Schuhgeschäft *n* 114
Schulbuch *n* 163
Schulbus *m* 196
schuldig 181
Schule *f* 162, 299
Schüler *m* 162
Schuljunge *m* 162
Schulleiter *m* 163
Schulmädchen *n* 162
Schultasche *f* 162
Schulter *f* 13
Schulterblatt *n* 17
Schulterpolster *n* 35
Schulterriemen *m* 37
Schuppe *f* 121, 294
Schuppen *f* 39, 293
Schuppen *m* 84
Schürze *f* 30, 69
Schuss *m* 151
Schüssel *f* 65
Schutz *m* 88
Schutzanstrich *m* 83
Schutzblech *n* 205
Schutzbrille *f* 81, 167
Schutzhelm *m* 95, 186, 224
Schutzkappe *f* 270
Schutzmaske *f* 228
schwach 321
Schwager *m* 23
Schwägerin *f* 23
Schwalbe *f* 292
Schwamm *m* 73, 74, 83
Schwan *m* 293
schwanger 52
Schwangerschaft *f* 52
Schwangerschaftstest *m* 52
Schwanz *m* 121, 242, 290, 294
Schwänzchen *n* 39
Schwarte *f* 119
schwarz 39, 272, 274
schwarze Gürtel *m* 237
schwarze Johannisbeere *f* 127
schwarze Kaffee *m* 148
schwarze Loch *n* 280
Schwarze Meer *n* 313
schwarze Olive *f* 143
schwarze Tee *m* 149
Schwebebalken *m* 235
Schweden 316
Schwefel *m* 289
Schweif *m* 280
Schweifsäge *f* 81
Schwein *n* 185
Schweinefarm *f* 183
Schweinefleisch *n* 118
Schweinestall *m* 185
Schweißband *n* 230
Schweiz *f* 316
schwer 321
Schwerkraft *f* 280
Schwert *n* 241
Schwertfisch *m* 120, 294
Schwester *f* 22
Schwiegermutter *f* 23
Schwiegersohn *m* 22
Schwiegertochter *f* 22
Schwiegervater *m* 23
Schwimmbad *n* 101
Schwimmbecken *n* 238, 250
Schwimmbrille *f* 238
schwimmen 238
Schwimmer *m* 61, 238
Schwimmfloß *n* 238
Schwimmflosse *f* 239
Schwimmflügel *m* 238
Schwimmreifen *m* 265
Schwimmsport *m* 238
Schwimmstile *m* 239
Schwimmweste *f* 240
schwingen 232
Science-Fiction-Film *m* 255
Scotch mit Wasser *m* 151
Scrabble *n* 272
Scrollbalken *m* 177
sechs 308
Sechseck *n* 164
sechshundert 308
sechster 309
sechzehn 308
sechzehnter 309
sechzig 308
sechzigster 309
sedimentär 288
See *m* 285
Seebarsch *m* 120
Seebrassen *m* 120
Seefischerei *f* 245
Seelöwe *m* 290
Seemann *m* 189
Seepferd *n* 294
Seepolyp *m* 121, 295
Seestern *m* 295
Seezunge *f* 120
Segel *n* 241
Segelboot *n* 215
Segelfliegen *n* 248
Segelflugzeug *n* 211, 248
Segeljacht *f* 240
Segelsport *m* 240
Sehenswürdigkeiten *f* 261
Sehkraft *f* 51
Sehne *f* 17
Sehnenband *n* 17
Sehnerv *m* 51
Sehtest *m* 51
Seide *f* 277
Seife *f* 73
Seifenoper *f* 178
Seifenschale *f* 73
Seil *n* 248
Seilspringen *n* 251
sein Testament machen 26
Seite *f* 164
Seitendeck *n* 240
Seitenleitwerk *n* 210
Seitenlinie *f* 220, 221, 226, 230
Seitenpferd *n* 235
Seitenruder *n* 210
Seitenspiegel *m* 198
Seitenstraße *f* 299
Seitenstreifen *m* 194
Seitfußstoß *m* 237
Sekretariat *n* 168
Sekunde *f* 304
Sekundenzeiger *m*
Selbstbräunungscreme *f* 41
selbstsicher 25
Selbstverteidigung *f* 237
Sellerie *m* 124
senden 177, 178
Sendung *f* 179
Senegal 317
Senf *m* 155
Senfkorn *n* 131
Senkblei *n* 82
senkrecht 165
Sepie *f* 121
September *m* 306
Server *m* 176
Serviceprovider *m* 177
servieren 64
Servierlöffel *m* 68
Serviette *f* 65
Serviettenring *m* 65
Sesamkorn *n* 131
Sesamöl *n* 134
Sessel *m* 63
Sessellift *m* 246
Set *n* 64, 179
Setzkasten *m* 89
Setzkescher *m* 244
seufzen 25
Shampoo *n* 38
Sherry *m* 145
Shiatsu *n* 54
Shorts 30, 33
Sibirien 313
sich aufwärmen 251
sich befreunden 26
sich übergeben 44
sich verlieben 26
Sicherheit *f* 75, 240
Sicherheitsbohrer *m* 80
Sicherheitsgurt *m* 198, 211
Sicherheitsnadel *f* 47
Sicherheitssperre *f* 246
Sicherheitsventil *n* 61
Sicherheitsvorkehrungen *f* 212
sichern 177
Sicherung *f* 60
Sicherungskasten *m* 60, 203
Sieb *n* 68, 89
sieben 91, 138, 308
siebenhundert 308
siebter 309
siebzehn 308
siebzehnter 309
siebzig 308
siebzigster 309
Siegerpodium *n* 235
Sierra Leone 317
Signal *n* 209
Silber *n* 235, 289
Silo *m* 183
Simbabwe 317
Singapur 319
Sinus *m* 19
Sirene *f* 94
Sitz *m* 204, 209, 210, 242
Sitzfläche *f* 64
Sitzung *f* 174
Sitzungsraum *m* 174
Sizilien 316
Skalpell *n* 81, 167
Skateboard *n* 249
Skateboardfahren *n* 249, 263
Skelett *n* 17
Ski *m* 246
Skibrille *f* 247
Skihang *m* 246
Skijacke *f* 246
Skiläuferin *f* 246
Skipiste *f* 246
Skisport *m* 246
Skisprung *m* 247
Skistiefel *m* 246
Skistock *m* 246
Skizze *f* 275
Skizzenblock *m* 275
Skorpion *m* 295
Slalom *m* 247
Slice *m* 230
Slip *m* 33, 35
Slipeinlage *f* 108
Slipper *m* 37
Slowakei 316
Slowenien 316
Smaragd *m* 288
Smartphone *n* 99, 176
SMS *f* 99
Snackbar *f* 148
Snooker *n* 249
Snowboarding *n* 247
Socken *f* 33
Sodabrot *n* 139
Sodawasser *n* 144
Sofa *n* 62
Sofakissen *n* 62
Software *f* 176
Sohle *f* 37
Sohn *m* 22
Sojabohnen *f* 131
Sojasprosse *f* 122
Soldat *m* 189
Somalia 317
Sommer *m* 31, 307
Sommersprosse *f* 15
Sonate *f* 256
Sonde *f* 50
Sonne *f* 280
Sonnenaufgang *m* 305
sonnenbaden 264
Sonnenbank *f* 41
Sonnenblock *m* 108, 265
Sonnenblume *f* 184, 297
Sonnenblumenkern *m* 131
Sonnenblumenöl *n* 134
Sonnenbrand *m* 46
Sonnenbräune *f* 41
Sonnenbrille *f* 51, 265
Sonnenhut *m* 30, 265
Sonnenmilch *f* 265
Sonnenschein *m* 286
Sonnenschirm *m* 264
Sonnenschutzcreme *f* 108
Sonnensystem *n* 280
Sonnenuhr *f* 262
Sonnenuntergang *m* 305
sonnig 286
Sonntag *m* 306
Sorbett *n* 141
Soße *f* 134, 143, 155
Soufflé *n* 158
Souffléform *f* 69
Soziussitz *m* 204
Spachtel *m* 68, 82
Spachtelmasse *f* 83
spachteln 82
Spalier *n* 84
Spanholz *n* 79
Spanien 316
Spann *m* 15
Spannung *f* 60
Spareinlagen *f* 96
Spargel *m* 124
Sparkonto *n* 97
Sparren *n* 237
spät 305
Spatel *m* 167
Spaten *m* 88, 265
später 304
Spatz *m* 292
Specht *m* 292
Speck *m* 118
Speckscheibe *f* 119
Speerfischen *n* 245
Speerwerfen *n* 234
Speibecken *n* 50
Speiche *f* 17, 207
Speicher *m* 176
Speisekarte *f* 148, 153, 154
Speiseröhre *f* 19
Speisewagen *m* 209
Spermium *n* 20
Sperrholz *n* 79
Spezialitäten *f* 152
Spiegel *m* 40, 71, 167
Spiegelei *n* 157
Spiel *n* 230, 273
Spielanzug *m* 30
Spielbahn *f* 225, 233
Spiele *n* 272
spielen 229, 273
Spielen *n* 75
Spieler *m* 273
Spielerbank *f* 229
Spielergebnis *n* 273
Spielernummer *f* 226
Spielfeld *n* 220, 221, 226, 228
Spielfeldgrenze *f* 225
Spielfilm *m* 269
Spielhaus *n* 75
Spielmarke *f* 272
Spielplatz *m* 263
Spielshow *f* 178
Spielstand *m* 220
Spielwaren *f* 105
Spielzeug *n* 75
Spielzeugkorb *m* 75
Spieß *m* 68
Spikes *m* 233
Spin *m* 230
Spinat *m* 123
Spinne *f* 295
Spinnerkasten *m* 244
Spion *m* 59
Spirale *f* 21
Spitze *f* 35, 37, 122, 165, 246
Spitzenklöppelei *f* 277
Spitzer *m* 163

deutsch

Spitzhacke *f* 187
Splitter *m* 46
Sport *m* 162, 220, 236
Sportangeln *n* 245
Sportartikel *m* 105
Sportjackett *n* 33
Sportkabriolett *n* 198
Sportler *m* 191
Sportplatz *m* 168
Sportschuh *m* 37
Sportschuhe *m* 31
Sportwagen *m* 75
Sprachen *f* 162
Sprachmitteilung *f* 99
Spray *m* 109
Sprechanlage *f* 59
Sprecher *m* 174
Sprechzimmer *n* 45
Springbrunnen *m* 85
springen *m* 227
springen lassen 227
Springer *m* 238, 272
Springreiten *n* 243
Sprinter *m* 234
Spritzbeutel *m* 69
Spritze 48, 109, 167, 311
Spritzschutz *m* 66
Sprühdose *f* 311
sprühen 91
Sprung *m* 235, 237, 239, 243
Sprungbrett *n* 235, 238
Sprungfeder *f* 71
Spülbecken *n* 66
Spule *f* 276
Spüle *f* 61
spülen 76, 77
Spuler *m* 276
Spülkasten *m* 61
Spülmaschine *f* 66
Squash *n* 231
Sri Lanka 318
Staat *m* 315
Staatsanwaltschaft *f* 180
Stab *m* 225, 235
Stabhochsprung *m* 234
Stachel *m* 295
Stachelbeere *f* 127
Stadien *n* 23
Stadion *n* 223
Stadt *f* 298, 299
Stadtplan *m* 261
Stadtrundfahrtbus *m* 260
Staffelei *f* 274
Staffellauf *m* 235
Stahlwolle *f* 81
Stake *f* 245
Stall *m* 185
Stallbursche *m* 243
Stamm *m* 296
Stammaktie *f* 97
Ständer *m* 88, 268
Stange *f* 90, 207, 250
Stangen *f* 133
Stangenbohne *f* 122
Stangensellerie *m* 122
stark 321
Start- und Landebahn *f* 212
Startblock *m* 234, 238
starten 211
Startlinie *f* 234
Startsprung *m* 239
Stativ *n* 166, 270, 281
Staub wischen 77
Staubgefäß *n* 297
Staubsauger *m* 77, 188
Staubtuch *n* 77
Staudamm *m* 300
Staudenrabatte *f* 85
stechen 90
Stechmücke *f* 295
Stechpalme *f* 296
Steckdose *f* 60
Stecker *m* 60
Stecknadel *f* 276
Steckschlüssel *m* 80
Steg *m* 258
Steigbügel *m* 242
Stein *m* 272, 275
Steingarten *m* 84
Steinobst *n* 126
Steiß- 52
Steißbein *n* 17
Stempel *m* 173
Stempelkissen *n* 173
Stengel *m* 111, 297
Steppdecke *f* 71
sterben 26
stereo 269
steril 20, 47
Stern *m* 280
Sternarnis *m* 133
Sternbild *n* 281
Sternfrucht *f* 128
Sternhyazinthen *f* 297
Stethoskop *n* 45
Steuer *f* 96
Steuerhebel *m* 269
Steuerrakete *f* 281
Steuerung *f* 204
Stich *m* 46, 277
Stichplatte *f* 276
Stichsäge *f* 78
Stichwähler *m* 276
Stickerei *f* 277
Stickrahmen *m* 277
Stiefel *m* 37, 220
Stiefmutter *f* 23
Stiefsohn *m* 23
Stieftochter *f* 23
Stiefvater *m* 23
Stiel *m* 112, 187, 297
Stier *m* 185
Stillbüstenhalter *m* 53
stillen 53
Stillen *n* 53
Stimmbänder *n* 19
Stipendium *n* 169
Stirn *f* 14
Stirnmuskel *m* 16
Stirnriemen *m* 242
Stirnrunzeln *n* 25
Stock *m* 58, 91
Stoff *m* 276, 277
Stoffdrücker *m* 276
Stoffwindel *f* 30
stolz 25
Stop *m* 269
stopfen 277
Stoppball *m* 230
Stoppuhr *f* 234
Stöpsel *m* 72, 166
Storch *m* 292
Stoß *m* 237, 239
Stößel *m* 68
Stoßstange *f* 198
Stoßzahn *m* 291
Stoßzeit *f* 209
Stout *m* 145
Strafmaß *n* 181
Strafraum *m* 223
Strafregister *n* 181
Straftäter *m* 181
Strähnen *f* 39
Strampelanzug *m* 30
Strand *m* 264
Strandhäuschen *n* 264
Strandsandale *f* 37
Strandtasche *f* 264
Strandtuch *n* 265
Strang *m* 277
Straße *f* 298
Straßen *f* 194
Straßenanzug *m* 32
Straßenarbeiten *f* 187
Straßenbahn *f* 196, 208
Straßenbaustelle *f* 195
Straßencafé *n* 148
Straßenecke *f* 298
Straßenlaterne *f* 298
Straßenmarkierungen *f* 194
Straßenrad *n* 206
Straßenschild *n* 298
Stratosphäre *f* 286
Strauß *m* 111, 292
Streaming *n* 269
Strebepfeiler *m* 301
Strecken *n* 251
Streichbürste *f* 83
Stress *m* 55
Strichkode *m* 106
Stricken *n* 277
Strickjacke *f* 32
Stricknadel *f* 277
Strohhalm *m* 144, 154
Strom *m* 60
Stromanschluss *m* 266
Stromausfall *m* 60
stromführende Schiene *f* 209
Stromkabel *n* 176
Stromnetz *n* 60
Stromschnellen *f* 284
Stromzähler *m* 60
Strumpf *m* 35
Strumpfband *n* 35
Strumpfhalter *m* 35
Strumpfhose *f* 35, 251
Strunk *m* 122
Stuck *m* 63
Stück *n* 140, 311
Student *m* 169
Studentenheim *n* 168
Studioeinrichtung *f* 178
Stufenbarren *m* 235
Stuhl *m* 64
Stunde *f* 163
Stundenzeiger *m*
Sturm *m* 286
Sturz *m* 186
Stütze *f* 187
stutzen 90
Stützräder *m* 207
subtrahieren 165
suchen 177
Südafrika 317
Sudan 317
Süden *m* 312
Südfrüchte *f* 128
Südkorea 318
südliche Halbkugel *f* 283
Südpolarmeer *n* 313
Südsudan 317
Sultanine *f* 129
Sumo *n* 237
Sumpf *m* 285
Supermarkt *m* 106
Suppe *f* 153, 158
Suppenlöffel *m* 65
Suppenteller *m* 65
Surfbrett *n* 241
Surfer *m* 241
Suriname 315
süß 124, 127, 155
süße Aufstrich *m* 134
Süßkartoffel *f* 125
Süßwaren *f* 107, 113
Süßwarengeschäft *n* 113
Süßwasserangeln *n* 245
Swasiland 317
Sweatshirt *n* 33
Symbol *n* 177
Symphonie *f* 256
Synagoge *f* 300
Synchronschwimmen *n* 239
synthetisch 31
Syrien 318
System *n* 176

T

Tabak *m* 112, 184
Tablett *n* 152, 154
Tachometer *m* 201, 204
Tadschikistan 318
Taekwondo *n* 236
Tafel *f* 162
Tafel Schokolade *f* 113
Tag *m* 306
Tagesdecke *f* 70
Tagesordnung *f* 174
Tai Chi *n* 236
Taille *f* 12
Taiwan 319
Takelung *f* 215, 240
Taktstock *m* 256
Taktstrich *m* 256
Tal *n* 284
Tamburin *n* 257
Tampon *m* 108
Tandem *n* 206
Tangelo *f* 126
Tankstelle *f* 199
Tankstellenplatz *m* 199
Tansania 317
Tante *f* 22
Tanzakademie *f* 169
Tänzerin *f* 191
Tanzmusik *f* 259
Tapedeck *n* 268
Tapete *f* 82, 177
Tapetenkleister *m* 82
Tapezierbürste *f* 82
Tapezieren *n* 82
tapezieren 82
Tapezierer *m* 82
Tapeziermesser *n* 82
Tapezierschere *f* 82
Tapeziertisch *m* 82
Tapisserie *f* 277
Tarowurzel *f* 124
Tasche *f* 32
Taschen *f* 37
Taschenlampe *f* 267
Taschenrechner *m* 165
Taschentuch *n* 36
Tasmanien 319
Tastatur *f* 176
Taste *f* 176
Tastenfeld *n* 97, 99
Tätigkeiten *f* 77, 183
Tätowierung *f* 41
Taube *f* 292
tauchen 238
Tauchen *n* 239
Taucheranzug *m* 239
Tauchermaske *f* 239
Taufe *f* 26
Tausendfüßler *m* 295
Taxifahrer *m* 190
Taxistand *m* 213
Team *n* 229
Techniken *f* 237
Teddy *m* 75
Tee *m* 144, 149, 184
Tee mit Milch *m* 149
Tee mit Zitrone *m* 149
Teebeutel *m* 144
Teeblätter *n* 144
Teekanne *f* 65
Teelöffel *m* 65
Teetasse *f* 65
Teich *m* 85
Teig *m* 138, 140
Teilchen *n* 140
Teiler *m* 173
teilnehmen 174
Teint *m* 41
Telefon *n* 99
Telefonzelle *f* 99
Telegramm *n* 98
Teleprompter *m* 179
Teleskop *n* 281
Tempel *m* 300
Temperatur *f* 286
Temperaturanzeige *f* 201
Tennis *n* 230
Tennisball *m* 230
Tennisplatz *m* 230
Tennisschläger *m* 230
Tennisschuhe *m* 231
Tennisspieler *m* 231
Teppich *m* 63, 71
Tequila *m* 145
Termin *m* 45, 175
Terminal *m* 212
Terminkalender *m* 173, 175
Terminplaner *m* 175
Termite *f* 295
Terparybohnen *f* 131
Terpentin *n* 83
Terrassencafé *n* 148
Territorium *n* 315
Tesafilm *m* 173
Tesafilmhalter *m* 173
Text *m* 259
Thailand 318
Thanksgiving Day *m* 27
Theater *n* 254, 299
Theaterkostüm *n* 255
Theaterstück *n* 254
Theke *f* 142, 150
Therapeutin *f* 55
Thermometer *n* 45, 167
Thermosflasche *f* 267
Thermosphäre *f* 286
Thermostat *m* 61
Thermounterwäsche *f* 35
Thermowäsche *f* 267
Thriller *m* 255
Thymian *m* 133
Tiefe *f* 165
tiefe Ende *n* 239
tiefgefroren 121, 124
Tiegel *m* 166
Tierärztin *f* 189
Tiere *n* 292, 294
Tierfutter *n* 107
Tierhandlung *f* 115
Tiger *m* 291
Tintenfisch *m* 121, 295
Tisch *m* 64, 148, 167
Tischdecke *f* 64

deutsch

Tischtennis *n* 231
Tischtennisschläger *m* 231
Titel *m* 168
Toast *m* 157
Toaster *m* 66
Tochter *f* 22
Toffee *n* 113
Togo 317
Toilette *f* 72
Toiletten *f* 104, 266
Toilettenartikel *m* 41, 107
Toilettenbürste *f* 72
Toilettensitz *m* 61, 72
Tomate *f* 125, 157
Tomatenketchup *m* 154
Tomatensaft *m* 144, 149
Ton *m* 275
Tonabnehmer *m* 258
Tonhöhe *f* 256
Tonicwater *n* 144
Tonleiter *f* 256
Tonmeister *m* 179
Tonne *f* 310
Tonspur *f* 255
Tonstudio *n* 179
Topas *m* 288
Töpfchen *n* 74
Töpferei *f* 275
Topfhandschuh *m* 69
Topfpflanze *f* 87, 110
Topinambur *m* 125
Tor *n* 85, 182, 221, 223, 224, 247
Torlinie *f* 220, 223, 224
Tornado *m* 287
Tornetz *n* 222
Torpfosten *m* 220, 222
Torraum *m* 221, 223
Törtchenform *f* 69
Torwächter *m* 225
Torwart *m* 222, 224
Touchdown *m* 220
Tourenfahrrad *n* 206
Tourer *m* 205
Tourist *m* 260
Touristenattraktion *f* 260
Touristenbus *m* 197
Touristeninformation *f* 261
Trab *m* 243
Trabrennen *n* 243
Tragbahre *f* 94
Tragebettchen *n* 75
Träger *m* 35, 186
trägerlos 34
Tragfläche *f* 210
Tragflügelboot *n* 215
trainieren 251
Trainingsanzug *m* 31, 32
Trainingsrad *n* 250
Trainingsschuhe *m* 251
Traktor *m* 182
Tranchiergabel *f* 68
Träne *f* 51
Transfer *m* 223
Transformator *m* 60
Transmission *f* 202
Trapez *n* 164
Traubenkernöl *n* 134
Traubensaft *m* 144
traurig 25
Trekking *n* 243
Treppe *f* 59
Treppenabsatz *m* 59
Treppengeländer *n* 59
Treppengitter *n* 75
treten 207
Trethebel *m* 61
Tretmaschine *f* 250
Triangel *m* 257
Trichter *m* 166
Triebwerk *n* 210
Trifle *n* 141
Trimester *n* 52
Trinidad und Tobago 314
Trittleiter *f* 82
Trizeps *m* 16
trocken 39, 41, 130, 145, 286, 321
Trockenblumen *f* 111
Trockendock *n* 217
trocknen 76
Trockner *m* 76
Trog *m* 183
Trommel *f* 258
Trompete *f* 257
Tropen *f* 283
Tropfen *m* 109
Tropfer *m* 109, 167
Tropfinfusion *f* 53
Troposphäre *f* 286
Trüffel *m* 113, 125
Truthahn *m* 185, 293
Tschad 317
Tschechische Republik 316
T-Shirt *n* 30, 33, 54
Tuba *f* 257
Tube *f* 311
Tülle *f* 80
Tulpe *f* 111
Tunesien 317
Tunfisch *m* 120
Tür *f* 196, 209
Turbolader *m* 203
Türgriff *m* 200
Türkei *f* 316
Türkette *f* 59
Türkis *m* 289
Türklingel *f* 59
Türklopfer *m* 59
Turkmenistan 318
Türknauf *m* 59
Turm *m* 272, 300
Turmalin *m* 288
Turmspitze *f* 300
Turmsprung *m* 239
Turnen *n* 235
Turnerin *f* 235
Turnierplatz *m* 243
Türriegel *m* 59
Türverriegelung *f* 200
Tüte *f* 311
Typen *m* 205

U

U-Bahn *m* 209
U-Bahnplan *m* 209
Übelkeit *f* 44
über 320
überbelichtet 271
Überdach *n* 266
Überführung *f* 194
Übergepäck *n* 212
überholen 195
Überholspur *f* 194
Überlauf *m* 61
übermorgen 307
Übernachtung mit Frühstück *f* 101
Überpar *n* 233
überrascht 25
Überschwemmung *f* 287
Überweisung *f* 49
U-Boot *n* 215
Übungen *f* 251
Übungsschwung *m* 233
Ufer *n* 284
Uganda 317
Uhr *f* 36, 304
Ukraine *f* 316
Ulme *f* 296
Ultraleichtflugzeug *n* 211
Ultraschall *m* 52
Ultraschallaufnahme *f* 52
Ultraviolettstrahlen *m* 286
um 320
Umfang *m* 164
Umhängetasche *f* 37
Umlaufbahn *f* 280
Umleitung *f* 195
umpflanzen 91
Umschlag *m* 98
umsteigen 209
Umwelt *f* 280
Umzug *m* 27
Unentschieden *n* 223
Unfall *m* 46
Ungarn 316
ungesalzen 137
ungültige Schlag *m* 228
Uniform *f* 94, 189
Universität *f* 299
Universum *n* 280
Unkraut *n* 86
Unkrautvernichter *m* 91
unpasteurisiert 137
unscharf 271
unschuldig 181
unsichere Fangen des Balls *n* 220
unter 320
Unterarm *m* 12
unterbelichtet 271
unterbrochen 99
untere Kuchenteil *m* 141
Unterführung *f* 194
Untergrund *m* 91
Unterhemd *n* 33, 35
Unterpar *n* 233
Unterrock *m* 35
Unterschrift *f* 96, 98
Untersetzer *m* 150
Untersuchung *f* 45, 49
Unterwäsche *f* 32, 35
Unze *f* 310
Uranus *m* 280
Urlaub *m* 212
Urlaubsprospekt *m* 212
Urologie *f* 49
Urteil *n* 181
Uruguay 315
Usbekistan 318

V

Vanille *f* 132
Vanillepudding *m* 140
Vanuatu 319
Vase *f* 63
Vater *m* 22
Vatikanstadt *f* 316
V-Ausschnitt *m* 33
vegetarische Hamburger *m* 155
Vene *f* 19
Venezuela 315
Ventil *n* 207
Ventilator *m* 60, 202
Venus *f* 280
Venusmuschel *f* 121
Verankerung *f* 217
Veranstaltungen *f* 243
verarbeiteten Getreidearten *f* 130
verärgert 25
Verband *m* 47
verbinden 177
verbleit 199
Verbrechen *n* 94
Verdächtige *m* 94, 181
Verdauungssystem *n* 19
Verdeck *n* 75
Verdünnungsmittel *n* 83
Vereinigte Arabische Emirate 318
Vereinigte Königreich *n* 316
Vereinigten Staaten von Amerika 314
Verfallsdatum *n* 109
Verfügung *f* 180
Vergiftung *f* 46
Vergnügungspark *m* 262
vergrößern *f* 172
Vergrößerung *f* 271
Verkäufer *m* 104
Verkäuferin *f* 188
Verkaufsabteilung *f* 175
Verkehr *m* 194
Verkehrsampel *f* 194
Verkehrsflugzeug *n* 210, 212
Verkehrsinsel *f* 194
Verkehrspolizist *m* 195
Verkehrsschilder *n* 195
Verkehrsstau *m* 195
verkleinern *f* 172
Verkühlung *f* 44
verlängern 168
verlängerte Limousine *f* 199
Verlängerung *f* 223
Verlängerungsschnur *f* 78
verlegen 25
Verletzung *f* 46
verlieren 273
Verlierer *m* 273
Verlobte *m* 24
Verlobte *f* 24
Verlobten m, *f* 24
vermehren 91
Vermieter *m* 58
Vermittlung *f* 99
Verordnung *f* 109
verputzen 82
verrühren 67, 138
Verschluss *m* 36
Versicherung *f* 203
Versiegelungsmittel *n* 83
Versorgungsfahrzeug *n* 212
Verspätung *f* 209
Verstärker *m* 268
Verstauchung *f* 46
verstellbare Schraubenschlüssel *m* 80
Versuch *m* 166, 221
Verteidiger *m* 223
Verteidigung *f* 181, 220
Verteidigungszone *f* 224
Verteiler *m* 203
Verwandten *m* 23
verwirrt 25
Vibraphon *n* 257
Videospiel *n* 269
Vieh *n* 183, 185
vier 308
vierhundert 308
vierter 309
viertürig 200
vierzehn 308
vierzehn Tage 307
vierzehnter 309
vierzig 308
vierzig Minuten 304
vierzigster 309
Vietnam 318
Violinschlüssel *m* 256
Virus *m* 44
Visier *n* 205
Visum *n* 213
Vitamintabletten *f* 108
Vögel *m* 292
Vögelbeobachten *n* 263
Vogelscheuche *f* 184
Volant *m* 71
voll 266, 321
Voll tanken, bitte 199
Volley *m* 231
Volleyball *m* 227
Vollkorn- 131
Vollkornbrot *n* 139
Vollkornmehl *n* 138
Vollmilch *f* 136
Vollmond *m* 280
Vollpension *f* 101
Volumen *n* 165, 311
vom Abschlag spielen 233
von Bord gehen 217
von, aus 320
vor 320
vorbestellen 168
Vordach *n* 58
vordere Backenzahn *m* 50
Vorderrad *n* 196
Vorderzwiesel *m* 242
Vorfeld *n* 212
vorgeburtlich 52
vorgestern 307
Vorhand *f* 231
Vorhang *m* 63, 254
Vorhaut *f* 21
vorher aufgezeichnet 178
Vorkriegsmodell *n* 199
Vorladung *f* 180
Vorlauf *m* 269
Vorort *m* 299
Vorschlaghammer *m* 187
Vorspeise *f* 153
Vorteil *m* 230
vorzeitig 52
Vulkan *m* 283

W

Waage *f* 98, 118, 310
Waagschale *f* 310
Wachtel *f* 119
Wachtelei *n* 137
Wächter *m* 189
Wade *f* 13
Wadenbein *n* 17
Wadenmuskel *m* 16
Waffeln *f* 157
Wagen *m* 208
Wagenheber *m* 203
Wagentypen *m* 199
wählen 99
Wal *m* 290
Wald *m* 285
Walnuss *f* 129
Walnussöl *n* 134
Walross *n* 290
Walze *f* 187
Wandern *n* 263
Wanderschuh *m* 37
Wanderschuhe *m* 267
Wandlampe *f* 62
Wanne *f* 83

deutsch

Warenlager *n* 216
Warenregal *n* 106
warm 286
Wärmflasche *f* 70
Warnlichter *n* 201
Wartehäuschen *n* 197
Warteraum *m* 45
Waschautomat mit Trockner *m* 76
Waschbär *m* 290
Waschbecken *n* 38, 72
Wäsche *f* 76, 105
Wäschedienst *m* 101
Wäscheklammer *f* 76
Wäschekorb *m* 76
Wäscheleine *f* 76
waschen 38
Wäscheschleuder *f* 76
Waschmaschine *f* 76
Waschmittel *n* 77
Waschsalon *m* 115
Wasser *n* 144, 238
Wasser treten 239
Wasserball *m* 239, 265
Wasserbehandlung *f* 55
Wasserfall *m* 285
Wasserflasche *f* 206, 267
Wasserflugzeug *n* 211
Wassergarten *m* 84
Wasserglas *n* 65
Wasserhahn *m* 66
Wasserhindernis *n* 232
Wasserkastanie *f* 124
Wassermelone *f* 127
Wassermotorradsport *m* 241
Wasserpflanze *f* 86
Wasserraum *m* 61
Wasserreis *m* 130
Wasserschildkröte *f* 293
Wasserski *n* 241
Wasserskifahrer *m* 241
Wassersport *m* 241
Wasserstrahl *m* 95
Wasserwaage *f* 80, 187
Watstiefel *m* 244
Wattebällchen *n* 41
Wattieren *n* 277
WC *n* 61
Weben *n* 277
Web-Site *f* 177
Webstuhl *m* 277
Wechselkurs *m* 97
Wechselstrom *m* 60
Wechselstube *f* 97
Wecker *m* 70
Wedge *n* 233
Weg *m* 58, 85
Wegschnecke *f* 295
Wegwerf- 109
Wegwerfwindel *f* 30
Wehe *f* 52
weiblich 20
weich 129, 321
weiche Brötchen *n* 139
Weichholz *n* 79
Weichkäse *m* 136
Weichspüler *m* 76
Weide *f* 182, 296
Weihnachten *n* 27
Wein *m* 145, 151
Weinberg *m* 183
Weinbrand *m* 145
weinen 25
Weinessig *m* 135
Weinglas *n* 65
Weinhandlung *f* 115
Weinkarte *f* 152
Weinstock *m* 183
weiß 39, 145, 272, 274
Weißbrot *n* 139
weiße Fleisch *n* 118
weiße Haut *f* 126
weiße Johannisbeere *f* 127
weiße Reis *m* 130
weiße Schokolade *f* 113
weißen Bohnen *f* 131
Weißfisch *m* 120
Weißrussland 316
weit 320
Weitsichtigkeit *f* 51
Weitsprung *m* 235
Weizen *m* 130, 184
Weizenmehl *n* 138
Weizenschrot *m* 130
Welle *f* 241, 264
Wellenlänge *f* 179
Wellenreiten *n* 241
Welpe *m* 290
Weltkarte *f* 312
Weltraum *m* 280
Wendekreis des Krebses *m* 283
Wendekreis des Steinbocks *m* 283
Werbung *f* 269
werdende Mutter *f* 52
werfen 221, 225, 227, 229
Werfer *m* 225, 229
Werferplatte *f* 228
Werft *f* 217
Werkbank *f* 78
Werkstatt *f* 199, 203
Werktag *m* 306
Werkzeuge *n* 187
Werkzeuggestell *n* 78
Werkzeuggürtel *m* 186
Werkzeugkasten *m* 80
Werkzeugleiste *f* 177
Wertpapiere *n* 97
Wespe *f* 295
Weste *f* 33
Westen *m* 312
Western *m* 255
Westsahara 317
Wette *f* 273
Wetter *n* 286
Wetzstein *m* 81
Whisky *m* 145
WLAN *n* 269
Wickelmatte *f* 74
Wickelraum *m* 104
Widerhaken *m* 244
Wiederbelebung *f* 47
wiegen 310
Wiese *f* 285
Wild *n* 118, 119
Wildwasser *n* 240
Wimper *f* 14, 51
Wimperntusche *f* 40
Wind *m* 241, 286
Windel *f* 75
windig 286
Windpocken *f* 44
Windschutz *m* 265
Windschutzscheibe *f* 198, 205
Windsurfer *m* 241
Windsurfing *n* 241
Winkel *m* 164
Winkelmesser *m* 165
Winter *m* 31, 307
Wintersport *m* 247
Wippe *f* 263
Wirbel *m* 259
Wirbellosen *n* 295
Wirbelsäule *f* 17
Wirtschaftsprüfer *m* 97, 190
Wirtschaftswissenschaft *f* 169
wischen 77
Wissenschaft *f* 166
Wissenschaftlerin *f* 190
Woche *f* 306
Wochenende *n* 306
wöchentlich 307
Wodka *m* 145
Wodka mit Orangensaft *m* 151
Wohnblock *m* 59, 298
Wohngegend *f* 299
Wohnmobil *n* 266
Wohnung *f* 59
Wohnwagen *m* 266
Wohnzimmer *n* 62
Wok *m* 69
Wolf *m* 290
Wolke *f* 287
Wolkenkratzer *m* 299, 300
Wolle *f* 277
Wörterbuch *n* 163
Wunde *f* 46
Wundsalbe *f* 74
Wurf *m* 237
Würfel *m* 164, 272
Wurflinie *f* 225
Wurm *m* 295
Wurst *f* 155
Würstchen *n* 118, 157
Wurzel *f* 124, 296
Wurzeln *f* 39
Wüste *f* 285

Y

Yard *n* 310
Yoga *n* 54

Z

Zahlen *f* 308
zählen 165
Zähler *m* 165, 270
Zahlung *f* 96
Zahn *m* 50
Zahnarzt *m* 50
Zahnärztin *f* 189
Zahnbelag *m* 50
Zahnbürste *f* 72
Zahnfleisch *n* 50
Zahnfüllung *f* 50
Zahnpasta *f* 72
Zahnpflege *f* 72, 108
Zahnprothese *f* 50
Zahnrad *m* 206
Zahnschmelz *m* 50
Zahnschmerzen *m* 50
Zahnseide *f* 50, 72
Zahnspange *f* 50
Zahnwurzel *f* 50
Zange *f* 167
Zäpfchen *n* 109
Zapfhahn *m* 150
Zapfsäule *f* 199
Zaumzeug *n* 242
Zaun *m* 85, 182
Zebra *n* 291
Zeder *f* 296
Zeh *m* 15
Zehe *f* 125
Zehennagel *m* 15
zehn 308
zehntausend 309
zehnter 309
Zeichendreieck *n* 165
Zeichentrickfilm *m* 178, 255
Zeichnen *n* 275
zeichnen 162
Zeigefinger *m* 15
Zeit *f* 234
Zeiten *f* 261
Zeitmesser *m* 166
Zeitschrift *f* 112, 168
Zeitschriften *f* 107
Zeitung *f* 112
Zeitungshändler *m* 112
Zelt *n* 267
Zeltboden *m* 267
zelten 266
Zeltplatz *m* 266
Zeltplätze frei 266
Zeltspannleine *f* 266
Zeltstange *f* 266
Zement *m* 186
Zentimeter *m* 310
Zentimetermaß *n* 276
Zentralafrikanische Republik 317
Zentrale *f* 175
zerbrechlich 98
zerstoßen 132
Zeuge *m* 180
Zicklein *n* 185
Ziege *f* 185
Ziegelstein *m* 187
Ziegenkäse *m* 142
Ziegenmilch *f* 136
ziehen 91
Ziellinie *f* 234
Zielscheibe *f* 249
Zier- 87
Zierstrauch *m* 87
Zigaretten *f* 112
Zigarre *f* 112
Zimmer *n* 58, 100
Zimmernummer *f* 100
Zimmerreinigung *f* 101
Zimmerschlüssel *m* 100
Zimmerservice *m* 101
Zimt *m* 133
Zink *n* 289
Zinn *n* 289
Zinssatz *m* 96
Zirkel *m* 165
Zirkeltraining *n* 251
Zitrone *f* 126
Zitronenaufstrich *m* 134
Zitronengras *n* 133
Zitrusfrüchte *f* 126
Zoll *m* 212, 310
Zollamt *n* 216
Zone *f* 315
Zoo *m* 262
Zoologie *f* 169
Zoom *n* 270
Zopf *m* 39
zu 320
zu, nach 320
zubereitet 121
Zubereitung *f* 159
Zubringer *m* 197
Zucchini *f* 125
züchten 91
Zuckerguss *m* 141
Zuckerkrankheit *f* 44
Zuckerrohr *n* 184
Zufahrtsstraße *f* 194
Zufahrtsstraße *f* 216
Zug *m* 208, 239, 273
Zugabe *f* 255
Zügel *m* 242
Zugfenster *n* 209
Zugtypen *m* 208
Zuleitung *f* 61
zum Mitnehmen 154
Zündkerze *f* 203
Zündung *f* 200
Zunge *f* 19, 37, 118
zur Schule kommen 26
Zuschauer *m* 233
Zustellung *f* 98
zwanzig 308
zwanzig Minuten 304
zwanzigster 309
zwanzigtausend 309
zwei 308
zwei Uhr 304
Zweibettzimmer *n* 100
Zweig *m* 296
Zweigstelle *f* 175
zweihundert 308
zweijährig 86
Zweispännerrennen *n* 243
zweitausend 307
zweitausendeins 307
zweitausendzwei 307
zweite Etage *f* 104
zweite Rang *m* 254
zweiter 309
zweitürig 200
zweiundzwanzig 308
zweiundzwanzigster 309
Zwerchfell *n* 19
Zwiebel *f* 86, 124
Zwillinge *m* 23
Zwinge *f* 78
Zwirn *m* 89
zwischen 320
Zwischenrippenmuskel *m* 16
zwölf 308
Zwölffingerdarm *m* 18
zwölfter 309
Zylinder *m* 164
Zylinderkopf *m* 202
Zypern 316

deutsch

Spanish index • index espagnol • spanisches Register • índice español • indice spagnolo

A

a 320
a la carta 152
a la plancha 159
a salvo 228
a través de 320
abadejo *m* 120
abajo 320
abdomen *m* 12
abdominal *m* 16, 251
abedul *m* 296
abeja *f* 295
abierta *f* 221
abierto 260, 321
abogado *m* 180, 190
abonar 91
abonar en la superficie 90
abono *m* 91
abono compuesto *m* 88
aborto espontáneo *m* 52
abrazadera *f* 78
abrebotellas *m* 68, 150
abrelatas *m* 68
abrigo *m* 32
abril 306
absuelto 181
abuela *f* 22
abuelo *m* 22
abuelos *m* 23
aburrido 25
acacia *f* 110
academia de danza *f* 169
acampar 266
acantilado *m* 285
accesorios *m* 36, 38
accidente *m* 46
accidente de coche *m* 203
acciones *f* 77, 97, 227, 229, 233
acebo *m* 296
acedera *f* 123
aceite *m* 142, 199
aceite aromatizado *m* 134
aceite de almendra *m* 134
aceite de avellanas *m* 134
aceite de cacahuete *m* 135
aceite de colza *m* 135
aceite de girasol *m* 134
aceite de maiz *m* 135
aceite de nueces *m* 134
aceite de oliva *m* 134
aceite de presión en frío *m* 135
aceite de semillas de uva *m* 134
aceite de sésamo *m* 134
aceite vegetal *m* 135
aceites *m* 134
aceites esenciales *m* 55
aceituna negra *f* 143
aceituna rellena *f* 143
aceituna verde *f* 143
aceitunas *f* 151
acelerador *m* 200, 204
acelga *f* 123
acelga china *f* 123
acera *f* 298
acero inoxidable *m* 79
aclarar 76
acolchado *m* 277
acomodador *m* 255
acompañamiento *m* 153
acontecimientos de una vida *m* 26
acostarse 71
acta *m* 174
actividades *f* 162, 183, 245, 263
actividades al aire libre *f* 262
actor *m* 191, 254
actores *m* 179
actriz *f* 254
acuarelas *f* 274
acupresión *f* 55
acupuntura *f* 55
acusación *f* 180
acusado *m* 180, 181
adelantar 195
adiós 322
adobado 143, 159
adolescente *f/m*23
adornos para el jardín *m* 84
adosado 58
adosado por un lado 58
aduana *f* 212
aduanas del puerto *f* 216
adulto *m* 23
adversario *m* 236
aerodeslizador *m* 215
aeropuerto *m* 212
afeitado *m* 73
Afganistán 318
afilador *m* 68, 118
África 317
aftershave *m* 73
agalla *f* 294
agarradera *f* 166
agarre *m* 237
ágata *f* 289
agencia de viajes *f* 114
agencia inmobiliaria *f* 115
agenda *f* 173, 175
agente de bolsa *m* 97
agente de policía *m* 94
agente de viajes *f* 190
agente inmobiliario *f* 189
agitador *m* 150
aglomerado *m* 79
agosto 306
agresión *f* 94
agricultor *m* 189
agua *m* 144, 238
agua de colonia *m* 41
agua de grifo *m* 144
agua embotellada *m* 144
agua mineral *m* 144
aguacate *m* 128
aguamarina *f* 288
aguanieve *f* 286
aguarrás *m* 83
águila *f* 292
aguja *f* 109, 276, 300
aguja de ganchillo *f* 277
aguja de la hora *f* 304
aguja de tejer *f* 277
agujero negro *m* 280
ahogarse 47, 239
ahora 304
ahorros *m* 96
ahumado 118, 121, 143, 159
aikido *m* 236
airbag *m* 201
aire acondicionado *m* 200
airear 91
aislamiento *m* 61
ajedrez *m* 272
ajo *m* 125, 132
al lado de 320
al otro lado de 320
al vapor 159
ala *f* 210, 293
ala *m* 119
ala delta *m* 248
alambre *m* 79, 89
álamo *m* 296
alargador *m* 78
alarma antirrobo *f* 58
alarma contra incendios *f* 95
Alaska 314
alba *m* 305
albahaca *f* 133
Albania 316
albañil *m* 186, 188
albaricoque *m* 126
albóndigas *f* 158
albornoz *m* 73
álbum de fotos *m* 271
alcachofa *f* 89, 124
alcachofa de la ducha *f* 72
alcantarilla *f* 299
alcaparras *f* 143
alcázar *m* 214
alcorza *f* 141
aldaba *f* 59
Alemania 316
alerce *m* 296
alergia *f* 44
alero *m* 58
alerón *m* 210
aleta *f* 210, 239, 292
aleta dorsal *f* 294
aleta pectoral *f* 294
aletas de raya *f* 120
alfalfa *f* 184
alfil *m* 272
alfiler *m* 276
alfiler de corbata *m* 36
alfiletero *m* 276
alfombra *f* 63
alfombrilla de baño *f* 72
Algeria 317
algodón *m* 184, 277
alguacil *m* 180
alhelí *m* 110
alicatar 82
alicates *m* 80
alimentos *m* 118, 130
alimentos embotellados *m* 134
aliñado 159
aliño *m* 158
alisar 39, 79
almacén *m* 216
almanaque *m* 306
almeja *f* 121
almendra *f* 122, 129
almendras *f* 151
almohada *f* 70
almohadilla de la tinta *f* 173
alquilar 58
alquiler *m* 58
alquiler de coches *m* 213
alrededor de 320
alta definición 269
altavoz *m* 176, 258, 268
alternador *m* 203
altitud *f* 211
alto 321
altura *f* 165
alubia blanca *f* 131
alubia blanca pequeña *f* 131
alubia de ojo negro *f* 131
alubia flageolet *f* 131
alubia morada *f* 131
alubia mung *f* 131
alubia pinta *f* 131
alubia roja *f* 131
alubias *f* 131
aluminio *m* 289
alumno *m* 162
amanecer *m*
amapola *f* 297
amargo 124, 127
amarillo 274
amarrar 217
amasar 138
amatista *f* 288
Amazonas *m* 312
ambulancero *m* 94
ambulancia *f* 94
América del Norte y Central 314
americana *f* 33
amigo *m* 24
amigo por correspondencia *m* 24
amniocentesis *f* 52
amperio *m* 60
ampliación *f* 58, 271
ampliar 172
amplificador *m* 268
ampolla *f* 46
anacardo *m* 129
anacardos *m* 151
analgésico *m* 109
analgésicos *m* 47
análisis *m* 49
análisis de sangre *m* 48
analógica 179
ancho 321
anchura *f* 165
ancla *f* 214, 240
andamio *m* 186
andén *m* 208
Andes *m* 312
Andorra 316
anestesista *m* 48
anfibios *m* 294
anfiteatro *m* 169
anfitrión *m* 64
anfitriona *f* 64
Angola 317
anguila *f* 294
ángulo *m* 164
anillas *f* 89, 235
anillo *m* 36
animadora *f* 220
animales *m* 292, 294
anís estrellado *m* 133
aniversario *m* 26
anochecer *m* 305
antebrazo *m* 12
antecedentes *m* 181
antena *f* 295
antena de radio *f* 214
antena parabólica *f* 269
antes 320
antes de 320
antes de ayer 307
antiadherente 69
antiarrugas 41
anticoncepción *f* 21, 52
anticongelante *m* 199, 203
Antigua y Barbuda 314
antiinflamatorio *m* 109
anual 86, 307
anular *m* 15
anuncio *m* 269
anzuelo *m* 244
año *m* 306
Año Nuevo *m* 27
apagado 99
apagar 141
apagar la televisión 269
apaisado 271
aparato corrector *m* 50
aparatos eléctricos *m* 105
aparcamiento *m* 298
aparcamiento para minusválidos *m* 195
aparcar 195
aparejos *m* 245
apelación *f* 181
apéndice *m* 18
aperitivo *m* 153
aperitivos *m* 151
ápice *m* 165
apio *m* 122
apio-nabo *m* 124
apisonadora *f* 187
aplaudir 255
aplicación *f* 99, 176
aplique *m* 62
apoyabrazos *m* 210
aprender 163
apuesta *f* 273
apuntalar 91
aquijón *m* 295
Arabia Saudita 318
arándano *m* 127
arándano rojo *m* 127
arandela *f* 80
araña *f* 295
arañazo *m* 46
arar 183
árbitro *m* 222, 225, 226, 229
árbol *m* 86, 296
arbusto de flor *m* 87
arce *m* 296
arcén *m* 194
archivador *m* 172
archivador suspendido *m* 173
arcilla *f* 85, 275
arco *m* 85, 164, 249, 301
arco del empeine *m* 15
arcoiris *m* 287
ardilla *f* 290
área *f* 165, 310

español

área de juegos *m* 263
área de meta *f* 223
área de penalty *f* 223
arena *f* 85, 264
arenques ahumados *m* 157
argamasa *f* 187
Argentina 315
aritmética *f* 165
armario *m* 66, 70
armario de las medicinas *m* 72
armario empotrado *m* 71
armario para clasificar la basura *m* 61
armazón *m* 230
Armenia 318
aro *m* 226
aromaterapia *f* 55
arquitecto *m* 190
arquitectura *f* 300
arquitrabe *m* 301
arrancar 82, 91
arrecife de coral *m* 285
arreglos *m* 111
arresto *m* 94
arriate de plantas herbáceas *m* 85
arriba 320
arroyo *m* 285
arroz *m* 130, 158, 184
arroz bomba *m* 130
arroz con leche *m* 140
arroz integral *m* 130
arroz largo *m* 130
arroz salvaje *m* 130
arruga *f* 15
art déco 301
arte *m* 162
arteria *f* 19
artes marciales *f* 237
articulación *f* 17
artículos de aseo *m* 107
artículos de tocador *m* 41
artículos deportivos *m* 105
artículos para el bebé *m* 107
as *m* 230, 273
asa *f* 88, 106
asa *m* 36
asado *m* 119, 158
asalto *m* 237
asar 67
asar a la parrilla 67
asas *f* 37
ascensor *m* 59, 100, 104
aseos *m* 104, 266
asesora financiera *f* 97
asesoría jurídica *f* 180
asfalto *m* 187
Asia 318
asiento *m* 64, 204, 209, 210
asiento del conductor *m* 196
asiento trasero *m* 200, 204
asistir 174
asma *m* 44
aspa *f* 211
aspecto *m* 30
aspersor *m* 89
aspiradora *f* 77, 188
asta *f* 291
asteroide *m* 280
astigmatismo *m* 51
astilla *f* 46
astillero *m* 217
astronauta *m* 281
astronomía *f* 281
asustado 25
ataque *m* 220
atasco de tráfico *m* 195
aterrizar 211
ático *m* 58
atleta *f* 234
atletismo *m* 234
atmósfera *f* 282, 286
atracar 217
atracción turistica *f* 260
atrio *m* 104
atún *m* 120
auditor *m* 180
aula *f* 162
auricular *m* 99
auriculares *m* 268
aurora *f* 286
Australasia 319
Australia 319
Austria 316
autobús *m* 196
autobús de dos pisos *m* 196
autobús de enlace *m* 197
autobús escolar *m* 196
autobús turístico *m* 197, 260
autobuses *m* 196
autocar *m* 196
autocue *m* 179
automático 200
automovilismo *m* 249
autopista *f* 194
autovía *f* 195
avalancha *f* 247
avance rápido *m* 269
avellana *f* 129
avena *f* 130
avenida *f* 299
avergonzado 25
avería *f* 203
aves *f* 292
avestruz *f* 292
avión *m* 210
avión de línea *m* 212
avión de pasajeros *m* 210
avioneta *f* 211
avispa *f* 295
axila *f* 13
ayer 306
ayudante *f* 24
ayudante del chef *m* 152
ayuntamiento *m* 299
ayurveda *f* 55
azabache *m* 288
azada *f* 88
azafata *f* 190
azafata de vuelo *f* 210
azafrán *m* 132
Azerbaiyán 318
azucena *f* 110
azufre *m* 289
azul 274
azul añil 274

B

babero *m* 30
babosa *f* 295
baca *f* 198
baca para bicicletas *f* 207
bacalao *m* 120
backgammon *m* 272
backswing *m* 233
bacon *m* 118, 157
bádminton *m* 231
baguette *f* 138
Bahamas 314
bailarina *f* 37, 191
bajar 177
bajo 320, 321
bajo par *m* 233
bala *f* 184
balancín *m* 263
balanza *f* 310
balanza de cocina *f* 69
balanza de muelle *f* 166
balcón *m* 59
baliza *f* 298
ballena *f* 290
ballet *m* 255
balón *m* 220, 221, 222, 226
baloncesto *m* 226
balonvolea *m* 227
balsa salvavidas *f* 240
bambú *m* 86, 122
banco *m* 96, 250, 262
banco de trabajo *m* 78
banda de paseo *f* 250
banda de rodadura *f* 207
banda sonora *f* 255
bandeja *f* 152, 154, 210, 310
bandeja de entrada *f* 172, 177
bandeja de horno *f* 69
bandeja de salida *f* 172
bandeja del desayuno *f* 101
bandeja para el papel *f* 172
bandeja para la pintura *f* 83
bandera *f* 221
bandera de esquina *f* 223
banderola *f* 232
Bangladesh 318
banquillo *m* 229
bañador *m* 238, 265
bañera *f* 72
bañera de plástico *f* 74
bar *m* 148, 150, 152
bar mitzvah *m* 26
baraja de cartas *f* 273
barajar 273
barandilla *f* 59, 196
barbacoa *f* 267
Barbados 314
barbero *m* 39, 188
barbilla *f* 14
barca de remos *m* 214
barco *f* 214
barco de vela *m* 215
barco de guerra *m* 215
barco de pesca *m* 217
barniz *m* 79, 83
barra *f* 139, 150, 250, 256
barra de acceso *f* 177
barra de desplazamiento *f* 177
barra de equilibrio *f* 235
barra de labios *f* 40
barra de pesas *f* 251
barra del menú *f* 177
barra fija *f* 235
barrer 77
barrera *f* 209, 222
barrera contra el viento *f* 265
barrera de seguidad *f* 75, 195, 246
barrita *f* 113
barroco 301
barrotes *m* 74
basalto *m* 288
báscula *f* 45, 69, 98, 166
base *f* 99, 164, 229
base *m* 228
base del bateador *f* 228
bastidor *m* 277
bastidores *m* 254
bastón *m* 246
bata *f* 31, 35, 38
bate *m* 225, 228
bateador *m* 225, 228
batear 225, 229
batería *f* 78, 202, 258
batería *m* 258
batido *m* 137
batido al café *m* 149
batido de chocolate *m* 149
batido de fresa *m* 149
batidor de varillas *m* 68
batir 67
batir un récord 234
batuta *f* 256
bautizo *m* 26
baya *m* 296
bazo *m* 18
bebé *m* 23, 30
bebida malteada *f* 144
bebidas *f* 144, 107, 156
bebidas alcohólicas *f* 145
bebidas calientes *f* 144
beca *f* 169
béisbol *m* 228
Belarús 316
Bélgica 316
Belice 314
belleza *f* 40
bemol 256
bengala *f* 240
Benin 317
berberecho *m* 121
berenjena *f* 125
berro *m* 123
berza *f* 123
besugo *m* 120
Bhutan 318
biatlón *m* 247
biberón *m* 75
biblioteca *f* 168, 299
bibliotecaria *f* 168
bibliotecario *m* 190
bíceps *m* 16
bicicleta *f* 206, 250
bicicleta de carreras *f* 206
bicicleta de montaña *f* 206
bicicleta de paseo *f* 206
bidé *m* 72
bienal 86
bifocal 51
bigotes *m* 290
bikini *m* 264
billar *m* 249
billar americano *m* 249
billete *m* 97, 209, 213
billete de autobús *m* 197
billetes de lotería *m* 112
biología *f* 162
biológico 91, 118, 122
biplano *m* 211
Birmania 318
bis *m* 255
biscote *m* 139
bisturí *m* 167
blanco 39, 145, 272, 274
blando 129, 321
bloc de apuntes *m* 173
bloc de dibujo *m* 275
bloque de hormigón *m* 187
bloquear 227
blues *m* 259
blusa *f* 34
bobina *f* 276
bobsleigh *m* 247
boca *f* 14
boca de agua *f* 95
boca de alcantarilla *f* 299
bocadillo *m* 155
bocado *m* 242
boceto *m* 275
bocina *f* 201
boda *f* 26, 35
bodega *f* 215
body *m* 30
bol *m* 65
bola *f* 149
bola de bowling *f* 249
bolas de algodón *f* 41
bolígrafo *m* 163
bolillo *m* 277
Bolivia 315
bollo *m* 139, 140, 155
bolo *m* 249
bolos *m* 249
bolsa *f* 291, 311
bolsa de agua caliente *f* 70
bolsa de golf *f* 233
bolsa de la compra *f* 106
bolsa de plástico *f* 122
bolsa de playa *f* 264
bolsa de valores *f* 97
bolsa de viaje *f* 37
bolsa del bebé *f* 75
bolsa para la hierba *f* 88
bolsillo *m* 32
bolsita de té *f* 144
bolso *m* 37
bolso de mano *m* 37
bolsos *m* 37
bomba *f* 207
bombardero *m* 211
bombero *m* 189
bomberos *m* 95
bombilla de ahorro de energía *f* 60
bombón *m* 113
bongos *m* 257
boniato *m* 125
boquilla *f* 89
bordado *m* 277
bordado en cañamazo *m* 277
borde del ocular *m* 269
bordillo *m* 298
borla *f* 40
borrén *m* 242
Bosnia y Herzegovina 316
bosque *m* 285
bostezar 25
bota *f* 37, 220, 223
bota de esquí *f* 246
bota de montar *f* 242
bota de trekking *f* 37
botar 227
botas altas de goma *f* 244
botas de agua *f* 31
botas de goma *f* 89
botas de trekking *f* 267
botavara *f* 240
bote salvavida *m* 214
botella *f* 61, 135, 311
botella de aire *f* 239
botella del agua *f* 206
botiquín *m* 47
botón *m* 32
botón de ajuste *m* 167
botón de parada *m* 197
botón para grabar *m* 269

botón para rebobinar *m* 269
botones *m* 100
Botswana 317
boutique *f* 115
bóveda *f* 300
boxeo *m* 236
boya *f* 217
bragas *f* 35
braguitas de plástico *f* 30
Brasil 315
braza *f* 239
brazada *f* 239
brazal *m* 45
brazo *m* 13, 95
brezo *m* 297
brida *f* 242
bridge *m* 273
brie *m* 142
brillo de labios *m* 40
brillo del sol *m* 286
broca *f* 78
broca de albañileriá *f* 80
broca de seguridad *f* 80
broca para madera *f* 80
broca para metal *f* 80
brocas *f* 80
brocas para madera *f* 80
brocha *f* 40, 83
brocha de cocina *f* 69
brocha de empapelador *f* 82
brocha de encolar *f* 82
broche *m* 36
brócoli *m* 123
bronce *m* 235
bronceado *m* 41
brotes de soja *m* 122
brújula *f* 240, 312
Brunei 319
buceo *m* 239
buenas noches 322
buenas tardes 322
bueno 321
buenos dias 322
bufanda *f* 31
bufete *m* 180
buffet *m* 152
buffet de desayuno *m* 156
buggy *m* 232
búho *m* 292
bujía *f* 203
bulbo *m* 86
Bulgaria 316
búnker *m* 232
buque de carga *m* 215
buque portacontenedores *f* 215
Burquina Faso 317
burro *m* 185
Burundi 317
buscar 177
butaca *f* 254
butacas *f* 254
buzo *m* 30
buzón *m* 58, 99
bytes *m* 176

C

caballa *f* 120
caballete *m* 174, 274
caballito de mar *m* 294
caballo *m* 185, 235, 242, 272
caballo con arcos *m* 235
caballo de carreras *m* 243
cabecero *m* 70
cabestrillo *m* 46
cabestro *m* 243
cabeza *f* 12, 19, 81, 230
cabezal *m* 78
cabezales de destornillador *m* 80
cabezuela *f* 122
cabina *f* 95, 210
cabina de pilotaje *f* 210
cabina del conductor *f* 208
cabina telefónica *f* 99
Cabinda 317
cable *m* 79, 207
cable de alimentación *m* 176
cables *m* 60
cabra *f* 185
cabrestante *m* 214
cabrito *m* 185
cacahuete *m* 129
cacahuetes *m* 151
cacao *m* 156
cacao en polvo *m* 148
cacatúa *f* 293
cachorro *m* 290
cactus *m* 87
caddy *m* 233
cadena *f* 36, 59, 206
cadena montañosa *f* 282
cadera *f* 12
café *m* 144, 148, 153, 156, 184
café con hielo *m* 148
café con leche *m* 148
café de cafetera eléctrica *m* 148
café molido *m* 144
café solo *m* 148
cafetera de émbolo *f* 65
cafetería *f* 148, 262
cafetería con mesas fuera *f* 148
caída *f* 237
caimán *m* 293
caja *f* 106, 150
caja archivador *f* 173
caja de aparejos *f* 244
caja de bombones *f* 113
caja de cambios *f* 202, 204
caja de fusibles *f* 203
caja de herramientas *f* 80
caja de los fusibles *f* 60
caja de pañuelos de papel 70
caja para cortar en inglete *f* 81
caja torácica *m* 17
cajero *m* 96, 106
cajero automático *m* 97
cajón *m* 66, 70, 172
cajón de las verduras *m* 67
cajón de salida *m* 234, 238
calabacín *m* 125
calabacín gigante *m* 124
calabaza *f* 125
calabaza bellota *f* 125
calamar *m* 121, 295
calambres *m* 44
calcetines *m* 33
calcio *m* 109
calcita *f* 289
calculadora *f* 165
caldera *f* 61
caldo *m* 158
calentador de convección *m* 60
cálido 286
caliente 321
cáliz *m* 297
calle *f* 232, 234, 238, 298
calle de sentido único *f* 298
calle lateral *f* 299
callejón *m* 298
calmante *m* 109
caluroso 286
calvo 39
calzapié *m* 207
calzoncillos *m* 33
calzoncillos de pata *m* 33
cama *f* 70
cama de matrimonio *f* 71
cama de rayos ultravioletas *f* 41
cama individual *f* 71
cámara *f* 178, 207, 283
cámara *m* 178
cámara de vídeo *f* 260, 269
cámara desechable *f* 270
cámara digital *f* 270
cámara Polaroid *f* 270
cámara réflex *f* 270
camarera *f* 191
camarero *m* 148, 150, 152, 191
camarote *f* 214
cambiador *m* 74
cambiar 209
cambiar de canal 269
cambiar de marcha 207
cambiar una rueda 203
Camboya 318
camello *m* 291
camembert *m* 142
Camerún 317
camilla *f* 48, 94
camino *m* 58, 85
camión *m* 194
camión volquete *m* 187
camionero *m* 190
camisa *f* 33
camiseta *f* 30, 33, 54
camiseta de tirantes *f* 35
camiseta interior *f* 33
camisola *f* 35
camisón *m* 31, 35
campari *m* 145
campeonato *m* 230
cámper *f* 266
camping *m* 268
campo *m* 182, 220, 222, 225, 228, 234
campo de críquet *m* 225
campo de deportes *m* 168
campo de golf *m* 232
campo de rugby *m* 221
campus *m* 168
Canadá 314
canal *m* 178, 269
canalón *m* 58
canario *m* 292
canasta *f* 226
cancha *f* 226
canción *f* 259
candado *m* 207
canela *f* 133
cangrejo *m* 121, 295
cangrejo de río *m* 121
canguro *m* 291
canoa *f* 214
cantante *m* 258
cantante *f* 191
cantidad *f* 96
cantimplora *f* 267
canto *m* 246
caña *f* 91
caña de azúcar *f* 184
caña de pescar *f* 244
caña del timón *f* 240
cañas *f* 89
capa de ozono *f* 286
capa superior de la tierra *f* 85
capacidad *f* 311
caparazón *m* 293
capazo *m* 75
capital *f* 315
capitán *m* 214
capitán del puerto *m* 217
capó *m* 198
capoeira *f* 237
capota *f* 75
cápsula *f* 109
cápsula de Petri *f* 166
captafaros *m* 204, 207
capuccino *m* 148
capucha *f* 31
capullo *m* 111, 295, 297
caqui *m* 128
cara *f* 14
carabola *f* 128
caracol *m* 295
carámbano *m* 287
caramelo *m* 113
caramelo blando *m* 113
caramelos *m* 113
caramelos duros *m* 113
carbón *m* 288
carbón vegetal *m* 266
carboncillo *m* 275
carcaj *m* 249
cárcel *f* 181
cardamono *m* 132
cardiología *f* 49
cardiovascular 19
cardo *m* 297
careta *f* 236
carga *f* 216
cargar 76
cargo *m* 94, 180
caries *f* 50
carnaval *m* 27
carne *f* 119
carne blanca *f* 118
carne de caza *f* 119
carne de vaca *f* 118
carne fresca *f* 142
carne magra *f* 118
carne picada *f* 119
carne roja *f* 118
carne y las aves *f* 106
carnicería *f* 114
carnicero *m* 118, 188
carpa koi *f* 294
carpeta *f* 177
carpeta de acordeón *f* 173
carpeta de anillas *f* 173
carpintero *m* 188
carrera *f* 169, 228, 234
carrera al trote *f* 243
carrera de caballos *f* 243
carrera de carrozas *f* 243
carrera de motoras *f* 241
carrera de obstáculos *f* 243
carrera de relevos *f* 235
carrera de vallas *f* 235
carrera sin obstáculos *f* 243
carrete *m* 244, 245, 271
carrete de hilo *m* 276
carretera de acceso *f* 216
carreteras *f* 194
carretilla *f* 88
carretilla elevadora *f* 186, 216
carril central *m* 194
carril de adelantamiento *m* 194
carril de bicicletas *m* 206
carril para el tráfico lento *m* 194
carrito *m* 100, 208
carrito de golf *m* 233
carrito de los postres *m* 152
carro *m* 106, 213
carta *f* 98, 148, 153
carta por avión *f* 98
cartas *f* 273
cartera *f* 37, 97, 162, 190
cartero *m* 98, 190
cartílago *m* 17
cartón de leche *m* 136
cartón madera *m* 79
cartulina *f* 275
carvi *m* 131
casa *f* 58
casa de juguete *f* 75
casa de labranza *f* 182
casa de muñecas *f* 75
casarse 26
cascada *f* 285
cáscara *f* 129, 130, 137
casco *m* 95, 186, 204, 206, 214, 220, 224, 228, 240, 242
caseta *f* 264
caseta de peaje *f* 194
casilla *f* 100, 272
casino *m* 261
caspa *f* 39
castaña *f* 129
castaña de agua *f* 124
castaño 39
castillo *m* 300
castillo de arena *m* 265
catamarán *m* 215
catarata *f* 51
catcher *m* 229
catedral *f* 300
catéter *m* 53
catorce 308
catre de campaña *m* 266
cavar 90
caza *m* 211
cazo *m* 69
cazoleta *f* 112
cazuela *f* 69
cazuela de barro *f* 69
cebada *f* 130, 184
cebar 245
cebo *m* 244
cebolla *f* 124
cebolleta *f* 125
cebollinos *m* 133
cebra *f* 291
cedro *m* 296
ceja *f* 14, 51
celda *f* 94, 181
celebración *f* 140
celebración de la boda *f* 26
celebraciones *f* 27
cemento *m* 186
cemento blanco *m* 83
cena *f* 64
cenicero *m* 150
ceniza *f* 283

centésimo 309
centímetro *m* 310
centrifugadora *f* 76
centrifugar 76
centro *m* 122, 164
centro comercial *m* 104
centro de la diana *m* 273
centro de salud *m* 168
centro del campo *m* 228
ceño fruncido *m* 25
cepillar 38
cepillarse los dientes 50
cepillo *m* 38, 77, 81
cepillo de dientes *m* 72
cepillo para la espalda *m* 73
cepillo para las cejas *m* 40
cera *f* 77
cerámica *f* 275
cerca 320
cerca *f* 182
cercado *m* 242
Cerdeña 316
cerdito *m* 185
cerdo *m* 118, 185
cereales *m* 107, 130, 156
cerebro *m* 19
ceremonia de graduación *f* 169
cereza *f* 126
cero 308
cerrado 260, 321
cerradura *f* 59
cerrojo *m* 59
cerveza *f* 145, 151
cerveza amarga *f* 145
cerveza negra *f* 145
cesárea *f* 52
césped *m* 85, 86, 90
cesta *m* 263
cesta *f* 95, 106, 207
cesta colgante *f* 84
cesta de fruta *f* 126
cesta de jardinero *f* 88
cesto de la colada *m* 76
cesto de la ropa sucia *m* 76
cesto de los juguetes *m* 75
ceta *f* 85
Chad 317
chaleco *m* 33
chaleco salvavidas *m* 240
chalote *m* 125
champán *m* 145
champanera *f* 150
champiñón *m* 125
champú *m* 38
chancla *f* 37
chándal *m* 31, 32
chapa *f* 202
chaqueta *f* 32, 34
chaqueta de esquí *m* 246
chaqueta sport *f* 33
chaquetón *m* 31, 33
charcutería *f* 107, 142
chasis *m* 203
cheddar *m* 142
chef *m* 152, 190
cheque *m* 96
cheque de viaje *m* 97
chica *f* 23
chichonera *f* 74
chicle *m* 113
chico *m* 23
Chile 315
chimenea *f* 58, 63, 214, 283
China 318
chincheta *f* 173
Chipre 316
chirivía *f* 125
chocolate blanco *m* 113
chocolate caliente *m* 144
chocolate con leche *m* 113
chocolate negro *m* 113
chocolate para untar *m* 135
chorizo *m* 143
chorro de agua *m* 95
chubasco *m* 286
chuleta *f* 119
chutar 221, 223
chutney *m* 134
ciclismo *m* 263
ciempiés *m* 295
cien 308
cien mil 308
ciencia *f* 162
ciencias *f* 166
ciencias económicas *f* 169
cieno *m* 85
cientifica *f* 190
ciento diez 308
cierre *m* 36, 37
cierre de seguridad *m* 75
ciervo *m* 291
cigarrillos *m* 112
cigüeña *f* 292
cilantro *m* 133
cilindro *m* 164
cincel *m* 81, 275
cincha *f* 242
cinco 308
cincuenta 308
cincuenta mil 309
cincuenta y cinco mil quinientos 309
cine *m* 255, 299
cinta *f* 27, 39, 111, 141, 235
cinta adhesiva protectora *f* 83
cinta aislante *f* 81
cinta métrica *f* 80, 276
cinta para el pie *f* 241
cinta reflectante *f* 205
cinta transportadora *f* 106, 212
cintura *f* 12
cinturilla *f* 35
cinturón *m* 32, 36, 236
cinturón de las herramientas *m* 186
cinturón de pesas *m* 239
cinturón de seguridad *m* 198, 211
cinturón negro *m* 237
círculo *m* 165
círculo central *m* 222, 224, 226
círculo de face-off *m* 224
círculo Polar Ártico *m* 283
circunferencia *f* 164
ciruela *f* 126
ciruela pasa *f* 129
cirugía *f* 48
cirugía plástica *f* 49
cirujano *m* 48
cisne *m* 293
cisterna *f* 61
cita *f* 45, 175
citación *f* 180
cítricos *m* 126
citronela *f* 133
ciudad *f* 298, 299
Ciudad del Vaticano 316
cizalla *f* 89
claqueta *f* 179
clara *f* 137
clarinete *m* 257
clarinete bajo *m* 257
claro 41, 321
clase preferente *f* 211
clase turista *f* 211
clavar con el martillo 79
clave de acceso *f* 99
clave de fa *f* 256
clave de sol *f* 256
clavel *m* 110
clavícula *f* 17
clavija *f* 60, 259, 266
clavo *m* 80
clavos *m* 133, 233
claxon *m* 204
cliente *m* 96, 104, 106, 152, 175, 180
cliente *f* 38
clínica *f* 48
clip *m* 173
clítoris *m* 20
club *m* 232
club sandwich *m* 155
cobertizo *m* 84, 182
cobrar 97
cobre *m* 289
cocer a fuego lento 67
cocer al horno 67
cocer al vapor 67
coche *m* 198, 200
coche de bomberos *m* 95
coche de cinco puertas *m* 199
coche de época *m* 199
coche de policía *m* 94
coche deportivo *m* 198
coche descapotable *m* 199
coche eléctrico *m* 199
coche ranchera *m* 199
cochecama *m* 209
cochecito de niños *m* 75
cocido en el horno 159
cocina *f* 66, 152, 214
cocinar 67
coco *m* 129
cocodrilo *m* 293
cóctel *m* 151
coctelera *f* 150
código de barras *m* 106
código postal *m* 98
codo *m* 13
codorniz *f* 119
coger 220, 227, 229, 245
coger con la red 245
coger prestado 168
coito *m* 20
cojín *m* 62
col *f* 123
col rizada *f* 123
cola *f* 35, 121, 144, 210, 242, 275, 280, 290, 294
cola de caballo *f* 39
cola de carpintero *f* 78
cola para empapelar *f* 82
colada *f* 76
colador *m* 68
colcha *f* 70, 71
colchón *m* 70, 74
colchoneta *f* 54, 235, 267
colegial *m* 162
colegiala *f* 162
colegio *m* 162, 299
colegio mayor *m* 168
coles de bruselas *f* 122
coletas *f* 39
colgante *m* 36
colibrí *m* 292
coliflor *f* 124
colina *f* 284
colinabo *m* 123
collage *m* 275
collar *m* 36
collar de perlas *m* 36
collarín *m* 46
colmillo *m* 50, 291
Colombia 315
colonia *f* 315
colores *m* 39, 274
colorete *m* 40
columna *f* 300
columpios *m* 263
colza *f* 184
comadrona *f* 53
combate *m* 237
combinación *f* 35
comedero *m* 183
comedia *f* 255
comedor *m* 64
comer 64
cometa *m* 280
comida *f* 64, 75, 149
comida de negocios *f* 175
comida para animales *f* 107
comida principal *f* 158
comida rápida *f* 154
comino *m* 132
comisario *m* 94
comisión *f* 97
comisión bancaria *f* 96
cómo se declara el acusado 180
cómoda *f* 70
comodín *m* 273
Comoros 317
compact disc *m* 269
compañero *m* 24
compañero/-a m/f 23
compartimento *m* 209
compartimento del carrete *m* 270
compartimento portaequipajes *m* 210
compás *m* 165
complejo vitamínico *m* 109
completo 266
compra *f* 106
compras *f* 104
compresa *f* 108
comunicaciones *f* 98
comunicando 99
con 320
con aros *m* 35
con brillo 83, 271
con corriente 60
con gas 144
con hielo y limón 151
con los hombros al aire 35
con plomo 199
concebir 20
concepción *f* 52
concha *f* 265
concierto *m* 255, 258
concierto de rock *m* 258
concurso *m* 178
concurso de saltos *m* 243
condón *m* 21
conducir 195
conducto seminal *m* 21
conductor *m* 196
conductor de autobús *m* 190
conectar 177
conejo *m* 118, 290
conexión *f* 212
confitería *f* 107, 114
confituras *f* 134
confuso 25
congelado 121, 124
congelador *m* 67
congelados *m* 107
congelar 67
conglomerado *m* 288
Congo 317
conífera *f* 86
conmoción *f* 46
conmutador de luces *m* 201
cono *m* 164, 187
conocido *m* 24
conseguir un trabajo 26
conservante *m* 83
conservas *f* 107
conservatorio *m* 169
consola *f* 269
constelación *f* 281
construcción *f* 186
construir 186
consulta *f* 45
contable *m* 97, 190
contador de la luz *m* 60
contar 165
contenedor *m* 216
contenedor de la basura *m* 266
contento 25
contestador automático *m* 99
contestar 99, 163
continente *m* 282, 315
contrabajo *m* 256, 258
contracción *f* 52
contrachapado *m* 79
contrafagote *m* 257
contrafuerte *m* 301
contraventana *f* 58
control de pasaportes *m* 213
controles *m* 201, 204, 269
coñac *m* 145
copa *f* 152
copa de vino *m* 65
copas *f* 150
copiloto *m* 211
corazón *m* 18, 119, 127, 273
corbata *f* 32
Córcega 316
corchete *m* 30, 276
corcho *m* 134
cordero *m* 118, 185
cordón umbilical *m* 52
cordonera *f* 37
Corea del Norte 318
Corea del Sur 318
córnea *f* 51
córner *m* 223
cornisa 300
corno de caza *m* 257
corno inglés *m* 257
coro *m* 301
corona *f* 50, 111
corral *m* 182
correa *f* 37
correa del calzapié *f* 207
correa del disco *f* 203
correa del ventilador *f* 203
correo certificado *m* 98
correo electrónico *m* 98, 177
correr 228
correr en parada 251

español

corriente alterna *f* 60
corriente continua *m* 60
corriente eléctrica *f* 60
corsé *m* 35
corsé con liguero *m* 35
cortaalambres *m* 80
cortacésped *m* 88, 90
cortar 38, 67, 79, 277
cortar el césped 90
cortar las puntas 39
cortatuberías *m* 81
cortaúñas *m* 41
corte *m* 46
corte de luz *m* 60
cortes *m* 119
corteza *f* 126, 127, 136, 139, 142, 282, 296
cortina *f* 63
cortina de ducha *f* 72
corto 33, 130, 151
cosecha *f* 183
cosechadora *f* 182
cosechar 91
cosechas *f* 184
coser 277
costa *f* 285
Costa de Marfil 317
Costa Rica 314
costilla *f* 17, 119
costillas *f* 155
costura *f* 34
costurera *f* 277
costurero *m* 276
coxis *m* 17
cráneo *m* 17
cráter *m* 283
crema *f* 109
crema autobronceadora *f* 41
crema bronceadora *f* 265
crema de limón *f* 134
crema hidratante *f* 41
crema para la cara *f* 73
crema para las escoceduras *f* 74
crema pastelera 140
crema protectora *f* 108, 265
crema protectora total *f* 108
cremallera *f* 277
crepe *f* 155
crepes *m* 157
cría *f* 290
criba *f* 89
cribar 91, 138
crimen *m* 94
criminal *m* 181
crin *f* 242
crin/melena *f* 291
críquet *m* 225
crisantemo *m* 110
crisol *m* 166
cristal *m* 51
cristalería *f* 64
cristaloterapia *m* 55
Croacia 316
croissant *m* 156
crol *m* 239
cronómetro *m* 166, 234
cruce *m* 194, 298
crudo 124, 129
cuaderno *m* 163, 172
cuadra *f* 243
cuadrado *m* 164
cuadragésimo 309
cuádriceps *m* 16
cuadro *m* 62, 206, 261, 274
cuarenta 308
cuarenta iguales *m* 230
cuarenta minutos 304
cuarto 309
cuarto de baño *m* 72
cuarto de baño privado *m* 100
cuarto de estar *m* 62
cuarto de galón *m* 311
cuarto oscuro *m* 271
cuarto para cambiar a los bebés *m* 104
cuarzo *m* 289
cuatro 308
cuatrocientos 308
Cuba 314
cubierta *f* 206, 214, 240
cubierto *m* 65
cubierto de chocolate 140
cubiertos *m* 64
cúbito *m* 17
cubito de hielo *m* 151
cubo *m* 77, 82, 164, 265
cubo de basura *m* 67
cubo de la basura *m* 61
cubo para reciclar *m* 61
cubrecanapé *m* 71
cubrir la tierra 91
cucaracha *f* 295
cuchara *f* 65
cuchara de madera *f* 68
cuchara de servir *f* 68
cuchara medidora *f* 109
cuchara para helado *f* 68
cuchara sopera *f* 65
cucharilla de café *f* 65, 153
cucharón *m* 68
cuchilla *f* 66, 78
cuchilla de afeitar desechable *f* 73
cuchillo *m* 65
cuchillo de cocina *m* 68
cuchillo de sierra *m* 68
cuello *m* 12, 32
cuello de pico *m* 33
cuello del útero *m* 20
cuello redondo *m* 33
cuello uterino *m* 52
cuenco *m* 69
cuenco mezclador *m* 66
cuenta *f* 152
cuenta corriente *f* 96
cuenta de ahorros *f* 97
cuenta de correo *f* 177
cuentagotas *m* 109, 167
cuentakilómetros *m* 201, 204
cuentarevoluciones *m* 201
cuerda *f* 230, 248, 256, 258, 266
cuerda de plomada *f* 82
cuerda para tender la ropa *f* 76
cuerdas vocales *f* 19
cuerno *m* 291
cuero cabelludo *m* 39
cuerpo *m* 12
cuerpos geométricos *m* 164
cuervo *m* 292
cueva *f* 284
cuidado de la piel *m* 108
cuidado del bebé *m* 74
cuidado dental *m* 108
cuidar 91
culata *f* 202
culpable 181
cultivador *m* 182
cultivar 91
cumpleaños *m* 27
cuna *f* 74
cuña f 37
cuñada *f* 23
cuñado *m* 23
cúpula *f* 300
curado 118, 143, 159
cúrcuma *f* 132
curling *m* 247
curry *m* 158
curry en polvo *m* 132
curso *m* 163
curvo 165
cuscús *m* 130
cúter *m* 80, 82
cutícula *f* 15
cutis *m* 41

D

dado de alta 48
dados *m* 272
damas *f* 272
dar 273
dar de comer 183
dar el pecho 53
dar marcha atrás 195
dardos *m* 273
darse un baño 72
darse una ducha 72
dársena *f* 216
dátil *m* 129
de 320
de cristal 69
de cuatro puertas 200
de fácil cocción 130
de granja 118
de hoja caduca 86
de hoja perenne 86
de mucho viento 286
de nada 322
de preparación al parto 52
de sentido único 194
de temporada 129
de tres puertas 200
de vestir 34
debajo de 320
deberes *m* 163
débil 321
década *f* 307
décimo 309
décimo noveno 309
décimo octavo 309
decimocuarto 309
decimoquinto 309
decimoséptimo 309
decimosexto 309
decimotercero 309
declaración *f* 180
decoración *f* 82, 141
decorado *m* 254
dedal *m* 276
dedalera *f* 297
dedo corazón *m* 15
dedo del pie *m* 15
dedo gordo del pie *m* 15
dedo pequeño del pie *m* 15
defender 229
defensa *m* 223
defensa *f* 181, 220
defensa personal *f* 237
dejada *f* 230
delantal *m* 30, 50, 69
delante de 320
delantero *m* 222
deletrear 162
delfín *m* 290
delgado 321
deltoides *m* 16
denominador *m* 165
dentadura postiza *f* 50
dentista *f* 189
dentista *m* 50
dentro 320
dentro de 320
denuncia *f* 94
departamento *m* 169
departamento de atención al cliente *m* 175
departamento de contabilidad *m* 175
departamento de márketing *m* 175
departamento de recursos humanos *m* 175
departamento de ventas *m* 175
departamento legal *m* 175
dependienta *f* 188
dependiente *m* 104
depilación a la cera *f* 41
deportes *m* 220, 236, 248
deportes acuáticos *m* 241
deportes de combate *m* 236
deportes de invierno *m* 247
deportista *m* 191
deportivo 200
depósito del aceite *m* 204
depósito del limpiaparabrisas *m* 202
depósito del líquido de frenos *m* 202
depósito del líquido refrigerante *m* 202
derecha *f* 260
derecho *m* 169, 180, 231
dermatología *f* 49
derrame cerebral *m* 44
derribo *m* 237
desagüe *m* 61, 72
desatascador *m* 81
desayuno *m* 64, 156
desayuno inglés *m* 157
descansillo *m* 59
descanso *m* 223
descarga eléctrica *f* 46
descenso *m* 247
descongelar 67
descorazonador *m* 68
descoser 277
descubierto 260
descubierto *m* 96
desde 320
desecado 129
desechable 109
desembarcar 217
desenfocado 271
desfiladero *m* 284
desfile *m* 27
desierto *m* 285
desinfectante *m* 47
desmayarse 25, 44
desodorante *m* 73
desodorantes *m* 108
despacho *m* 63
despegar 211
desperdicios orgánicos *m* 61
despertarse 71
desplantador *m* 89
después 320
destino *m* 213
destornillador *m* 80
destornillador de estrella *m* 81
desvío *m* 195
detective *m* 94
detector de humos *m* 95
detergente *m* 77
detrás de 320
día *m* 305, 306
día de Acción de Gracias *m* 27
día de Halloween *m* 27
día laborable 304
diabetes *f* 44
diadema *f* 38
diafragma *m* 19, 21
diagonal *f* 164
diamante *m* 288
diámetro *m* 164
diana *f* 249, 273
diarrea *f* 44, 109
dibujar 162
dibujo *m* 275
dibujos animados *m* 178
diccionario *m* 163
diciembre 306
diecinueve 308
dieciocho 308
dieciséis 308
diecisiete 308
diente *m* 50, 125
diente de la rueda *m* 206
diente de león *m* 123, 297
diesel *m* 199
diez 308
diez mil 309
difícil 321
digestivo 19
digital 179, 269
dilatación *f* 52
Dinamarca 316
dinamo *f* 207
dinero *m* 97
dintel *m* 186
dioptría *f* 51
diploma *m* 169
dique seco *m* 217
dirección *f* 98
dirección electrónica *f* 177
director *m* 163, 174, 254
director de banco *m* 96
director de orquesta *m* 256
director general *m* 175
directorio *m* 104
disco *m* 224
disco de DVD *m* 269
disco duro externo *m* 176
discos protectores *m* 53
discutir 163
diseñador *m* 191, 277
diseñar 91
disolvente *m* 83
disparador *m* 270
dispensario *m* 108
dispositivo intrauterino DIU *m* 21
distancia *f* 310
distribuidor *m* 203
distrito *m* 315
dividendos *m* 97
dividido por 165
dividir 165
divisas *f* 97
divisor *m* 173
divorcio *m* 26
Diwali *m* 27

Djibouti 317
dobladillo *m* 34
doble techo *m* 266
doce 308
doctorado *m* 169
documental *m* 178
documento adjunto *m* 177
dolor de cabeza *m* 44
dolor de estómago *m* 44
dolor de muelas *m* 50
doma y monta *f* 243
domiciliación bancaria *f* 96
domingo 306
Dominica 314
dominó *m* 273
dormirse 71
dormitorio *m* 70
dorsal *m* 16
dos 308
dos en punto 304
dos mil 307
dos mil uno 307
doscientos 308
dosis *f* 109
drenaje *m* 91
ducha *f* 72
duchas *f* 266
dulce 124, 127,155
duodécimo 309
duodeno *m* 18
duro 129, 321

E

eccema *m* 44
echar 67
eclipse *m* 280
ecografía *f* 48, 52
ecuación *f* 165
Ecuador 315
ecuador *m* 283
edificio *m* 59
edificio de oficinas *m* 298
edificio de pisos *m* 298
edificio histórico *m* 261
edificios *m* 299
edredón *m* 71
educación física *f* 162
efecto *m* 230
efectos secundarios *m* 109
Egipto 317
eje *m* 205, 206
eje de la transmisión *m* 202
ejecutivo *m* 174
ejercicio de bíceps *m* 251
ejercicios *f* 251
ejercicios de piernas *m* 251
ejercicios de suelo *m* 235
ejercicios pectorales *f* 251
El Salvador 314
electricidad *f* 60
electricista *m* 188
electrodo negativo *m* 167
electrodo positivo *m* 167
electrodomésticos *m* 66, 107
elefante *m* 291
eliminación de desechos *f* 61
embalse *m* 300
embarazada 52
embarazo *m* 52
embarcaciones *f* 215
embarcadero *m* 217
embarcar 217
embrague *m* 200, 204
embrión *m* 52
embudo *m* 166
emigrar 26
Emiratos Árabes Unidos 318
emisión *f* 179
emitir 178
emociones *f* 25
empapelar 82
empaste *m* 50
empate *m* 223
empeine *m* 15
empezar el colegio 26
empleado *m* 24
empleado de correos *m* 98
empleado de la limpieza *m* 188
empresa *f* 175
empresaria *f* 24
en 320
en aceite 143
en almíbar 159
en directo 178
en diferido 178
en filetes 121
en formato vertical 271
en frente de 320
en línea 177
en polvo 77
en salmuera 143
en salsa 159
en vinagre 159
enamorarse 26
encaje *m* 35, 80
encender la televisión 269
encender una hoguera 266
encendido *m* 200
enchufe hembra *m* 60
enchufe macho *m* 60
encía *f* 50
enciclopedia *f* 163
encima de 320
encimera *f* 66
encinta 52
endibia *f* 122
endocrino 19
endocrinología *f* 49
eneldo *m* 133
enero 306
enfadado 25
enfermedad *f* 44
enfermedad de transmisión sexual *f* 20
enfermera *f* 45, 48, 189
enfocar 271
enhebrar 277
enjuagar 38
enjuague bucal *m* 72
enrollador de manguera *m* 89
ensalada *f* 149
ensalada mixta *f* 158
ensalada verde *f* 158
ensayo *m* 221
enseñanza superior *f* 168
entarimado *m* 85
entero 129, 132
entrada *f* 59
entrante *m* 153
entrar en el sistema 177
entrar en erupción 283
entre 320
entrega a domicilio *f* 154
entrenadora personal *f* 250
entrenamiento *m* 237
entrenar 251
entrevistador *m* 179
entusiasmado 25
envenenamiento *m* 46
enviar 177
envoltorio *m* 111
enyesar 82
epidural *f* 52
epiglotis *f* 19
epilepsia *f* 44
episiotomía *f* 52
equipaje *m* 100, 198, 213
equipaje de mano *m* 211, 213
equipo *m* 205, 220, 229, 233, 238
equipo de alta fidelidad *m* 268
equipo de limpieza *m* 77
equipo de oficina *m* 172
equitación *f* 242, 263
Eritrea 317
erizo *m* 290
escala *f* 256
escalada *f* 248
escalada en hielo *f* 247
escalera *f* 59, 95, 186
escalera de mano *f* 82
escalera mecánica *f* 104
escalfar 67
escalfado 159
escalpelo *f* 81
escama *f* 121, 294
escamas *f* 293
escáner *m* 106
escarabajo *m* 295
escarcha *f* 287
escardar 91
escariador *m* 80
escarola *f* 123
escenario *m* 254
escoba *f* 77
escobilla del wáter *f* 72
escorpión *m* 295
escota *f* 241
escotera *f* 240
escotilla *f* 281
escribir 162
escritorio *m* 172, 177
escroto *m* 21
escuadra *f* 165
escucha-bebés *m* 75
escuela de Bellas Artes *f* 169
escuelas *f* 169
escultor *m* 191
escultura *f* 275
escurridor *m* 67, 68
esfera *f* 164
esgrima *m* 249
eslabón *m* 36
Eslovaquia 316
Eslovenia 316
esmalte *m* 50
esmalte de uñas *m* 41
esmeralda *f* 288
esófago *m* 19
espacio *m* 280
espada *f* 236
espalda *f* 13, 239
espaldera *f* 84
espantapájaros *m* 184
España 316
esparadrapo *m* 47
espárrago *m* 124
espátula *f* 68, 167
especialista *m* 49
especias *f* 132
espectadores *m* 233
espejo *m* 40, 71, 167
espejo retrovisor *m* 198
esperma *m* 20
espigón *m* 217
espina *f* 121
espina dorsal *f* 17
espinaca *f* 123
espinilla *f* 12
esponja *f* 73, 74, 83
esposas *f* 94
esprinter *m* 234
espuma *f* 148
espuma de afeitar *f* 73
espumadera *f* 68
esqueje *m* 91
esqueleto *m* 17
esquí *m* 241, 246
esquí acuático *m* 241
esquí alpino *m* 247
esquí de fondo *m* 247
esquiador acuático *m* 241
esquiadora *f* 246
esquina *f* 298
esquisto *m* 288
esta semana 307
estabilizador horizontal *m* 210
establo *m* 185
estaca *f* 90
estación de autobuses *f* 197
estación de policía *f* 94
estación de radio *f* 179
estación de tren *f* 208
estación espacial *f* 281
estaciones *f* 306
estadio 223
estado *m* 315
Estados Unidos de América 314
estambre *m* 297
estanque *m* 67, 85, 106, 232
estantería *f* 63, 168
estantes *m* 66
estaño *m* 289
estatuilla *f* 260
este *m* 312
estéreo 269
estéril 20, 47
esterilla *f* 267
esternón *m* 17
estetoscopio *m* 45
estilo modernista *m* 301
estilos *m* 39, 239, 301
estilos de jardín *m* 84
estilos musicales *m* 259
estiramiento *m* 251
estirar 251
estómago *m* 18
Estonia 316
estor *m* 63
estor de láminas *m* 63
estornudo *m* 44
estragón *m* 133
estratosfera *f* 286
estrecho 321
estrella *f* 280
estrella de mar *f* 295
estreno *m* 254
estrés *m* 55
estribo *m* 71, 242
estructura *f* 267
estructura para escalar *f* 263
estuario *m* 285
estuche *m* 163
estuche para las lentillas *m* 51
estudiante *m* 169
estudio *m* 162
estudio de grabación *m* 179
estudio de televisión *m* 178
estufa *f* 60
etapas *f* 23
Etiopía 317
etiquetas *f* 89
eucalipto *m* 296
Europa 316
examen *m* 163
examen de ojos *m* 51
examen médico *m* 45
excavadora mecánica *f* 187
exceso de equipaje *m* 212
exfoliar 41
exósfera *f* 286
experimento *m* 166
exploración espacial *f* 281
exposición *f* 261, 271
expulsión *f* 223
extender con el rodillo 67
exterior *m* 198, 229
exterior derecho *m* 229
exterior izquierdo *m* 228
extintor *m* 95
extracción *f* 50
extractor *m* 66

F

fábrica *f* 299
fácil 321
facturar 212
fagote *m* 257
faisán *m* 119, 293
falda *f* 30, 34
fallo *m* 228
falsa torre *f* 215
falta *f* 222, 226, 230
familia *f* 22
fans *m* 258
faringe *f* 19
farmacéutica *f* 189
farmacéutico *m* 108
farmacia *f* 108
faro *m* 198, 205, 207, 217
faro trasero *m* 207
farola *f* 298
fax *m* 98
febrero 306
fecha *f* 306
fecha de caducidad *f* 109
fecha de devolución *f* 168
fecha del juicio *f* 180
Federación Rusa 318
feijoa *f* 128
felpudo *m* 59
femenino 20
fémur *m* 17
feng shui *m* 55
feria *f* 262
ferretería *f* 114
ferry *m* 215, 216
fertilización *f* 20
festivales *m* 27
feto *m* 52
fiambre *m* 118, 142, 143
fianza *f* 181
fibra *f* 127
fibra natural *f* 31
ficha *f* 272
fichero *m* 177
fideos *m* 158
fiebre *f* 44
fiebre del heno *f* 44
fiesta de cumpleaños *f* 27
Fiji 319

español

fila *f* 210, 254
filatelia *f* 273
filete *m* 119, 121
filete de lomo *m* 119
filete de solomillo *m* 119
filetes de mero *m* 120
Filipinas 319
filosofía *f* 169
filtro *m* 270
filtro de papel *m* 167
filtro del aire *m* 202, 204
fin de semana *m* 306
final *m* 321
finanzas *f* 97
Finlandia 316
firma *f* 96, 98
firme 124
física *f* 162, 169
fisioterapia *f* 49
flamenco *m* 292
flanera *f* 69
flash *m* 270
flash electrónico *m* 270
flauta *f* 257
flautín *m* 257
flecha *f* 249
flexión *f* 251
flexión con estiramiento *f* 251
flexionar 251
flor *f* 297
florentina *f* 141
flores *f* 110
flores secas *f* 111
florete *m* 249
florista *f* 188
floristería *f* 110
florón 300
flotador *m* 61, 238, 244, 265
flotador de brazo *m* 238
foca *f* 290
foco *m* 50, 178, 259
folículo *m* 20
follaje *m* 110
folleto *m* 175
folleto de viajes *m* 212
folletos *m* 96
fondear 217
fondo *m* 177
fontanería *f* 61
fontanero *m* 188
footing *m* 251, 263
foque *m* 240
fórceps *m* 53, 167
forma física *f* 250
formas *f* 164
forro *m* 32
foso *m* 300
foso de la orquesta *m* 254
foto *f* 271
foto (revelada) *f* 271
fotocopiar 172
fotofinish *f* 234
fotografía *f* 270
fotografiar 271
fotógrafo *m* 191
fotómetro *m* 270
fractura *f* 46
frágil 98
frambuesa *f* 127
frambuesa Logan *f* 127
Francia 316
franqueo *m* 98
frasco de cristal *m* 166
frecuencia *f* 179
fregadero *m* 66
fregador *m* 61
fregar 77
fregona *f* 77
freír 67
frenar 207
freno *m* 200, 204, 206
freno de mano *m* 203
frente *f* 14
frente de la cocina *m* 66
fresa *f* 127
fresco 121, 127, 130
fresia *f* 110
friegaplatos *m* 66
frigorífico *m* 67
frigorífico congelador *m* 67
frío 286, 321
friso *m* 301
frito 159
frito con mucho aceite 159
frito con poco aceite 159
frontal *m* 16
frontalera *f* 242
frontón *m* 300, 301
fruta *f* 107, 126, 128
fruta con hueso *f* 126
fruta desecada *f* 156
fruta en conserva *f* 134
fruta escarchada *f* 129
fruta fresca *f* 157
frutas tropicales *f* 128
frutero *m* 188
fruto del pan *m* 124
frutos secos *m* 129, 151
fuente *f* 85, 177
reloj de sol *m* 262
fuente para gratinar *f* 69
fuera 225, 228, 320
fuera de banda 226
fuera de juego *m* 223
fuera de pista 247
fuerte 321
full contact *m* 236
fumar 112
funcionario de prisiones *m* 181
funda *f* 51
funda de la almohada *f* 71
funda de la cámara *f* 271
funeral *m* 26
fuselaje *m* 210
fusible *m* 60
fusta *f* 242
fútbol *m* 222
fútbol americano *m* 220
futbolista *m* 222

G

gabardina *f* 32
Gabón 317
gachas de avena *f* 157
gafas *f* 51, 239, 247
gafas de natación *f* 238
gafas de seguridad *f* 81
gafas de sol *f* 51, 265
gafas protectoras *f* 167
gajo *m* 126
galápago *m* 293
galaxia *f* 280
galería *f* 254
galleta *f* 113
galleta de centeno *f* 156
galletas *f* 141
gallina *f* 185
gallinero *m* 185
gallo *m* 185
galón *m* 311
galope *m* 243
galvanizado 79
gambas peladas *f* 120
Gambia 317
ganado *m* 183, 185
ganador *m* 273
ganar 273
ganchillo *m* 277
gancho *m* 118, 187
garaje *m* 58
garbanzos *m* 131
garganta *f* 19
garra *f* 293
gasa *f* 47
gasolina *f* 199
gasolinera *f* 199
gatito *m* 290
gato *m* 290
gaviota *f* 292
géiser *m* 285
gel *m* 38, 109
gel de baño *m* 73
gel de ducha *m* 73
gemas *f* 288
gemelo *m* 36
gemelos *m* 23
generación *f* 23
generador *m* 60
genitales *m* 12
gente *f* 12, 16
geografía *f* 162
geometría *f* 165
Georgia 318
gerbera *f* 110
Ghana 317
giba *f* 291
gimnasia *f* 235
gimnasia prepugilística *f* 251
gimnasia rítmica *f* 235
gimnasio *m* 101, 250
gimnasta *f* 235
gin tonic *m* 151
ginebra *f* 145
ginecología *f* 49
ginecólogo *m* 52
girasol *m* 184, 297
giro *m* 238
giro postal *m* 98
glaciar *m* 284
gladiolo *m* 110
glándula *f* 19
glándula del tiroides *f* 18
glasear 139
globo *m* 230
globo aerostático *m* 211
glorieta *f* 195
gneis *m* 288
gofres *m* 157
golf *m* 232
golfista *f* 232
golondrina *f* 292
golosinas *f* 113
golosinas a granel *f* 113
golpe *m* 233, 237
golpear 224
golpes *m* 231
goma *f* 163
goma del pelo *f* 39
goma elástica *f* 173
gominola *f* 113
gong *m* 257
gordo 321
gorila *m* 291
gorra *f* 36
gorra de montar *f* 242
gorrión *m* 292
gorro de baño *m* 238
gorro de cocinero *m* 190
gorro para el sol *m* 30
gotas *f* 109
gotero *m* 53
gótico 301
grabado *m* 275
grabado con antelación 178
gracias 322
gráfica del paciente *f* 48
grafito *m* 289
gramo *m* 310
Granada 314
granada *f* 128
granate *m* 288
grande 321
grandes almacenes *m* 105
granero *m* 182
granito *m* 288
granizo *m* 286
granja *f* 182, 184
granja de ganado porcino *f* 183
granja avícola *f* 183
granja de frutales *f* 183
granja de ganado ovino *f* 183
granja de tierras cultivables *f* 183
granjero *m* 182
grano *m* 130
granos *m* 130, 144
granos procesados *m* 130
grapadora *f* 173
grapas *f* 173
grasa *f* 119
graso 39, 41
grava *f* 88
gravedad *f* 280
Grecia 316
green *m* 232
grifo *m* 61, 66
grifo de agua caliente *m* 72
grifo de agua fría *m* 72
grifo de la cerveza *m* 150
grillo *m* 295
gripe *f* 44
gris 39, 274
gritar 25
Groenlandia 314
grosella blanca *f* 127
grosella espinosa *f* 127
grosella negra *f* 127
grúa *f* 187, 203, 216
grúa de la cámara *f* 178
grueso 321
grulla *f* 292
guante *m* 224, 228, 233, 236, 246
guantes *m* 36
guantes de boxeo *m* 237
guantes de jardín *m* 89
guardabarros *m* 205
guardacostas *m* 217
guardar 177
guardia de seguridad *m* 189
guardián del rastrillo *m* 225
guarnecedor *m* 88
Guatemala 314
guayaba *f* 128
Guayana Francesa 315
guía del hilo *f* 276
guía del viajero *f* 260
guía turístico *m* 260
guiar 91
guimbarda *f* 78
guindilla *f* 124, 132, 143
Guinea 317
Guinea Ecuatorial 317
Guinea-Bissau 317
guión *m* 254
guirnalda *f* 111
guisante *m* 122
guisantes *m* 131
guisantes secos *m* 131
guisantes tiernos *m* 131
guiso *m* 158
guitarra eléctrica *f* 258
guitarrista *m* 258
gusano *m* 295
Guyana 315
gypsofila 110

H

haba *f* 122
habas *f* 131
habitación *f* 58
habitación con desayuno incluido *f* 101
habitación con dos camas individuales *f* 100
habitación de los niños *f* 74
habitación doble *f* 100
habitación individual *f* 100
habitación privada *f* 48
habitaciones *f* 100
hacer agua 239
hacer agujeros con la horquilla 90
hacer amigos 26
hacer ejercicios de calentamiento 251
hacer la cama 71
hacer testamento 26
hacer un chip 233
hacer un drive 233
hacer un pase 223
hacer un swing 232
hacer una entrada 223
hacer una parada 223
hacha *f* 95
hacha de cocina *f* 68
hacia 320
hacia arriba 98
haciendo pan 138
Haití 314
halcón *m* 292
hamaca *f* 265, 266
hambriento 64
hamburguesa *f* 154
hamburguesa con patatas fritas *f* 154
hamburguesa de pollo *f* 155
hamburguesa vegetariana *f* 155
hamburguesería *f* 154
hámster *m* 290
handicap *m* 233
hardware *m* 176
harina blanca *f* 138, 139
harina con levadura *f* 139
harina de huesos *f* 88
harina integral *f* 138
harina morena *f* 138
harina para pan *f* 139
harinas *f* 138
harpa *f* 256

hasta 320
hasta la rodilla 34
Hawaii 314
haya *f* 296
heavy metal *m* 259
hebilla *f* 36
hecho puré 159
helada *f* 287
helado *m* 137, 149
helecho *m* 86
hélice *f* 211, 214
helicóptero *m* 211
hematites *m* 289
hematoma *m* 46
hemisferio norte *m* 283
hemisferio sur *m* 283
hemorragia *f* 46
hemorragia nasal *f* 44
heno *m* 184
heno griego *m* 132
herbicida *m* 91, 183
herbolario *m* 55
herboristería *f* 115
herida *f* 46
hermana *f* 22
hermano *m* 22
herradura *f* 242
herramienta para modelar *f* 275
herramientas *f* 187
herramientas de jardinería *f* 88
hervidor *m* 66
hervir a fuego lento 67
hexágono *m* 164
hidroavión *m* 211
hidrodeslizador *m* 215
hidroterapia *f* 55
hielo *m* 120, 287
hierba *f* 55, 86, 262
hierbas *f* 133, 134
hierbas y las especias *f* 132
hierro *m* 109, 289
hígado *m* 18, 118
higiene dental *f* 72
higiene femenina *f* 108
higo *m* 129
higo chumbo *m* 128
hija *f* 22
hijastra *f* 23
hijastro *m* 23
hijo *m* 22
hilo *m* 276
hilo de bramante *m* 89
hilo de estaño *m* 79, 80
hilo dental *m* 50, 72
hilvanar 277
Himalaya *m* 313
hinojo *m* 122, 133
hipermetropía *f* 51
hipnoterapia *f* 55
hipoalergénico 41
hipódromo *m* 243
hipopótamo *m* 291
hipoteca *f* 96
hipotenusa *f* 164
historia *f* 162
historia del arte *f* 169
hocico *m* 293
hockey *m* 224
hockey sobre hielo *m* 224
hockey sobre hierba *m* 224
hogaza *f* 139
hoguera *f* 266
hoja *f* 60, 89, 122, 296
hoja de afeitar *f* 73
hoja de ingreso *f* 96
hoja de reintegro *f* 96
hojaldre *m* 140
hola 322
hombre *m* 12, 23
hombre de negocios *m* 175
hombrera *f* 35, 225
hombro *m* 13
homeopatía *f* 55
homogeneizado 137
Honduras 314
hora *f* 304
hora de dormir *f* 74
hora punta *f* 209
horario *m* 197, 209, 261
horas *f* 261
horas de visita *f* 48
horca *f* 88
hormiga *f* 295
hormigonera *f* 186
hormona *f* 20
hornear 138
hornillo *m* 267
horno *m* 66
horno microondas *m* 66
horquilla *f* 38, 89, 207
horrorizado 25
hospital *m* 48
hotel *m* 100, 264
hoy 306
hoyo *m* 232
hoyo en uno *m* 233
hoyuelo *m* 15
huella dactilar *f* 94
huerto *m* 85, 182
hueso *m* 17, 119
huésped *m* 100
huevera *f* 65, 137
huevo de codorniz *m* 137
huevo de gallina *m* 137
huevo de oca *m* 137
huevo de pato *m* 137
huevo frito *m* 157
huevo pasado por agua *m* 137, 157
huevos *m* 137
huevos revueltos *m* 157
húmedo 286, 321
húmero *m* 17
humo *m* 95
Hungría 316
huracán *m* 287

I

icono *m* 177
idiomas *m* 162
iglesia *f* 298, 300
ígneo 288
igual a 165
iguana *f* 293
iluminación *f* 105
imán *m* 167
imperdible *m* 47
impermeable *m* 31
impotente 20
impresión *f* 275
impresora *f* 172, 176
imprimación *f* 83
imprimir 172
impuestos *m* 96
incendio *m* 95
incisivo *m* 50
inconsciente 47
incubadora *f* 53
India 318
indicaciones *f* 260
indicador de fotos *m* 270
indicador de la gasolina *m* 201
indicador de temperatura *m* 201
indicador de velocidad *m* 201
índice *m* 15
Indonesia 319
infarto de miocardio *m* 44
infección *f* 44
información *f* 168, 261
informe *m* 174
infusión *f* 149
ingeniería *f* 169
ingle *f* 12
ingredientes *m* 155
ingresado 48
ingresar 96
inhalador *m* 44, 109
injertar 91
inmigración 212
inmovilización *f* 237
inocente 181
inoculación *f* 45
inquilino *m* 58
insomnio *m* 71
instalaciones internas *f* 60
instalar 177
instrumentos *m* 256, 258
insulina *f* 109
integral 131
interceptar y devolver 225
intercostal *m* 16
interfono *m* 59
interior *m* 200, 228
intermitente *m* 198, 204
internet *m* 177
interruptor *m* 60
intestino delgado *m* 18
intestino grueso *m* 18
inundación *f* 287
invernadero *m* 85
inversión *f* 97
invertebrados *m* 295
investigación *f* 94, 169
invierno *m* 31, 307
invitado *m* 64
inyección *f* 48
iPad *m* 176
iPod *m* 268
ionosfera *f* 286
ir en bicicleta 207
Irán 318
Iraq 318
iris *m* 51, 110
Irlanda 316
isla *f* 282
Islandia 316
Islas Baleares 316
Islas Galápagos 315
Islas Salomón 319
Israel 318
Italia 316
itinerario *m* 260
izquierda 260

J

jabón *m* 73
jaboncillo *m* 276
jabonera *f* 73
jade *m* 288
Jamaica 314
jamón *m* 119, 143, 156
jamón serrano *m* 143
Japón 318
jaqueca *f* 44
jarabe *m* 109
jarabe de arce *m* 134
jarabe para la tos *m* 108
jarcias *f* 240
jarcias *f* 215
jardín *m* 84
jardín acuático *m* 84
jardín campestre *m* 84
jardín clásico *m* 84
jardín de plantas herbáceas *m* 84
jardín en la azotea *m* 84
jardinería *f* 90
jardinero *m* 188
jardines *m* 261
jardines clásicos *m* 262
jarra *f* 65, 151
jarra graduada *f* 69, 311
jarrón *m* 63, 111
jazz *m* 259
jefe *m* 24
jengibre *m* 125, 133
jeringuilla *f* 109, 167
jersey *m* 33
jet privado *m* 211
jinete *m* 242
jirafa *f* 179, 291
Jordania 318
jota *f* 273
joyas *f* 36
joyería *f* 114
joyero *m* 36, 188
jubilarse 26
judía verde *f* 122
judo *m* 236
juego *m* 230
juego de dobles *m* 230
juego individual *m* 230
juegos *m* 75, 272
juegos de mesa *m* 272
juegos de raqueta *m* 231
jueves 306
juez *m* 180
juez de línea *m* 220, 223, 230
juez de silla *m* 230
jugador *m* 220, 221, 231, 273
jugador de baloncesto *m* 226
jugador de críquet *m* 225
jugador de hockey sobre hielo *m* 224
jugar 229, 273
jugoso 127
juguete *m* 75
juguetería *f* 105
juicio *m* 180
julio 306
junco *m* 86
junio 306
junta *f* 61
Júpiter *m* 280
jurado *m* 180

K

K. O. *m* 237
Kaliningrado 316
karate *m* 236
kayak *m* 241
Kazajstán 318
kendo *m* 236
Kenya 317
ketchup *m* 135, 154
kilogramo *m* 310
kilómetro *m* 310
Kirguistán 318
kit de reparaciones *m* 207
kiwi *m* 128
koala *m* 291
Kosovo 316
kumquat *m* 126
kung fu *m* 236
Kuwait 318

L

labio *m* 14
labios *m* 20
labor de encaje *f* 277
labor de punto *f* 277
labor de retales *f* 277
laboratorio *m* 166
laca *f* 38
lacio 39
lacrosse *f* 249
lactancia *m* 53
lácteos *m* 107
lactosa *f* 137
ladera *f* 284
lado *m* 164
ladrillo *m* 187
lagarto *m* 293
lago *m* 285
lágrima *f* 51
laminado 132
lámpara *f* 62, 217
lámpara de la mesilla *f* 70
lana *f* 277
lana de acero *f* 81
lancha motora *f* 214
langosta *f* 121, 295
langostino *m* 121
lanzacohetes *m* 281
lanzador *m* 225
lanzamiento *m* 281
lanzamiento de disco *m* 234
lanzamiento de jabalina *m* 234
lanzamiento de peso *m* 234
lanzar 221, 225, 227, 229, 245
Laos 318
lápiz *m* 163, 275
lápiz corrector *m* 40
lápiz de cejas *m* 40
lápiz de colores *m* 163
lápiz de labios *m* 40
lápiz de ojos *m* 40
largo 32, 34, 130, 151
largometraje *m* 269
larguero *m* 222
laringe *f* 19
lata *f* 145, 311
lata de bebida *f* 154
lata de pintura *f* 83
latitud *f* 283
laurel *m* 133
lava *f* 283
lavabo *m* 38, 50, 72
lavadero *m* 76
lavadero de coches *m* 198
lavadora *f* 76
lavadora secadora *f* 76
lavandería *f* 115
lavar 38
laxante *m* 109
lección *f* 163

español

leche *f* 136, 156
leche condensada *f* 136
leche de cabra *f* 136
leche de oveja *f* 137
leche de vaca *f* 136
leche del cuerpo *f* 73
leche desnatada *f* 136
leche en polvo *f* 137
leche entera *f* 136
leche limpiadora *f* 41
leche semidesnatada *f* 136
lechuga *f* 123
lector de compact discs *m* 268
lector de rayos x *m* 45
leer 162
legumbres *f* 130
lejía *f* 77
lejos 320
lencería *f* 35, 105
lengua *f* 19
lengua *f* 118
lenguado *m* 120
lengüeta *f* 37, 244
lente del objetivo *f* 167
lenteja castellana *f* 131
lenteja roja *f* 131
lentes de contacto *f* 51
lentilla *f* 51
lento 321
león *m* 291
león marino *m* 290
leotardos *m* 251
lesión *f* 46
lesión en la cabeza *f* 46
Lesotho 317
Letonia 316
letra *f* 259
letrero *m* 104
levadura *f* 138
levantamiento de pesas *m* 251
levantar 251
levantarse 71
levar 139
Líbano 318
libélula *f* 295
Liberia 317
libertad condicional *f* 181
Libia 317
libra *f* 310
libre 321
librería *f* 115
libro *m* 168
libro de texto *m* 163
licencia de pesca *f* 245
licenciada *f* 169
licenciarse 26
lichi *m* 128
licor *m* 145
licuadora *f* 66
Liechtenstein 316
lienzo *m* 274
liga *f* 35, 223
ligamento *m* 17
ligas *f* 35
ligero 321
lijadora *f* 78
lijar 82
lima *f* 81, 126
lima de uñas *f* 41
límite de velocidad *m* 195
limón *m* 126
limonada *f* 144
limousine *f* 199
limpiaparabrisas *m* 198
limpiar 77
limpiar el polvo 77
limpieza de cutis *f* 41
limpio 121
línea central *f* 226
línea de banda *f* 220, 221, 226, 230
línea de falta *f* 229
línea de flotación *f* 214
línea de fondo *f* 221, 225, 226, 230
línea de gol *f* 220
línea de juego *f* 233
línea de meta *f* 223, 224, 234
línea de salida *f* 234
línea de servicio *f* 230
línea de tiro libre *f* 226
línea de tres *f* 226
línea del bateador *f* 225
línea divisoria *f* 194
líneas *f* 165
linfático 19
lino *m* 184, 277
linterna *f* 267
líquido 77
líquido amniótico *m* 52
líquido limpiador *m* 51
líquido limpiaparabrisas *m* 199
lista de lecturas *f* 168
lista de precios *f* 154
lista de vinos *f* 152
listón *m* 235
literatura *f* 162, 169
litro *m* 311
Lituania 316
llanta *f* 206
llanura *f* 285
llave *f* 59, 80, 203, 207
llave de boca *f* 80
llave de la habitación *f* 100
llave de memoria *f* 176
llave de paso *f* 61
llave de tubo *f* 80
llave del desagüe *f* 61
llave inglesa *f* 80
llegadas *f* 213
lleno 64, 321
llorar 25
lluvia *f* 287
lo siento 322
lobo *m* 290
loción *f* 109
loción contra los insectos *f* 267
loción para después del sol *f* 108
locomotora *f* 208
logotipo *m* 31
lomo *m* 121
loncha *f* 119
longitud *f* 165, 283, 310
longitud de onda *f* 179
loro *m* 293
lubina *f* 120
luces *f* 94
luces de emergencia *f* 201
lucha libre *f* 236
lugares de interés *m* 261
luge *m* 247
luna *f* 280
luna de miel *f* 26
luna llena *f* 280
luna nueva *f* 280
lunar *m* 14
lunes 306
lupino *m* 297
Luxemburgo 316
luz de lectura *f* 210
luz del porche *f* 58
luz trasera *f* 204

M

macadamia *f* 129
Macedonia 316
maceta *f* 89, 110
machacado 132
macis *f* 132
macramé *m* 277
Madagascar 317
madeja *f* 277
madera *f* 79, 187, 275
madera de pino *f* 79
madera noble *f* 79
madrastra *f* 23
madre *f* 22
madreselva *f* 297
maduro 129
maestro *f* 190
magdalena *f* 140
magma *m* 283
magnesio *m* 109
maíz *m* 124, 130, 184
maíz dulce *m* 122
mal pase de balón *m* 220
malaquita *f* 288
malas hierbas *f* 86
Malasia 318
Malawi 317
Maldivas 318
maletero *m* 198
maletín *m* 37
Malí 317
mallas *f* 31
malo 321
Malta 316
Malvinas 315
mamíferos *m* 290
manada *f* 183
manchego *m* 142
mandarina *f* 126
mandarina clementina *f* 126
mandarina satsuma *f* 126
mandíbula *f* 14, 17
mandioca *f* 124
mando a distancia *m* 269
mandos de la calefacción *m* 201
manga *f* 34
manga pastelera *f* 69
mango *m* 128, 187, 230
mangostán *m* 128
manguera *f* 89, 95
manicura *f* 41
manillar *m* 207
maniquí *m* 276
mano *f* 13, 15
mano de mortero *f* 68, 167
manopla de cocina *f* 69
manoplas *f* 30
manta *f* 71, 74
manta eléctrica *f* 71
mantel *m* 64
mantel individual *m* 64
mantequilla *f* 137, 156
mantequilla de cacahuetes *f* 135
mantis religiosa *f* 295
manto *m* 282
manual 200
manualidades *f* 274, 275, 276
manzana *f* 126
manzanilla *f* 149
mañana *f* 305
mañana 306
mapache *m* 290
mapamundi *m* 312
maqueta *f* 190
maquillaje *m* 40
maquillaje de fondo *m* 40
máquina de coser *f* 276
máquina de cross *f* 250
máquina de ejercicios *f* 250
máquina de los cubitos *f* 67
máquina de rayos x *f* 212
máquina de remos *f* 250
máquina de step *f* 250
máquina del café *f* 148, 150
máquina del fax *f* 172
máquina fotográfica *f* 260
maquinaria *f* 187
maquinilla de afeitar eléctrica *f* 73
mar *m* 264, 282
Mar Báltico *m* 313
Mar Caribe *m* 312
Mar Caspio *m* 313
Mar de Omán *m* 313
Mar del Norte *m* 312
Mar Mediterráneo *m* 313
Mar Negro *m* 313
Mar Rojo *m* 313
maracas *f* 257
maracuyá *m* 128
maratón *f* 234
marca personal *f* 234
marcador *m* 225
marcar 38, 99, 227
marcar un gol 223
marchas *f* 206
marco *m* 62
margarina *f* 137
margarita *f* 110, 297
marido *m* 22
marino *m* 189
mariposa *f* 239, 295
mariquita *f* 295
marisco *m* 121
mármol *m* 288
marquesina *f* 197
marrón 274
Marruecos 317
Marte 280
martes 306
martillo *m* 80
martillo neumático *m* 187
martini *m* 151
marzo 306
más 165
más allá de 320
más tarde
masa *f* 138, 140
masa brisa *f* 140
masa de profiteroles *f* 140
masaje *m* 54
máscara *f* 228, 249
mascarilla *f* 41, 189
masculino 21
masilla *f* 83
máster *m* 169
mástil *m* 240, 258
matasellos *m* 98
mate 83, 271
mate *m* 231
matemáticas *f* 162, 164
materiales *m* 79, 165, 187
materiales de oficina *m* 173
maternidad *f* 49
matraz *m* 166
matrícula *f* 198
matriz *f* 52, 96
Mauricio 317
Mauritania 317
mayo 306
mayonesa *f* 135
mazapán *m* 141
mazo *m* 187, 275
mazo de cocina *m* 68
mazo para puré de patatas *m* 68
mecánica *f* 202
mecánico *m* 188, 203
mechero *m* 112
mechero Bunsen *m* 166
medallas *f* 235
media luna *f* 280
media pensión *f* 101
mediana *f* 194
medianoche *f*
media *f* 35
medias *f* 35
medias de liguero *f* 35
medicación *f* 109
medicamento *m* 109
medicina *f* 169
médico *m* 45, 189
medida *f* 151
medida de capacidad *f* 311
medidas *f* 165
medidor *m* 150
medidor óptico *m* 150
medio ambiente *m* 280
medio galope *m* 243
medio litro *m* 311
mediodía *m* 305
medios de comunicación *m* 178
medir 310
meditación *f* 54
médula *f* 126
medusa *f* 295
mejilla *f* 14
mejillón *m* 121, 295
mejorana *f* 133
melée *f* 221
melena *f* 39, 291
melocotón *m* 126, 128
melodía *f* 259
melón *m* 127
membrete *m* 173
membrillo *m* 128
memoria *f* 176
menaje de hogar *m* 105
menos 165
mensaje de texto (SMS) *m* 99
mensaje de voz *m* 99
mensajero *m* 99
mensajes *m* 100
menstruación *f* 20
mensualmente 307
menta *f* 133
menta poleo *f* 149
menú *m* 154
menú de la cena *m* 152
menú de la comida *m* 152
menú para niños *m* 153
menudillos *m* 118
meñique *m* 15
mercado *m* 115
mercería *f* 105

español

mercurio *m* 289
Mercurio *m* 280
merengue *m* 140
mermelada *f* 134, 156
mermelada de frambuesa *f* 134
mermelada de naranja *f* 134, 156
mes *m* 306
mesa *f* 64, 148
mesa de café *f* 62
mesa de encolar *f* 82
mesa de mezclas *f* 179
mesa de picnic *f* 266
mesa del desayuno *f* 156
meseta *f* 284
mesilla de noche *m* 70
mesoesfera *f* 286
metacarpo *m* 17
metal *m* 79
metales *m* 289
metamórfico 288
metatarso *m* 17
meteorito *m* 280
metralleta *f* 189
metro *m* 209, 310
metro cuadrado *m* 310
México 314
mezclar 67, 138
mezquita *f* 300
mica *f* 289
microbús *m* 197
micrófono *m* 179, 258
microscopio *m* 167
miel compacta *f* 134
miel líquida *f* 134
miércoles 306
mijo *m* 130
mil 309
mil millones 309
mil novecientos 307
mil novecientos diez 307
mil novecientos uno 307
milenio *m* 307
miligramo *m* 310
mililitro *m* 311
milímetro *m* 310
milla *f* 310
millón *m* 309
minerales *m* 289
mini bar *m* 101
minutero *m* 304
minuto *m* 304
miopía *f* 51
mirilla *f* 59
misil *m* 211
mobiliario para el hogar *m* 105
mocasín *m* 37
mochila *f* 31, 37, 267
mochila del bebé *f* 75
moda *f* 277
modalidades *f* 243
modelismo *m* 275
modelo *f* 169
modelos *m* 199
modista *f* 191
modo de empleo *m* 109
módulo lunar *m* 281
moisés *m* 74
Moldavia 316
molde individual *m* 69
molde para bizcocho *m* 69
molde para magdalenas *m* 69
molde para suflé *m* 69
molde redondo *m* 69
moldura *f* 63
molido 132
Mónaco 316
mondador *m* 68
moneda *f* 97
monedas devueltas *f* 99
monedero *m* 37
Mongolia 318
monitor *m* 53
monitor eléctrico de la presión sanguínea *m* 45
mono *m* 82, 291
monopatín *m* 249
monopoly *m* 272
monorraíl *m* 208
monovolumen *m* 199
montaña *f* 284
montaña rusa *f* 262
Montañas Rocosas *f* 312
montar en monopatín 249
montar en patinete 263
montar una tienda 266
montón de abono compuesto *m* 85
montura *f* 51
monumento *m* 261
monzón *m* 287
moño *m* 39
moño francés *m* 39
moqueta *f* 71
mora *f* 127
morado 274
morcilla *f* 157
mordisco *m* 46
moreno 41
morir 26
morro *m* 210
morsa *f* 290
mortero *m* 68, 167
mosca *f* 244, 295
mosquitera *f* 267
mosquito *m* 295
mostaza *f* 155
mostaza en grano *f* 131, 135
mostaza francesa *f* 135
mostaza inglesa *f* 135
mostrador *m* 96, 98, 100, 142
mostrador de bocadillos *m* 143
mostrador de facturación *m* 213
mostrador de préstamos *m* 168
moto acuática *f* 241
moto de carreras *f* 205
moto de carretera *f* 205
moto de cross *f* 205
moto de nieve *f* 247
motocicleta *f* 204
motociclismo *m* 249
motocross *m* 249
motor *m* 88, 202, 204, 210
motor fueraborda *m* 215
mousse *f* 141
móvil *m* 74
movimientos *m* 237
Mozambique 317
mozo de cuadra *m* 243
mozzarella *f* 142
mueble *m* 268
muela *f* 50
muelle *m* 71, 214, 216
muelle comercial *m* 216
muelle de pasajeros 216
muerte súbita *f* 230
muestra *f* 261
muffin *m* 140
mujer *f* 12, 22, 23
mujer de negocios *f* 175
muletilla *f* 31
multiplicado por 165
multiplicar 165
muñeca *f* 13, 15, 75
muñeco de peluche *m* 75
muñequera *f* 230
murciélago *m* 290
músculos *m* 16
museo *m* 261
muserola *f* 242
música *f* 162
música clásica *f* 255, 259
música country *f* 259
música de baile *f* 259
música folk *f* 259
musical *m* 255
músico *m* 191
muslo *m* 12, 119
Myanmar 318

N, Ñ

naan *m* 139
nabo *m* 124
nabo sueco *m* 125
nacer 26
nacimiento *m* 52
nación *f* 315
nada *f* 230
nadador *m* 238
nadar 238
nailon *m* 277
nalga *f* 13, 16
Namibia 317
naranja 274
naranja *f* 126
naranjada *f* 144
narciso *m* 111
narcisos silvestres *m* 297
nariz *f* 14
nasa *f* 245
nata *f* 137, 140, 157
nata agria *f* 137
nata líquida *f* 137
nata montada *f* 137
nata para montar *f* 137
natación *f* 238
natación sincronizada *f* 239
natillas *f* 140
natural 256
naturopatía *f* 55
náusea *f* 44
navaja *f* 121
navegación por satélite *f* 201
navegador *m* 177
navegador por satélite *m* 195
navegar 177, 240
Navidad *f* 27
neblina *f* 287
nebulosa *f* 280
nectarina *f* 126
negativo *m* 271
negocio *m* 175
negocios *m* 175
negro 39, 272, 274
neoclásico 301
Nepal 318
Neptuno *m* 280
nervio *m* 19, 50
nervio óptico *m* 51
nervioso 19, 25
neumático *m* 198, 205
neurología *f* 49
neutro 60
Nicaragua 314
niebla *f* 287
nieta *f* 22
nieto *m* 22
nietos *m* 23
nieve *f* 287
Níger 317
Nigeria 317
niño *m* 23, 31
niño pequeño *m* 30
niños *m* 23
níquel *m* 289
nivel *m* 80, 187
no 322
no adosado 58
no doblar 98
no torcer a la derecha 195
noche *f* 305
nómina *f* 175
nonagésimo 309
noray *m* 214
normal 39
norte *m* 312
Noruega 316
nota *f* 163, 256
nota con saludos *f* 173
notación *f* 256
notas *f* 191
noticias *f* 178
novecientos 308
noveno 309
noventa 308
novia *f* 24
noviembre 306
novio *m* 24
nube *f* 113, 287
nublado 286
nuca *f* 13
núcleo externo *m* 282
núcleo interno *m* 282
nudillo *m* 15
nuera *f* 22
Nueva Zelandia 319
nueve 308
nuevo 321
nuez *f* 19, 129
nuez del Brasil *f* 129
nuez moscada *f* 132
numerador *m* 165
número *m* 226
número de andén *m* 208
número de cuenta *m* 96
número de la habitación *m* 100
número de puerta de embarque *m* 213
número de ruta *m* 196
número de vuelo *m* 213
números *m* 308
nutria *f* 290
ñame *m* 125

O

obertura *f* 256
objetivo *m* 270
oboe *m* 257
obra *f* 186, 254
obras *f* 187, 195
obsidiana *f* 288
oca *f* 119, 293
océano *m* 282
Océano Antártico *m* 313
Océano Ártico *m* 312
Océano Atlántico *m* 312
Océano Índico *m* 312
Océano Pacífico *m* 312
ochenta 308
ocho 308
ochocientos 308
ocio *m* 254, 258, 264
ocio en el hogar *m* 268
octágono *m* 164
octavo 309
octogésimo 309
octubre 306
ocular *m* 167
ocupado 321
oeste *m* 312
ofertas *f* 106
oficina *f* 24, 172, 174
oficina central *f* 175
oficina de cambio *f* 97
oficina de correos *f* 98
oficina de información *f* 261
oficina del director del camping *f* 266
oftalmología *f* 49
ojal *m* 32, 37
ojo *m* 14, 51, 244, 276
ojo de buey *m* 214
ojos rojos *m* 271
ola *f* 241, 264
olmo *m* 296
Omán 318
ombligo *m* 12
omoplato *m* 17
once 308
oncología *f* 49
onda larga *f* 179
ónice *m* 289
onza *f* 310
ópera *m* 255
operación *f* 48
operador *m* 99
óptico *m* 51, 189
orador *m* 174
órbita *f* 280
orden del día *m* 174
orden judicial *f* 180, 180
ordenador *m* 176
ordenador portátil *m* 176
ordeñar 183
orégano *m* 133
oreja *f* 14
orfebrería *f* 275
organizador de las herramientas *m* 78
órganos reproductores *m* 20
orgulloso 25
orificio nasal *m* 290
orilla *f* 284
orinal *m* 74
ornamental 87
ornitología *f* 263
oro *m* 235, 289
orquesta *f* 254, 256
orquídea *f* 111
ortiga *f* 297
ortopedia *f* 49
oruga *f* 295
orza v 241
oscuro 321
oso *m* 291
oso de peluche *m* 75
oso panda *m* 291

oso polar *m* 291
osteopatía *f* 54
ostra *f* 121
otoño *m* 31, 307
otorrinolaringología *f* 49
otras embarcaciones *f* 215
otras manualidades 275
otras tiendas *f* 114
otros deportes *m* 248
óvalo *m* 164
ovario *m* 20
oveja *f* 185
ovulación *f* 20, 52
óvulo *m* 20

P

pacana *f* 129
paciente *f* 45
paciente externo *m* 48
paddle *m* 231
padrastro *m* 23
padre *m* 22
padres *m* 23
pagar 153
pago *m* 96
país *m* 315
paisaje *m* 284
Países Bajos 316
pajarería *f* 115
pajarita *f* 36
pájaro carpintero *m* 292
pajita *f* 144, 154
Pakistán 318
pala *f* 88, 187, 231, 265
pala para pescado *f* 68
paladar *m* 19
palanca *f* 61, 150
palanca de cambio *f* 201, 207
palanca de emergencia *f* 209
palanca de frenos *f* 207
palanca de la llanta *f* 207
palco *m* 254
paleta *f* 186, 187, 274
palma de la mano *f* 15
palmera *f* 86, 296
palmitos *m* 122
palo *m* 224, 225, 249, 273
palo de hierro *m* 233
palo de hockey *m* 224
palo de la tienda *m* 266
palo de madera *m* 233
paloma *f* 292
palomitas *f* 255
palos de golf *m* 233
pan *m* 138, 157
pan al bicarbonato sódico *m* 139
pan blanco *m* 139
pan con grano *m* 139
pan con semillas *m* 139
pan de centeno *m* 138
pan de maíz *m* 139
pan de molde *m* 138
pan de pita *m* 139
pan dulce francés *m* 157
pan fermentado *m* 139
pan integral *m* 139, 149
pan moreno *m* 139
pan rallado *m* 139
pan sin levadura *m* 139
panadería *f* 107, 114, 138
panadero *m* 139
panal *m* 135
Panamá 314
páncreas *m* 18
pandereta *f* 257
panecillo *m* 139, 143
pantalla *f* 97, 172, 176, 255, 269
pantalla informativa *f* 213
pantalón de montar *m* 242
pantalones *m* 32, 34
pantalones con peto *m* 30
pantalones cortos *m* 30, 33
pantalones vaqueros *m* 31
pantano *m* 285
pantorrilla *f* 13, 16
pañal *m* 75
pañal de felpa *m* 30
pañal desechable *m* 30
pañuelo *m* 36
pañuelo de papel *m* 108
papaya *f* 128
papel celo *m* 173
papel de apresto *m* 83
papel de lija *m* 81, 83
papel estampado en relieve *m* 83
papel maché *m* 275
papel pintado *m* 82
papelera *f* 172, 177
papelería *f* 105
paperas *f* 44
papiroflexia *f* 275
Papua Nueva Guinea 319
paquete *m* 99, 311, 311
paquete de tabaco *m* 112
par *m* 233
para 320
para comer en el local 154
para llevar 154
parabrisas *m* 198, 205
paracaídas *m* 248
paracaidismo 248
paracaidismo en caída libre *m* 248
parachoques *m* 198
parada *f* 237
parada de autobús *f* 197, 299
parada de taxis *f* 213
paraguas *m* 36
Paraguay 315
paragüero *m* 59
paralelas *f* 235
paralelas asimétricas *f* 235
paralelo 165
paralelogramo *m* 164
parapente *m* 248
parche *m* 207
pared *f* 58, 186
pareja *f* 24
pareja prometida *f* 24
parientes *m* 23
parmesano *m* 142
párpado *m* 51
parque *m* 75, 262
parque de atracciones *m* 262
parque de bomberos *m* 95
parque nacional *m* 261
parquímetro *m* 195
parrilla *f* 69, 69
parterre *m* 85, 90
partida *f* 273
partida de nacimiento *f* 26
partido *m* 230
partitura *f* 255, 256
parto *m* 52, 53
parto asistido *m* 53
parto de nalgas *m* 52
pasa *f* 129
pasa de Corinto *f* 129
pasa sultana *f* 129
pasado mañana 307
pasajero *m* 216
pasamanos *m* 59
pasaporte *m* 213
pasar 220
pasar la bayeta 77
pasarela *f* 212, 214
Pascua judía *f* 27
pase *m* 226
paseo *m* 75, 243
paseo marítimo *m* 265
pasillo *m* 106, 168, 210, 254
paso *m* 243
paso de peatones *m* 195
paso elevado *m* 194
paso subterráneo *m* 194
pasta *f* 158
pasta de dientes *f* 72
pastel *m* 149, 158
pastel de nata *m* 141
pasteles *m* 140, 274
pasteles de carne *m* 143
pasteurizado 137
pastilla *f* 258, 311
pastilla de menta *f* 113
pastilla para hogueras *f* 266
pastilla para la garganta *f* 109
pasto *m* 182
pata *f* 64
patada *f* 124, 237, 239
patata nueva *f* 124
patatas fritas *f* 113, 151, 154
paté *m* 142, 156
patilla de apoyo *f* 207
patín *m* 247
patín de cuchilla *m* 224
patinaje *m* 263
patinaje artístico *m* 247
patinaje de velocidad *m* 247
patinaje en línea *m* 249
patinaje sobre hielo *m* 247
patinar 224
patio *m* 58, 84
patio de butacas *m* 254
patito *m* 185
pato *m* 119, 185
patología *f* 49
patrimonio neto *m* 97
patrón *m* 276
patucos *m* 30
pausa *f* 256, 269
pavo *m* 119, 185, 293
pavo real *m* 293
peca *f* 15
peces *m* 294
pecho *m* 12
pechuga *f* 119
pectoral *m* 16
pedal *m* 61, 206, 257
pedal de los frenos *m* 205
pedalear 207
pedernal *m* 288
pediatría *f* 49
pedicura *f* 41
pedir 153
peinar 38
peine *m* 38
pelacables *m* 81
pelado 129
pelar 67
pelele *m* 30
pelele sin pies *m* 30
pelícano *m* 292
película *f* 260, 271
película de aventuras *f* 255
película de ciencia ficción *f* 255
película de dibujos animados *f* 255
película de miedo *f* 255
película de suspense *f* 255
película del oeste *f* 255
película romántica *f* 255
peligro *m* 195
pelirrojo 39
pelo *m* 14, 38
pelo corto *m* 39
pelota *f* 75, 224, 228, 230
pelota de críquet *f* 225
pelota de golf *f* 233
pelota de playa *f* 265
peloteo *m* 230
peluca *f* 39
peluquera *f* 38
peluquería *f* 115
peluquero *m* 188
pelvis *f* 17
penalti *m* 222
pendiente *m* 36
pene *m* 21
península *f* 282
pensión completa *f* 101
pentágono *m* 164
pentagrama *f* 256
peón *m* 272
peonía *f* 111
pepino *m* 125
pepita *f* 127, 128
pequeño 321
pera *f* 127
percha *f* 70
percusión *f* 257
perdedor *m* 273
perder 273
perdone 322
perejil *m* 133
perenne 86
perforadora *f* 173
perfumado 130
perfume *m* 41
perfumería *f* 105
pérgola *f* 84
periferia *f* 299
periódico *m* 112, 168
periodista *m* 190
permanente *f* 39
peroné *m* 17
perpendicular 165
perrito caliente *m* 155
perro *m* 290
perseguir 229
personal *m* 175
pértiga *f* 245
Perú 315
pesa *f* 166, 251
pesado 321
pesar 310
pesas *f* 250
pesca *f* 244
pesca con arpón *f* 245
pesca con mosca *f* 245
pesca de altura *f* 245
pesca deportiva *f* 245
pesca en agua dulce *f* 245
pesca en alta mar *f* 245
pesca en la orilla *f* 245
pescadera *f* 188
pescadería *f* 114, 120
pescadilla *f* 120
pescado *m* 107, 120
pescado ahumado *m* 143
pescado y las patatas fritas *m* 155
pescador *m* 189
pescador de caña *m* 244
peso *m* 118
peso al nacer *m* 53
pestaña *f* 14, 51
pesticida *m* 89, 183
pestillo *m* 200
pétalo *m* 297
petrolero *m* 215
pez de colores *m* 294
pez espada *m* 120, 294
pezón *m* 12
pezuña *f* 291
phisicallis *m* 128
piano *m* 256
pica *f* 273
picadura *f* 46
picante 124
picar 245
picnic *m* 263
pico *m* 187, 293
pie *m* 12, 15, 310
pie cuadrado *m* 310
pie de la aguja *m* 276
pie del altavoz *m* 268
piedra *f* 36, 275
piedra afiladora *f* 81
piedra arenisca *f* 288
piedra caliza *f* 288
piedra lunar *f* 288
piedra pómez *f* 73, 288
piel *f* 14, 119, 128
pierna *f* 12, 119
pijama *m* 33
pijama enterizo *m* 30
pila *f* 167
pilas *f* 260
pilates *m* 251
píldora *f* 21, 109
píldoras para el mareo *f* 109
piloto *m* 190, 211
piloto de carreras *m* 249
pimentón *m* 132
pimienta *f* 64, 152
pimienta de Jamaica *f* 132
pimienta en grano *f* 132
pimiento *m* 124
pin *m* 96
pincel *m* 274
pincel de labios *m* 40
pinchadiscos *m* 179
pinchazo *m* 203, 207
pincho *m* 68, 158
pincho moruno *m* 155
ping-pong *m* 231
pingüino *m* 292
pino *m* 296
pinta *f* 311
pintar 83
pintor *m* 82
pintora *f* 191, 274
pintura *f* 83, 274
pintura acrílica *f* 274
pintura al agua *f* 83
pinturas *f* 274
pinturas al óleo *f* 274
pinza *f* 167
pinza para la nariz *f* 238
pinza para la ropa *f* 76
pinzas *f* 40, 47, 150, 167

piña *f* 128
piñón *m* 129, 207
pipa *f* 112
pipa de calabaza *f* 131
pipa de girasol *f* 131
pipeta *f* 167
piragüismo *m* 241
pirámide *f* 164
piruleta *f* 113
piscifactoría *f* 183
piscina *f* 101, 238, 250
piscina de plástico *f* 263
piso *m* 58, 59
pista *f* 212, 234, 246
pista de esquí *f* 246
pista de estacionamiento *f* 212
pista de hockey sobre hielo *f* 224
pista de tenis *f* 230
pistacho *m* 129
pistola *f* 94
pistola para encolar *f* 78
pitcher *m* 229
pizarra *f* 162, 174, 288
pizza *f* 154
placa *f* 67, 94, 283
placa bacteriana *f* 50
placa de identificación *f* 189
placa de la aguja *f* 276
placa vitrocerámica *f* 66
placar 220
placenta *f* 52
plancha *f* 76
plancha de pelo *f* 38
planchar 76
planeador *m* 211, 248
planeta *m* 280, 282
plano *m* 261
plano de la planta *m* 261
plano del metro *m* 209
planta *f* 48
planta acuática *f* 86
planta alpestre *f* 87
planta baja *f* 104
planta de flor *f* 297
planta de maceta *f* 87
planta de sombra *f* 87
planta del pie *f* 15
planta para cubrir suelo *f* 87
planta suculenta *f* 87
planta trepadora *f* 87
plantar 183
plantar en tiesto 91
plantas *f* 296
plantas de jardín *f* 86
plantas podadas con formas *f* 87
plantilla *f* 83
plantón *m* 91
plata *f* 235, 289
plataforma de lanzamiento *f* 228
plátano *m* 128
platea *f* 254
platea alta *f* 254
platija *f* 120
platillos *m* 257
platina portaobjeto *f* 167
platino *m* 289
platito *m* 65
plató *m* 178
plató de rodaje *m* 179
plato llano *m* 65
plato principal *m* 153
plato sopero *m* 65
platos *m* 153
platos del día *m* 152
platos preparados *m* 107
play *m* 269
playa *f* 264
plaza *f* 266, 299
pletina *f* 268
plomo *m* 244
pluma *f* 293
plumcake *m* 139
plum-cake *m* 140
Plutón *m* 280
pocilga *f* 185
podadera de mango largo *f* 88
podar 90, 91
podio *m* 235, 256
podrido 127
póker *m* 273
policía *m* 189
policía *f* 94
policía de tráfico *m* 195
poliéster *m* 277
polilla *f* 295
política *f* 169
pollo *m* 119
pollo frito *m* 155
pollo preparado *m* 119
polluelo *m* 185
polo *m* 243, 282
Polo Norte *m* 283
Polonia 316
polvera *f* 40
polvos *m* 109
polvos compactos *m* 40
polvos de talco *m* 73
pomada *f* 47, 109
pomelo *m* 126
pomo de la puerta *m* 59
poner césped 90
poner el despertador 71
poner en remojo 130
poner la mesa 64
pop *m* 259
popa *f* 240
popurrí *m* 111
por 320
por avión 98
por favor 322
porcentaje *m* 165
porche *m* 58
porciones de pollo *f* 155
poro *m* 15
porra *f* 94
portaaviones *m* 215
portabolígrafo *m* 172
portaequipaje *m* 196, 204
portaequipajes *m* 209
portaobjetos *m* 167
portarretratos *m* 271
portería *f* 221, 223, 224
portero *m* 222, 224
Portugal 316
posavasos *m* 150
posgrado 169
poste *m* 222, 247
poste de la portería *m* 220
póster *m* 255
postre *m* 153
postre de soletillas, gelatina de frutas y nata *m* 141
postura *f* 232
potro *m* 185
pradera *f* 285
prado *m* 285
precio *m* 152, 199, 209
precio de entrada *m* 260
pregunta 163
preguntar 163
prematuro 52
premolar *m* 50
prensa *f* 178
prensaajos *m* 68
preocupado 25
prepucio *m* 21
presentación *f* 174
presentador *m* 178
presentadora *f* 191
presentadora de las noticias *f* 179
presidir 174
presión del neumático *f* 203
préstamo *m* 96, 168
primavera *f* 307
primer piso *m* 141
primera mano *f* 83
primera planta *f* 104
primero 309
primeros auxilios *m* 47
primo *m* 22
prímula *f* 297
principado *m* 315
principio *m* 321
prismáticos *m* 281
proa *f* 215, 240
probadores *m* 104
problemas *m* 271
procesador *m* 176
productor *m* 254
productos de belleza *m* 105
productos de limpieza *m* 107
productos lácteos *m* 136
profesiones *f* 188, 190
profesor *m* 169
profesora *f* 162
profiterol *m* 140
profundidad *f* 165
programa *m* 176, 254, 269
programación *f* 178
prohibido el paso *m* 195
prohibido parar 195
prometida *f* 24
prometido *m* 24
propagar 91
propietario *m* 58
propuesta *f* 174
propulsor *m* 281
prórroga *f* 223
próstata *f* 21
protector *m* 83, 88, 236
protector de la cara *m* 225
protector de la pierna *m* 225
protegedientes *m* 237
proveedor de servicios *m* 177
provincia *f* 315
provocar el parto 53
proyector digital *m* 163
prueba *f* 181
prueba del embarazo *f* 52
pruebas *f* 247
psicoterapia *f* 55
psiquiatría *f* 49
público *m* 254
pueblo *m* 299
puente *m* 15, 214, 258, 300
puenting *m* 248
puerro *m* 125
puerta *f* 85, 182, 196, 198, 209
puerta automática *f* 196
puerta de la ducha *f* 72
puerta del maletero *f* 198
puerta exterior *f* 59
puerta principal *f* 58
puerto *m* 176, 214, 216, 217
puerto de pesca *m* 217
puerto deportivo *m* 217
Puerto Rico 314
puesta de sol *f* 305
puesto callejero *m* 154
pulgada *f* 310
pulgar *m* 15
pulmón *m* 18
pulpa *f* 124, 127, 129
pulpejo *m* 15
pulpo *m* 121, 295
pulsera *f* 36
pulsera de identificación *f* 53
pulso *m* 47
pulverizador *m* 89, 311
punta *f* 36, 122, 163, 246
puntada *f* 277
puntas abiertas *f* 39
punto *m* 273
punto de amarre *m* 217
puntos *m* 52
puntuación *f* 220, 273
puntual 305
puñetazo *m* 237
puño *m* 15, 32, 237
pupila *f* 51
pupitre *m* 162
puro *m* 112
putter *m* 233
puzle *m* 273

Q

Qatar 318
quebrado *m* 165
quemador *m* 61, 67
quemadura *f* 46
quemadura de sol *f* 46
queso *m* 136, 156
queso azul *m* 136
queso cremoso *m* 136
queso cremoso semicurado *m* 136
queso curado *m* 136
queso de bola *m* 142
queso de cabra *m* 142
queso fresco *m* 136
queso rallado *m* 136
queso semicurado *m* 136
quiche *f* 142
quilla *f* 214
química *f* 162
quince 308
quince días 307
quincuagésimo 309
quingombó *m* 122
quinientos 308
quinoa *f* 130
quinto 309
quirófano *m* 48
quiropráctica *f* 54
quitaesmalte *m* 41
quitar las flores muertas 91
quizá 322

R

rábano *m* 124
rábano picante *m* 125
ración *f* 64
radar 281
radar *m* 214
radiador *m* 60, 202
radicchio *m* 123
radio *m* 17, 164, 207
radio *f* 179, 268
radio del coche *f* 201
radio despertador *f* 70
radio digital *f* 268
radiografía *f* 48, 50
radiología *f* 49
rafting *m* 241
raices *f* 39
raíl *m* 208
raíl electrificado *m* 209
raíz *f* 50, 124, 296
raíz del taro *f* 124
ralentí *m* 203
rallador *m* 68
rallar 67
rally *m* 249
RAM *m* 176
rama *f* 296
ramadán *m* 26
ramas *f* 133
ramillete aromático *m* 132
ramita *f* 296
ramo *m* 111
ramo de flores *m* 35
rampa de lanzamiento *f* 281
rampa para sillas de ruedas *f* 197
rana *f* 294
ranúnculo *m* 297
ranura de la tarjeta *f* 97
rap *m* 259
rape *m* 120
rápido 321
rápidos *m* 240, 284
rappel *m* 248
raqueta *f* 230
rascacielos *m* 299, 300
raspador *m* 82
raspar 77
rastrillar 90
rastrillo *m* 88, 225
rastrillo para el césped *m* 88
rata *f* 290
ratón *m* 176, 290
raya *f* 120, 294
rayos ultravioleta *m* 286
rayos x dentales *m* 50
reanimación *f* 47
rebanada *f* 139
rebanador *m* 139
rebaño *m* 183
rebeca *f* 32
recalentar 154
recepción *f* 100
recepcionista *f* 100, 190
receta *f* 45
recibir 177, 227
recibo *m* 152
recién nacido *m* 53
recipiente *m* 311
recogedor *m* 77
recogepelotas *m* 231
recoger 245
recogida *f* 98
recogida de equipajes *f* 213
recolectar 183
récord *m* 234
rectángulo *m* 164
recto *m* 21
recto 165, 260
recuerdos *m* 260

red *f* 176, 217, 222, 226, 227, 231
red! 231
red ferroviaria *f* 209
red para las capturas *f* 244
red para recoger *f* 244
redacción *f* 163
redactora *f* 191
redil *m* 185
reducir 172
refectorio *m* 168
reflejos *m* 39
reflexología *f* 54
refresco *m* 154
refrescos *m* 144
regadera *f* 89
regaliz *m* 113
regalo *m* 27
regar 90, 183
regatear 223
reggae *m* 259
región *f* 315
registro *m* 100
regla *f* 163, 165
regulador *m* 239
reiki *m* 55
reina *f* 272, 273
Reino Unido 316
reír 25
rejilla *f* 69
relaciones *f* 24
relajación *f* 55
relámpago *m* 287
rellenar 82
relleno 159
relleno *m* 140, 155
reloj *m* 36, 304
reloj despertador *m* 70
remar 241
remedios de herbolario *m* 108
remero *m* 241
remite *m* 98
remo *m* 241
remolacha *f* 125
remolcador *m* 215
remolcar 195
remolque *m* 266
remolque del equipaje *m* 212
remover 67
Renacimiento 301
renacuajo *m* 294
renovar 168
reparto *m* 98, 254
repelente de insectos *m* 108
reportera *f* 179
reposabrazos *m* 200
reposacabezas *m* 200
repostería *f* 69, 140
reproducción *f* 20
reproductor 19
reproductor de DVD *m* 268
reptiles *m* 293
República Centroafricana 317
República Checa 316
República Democrática del Congo 317
República Dominicana 314
requesón *m* 136
resbalar 229
reserva *m* 223
reservar 168
reservar un vuelo 212
resfriado *m* 44
resistencia *f* 61
resistente al horno 69
respaldo *m* 64, 210
respiración *f* 47
respiratorio 19
respuesta *f* 163
restar 165
restaurante *m* 101, 152
resto *m* 231
restregar 77
resultado *m* 49
retina *f* 51
retraso *m* 209
retrato robot *m* 181
retrete *m* 61
retrovisor exterior *m* 198
reunión *f* 174
revelar 271
revés *m* 231
revestimiento *m* 187
revisión *f* 50
revisor *m* 209
revista *f* 112, 168
revistas *f* 107
revuelto *m* 158
rey *m* 272, 273
riego *f* 89
riendas *f* 242
rímel *m* 40
ring *m* 237
rinoceronte *m* 291
riñon *m* 18, 119
río *m* 284
ritmo *m* 259
rizado 39
roble *m* 296
robo *m* 94
robot de cocina *m* 66
rocalla *f* 84
rocas *f* 284, 288
rociar 91
rococó 301
rodaja *f* 121
rodeo *m* 243
rodilla *f* 12
rodillera *f* 205, 227
rodilleras *f* 220
rodillo *m* 83
rodillo de cocina *m* 69
rojizo 39
rojo 274
rollo *m* 311
rollo de papel higiénico *m* 72
rombo *m* 164, 273
romero *m* 133
romper aguas 52
rompiente *f* 241
ron *m* 145
ron con Coca-Cola *m* 151
roncar 71
ropa de caballero *f* 32, 105
ropa de cama *f* 71, 74
ropa de hogar *f* 105
ropa de niño *f* 30
ropa de señora *f* 34, 105
ropa impermeable *f* 245, 267
ropa interior *f* 32
ropa interior térmica *f* 35
ropa limpia *f* 76
ropa para dormir *f* 31
ropa casual *f* 33
ropa sucia *f* 76
ropa termoaislante *f* 267
roqueta *f* 123
rosa 274
rosa *f* 110
rosado 145
rosquilla *f* 139
rótula *f* 17
rótulo *m* 173
rough *m* 232
roulotte *f* 266
rubí *m* 288
rubio 39
rueda *f* 198, 207
rueda de ajuste *f* 276
rueda de repuesto *f* 203
rueda delantera *f* 196
rueda del diafragma *f* 270
rueda trasera *f* 197
ruedas de apoyo *f* 207
ruedo *m* 243
rugby *m* 221
ruibarbo *m* 127
ruina famosa *f* 261
Rumanía 316
Rwanda 317

S

sábado 306
sábana *f* 71, 74
saca postal *f* 98
sacacorchos *m* 150
sacaleches *m* 53
sacapuntas *m* 163
sacar 231
sacar brillo 77
saco de arena *m* 237
saco de dormir *m* 267
safari park *m* 262
Sáhara *m* 313
Sáhara Occidental 317
Saint Kitts y Nevis 314
sal *f* 64, 152
sala de embarque *f* 213
sala de espera *f* 45
sala de lecturas *f* 168
sala de máquinas *f* 214
sala de maternidad *f* 48
sala de pediatría *f* 48
sala de reuniones *f* 174
sala de urgencias *f* 48
sala del tribunal *f* 180
salado 121, 129, 137, 143, 155
salamandra *f* 294
salami *m* 142
salchicha *f* 155, 157
salchichas *f* 118
salchichón *m* 142
salida *f* 61, 210, 232
salida de emergencia *f* 210
salida de incendios *f* 95
salidas *f* 213
salir 233
salmón *m* 120
salmonete *m* 120
salpicadero *m* 201
salsa *f* 134, 143, 155
saltador *m* 238
saltamontes *m* 295
saltar 227
saltar a la comba 251
saltear 67
salto *m* 235, 237, 239, 243, 247
salto alto *m* 239
salto con pértiga *m* 234
salto de altura *m* 235
salto de longitud *m* 235
salto de salida *m* 239
salto entre dos *m* 226
salto mortal *m* 235
salud *f* 44
salvado *m* 130
salvaslip *m* 108
salvavidas *m* 240
salvia *f* 133
San Marino 316
San Vicente y las Granadinas 314
sandalia *f* 37
sandalias *f* 31
sandía *f* 127
sandwich abierto *m* 155
sandwich tostado *m* 149
Santa Lucía 314
Santo Tomé y Príncipe 317
sapo *m* 294
saque de banda *m* 223, 226
sarampión *m* 44
sardina *f* 120
sarpullido *m* 44
sartén *f* 69
sastre *m* 191
sastre 35
sastrería *f* 115
satélite *m* 281
Saturno *m* 280
sauce *m* 296
sauna *f* 250
saxofón *m* 257
scanner *m* 176
scrabble *m* 272
secador *m* 38
secadora *f* 76
secar 76
secar con el secador 38
sección *f* 282
sección de equipajes *f* 104
sección de zapatería *f* 104
sección infantil *f* 104
seco 39, 41, 130, 145, 286, 321
secretaría *f* 168
seda *f* 277
sedal *m* 244
sedimentario 288
segunda planta *f* 104
segundero *m* 304
segundo *m* 304
segundo 309
seguridad *f* 212, 240
seguridad *f* 75
seguro *m* 203
seguro de sí mismo 25
seis 308
seiscientos 308
selector de puntada *m* 276
sellante *m* 83
sello *m* 98, 173
sellos *m* 112
selva tropical *f* 285
semáforo *m* 194
semana *f* 306
semana pasada *f* 307
semana que viene *f* 306
Semana Santa *f* 27
semanalmente 307
sembrar 90, 183
semilla *f* 122, 130
semilla de sésamo *f* 131
semilla de soja *f* 131
semillas *f* 88, 131
semillas de amapola *f* 138
semillas de hinojo *f* 133
semillero *m* 89
sémola *f* 130
senderismo *m* 263
sendero *m* 262
sendero para caballos *m* 263
Senegal 317
seno *m* 19
sensible 41
sentarse en cuclillas 251
sentencia *f* 181
señal *m* 209
señal de tráfico *f* 298
señales de tráfico *f* 195
señales horizontales *f* 194
Señor *m* 23
Señora *f* 23
Señorita *f* 23
señuelo *m* 244
sepia *f* 121
septiembre 306
séptimo 309
septuagésimo 309
serie *f* 179
serie televisiva *f* 178
serpiente *f* 293
serrar 79
serrucho *m* 80
serrucho de costilla *m* 81
servicio *m* 231
servicio al cliente *m* 104
servicio de habitaciones *m* 101
servicio de lavandería *m* 101
servicio de limpieza *m* 101
servicio incluido 152
servicio no incluido 152
servicios *m* 49
servicios de emergencia *m* 94
servidor *m* 176
servilleta *f* 65
servilleta de papel *f* 154
servilletero *m* 65
servir 64
sesenta 308
set *m* 230
setecientos 308
setenta 308
seto *m* 85, 90, 182
sexagésimo 309
sexto 309
shiatsu *m* 54
shock *m* 47
sí 322
Siberia 313
Sicilia 316
sidra *f* 145
sien *f* 14
sierra circular *f* 78
sierra de calar *f* 81
sierra de mano *f* 89
sierra de vaivén *f* 78
Sierra Leona 317
sierra para metales *f* 81
siete 308
siglo *m* 307
silenciador *m* 203, 204
silla *f* 64
silla de montar *f* 242
silla de montar de señora *f* 242
silla de ruedas *f* 48
silla giratoria *f* 172
silla para el niño *f* 207
silla para niños *f* 198

español

silleta de paseo *f* 75
sillín *m* 206, 242
sillón *m* 63
sillón del dentista *m* 50
silo *m* 183
sin 320
sin escamas 121
sin espinas 121
sin gas 144
sin grasa 137
sin mangas 34
sin pasteurizar 137
sin pepitas 127
sin piel 121
sin plomo 199
sin sal 137
sin tirantes 34
sinagoga *f* 300
sinfonía *f* 256
Singapur 319
sintético 31
sintonizar 179
sintonizar la radio 269
sintonizador digital *m* 269
sirena *f* 94
Siria 318
sistema *m* 176
sistema de megafonía *f* 209
sistema solar *m* 280
sistemas *m* 19
sitio web *m* 177
slálom *m* 247
slálom gigante *m* 247
snowboard *m* 247
sobre 320
sobre *m* 98, 173
sobre par *m* 233
sobreexpuesto 271
sobrina *f* 23
sobrino *m* 23
socia *f* 24
socorrista *m* 239, 265
soda *f* 144
sofá *m* 62
sofá-cama *m* 63
software *m* 176
sol *m* 280
solapa *m* 32
soldado *m* 189
soldador *m* 81
soldar 79
soleado 286
soletillas *f* 141
soltar 245
soluble 109
solución desinfectante *f* 51
Somalia 317
sombra de ojos *f* 40
sombrero *m* 36
sombrero para el sol *m* 265
sombrilla *f* 264
somnífero *m* 109
sonajero *m* 74
sonata *f* 256
sonda *f* 50
sonrisa *f* 25
sopa *f* 153, 158
soporte *m* 88, 166, 187, 205
soporte de la agarradera *m* 166
soporte del papel celo *m* 173
soporte del sillín *m* 206
sorbete *m* 141
sorprendido 25
sospechoso *m* 94, 181
sostenido 256
sótano *m* 58
soufflé *m* 158
sport 34
spray *m* 109, 311
squash *m* 231
Sri Lanka 318
stop *m* 269
strike *m* 228
suavizante *m* 38, 76
subexpuesto 271
subibaja *m* 263
subir 139
submarino *m* 215
subsuelo *m* 91
sucursal *f* 175
sudadera *f* 33
Sudáfrica 317
Sudán 317
Sudán del Sur 317
Suecia 316
suegra *f* 23
suegro *m* 23
suela *f* 37
sueldo *m* 175
suelo *m* 62, 71
suelo aislante *m* 267
suero de la leche *m* 137
Suiza 316
sujetador *m* 35
sujetador para la lactancia *m* 53
sujetapapeles *m* 173
sumar 165
sumidero *m* 299
suministro de electricidad *m* 60
sumo *m* 237
supermercado *m* 105, 106
suplemento *m* 55
supositorio *m* 109
sur *m* 312
surco *m* 183
surfing *m* 241
surfista *m* 241
Suriname 315
surtidor *m* 199
suspensión *f* 203, 205
suspirar 25
sustitución *f* 223
Swazilandia 317
swing de práctica *m* 233

T

tabaco *m* 112, 184
tabla *f* 241
tabla de gimnasia *m* 251
tabla de la plancha *f* 76
tabla de surf *f* 241
tabla para cortar *f* 68
tablero *m* 226
tablero de ajedrez *m* 272
tablero de densidad media *m* 79
tableta de chocolate *f* 113
tablilla *f* 47
tablilla con sujetapapeles *f* 173
tablón de anuncios *m* 173
taburete *m* 150
taco *m* 155
taco del freno *m* 207
tacón *m* 37
taekwondo *m* 236
tai-chi *m* 236
Tailandia 318
Taiwán 319
taladrar 79
taladro eléctrico *m* 78
taladro inalámbrico *m* 78
taladro manual *m* 78, 81
talla en madera *f* 275
tallar 79
taller *m* 78, 199, 203
tallo *m* 111, 122, 297
talón *m* 13,15
talonario de cheques *m* 96
tambor pequeño *m* 257
tampón *m* 108
tándem *m* 206
tanque *m* 61
tanque de la gasolina *m* 203, 204
tanque del agua *m* 61
Tanzania 317
tapa *f* 61, 66
tapa del objetivo *f* 270
tapa del wáter *f* 72
tapacubo *m* 202
tapadera *f* 69
tapón *m* 72, 166
taquígrafa *f* 181
taquilla *f* 209, 255
taquillas *f* 239
tarde *f* 305
tarde 305
tarifa *f* 197
tarjeta *f* 27
tarjeta amarilla *f* 223
tarjeta de crédito *f* 96
tarjeta de débito *f* 96
tarjeta de embarque *f* 213
tarjeta de la biblioteca *f* 168
tarjeta postal *f* 112
tarjeta roja *f* 223
tarrina *f* 311
tarro *m* 134, 311
tarro hermético *m* 135
tarta nupcial *f* 141
tarta de chocolate *f* 140
tarta de cumpleaños *f* 141
tartaleta de fruta *f* 140
tartas para celebraciones *f* 141
Tasmania 319
tatuaje *m* 41
taxista *m* 190
Tayikistán 318
taza *f* 61, 65, 75
taza de café *f* 65
taza de té *f* 65
té *m* 144, 149, 184
té con hielo *m* 149
té con leche *m* 149
té con limón *m* 149
té en hoja *m* 144
té solo *m* 149
té verde *m* 149
teatro *m* 254, 299
tebeo *m* 112
techo *m* 62, 203
techo solar *m* 202
tecla *f* 176
teclado *m* 97, 99, 176, 258
técnicas *f* 79, 159
técnico de sonido *m* 179
tee *m* 233
teja *f* 58, 187
tejado *m* 58
tejer 277
tela *f* 276, 277
tela metálica *f* 167
telar *m* 277
teleférico *m* 246
teléfono *m* 99
teléfono con cámara *m* 270
teléfono de emergencia *m* 195
teléfono inalámbrico *m* 99
teléfono inteligente *m* 99, 176
teléfono móvil *m* 99
teléfono público *m* 99
telegrama *m* 98
telenovela *f* 178
teleobjetivo *m* 270
telepizzería *f* 154
telescopio *m* 281
telesilla *f* 246
televisión *f* 268
televisión por cable *f* 269
telón *m* 254
telón de fondo *m* 254
televisor de pantalla *m* 269
temblor *m* 283
témpera *f* 274
temperatura *f* 286
templo *m* 300
temprano 305
tenacillas *f* 38
tenazas *f* 81, 167
tenazas de alambre *f* 80
tendón *m* 17
tendón de Aquiles *m* 16
tendón de la corva *m* 16
tenedor *m* 65, 153
tenedor para trinchar *m* 68
tener un hijo 26
tenis *m* 230, 231
tensión arterial *f* 44
teñido 39
tequila *m* 145
terapeuta *m* 55
terapeuta *f* 55
terapia de grupo *f* 55
terapias alternativas *f* 54
tercero 309
terminal *f* 212
terminal del ferry *f* 216
termita *f* 295
termo *m* 267
termoesfera *f* 286
termómetro *m* 45, 167
termostato *m* 61
ternera *f* 118
ternero *m* 185
terraza *f* 85, 148
terraza ajardinada *f* 85
terremoto *m* 283
territorio *m* 315
tesina *f* 169
tesis *f* 169
testículo *m* 21
testigo *m* 180, 235
tetera *f* 65
tetina *f* 75
tetrabrik *m* 311
tía *f* 22
tibia *f* 17
tiburón *m* 294
tiempo *m* 234, 286, 304
tiempo muerto *m* 220
tienda *f* 298
tienda de antigüedades *f* 114
tienda de artículos de ragalo *f* 114
tienda de campaña *f* 267
tienda de discos *f* 115
tienda de fotografía *f* 115
tienda de golosinas *f* 113
tienda de licores *f* 115
tienda de materiales de arte *f* 115
tienda de muebles *f* 115
tienda de artículos usados *f* 115
tienda libre de impuestos *f* 213
tiendas *f* 114
Tierra *f* 280, 282
tierra *f* 85
tierra firme *f* 282
tierras de labranza *f* 182
tigre *m* 291
tijeras *f* 38, 47, 82, 276
tijeras de podar *f* 89
tijeras de uñas *f* 41
tilo *m* 296
timbal *m* 257
timbre *m* 48, 59, 197
tímido 25
timón *m* 210, 241
Timor Oriental 319
tinta *f* 275
tinte para el pelo *m* 40
tinte para madera *m* 79
tinto 145
tintorería *f* 115
tío *m* 22
tipo de cambio *m* 97
tipo de interés *m* 96
tipos *m* 205
tipos de autobuses *m* 196
tipos de cámara *m* 270
tipos de granja *m* 183
tipos de pesca *m* 245
tipos de plantas *m* 86
tipos de tren *m* 208
tirador *m* 200
tirante *m* 35
tirar 223, 227
tirar al hoyo con un putter *m* 233
tirar de cabeza 222
tirarse de cabeza 238
tirarse en trineo 247
tirita *f* 47
tiro *m* 249
tiro con arco *m* 249
tiro con efecto *m* 230
tiro libre *m* 222
tirón *f* 239
tirón en el cuello *m* 46
título *m* 168
tiza *f* 162, 288
toalla de ducha *f* 73
toalla de lavabo *f* 73
toalla de playa *f* 265
toallas *f* 73
toallero *m* 72
toallita antiséptica *f* 47
toallita húmeda *f* 108
toallitas húmedas *f* 75
tobillo *m* 13, 15
tobogán *m* 263
tocadiscos *m* 268
tocador *m* 71
tocólogo *m* 52
todoterreno *m* 199
toffee *m* 113
toga *f* 169
Togo 317
toldo *m* 148
toma *f* 61

español

toma de tierra *f* 60
toma del agua *f* 61
tomar apuntes 163
tomar el sol 264
tomate *m* 125, 157
tomate cherry *m* 124
tomillo *m* 133
tonelada *f* 310
tónica *f* 144
tónico *m* 41
tono *m* 41, 256
topacio *m* 288
topinambur *m* 125
torcedura *f* 46
tormenta *f* 287
tornado *m* 287
tornear 79
torneo *m* 233
tornillo *m* 80
tornillos de la rueda *m* 203
torno de alfarero *m* 275
torno de banco *m* 78
torno de dentista *m* 50
toro *m* 185
torre *f* 272, 300
torre de control *f* 212
torre de vigilancia *f* 265
torreón *m* 300
torrija *f* 157
tortilla *f* 158
tortuga *f* 293
tos *f* 44
tostada *f* 157
tostado 129
tostador *m* 66
trabajo *m* 172
tractor *m* 182
tráfico *m* 194
trago *m* 151
traje *m* 255
traje de baño *m* 238
traje de buzo *m* 239
traje de chaqueta *m* 32
traje de cuero *m* 205
traje de noche *m* 34
traje espacial *m* 281
traje minifaldero *m* 34
trampolín *m* 235, 238
transatlántico *m* 215
transferencia bancaria *f* 96
transformador *m* 60
transmisión *f* 202
transmisión por secuencias *f* 269
transplantar 91
transportador *m* 165
transporte *m* 194
tranvía *m* 196, 208
trapecio *m* 16, 164
trapo del polvo *m* 77
tráquea *f* 18
trasbordador espacial *m* 281
traspaso *m* 223
traste *f* 258
tratamientos *m* 23
tratamientos de belleza *m* 41
trébol *m* 273, 297
trece 308
treinta 308
trementina *f* 83
tren *m* 208
tren de alta velocidad *m* 208
tren de aterrizaje *m* 210
tren de mercancías *m* 208
tren de vapor *m* 208
tren delantero *m* 210
tren diesel *m* 208
tren eléctrico *m* 208
tren intercity *m* 209
trenca *f* 31
trenza *f* 39
tres 308
trescientos 308
triángulo *m* 164, 257
tribuna del jurado *f* 180
tríceps *m* 16
trigésimo 309
trigo *m* 130, 184
trigo partido *m* 130
trimestre *m* 52
trineo con perros *m* 247
Trinidad y Tobago 314
trípode *m* 166, 270, 281
tripulación *f* 241
triste 25
triturador de basuras *m* 61
trocitos de chocolate *m* 141
trolebús *m* 196
trombón de varas *m* 257
trompa *f* 291
trompa de Falopio *f* 20
trompeta *f* 257
trona *f* 75
tronco *m* 296
trópico de Cáncer *m* 283
trópico de Capricornio *m* 283
trópicos *m* 283
troposfera *f* 286
trote *m* 243
trozo *m* 140
trucha *f* 120
trucha arco iris *f* 120
trueno *m* 286
trufa *f* 113, 125
tuba *f* 257
tubo *m* 112, 202, 239, 311
tubo de desagüe *m* 61
tubo de ensayo *m* 166
tubo de escape *m* 203, 204
tubo de la aspiradora *m* 77
tubo superior *m* 207
tuerca *f* 80
tulipán *m* 111
Túnez 317
turbo *m* 203
turismo *m* 199, 260
turista *m* 260
Turkmenistán 318
turmalina *f* 288
turno *m* 228, 273
turquesa *f* 289
Turquía 316
turrón *m* 113
tutú *m* 191

U

Ucrania 316
Uganda 317
ugli *m* 126
última mano *f* 83
último piso *m* 141
ultraligero *m* 211
ultramarinos *m* 114
ultrasonido *m* 52
un cuarto de hora 304
una media hora 304
undécimo 309
unidad de cuidados intensivos *f* 48
uniforme *m* 94, 189, 222
uniforme de rugby *m* 221
uniforme del equipo *m* 31
universidad *f* 299
universo *m* 280
uno 308
uña *f* 15
uña del pie *f* 15
Urano *m* 280
uréter *m* 21
uretra *f* 20
urgencia *f* 46
urinario 19
urología *f* 49
Uruguay 315
usar el hilo dental 50
utensilios de cocina *m* 68
útero *m* 20, 52
Uzbekistán 318

V

vaca *f* 185
vacaciones *f* 212
vacío 321
vagina *f* 20
vagón *m* 208
vagón restaurante *m* 209
vaina *f* 122
vainilla *f* 132
vajilla *f* 64
vajilla y los cubiertos f/*m* 65
vajillas *f* 105
vale 322
valla *f* 85, 243
valle *m* 284
valor de las acciones *m* 97
valor nominal *f* 97
válvula *f* 207
válvula de la presión *f* 61
Vanuatu 319
vaquería *f* 183
varicela *f* 44
varilla de cristal *f* 167
varilla del nivel del aceite *f* 202
vaso *m* 65
vaso de precipitados *m* 167
vecino *m* 24
vehículo de servicio *m* 212
veinte 308
veinte mil 309
veinte minutos 304
veintidós 308
veintiuno 308
vejiga *f* 20
vela *f* 240, 241
vela mayor *f* 240
velas de cumpleanos *f* 141
vellón *m* 74
velo 35
vena *f* 19
venado *m* 118
venda *f* 47
vendaje *m* 47
vendedor de golosinas *m* 113
vendedor de periódicos *m* 112
Venezuela 315
ventaja *f* 230
ventana *f* 58, 177, 186
ventana de la buhardilla *f* 58
ventana de la nariz *f* 14
ventanilla *f* 96, 98, 197, 209, 210
ventanilla de pasajes *f* 216
ventarrón 286
ventilador *m* 60, 202, 210
ventosa *f* 53
Venus 280
ver la televisiòn 269
verano *m* 31, 307
verde 129, 274
verdulería *f* 114
verdura *f* 107
verduras *f* 122, 124
veredicto *m* 181
vértebras cervicales *f* 17
vértebras dorsales *f* 17
vértebras lumbares *f* 17
vesícula seminal *f* 21
vespa *f* 205
vestíbulo *m* 59, 100, 209, 255
vestido *m* 31, 34
vestido de novia *m* 35
veterinaria *f* 189
vía *f* 208
vía de acceso *f* 194
vía de salida *f* 194
viaje de negocios *m* 175
viajero de cercanías *m* 208
vibráfono *m* 257
videojuego *m* 269
videoteléfono *m* 99
vieira *f* 121
viejo 321
viento *m* 241, 286
viento-madera *m* 257
viento-metal *m* 256
viernes 306
Viet Nam 318
viga de acero *f* 186
viga de madera *f* 186
viga del tejado *f* 186
vigésimo 309
vigésimo primero 309
vigésimo segundo 309
vigésimo tercero 309
vinagre *m* 135, 142
vinagre balsámico *m* 135
vinagre de malta *m* 135
vinagre de sidra *m* 135
vinagre de vino *m* 135
vino *m* 145, 151
vino de jerez *m* 145
vino de oporto *m* 145
viña *f* 183
viñedo *m* 183
viola *f* 256
violín *m* 256
violoncelo *m* 256
virar 241
virus *m* 44
virutas de madera *f* 78
visado *m* 213
visera *f* 205
visillo *m* 63
visita *f* 45
visita con guía *f* 260
visor *m* 271
vista *f* 51
vitaminas *f* 108
vivero *m* 115
vivienda de una planta *f* 58
vivienda urbana *f* 58
vodka *m* 145
vodka con naranja *m* 151
volante *m* 49, 201, 231
volante a la derecha *m* 201
volante a la izquierda *m* 201
volar 211
volcán *m* 283
volcar 241
volea *f* 231
voltaje *m* 60
voltereta lateral *f* 235
volumen *m* 165, 179, 269, 311
vomitar 44
vuelo con ala delta *m* 248
vuelo internacional *m* 212
vuelo nacional *m* 212
vuelo sin motor *m* 248

W

wáter *m* 72
waterpolo *m* 239
wedge *m* 233
whisky *m* 145
whisky escocés con agua *m* 151
Wi-Fi *m* 269
windsurfing *m* 241
windsurfista *m* 241
wok *m* 69

Y

yarda *f* 310
yate *m* 215, 240
yema *f* 137, 157
Yemen 318
yerno *m* 22
yeso *m* 83
yoga *m* 54
yogurt *m* 137
yogurt de frutas *m* 157
yogurt helado *m* 137
Yugoslavia 316

Z

zafiro *m* 288
Zambia 317
zanahoria *f* 124
zapatería *f* 114
zapatilla deportiva *f* 37
zapatillas *f* 31, 251
zapatillas de deporte *f* 31
zapato de caballero *m* 37
zapato de cordoneras *m* 37
zapato de golf *m* 233
zapato de tacón *m* 37
zapatos *m* 34, 37
zapatos de piel *m* 32
zarpa *f* 291
zarpar 217
Zimbabwe 317
zinc *m* 289
zodiac *m* 215
zona *f* 315
zona de abastecimiento *f* 199
zona de ataque *f* 224
zona de defensa *f* 224
zona de marca *f* 221
zona final *f* 220
zona industrial *f* 299
zona lumbar *f* 13
zona neutral *f* 224
zona peatonal *f* 299
zona poco profunda *f* 239
zona profunda *f* 239
zonas *f* 283, 299
zoo *m* 262

zoología *f* 169
zorro *m* 290
zumo *m* 127
zumo de frutas *m* 156
zumo de manzana *m* 149
zumo de naranja *m* 148
zumo de piña *m* 149
zumo de tomate *m* 144, 149
zumo de uva *m* 144
zumos y los batidos *m* 149
zurcir 277

Italian index • index italien • italienisches Register • índice italiano • indice italiano

A

a 320
a chicco corto 130
a chicco lungo 130
a due porte 200
a folglie caduche 86
a la carte 152
a quattro porte 200
a schiera 58
a tre porte 200
a zero 230
abbaino *m* 58
abbigliamento *m* 205
abbigliamento da donna *m* 105, 34
abbigliamento da uomo *m* 105, 32
abboccare 245
abbronzatura *f* 41
abiti per il bambino *m* 30
abito *m* 32
abito da sera *m* 34
abito da sposa *m* 35
aborto spontaneo *m* 52
acacia *f* 110
accademia di danza *f* 169
accanto 320
accappatoio *m* 73
acceleratore *m* 200, 204
accendere la televisione 269
accendere un fuoco 266
accendino *m* 112
accensione *f* 200
accesso per sedie a rotelle *m* 197
accessori *m* 36, 38
accessori per la pulizia *m* 77
acchiappare 227, 229
acciaio inossidabile *m* 79
acconciature *f* 39
accordo di affari *m* 175
account di posta elettronica *m* 177
accusa *m* 94
accusato *m* 180
acerbo 129
acero *m* 296
aceto *m* 135, 142
aceto balsamico *m* 135
aceto di malto *m* 135
aceto di sidro *m* 135
aceto di vino *m* 135
acetone *m* 41
acetosa *f* 123
acqua *f* 144, 238
acqua dal rubinetto *f* 144
acqua di colonia *f* 41
acqua in bottiglia *f* 144
acqua minerale *m* 144
acqua naturale *f* 144
acqua tonica *f* 144
acquaio *m* 61
acquamarina *f* 288
acquaragia *f* 83
acquarello *m* 274
acquascooter *m* 241
acquisti *m* 104
addebito diretto *m* 96
addetta alla ricezione *f* 100, 190
addetto alle pulizie *m* 188
addome *m* 12
addominali *m* 16
addormentarsi 71
adesso 304
adolescente *m* 23
adulto *m* 23
aerare 91
aereo biposto *m* 211
aereo da caccia *m* 211
aereo da diporto *m* 211
aereo di linea *m* 210, 212
aereo privato *m* 211
aereoplano *m* 210
aeroporto *m* 212
affamato 64
affari *m* 175
affettare 67
affettatrice *f* 139
affilacoltelli *m* 68, 118
affilatore *m* 81
affittare 58
affitto *m* 58
affogare 67
affogato 159
affrancatura *f* 98
affumicato 118, 121, 143, 159
Afghanistan 318
Africa 317
agata *m* 289
agenda *f* 173, 175
agente *m* 94
agente di viaggio *m* 190
agente immobiliare *f* 189
agenzia di viaggi *f* 114
agenzia immobiliare *f* 115
aggressione *f* 94
aggrottare le ciglia 25
aglio *m* 125, 132
agnello *m* 118, 185
ago *m* 109, 276
agopressione *f* 55
agopuntura *f* 55
agosto 306
agre 127
agricoltore *m* 182, 189
agrifoglio *m* 296
agrumi *m* 126
aia *f* 182
aikido *m* 236
airbag *m* 201
aiuola *f* 85, 90
aiuto cuoco *m* 152
al ginocchio 34
al sugo 159
al vapore 159
ala *f* 119, 210, 293
Alaska 314
alba *f* 305
Albania 316
albergo *m* 100, 264
albero *m* 86, 240, 296
albero di trasmissione *m* 202
albicocca *f* 126
album fotografico *m* 271
alchechengi *m* 128
alesatore *m* 80
aletta *f* 210
alettone *m* 210
alfalfa *m* 184
alfiere *m* 272
Algeria 317
aliante *m* 211, 248
alimentazione di rete *f* 60
aliscafo *m* 215
all'esterno 320
all'interno 320
alla caviglia 34
alla griglia 159
allarme antifumo *m* 95
allarme antifurto *m* 58
allarme antincendio *m* 95
allattamento *m* 53
allattamento al seno *m* 53
allegato *m* 177
allenamento *m* 237
allenamento a circuito *m* 251
allenamento con i pesi *m* 251
allenarsi 251
allergia *f* 44
allevamento di maiali *m* 183
allevamento di pecore *m* 183
alligatore *m* 293
allisciare 39
allo sciroppo 159
alloro *m* 133
alluce *m* 15
alluminio *m* 289
alpinismo in parete *m* 248
alta definizione (HD) 269
altalena *f* 263
alternatore *m* 203
altezza *f* 165
altipiano *m* 284
alto 98, 321
altoparlante *m* 176, 258, 268
altre imbarcazioni *f* 215
altri lavori artigianali 275
altri negozi *m* 114
altri sport *m* 248
altroieri *m* 307
alunno *m* 162
alzarsi 71
alzarsi a sedere 251
alzate con il manubrio *f* 251
alzatina paraspruzzi *f* 66
amaca *f* 266
amaro 124, 127
Amazzonia *f* 312
ambiente *m* 280
ambulanza *f* 94
ambulatorio *m* 45, 168
America Centrale 314
America del Nord 314
America del Sud 315
ametista *f* 288
amico *m* 24
amico di penna *m* 24
amministratore delegato *m* 175
ammorbidente *m* 76
ammortizzatore *m* 205
amniocentesi *f* 52
amo *m* 244
ampere *m* 60
amplificatore *m* 268
ampolla *f* 166
anacardi *m* 151
anacardio *m* 129
analisi *f* 49
analisi del sangue *f* 48
analogica 179
ananas *m* 128
anatra *f* 119, 185
anatroccolo *m* 185
anca *f* 121
ancora *f* 214, 240
andare a letto 71
andare in bici 207
andare in pensione 26
Ande *f* 312
Andorra 316
anelli *m* 89, 235
anello *m* 36, 226
anestetista *m* 48
aneto *m* 133
anfibi *m* 294
Angola 317
angolo *m* 164, 223
angolo della strada *m* 298
anguilla *f* 294
anguria *f* 127
anice stellato *m* 133
animale *m* 292
animali *m* 292, 294
animazione *f* 255
annaffiare 90
annaffiatoio *m* 89
annaffiatura *f* 89
annegare 239
annesso *m* 58
anniversario *m* 26
anno *m* 306
annoiato 25
annotazione *f* 256
annuale 86
annunciatrice *f* 191
annuo 307
antenna *f* 295
antenna della radio *f* 214
antenna parabolica *f* 269
antiaderente 69
antidolorifici *m* 47
antidolorifico *m* 109
antigelo *m* 199, 203
Antigua e Barbuda 314
antinfiammatorio *m* 109
antipasto *m* 153
antirughe 41
anulare *m* 15
ape *f* 295
aperitivo *m* 153
aperto 260, 321
apice *m* 165
app *m* 99
apparecchiare 64
apparecchiature da ufficio *f* 172
apparecchio a raggi x *m* 212
apparecchio correttore *m* 50
appartamento *m* 59, 298
appellativi *m* 23
appendice *f* 18
applaudire 255
applicazione *f* 176
applique *f* 62
appuntamento *m* 45, 175
appunti *m* 191
apribottiglie *m* 68, 150
aprile 306
apriscatole *m* 68
aquila *f* 292
Arabia Saudita 318
arachide *f* 129
aragosta *f* 121, 29
arancia *f* 126
arancia *f* 126
aranciata *f* 144
arancino cinese *m* 126
arancione 274
arare 183
aratro *m* 182
arbitro *m* 222, 225, 226, 229, 230
arbusto da fiore *m* 87
architettare 91
architetto *m* 190
architettura *f* 300
architrave *m* 186, 301
arco *m* 85, 164, 249, 301
arco plantare *m* 15
arcobaleno *m* 287
ardesia *f* 288
area della porta *f* 221, 223
area di attacco *f* 224
area di difesa *f* 224
area di rigore *f* 223
area di stazionamento *f* 199, 212
area neutrale *f* 224
arena *f* 243
arenaria *f* 288
Argentina 315
argento *m* 235, 289
argilla *f* 85, 275
aria condizionata *f* 200
aringhe affumicate *f* 157
aritmetica *f* 165
armadietti *m* 239
armadietto *m* 66
armadietto dei medicinali *m* 72
armadio *m* 70
armadio a muro *m* 71
Armenia 318
aromaterapia *f* 55
arpa *f* 256
arrabbiato 25
arrampicata su ghiaccio *f* 247
arrangiamenti *m* 111
arredamento per casa *m* 105
arresto *m* 94
arricciacapelli *m* 38
arrivederci 322
arrivi *m* 213
arrostire 67
arrostito 129
arrosto *m* 119, 158
art déco *m* 301
art nouveau *m* 301
arte *f* 162
arte e artigianato 274
arte topiaria *f* 87
arteria *f* 19
arti marziali *f* 237
articolazione *f* 17
articoli da cucina *m* 105
articoli da toilette *m* 41
articoli di cancelleria *m* 173
articoli elettronici *m* 105
articoli sportivi *m* 105
artigianato *m* 276
artiglio *m* 291
artista *f* 274

italiano

ascella f 13
ascensore m 59, 100, 104
ascia f 95
asciugabiancheria f 76
asciugacapelli m 38
asciugamani m 73
asciugamano da spiaggia m 265
asciugamano grande m 73
asciugamano piccolo m 73
asciugare 76, 77
asciugare con il phon 38
asciutto 321
Asia 318
asino m 185
asma f 44
asola f 32
asparago m 124
aspetto m 30
aspirapolvere m 188
aspirapolvere m 77
assaggiare 139
asse m 205
asse da stiro f 76
assegno m 96
assicurazione f 203
assistente m/f 24
assistente di volo f 190, 210
assistente socio-psicologico m 55
assistenza ai clienti f 104
asso m 230, 273
assolto 181
assorbente f 108
asteroide m 280
asticella f 225
astigmatismo m 51
astronauta m 281
astronomia f 281
astuccio m *163*, 271
atleta m 191, 234
atletica f 234
atmosfera f 282, 286
atrio m 104, 209, 255
attaccante m 222
attacco m 220
atterrare 211
attico m 58
attillato 35
attività f 77, 162, 183, 245, 263
attività all'aria aperta f 262
attore m 191, 254
attori m 179
attorno 320
attraverso 320
attrezzatura f 165, 238, 245
attrezzature f 233
attrezzi m 187
attrezzi da giardino m 88
attrezzo per modellare m 275
attrice f 254
aula f 162, 169
aula del tribunale f 180
aurora m 286
Australia 319
Austria 316
autista m 190, 196
auto a tre/cinque porte f 199
auto decappottabile f 199
auto della polizia f 94
auto d'epoca f 199
auto familiare f 199
auto sportiva f 198
autobus m 196
autobus a due piani m 196
autodifesa f 237
autolavaggio m 198
automatico 200
automobile f 198, 200
automobile elettrica f 199
autonoleggio m 213
autopompa f 95
autoradio f 201
autostazione f 197
autostrada f 194
autunno m 31, 307
avambraccio m 12
avampiede m 15
avanzamento veloce m 269
avena f 130
avere un bambino 26
avocado m 128
avvelenamento m 46
avvenimenti della vita m 26
avventura f 255
avversario m 236
avvitamento m 230
avvocato m 180, 190
avvolgibile m 63
avvolgitubo m 89
Azerbaigian 318
azienda agricola f 183
azienda avicola f 183
azienda ortofrutticola f 183
azioni f 97, 227, 233, 229

B

bacca f 296
baccello m 122
bacchetta f 256
bacchetta di vetro f 167
bacheca f 173
bacino m 17, 214
bacino per riparazioni m 217
back-swing m 233
badminton m 231
baffi m 290
bagagli m 198
bagagliaio m 196, 198
bagaglio m 100, 213
bagaglio a mano m 211, 213
bagaglio in eccedenza m 212
bagel m 139
bagnato 321
bagni m 266
bagnino m 239, 265
bagno privato m 100
bagnoschiuma m 73
Bahamas 314
Bahrain 318
balconata f 254
balcone m 59
balena f 290
balla f 184
ballerina f 37, 191
balletto m 255
balsamo m 38
balza f 71
bambini m 23
bambino m 23, 31
bambino piccolo m 30
bambola f 75
bambù m 86, 122
banana f 128
banca f 96
banchina f 216
banchina spartitraffico f 194
banco m 96, 98, 100, 142, 150, 162, 216
banco accettazione m 213
banco da lavoro m 78
banco della giuria m 180
banco informazioni m 168
banco prestiti m 168
banconote f 97
bandierina f 221, 223, 232
Bangladesh 318
bar m 150, 152
bar all'aperto m 148
bar con terrazza m 148
bar mitzvah m 26
barattolo m 134, 311
barattolo a chiusura ermetica m 135
barattolo di vernice m 83
barbabietola f 125
Barbados 314
barbiere m 39, 188
barca a remi f 214
barca a vela f 215
barca da pesca f 217
barella f 94
barista m 150, 191
barocco 301
barra f 240
barra degli strumenti f 177
barra del menu f 177
barra di scorrimento f 177
barriera f 209
barriera corallina f 285
basalto m 288
base f 99, 164, 229
base di battuta f 228
baseball m 228
basilico m 133
basso 321
bastoncini m 133
bastoncino m 90, 91
bastone da sci m 246
battente m 59
battere 225, 229
battere un primato 234
batteria f 78, 167, 202, 260, 258
batterista m 258
battesimo m 26
battistrada m 207
battitore m 225, 228
battuta f 256
batuffoli di ovatta m 41
bavaglino m 30, 50
becco m 89, 293
becco Bunsen m 166
becher m 167
Belgio 316
Belize 314
bellezza f 40, 105
bemolle 256
benda f 47
bendatura f 47
Benin 317
benzina f 199
berlina f 199
berretto m 36
bersaglio m 249, 273
bestiame m 183, 185
betoniera f 186
betulla f 296
bevanda al malto f 144
bevande f 144, 156
bevande alcoliche f 145
bevande calde f 144
Bhutan 318
biancheria f 105
biancheria da letto f 71, 74
biancheria intima f 32, 35, 105
biancheria termica f 35
bianchi 39
bianco 145, 272, 274
biathlon m 247
biberon m 75
bibita f 154
bibita in lattina f 154
bibite f 107, 144
biblioteca f 168, 299
bibliotecaria f 168
bibliotecario m 190
bicchiere m 65, 151, 152
bicchieri m 150
bicicletta f 206
bicicletta da corsa f 206
bicicletta da strada f 206
bicicletta da turismo f 206
bicipite m 16
bidè m 72
Bielorussia 316
biennale 86
bieta f 123
bietola f 123
bifamiliare 58
bifocale 51
biglietteria f 209, 216, 255
biglietti della lotteria m 112
biglietto m 197, 213, 209
biglietto d'auguri m 27
biglietto di accompagnamento m 173
bignè al cioccolato m 140
bignè ripieno m 140
bikini m 264
bilancia f 45, 69, 98, 118, 166, 310
bilancia a molla f 166
bilanciere m 251, 263
biliardo m 249
bimbo m 23, 30
binario m 208
binario elettrificato m 209
binocolo m 281
biologia f 162
biologico 91, 118, 122
biondo 39
biplano m 211
birillo m 187, 249
Birmania 318
birra f 145, 151
birra amara f 145
birra scura f 145
bis m 255
biscotti m 141
biscotto m 113
biscotto alle noci m 141
biscotto con scaglie di cioccolato 141
bistecca di culaccio f 119
bisturi m 81, 167
blatta f 295
blazer m 33
blocca freni m 207
bloccare 227
blocco m 172
blocco di partenza m 234
blocco per appunti m 173
blocco per schizzi m 275
blu 274
blues m 259
boa f 217
bob m 247
bobina f 245, 276
bocca f 14
boccaglio m 239
bocchino m 112
bocciolo m 111, 297
bocconcini di pollo m 155
Bolivia 315
bollire 67
bollitore m 66
boma m 240
bombardiere m 211
bombola f 239
bomboletta spray f 311
bongo m 257
bonifico bancario m 96
bordeggiare 241
bordo m 230
bordo erbaceo m 85
borraccia f 206, 267
borsa f 190
borsa a tracolla f 37
borsa calda f 70
borsa da spiaggia f 264
borsa dei ricambi f 75
borsa di studio f 169
borsa per il cambio f 75
borsa valori f 97
borse f 37
borsetta f 37
bosco m 285
Bosnia ed Erzegovina 316
Botswana 317
bottiglia f 61, 135, 311
bottiglia di vetro f 166
bottone m 32
bottone automatico m 30
bouquet m 35
boutique f 115
bowling m 249
box m 75
boxer m 33
bozzolo m 295
bracciale m 36
bracciata f 239
braccio m 13, 95
bracciolo m 200, 210, 238
branchia f 294
brandy m 145
Brasile 315
bretella f 37
bricco misuratore m 69
briciole f 139
bridge m 273
brie m 142
briglia f 242
brioche f 157
brocca f 65, 151
brocca graduata f 311
broccolo m 123
broker m 97
bronzo m 235
browser m 177
bruciatore a gas m 61
bruco m 295
Brunei 319
buca f 232
buca delle lettere f 99
buca in uno f 233
buccia f 126, 127, 128
buco nero m 280
budino di riso m 140
bufera f 286
buffet m 152
buffet della colazione m 156
buggy m 232
bulbo m 86
Bulgaria 316
bulloni della ruota m 203
bungalow m 58
bungee jumping m 248
bunker m 232

italiano

buongiorno 322
buono 321
Burkina Faso 317
burro *m* 137, 156
burro di arachidi *m* 135
Burundi 317
business class *f* 211
bussola *f* 80, 240, 312
busta *f* 98, 173
busta della spesa *f* 106
busta di plastica *f* 122
bustina di tè *f* 144
byte *m* 176

C

cabina *f* 95, 210, 214, 264
cabina del conducente *f* 208
cabina di pilotaggio *f* 210
cabina telefonica *f* 99
Cabinda 317
cacatoa *m* 293
cacciagione *f* 119
cacciavite *m* 80
cacciavite a croce *m* 81
cachi *m* 128
cactus *m* 87
caddy *m* 233
caduta *f* 237
caffè *m* 144, 148, 153, 156, 184, 262
caffè filtrato *m* 148
caffè freddo *m* 148
caffè macchiato *m* 148
caffè nero *m* 148
caffettiera *f* 65
calamaro *m* 121, 295
calamita *f* 167
calcare *m* 85, 288
calcestruzzo *m* 187
calciare 223
calciatore *m* 222
calcio *m* 109, 221, 222, 237
calcio di punizione *m* 222
calcite *f* 289
calcolatrice *f* 165
caldo 286, 321
calendario *m* 306
calice *m* 297
calice da vino *m* 65
calorifero *m* 60
calvo 39
calza *f* 35
calzini *m* 33
calzoncini *m* 33
cambiare 209
cambiare canale 269
cambiare marcia 207
cambiare una ruota 203
Cambogia 318
camembert *m* 142
camera *f* 283
camera a due letti *f* 100
camera da letto *f* 70
camera d'aria *f* 207
camera dei bambini *f* 74
camera doppia *f* 100
camera oscura *f* 271
camera privata *f* 48
camera singola *f* 100
cameraman *m* 178
camere *f* 100
cameriera *f* 191
cameriere *m* 148, 152
camerino *m* 104
Camerun 317
camicetta *f* 34
camicia *f* 33
camicia da notte *f* 31, 35
caminetto *m* 63
camino *m* 58
camion *m* 194
camion con cassone ribaltabile *m* 187
camionista *m* 190
cammello *m* 291
camomilla *f* 149
campanello *m* 59, 197
Campari *m* 145
campeggiare 266
campeggio *m* 266
camper *m* 266
campionato *m* 223, 230
campo *m* 182, 220, 222, 226, 228, 230, 234
campo da golf *m* 232
campo destro *m* 229
campo di cricket *m* 225
campo di rugby *m* 221
campo esterno *m* 229
campo sinistro *m* 228
campo sportivo *m* 168
campus *m* 168
Canada 314
canale *m* 178, 269
canale di scolo *m* 299
canale radiofonico *m* 179
canarino *m* 292
cancelleria *f* 105
cancello *m* 85, 182
candela *f* 203
candeline *f* 141
cane *m* 290
canestro *m* 226
canguro *m* 291
canino *m* 50
canna *f* 91, 207
canna da pesca *f* 244
canna da zucchero *f* 184
canne *f* 89
cannella *f* 133
cannolicchio *m* 121
cannuccia *f* 112, 144, 154
canoa *f* 214
canottaggio *m* 241
canottiera *f* 33, 35
cantante *m* 258
cantante *f* 191
cantiere *m* 186
cantiere navale *m* 217
canzone *f* 259
capacità *f* 311
capanno *m* 182
capelli *m* 14, 38
capezzolo *m* 12
capitale *f* 315
capitale netto *m* 97
capitaneria di porto *f* 217
capitano *m* 214
capitano di porto *m* 217
capo *m* 24
Capodanno *m* 27
capoeira *f* 237
capote *f* 75
capovolgersi 241
cappa *f* 66
cappello *m* 36, 190
cappello da equitazione *m* 242
cappello da spiaggia *m* 265
cappello per il sole *m* 30
capperi *m* 143
cappotto *m* 32
cappuccino *m* 148
cappuccio *m* 31
cappuccio cervicale *m* 21
capra *f* 185
capretto *m* 185
caprifoglio *m* 297
capriola *f* 235
capsula *f* 50, 109
capsula di Petri *f* 166
carambola *f* 128
caramella alla frutta *f* 113
caramella di gelatina *f* 113
caramella gommosa *f* 113
caramella mou *f* 113
caramelle *f* 113
caramelle assortite *f* 113
caramello *m* 113
carattere *m* 177
carboncino *m* 275
carbone *m* 288
carbonella *f* 266
carcere *m* 181
carciofo *m* 124
cardamomo *m* 132
cardio *m* 121
cardiologia *f* 49
cardiovascolare 19
cardo *m* 297
caricare 76
carico *m* 216
carie *f* 50
carnagione *f* 41
carne *f* 119
carne bianca *f* 118
carne cotta *f* 118, 143
carne cruda *f* 142
carne e pollame f\m 106
carne macinata *f* 119
carne magra *f* 118
carne rossa *f* 118
carnevale *m* 27
carota *f* 124
carpa koi *f* 294
carrellino *m* 233
carrello *m* 106, 208, 213
carrello d'atterraggio *m* 210
carrello dei dolci *m* 152
carrello della telecamera *m* 178
carrello elevatore *m* 186, 216
carrello portabagagli *m* 212
carriola *f* 88
carro attrezzi *m* 203
carrozzeria *f* 202
carrozzina *f* 75
carta a rilievo *f* 83
carta da parati *f* 82
carta di credito *f* 96
carta di debito *f* 96
carta di fondo *f* 83
carta d'imbarco *f* 213
carta igienica *f* 72
carta intestata *f* 173
carta vetrata *f* 81, 83
cartapesta *f* 275
carte *f* 273
cartella *f* 162, 177
cartella sospesa *f* 173
cartellino giallo *m* 223
cartellino rosso *m* 223
cartello stradale *m* 195
cartilagine *f* 17
cartolina *f* 112
cartone *m* 275, 311
cartone animato *m* 178
cartone di latte *m* 136
casa *f* 58
casa da gioco *f* 75
casa delle bambole *f* 75
casa dello studente *f* 168
casa di città *f* 58
casalinghi *m* 107
cascata *f* 285
caschetto 39
casco *m* 95, 186, 204, 206, 220, 228, 236
caseificio *m* 183
casella *f* 100, 272
casello *m* 194
caserma dei vigili del fuoco *f* 95
casinò *m* 261
casolare *m* 182
cassa *f* 106, 150
cassa automatica *f* 97
cassa toracica *f* 17
cassava *f* 124
casseretto *m* 214
casseruola *f* 69
casseruola di terracotta *f* 69
cassetta *f* 61
cassetta delle lettere *f* 99
cassetta di pronto soccorso *f* 47
cassetta guidalama per ugnature *f* 81
cassetta per le lettere *f* 58
cassetto *m* 66, 70, 172
cassetto per la verdura *m* 67
cassettone *m* 70
cassiere *m* 96, 106
cast *m* 254
castagna *f* 129
castagna d'acqua *f* 124
castano 39
castello *m* 300
castello di sabbia *m* 265
casual *m* 33, 34
catamarano *m* 215
cataratta *f* 51
catarifrangente *m* 207
catena *f* 36, 206
catena montuosa *f* 282
catenella *f* 59
catetere *m* 53
catrame *m* 187
cattedrale *f* 300
cattivo 321
cauzione *f* 181
cavalcavia *m* 194
cavalletta *f* 295
cavalletto *m* 174, 205, 207, 274
cavallo *m* 185, 235, 242, 272
cavallo da corsa *m* 243
cavalluccio marino *m* 294
cavatappi *m* 150
cavatorsoli *m* 68
caverna *f* 284
cavezza *f* 243
caviglia *f* 13, 15
cavo *m* 79, 207
cavo di alimentazione *m* 176
cavolfiore *m* 124
cavolino di Bruxelles *m* 122
cavolo *m* 123
cavolo rapa *m* 123
cavolo riccio *m* 123
cazzuola *f* 187
ceci *m* 131
cedro *m* 296
celebrazioni *f* 27
cella *f* 94, 181
cembali *m* 257
cemento *m* 186
cena *f* 64, 158
cenere *f* 283
centesimo 309
centimetro *m* 310
cento 308
centodieci 308
centomila 308
centrifuga *f* 76
centrifugare 76
centro *m* 164, 273
centro campo *m* 222
centro commerciale *m* 104
centro della tavola *m* 241
centrocampo *m* 228
cera *f* 77
ceramica *f* 275
cercare 177
cerchietto *m* 38
cerchio *m* 165, 277
cerchio centrale *m* 224
cerchione *m* 206
cereale *m* 130, 156
cereali da colazione *m* 107
cereali trattati *m* 130
ceretta *f* 41
cerotto *m* 47
certificato di nascita *m* 26
cervello *m* 19
cervice *f* 52
cervo *m* 118, 291
cesoie *f* 89
cesta *f* 263
cesta dei giocattoli *f* 75
cesta del cucito *f* 276
cestello *m* 88, 207
cestino *m* 106, 172, 177
cestino di frutta *m* 126
cesto della biancheria da lavare *m* 76
cesto della biancheria pulita *m* 76
cesto sospeso *m* 84
cetriolo *m* 125
champagne *m* 145
cheddar *m* 142
cheerleader *f* 220
chiara *f* 137
chiaro 41, 321
chiave *f* 59, 80, 203, 207
chiavetta USB *f* 176
chiave a tubo *f* 80
chiave della camera *f* 100
chiave di basso *f* 256
chiave di sol *f* 256
chiave inglese *f* 81
chiave regolabile *f* 80
chiavistello *m* 59
chicchi *m* 144
chiesa *f* 298, 300
chiglia *f* 214
chilogrammo *m* 310
chilometro *m* 310
chimica *f* 162
chiocciola *f* 295
chiodi *m* 233
chiodi di garofano *m* 133
chiodo *m* 80
chiropratica *f* 54
chirurgia *f* 48
chirurgia plastica *f* 49
chirurgo *m* 48
chitarra elettrica *f* 258
chitarrista *m* 258
chiuso 260, 321
chiusura lampo *f* 277

italiano

chorizo *m* 143
chutney *m* 134
ciabatta *f* 37
ciac *m* 179
Ciad 317
ciambella *f* 139, 265
cibi imbottigliati *m* 134
cibi pronti *m* 107
cibo *m* 118, 130, 149
cibo per animali *m* 107
ciclismo *m* 263
cicogna *f* 292
cicoria *f* 122
ciglio *m* 14, 51, 298
cigno *m* 293
Cile 315
ciliegia *f* 126
cilindro *m* 164
Cina 318
cinema *m* 255, 299
cinghia *f* 37, 242
cinghia della camma *f* 203
cinghia della ventola *f* 203
cinghia frontale *f* 242
cinghia nasale *f* 242
cinghietto *m* 207
cinquanta 308
cinquantacinquemilacinquecento 309
cinquantamila 309
cinquantesimo 309
cinque 308
cinquecento 308
cinta per gli attrezzi *f* 186
cintura *f* 32, 36, 236
cintura dei pesi *f* 239
cintura di sicurezza *f* 198, 211
cintura nera *f* 237
cintura porta attrezzi *f* 186
cioccolata calda *f* 156
cioccolata spalmabile *f* 135
cioccolatino *m* 113
cioccolato al latte *m* 113
cioccolato bianco *m* 113
cioccolato caldo *m* 144
cioccolato fondente *m* 113
ciotola *f* 65
cipolla *f* 124
cipollina *f* 125
cipria *f* 40
Cipro 316
circolo di confronto *m* 224
circolo polare artico *m* 283
circonferenza *f* 164
citazione *f* 180
citofono *m* 59
citronella *f* 133
città *f* 298, 299
Città del Vaticano *f* 316
clacson *m* 201, 204
clarinetto *m* 257
clarinetto basso *m* 257
classe *f* 163
classe economica *f* 211
clavicola *f* 17
clementina *f* 126
cliente *m* 38, 96, 104, 106, 152, 175, 180
clinica *f* 48
clitoride *m* 20
coca *f* 144
coccige *f* 17
coccinella *f* 295
coccodrillo *m* 293
cocktail *m* 151
coda *f* 121, 210, 242, 280, 290, 294
coda di cavallo *f* 39
codice a barre *m* 106
codice d'accesso *m* 99
codice di avviamento postale *m* 98
codini *m* 39
cofanetto portagioie *m* 36
cofano *m* 198
cogliere 91
cognata *f* 23
cognato *m* 23
coincidenza *f* 212
coito *m* 20
colazione *f* 64, 156
colazione all'inglese *f* 157
coleottero *m* 295
colibrì *m* 292
colino *m* 68
colla *f* 275
colla da legno *f* 78
colla da parati *f* 82
collage *m* 275
collana *f* 36
collant *m* 35, 251
collare *m* 46
collega m/f 24
collegare 177
collegarsi 177
colletto *m* 32
collina *f* 284
collo *m* 12
collo a V *m* 33
collo del piede *m* 15
collo dell'utero *m* 20
collutorio *m* 72
Colombia 315
colonia *f* 315
colonna *f* 300
colonna d'ormeggio *f* 214
colonna sonora *f* 255
colonnina *f* 298
colore *m* 273
colori *m* 39, 274
colori acrilici *m* 274
colori ad olio *m* 274
colpi *m* 231
colpi di sole *m* 39
colpire 224
colpire a distanza *f* 233
colpire da vicino 233
colpire di testa 222
colpire leggermente 233
colpo *m* 233, 237
colpo di frusta *m* 46
colpo di taglio *m* 237
colpo nullo! 231
coltello *m* 65, 80
coltello da cucina *m* 68
coltello da pacchi *m* 82
coltello da pane *m* 68
coltivare 91
colture *m* 184
colza *f* 184
comandi *m* 201, 204
comandi per il riscaldamento *m* 201
comando *m* 269
cometa *f* 280
cominciare la partita 233
commedia *f* 255
commercialista *m* 190
commessa *f* 188
commesso *m* 104
commissario *m* 94
commissione *f* 97
commissione bancaria *f* 96
commozione *f* 46
comodino *m* 70
Comore 317
compact disc *m* 269
compagno/-a m/f 23
compartimento portabagagli *m* 210
compasso *m* 165
compensato *m* 79
compiti *m* 163
compleanno *m* 27
complesso di uffici *m* 298
completo 266
comporre 99
computer *m* 176
computer portatile *m* 176
comunicazioni *f* 98
con 320
con armatura 35
concepire 20
concerto *m* 255, 258
concerto rock *m* 258
concezione *f* 52
conchiglia *f* 265
concimaia *f* 85
concimare 91
concimare a spandimento 90
concime *m* 91
concorso di salto a ostacoli *m* 243
condimento *m* 155, 158
condito 159
confetiere *m* 113
confetture *f* 134
confuso 25
congelare 67
congelato 121, 124
congelatore *m* 67
conglomerato *m* 288
Congo 317
conifera *f* 86
coniglio *m* 118, 290
cono *m* 164
conoscente *m* 24
consegna *f* 98
consegna a domicilio *f* 154
consegna delle lauree *f* 169
conserva di frutta *f* 134
conservante *m* 83
conservatorio *m* 169
console *f* 269
consulente finanziaria *m* 97
consulenza legale *f* 180
contabile *m* 97
contachilometri *m* 201, 204
contafotogrammi *m* 270
contagiri *m* 201
contagocce *m* 109, 167
container *m* 216
contante *m* 97
contare 165
contatore di corrente *m* 60
contenitore *m* 311
contenitore di riciclaggio *m* 61
continente *m* 282, 315
conto *m* 152
conto corrente *m* 96
conto di risparmio *m* 97
contornitrice *f* 78
contorno *m* 153
contrabbasso *m* 256
contraccezione *f* 21, 52
contrafforte *m* 301
contrastare 223
contrazione *f* 52
controfagotto 257
controfiletto di manzo *m* 119
controllo *m* 50
controllo passaporti *m* 212, 213
controllore *m* 209
coperchio *m* 61, 66
coperta *f* 71, 74
coperto *m* 65
copiare 172
copilota *m* 211
copione *m* 254
coppe *f* 53
coppia *f* 24
copriletto *m* 70
coprimozzo *m* 202
copriobiettivo *m* 270
coprire con strato protettivo 91
corda *f* 230, 248, 266
corda per bucato *f* 76
corda tirante *f* 266
cordata *f* 248
corde *f* 256
corde vocali *f* 19
cordone ombelicale *m* 52
Corea del Nord 318
Corea del Sud 318
coriandolo *m* 133
corna *f* 291
cornacchia *f* 292
cornea *f* 51
cornetto *m* 156
cornice *f* 62, 63, 271
cornicione *m* 300
corno *m* 257, 291
corno inglese *m* 257
coro *m* 301
corona *f* 111
corpetto *m* 35
corpo *m* 12
corrente alternata *f* 60
corrente continua *f* 60
correre 228
correttore *m* 40
corridoio *m* 210, 254
corriere *m* 99
corrimano *m* 59
corsa a ostacoli *f* 235, 243
corsa al trotto *f* 243
corsa automobilistica *f* 249
corsa di carrozze *f* 243
corsa di cavalli *f* 243
corsa in motoscafo *f* 241
corsa in piano 243
corsa su slitta *f* 247
corsa su slitta trainata da cani *f* 247
corsa sul posto *f* 251
corse *f* 243
corsetto *m* 35
corsia *f* 168, 234, 238
corsia centrale *f* 194
corsia d'emergenza *f* 194
corsia esterna *f* 194
corsia interna *f* 194
Corsica 316
corso per azione *m* 97
corteccia *f* 296
cortile *m* 58, 84
corto 32
coscia *f* 12, 119
costa *f* 285
Costa d'Avorio 317
Costa Rica 314
costata *f* 119
costellazione *f* 281
costola *f* 17
costoletta *f* 119
costolette *f* 155
costruire 186
costume *m* 255
costume da bagno *m* 238, 265
costumista *f* 191
cotenna *f* 119
cotone *m* 184, 277
cotto al forno 159
cottura dei dolci *f* 69
cottura facile 130
country *f* 259
cozza *f* 121, 295
crampi *m* 44
crampo *m* 239
cranio *m* 17
cratere *m* 283
cravatta *f* 32
crema *f* 140
crema abbronzante *f* 265
crema al limone *f* 134
crema autoabbronzante *f* 41
crema idratante *f* 41
crema pasticcera *f* 140
crema per il viso *f* 73
crema protettiva *f* 265
crema schermo totale *f* 108
crema solare *f* 108
crêpe *f* 155,
crêpes *f* 157
crescione *m* 123
cresta dell'onda *f* 241
cric *m* 203
criceto *m* 290
cricket *m* 225
criminale *m* 180
criniera *f* 242, 291
crisantemo *m* 110
cristalleria *f* 64
cristallino *m* 51
cristalloterapia *f* 55
Croazia 316
croccante 127
crocchia *f* 39
crocevia *m* 298
crogiolo *m* 166
cronista *f* 179
cronometro *m* 166, 234
cross trainer *m* 250
crosta *f* 136, 139, 282
crostatina *f* 140
crudo 124, 129
crusca *f* 130
cruscotto *m* 201
Cuba 314
cubetto di ghiaccio *m* 151
cubo *m* 164
cucchiaino *m* 65
cucchiaino da caffè *m* 153
cucchiaio *m* 65
cucchiaio da minestra *m* 65
cucchiaio da portata *m* 68
cucchiaio di legno *m* 68
cucchiaio dosatore *m* 68, 109
cucciolo *m* 290
cucina *f* 66, 152
cucina di bordo *f* 214
cucinare 67
cucire 277
cucitrice *f* 173
cucitura *f* 34
cuffia *f* 238
cuffie *f* 268
cugino *m* 22
culla portatile *f* 75

italiano

cumino *m* 132
cunetta *f* 299
cuocere a fuoco lento 67
cuocere al forno 67, 138
cuocere al vapore 67
cuocere alla griglia 67
cuoco *m* 152, 190
cuoio capelluto *m* 39
cuore *m* 18, 119, 122, 273
cuori di palma *m* 122
cupola *f* 300
curare 91
curcuma *f* 132
curling *m* 247
curry *m* 158
curva 165
cuscino *m* 62
cuscus *m* 130
custodia *f* 51
custodia degli occhiali *f* 51
cyclette *f* 250

D

d'accordo 322
da 320
da asporto154
dado *m* 80, 272
dama *f* 272
Danimarca 316
dar da mangiare 183
data *f* 306
data di comparizione *f* 180
data di restituzione *f* 168
data di scadenza *f* 109
datore di lavoro *m* 24
dattero *m* 129
davanti 320
debole 321
decade *f* 307
decimale *m* 165
decimo 309
decoder *m* 269
decollare 211
decoratore *m* 82
decorazione *f* 82, 141
delfino *m* 290
deltaplano *m* 248
deltoide *m* 16
denominatore *m* 165
denominazione *f* 97
dente *m* 50, 207
dente di leone *m* 123, 297
dentiera *f* 50
dentifricio *m* 72
dentista *m/f* 50, 189
dentro 320
denuncia *f* 94
deodorante *m* 73
deodoranti *m* 108
dépliants *m* 96
dermatologia *f* 49
deserto *m* 285
desktop *m* 177
desquamato 121
dessert *m* 140, 153
destinazione *f* 213
destra 260
detergente *m* 77
detergente per vetri *m* 199
deuce *m* 230
deviazione *f* 195
di fronte 320
di vetro 69
diabete *m* 44
diaframma *m* 19, 21
diagonale *f* 164
diamante *m* 288
diametro *m* 164
diarrea *f* 44, 109
dicembre 306
dichiarazione *f* 180
diciannove 308
diciannovesimo 309
diciassette 308
diciassettesimo 309
diciottesimo 309
diciotto 308
dieci 308
diecimila 309
diesel *m* 199
diesis *m* 256
dietro 320
difendere 225, 227, 229
difensore *m* 223
difesa *f* 181, 220
difetti *m* 271
difficile 321
diffusore *m* 89
diga *f* 300
digerente 19
digitale 179, 269
digitali *m* 297
dilatazione *f* 52
dimensioni *f* 165
dimesso 48
dinamo *f* 207
diottria *f* 51
dipartimento *m* 169
dipendente *m* 24
diploma *m* 169
direttore *m* 96, 174
direttore di orchestra *m* 256
dirigente *m* 174
diritto *m* 169
discesa *f* 247
dischetto *m* 224, 226
disco DVD *m* 269
disco rigido esterno *m* 176
discutere 163
disegnare 162
disegnatore *m* 191
disegno *m* 275
diserbante *m* 91
disinfettante *m* 47
dispensario *m* 108
dispenser *m* 173
dispositivo intrauterino *m* 21
dissertazione *f* 169
distanza *f* 310
distintivo *m* 31, 94, 189
distretto *m* 315
distribuire 273
distributore *m* 203
ditale *m* 276
dito del piede *m* 15
Divali *m* 27
divano *m* 62
divano letto *m* 63
dividendi *m* 97
dividere 165
divisa *f* 189, 222
divisa da rugby *f* 221
diviso per 165
divisore *m* 173
divorzio *m* 26
dizionario *m* 163
DJ *m* 179
docce *f* 266
doccia *f* 72
docente *m* 169
documentario *m* 178
dodicesimo 309
dodici 308
dogana *f* 212
dolce 124, 127, 155
dolce di frutta *m* 140
dolci *m* 107, 140
dolciumi *m* 113
domanda *f* 163
domandare 163
domani 306
domenica 306
Dominica 314
domino *m* 273
donna *f* 12, 23
donna d'affari *f* 175
dopo 320
dopobarba *m* 73
dopodomani *m* 307
doposole *m* 108
doppia carreggiata *f* 195
doppie punte *f* 39
doppio *m* 230
doppio 151
dormire *f* 74
dorso *m* 239
dorso del piede *m* 15
dosaggio *m* 109
dotto deferente *m* 21
dotto eiaculatore *m* 21
dottorato *m* 169
dragoncello *m* 133
dressage *m* 243
dribblare 222
dritto 165, 260
dritto *m* 231
drogheria *f* 114
due 308
duecento 308
duemila 307
duemilauno 307
duodeno *m* 18
duro 129, 321

E

eccitato 25
éclair *f* 140
eclisse *f* 280
ecografia *f* 48, 52
economia *f* 169
Ecuador 315
eczema *m* 44
edam *m* 142
edicola *f* 112
edifici *m* 299
edificio storico *m* 261
edilizia *f* 186
educazione fisica *f* 162
effetti collaterali *m* 109
Egitto 317
eglefino *m* 120
El Salvador 314
elastico *m* 39, 173
elefante *m* 291
elegante 34
elemento riscaldante *m* 61
elettricista *m* 188
elettricità *f* 60
elettrodo negativo *m* 167
elettrodo positivo *m* 167
elettrodomestici *m* 107
elica *f* 211, 214
elicottero *m* 211
ematite *f* 289
embrione *m* 52
emergenza *f* 46
emicrania *f* 44
emigrare 26
Emirati Arabi Uniti 318
emisfero meridionale *m* 283
emisfero settentrionale *m* 283
emorragia *f* 46
emorragia nasale *f* 44
emozioni *f* 25
enciclopedia *f* 163
endocrino 19
endocrinologia *f* 49
entrare in bacino 217
entrata *f* 59, 61
entro 320
epidurale *f* 52
epiglottide *m* 19
epilessia *f* 44
episiotomia *f* 52
equatore *m* 283
equazione *f* 165
equipaggio *m* 241
equitazione *f* 263, 242
erba *f* 55, 86
erba aromatica *f* 86
erba cipollina *f* 133
erbacce *f* 86
erbalismo *f* 55
erbe *f* 133
erbe aromatiche *f* 134
erbe e spezie *f* 132
erbicida *f* 183
erica *f* 297
Eritrea 317
eruttare 283
esagono *m* 164
esame *m* 163
esame della vista *m* 51
esca *f* 244
esca per il fuoco *f* 266
escavatrice meccanica *f* 187
escursione a cavallo *f* 243
escursionismo *m* 263
esercizi *m* 251
esfoliare 41
eskimo *m* 31
esofago *m* 19
esosfera *f* 286
esperimento *m* 166
esplorazione dello spazio *f* 281
esposimetro *m* 270
esposizione *f* 261, 271
espresso *m* 148
espulsione *f* 223
essiccato 129
est *m* 312
estate *f* 31, 307
esterno *m* 198
estintore *m* 95
Estonia 316
estrazione *f* 50
estuario *m* 285
etichetta *f* 173
etichette *f* 89
Etiopia 317
eucalipto *m* 296
Europa *f* 316

F

fabbrica *f* 299
fabbrica-ghiaccio *m* 67
fabbricazione dei merletti *f* 277
facchino *m* 100
faccia *f* 14
facile 321
faggio *m* 296
fagiano *m* 119, 293
fagioli *m* 131
fagioli aduki *m* 131
fagioli bianchi *m* 131
fagioli borlotti *m* 131
fagioli cannellini *m* 131
fagioli dall'occhio nero *m* 131
fagioli di Spagna *m* 131
fagioli mung *m* 131
fagioli nani *m* 131
fagiolino *m* 122
fagotto *m* 257
fairway *m* 232
falco *m* 292
falegname *m* 188
falegnameria *f* 275
falena *f* 295
fallo *m* 222, 226, 228, 230
famiglia *f* 22
fanale *m* 207
fanale posteriore *m* 204, 207
fans *m* 258
fante *m* 273
fantino *m* 242
far crescere 91
fard *m* 40
fare amicizia 26
fare il check-in 212
fare il letto 71
fare il pane 138
fare lo swing 232
fare marcia indietro 195
fare testamento 26
faretra *f* 249
farfalla *f* 36, 239, 295
farina autolievitante *f* 139
farina bianca *f* 138
farina di ossa *f* 88
farina integrale *f* 138
farina nera *f* 139
farina per il pane *f* 139
farina semplice *f* 139
farine *f* 138
faringe *f* 19
farmacia *f* 108
farmacista *m* 108, 189
faro *m* 217
farsi il bagno 72
farsi la doccia 72
fascia a tracolla *f* 46
fascia rifrangente *f* 205
fasi *f* 23
fattoria *f* 182, 184
fava *f* 122
fave *f* 131
favo *m* 135
fax *m* 98
fazzolettino *m* 108
fazzoletto *m* 36
febbraio 306
febbre *f* 44
febbre da fieno *f* 44
fecondazione *f* 20
federa *f* 71
Federazione Russa 318
fedina penale *f* 181
fegato *m* 18, 118
feijoa *f* 128
felce *f* 86
felice 25
felpa *f* 74
femminili 20
femore *m* 17
feng shui *m* 55
fenicottero *m* 292
ferita *f* 46
ferita alla testa *f* 46
fermacravatta *m* 36

italiano

fermafogli *m* 173
fermaglio *m* 36
fermapiedi *m* 207
fermata dell'autobus *f* 197, 299
fermo di sicurezza *m* 75
ferro *m* 109, 289
ferro da calza *m* 277
ferro da cavallo *m* 242
ferro da stiro *m* 76
fessura *f* 283
festa *f* 140
festa di compleanno *f* 27
Festa di Halloween *f* 27
feste *f* 27
feto *m* 52
fetta *f* 119, 139, 140
fettucce *f* 89
fibbia *f* 36
fibra *f* 127
fibra naturale *f* 31
fico *m* 129
fico d'india *m* 128
fidanzata *f* 24
fidanzati *m* 24
fidanzato *m* 24
fiducioso 25
fieno *m* 184
fieno greco *m* 132
fiero 25
Figi 319
figlia *f* 22
figliastra *f* 23
figliastro *m* 23
figlio *m* 22
fila *f* 210, 254
filatelia *f* 273
file *m* 177
filetti 121
filetto *m* 119, 121
fili *m* 60
Filippine 319
film d'amore *m* 255
film di fantascienza *m* 255
film di orrore *m* 255
filo *m* 79, 276
filo a piombo *m* 82
filo dentale *m* 50
filo di perle *m* 36
filo interdentale *m* 72
filobus *m* 196
filone *m* 138, 139
filosofia *f* 169
filtro *m* 270
filtro dell'aria *m* 202, 204
filtro di carta *m* 167
finanza *f* 97
fine *m* 321
fine settimana *m* 306
finestra *f* 58, 177, 186
finestrino *m* 197, 209, 210
Finlandia 316
fino 320
finocchio *m* 122, 133
fioraia *f* 188
fioraio *m* 110
fiore *m* 273, 297
fioretto *m* 249
fiori *m* 110
fiori secchi *m* 111
firma *f* 96, 98
fisica *f* 162, 169
fisioterapia *f* 49
fitness *m* 250
fiume *m* 284
flan *m* 141
flash *m* 270
flauto *m* 257
flebo *f* 53
flessioni *f* 251
flettere 251
foca *f* 290
focaccina *f* 140
fodera *f* 32
foglia *f* 122, 296
fogliame *m* 110
follicolo *m* 20
fondale *m* 254
fondo campo *m* 220
fondotinta *m* 40
fontana *f* 85
football americano *m* 220
footing *m* 251, 263
foratura *f* 203, 207
forbici *f* 38, 47, 82, 276
forbici da giardino *f* 89
forbici tagliabordi *f* 88
forbicine per le unghie *f* 41
forcella *f* 207
forchetta *f* 65, 89, 153
forchettone *m* 68
forcina *f* 38
forcipe *m* 53, 167
forcone *m* 88, 89
foresta *f* 285
foresta pluviale *f* 285
forfora *f* 39
formaggio *m* 136, 156
formaggio cremoso *m* 136
formaggio di capra *m* 142
formaggio duro *m* 136
formaggion erborinato *m* 136
formaggio fresco *m* 136
formaggio grattugiato *m* 136
formaggio molle fresco *m* 136
formaggio morbido *m* 136
formaggio semiduro *m* 136
formaggio semimorbido *m* 136
forme *f* 164
formica *f* 295
fornelletto da campeggio *m* 267
fornello *m* 67, 112
fornello di ceramica *m* 66
fornire di esca 245
fornitore di servizi *m* 177
forno *m* 66
forno a microonde *m* 66
forse 322
forte 321
foschia *f* 287
fossa *f* 229
fossa di sabbia *f* 263
fossato *m* 300
fossetta *f* 15
fotofinish *m* 234
fotofit *m* 181
fotografare 271
fotografia *f* 270, 271
fotografo *m* 191
foulard *m* 36
fragile 98
fragola *f* 127, 149
Francia 316
francobolli *m* 112
francobollo *m* 98
frappé al caffè 149
fratello *m* 22
frattaglie *f* 118
frattura *f* 46
frazione *f* 165
freccette *f* 273
freccia *f* 198, 204, 249
freddo 286, 321
fregare 77
fregio *m* 301
frenare 207
freno *m* 200, 204, 206
freno a mano *m* 203
frequenza *f* 179
fresco 121, 127, 130
fresia *f* 110
friggere 67
frigocongelatore *m* 67
frigorifero *m* 67
frittata *f* 158
fritto 159
fritto in olio abbondante 159
fritto in padella 159
frittura *f* 158
frizione *f* 200, 204
frizzante 144
frontale *m* 16
fronte *f* 14
frontone *m* 300, 301
frullato *m* 137
frullatore *m* 66
frusta *f* 68
frustino *m* 242
frutta *f* 107, 126, 128
frutta candita *f* 129
frutta con nocciolo *f* 126
frutta fresca *f* 157
frutta secca *f* 129, 156
frutta snocciolata *f* 126
frutta tropicale *f* 128
frutti di mare *m* 121
fruttivendolo *m* 114, 188
frutto della passione *m* 128
frutto dell'albero del pane *m* 124
fulmine *m* 287
fumaiolo *m* 214
fumare 112
fumble *m* 220
fumo *m* 95
funerale *m* 26
fungo *m* 125
funivia *f* 246
fuoco *m* 266
fuori 225, 228, 320
fuori campo 226
fuorigioco *m* 223
fuoripista 247
fuoristrada *m* 199
furto *m* 94
fusibile *m* 60
fusoliera *f* 210

G

gabbia *f* 95
gabbiano *m* 292
Gabon 317
galassia *f* 280
galleggiante *m* 61, 244
galleria *f* 254
galleria d'arte *f* 261
gallina *f* 185
gallo *m* 185
galloccia *f* 240
gallone *m* 311
galoppo *m* 243
galosce *f* 31, 89
gamba *f* 12, 64
gambata *f* 239
gamberi sgusciati *m* 120
gambero *m* 121
gambero d'acqua dolce *m* 121
Gambia 317
gambo *m* 297
gancio *m* 118, 187, 276
gara *f* 234
garage *m* 58, 199, 203
gare *f* 247
garofano *m* 110
garza *f* 47
gattino *m* 290
gatto *m* 290
gel *m* 38, 109
gel per doccia *m* 63
gelata *f* 287
gelato *m* 137, 149
gelo *m* 287
gemelli *m* 23
gemello *m* 36
gemme *f* 288
generatore *m* 60
generazione *f* 23
genero *m* 22
gengiva *f* 50
genitali *m* 12
genitori *m* 23
gennaio 306
geografia *f* 162
geometria *f* 165
Georgia 318
gerbera *f* 110
Germania 316
germoglio *m* 122
germoglio di soia *m* 122
gesso *m* 85, 162, 276, 288
getto d'acqua *m* 95
geyser *m* 285
Ghana 317
ghiacciaio *m* 284
ghiaccio *m* 120, 287
ghiaccio e limone 151
ghiacciolo *m* 287
ghiaia *f* 85, 88
ghiandola *f* 19
ghirlanda *f* 111
giacca *f* 32, 34
giaccone *m* 33
giacinti di bosco *m* 297
giada *f* 288
giaietto *m* 288
giallo 274
Giamaica 314
Giappone 318
giardinaggio *m* 90
giardini *m* 261
giardiniere *m* 188
giardino *m* 84
giardino acquatico *m* 84
giardino all'inglese *m* 84
giardino all'italiana *m* 262
giardino all'italiana *m* 84
giardino di erbe *m* 84
giardino di rocce *m* 84
giardino pensile *m* 84
giarrettiera *f* 35
Gibuti 317
giglio *m* 110
gilet *m* 33
gin *m* 145
gin tonic *m* 151
ginecologia *f* 49
ginecologo *m* 52
ginnasta *f* 235
ginnastica *f* 235
ginnastica a corpo libero *f* 235
ginnastica prepugilistica *f* 251
ginnastica ritmica *f* 235
ginocchiera *f* 227
ginocchiere *f* 220
ginocchio *m* 12
giocare 229, 273
giocatore *m* 220, 221, 231, 273
giocatore di base *m* 228
giocatore di cricket *m* 225
giocatore di hockey su ghiaccio *m* 224
giocatore di pallacanestro *m* 226
giocattoli *m* 105
giocattolo *m* 75
giocattolo di pezza *m* 75
giochi *m* 272
giochi con la racchetta *m* 231
giochi da tavolo *m* 272
gioco *m* 75, 230, 273
gioco a premi *m* 178
gioielleria *f* 114
gioielli *m* 36
gioielliere *m* 188
Giordania 318
giornale *m* 112
giornalino a fumetti *m* 112
giornalista *m* 190
giorno *m* 306
Giorno del Ringraziamento *m* 27
giorno feriale *m* 306
Giove 280
giovedì 306
gipsofila *f* 110
girabacchino *m* 78
giradischi *m* 268
giraffa *f* 179, 291
girasole *m* 184, 297
giravolta *f* 238
girino *m* 294
giro *m* 228
girocollo *m* 33
girovita *m* 35
giù 320
giubbotto da sport *m* 33
giubbotto di salvataggio *m* 240
giudice *m* 181
giudice di linea *m* 220, 230
giugno 306
giunco *m* 86
giuria *f* 180
gladiolo *m* 110
glassare 139
glassatura *f* 141
gluteo *m* 16
gneiss *m* 288
gobba *f* 291
gobbo *m* 179
gocce *f* 109
gocciolatoio *m* 67
gocciolatore *m* 53
gola *f* 19, 284
golf *m* 32, 232
golfista *m/f* 232
golfo mistico *m* 254
gomito *m* 13
gomma *f* 163
gomma da masticare *f* 113
gommone *m* 215
gong *m* 257
goniometro *m* 165
gonna *f* 30, 34
gorilla *m* 291
gotico 301
grafite *f* 289
grammo *m* 310
granaglie *f* 130
granaio *m* 182

italiano

granato *m* 288
granchio *m* 121, 295
grande 321
grande magazzino *m* 105
grandine *f* 286
granito *m* 288
grano *m* 130, 184
grano di pepe *m* 132
grano spezzato *m* 130
granturco *m* 122, 130, 184
grappetta *f* 173
grassi 39
grasso 41, 321
grasso *m* 119
gratella *f* 69
graticcio *m* 84
grattacielo *m* 299, 300
grattugia *f* 68
grattugiare 67
gravidanza *f* 52
gravità *f* 280
grazie 322
Grecia 316
green *m* 232
gregge *m* 183
grembiule *m* 38, 69
grembiulino *m* 30
grembo *m* 52
Grenada 314
gridare 25
grigi 39
grigio 274
griglia per barbecue *f* 267
grillo *m* 295
Groenlandia 314
gronda *f* 58
grondaia *f* 58
gru *f* 187, 216, 292
gruccia *f* 70
guaiava *f* 128
guancia *f* 14
guanciale *m* 70
guanti *m* 30, 36, 237
guanti da giardinaggio *m* 89
guanto *m* 224, 233, 236, 246
guanto da forno *m* 69
guantone *m* 228
guardare la televisione 269
guardia *f* 180
guardia carceraria *f* 181
guardia di sicurezza *f* 189
guardialinee *m* 223
guardrail *m* 195
guarnizione *f* 61
Guatemala 314
guêpière *f* 35
gufo *m* 292
guida *f* 260
guida a destra *f* 201
guida a sinistra *f* 201
guida al negozio *f* 104
guida turistica *f* 260
guidafilo *m* 276
guidare 195
Guinea 317
Guinea Bissau 317
Guinea Equatoriale 317
guscio *m* 129, 137, 293
Guyana 315
Guyana Francese 315

H

Haiti 314
hamburger *m* 154
hamburger di pollo *m* 155
hamburger vegetariano *m* 155
handicap *m* 233
hardware *m* 176
Hawaii 314
heavy metal *m* 259
Himalaia *m* 313
hockey *m* 224
hockey su ghiaccio *m* 224
hockey sull'erba *m* 224
Honduras 314
hot dog *m* 155
hovercraft *m* 215

I

iarda *f* 310
icona *f* 177
idrante *m* 95
idraulico *m* 188
idroterapia *f* 55
idrovolante *m* 211
ieri 306
igiene del neonato *f* 74
igiene dentale *f* 72
igiene femminile *m* 108
igname *m* 125
igneo 288
iguana *f* 293
illuminazione *f* 105
imbarazzato 25
imbarcare 217
imbarcazioni *f* 215
imbastire 277
imbottito 159
imbrunire *m* 304
imbuto *m* 166
impalcatura *f* 186
imparare 163
impastare 138
impermeabile *m* 31, 32
impianto idraulico *m* 61
impianto stereo *m* 268
impiegato *m* 24
impiegato delle poste *m* 98
importo *m* 96
imposta *f* 96
impotente 20
impronta digitale *f* 94
impugnatura *f* 230
imputato *m* 181
imputazione *f* 180
in cima 320
in differita 178
in diretta 178
in orario 305
in polvere 77
in rete 177
in salamoia 143
in stato interessante 52
in tensione 60
inalatore *m* 44, 109
incarto *m* 111
incassare 97
incendio *m* 95
inchiostro *m* 275
incidente *m* 46
incidente stradale *m* 203
incidere 79
incinta 52
incisione *f* 275
incisivo *m* 50
incollare 82
incontro *m* 237
incubatrice *f* 53
indaco 274
indagine *f* 94
India 318
indicatore di livello dell'olio *m* 202
indicazioni *f* 260
indice *m* 15
indirizzo *m* 98
indirizzo e-mail *m* 177
indivia *f* 123
Indonesia 319
indumenti impermeabili *m* 267
indumenti per la notte *m* 31
indumenti termici *m* 267
infarto *m* 44
infermiera *f* 45, 48, 189
infezione *f* 44
infilare 277
influenza *f* 44
inforcare 90
informazione *f* 261
informazione turistica *f* 261
infreddatura *f* 44
ingegneria *f* 169
ingorgo *m* 195
ingrandimento *m* 271
ingrandire 172
ingresso *m* 59, 100
ingresso vietato *m* 195
inguine *m* 12
iniezione *f* 48
iniziare la scuola 26
inizio *m* 321
innamorarsi 26
innestare 91
innocente 181
inoculazione *f* 45
inondazione *f* 287
inquilino *m* 58
insalata *f* 149
insalata mista *f* 158
insalata verde *f* 158
insegna *f* 104
insegnante *f* 190
insegnante *m/f* 162
inseguire 229
insettifugo *m* 108
insonnia *f* 71
installazione *f* 177
insulina *f* 109
integrale 131
integratore *m* 55
intercostale *m* 16
Internet 177
interno *m* 200
intero 129, 132
interruttore *m* 60
interruttore per le luci *m* 201
interruzione di corrente *f* 60
intervallo *m* 223, 254
intervistatore *m* 179
intestino crasso *m* 18
intestino tenue *m* 18
intonacare 83
intonaco *m* 82
intrattenimenti in casa *m* 268
invasare 91
inverno *m* 31, 307
invertebrati *m* 295
investigatore *m* 94
investimento *m* 97
ionosfera *f* 286
iPad *m* 176
ipnositerapia *f* 55
ipoallergenico 41
iPod *m* 268
ipoteca *f* 96
ipotenusa *f* 164
ippodromo *m* 243
ippoglosso *m* 120
ippopotamo *m* 291
Iran 318
Iraq 318
iride *f* 51
iris *m* 110
Irlanda 316
irrigare 183
irrigatore *m* 89
Islanda 316
isola *f* 282
Isola Falkland 315
Isola Galapagos 315
isolamento *m* 61
Isole Baleari 316
Isole Salomone 319
Israele 318
istruttore individuale *m* 250
istruzioni *f* 109
Italia 316
itinerario *m* 260

J

jazz *m* 259
jeans *m* 31
jolly *m* 273
judo *m* 236
Jugoslavia 316

K

k.o. *m* 237
Kaliningrad 316
karate *m* 236
kayak *m* 241
Kazakistan 318
kendo *m* 236
Kenya 317
ketchup *m* 135
kickboxing *m* 236
Kirghizistan 318
kit per riparazioni *m* 207
kiwi *m* 128
koala *m* 291
Kosovo 316
kung-fu *m* 236
Kuwait 318

L

labbra *f* 20
labbro *m* 14
laboratorio *m* 78, 166
lacca *f* 38, 79
laccio *m* 37
lacrima *f* 51
lacrosse *m* 249
lago *m* 285
lama *f* 60, 66, 78, 89, 246
lama rotante *f* 211
lametta *f* 73
lampada *f* 50, 62, 178
lampadina *f* 70
lampadina a risparmio energetico *f* 60
lampeggiatore *m* 270
lampone *m* 127
lana *f* 277
lana d'acciaio *f* 81
lancetta dei minuti *f* 304
lancetta dei secondi *f* 304
lancetta delle ore *f* 304
lancia di salvataggio *f* 214
lanciarazzi *m* 281
lanciare 225, 229, 245
lanciatore *m* 225
lancio *m* 281
lancio del disco *m* 234
lancio del giavellotto *m* 234
lancio del peso *m* 234
Laos 318
larghezza *f* 165
largo 321
larice *m* 296
laringe *f* 19
lassativo *m* 109
lastrina *f* 167
latitudine *f* 283
lato *m* 164
latte *m* 136, 156
latte condensato *m* 136
latte detergente *m* 41
latte di capra *m* 136
latte di mucca *m* 136
latte di pecora *m* 137
latte in polvere *m* 137
latte intero *m* 136
latte parzialmente scremato *m* 136
latte scremato *m* 136
latticini *m* 107, 136
lattina *f* 145, 311
lattosio *m* 137
lattuga *f* 123
laurea *f* 169
laurearsi 26
laureata *f* 169
lava *f* 283
lavagna *f* 162
lavanderia *f* 76, 115
lavandino *m* 38, 66, 72
lavare 38, 77
lavasciuga *m* 76
lavasecco *m* 115
lavastoviglie *f* 66
lavatrice *f* 76
lavori stradali *m* 187, 195
lavoro *m* 172
lavoro a maglia *m* 277
lecca lecca *m* 113
lega per saldatura *f* 79, 81
legamento *m* 17
legge *f* 180
leggere 162
leggero 321
legno *m* 79, 187, 275
legno dolce *m* 79
legno duro *m* 79
legumi secchi *m* 130
lente *f* 51
lenti a contatto *f* 51
lenticchie marroni *f* 131
lenticchie rosse *f* 131
lentiggine *f* 15
lento 321
lenza *f* 244
lenzuolo *m* 71, 74
leone *m* 291
leone marino *m* 290
Lesotho 317
lettera *f* 98, 272
lettera per posta aerea *f* 98
letteratura *f* 162, 169
lettiga *f* 48
lettino *m* 74
lettino da campeggio *m* 266
lettino solare *m* 41
letto *m* 70
letto matrimoniale *m* 71
letto singolo *m* 71
Lettonia 316
lettore di cd *m* 268
lettore di dvd *m* 268
lettore ottico *m* 106

leva *f* 61, 150
leva del cambio *f* 201, 207
leva del freno *f* 207
leva di emergenza *f* 209
leva per il pneumatico *f* 207
lezione *f* 163
Libano 318
libbra *f* 310
libellula *f* 295
Liberia 317
libero 321
libertà per buona condotta *f* 181
Libia 317
libreria *f* 63, 115
libretto degli assegni *m* 96
libro *m* 168
libro di testo *m* 163
libro paga *m* 175
licenza di pesca *f* 245
Liechtenstein 316
lievito *m* 138
lima *f* 81
limetta *f* 41, 126
limite *m* 225
limite di velocità *m* 195
limo *m* 85
limonata *f* 144
limone *m* 126
limousine *f* 199
linea *f* 225
linea dei tre punti *f* 226
linea del gol *f* 220
linea della porta *f* 224
linea di centro *f* 226
linea di fallo *f* 229
linea di fondo *f* 223, 226, 230
linea di gioco *f* 233
linea di palla morta *f* 221
linea di partenza *f* 234
linea di servizio *f* 230
linea di tiro libero *f* 226
linea di touch *f* 221
linea divisoria *f* 194
linea laterale *f* 220, 226, 230
linee *f* 165
linfatico 19
lingua *f* 19, 37, 118, 162
lino *m* 184, 277
liquido 77
liquido amniotico *m* 52
liquirizia *f* 113
liquore *m* 145
lisci 39
lista dei libri *f* 168
lista dei vini *f* 152
listino *m* 154
litchi *m* 128
litro *m* 311
Lituania 316
livella *f* 80, 187
livello *m* 163
livido *m* 46
locomotiva *f* 208
lombo *m* 121
longitudine *f* 283
lontano 320
lontra *f* 290
lotta greco-romana *f* 236
lozione *f* 109
lozione per il corpo *f* 73
lozione tonificante *f* 41
lucchetto *m* 207
luce *f* 217
luce del portico *f* 58
luce del sole *f* 286
luce di lettura *f* 210
lucertola *f* 293
luci *f* 94
luci intermittenti *f* 201
lucidare 77
lucidatore *m* 78
lucido 83, 271
luglio 306
lumaca *f* 295
luna *f* 280
luna nuova *f* 280
luna park *m* 262
luna piena *f* 280
lunaria *f* 288
lunedì 306
lunghezza *f* 165, 310
lunghezza d'onda *f* 179
lungo 32, 320
lungomare *m* 265
lungometraggio *m* 269
luoghi d'interesse *m* 261
luogo d'interesse turistico *m* 260
lupini *m* 297
lupo *m* 290
Lussemburgo 316

M

macadamia *f* 129
macchina da caffè *f* 150
macchina da cucire *f* 276
macchina del caffè *f* 148
macchina fotografica *f* 260
macchina fotografica digitale *f* 270
macchina fotografica Polaroid *f* 270
macchina fotografica usa e getta *f* 270
macchina per esercizi *f* 250
macchina per step *f* 250
macchinari *m* 187
Macedonia 316
macellaio *m* 118, 188
macelleria *f* 114
macinato 132, 144
macinatore di rifiuti *m* 61
macis *m* 132
macramè *m* 277
Madagascar 317
madre *f* 22
magazzino *m* 216
maggio 306
maggiorana *f* 133
maglia *f* 36
maglietta *f* 30, 33, 54
maglione *m* 33
magma *f* 283
magnesio *m* 109
magro 321
maiale *m* 118, 185
maialino *m* 185
maionese *f* 135
mais *m* 124
mal di denti *m* 50
mal di stomaco *m* 44
mal di testa *m* 44
malachite *f* 288
malattia *f* 44
malattia trasmissibile per via sessuale *f* 20
Malawi 317
Malaysia 318
Maldive 318
Mali 317
Malta 316
malta *f* 83, 187
mammiferi *m* 290
manchego *m* 142
mandare da uno specialista 49
mandarino *m* 126
mandato *m* 180
mandibola *f* 14, 17
mandorla *f* 129
mandorla brasiliana *f* 129
mandorle *f* 151
mandria *f* 183
mandrino *m* 78
manette *f* 94
manganello *m* 94
mangiare 64
mangiare sul posto 154
mangiatoia *f* 183
mango *m* 128
mangostina *f* 128
manica *f* 34
manichino *m* 276
manici *m* 37
manico *m* 36, 88, 106, 187, 258
manicotto *m* 45
manicure *f* 41
maniglia *f* 196, 200
mannaia *f* 68
mano *f* 13, 15
mano di fondo *f* 83
mano finale *f* 83
manopola di messa a fuoco *f* 167
mantello *m* 282
mantide religiosa *f* 295
manuale 200
manubri *m* 250
manubrio *m* 207, 251
manzo *m* 118
mapo *m* 126
mappa *f* 261
mappa della metropolitana *f* 209
mappamondo *m* 312
Mar Baltico *m* 313
Mar Caspio *m* 313
Mar dei Caraibi *m* 312
Mar Mediterraneo *m* 313
Mar Nero *m* 313
Mar Rosso *m* 313
maracas *m* 257
maratona *f* 234
marca di bordo libero *f* 214
marcare 227
marcatore per le labbra *m* 40
marce *f* 206
marciapiede *m* 298
marcio 127
mare *m* 264, 282
Mare Arabico *m* 313
Mare del Nord *m* 312
margarina *f* 137
margherita *f* 110, 297
marinaio *m* 189
marinato 143, 159
marito *m* 22
marmellata *f* 134, 156
marmellata agli agrumi *f* 156
marmellata di agrumi *f* 134
marmellata di lamponi *f* 134
marmo *m* 288
Marocco 317
marrone 274
marsupio *m* 75, 291
Marte 280
martedì 306
martelletto *m* 181
martello *m* 68, 79, 80, 275
martello pneumatico *m* 187
martini *m* 151
marzapane *m* 141
marzo 306
mascara *m* 40
maschera *f* 228, 236, 239, 249, 255
maschera di bellezza *f* 41
maschera protettiva *f* 225
mascherina *f* 189
maschili 21
mass media *m* 178
massaggio *m* 54
masters *m* 169
matassa *f* 277
matematica *f* 162, 164
materassino *m* 74, 267
materassino ad aria *m* 267
materasso *m* 70, 74
materiali *m* 79, 187
maternità *f* 49
matita *f* 163, 275
matita colorata *f* 163
matita per gli occhi *f* 40
matita per le sopracciglia *f* 40
matrice *f* 96
matrigna *f* 23
matrimonio *m* 26, 35
mattarello *m* 69
mattino *m* 305
mattone *m* 187
maturo 129
Mauritania 317
Maurizio 317
mazza *f* 187, 224, 225, 228, 249
mazza da hockey *f* 224
mazza di ferro *f* 233
mazza di legno *f* 233
mazza ricurva *f* 233
mazze da golf *f* 233
mazzetto *m* 111
mazzetto odoroso *m* 132
mazzo di carte *m* 273
mazzo di fiori *m* 111
mazzuolo *m* 78
MDF *m* 79
meccanica *f* 202
meccanico *m* 188, 203
medaglie *f* 235
medicamento *m* 109
medicina *f* 109, 169
medicina aiurvedica *f* 55
medicina per la tosse *f* 108
medico *m* 45, 189
medio *m* 15
meditazione *f* 54
medusa *f* 295
mela *f* 126
mela cotogna *f* 128
melanzana *f* 125
melodia *f* 259
melograno *m* 128
melone *m* 127
memoria *f* 176
meno 165
mensile 307
mensola *f* 67
mensole *f* 66
menta *f* 133
mentina *f* 113
mento *m* 14
menù *m* 148, 153, 154
menù del pranzo *m* 152
menù della cena *m* 152
menù per bambini *m* 153
mercato *m* 97, 115
merceria *f* 105
mercoledì 306
mercurio *m* 289
Mercurio 280
meridiana *f* 262
meringa *f* 140
merlango *m* 120
merluzzo *m* 120
mescolare 138, 273
mese *m* 306
mesosfera *f* 286
messa a terra *f* 60
messa in fase *f* 203
messaggi *m* 100
messaggio (SMS) *m* 99
messaggio vocale *m* 99
Messico 314
mestieri *m* 188, 190
mestolo *m* 68
mestruazione *f* 20
meta *f* 221
metacarpo *m* 17
metalli *m* 289
metallo *m* 79
metamorfico 288
metatarso *m* 17
meteora *f* 280
metodi *m* 159
metro *m* 80, 276, 310
metro quadro *m* 310
metropolitana *f* 209
mettere a bagno 130
mettere a fuoco 271
mettere in piega 38
mettere la sveglia 71
mezza pensione *f* 101
mezzaluna *f* 280
mezzanotte *f* 305
mezzo litro *m* 311
mezzogiorno *m* 305
mica *f* 289
microfono *m* 179, 258
microscopio *m* 167
miele condensato *m* 134
miele sciolto *m* 134
mietitrebbia *f* 182
miglio *m* 130, 310
mignolo *m* 15
mignolo del piede *m* 15
miliardo 309
milione *m* 309
mille 309
millennio *m* 307
millenovecento 307
millenovecentodieci 307
millenovecentouno 307
millepiedi *m* 295
milligrammo *m* 310
millilitro *m* 311
millimetro *m* 310
milza *f* 18
minerali *m* 289
minestra *f* 153, 158
minibar *m* 101
minigonna *f* 34
minuto *m* 304
miopia *f* 51
mirino *m* 271
mirtillo *m* 127
miscelatore *m* 66, 150
mischia *f* 221
missile *m* 211
misura *f* 151
misura di liquido *f* 311

italiano

misurare 310
misuratore elettronico della pressione *m* 45
misure *f* 165
misurino *m* 150
mitragliatrice *f* 189
mittente *m* 98
mobile *m* 74
mocassino *m* 37
moda *f* 277
modella *f* 169
modellismo *m* 275
modello *m* 190, 276
modulo di prelievo *m* 96
modulo di versamento *m* 96
modulo lunare *m* 281
moglie *f* 22
molare *m* 50
Moldavia 316
mollare l'ancora *f* 217
molletta *f* 38, 76, 173
molletta per il naso *f* 238
molo *m* 217
moltiplicare 165
moltiplicato per 165
Monaco 316
monete *f* 97
monete non utilizzate *f* 99
mongolfiera *f* 211
Mongolia 318
monitor *m* 53, 172
monopoly *m* 272
monorotaia *f* 208
monouso 109
monovolume *f* 199
monsone *m* 287
montagna *f* 284
Montagne Rocciose *f* 312
montagne russe *m* 262
montatura *f* 51
montgomery *m* 31
monumento *m* 261
mora *f* 127
mora-lampone *f* 127
morbido 129, 321
morbillo *m* 44
mordente per legno *m* 79
morire 26
morsa *f* 78
morsetto *m* 78, 166, 167
morso *m* 46, 78, 242
mortaio *m* 68, 167
mosca *f* 244, 295
moschea *f* 300
mossa *f* 273
mosse *f* 237
mostarda *f* 135
mostarda con semi *f* 135
moto da corsa *f* 205
moto da cross *f* 205
moto da turismo *f* 205
motocicletta *f* 204
motociclismo *m* 249
motocross *m* 249
motore *m* 88, 202, 204, 210
motore fuoribordo *m* 215
motoscafo *m* 214
motoslitta *f* 247
mountain bike *f* 206
mouse *m* 176
mousse *m* 141
Mozambico 317
mozzarella *f* 142
mozzo *m* 206
mucca *f* 185
muffin *m* 140
mulinello *m* 214, 244
multivitamina *f* 109
mungere 183
municipio *m* 299
muratore *m* 186, 188
muro *m* 58, 186, 222
muscoli *m* 16
museo *m* 261
musica *f* 162
musica classica *f* 255, 259
musica da ballo *f* 259
musica folk *f* 259
musical *m* 255
musicista *m* 191
muso *m* 210, 293
mutande di plastica *f* 30
mutandine *f* 35
Myanmar 318

N

naan *m* 139
nailon *m* 277
Namibia 317
narciso *m* 111
narice *f* 14
nascere 26
nascita *f* 52
naso *m* 14
nassa *f* 245
nastro *m* 27, 39, 111, 141, 235
nastro adesivo *m* 47, 173
nastro adesivo coprente *m* 83
nastro convogliatore *m* 106
nastro isolante *m* 81
nastro trasportatore *m* 212
Natale *m* 27
natica *f* 13
naturale 256
naturopatia *f* 55
nausea *f* 44
nave *f* 214
nave da crociera *f* 215
nave da guerra *f* 215
nave da trasporto *f* 215
nave porta container *f* 215
navetta *f* 197
navigare 240
navigatore satellitare *m* 195
navigazione *f* 177
navigazione via satellite *f* 201
nazione *f* 315
nebbia *f* 287
nebulizzatore *m* 311
nebulosa *f* 280
negativo *m* 271
negatoscopio *m* 45
negozio *m* 298
negozio dell'usato *m* 115
negozio di alimenti biologici *m* 115
negozio di animali *m* 115
negozio di antiquariato *m* 114
negozio di articoli da regalo *m* 114
negozio di articoli fotografici *m* 115
negozio di articoli per l'arte *m* 115
negozio di calzature *m* 114
negozio di dischi *m* 115
negozio di dolciumi *m* 113
negozio di ferramenta *m* 114
negozio di liquori *m* 115
negozio di mobili *m* 115
negozio duty free *m* 213
neo *m* 14
neoclassico 301
neonato *m* 53
Nepal 318
nero 39, 272, 274
nervo *m* 19, 50
nervo ottico *m* 51
nervoso 19, 25
Nettuno 280
neurologia *f* 49
neutro 60
neve *f* 287
nevischio *m* 286
Nicaragua 314
nichel *m* 289
Niger 317
Nigeria 317
nipote *f* 22, 23
nipote *m* 22, 23
nipoti *m* 23
no 322
nocca *f* 15
nocciola *f* 129
noccioline *f* 151
noccioline americane *f* 151
nocciolo *m* 122, 129
noce *f* 129
noce di cocco *f* 129
noce moscata *f* 132
non pastorizzato 137
non piegare 98
nonna *f* 22
nonni *m* 23
nonno *m* 22
nono 309
nord *m* 312
normale 39
Norvegia 316
nota *f* 256
notte *f* 305
novanta 308
novantesimo 309
nove 308
novecento 308
novembre 306
nuca *f* 13
nucleo esterno *m* 282
nucleo interno *m* 282
numeratore *m* 165
numeri *m* 308
numero *m* 226
numero del binario *m* 208
numero del percorso *m* 196
numero del volo *m* 213
numero della camera *m* 100
numero dell'uscita *m* 213
numero di conto *m* 96
nuora *f* 22
nuotare 238
nuotatore *m* 238
nuoto *m* 238
nuoto sincronizzato *m* 239
nuoto subacqueo *m* 239
Nuova Zelanda 319
nuovo 321
nuvola *f* 287
nuvoloso 286

O

obiettivo *m* 167, 270
oblò *m* 214
oboe *m* 257
oca *f* 119, 293
occhialetti *m* 238
occhiali *m* 51, 247
occhiali da sole *m* 51, 265
occhiali protettivi *m* 81, 167
occhiello *m* 37, 244, 276
occhio *m* 14, 51
occhio rosso *m* 271
occupato 99, 321
Oceania 319
oceano *m* 282
Oceano Antartico *m* 313
Oceano Artico *m* 312
Oceano Atlantico *m* 312
Oceano Indiano *m* 312
Oceano Pacifico *m* 312
oculare *m* 167, 269
odometro *m* 201
offerte *f* 106
oftalmologia *f* 49
oggetto *m* 261
oggi 306
okra *f* 122
oli *m* 134
olii essenziali *m* 55
olio *m* 142, 199
olio aromatizzato *m* 134
olio di colza *m* 135
olio di mais *m* 135
olio di mandorla *m* 134
olio di noccioline *m* 134
olio di noce *m* 134
olio di semi di arachide *m* 135
olio di semi di girasole *m* 134
olio di semi di sesamo *m* 134
olio di semi d'uva *m* 134
olio d'oliva *m* 134
olio spremuto a freddo *m* 135
olio vegetale *m* 135
oliva nera *f* 143
oliva ripiena *f* 143
oliva verde *f* 143
olive *f* 151
olivetta *f* 31
olmo *m* 296
oltre 320
Oman 318
ombelico *m* 12
ombrello *m* 36
ombrellone *m* 264
ombretto *m* 40
omeopatia *f* 55
omero *m* 17
omogeneizzato 137
oncia *f* 310
oncologia *f* 49
onda *f* 241, 264
onda lunga *f* 179
onice *f* 289
opaco 83, 271
opale *m* 288
opera *f* 255
opera teatrale *f* 254
operatore *m* 99
operazione *f* 48
opuscolo *m* 175
opuscolo vacanza *m* 212
ora *f* 304, 304
ora di punta *f* 209
orari *m* 261
orario *m* 197, 209, 261
orario delle visite *m* 48
orbita *f* 280
orchestra *f* 254, 256
orchidea *f* 111
ordinare 153
ordine *m* 180
ordine del giorno *m* 174
orecchino *m* 36
orecchio *m* 14
orecchioni *m* 44
oreficeria *f* 275
organi riproduttivi *m* 20
origami *m* 275
origano *m* 133
orizzontale 271
orlo *m* 34
ormeggiare 217
ormeggio *m* 217
ormone *m* 20
ornamentale 87
ornamenti oggetti per giardini *m* 84
ornitologia *f* 263
oro *m* 289
oro *f* 235
orologio *m* 304
orologio da polso *m* 36
orsacchiotto *m* 75
orso *m* 291
orso polare *m* 291
ortica *f* 297
orto *m* 85, 182
ortopedia *f* 49
orzo *m* 130, 184
ospedale *m* 48
ospite *m* 64, 100
ossicocco *m* 127
ossidiana *f* 288
osso *m* 17, 119
ostacolo *m* 243
osteopatia *f* 54
ostetrica *f* 53
ostetrico *m* 52
ostrica *f* 121
otorinolaringologia *f* 49
ottagono *m* 164
ottanta 308
ottantesimo 309
ottavo 309
ottico *m* 51, 189
otto 308
ottobre 306
ottocento 308
ottoni *m* 256
otturare 82
otturazione *f* 50
ouverture *f* 256
ovaia *f* 20
ovale *m* 164
overpar *m* 233
ovest *m* 312
ovulazione *f* 20, 52
ovulo *m* 20

P

pacchetto *m* 311
pacchetto di sigarette *m* 112
pacco *m* 99
padella *f* 69
padella per grigliare *f* 69
padre *m* 22
padrona di casa *f* 64
padrone di casa *m* 58, 64
paesaggio *m* 284
paese *m* 315
Paesi Bassi 316
pagaia *f* 241
pagamento *m* 96
pagare 153
Pakistan 318
pala *f* 187
palafreniere *m* 243
palato *m* 19
palco *m* 254
palcoscenico *m* 254
palestra *f* 101, 250

paletta *f* 77, 89, 265
paletta forata *f* 68
palla *f* 75, 228, 230
palla da bowling *f* 249
pallacanestro *f* 226
pallanuoto *f* 239
pallavolo *f* 227
palleggiare 223
palleggio *m* 230, 231
pallet *m* 186
pallina *f* 149, 224
pallina da cricket *f* 225
pallina da golf *f* 233
pallone *m* 220, 221, 222, 226
pallone da spiaggia *m* 265
palma *f* 86, 296
palmo *m* 15
palo *m* 222, 245, 266
palo della porta *m* 220
palpebra *f* 51
palude *f* 285
pan di Spagna *m* 140
Panama 314
panca *f* 250
pancetta *f* 118, 157
panchina *f* 262
pancreas *m* 18
panda *m* 291
pane *m* 107, 157
pane affettato *m* 138
pane alla frutta *m* 139
pane bianco *m* 139
pane biscottato *m* 139, 156
pane con lievito naturale *m* 139
pane con semi *m* 139
pane di granaio *m* 139
pane di mais *m* 139
pane di segale *m* 138
pane e le farine *m* 138
pane fritto all'uovo *m* 157
pane integrale *m* 139, 149
pane lievitato con bicarbonato di sodio *m* 139
pane tostato *m* 157
panettiere *m* 139
panificio *m* 114, 138
panino *m* 139, 143, 155
paninoteca *f* 143
panna *f* 137, 140, 157
panna acida *f* 137
panna densa *f* 137
panna fresca *f* 137
panna liquida *f* 137
panna montata *f* 137
panne *f* 203
pannello degli orari *m* 213
pannello di protezione *m* 66
panni sporchi *m* 76
pannolino *m* 75
pannolino di spugna *m* 30
pannolino usa e getta *m* 30
pantacollant *m* 31
pantaloncini *m* 30
pantaloni *m* 32, 34
pantaloni da equitazione *m* 242
pantaloni di felpa *m* 33
pantofole *f* 31
papaia *f* 128
papavero *m* 297
pappagallo *m* 293
paprica *f* 132
Papua Nuova Guinea 319
par *m* 233
parabrezza *m* 198, 205
paracadute *m* 248
paracadutismo *m* 248
paracadutismo libero *m* 248
paracolpi *m* 74
paradenti *m* 237
parafango *m* 205
paraginocchio *m* 205
Paraguay 315
parallelo 165
parallelogramma *m* 164
paramedico *m* 94
parapendio *m* 248
parare 223
parastinchi *m* 224, 225
parata *f* 237
paraurti *m* 198
paravento *m* 265
parcheggiare 195
parcheggio *m* 298
parcheggio per disabili *m* 195
parchimetro *m* 195
parco *m* 262
parco a tema *m* 262
parco giochi *m* 263
parco nazionale *m* 261
pareggio *m* 223
parenti *m* 23
parmigiano *m* 142
parrucca *f* 39
parrucchiere *m* 38, 115, 188
parte bassa *f* 239
parte profonda *f* 239
partecipare 174
partenze *f* 213
partita *f* 230
partitura musicale *f* 255
partner di affari m/f 24
parto *m* 52, 53
parto assistito *m* 53
pascolo *m* 182, 285
Pasqua *f* 27
Pasqua ebraica *f* 27
passaggio *m* 106, 226
passaggio pedonale *m* 195, 212
passaporto *m* 213
passare 220, 223
passeggero *m* 216
passeggiata *f* 75
passeggino *m* 75
passerella *f* 214
passero *m* 292
passo *m* 243
pasta *f* 138, 140, 149, 158
pasta filo *f* 140
pasta sfoglia *f* 140
pastelli *m* 274
pasticca *f* 109
pasticca per la gola *f* 109
pasticceria *f* 114
pasticche per il mal d'auto *f* 109
pasticci di carne *m* 143
pasticcio *m* 158
pastinaca *f* 125
pasto *m* 64, 75
pasto con hamburger *m* 154
pastorizzato 137
patata *f* 124
patata dolce *f* 125
patata novella *f* 124
patate frite *f* 154
patatine *f* 113, 151
patchwork *m* 277
pâté *m* 142, 156
patio *m* 85
patio in legno *m* 85
patologia *f* 49
patrigno *m* 23
pattinaggio *m* 263
pattinaggio artistico *m* 247
pattinaggio di velocità *m* 247
pattinaggio in linea *m* 249
pattinaggio su ghiaccio *m* 247
pattinare 224
pattino *m* 224, 247
pattumiera *f* 61, 67
pausa *f* 256, 269
pavimentazione *f* 85
pavimento *m* 62, 71
pavone *m* 293
paziente *m* 45
paziente esterno *m* 48
pecan *m* 129
pecora *f* 185
pedalare 207
pedale *m* 61, 206
pedale del freno *m* 205
pedali *m* 257
pedana *f* 235
pedana del letto *f* 71
pedana di lancio *f* 228
pedana elastica *f* 235
pediatria *f* 49
pedicure *f* 41
pedina *f* 272
pedone *m* 272
pelapatate *m* 68
pelle *f* 14, 119
pellicano *m* 292
pellicina *f* 15
pellicola *f* 260, 271
pellicola radiografica *f* 50
pendaglio *m* 36
pendice *f* 284
pendolare *m* 208
pene *m* 21
penisola *f* 282
penna *f* 163
pennello *m* 40, 83, 274
pennello da colla *m* 82
pennello da cucina *m* 69
pennello per le labbra *m* 40
pensilina *f* 197
pensione completa *f* 101
pensione con colazione *f* 101
pentagono *m* 164
pentagramma *m* 256
pentola *f* 69
peonia *f* 111
pepe *m* 64, 152
pepe della Giamaica *m* 132
peperoncino *m* 124, 132, 143
peperone *m* 124
per 320
per favore 322
pera *f* 127
percentuale *f* 165
percussione *f* 257
perdente *m* 273
perdere 273
perenne 86
perfezionamento *m* 169
perforatore *m* 173
pergola *f* 84
pericolo *m* 195
periferia *f* 299
periodico *m* 168
permanente *f* 39
permesso 322
perone *m* 17
perpendicolare 165
persiana *f* 58
persona suspetta *f* 181
personale *m* 175
persone *f* 12, 16
Perù 315
pesante 321
pesare 310
pesca *f* 126, 128, 244, 245
pesca con la fiocina *f* 245
pesca con la mosca *f* 245
pesca dalla riva *f* 245
pesca in acqua dolce *f* 245
pesca in alto mare *f* 245
pesca in mare *f* 245
pesca noce *f* 126
pesca sportiva *f* 245
pescare con la rete 245
pescatore *m* 189, 244
pesce *m* 107, 120
pesce affumicato *m* 143
pesce con patatine *m* 155
pesce rosso *m* 294
pesce spada *m* 120, 294
pescheria *f* 114, 120
pesci *m* 294
pescivendola *f* 188
peso *m* 166, 244
peso alla nascita *m* 53
pestello *m* 68, 167
pesticida *m* 89, 183
petalo *m* 297
petizione *f* 180
petroliera *f* 215
pettinare 38
pettine *m* 38, 121
petto *m* 119
pettorale *m* 16
piadina *f* 155
pialla *f* 81
piallare 79
pianerottolo *m* 59
pianeta *m* 280, 282
piangere 25
piano *m* 58
piano di lavoro *m* 66
piano di mixaggio *m* 179
piano inferiore *m* 141
piano superiore *m* 141
piano terra *m* 104
pianoforte *m* 256
pianta acquatica *f* 86
pianta adatta all'ombra *f* 87
pianta copriterreno *f* 87
pianta da fiore *f* 87
pianta da fiori *f* 297
pianta da vaso *f* 87, 110
pianta del piano *f* 261
pianta del piede *f* 15
pianta grassa *f* 87
piantare 183
piantare una tenda 266
piante *f* 86, 296
piante da giardino *f* 86
piante da roccia *f* 87
pianura *f* 285
piastra per i capelli *f* 38
piastra *f* 67
piastrellare 82
piastrina dell'ago *f* 276
piatti *m* 64
piatti del giorno *m* 152
piattino *m* 65
piatto *m* 310
piatto da gratin *m* 69
piatto piano *m* 65
piatto principale *m* 153
piazza *f* 299
piazzole disponibili *f* 266
picca *f* 273
piccante 124
picchio *m* 292
piccione *m* 292
piccolo 321
piccolo galoppo *m* 243
piccone *m* 187
picnic *m* 263
piede *m* 12, 15, 310
piede quadro *m* 310
piedino *m* 60, 276
piega alla francese *f* 39
pieno 321
pietra *f* 36
piffero *m* 257
pigiama *m* 33
pigiamino *m* 30
pilates *m* 251
pillola *f* 21, 109
pilota *m* 190, 211
pilota da corsa *m* 249
pin *m* 96
ping pong *m* 231
pinguino *m* 292
pinna *f* 239, 292
pinna dorsale *f* 294
pinna pettorale *f* 294
pinnacolo *m* 300
pinne di razza *f* 120
pino *m* 296
pinolo *m* 129
pinta *f* 311
pinza spelafilo *f* 81
pinza tagliafilo *f* 80
pinze *f* 150
pinze tonde *f* 80
pinzette *f* 40, 47, 167
pioggia *f* 287
piolo *m* 266
piombata 199
pioppo *m* 296
piovoso 286
piovra *f* 295
pipa *f* 112
pipetta *f* 167
pipistrello *m* 290
piramide *f* 164
pirofilo 69
pirolo *m* 258
piscina *f* 101, 238, 250
piscina gonfiabile *f* 263
piselli *m* 131
piselli spaccati *m* 131
pisello *m* 122
pista *f* 212, 234
pista ciclabile *f* 206
pista da hockey su ghiaccio *f* 224
pista da sci *f* 246
pistacchio *m* 129
pistola *f* 94
pistola per colla *f* 78
pita *f* 139
pitcher *m* 229
pittrice *f* 191
pittura *f* 83, 274
più 165
più tardi 304
piuma *f* 293
piumino *m* 40
pizza *f* 154
pizzeria *f* 154
pizzo *m* 35
placca *f* 50

italiano

placca da forno *f* 69
placcare 220
placenta *f* 52
platino *m* 289
play *m* 269
Plutone 280
pneumatico *m* 198, 205, 206
podalico 52
podio *m* 235, 256
podio di partenza *m* 238
poggiatesta *m* 200
poker *m* 273
poli *m* 282
poliestere *m* 277
politica *f* 169
polizia *f* 94
poliziotto *m* 189
pollaio *m* 185
pollame *m* 119
pollice *m* 15, 310
pollo *m* 119
pollo fritto *m* 155
pollo preparato *m* 119
polmone *m* 18
polo *m* 243
Polo Nord *m* 283
Polonia 316
polpa *f* 124, 127, 129
polpaccio *m* 13, 16
polpette *f* 158
polpo *m* 121
polsino *m* 32, 230
polso *m* 13, 15
poltrona *f* 63, 254
poltrona da dentista *f* 50
poltrone *f* 254
poltrone di platea *f* 254
polvere *f* 109
polvere di cacao *f* 148
polvere di curry *f* 132
pomata *f* 47
pomata antirossore *f* 74
pomello *m* 59
pomeriggio *m* 305
pomice *f* 73, 288
pomo *m* 242
pomo di Adamo *m* 19
pomodorino *m* 124
pomodoro *m* 125, 149, 157
pompa *f* 207
pompa da seno *f* 53
pompa di benzina *f* 199
pompelmo *m* 126
ponte *m* 214, 258, 300
ponte di comando *m* 214
ponte laterale *m* 240
pontile *m* 217
pop *m* 259
popcorn *m* 255
poppa *f* 240
porcellana *f* 105
porcile *m* 185
poro *m* 15
porridge *m* 157
porro *m* 125
porta *f* 176, 196, 209, 221, 223, 224, 247
porta a soffietto *f* 196
porta cipria *m* 40
porta della doccia *f* 72
porta esterna *f* 59
porta uovo *m* 137
portabagagli *m* 198, 209
portabebè *m* 74
portablocco con fermaglio *m* 173
portacarte a fisarmonica *m* 173
portaerei *f* 215
portafoglio *m* 37, 97
portaghiaccio *m* 150
portamonete *m* 37
portaombrelli *m* 59
portapacchi *m* 204
portapenne *m* 172
portasapone *m* 73
portasciugamani *m* 72
portate *f* 153
portatovagliolo *m* 65
portauovo *m* 65
portellone *m* 198
portico *m* 58
portiere *m* 222, 224
porto *m* 145, 214, 216, 217
porto da pesca *m* 217
porto per container *m* 216
porto per passeggeri *m* 216
Portogallo 316
portone *m* 58
porzione *f* 64
posacenere *m* 150
posate *f* 64
posizione *f* 232
posta aerea 98
posta elettronica *f* 98, 177
posta in arrivo *f* 177
posteggio *m* 266
posteggio dei taxi *m* 213
posteggio per bici *m* 207
poster *m* 255
poster scorrevole *m* 174
postino *m* 98, 190
potare 91
poto turistico *m* 217
pot-pourri *m* 111
pranzo *m* 64
pranzo di affari *m* 175
prateria *f* 285
prato *m* 85, 90, 262
prego 322
prematuro 52
premolare *m* 50
prenatale 52
prendere 220, 245
prendere appunti 163
prendere il sole 264
prendere in prestito 168
prenotare 168
prenotare un volo 212
preoccupato 25
prepuzio *m* 21
presa *f* 60, 237
presa di corrente *f* 266
presa per il piede *f* 241
presbiopia *f* 51
presentatore *m* 178
presentatrice *f* 179
presentazione *f* 174
preservativo *m* 21
preside *f* 163
presiedere 174
pressa per le gambe *f* 251
pressa per pettorali *f* 251
pressione dei pneumatici *f* 203
pressione del sangue *f* 44
prestito *m* 96, 168
presto 305
prezzemolo *m* 133
prezzo *m* 152, 199
prima 320
prima *f* 254
primato *m* 234
primato personale *m* 234
primavera *f* 307
primo 309
primo piano *m* 104
primula *f* 297
principato *m* 315
privo di sensi 47
proboscide *f* 291
procedimento *m* 180
processione *f* 27
processore *m* 176
procione *m* 290
prodotti per bambini *m* 107
prodotti per i denti *m* 108
prodotti per il bagno *m* 107
prodotti per la pelle *m* 108
produttore *m* 254
profondità *f* 165
profumato 130
profumeria *f* 105
profumo *m* 41
programma *m* 176, 254, 269
programmazione *f* 178
proiettore *m* 205, 259
proiettore digitale *m* 163
proiezione *f* 237
prolunga *f* 78
pronto soccorso *m* 47
propagare 91
proposta *f* 174
prosciutto *m* 119, 143, 156
prosciutto crudo *m* 143
prostata *f* 21
protezione *f* 88
prova *f* 181
provetta *f* 166
provincia *f* 315
prua *f* 215, 240
prugna *f* 126
prugna secca *f* 129
psichiatria *f* 49
psicoterapia *f* 55
pubblicità *f* 269
pubblico *m* 254
pubblico ministero *m* 180
Puerto Rico 314
pugilato *m* 236
pugno *m* 15, 237
pula *f* 130
pulcino *m* 185
puledro *m* 185
pulire 77
pulito 121
pullman *m* 196
pullman turistico *m* 197, 260
pulmino *m* 197
pulsante di chiamata *m* 48, 197
pulsante di scatto *m* 270
pulsazioni *f* 47
pungiglione *m* 295
punta *f* 36, 78, 122, 163, 246
punta dell'ago *f* 277
punta di sicurezza *f* 80
punta per metalli *f* 80
punta per muratura *f* 80
punta piana per legno *f* 80
puntaspilli *m* 276
punte *m* 80
punte da falegnameria *f* 80
punte per cacciavite *f* 80
punteggio *m* 220, 273
punti *m* 52, 173
puntina *f* 173
punto *m* 273, 277
puntura *f* 46
punze ad ago *f* 80
pupilla *f* 51
putter *m* 233
puzzle *m* 273

Q

Qatar 318
quaderno *m* 163
quadrato *m* 164
quadricipite *m* 16
quadro *m* 62, 261, 273, 274
quaglia *f* 119
quaranta 308
quaranta minuti 304
quarantesimo 309
quarto 309
quarto di gallone *m* 311
quarzo *m* 289
quattordicesimo 309
quattordici 308
quattro 308
quattrocento 308
quercia *f* 296
questa settimana 307
quindicesimo 309
quindici 308
quindici giorni 307
quinoa *f* 130
quinte *f* 254
quinto 309
quota *f* 211

R

rabarbaro *m* 127
raccattapalle *m* 231
racchetta *f* 230, 231
raccoglierba *m* 88
raccogliere 91, 183, 229
raccoglitore a leva *m* 173
raccolta *f* 98
raccolto *m* 183
raccomandata *f* 98
racquetball *m* 231
radar *m* 214, 281
radiatore *m* 202
radicchio *m* 123
radice *f* 50, 124, 296
radice di taro *f* 124
radici *f* 39
radio *m* 17
radio *f* 179, 268
radio digitale *f* 268
radiografia *f* 48
radiografia dentale *f* 50
radiologia *f* 49
radiosveglia *f* 70
rafano *m* 125
raffreddore *m* 44
rafting *m* 241
ragazza *f* 23, 24
ragazzo *m* 23, 24
raggi ultravioletti *m* 286
raggio *m* 164, 207
ragno *m* 295
rally *m* 249
RAM *f* 176
Ramadan *m* 26
rame *m* 289
rammendare 277
ramo *m* 296
ramoscello *m* 296
rampa di accesso *f* 194
rampa di lancio *f* 281
rampa di uscita *f* 194
rampicante *m* 87
rana *f* 239, 294
rana pescatrice *f* 120
ranuncolo *m* 297
rap *m* 259
rapa *f* 124
rapa svedese *f* 125
rapide *f* 284
rapide *m* 240
rapporti *m* 24
rasatura *f* 73
raschiare 77
raschietto *m* 82
rasoio elettrico *m* 73
rasoio usa e getta *m* 73
rastrellare 90
rastrelliera *f* 166
rastrelliera per gli arnesi *f* 78
rastrello *m* 88
ratto *m* 290
ravanello *m* 124
razza *f* 120, 294
razzo illuminante *m* 240
re *m* 272, 273
reato *m* 94
reattore *m* 281
recinto *m* 85, 182, 185, 242
recipiente *m* 66
redattrice *f* 191
redini *f* 242
refettorio *m* 168
regalo *m* 27
reggae *m* 259
reggicalze *m* 35
reggiseno *m* 35
reggiseno da allattamento *m* 53
regina *f* 272, 273
regione *f* 315
regista *m* 254
registrazione *f* 269
registro *m* 100
Regno Unito *m* 316
regolatore *m* 239
regolatore di esposizione *m* 270
reiki *m* 55
relatore *m* 174
relazione *f* 174
remare 241
rematore *m* 241
remo *m* 241
rene *m* 18
reni *f* 13
reparti *m* 49
reparto *m* 48
reparto alimentari *m* 105
reparto bagagli *m* 104
reparto bambini *m* 104
reparto calzature *m* 104
reparto di cura intensiva *m* 48
reparto maternità *m* 48
reparto pediatrico *m* 48
repellente per insetti *m* 267
Repubblica Ceca 316
Repubblica Centrafricana 317
Repubblica Democratica del Congo 317
Repubblica Dominicana 314
respiratorio 19
respirazione *f* 47
rete *f* 176, 217, 222, 226, 227, 231
rete da pesca *f* 244
rete del letto *f* 71
rete ferroviaria *f* 209
reticella *f* 167
retina *f* 51, 244

italiano

rettangolo *m* 164
rettili *m* 293
retto *m* 21
rianimazione *f* 47
riasfaltatura *f* 187
riavvolgimento *m* 269
ribes bianco *m* 127
ribes nero *m* 127
ricamo *m* 277
ricci 39
riccio *m* 290
ricerca *f* 169
ricetta *f* 45
ricevere 177
ricevimento nuziale *m* 26
ricevitore *m* 99, 225, 229
ricevuta *f* 152
ricezione *f* 100
ricoperto di cioccolato 140
ricoprire di zolle erbose 90
ricordi *m* 260
ricorso *m* 181
ricoverato 48
ricupero bagagli *m* 213
ridere 25
ridurre 172
rifiuti *m* 266
rifiuti organici *m* 61
riflessologia *f* 54
righello *m* 163, 165
rigore *m* 222
rilasciare 245
rilassamento *m* 55
rimbalzare 227
rimedi alle erbe *m* 108
rimessa *f* 226
rimessa in gioco *f* 223
rimestare 67
rimorchiare 195
rimorchiatore *m* 215
rimorchio *m* 266
Rinascimento 301
ring *m* 237
ringhiera *f* 59
rinnovare 168
rinoceronte *m* 291
ripiano *m* 167
ripieno *m* 140, 155
riproduttivo 19
riproduttore acustico *m* 258
riproduzione *f* 20
riscaldare 154
riscaldarsi 251
riso *m* 130, 158, 184
riso bianco *m* 130
riso da budino *m* 130
riso integrale *m* 130
riso selvatico *m* 130
risparmi *m* 96
rispondere 99, 163
risposta *f* 163
ristorante *m* 101, 152
risultato *m* 49
risvolto *m* 32
ritardo *m* 209
ritmo *m* 259
ritorno *m* 231
riunione *f* 174
riva *f* 284
rivista *f* 112, 168
riviste *f* 107
rocce *f* 284, 288
rocchetto del filo *m* 276
rococò 301
rodeo *m* 243
rognone *m* 119
rollino *m* 271
Romania 316
rombo *m* 164
rompere le acque 52
rondella *f* 80
rondine *f* 292
rosa 274
rosa *f* 89, 110
rosé 145
rosmarino *m* 133
rospo *m* 294
rossetto *m* 40
rossi 39
rosso 145, 274
rotaia *f* 208
rotatoria *f* 195
rotelle *f* 207
rotolo *m* 311
rotula *f* 17
rough *m* 232
roulotte *f* 266
round *m* 237
rovescio *m* 231, 286
rovina famosa *f* 261
Ruanda 317
rubinetto *m* 61, 66
rubinetto dell'acqua calda *m* 72
rubinetto dell'acqua fredda *m* 72
rubinetto di arresto *m* 61
rubinetto di scarico *m* 61
rubino *m* 288
ruck *m* 221
rucola *f* 123
ruga *f* 15
rugby *m* 221
rullo *m* 83
rullo compressore *m* 187
rum *m* 145
rum con coca cola *m* 151
ruota *f* 198, 207, 235, 276
ruota anteriore *f* 196, 210
ruota dentata *f* 206
ruota di scorta *f* 203
ruota posteriore *f* 197
ruspante 118
russare 71

S

sabato 306
sabbia *f* 85, 264
sacca *f* 37
sacca da golf *f* 233
sacchetto *m* 311
sacco *m* 237
sacco a pelo *m* 267
sacco postale *m* 98
Sahara *m* 313
Sahara Occidentale 317
Saint Kitts-Nevis 314
Saint Lucia 314
Saint Vincent e Grenadine 314
sala da pranzo *f* 64
sala da riunione *f* 174
sala d'attesa *f* 45
sala delle partenze *f* 213
sala di lettura *f* 168
sala emergenze *f* 48
sala macchine *f* 214
sala operatoria *f* 48
salamandra *f* 294
salame *m* 142
salame piccante *m* 142
salato 121, 129, 137, 143, 155
saldare 79
saldatore *m* 80
sale *m* 64, 152
salice *m* 296
salmone *m* 120
salopette *f* 30
salotto *m* 62
salpare 217
salsa *f* 134, 143, 155
salsa di pomodoro *f* 154
salsiccia *f* 118, 157
salsiccia piccante *f* 142
saltare 227
saltare con la corda 251
saltare in padella 67
salto *m* 235, 237, 243, 247
salto con l'asta *m* 234
salto in alto *m* 235
salto in lungo *m* 235
salumeria *f* 142
salumi *f* 107
salute *f* 44
salvagente *m* 240
salvare 177
salvaslip *m* 108
salvia *f* 133
salvietta antisettica *f* 47
salviettina umidificata *f* 75, 108
San Marino 316
sandali *m* 31
sandalo *m* 37
sanguinaccio *m* 157
São Tomé e Príncipe 317
sapone *m* 73
saponetta *f* 311
Sardegna 316
sardina *f* 120
sarta *f* 277
sartiame *m* 215, 240
sarto *m* 191
sartoria *f* 115
sassofono *m* 257
satellite *m* 281
satsuma *m* 126
Saturno 280
sauna *f* 250
savoiardi *m* 141
sazio 64
sbadigliare 25
sbarcare 217
sbarra *f* 235, 250
sbarramento *m* 75
sbarre *f* 74
sbarre asimmetriche *f* 235
sbarre parallele *f* 235
sbattere 67
sbucciare 67
sbucciatura *f* 46
scacchi *m* 272
scacchiera *f* 272
scaffale *m* 106, 168
scafo *m* 214, 240
scaglia *f* 294
scaglie *f* 132, 293
scala *f* 95, 186, 256
scala a pioli *f* 82
scala di sicurezza *f* 95
scala mobile *f* 104
scaldaacqua *m* 61
scale *f* 59
scalogno *m* 125
scalpello *m* 81, 275
scandalizzato 25
scandire 162
scanner *m* 176
scapola *f* 17
scarafaggio *m* 295
scarcerazione sulla parola *f* 180
scaricare 177
scarpa con i lacci *f* 37
scarpa con tacco alto *f* 37
scarpa da ginnastica *f* 37
scarpa da golf *f* 233
scarpa da trekking *f* 37
scarpa da uomo *f* 37
scarpe *f* 34, 37
scarpe da escursionismo *f* 267
scarpe da ginnastica *f* 31
scarpe da tennis *f* 231
scarpe di cuoio *f* 32
scarpette *f* 30
scarpino *m* 220, 223
scarponcini *m* 251
scarpone da sci *m* 246
scartavetrare 82
scatola d'archivio *f* 173
scatola degli attrezzi *f* 80, 244
scatola dei fusibili *f* 203
scatola del cambio *f* 202, 204
scatola di cioccolatini *f* 113
scatola di fazzolettini *f* 70
scatolame *m* 107
scatoletta *f* 311
scavare 90
scendibagno *m* 72
scenografia *f* 254
scheda del paziente *f* 48
schedario *m* 172
scheggia *f* 46
scheletro *m* 17
scherma *f* 249
schermo *m* 97, 176, 255, 267
schiacciapatate *m* 68
schiacciata *f* 139, 231
schiacciato 159
schiena *f* 13
schienale *m* 64, 210
schiuma *f* 148
schiuma da barba *f* 73
schizzo *m* 275
sci *m* 241, 246
sci alpino *m* 247
sci d'acqua *m* 241
sci di fondo *m* 247
sciabola *f* 236
sciacquare 38, 76
sciarpa *f* 31
sciatore d'acqua *m* 241
sciatrice *m* 246
scienza *f* 162, 166
scienziata *f* 190
scimmia *f* 291
sciroppo *m* 109
sciroppo d'acero *m* 134
scisto *m* 288
scivolare 229
scivolata *f* 237
scivolo *m* 263
scodella *f* 65
scogliera *f* 285
scoiattolo *m* 290
scolapasta *m* 68
scolara *f* 162
scolaro *m* 162
scolo *m* 61, 72, 91
scommessa *f* 273
scompartimento *m* 209
scompartimento a cuccette *m* 209
scongelare 67
scopa *f* 77
scopa di spugna *f* 77
scoperto 260
scoperto *m* 96
scorpione *m* 295
scorza *f* 142
scorza interna *f* 126
scossa elettrica *f* 46
scotta *f* 241
scottatura *f* 46
scrabble *m* 272
scrivania *f* 172
scrivere 162
scroto *m* 21
scucire 277
scultore *m* 191
scultura *f* 275
scuola *f* 162, 299
scuola d'arte *f* 169
scuolabus *m* 196
scuole *f* 169
scuro 41, 321
seccato 159
secchi 39
secchiello *m* 265
secchio *m* 77, 82
secchio di riciclaggio *m* 61
secco 41, 130, 145, 286
secolo *m* 307
seconda galleria *f* 254
secondo *m* 304
secondo 309
secondo piano *m* 104
sedano *m* 122
sedano rapa *m* 124
sedativo *m* 109
sede *f* 175
sede del circolo *f* 232
sedia *f* 64
sedia a rotelle *f* 48
sedia a sdraio *f* 265
sedia girevole *f* 172
sedicesimo 309
sedici 308
sedile *m* 61, 64, 204, 209, 210, 242
sedile del water *m* 72
sedile dell'autista *m* 196
sedile posteriore *m* 200
sedimentario 288
sega *f* 89
sega circolare *f* 78
sega da traforo *f* 78, 81
sega manuale *f* 80
sega per tenoni *f* 81
segare 79
seggiolino per bambini *m* 207
seggiolino per bambino *m* 198
seggiolone *m* 75
seggiovia *f* 246
seghetto per metalli *m* 81
segnale *m* 209
segnale stradale *m* 298
segnaletica orizzontale *f* 194
segnare 223, 227
segreteria telefonica *f* 99
sei 308
seicento 308
selce *f* 288
selezionatore dei punti *m* 276
sella *f* 242
sella da signora *f* 242
sellino *m* 206
sellino posteriore *m* 204
semaforo *m* 194, 298
seme *m* 122, 127, 128, 130

italiano

seme di girasole *m* 131
seme di sesamo *m* 131
seme di zucca *m* 131
semenzaio *m* 89
semenzale *m* 91
semi *m* 88, 131
semi di carvi *m* 131
semi di finocchio *m* 133
semi di mostarda *m* 131
semi di papavero *m* 138
semi di soia *m* 131
seminare 90, 183
seminterrato *m* 58
semola *f* 130
sempreverde 86
senape *f* 135, 155
Senegal 317
seno *m* 12, 19
sensibile 41
senso unico *m* 194, 298
sentenza *f* 181
sentiero *m* 85, 262
sentiero per cavalli *m* 263
senza 320
senza grassi 137
senza maniche 34
senza piombo 199
senza sale 137
senza semi 127
senza spalline 34
seppia *f* 121
sera *f* 305
serbatoio *m* 61, 204
serbatoio del liquido lavavetri *m* 202
serbatoio del liquido per i freni *m* 202
serbatoio della benzina *m* 203
serbatoio dell'acqua *m* 61
serbatoio dell'olio *m* 204
serbatoio per il liquido refrigerante *m* 202
serie *f* 179
serie televisiva *f* 178
serpente *m* 293
serratura *f* 59
server *m* 176
servire 64, 229
servizi di emergenza *m* 94
servizio *m* 231, 231
servizio compreso 152
servizio di lavanderia *m* 101
servizio di pulizia *m* 101
servizio in camera *m* 101
servizio non compreso 152
sessanta 308
sessantesimo 309
sesto 309
set *m* 178, 179, 230
seta *f* 277
setacciare 91, 138
setaccio *m* 89
settanta 308
settantesimo 309
sette 308
settecento 308
settembre 306
settimana *f* 306
settimana prossima *f* 306
settimana scorsa *f* 307
settimanale 307
settimo 309
sfera *f* 164
sfiatatoio *m* 290
sfocato 271
sfogo *m* 44
sfondo *m* 177
sformato *m* 142
sfumatura alta *f* 39
sgabello *m* 150
sgombro *m* 120
sgusciato 129
shaker *m* 150
shampoo *m* 38
sherry *m* 145
shiatsu *m* 54
shock *m* 47
shuttle *m* 281
si 322
Siberia *f* 313
Sicilia 316
sicura *f* 200
sicurezza *f* 75, 212, 240
sicuro 228
sidro *m* 145
siepe *f* 85, 90, 182
siero di latte *m* 137
Sierra Leone 317
sigarette *f* 112
sigaro *m* 112
sigillante *m* 83
Signora *f* 23
Signore *m* 23
Signorina *f* 23
silenziatore *m* 203, 204
silos *m* 183
sinagoga *f* 300
sinfonia *f* 256
Singapore 319
singolo *m* 230
singolo 151
sinistra 260
sintetico 31
sintonizzare 179
sintonizzare la radio 269
sipario *m* 254
sirena *f* 94
Siria 318
siringa *f* 109, 167
sistema *m* 176
sistema di altoparlanti *m* 209
sistema solare *m* 280
sistemi corporali *m* 19
sistemi interni *m* 60
sito web *m* 177
skateboard *m* 249, 263
slalom *m* 247
slalom gigante *f* 247
slip *m* 33, 35
slittino *m* 247
slogatura *f* 46
Slovacchia 316
Slovenia 316
smaltimento dei rifiuti *m* 61
smalto *m* 50
smalto per le labbra *m* 40
smalto per unghie *m* 41
smartphone *m* 99, 176
smeraldo *m* 288
smorzata *f* 230
snack bar *m* 148
snooker *m* 249
snowboard *m* 247
società *f* 175
soda *f* 144
sodo 124
soffiare 141
soffione della doccia *m* 72
soffitto *m* 62
soffocare 47
software *m* 176
sogliola *f* 120
sogliola limanda *f* 120
solco *m* 183
soldato *m* 189
sole *m* 280
soleggiato 286
solidi *m* 164
sollevare 251
solubile 109
soluzione disinfettante *f* 51
soluzione per la pulizia *f* 51
solvente *m* 83
Somalia 317
sommare 165
sonaglio *m* 74
sonata *f* 256
sonda *f* 50
sonnifero *m* 109
sopra 320
sopracciglio *m* 14, 51
sorbetto *m* 141
sorella *f* 22
sorgere del sole *m* 305
sorpassare 195
sorpreso 25
sorriso *m* 25
sospensione *f* 203
sospetto *m* 94
sospirare 25
sosta vietata 195
sostegno *m* 88
sostegno del morsetto *m* 166
sostituto *m* 223
sostituzione *f* 223
sottaceto 159
sottile 321
sotto 320
sottobicchiere *m* 150
sottoesposto 271
sott'olio 143
sottomarino *m* 215
sottopassaggio *m* 194
sottosuolo *m* 91
sottoveste *f* 35
sottrarre 165
soufflé *m* 158
sovraesposto 271
spaccato *m* 282
Spagna 316
spalla *f* 13
spallina *f* 35
spartito *m* 256
spatola *f* 68, 167
spaventapasseri *m* 184
spaventato 25
spazio *m* 280
spazzare 77
spazzola *f* 38, 77, 82
spazzola da water *m* 72
spazzola per la schiena *f* 73
spazzolare 38
spazzolina per le sopracciglia *f* 40
spazzolino *m* 50
spazzolino da denti *m* 72
specchietto laterale *m* 198
specchietto retrovisore *m* 198
specchio *m* 40, 71, 167
specialista *m* 49
spedire 177
spegnere la televisione 269
spellato 121
sperma *m* 20
spesa *f* 106
spesso 321
spettatori *m* 233
spezie *f* 132
spia del carburante *f* 201
spia della temperatura *f* 201
spiaggia *f* 264
spianare 67
spicchio *m* 125, 126
spiedino *m* 68, 155, 158
spigola *f* 120
spilla *f* 36
spilla da balia *f* 47
spillatore di birra *m* 150
spillo *m* 276
spina *f* 60, 121
spina dorsale *f* 17
spinaci *m* 123
spinato 121
spioncino *m* 59
spira *f* 300
spoletta *f* 277
spolverare 77
spolverino *m* 77
sport *m* 220
sport acquatici *m* 241
sport da combattimento *m* 236
sport e il tempo libero *m* 236
sport invernali *m* 247
sportello *m* 96, 98, 198
sportello dell'equipaggio *m* 281
sposarsi 26
spray *m* 109
spremiaglio *m* 68
spremuta d'arancia *f* 144
spremute e i frappé f/m 149
spruzzare 91
spugna *f* 73, 74, 83
spuntare 39, 90
sputacchiera *f* 50
squadra *f* 165, 220, 229
squalo *m* 294
squama *f* 121
squash *m* 231
squat *m* 251
sradicare le erbacce 91
Sri Lanka 318
stabilizzatore *m* 210
staccare 82
staccato 99
stadio *m* 223
staffa *f* 242
staffetta *f* 235
stagionale 129
stagioni *f* 306
stagno *m* 85, 232, 289
stalla *f* 185, 243
stame *m* 297
stampa *f* 178, 275
stampante *f* 172, 176
stampare 172
stampino *m* 83
stampo *m* 69
stampo per dolci *m* 69
stampo per flan *m* 69
stampo per soufflé *m* 69
stampo per torte *m* 69
stanza *f* 58
stanza da bagno *f* 72
stanza di cambio pannolini *f* 104
starnuto *m* 44
Stati Uniti d'America 314
stato *m* 315
statuina *f* 260
stazione di polizia *f* 94
stazione di servizio *f* 199
stazione ferroviaria *f* 208
stazione spaziale *f* 281
stecca *f* 47
stella *f* 280
stella di mare *f* 295
stelo *m* 111, 122, 297
stendere 251
stenografo *m* 181
stereo 269
sterile 20, 47
sterno *m* 17
stetoscopio *m* 45
stile libero *m* 239
stili *m* 239, 301
stili musicali *m* 259
stilista *m* 277
stinco *m* 12
stipendio *m* 175
stiramento *m* 251
stirare 76
stiva *f* 215
stivale m 37
stivale da equitazione *m* 242
stivaloni di gomma *m* 244
stoffa *f* 276
stomaco *m* 18
stop *m* 269
storia *f* 162
storia dell'arte *f* 169
stoviglie e posate *f* 65
strada *f* 298
strada di accesso *f* 216
strade *f* 194
strascico *m* 35
strato di ozono *m* 286
strato superficiale *m* 85
stratosfera *f* 286
streaming *m* 269
stress *m* 55
stretching *m* 251
stretto 321
strike *m* 228
strumenti *m* 256, 258
strumenti a fiato *m* 257
struttura *f* 267
struttura per arrampicarsi *f* 263
struzzo *m* 292
stucco *m* 83
studente universitario *m* 169
studio *m* 63, 162
studio dell'avvocato *m* 180
studio di registrazione *m* 179
studio televisivo *m* 178
stufa *f* 60
stufa a convezione *f* 60
stufato *m* 158
sturalavandini *m* 81
stuzzichini *m* 151
su 320
succo *m* 127
succo d'ananas *m* 149
succo d'arancia *m* 148
succo di frutta *m* 156
succo di mela *m* 149
succo di pomodoro *m* 144
succo d'uva *m* 144
succursale *f* 175
sud *m* 312
Sud Africa 317
Sudan 317
Sudan del Sud 317
sugoso 127
sumo *m* 237
suocera *f* 23
suocero *m* 23
suola *f* 37
superficie *f* 165, 310
supermercato *m* 106

supplemento *m* 55
supporto *m* 187, 268
supporto per l'altoparlante *m* 268
supposta *f* 109
surf *m* 241
surfing *m* 241
surfista *m* 241
surgelati *m* 107
Suriname 315
sveglia *f* 70
svegliarsi 71
svenire 25, 44
Svezia 316
sviluppare 271
svincolo *m* 194
Svizzera *f* 316
svolta a destra vietata 195
Swaziland 317
swing di pratica *m* 233

T

tabacco *m* 112, 184
tabellone *m* 173, 226
tabellone dei risultati *m* 225
tacchino *m* 119, 185, 293
tacco *m* 37
tae kwondo *m* 236
Tagikistan 318
tagli *m* 119
tagliabordi *m* 88
tagliare 38, 79, 277
tagliatubi *m* 81
tagliaunghie *m* 41
tagliere *m* 68
taglierini *m* 158
taglio *m* 46, 230
taglio cesareo *m* 52
tai-chi *m* 236
Tailandia 318
Taiwan 319
talco *m* 73
talea *f* 91
tallone *m* 13, 15
tamburino *m* 257
tamburo militare *m* 257
tampone di inchiostro *m* 173
tamponi *m* 108
tandem *m* 206
Tanzania *f* 317
tappetino *m* 54
tappeto *m* 63, 71
tappezzare 82
tappo *m* 72, 134, 166
tardi 305
targa *f* 198
targhetta d'identità *f* 53
tariffa *f* 197, 209
tariffa d'ingresso *f* 260
tartaruga *f* 293
tartufo *m* 113, 125
tasca *f* 32
tasca da pasticciere *f* 69
Tasmania 319
tassista *m* 190
tasso di cambio *m* 97
tasso d'interesse *m* 96
tastiera *f* 97, 99, 176, 258
tasto *m* 176, 258
tatuaggio *m* 41
tavola *f* 241
tavola da skateboard *f* 249
tavoletta *f* 238
tavoletta di cioccolata *f* 113
tavoletta spuntino *f* 113
tavolino *m* 62
tavolo *m* 64, 148
tavolo da lavoro *m* 82
tavolo da picnic *m* 266
tavolo della colazione *m* 156
tavolozza *f* 274
tazza *f* 61, 65
tazza da tè *f* 65
tazza per bere *f* 75
tazzina da caffè *f* 65
tè *m* 144, 149, 184
tè al limone *m* 149
tè alla menta *m* 149
tè alle erbe *m* 149
tè con latte *m* 149
tè freddo *m* 149
tè nero *m* 149
tè sciolto *m* 144
tè verde *m* 149
teatro *m* 254, 299
tecniche *f* 79
tecnico del suono *m* 179
tee *m* 233
teeing-ground *m* 232
teglia *f* 69
teglia per pasticcini *f* 69
tegola *f* 58, 187
teiera *f* 65
tela *f* 274
telaio *m* 203, 206, 277
telecamera *m* 178
telecomando *m* 269
telefonino *m* 99
telefono *m* 99
telefono con macchina fotografica *m* 270
telefono per emergenze *m* 195
telefono pubblico *m* 99
telefono senza fili *m* 99
telegiornale *m* 178
telegramma *m* 98
telenovela *f* 178
telescopio *m* 281
televisione via cavo *f* 269
televisore *m* 268
telo di protezione *m* 83
telo isolante *m* 267
telo protettivo *m* 266
tema *m* 163
tempera *f* 274
temperamatite *m* 163
temperatura *f* 286
tempesta *f* 287
tempia *f* 14
tempio *m* 300
tempo *m* 234, 286
tempo libero *m* 254, 258, 264
tempo supplementare *m* 223
tenaglie *f* 167
tenda *f* 63, 148, 267
tenda da doccia *f* 72
tendina *f* 63
tendine *m* 16, 17
tendine di achille *m* 16
tenersi a galla 239
tennis *m* 230
tensione *f* 60
tenuta da calcio *f* 31
tequila *f* 145
terapia di gruppo *f* 55
terapie alternative *f* 54
terapista *f* 55
tergicristallo *m* 198
terminale *m* 212
terminale di carenaggio *m* 216
termite *f* 295
termocoperta *f* 71
termometro *m* 45, 167
termosfera *f* 286
termostato *m* 61
terra *f* 282
Terra *f* 280
terraferma *f* 282
terremoto *m* 283
terreno *m* 85
terreno agricolo *m* 182
terriccio *m* 88
terrina *f* 69
territorio *m* 315
terzo 309
tesi *f* 169
tesserino *m* 168
tessitura *f* 277
tessuto *m* 277
test di gravidanza *m* 52
testa *f* 12, 19, 81, 230
testa del cilindro *f* 202
testata *f* 70
testicolo *m* 21
testimone *m* 180, 235
testo *m* 259
testuggine *f* 293
tettarella *f* 75
tetto *m* 58, 203
tettuccio *m* 202
thermos *m* 267
thriller *m* 255
tibia *f* 17
tiebreak *m* 230
tiepido 286
tiglio *m* 296
tigre *f* 291
timbro a umido *m* 173
timbro postale *m* 98
timido 25
timo *m* 133
timone *m* 210, 241
Timor Est 319
timpano *m* 257
tinti 39
tintura per capelli *f* 40
tipi *m* 199, 205
tipi di autobus *m* 196
tipi di fattoria *m* 183
tipi di giardino *m* 84
tipi di macchina fotografica *m* 270
tipi di pesca *m* 245
tipi di piante 86
tipi di treno *m* 208
tirare 221, 223, 227
tirare con il mulinello 245
tiro al bersaglio *m* 249
tiro alto *m* 230
tiro con l'arco *m* 249
tiro insospensione *m* 226
tiroide *f* 18
titoli *m* 97
titolo *m* 168
toeletta *f* 71
toga *f* 169
togliere i fiori appassiti 91
Togo *m* 317
toilettes *f* 104
tombino *m* 299
tonalità 41
tonnellata *f* 310
tonno *m* 120
tono *m* 256
topazio *m* 288
topinambur *m* 125
topo *m* 290
toppa *f* 207
torace *m* 12
torcia *f* 267
tormalina *f* 288
tornado *m* 287
torneo *m* 233
tornio da vasaio *m* 275
tornire 79
toro *m* 185
torre *f* 272, 300
torre di controllo *f* 212
torre di sorveglianza *f* 265
torrente *m* 285
torretta *f* 300
torretta di comando *f* 215
torrone *m* 113
torsolo *m* 127
torta al cioccolato *f* 140
torta alla crema *f* 141
torta di compleanno *f* 141
torta nuziale *f* 141
torte per celebrazioni *f* 141
tosaerba *m* 88, 90
tosare l'erba 90
tosse *f* 44
tostapane *m* 66
touch-down *m* 220
tovaglia *f* 64
tovaglia individuale *f* 64
tovagliolo *m* 65
tovagliolo di carta *m* 154
tra 320
trachea *f* 18
traffico *m* 194
traghetto *m* 215, 216
traguardo *m* 234
tram *m* 196, 208
tramezzino *m* 155
tramezzino a strati *m* 155
tramezzino aperto *m* 155
tramezzino tostato *m* 149
tramonto *m* 305
trampolino *m* 238
trancia *f* 121
transenna di sicurezza *f* 246
trapanare 79
trapano *m* 50
trapano elettrico *m* 78
trapano manuale *m* 81
trapano ricaricabile *m* 78
trapezio *m* 16, 164
trapiantare 91
trapunta *f* 71
trapunto *m* 277
trasferta *f* 223
trasformatore *m* 60
trasmettere 178, 179
trasmissione *f* 202
trasmittente *f* 75
trasporti *m* 194
trattamenti di bellezza *m* 41
trattamento per il viso *m* 41
trattato 118, 143
trattore *m* 182
travaglio indotto *m* 53
trave *f* 186, 235
travel cheque *m* 97
traversa *f* 222
tre 308
treadmill *m* 250
treccia *f* 39
trecento 308
tredicesimo 309
tredici 308
trementina *f* 83
tremore *m* 283
treno *m* 208
treno a vapore *m* 208
treno ad alta velocità *m* 208
treno diesel *m* 208
treno elettrico *m* 208
treno intercity *m* 209
treno merci *m* 208
trenta 308
trentesimo 309
treppiede *m* 166, 270, 281
triangolo *m* 164, 257
tric trac (la tavola reale) m 272
tricheco *m* 290
tricipite *m* 16
trifoglio *m* 297
triglia *f* 120
trimestre *m* 52
Trinidad e Tobago 314
triste 25
tritato 132
tromba *f* 257
trombone *m* 257
tronco *m* 296
tropici *m* 283
tropico del cancro *m* 283
tropico del capricorno *m* 283
troposfera *f* 286
trota *f* 120
trotto *m* 243
trovare un lavoro 26
trucco *m* 40
truciolato *m* 79
trucioli *m* 78
tuba *f* 257
tubetto *m* 311
tubo *m* 89, 202
tubo dell'acqua *m* 61
tubo di aspirazione *m* 77
tubo di Fallopio *m* 20
tubo di scappamento *m* 203, 204
tubo di scolo *m* 61
tubo di troppopieno *m* 61
tubo reggisella *m* 206
tuffarsi 238, 239
tuffatore *m* 238
tuffo alto *m* 239
tuffo di rincorsa *m* 239
tulipano *m* 111
Tunisia *f* 317
tuono *m* 286
tuorlo *m* 137, 157
turbato 25
turbocompressore *m* 203
turchese *m* 289
Turchia *f* 316
turismo *m* 260
turista *m* 260
Turkmenistan 318
turno di battuta *m* 228
tuta *f* 31, 82
tuta da sport *f* 32
tuta di pelle *f* 205
tuta spaziale *f* 281
tuta subacquea *f* 239
tutina *f* 30
tutina da neve *f* 30
tutina senza maniche *f* 30
tutù *m* 191
TV a schermo piatto *f* 269

U

uccelli *m* 292
Ucraina *f* 316
ufficio *m* 24, 172, 174
ufficio contabilità *m* 175
ufficio del direttore *m* 266

italiano

ufficio del personale *m* 175
ufficio della dogana *m* 216
ufficio di assistenza al cliente *m* 175
ufficio di cambio *m* 97
ufficio iscrizioni *m* 168
ufficio legale *m* 175
ufficio marketing *m* 175
ufficio postale *m* 98
ufficio vendite *m* 175
Uganda *m* 317
uguale 165
ulna *f* 17
ultrasuono *m* 52
un quarto d'ora 304
una mezzora 304
uncinetto *m* 277
uncino *m* 244
underpar *m* 233
undicesimo 309
undici 308
Ungheria 316
unghia *f* 15
unghia del piede *f* 15
unguento *m* 109
unifamiliare 58
uniforme *f* 94
unità di smistamento *f* 61
università *f* 168, 299
universo *m* 280
uno 308
uomo *m* 12, 23
uomo di affari *m* 175
uova *f* 137
uova strappazzate *f* 157
uovo alla coque *m* 137, 157
uovo di anatra *m* 137
uovo di gallina *m* 137
uovo di quaglia *m* 137
uovo d'oca *m* 137
uovo fritto *m* 157
uragano *m* 287
Uranio 280
uretere *m* 21
uretra *f* 20
urinario 19
urologia *f* 49
Uruguay 315
uscita *f* 61, 210
uscita di emergenza *f* 210
ustione *f* 46
utensili *m* 66
utensili da cucina *m* 68
utero *m* 20, 52
uva passa *f* 129
uva spina *f* 127
uva sultanina *f* 129
uvetta *f* 129
Uzbekistan 318

V

vacanza *f* 212
vagina *f* 20
vaglia postale *m* 98
vagone *m* 208
vagone ristorante *m* 209
valanga *f* 247
valigetta *f* 37
valle *f* 284
valuta estera *f* 97
valvola *f* 207
valvola della pressione *f* 61
valvoliera *f* 60
vanga *f* 88
vaniglia *f* 132
vano della pellicola *m* 270
vantaggio *m* 230
Vanuatu 319
varechina *f* //
varicella *f* 44
vasca *f* 72
vaschetta *f* 74, 311
vaschetta per la vernice *f* 83
vasino *m* 74
vaso *m* 63, 111
vaso da fiori *m* 89
vassoio *m* 152, 154, 210
vassoio della colazione *m* 101
vassoio in arrivo *f* 172
vassoio in partenza *m* 172
vecchio 321
veicolo di servizio *m* 212
vela *f* 240, 241
vela di maestra *f* 240
vela di prua *f* 240
velo *m* 35
veloce 321
velocista *m* 234
vena *f* 19
venditore ambulante *m* 154
venerdì 306
Venere 280
veneziana *f* 63
Venezuela 315
ventesimo 309
venti 308
venti minuti 304
ventidue 308
ventiduesimo 309
ventilatore *m* 60
ventimila 309
ventitreesimo 309
vento *m* 241, 286
ventola *f* 202
ventola per l'aria *f* 210
ventosa *f* 53
ventoso 286
ventunesimo 309
ventuno 308
verbale *m* 174
verde 274
verdetto *m* 181
verdura *f* 122
verdure *f* 107, 124
verme *m* 295
vernice di base *f* 83
vernice trasparente *f* 83
verniciare 83
versare 67, 96
verso 320
vertebra cervicale *f* 17
vertebra lombare *f* 17
vertebra toracica *f* 17
verticale 271
verza *f* 123
vescica *f* 20, 46
vescicola seminale *f* 21
vespa *f* 205, 295
vestaglia *f* 31, 32, 35
vestiti puliti *m* 76
vestito *m* 31, 34
veterinaria *f* 189
via laterale *f* 299
viaggio di affari *m* 175
viaggio di nozze *m* 26
viale *m* 299
vibrafono *m* 257
vicino 320
vicino *m* 24
vicolo *m* 298
videocamera *f* 260, 269
videogioco *m* 269
videotelefono *m* 99
Vietnam 318
vigile del fuoco *m* 189
vigile urbano *m* 195
vigili del fuoco *m* 95
vigilia di Ognissanti *f* 27
vigna *f* 183
vigneto *m* 183
villaggio *m* 299
villino *m* 58
vincere 273
vincitore *m* 273
vino *m* 145, 151
viola 274
viola *f* 256
violacciocca *f* 110
violino *m* 256
violoncello *m* 256
viottolo *m* 58
virus *m* 44
visiera *f* 205
visita *f* 45
visita guidata *f* 260
visita medica *f* 45
vista *f* 51
visto *m* 213
vita *f* 12
vitamine *f* 108
vite *f* 80
vitello *m* 118, 185
vivaio *m* 84, 115
vivaio ittico *m* 183
vodka *f* 145
vodka all'arancia *f* 151
vogatore *m* 250
volano *m* 231
volant *m* 71
volante *m* 201
volare 211
volo in deltaplano *m* 248
volo internazionale *m* 212
volo nazionale *m* 212
volo senza motore *m* 248
volpe *f* 290
volta *f* 300
volume *m* 165, 179, 269, 311
vomitare 44
vongola *f* 121
vulcano *m* 283
vuoto 321

W

waffle *m* 157
water *m* 61, 72
western *m* 255
whisky *m* 145
whisky con acqua *m* 151
wicket *m* 225
Wifi *m* 269
windsurf *m* 241
wok *m* 69
wurstel *m* 155

Y

yacht *m* 215, 240
Yemen 318
yoga *m* 54
yogurt *m* 137
yogurt alla frutta *m* 157
yogurt gelato *m* 137

Z

zafferano *m* 132
zaffiro *m* 288
zainetto *m* 37
zaino *m* 31, 267
Zambia *m* 317
zampa *f* 119
zanna *f* 291
zanzara *f* 295
zanzariera *f* 267
zappa *f* 88
zattera di salvataggio *f* 240
zebra *f* 291
zenzero *m* 125, 133
zeppa *f* 37
zerbino *m* 59
zero 308
zia *f* 22
Zimbabwe *m* 317
zincato 79
zinco *m* 289
zio *m* 22
zoccolo *m* 242, 291
zolfo *m* 289
zolla *f* 283
zona *f* 315
zona industriale *f* 299
zona pedonale *f* 299
zone *f* 283, 299
zoo *m* 262
zoologia 169
zoom *m* 270
zoosafari *m* 262
zucca *f* 124, 125
zucca a ghianda *f* 125
zucca butternut *f* 125
zucchina *f* 125
zuppa *f* 158
zuppa inglese *f* 141

italiano

acknowledgments • remerciements • Dank • agradecimientos • ringraziamenti

DORLING KINDERSLEY would like to thank Tracey Miles and Christine Lacey for design assistance, Georgina Garner for editorial and administrative help, Sonia Gavira, Polly Boyd, and Cathy Meeus for editorial help, Claire Bowers for compiling the DK picture credits, and Surabhi Wadhwa, Harish Aggarwal, and Saloni Singh for jacket design.

The publisher would like to thank the following for their kind permission to reproduce their photographs:
Abbreviations key:
t=top, b=bottom, r=right, l=left, c=centre

123RF.com: Andriy Popov 34tl; Daniel Ernst 179tc; Hongqi Zhang 24cla. 175cr; Ingvar Bjork 60c; Kobby Dagan 259c; leonardo255 269c; Liubov Vadimovna (Luba) Nel 39cla; Ljupco Smokovski 75crb; Oleksandr Marynchenko 60bl; Olga Popova 33c; oneblink 49bc; Racorn 162tl; Robert Churchill 94c; Roman Gorielov 33bc; Ruslan Kudrin 35bc, 35br; Subbotina 39cra; Sutichak Yachaingkham 39tc; Tarzhanova 37tc; Vitaly Valua 39tl; Wavebreak Media Ltd 188bl; Wilawan Khasawong 75cb; **Action Plus:** 224bc; **Alamy Images:** 154t; A.T. Willett 287bcl; Alex Segre 105ca, 105cb, 195cl; Ambrophoto 24cra; Blend Images 168cr; Cultura RM 33r; Doug Houghton 107fbr; Ekkapon Sriharun 172bl; Hugh Threlfall 35tl; 176tr; Ian Allenden 48br; Ian Dagnall (iPod is a trademark of Apple Inc., registered in the U.S. and other countries) 268tc, 270t; Ievgen Chepil 250bc; imagebroker 199tl, 249c; keith morris 178c; Martyn Evans 210b; MBI 175tl; Michael Burrell 213cra; Michael Foyle 184bl; Oleksiy Maksymenko 105tc; Paul Weston 168br; Prisma Bildagentur AG 246b; Radharc Images 197tr; RBtravel 112tl; Ruslan Kudrin 176tl; Sasa Huzjak 258t; Sergey Kravchenko 37ca; Sergio Azenha 270bc; Stanca Sanda (iPad is a trademark of Apple Inc., registered in the U.S. and other countries) 176bc; Stock Connection 287bcr; tarczas 35cr; vitaly suprun 176cl; Wavebreak Media ltd 39cl, 174b, 175tr; **Allsport/Getty Images:** 238cl; **Alvey and Towers:** 209 acr, 215bcl, 215bcr, 241cr; **Peter Anderson:** 188cbr, 271br. **Anthony Blake Photo Library:** Charlie Stebbings 114cl; John Sims 114tcl; **Andyalte:** 98tl; **apple mac computers:** 268tcr; **Arcaid:** John Edward Linden 301bl; Martine Hamilton Knight, Architects: Chapman Taylor Partners, 213cl; Richard Bryant 301br; **Argos:** 41tcl, 66cbl, 66cl, 66br, 66bcl, 69cl, 70bcl, 71t, 77tl, 269tc, 270tl; **Axiom:** Eitan Simanor 105bcr; Ian Cumming 104; Vicki Couchman 148cr; **Beken Of Cowes Ltd:** 215cbc; **Bosch:** 76tcr, 76tc, 76tcl; **Camera Press:** 38tr, 256t, 257cr; Barry J. Holmes 148tr; Jane Hanger 159cr; Mary Germanou 259bc; **Corbis:** 78b; Anna Clopet 247tr; Ariel Skelley / Blend Images 52l; Bettmann 181tl, 181tr; Blue Jean Images 48bl; Bo Zauders 156t; Bob Rowan 152bl; Bob Winsett 247cbl; Brian Bailey 247br; Carl and Ann Purcell 162l; Chris Rainer 247ctl; Craig Aurness 215bl; David H. Wells 249cbr; Dennis Marsico 274bl; Dimitri Lundt 236bc; Duomo 211tl; Gail Mooney 277ctcr; George Lepp 248c; Gerald Nowak 239b; Gunter Marx 248cr; Jack Hollingsworth 231bl; Jacqui Hurst 277cbr; James L. Amos 247bl, 191ctr, 220bcr; Jan Butchofsky 277cbc; Johnathan Blair 243cr; Jose F. Poblete 191br; Jose Luis Pelaez.Inc 153tc; Karl Weatherly 220bl, 247tcr; Kelly Mooney Photography 259tl; Kevin Fleming 249bc; Kevin R. Morris 105tr, 243tl, 243tc; Kim Sayer 249tcr; Lynn Goldsmith 258t; Macduff Everton 231bcl; Mark Gibson 249bl; Mark L. Stephenson 249tcl; Michael Pole 115tr; Michael S. Yamashita 247ctcl; Mike King 247cbl; Neil Rabinowitz 214br; Pablo Corral 115bc; Paul A. Sounders 169br, 249ctcl; Paul J. Sutton 224c, 224br; Phil Schermeister 227b, 248tr; R.W Jones 309; Richard Morrell 189bc; Rick Doyle 241ctr; Robert Holmes 97br, 277ctc; Roger Ressmeyer 169tr; Russ Schleipman 229; The Purcell Team 211ctr; Vince Streano 194t; Wally McNamee 220br, 220bcl, 224bl; Wavebreak Media LTD 191bc; Yann Arhus-Bertrand 249tl; **Demetrio Carrasco / Dorling Kindersley (c) Herge / Les Editions Casterman:** 112ccl; **Dorling Kindersley:** Banbury Museum 35c; Five Napkin Burger 152t; **Dixons:** 270cl, 270cr, 270bl, 270bcl, 270bcr, 270ccr; **Dreamstime.com:** Alexander Podshivalov 179tr, 191cr; Alexxl66 268tl; Andersastphoto 176tc; Andrey Popov 191bl; Arne9001 190tl; Chaoss 26c; Designsstock 269cl; Monkey Business Images 26clb; Paul Michael Hughes 162tr; Serghei Starus 190bc; **Education Photos:** John Walmsley 26tl; **Empics Ltd:** Adam Day 236br; Andy Heading 243c; Steve White 249cbc; **Getty Images:** 48bcl, 100t, 114bcr, 154bl, 287tr; 94tr; Don Farrall / Digital Vision 176c; Ethan Miller 270bl; Inti St Clair 179bl; Liam Norris 188br; Sean Justice / Digital Vision 24br; **Dennis Gilbert:** 106tc; **Hulsta:** 70t; **Ideal Standard Ltd:** 72r; **The Image Bank/Getty Images:** 58; **Impact Photos:** Eliza Armstrong 115cr; Philip Achache 246t; **The Interior Archive:** Henry Wilson, Alfie's Market 114bl; Luke White, Architect: David Mikhail, 59tl; Simon Upton, Architect: Phillippe Starck, St Martins Lane Hotel 100bcr, 100br; **iStockphoto.com:** asterix0597 163tl; EdStock 190br; RichLegg 26bc; SorinVidis 27cr; **Jason Hawkes Aerial Photography:** 216t; Dan Johnson: 35r; **Kos Pictures Source:** 215cbl, 240tc, 240tr; David Williams 216b; **Lebrecht Collection:** Kate Mount 169bc; **MP Visual.com:** Mark Swallow 202t; **NASA:** 280cr, 280ccl, 281tl; P&O **Princess Cruises:** 214bl; **P A Photos:** 181br; **The Photographers' Library:** 186bl, 186bc, 186t; **Plain and Simple Kitchens:** 66t; **Powerstock Photolibrary:** 169tl, 256t, 287tc; **PunchStock:** Image Source 195tr; **Rail Images:** 208c, 208 cbl, 209br; **Red Consultancy:** Odeon cinemas 257br; **Redferns:** 259br; Nigel Crane 259c; **Rex Features:** 106br, 259tc, 259tr, 259bl, 280b; Charles Ommaney 114tcr; J.F.F Whitehead 243cl; Patrick Barth 101tl; Patrick Frilet 189cbl; Scott Wiseman 287bl; **Royalty Free Images:** Getty Images/Eyewire 154bl; **Science & Society Picture Library:** Science Museum 202b; Science Photo Library: IBM Research 190cla; NASA 281cr; **SuperStock:** Ingram Publishing 62; Juanma Aparicio / age fotostock 172t; Nordic Photos 269tl; **Skyscan:** 168t, 182c, 298; Quick UK Ltd 212; **Sony:** 268bc; **Robert Streeter:** 154br; **Neil Sutherland:** 82tr, 83tl, 90t, 118, 188ctr, 196tl, 196tr, 299cl, 299bl; **The Travel Library:** Stuart Black 264t; **Travelex:** 97cl; **Vauxhall:** Technik 198t, 199tl, 199tr, 199cl, 199cr, 199ctcl, 199ctcr, 199tcl, 199tcr, 200; **View Pictures:** Dennis Gilbert, Architects: ACDP Consulting, 106t; Dennis Gilbert, Chris Wilkinson Architects, 209tr; Peter Cook, Architects: Nicholas Crimshaw and partners, 208t; **Betty Walton:** 185br; **Colin Walton:** 2, 4, 7, 9, 10, 28, 42, 56, 92, 95c, 99tl, 99tcl, 102, 116, 120t, 138t, 146, 150t, 160, 170, 191ctcl, 192, 218, 252, 260br, 260l, 261tr, 261c, 261cr, 271cbl, 271cbr, 271ctl, 278, 287br, 302, 401.

DK PICTURE LIBRARY:
Akhil Bahkshi; Patrick Baldwin; Geoff Brightling; British Museum; John Bulmer; Andrew Butler; Joe Cornish; Brian Cosgrove; Andy Crawford and Kit Hougton; Philip Dowell; Alistair Duncan; Gables; Bob Gathany; Norman Hollands; Kew Gardens; Peter James Kindersley; Vladimir Kozlik; Sam Lloyd; London Northern Bus Company Ltd; Tracy Morgan; David Murray and Jules Selmes; Musée Vivant du Cheval, France; Museum of Broadcast Communications; Museum of Natural History; NASA; National History Museum; Norfolk Rural Life Museum; Stephen Oliver; RNLI; Royal Ballet School; Guy Ryecart; Science Museum; Neil Setchfield; Ross Simms and the Winchcombe Folk Police Museum; Singapore Symphony Orchestra; Smart Museum of Art; Tony Souter; Erik Svensson and Jeppe Wikstrom; Sam Tree of Keygrove Marketing Ltd; Barrie Watts; Alan Williams; Jerry Young.

Additional Photography by Colin Walton.

Colin Walton would like to thank:
A&A News, Uckfield; Abbey Music, Tunbridge Wells; Arena Mens Clothing, Tunbridge Wells; Burrells of Tunbridge Wells; Gary at Di Marco's; Jeremy's Home Store, Tunbridge Wells; Noakes of Tunbridge Wells; Ottakar's, Tunbridge Wells; Selby's of Uckfield; Sevenoaks Sound and Vision; Westfield, Royal Victoria Place, Tunbridge Wells.